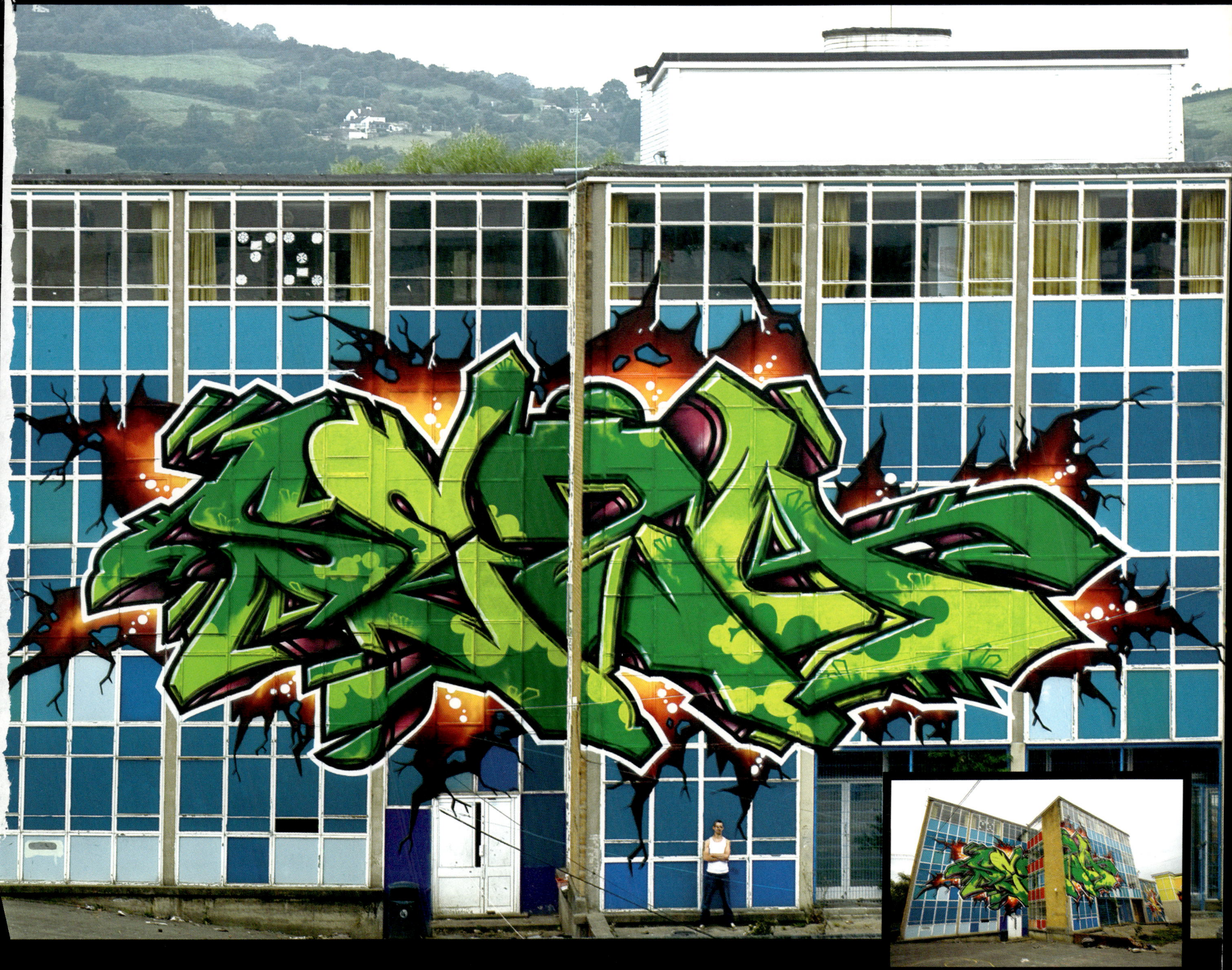

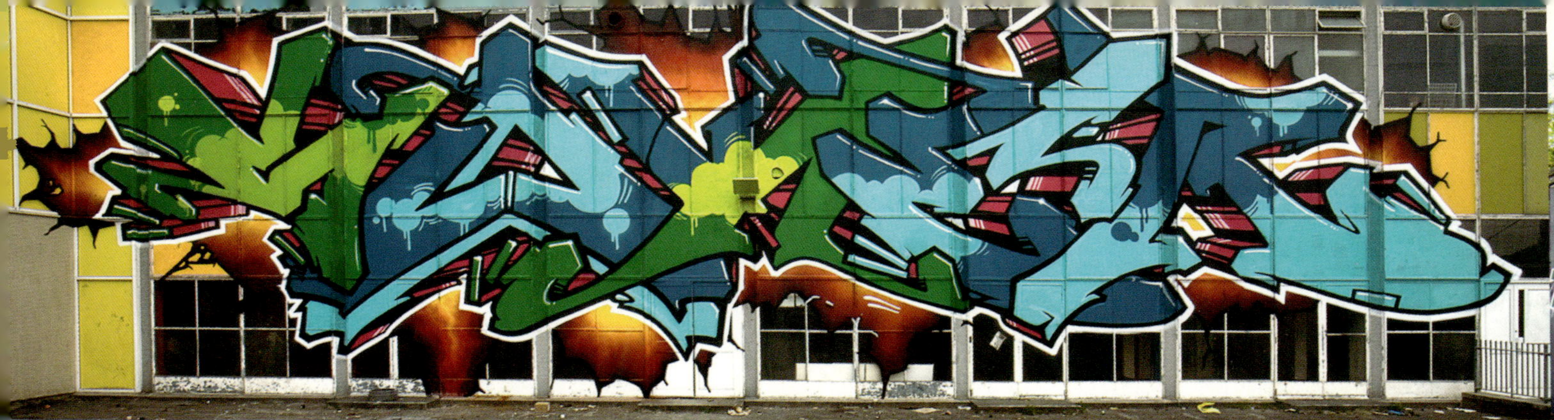
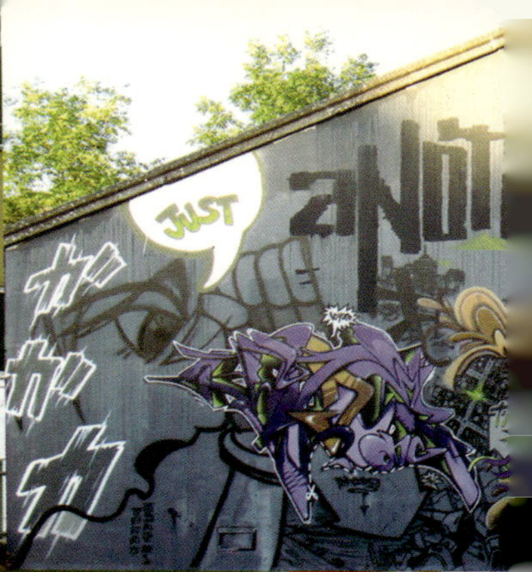
JUST
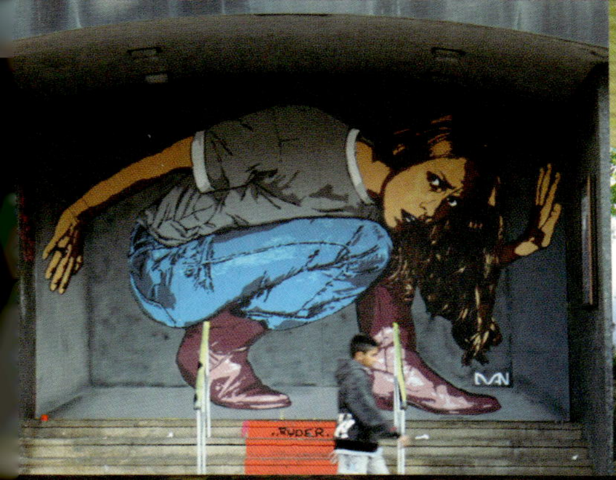
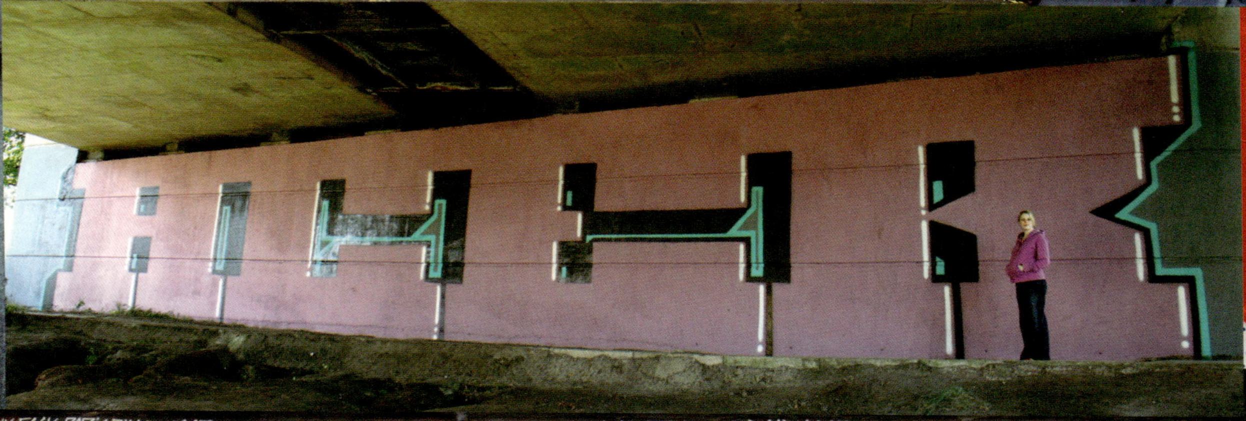
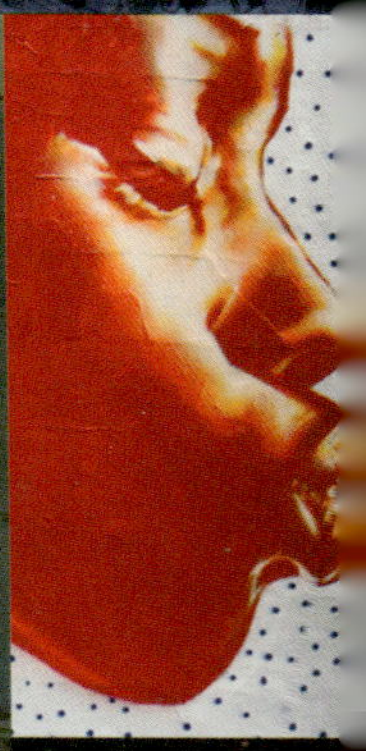
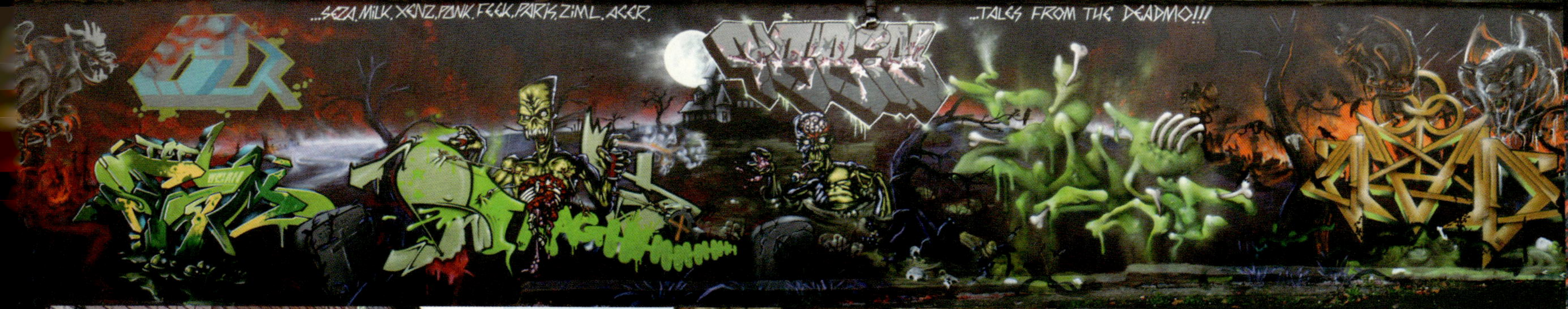
...SEZA.MILK.XENZ.PONK.FECK.PARIS.ZIML.ACER.
...TALES FROM THE DEADMO!!!
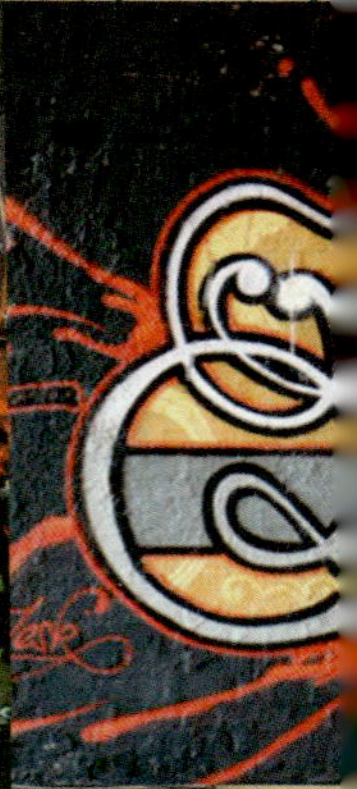
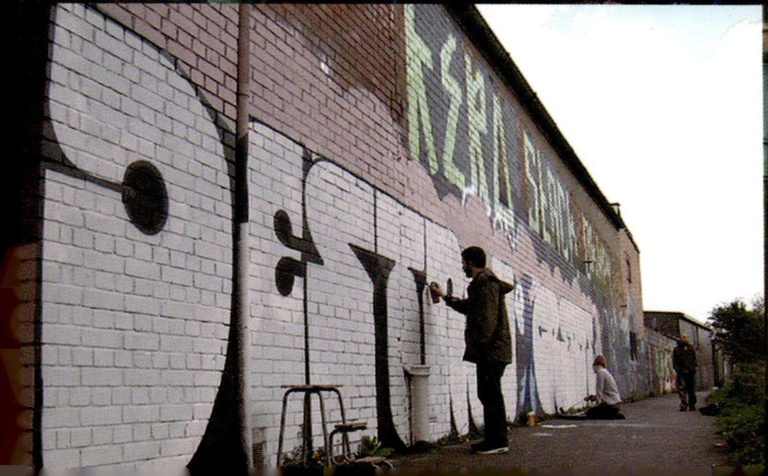
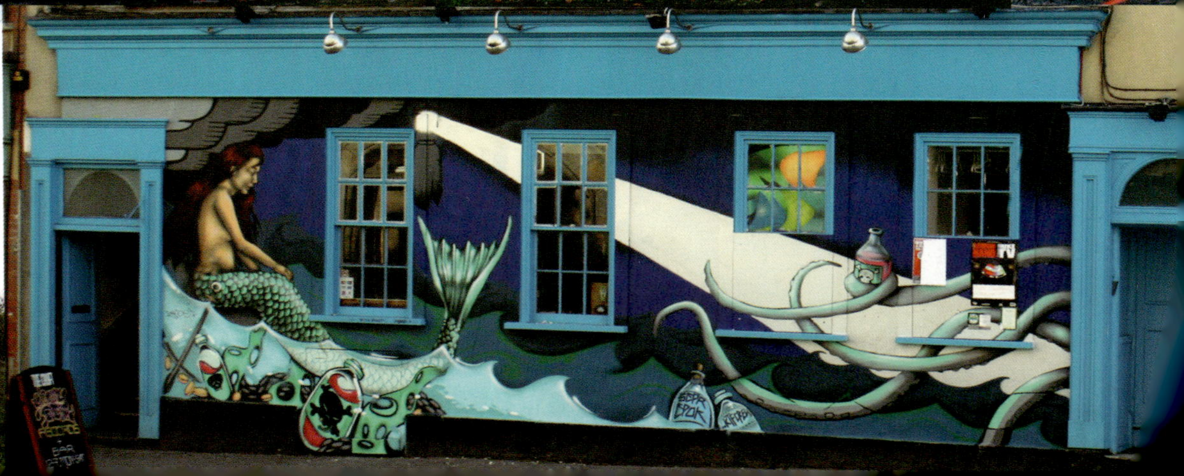

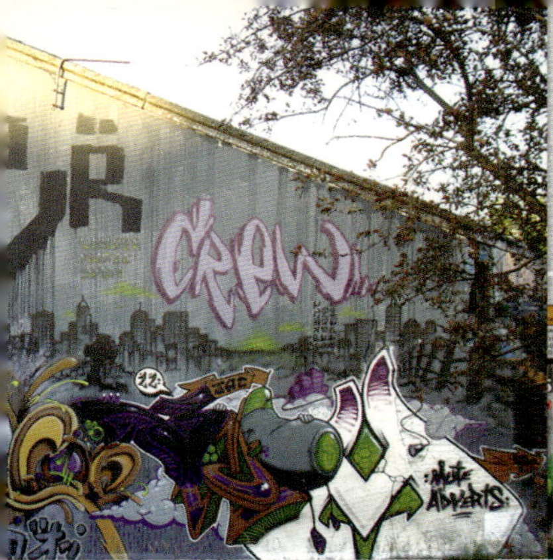
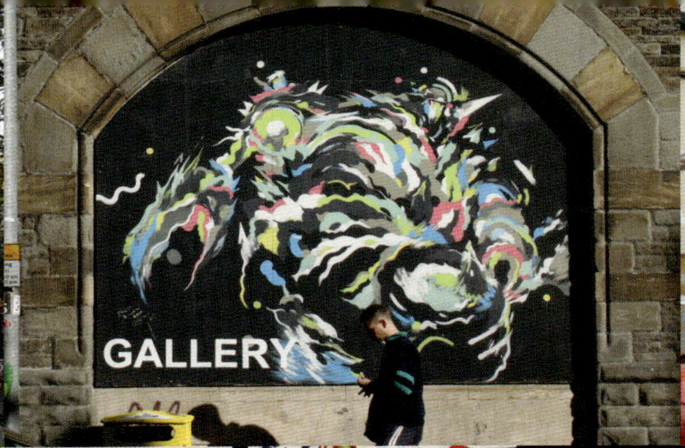
GALLERY
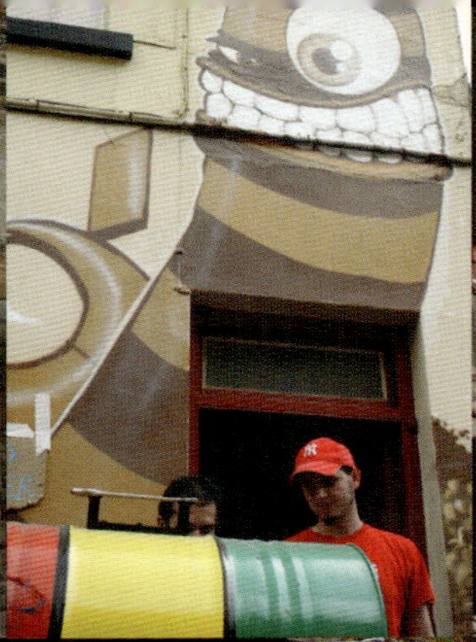
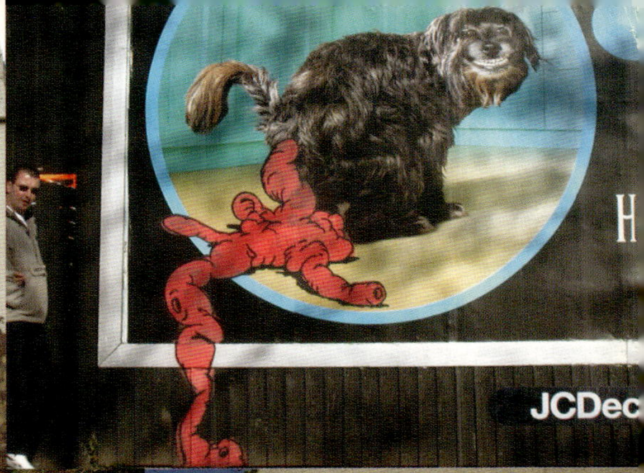
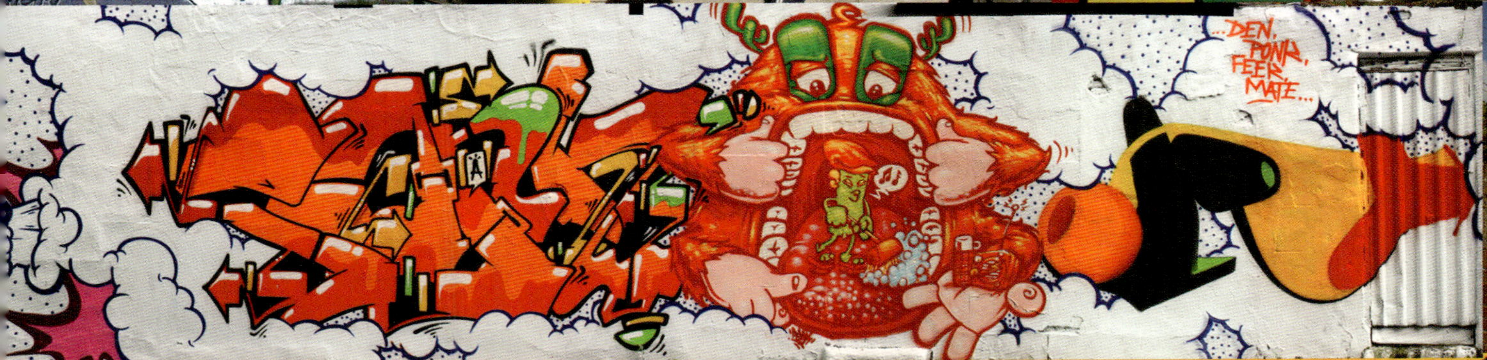
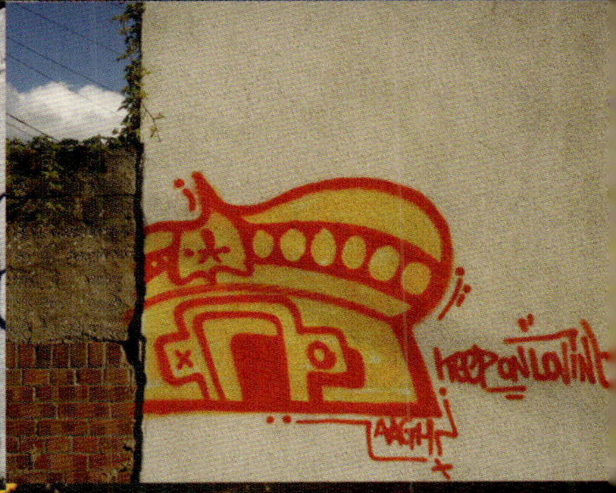
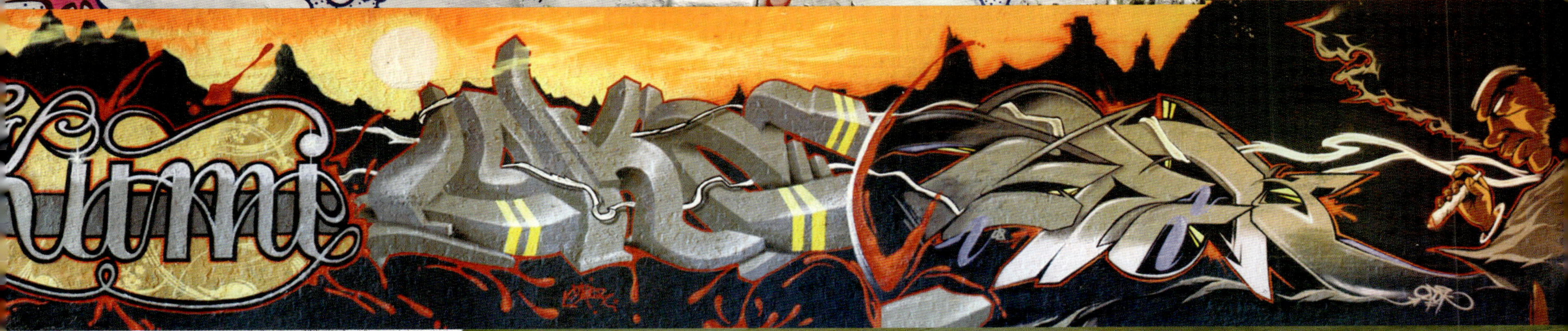
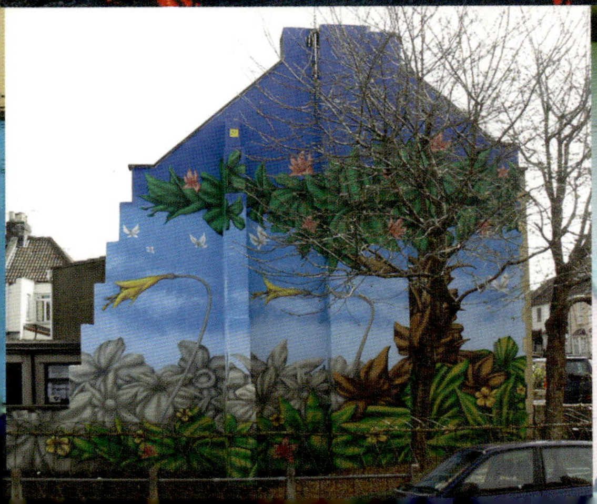
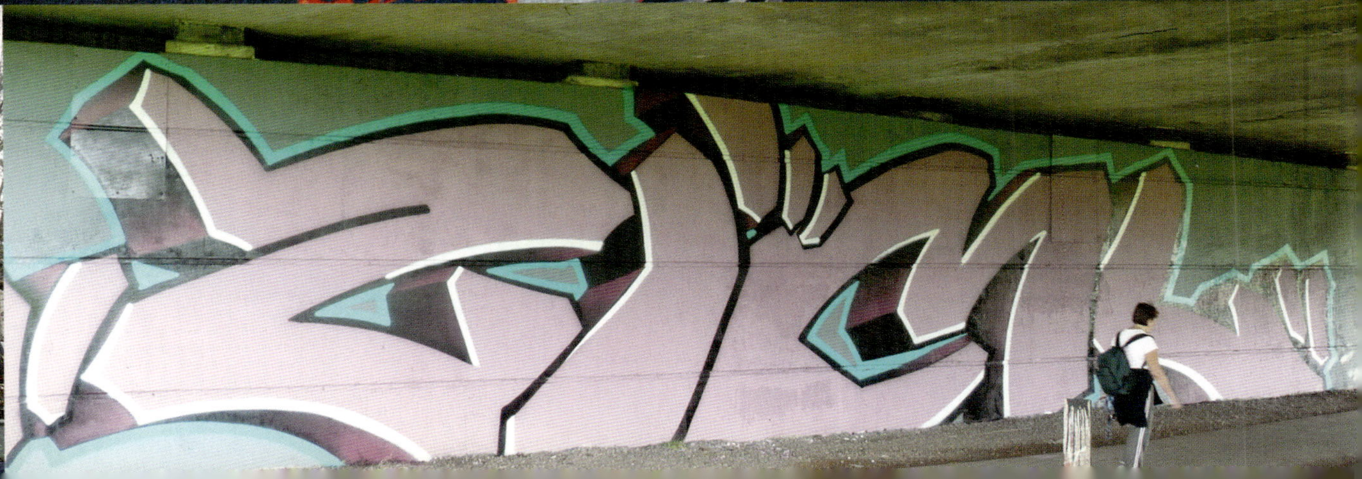

For Daniela, for helping me to believe in myself enough to do this. And for Joe - aka Jinx - if this doesn't get you painting again, nothing will.

In memory of Toby 'Jaffa' Pascoe
and Terry Brace

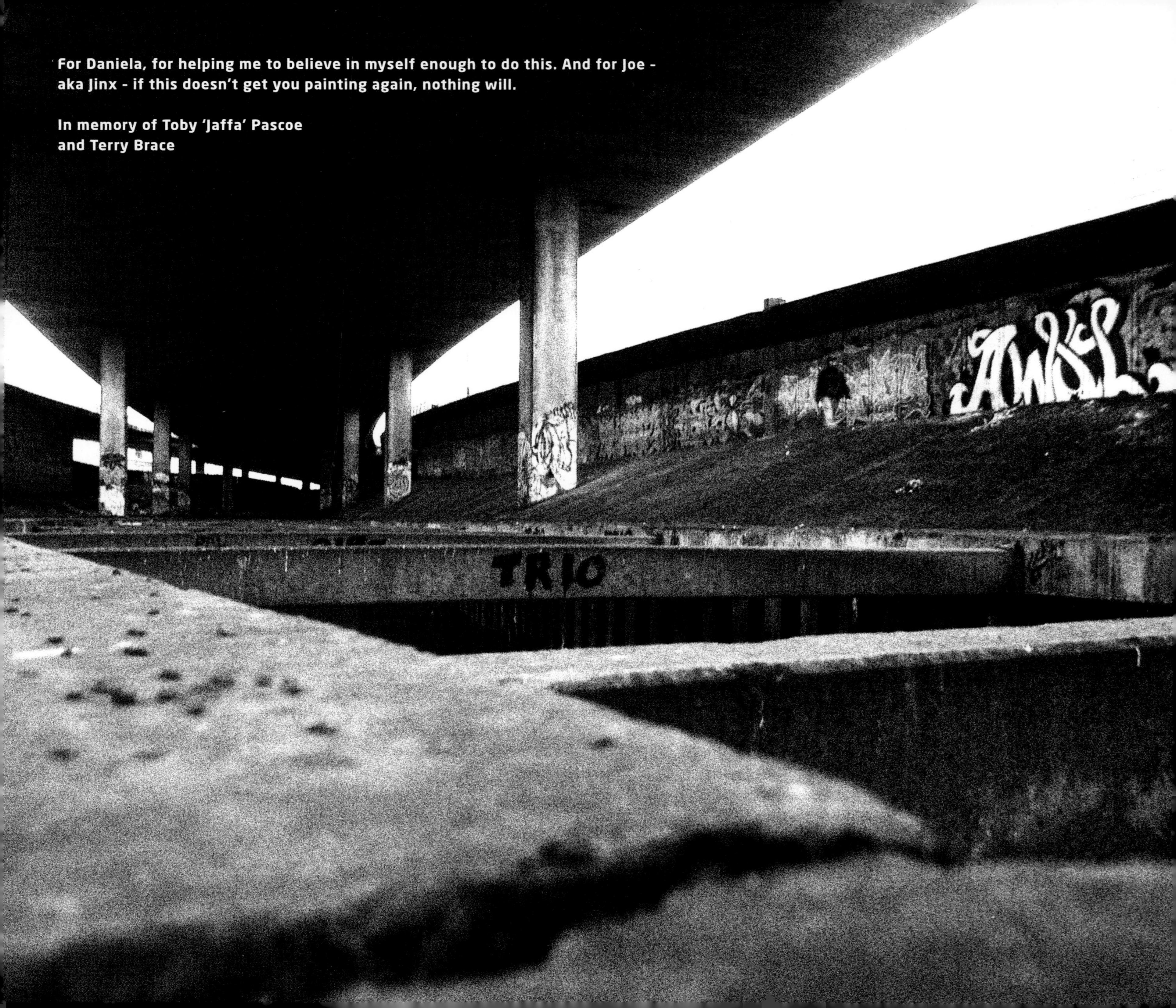

CHILDREN OF THE CAN

...25 YEARS OF BRISTOL GRAFFITI...

BY FELIX 'FLX' BRAUN

Published 2008 by Tangent Books

Tangent Towers
5.16, Paintworks
Bristol BS4 3EH

T: 0117 972 0645
www.tangentbooks.co.uk

Children of the Can: 25 Years of Bristol Graffiti
by Felix Braun (ISBN 9781906477073)

Editor: Steve Wright

Design: Cheba and Felix Braun, Cover Graphics by Feek, Paris and Soker

Publisher: Richard Jones

Production: Nick Law, Nicky Johns

Print management: Jon Lewis, Essential Print Management

Packaging: Faragher Jones www.faragherjones.com

Photography:

P1: Gina Lundy; P2-3 various; P4: Paul Whitfield ; P9: Sarah Connolly; P10: Map by Cheba, characters by Cheo; P11: Felix Braun; P12-13: Felix Braun; P15-25: All pictures in the 3D chapter provided by Robert (3D) Del Naja, except Law P17: Frank Drake, It's No Great Crime P17: Beezer; P26-31: All pictures for the Z-Boys chapter provided by Ian Dark, except: P26, top left: Beezer, P28, top right: Julian Monaghan; P36-43: All pictures provided by Nick Walker; P44-45: All pictures provided by Felix Braun; P46: Main picture Scarce, others John Nation; P48: Top: Felix Braun, bottom: John Nation; P50: John Nation; P51: Pictures provided by Inkie, except Barton Hill images provided by John Nation; P52: Top: Lokey, middle: John Nation, bottom: Felix Braun; P55: Sarah Connolly; P57: Deed; P58: Top left and bottom left: Deed; top right: Deed, middle right: Teao; P59: Deed; P62: Main picture: Wayne 'Chu' Edwards, others: John Nation; P63: John Nation; P64-70: John Nation; P72: All provided by John Nation except P72 top right: Turo; P74: John Nation; P75: John Nation except top left: Scarce; P76-77: Scarce; P78-81: Sarah Connolly; P82-3: Scarce and John Nation; P84-85: Turo; P86-87: All Turo except P96 main pic by Scarce; P88: Turo; P89-93: Teao; P94-97: All Sorse except P94 top left: Scarce; P98-105: Jody except P102: John Nation; P106: John Nation; P107: Lokey and Kato; P108-117: Kato, except p114 bottom left: Turo; P118: right: Telbert James P118-P124: Soker; P125: right: Telbert James; P125-131: Lokey; P130: bottom right Alice Lowndes; P132: top left: S.Chapple, bottom left: L.Palmer, right: Turo; P133: Lokey and Kato; P134: Jeff Row and Lokey P135: Jeff Row and Iyers; P136: Top SoF, bottom: Soker; P137; All SoF Except bottom left: Turo; P138: Top: SoF; bottom: Soker; P139: top: Soker; bottom: Luke Palmer; P140-141: SoF; P142-145: All SoF except P145 top: Soker; P146-152: Rowdy except P147 top left: Soker; P150 bottom right: Steve Chapple, left: Paul Whitfield; P151: right: Craig Body English ; P153-158: Shimz except P157 top: Scarce; P159-164: Dicy; P165-171: Paris, except P165: Karen Dews P166: Lokey; P172-177: Acer; P179-184: Feek; P185-191: Seza; P192-193: China Mike; P196-197: Top and middle: Lokey; bottom: Luke Palmer; P199: Fantastic Super Heroes; P200-202: All Awkward except P201 main pic: Karen Dews; P203-208: Will Barras; P209: bottom left: Telbert James; P209-214: Mr Jago except P209 top left: Karen Dews, bottom left: Telbert James; top right: Lokey, P210 top right: Karen Dews; P215: top left and right top and bottom: Luke Palmer, bottom right: Karen Dews; P216-220: Xenz except P219 main image: Luke Palmer; P221: Main image: Eko; left: Karen Dews; P222: Sarah Connolly; P223: Top: Lokey, bottom: Karen Dews; P224: Karen Dews; P225: Top left: Eko; top right: Turo; bottom: Karen Dews; P226-227: Eko; P228: Ziml; P229: Iyers; P230-233 Ziml; P234-237: Jeff Row; P238: Dr. Dog; P239: left: Karen Dews, right: Dr. Dog; P240: Dr. Dog; P241-246: Sarah Connolly except P244 top left: Iyers, P245 bottom left: Iyers; P247-252: Ponk, P253-255: Haka; P256: left: Demz; right Paul Whitfield; P257: Telbert James; P258: Top: Demz, middle: A Milsom, bottom: Little Pete, P259: Demz; P260: Little Pete; P261-263: Space; P264-265: Cheba; P266-267 cargo image by Ben Mason, stokes croft image Alice Lowndes: Mudwig; P268-271: TNP; P272-274: SEPR; P275: Little Pete; P276: Top left: Paul Whitfield, top right: JAC, bottom: A Milsom; P277: JAC; P278: Top left: Paul Whitfield, top right: JAC; P279: JAC; P280-281: KTF; P282-283: What Collective, Laura Thorne; P284-285: Filthy Luker, Dan Prior, Ross James; P286: Milk except top middle: Karen Dews; bottom right Jeff Row; P287: Dan

Thanks to: All the city's graffiti writers and documenters for their time, energy and passion for the art form and without whom you would now be looking at blank pages, which is about as inspiring as staring at a blank, grey wall; Steve Faragher and all at Faragher Jones

Limited first edition of 3,000 copies printed in Italy by G. Canale & C S.p.A

Font: Neo Sans Family.

CONTENTS

1983-1987 - LAYING THE FOUNDATIONS

1987-1998 - THE VIEW FROM THE HILL

1998-2009 - THE RENAISSANCE

Opposite page: Soker and Cheo in the shadow of the old Robinson Building, Bedminster, 2008

FOREWORD

Ever since what we understand as 'graffiti art' arrived from the USA in books, films and music videos in the early 1980s, Bristol has consistently been a vibrant and fertile breeding ground for graffiti writers and street artists of every persuasion. The city's reputation as a hotbed for creativity has long been international (thanks in no small part to its music scene) and has both spawned and attracted artists, who together have made this one of the most colourful cities in the UK. Over the last 25 years, the art form has mutated and matured with its practitioners, and these days it is not uncommon to meet graffiti artists (and graffiti-influenced artists, more of whom later) who make a reasonable living from their art. A few Bristol graffiti artists are doing extremely well for themselves - one of them is arguably the best known artist of his generation, graffiti or otherwise.

This, then, is the story of Bristol's graffiti as told by those who know it best - the artists - and charts its development from the early 1980s through to the present day. Alongside colour photos of their pieces, I have offered them a platform to talk about their work, their lives, what motivates them, and how they feel about Bristol. I have found some to be bemused and aggravated by the city (or, more specifically, those who govern and police it), while others are in love with the place, and infatuated with its lively scene. Some paint purely and simply for the buzz of it, some because they feel a strange compulsion to do so, and others because it has become a huge part of who they are and is central to their daily lives. It can be a hobby, a job, a mission to destroy, or an expression of the primal need to create.

Graffiti in the 21st century has splintered into various factions, each reacting to what has gone before, re-inventing and re-naming itself (or having the media do it for us) and all too often hating on itself. This, however, does not detract from the fact that all of its various facets essentially amount to the same thing - as a means of commenting on the space we live in, graffiti remains largely unchanged in its motivation and purpose.

There are, however, essentially two entirely separate defining components to modern day graffiti, and, while they often overlap, they also exist totally independently from one another. Firstly there is the process, which can include anything from putting up a tag or painting a full-colour piece, to using a stencil, a sticker, or even the sharp edge of a stone to make your mark on society. Secondly there is the aesthetic: the angles, the quality of line, the juxtapositions of forms and colours - all derived from graffiti's formative expressions in New York and Philadelphia in the 1970s and 1980s. These days, the latter is not exclusively confined to walls, or even public space in general, and some of the artists featured in this book acknowledge the aesthetic and the practice as having been merely their starting point, or their inspiration.

In fact, as graffiti has become the art movement du jour, fetching unprecedented prices on the international art market, hardcore and underground graffiti writers have become increasingly polarised from the more acceptable (read 'marketable') face of graffiti, which has been conveniently re-labelled 'street art' to make it more digestible. However, although a character, logo, or stencil is easier for the general public to comprehend, it is essentially performing the same role.

That said, in Bristol - where the unstoppable march of 'redevelopment' is steamrollering the city's intrinsic character and turning it into a giant mall surrounded by ugly, unaffordable Lego apartment blocks - perhaps raw, untamed tagging and bombing are the sanest, most honest of all responses to the city. Few (if any) of the artists featured in this book would question the importance of the young bombers who continue to mark their territory on concrete, brick, steel and glass.

The book you hold in your hands, therefore, features the work and words of graffiti artists and writers both young and old, who paint both illegally and legally, and ultimately have a lot more in common with one another than might initially be apparent. It also features the work of artists who defy (and willfully avoid) categorisation, but who nonetheless are inspired by, or started out, painting graffiti. As artists we are all, ultimately, carving out our own paths and satisfying the urge to create a new identity for ourselves through our art. An identity, crucially, which is not prescribed or manufactured by any third party. I paint therefore I am.

Felix Braun, Bristol, 2008

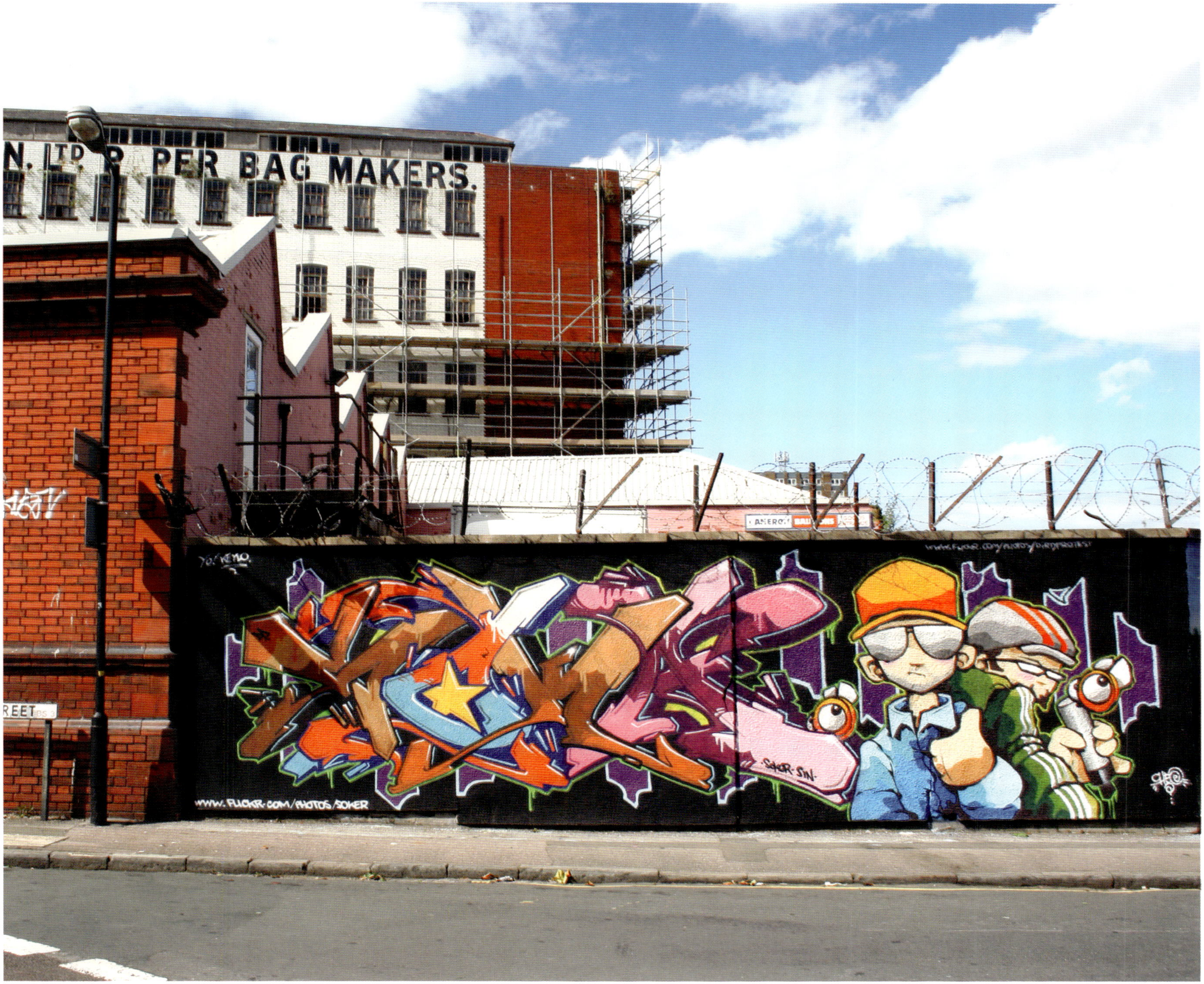
PER BAG MAKERS.
WWW.FLICKR.COM/PHOTOS/SOKER

KEY

1) Barton Hill Youth Club
2) M32 hall of fame
3) Bedminster Skate Park
4) Brislington warehouse
5) Westmoreland House
6) Bath Road Esso
7) Millionaire's
8) Riverside Park HOF

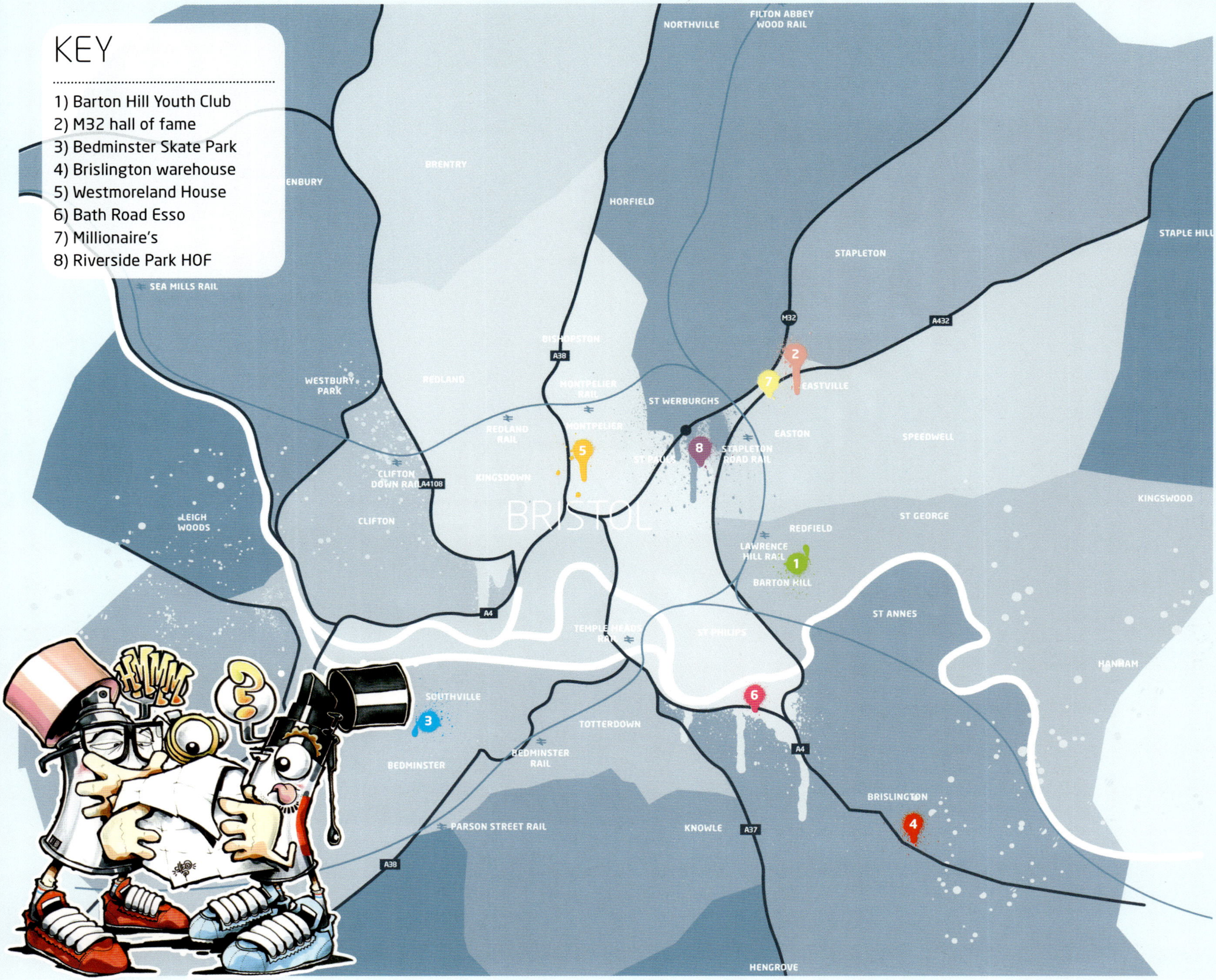

INTRODUCTION

"Here's a little story that must be told..."*

July 1983: My friends and me sit goggle-eyed in the ancient wooden seats of the Arts Centre Cinema on King Square in Bristol, as Charlie Ahearn's film *Wild Style* plays to a noisy, half-full auditorium. We react loudly with the rest of the young audience at the sight of the Rocksteady Crew B-boying (or break-dancing) in a circle while the Cold Crush Brothers speak the new rap language over a new kind of beat:

My goal is the same
I aim for fame
I don't pop no game
I don't have no chain. **

For us, though, it is the opening scene of Lee Quinones' character, Zoro, breaking into the yards to paint the side of a subway train that really mesmerises. None of us dares to blink as Zoro slides down a rope into the darkness, looking like an urban ninja on a mission of creative destruction. The painted letters on the wall behind him come to life, and introduce the film's animated title sequence; the words 'Wild Style' writhe and contort in time with the off-key funky soundtrack, growing ever more complex and eventually exploding. I sit gob-smacked, unable to wipe the demented grin off my face and savouring every moment. We are hungry teenagers, always hunting for the next thing – and this is exactly what we need.

On our way out of the auditorium there is a collective moment of recognition: the corridor outside has been painted in a style similar to that in the film by artists who have signed their work 3D and The Z-Boys. This is it, we think: and it's already here! The urge to emulate, to be involved, is instant, intoxicating and powerful. My friends, my brother and me talk about nothing else for months; we doodle incessantly in school, trying to recreate styles that are gradually fading from the backs of our retinas. The addiction has taken hold and it feels incredible. In our hearts and minds we are already graffiti artists. Or, more correctly, 'writers', because that's what it's all about: writing your name, letting the world know that you exist: I write therefore I am.

Other elements of this new creative subculture had arrived not long before, albeit in a somewhat watered-down form. Herbie Hancock's *Rockit* and Malcolm McLaren's *Buffalo Gals* both featured embryonic scratching, the latter accompanied by a promo video featuring legendary style master Dondi painting the song's title in yellow and orange letters, and outlining them in black with seemingly effortless hand movements. We wore out the pause buttons on suitcase-sized VCRs waiting to catch these and other early gems on tape.

Most important to us, though, was the arrival of Henry Chalfant and Martha Cooper's book *Subway Art* in 1984. The graffiti in *Wild Style*, memorable as it was, had been hard to grab hold of – moving, hidden in the shadows, cut short by an edit to another scene. *Subway Art*, by contrast, distilled the ephemeral and turned it into something timeless, freezing forever the days when subway trains used to glide across New York City, adorned with full-colour, intricate ornamentation, straight from the minds and hands of inner-city kids.

We would sit examining the front and back covers for hours on end, getting a heavy fix of what we craved before even opening it. The inside was almost too much – the giant, fold-out photos of whole

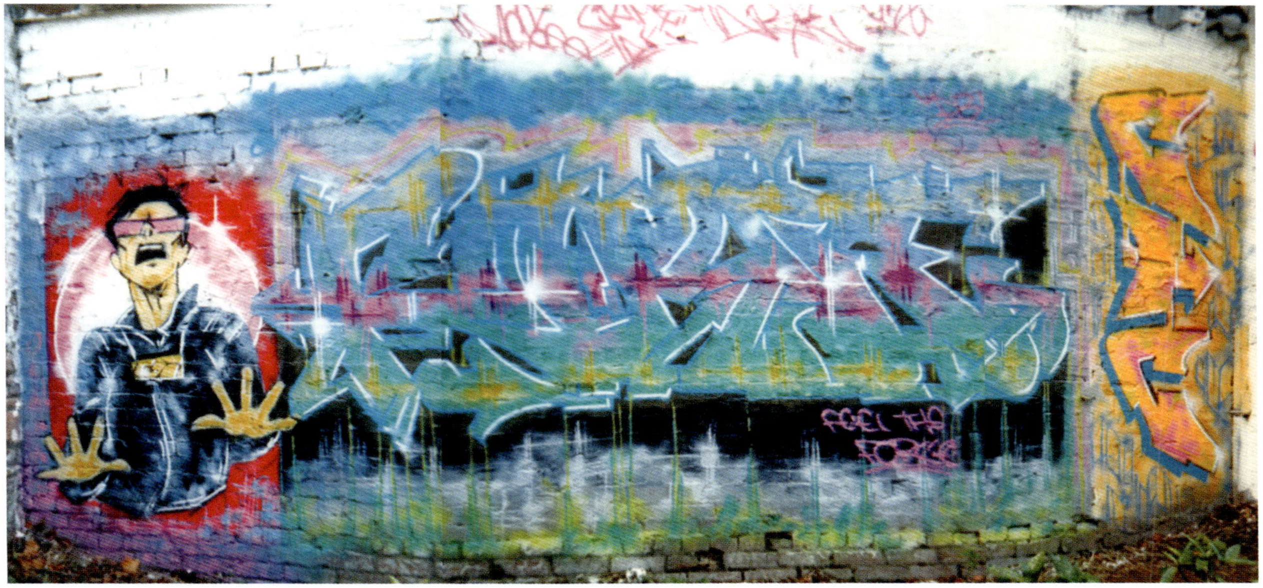

Above: 'Force CIC' by Crime Inc. Character: FLX, letters: Inkie, 1986

Opposite Page: Map by Cheba, characters by Cheo

Left: 'Crime Inc 3', 1986

Right: The Crime Inc Crew: Jinx, Nick Walker, FLX, Inkie

Opposite Page: 'Crime Wild Style' Filton College Commission, 1986

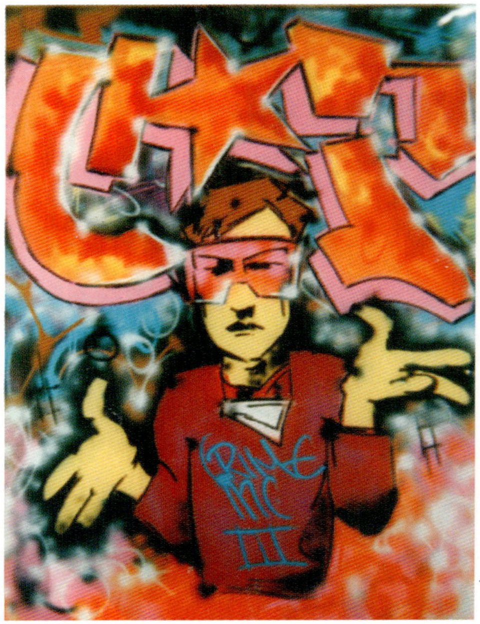

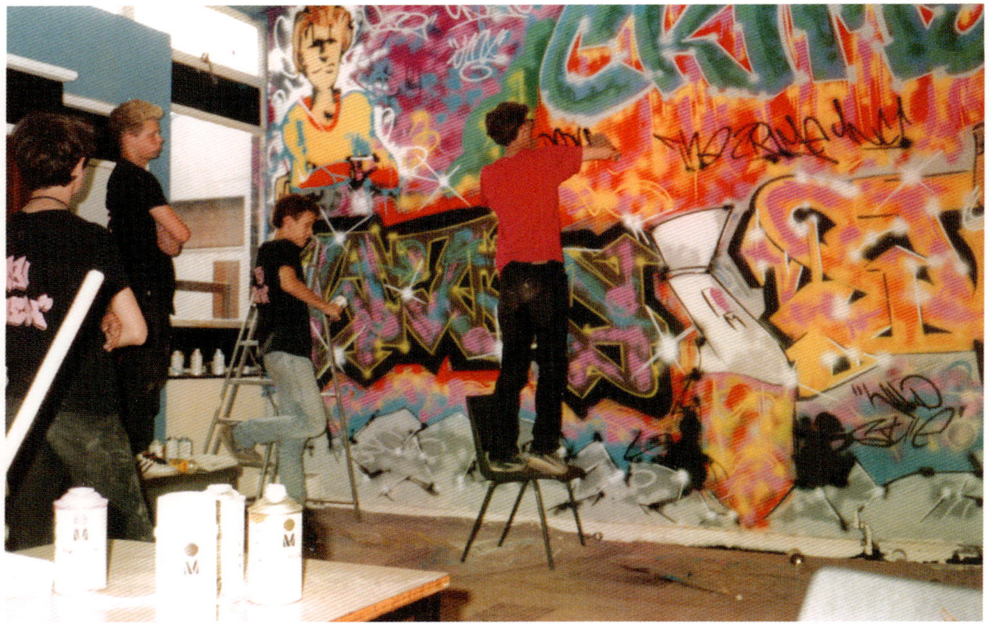

subway cars painted from top to bottom were to become iconic images in their own right. As for the artists photographed - Skeme reclining on the third rail; Case, the one-armed master of the computer rock style, looking sagely up at a passing train - these images assured them legendary status. Pop and film stars just weren't doing it for us anymore - compared to these guys they were straight-up frauds. Even punk seemed fake compared to what we were now immersed in. Graffiti writers were real living heroes and teenagers like us. They didn't come any cooler than this.

Our first crew was born soon after and initially, I wasn't even a member. I had been designing for months, lying on my front on the floor practising full-colour outlines, content in my own imaginary world, when one afternoon I smelt a vaguely familiar scent coming from the back yard, accompanied by laughter and the occasional 'psh-pshhhht' sound. I looked out the back window and saw my brother and his friend Tom painting an old wooden board with spray paint. They had painted the letters ID (which, they told me, stood for Inkie and Drips) in yellow and orange with a black outline, complete with shadow, fade, white highlights and everything. I tried to hide how impressed I was.

We painted our first proper illegal piece soon after, in broad daylight. It didn't even occur to us at the time that we might get arrested. We just figured that, since there was already a piece on the same wall (3D's incredible 'Phase 2', complete with a B-boy character in a freeze), it would be fine to paint something next to it. The fact that we had the balls to put up our first, completely wack effort next to one of 3D's extremely accomplished pieces says a lot about how young and naïve we were. I remember a few curtains twitching across the street, but no police appeared, so we walked away unfazed, feeling bigger, stronger and a whole lot cooler. We named the crew Crime Inc (a name borrowed from a TV documentary about the Mafia) and together Inky, Jinx (aka Drips) and FLX started hitting the city's walls on a regular basis, tagging our names whenever we went out and painting full-colour pieces every weekend. Our activities soon caught the attention of a fellow Bristol writer by the name of Nick Walker (at that time using the tag Wizardo) who was painting solo on the other side of town, and Crime Inc soon inducted its fourth member over bottles of Holsten Pils and big spliffs of squidgy black.

Racking (stealing) paint, planning nocturnal missions, enlisting lookouts, getting drunk for Dutch courage, guessing paint colours under yellow streetlights in the dead of night; all were a part of our everyday existence. Crime Inc's exploits soon became common knowledge amongst our peers and came to define us as a group. We were graffiti writers - audacious,

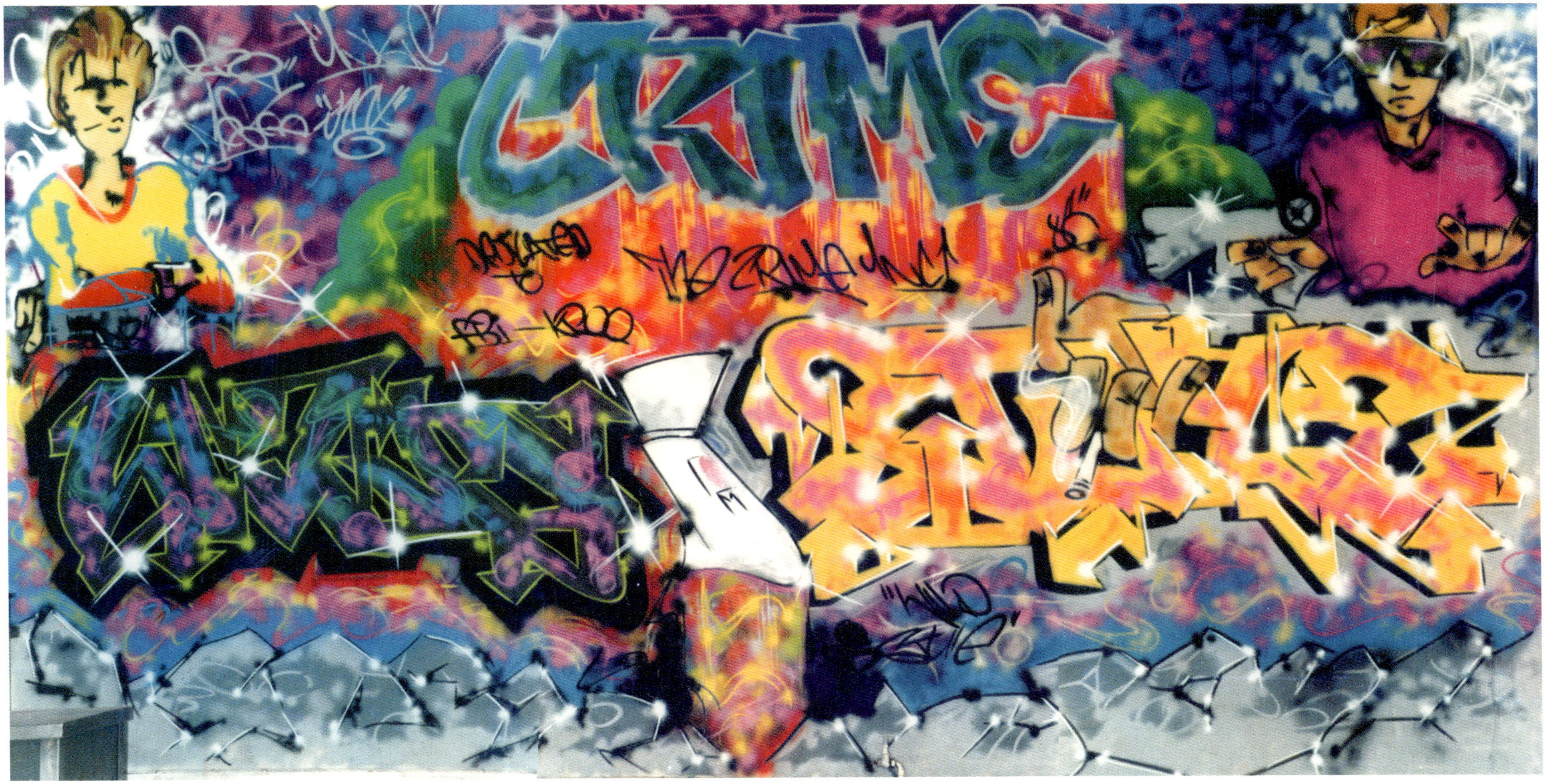

inventive, fearless teenagers – just like our heroes from New York. Or so we thought.

Meanwhile, 3D and the Z-Boys had turned legit under threat of imprisonment, having been arrested twice, before we had even started; an anonymous early style-writer whose tag was Tarzan painted two phenomenal pieces and then seemed to vanish. The Aerosoul Idiots only painted a handful of pieces that we were aware of, as did Rikki D. In short, we had little competition. That was all about to change.

New names were going up, and pieces started appearing across Bristol. The Dynamic 2 (aka Zion and Healer, also the MCs with local sound system UD4) were painting bold, basic pieces around Montpelier; Fade & Jaffa, Style and TPA (Bandito and DMK) were active in and around the neighbourhoods of St Paul's and St Andrew's; the TCP crew were finding their feet in Kingswood, on the city's eastern edge.

By now, the subculture had a name: hip hop. At parties hosted by the likes of the Wild Bunch, 2 Bad, UD4, FBI and City Rockers, Bristol was embracing hip hop with open arms, and for many kids it was the first time they had partied side by side with people of a different skin colour. But it didn't seem like a big deal: it was what it was. We were so wrapped up in being teenagers and writing graffiti that the significance of what was happening – the building of a UK branch of a new, global, multi-cultural subculture – went straight over our heads. We just carried on painting, partying and having the time of our lives.

FB

***Double Trouble:** Stoop Rap, from Charlie Ahearn's film Wild Style, 1982, First Run Features

****Cold Crush Brothers:** Cold Crush Brothers At The Dixie, from Charlie Ahearn's film Wild Style, 1982, First Run Features

1983-87:
Laying The Foundations

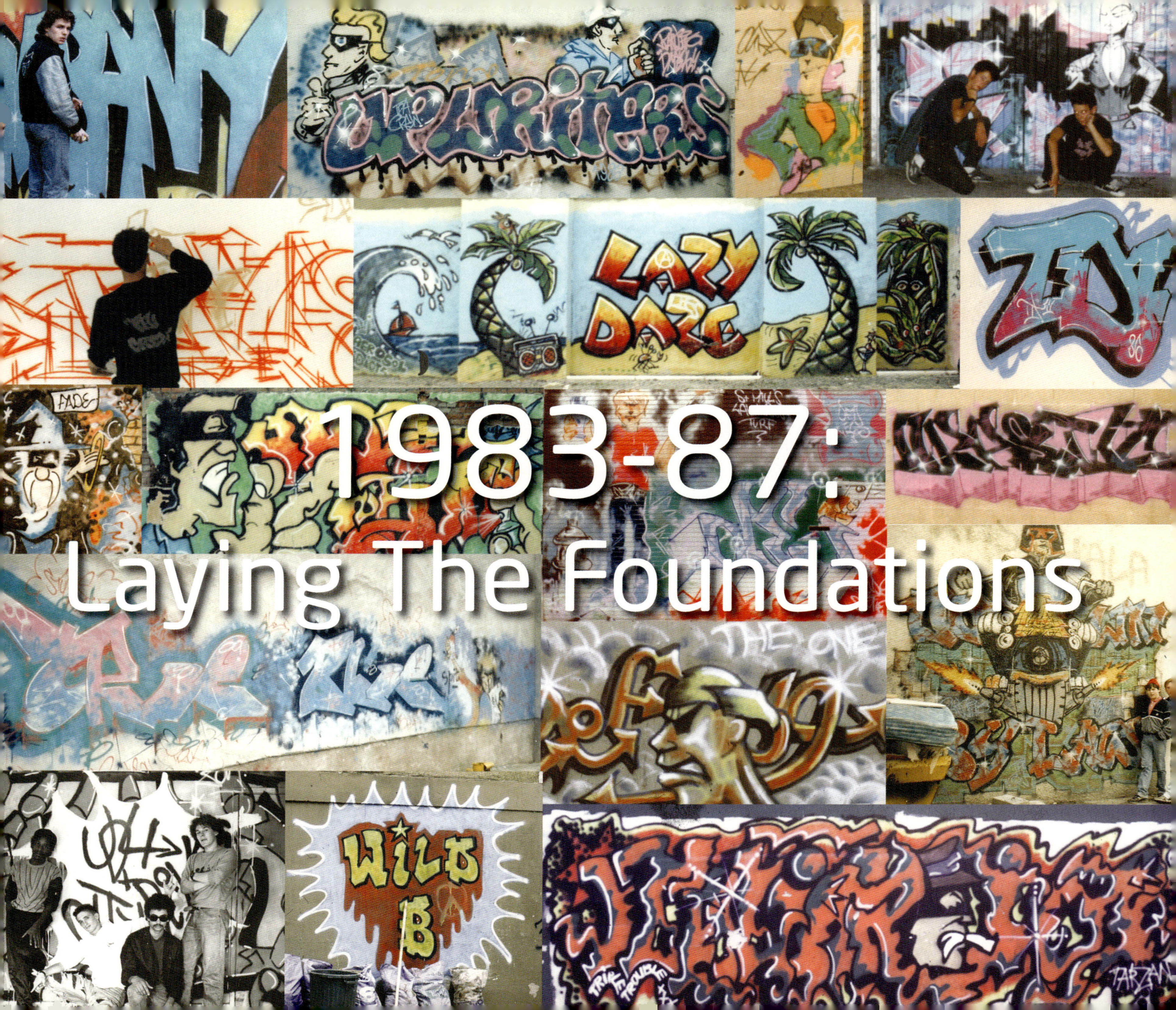

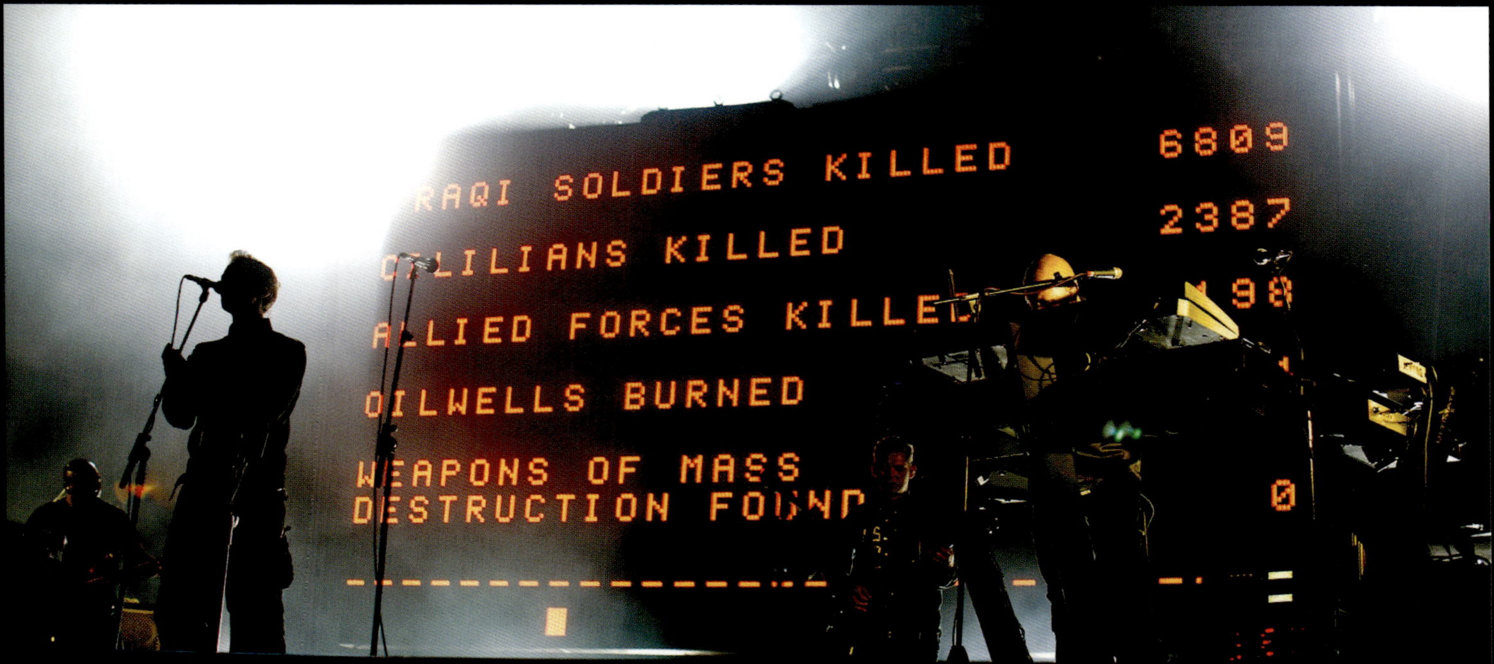

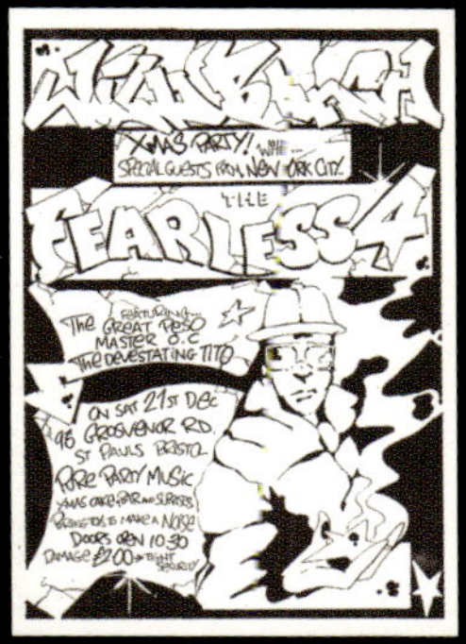

Above: Wild Bunch Xmas party flyer. Old school New York legends Fearless 4 brought The Bronx to Bristol. Character on flyer based on DJ Mushroom (see photograph bottom left). Before 1985

Left: 3D on stage in front of the 'graphic information transmitter' with Massive Attack, 2004. 3D continues to define the band's visual identity, through sleeve design and on-stage 'LED graffiti,' in collaboration with United Visual Artists

Bottom left: Life imitating art. 3D and DJ Mushroom recreate two of 3D's painted characters before 1985

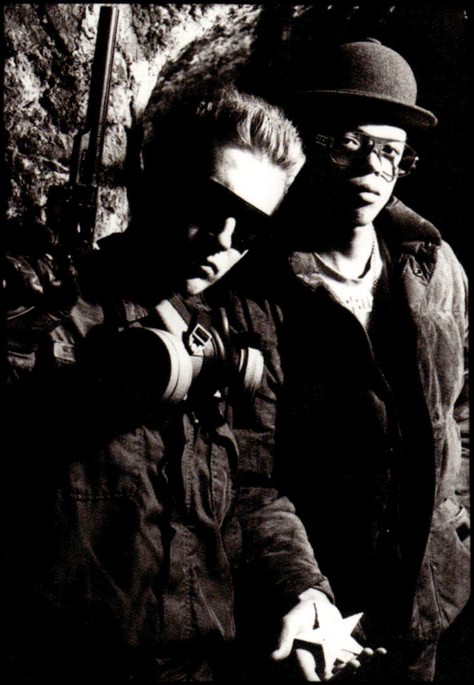

3D

• **"My whole thing was that I liked the idea of being the 'lone wolf', wandering out with the rain sizzling off his shadow.** As a kid I was obsessed with comics, and I surrounded myself with images of Daredevil and Spiderman. Crouched, poised to spring off buildings in New York, in the rain and the moonlight. To me that was like fucking glamour! I loved the idea of the whole secret identity, and to me the whole graffiti thing appealed on that level."

1981:

A teenage punk and die-hard Clash fan named Robert Del Naja sees the scratchy video for the band's *This Is Radio Clash* single for the first time and something clicks. The video is a montage that includes news footage of political protests, troops in Nicaragua and armed police on rooftops juxtaposed with scenes of youths spinning on their backs and heads, and graffiti-coated New York subway trains, while the band bounce across rooftops and down streets carrying huge portable stereos. But there is another, more elusive character present in the soup of images, his eyes concealed behind a huge pair of Wayfarers, he floats around a hardware store, stuffing cans of spray paint into his windcheater, before running outside and spraying 'TV LAND' on a wall. Later he is seen pointing at a subway car going by with the message 'ART IS THE WORD' painted onto its panels in bold silver letters. The video closes with the unfurling of a huge banner with the

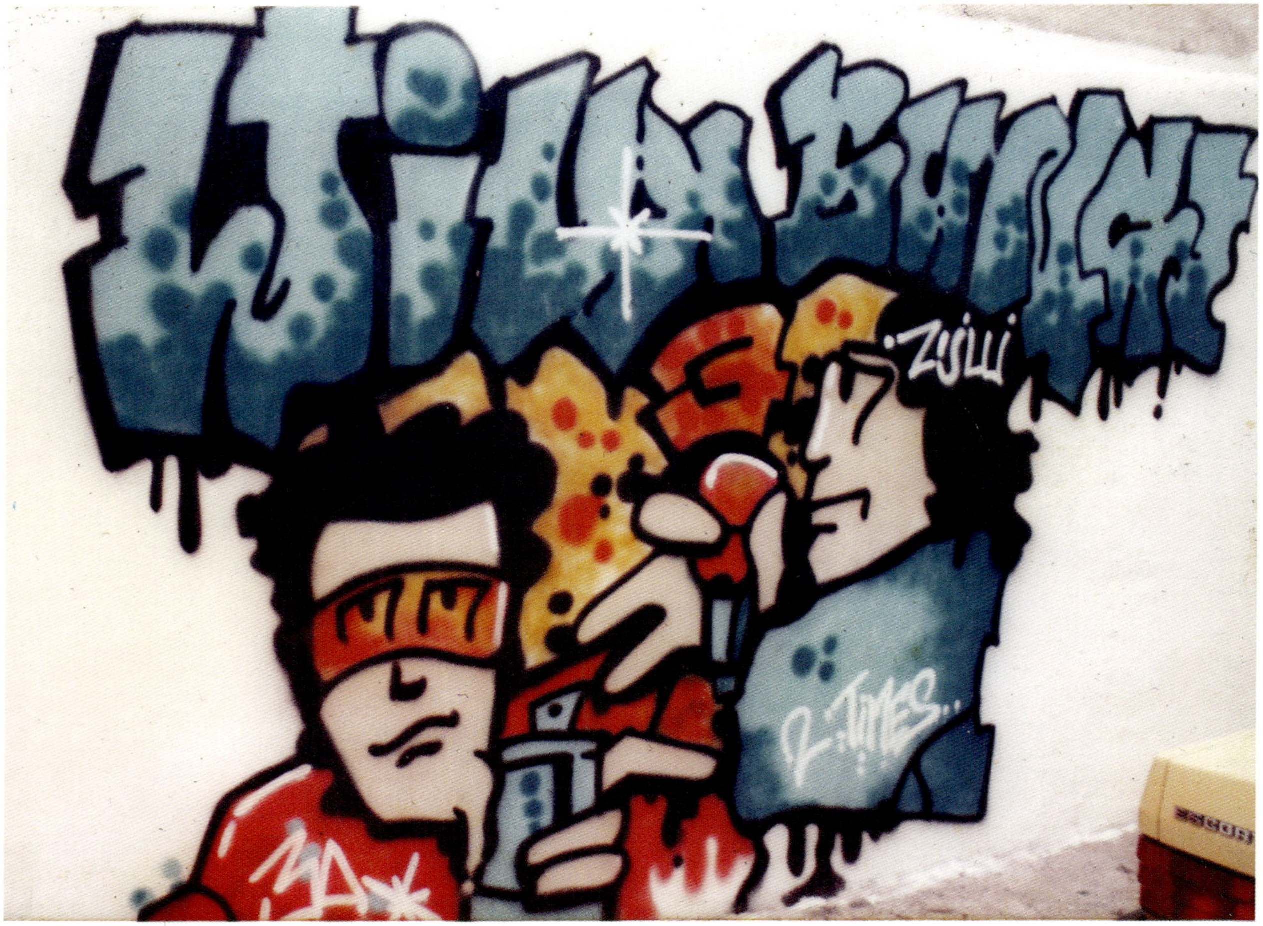

Above: 'Wild Bunch' piece, Frogmore Street, Aug1984

Opposite page. Top left: 'King' Clifton Village, September 1984

Top right: 'It's No Great Crime' B-boys get busy while 3D looks on, January 1984

Middle left: 'Tuf (State Of Art)' Thekla, Bristol. DJ Milo from The Wild Bunch, centre, in yellow, October 1984

Bottom right: '3D' Triangle, December 1984

Bottom: Original sketch for '3D' piece

band's name painted in enormous red graffiti letters as Joe Strummer shouts: "Go back to urban 'Nam!"

The character in the shades was Futura 2000, the legendary New York graffiti artist who also designed the sleeve for *This Is Radio Clash* and later the sleeve notes and lyric sheet for the band's *Combat Rock* LP. As The Clash had recognised by adopting the young music and art of the New York ghettoes, a new cultural force was coming to the fore. Robert saw the signs and they echoed his own feelings. Change was in the air.

"When punk started to lose its impact on people, when it became the norm, it didn't really have any power any more. Suddenly hip hop held the power. It was its own self-contained subculture, which was really exciting, and for people like me coming out of punk it was like 'wow, this is fucking amazing', it was another way of expressing yourself. And the graffiti thing, I guess, was the most exciting part of it, because it was using the trains to transmit messages around the city in a completely uncontrollable way. That was the thing that really struck me."

Prior to this sub-cultural shift, however, the potential of the spray can as a tool for making high-impact, quick-hit statements had already been realised by the punk movement – notably in Gee Vaucher's guerrilla art campaigns for seminal anarchist band Crass, whose spray-painted stencils appeared on the London Underground system and on billboards across the city. For young punks like Robert, stencils were simply a quick way of getting your favourite band's logo onto the back of your biker jacket, or onto a T-shirt, and were part and parcel of punk's DIY approach to music and art.

"I think the first thing I ever sprayed was 'God Is Love' – which I took off the church round the corner– on a T-shirt with a stencil, just to annoy my mum. I put a zip next to it. Then it was the stencil that came with The Clash's *Straight To Hell* single. As a kid I was a typical numbskull, whether it was knocking off school, or hanging out in squats when I had a middle class home to go to. And the usual shit, you know, sniffing glue and drinking cider in the park, and sleeping under bushes, just for the hell of it. Punk to me was a great way of expressing that teenage rebellion. I was the classic rebel without a clue."

Further visual cues from what would soon become labelled as hip hop began to seep into British youth's collective consciousness and Robert was among the first to translate punk's DIY ethos into a more colourful and stylised visual statement of discontent. The country was drowning in political unrest and its factionalised teenage tribes needed somewhere new, and perhaps less serious, to go to express themselves. "At that point, if I was down watching Bristol City we were

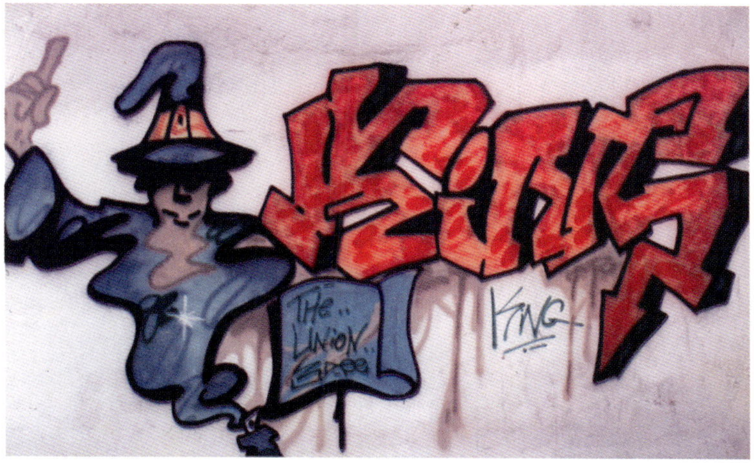
King

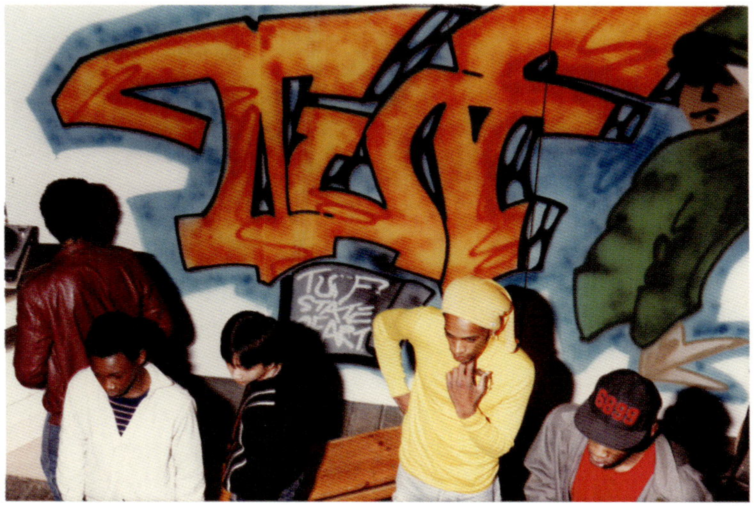

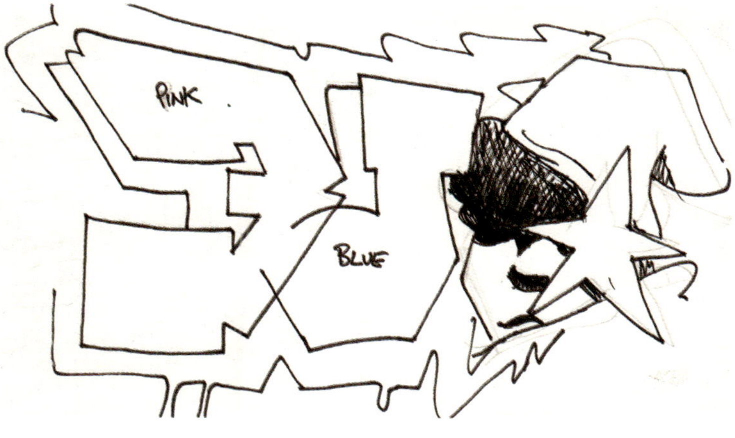
PINK
BLUE

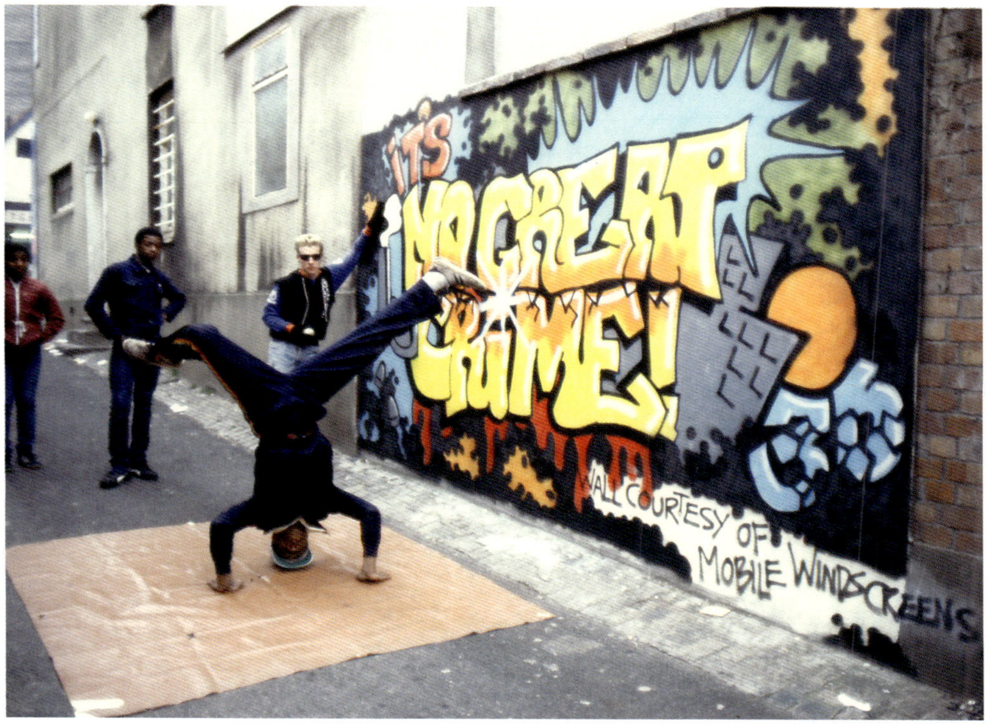
IT'S NO GREAT CRIME!
WALL COURTESY OF MOBILE WINDSCREENS

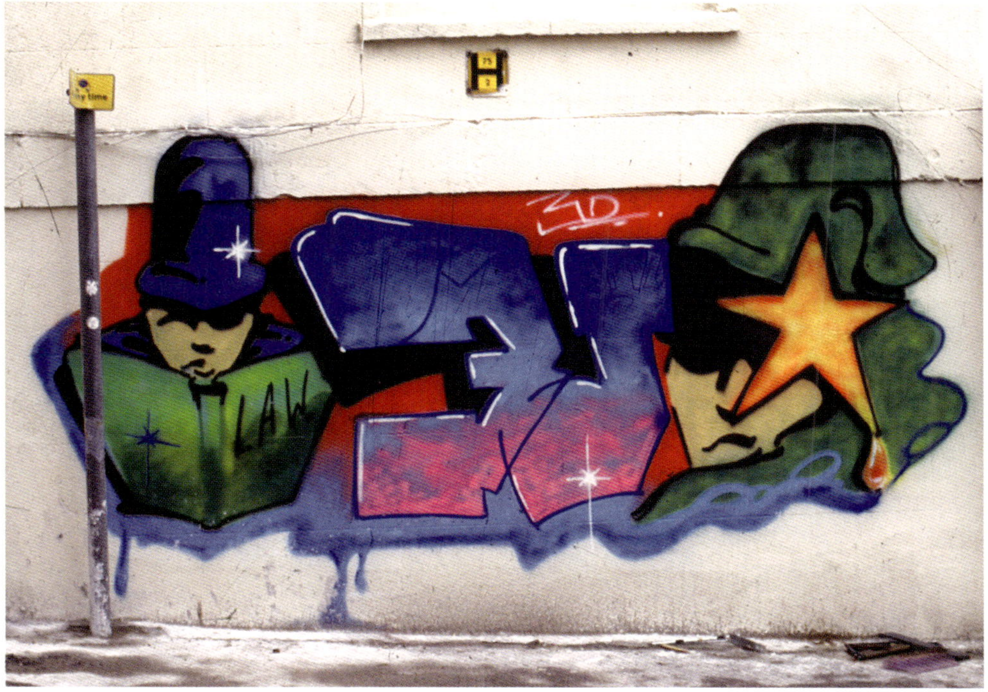
LAW
3D

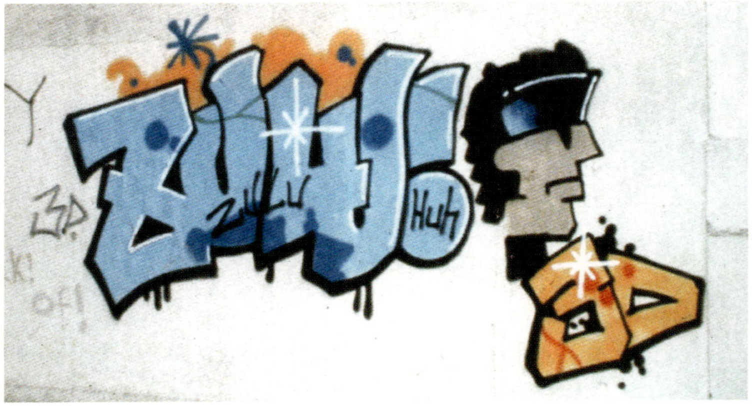

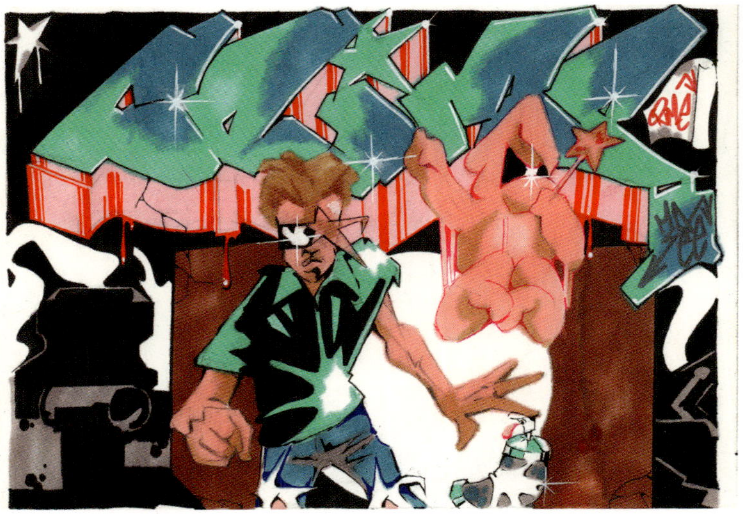

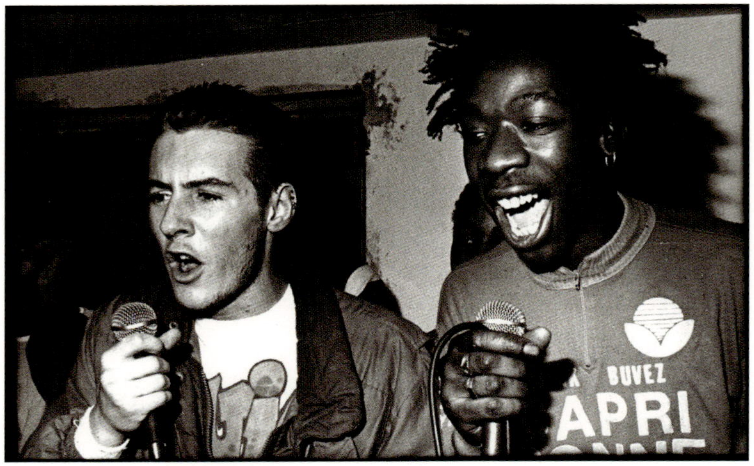

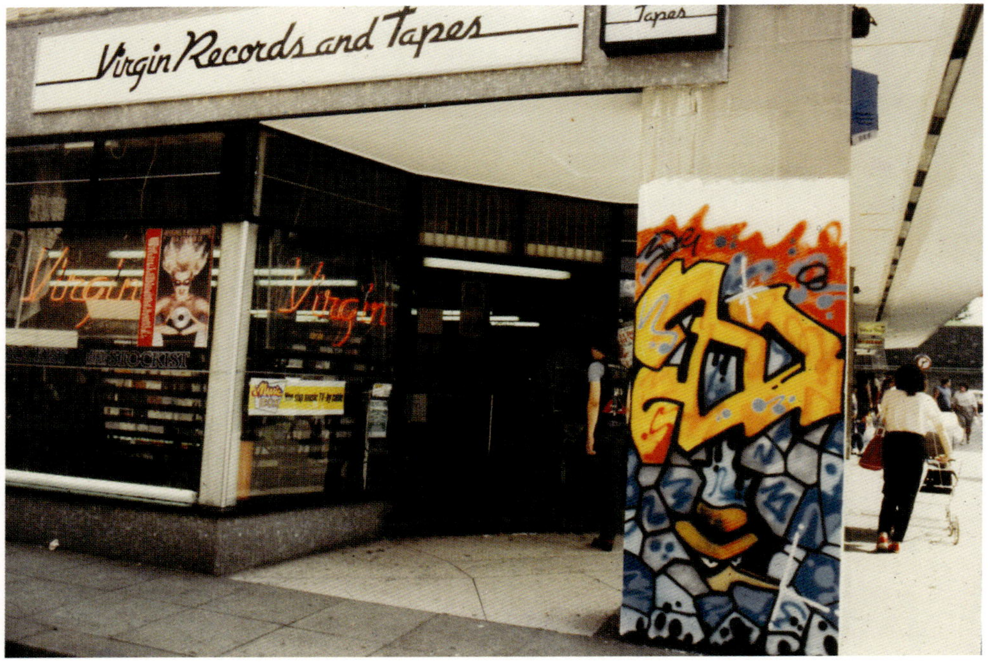

shouting 'MAGGIE-MAGGIE-MAGGIE! OUT-OUT-OUT!' every week, and on the walls everywhere was 'Support The Miners' and 'Fuck The Tories', and we were surrounded by billboards with all that on. To me graffiti was like an alternative to that, and in a strange way the hip hop thing was a type of escapism, as well as being totally anti-establishment."

June 1983

The Avon and Somerset Constabulary find themselves over-stretched by the demands of policing the city's racially mixed St. Paul's area, following the third bout of rioting there in as many years. Some see the riots as a response to the re-election of the Conservatives, others blame heavy-handed and racist policing as the cause. Robert sees the quiet streets on the other side of town as an opportunity too good to be missed.

"The first time I decided to go out and paint was in the summer of 1983. I'd planned it, but had no one with me, so I stepped out the house at two or three in the morning and just walked up Hotwell Road on my own. I set up by a big fucking wall, dropped this bag of cans, with barely a design in my pocket, and just started painting.

"I actually took a stencil with me as well, of a breakdancer, and stencilled some stars and things, and put this 'Graffiti Stylee' thing up. It was just really basic; I'd not even attempted to paint in my bedroom or on a wall before I took it onto the street. I didn't even think of the consequences of getting arrested, although I probably should have been more worried about how embarrassing it would have been if I'd fucked it up!

"My tag just came about that night, I just thought 'what should I call myself?' and so I wrote 3D – as in three separate Ds – and I

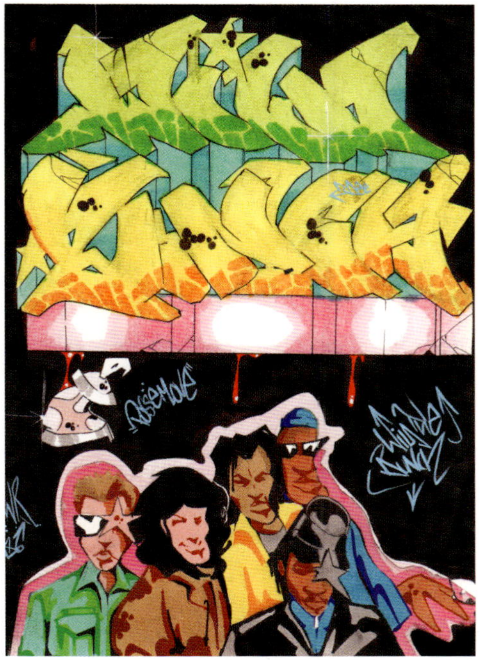

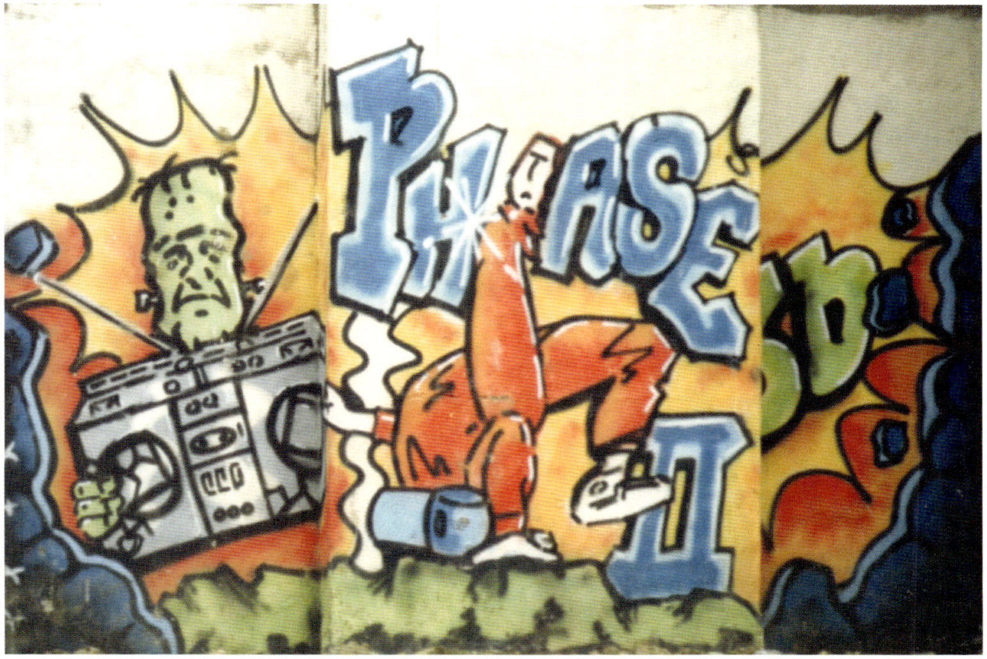

Opposite page. Top left: 'Zulu' St.Paul's, 1984

Top right: '3D' outside Virgin Records in Broadmead, 1985

Middle: 'Crime' Magic Marker on paper, 1984

Bottom: MCs in unison, 3D and Willie Wee rock a Wild Bunch party, 1984

This page. Top left: 'Wild Bunch' (left to right: 3D, Nellee, DJ Milo, Willie Wee, Daddy G) Magic Marker and Posca paint pen on paper, Special K's Café, 1985

Top right: 'Phase 2' St.Michael's Hill, 1984

thought 'oh, that'll do, 3D' it was as simple as that."

Without any real idea of what he had set in motion, Robert became 3D overnight. He had made his mark, he was up, and he knew that he had to do it again. He had caught the graffiti bug that would see him go on to create a string of increasingly accomplished and fresh full-colour illegal pieces. These, in turn, would soon establish him as a leading light in the emerging UK hip hop scene.

"Once I'd done it and saw it the next day, I was like 'that's fucking mad, it's there' and then the buzz had me, totally, and from then I spent every day working on sketches and designs. Then I got obsessed with Magic Markers, I wanted the whole set, and the Uni Poscas, the fat markers. It was just a total buzz, constantly thinking what to do next, and where to hit next.

"One of my proudest moments of illegal painting was the 3D piece opposite Swanton's Barbers, right off the Triangle (in Clifton). Not only did it turn out to be a really nice piece, but I had pink spray paint for the first time! You couldn't get it in car paint, and suddenly there was Buntlack Pink and I was like 'fucking hell, this is artists' paint'.

"That one was difficult because I kept getting interrupted and I had to keep running, chucking my cans down – I had to get my stash away from the piece, obviously – and then if it wasn't cars, which sounded like potential cops, it was people stopping and chatting to me, and I was like 'for fuck's sake' because I just wanted to finish and I could see it was getting light. Eventually there were a load of people coming out of their houses offering me drinks and watching! I was shitting myself because I didn't want them to watch in the first place plus I was worried about the Old Bill, and I had an audience. It was surreal."

Graffiti also provided 3D with an introduction to the coolest sound system, or crew, in town: The Wild Bunch, whose nights at the Dug Out Club have now become the stuff of Bristol legend.

"What I used to do was take my paint with me to the Dug Out, put it in the DJ box, and then I'd leave the club pretty much pissed, and go out and hit a site.

"The funniest one was doing the Wild Bunch piece at the bottom of Park Street, and ironically hitting what is now the wall of our club (The Tube). It was pissing with rain, and I can remember even to this day the smell of the bins, they were those black rubber ones, and I had to stand on them to get the height, and they were sinking under my weight. I had Rob Merrell helping me and it was the most miserable couple of hours he'd ever spent, I'm sure. The only thing I could keep him going with was some beer I'd brought from the Dug Out. I just

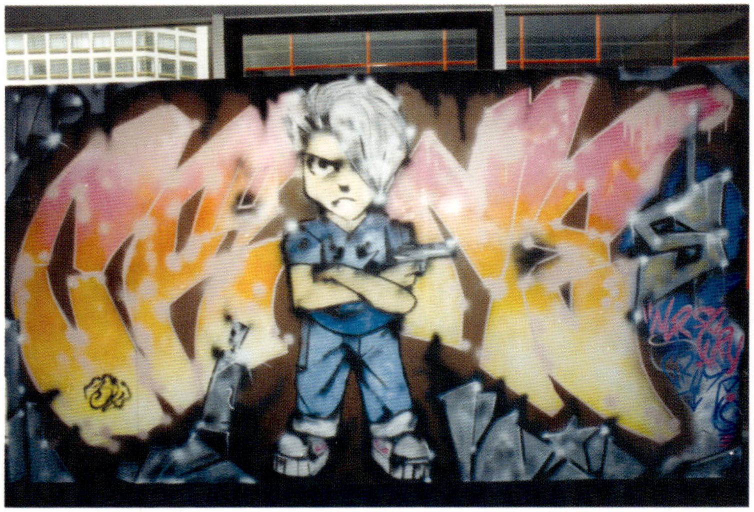

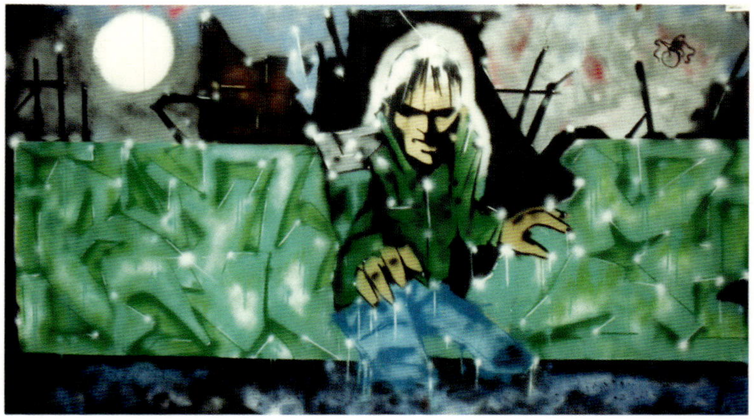

Top: 'Crimes' Birmingham Central Library exhibition, 1987

Above: 'Ruins' Birmingham Central Library exhibition, 1987

kept saying 'have another beer Rob, have another beer'. That was funny man!

"The Dug Out Club was almost like a strange oasis outside of the norm. If you went into town it was pretty much all these 'Saturday night' clubs, or in St.Paul's it was all these blues clubs… but going to the Dug Out when I was 16 was like 'fucking hell, this is it! I can listen to hip hop, soul, reggae, and punk.' And it kind of made sense, it all came together, because once I started hanging with The Wild Bunch boys and I'd started doing a bit of graffiti, that was my invitation into the Bunch, really, because I had a purpose and a role, before I started to rap.

"At the beginning it was just two turntables and a microphone, and the whole fucking thing was a laugh, and putting on gigs and sound systems was a night out and an event that was fun. We were just escaping into the American hip hop scene, which was this wonderful place - the music, the dancing, the graffiti, the rap, the scratching - it had so much, it was just unique."

The Wild Bunch used to host the biggest jams in Bristol. They were often off the beaten track in squats or empty warehouses, and yet everyone would be there, they would be packed to the rafters with sweat dripping down the walls all night. And they were all publicised by the humble hand-made flyer, which is where 3D came in.

"I'd be sitting up all night, hand-drawing a flyer, using Letraset rub-down letters, taking it down the photocopy shop in the morning, getting the Tippex out, retouching it, and getting them printed onto card and cutting them up on the guillotine, doing all that myself. Flyers and fly posting, and spreading things word-of-mouth about gigs, that sort of grapevine was the most powerful thing in the city. All our gigs were publicised on the grapevine, we didn't really do publicity apart from flyers and a few things pasted on walls, but it was mostly handouts. It was a very different time, back then you really had to go out there and put yourself about. The only way you could call someone in those days was to go into a red phone box or borrow your mum's phone! It seems prehistoric now, but that was how we communicated."

All across the city, crews were springing up, and the sound system scene became highly competitive, with the likes of 2 Bad Crew, UD4, City Rockas and the FBI Crew all hosting their own packed jams. The graffiti scene was also becoming competitive, and the first writers to emerge after 3D named themselves The Z-Boys, after the maverick American West Coast skaters.

"When Z-Boys came out, I suddenly had competition and I was fucked right off. I was like 'who are these dudes?' because I wanted all the glory! To be honest I was a bit impressed with their stuff, like that 'Take The Train' piece on that little alley. I remember standing there, staring at that for pretty much a whole afternoon, going 'how the fuck did they get that white shine so nice next to the black?'"

After initial reservations 3D and the Z-Boys teamed-up and soon found themselves splashed across the pages of the local press and, inevitably, catching the eye of the local Constabulary.

"I don't remember who approached who, but it was one smoky night in the Dug Out, and we became friends and went out and painted together after that. In fact my second arrest was with Ian (Dark of the Z-Boys), we both got caught. We did this piece, 'The Day Law Died', with a Robert De Niro character on it, up in Clifton. I had this character that I'd drawn from the Deer Hunter poster and I painted it on the outside edge and it was fucking wicked, for some reason every stroke was perfect. But the cops got us man; we legged it behind this wall and a whole team of them came out of nowhere and got us.

"Then I did a piece for the cover of Venue [Bristol's listings magazine] which was based on the fact that I didn't finish the one we got arrested for. I remember showing Henry Chalfant a picture of the De Niro character, and asked if he wanted to use it for *Spraycan Art*. He said 'no, it's a stencil' and I said 'it's not a fucking stencil, it was hand painted' – but he wouldn't believe me!

"When I got done the second time it was pretty harsh – I had to do community service on the weekends plus pay the fines – back then it was 'three strikes and you're out' (sent to prison) that was the policy, so if I'd been done again that would have been me. After the first arrest I was loving taking on the challenge, and it was a good crack, it was 'us and them'. The problem was that without the benefit of anonymity, because I was '3D of the Wild Bunch' and we were doing press and papers, there could be no bullshit. It was like 'we know who you are and we've caught you red-handed', so there was no game to play."

1985

Media interest in the UK hip hop scene has mushroomed, with both the BBC and Channel 4 commissioning major documentaries on the subject. The Arnolfini arts centre in Bristol stages the first group show of work by British graffiti artists, which, among others, features work by the Z-Boys, 3D and London writer Pride. As a pioneer of the British graffiti scene and a member of the Wild Bunch, 3D finds himself firmly in the public eye, with Bristol at the cutting edge of what's happening across the country.

"Henry Chalfant was in town taking pictures for *Spraycan Art*, and everyone suddenly arrived in Bristol out of nowhere. It was a pretty strange thing, because if you think about it there wasn't a lot to look at, but even still it was the first UK graffiti exhibition, and it was in Bristol. I think a lot of it had to do with the music scene; that really helped to develop the graffiti.

"I met Pride at one of the hip hop nights Wild Bunch did in London. We started doing nights in Soho, at this club called Krush Groove, and it was either there or at one of Westwood's rap all-dayers. There were only a few artists in London then: Pride, Zaki Dee, Mode 2. This was before the Chrome Angels [seminal London graffiti crew] formed, and not long after that I met Goldie, who came to the exhibition at the Arnolfini. He just came up to me in a whirlwind of manic energy! We became mates after that."

One link led to another and after being involved in Channel 4's documentary *Bombin'*, 3D was invited to include work in an international group show at Birmingham's Central Library. The show, organised by Goldie's manager at the time, heralded a change in style for 3D and saw him experimenting with stencils for the first time. It also featured work by New York legends Vulcan and T-Kid, amongst others.

"The first time I really used stencils was in 1986, for the Birmingham exhibition. I did the Mona Lisa painting without the mouth. I painted the rest freehand, and I tried to be quite painterly about it. It had a blue face. I was sitting there thinking 'Da Vinci, flesh tones, I don't want to even try and match that!'

"The graffiti boys hated it. I remember sitting in the *Bombin'* preview with Brim, Bio, T-Kid, Nicer, Vulcan and Goldie and his boys, and I'd sent all my pictures up to the exhibition, and I was sat there with Miles [Johnson, DJ with the Wild Bunch] and one of them said 'yeah, somebody's been using

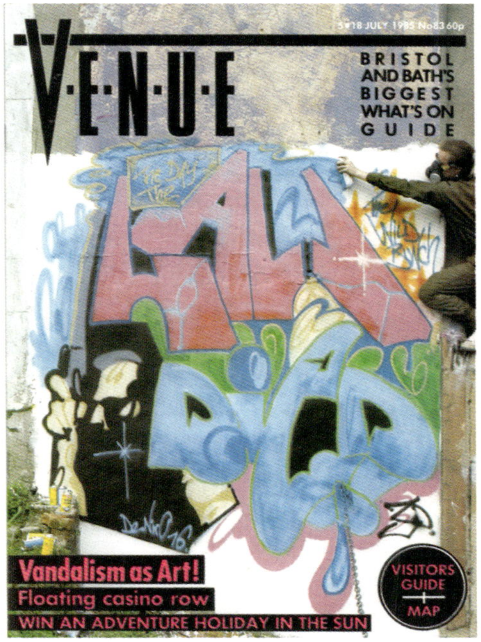

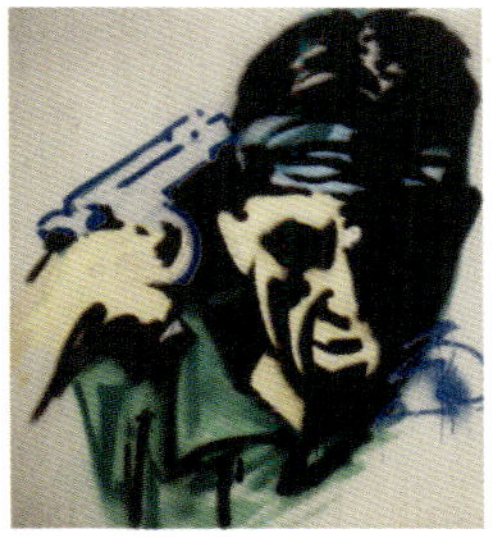

Above: Robert De Niro character based on a still from The Deer Hunter, 1984

Top left: 'The Day The Law Died' painted on the outside of the Venue magazine office, Jamaica Street. Venue cover, 1985

Left: 'The Day The Law Died' sketch that 3D was painting from when he was arrested for the second time, 1984

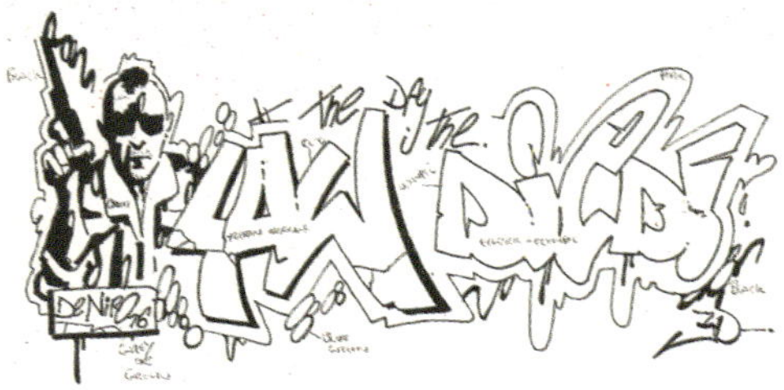

stencils.' The rest of them were like 'yeah, that's wack man' obviously taking the piss out of me, and Miles gave me an elbow in the ribs and whispered 'you wanker Jack'."

Unpopular as stencils may have been with the hardcore old school writers, 3D seemed to be taking a step to the side in an attempt to push his work forward and set himself apart from what had by now become, as he saw it, an overcrowded scene.

"What drove me away from graffiti was the fact that we all were all drawing from the same well. I loved the American hip hop

Top row: 'Iron Mike' 'Maggie Monroe' and 'Bristol Taxis'. Early stencil pieces, Montpelier Hotel pub, 1988

Below: 'Mute Mona' Birmingham Central Library exhibition, 1987

Bottom middle: 'Lightning Hopkins' first 'white on black' stencil, 1987

Bottom right: 'Noodles' 1987

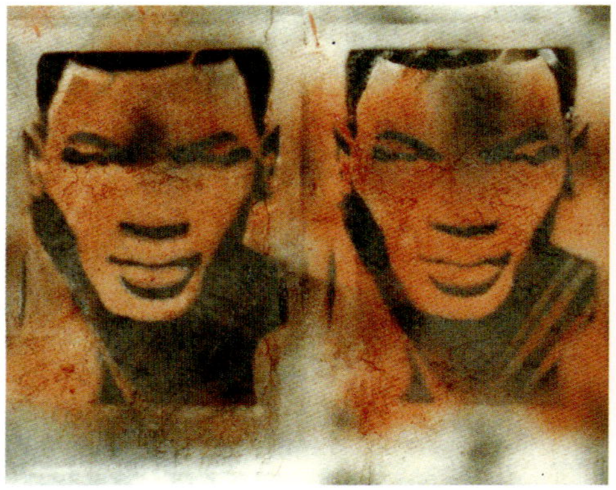

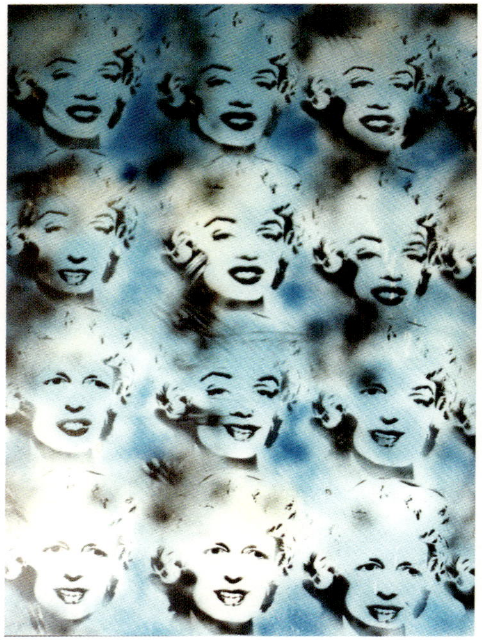

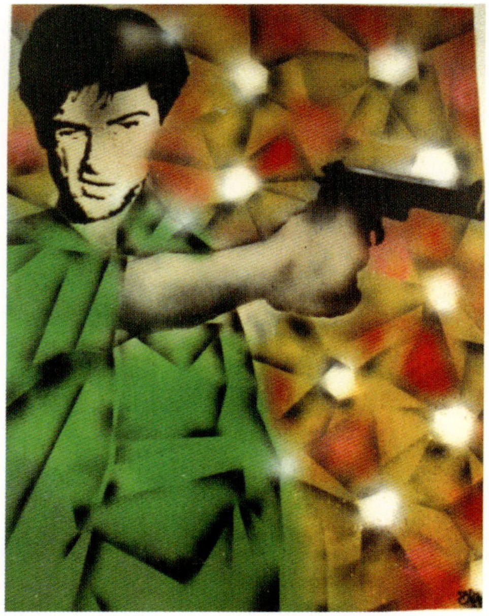

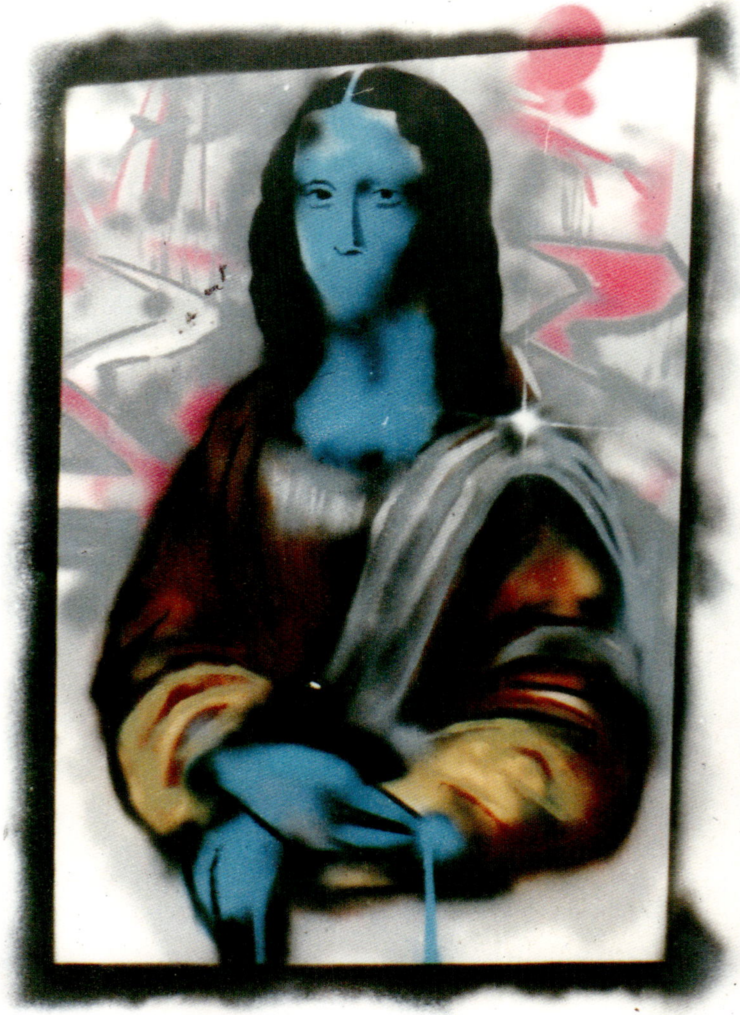

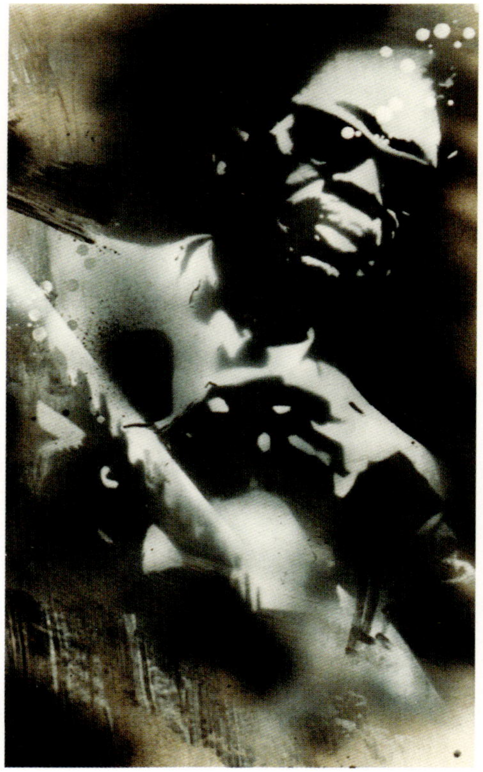

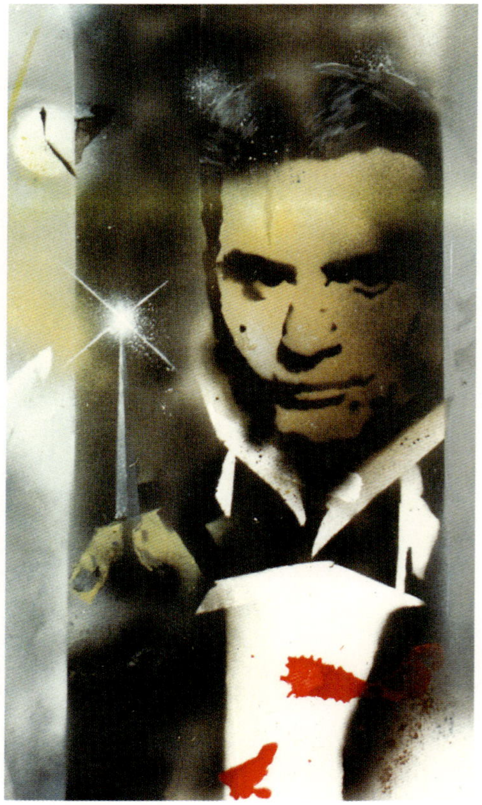

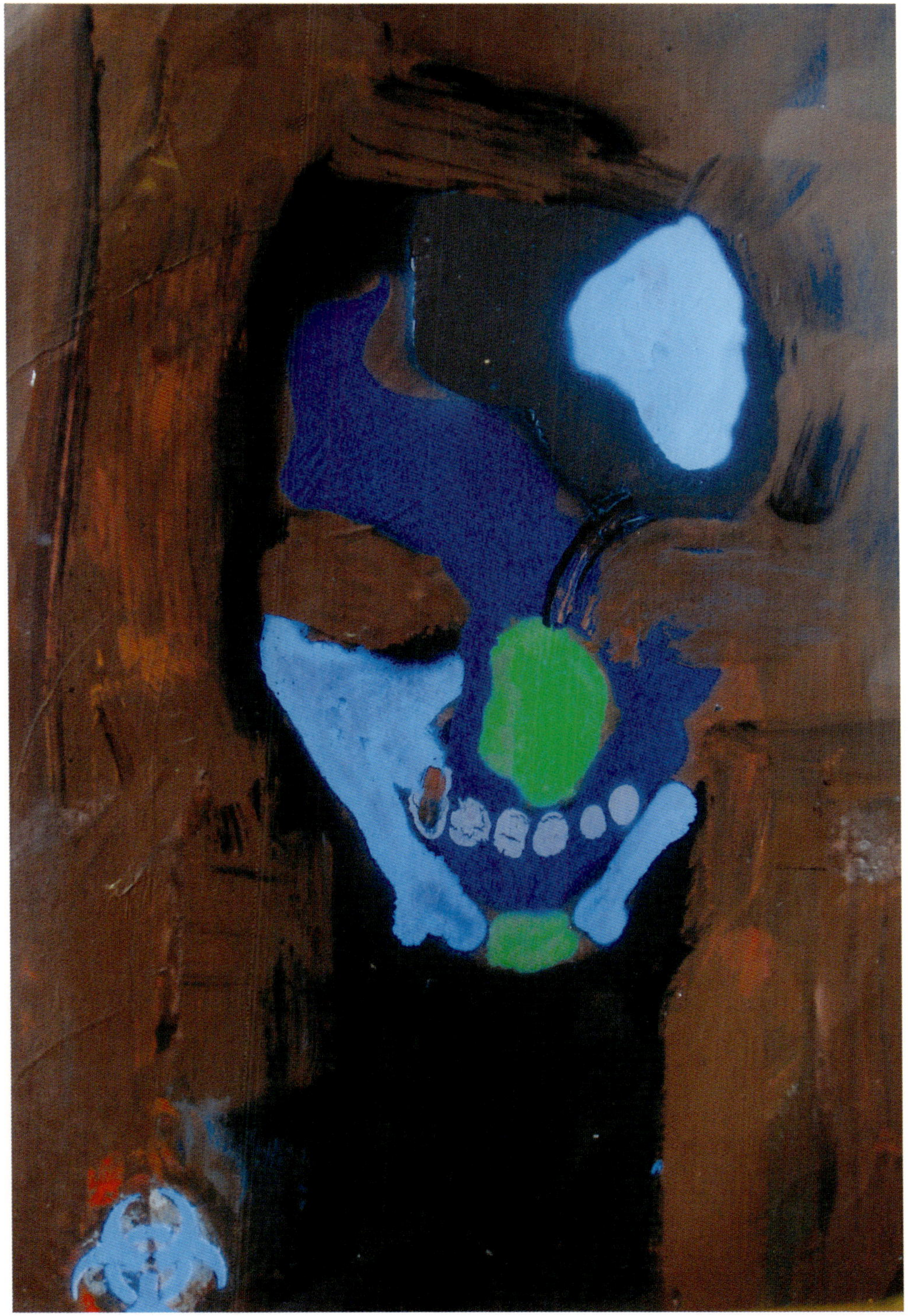

scene - it was my absolute inspiration - but the scene had changed, and I wanted to do something different. For the Wild Bunch, the era of independent inner city warehouse jams was over. New legislation had killed them off. And in the same way that punk lost its power for me, so had graffiti: everyone had a sketchbook and a tag, which was cool, but only a few people were hitting high-profile central spaces.So I started experimenting with stencils, fucking around doing stuff on canvas, or metal, or board, or whatever I could get my hands on. That became the stuff I did in the Montpelier Hotel. I did a Maggie Monroe, a Mike Tyson, and a few DeNiro things as well. I started to paint more figuratively and began experimenting with abstraction."

April 1991

Three months after UN coalition forces led by the US and the UK invade Iraq under the banner of Operation Desert Storm, a band called Massive Attack release their first LP on Circa/Virgin Records, entitled *Blue Lines*. It is no ordinary record, and Massive Attack aren't even a band in the traditional sense, growing as they have out of the ashes of the Wild Bunch sound system, which has split into two separate camps: one based in London, the other in Tokyo.

"When we went to get our record deal we told Virgin 'this is our history,' and Wild Bunch had quite a good reputation. Everyone had heard about us even if they hadn't been to Bristol. It was quite bizarre how a bunch of blokes doing sound system parties had such a big rep. So when we met with the label we were like 'yeah, this is what we want to do, we want to design the sleeves, we want to talk about the videos, we're into films, and we want to work

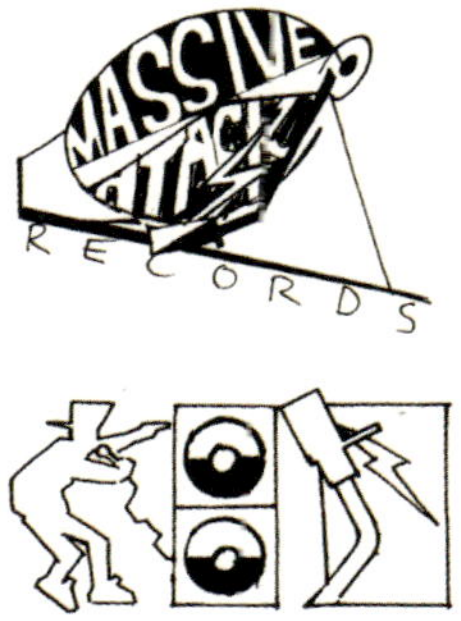

Left: 'Kate', stencil spray paint on board, 1993

Above: 'Massive Attack Records' sketches, c.1987

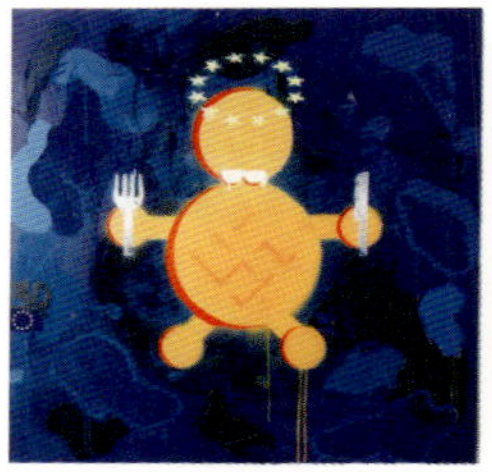

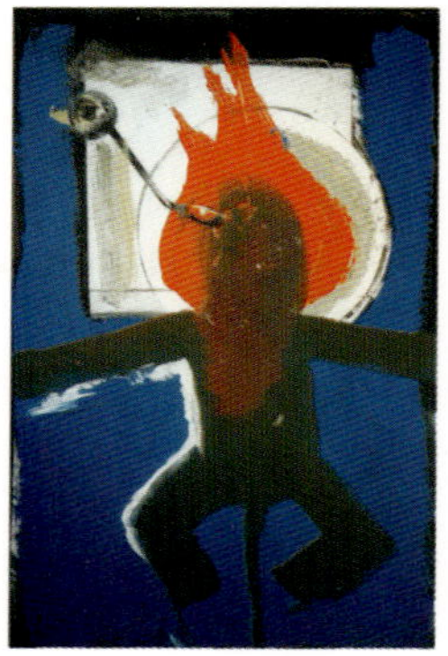

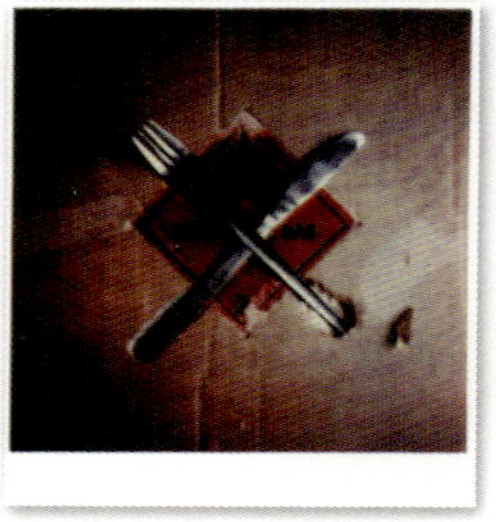

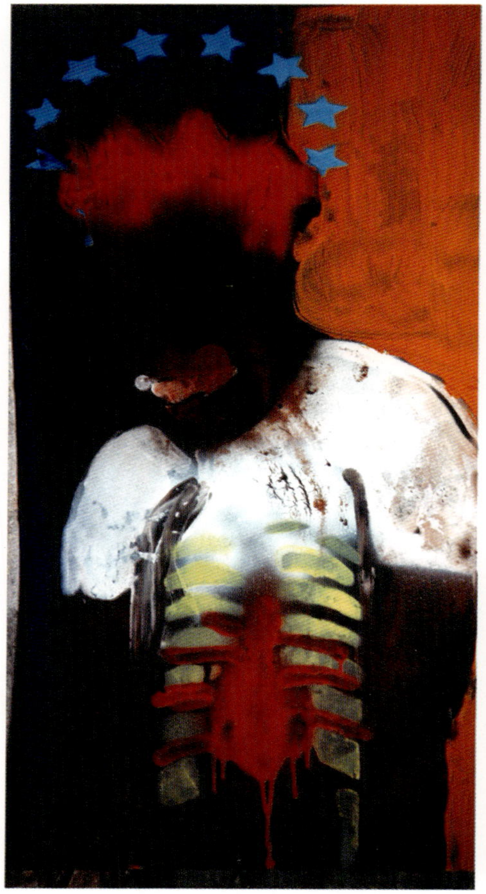

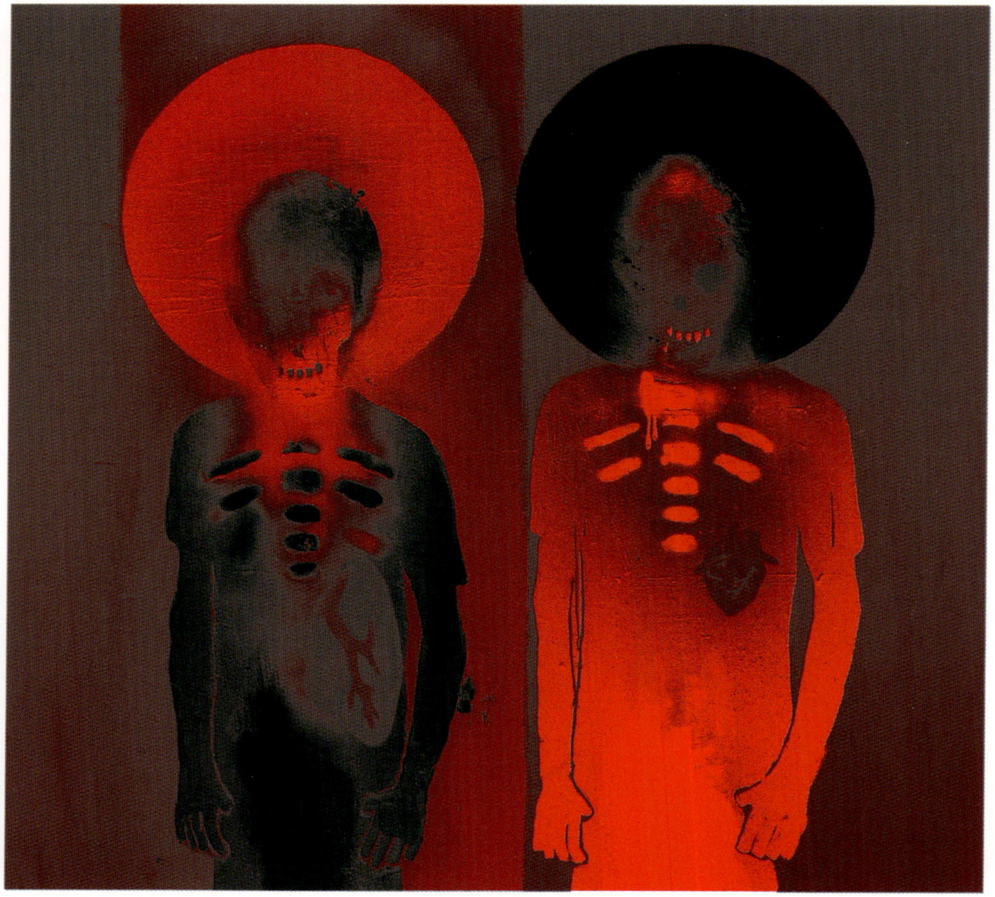

Top: 'Eurochild' (original version) spray paint on board, for an anti-fascism in Europe piece, Face Magazine,1993

Above Middle: 'Blue Lines' mixed media on board, c.1989

Above: 'Massive Attack sleeve concept' Polaroid, c.1994

Middle: 'European Male' spray paint onboard, c.1993

with directors that are into film.' Working with [director] Bailey Walsh was all about working with 35mm film, and I wanted to include the paintings with the sleeves, but at the same time I was also excited at that point about graphic information.

"I think coming out of the painting thing, into the stencilling, my ideas had become more graphic, and less free hand. We wanted to make it look like a scrapbook, with everything in it: photographs, snapshots, graphic information, and paintings as well.

"The cover, the inflammable material logo – I had pretty much ripped it off from Stiff Little Fingers' *Inflammable Material*, which was my favourite sleeve from the punk era. It was all about making a kind of collage, and the use of products and popular iconography as art totally informed all the Massive sleeve artwork, and later the stage lighting information board concept."

3D's independent outlook and have-a-go ethos have remained the defining characteristics of his work throughout his career. Whether he's making music or art, the most important point seems to be that he continues to produce unique, original artistic statements that have some resonance and individuality.

"I know I'm not the best painter or graffiti artist in the world, but I also know that I trust my imagination, which has taken me through everything I've ever done. It was what took me out of my house at three o'clock in the morning to paint on the street, took me into a studio situation without a clue what I was doing, took me onto a stage where I may have had no real right to be, and that's what it's about at the end of the day. For me the underlying motivation is to do something that is identifiably yours. Graffiti as an art form gave me the confidence to do that, and taught me the art history I missed out on in school: Warhol, Basquiat, Futura 2000."

Making a mark on society that sets you apart from your peers, sticking your neck out far enough to get noticed - the energy and the buzz with which 3D kick-started the graffiti scene in Bristol - a scene that has produced numerous highly accomplished artists - has stayed with him. The artists, for whom graffiti has been the thing that made them really believe in themselves, all share in 3D's need to be out there - getting up and getting noticed. Taking on the city is the ultimate rehearsal for taking on the world.

"Originally in New York people were taking their messages out from the ghetto and into the city, and making people confront the fact that they existed in the first place. I think that was really important, it still is. It's just people wanting to express themselves. Whether it's purely for the thrill, or out of a sense of complete frustration and unhappiness, you can't stop it happening. What's going to happen if you suppress everyone's feelings, what do they expect to happen then?

"In the city I live in half the public spaces have been sold by my elected Council so private companies can then advertise their products. Every available space is now given up to adverts and products, to sell me something, and to completely invade my space.

"Anyone who goes out painting on a wall whether it's on public or private property - they're actually just expressing themselves, they're not trying to sell you something, they're just expressing an opinion. It shouldn't be controlled or contained. Suppressing people's opinions, art and creativity - that's what should be illegal.

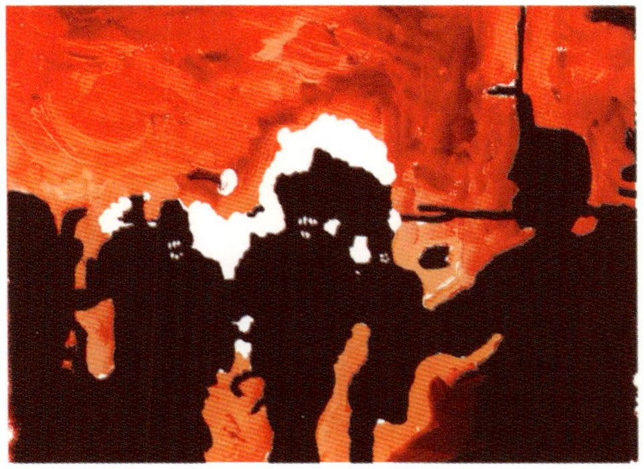

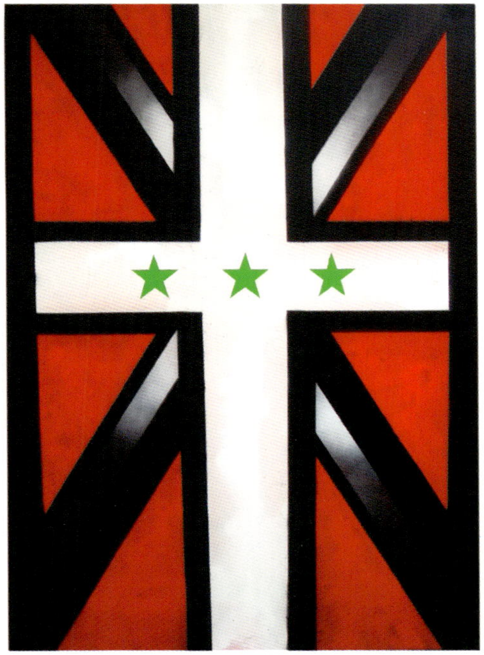

"I decided to redecorate parts of my city, a city that had been vandalised by advertising, bad architecture and commerce, and in doing so I became 'the criminal'. The row should be about personal liberty versus the privatisation and ownership of property, public space and the media. But fuck me! I have become an even greater hypocrite now by selling my work privately through an agent and a gallery!"

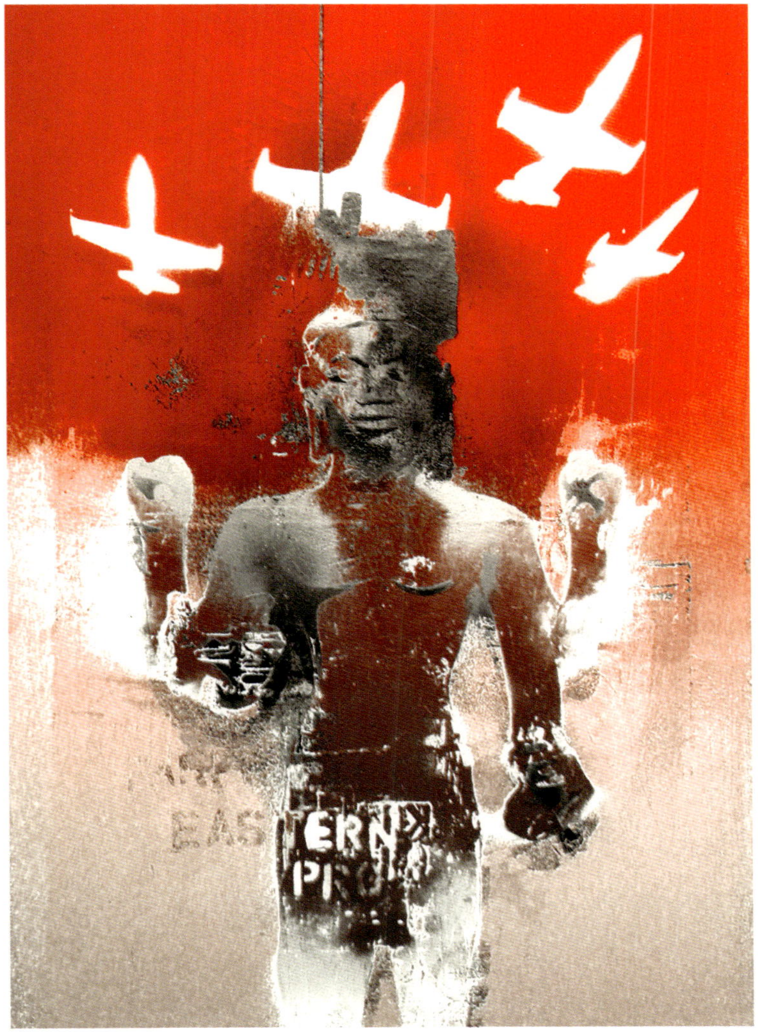

Opposite page. Right: 'Peace At Last' War Stories UNKLE LP cover, 2007. "I was proud to paint the War Stories cover, following Futura's brilliant work for Mo'Wax in the 90s. It felt like a cool symmetry."

Top left: 'The Future Is Behind You' mixed media, 2007

Bottom left: 'United Kingdoms' stencil spray paint on canvas. Painted for New Statesman magazine article on Iraq, 2007

Above: 'Four Noble Truths' mixed media, 2007

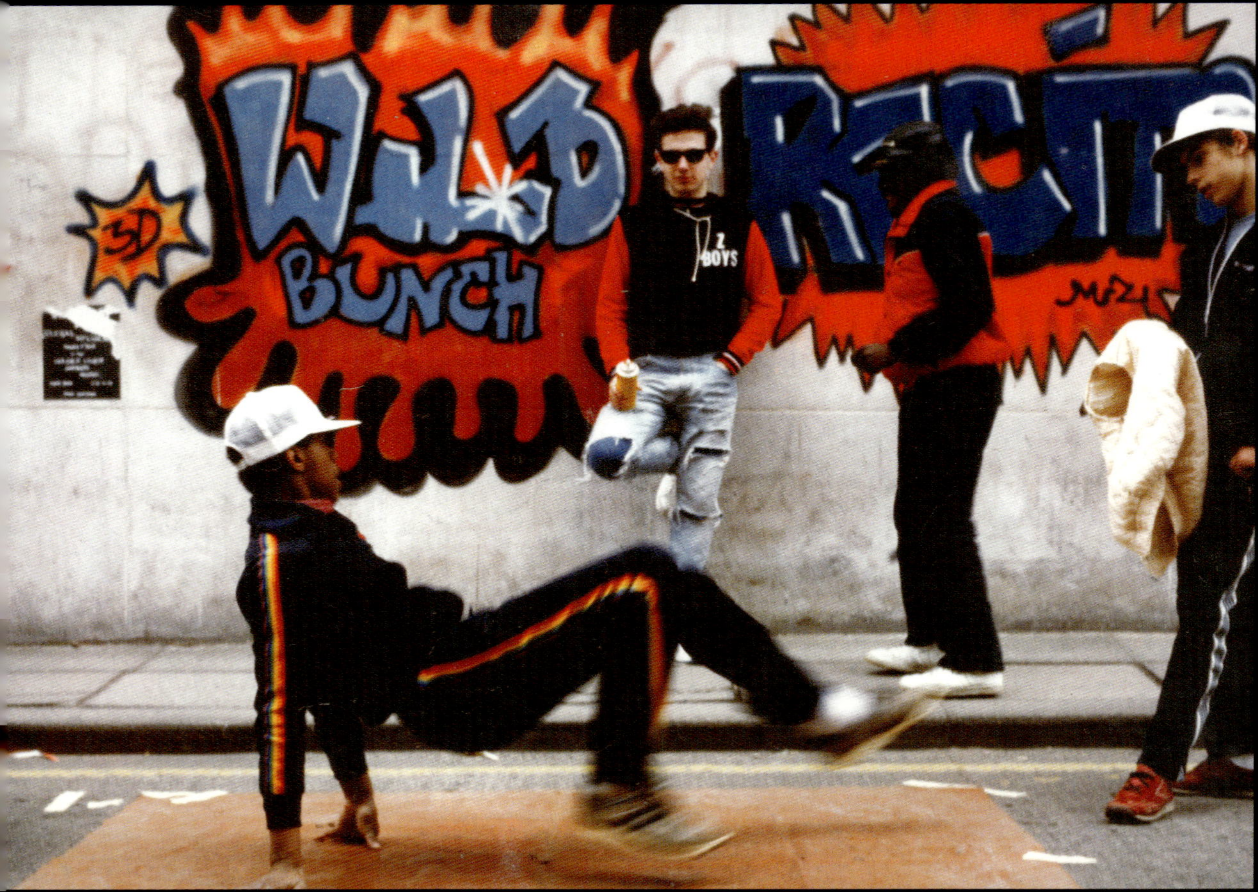

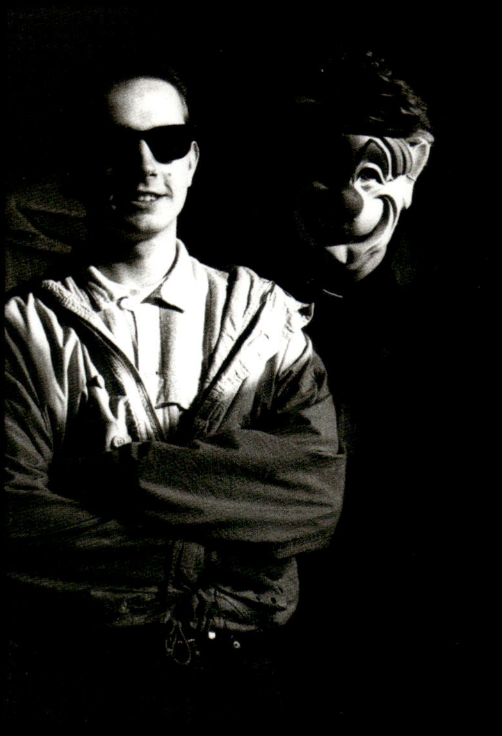

Above: Ian Dark and Bristol B-boys in front of 'Wild Bunch' by 3D and 'Roc It' by The Z-Boys,1983

Top Right: Ian and Alan (in clown mask)

IAN DARK THE Z-BOYS

Despite undoubtedly being inspired by the New York subway writing scene, Bristol's embryonic graffiti nonetheless had a character that was distinctly its own. With precious little in the way of source material, the city's pioneering writers made it up as they went along. If 3D was the first graffiti writer in Bristol, then the Z-Boys were the first crew, following hot on his heels within a couple of months. Faced with competition, both parties pushed up the standard of the pieces that they were painting rapidly, before joining forces to build a firm foundation for Bristol's graffiti scene.

Can you describe what the pre-hip hop scene in Bristol was like in the early 80s?
"Bristol was dire in the early 80s. There was just one club to go to that was any good (The Dug Out) and some local jazz funk bands like Pigbag, Animal Magic and Mouth – who Nellee Hooper (Wild Bunch DJ) played with. There was a tight scene, though, and it was nicely separated from London. Not that I knew it at the time, but I later realised that Bristol was different from other places – I thought everyone liked dub, rap and funk tunes, but not so apparently."

What were you into before hip hop started to seep into the UK? Were you a punk, a skater, a soul boy?
"At the time I was a skater but loved my soul and funk music and had already been buying rap records since about 1980; and before that I was influenced by the 'do it yourself' attitude of punk. I was a big Clash fan and they started moving towards funk in about 1980. I'd been aware of reggae from about the age of eleven, I guess. My tastes were a bit all over the shop then! At the time I was buying all sorts of stuff, but not loads because I only had a paper round; I could buy a tune a week maximum. I think Grandmaster Flash's *Adventures On The*

Wheels Of Steel was probably the first hip hop record I bought. The first pieces we did were all words from those early hip hop tunes: Body Rock, Take The Train, Fresh."

Do you remember when you first saw New York graffiti, and how it made you feel?
"It was probably on a record sleeve. I was aware of seeing some Futura 2000 stuff on a Clash record, but the first time I saw it up close was in *Wild Style* at the Arts Centre cinema in King Square, in about 1982. That stuff was amazing. You came away with a feel for something that you wanted to do, but that was it, so I just got some pens and paper and started mucking about."

1982 was pre-Subway Art, in fact apart from the odd record sleeve, there wasn't really any graffiti in print to look at, was there? Were you drawing influences from other sources, or was it all from your imagination?
"Stuff like comics were a big influence, the Marvel and DC comics, because it had the same elements: block letters, shading, shadows, highlighting, and bubbles and stars and stuff. I used to copy the characters and the writing from things like Batman and Iron Man, and read lots when I was younger: Dare Devil, Swamp Thing and Howard the Duck."

Where did the name Z-Boys come from?
"Z-Boys came from the skate scene – from the Zephyr Boys from California."

How did the Z-Boys get started?
"Skateboarding had died by '79, and only a few people had carried on: there was Specks, this guy Alan, and a couple of others, but that was it. Me and my mate Oli went down the skate park one day, and there were these guys there skating and that's where I met Alan. We just started going down on a regular basis and hanging out, because we were into the same things. I'd been talking to those guys about graffiti for a while, obviously without having any idea how to do it.

"I think it was just a case of saying 'why don't we just give it a go? Let's get some spray cans, draw something on some paper and let's see if we can make it happen.' We did it in broad daylight. It said 'Hip Hop', and was the first piece there ever. It was three colours as I remember, with a kind of comic splash behind it. It was quite simple but we were very happy with it."

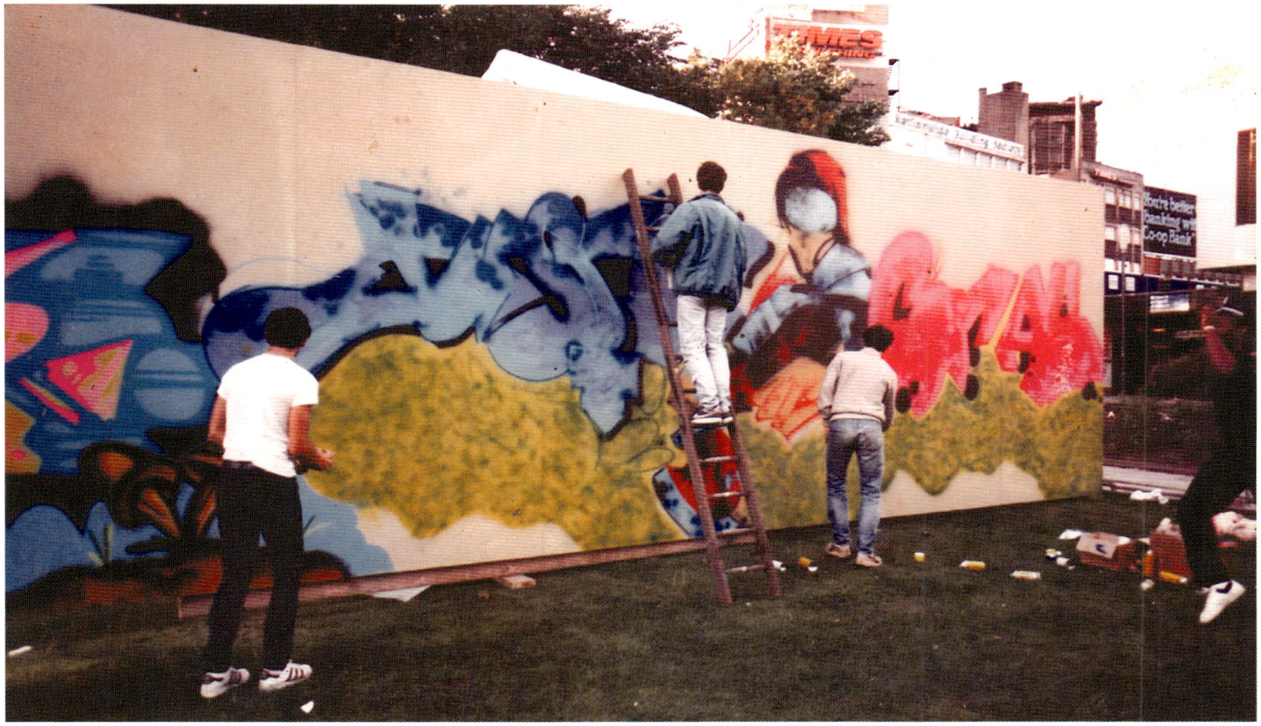

Above: Ian and 3D painting 'Justice For All' at Birmingham Bull Ring for Channel 4's *Bombin'* documentary, 1985

Did you paint it on one of the ramps, or on the walls?
"On one of the slopes below the five-a-side football court. Being skaters it felt right to paint on a ramp, we were used to being at an angle."

So you started the longest-standing graffiti halls of fame in Bristol?
"I know. People still paint down there, don't they? That's really cool. We did a couple of pieces down there, we did one saying Off The Wall – you know,the Vans logo – we did that as well. But the thing about the skate park was we did it in the daytime and it was safe. We were there every weekend and on nights during the week, so it was our place, really. There were a few BMXers around and that was it. People didn't walk through there, we never saw a policeman or

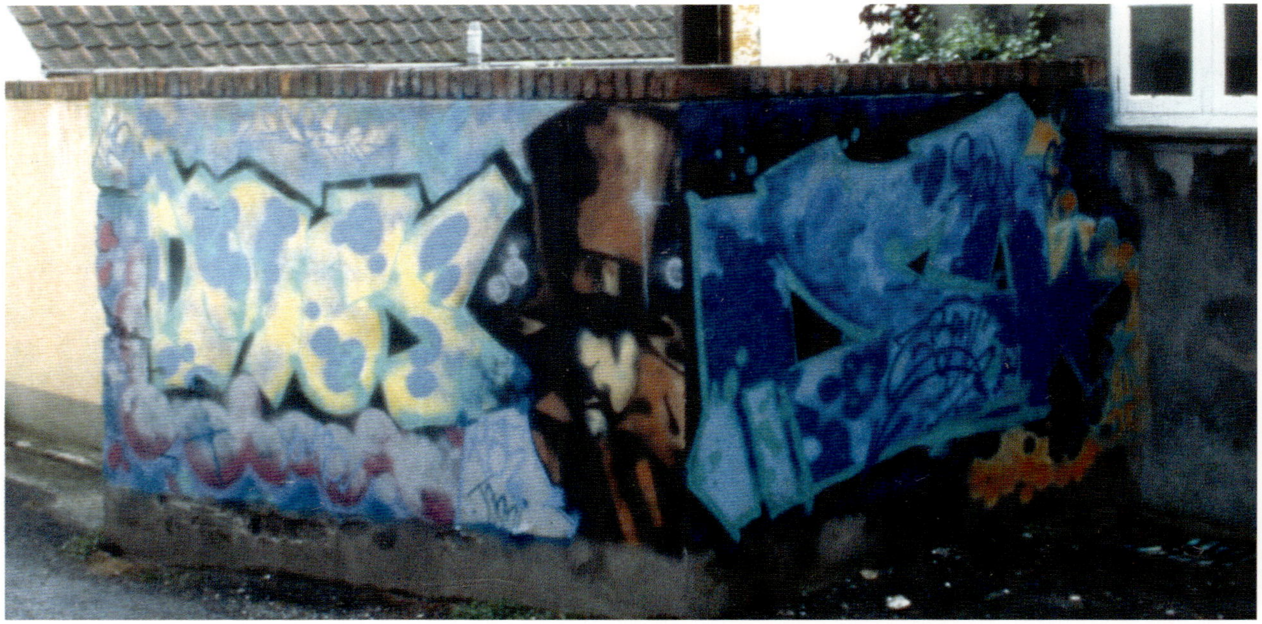

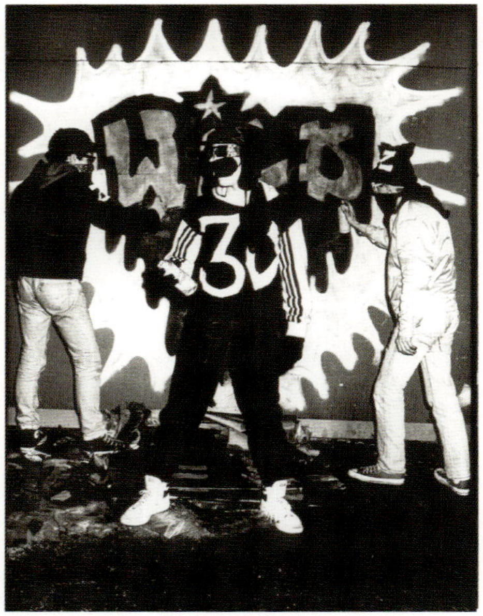

THIS EXCLUSIVE picture of Bristol's phantom Wild Style graffiti artists was delivered anonymously to the Venue offices this week. A masked figure walked in, delivered a brown envelope and left without a word. An explanatory note says "Graffiti Outlaw Supreme" 3D is in the foreground, with the "Double Trouble" Z Boys at work behind him. Signed works of art by these three now adorn many walls in Bristol, mainly in the Clifton area - in Pro-Cathedral Lane for example. What they are doing is, of course, outside the law and is diametrically opposed to Bristol City Council's new campaign to keep the area's walls bare of graffiti and posters. Asked by the BBC's RPM programme whether any distinction between art and graffiti would be made when cleaning off walls, the council spokesman wouldn't commit himself. Will the ultimate fate for the Z Boys and 3D be court appearances and a bucket of whitewash? Watch this space...and watch those walls!

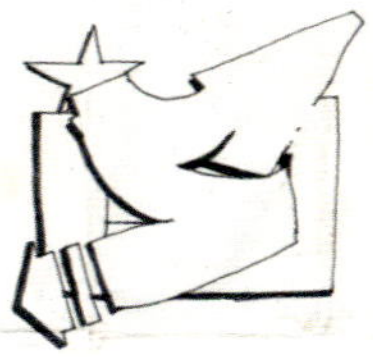

Top Left: '1965' by 3D, 'S' by Z-Boys, 1985

Above: Design for 'S' piece by Ian Dark, Z-Boys

Top Right: First press photo of 3D and The Z-Boys, Venue Magazine, 1983

anything. So then we thought 'we need to expand from here' because it was only us seeing it."

What was your first, proper, night time bombing mission?

"We went and did this Body Rock piece in Clifton. We did it at three, four o'clock in the morning. Alan had a car – because he actually had a job – and he parked it next to the wall and we hid behind it to paint. It was terrifying to be honest, and a police car did go past and stopped, but they didn't get out the car. We were ducked down hiding behind Alan's car."

How did it make you feel doing your first street piece? Did you get a real buzz off it?

"Oh yeah, you go back as soon as you can, don't you? You go home, five in the morning or whatever, and as soon as you get up you go and have a look. I was straight on the bus back to Clifton, as I remember. And it's wicked, looking at this massive thing you did on the wall. Yeah, I got a real buzz off that. Also you had to keep it secret, you couldn't just tell anybody."

Take The Train was a classic piece of yours, my favorite. Can you tell me the story behind doing that one?

"Take The Train is a line in a Grandmaster Flash tune, *Super Rapping Part 2*. It just sounded cool to me at the time, so we sketched an outline and went out one Tuesday night to paint. It was a good place to paint because the wall was long and the lane was quiet at four in the morning, so we weren't about to get caught. Funny thing was when we went back to check the next day it was really faded because the concrete soaked the paint up. So annoying! We had to go back again and redo it the next night – back to the scene of the crime. After that it was ok and it lasted for years."

But you did Take The Train before you met up with 3D?

"I'd met him but we weren't painting together then. But it was only a matter of months, and then we started working together quite quickly. There were only three people in Bristol that were doing it, and it's nice to collaborate with people. That was when there was still the healthy competition. We'd go out and do a piece and D would see it, or we'd see one of his, and we pushed each other on in that way. Then we ended up working together for a bit. We had a mutual friend called Rich and we met through him. The first piece we painted as 3D and the Z-Boys was a thing in Hotwells. It was nice working with someone else. I

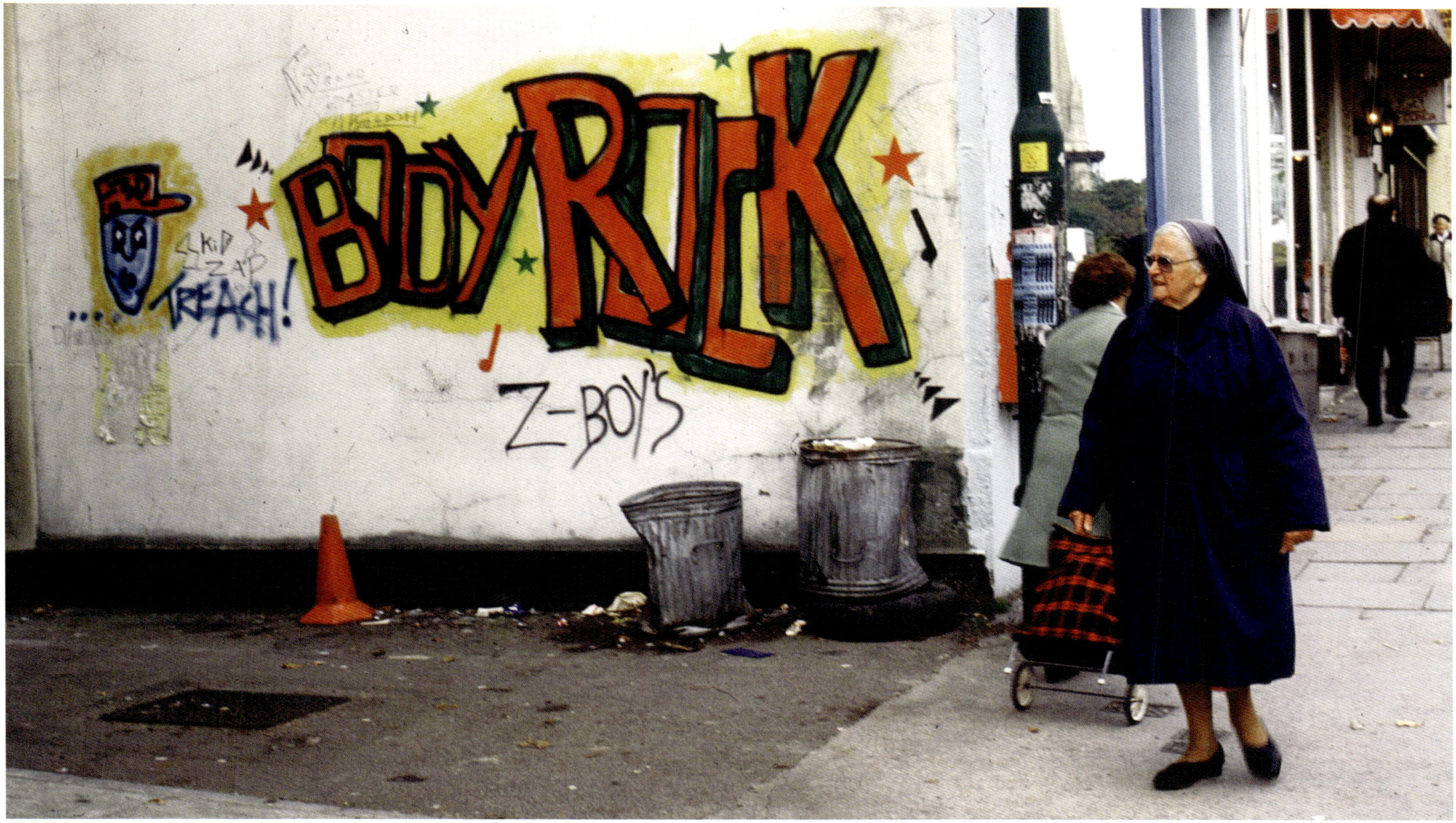

think D was quite happy to have someone else around as well, you know, just to share, and if you get arrested it's not just you."

The local media started taking an interest pretty early on as well.
"We took a picture and got someone to hand it in to *Venue* magazine, to just kind of build it up a bit, I guess. They seemed quite interested, I don't know why.

Probably because graffiti was new to this country, nobody else was doing it. There was also a connection to the whole hip hop scene, with 3D putting up Wild Bunch pieces. Tell me about when you and 3D got arrested.
"Yeah, we got stopped several times by police in our car, with a trunk full of paint. They knew that someone was out painting because they'd had a phone call but they had no proof. Really funny times. D and I got caught doing a piece in Clifton, someone saw us and dialed 999. We ran but we were surrounded .It was like a movie scene, scary but fucking excellent fun. The coppers had this file with all sorts of stuff, and he pulled out the cutting from *Venue* and he said 'that's you, right?' I didn't know what to say, really! They had photos of everything we had done up to that point and D had been arrested before, so they had his file out as well. It was funny. You don't want to get arrested, right, but if you're going to get arrested for anything... It was a good one, you know?

Above: 'Body Rock' by Z-Boys, first illegal piece, 1983. 'Treach' character added later by 3D. Note early use of stencils for stars and musical notes

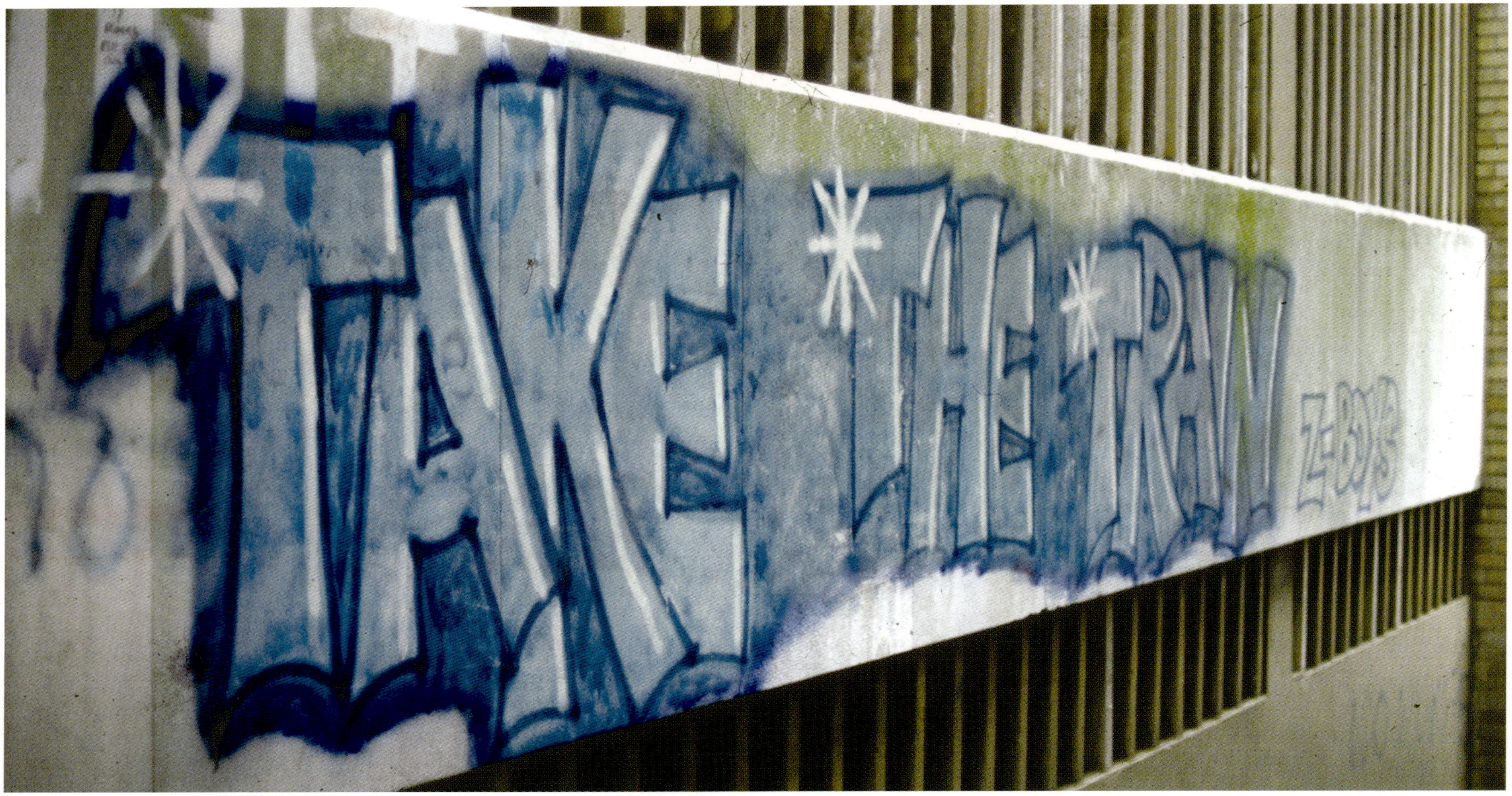

Above: 'Take The Train', 1983, which after being painted a second time remained on this wall for many years

And the luxury of it was they had been investigating us, we weren't just caught with a can; they were after us, they wanted us. That was quite a nice feeling, really. We had our own *Wild Style* movie going on, didn't we? It felt like that, anyway."

What was the result of the arrest? Did the case go to court?

"Yeah, we went to court and they gave us however many hours community service and we had to go for three hours every other Saturday. An hour of it was spent running around a gym in some shorts they gave us, then the second hour was spent cutting out jigsaws: rabbits and tractors and balloons and stuff. Then for another hour we had to paint the jigsaws we had just cut, but you would never get your own one to make, there was no creative process.

"So D and I decided we would ask if we could make our own jigsaws - and these coppers didn't know what to do with us, because we weren't the traditional criminals - and they said yeah, so we made these graffiti jigsaws. And we got to cut them out and paint them and take them home with us.

I remember that community service fondly now. It was really funny."

What about the Arnolfini exhibition in '85, do you have clear memories of painting there?

"The Arnolfini thing was great, it felt like acceptance from serious art people and we got paid to do it! The graffiti was big; I'd never done anything that big, everybody's pieces were massive. Then there was the opening party, with the Wild Bunch playing, really good night that was. You were there, right? I remember just bubbling around, drinking, everybody wanted to chat to you. It was a bit like being a celebrity, which is partly why I painted the 'Traitor' piece there: I wanted it to say something, because beforehand it had been about being secretive and going out and doing it illegally; and quite quickly it had become this thing where you got accepted, even though that was exciting, there was a bit of 'actually that's not what it's about, it's not about being on TV.' It all happened at the same time: we got arrested, there was the Arnolfini, and the guys came to film *Bombin'* with Brim and Bio from New York."

So did you feel like a traitor doing the Bombin' documentary?
"No it was really good fun actually, because they pay your bus fares and train fares to places and then they film you. It was wicked, although I'm not in it that much in the final film."

There's that scene with you guys doing a piece then running in the abandoned cinema in St. Paul's.
"Yeah, D came up with this idea that this hand would come out of a spray can. We had this plastic hand and melted stuff all over it, to make it look like a horror movie, I think. It was supposed to be like our introduction to graffiti or something."

Did you do any commissions, or other legal stuff?
"I did a wall for the Upstairs Club, above the Dug Out club. Do you remember that? I also did Tim Westwood's front room with D. The Wild Bunch did a night at Gossip's in Soho, in London and we painted the outside of the club. I remember Westwood turned up at the club in a full safari suit; he loved what we'd done and asked us to come and paint in his house."

I remember you best as half of the Def Con sound system, with John Stapleton. Your nights at places like the Rummer, the Thekla and the Moon Club were legendary during the big rare groove scene in the late '80s. Did music pull you away from painting?
"I knew John Stapleton already, because he used to work in Tony's Records, and he persuaded Tony to start bringing in some American imports, so I would buy stuff off him. I'd been buying tunes for ages and eventually got my first chance to DJ in about '84 down at the Tropic Club. Yeah, I think music did pull me from painting, but also a little later Alan went to Australia and more people started painting and it got horribly snide and over competitive to be honest and after being arrested for it once, I was looking at time in prison if I got caught again, so I was glad to be playing tunes and still having fun."

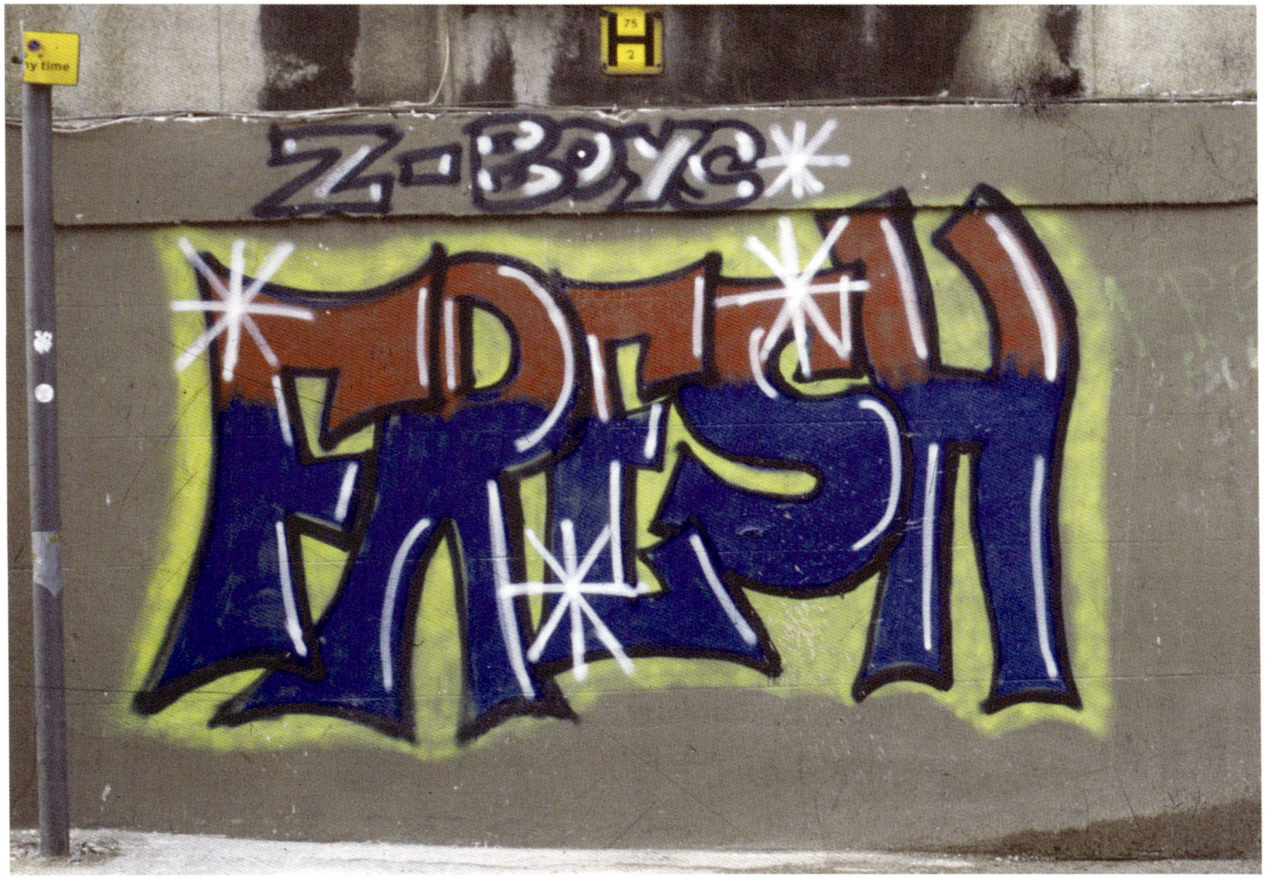

Above: 'Fresh', Clifton, 1983

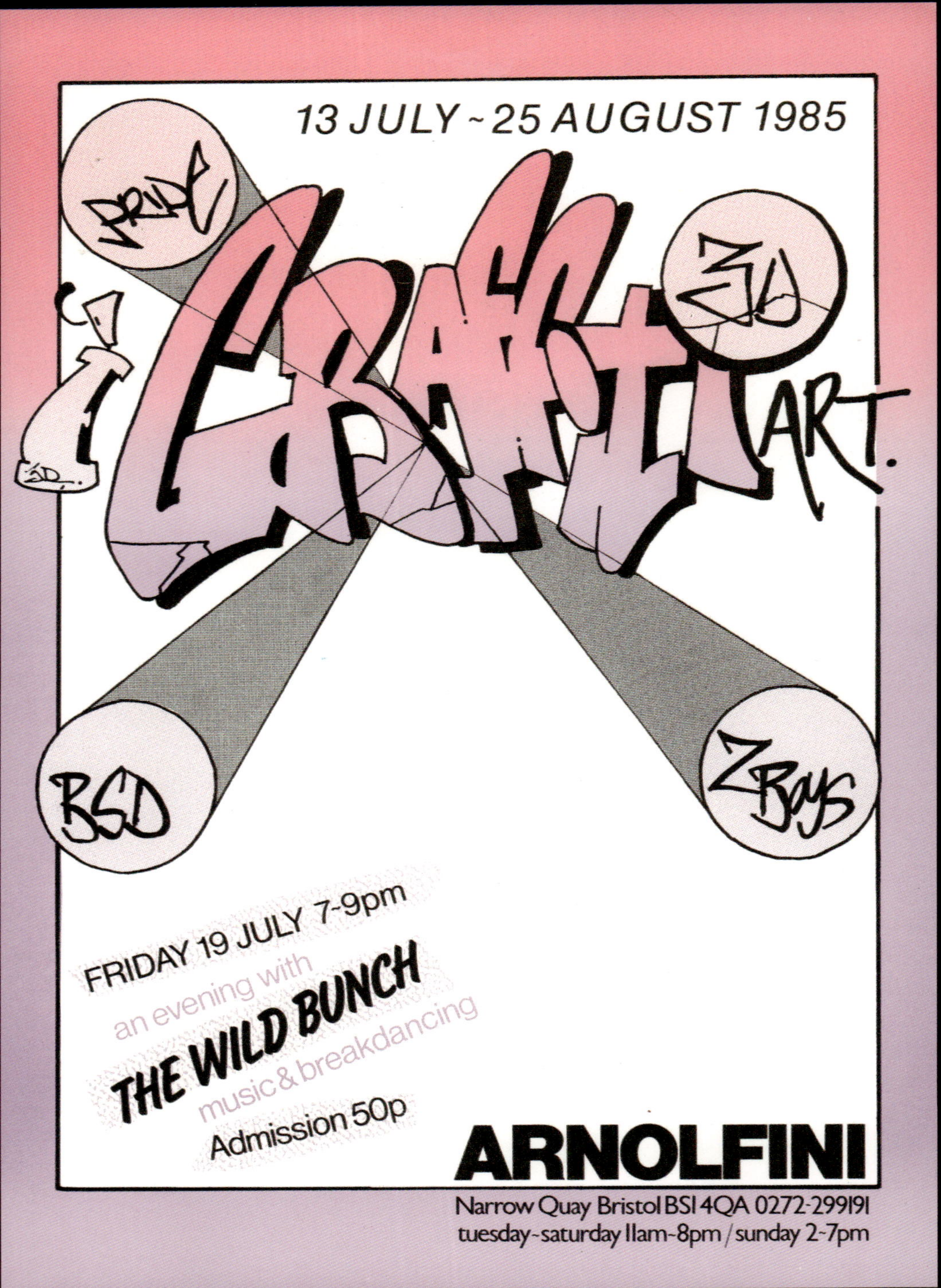
13 JULY ~ 25 AUGUST 1985
ART.
BSD
Z Boys
FRIDAY 19 JULY 7-9pm
an evening with
THE WILD BUNCH
music & breakdancing
Admission 50p
ARNOLFINI
Narrow Quay Bristol BS1 4QA 0272-299191
tuesday~saturday 11am-8pm / sunday 2-7pm

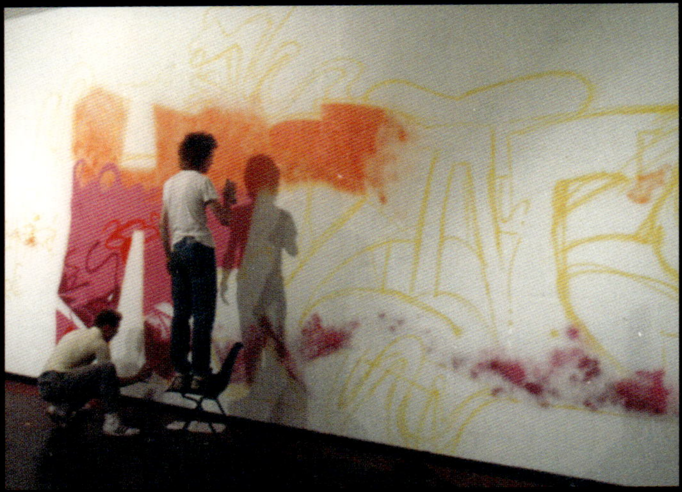

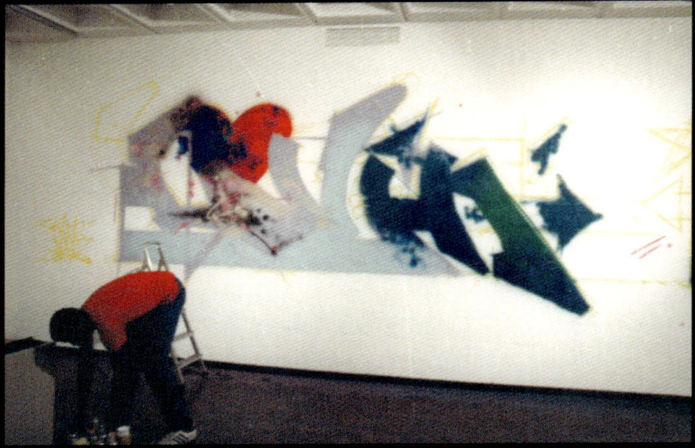

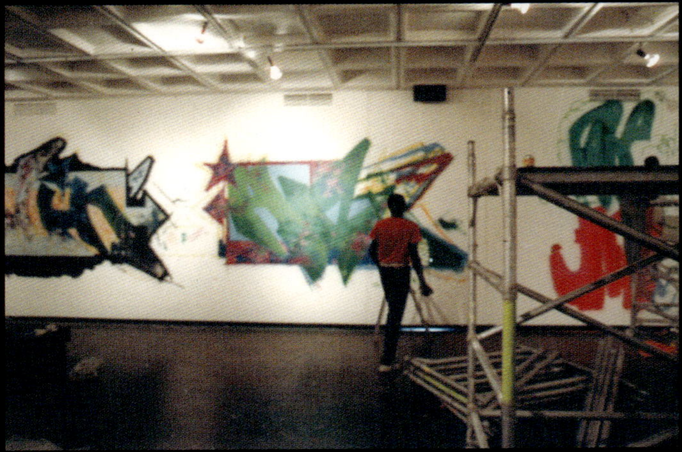

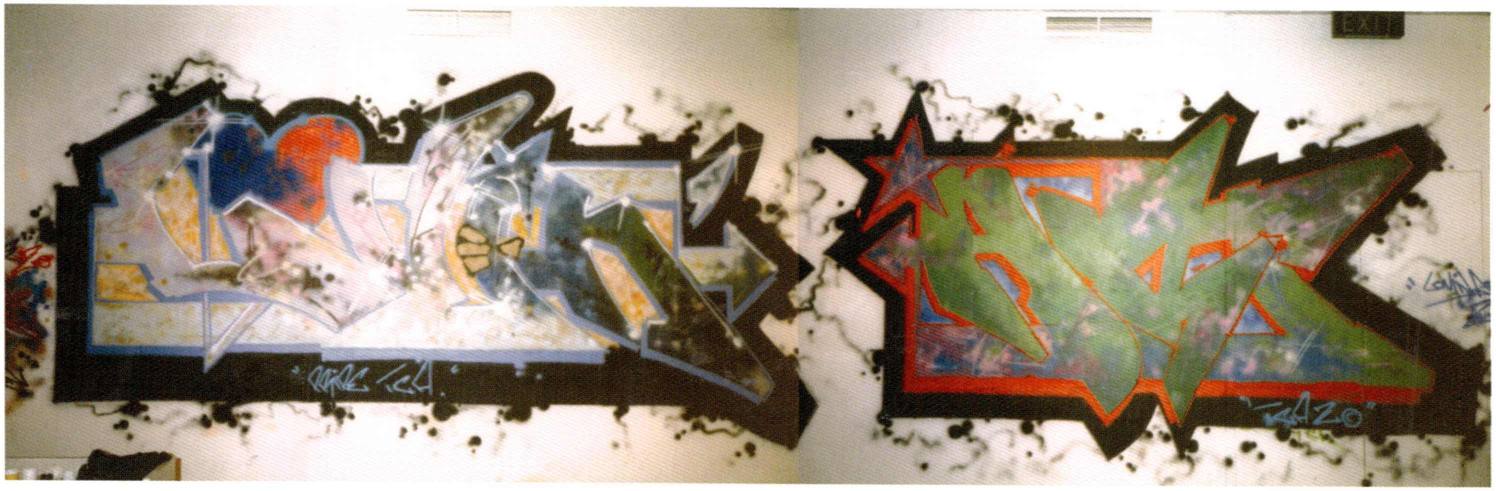

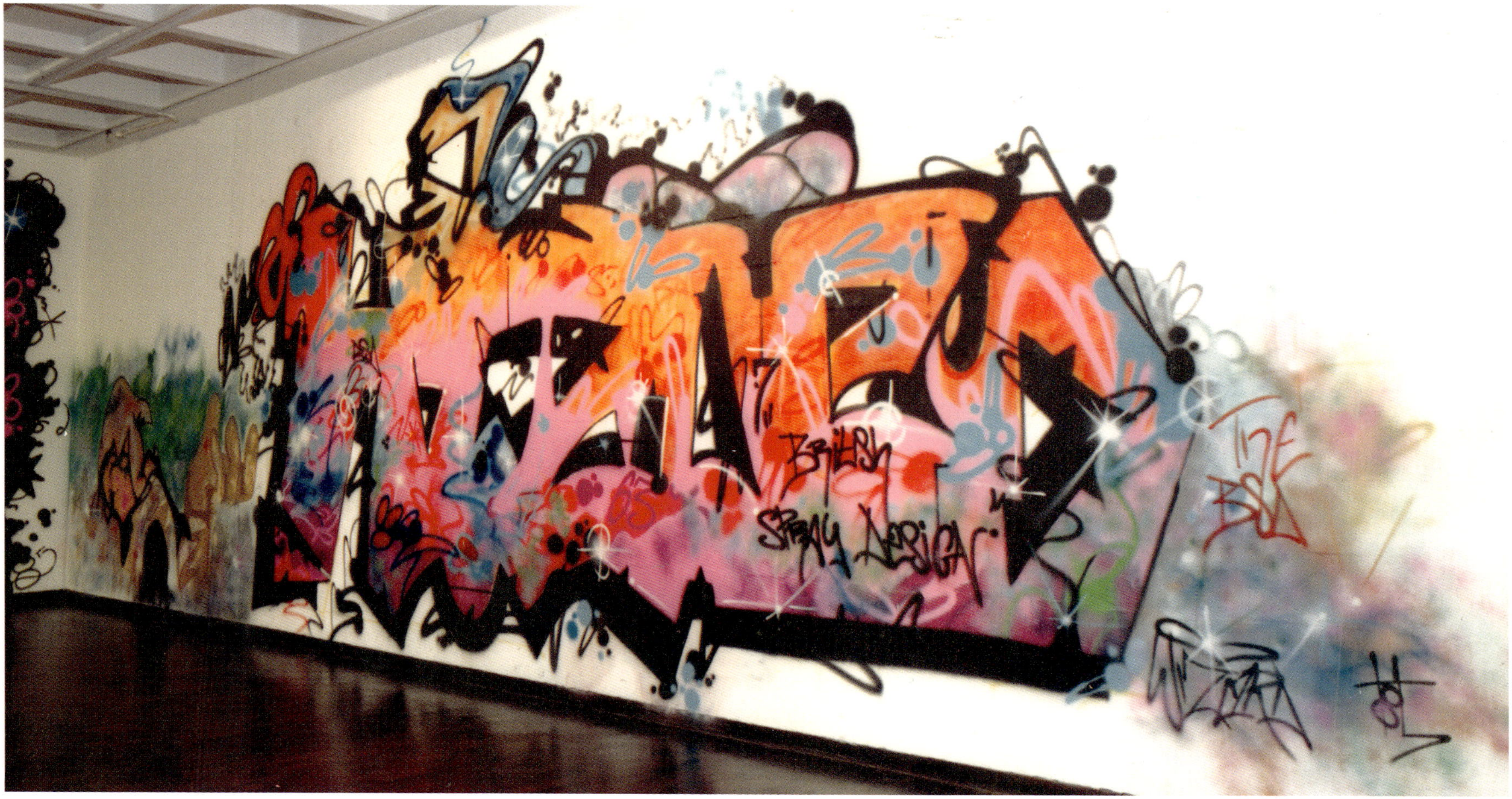

Opposite page. Top: BSD: Wizardo, (Nick Walker) and Tootz painting

Middle and bottom: Pride Inc (The Chrome Angelz) painting and contemplating

This page. Top: 'Lovin' Art' by Pride Inc

Bottom: 'Wizard' by BSD (British Spray Design)

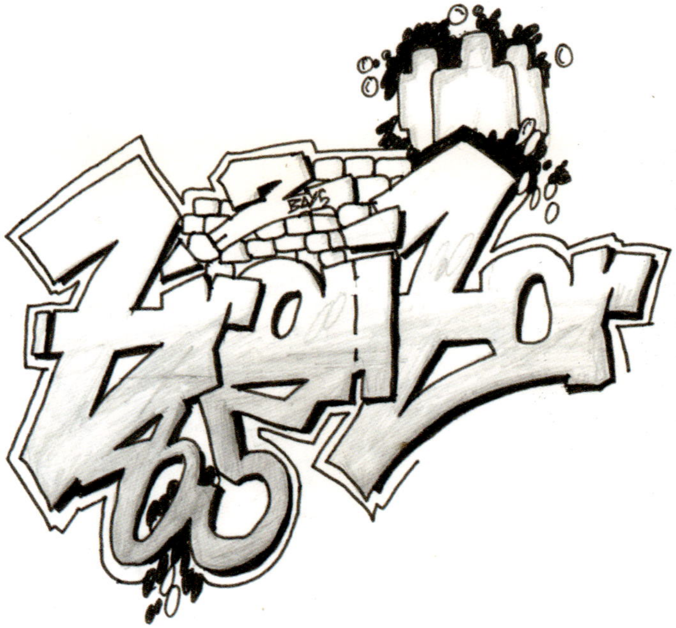

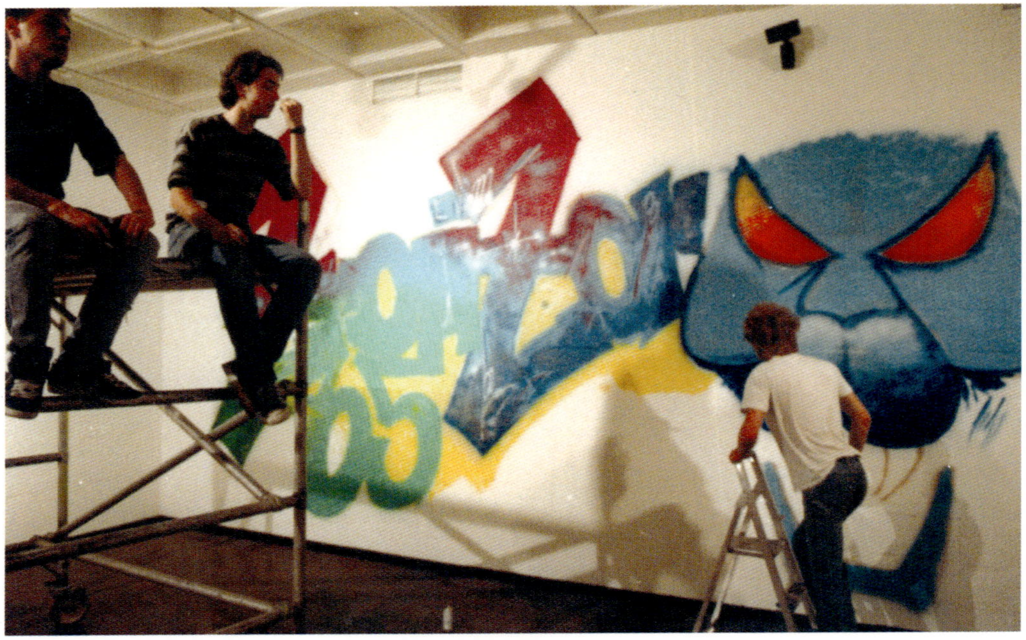

Above: 'Traitor 85' original design (pen and pencil)

Top right: Z-Boys work in progress.

Right: 'Traitor 85' finished piece. Letters by Ian, character by Alan

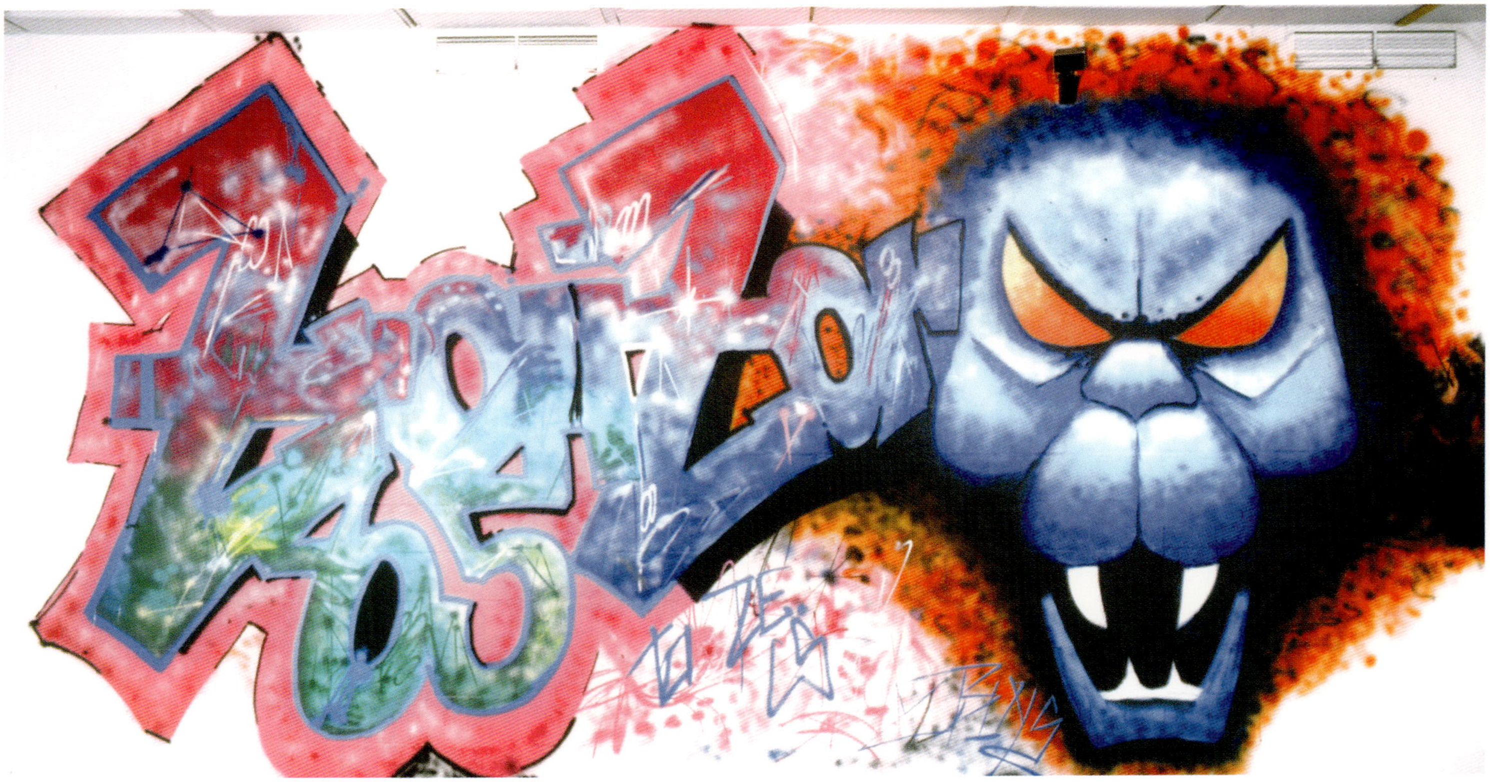

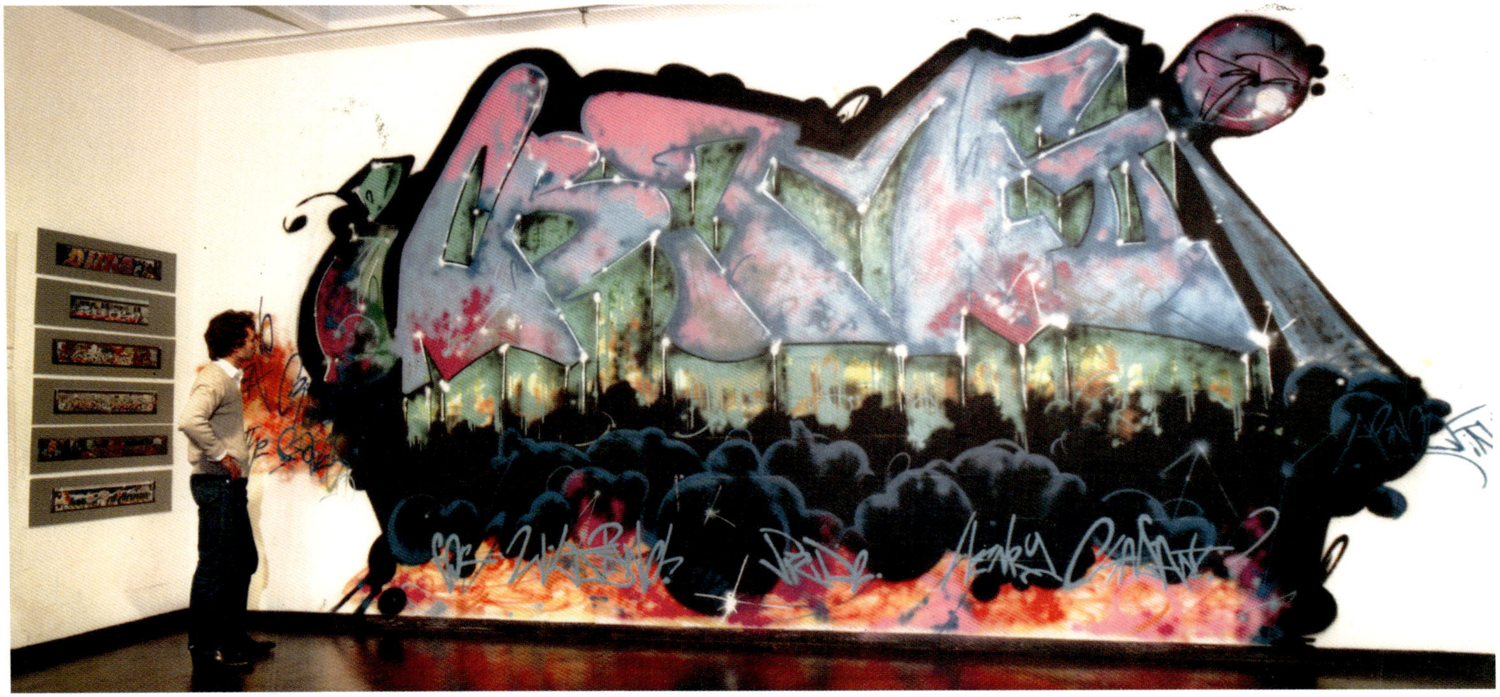

Left: 'Crime 2' by 3D. Note dedication to Henry Chalfant, who was in Bristol taking photographs for *Spraycan Art* at the time of the exhibition

Below left: Pride's distinctive tag style

Below: 'Fade and Jaffa'

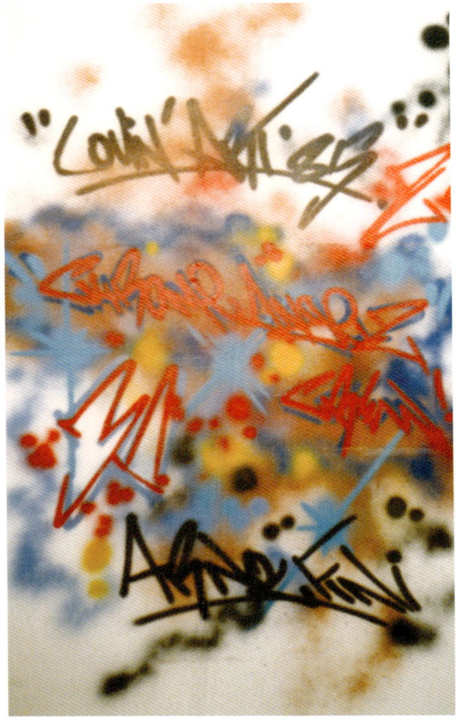

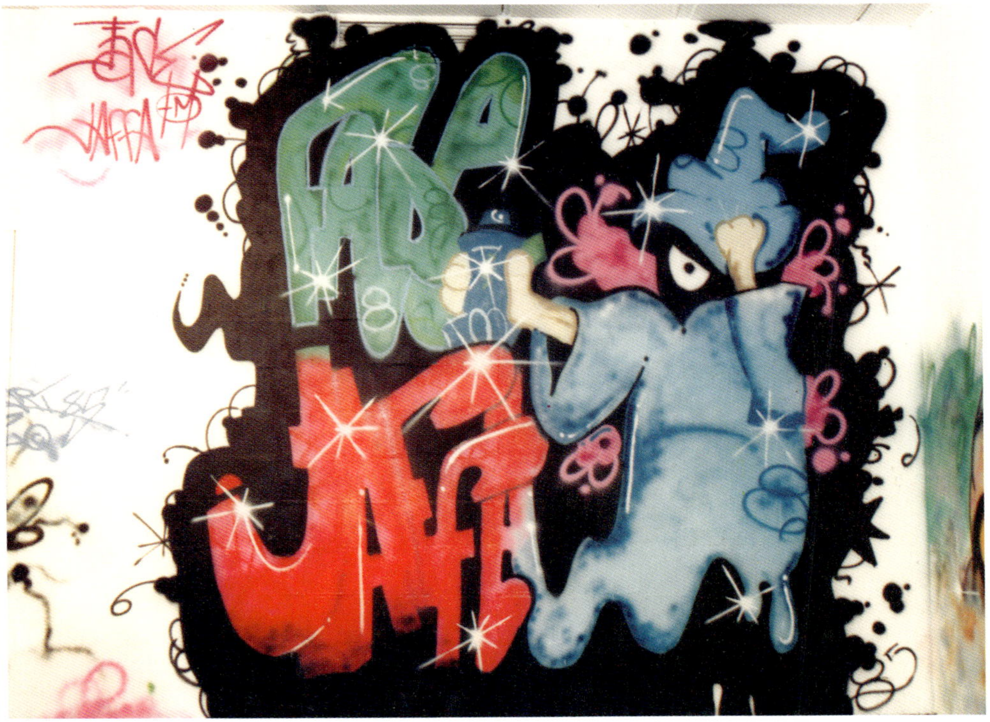

This page:

Left: 'Self portrait' spray paint on board. Freehand and stencil, 1992

Right: Nick stands firm with an old-school freehand canvas.

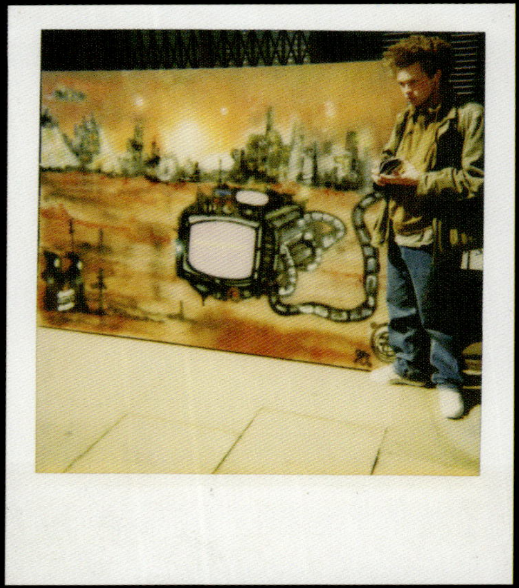

NICK WALKER

• **"It's almost like there was some kind of secret doorway to New York somewhere in the woods on the outskirts of Bristol.** That's how it always seemed to me. There's that direct link, that immediate association that's been there since the birth of hip hop in this country. It felt like it was meant to be."

Counting himself amongst the first wave of graffiti writers in Bristol, Nick Walker always approached the art form on his own terms. Whilst mindful of the pervading styles of the time, he simultaneously adopted his own stance: part B-boy, part fantasy artist, always distinctly different. More recently, his blend of freehand and stencil painting has caught the attention of a worldwide audience, with solo shows in both the United States and Japan.

Do you remember when you first saw a piece of graffiti?

"Remember the 'number guy' from

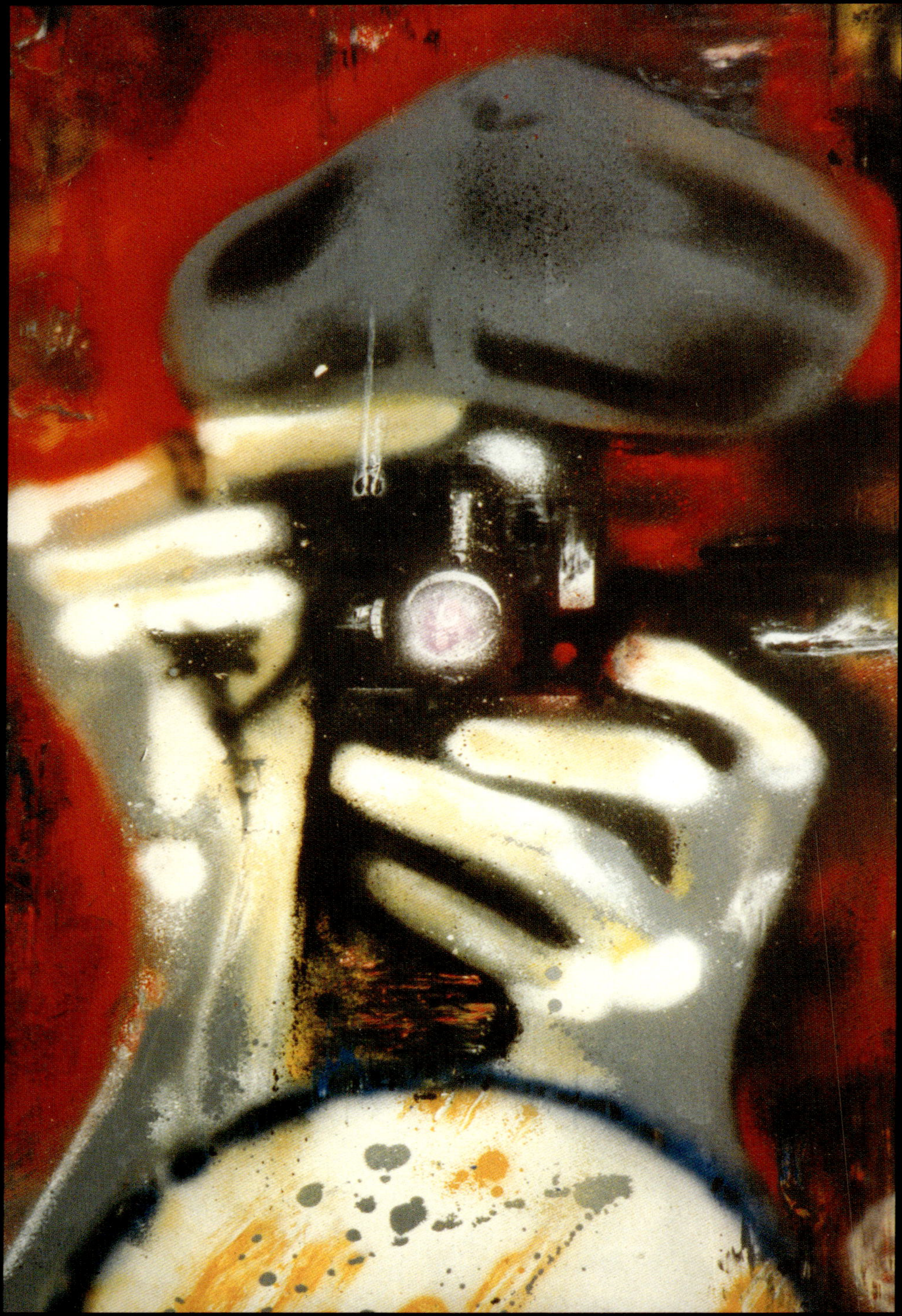

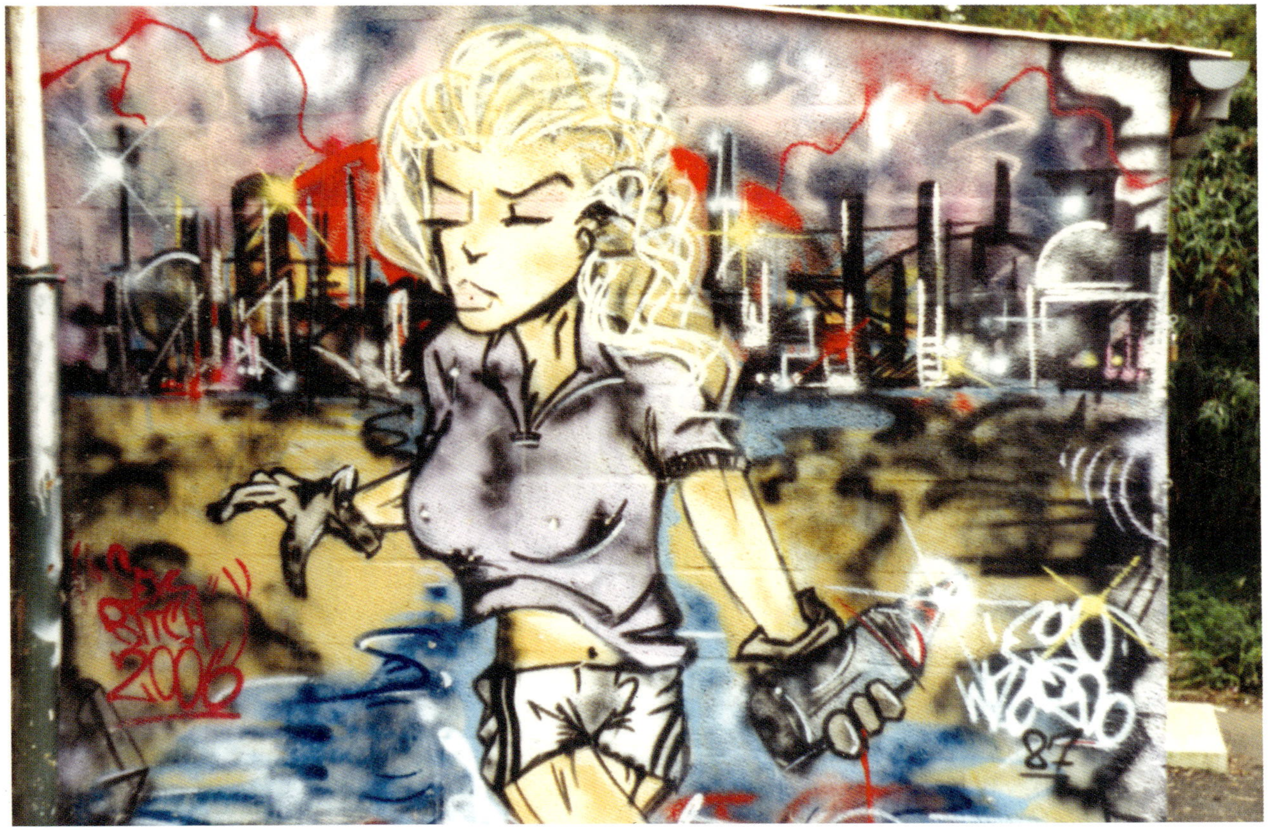

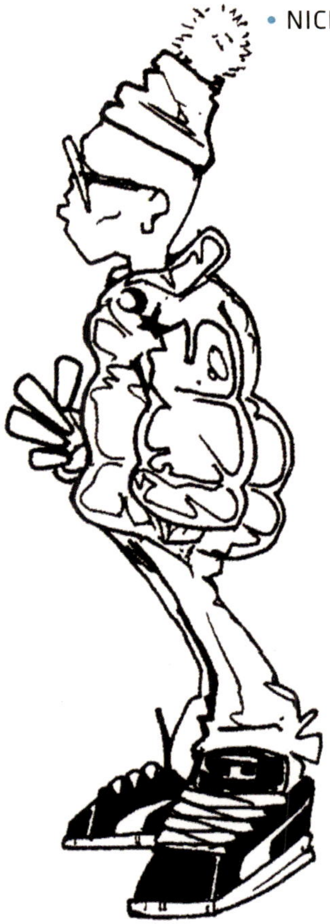

Sesame Street back in the '70s? He was this random gangly dude in a bowler hat and raincoat who would paint numbers anywhere he liked and was always being chased – or his number would get buffed at the end in some random way."

That doesn't count. For a start he didn't use spray paint.
"But he was a street artist in some sense."

Touché. But what about hip hop, and New York graffiti?
"In the early '80s I remember seeing snippets of stuff – in the Blondie video for *Rapture*, or Dondi outlining the letters perfectly in the *Buffalo Gals* video – without really knowing what graffiti was. Then, later on, it was seeing *Wild Style*, of course. Seeing those kind of things was like, 'Damn! Look at that!' But I was painting even before that. I remember going to see *Wild Style* and I had fat laces in even then. They probably weren't laces at all, I think they came from a curtain shop. We were just bobbing our heads all the way through, and the cinema was full of tracksuits."

Dancing – that's what I remember about you. You were already B-boying when we first met, I think?
"I was breaking before I was writing, and that arrived even before the videos. There were things in *The Face* magazine; I remember seeing photos of a breaker in Red Square. I used to go into town and go to the bandstand in Castle Park and get into B-boy battles. That was when E-Force were about and I got to know characters like [Bristol B-boy legend] Smurf, and I also first met Tricky around those days."

Were you buying early hip hop and electro with your pocket money?
"I was into the music right from an early age, from hearing John Peel playing things like Sucker MCs. I remember going to Focus in Clifton when Tony's Records was in the basement, and seeing the Z-Boys in there. That was just after 3D had started and only a handful of pieces had gone up in Bristol."

Top left: 'Sexy bitch 2006', 1987

Top right: B-boy design for Magic Pudding Avenue stickers and T-shirts, 1986

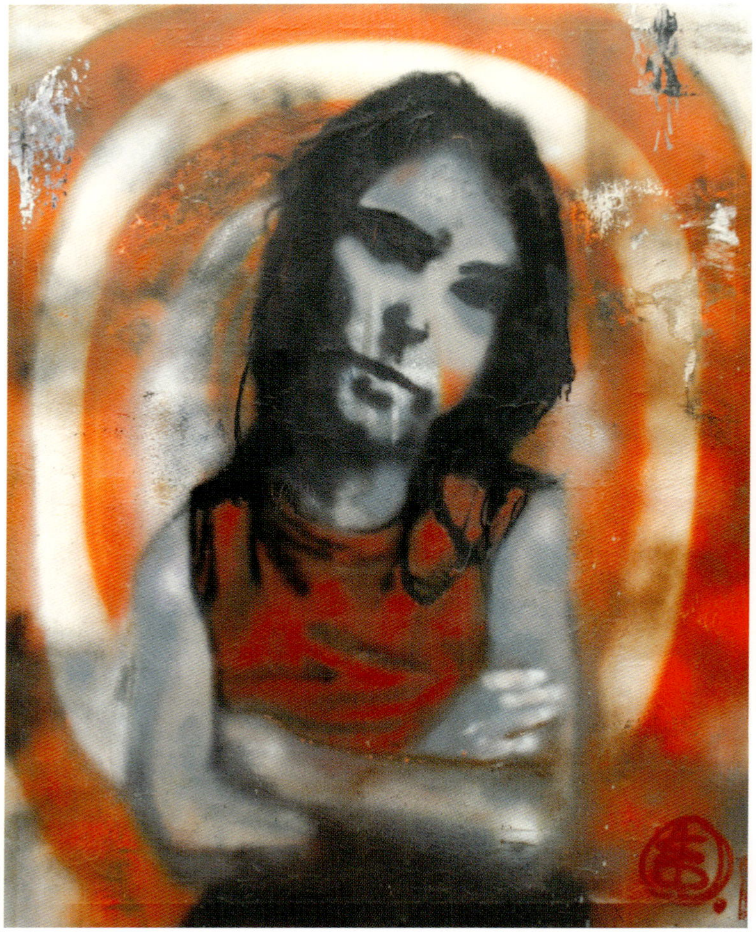

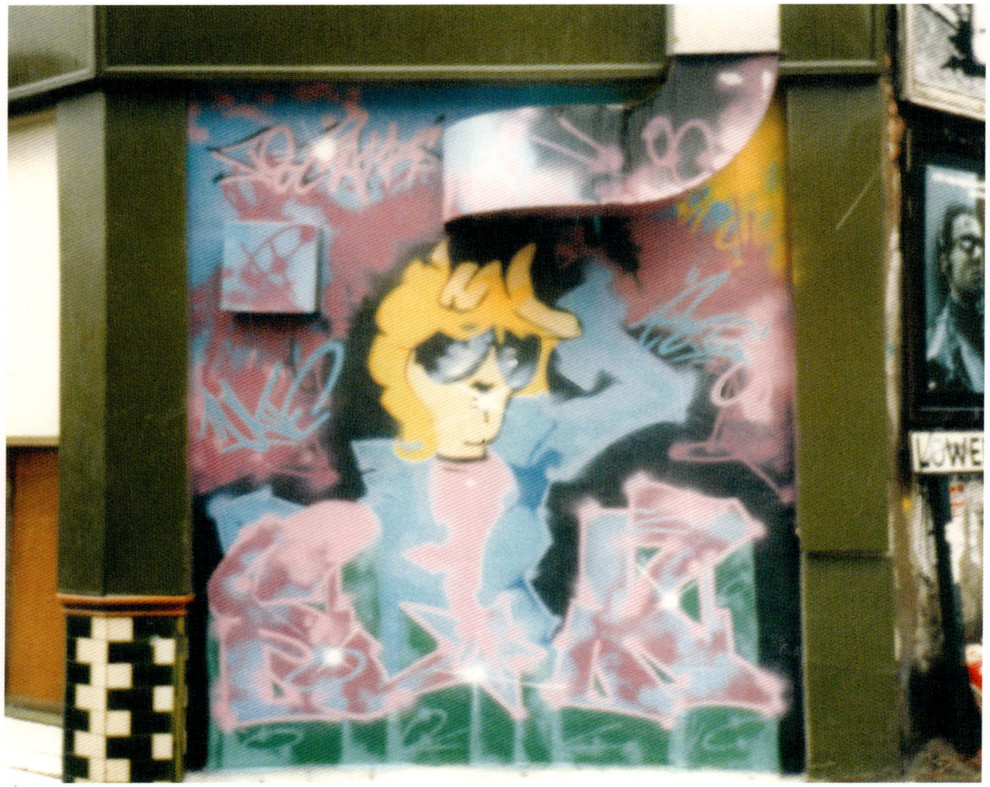

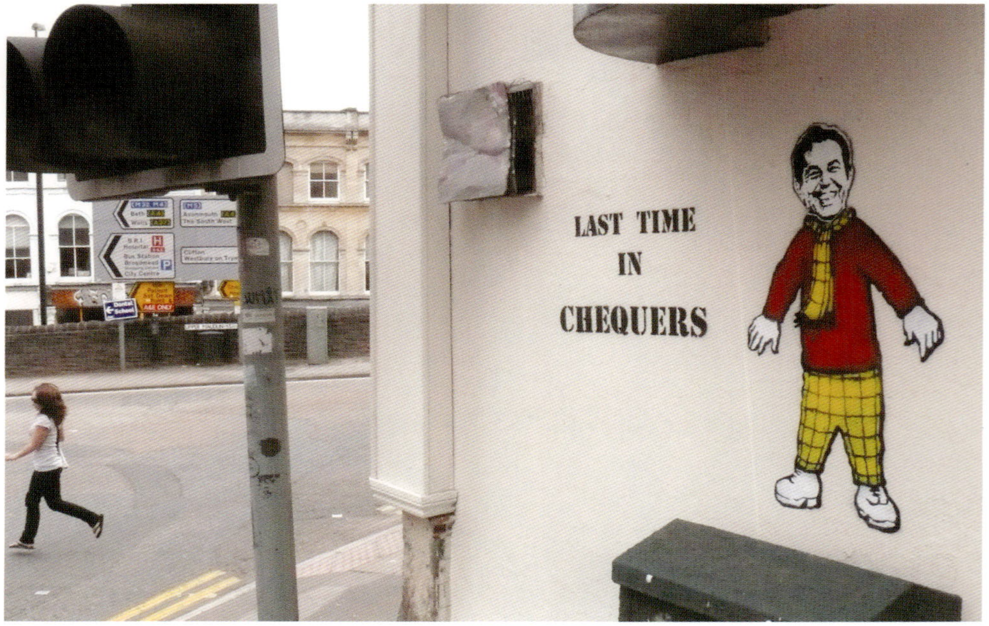

Above: 'Girl' freehand spray paint on canvas, 1994

Top right: 'SK' with Inkie on the outside of Special K's Cafe, 1986

Bottom: 'Last Time In Chequers' on the same wall as 'SK', 2007

So you were mesmerised by all the elements of hip hop?
"I think it was the music and the graffiti together, the whole package. But you had to choose your weapon, and I was no DJ, although I'd try to scratch up Herbie Hancock's *Rock It* on one turntable. I'd be pause-button tape mixing and stuff, until I killed the tape machine."

Where did you paint your first piece? Can you remember what it said?
"Westbury Village, on the side of a Kiosk. I painted it around 10.30 at night, maybe

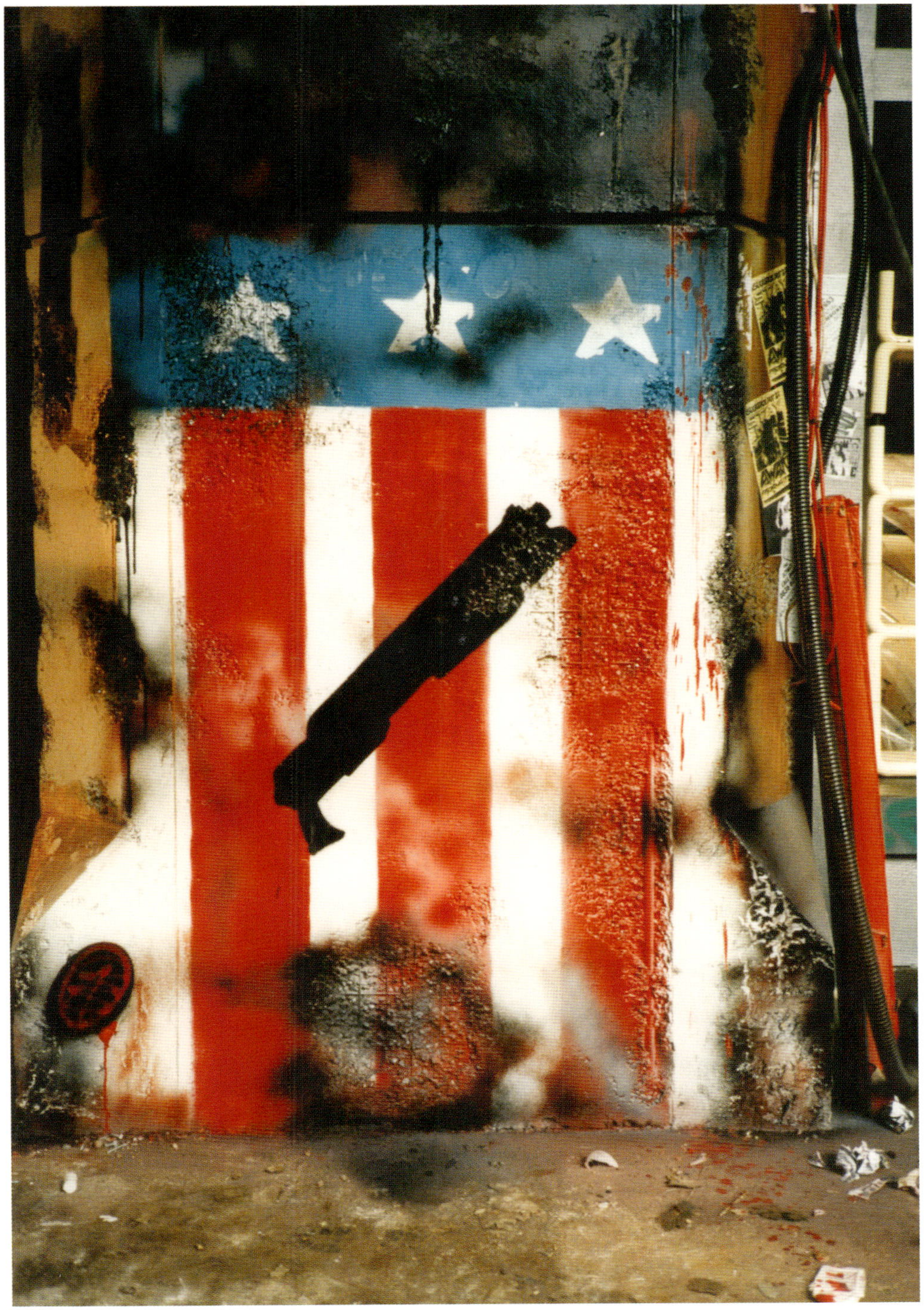

even earlier. It said Crazy Crew. It had blue letters and a yellow 3-D. I went in the shop the next day, buzzing because it was there and they didn't know I'd done it. Then once you've done one you want to get your can control up to par, in the same way that Dondi outlined the Buffalo Gals letters: that was the goal. I'd be practising in my dad's garage, inhaling pure Car Plan. I still use that stuff – the Electric Blue is spot on."

Were you racking paint as soon as you started painting?
"That was all part of it, and besides, we didn't have any money. The paint was stolen from car accessory establishments. You had to find a way to go in there and get as much paint as possible, and you couldn't do that with a jacket. So you'd go in there with a big sports bag, with a towel and a tennis racket sticking out, so you looked liked Mr Sporty, and then just get as many as you could, without rattling."

Can you remember your first tag, or is it too embarrassing to share?
"Chilly B. I used to play with all sorts of names. Then it was Wizardo, but where that came from I've no idea. And then it was Ego Wizardo. It took me quite a while to get to a point where I was happy with a name."

Were you in a crew before you hooked up with us and joined Crime Inc?
"Yeah, we were called the Bomb Squad, but the names changed every other week. That was with this guy Scott, who wrote Tootz. We did a piece in the sixth-form common room at school: it had subway trains on it and was a complete rip-off out of *Subway Art*, basically."

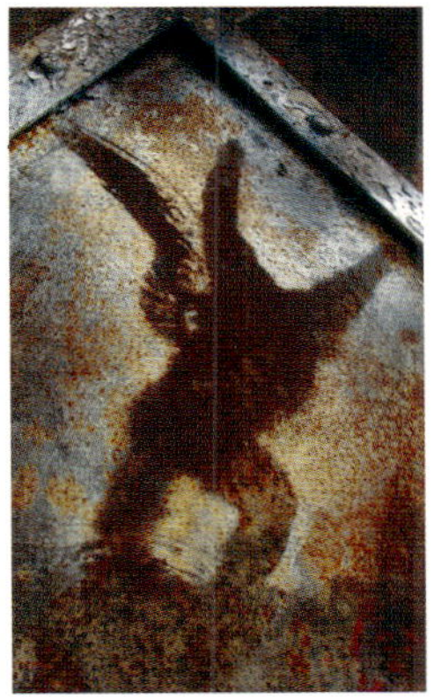

Above: 'Apish Angel', 2006

Left: Set painting from *Judge Dredd* (copyright Hollywood Pictures, 1995)

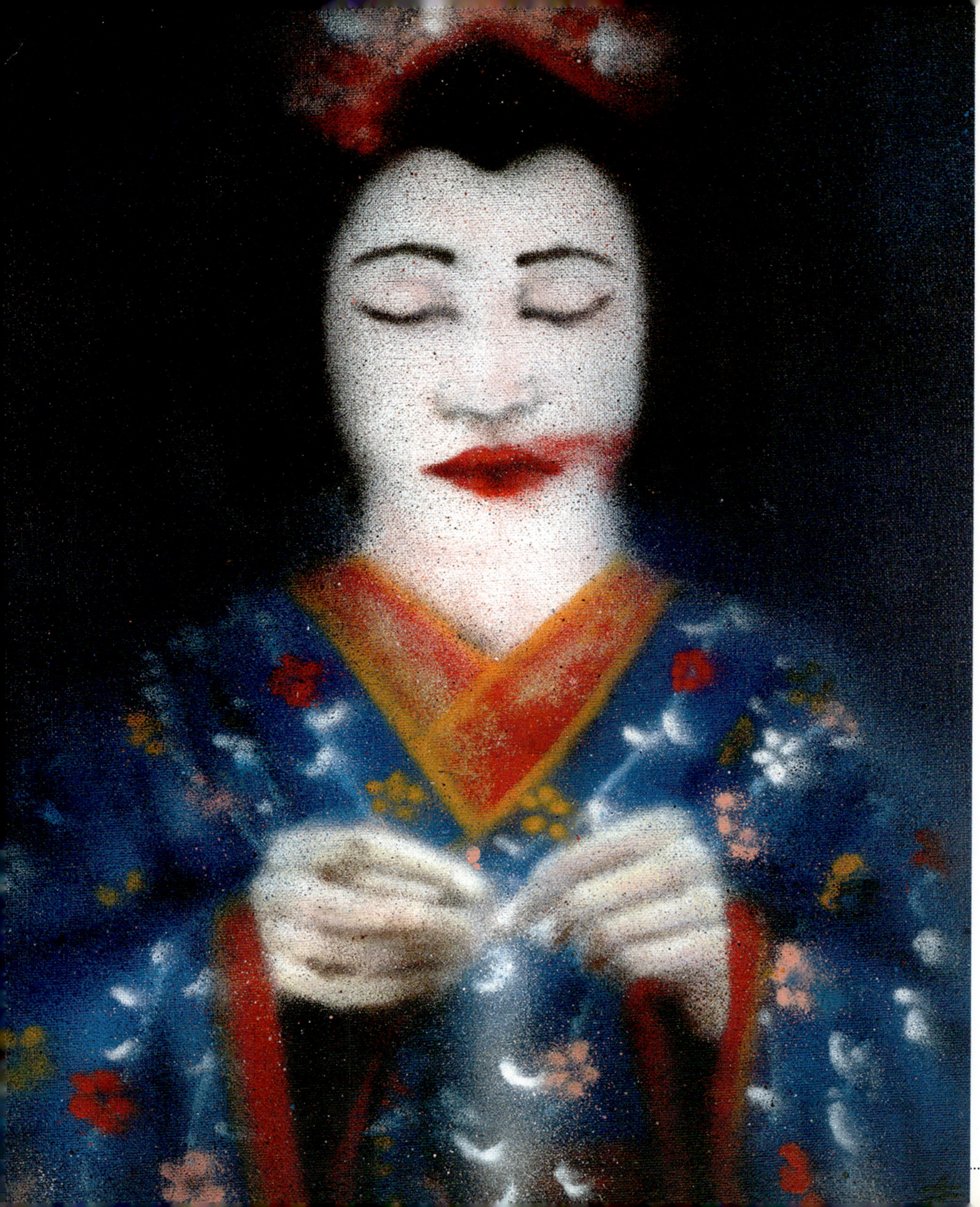

How did you get involved in the Arnolfini Graffiti Art exhibition in 1985?
"Me and Scott just walked into the Arnolfini and met Jeremy Rees, who was the director at the time, and we proposed that they have a graffiti art exhibition. He was an open-minded character so we spoke about it, and he seemed very interested in the idea. But when it happened it was on a much greater scale than I had anticipated.

"I guess with me being a 15-year-old, the Arnolfini didn't have much faith in me getting anything together. And so after I proposed the idea, 3D pretty much took over, which wasn't a bad thing. It was cool, he spurred people on, and he was a lot more connected than I was. It made it happen to the extent that it did."

The Arnolfini's a pretty big, white space: what was it like painting in there?
"Everyone painted on the same day, and it was pungent in there. We painted ridiculously big pieces, they were massive for the time. We had loads of Buntlack. In hindsight I could have done something better. I remember finishing it and thinking, 'Wow, that's a lot of orange.'"

Buntlack was the Rolls Royce of spray paint – the colours were so bright.
"It was the Holy Grail. They had pink and purple, and sort of blancmange colours. And there were only certain places that you could... acquire it. The main difference was that it dried really quick. It wasn't like it came out any thinner or anything, it was still pretty high-pressure shit. But once we started to get Buntlack our pieces just started to look more vibrant. It was a new era – a page had been turned."

The following year we started going out painting as Crime Inc. I remember it being a laugh most of the time.
"Back then everyone was a lot less jumpy. It's only after you get caught that you start thinking, 'We could go down for this', having been told that it's a punishable offence. It's the fear of what you don't know as well, and we were never sure what could happen. So really we should have hit a lot more spots than we did. Looking back, it's like, 'fuck, what were we doing?'

"I remember one time we wandered out with two bags of paint and we were walking through Kingsdown, and the police stopped us and we hadn't even painted anything. But I think they took our names and told us, 'You'd best be going back inside now.' But we just went back to your house for half an hour and then went back out again."

Have you ever had any major run-ins with the police for painting illegally?
"I think I was the last person to be arrested during Operation Anderson. I was in London and I was running around, a bit drunk. We tagged up Trafalgar Square and we got chased by a copper, PC Fat Nigel. I'll never forget it. He chased us down this road, then round the back of these shops and into this dead end where he caught up with us. We literally ducked under his arms, outran him and got into a cab.

"The driver refused to move at first, guessing we'd been up to no good. We told him we were being chased by skinheads, so he reluctantly pulled away at which point three police cars intercepted the cab and we got taken to Bow Street police station and got locked up overnight. We were picked up the next day by Bristol Transport Police, who had driven up to London, because there was a warrant out for my arrest. I got a £75 fine. All that for £75."

You were mostly painting characters back then. What was it that got you interested in doing figurative work?
"From reading comics and being into it for the art, you search high and low for that kind of stuff. I used to spend a lot of time in Holland as a kid and I found this underground fantasy comic called 1984. The artwork in them was incredible, particularly this guy Alex Nino, who drew some of the most amazing characters I'd ever seen. I was trying to emulate the stuff I'd seen, and digging into my own style and being inspired enough to go away and not just copy. I got into drawing facial expressions in order to create a certain mood. Coming across those comics was almost like finding something no one else knew about."

How did you get into using stencils in your paintings?
"The first person I saw doing them was 3D, and I thought he was a lunatic at the time. We all did. We were still concentrating on the old format then, doing B-boy characters and letters and that kind of thing. But he had moved on, and that must have inspired me to take a step in that direction."

Things really started to happen after you moved to London in the early '90s. No one else in Bristol had done that, was it a career move on your part?
"Yeah, I wanted to just go and do my own thing and concentrate on producing work on canvas. From '92-'96 I was living there and working hard towards doing my first

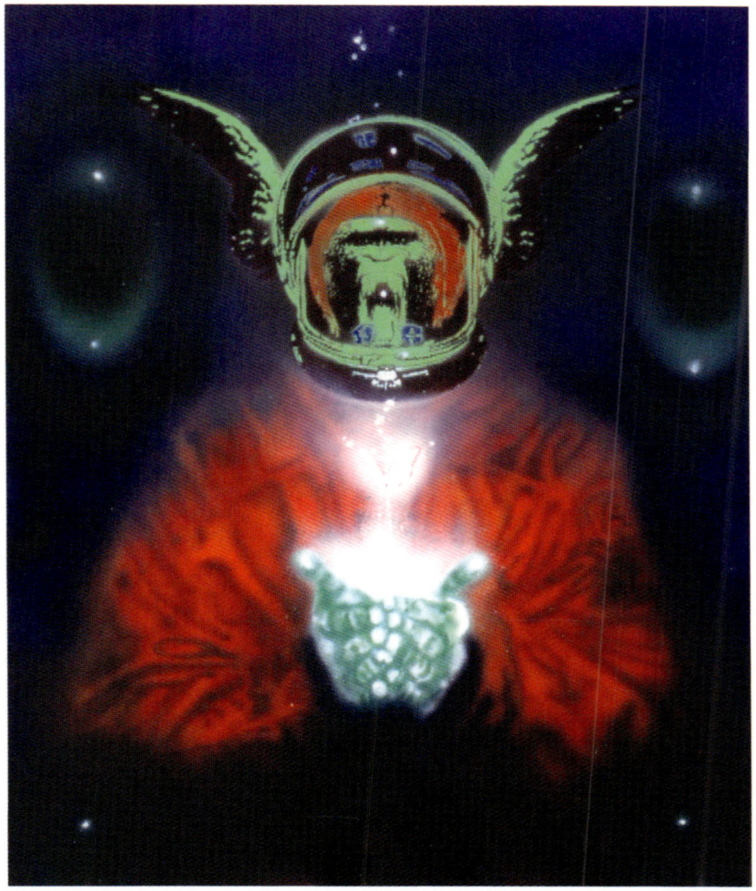

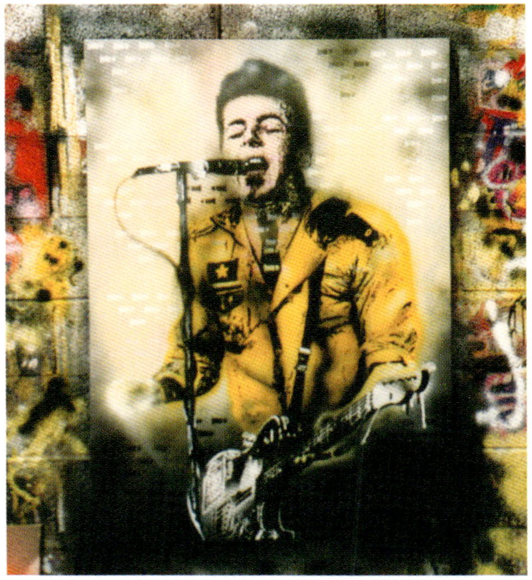

Opposite page: 'Geisha' freehand spray paint on canvas, 2003

This page. Above: 'The Angel And The Butterfly' stencil and freehand spray paint on canvas, 2002

Left: 'Strummer' stencil and freehand spray paint on board, 2004

Top right: 'Traffic King' Stencil and freehand spray paint on board, 1994

Bottom right: Selection of stencil pieces on ceramic tiles, 2005

solo shows. I was basically carving out something for myself, and concentrating on developing a style, a combination of freehand and intricate stencils."

What was your first big commercial job?
"In '94 I did an advertising campaign for Snapple. That was the first intricate stencil that I'd done – it was three or four different layers. The image was a Snapple bottle, and it was heavily influenced by Andy Warhol's 210 Coca Cola Bottles piece. I saw what I was capable of doing and then carried on trying to develop that into something.

"Then I heard about this film being made of Judge Dredd, which was still in pre-production. So I contacted them – just cold-called them – and gave them a concept of how I could be a part of the movie. I devised this idea of how in the future there would be a style of graffiti that would be totally different from styles that were on the streets at the time, fusing Hebrew, Japanese and English words all together. I created a lot of futuristic symbols as well, the idea being that 200 years from now maybe words won't be used so much.

"One film led to another film, and another, and the media picked up on it, so I got magazine coverage. And that was necessary at the time. I didn't have an agent or anything, I just did it all myself. I've only ever had an agent for six months and nothing ever came of it, really. I walked it alone and have been doing so ever since."

Where was your first solo show?
"My first show was at the Thomas Kettle Gallery in Covent Garden, in '94. The show featured a series of paintings based on 'the underclass,' which was something I read about, with the youth being involved

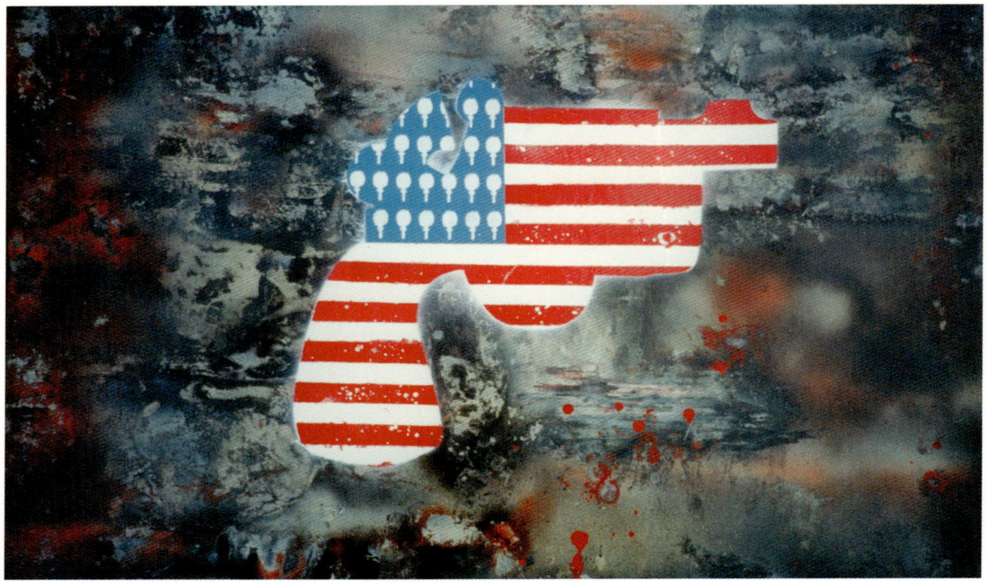

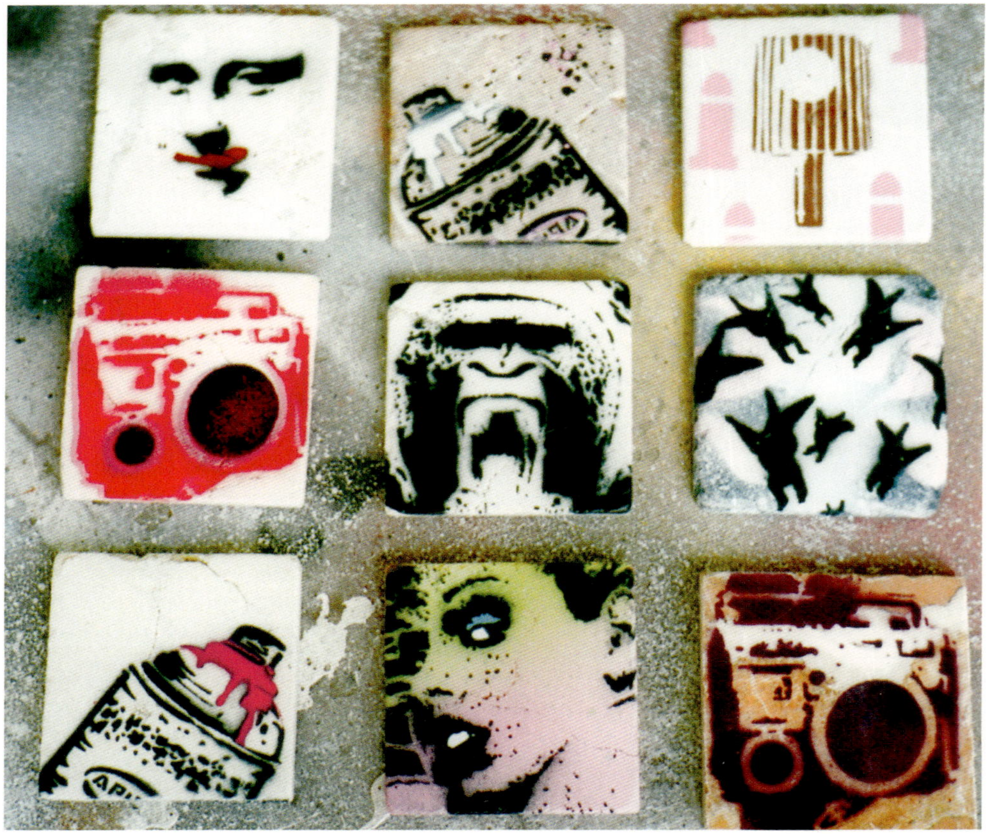

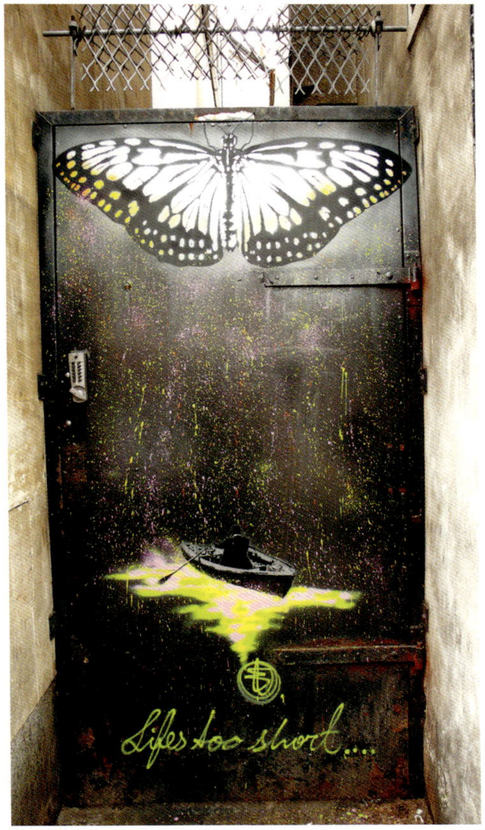

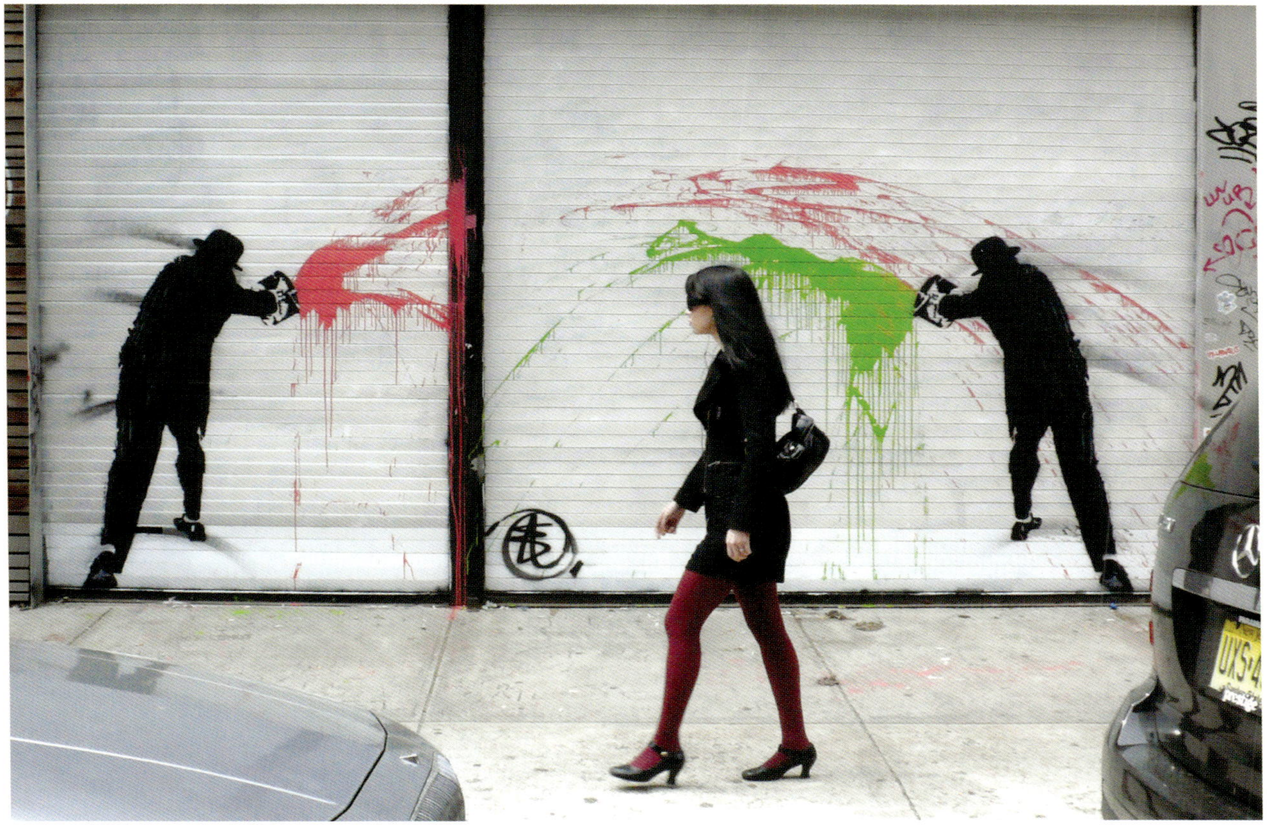

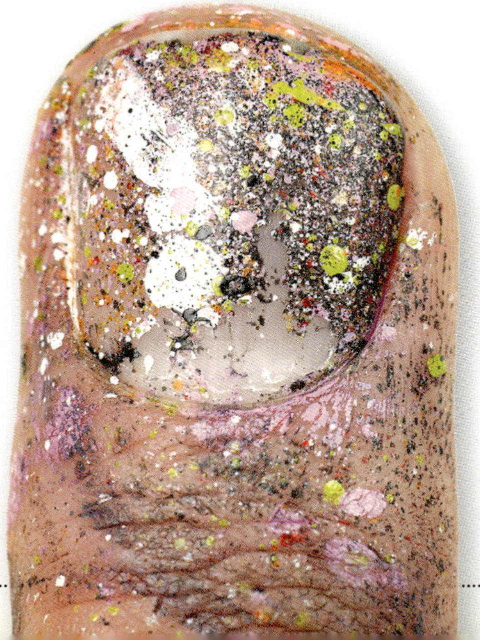

in serious crime and how it was a warning for the future. It was the first one that I did that had a concise theme."

Those transitional pieces using freehand and stencils really set your work apart.

"If you add a stencil to a rough background it has an immediate impact - it sits better than a freehand image would. It's the marriage of two different styles. For me anything that's kind of one-track becomes too clinical, or technical. When I did the Snapple stencils, I realised that you could produce a piece of work that's kind of photo-realistic, and that if you combine that with a rough, scratchy freehand background - which has a lot of energy and soul - the juxtaposition gave the images longevity."

Of all the old-school Bristol writers you are the one person who has stuck at it constantly and kept chipping away. What keeps you going?

"It's the influx of ideas that come to me and that have to be executed. It's been constant, I've painted with a goal in mind all the way. And the goal has been to live off my art, at the end of the day. There's an element inside me that makes me we want to keep raising the bar each time I come up with a new concept, and you can't do that without a purpose in life. Plus, everyone wants to make their mark on society."

Top left: 'Life's Too Short', 2007

Above: 'Chuckers' Elizabeth Street, New York, 2008

Bottom left: 'By-Product' from the Origin Of The Species show

FLX CIC

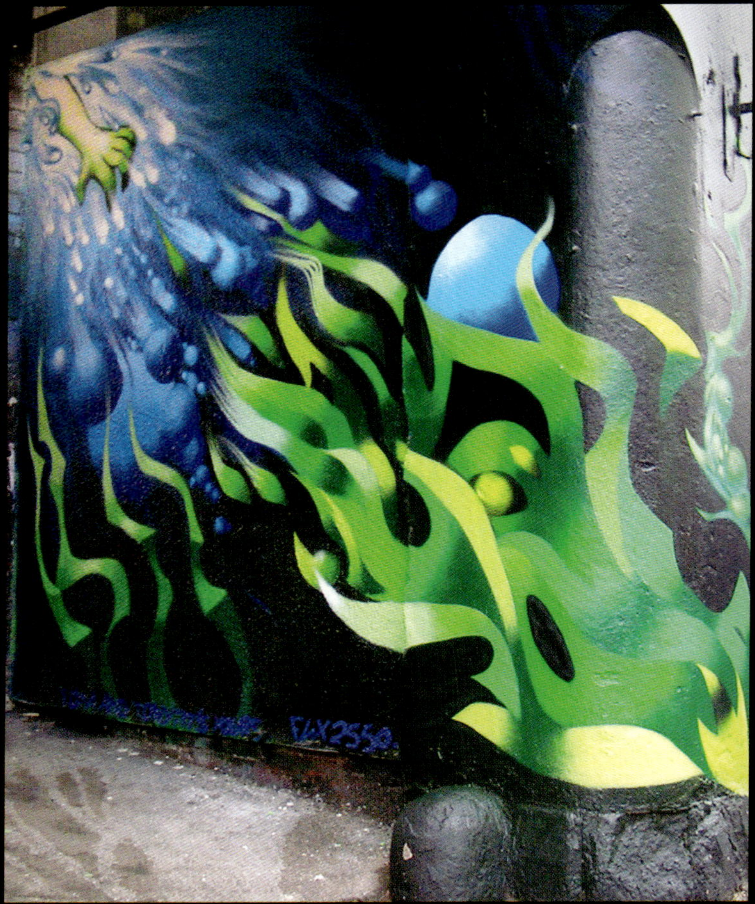

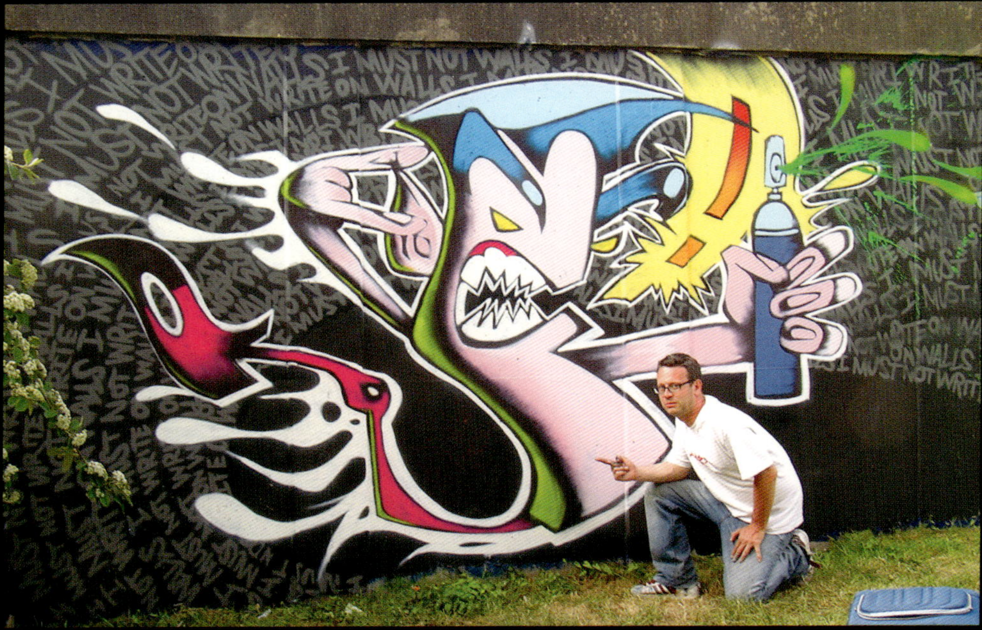

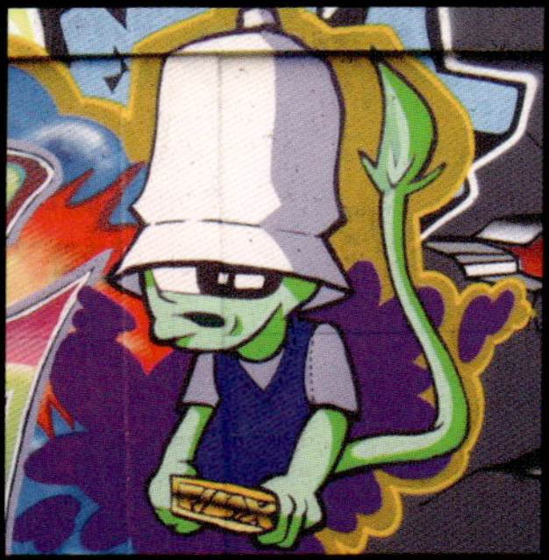

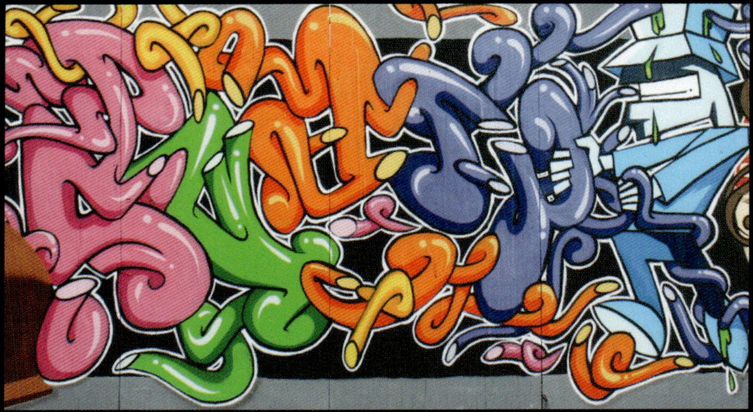

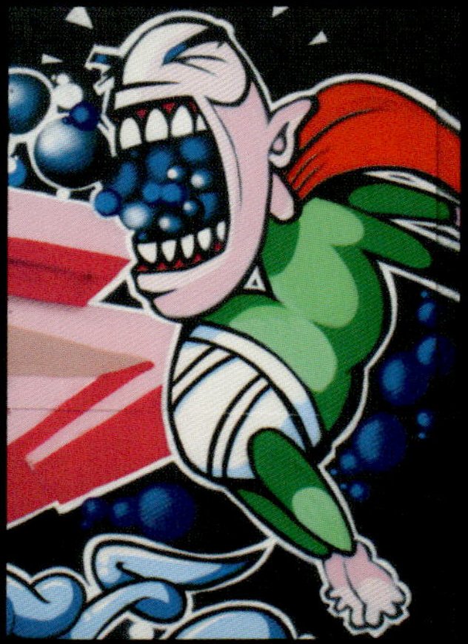

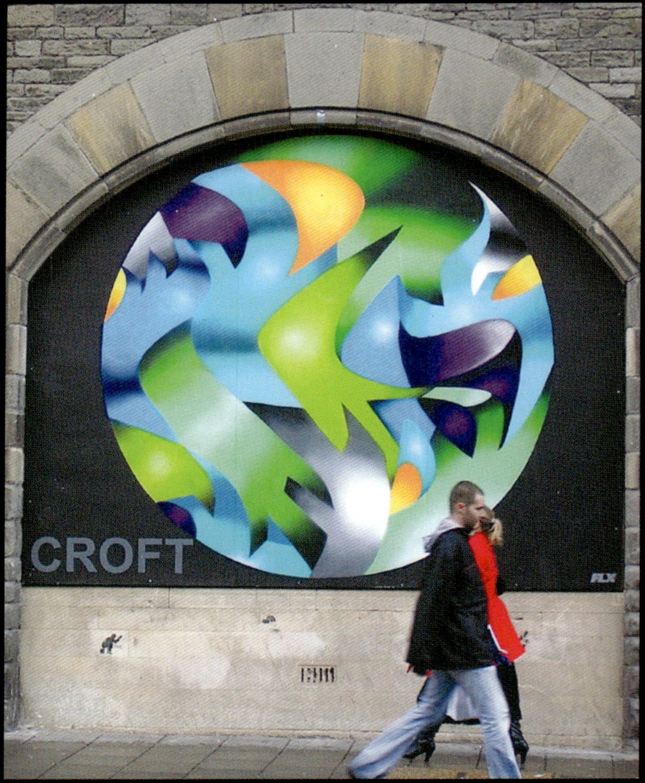

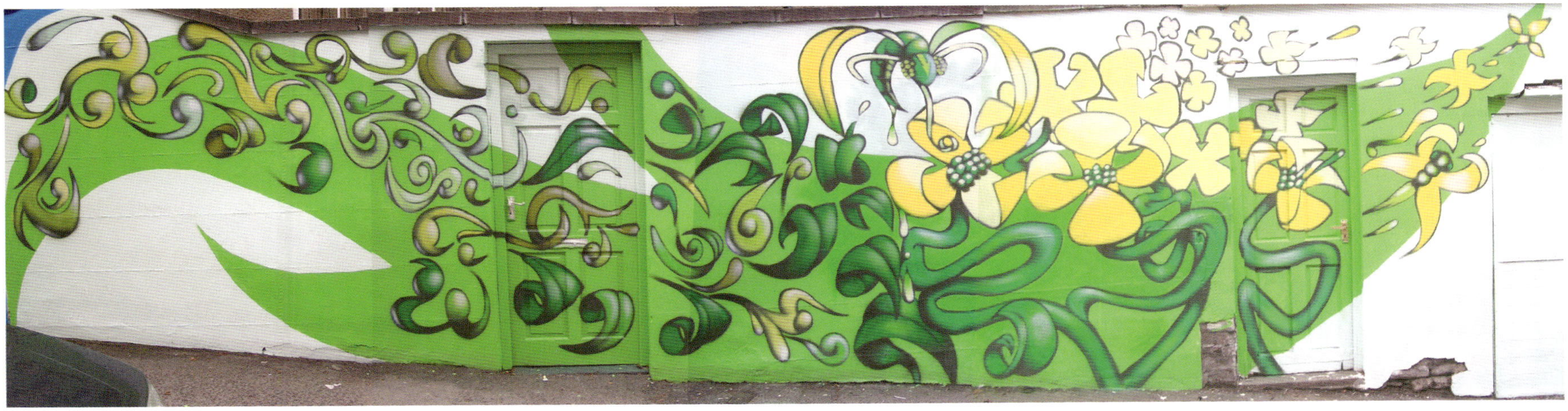

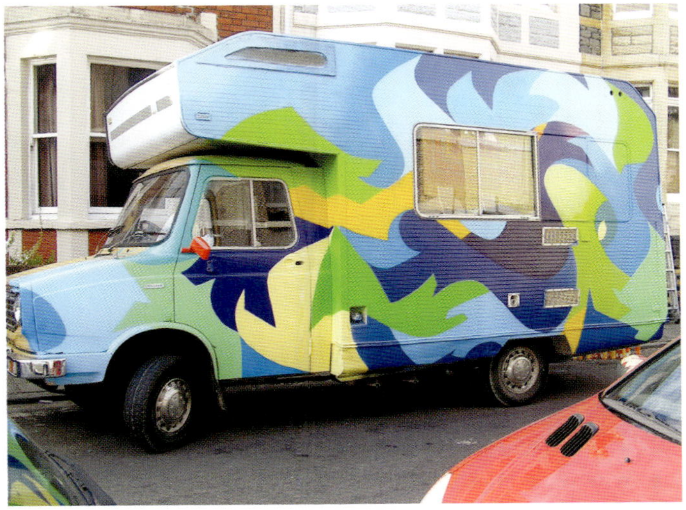

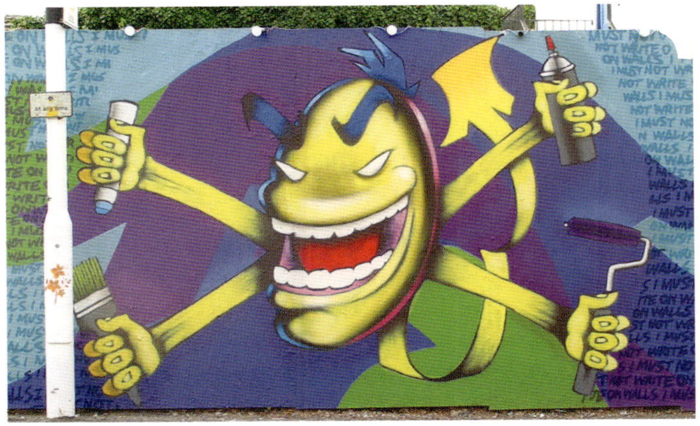

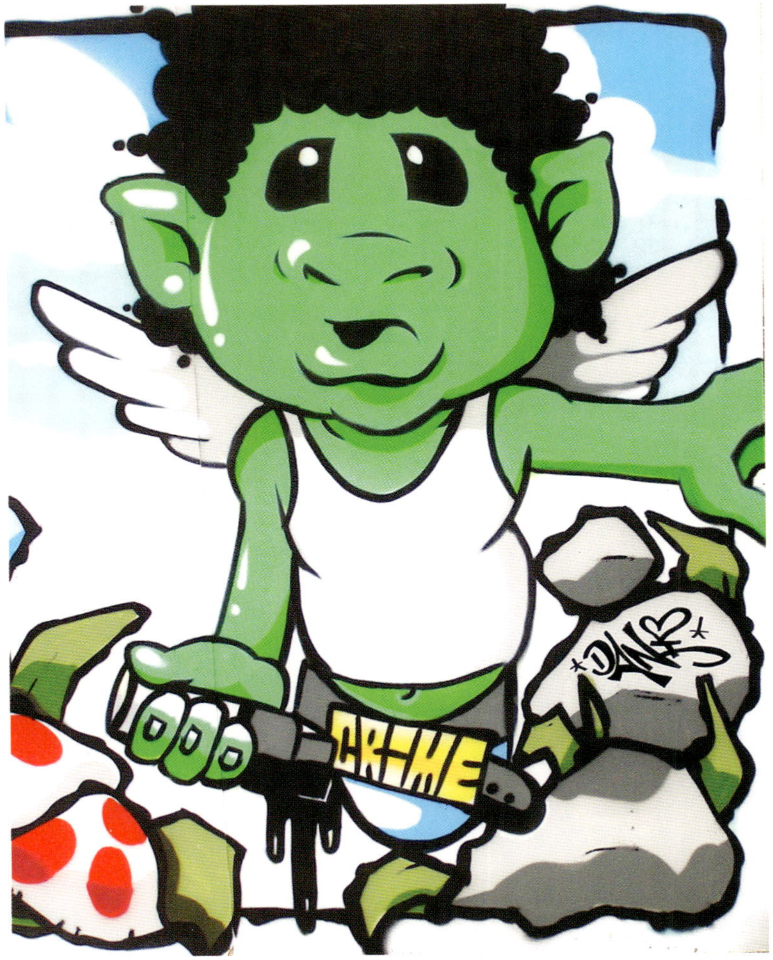

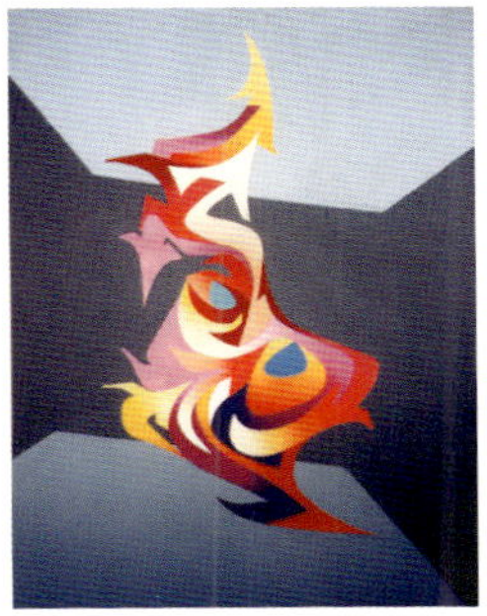

This spread: FLX's work oscilates between the abstract and the traditional character-based painting, reflecting both his experimental and old-school roots

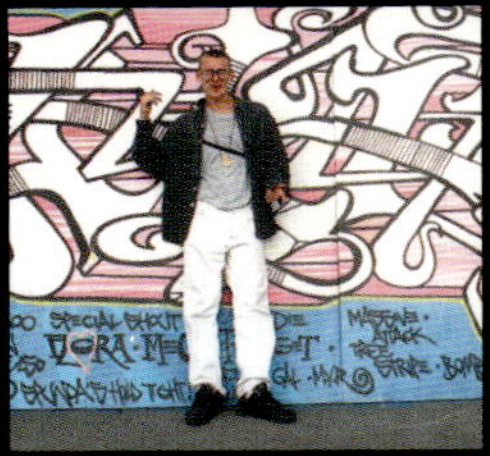

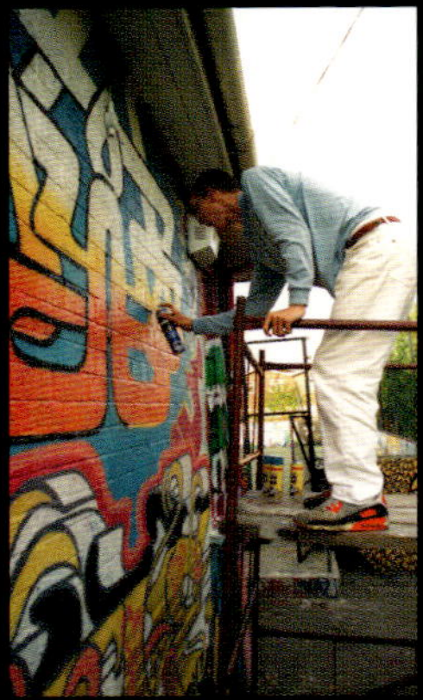

Top: Inkie in Livingstone, Scotland in 1990

Above: Painting the front wall at Barton Hill Youth Club, in 1989

Top right: Inkie and FLX painting at the Southside Freestyle event at Bedminster skate park in 1989

Bottom right: 'IE' Barton Hill Youth Club, 1989

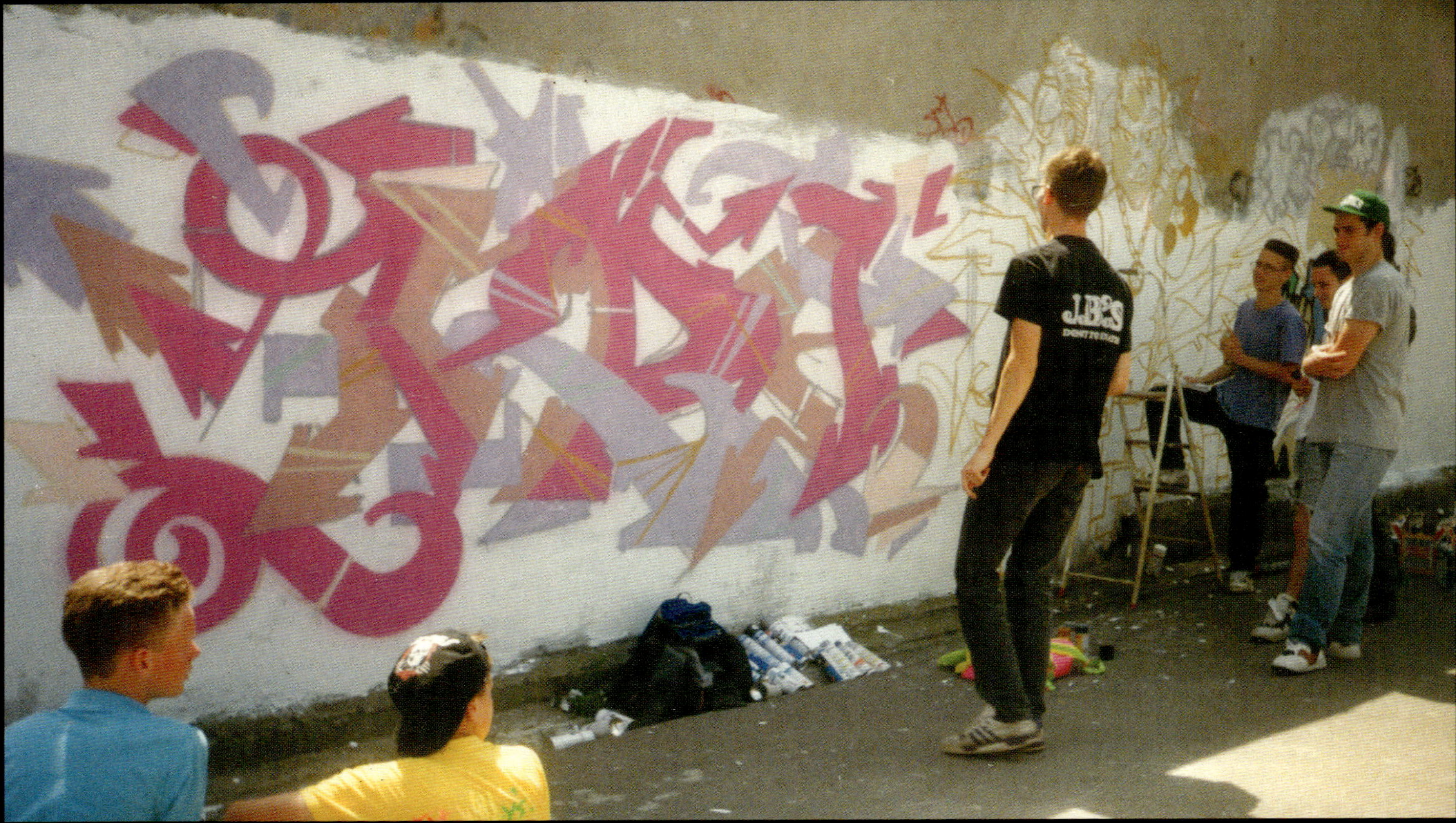

INKIE CIC/TUA/TUB/KTS/NOT/XXX/OGOG/GK

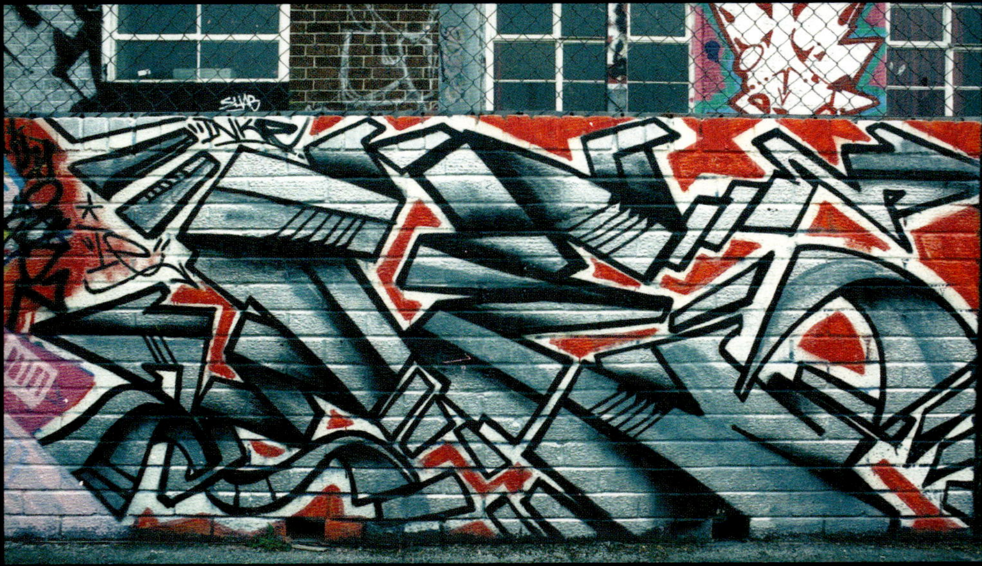

• **1981: A tall, bespectacled ten year-old kid is clutching the joystick on a Pac-Man machine as if his life depends on it.** With a new high score in sight his tongue pokes out of the side of his mouth in intense concentration. On the screen the yellow Pac-Man's mouth opens and closes furiously, eating up the dots in the maze until it reaches a 'power pellet.' The titular yellow circle hovers, tempting the four ghosts to come ever nearer and, just before being attacked by its adversaries, the kid

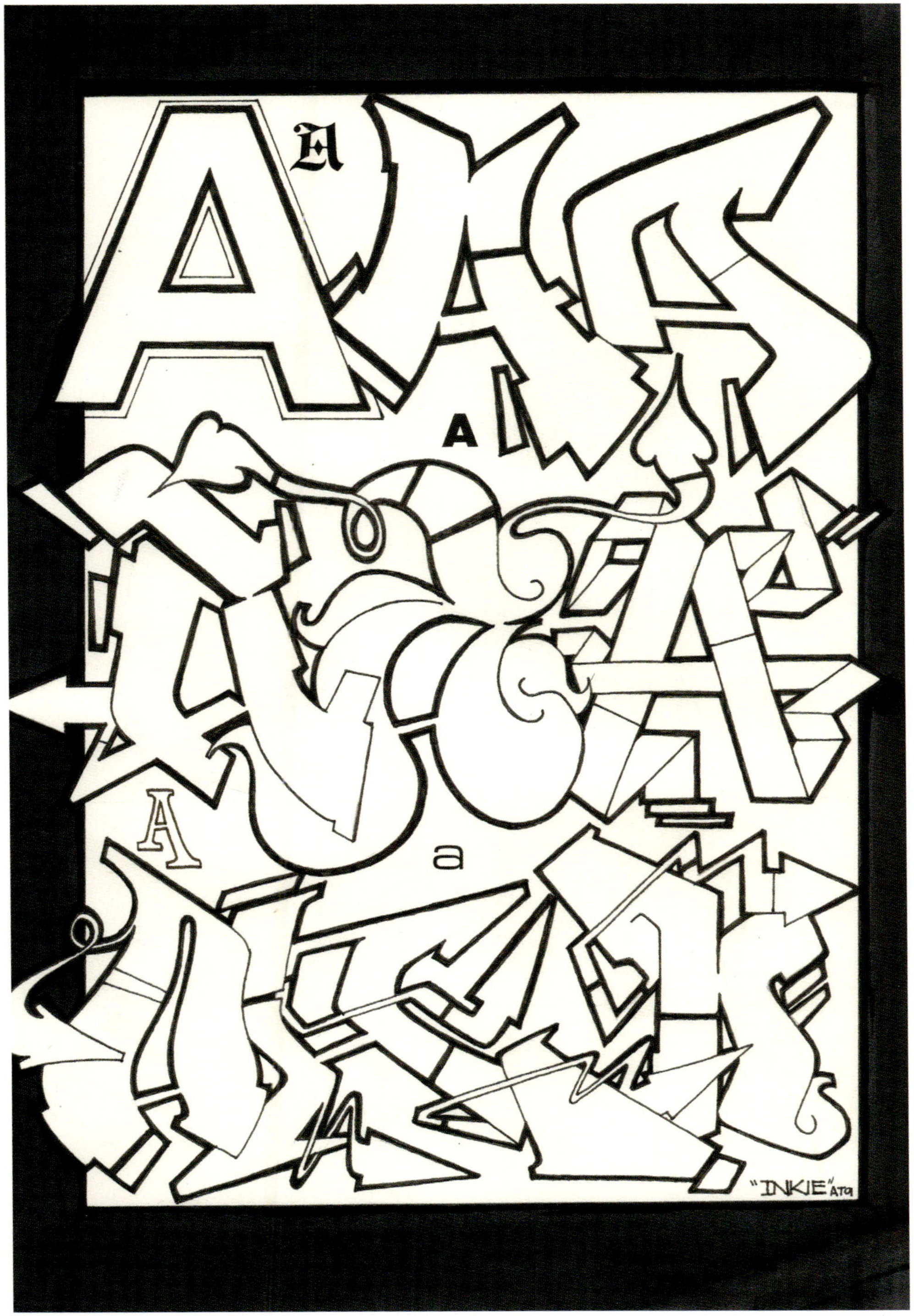

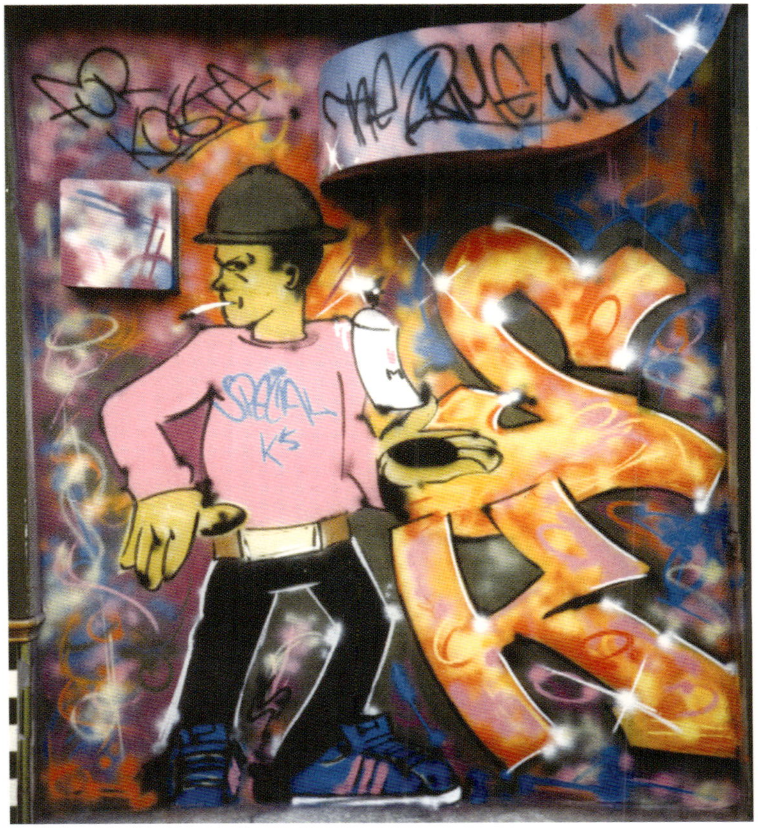

Above: 'SK' Inkie and FLX on Special K's Cafe, 1986

Left: 'Letter A studies' Ink on paper, 1988

slams the joystick to the right and Pac-Man eats the pellet. The ghosts turn blue, and Pac-Man eats them up: first Blinky, then Pinky, Clyde and finally Inky. A new high score is achieved for the local king of the arcades and the name of the last ghost sticks in the kid's head.

"When I was young – just after I'd started doing graffiti – I bought a Bazooka Joe bubble gum and inside it was like a proverb thing that came with a little cartoon that said 'you will become famous for writing on walls.' And I thought to myself 'right, I'm going to do this.'"

Competitive from an early age, and a video-game king long before he discovered his abilities with a spray can, Inkie is a

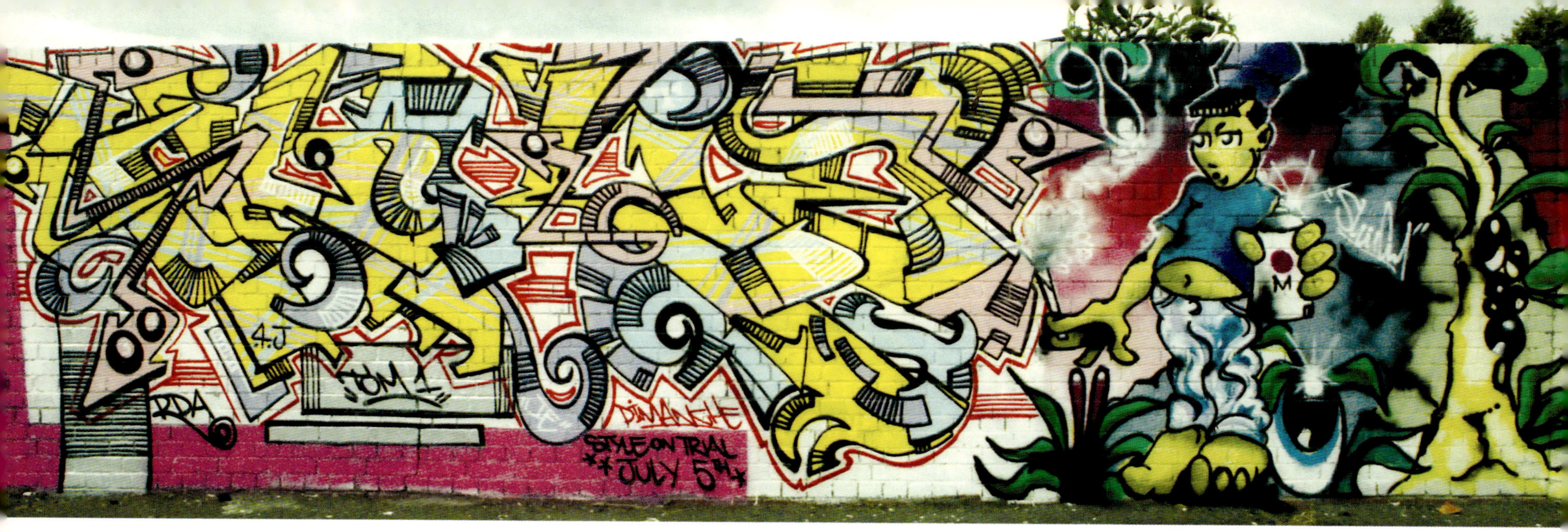
RDA
STYLE ON TRIAL
JULY 5th

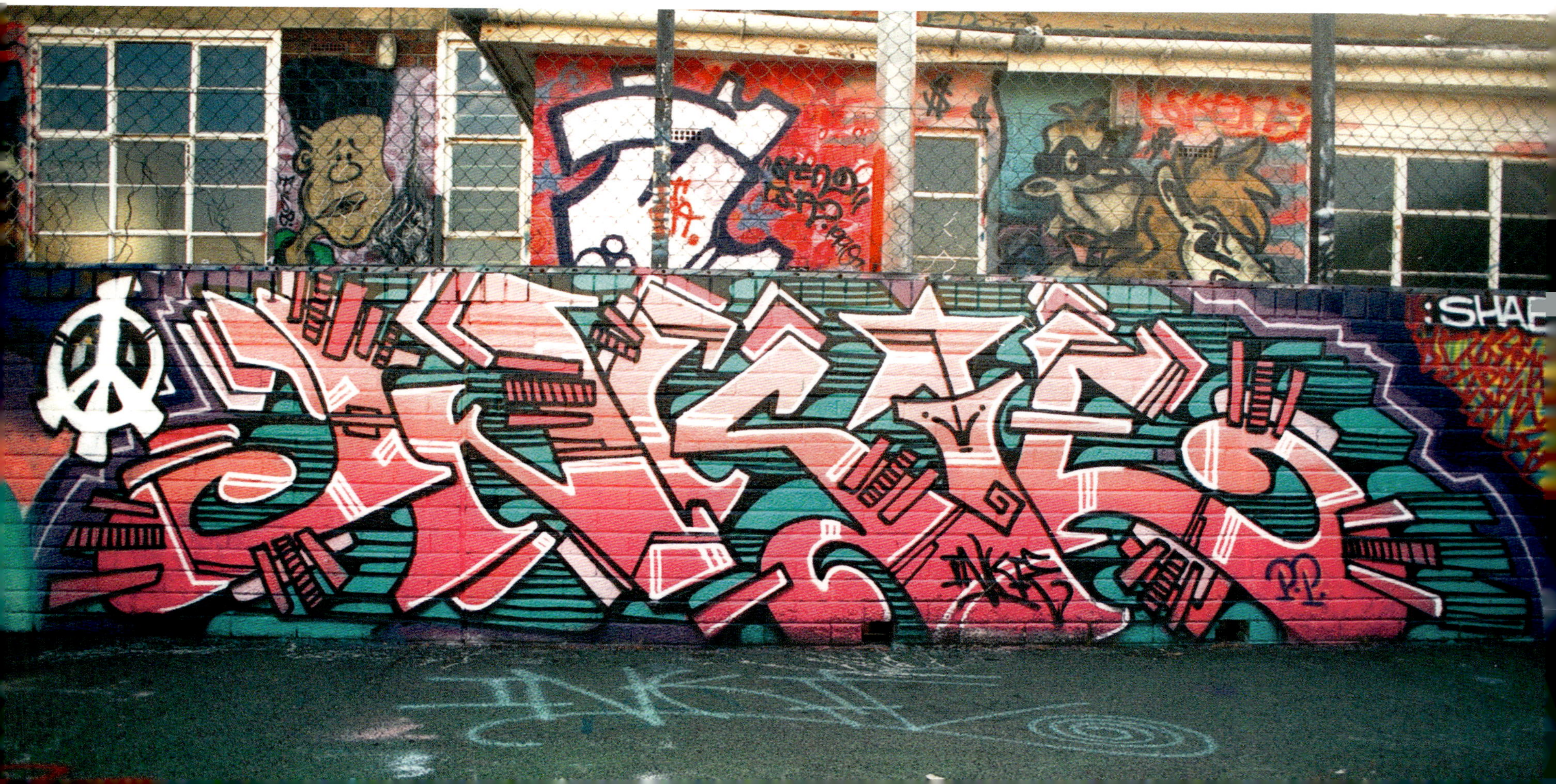
:SHAB

household name on the graffiti scene. His experimental and progressive approach to designing and painting pieces saw him taking the concept of wildstyle letter design to a new level, introducing elements from influences as diverse as Ancient Egyptian and Mayan friezes to Art Nouveau, circuit board diagrams and plant forms.

"Definitely my dad's architecture design inspired me, and as a child there was always art in the house. He did art with us on Saturdays, and we were encouraged to go to art galleries and museums when we went on holiday. My dad saw that I was into it and helped me push that a bit further. Meeting your mum as well, that's why I think Crime Inc developed so quickly, because we were all from creative backgrounds."

Clearly it is difficult for me to write about Inkie's life in graffiti and his achievements objectively because I know him so well, but his pedigree and stature on the scene clearly speak for themselves. He's talking about my mother in the previous quote, and my brother and I were both members of his original crew. So what follows is as much a conversation between a couple of old friends as it is an interview with one of the country's longest-established graffiti writers.

Starry-eyed city duo switch on to TV fame

TOM MAKES HIS MARK WRITING ON WALL

TOM Bingle is set is be a TV star — because of his skills as a graffiti artist.

He has been filmed painting the logo that will be used for the opening credits of the popular kids TV show Can You Do It On TV? presented by Michaela Strachan.

And he has been signed up to design and paint the set for next month's new series.

Story: CHRISTINE ALSFORD
Picture: NIGEL TAILBY

Can You Do It On TV? producer Ludo Graham said: "His work is absolutely brilliant.

"It's lively and exciting and modern and really in keeping with the style of the show."

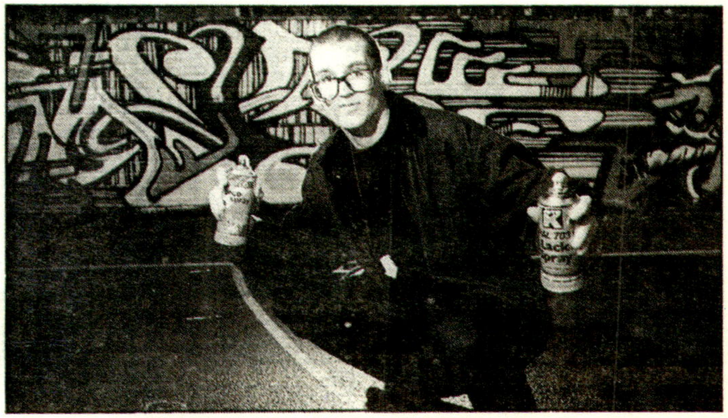

DRAWING ON TALENT: Graffiti artist Tom Bingle in front of his work

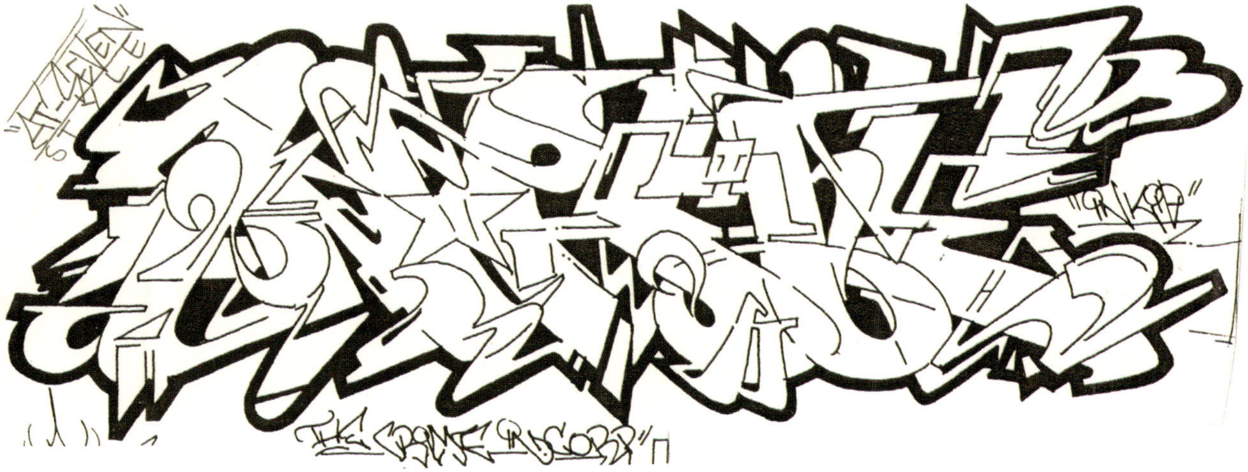

What inspired you to start painting?

"Seeing *Subway Art*. It was just instant, I just thought 'fuck me, this is the most amazing art form I've seen in my life and it's perfect for what I want to do with my drawing.' Creatively I think it was your drawing, the lettering and stuff you were doing really was like 'wow.' It was so immediate because I saw you doing it in front of me, and that really pushed me into it. Then seeing 3D's stuff, I was really amazed by some of his early work."

I remember you embraced the challenge pretty much from the start, and became like a designing machine.

"It was that whole trying to perfect something, and honing it by just practising, and practising. You're always trying to better yourself, and every time you do a bit of drawing you learn something from it; you can do a drawing, see it, do another one, and it's better. That kind of organic growth of the art form where you're inspired by

Opposite page. Top: 'Style On Trial' Inkie and FLX, Newtown estate, 1989

Bottom: Barton Hill, 1989

This page. Top: Inkie makes the headlines, 1989

Bottom: 'Inkie', pen on paper, 1987

This page. Top: Livingstone jam, Scotland, 1989

Bottom: DB Records, London Spraypaint and paint pen, 2003

Opposite page. Top right: Inkie and Cheo, front wall at Barton Hill youth club, 1989

Bottom right: Outlining with Smoothrite at Barton Hill, 1989

Top left: Three of the four seasons, Latitude Festival. Spray paint and paint pen on board, 2007

Bottom left: 'Ink Nouveau' at Cargo, London. Paint pen on board, 2008

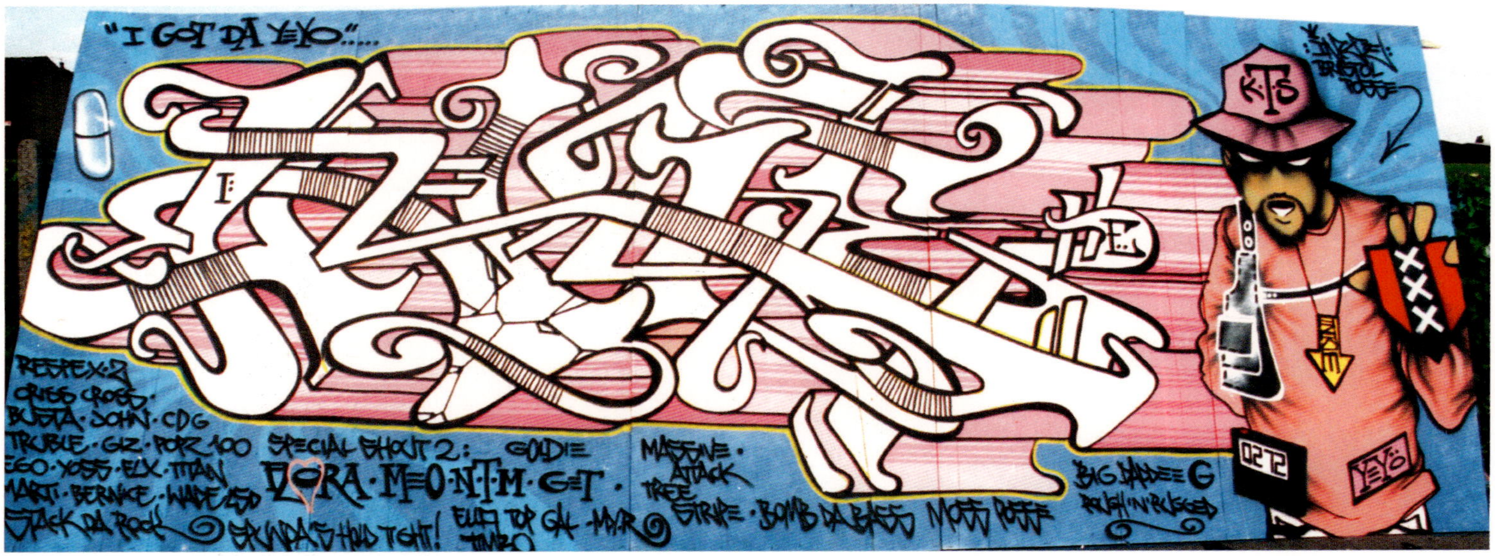

everyone else's work, without copying them, and that competitiveness that we used to have in the early days: those were the things that sucked me in."

I think you were out to burn my brother and me as soon as you got into it. In fact, we didn't really start to go out bombing properly until it became obvious that you were going to be the letters man in the crew. Tell me about those early bombing missions.
"We'd all stay in, get stoned and then go out, a whole load of us. First we would shoplift the paint, then smoke some spliffs and draw a design up, then finally hit a wall. We were doing pieces all around Kingsdown, Montpelier, Redland, Clifton and Cotham. We actually did a fair bit in quite a short space of time. That was after 3D and the Z-Boys had stopped, so there was no one else really doing the illegal stuff then."

That helped us get a lot of attention for what we were doing, I think - and the fact that we were smashing it, of course. I can still remember vividly the buzz of seeing one of our pieces up on a wall the day after we had painted it.
"Even just seeing a tag I'd done would get me so excited that I'd have to go back and walk past it like four or five times. I'd go out of my way to check out my tags and make sure they were still there. I'd just get a feeling of immense pride. With doing pieces, it was the fact that you could show someone your abilities and it was in a public place. It builds up your confidence, doing illegal stuff and people commenting on it, and you start to move on. It's that whole 'practice makes perfect' thing. Because you're getting an ego boost with people patting you on the back, you end up doing more and more."

Nick Walker was also coming out bombing with us by then. Can you remember where you guys first met?
"At Special K's Café, I think that was where I first bumped into Nick. That's also where

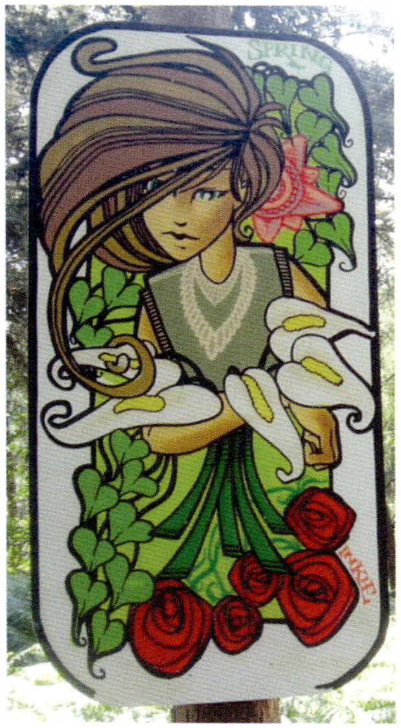
SPRING
INKIE

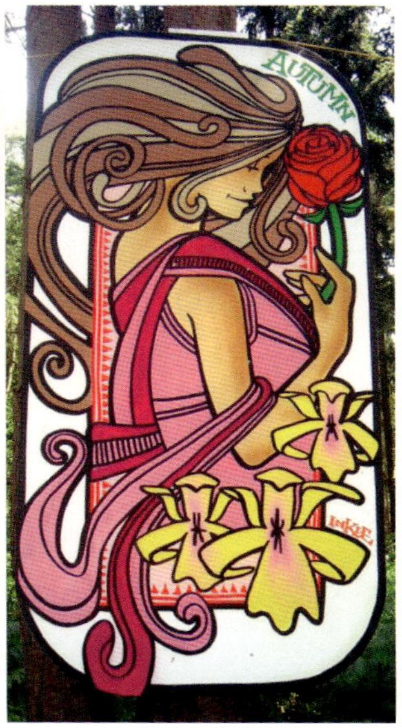
AUTUMN

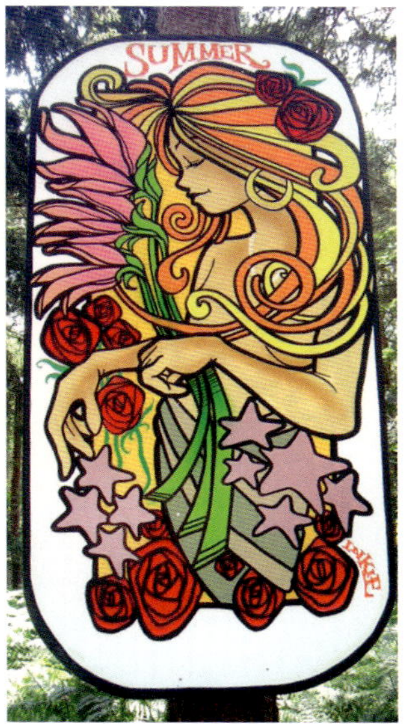
SUMMER
INKIE

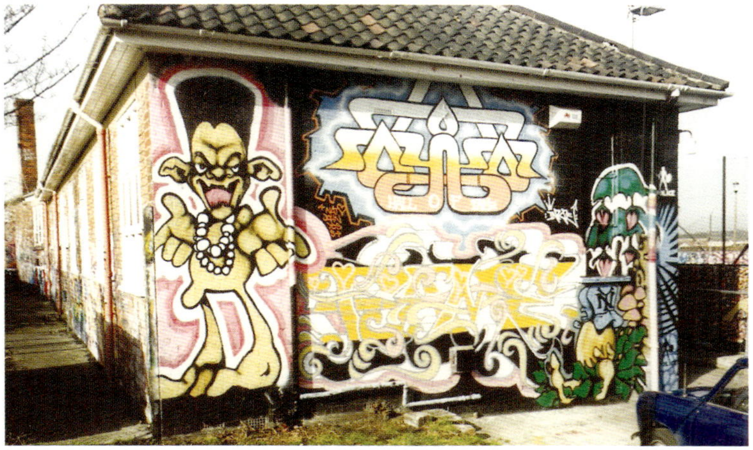

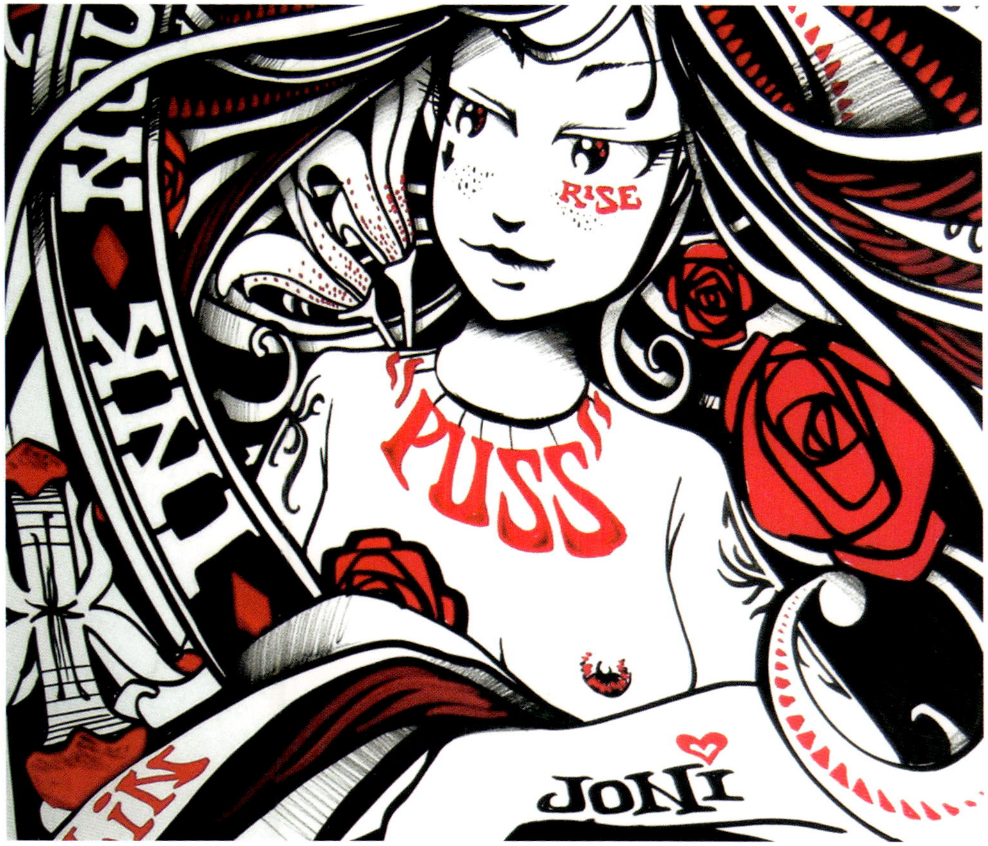
RISE
PUSS
JONI

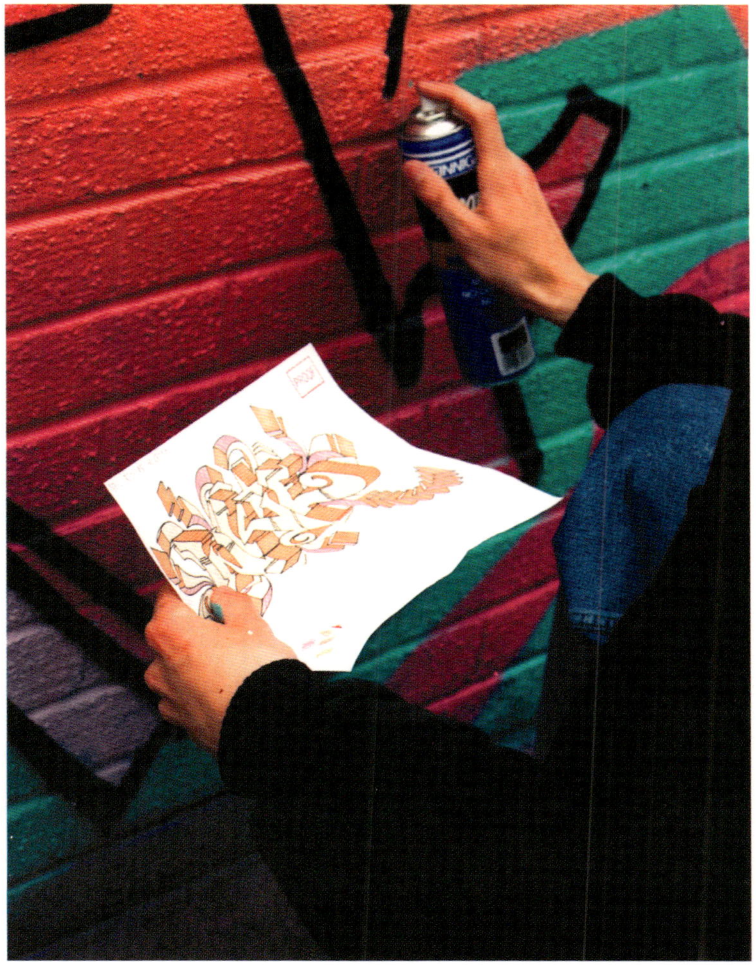

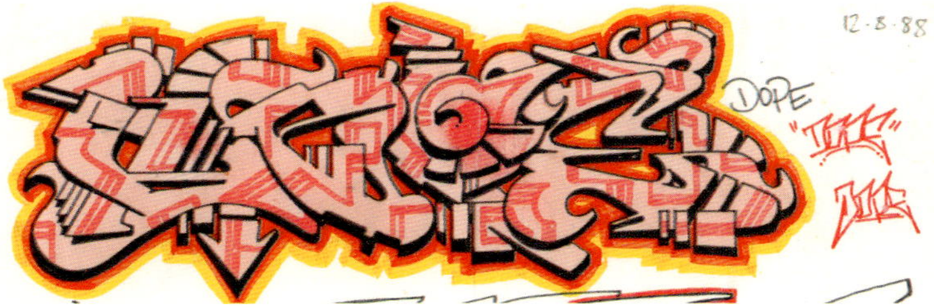
12-8-88
DOPE

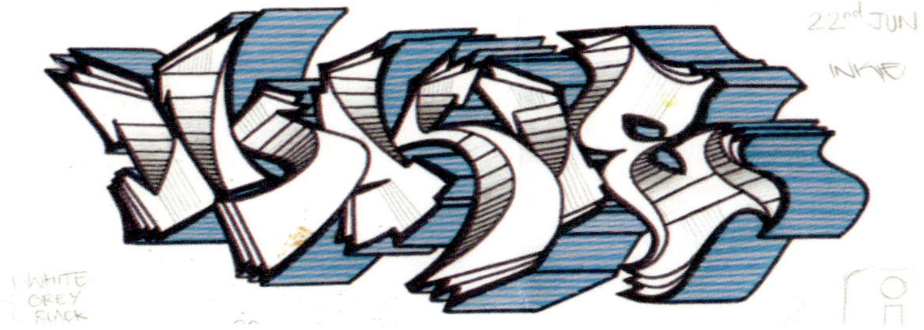
22nd JUN
INKIE
WHITE
GREY
BLACK

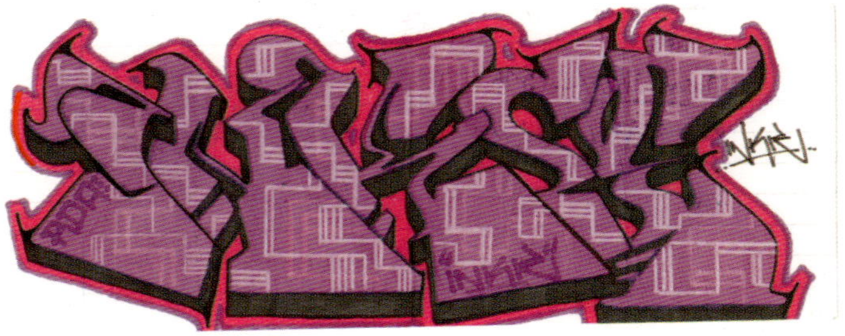

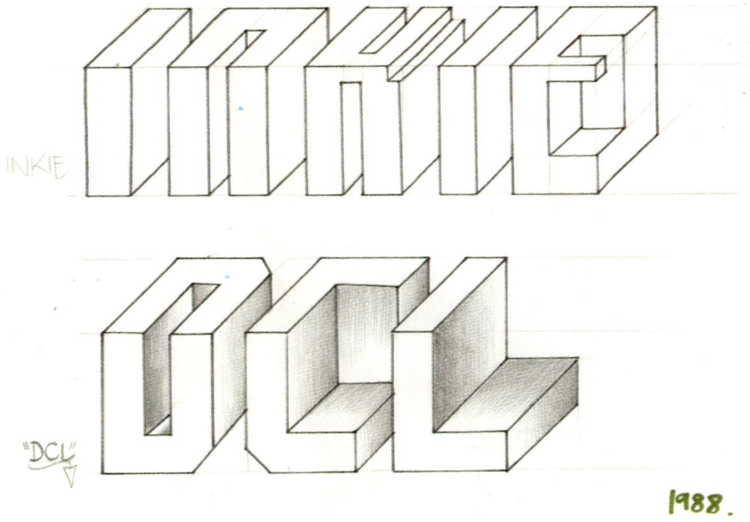
INKIE
"DCL"
1988.

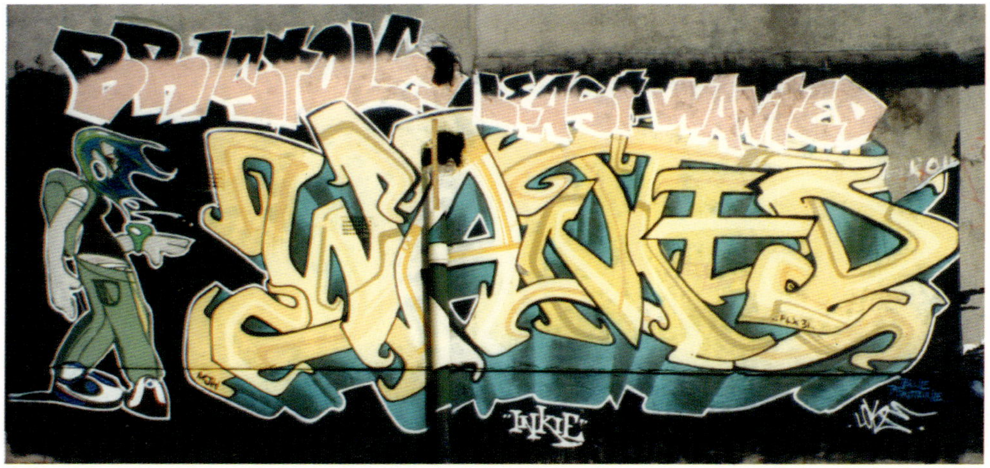
INKIE

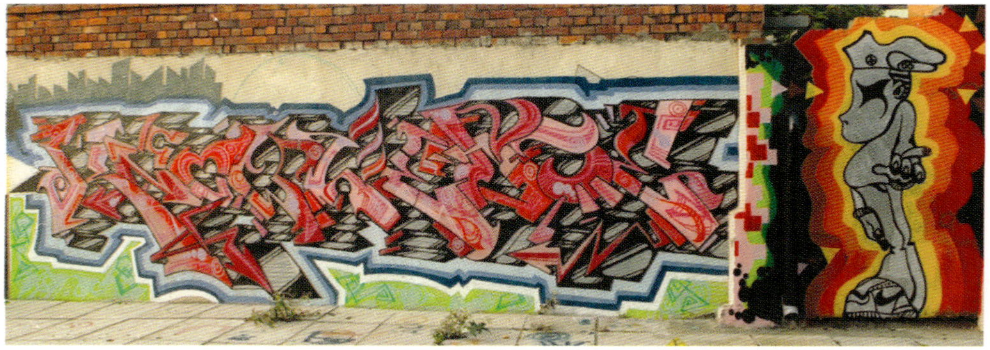

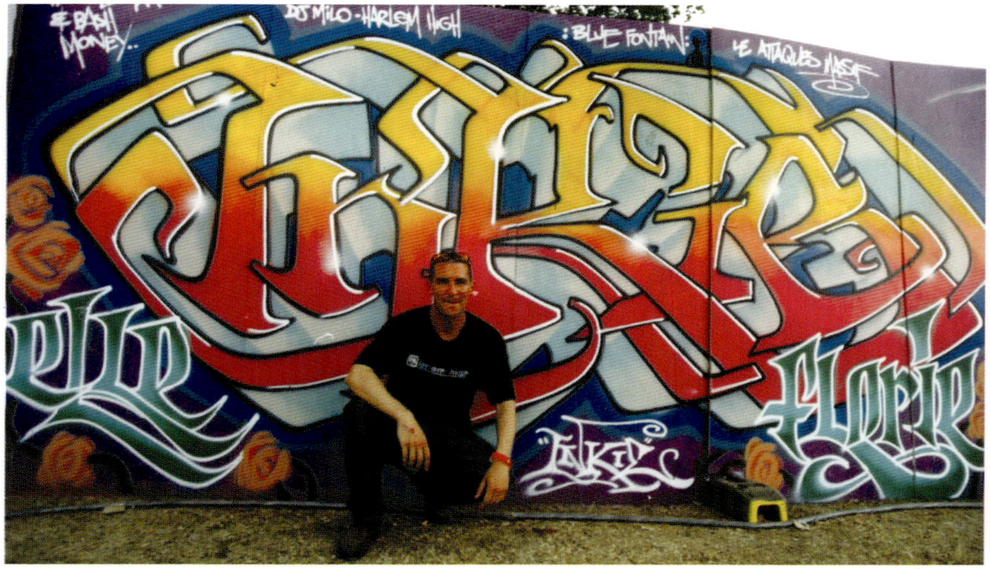
& BASH MONEY
DJ MILO - HARLEM HIGH
BLUE FONTAIN
INKIE

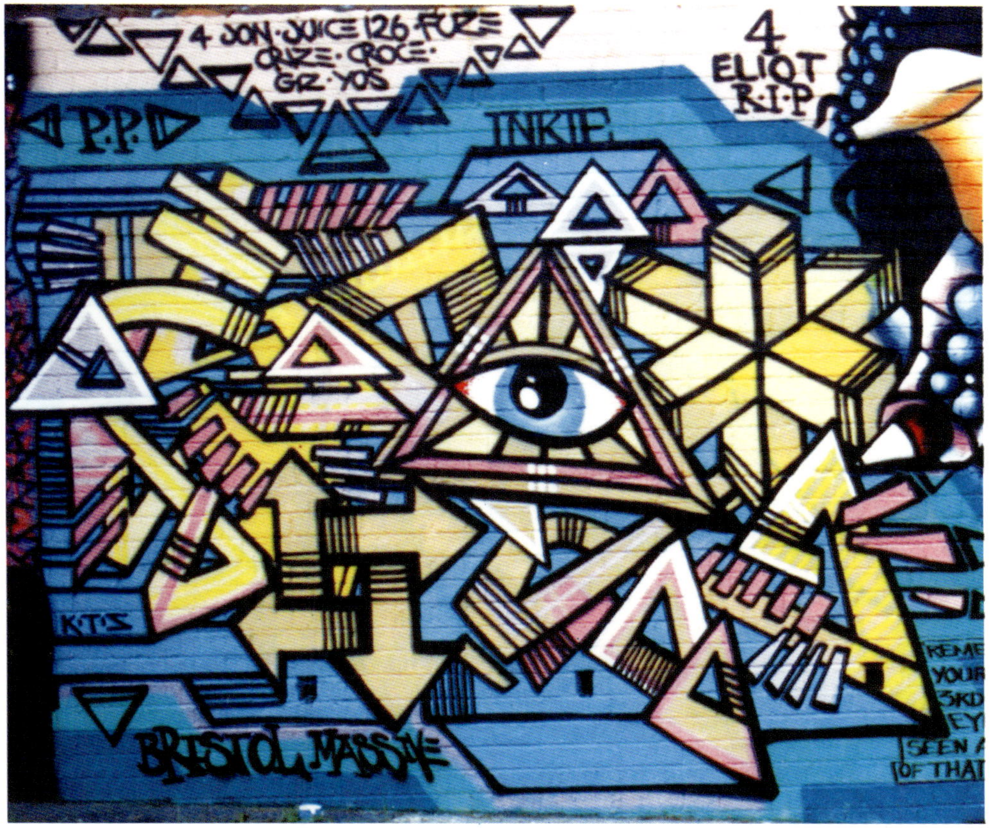

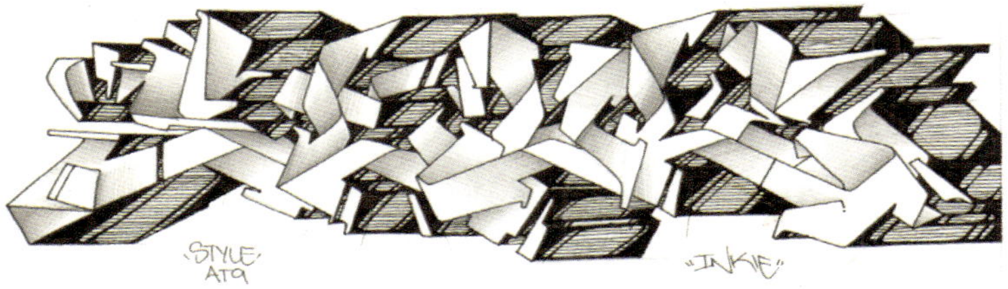

I first met 3D. We'd go to D's house and do drawings. Toots was around at that time as well, we'd see him in there. He was quite a big part of all that because he had that van and he used to drive around to go painting."

3D put up a lot of pieces in a couple of years. His work seemed so accomplished from early on. Do you have any favourite pieces of his?
"The standout pieces for me from that time were definitely his Wild Bunch piece at the bottom of Park Street, his one outside Virgin Records in Broadmead, and the King one that he did with Pride (Chrome Angels) in Clifton Village."

His connection with the Wild Bunch made their whole thing complete. At the Wild Bunch jams you would often get all the different aspects of hip hop under one roof. Didn't you paint at some of their parties?
"Yeah, me and D used to paint boards at Wild Bunch jams in Bristol, and I think that was integral to the whole scene, the fact that all their flyers had graff on them. You and me were doing flyers for FBI Crew parties as well, and the fact that people were seeing those was quite a big drive for us. People were getting to know who we were. The whole link to the sound systems and the party scene was a big part of it."

I guess probably the next significant factor for you was painting at the Barton Hill Youth Club. How did you hear about it, and what were your first impressions of the place?
"I think I met [Barton Hill youth worker] John Nation at a party or something and he just invited me to come up there one time. I remember walking in there the first time and seeing the whole place covered in graff, it was like, 'I fucking love this place!'"

That would have been around 1987. It quickly became the centre for graffiti in the city. Can you mention some of the writers that you met up there?
"Cheo, Turo, Shab, Chaos, Junks and Jody, but the people I'd go out bombing with was mostly Teao, Slo, SP27 and Era. I used to go over there probably two or three times a week and then go out bombing with the TUB boys. We'd get a City Rider ticket, go out armed with paint and just go all across the city, getting off the bus doing stuff, putting up tags and doing throw-ups. We'd get the bus up to a remote train station and walk back down the train track into town, basically hitting everything on the way - trains, walls, the workers' huts, all the little electrical boxes. At one point I had it caned all the way from Clifton Down right over to Barton Hill, and out past the other side of Temple Meads."

Opposite page. Left top to bottom: 'Dope' pen on paper, 1988, 'Inkie' pen and pencil on paper, 1987, 'Inkie' pen and pencil crayon on paper, 1987, 'Inkie/DCL' pen and pencil on paper, 1988

Top right: 'Bristol's Least Wanted' Inkie, Will Barras, Banksy, Lokey (Banksy characters removed), 1999

Middle right: 'Knowledge' Inkie and FLX, 1988

Bottom right: 'Inkie' Urban Games, Clapham Common, London, 1999

This page. Left: Selly Oak youth club, Birmingham, 1990

Above: 'Style' outline for Bridlington World Championships. Pen and pencil on paper, 1989

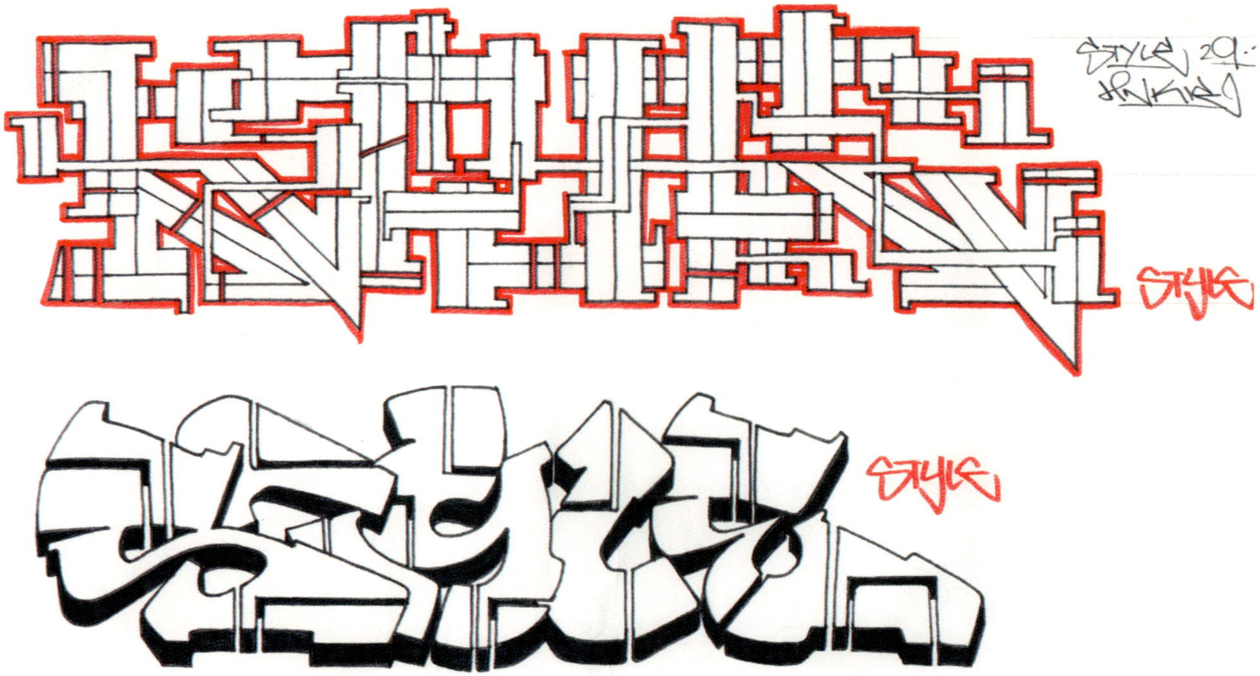

Above: 'Style' in two different styles. Pen on paper, 1989

Barton Hill was basically a microcosm of the whole graffiti scene back then, and you had a foot in both camps - the legal and illegal painting. Tell me about the legal side of things: what was the vibe like painting at the club?
"It was just about meeting up with other guys and drawing and constantly repainting the ball court, experimenting with different styles of lettering and stuff. Barton Hill gave you the freedom to completely experiment and you knew that if you wanted to do another one next week you could just come back and paint over it. The thing about Bristol back then is that everyone was doing different styles."

The youth club seemed to be where you really came into your own. You progressed in leaps and bounds once you had somewhere to try out new things.
"I think it was also going to college, and what I learnt in graphics about the negative spaces between letters. They almost became more important than the letters themselves; when you've got the letters joined up, it's making the gaps between them work. I also learnt early on that it's about drawing the whole word, rather than doing good individual letters and trying to get them to stick together. That's what balances a piece and without that it doesn't look right to me; that's what makes a piece stand out and gives it that more soulful feel. The funk, basically."

You seemed to have an endless supply of outlines, and the ideas just kept on coming.
"From about the age of 13 until I was nineteen, pretty much all I did was draw. Nearly every night for six years I'd just stay in and draw. Once I got into graffiti it just took my life over. I'd be hanging out with you guys, or Fade and Jaffa, or 3D, or Nick, and we'd be designing the whole time. It was totally consuming, every minute of every day: at school, through college, it was just about drawing, basically. Taking (magic) mushrooms and drawing: that's where the wildstyle really took off, I was coming up with crazier and crazier, more complex, intricate and fucking random stuff."

Can you tell me a bit more about John Nation's role at Barton Hill? It wasn't just about providing people with space to paint, was it?
"John was the documenter of the scene. He was getting photos from all around the UK and Europe, giving us information and encouraging us, showing us pictures and different styles from all over. It was really unfair when he got busted, because he didn't really do anything bad, he could see it was a good way out for kids from being naughty, and he was basically just totally into the art form."

John's arrest was part of Operation Anderson early in 1989.The police and the tabloid press portrayed John as some kind of Fagin figure, and you were described as the 'Kingpin' of the whole case. Tell me what happened.
"I'd already been nicked three times before it all kicked off, and I was away when the

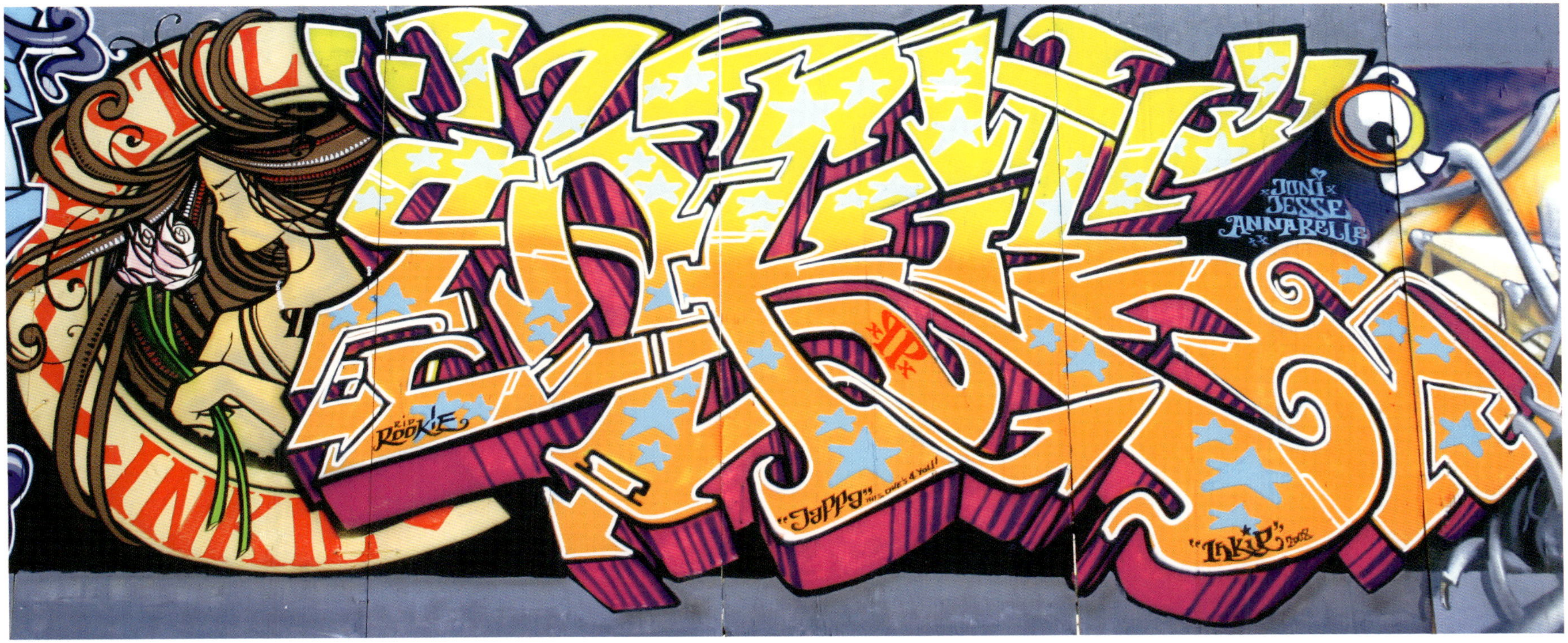

Above: Inkie at the Bristol Festival, 2008

police raided my mum and dad's house, so when I came back to Bristol I went to turn myself in. I didn't think it was going to be that serious, but while I was there they just brought out more and more stuff, and they laid out a massive charge sheet. The first one was for £25,000 worth of criminal damage, and they just went up and up from that. They had a photo of every tag and every piece I'd done from Clifton Down train station all the way down to Temple Meads. They told me, 'once we've got you for Clifton Down we're going to nail this whole lot on you.'"

"We took it all as a bit of a joke, but it did get quite serious, even though we did get off fucking lightly, basically because the police were very amateur in how they presented their case. I think they were so intent on getting us that they shot themselves in the foot. I ended up with a £100 fine."

I think the police learnt their lesson the hard way. While the case was still going on, you and Cheo went to Bridlington and came second in the World Graffiti Championships, behind Slick and Risky from LA. Those two are real legends -that must have been incredible.

"It was amazing. Pretty much the best writers in Europe at the time were there, apart from Mode.2 (Chrome Angels) who had entered the year before. You had Bates and Romance from Copenhagen, System from North Wales, Part.2, Desire, Pops 100, Lokiss from Paris, and Meo and Jon 156 - both New Yorkers who had moved to Paris. Seeing Slick and Risky's piece, with their kind of 3-D, faded stuff, was quite an eye-opener. That was the first time we'd seen any LA stuff."

After Bridlington and getting off relatively lightly with the court case, the media were having a field day. You were on all these TV programmes. There was even a BBC2 documentary about Barton Hill and Operation Anderson. I'd have thought you would have been on a real high and things would have completely taken off.

"Not really. After Bridlington and doing TV and stuff I was a bit like 'well, where am I going to go from here?' I'd basically done all I wanted to do; I didn't really know where to go next. It got to the point, after all the press and media stuff kicked off, where everyone knew what we were doing and I was getting a lot of the whole

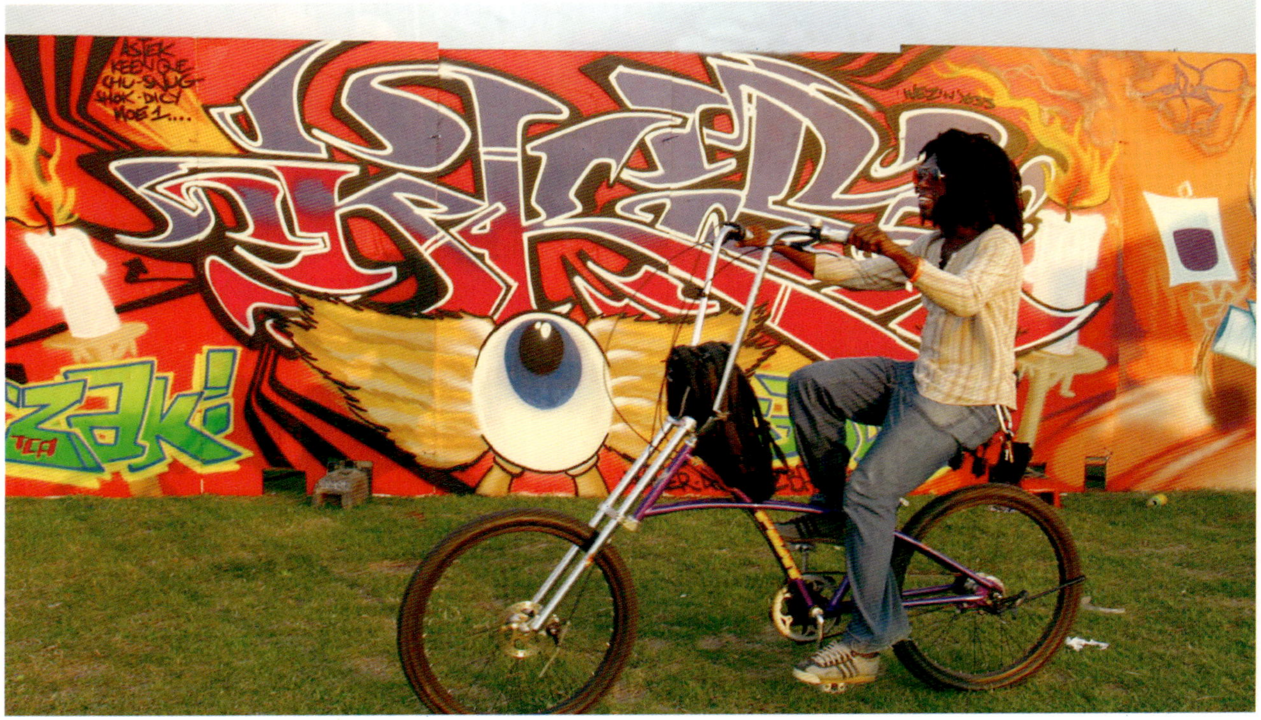

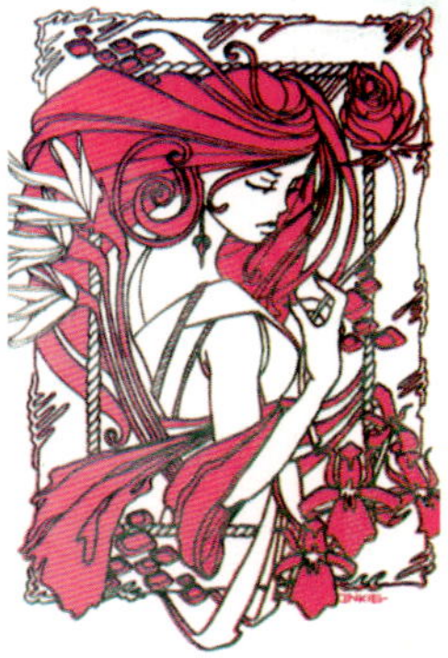

Top: 'Inkie' Urban Games, Clapham Common, London, 2002

Above: 'Ink Nouveau' screen print on paper, 2004

back-slapping thing going on; and in a way it almost hinders you because you end up resting on your laurels and getting a bit complacent. I wasn't keeping ahead of the game. Whereas when I was younger I was just so keen. I've got that back now - but for a while I sat back."

But you weren't unproductive - you were just painting less, weren't you?
"Yeah, I got more into graphics. I was 19, I'd just left college, so I had to do something to get some money coming in. I was doing T-shirts and flyers, I got an Apple Mac, and I did a few record label things. I was still drawing graffiti, just not painting so much."

You were involved in the Walls on Fire jam on Bristol Harbourside in '98. What was it that got you painting again?
"The turning point for me was when Banksy was painting the shutters of Rollermania (skate shop), and I walked past and he invited me to go and paint at Glastonbury Festival. That was when things kicked off again; it was like 'hang on a minute, there's another wave of people coming through,' like FSH [Fantastic Super Heroes] and the TCF lot. Me and Banksy got on really well. We were doing a lot of painting and he pretty much gave me a boot up the arse. At the same time I was also helping him by having a lot of contacts."

Walls on Fire was massive, what was your involvement in that event?
"Banksy was driving it, and I was helping him out by contacting *Graphotism* and all the writers and stuff. There were all these writers there that I knew and it was basically an excuse for everyone to get back together. That was when I first met Will Barras and Snug, and also hooked back up with Chu, who I knew from Selly Oak, through Juice and Desire and all those guys. I hadn't seen him for like ten years. That jam really put Bristol back on the map."

Then, when things were picking up again in Bristol you moved to London?
"Yeah, I moved to London in 1999 and got a job with Sega, and was still doing bits of painting here and there. Video games to me were the perfect form of graphics to get into, because doing all the logos was just like drawing graffiti. As a graffiti artist I really appreciated doing that work. I was doing logo-type design and stuff. I still love doing Mac-based stuff now, just as much as doing a piece. There's a certain tightness that a graffiti artist will bring to graphics that I think maybe a normal graphic designer wouldn't. It's something I've carried over into the Flying Eyeball T-shirts I've been doing with Zaki Dee [old school Chrome Angels writer]."

Looking back over nearly 25 years of painting, what is it that keeps you passionate about graffiti?
"For me the essence of the whole feeling behind graffiti is that you can get so inspired by someone else's drawing. No other art form has had that impact. I get inspired by old artists and different influences and that, but to get that buzz from someone else's work and to just see something and think 'fucking hell, that is totally wicked', is the best. It's almost like you're gutted that you're not that good, but at the same time it inspires you to make yourself better."

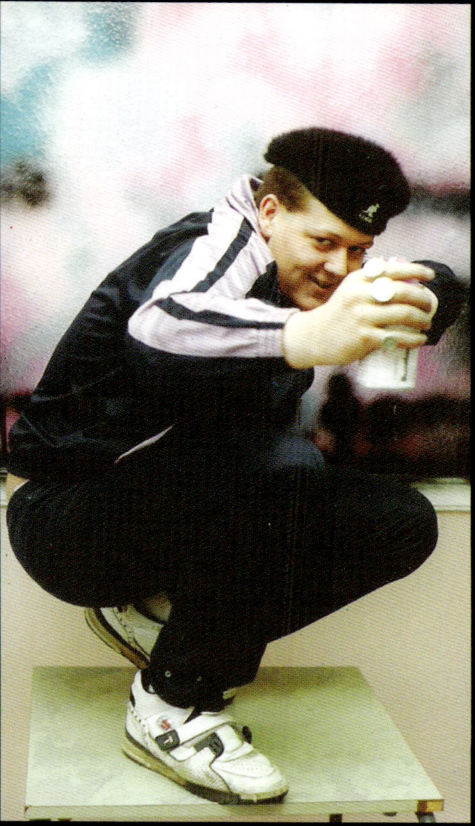

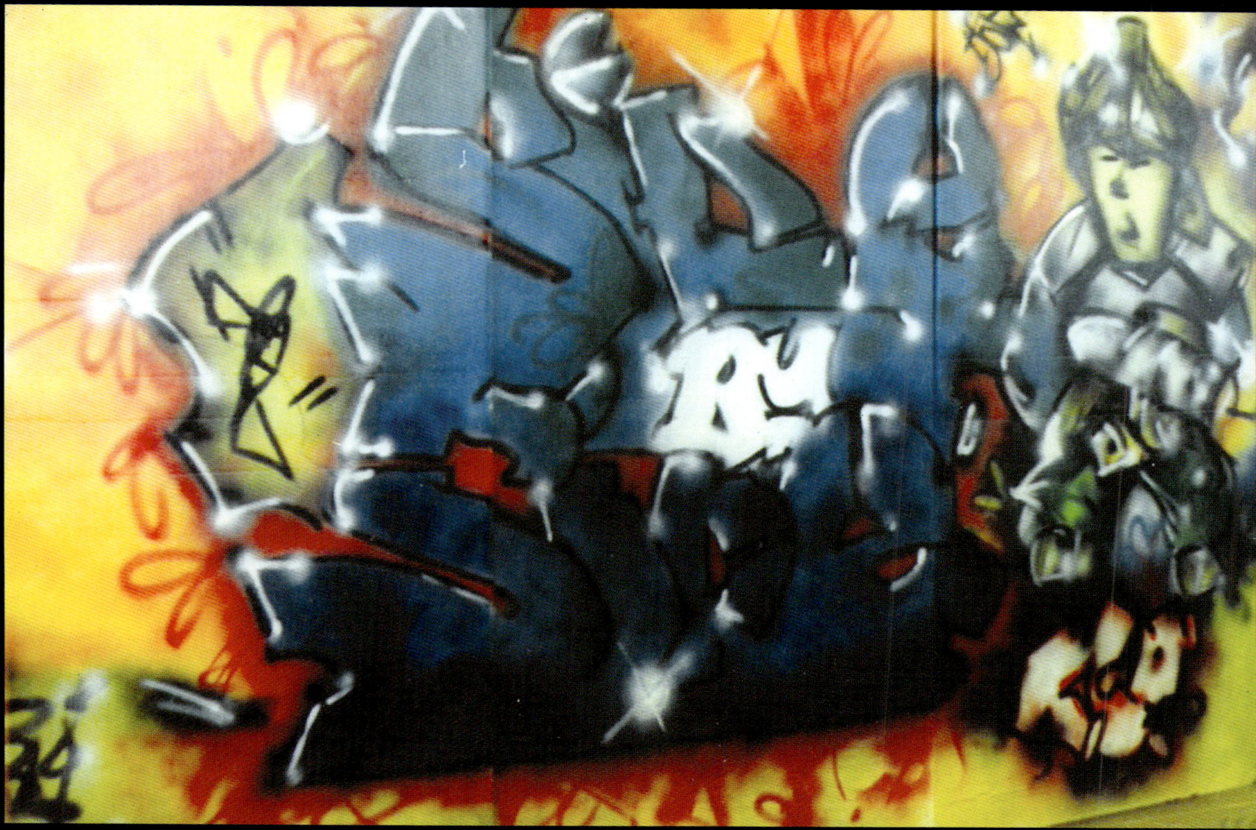

DEED TCP

• **Deed – better known by his full moniker, Scout Leader Deed – has been a part of the Bristol hip hop scene since its humble beginnings in the early 1980s, and is still actively involved today.** He's among a handful of individuals to have made his mark in all four elements of the subculture at one time or another. The beats and rhymes he creates for the Hairy Parents label and extended family (which has included Parlour Talk, Undivided Attention and, more recently, All Creatures) are the stuff of UK hip hop legend.

When and where were you introduced to graffiti? Who did you paint your first piece with?
"I was introduced to graf and hip hop as a whole at the end of 1983, aged 11, during the electro boom when every bastard was breaking. Cheo – who I've known since playschool – and me spent many hours drawing together, copying characters from *Nutty Comic* and inventing our own superheroes.

"One day, he brought some drawings into school that turned out to be copies of Doze's famous Rocksteady Crew portraits from the cover of *Hey You (The Rocksteady Crew)* – which he promptly passed off as his own work. Biting bastard, bless him.

"Shortly afterwards, we were all 'biting' stuff from a copy of *Subway Art*. Linda, a youth worker at The Summit youth club in Kingswood, had brought it – not realising what levels of vandalism it would lead to!"

You were also a B-boy. Which came first?
"I started breaking seriously midway through 1984 with Twilight Rockers – having been inspired by local B-boy heroes Street Masters, who also painted quite a few pieces themselves. That prompted me to do my first illegal pieces, with paint bought from a bloke who had burgled Kingswood Autoparts and stashed boxes of Car Plan and Holt's Dupli-Colour

Above: 'Side By Side' by Deed and Cheo wins the 1987 National Association Of Boys' Clubs graff competition.

Top left: Deed rocking a B-boy crouch. Note 'furgora' black Kangol cap and sovereign rings

Next page. Top left: 'Crazy Vision' Deed and Cheo at Barton Hill, 1987. Cheo (centre) in red Puma States, Deed (right) in red Kangol hat.

Top right: Secs 1993

Middle left: Deed track side, Barton Hill, c.1988. Dedication to John (Nation) and Lenny, John's dog.

Right: 'Won't Be 2 Bad' c.1986

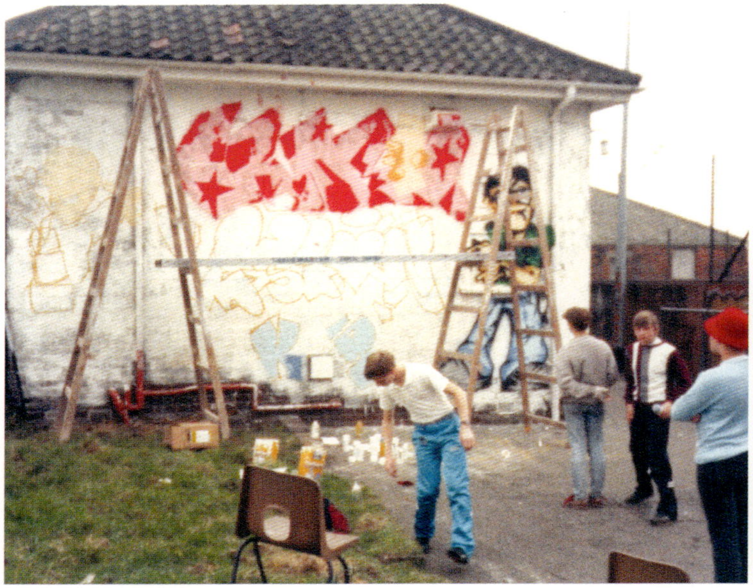

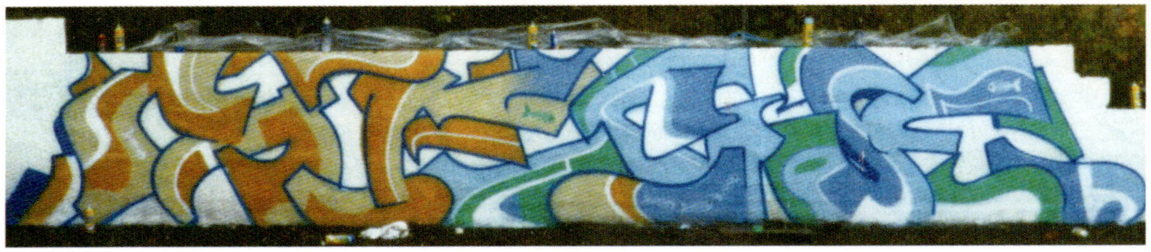

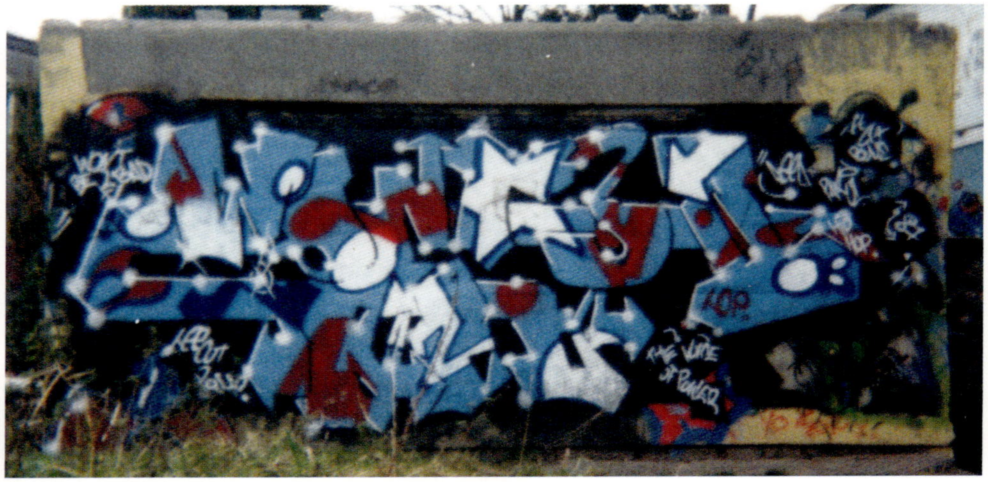

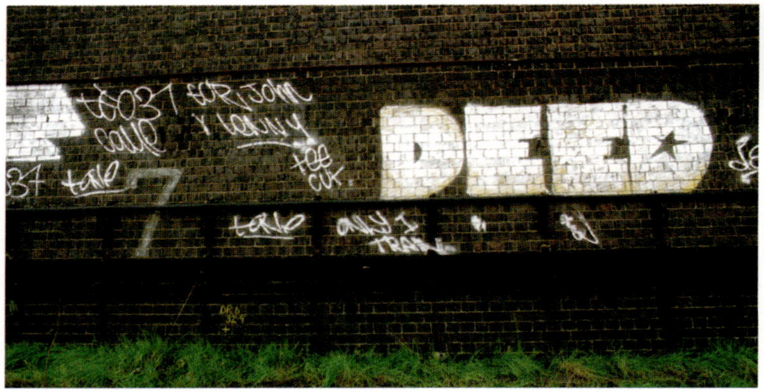

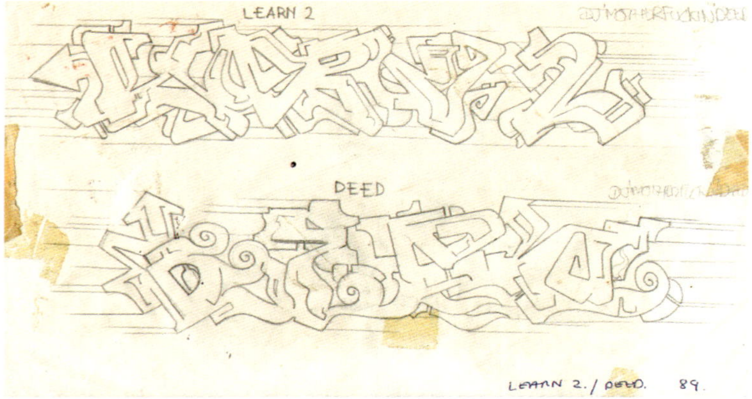

in a discreet cubbyhole under his doormat, and was selling it for 25p a small can."

Can you describe your earliest memories of painting illegally?
"Doing illegal bombing around Kingswood was pretty easy, and although we got chased and caught a few times by members of the public, our inquisitors were more worried that we were breaking into their property: they were not that concerned with us spraying places up."

We all had some pretty embarrassing tags when we started painting. Are you brave enough to disclose any of yours?
"After experimenting with the amazing tags Dr. Graffiti Spraycan and Master Graffiti, I settled on Shine, which I kept until I started painting with Cozie (aka Cheo) under the new guise of Psycho, in 1986. Then, early in 1987, after trying numerous other tags (Wizzard, 2bad, Em 2) and crew names (Sioux Warriors, Dubbed Arts) I adopted the tag Deed, which stuck."

Who were the original members of your crew, TCP?
"I started Tee Cut Posse (TCP) with Cheo, Paris (not to be confused with Paris TCF) and Fuze. Before long, some youngsters joined the crew: Teao, Cema and Era (before they started the infamous TUB). They were master rackers, (paint thieves) and were into travelling around getting fame. I was more into keeping up in Kingswood and have seldom pieced beyond walking distance of my house. Bus trips were for tagging and looking for other pieces around Bristol."

Tell us about winning the 1987 NABC Graffiti Championships.
"As well as illegal work we got funding for graf projects with The Summit and Kingswood YMCA. That led to us entering the NABC Graffiti Championships, taking on five other crews from all over Britain. At this event we discovered the all-conquering Smoothrite paint. We'd never seen white cover black like that! We already knew of [German spray paint] Buntlack, but it was great to see a can in the flesh, although all crews were only supposed to use the 12 small cans of Car Plan provided.

"We won the competition with our piece 'Side By Side'. In fact, we knew we'd been taken out by the Nottingham crew, but being a youth event, their piece (titled 'Lust', with a semi-naked bird painted on it) wasn't viewed as appropriate. They definitely took us out from a graf perspective, which was probably why they kicked our boards over and acted like juvenile suckers. But we won the airbrush equipment and medals and got our piece in the Evening Post, with us stood next to our tags. Oops!"

When did you start getting into music?
"I started DJing at the end of '87, when Tee Cut turned into an MC/DJ/dance crew, and started to rap a few years later.

Was it music or getting busted for graffiti that caused you to stop painting?
"Records won the battle of the wallet over paint, so I was mostly tagging and doing the odd chromer with TUB until I got caught tagging, when I somehow managed to smudge it out with spit. Subsequently I received a visit from the boys in blue, who found graf all around my neighborhood bearing my tag, Deed. But I convinced them I was DJ Deed, not Deed TUB – who, I claimed, was someone else who had nicked my tag.

"All the same I ended up in court with the rest of them, after Operation Anderson, and got a £400 fine and 24 hours at the attendance centre, doing military police training and making jigsaws. I always continued penning outlines but stopped painting totally for a few years, until I caught the bug again in 1993 and continued – using the tag Ed – in a crew called BDF (Big Dicked Fish) with Soak (Cheo, again!) Bouldi, Fine, Brow and Quin.

"We painted small colour pieces and chrome bits around Kingswood (keep it local) and I did the most illegal bombing I've ever done, even making an appearance in Graphotism. It was good fun!"

And since then?
"I continued through the Transcript Carriers era but fizzled out again with the start of Parlour Talk/Undivided Attention. And that, in turn, was replaced with looking after a wife and three nippers. My eldest boy has studied *Subway Art* and *Spraycan Art* and is now doing some nifty outlines, but I'm definitely promoting legal painting to him, and if I catch him racking paint and bombing I'm going to get totally and utterly 'dad' on his ass; although I may join him when I can get a day off from working like a bastard."

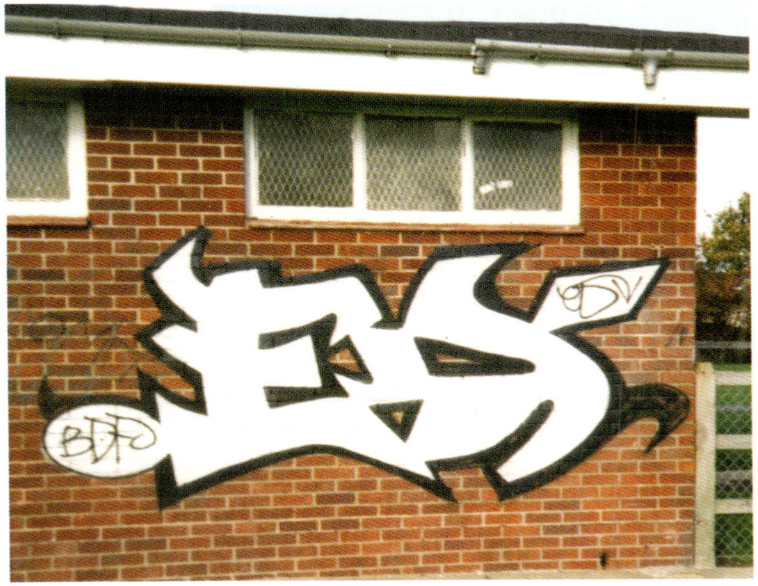

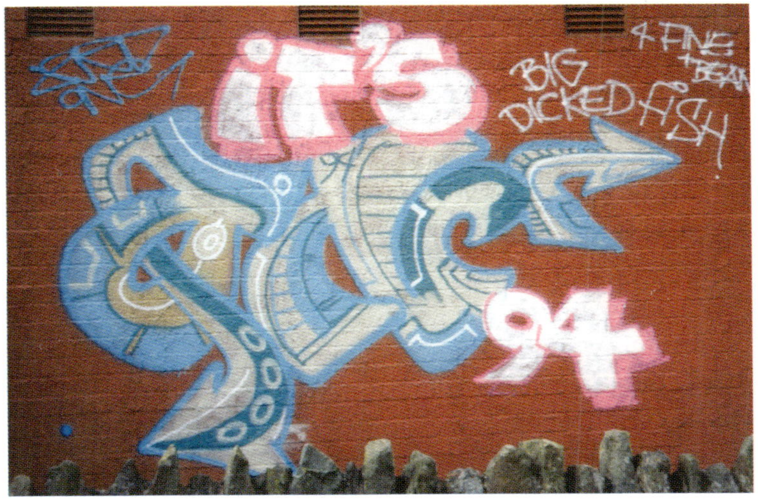

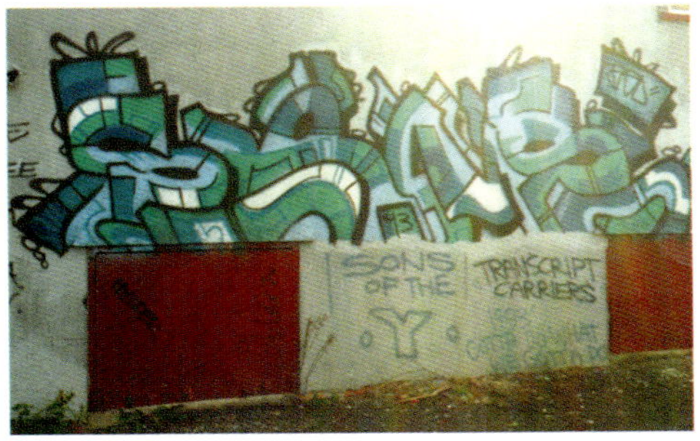

Top: 'Ed BDF (Big Dicked Fish)', 1994.

Middle: 'It's On 94', 1994

Bottom: 'Sons (of the Y)', 1993

Opposite page. Bottom left: 'Learn2' and 'Deed' pencil outlines on paper tagged DJ 'Motherfuckin' Deed, 1989.

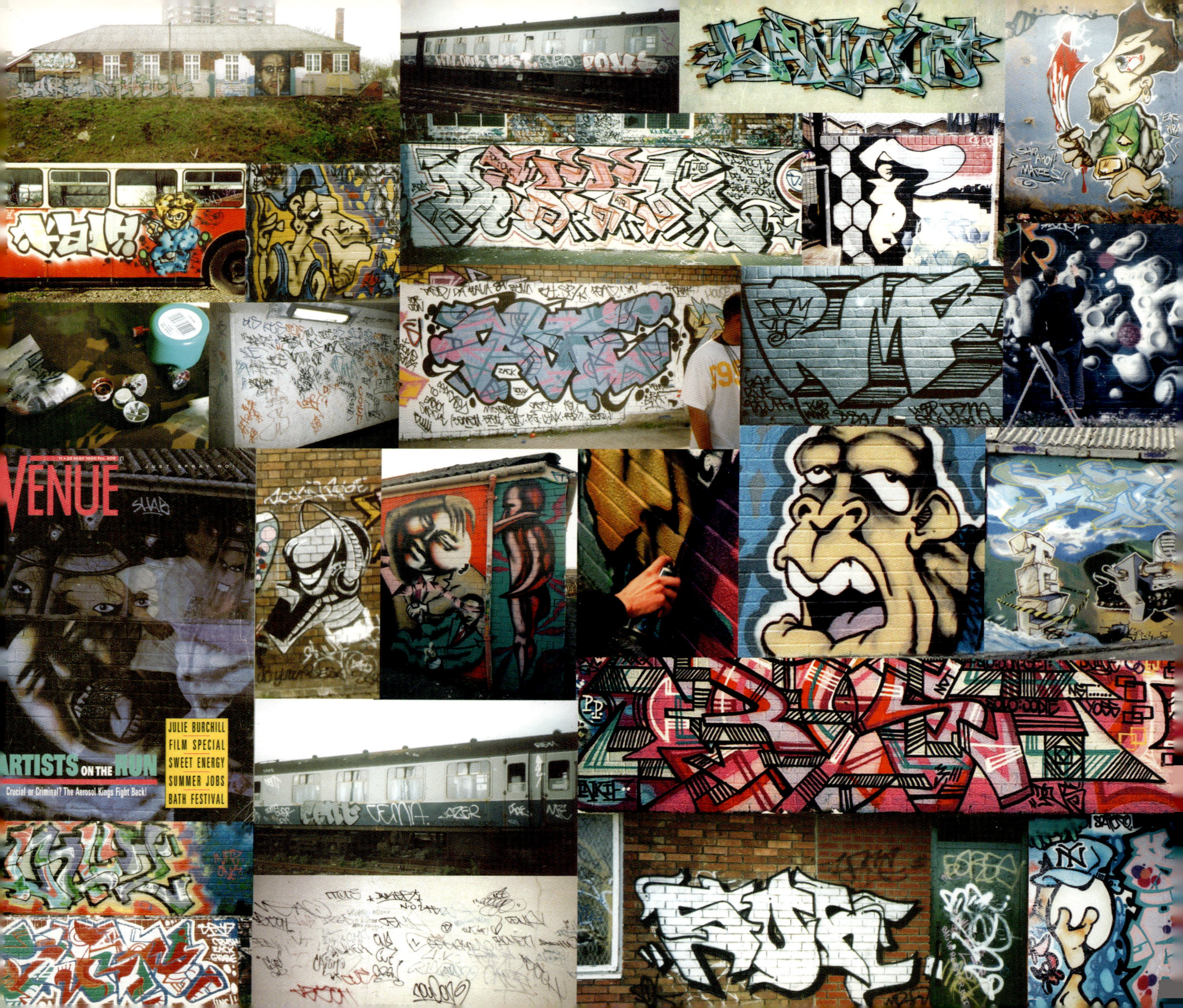
VENUE
JULIE BURCHILL
FILM SPECIAL
SWEET ENERGY
SUMMER JOBS
BATH FESTIVAL
ARTISTS ON THE RUN
Crucial or Criminal? The Aerosol Kings Fight Back!

1987-98: The View From The Hill

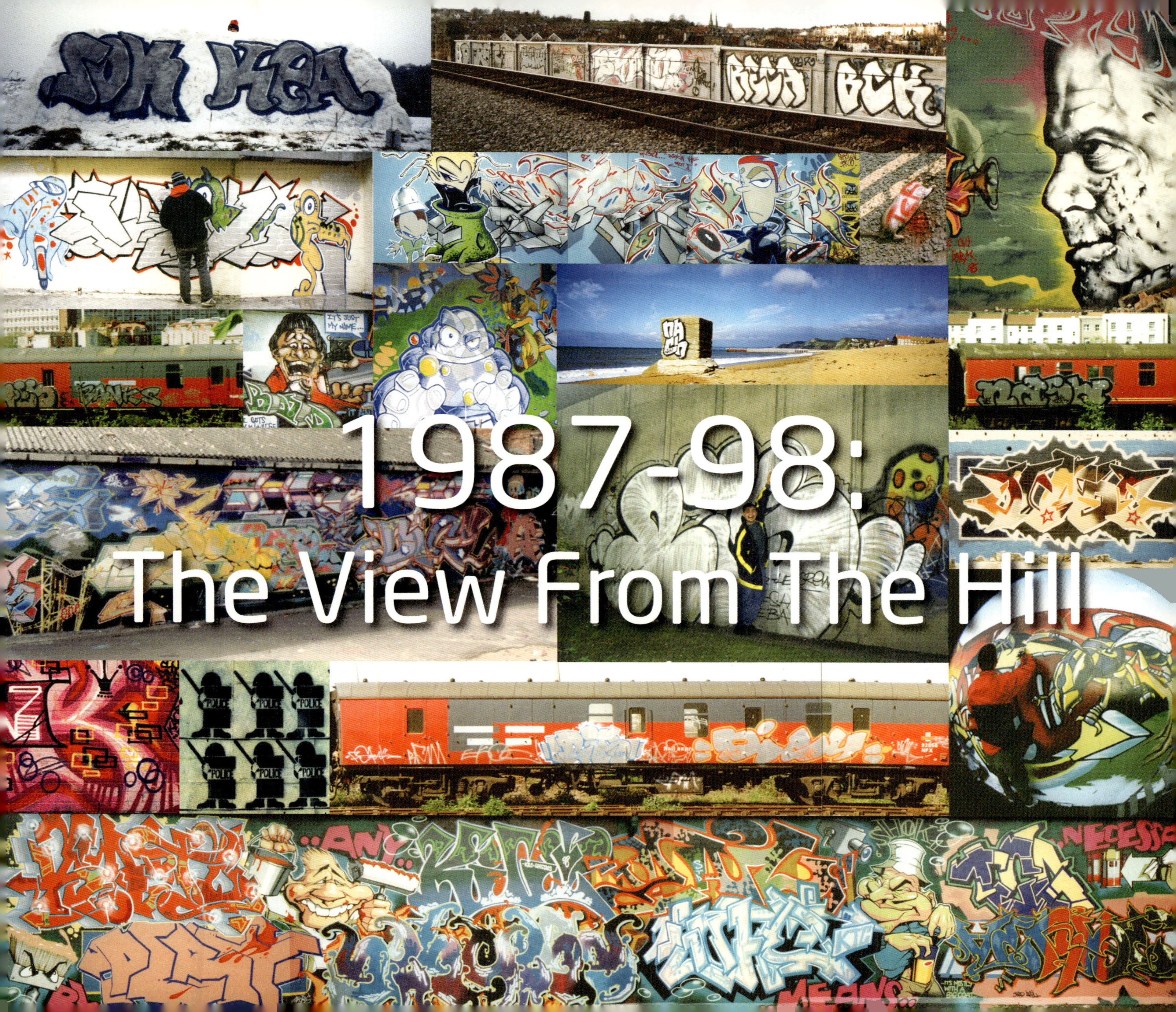

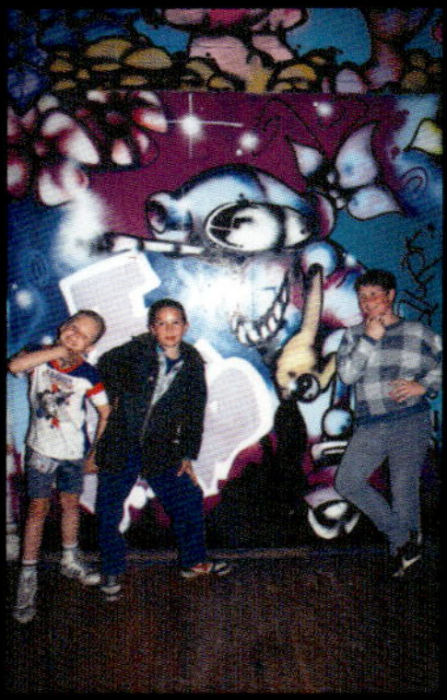

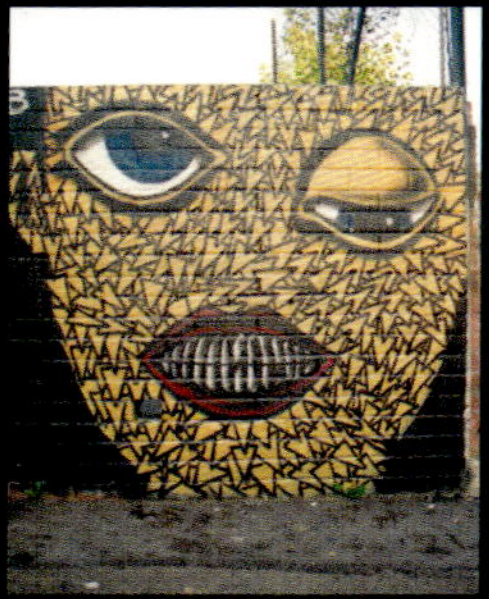

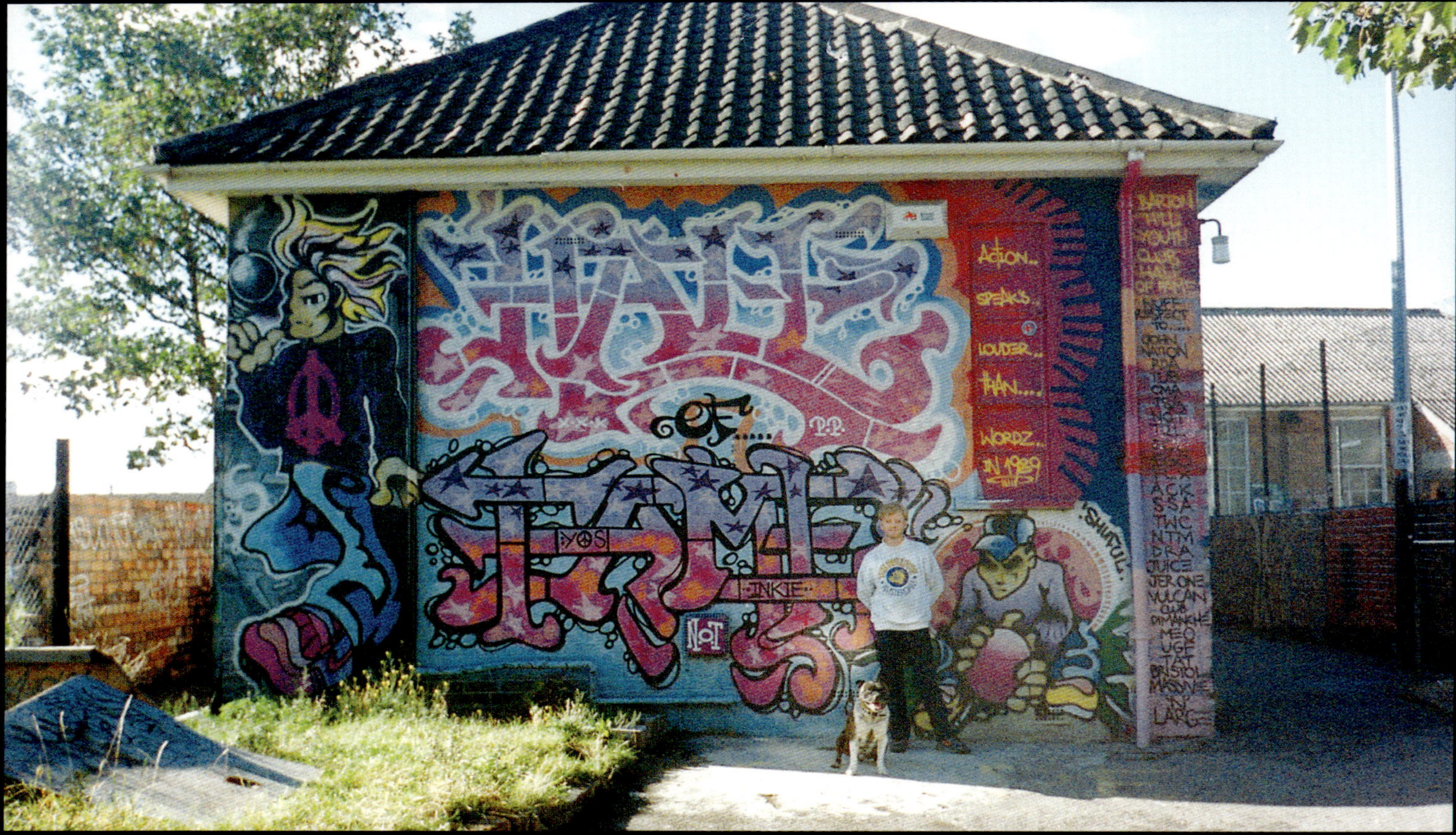

This page. Top left: Local Barton Hill kids pose in front of a Cheo character, c.1989

Above: Winking face by Shab, c.1989

Right: John and Lenny outside Barton Hill Youth Club. Piece by Inkie and FLX, 1989

Opposite page. Top left: Young people congregate in front of the first ever piece on the front wall of

Barton Hill Youth Club, 1985

Top right: Era tag on Barton Hill street sign

Middle right: The paint cupboard in the youth club, full to the brim

Bottom right: Lenny and his ball

JOHN NATION

• **The history of graffiti is scattered with key players who have never painted a single piece in their lives, but whose impact as documenters, advocates and all-round fans of the art form has been enormous.** Had Martha Cooper and Henry Chalfant not written their book *Subway Art*, for example, New York subway graffiti's transformation into a global art movement may well have been very different. Likewise, without the involvement of John Nation, a youth worker from the Barton Hill neighbourhood of Bristol, the city's graffiti scene would not be what it is today. In fact, John's influence was felt throughout the UK scene, and he was in regular contact with writers from around the world long before the Internet made it easy.

John's introduction to the art form occurred not in Bristol but in Amsterdam, one of the first European cities to have a graffiti scene. This was largely thanks to visionary Dutch gallery owner Yaki Kornblit, who staged solo shows by ten New York subway graffiti legends – including wild style master craftsman Dondi, whose show in January 1983 attracted art collectors and curious kids alike. The seeds of the homegrown Dutch graffiti scene were sown and when John arrived, Amsterdam and its environs were in full bloom.

"I caught the train from Schiphol airport to Amsterdam Central Station, and the place was bombed out with graffiti. I was like 'wow, what's this all about?' I spent a whole week taking photographs, rather than smoking in the cafes. I would go out riding the metro just looking for graff. I went to all their halls of fame, and I got to meet all of the early Dutch guys: Delta, Cat 22, Shoe. Shoe had a workshop in central Amsterdam, doing airbrush on denim jackets and prints, and was getting commissions as well. He and his crew were very prolific bombers,

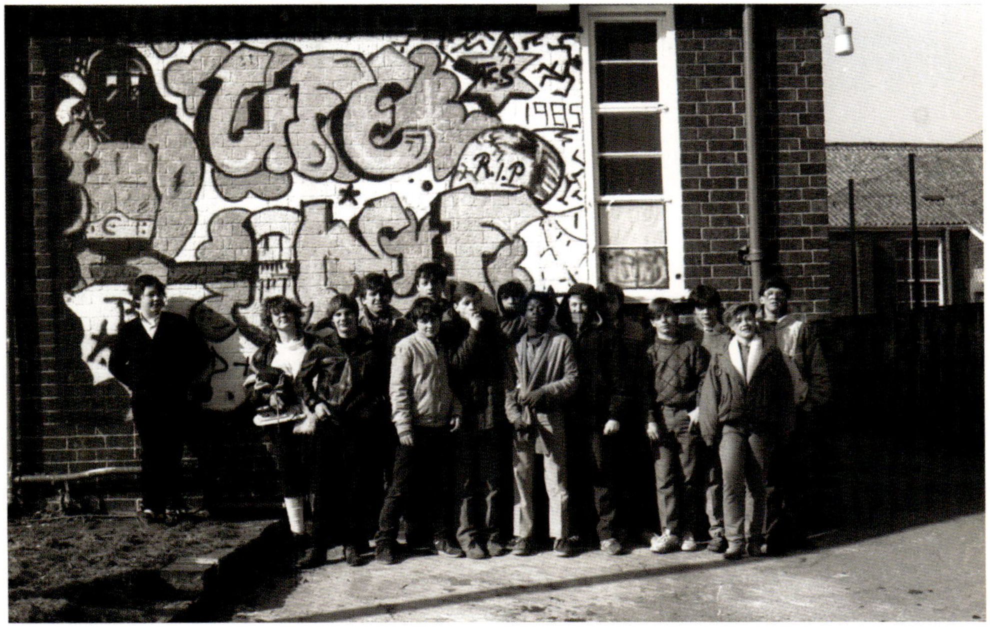

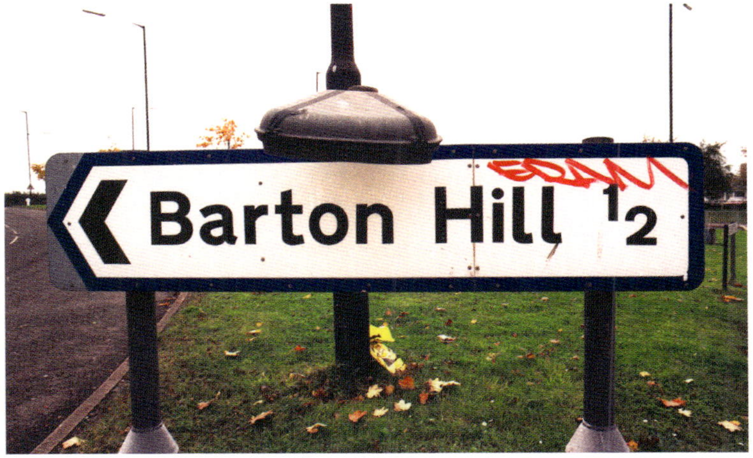

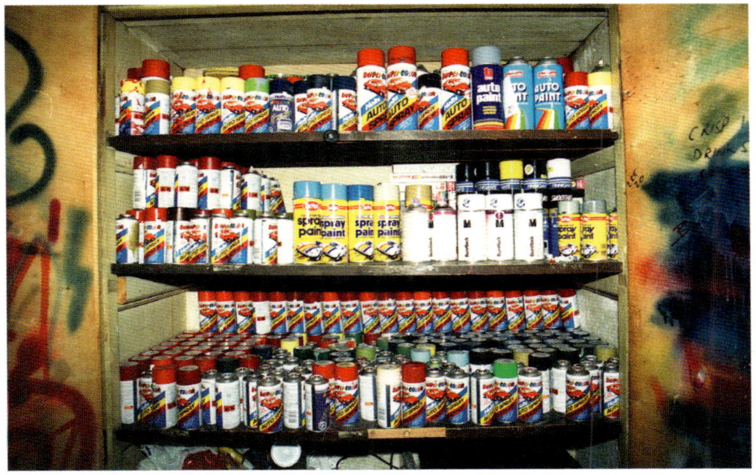

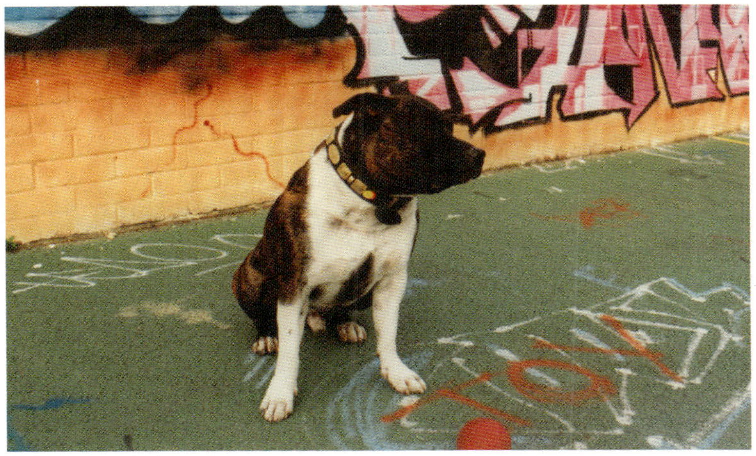

but they were also organised in terms of marketing themselves as legal artists. For me, that was the moment that graffiti turned from an interest into an obsession."

Locked up for football violence four years earlier, John had been among the first British young offenders to find out what Tory Home Secretary William Whitelaw meant when he announced a 'short, sharp shock' approach to youth detention. It gave the 15-year-old Barton Hill boy time to reflect, and he took his GCE exams while incarcerated.

"When I got there I was met with a far greater degree of violence than I'd seen on the outside – from everyone: screws and inmates. It was an eye-opening experience. It gave me six months to evaluate myself."

After release, John returned to his old neighbourhood of Barton Hill. There, he found changes afoot at the local youth club, the Dug Out, and was encouraged by staff to volunteer as a junior youth worker.

"It was a case of local people helping local people. I did a few sessions, and liked it. It gave me something to do a couple of nights a week. I did some voluntary work for a while and then from there on in it grabbed me. It was something I was really interested in."

When not studying to qualify as a youth worker, John was a religious fan of Bristol City Football Club, spending time on the terraces at Ashton Gate. He also became a regular visitor to Bristol's other Dug Out club, on Park Row in the centre of town, where familiar faces from the Gate terraces – Miles Johnson, Claude Williams, Robert Del Naja and fellow Barton Hill boy Paul 'Nellee' Hooper – were holding court as part of the Wild Bunch Crew. Hip hop had arrived and, having had his eyes opened to graffiti in Holland, John started to seek it out in Bristol.

"I wouldn't go anywhere without my camera and I would literally go all around

This page: Top: Junks painting the outside the youth club, c.1989

Bottom: Tuma character inside the club. Tuma was one of many visiting artists who came from outside Bristol to leave their mark on the club. Tuma was from Walsall. He later became Chu, c.1989

Opposite page. Left: Junks character inside the youth club, c.1989

Top right: Bus shelter on Lawrence Hill tagged with paint pens

Bottom right: 'British Transport Police Eat My Shorts' by Bart 'N' Hill (aka Junks), c.1989

the city photographing graff. At that time I didn't really know any of the artists – other than 3D, through the Wild Bunch. I went to the Arnolfini exhibition in 1985 and for me that was the thing that made me think 'yeah, something's happening in this city.'"

Inspired by his visits to Amsterdam and, increasingly, the pieces appearing on the streets of Bristol, John began to form a vision of how hip hop's visual language might be harnessed to brighten up the Barton Hill Youth Club. The latter, at the time, was still very much a microcosm of the neighbourhood around it: tough, scary and far from welcoming.

"Barton Hill was very territorial, very white, very right wing. Outsiders weren't welcome. A lot of people from outside the area would get mugged or attacked. So we decided that the youth club needed brightening up, to get away from how it looked and was perceived by outsiders. The walls at the time were sprayed up with 'BARTON HILL BOOT BOYS' and 'UDA: FUCK THE POPE AND THE IRA', all that sort of stuff. There was a lot of political graffiti, a lot of right-wing slogans, and loads of football graffiti."

With John's encouragement, a couple of local teenagers spray-painted the first New York-style graffiti piece in the sports hall at the club. It read 'GAS BUSTERS', and was both a pastiche of the Ghostbusters film logo and a reference to Bristol City's arch rivals Bristol Rovers, also known as 'The Gas.' Basic even by the standards of the time, it was nonetheless a start, and graffiti writers from across the city began telling each other that if you were brave enough to venture into Barton Hill, you would be rewarded with a safe, legal spot to paint – the city's first subsidised 'hall of fame.'

"Word started getting out that Barton Hill was a bit safer to venture into, and that you could go to the youth club without being attacked. People from other parts of Bristol knew that there was graff starting to appear at Barton Hill, but were wary that it was an unwelcoming place. As a youth worker there, I wanted to channel people's responses to Barton Hill in a positive way and because I was into the art, I could share that interest with anybody who dared set foot into the area."

Barton Hill Youth Club soon became the place to meet and paint in Bristol, and the low brick walls of its ball court were constantly being repainted by the likes of Shab, Chaos, Inkie, Jody, Junks, Turo, Era, SP27, Teao, Choam, Slo, Cheo, myself and countless others. The demand for wall space eventually saw the entire club being painted – inside and out – under John's laid-back supervision. Inevitably, however, with all this artistic freedom came problems.

"The railway lines near the club were starting to get bombed," John recalls. "There were tags all along the route to the youth club, and the residents of the housing estate next door started getting a bit pissed off with people coming through the estate tagging on their front doors and bins.

"Another problem was that the car accessory shop just down the road, AutoQuip, was getting robbed silly most weekends. The manager came to the youth club saying that the club was a hangout for thieves; he made a link between the graffiti that was appearing in the area, the paint being robbed from his shop and the youth club. I turned that around by saying 'wouldn't you prefer to be involved in a positive way by donating some of your

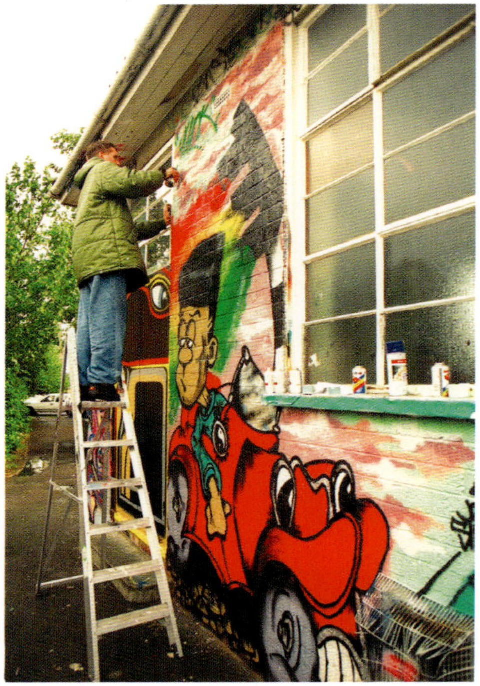

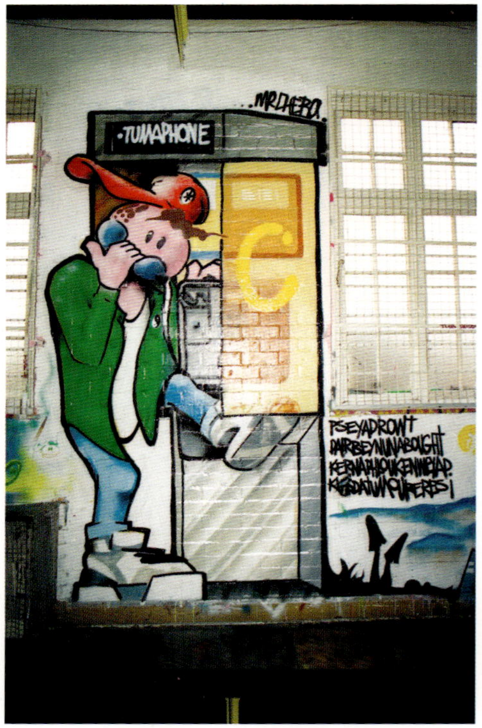

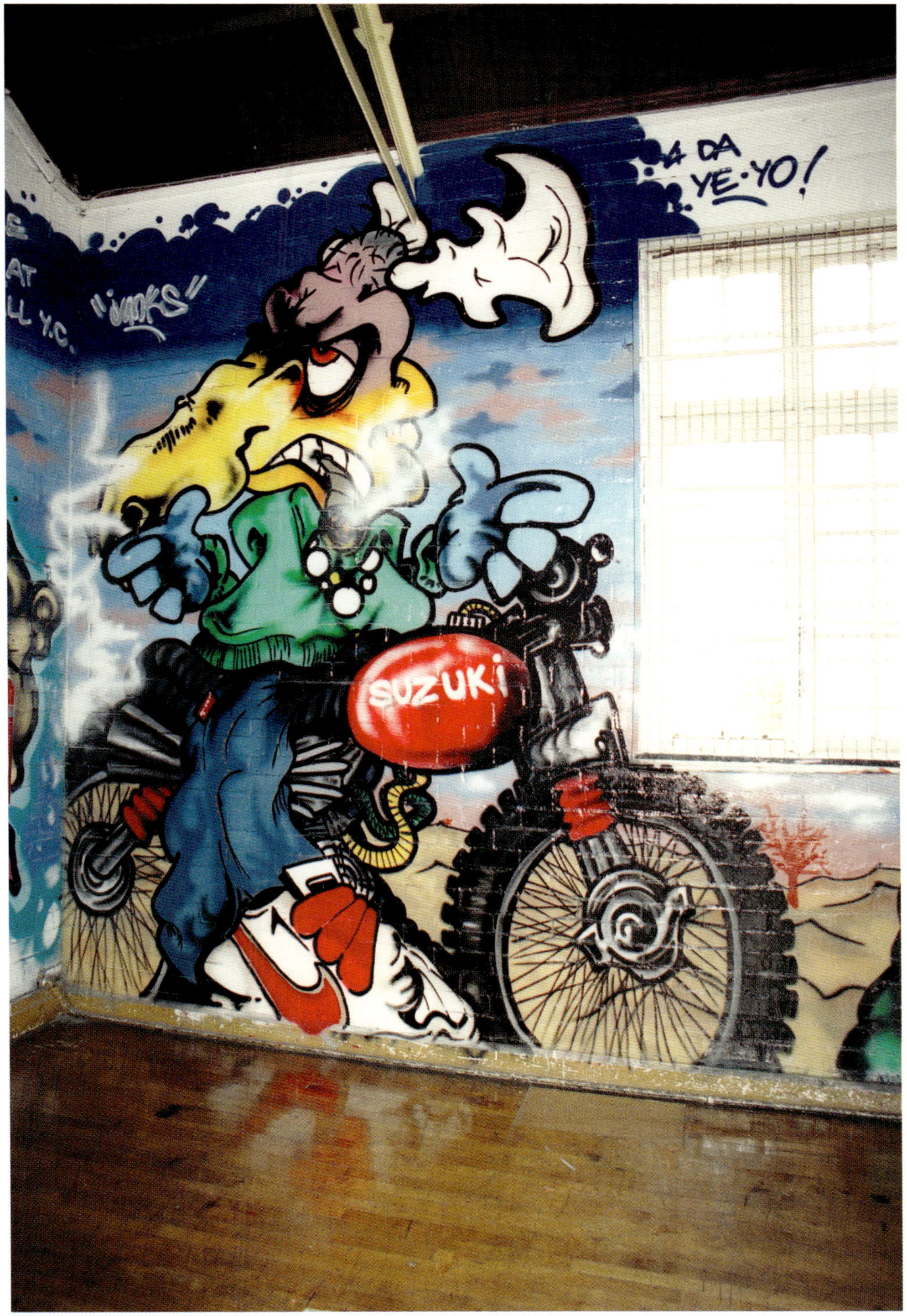
4 DA YE-YO!
SUZUKi

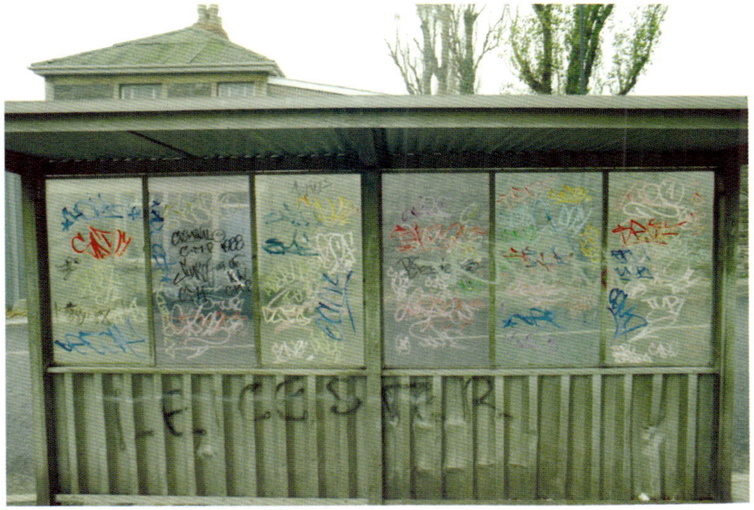

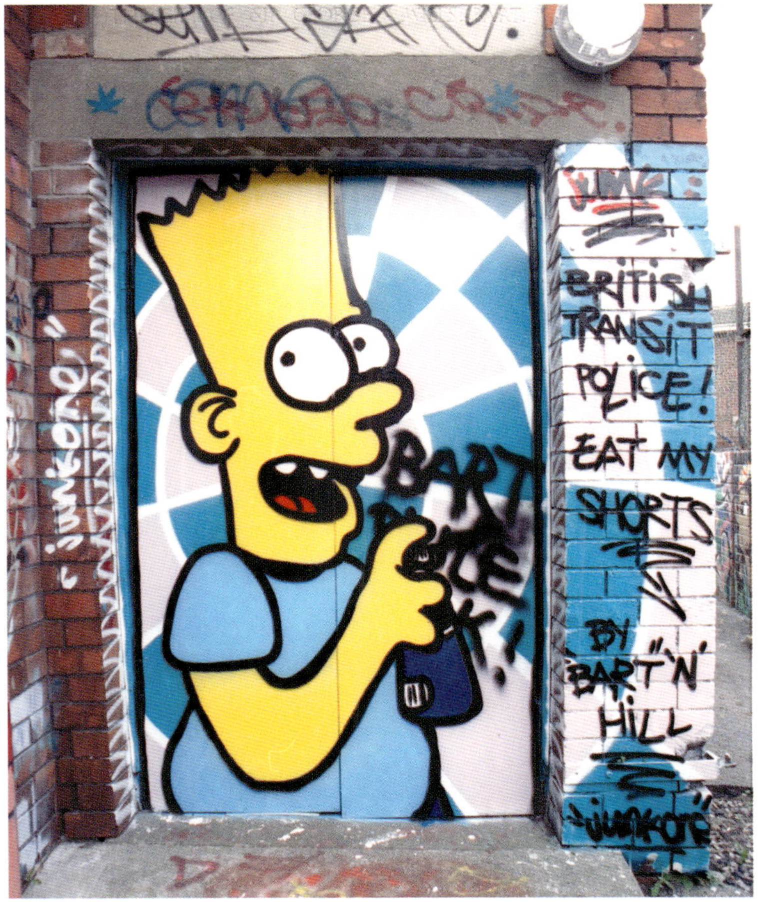
BRITISH TRANSIT POLICE! EAT MY SHORTS
BY BART 'N' HILL

outdated stock, and maybe doing me a discount of, say, 20 per cent on a job lot?' I thought that might lessen the chances of him being robbed."

Surprisingly, the shop manager was open to the idea. He even went as far as putting John in touch with spray paint manufacturers, with a view to acquiring some free paint. Some were keen, others weren't, but a precedent had been set, and the idea that Barton Hill Youth Club had something to offer had been born.

"I started approaching paint manufacturers like Car Plan, Holts, and Dupli Colour. I'd put a proposal together, saying, 'this is the work artists are producing at the moment,' and I'd send them photographs showing the club as it was before, and how it looked freshly painted. It was quite fruitful."

Barton Hill Dug Out had become a centre for what John referred to as 'aerosol art,' rather than graffiti. It needed financial support to sustain its growth, and to continue to nurture the young talent it was attracting.

"It wasn't like a normal youth club where it was only open set hours, the Dug Out was open 24/7, even at weekends. I worked there to offer people the opportunity to come and paint, or do whatever. I knew there was a need for provision of legal wall space and understanding, not intolerance, for the art form in Bristol."

Ever the football fanatic, John's second team after City were Aston Villa, and every fortnight he'd travel to Birmingham to see them play. It was on one of these trips, in 1985, that he stumbled across another graffiti hall of fame in a Birmingham suburb.

"One week I got off the train a couple of stops early and went to a place called Selly Oak, which had a big, important hall of fame. I was wandering around taking pictures and this guy came up to me. He was a youth worker at the Selly Oak Youth Club, and also an artist by the name of Juice. I went up two weeks later and met these two writers, Crise and Desire. Desire, who was from Walsall just up the road, told me about this big graffiti convention that Channel 4 were filming for a documentary called *Bombin'*, for which the main focus was going to be Goldie. So I went up to the convention – missing Villa-Liverpool as a result. Goldie painted there, as well as [New York writer] Brim, The Chrome Angels, and 3D. I forged links with all of them, and got to know Goldie."

The latter's manager, Martin Jones, told John about an exhibition he was planning for the following year, featuring UK artists alongside Brim, Bio, T-Kid, Nicer and Vulcan from New York.

"That exhibition – at Birmingham Central Library – was where I really got hooked up. We met a lot of writers there who had travelled up from around the country, and it dawned on me that there was a load of people doing graff who weren't just doing illegal stuff: they were trying to push it forward, doing exhibitions and commissions, and trying to promote aerosol art in a legitimate way."

Inspired by seeing work of such a high standard – and by meeting like-minded individuals – John began to use his infectious enthusiasm and renowned gift of the gab to broadcast what was going on in Barton Hill – and to push for graffiti's legal acceptance. Locally, this was an uphill struggle that met with a lot of negativity. Across the country, however, John's network of contacts shared a vision of aerosol art's potential and importance. Barton Hill became a mecca for graffiti artists, the allure of its walls attracting visitors from as far afield as Walsall and Hull, Amsterdam and New York.

"Things mushroomed. I had a lot of contact with people outside Bristol, exchanging photographs, addresses and so on. And it was all done by post, obviously, since there was no Internet back then. Word got out that Bristol was a happening place and that there was somewhere that you could paint legally. By 1989 Barton Hill Youth Club was at its peak, and the connections that I had were increasing week by week. From there a lot of links and friendships were formed, not just with artists but also other youth workers who were interested in the work I was doing, and wanted to find out about getting sponsorship and funding."

Nationally, Barton Hill was now firmly established as the hub of Bristol's diverse, experimental graffiti scene. Locally though, it was notorious as the centre for the city's illegal graffiti activities. The infamous TUB crew (The United Bombers) often started or finished their frenzied tagging and piecing missions in Barton Hill and, as artists regularly expressed their disdain for the forces of law and order in their work at the youth club. Sooner or later the shit was going to hit the fan.

"Bristol was really badly hit – bus stations, train stations, bus shelters, the buses themselves – anything and everything was just getting absolutely whacked. It couldn't continue the way it was going, something had to give. TUB were so brazen: they wanted to paint legally at Barton Hill Youth Club but they were still painting illegally elsewhere. They were very active at the time.

"The youth club was under surveillance, and people were being followed by plain clothes police officers. Then a couple of lads were caught tagging but were released without charge, which I thought was a bit weird at the time. In fact, what the British Transport Police had done was to get their addresses. We should have taken that as a warning of what was coming, but it didn't sink in at the time."

John was in an impossible situation. Relations between the local police and the people of Barton Hill had never been good, and attempts to integrate community policing into the daily life of the youth club had failed miserably. Moreover, he'd inevitably got to know the young graffiti artists well, and they made no bones about their city-wide illegal bombing missions. But John wasn't about to betray their confidence to anybody, least of all the local community beat officer, PC George Wlaznik, with whom he'd already had at least one run-in.

"The relationship between Barton Hill Youth Club and the local police was less than cordial. At the time community policing was being touted as the way forward, and the government were saying that the police needed to have greater involvement with communities. But when the raids finally happened, the community copper for Barton Hill was at the forefront of it, even though he wasn't a British Transport Police Officer. He could see what was going on, he could see the artwork going up on the walls of the club. I'd had dealings with him before – for allegedly organising an illegal acid house rave, which in fact I'd had no involvement with."

At 6am on Monday 20 March 1989, the joint forces of Avon and Somerset Constabulary and the British Transport Police carried out simultaneous raids on the houses of 72 individuals in Bristol, Bath, Exeter and Cardiff. The raids were the culmination of months of intelligence gathering, under the name of Operation Anderson. It was the biggest anti-graffiti operation in the history of British policing, and at the centre of it all was an evil criminal mastermind cleverly posing as an Avon County Council youth worker: none other than John Nation. Or so the police thought.

"The police turned up at my mum's house, where I lived at the time, with a warrant to search the house and another to search the youth club. I was arrested for 'conspiracy to incite individuals to commit criminal damage.' The police warrant stated that they were looking for 'materials that relate to illegal graffiti'. What they found was documentation of graffiti, literature relating to graffiti, and nothing much else. They bagged it all, handcuffed me, took me up to the youth club, where they literally swarmed all over it. There must have been 20 of them there. They also had a sniffer dog looking for drugs – because of course all graffiti artists were on drugs. How else could you explain those wacky designs they came up with?

"They were so full of themselves, they thought they'd struck gold: 'here we are, at the hub of the axis of evil!' They went through the whole club. I had a photograph collection, with thousands of photographs of pieces from all around the UK, Europe, the States and Australia. They photographed every single piece on the inside and outside of the building. They

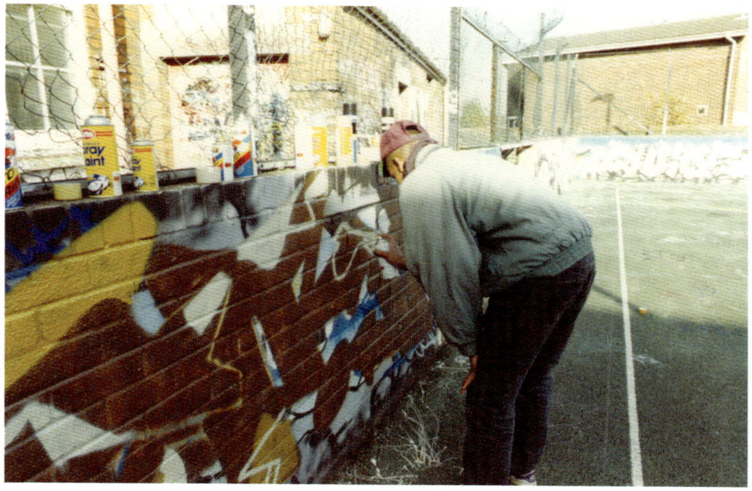

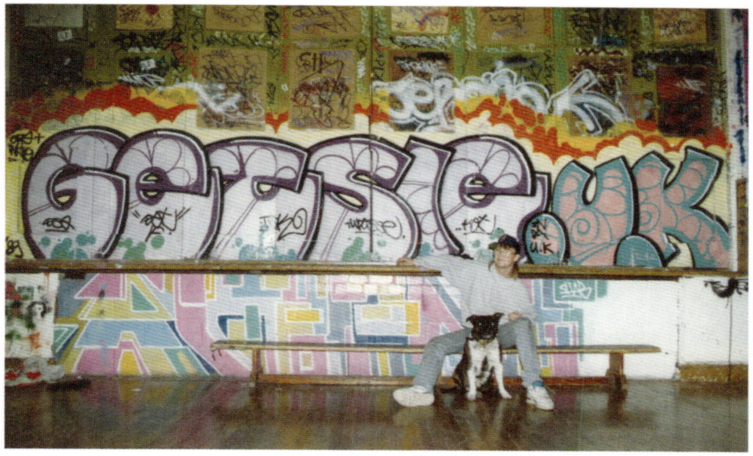

Top right: SP 27 painting in the ball court at the youth club, c.1989

Bottom right: Regular visitor Gets from Amsterdam with Lenny

made links between tags on the artwork at the club, and tags on illegal work. So the police took away all my photos, all my magazines, marker pens and sketchbooks full of designs. They took anything and everything. They must have had two van loads full of material."

Amongst the potentially incriminating material the police seized was John's 20,000-word dissertation that he had been writing for his Youth and Community Work Diploma. Despite his protests the police insisted that this, too, was relevant

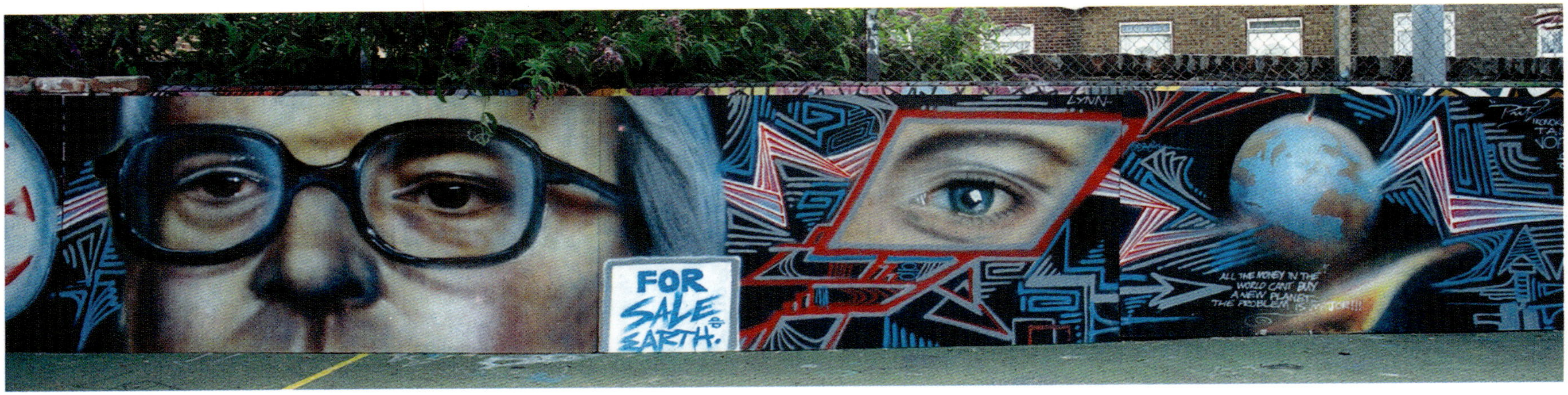

Above: 'For Sale: Earth' by Part.2, c.1990

to the case against him. The sum of his experiences and thoughts on the subject of graffiti and life in the inner city, its title – ironically – was 'Art Or Crime In Bristol?'.

"The dissertation asked where we draw the line between an acceptable art form and an unacceptable crime. I explained to the coppers that this was a major volume of work, which counted towards my diploma, and that they had no right to take it. Their response was simple: 'we're taking it as evidence in relation to your charge.'"

During questioning, it became clear how and why the police had dreamt up the conspiracy charge: they needed a figurehead, someone to make an example of. And all the evidence, as they saw it, pointed to one person.

"They called me a subversive, a pied piper, the Fagin of the graffiti world. So I told them, 'you can make all the accusations you want, but I know that the only thing I'm guilty of is trying to channel the activities of people that were working illegally into working legally. Trying to show them that, to be accepted through your art, you've got to try and lessen the illegal side of things.' But the police argument was that I knew everybody responsible for the illegal work going on in Bristol. Which, it's true, I did."

Using John's own photographs as evidence against him held a certain irony (it is a tactic employed by BTP to the present day), but at no point did he try to deny that he was the John to whom countless pieces had been dedicated. The police were even more determined to track down another individual regularly name-checked on pieces at the youth club – the mysterious Lenny.

"When the police produced their evidence against me, they kept showing me photos of dedications on the pieces that said 'FOR JOHN AND LENNY.' Of course, they wanted to know who this Lenny was, which made me chuckle. At first I just said 'no comment', but then I explained that Lenny was my Staffordshire Bull Terrier, who was always at my side.

"Everyone knew Lenny, he went everywhere with me, but the police thought I was taking the piss. Who would write a dedication to a dog when it can't read? They'd mounted this undercover operation costing half a million quid of taxpayers' money, and they hadn't even worked out that Lenny was a Staffordshire bull terrier. It was farcical."

Undeterred by their apparent failure to acquire even the most basic intelligence, PCs Edwards and Wlaznik – under the watchful eye of Superintendent Tony Thompson – pursued their conspiracy theory with gusto.

"Their argument was that if all this material I had was shown to a young person of impressionable mind, it could incite them to go out and act criminally. Which was complete bollocks, because at the end of the day people are responsible for their own actions, simple as that."

Conspiracy is potentially a very serious charge. John's solicitors Douglas and Partners approached the case accordingly, researching the history of graffiti and examining contemporary thought on the subject. And, when it came to approaching someone to act as character referee for John, they pulled off a massive coup.

"James Prigoff [co-author of *Spraycan Art*] gave me a wicked reference, saying that he was aware of the work that I was doing at the time. He said that, like him, I knew that you have to document the art to be able to publicise it. He added that, if I was going to be charged with conspiracy for what I was doing, maybe they should be looking at charging him and his publishers with the same thing. It was a very valid point."

The media had a field day. Taxpayers' money had been used by Avon County Council to employ an ex-convict to incite young people to commit wanton acts of criminal damage! Within days, the national press caught wind of the case and everyone from *The Independent* to *The Sun* ran the story. Serious questions were asked in Avon House, the centre of local government at the time. Local Tory MPs Jonathan Said and William Waldegrave used the case as ammunition against the Labour-controlled Council. John found himself fearing for his job - and for the liberty of both himself and the young people who had grown to trust him. The job, however, was safe - for the time being, at least.

"I received a lot of support from the Council. They had employed me to do that job, so they couldn't hang me out to dry. I was working to a job description that they wrote, and that I adhered to, so I had the support of my line manager and my area boss. But there were rumblings in Avon House, there was great embarrassment that a project that they had set up was being cast as the hub of illegal graffiti in Bristol."

In the midst of all the madness came a call from Martin Jones, Goldie's manager, who contacted John with a view to inviting some artists to represent Bristol at an international graffiti competition being held in Bridlington, a sleepy seaside town in East Yorkshire. Cheo and Inkie were chosen to paint on the day, John organised a coach, and the trio headed north with most of the youth club's regulars leaving the impending case behind them. They were on a mission to let people know what was really happening in Bristol: a thriving graffiti scene that was by now producing some world-class talent.

"It wasn't a case of Bristol going there and saying 'we're the best.' It was just the fact of taking part," John recalls. "There were all these international artists going there to paint, like Meo, Jon 156, Lokiss, Bates from Denmark, and Risky and Slick from LA. So we decided we were going to go there and make an impression, show people that Barton Hill, and Bristol, was doing it. Inkie did these flyers with some Hall Of Fame lettering and a character, and our telephone number.

"The boards that they painted generated a lot of interest throughout the day, mostly because Inkie's work was known throughout the country by then. That day I nearly lost my voice from speaking to so many people, bigging up Bristol all day long. I had mountains of photos of pieces from the club to give out."

The Bristol Massive - as they called themselves on the day - came second in the crew category - surprising everyone including themselves. Bristol had well and truly arrived and made its mark, both on the national and international scenes.

"The fact that they came second after Slick and Risky added a lot of credibility to the Bristol graff scene, without a doubt. After that event the interest in Bristol exploded. For months after that I was getting requests for photos from all over, and loads of people coming down to paint."

Back in Bristol, however, the court case loomed large in everyone's minds, and when it finally came to trial the judiciary found it impossible to make the charge against John stick. From those that were unfortunate enough to be convicted, the responses were mixed: some quit graffiti and got jobs to pay off their fines, some concentrated on painting legally, others simply came up with new tags and carried on regardless.

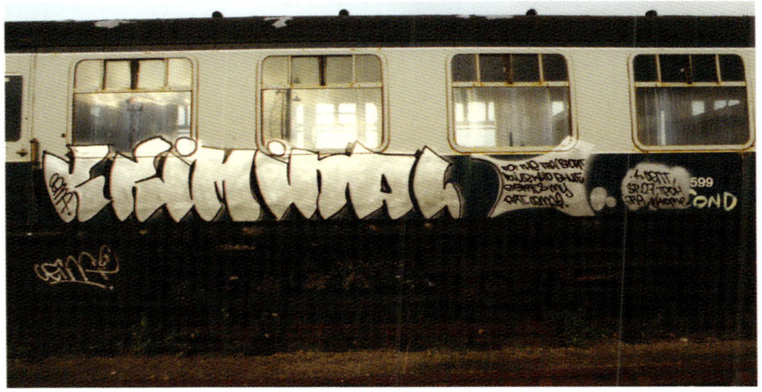

Above: 'Kriminal' piece by Cema on British Rail passenger carriage, c.1989

"One by one everyone was dealt with, then we had a trial hearing at the magistrates' court, and they charged Inkie, SP27, Era, Chaos, and a couple of others with me on the conspiracy charge. But the magistrates had such a wealth of material presented to them that they decided it was just too complicated for them to handle, so it was referred to the Crown Court. They couldn't prove the conspiracy charge, because there was no conspiracy! I could match up people's tags to their real names, but there was no conspiracy. The authorities thought that they could police Bristol's graffiti out of existence, but it was never going to happen, and it never will. All it achieved, in fact, was to increase Bristol's notoriety in the UK as a graffiti city."

Indeed. After John's acquittal, media interest went into hyperdrive. Never one to miss an opportunity, John appeared on TV - accompanied by various artists including Cheo, Inkie and Junks - on such programmes as *This Morning With Richard and Judy*,

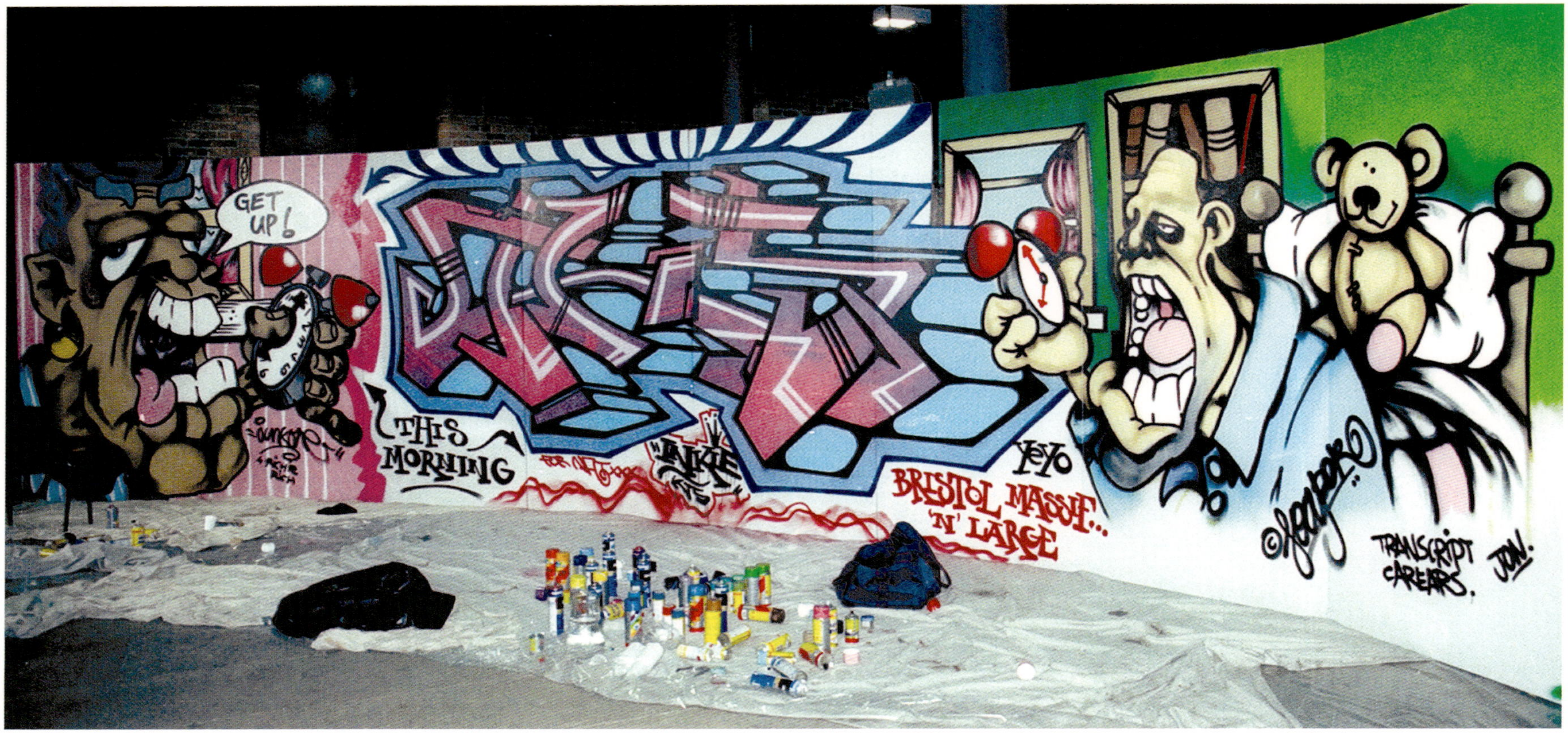

Above: 'This Morning' by Inkie, Cheo and Junks, painted for the Granada TV programme of the same name, 1989

Opposite page: A small selection of the press coverage of Operation Anderson, including an editorial from Barton Hill Youth Club's magazine Clean Slate (middle right)

Sky TV's *Cool Cube* and the BBC kids' news magazine *Newsround*. Then there was *Drawing The Line*, a half-hour BBC documentary which followed the case and the plight of John and the artists caught up in it.

"I was like a dog with a bone. There was no way that I wasn't going to use this situation to our advantage, to publicise the art that was going on here. No other city had ever had that much coverage of their graff scene. For six months after the case we milked it and proved that, given an opportunity to express themselves in a legal context, these young people – the ones with the talent – would gain recognition."

John Nation's legacy is visible on the walls of youth centres and in halls of fame in Bristol and across the country. Graffiti is now taken seriously as a form of alternative education in schools and youth centres throughout the UK – enabling many graffiti artists to make a living doing what they enjoy most, and to keep themselves in paint long after they've stopped stealing it.

Still living and working in Bristol, John has remained passionate about graffiti (or aerosol art, as he would have it) throughout the two decades since the events of 1989.

"Barton Hill was a drab, grey backdrop to the bright and colourful place that the Dug Out became. It was invigorating. Most importantly it showed that, given the opportunity, you could channel young people's talents in a positive way, and that you could showcase what young people were capable of artistically. They had talent – but no one else in Bristol was working to harness that talent. That was where I stepped in. I've got pride in Bristol, always have had. I'm a Bristol boy born and bred."

Graffiti gang's trail led to club

'Spray-can spree'

MEMBERS of a "hip-hop" graffiti gang who met at a council-backed club to practise their art on a special wall, were charged yesterday with causing £250,000 criminal damage.

Court rap for hip-hop graffiti gang

Youth on £17,000 damage charges

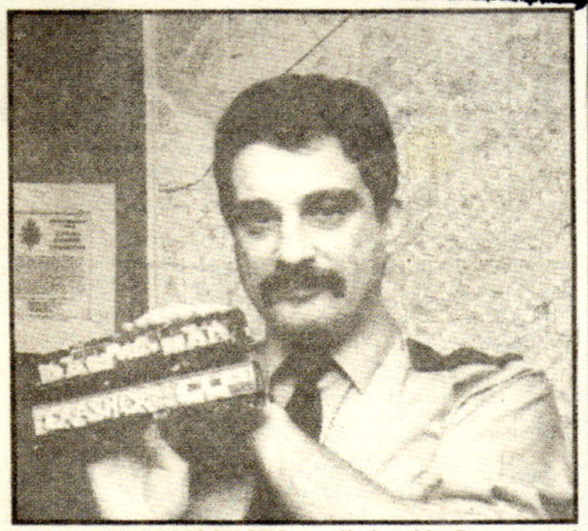

MODEL TRAIN MOCK-UPS . . . displayed by Somerset and Avon Pc George Wlaznik who liaised with the BT police during Operation Anderson.

GRAFFITI SWOOP

POLICE today arrested several paint spraying graffiti artists in Bristol who have caused more than £200,000 damage to property.

The majority of damage was caused to railway property and the swoop was a joint operation with Transport police.

The arrested have been detained for questioning at Trinity Road police station.

Railnews, February 1990

7

WRITING'S ON THE WALL FOR THE 'BOMBERS'

Undercover cops trap spray gang

TRANSPORT police went undercover to attend "graffiti conventions" as part of a campaign to trap a gang of spray can vandals.

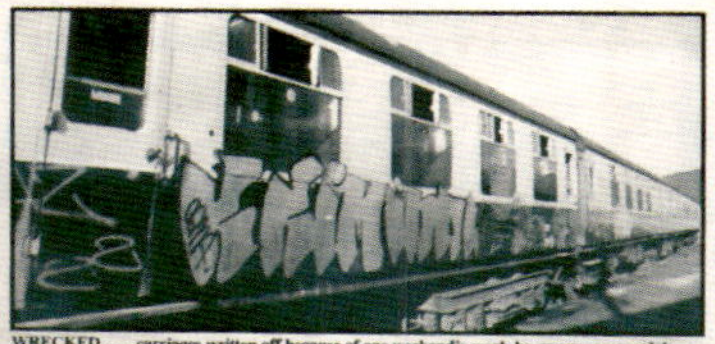

WRECKED . . . carriages written off because of one weekend's work by spray-can vandals.

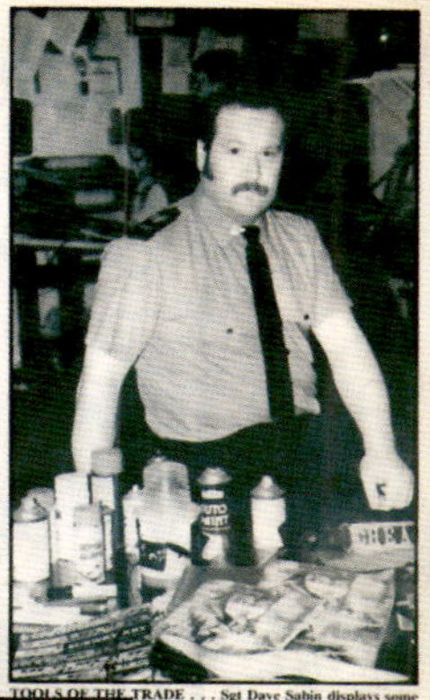

TOOLS OF THE TRADE . . . Sgt Dave Sabin displays some ...nfiscated, while below is an example of street ... Criminal Minded Artists.

£250,000 graffiti 'Bombers'

View from the hill

STOP THIS CRAZY THING

If the police want to drive the vast majority of writers back into illegaility that's their responsibility. The writers must be encouraged by workers to stop "tagging" and "piercing" illegally and be shown the benefits of a legal site. They just won't bother if the police hassle the legal sites.

When those writers do go back on the streets, then Bristol will realise what a good job of containment Barton Hill has achieved. Believe us Bristol will be plagued.

Whatever the police try to do, us who produce Clean Slate know that this will only make us more determined to carry on. The police threat in terms of trying to stop Clean Slate going to print and giving the people the chance to voice their opinions in matters that effect them, is oppressive and unwarranted.

Our right to freedom of speech is slowly being eroded. Compared to Russia, these rights are always being highlighted as part of the fundamental freedom to which every individual in this country is entitled. So lets fight for our rights, because when the pen is a weapon, use it, it's yours!

Clean Slate

YOUTH MAG FROM BARTON HILL, EAST BRISTOL

GRAFFITI YOUTH IS CAUGHT IN ACT

A POLICEMAN in plain clothes kept watch through binoculars as a 17-year-old youth painted graffiti on a wall, Bristol magistrates were told.

He kept observation from the top of St James Barton roundabout while the youth wrote on the underpass wall with a marker pen.

Barry Walsh of Lanaway Road, Oldbury Court, Fishponds, admitted two charges of causing criminal damage.

Yesterday, he was put on probation for 18 months, and ordered to pay £5 compensation.

Youth worker held in graffiti clampdown

By Mike Prestage

A PART-TIME youth worker employed to promote "aerosol art" was one of 72 people arrested by British Transport Police in a crackdown on illegal graffiti.

The arrest of John Nation, 27, of Barton Hill, Bristol, is an embarrassment for his employers, Avon County Council, and has put a question mark over its efforts to promote aerosol art — the phrase preferred by the writers — on legal sites.

Mr Nation has been charged with inciting others to commit criminal damage. The case will be heard at crown court, where he will plead not guilty.

He still works at Barton Hill youth club, which has a national reputation among aerosol artists as a meeting place, but has been told not to talk about the case.

The police operation, codenamed Anderson, began last October in an attempt to catch what the authorities regard as vandals.

The 72 arrested, who came from Cardiff, Exeter, and Bath, as well as Bristol, are not linked, but know each other by their "tags" (signatures).

Sgt David Edwards led a team of six officers in the operation, which involved taking out search warrants to look for paint sprays, photographs, stencils and albums in artists' homes. "You could say some of the people who do it are quite talented, but the thing is, would you like it painted on the walls of your house?" he said.

Those already dealt with by the courts have faced heavy fines and damages.

Last week Mark Tudor, 20, from Bath, was ordered to pay £1,200 in fines and damages for his work on railway sidings.

"The police are only doing their job, but it's a bit over the top. We are not robbing anyone or breaking into cars. We are going to do art," Mr Tudor, whose tag is Catch 22, said.

Ms Flo McGowan, full-time youth worker at Barton Hill, said: "The difficulty we face is that the centre has to meet the needs expressed by young people and sometimes we have to walk a tightrope between what is legal and not legal.

"We have to make contact with artists working illegally and let them know there is a place here where they can work. Many of the writers who come here will also do illegal work, but in areas where there is no place for kids to go there is far more illegal work done."

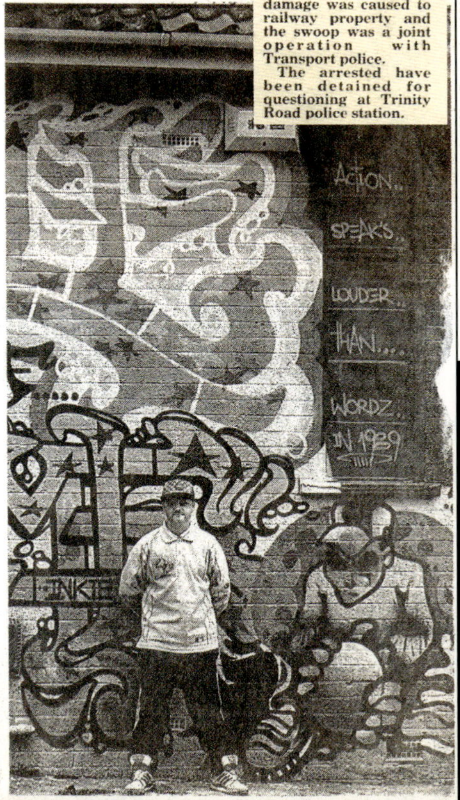

HONOURS FOR POLICE WHO TRACKED VANDALS

Graffiti squad makes its mark

By Bob Corfield

FIVE police heroes who targetted graffiti-scrawling vandals in Bristol were honoured today.

Their year-long efforts brought more than 50 people to book for daubing public buildings and trains with unsightly 'street art'.

But while their operation, code named Anderson, has kept trains and stations clear of graffiti, the spray can and marker pen vandals are still in action around Bristol.

Suspects

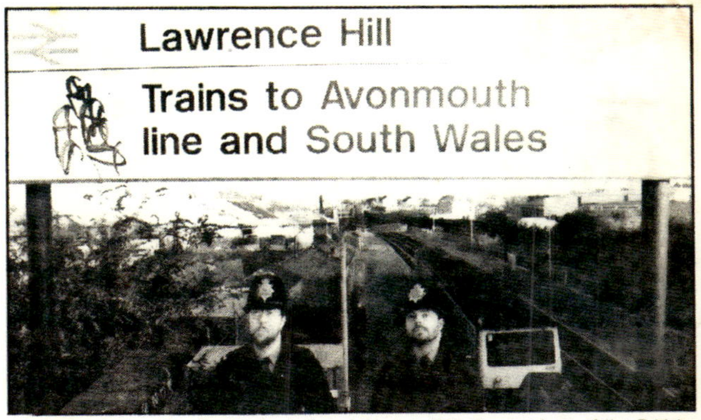

Platform patrol . . . PCs Jim Marks, left, and Stephen Wheale, members of the British

SHAB

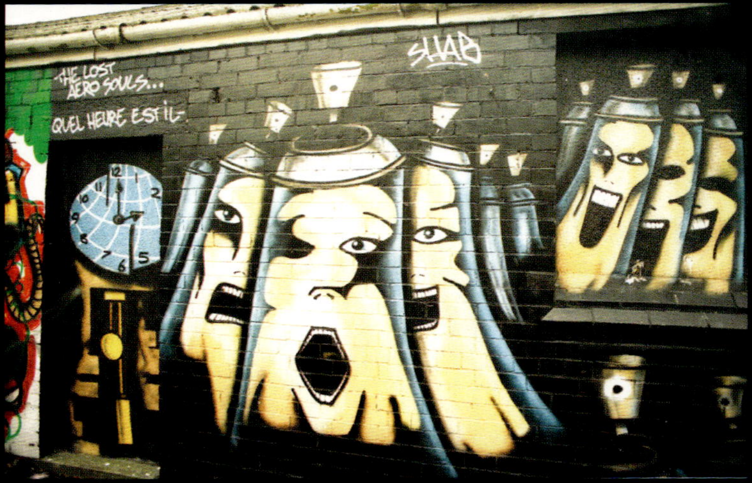

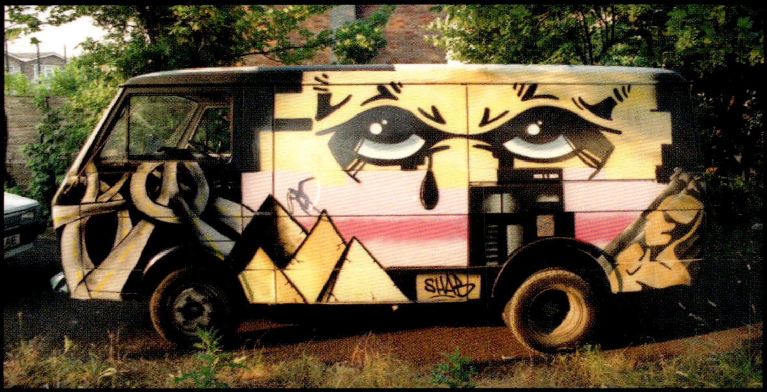

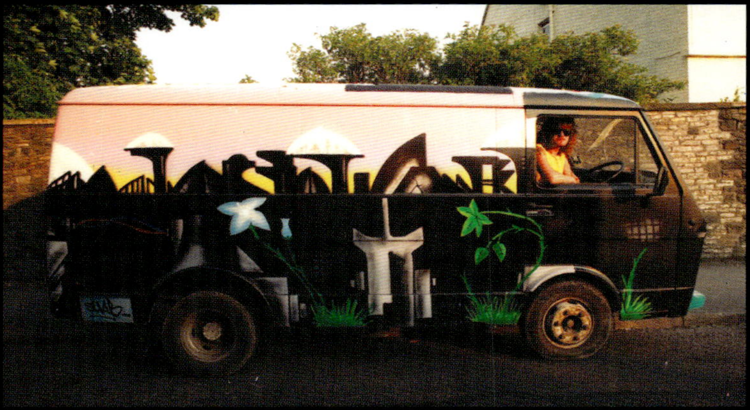

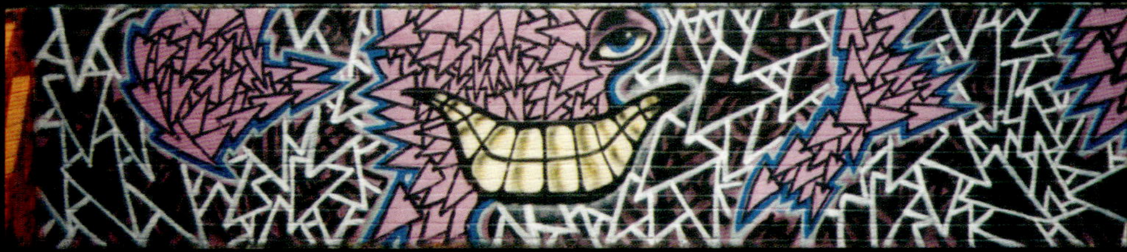

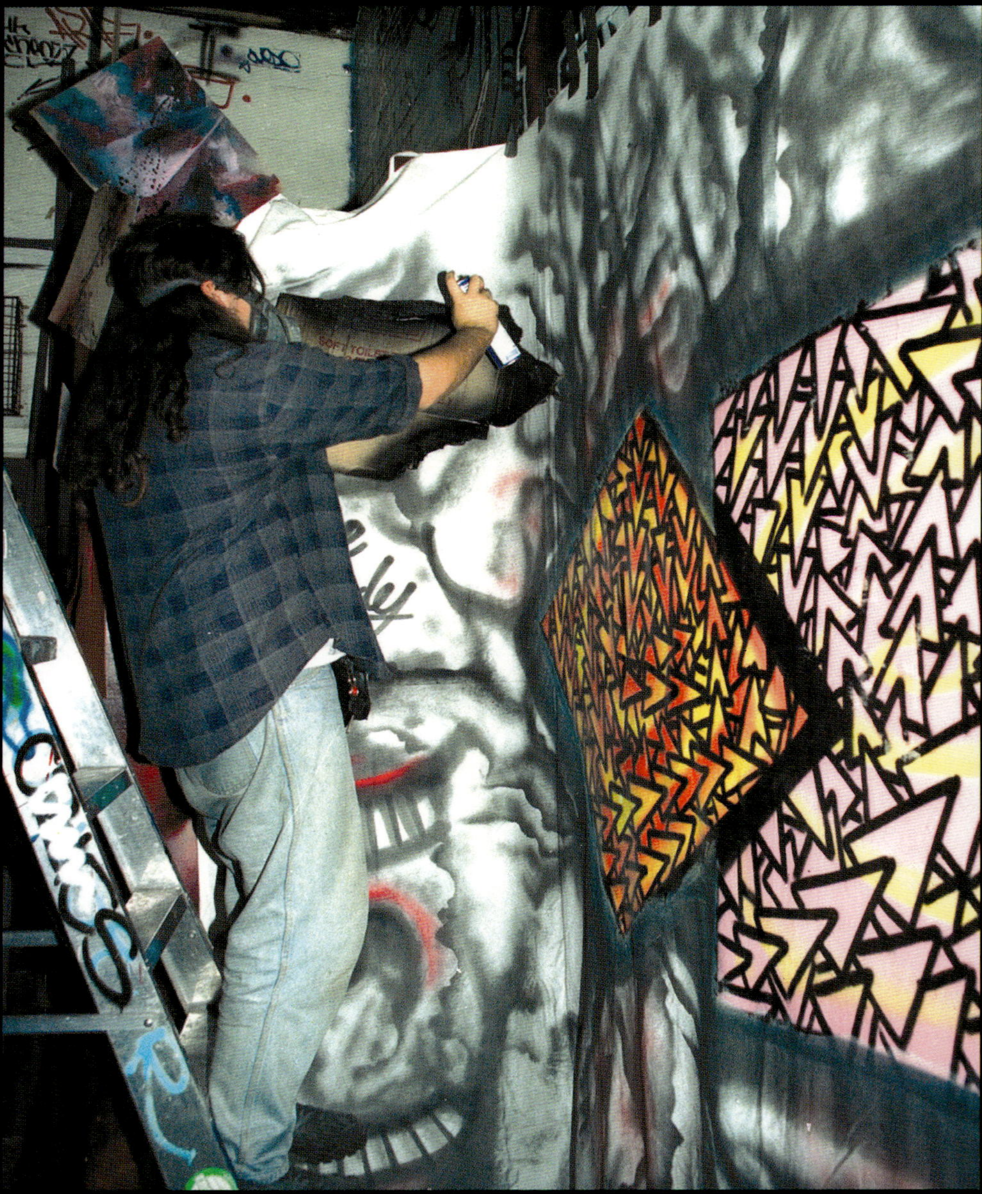

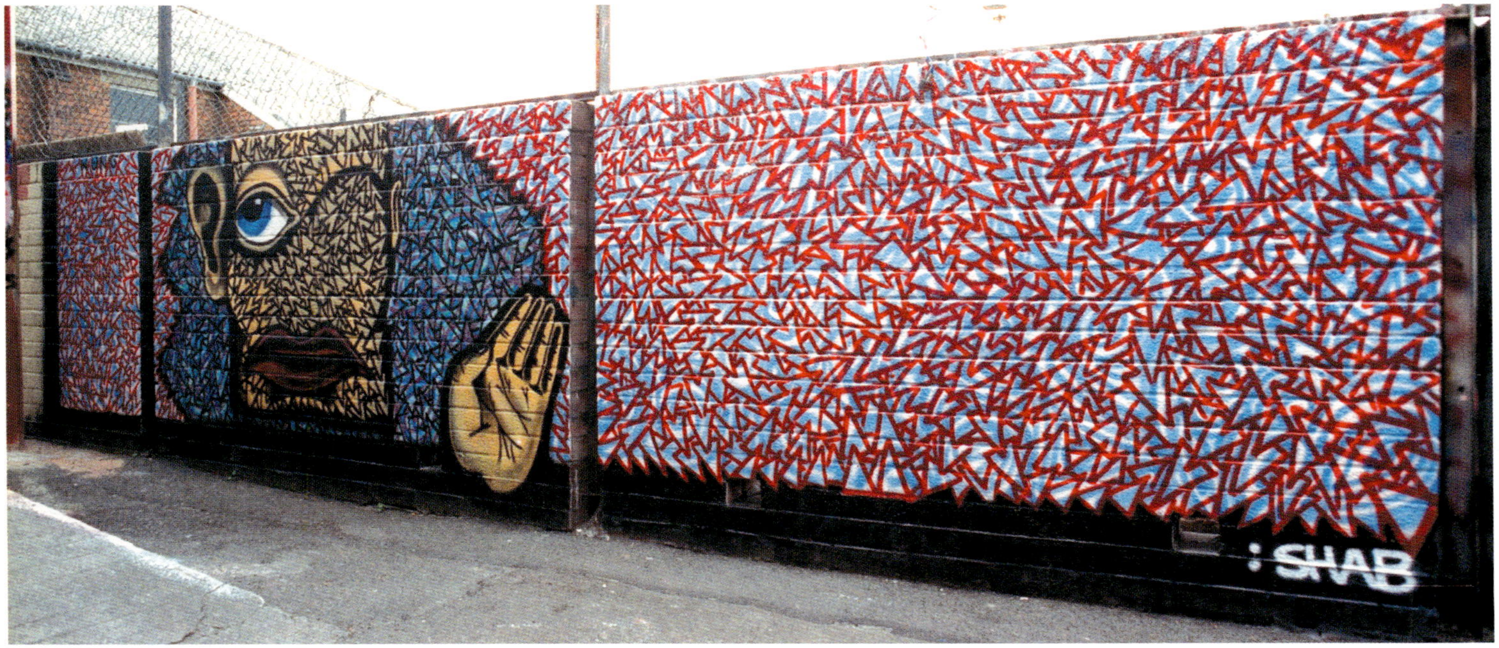

A selection of pieces by Shab from Barton Hill, c.1989-90. His distinctive interlocking-triangles became his trademark and made his style stand out at a time of intense experimentation and development at Barton Hill Youth Club. Shab was originally a member of CMA (Criminally Minded Artists) alongside Chaos

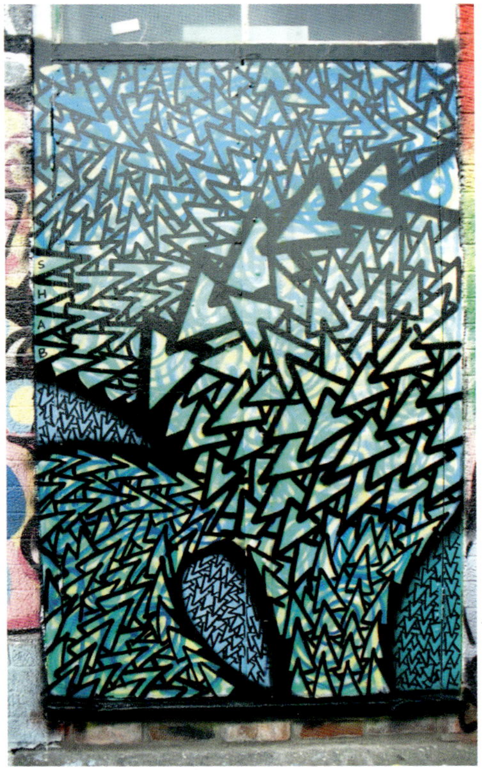

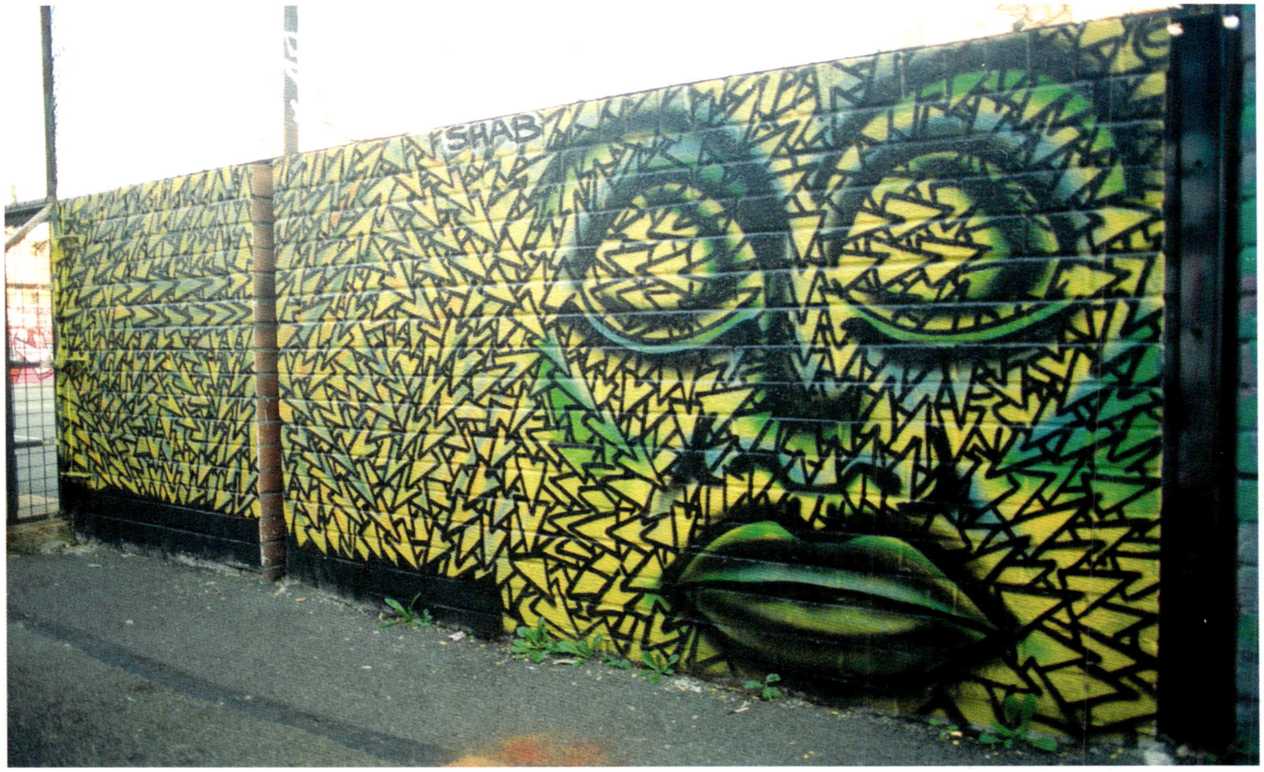

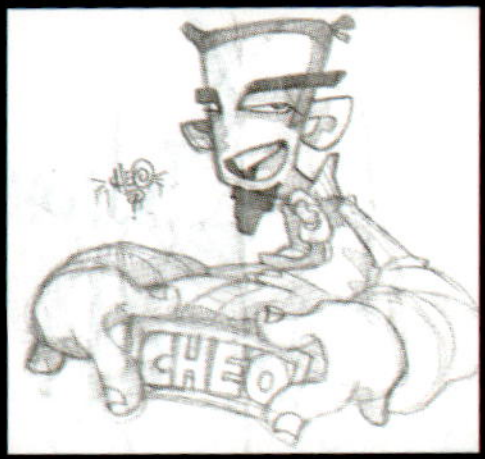

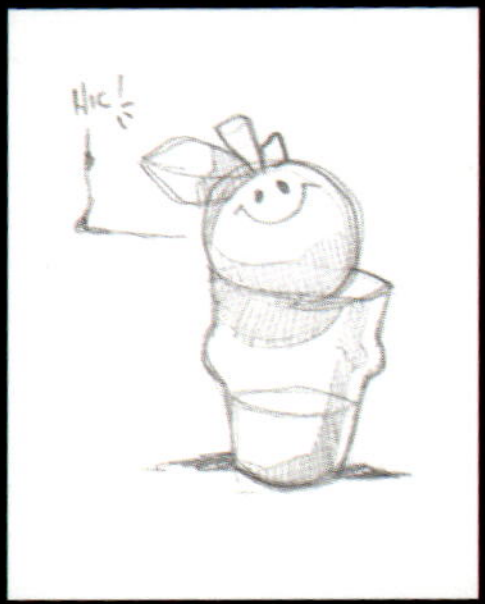

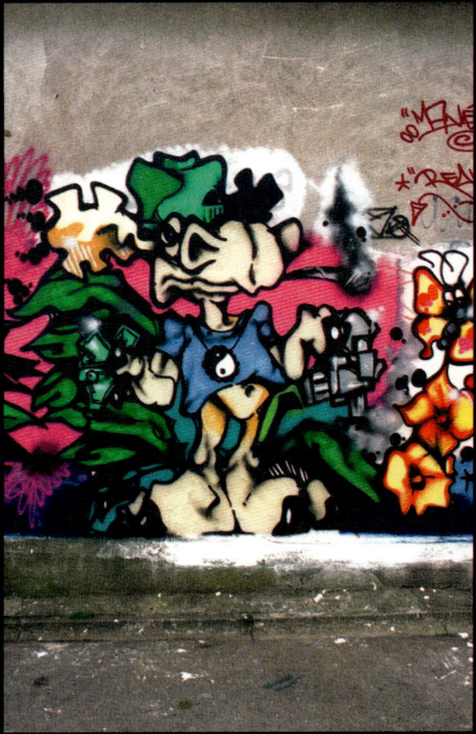

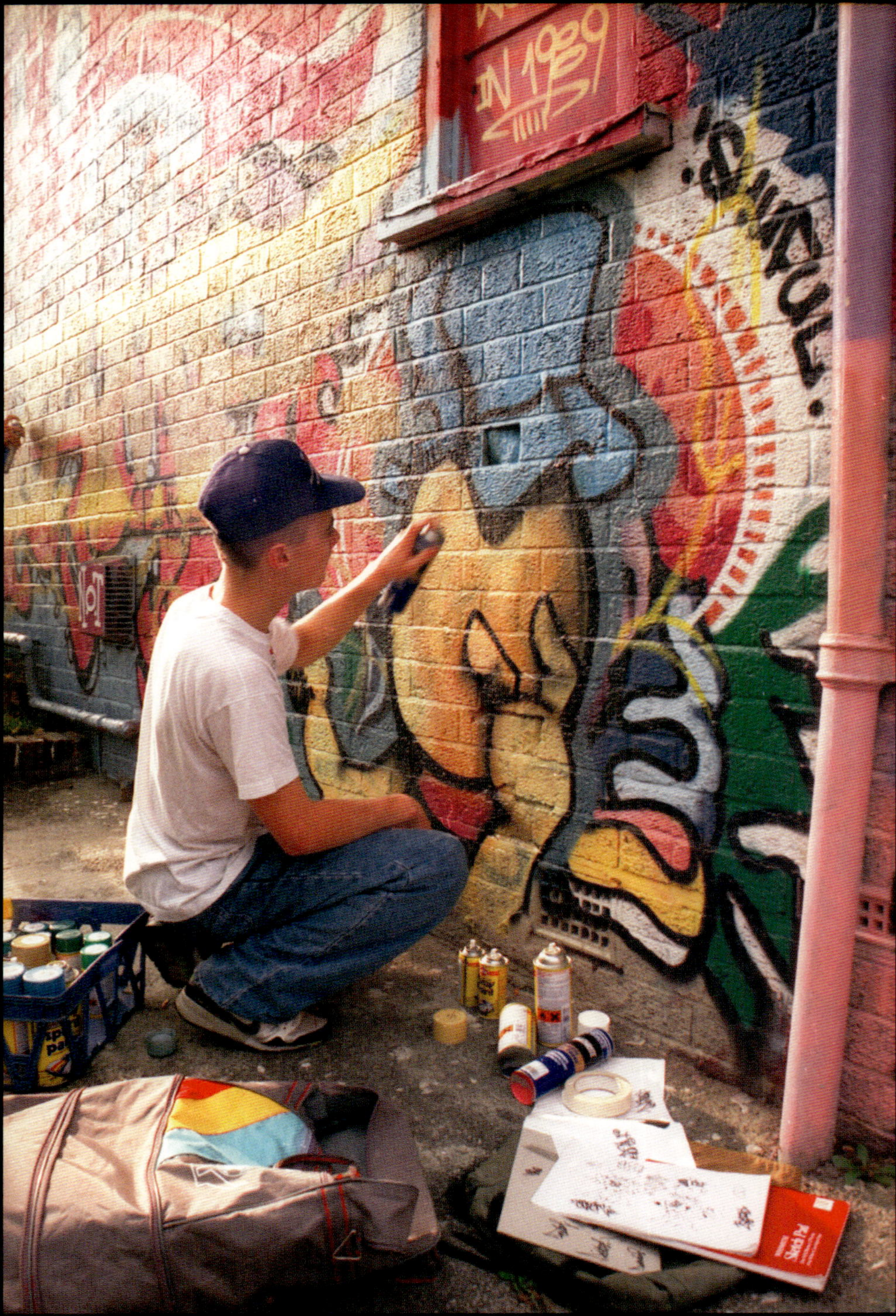

Above: Pencil sketch of a drunken cider apple

Top left: Cheo B-boy pencil sketch displaying archetypal hip hop angles

Top middle: 'The Badass Moose' on the wall in Bedminster, 1989

Right: Cheo painting his 'Egg Man' character on the front wall at Barton Hill Youth Club in 1989

Opposite page. Top left: Cheo lettering piece in the ball court at Barton Hill Youth Club, c.1989

Top right: 'FTP (Fuck The Police)' by Cheo and SP 27, Barton Hill ball court, c.1989

Bottom right: Skate ramp inside Barton Hill Youth Club, c.1989

Bottom left: 'Egg Head' cartoon strip by Soaper (aka Cheo) 1990.

CHEO TCP/TUB/DP/ASK

• **Half cute, half twisted, Cheo's characters occupy their own world, like those of all visionary cartoonists.** His creations appear to come to life fully formed and with little interference from their creator – a feat so apparently effortless that you know it must have taken years to perfect. It's an approach that owes a great deal to his single biggest influence, the late underground comics genius Vaughn Bode – creator of such characters as Cheech Wizard and Cobalt 60.

"I first saw his stuff in *Subway Art*, and then I heard his name mentioned in *Wild Style* and I just fell in love with his work, really. It's the most amazing art ever. Then I went up to Forever People, the comic

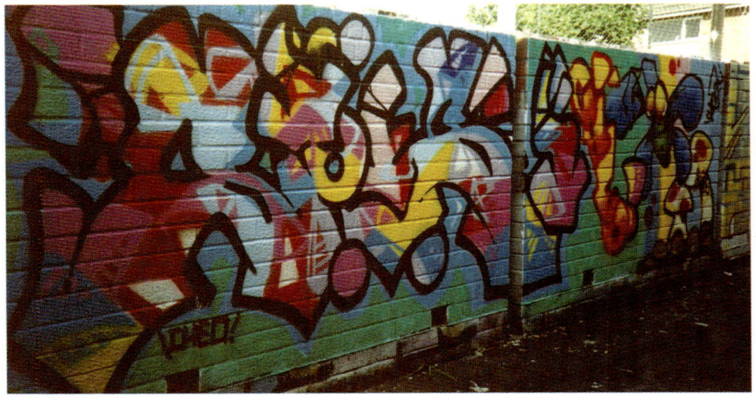

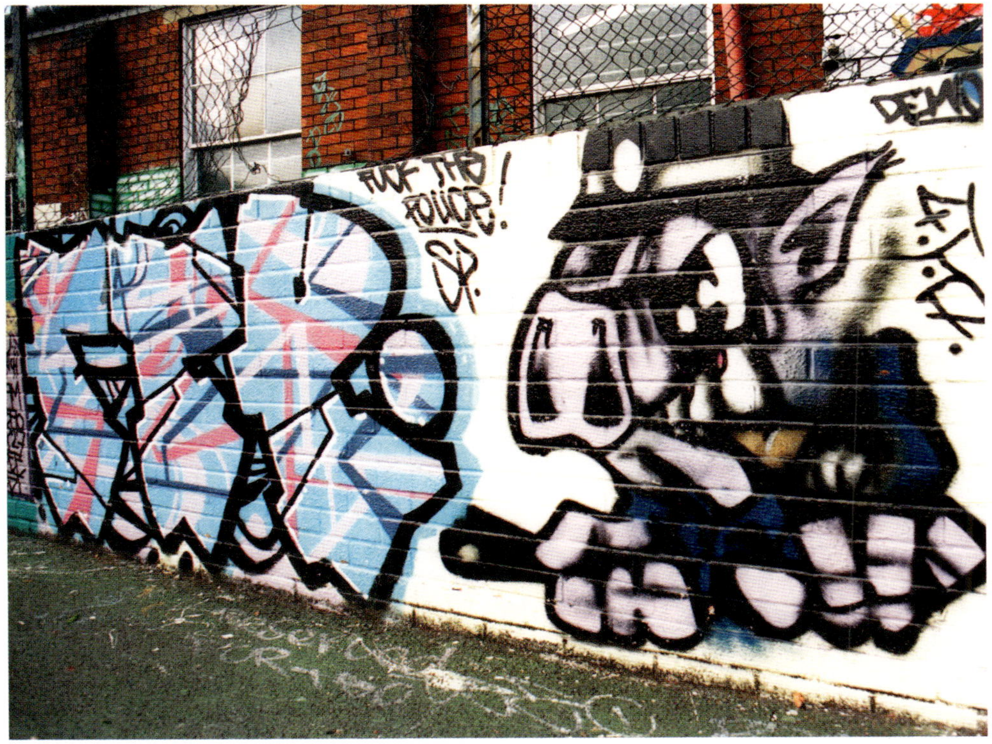

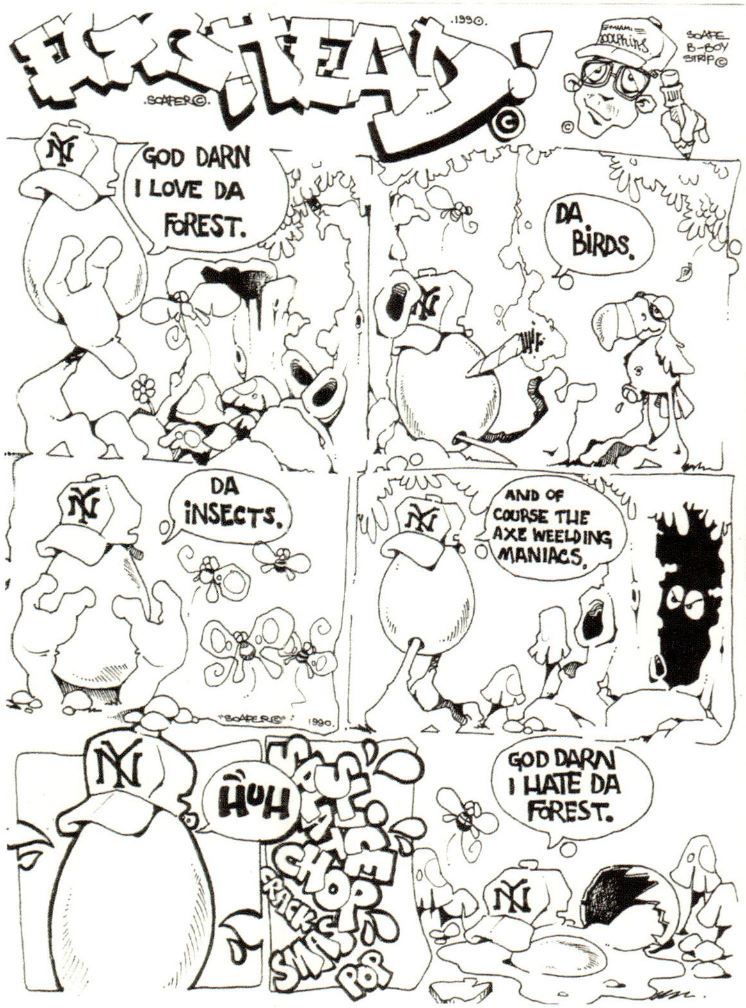
SOAPE B-BOY STRIP ©
.1990.
GOD DARN I LOVE DA FOREST.
DA BIRDS.
DA INSECTS.
AND OF COURSE THE AXE WEELDING MANIACS.
HUH
CHOP
POP
GOD DARN I HATE DA FOREST.

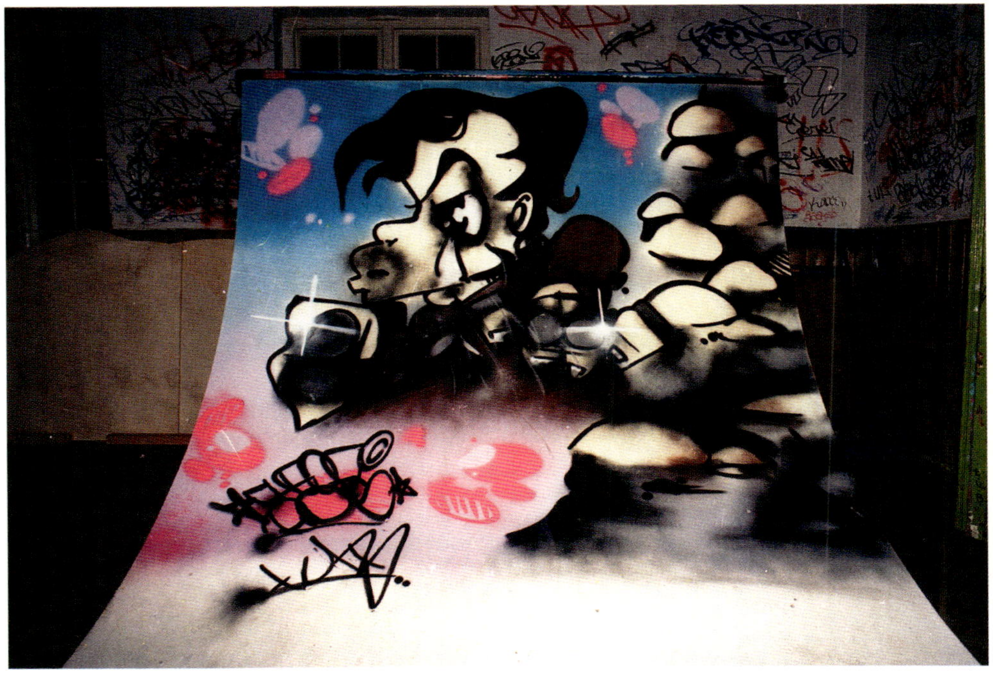

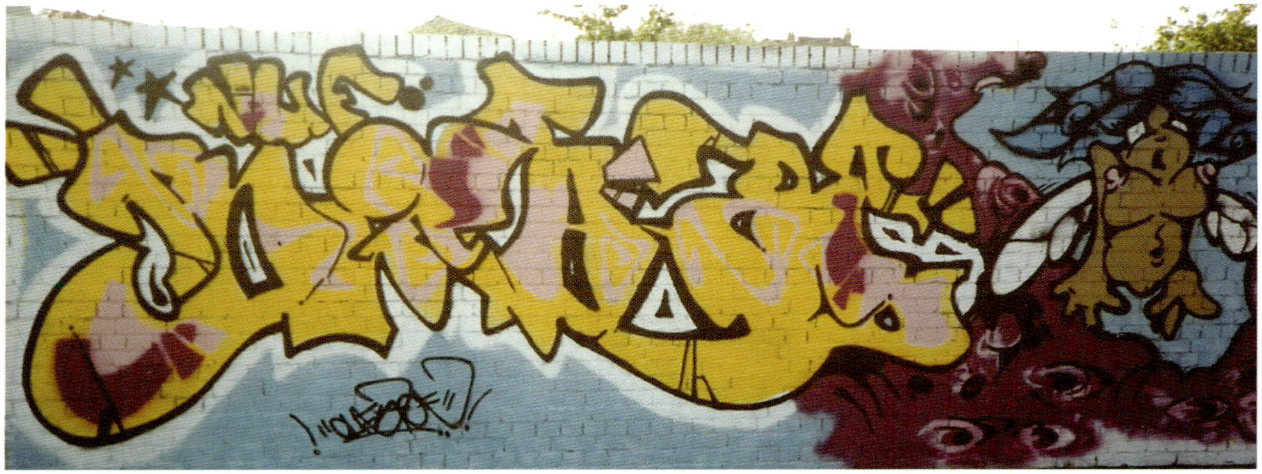

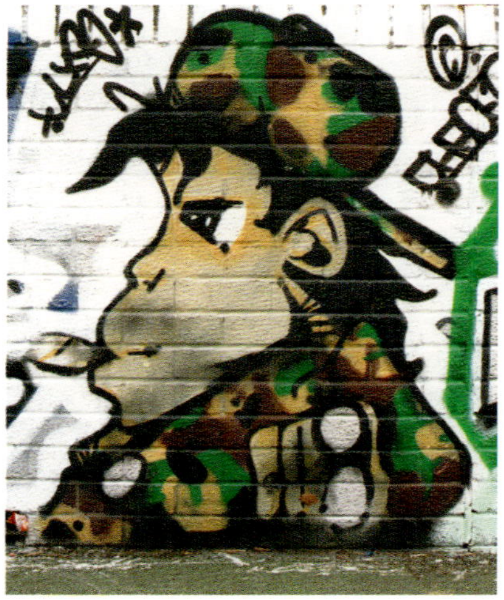

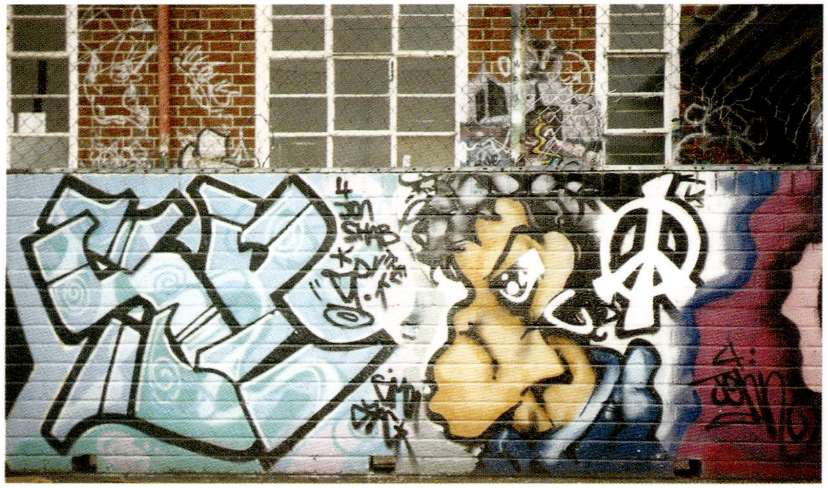

Top: 'Nuf Nikaz' Newtown housing estate wall, Bristol, c.1989-90

Above left: Camouflage B-boy, c.1989

Above right: Another Cheo/SP 27 collaboration, c.1989

shop on Park Street, and nearly soiled my trousers when I saw that they had a couple of his comics in there. I didn't care how much it cost, it was like 'you're coming with me.' It was amazing. I had a bit of a twitch on looking through that lot. It was weird looking through it and seeing characters that Dondi used and stuff: it's almost like Bode did the drawings for graffiti artists. The guy was a friggin' genius. If somebody said my stuff reminded them of Vaughn Bode's it wouldn't bother me one bit, in fact that would be the ultimate compliment."

Bode's influence is clearly visible in the work of many graffiti writers and Cheo's early characters owe much to that influence, but Cheo has taken the great man's angles and proportions on a journey and made them his own. Like old-school New York character writers before him (such as Tack of FBA, Skeme TNT and, perhaps most notably, Doze TC5), Cheo studied Vaughn's creations hard, examining their postures, their facial expressions and how they are weighted; trying to unearth what makes them so damned funky, and so fitting to the whole classic graffiti aesthetic.

"I've no idea why it is but you can look at a character and say 'yeah, that's B-boy.' It must be the stance or something, and a bit of the attitude and what have you. It's how they're stood, maybe, with one leg forward and one leg back. It's a little front-to-back lean. It's weird how a stance can represent the whole of hip hop!"

Like Doze - who found fame B-boying as a member of the Rocksteady Crew - Cheo also started out dancing before he picked up a spray can. When hip hop in the UK was in its infancy, it seemed natural to explore its various elements before becoming comfortable with aspect or another.

"I used to breakdance in a friend's garage and we had a little crew, which we started after seeing *Beat Street* and we tried out doing some spraying in his garage as well. We were only kids, it was very naïve. It was looking at things like the [Street Sounds] *Electro* albums and things like that, and just getting little snippets of stuff here and there, because back then you didn't see anything, apart from things like the [Artful Dodger's] Weetabix billboards and Brim doing stuff in *Bombin'*.

"Those kinds of things got me excited and got me right into it, and I've always been more comfortable with doing cartoon characters, so I stepped away from the letters. I was painting with people who could really do letters, so I thought, 'well I'll just do a character on the end of the piece.'"

After forming his first crew TCP (T-Cut Posse) with childhood friend Deed and honing their skills in and around their neighbourhood of Kingswood, Cheo and

Deed stumbled across the then relatively virgin walls of Barton Hill Youth Club. Still in its infancy as a hall of fame, Barton Hill's reputation as being unwelcoming was not unfounded. Not that it bothered them much: they had found somewhere to paint legally, hang out and meet other juvenile delinquents obsessed with hip hop. It soon became a home from home for the Kingswood boys.

"Me and Deed went to Barton Hill Dug Out one day, just to look at the front wall, and then Johnny Nation walked up to us and said 'do you like that?' And he said 'if you want to do graffiti, come and do the front wall.' I think after the very first piece on there, it was me and Deed who did the front wall next. We went out and bought a load of paint and did it in a day, which was pretty cool. But John wasn't really welcoming at first, he was really brash and set his dog on us, but we were young and didn't give a shit, so we just went along with it.

"It was just somewhere to go and be bad little shithouses, and a lot of the time you didn't really have to buy or steal paint. It was a congregation of like-minded people. You'd get people coming from all over to this one hub, where people felt comfortable painting without any hassle. We just fannied about, talking about girls and doing spraying. What more do you want when you're a kid? It was perfect. I used to travel from Kingswood to Barton Hill just to do that on a daily basis."

Soon after, Cheo and Deed bumped into Era and Teao - two other young writers they recognised from Barton Hill - at Soundwell Swimming Pool. Petty grievances were soon forgotten over talk of graffiti, and The United Bombers (TUB) were formed. Their name essentially sums up their collective goal - to destroy Bristol with spray paint, marker pens, stones, keys and anything else that could be used to make a mark.

"It was a progressive thing, it took a while to feel confident enough to go and do it at night. But because you're a kid you're yearning for a buzz, you need that adrenaline rush, and going out and doing the trains was fucking amazing. There's an area of Bristol where the Showcase Cinema is now that used to be a big coach yard. They'd stop the Royal Mail trains there, and the passenger trains would slow down there as well. We used to wait for trains to slow down and then run up the side of the hill and bomb the crap out of them while they were still moving. There'd be people banging on the window, saying 'Oi, you, what do you think you're doing?'

"They were crazy times. I can't believe I did it sometimes. I can remember sleeping in the carriages, then waking up hearing people coming to work, thinking 'shit, we've got to get out of here!', and just running off after we'd destroyed the place.

"I was at a stage of my life where I couldn't be arsed with college, and I was in and out of jobs. I didn't really know what to do with myself, so I had all the time in the world. There was usually about three or four of us going out. TUB wasn't that big in numbers, it was just what we did, really, we were stupid enough to go all over the place destroying it. It looked like we went mob-handed, but we didn't really."

Cheo's experiences were much like those of most other Bristol graffiti writers in the late 1980s. On the one hand there was the madness that was the bombing missions, on the other the relatively relaxed sessions painting full-colour pieces at the Barton Hill Dug Out. But in 1989 the legal and the illegal collided within a matter of months, making a huge impact on all those involved. In March the British Transport Police carried out a series of raids on the homes of graffiti writers across the south-west - including Cheo's - as part of Operation Anderson. Two months later the bailed 17-year-old graffiti artist was the proud winner, alongside Inkie, of second prize in the crew category at the World Graffiti Championships in Bridlington, North Yorkshire.

"I didn't actually do that much illegal painting, really. With the Operation Anderson thing they pulled out all my stuff and it was pretty meagre, it was quite pathetic. It was like 'actually I want to be a bad boy, this is crap!' I did the odd train, but

Below: Money folding gold-toothed skinhead gets a disapproving look from his butterfly companion, Barton Hill, c.1989

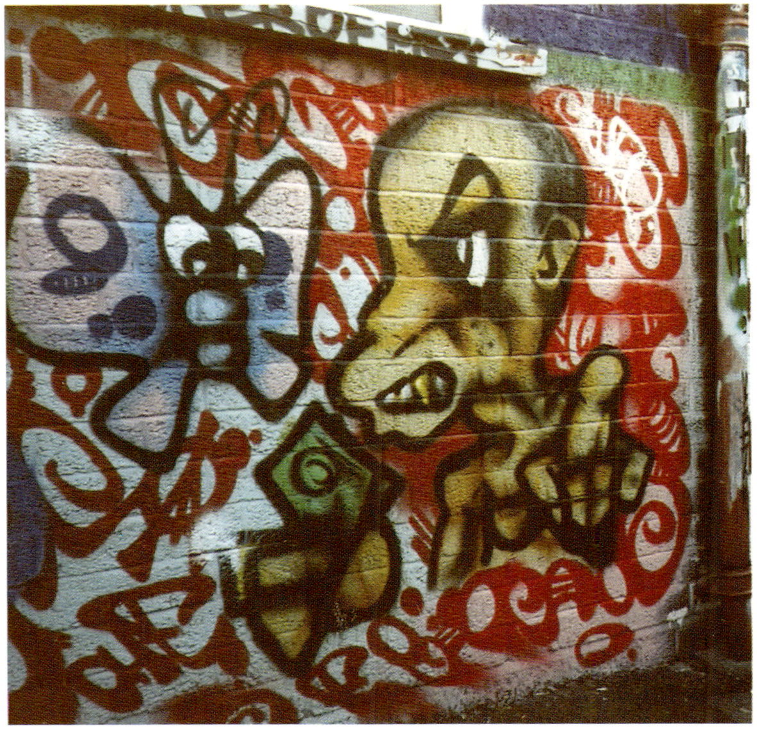

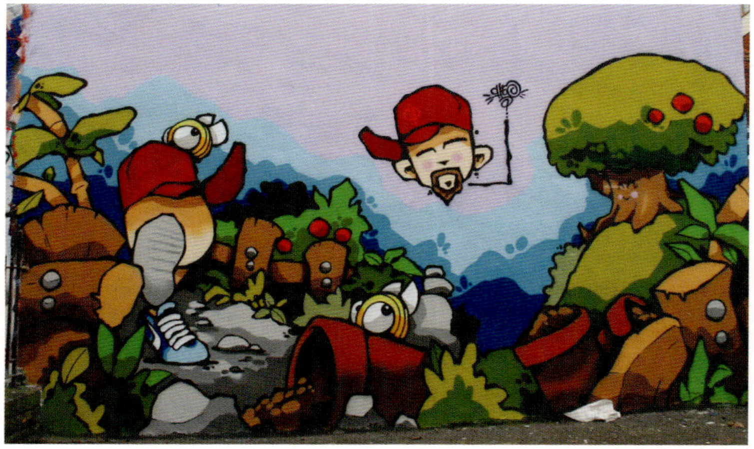

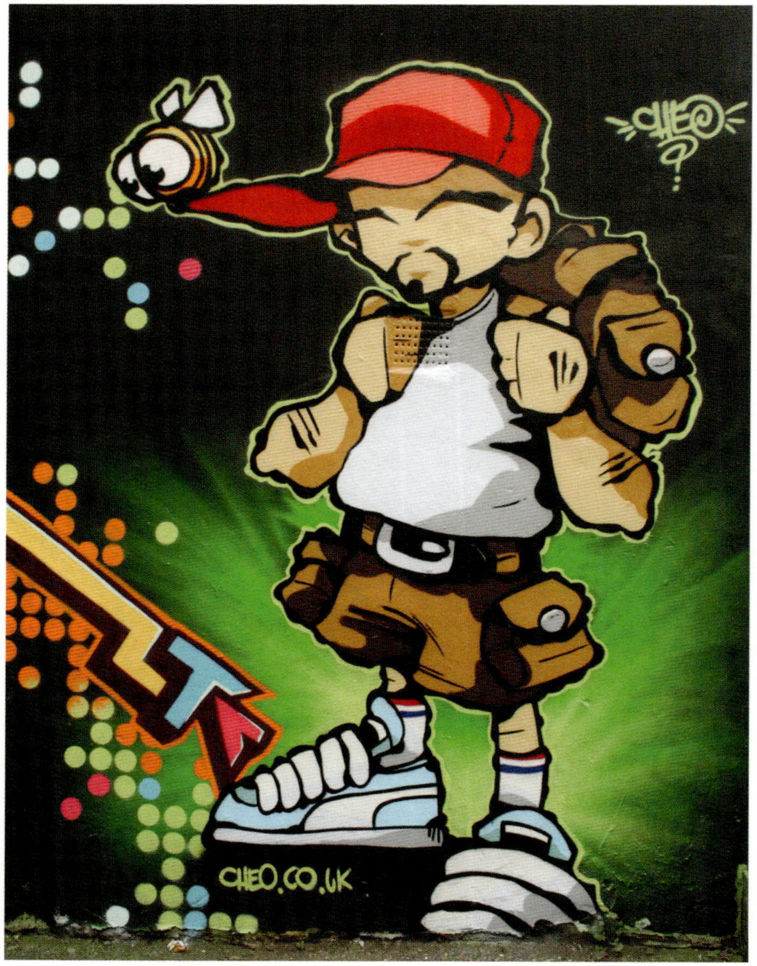

I didn't hit Bristol as much as most of the others. I was too busy - as I am now - doing things that I could take my time on, and making something that I was proud of. I'd sooner sit there with ten cans and take all day doing something."

To the BTP, however, Cheo's relatively low level of involvement in TUB's city-wide campaign was irrelevant. He had been active enough to be hauled in alongside everyone else, and that meant confiscating as evidence every last item even vaguely connected with graffiti.

"I had everything taken and I never got any of it back - photo albums, magazines with my tag on, they even took porn mags that I'd tagged the front of! They took my Cheo name belt, they took the lot. They even took examples of my handwriting so they could get some handwriting specialist in to see if it was my tag.

"My father took photographs of a lot of my stuff - the legal stuff - and he was quite proud of it. He filled photo albums with it, but the police swiped the lot and I never saw any of it again. I have no history on paper of anything, it was all taken at the time. It was all destroyed 'for the good of the nation.' It may all still be down there, but I can remember it was on the local news and I swear I saw my buckle belt on that fire. They were throwing on photo albums and sketches, everything. It all just went up into the ether. But what can you do? You were a bad boy and you were destroying the city, you get everything that comes to you."

Bridlington, however, raised the spirits and gave Cheo and Inkie a chance to paint with the big boys. Slick and Risk from Los Angeles came half way across the planet to push the Bristol Massive into second place, a result that Cheo was more than happy with. "Bridlington was a bit of an anti-climax after the raids, but at the same time we all still wanted to paint. And it was a good experience. We got to see a lot of other writers from all over the place. Slick and Risk, their stuff just blew me away, it was on a whole new level. It just freaked me out, almost to the point of making me want to give up. I felt quite privileged to be there, but I also felt quite humbled by the whole affair. It made me look at my stuff and think 'are we worthy?' - but obviously we were, because we came second. It was only Slick and Risk turning up that knocked us off the first place spot. But fair play to them, because their piece was fantastic, really crazy stuff. I had never seen people doing stuff like that with paint - throwing in colours you just wouldn't expect and doing that second highlight thing."

Despite the positive aspects of Bridlington, and the subsequent exposure enjoyed by a few of those convicted, for many the aftershock of Operation Anderson ran deep. Cheo thought himself one of the lucky ones, but the knock-on effect was nonetheless devastating for him in the long term. "As soon as it happened there was a cut-off. Virtually everybody stopped being friends, and a few people went down a bad road - towards drugs and stuff. I was fortunate enough to have a girlfriend at the time and that was my life, really, even though I was living like a 40-year-old when I was 20. But it got to a point with TUB - because people were going off and smoking crack and what have you - when the whole enjoyment, the whole feel of it was gone, so I thought 'fuck it, I'm going to stop.' It took the edge off it. I completely cut it off. And sometimes for six months at

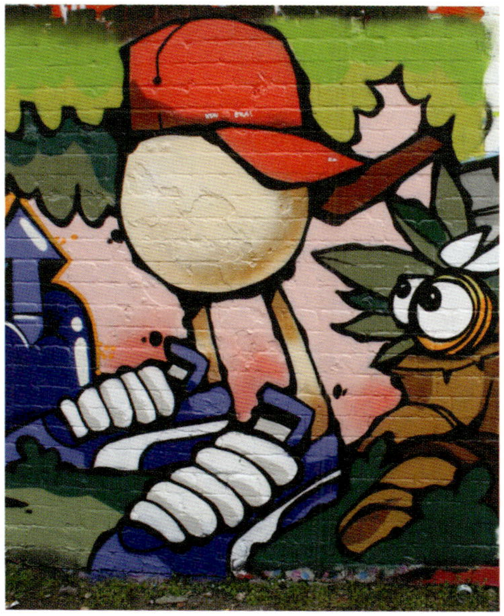

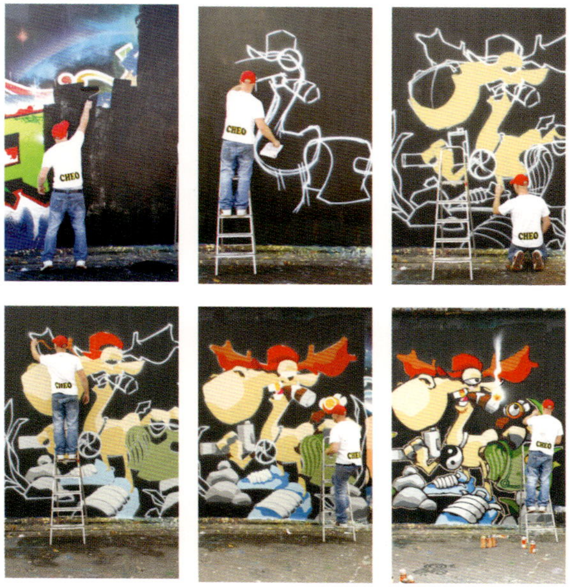

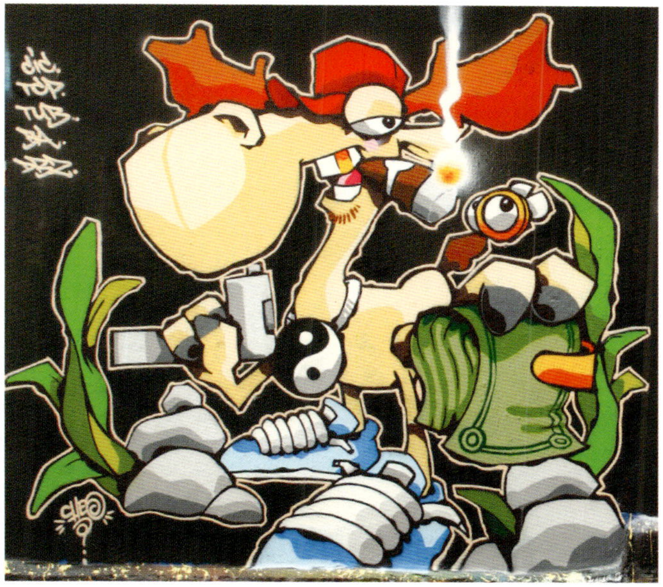

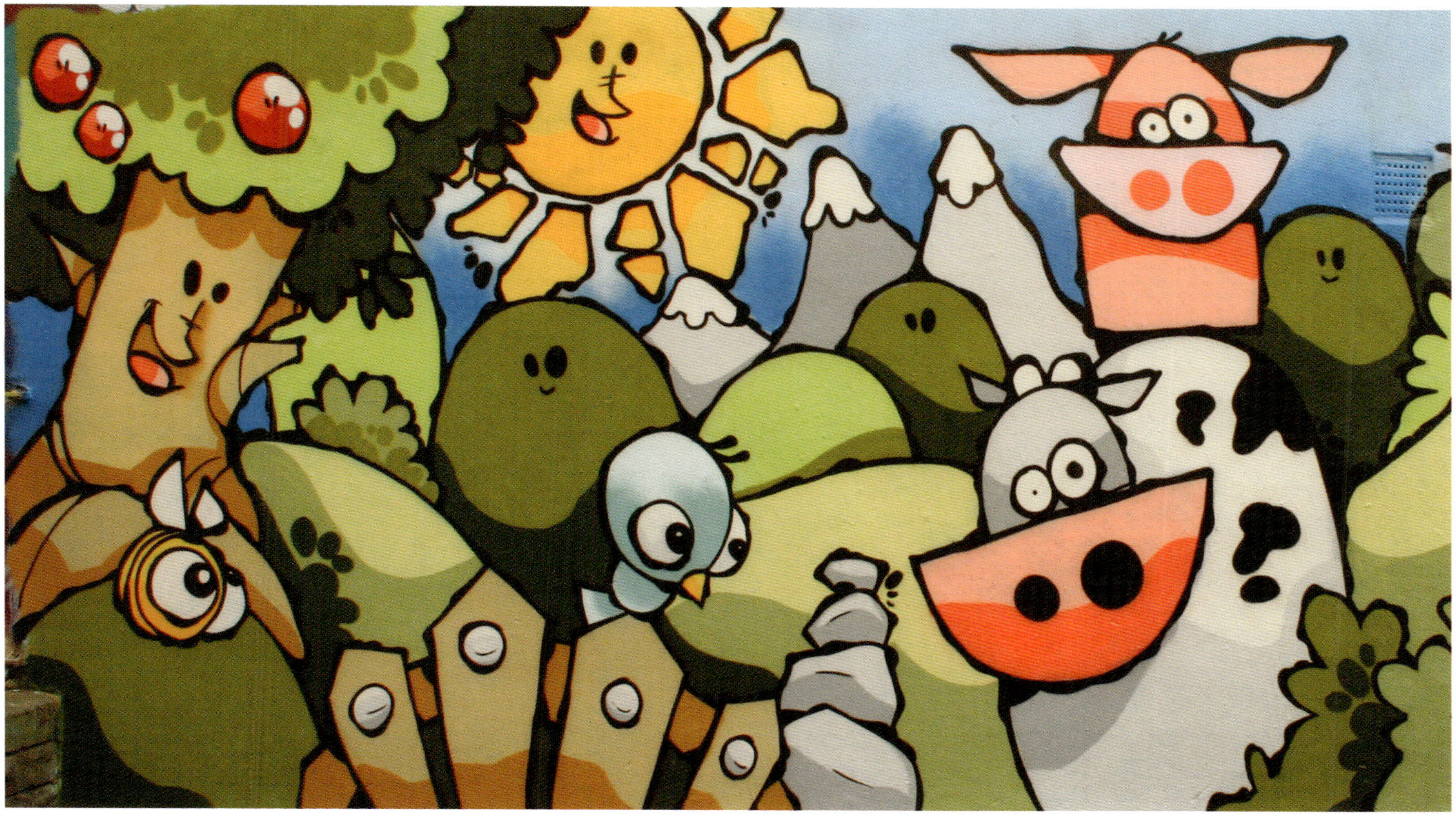

Opposite page: More recent Cheo characters sporting his ubiquitous red baseball cap and accompanied by the ever-present bee character. The 'bumpy' outline is another of his trademarks. 2007-08

This page. Top row: Familiar old faces 'Egg Head' and 'The Badass Moose' are brought out of retirement, 2007-8

Bottom: The hills have eyes. Even the tiny apples in the trees are given characteristics in Cheo World, 2008

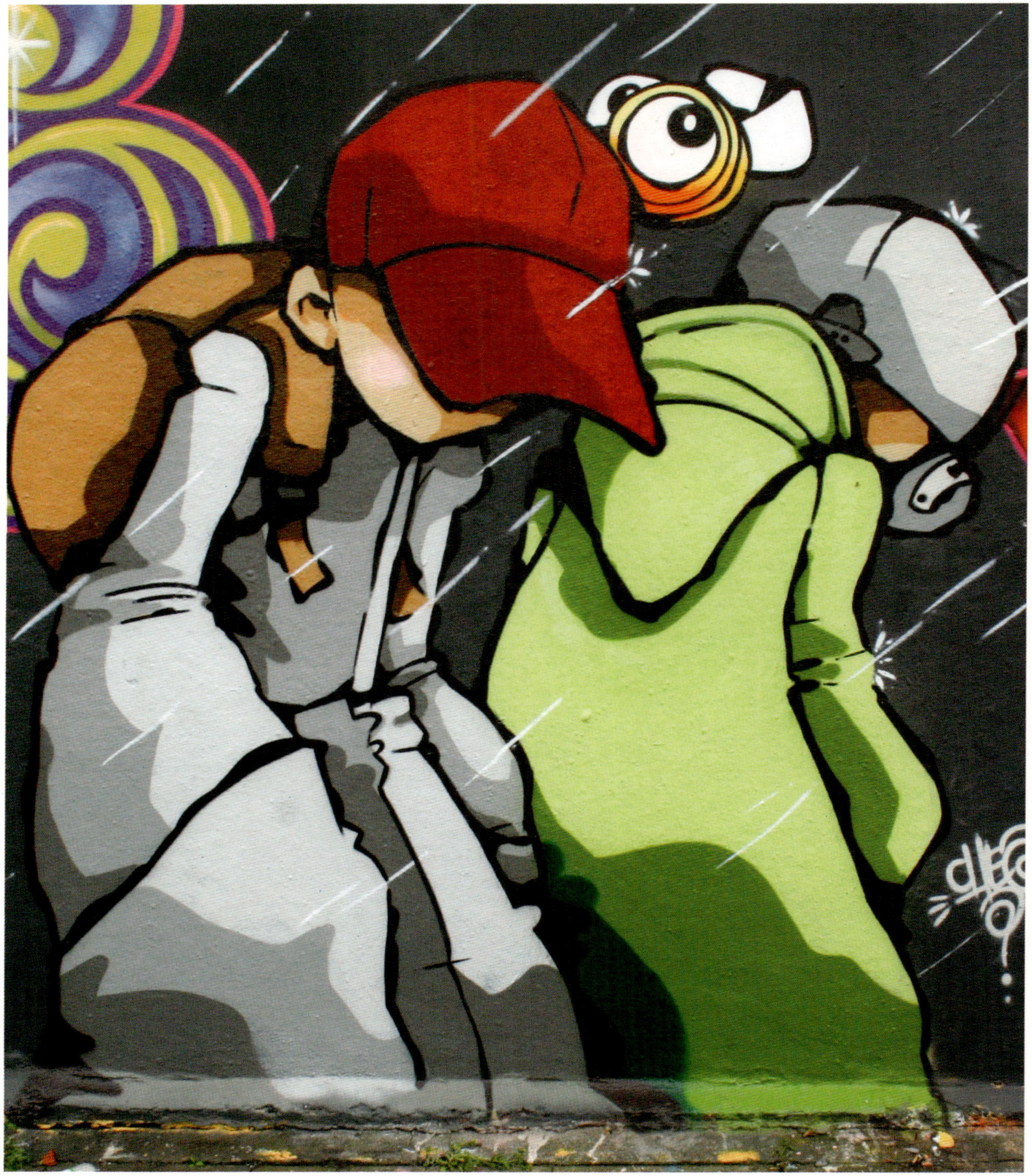

a time after that I wouldn't pick up a pen. I'd get a flash of inspiration from something and then I'd give up for months and months again. I didn't paint at all for at least ten years; I didn't even pick up a can. It pretty much stopped me in my tracks."

By the turn of the decade the whole country was changing and uptempo dance music was starting to dominate, bringing new drugs and a changed youth culture. An old school B-boy at heart, Cheo found himself drifting away from his old crew and eventually lost touch with them completely.

"I used to go to the Fresh Four warehouse raves with the TUB lot, down in Bedminster, and I used to go and spray out the back, to keep me hand in. But then the whole thing changed, and everyone found drugs and started doing the whole rave thing. But I didn't follow that, I'm too into my hip hop to want to stand in a muddy field off me tits loving everyone and dancing like a twat for ten hours. That wasn't my scene. The whole Bristol graffiti scene was starting to crumble and life took precedence over what I had been doing."

And things might well have stayed that way. Cheo could easily have gone back to being Scott Priddy and left his creativity in the past, forever tainted by the experience of having the sum of his efforts confiscated at the age of 17. That is, if it hadn't been for one of his younger contemporaries and one-time biggest fan – another Kingswood writer fresh out of retirement, by the name of Soker.

"I bumped into Soker in Asda and he said 'alright?' and I thought 'who the hell are you?' Then we went out for a beer and we just started talking about graff again, and he said 'we ought to go out and do something.' I didn't know anything about

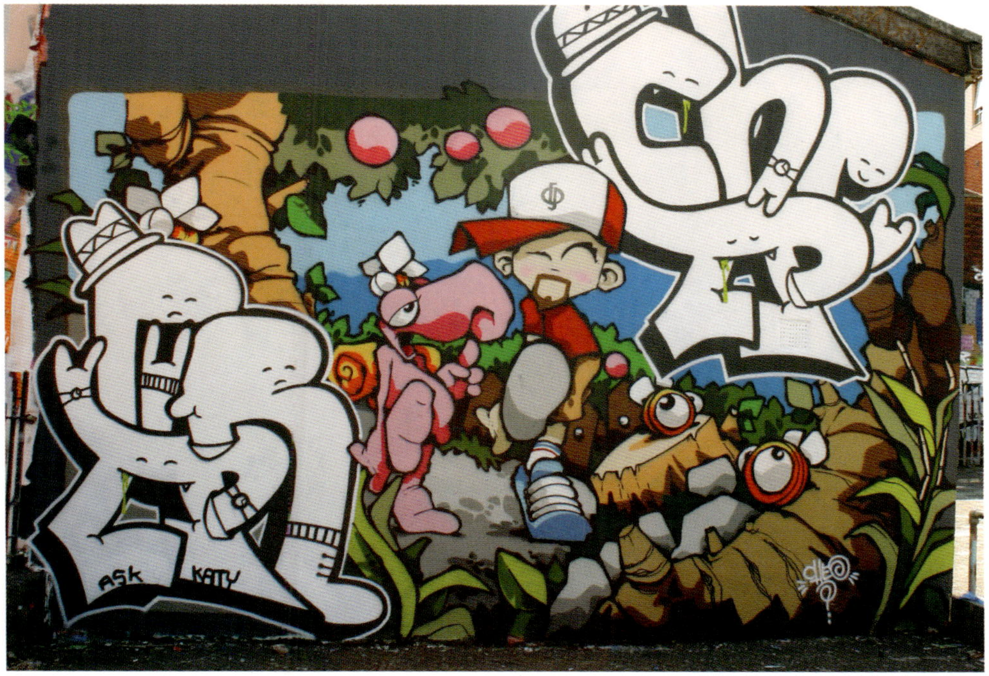

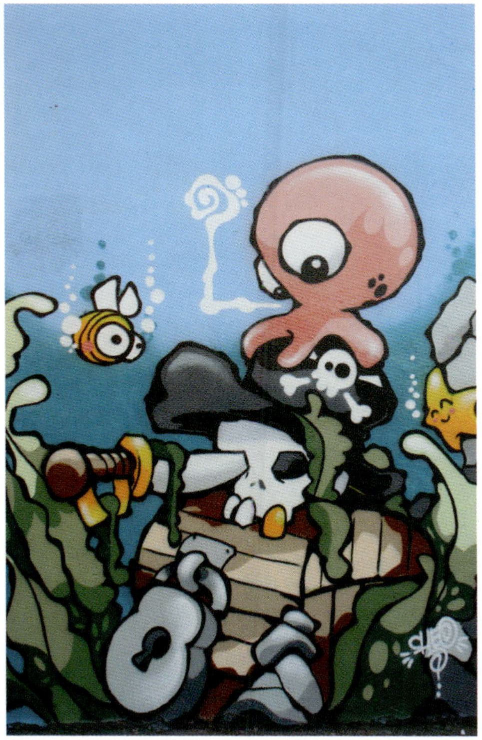

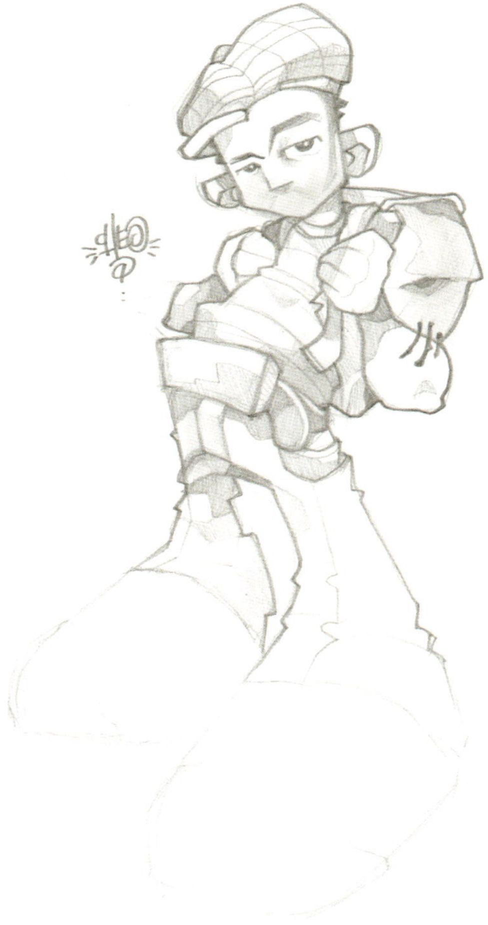

the new paint, like Belton, or anything. I didn't know that there was this magic paint and all these different nozzles. That's why getting back into it was almost like starting again. Then when you find all these new colours, it opens your mind. It got me thinking, 'what can I do with this? It's fucking brilliant'. I can remember Soker sending me a text saying 'yeah, let's go out and paint and serve these dudes!'"

But things are never that simple, and it took Cheo quite some time to regain his confidence, and to re-invent his style, synthesizing his love of Japanese manga comics and computer game graphics with the old Vaughn Bode influences to come up with something entirely his own. Always a prolific sketcher, Cheo's A4 pencil drawings began to pile back up again, giving him plenty of visual ammunition. 21st century innovations in spray paint technology helped him get back up to speed, and to watch Cheo paint now you would never guess he had ever put his cans down.

"To start with, when I started again, I was scared I was going to fuck it up, but now I don't give a monkey's. I feel confident enough to walk up to a wall with a bag full of cans and do something. But it took a long time. Now I can't think of anything better than standing next to a wall with a friend, drinking cider and doing something you enjoy, with the sun on your back, getting your hands covered in paint and getting arseholed. It's brilliant."

Opposite page: Bottom-heavy B-boy characters hunker down to avoid the rain, 2008

This page. Top left: Vaughn Bode-inspired collaboration with Piro, 1989

Top right: Bottom-heavy B-boy pencil sketch displays archetypal lean and proportions

Bottom left: The starfish seems happy but the bee is drowning! Undersea capers, 2008

Top right: Inkie and Cheo's piece that won second place

Middle left: 'Street 89' flyer front, the 'international street art competition' avoiding using the word 'graffiti' even then

Middle right: Inkie in deep concentration

Bottom left: Inkie's character design

Middle: Cheo's character design

Bottom right: An account of the event from Barton Hill's Clean Slate magazine

Opposie page. Left top to bottom: Risky and Slick from Los Angeles' winning piece; Meo's abstract stylings (New York/Paris); Style Wars Crew (Manchester)

Right top to bottom: TDK crew (Shefield); Young people from the Bristol contingent (top two pictures); Raide and Spade's piece (Oslo); Dezire's piece (Wolverhampton)

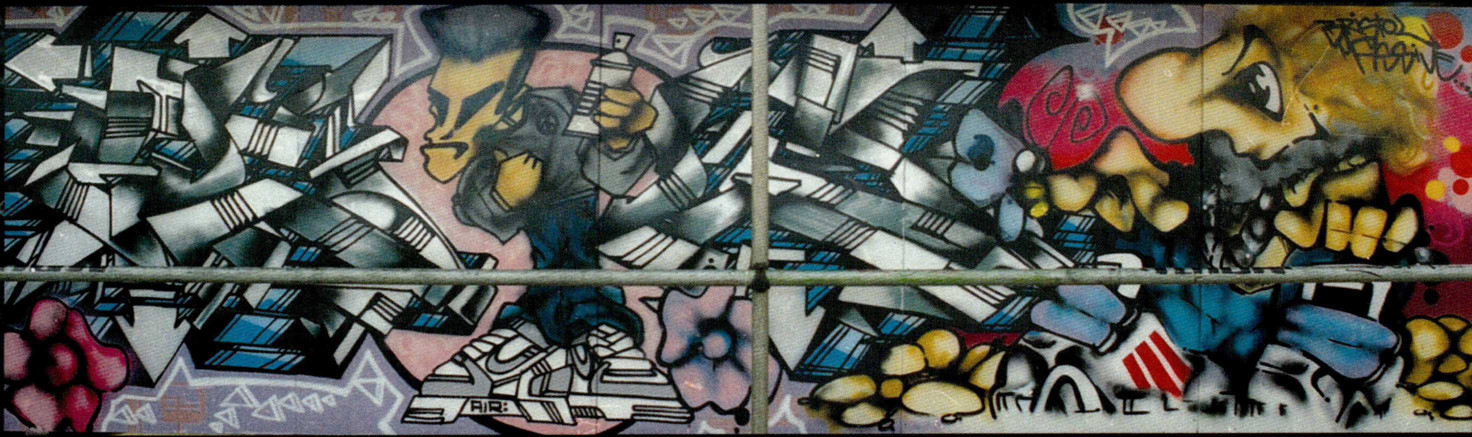

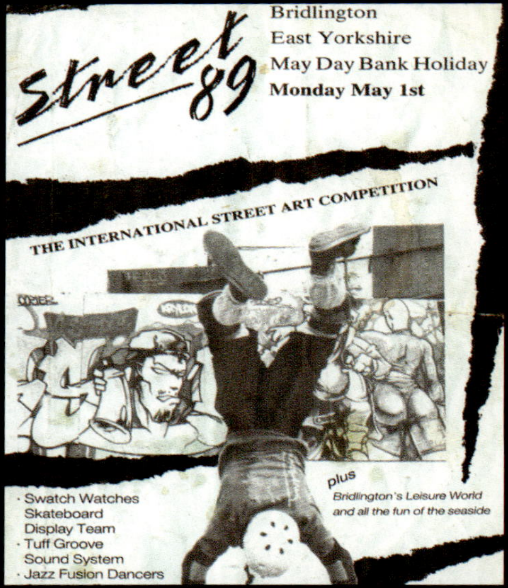

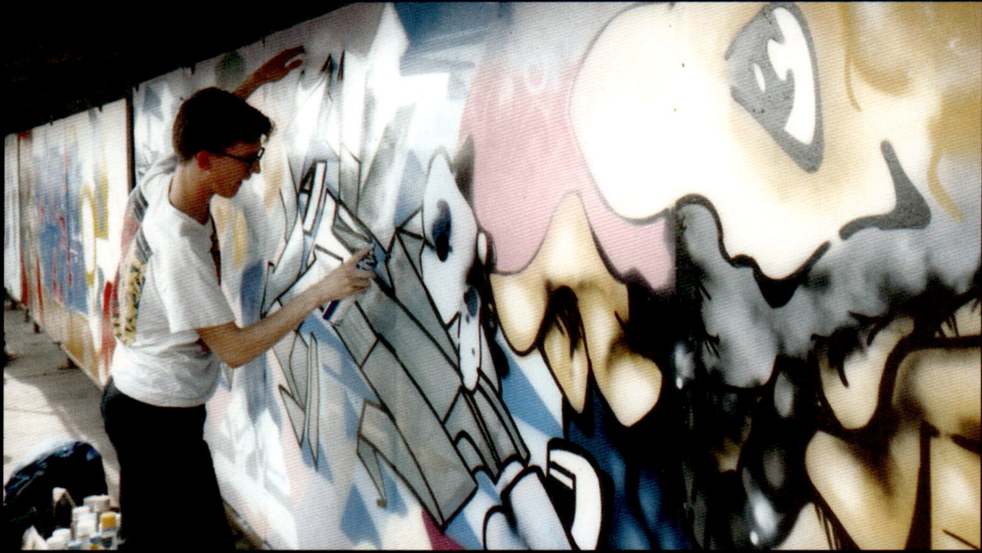

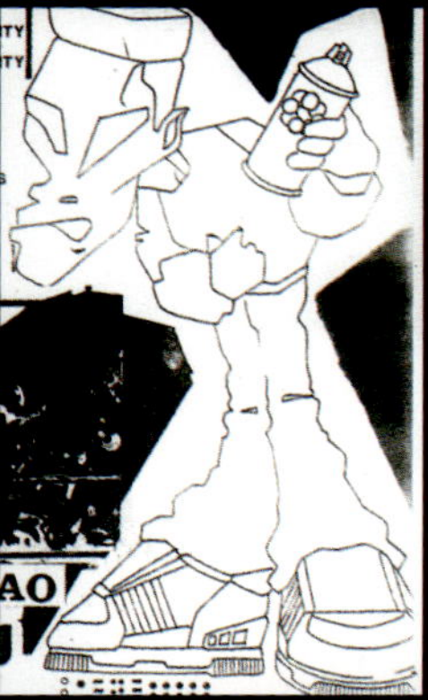

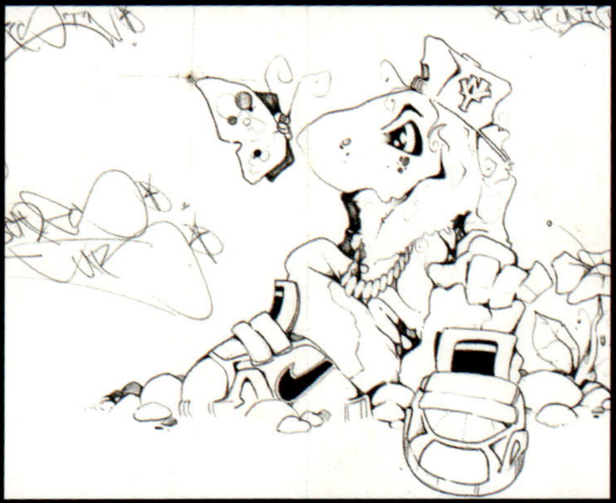

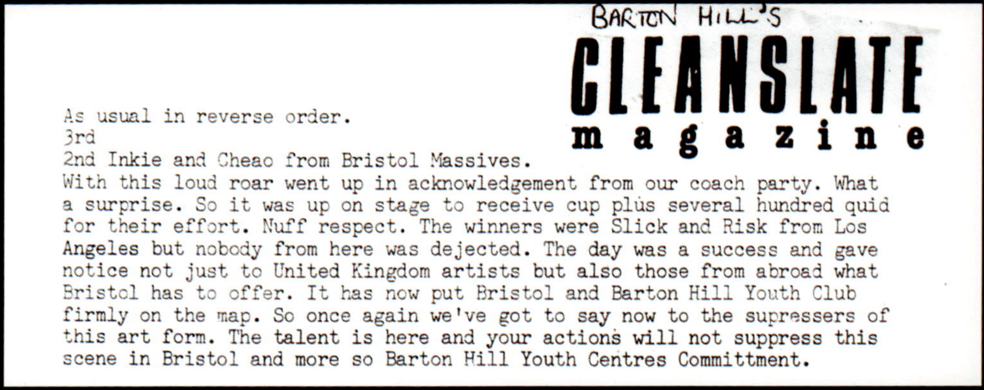

BARTON HILL'S

CLEANSLATE

magazine

As usual in reverse order.
3rd
2nd Inkie and Cheao from Bristol Massives.
With this loud roar went up in acknowledgement from our coach party. What a surprise. So it was up on stage to receive cup plus several hundred quid for their effort. Nuff respect. The winners were Slick and Risk from Los Angeles but nobody from here was dejected. The day was a success and gave notice not just to United Kingdom artists but also those from abroad what Bristol has to offer. It has now put Bristol and Barton Hill Youth Club firmly on the map. So once again we've got to say now to the supressers of this art form. The talent is here and your actions will not suppress this scene in Bristol and more so Barton Hill Youth Centres Committment.

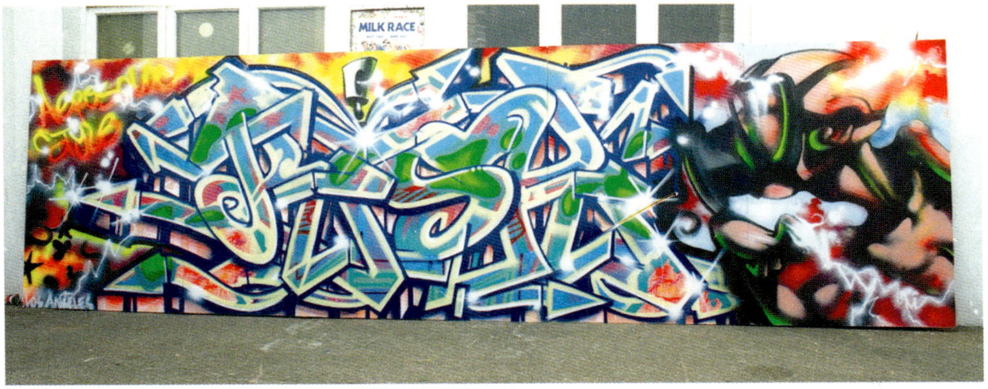
MILK RACE

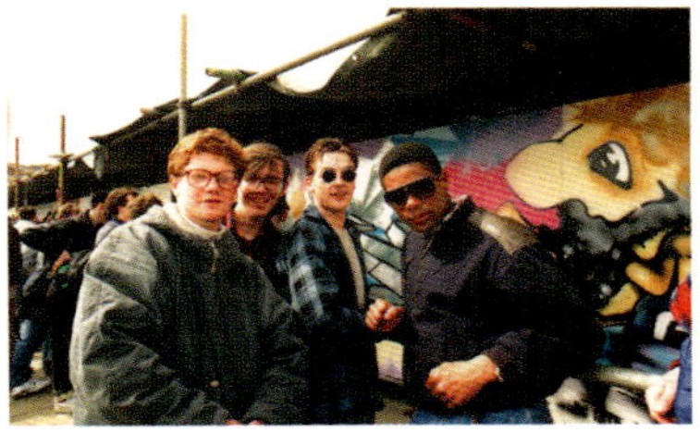

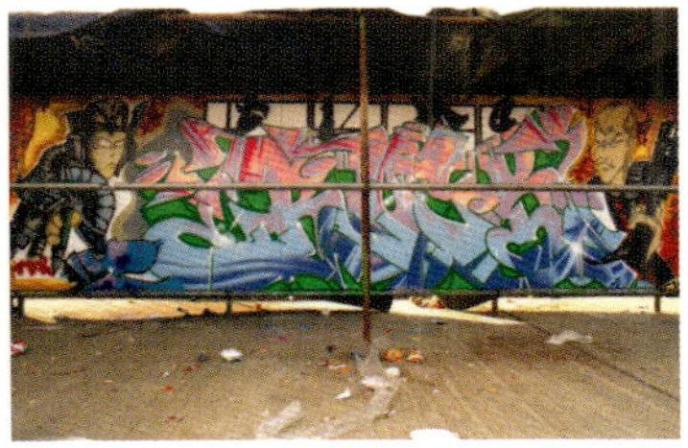

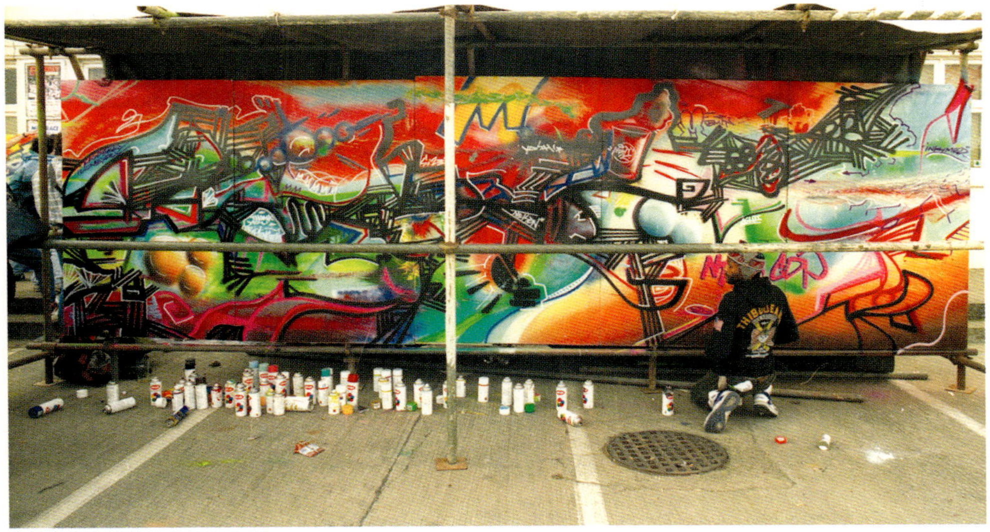

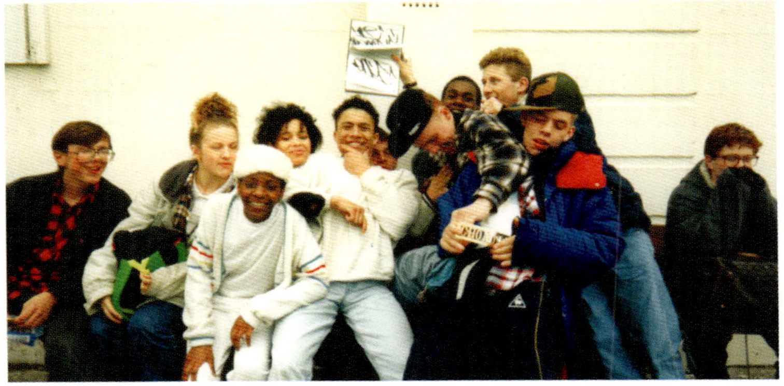

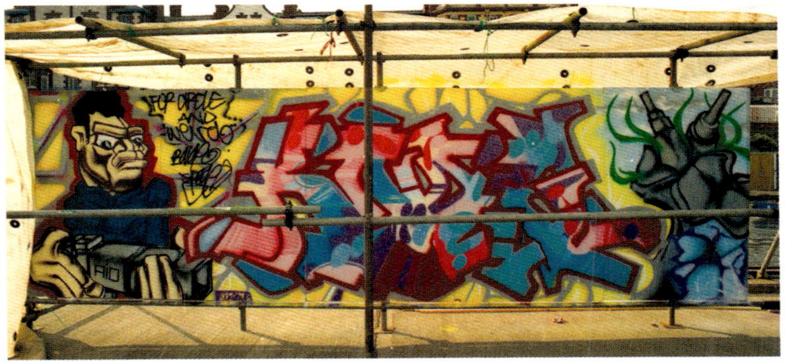

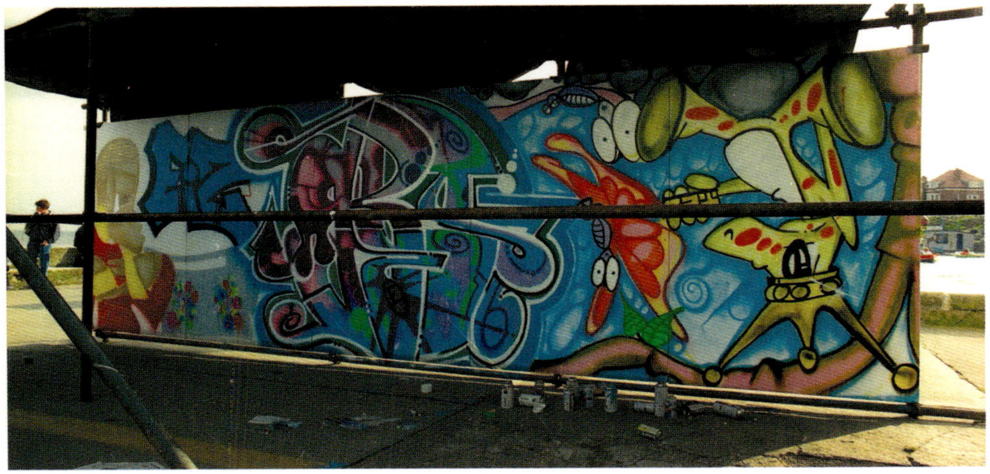

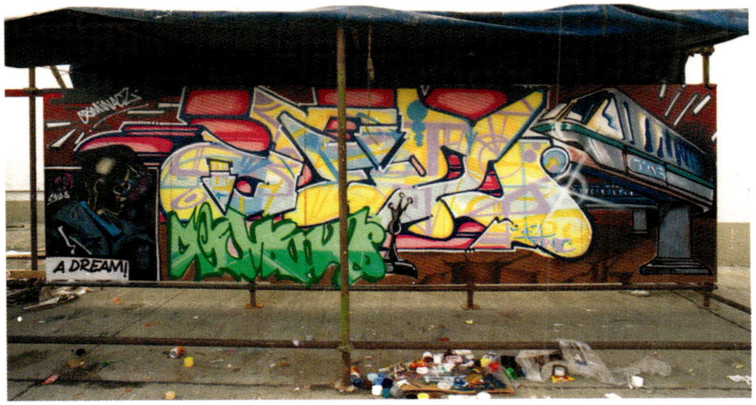
A DREAM!

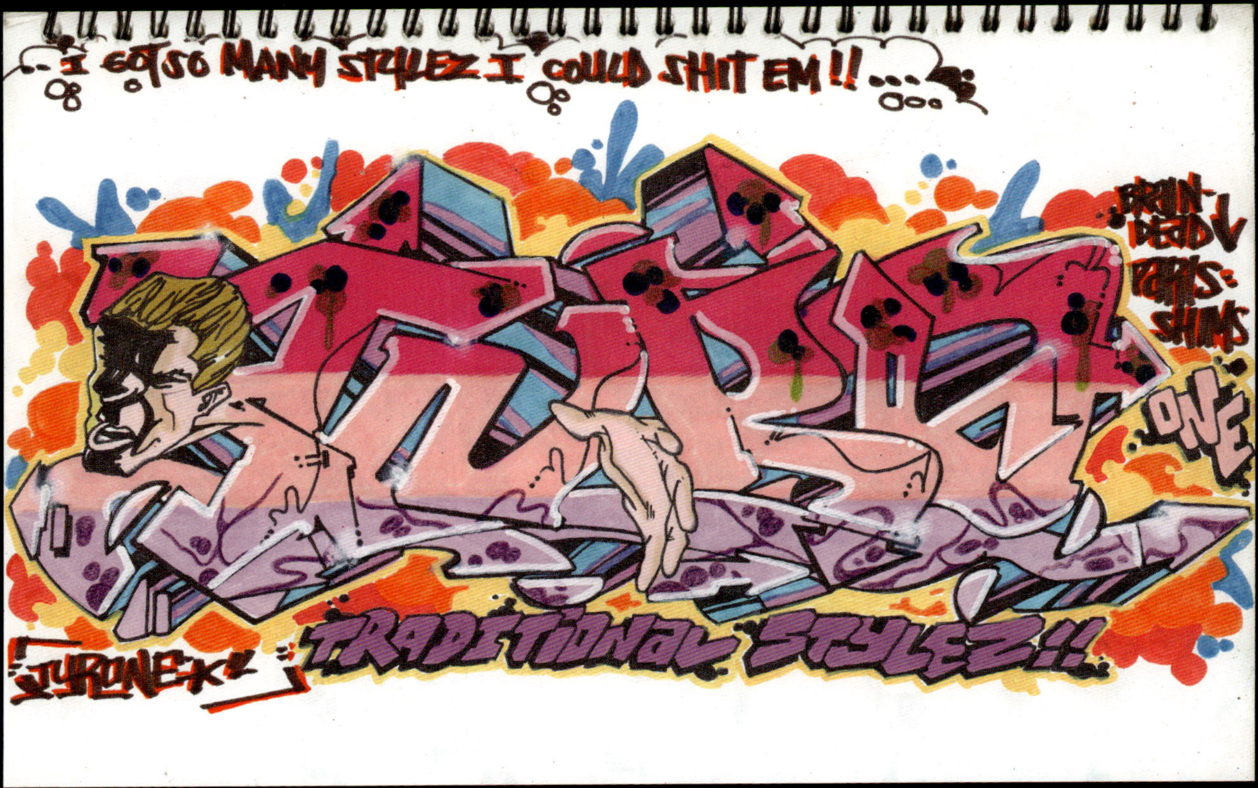

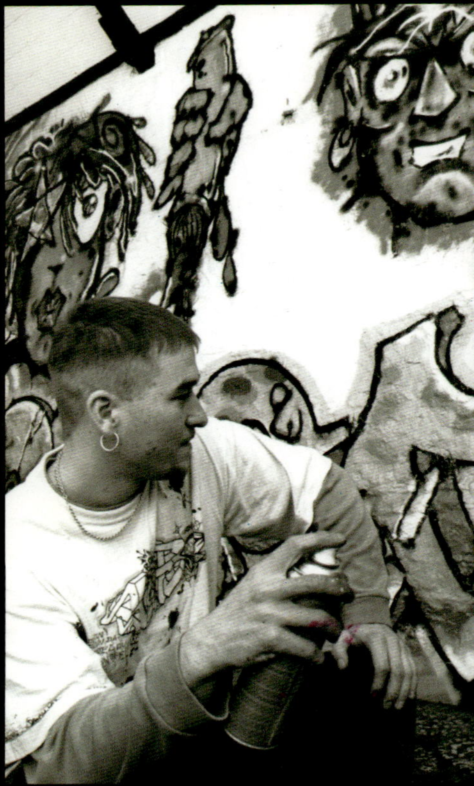

Top left: Black book page, c.1997

Top right: Turo strikes a reflective pose for the press

TURO OMBD/TUB

• **Turo has been a prominent figure on the Bristol hip hop scene for over 20 years.** From the 1980s through to the present day, he has painted with practically every crew in the city. Also an MC of some stature, he has performed and recorded with the likes of Monk, Aspects, Numskullz, Headcase Lads, Souljah Clique, Beat Route 38, Junior Disprol and Sir Beans OBE to name a few.

When did you first see graffiti, and what impact did it have on you?
"Around '83 or '84. I must have been 11 or 12 at the time. Me and my mate got into electro, and I went round his house to tape the *Electro* albums. And he goes, 'have a look at this' and pulls out *Subway Art*. I was just like 'what the fuck is this?' Then he goes, 'look in my brother's bedroom.' He had all these designs on his wall, which he'd done. It was clouds, lightning, arrows, and words like 'Electro Rock', 'Pop' and 'Break.' They were all coloured in with pencil crayon. He'd obviously taken his time, 'cos they were very intricate. I thought 'fucking hell, that's mint.'"

So you were there right from the start. Can you remember the first graffiti in Bristol that you came across?
"The same kiddie that had showed me his brother's pieces told me there was this exhibition happening, at the Arnolfini in town. He said, 'you've got to come: there's going to be all these people painting there,' but I hadn't even been into town by then, I was too young. I really wanted to go, but I wasn't allowed. He came back and told me all about it and I was just devastated. I got the flyer, and I saw photos of it, but that was it.

"Then we started riding round, three or four of us on our little bikes, looking for graffiti. I don't really know how we knew where to find it, we just had a sixth sense of where it would be, we'd just follow tags and whatever. We'd be sniffing it out, going all over to these dodgy little areas. We would take photos, come back and we'd just collect them."

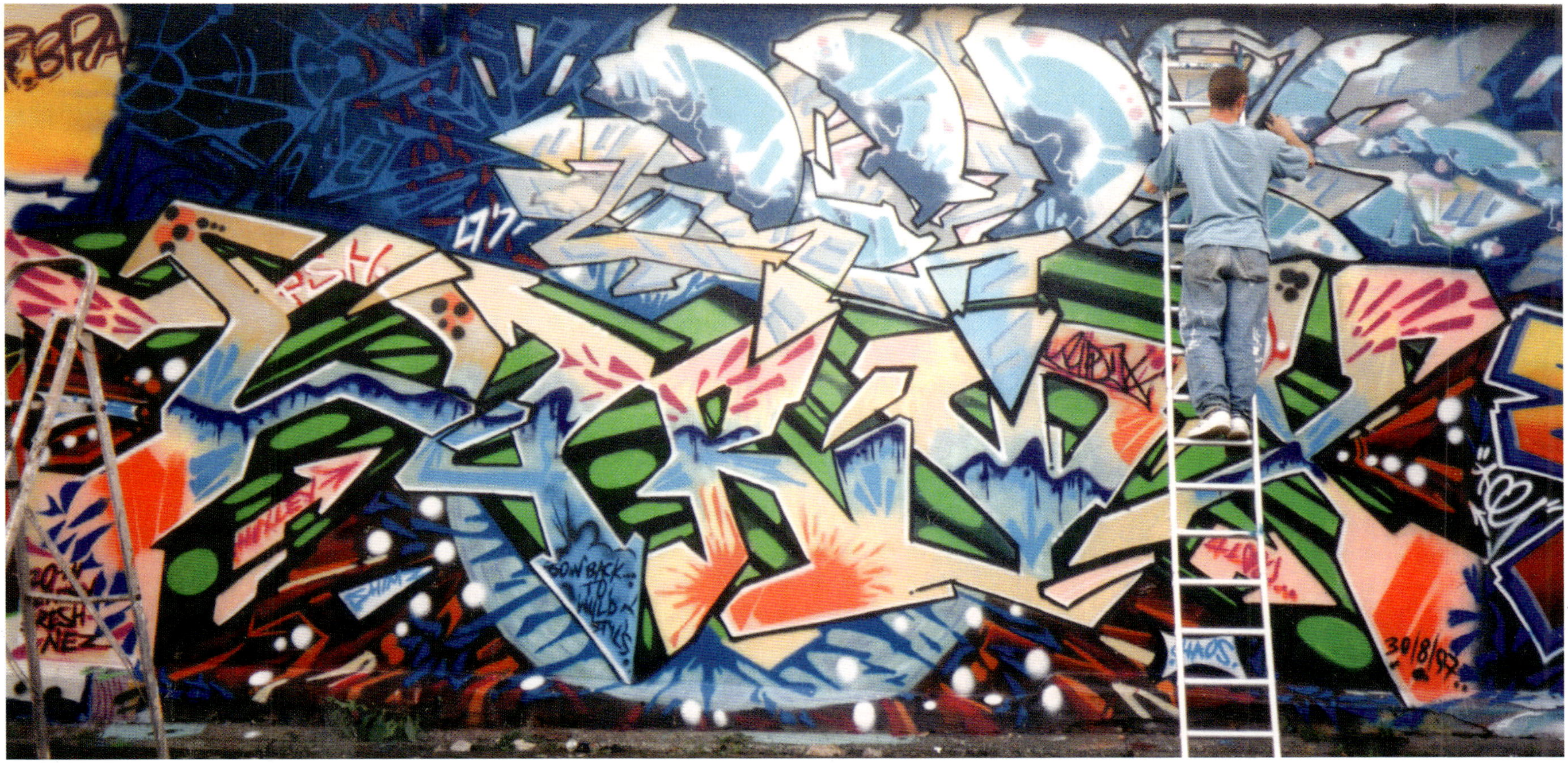

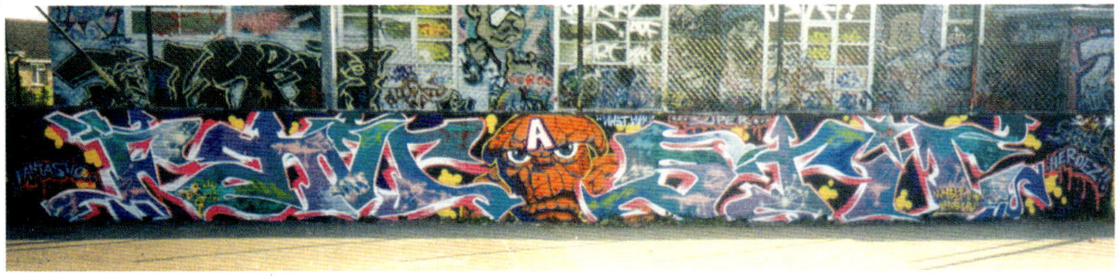

Top: Paris and Turo, 1997

Bottom: 'Fantastic' c.1997

Did you start off tagging or did you go straight into trying to paint pieces?
"Me and my mate Risk would go and just tag anything. We'd literally see tags, cross them out, put ours over them. We didn't know no better back then, we were just finding our feet. Then we decided to do our first piece, one night it was just like 'right, let's go out and do it.' Risky would go and do something, then we'd do something together. Then we fell out, as you do, and I hooked up with another mate and we'd go out and cross out all his stuff. It was like schoolkids' 'I'm better than you' stuff. We must have been about 14 or 15 by then. Our first crew was the BD crew: me, Risky, Sane, Rimer. And a few other mates were affiliated, they used to DJ and that. It was Bedminster Down Posse, BDP. Then we changed it to Brain Dead. We were like, 'we're going to go out and do proper pieces.' We decided we'd find a big concrete wall along the tracks and do it from end to end. We knew what was going on at Barton Hill, because I'd ventured over that way, and we were like 'we're going to do something to show they fuckers that we can do it just as well on this side of town.'"

There's nothing quite like a bit of healthy competition between writers...
"We'd planned to do it on a Friday, Saturday

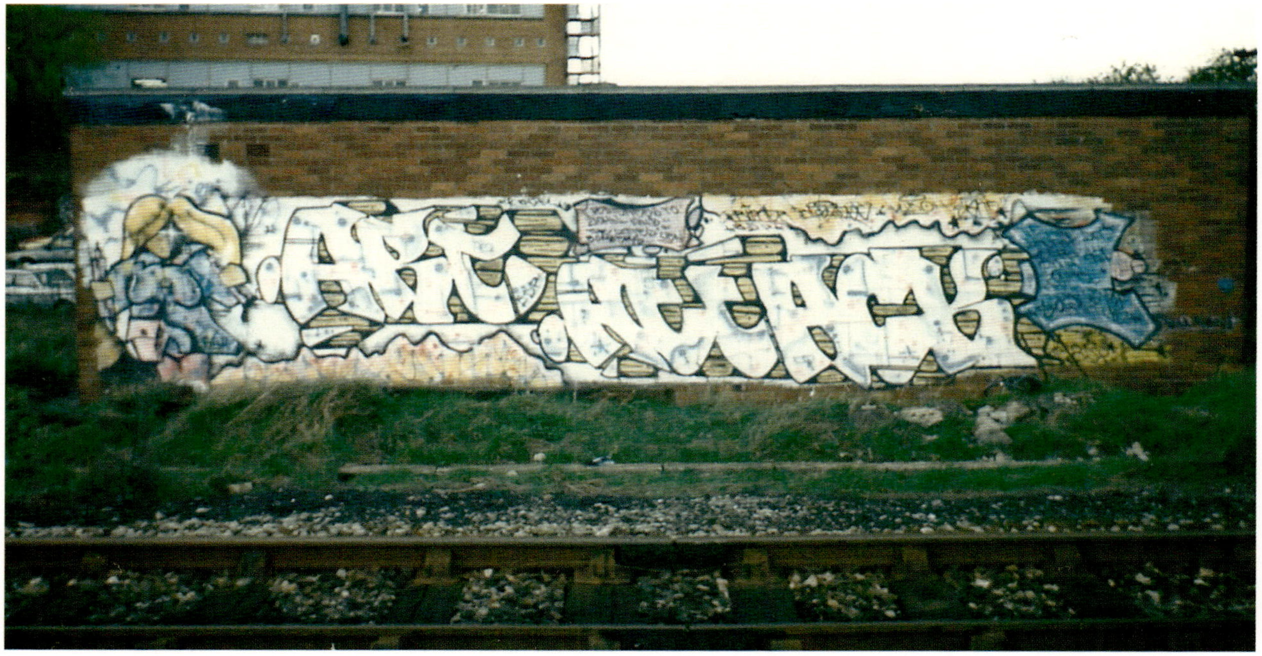

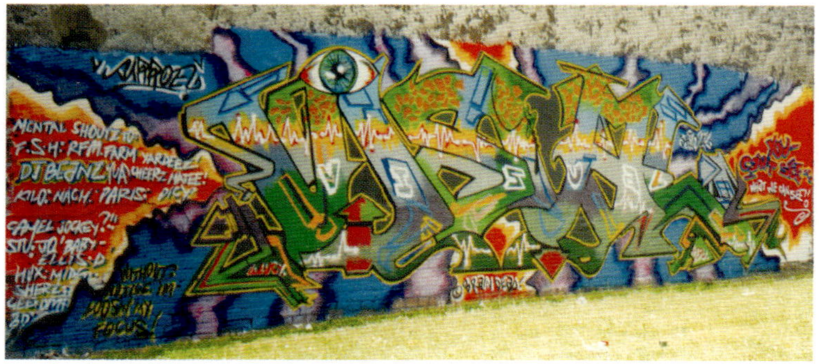

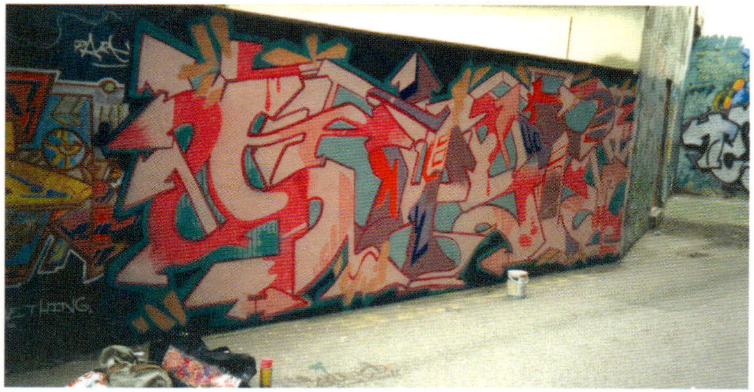

night. I remember it clearly: the 11th of February 1989. We went and emulsioned the wall at about ten o'clock, and we decided we'd wait till three in the morning to do it. We sat in this little hut by the tracks until about twelve o'clock, when everything was quiet, and then we were like 'fuck it, we can't wait no more.' We walked across the track and the wall was literally just lit up, because it was white. We were there three, maybe four hours, totally into it; but Risky was taking like three hours to do one character, and I'm saying, 'fucking give us a hand' doing the letters, and it was massive. I couldn't believe how it fitted onto the wall: it was spot on, perfect, end-to-end. That's how we went on."

You'd got the bug for painting big illegal burners. Was the Art Attack piece as big as the illegal stuff got for you guys?
"No, we actually did another one that was bigger and better. It was incredible, but the emulsion was still wet when we walked away from it, and it rained. It literally washed all the emulsion off and left the piece on the wall, still all filled in, but it looked like it had been there for ten years by the next day. We were just like 'NOOOOOO!!!!!' So we did the same thing again, this one said 'Untouchables' and I did all the lettering on my own again, and it took me like four hours. That was a good night, it was Christmas Eve."

You mentioned Barton Hill. I know you used to go bombing with TUB. Those must have been pretty hectic times?
"I'd been to Barton Hill a couple of times and posted a few little drawings through the letter box, but I didn't really go in. I was like 'I'm such a fucking toy, what am I doing?' Then I started going up there and hooking up with all the TUB lot, and we were just basically destroying the city, probably about 30 of us in all. I met Teao, Era, Chome, SP27, Cema, Cuba, Cheo; there was loads and loads of them, I'm probably forgetting a couple. Everybody would go tagging, we all had Torch pens and Posterman paint pens, and those lush silver markers. And we all looked the same - hats on sideways, Berghaus jackets, bum bags.

"Everyone would meet in Barton Hill, do pieces in the day then go out at night and do illegal pieces. That's how we went on, for about a year. There wasn't much of a train scene in Bristol, it was more like, anything else that moved, we'd try to destroy it. We knew what was going on with the Tubes in London, but it wasn't like that here. I wanted the biggest and best piece on the side of the track that people going by on a train could actually see."

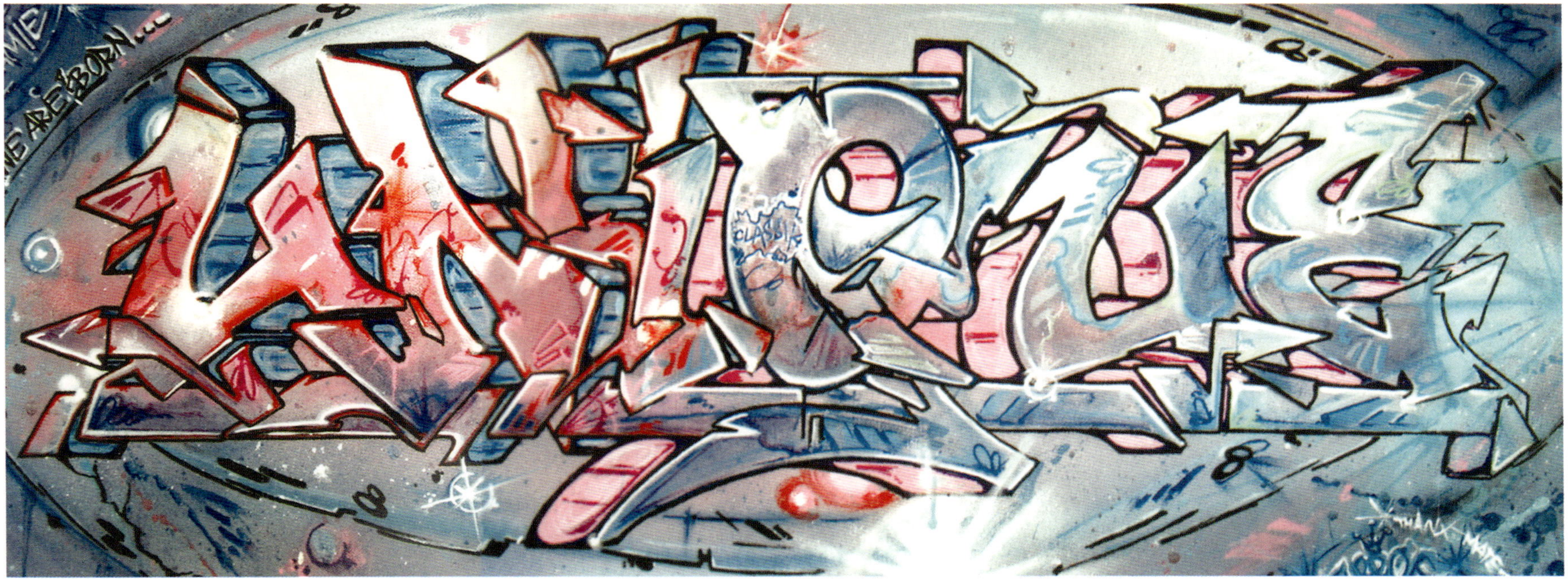

Pretty much everybody who was active at that time got arrested in Operation Anderson. Did you get into much trouble with the police before that?
"Yeah, I'd already been caught three times tagging. I was the dumbest tagger you could meet – I'd literally just see a billboard, or a bus, or whatever, and look round, and if no one was coming I'd pull out my marker and tag it. And then suddenly I'd hear brakes screech: copper car! Every time I pulled out a marker there seemed to be a copper behind me."

When Operation Anderson finally happened it was inevitable, and perhaps people should have seen it coming. Were there warning signs?
"I remember one time we were up at the club and Shab goes 'I got followed last night', and no one believed him, but he says 'I did, I got chased. I did a piece at Stapleton Road Station, I had to jump through bushes. They had dogs, everything.' Everyone just thought he was being paranoid. Next thing you know – bang-bang-bang at the front door, everyone gets raided at the same time. They came to my house with five copper cars, everyone in my street thought I'd done a murder, or a bank robbery or something. All the neighbours' curtains were twitching. But I wasn't there, I was at work. I was doing work experience opposite Barton Hill Youth Club, working down on the railway tracks building signs with this old bloke. How close can you get?

"My mum got hold of me and says, 'you've got to come home, the police have been round.' My bedroom was covered floor to ceiling in photos, pieces, you name it, if it was to do with graffiti it was in my bedroom. I had brick wall wallpaper, with tags all over it. It was B-boy heaven."

The case went to Crown Court, didn't it? Did you get a hefty fine?
"Yeah, the case kept getting adjourned and in the end it went to Crown Court, and the solicitors said 'you could go down for this, it's getting serious.' I was just like 'you're kidding me aren't you?' Anyway, they tried us one by one and I ended up with 136 hours' community service, which I did with SP, and an £800 fine – which for a sixteen-year-old kid in 1989 was a fucking stupid amount of money. I was on YTS [Youth Training Scheme] at the time, so I said 'I can't pay it, I'll give you a fiver a week.' It took me six years to pay it."

Although things calmed down for a while, after the dust had settled people just carried on painting, didn't they?
"They thought that would be the end of Bristol graffiti, but I couldn't not do it. What was I going to do instead, take drugs,

Opposite page. Top: 'Art Attack' full-colour track side by Turo and Risk, 1989

Middle: 'Visual' by Turo and Shimz, Bedminster Skate Park, 1997

Bottom: 'Shyte' (work in progress) c.1998

This page: Above: 'Unique' Spray paint and paint pens on canvas, 2007

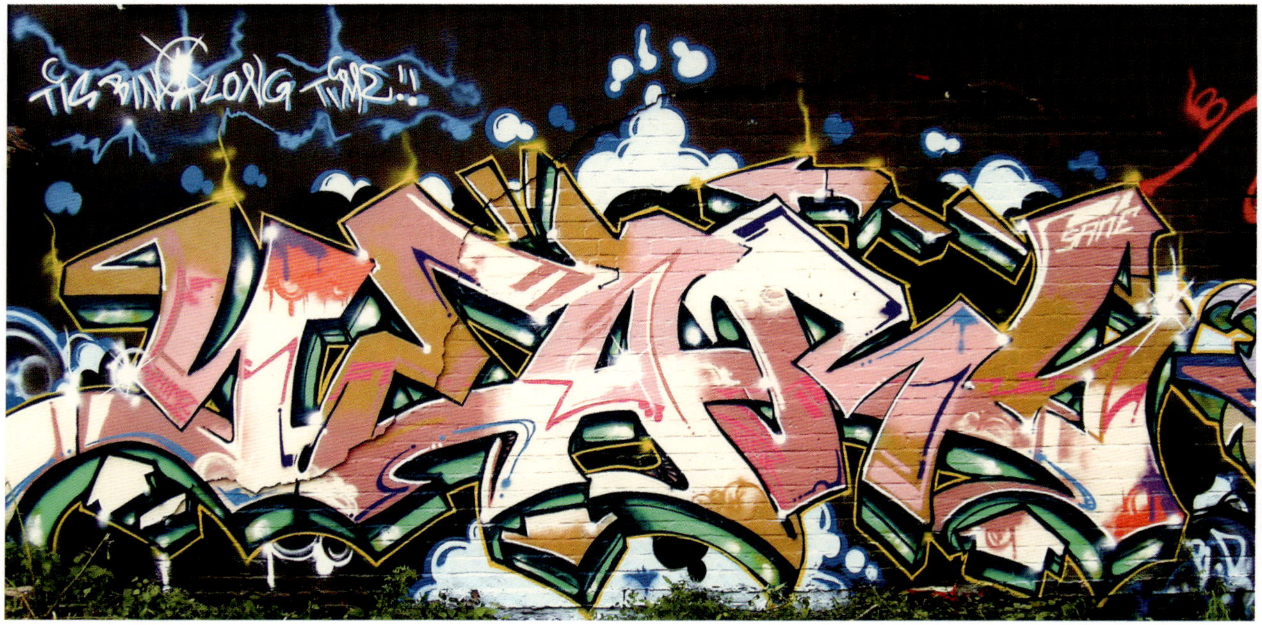

Above: 'Years (Tis Bin A Long Time)', 2008

steal cars? No. So we sat down and were quiet for six months, but after that, having promised my mum and dad to stay away from John Nation and Barton Hill, I was straight back up there. And everybody else who didn't get caught, they were still out doing pieces everywhere in protest, and it carried on. Out goes one, in comes another."

Your other great passion is music. When did you start MCing at parties? Did you paint at the parties as well as rocking the mic?

"I started rhyming in 1989, and I always juggled the two after that. DJ Bunjy (Une Deux Trois Crew) used to do me tapes, and I used to write rhymes and just fuck about, really. I did a little jam at the YMCA, got to know a few people who were DJing, and just started rhyming, just free-styling at jams and that. I remember me and SP went to this warehouse jam at Whitehouse Street in Bedminster, and everyone painted there. We used to go to the Fresh Four jams as well, and Chaos used to paint the backdrops. It always went hand in hand for me. At Whitehouse Street there were two warehouses back-to-back, and they were just down the road from where we lived, so we went in there and claimed it as our own. Then we did a jam in the warehouse behind it, and they set up spotlights and me and Risky did a piece on the night. We did a nice piece in there. This was just before the Bedminster Skate Park jams were going on, and we pieced there as well. It all just coincided."

Towards the mid-90s, a whole wave of new talent was emerging. Who were you painting and MCing with then?

"I carried on piecing and then Shimz came up, and I sort of took him under my wing and started piecing with him. Next to SP he was one of the worst for tagging. I could go miles and miles away and there'd be a Shimz tag. He was everywhere.

Around the same time, I met Paris, and he was part of the FSH [Fantastic Super Heroes] thing then. Aspects had arrived in Bristol, and I started doing ciphers and MCing with them. Me and Paris were going and doing a lot of piecing, and throughout the mid-to-late 90s I carried on and got even more prolific. After John left Barton Hill, Bunjy was working there, so I also got a load of commissions through that."

Sooner or later life and commitments take over, though, don't they? What caused you to focus on the music and put the graffiti on the back burner?

"After we had the little 'un I just thought, 'this takes up too much time' and I couldn't be doing both. So I eased off the painting."

Yet it stays with you. Would you agree that if you've grown up painting graffiti, the urge never really goes away?

"Most of my mates do something creative. I never did the football thing, we did the B-boy thing or the graff thing. A few of my mates dabbled and then went off into rave and stuff, but we stuck at it. And the reason it grabbed me in the first place is the reason it still grabs me now. Being thirtysomething, if you're creative you still need that thing to do, and if you take it away from yourself, you're like 'well, who am I now?' This is me: the B-boy persona and the tag is me now, people know me as Turo, there's a lot of people that don't even know my real name. This persona I've created is actually me."

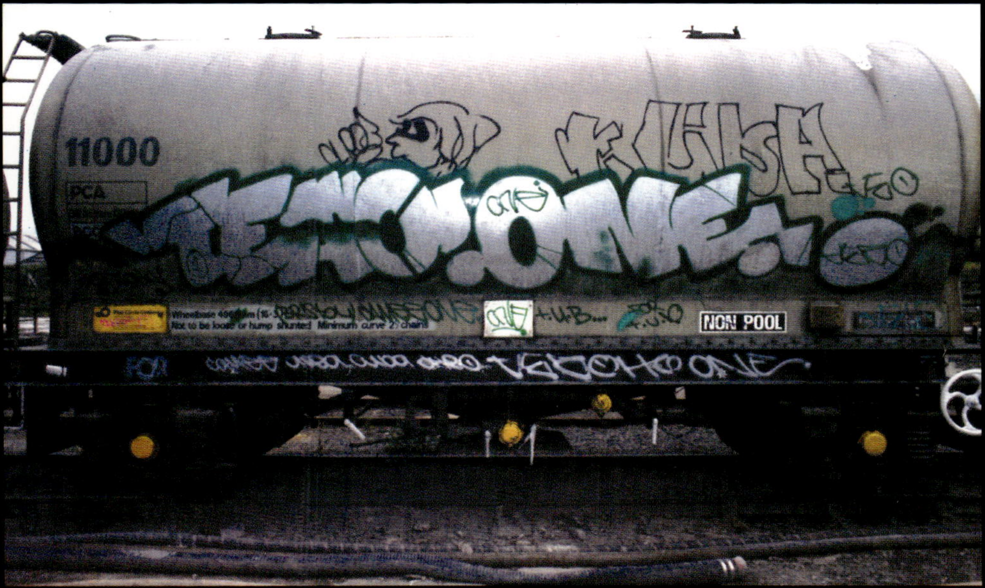

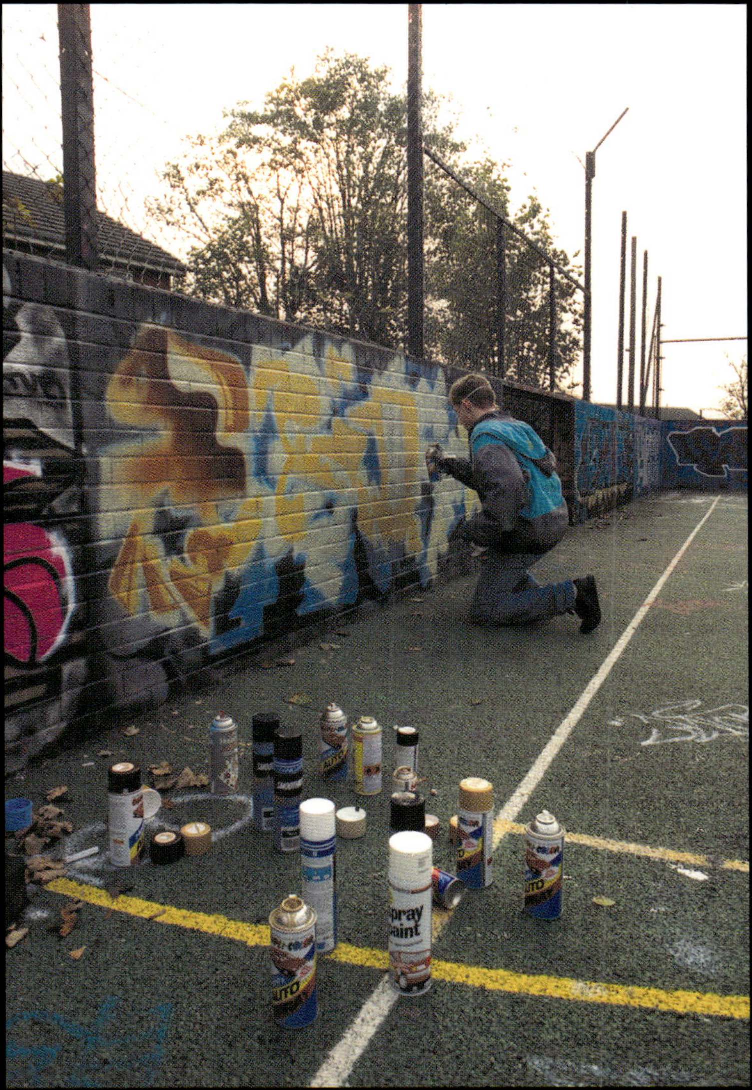

TEAO TUB

• As a writer with The United Bombers (TUB) in the late 80s, Teao was amongst the most prolific and versatile of the crew's members: equally comfortable bombing railway tracksides, tagging buses or creating something a bit more considered on the low walls of the ball court at the Barton Hill Dug Out.

When did you first start bombing?
"It really started at the Barton Hill Dug Out. Everyone used to go down there and do a bit of graffiti, and then we all started going out tagging. Because the railway line ran right beside it, we thought 'we have to get down on the lines and do something.' Before long the whole side of the lines was just taken up with chromers down there."

John Nation was instrumental in making the youth club into a centre for graffiti art. Did you have a lot of time for him?
"Fucking amazing mate, best bloke, fucking proper. He wanted the whole building painted. At the end of the day he gave us enough wall space to paint on, and it wasn't down to him what we'd go and do afterwards. Most days we would be there painting, and if we hadn't had that place we would have been painting elsewhere."

As I remember TUB were pretty much running things in Bristol at that time, as far as illegal graffiti writing was concerned. Were there many rival crews?
"We chased after a few people for going over our pieces. The Bedminster lot used to come over and at first we didn't know who they were. They would come over, do a piece and then vanish. But when we finally met them, TUB just kind of swallowed them up into the crew. Like with T-Cut, Cheo and Deed and them, they ended up in TUB as well. We were all from Bristol, I suppose, we were all united. That's why we were The United Bombers! We called it that without realising how much it was going to spread and how many people were going to end up in the crew. It's only looking back I realise how big TUB was. It was a proper firm."

So did you prefer the bombing missions to the legal painting at the club?
"Yeah, you had to be sneaking out there. We

Top left: Tanker carriage, c.1989

Above: Teao painting in the Barton Hill Youth Club ball court

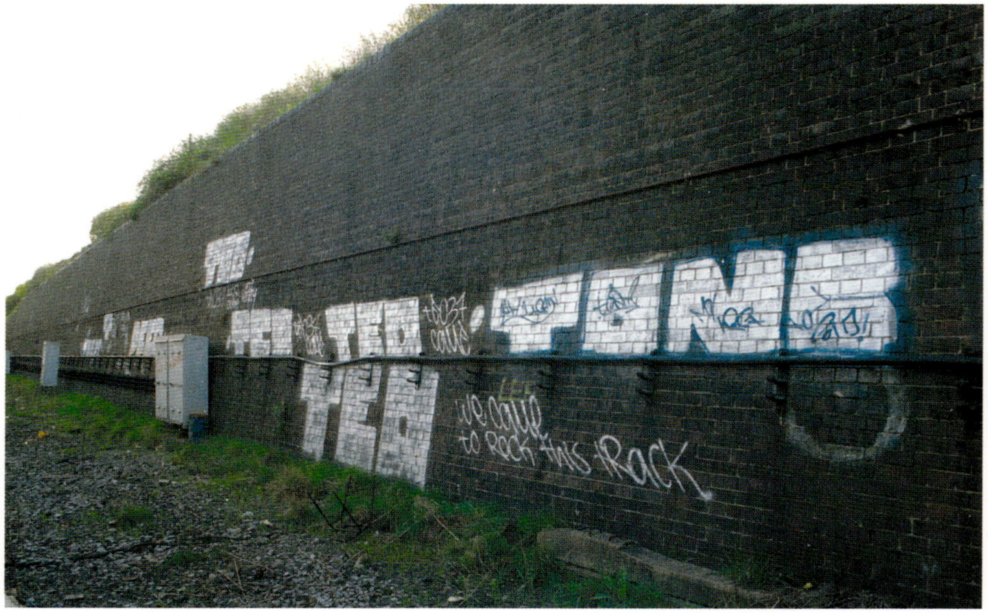

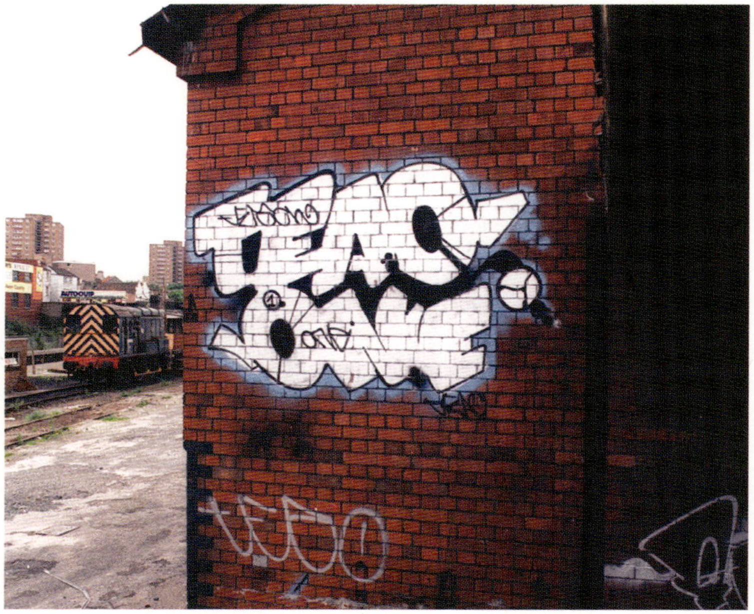

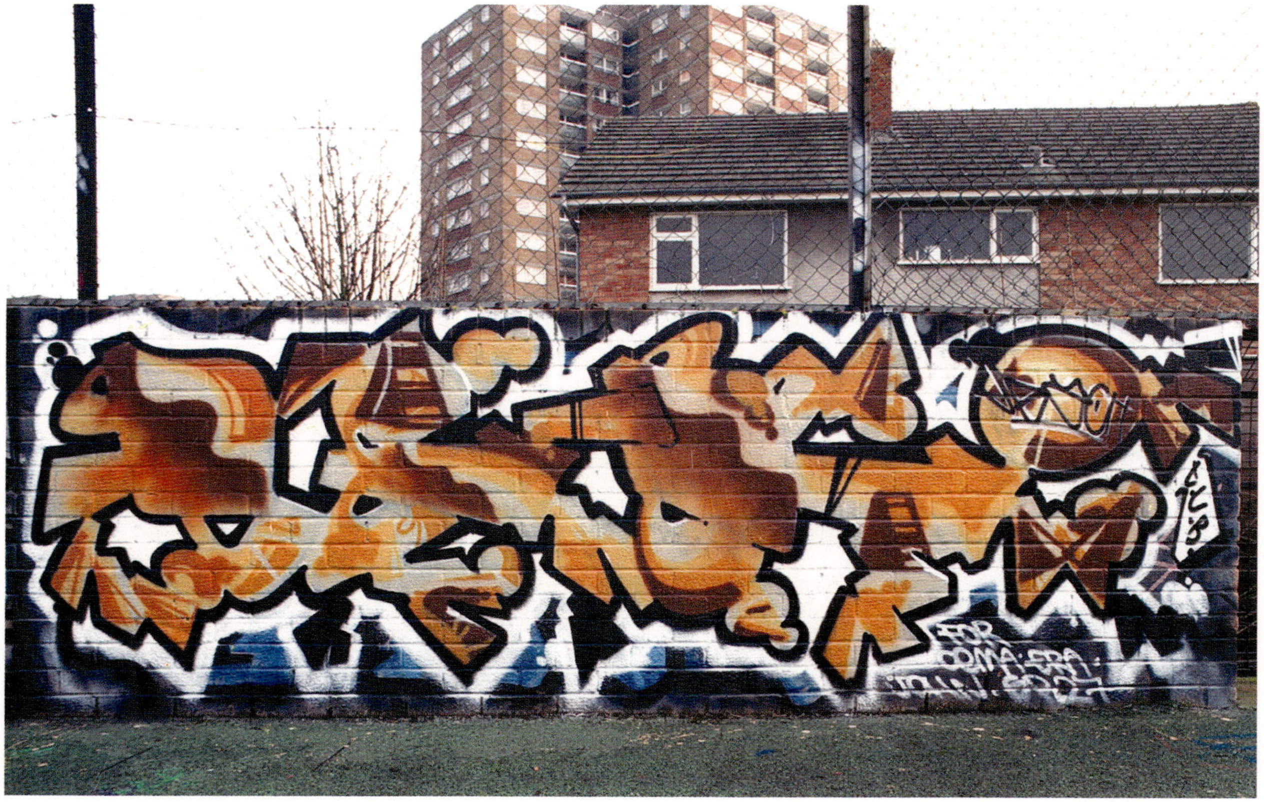

would get down onto the tracks at Temple Meads Station when it was really busy, and just walk up the lines. Sometimes, if a train pulled into Lawrence Hill during the day, we'd just jump down onto the track, tag the side of the train up and do throw ups and everything. Then we'd watch it pull out, and shift back up to the Dug Out."

You were known for being extremely prolific back then, especially on the Bristol buses.

"I can remember I used to knock off school and get a Day Rider [all-day bus ticket]. Then I'd get on one bus, tag all the upstairs windows, and then get off at the next stop and get on another bus. I'd do that constantly for four or five hours, until I'd tagged pretty much every number 40 running.

"Then at night we used to go back down to Lawrence Hill and sit around, all the writers, and every bus that went past had

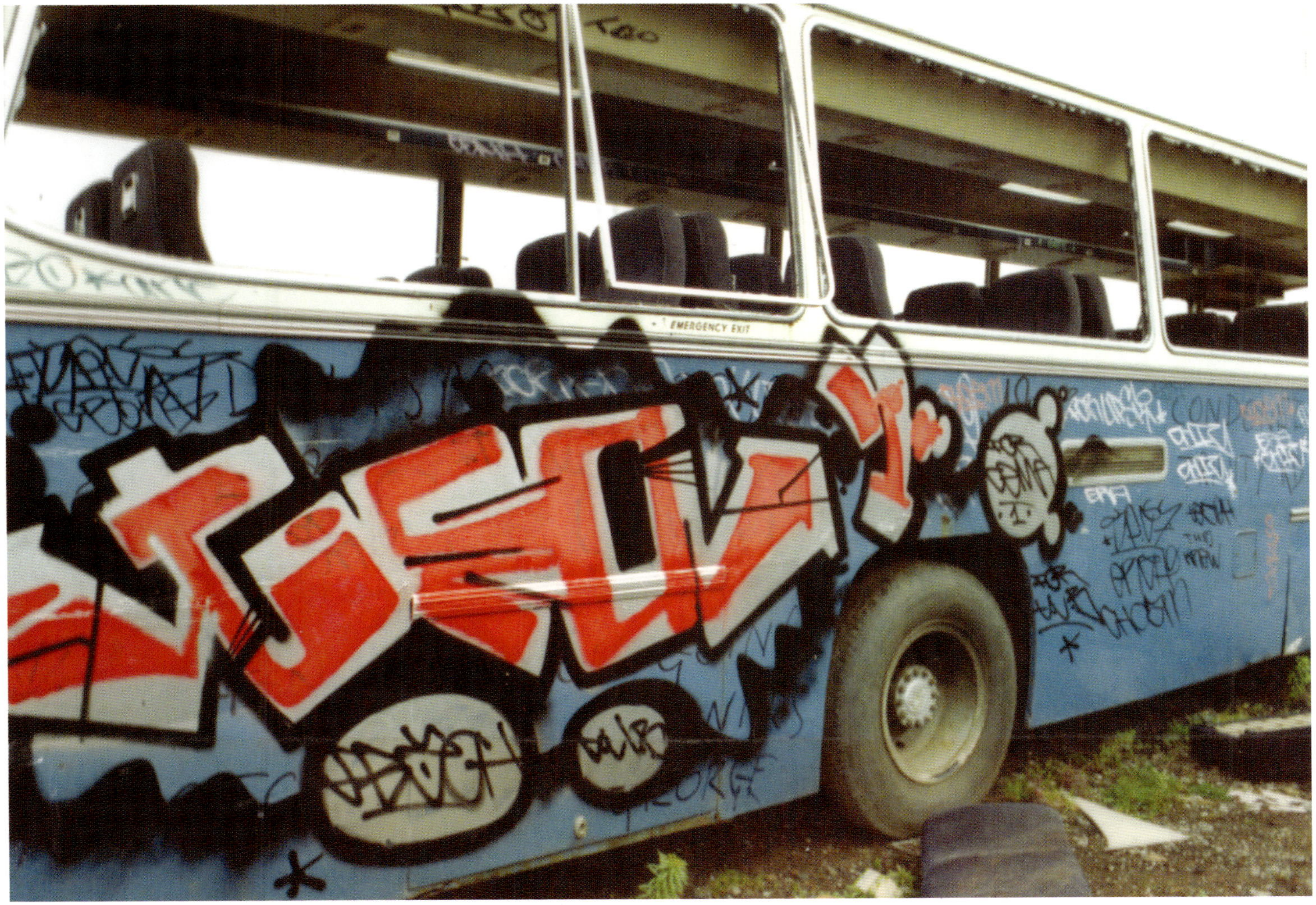

Opposite page. Top left and right: 'We came to rock this track' Teao hits the track sides hard, c.1989

Left: Experimenting with style, Barton Hill, c.1989

This page: A bombed, disused coach at Lawrence Hill coach station, c.1989

Teao tags all inside it, every bus. I'd done so many 40s and 45s that every bus that pulled up was just blasted with tags."

I remember seeing the tags high up on the back of the double-decker buses and wondering how they had been done. How did you do it?

"If you opened the back window the alarm would go off downstairs, but a kiddie from Birmingham told us that if you put a matchstick in where the alarm is, it wouldn't go off. Once we knew that, we'd be hanging out the window, writing on the back of the bus, tagging upside down. Then we started just hanging out the back window and jumping down onto the road when the bus stopped. We were a bit mad. Mad days, they were.

"The City Darts came in next, those little buses, and when they'd pull up at the bus stop we'd just have enough time to do a quick throw up on the back before they pulled away again."

Did you have a favourite surface for tagging on?

"Anything we could put our pens on, man. I pinched all my pens so I never minded writing on walls, even though it fucked your pen right up. Because I had so many pens, I would write on any wall. As long as I was on there, that was all that mattered."

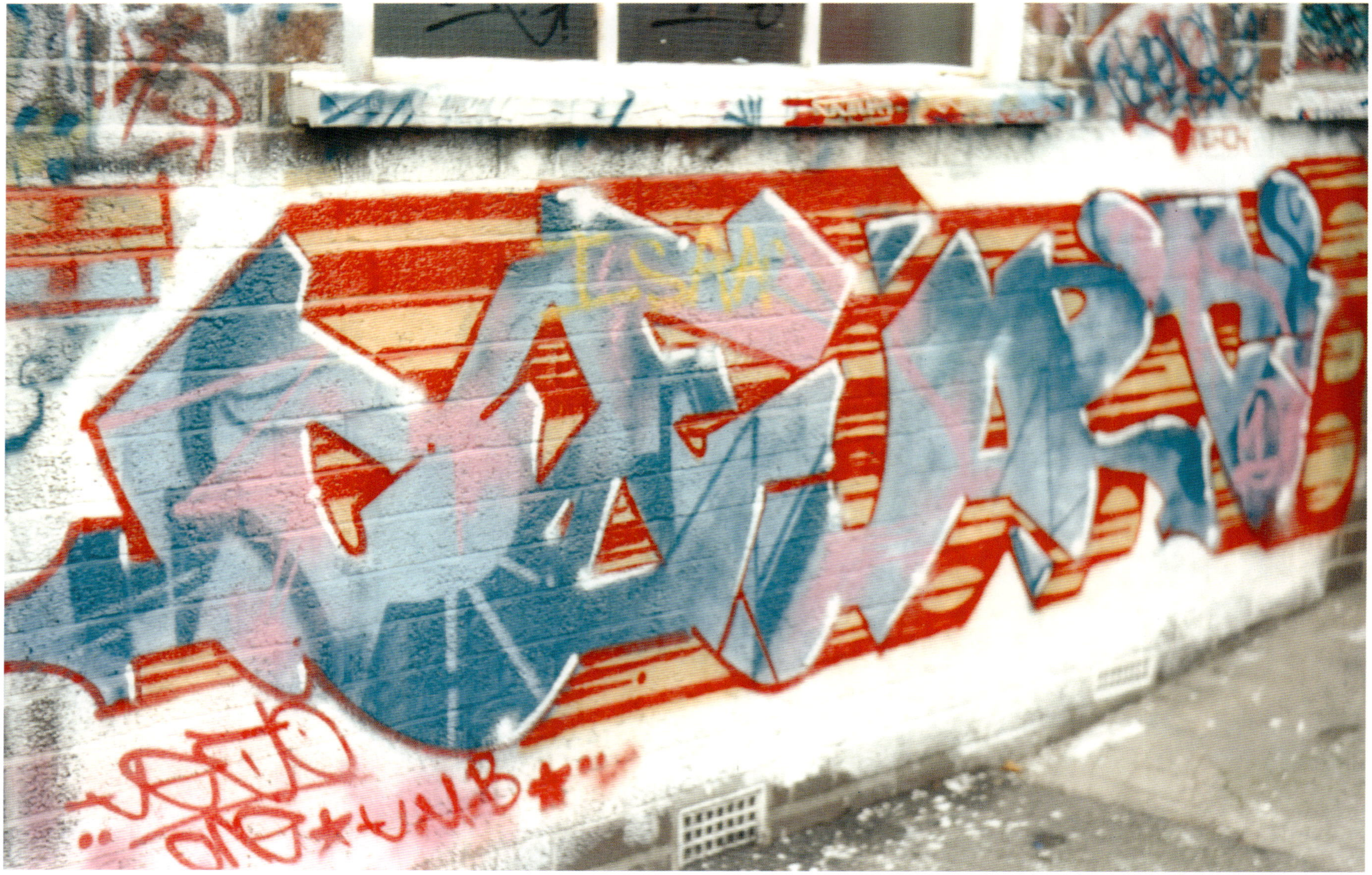

Above: Pink Buntlack used sparingly on the outside of Barton Hill Youth Club, c.1989

Who was the most brazen bomber in TUB?
"It was between SP 27, Cuba and me. Cuba was never that good, he was just a tagger, but he would tag up on the police station and all sorts. A few of us did, but he was proper blatant. Era was good, but he kept changing his name. In the end I said 'I'm not even going to put your name up, why should I bother when you're going to change it next week?' I used to get that a lot, 'put me up, put my name up' but I stopped after a while; it's too risky when you're hanging off of something or whatever."

You painted in some pretty visible spots back then.
"It had to be on the main road sometimes, just so people would think 'how the hell did he do that?' I'd just do a quick outline and then hide in a hedge until a car went past, then get back out again and psshhhhhht! It might take a bit longer, but if you did

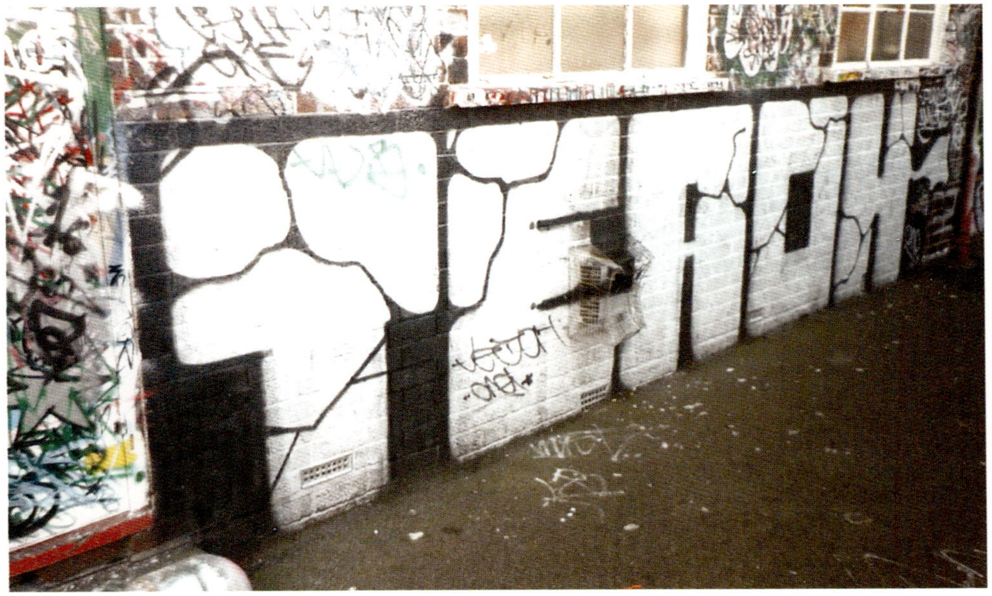

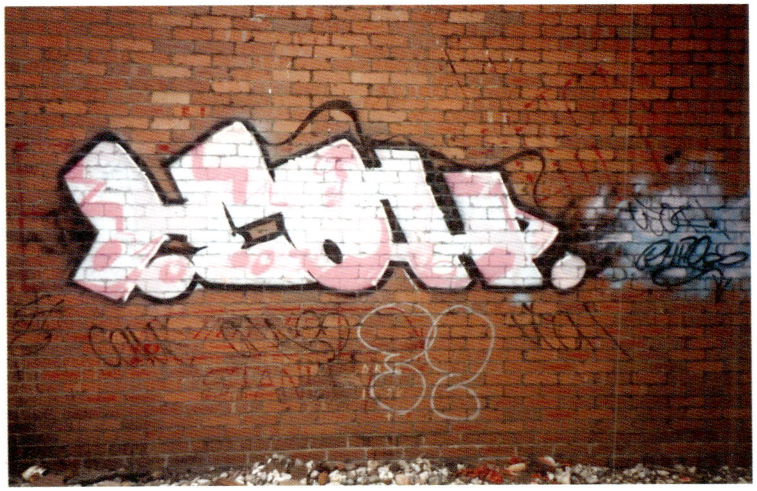

Top left: Block buster letters normally reserved for track sides on the outside of Barton Hill Youth Club, c.1989

Above: Full colour track side on a track worker's building that was visible from the youth club. The club's location made for many an easy escape after bombing on the lines

a little at a time it worked well. I can remember one wall that was at the top of my street, and there was no way you could do it, so I just did a tiny bit each night. It took about a week, but it was worth it. Saying that, though, the next week it got whitewashed off."

What about stealing paint? Were you one of those writers who refused to buy it on principle?
"Yeah, we were nicking all our paint. We used to meet up on Lawrence Hill and get the bus up to Clifton, and we would stop off in every shop pinching paint. We used to go to Homebase as well, when we found out that they'd started selling pink paint there. That was a big part of it, really, pinching the paint. Personally I used to pinch all my paint. I was never short of paint. Never."

Can you recall any particularly memorable paint-racking missions?
"One night we were on Lawrence Hill, me and Era. We were round the back of the shops, tagging or something, and we noticed the back door of this auto parts shop was open. So we went in – we were proper trembling. There were no shutters on the shops back then, so you could be seen from the road. We were crawling along, passing all these cans of chrome back and out the back door. We nicked every single can of chrome paint that was in there – I think we had about 30 cans each, or something like that. We never touched anything else, mind. All we were interested in was the paint. We had loads of it. That was a good hit, that was."

By 1989, TUB were so prolific that the Council and British Rail felt they had to intervene. The volume of graffiti going up was unprecedented: it had never been as extreme as that before, and it definitely hasn't been since.
"When I think of the amount of damage we did, after graffiti really took off... we were just spraying on everything. I think the Council and the Transport Police didn't know what hit them, because we were just going so mad, every night, just painting everywhere. And if there's ten of you, that's a lot of graffiti going up every day, for months on end."

With the benefit of hindsight are you more proud of the colour pieces you painted at the Dug Out, or the track-side and street bombing?
"When I first saw a piece that I'd done at the Dug Out on Flickr I couldn't believe it. Kato had written 'one of my all-time favourite pieces: a Bristol legend.' That makes me feel more proud than any chromer on any track-side. I said to my missus, 'come and look at this, they're talking about me on here! You don't even know the world I was in.'"

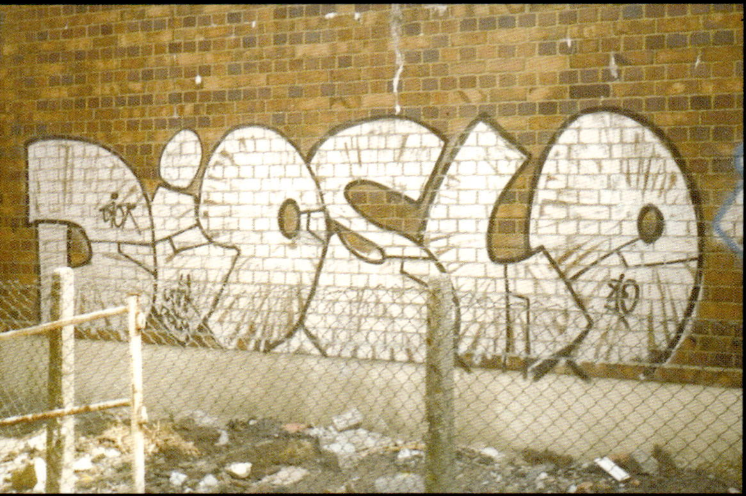

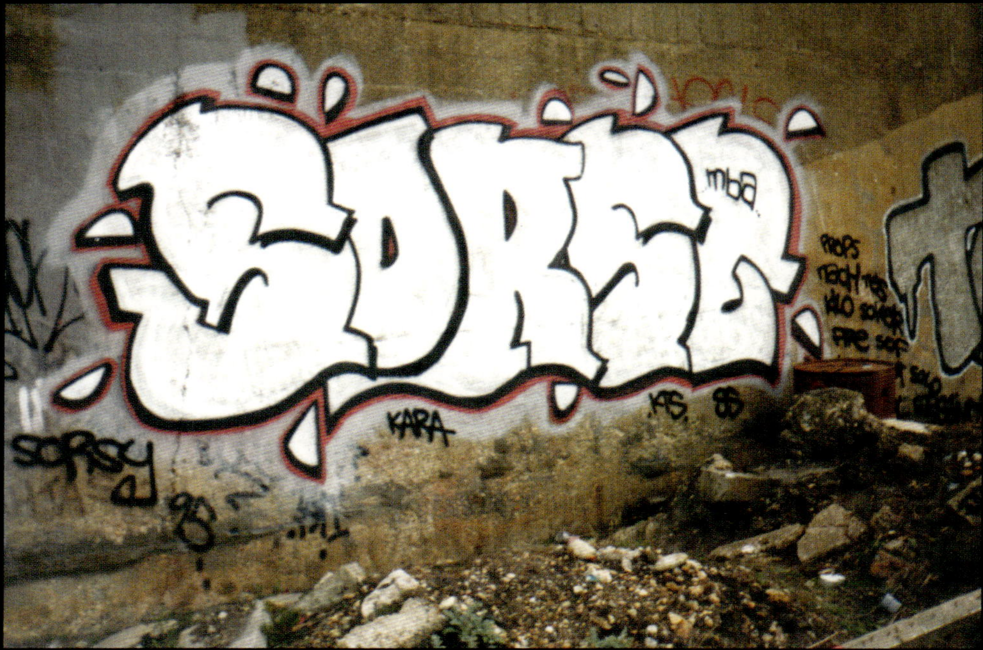

Above: Dio/Slo track side action, 1989

Top right: 'Sorsy' chrome throw up in the distinctive 'spiky' MBA-style. MBA became Bad Applez and The Dry Breadz, 1995

Opposite page. Top: 'Mad Bastard Animals?' just one of many possible acronyms for MBA. Brislington warehouse, 1995

Left: Radioactive Sorse, Bedminster skate park, 1996

Right: Dedicated to 'Those residing at her majesty's pleasure', 1995

SORSE OCP/SET/TUB/DBZ

• **As a member of TUB and later DBZ (Dry Breadz), Sorse (aka Sloe) was amongst the more active graffiti writers in Bristol in the late 1980s.** A regular at the Barton Hill Youth Club with a taste for bombing, he inevitably became involved in both the illegal and legal sides of the graffiti scene. Given the opportunity to reflect on his experiences 20 years down the line, however, he's found that it's the less obvious aspects of life at the Barton Hill Dug Out that have stayed with him.

When and why did you first get into painting graffiti?
"I got into graffiti from listening to hip hop from '82 onwards. The first thing I remember seeing was the cover of Rocksteady Crew's *Hey You (The Rocksteady Crew)*, me and my mates all used to copy it, and do our own versions of the characters; that and the graffiti on the cover of *Cold Crush Brothers* on Tuff City Records."

So were you into hip hop right from the very start?
"A few of my mates were heavily into break dancing and popping. I remember going to Roxy's on Fairfax Street and having little battles with people like E-Force and a few other crews. We used to go to Dolphin Square in Weston-super-Mare. We would take our lino and everything, set up, put on some music and people would chuck us money. I remember going to watch [legendary 1984 hip hop film] *Beat Street* at the old cinema by the Millionaire's Club in Easton: I think I must have been about 15. It was the same as going to see a Bruce Lee film, and you come out afterwards wanting to do martial arts. We came out just wanting to tag up on everything."

What was it that opened your eyes to the graffiti scene in Bristol?
"Going to the Dug Out in Barton Hill, I think, and seeing a totally different side to it all and meeting with John Nation, seeing how influential he was, providing paints and a venue for us to paint in."

As well as painting at the youth club, you were also a member of TUB. How did that come about?
"It was meeting up with Cema, Teao and Remer. Because I was just tagging everywhere - doing the buses, going to the bus depots, and using a stone to scratch tags and all sorts - those guys were like: 'shit we've seen a lot of your stuff', and I got the kudos that comes with that and they invited me to paint with them."

How did you feel the first time you went out on a mission with those guys?
"Going to the Bone Yard [a train yard near Temple Meads station], I was shitting bricks. You had to climb over this massive

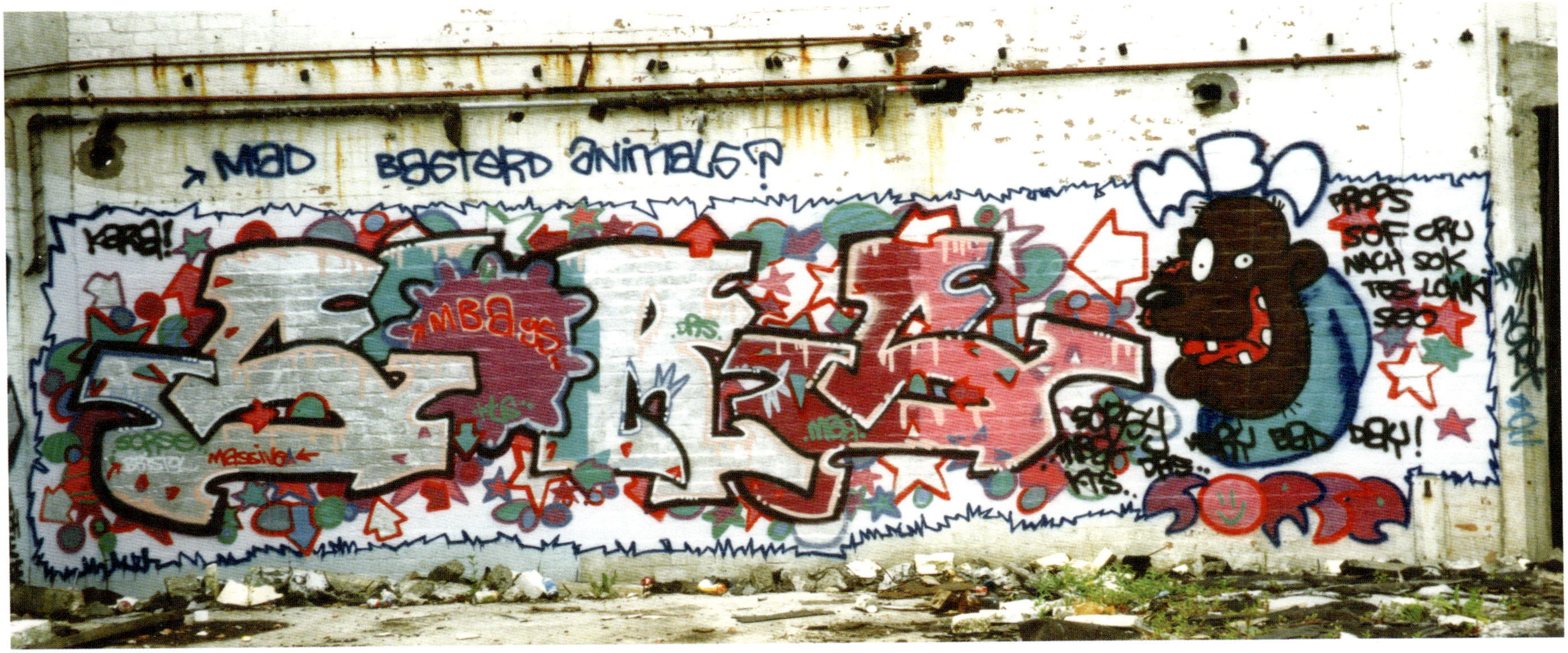

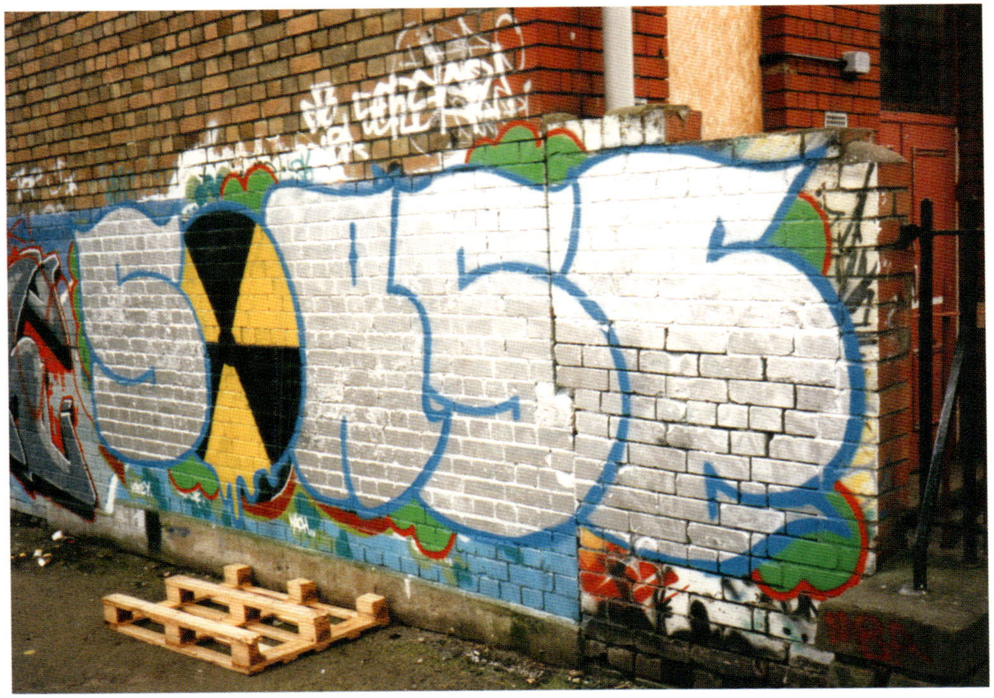

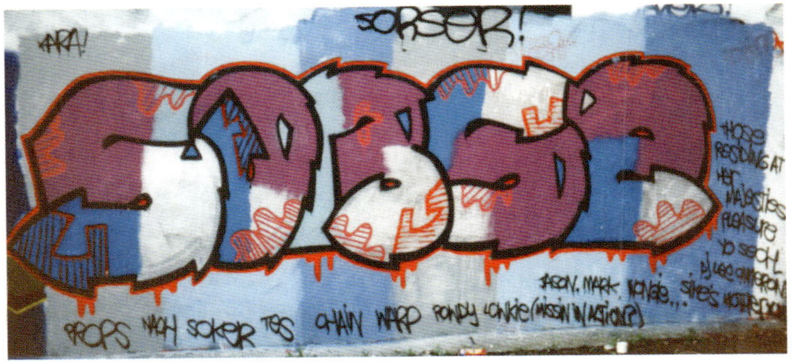

wall, and it was all pretty rushed and was done very quick. It was quite sketchy at the time, but the buzz I got from it was up there with what we were getting with the pills later on. But this was a totally natural high."

What were you writing at that point?
"The first train I did, I used Rome, I don't

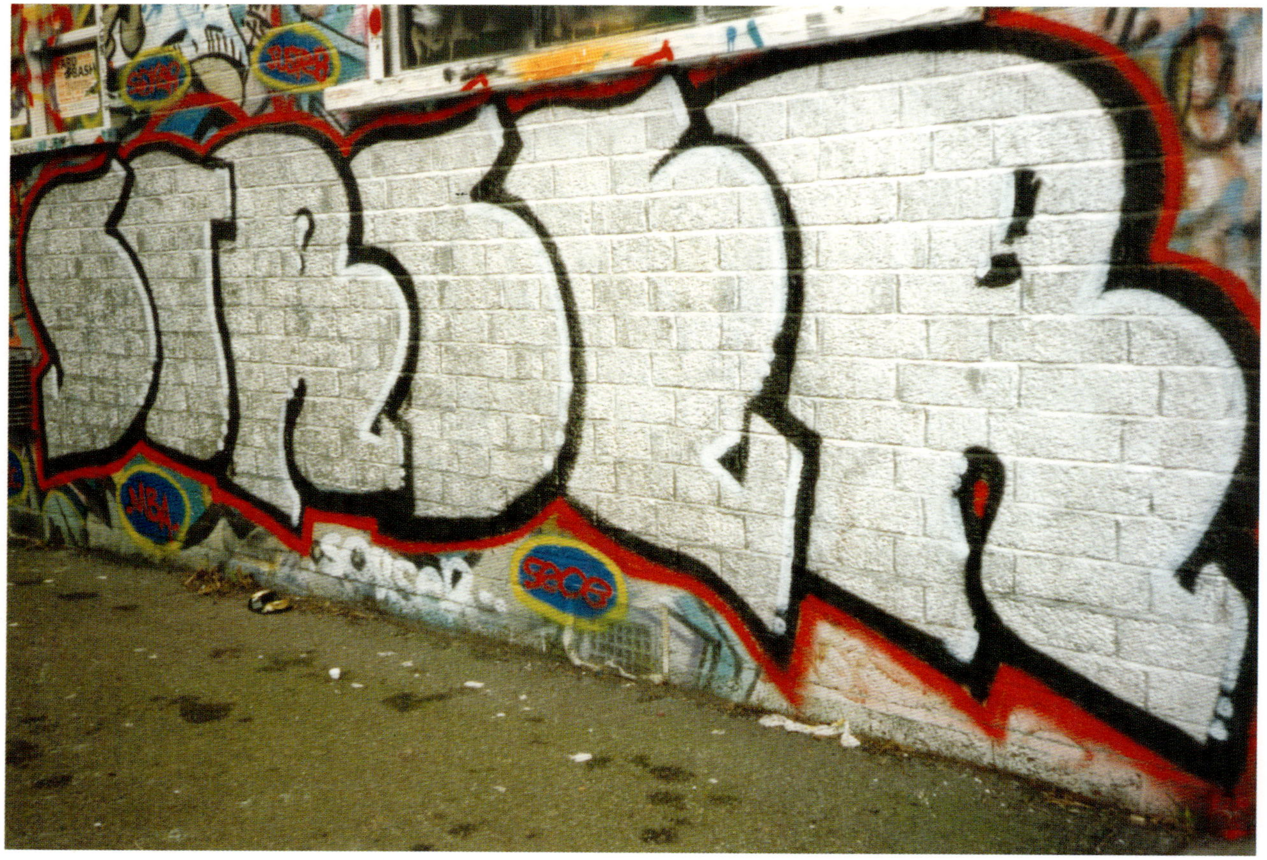

Above: Chrome on the outside of Barton Hill Youth Club, which continued to be used as a hall of fame long after the Council left it for dead, circa mid 90s. It has since been re-opened as a youth centre

know why I chose it, maybe it's the Catholic in me? Although more than likely it was because of other people, like Chome, basically."

What was it that encouraged you to start doing more legal painting, and developing your style?

"When I started puffing out (smoking weed) my style changed straight away and I got more into taking my time over a piece, doing a bit, going off, coming back, taking photos throughout, whereas painting illegally you'd just put it up and that's it. It was a blessing on the one hand, that you could get more methodical with it, and I mastered a few of my own styles doing that. But at the same time I know that if it had been illegal, I'd have got it done real quick. It was cool because you could develop a piece more, do intricate flowers and stuff like that. At the same time it would have been nice to have someone saying 'come on, let's get this finished.'"

I remember Barton Hill being a real oasis of creativity, somewhere to learn from what others were painting and experimenting with.

"It was. There was a room full of paint and you could go to John, 'can I have some of them?' Juice from Birmingham told us about mixing paints, and that was crazy, because you could start making your own shades. It was like you didn't just have to use spray, you could use emulsion to do the background. I'd get a red, a blue and a white and make various violets as a base coat."

It does make me come over a bit misty-eyed talking about it...

"I've got nothing but fond memories of Barton Hill, just for the fact that you had a youth worker there who was facilitating you doing art, encouraging you not to do it illegally, providing you with paint, getting all these people down to come and visit - like Vulcan from America, Get from Amsterdam and all the other English artists. It was like a family. You'd get the camaraderie, although some people did get stick for what they were doing, like Shab and Jody. Reflecting on it now, I've got nothing but love for Shab, really, because what he was doing was something you just wouldn't see anywhere else. Same as Jody's stuff, it was totally new. It was a breath of fresh air."

It's interesting that you describe it as a family.

"You had people who could understand your scenario, they'd been through what you'd been through and so you could learn from them. They made you aware of different stuff that was going on, they made you realise that all those around were in a similar situation. They wouldn't ram it down your throat or anything, but through the conversations you were having you'd become aware of stuff. You might have a guy coming in who's an old-school racist, and we'd be like: 'You can't be like that in here, mate.' And it'd be like: 'What music do we all like listening to? Hip hop? And where does that come from?'"

Hip hop in general was a response to terrible inner-city conditions, and a lot of the young people at Barton Hill Dug Out were from socially deprived neighbourhoods.
"Certainly looking back on it now, and to an extent at that time, I remember thinking 'where does it come from, the graffiti side of it?' I remember that 'Concrete Jungle' piece in St Paul's: that piece told it how it was. It's like you've got to make your mark on society, rather than have society mark you out. It might not have linked directly to the youth workers talking to us about politics, but at the same time you can't ignore the ethos of where graffiti came from. It's like with hip hop in general; it was a two fingers up to the status quo at the time. It was like 'nah, we're going to paint, and we're going to put it anywhere we want. You didn't ask us about this building you're putting up.' It's the same as how Bristol is now with all the new buildings going up. No one's asked us, 'is that aesthetically pleasing? Is that nice to look at?' Most of the time the answer's 'no'."

That was what the Kane The System (KTS) crew stood for, wasn't it? Albeit in a very blunt and non-political way, but the sentiment was still there.
"For me KTS was the best because of what it was saying. It was mainly the same peeps as TUB, but the thing about KTS was that you had all the lot from the Dug Out writing it, and then you also had Inkie – who for me was the dog's bollocks from Bristol – and seeing him writing the words 'Kane The System was proper. That was what we were doing, we were like 'yeah, sod it'; That's what we do, we're kaning it'."

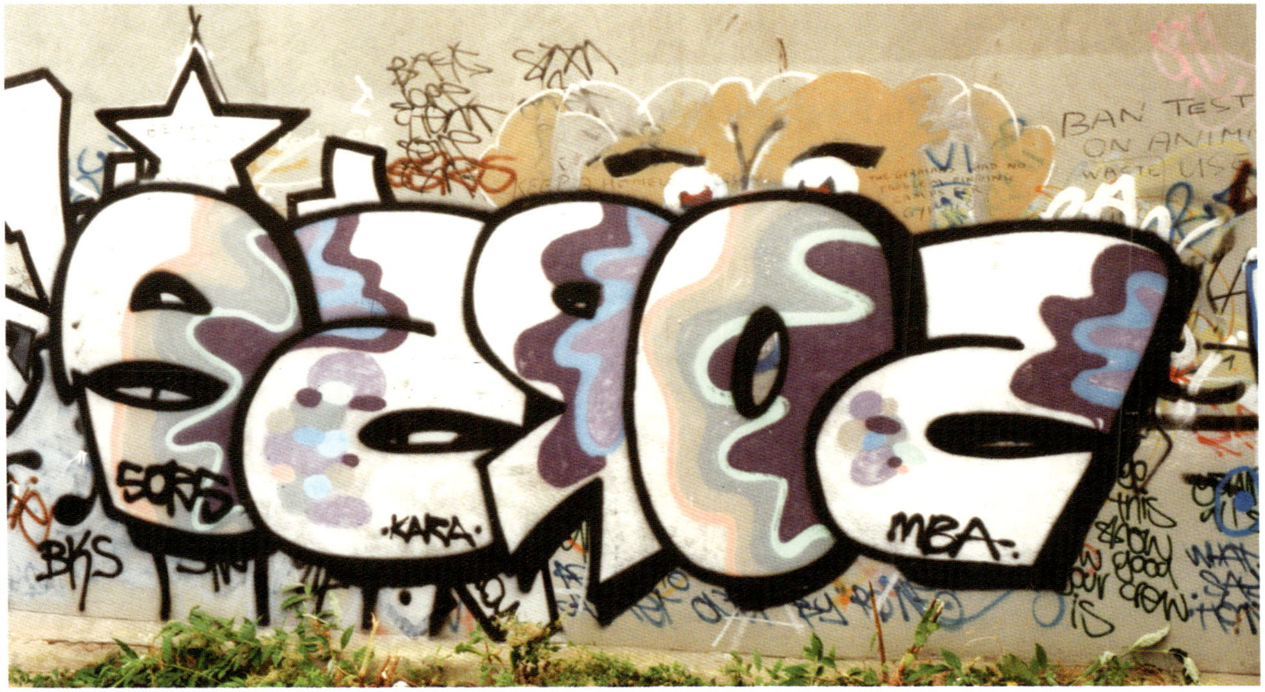

Above: Reverse piece, another MBA/DBZ trademark style, 1994

You said the staff at the club didn't ram their views down our throats, but at the same time they didn't exactly keep their political opinions to themselves, did they?
"I think everyone was more politically aware back then, especially young people. I remember going along to the Poll Tax demonstrations and I saw all the guys that worked at the club. There was a sense that it was going to kick off and we were like 'yeah, we don't care, we'll stand up; we'll represent.' I remember one of the workers telling me to go careful, and it was almost like a football riot in a sense. They had fences in front of the Council House on College Green, and we were all along the front of the fence when we suddenly saw the police come along and people getting arrested, and it got a bit crazy. One of the guys I was with punched a police horse, which I don't condone, but at the same time it was like 'fuck this, we're not going to have them up on their horses telling us what to do.' The barriers came down, it all sort of kicked off."

I get the impression that the times you spent at the Dug Out have really stayed with you, and that John Nation and the rest of the staff made a lasting impression on you?
"Definitely. The career I've chosen now, working with young people, is as a direct result of those influential characters from those days."

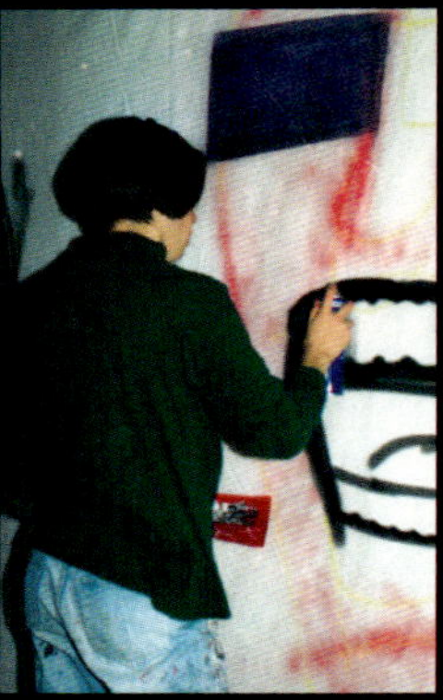

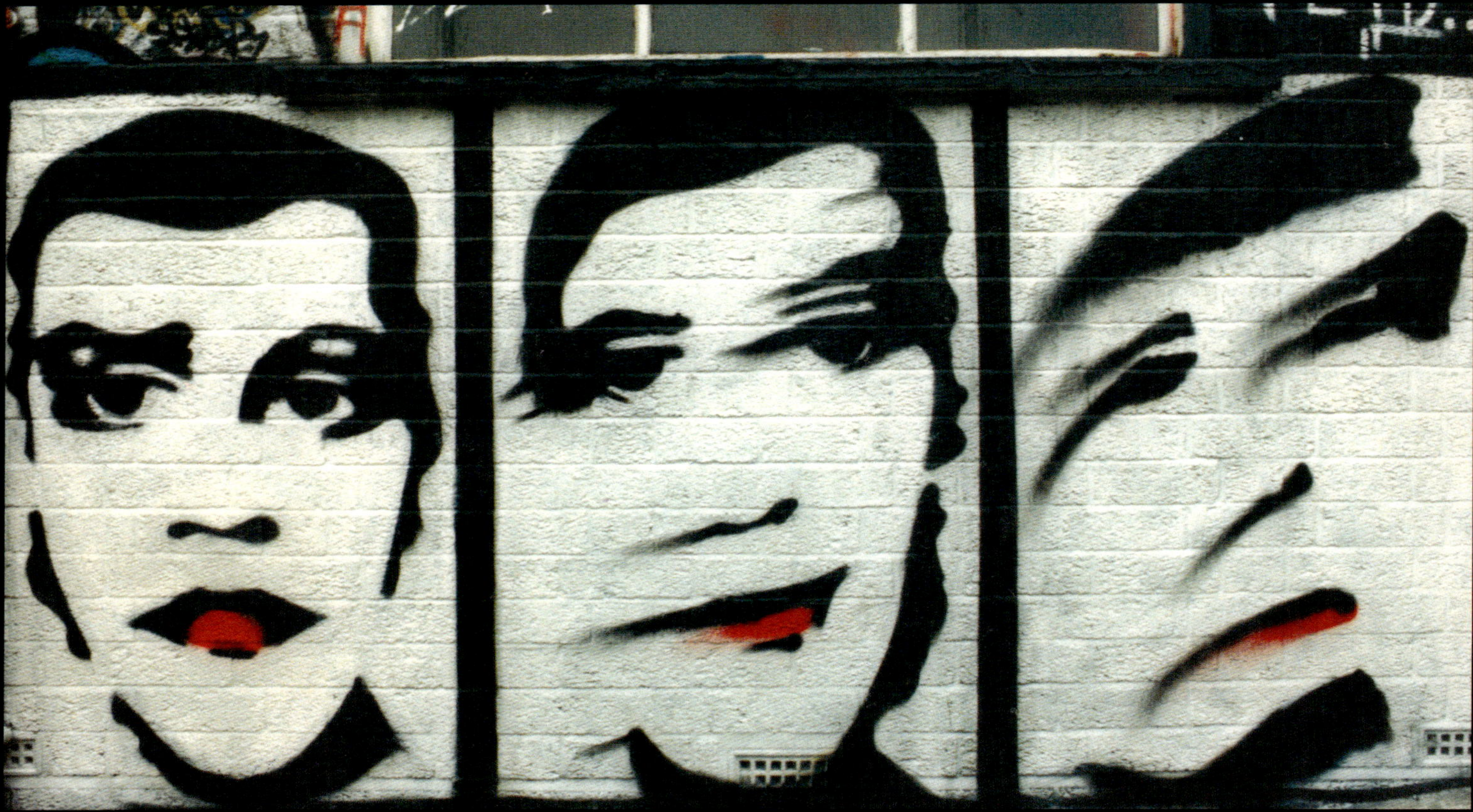

Above: Jody painting a backdrop on a sheet, one of many commissions arranged by John Nation, c.1990

Top right: Jody's graphic style given the 'photocopier blur' treatment on the outside of Barton Hill Youth Club

Bottom right: Mixing up the styles and techniques on a board for Birdland's nightclub in Bristol

JODY

• **At the height of creative activity in Barton Hill a shy, self-effacing 15-year-old called Jody turned up at the youth club, clutching a folder full of drawings under one arm.** Jody was at school with Chome, a member of TUB, who had told him about the club and encouraged him to come down and have a look.

Within a matter of weeks he was producing unique, arresting sprayed paintings. Not exactly 'graffiti' as anyone understood it at the time, they were nonetheless entirely in keeping with the experimental attitude towards the art form

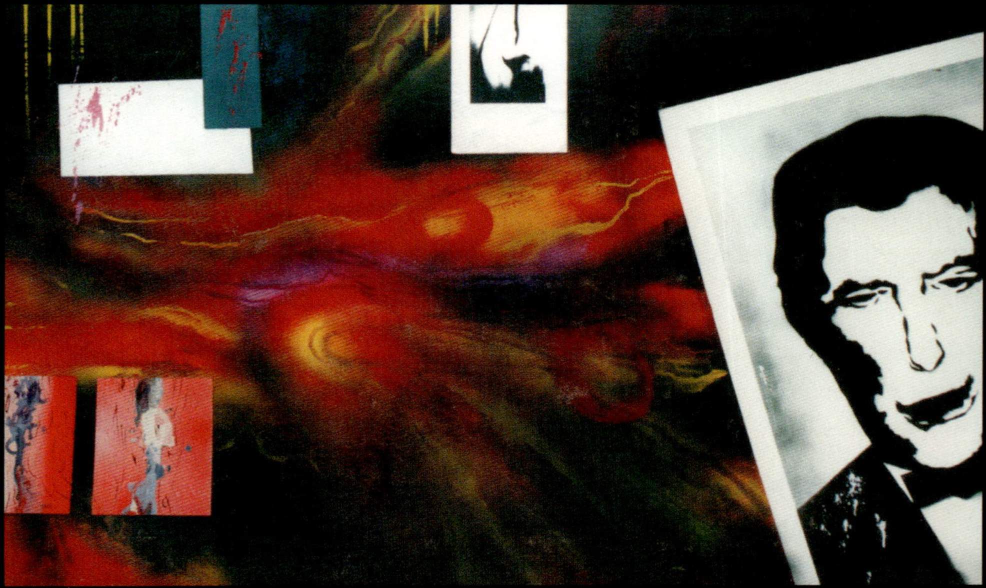

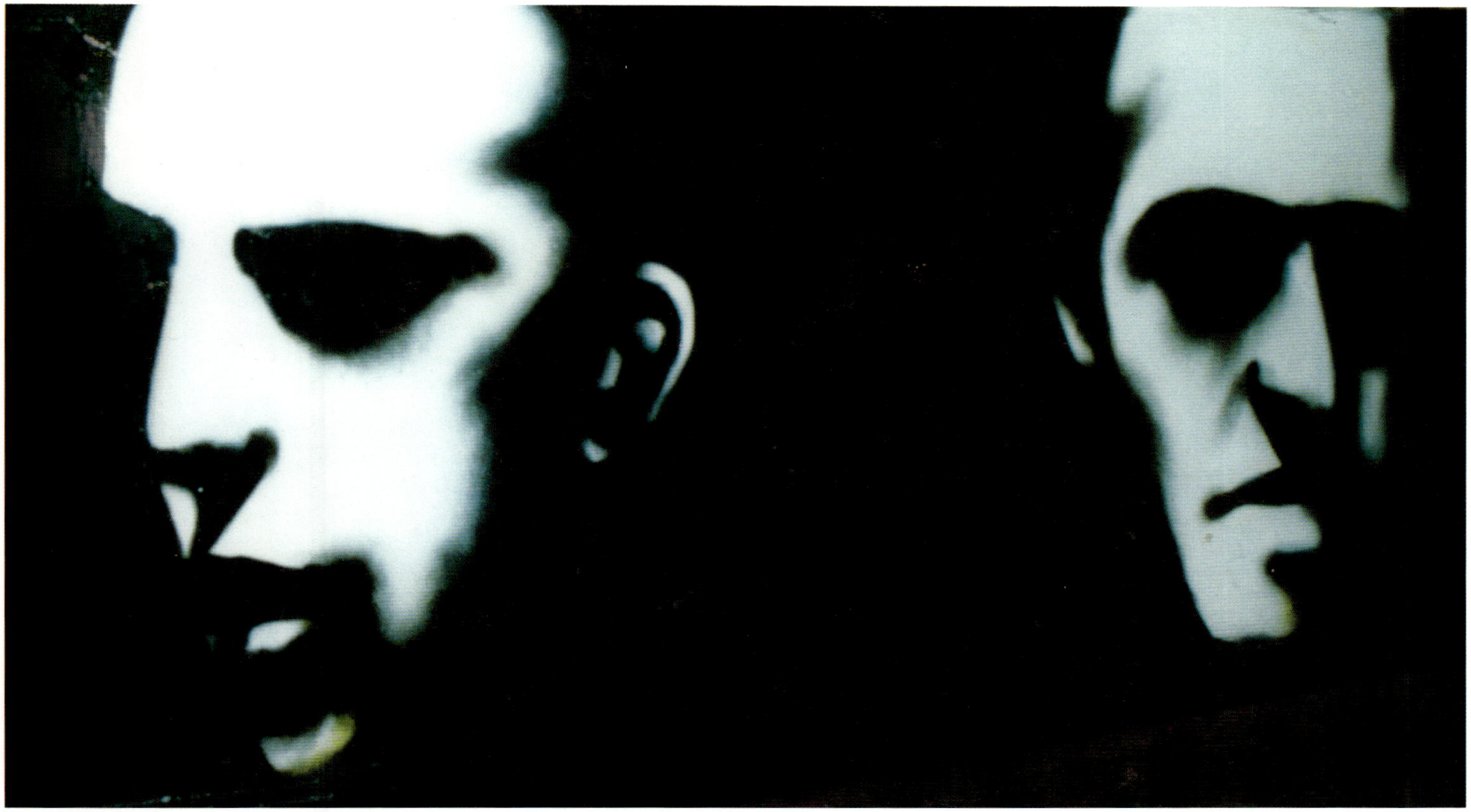

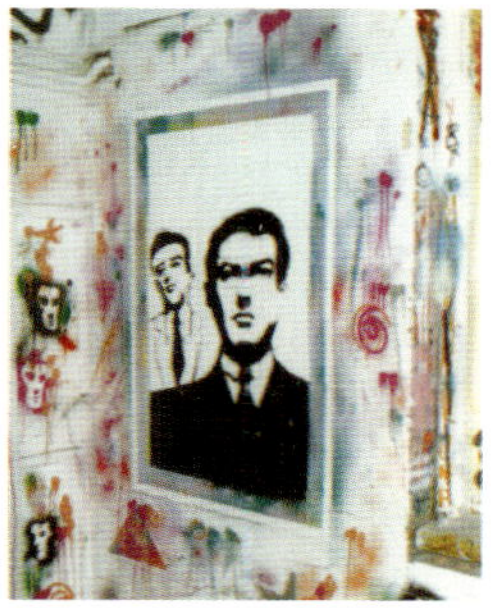

Top left: Two of Jody's trademark faces looming out of the shadows, interior Barton Hill Youth Club, 1989

Above: Stencil piece of the Kray brothers, based on David Bailey's iconic portrait. Subject matter as suggested by John Nation, 1989

Bottom left: Moors murderer Ian Brady gets the Warhol/3D-style treatment, 1990

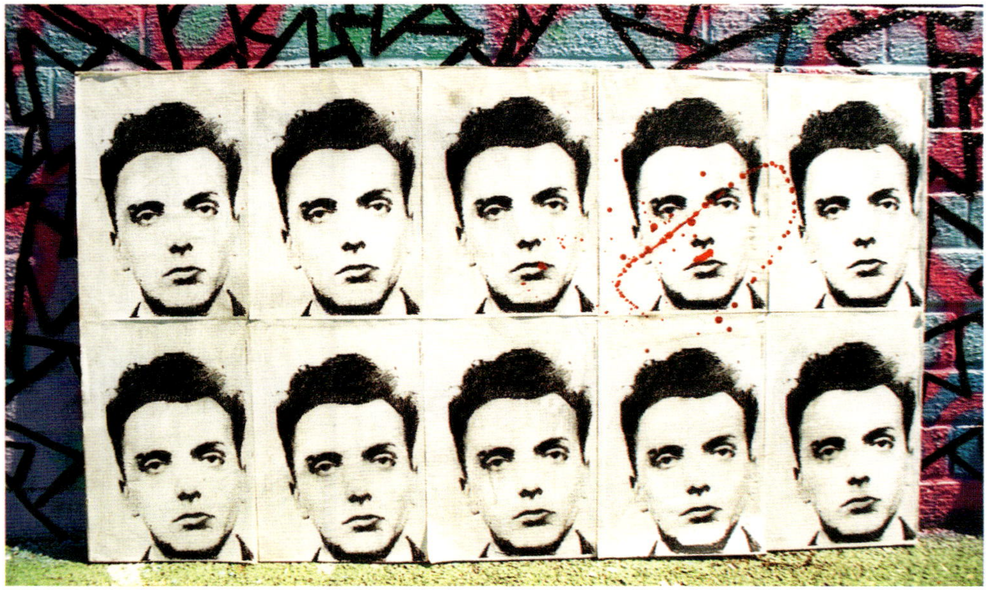

being encouraged at Barton Hill Youth Club in the late 80s. Arguably the second artist in Bristol to adopt stencilling as one of his tools, Jody's work was in many ways ahead of his time."

What were your initial impressions of Barton Hill Youth Club and the kids who hung out there?
"You take people at face value, and these kids were kind of tough, street-wise kids, while I was a skinny, arty kind of guy. I had a lot of respect for these guys, and I knew I wasn't from the street, even though I was a working class kid. I had always had an interest in art."

Right: Jody's groundbreaking monotone stencil pieces pre-dated later trends in street art by the best part of ten years and gave his work an unmistakable flavour, c.1989

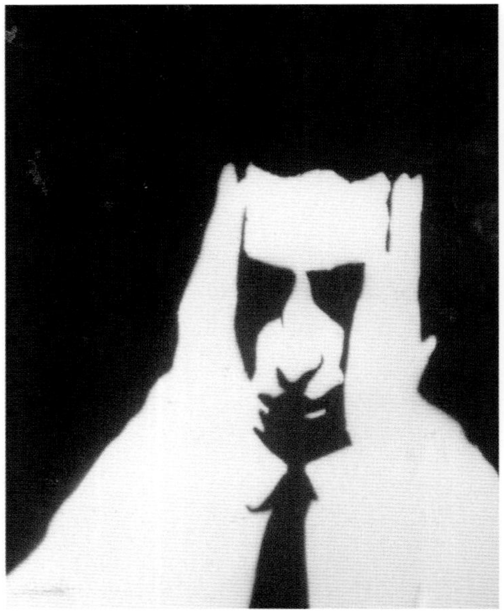

When did you get involved in painting there?

"I turned up at the club in '89 and I met John. He was a bit of a formidable character, and the only thing I had to show him was my GCSE art project. I said, 'look, I haven't really done anything but I want to get into painting.' And John said, 'If you want to practise on that little wall down there, you can'. It was this little 'courtesy panel' for the ladies' toilet.

"The first piece I ever did was half graffiti and half my own style. What I was basically doing was trying to show the graffiti guys that I could do letters, outlines, this, that and the other – but I was also experimenting with my own stuff. I remember people coming up to me while I was painting and saying 'hey, that looks really good, but why are you doing that letter with it?' It was kind of divided in half. Anyway, John came over and he said 'if that's your first piece, I rate that. If you're going to do something like that, you can do

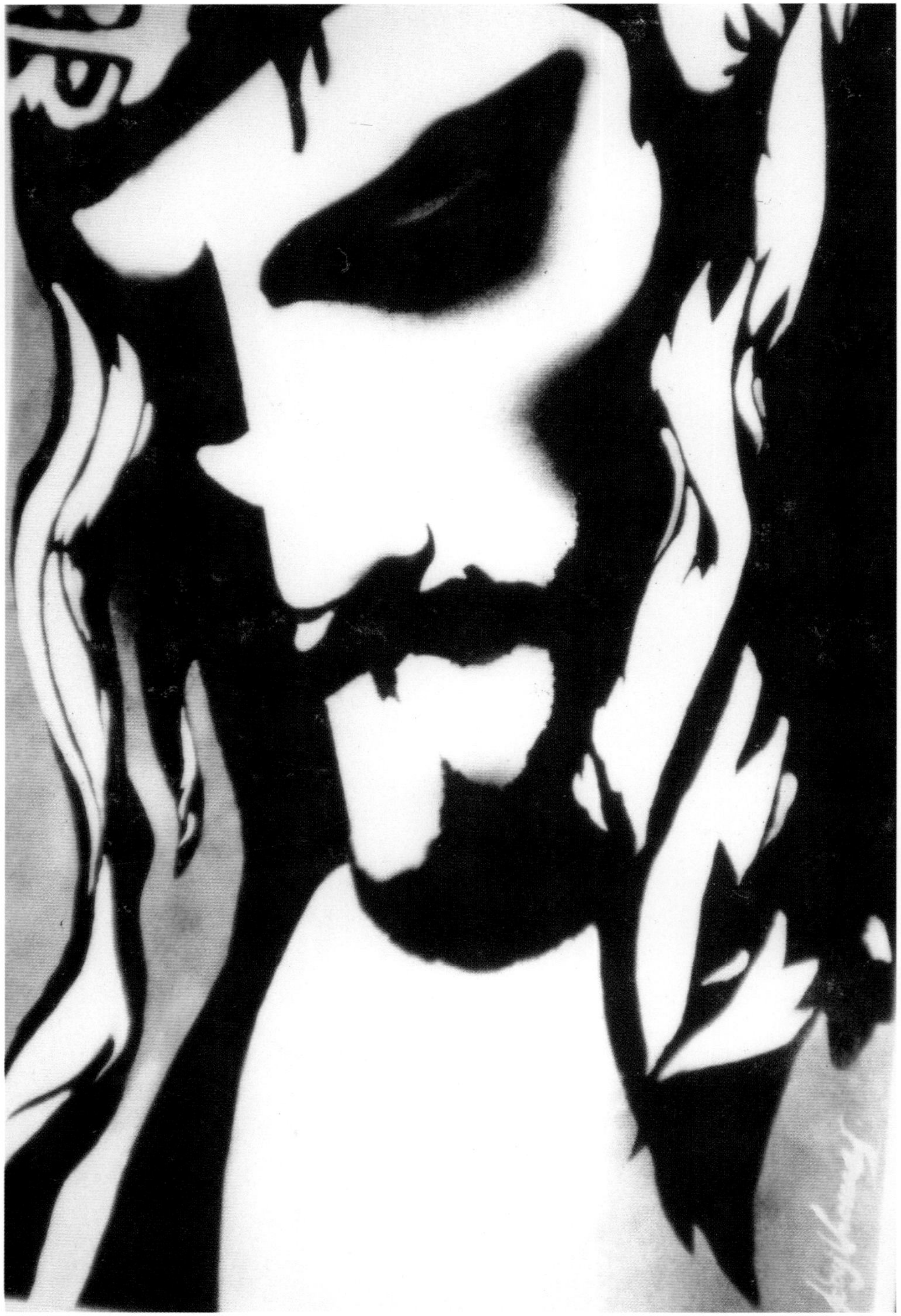

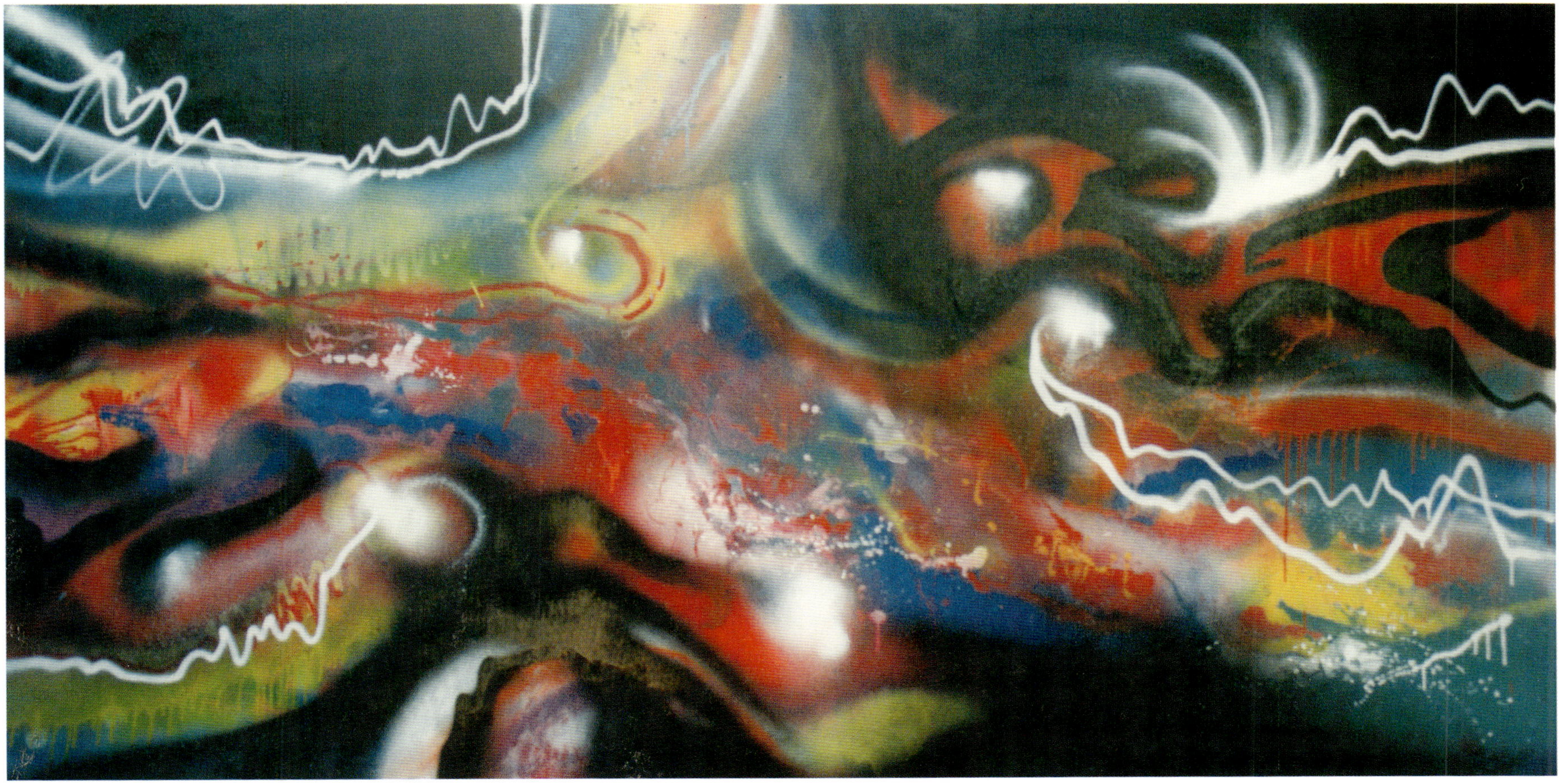

it out there.' Which was amazing, because the actual hall of fame was the football court, and if you could get a piece out there you had the respect of everybody."

From the start your work was a million miles from what most people were doing. How were your early paintings received by the writers at the club?
"I think the real hardcore writers thought, 'this kid is good enough to paint in the court, but we don't quite get where he's coming from', and people like Cema and those guys would all say 'it's a waste of space!' But as a newcomer I was very aware that I had to do a certain amount of proving myself among these guys. I immediately struck up a friendship with Shab, he was very similar to me in that he was coming from a very artistic perspective. He wasn't exactly derided by the other writers, but there was a lot of piss-taking going on."

What influenced the development of your style? Were there artists in Bristol at the time who influenced you?
"I saw some of 3D's stuff – outside of [clothing shop] Westworld, and I saw the piece at the back of Special K's Café, with the face that had been stencilled. It's very easy to get it wrong when you're painting a face freehand, to get the proportions and features right. I remember seeing that piece and thinking 'he's got that just right, he's got the eyes right.'"

I think 3D influenced all the early graffiti artists in the city. When did you first see graffiti in Bristol?
"There was the Weetabix billboard advert that Artful Dodger did '80s. I remember a friend of mine saying 'there's a really wicked piece of graffiti down by the swimming baths' which was about two miles away, so we all got on our BMXs and

Above: Freestyle abstract piece for Birdland's nightclub, strongly influenced by Jon 156 and Meo's pieces at the Bridlington 1989 world championships

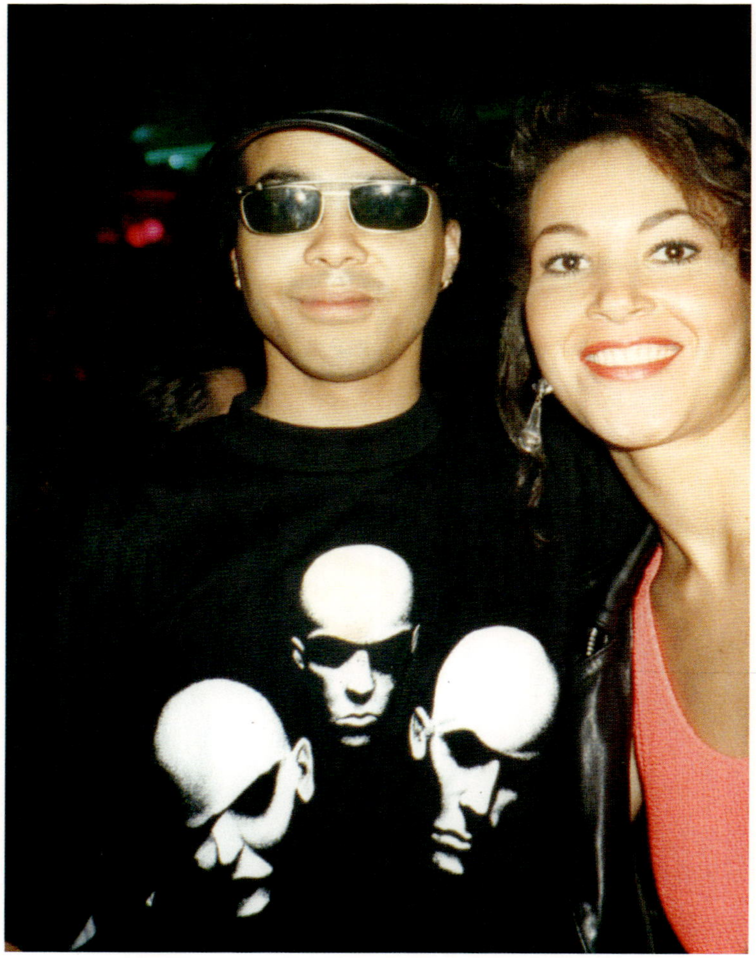

Above: Barton Hill youth worker Lee Jones in one of Jody's much sought-after t-shirts, with the distinctive design based on a scene from Terry Gilliam's film Brazil

Opposite page: Freehand piece of one of the Brazil faces, 1989

we piled down there, and when we got there it was like... 'Wow!'. None of us had cameras at the time. I remember standing there trying to memorise it, and then I went home and tried to recreate it.
Then when I went down to the Arnolfini exhibition, I bought *Subway Art*. I remember the smell of the book – you know that print smell that you get? And I remember opening it only so far, because I didn't want to crack the spine on it. It was like a Bible. When that came out, that was it."

I remember seeing you tag your pieces 'DVant' but then you switched to using your real name. Why was that?
"I messed around with a couple of names. I don't know whether I was trying to throw people or if I was having some kind of identity crisis at the time, or a bit of both. I remember having a conversation with John about it, and he said, 'why don't you just use Jody? You've got to let people know that you're an artist per se'. John was always a very persuasive kind of guy. And from then on I'd either leave it unsigned – because it was pretty obvious who did it – or I'd write my name, just like an artist would sign a painting."

Where did the idea for the faces coming out of the darkness come from? They were so different to anything anyone else was doing at that time.
"There was a particular scene in Terry Gilliam's film *Brazil* where these guys come into an office and they're all staring at the camera. I kept rewinding it until I got the right pose and I paused it, and I thought, 'yeah, that's what I want to create on the wall, that look of intensity in their faces.' Then I got a piece of paper, taped it over the screen and traced around their faces. It was that feeling of emerging from the darkness that I wanted to recreate."

It's a very arresting image, quite dark. Do you remember people's responses to those pieces?
"We were all in the football courts one evening and there was this old guy there for a residents' meeting. He looked at one of my pieces and he said, 'did you do that? That man in that picture, he looks like he's been in Belsen.' Then one of the youth workers came up to me and he said, 'you see that old guy there? He's generations away from you, but he came over and he spoke to you. You've got to remember, if it wasn't for them there would be no you.'
It was clear that my work could span generational gaps as well as cultural differences because of its immediacy – there were no complicated letter forms or colours to decode visually, people could relate to the simplicity of what I was trying to create and that is maybe what made my work popular."

John Nation was clearly an influential figure in your life at that time. I get the impression he warmed to you?
"Pretty early on I had John's ear, and eye, in terms of doing stuff around the club. So if there were any awkward spaces, I'd take them and try to do something interesting. He would come up with little projects for me: he would say things like, 'I really like that David Bailey photo of the Krays, do you reckon you could do that?'"

Those little stencilled pieces were all over the club. Back then you must have produced all the images from scratch...?
"The thing about painting stencils is that they're instant, but you do all the hard work at home. I used to do them in my dad's garage on the floor, because I had lots of space. I'd do all the work there, so that on the day I could just rock up, lay it all up and do it – it was instant. But there was also an element of chance in there, because I never used to test them out as much as I should have, so I never knew quite how they would come out. I would use the worst, roughest photocopier I could find to produce the effect I was after. I

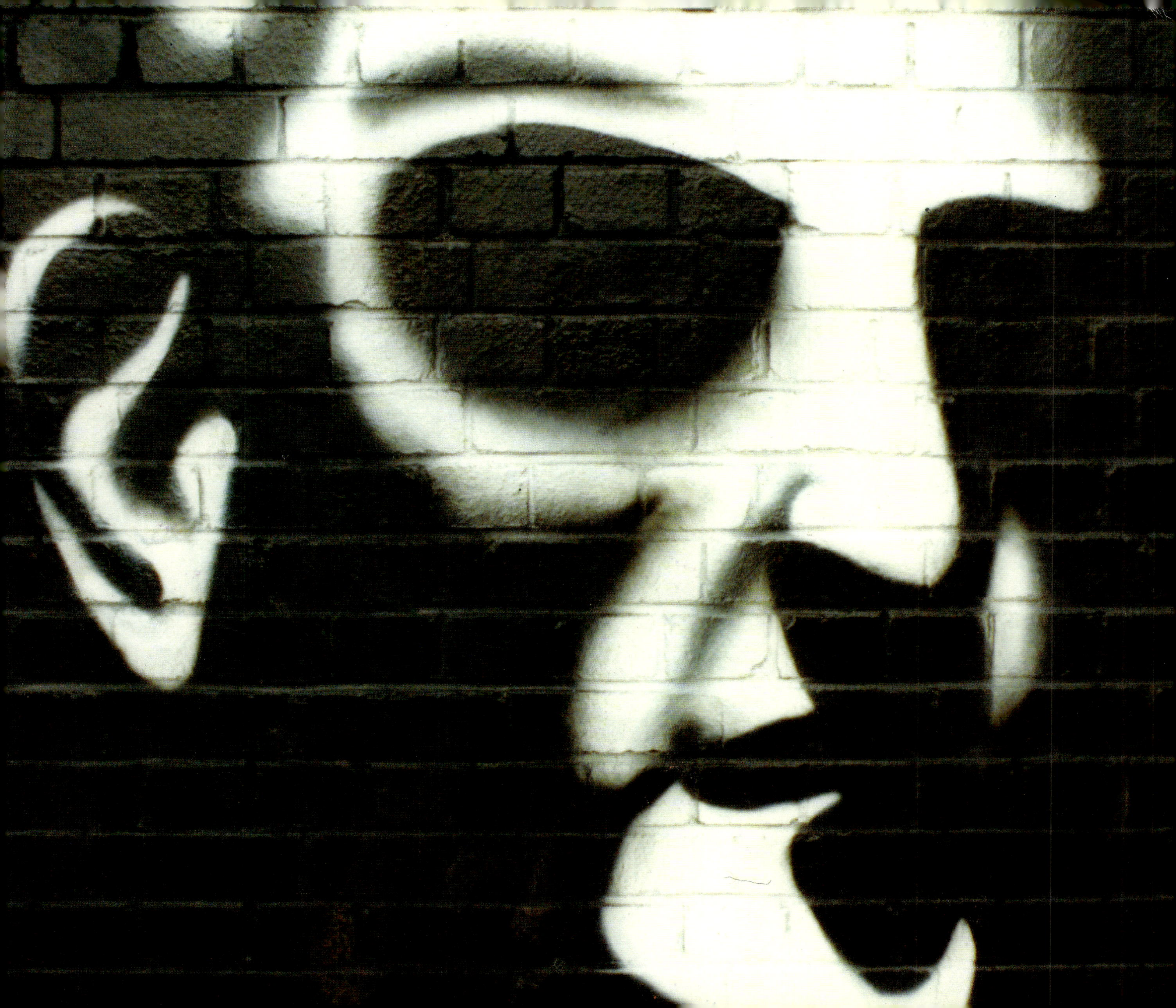

didn't have 'Posterize Filter' in Photoshop back then, I was nowhere near computers at this time. I'd get a picture and blow it up so it would distort, and it would give me the edge of the shadows, and that's where – with the combination of looking at Andy Warhol's screen prints and 3D's stuff – I got my approach to stencilling. But the stencil stuff, more than anything, got people taking the piss because to the graffiti guys it just wasn't graffiti, it was 'cheating.'"

The abstract stuff was another, very different aspect to your work. What inspired you to start throwing paint around and being more experimental?
"I got into doing all these abstract textures after seeing the work of this guy Vaughn Oliver. He did all the artwork for 4AD Records, who put out stuff by the Cocteau Twins, Colourbox, and all these weird bands. John put me onto these bands, and they had these fantastic album covers with infinite textures and images. Those covers were one of the things that really got me thinking about going into design. I also remember how, at Bridlington in 1989, John 156 created this crazy piece that was half graffiti, half sculpture. It was basically where art and graffiti met, and that for me was inspiring. It also gave me a bit more confidence, because I could see there were other guys going out there and doing it. They were blurring that line between art and graffiti, and that was important to me. I liked to mix it up – it was me doing my John 156 thing, basically – I liked the contrast between the organic, abstract forms and the stencils. I used to sit in the garage, pouring paint onto boards and then adding these other bits in, like photocopies or bits of plywood."

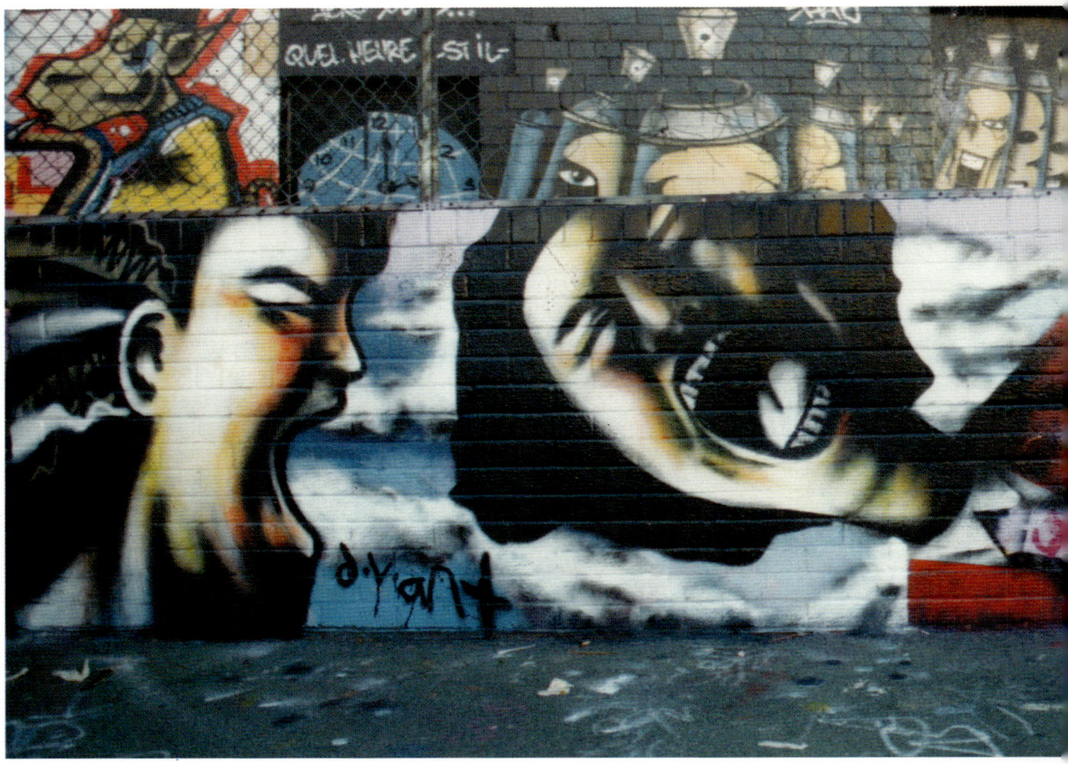

You became quite the entrepreneur along the way. How did that start?
"People would always ask me to design T-shirts for them. I had an airbrush setup at home and would do one-offs – but the time involved in doing them wasn't really worth it, so I got in contact with a screen printer and showed them the effect I wanted to achieve. The black-and-whites were perfect to make the jump onto T-shirts, and I went around town selling them, and they went like hot cakes. I remember going to pick a batch up from the printers and the three guys that worked there were all wearing them – they'd brought in their own T-shirts and done them.

"A war broke out between shops, I took them into about four or five different places, and I remember one of the shop managers at the time went bananas at me, saying 'you should be selling them exclusively to me, not to these other guys!' Anyway, the money I made from those shirts got me through college, where I studied graphic design. It also paid for my first car, which I've still got, a '67 Volkswagen Beetle. I remember the day I finished college, I checked my balance and it was £00.00. I had no money but I had no debt, and I had a car. I'd broken even."

What effect did Operation Anderson have on the more legally inclined among the artists painting there?
"I think the raids gave people a bit of a knock, and it forced the focus onto the more positive aspects of the club, mainly the artistic side of things. I got a lot of

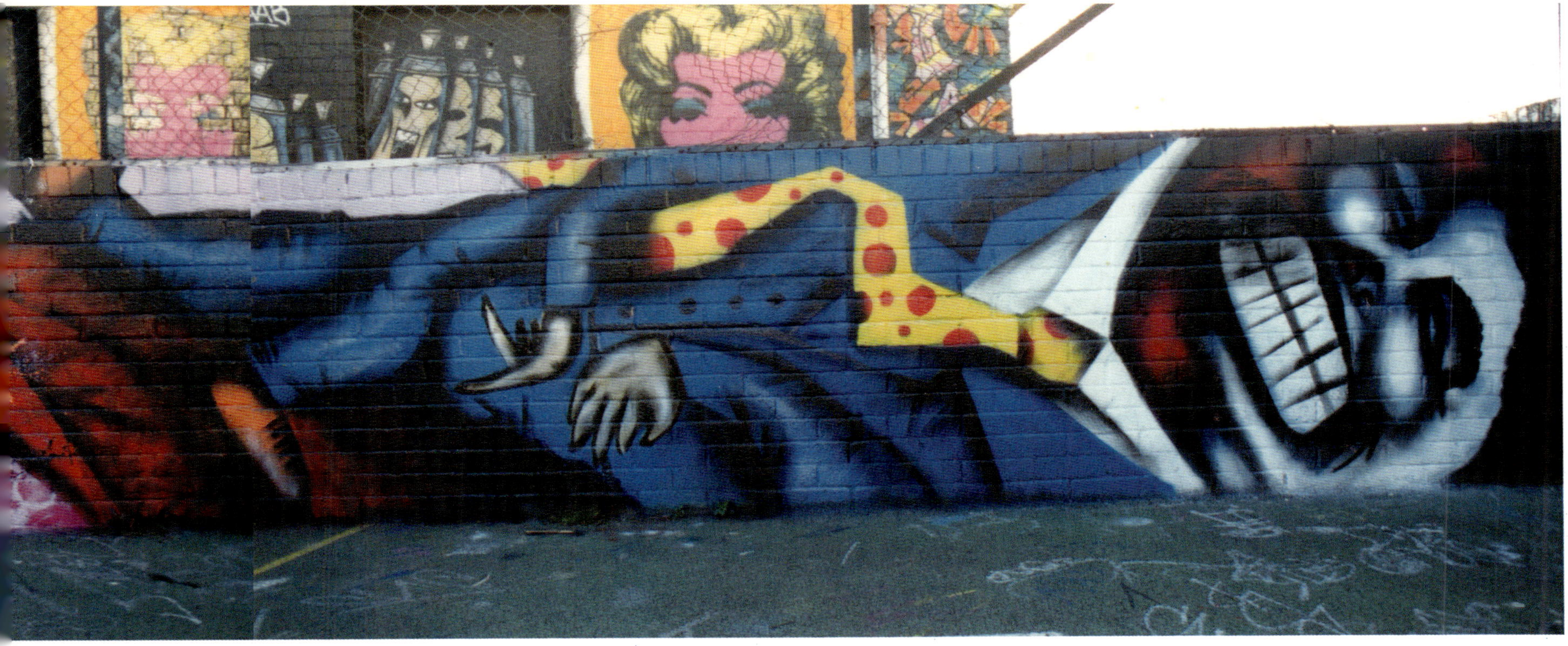

exposure. The *Independent* ran an article on me; Inkie, Shabs and me were in Venue and i-D magazines; and John, Inkie and me were on the original Sky TV (which was called BSkyB back then), on a TV programme called Swing Shift, hosted by Suggs from Madness.

"I remember when Inkie turned up at Barton Hill it was like the Pope coming to visit, the red carpet came out. People would be like, 'what's he going to be painting?' I was young and I looked up to him in a lot of ways, but he always had a lot of time for me. He had a presence about him – and, of course, a reputation as a really good writer."

The youth workers and young people used to talk about stuff in a way I couldn't imagine people doing today.

"Lee, who used to work with John at the club, said something to me once about drugs. It was in the very early days of MDMA and Ecstasy, and he said, 'I can see from what you put on the walls that you think about things a lot. You've got a very, very sensitive mind. If you ever want to take drugs, if you even have the slightest doubt in your mind, don't do it, because for someone like you it will exponentially get worse, and you will almost definitely have a bad time.' He said, 'to be honest with you, I would leave your mind intact. Don't fuck about with it.' I still tell my nieces and nephews that story to this day.

"Barton Hill brought a lot of people together from all around the city and from different backgrounds, and gave them an opportunity to paint. The Dug Out became a centre for everyone to meet, paint and talk about graffiti art, and for someone like me...I wouldn't have painted anywhere else. Barton Hill Youth Club gave me the outlet that I needed."

Does all this reminiscing get your nozzle finger twitching?

"Yes, I still hanker after painting but my job now as a design and brand consultant takes up a lot of my creative energy. I still have an eye for it, and always look out for new graf going up around the city. I really owe a lot to the club and John, it was a big turning point in my life meeting those people in Barton Hill. I'm working up some new ideas at the moment and will be back painting again soon."

Above: Making good use of the low walls surrounding the Barton Hill Youth Club's ball court, c.1990

CHAOS CMA

• **As well as being a long-standing resident on Barton Hill Youth Club's walls, Barton Hill legend Chaos gets a mention on Fresh 4's 1989 single *Wishing On A Star* and regularly painted at their St. Luke's Road warehouse parties.**

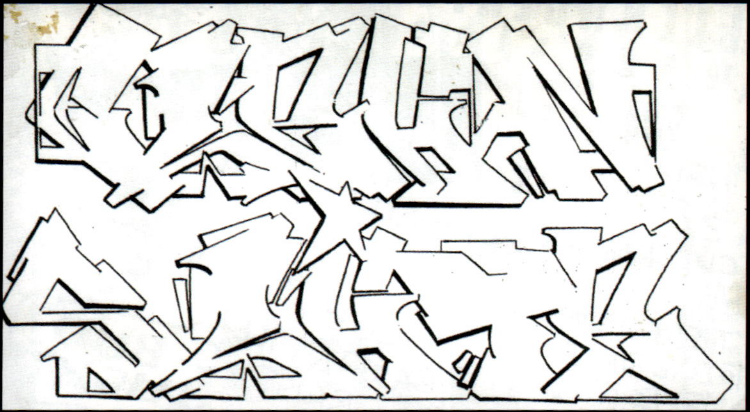

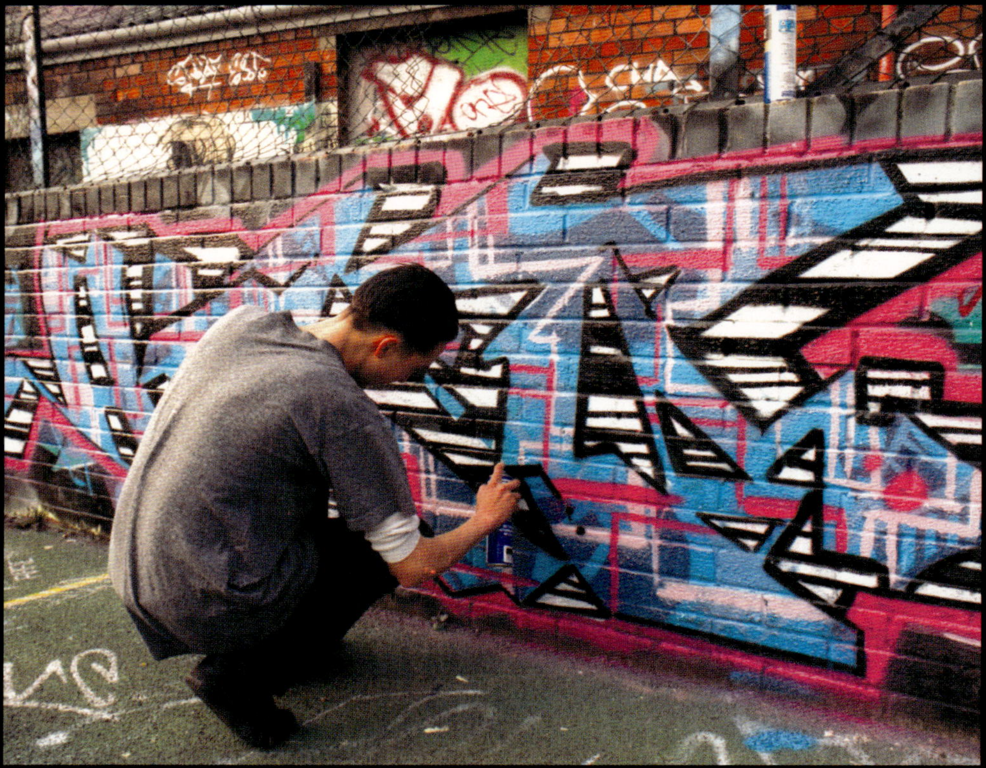

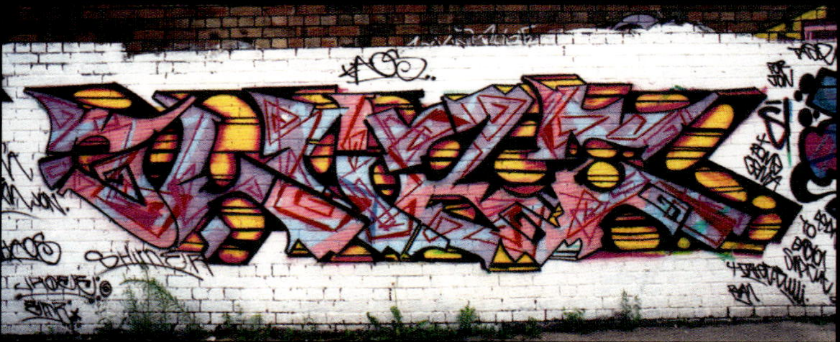

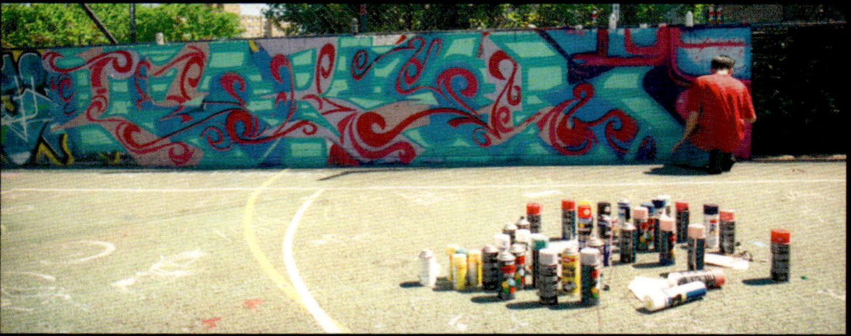

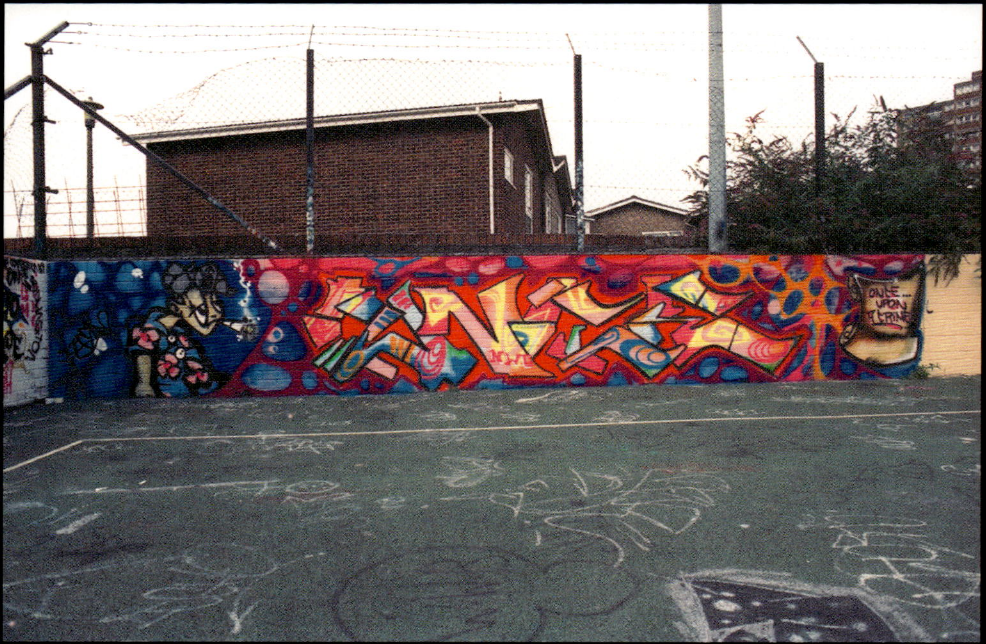

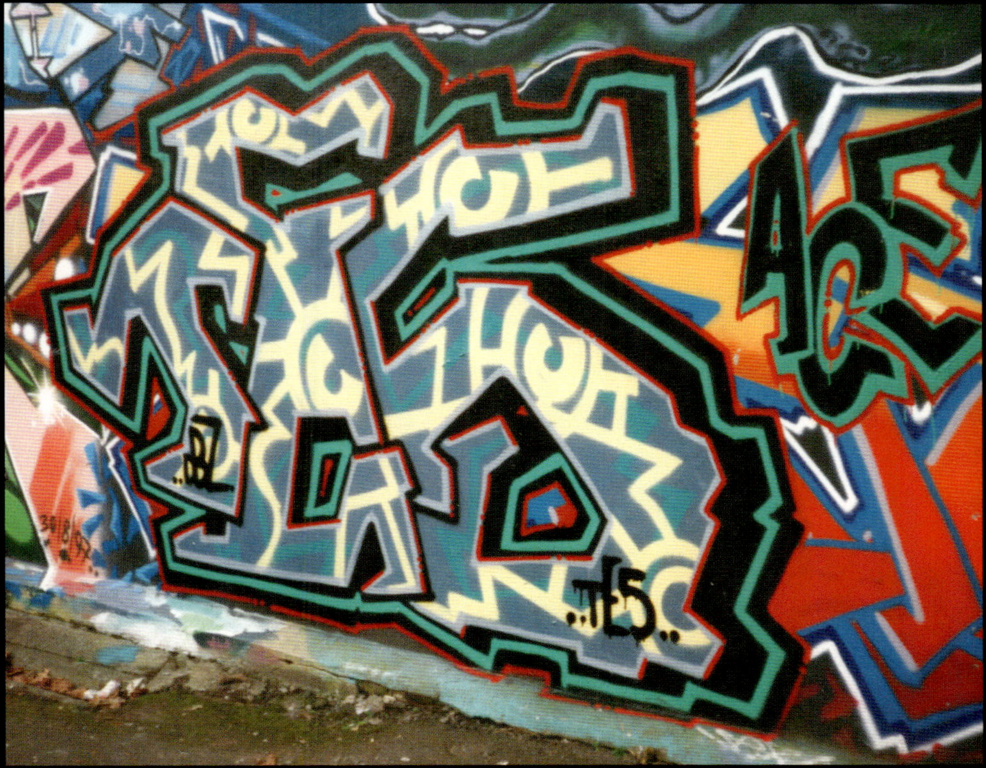

TES TUB/DBZ/TNP

• "I never gave a fuck and still don't." Describing himself as "a simple person with simple rules" Tes has been a long-standing and prolific letter writer and bomber with a militant attitude who began writing with TUB in the late 1980s.

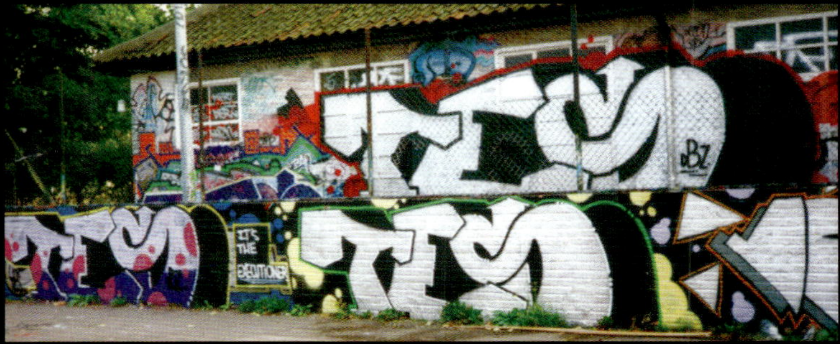

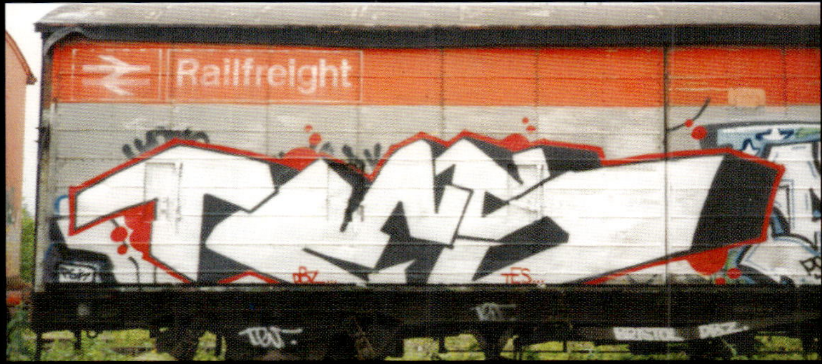

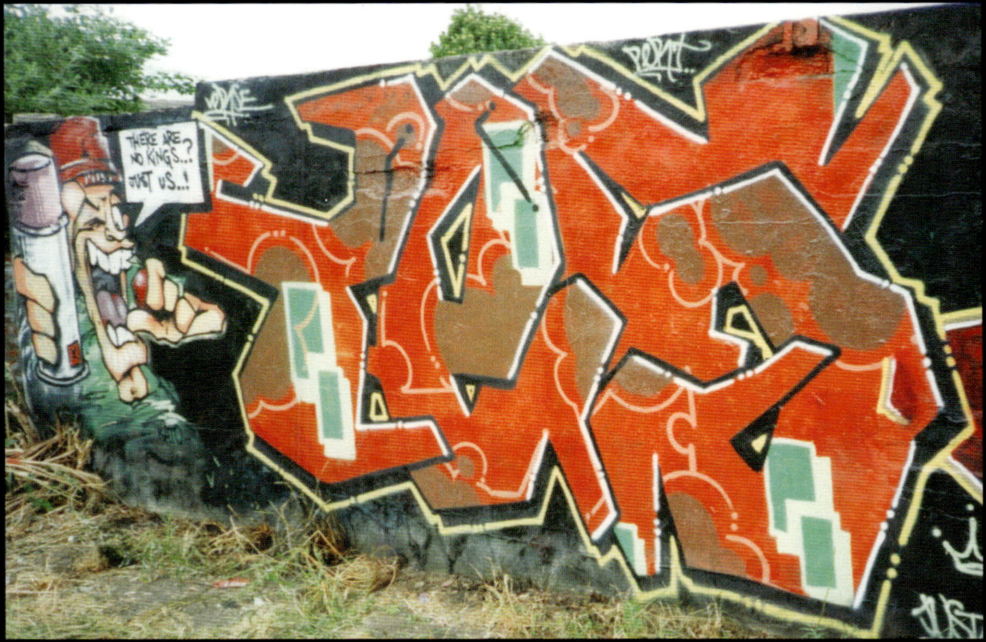

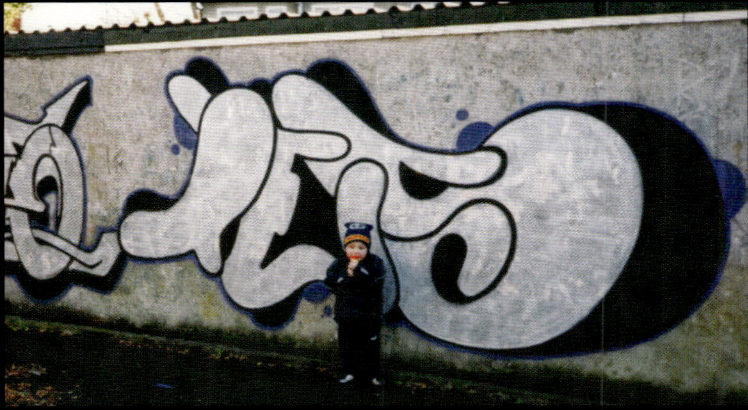

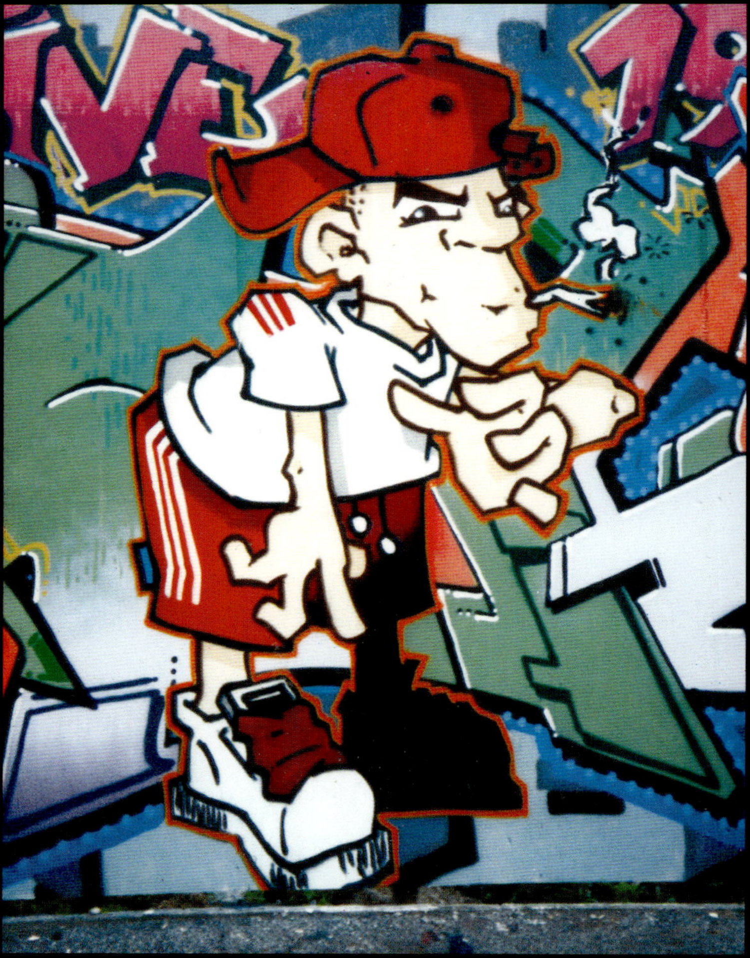

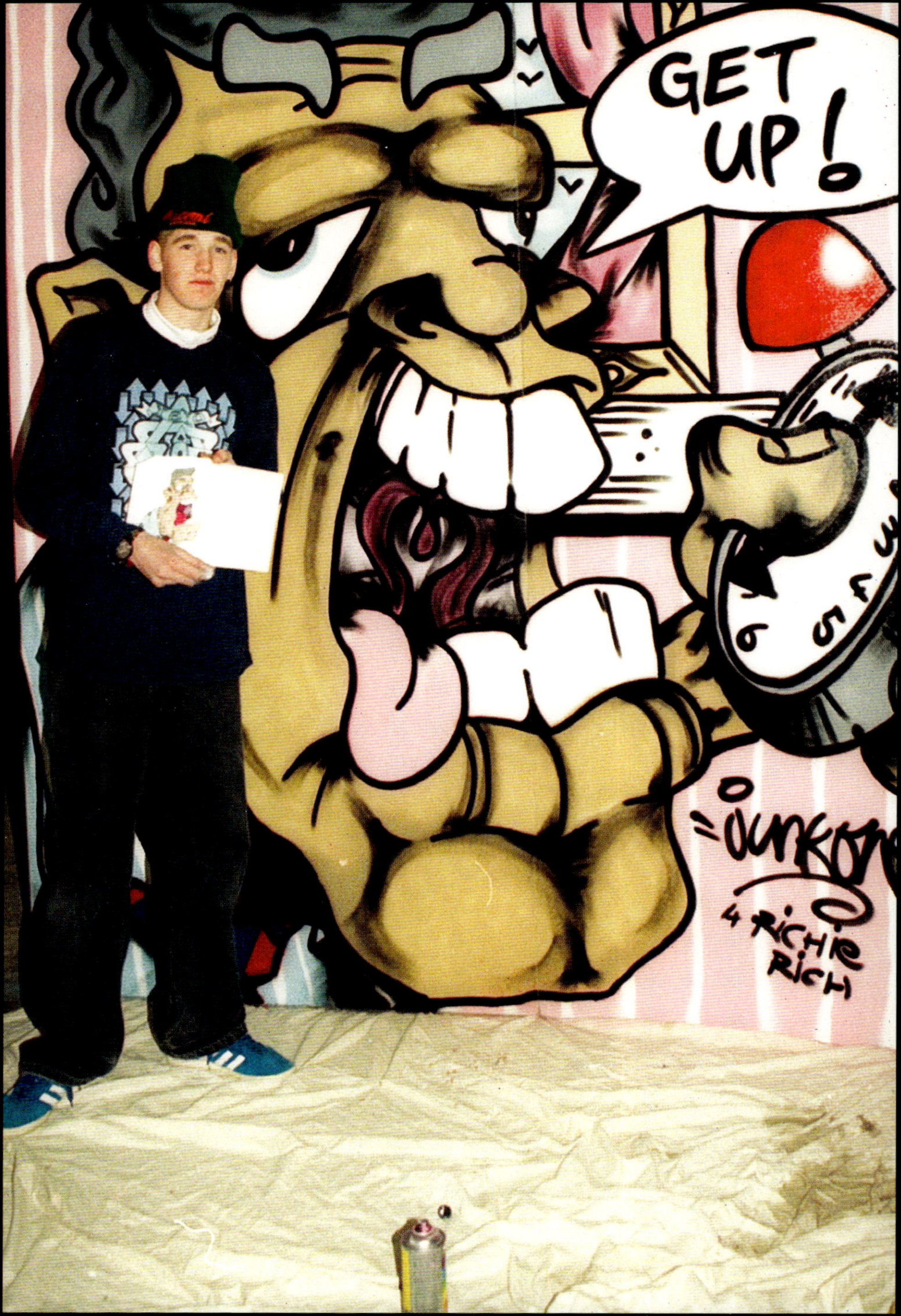

Above: Spliff-smoking B-boy dipped-out in Adidas, Leicester Return Of The Macks jam, 1996

Right: Kato, character and sketch, This Morning With Richard And Judy, Granada TV, 1989

KATO TUB/ESR/MBA/BA/DBZ/SINSTARS/ASK

• **Kato can safely claim to have been there, done that and seen it all over the 20-odd years he has been writing graffiti.** From crazed bombing missions to painting live on TV, from chrome and black track-sides to intricate character work and extravagant productions, Kato has covered a lot of ground, both literally and figuratively.

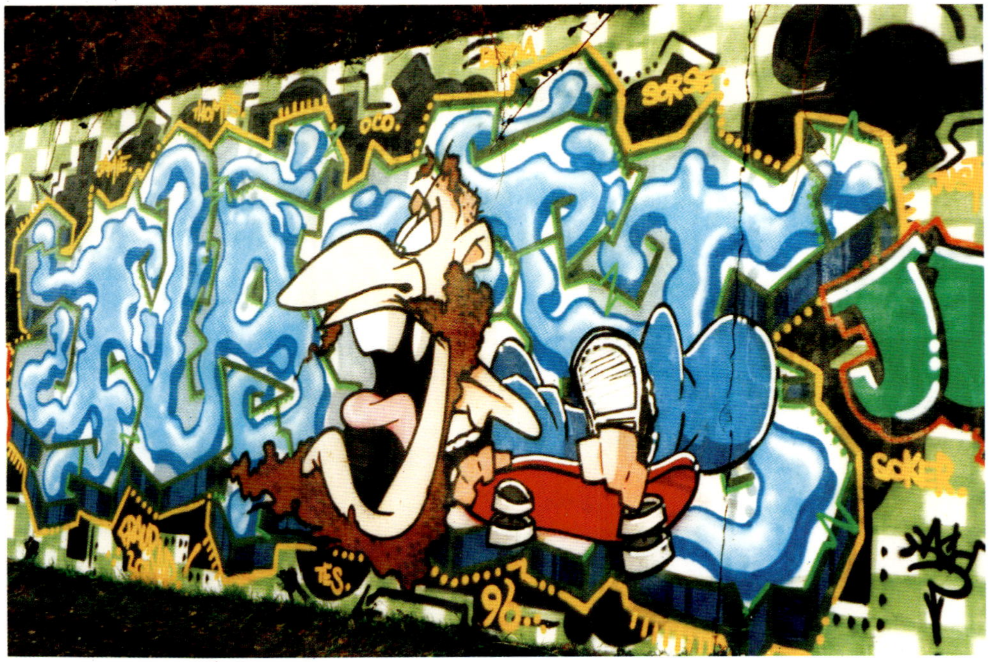

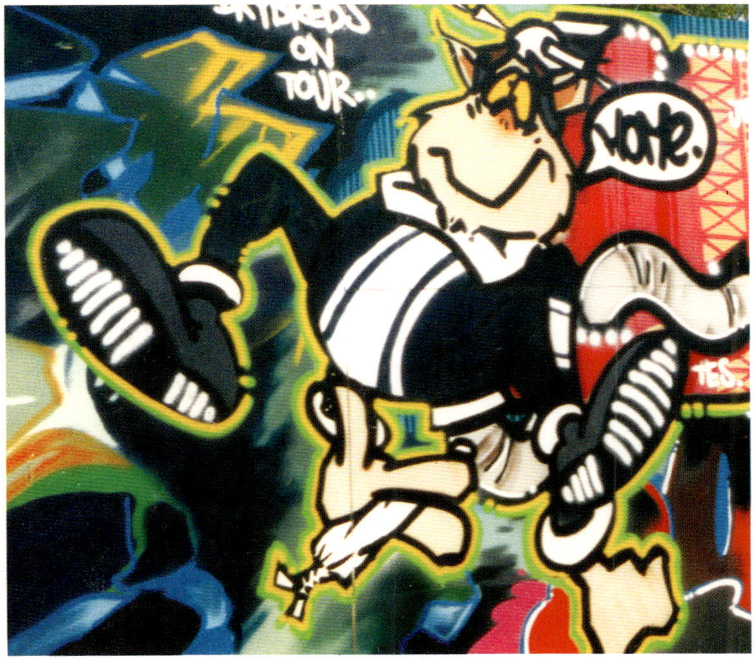

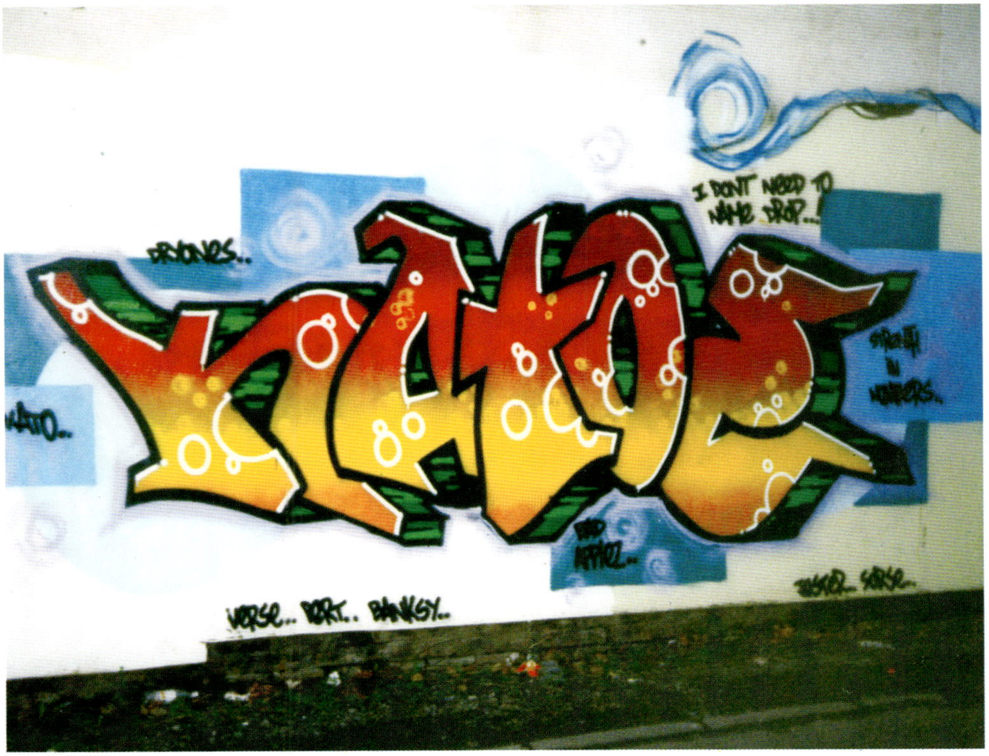

This page: A man of many styles and names, Kato/Nach pieces and characters from the mid '90s

Like so many kids who developed a passion for graffiti in Bristol in the '80s, Kato's initial spark was seeing the work of UK graffiti pioneer 3D on the city's walls. They always seemed to be in the right places – usually downtown or around Clifton.

"I remember going to an auto parts shop in the summer holidays between primary and secondary school, and getting a can of Dupli Colour Dark Green. I went down a lane and did a piece of my initials, and I blatantly ripped it off from this 3D 'Wild Style' piece I'd seen downtown. I had a photo of it that I'd taken on my mum and dad's old 110mm camera. Then I did the same letters on the flap of my school satchel with Airfix paints, ripping off the blue and orange colour scheme from the 'Wild Style' piece again.

"Then one of the breakers from up round our way saw it, and that's when I realised all the grief you can get from what he called 'biting.' I'd not even stepped into the

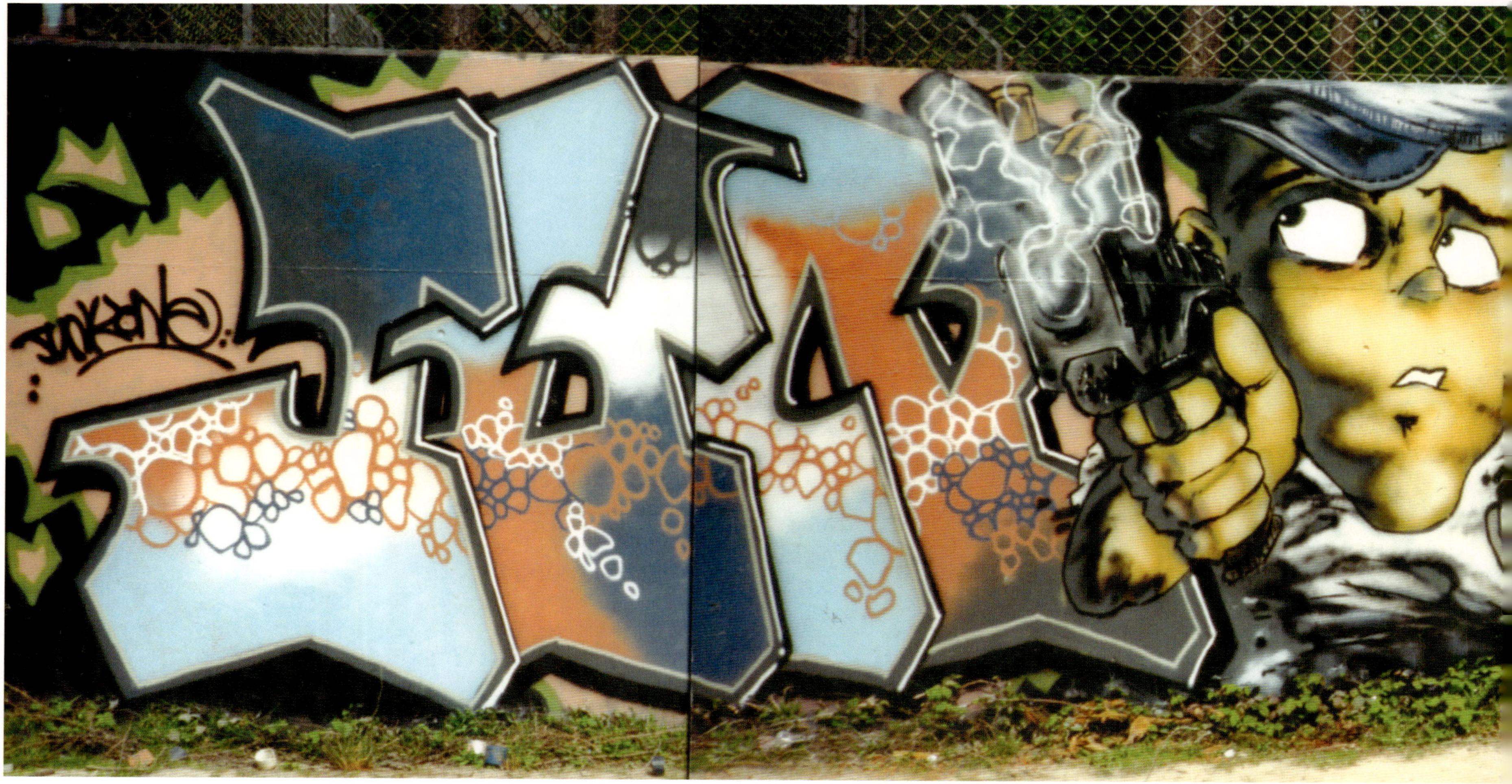

graffiti world but I realised then what I was getting into. Some people call it 'influence', and ultimately it's just about finding your own style – but back then you were 'biting', there were no two ways about it."

Soon afterwards Kato started secondary school, where a hardcore hip hop mindset was already well established, and where copying other writers' work meant paying painful dues.

"I had a friend in my art class who gave me some drawings of these really nice characters that his friend had drawn. I was 'influenced' by them, or whatever you want to call it! Anyway, I did some drawings that were blatantly similar to them, because that's all I'd seen, but they turned out to be Cheo's characters. I later got beaten up by a mate of Cheo's for doing that. But that was what influenced me, I looked up to him at the time.

"As a kid, getting beaten up at school when you're just finding your feet in the graffiti culture was quite a blow. Having older kids from another school walking into the playground and hitting you in front of your mates, it fucked me up for a little bit. Then I saw *Subway Art* and *Spraycan Art* in the school library and saw where Cheo's influences came from – Vaughn Bode, the Mode 2 characters, the hand poses, the leg stances. I thought, 'why did I get a beating for that when somebody's already been inspired by someone else?'"

Kato had always been a big fan of comic art, and he wasn't going to let being beaten up and humiliated put him off his growing passion for graffiti. Graffiti made drawing cool, and collecting comics gained a new

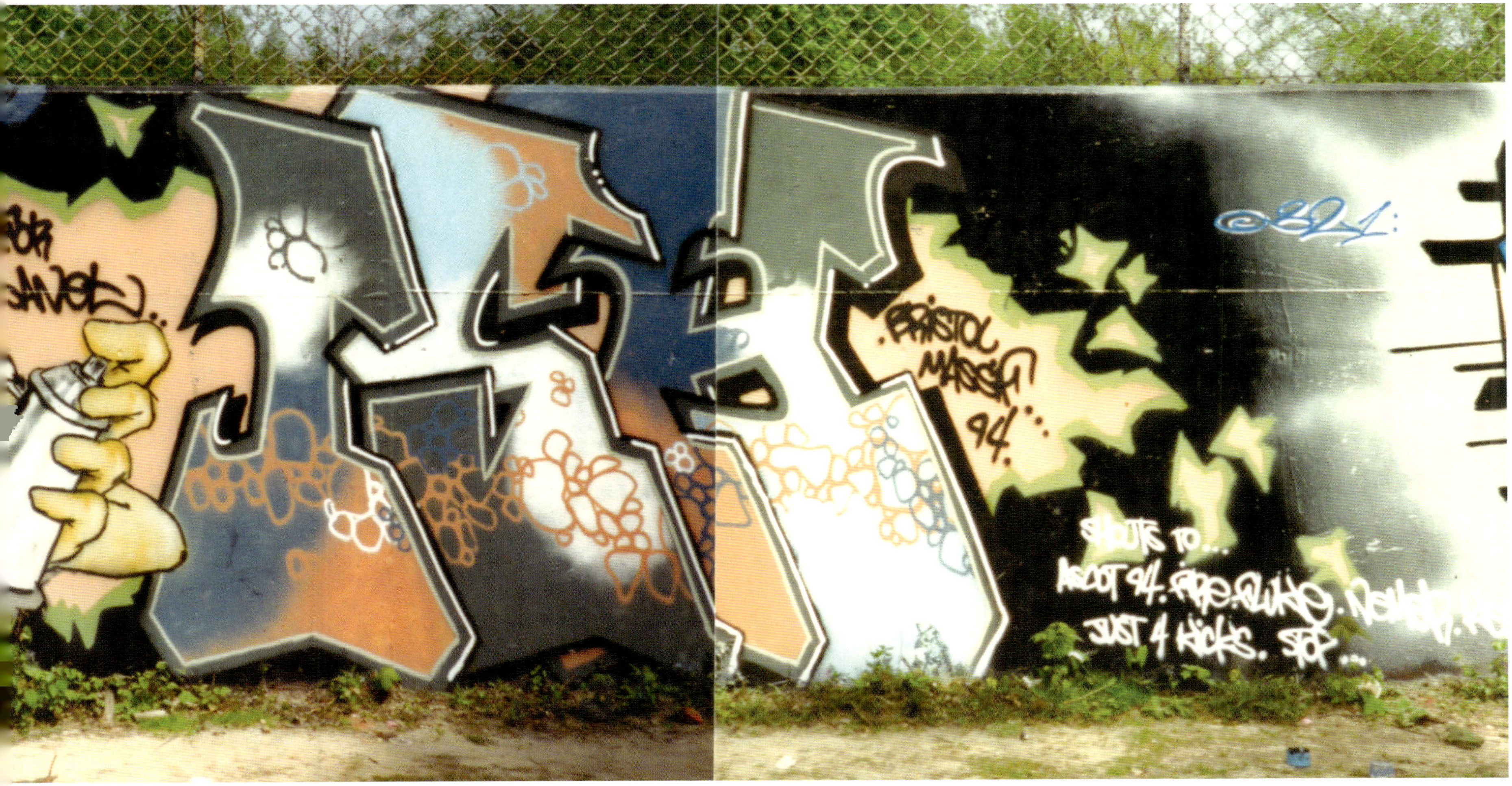

purpose for him. "I always wanted to be a cartoonist when I was a kid, and when I got into graffiti I saw that there was a niche for people who wanted to paint characters. It was Mode 2 who influenced me the most – the structures of the characters he painted and the poses of the figures, particularly the faces and hands. Also Doze's B-boy characters on the covers of the Rocksteady Crew records: the fat trainers, the way they were stood. I still dabble with that style now. It's about the stance of a particular leg, or the flare of the jeans.

"Vaughn Bode, of course, he's always been a part of it. Seeing his comics and making the connection with *Subway Art* was a big thing, realising where Dondi got his stuff from. I was also heavily into Simon Bisley's ABC Warriors stuff in [seminal British sci-fi comic] *2000 AD*. [Fantasy artist] Rodney Matthews was a big influence as well. It's the way he colours his work, he has a kind of graff-type, graphic look to his stuff. It's really about structuring the shapes and the composition of the characters."

Supportive parents encouraged the not-so-academic Kato to take every opportunity to develop his art skills. That led to a chance meeting with younger, like-minded writers who went on to become crew-mates and lifelong friends. "I've got nothing upstairs, but I could always draw and paint, so my mum sent me to the after-school art classes. Soker and Lokey were both there, sat at the back, with five or six other writers from around our way, which was a little intimidating; but eventually the black books came out and that was that."

Above: 'Junkish' painted at the Ascot '94 Jam. Letters and characters by Kato

Above: Classic Kato cartoon stylings. Leicester Return Of The Macks jam, 1996

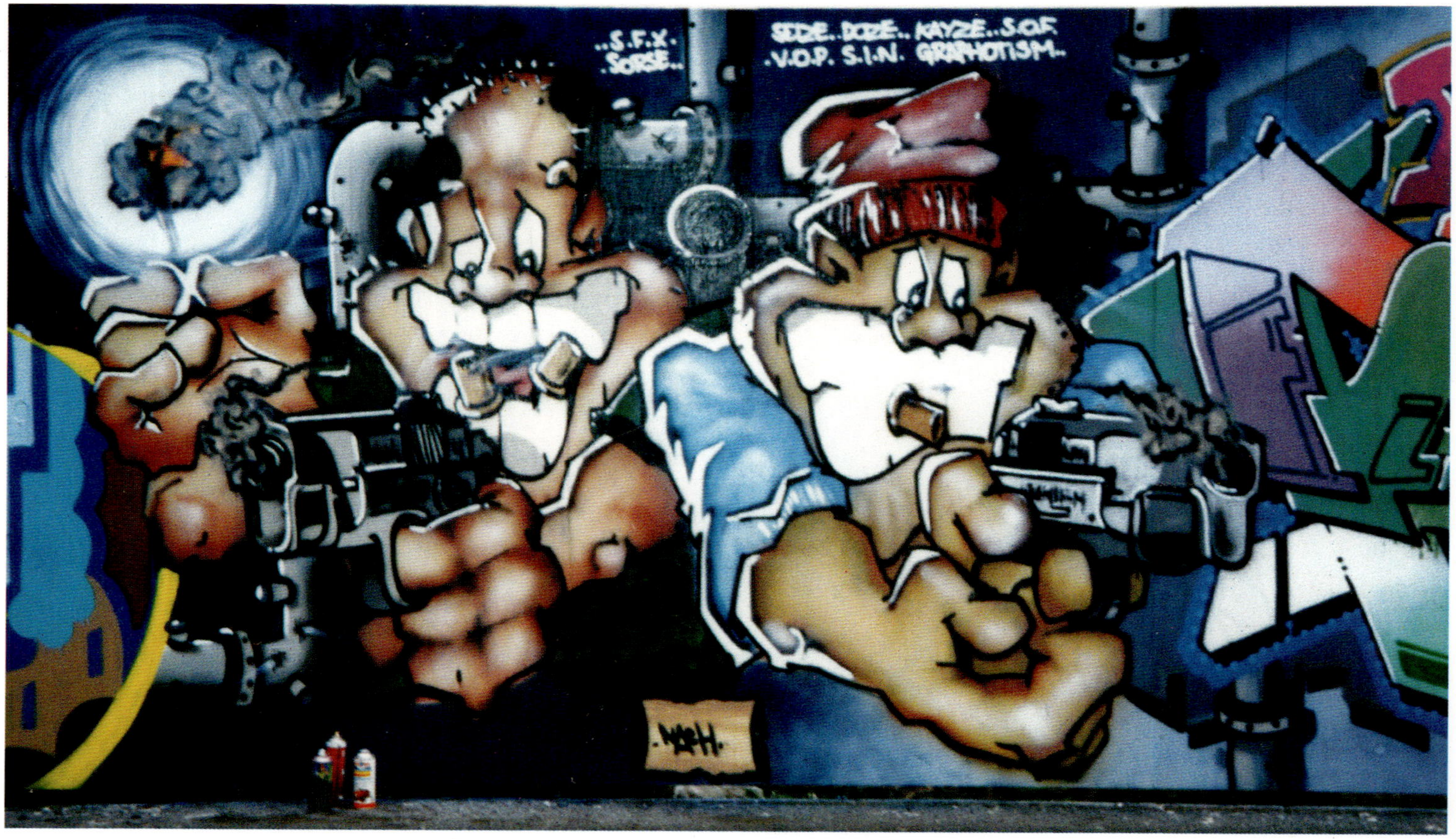

For kids discovering graffiti, its appeal has two very different, yet complementary aspects. Learning to paint with a spray can is all well and good, but going out at night bombing has always been where the adrenaline comes from. Kato discovered the latter in a big way in 1989, just before Operation Anderson kicked off.

"I got put in TUB by Era, but I was literally in the crew for about two weeks before everyone got busted. After that, a lot of people died off and some carried on. TUB basically became ESR (East Side Rebels) and everybody had new tags. Everything changed and became secret again. A lot of time was spent bombing with ESR, mainly on the 40 and 45 bus routes. There would be tagging with markers and Poscas (paint pens) on the windows, scratching on them with stones to engrave tags. Everyone would get on and off the buses with a Day Rider ticket, tagging everywhere. It was proper graffiti writing – nobody gave a monkey's, they'd do whatever they had to do to get that tag up, with or without passengers on the bus."

Operation Anderson was intended to stop the plague of bombing in Bristol in its tracks, and for many writers it worked. For the hardcore few, however, it was a minor glitch in a relentless wave that continued to spread across the city and beyond. "We'd get on the trains down to Weston-super-Mare or Avonmouth, and then go and find walls along the tracks. Barton Hill was like a central point and the train lines ran near there. We were just like any teenagers hanging around on the streets, except we were carrying markers and spray paints. We'd hit anything, whatever we fancied. The more neck you had on you, the less you cared who was watching you or whatever the other risks might be. Each member of the crew wanted to get up more than the next man, each one wanted to get up higher, and bigger. There was healthy competition within the crew, as well as with other crews."

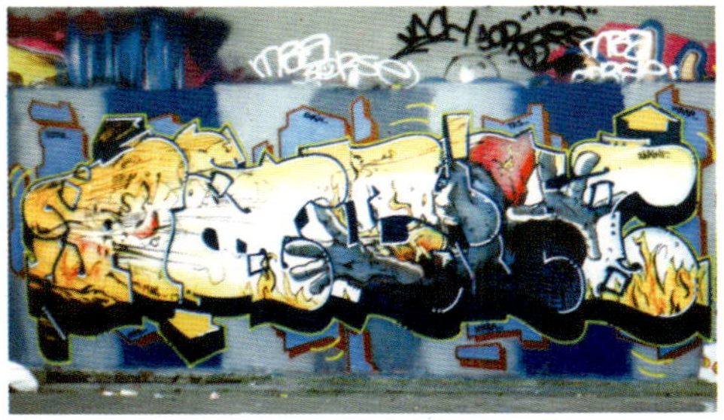

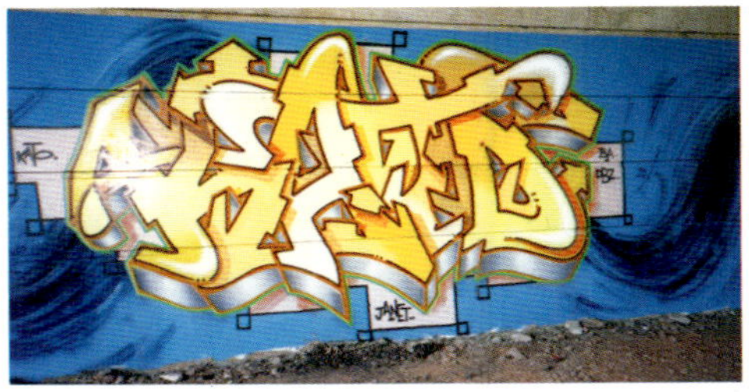

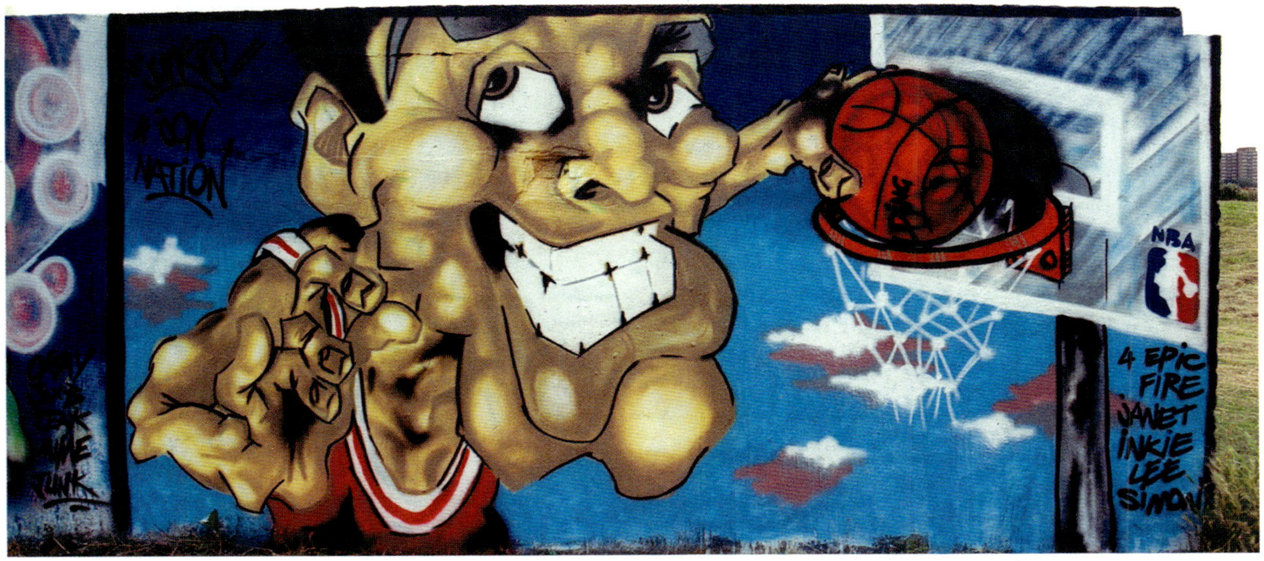

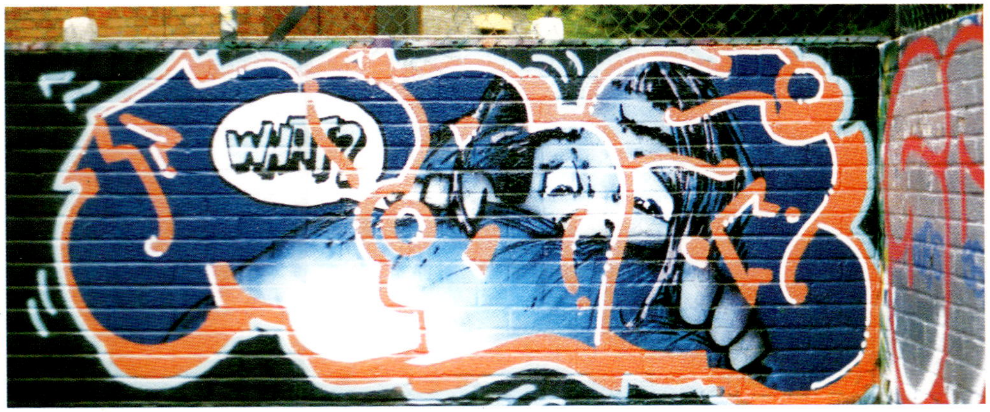

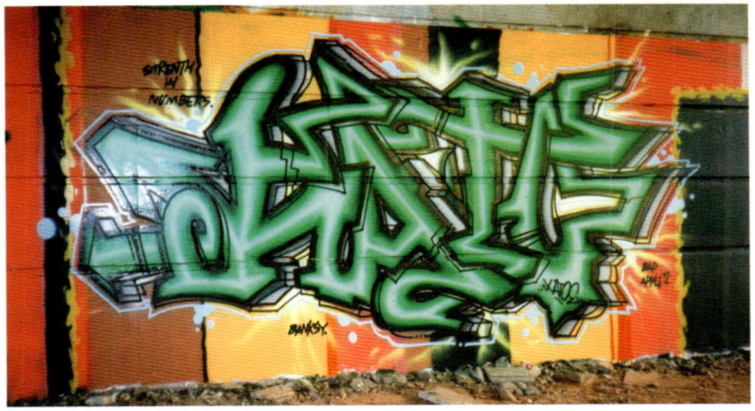

Criminal activities also included stealing paint – and the most sought-after at the time was the German paint brand Buntlack, which cost an astronomical £7.00 per can (plus VAT) and was only available from one shop in the whole of Bristol.

"We got caught nicking paint in Euro Graphics, all wearing Kangol hats, checkered shirts, baggy jeans and fat-laced trainers, and thinking we didn't look suspicious! I got locked in the office with the manager. He was fed up with all the graffiti writers nicking the Buntlack. I know of one writer who used to get in there through the roof, by pulling the glass slats out of the skylights."

In the early 90s, Barton Hill Youth Club continued to be a meeting place for Bristol graffiti writers. Increasingly, it also attracted people from around the country and abroad, visiting to paint, swap photos and on occasion impart DIY trade secrets.

"To mix two colours of spray paint, you'd either freeze a can or you'd boil one up, then you'd stick two WD-40 nozzles together with a load of glue and blast paint through the straw from one can into another. I learned all that shit. The easiest way to do it, though, was with the tube from a Bic biro with a couple of slits in, joining the two cans. Juice and Krise from Selly Oak showed us how to do that.

"We met a lot of writers from all over, including Kilo, Fuse, Boyd, Remer, Part.2, System, Chu, Get from Amsterdam; they were all visiting Bristol regularly and

This page: Characters inside letters, off-set outlines and boldly sculpted faces are all typical of Kato's experimental and fun-loving approach

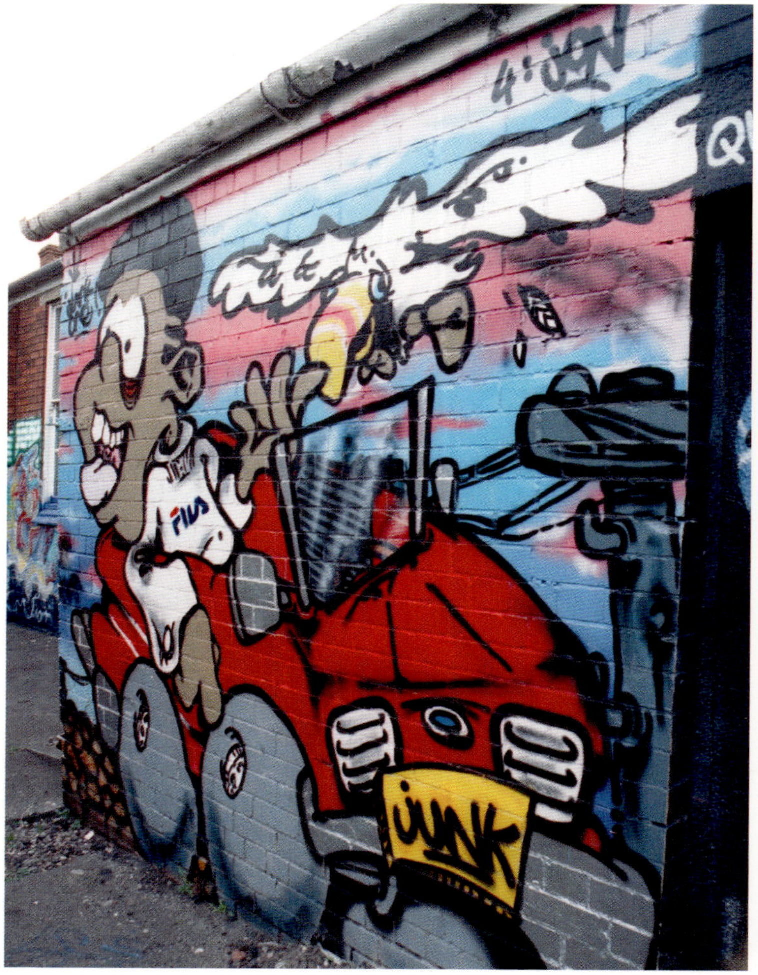
FILA
JUNK

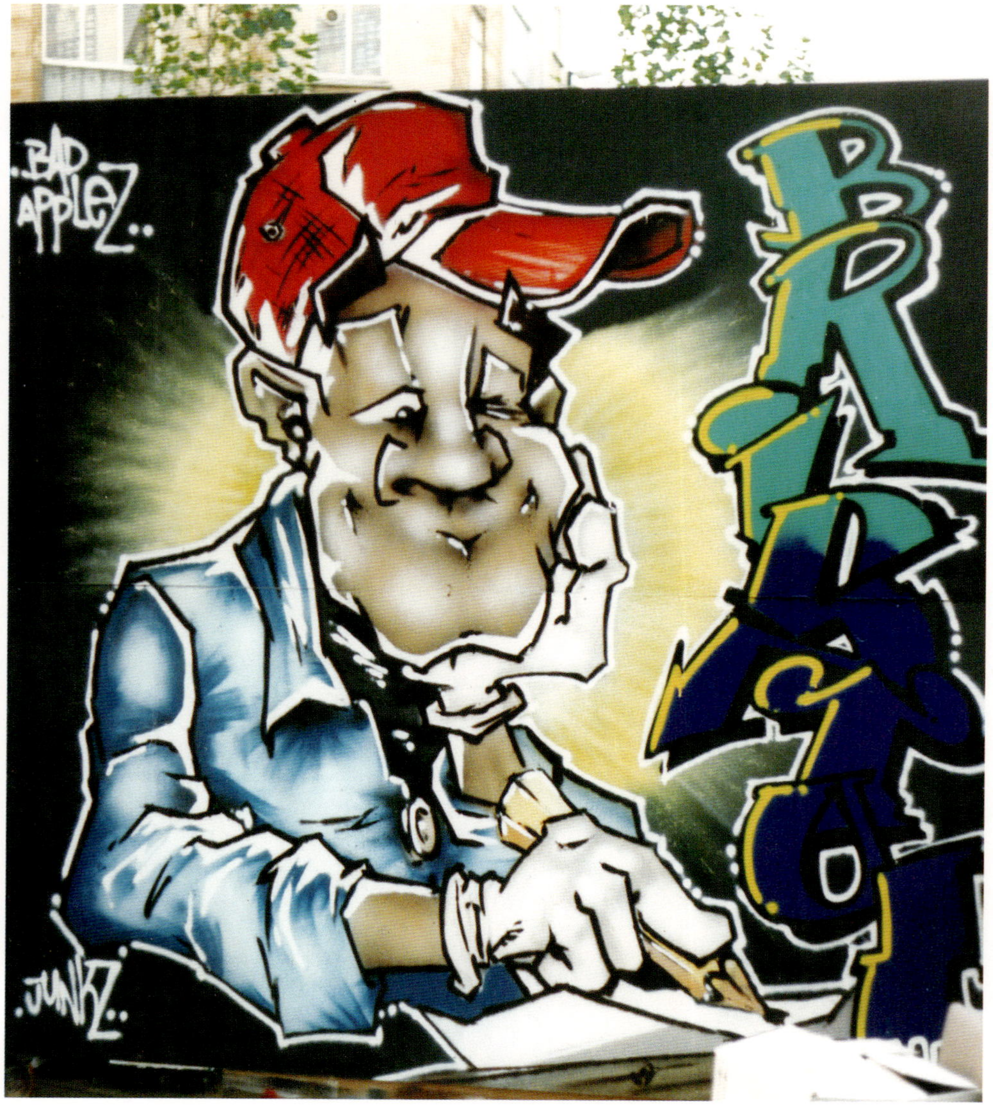
..BAD
APPLEZ..
.JUNKZ..

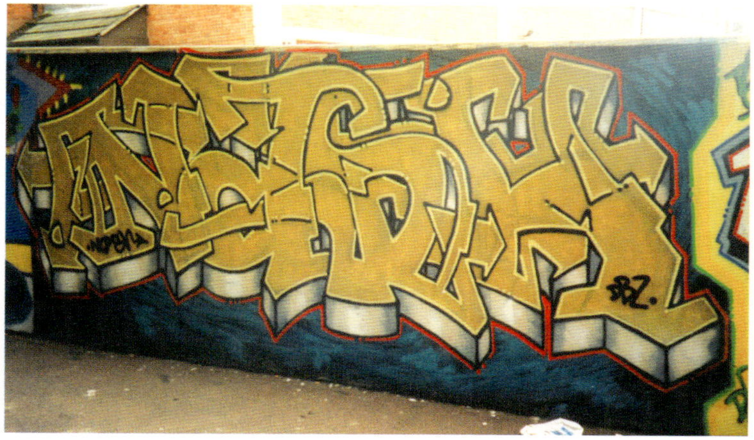

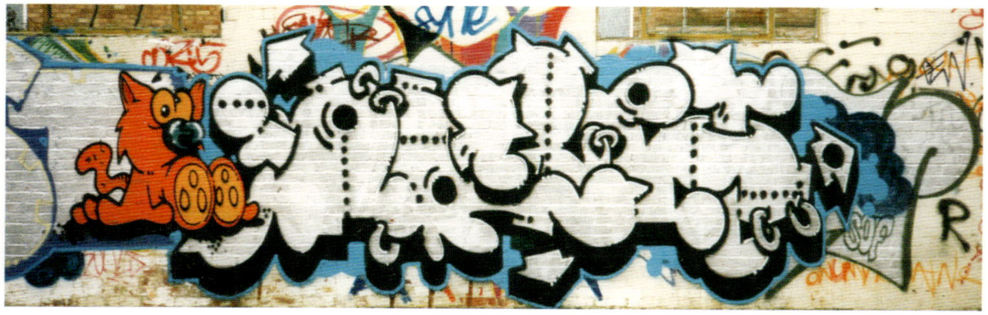

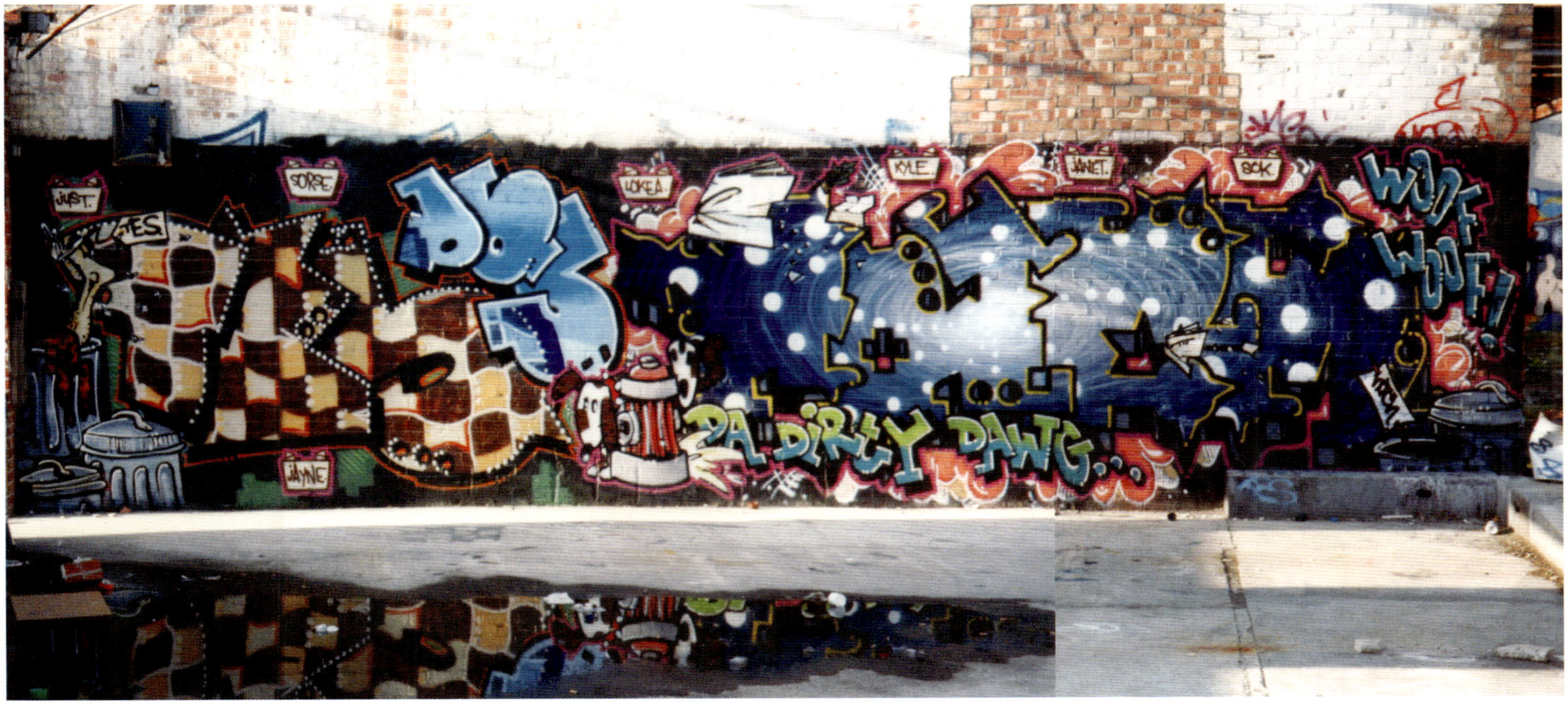

coming to Barton Hill. And, being a youth club, we were there pretty much every night. You had the hard core of seven or eight of us who would just go and sit in the office, looking at the photos John had been sent that day."

It was at Barton Hill that Kato, like so many others, was given a chance to hone his skills. Thanks to the flood of media interest after Operation Anderson, he was soon being offered opportunities to paint professionally. "That's when John started to get us commissions and stuff. I was writing Junk at the time, doing characters alongside the letter writers, and that was when I first met Inkie."

After a nerve-wracking appearance painting live on Granada TV's *This Morning* programme in 1990 alongside Inkie and Cheo, and a second on children's programme *Motor Mouth* (painting behind 9-year old Bristolian scratch DJ Kev.E Kev and that year's DMC World Mixing Champion DJ Wreckless), Kato readily accepted his third invitation to paint on TV. This time, he took his old school collaborator Soker.

"I did a programme called *Wolf It*, with Soker. We got put up in a hotel, and instead of going out for a drink we thought we'd save our money and hang out at the hotel. We watched a badly dubbed kung fu movie and found the mini-bars in our rooms and drank the lot because we thought it was free. When we came back from doing the programme the next day the mini-bar had been filled up again, so we emptied it into our bags, only to have to give it all back at reception when they said the TV company were only paying for the rooms and that the drinks weren't free. Well embarrassing. We came back with no money, glum faces, and half tins of Car Plan paint."

Mini-bar disasters aside, Kato was beginning to get a taste for where graffiti (or, perhaps more specifically, his own characters) could take him. Disheartened with the quietness of the scene in Bristol, he moved to Bournemouth to study animation, where he met Brighton writer Fyre. "Fyre had been a pen pal back in the day - we used to exchange photos and outlines - but we'd lost touch. He introduced me to the Brighton scene, and soon I was going down there and painting.

Opposite page. Top left: Character in the fashion of the time: Fila roll neck and a flat-top with tram-lines, Barton Hill, c.1989

Top right: Distinctive 'second light' white highlight pushes this 1996 character off the wall and into your face

Bottom left: 'Nash' piece on the wall behind the Millionaire's Club, Easton, '96

Bottom right: 'Nach' piece, all bubbles, spikes and piercings: as much knockabout cartoon as it is graffiti, 1995

Above: Tes and Nach 'Da Dirty Dawg' Brislington warehouse, 1995

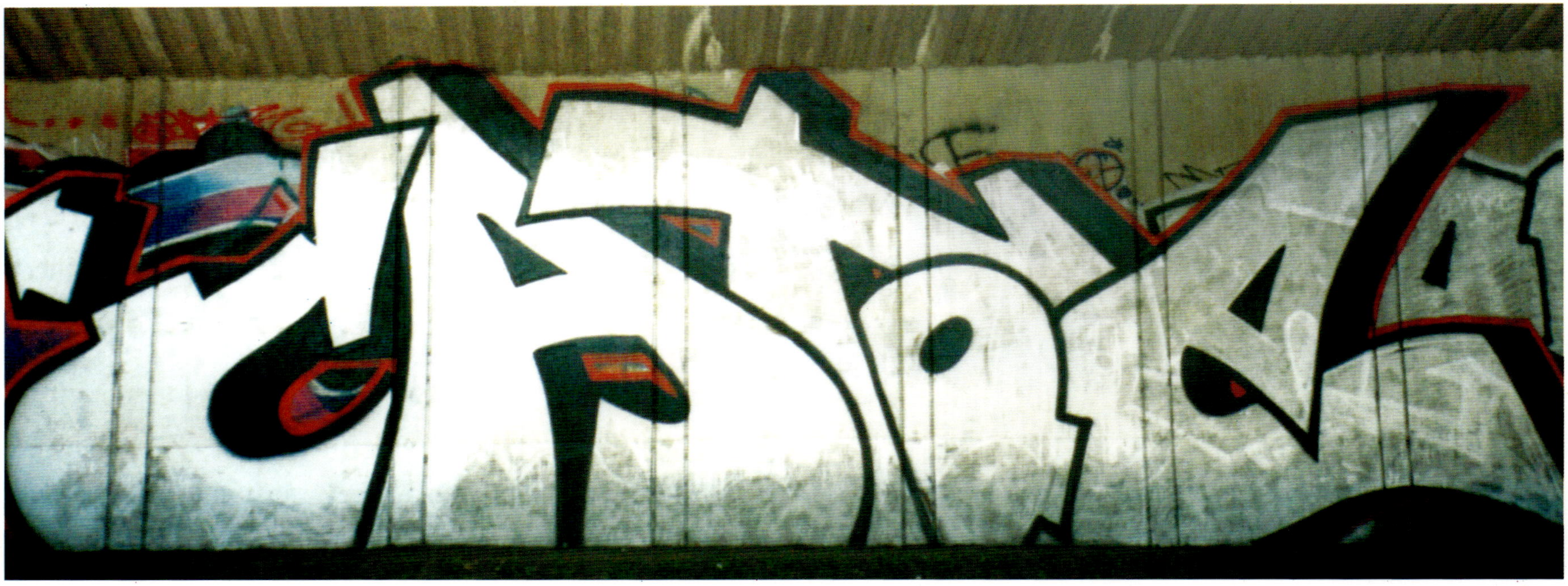

Above: Top-to-bottom, M32 hall of fame, 2001

Right: 'Nach...to the west!' Bedminster skate park, 1996

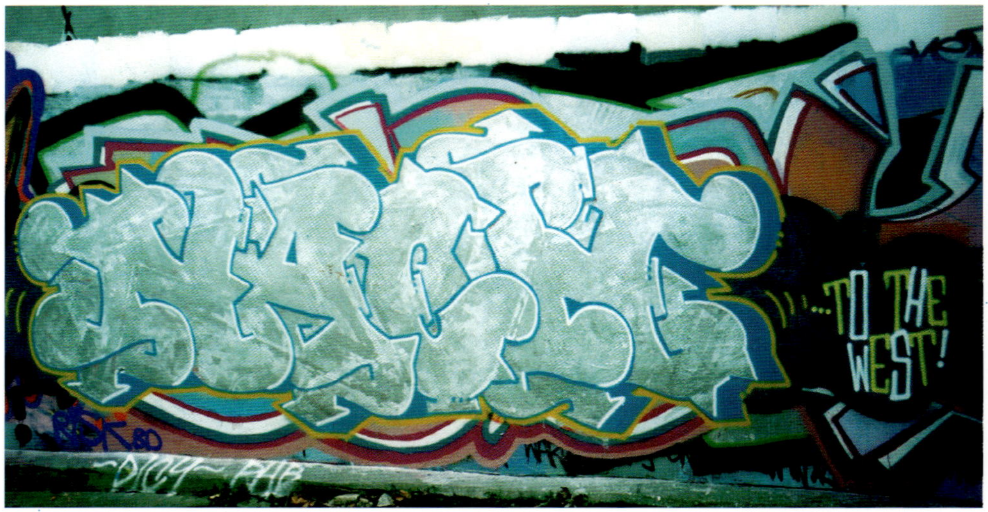

When I came back to Bristol I'd hook up with Soker again and do some proper painting, and sometimes Fyre would come with me. We started going back up to Barton Hill, and Tes popped up – doing some block letters, going over people's pieces and stuff – and Lokey, who we'd been at school with. That's when we started Bad Applez, and started making all kinds of connections and going places with graf.

"When I came back from college the Bristol scene was pretty much dead, and we seemed to be the only people who had a passion for painting spots that had been established years before, like Bedminster Skate Park. We also started painting Champion Park, Brislington warehouse, and under the Esso garage on the Bath Road, and these all became recognised halls of fame. We were also going down to Brighton and painting with Fyre, and going to jams around the country and meeting other writers. We used to go and paint the halls of fame in London, Ascot, Brighton and Reading, because Tes had a van. We were building up a name for ourselves as a crew – usually for being disorganised and casual, but we would always rock it anyway."

Once established under the new moniker of Dry Breadz – a reference to the fact that none of them ever had any money – the crew kept growing. Former TUB and ESR collaborator Sorse (previously Sloe) was next to join, followed by Bath writer Juster

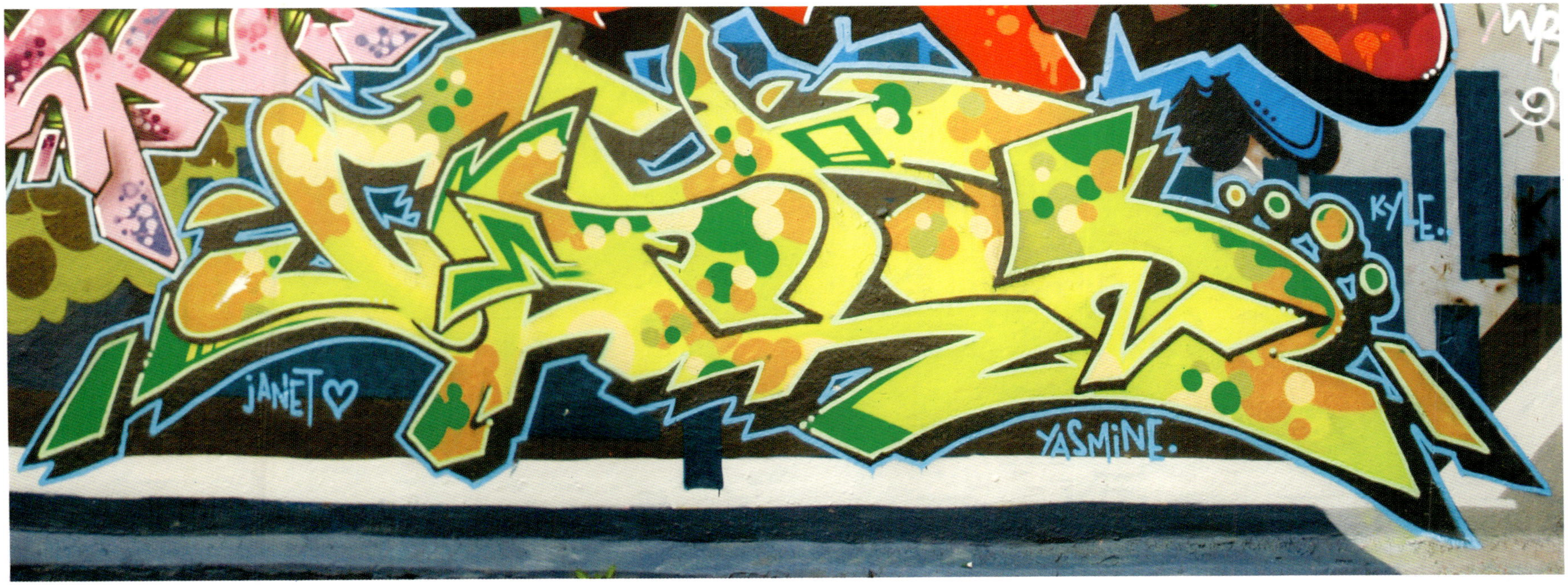

Above: Camouflage burner, Bedminster skate park, 2006

– and lastly, a young writer who called himself Banksy.

"Banksy didn't come in until about '97. He just turned up when we were painting behind the Millionaire's Club in Easton, and said he was into graf and wanted to paint with us. He was already doing stencils by then. He had a knack for putting them in the right places, and they always had just the right content. He invited us to do workshops and stuff, and he always seemed to be able to blag good spots. He sorted out for us to do Glastonbury Festival a few times as well... good times."

The following year DBZ painted at the Walls On Fire graffiti jam on Bristol's harbourside, which Banksy and Inkie organised. It was the biggest event of its kind that the city had ever seen, and the crew painted at full strength. Kato remembers it fondly. "A lot of people were happy, it was a really good vibe. It was the first really big event in Bristol, and it introduced a lot of the public to graffiti on a large scale for the first time.

"We used to go to a lot of jams in London – like Unity, for example – and often there wasn't enough wall space for us, so to have this jam in Bristol that Banksy had organised was nice. He let us have all the space we wanted. The full crew turned out and it all gelled really well. I think it shows in what we painted. It was good to see a lot of writers come to Bristol and shake our hands and say 'hello' again."

A crew writer who has mellowed with age, Kato is an old school Bristolian who paints, nowadays, simply for the pleasure of it. He is genuinely surprised and flattered when younger writers remember his work, and remains philosophical about his experiences and the way graffiti has changed over the years.

"It's all about feelings between friends, mates getting together, and having mutual respect. It's not about, 'I've been doing it longer than you, I'm better than you.' It's nothing to do with that for me, it's just about people appreciating each other's work. Let's talk and get on with one another. It doesn't have to be secretive and competitive. With a job and two lovely kids, I've got nothing to prove, I'm just into painting and I'm happy to paint with you. Graffiti's very important to some people but it's taken too seriously.

"People say to me 'yeah man, I remember your stuff!' And to get that 15 years later, it's like somebody somewhere has taken that in – and, just as we were inspired by the previous generation of writers, they've been inspired by us. And that's when I'm like, 'wow! Thanks man.' To be an inspiration to someone is a good feeling."

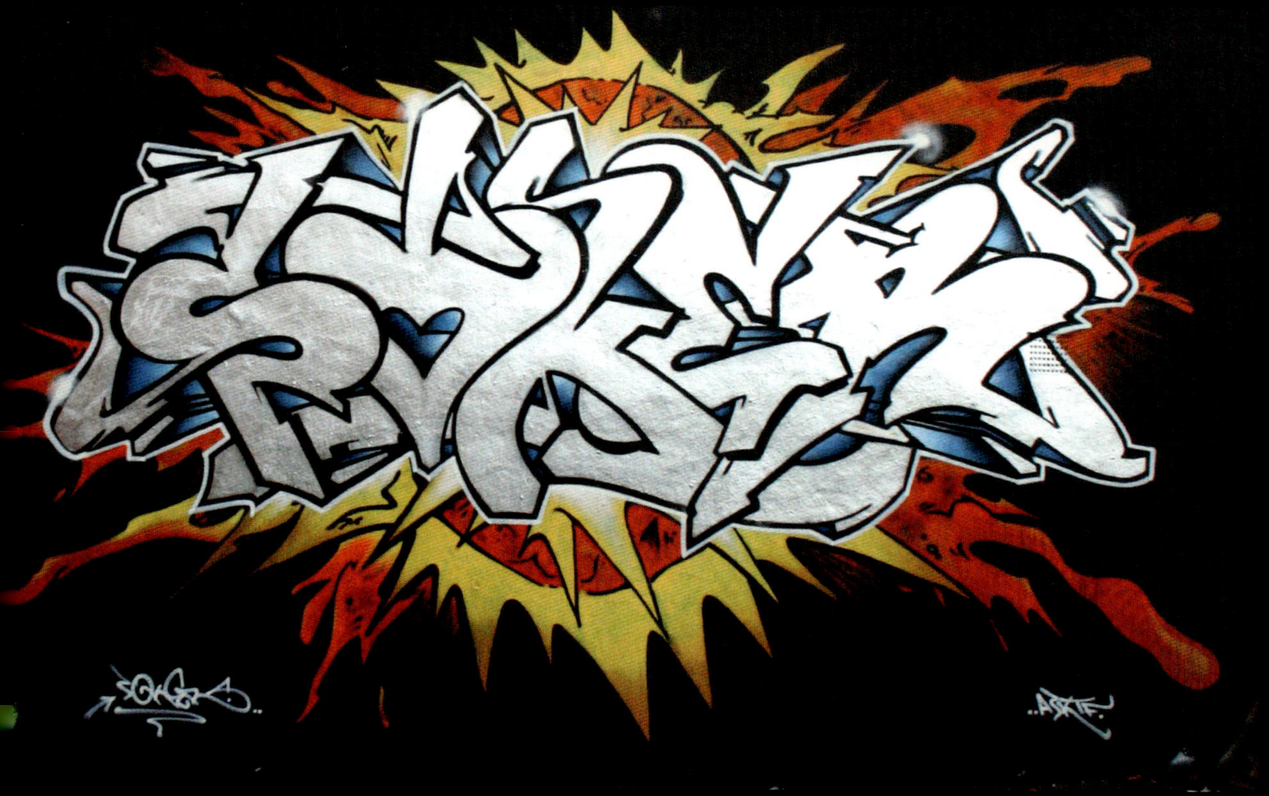

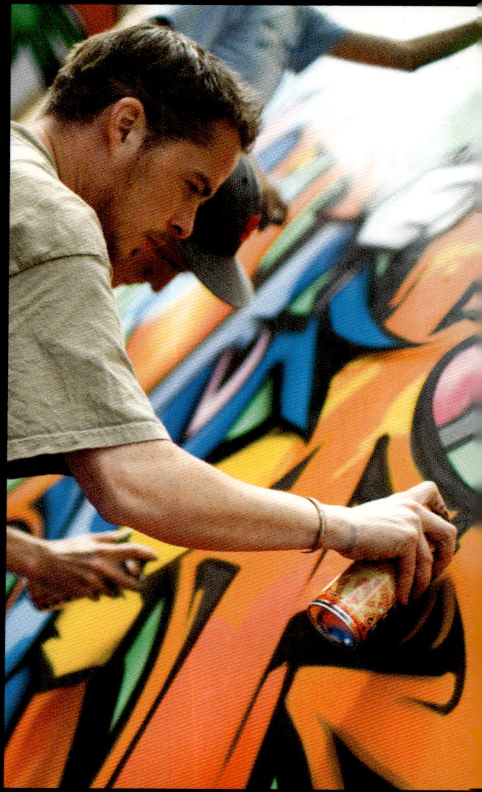

Above: Soker super nova, Bedminster skate park, 2007

Above right: Soker in deep concentration at the Glostonbury street party, Gloucester Road, 2008

Opposite: Straight to the point chrome dubs, 1995

Page 120: Ren and Stimpy get the wildstyle treatment from Soker and Kato, B'mouth 94

Middle left: Working the colours on a chunky, 1995

Bottom left: Two for the price of one, double Verse burner, 1998

SOKER JFK/JKC/MBA/BA/DBZ/SIN/DP/ASK

• **Perpetually rocking back and fourth, stretching and twisting, seemingly caught mid-flow, Soker's pieces come close to the essence of how a truly funky piece should look.** Like a still frame from Zephyr's animated sequence at the start of *Wild Style*, his symmetrical stylings tap into the intricate science of making letters appear to move whilst standing still – a Bristolian take on the New York bounce.

"Wildstyle pieces for me were always what it was all about. I got into graffiti for the Wildstyle letters and B-boy characters – the classic graff. It's what I've always been into and probably always will be. If you look back at my outlines from school you can see in there some of what I'm still doing now. I've never changed what I do that drastically. I like balancing a piece; I like letters to fit, to lock, to all come together."

Soker's approach to painting has been with him since he first picked up a can in the mid 80s, and since coming out of retirement a few years back he has found a renewed hunger for his craft. Bold and confident in their juxtaposition of colours and forms, his pieces are like an advertisement for the advances made in aerosol technology.

"When I saw *Style Wars* and got to look at *Subway Art*, it influenced me so much that it stuck with me – and it's where my heart is to this day. Classic pure style is what I love more than anything else; and although I've tried doing other things, like portraits and canvases for exhibitions, this is more natural to me than any other form of art. I know what I can do best and that's what I'm sticking to."

Soker – like a number of other prominent older Bristol graffiti writers – is currently in the ascendant for the second time in his career. He was introduced to graffiti at the age of 11 and grew up painting with schoolfriends Kato and Lokey, who together went on to form the nucleus of the crews BA, (Bad Applez) and DBZ (Dry Breadz). The latter hit their stride in the mid-Nineties, gaining national recognition through their appearances in Kilo's groundbreaking Visual Grafix videos and the seminal British graffiti magazine *Graphotism*, and were inducted to the country-wide hip hop collective SIN (Strength In Numbers).

Like most writers, Soker found graffiti becoming an intrinsic part of his personality, the manifestation of his more confident, expressive side; but when the crew found themselves drifting apart in the late Nineties, the writer in him went to sleep. Back now for the second time, he is hungrier and sharper than ever before.

"When I started going out painting again, I'd just come out of a long-term relationship. I was bored, and I was missing graf. I was missing being a writer. That was a big thing for me; I felt like I'd lost my identity a bit, I'd just blended into the background. I think the most frightening thing – and it's probably the same for any writer – is being forgotten about. When you've had your day and then it's gone, that's not a nice feeling for anyone. So it was about getting back out there, getting a little bit of that feeling back, that rush, that you used to get back in the day. The challenge comes back, and you can't just step back into it and be bad as fuck. You've got to work at it, you've got to make it happen. The thing is to stay there and keep plugging away. Each piece you do, you want the next one to be better. For me it's like you're pushing yourself again – it brings that focus back into your life."

Soker works constantly to hone the way his chosen letters work together. This is why, for letter writers, the relationship between painting pieces and the letters in your tag is so close. The sculpting and manipulating of the individual elements into a cohesive, flowing whole is at the core

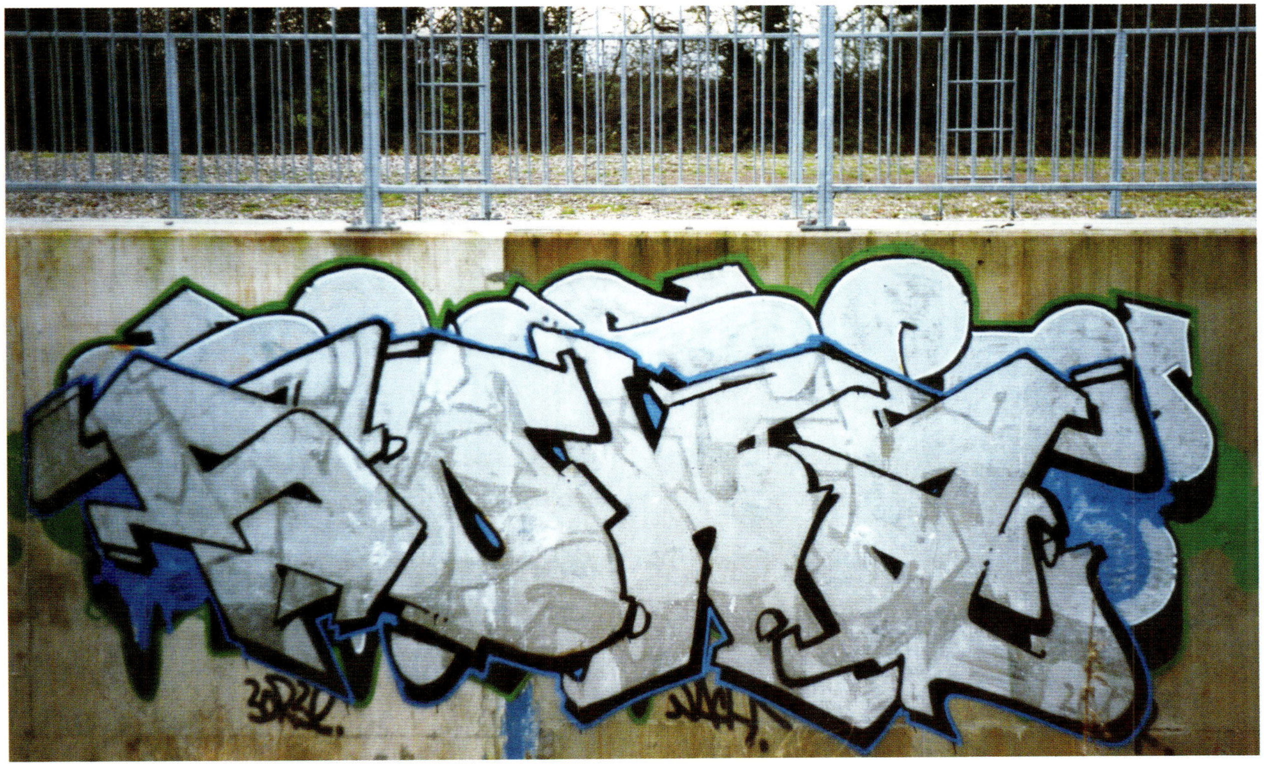

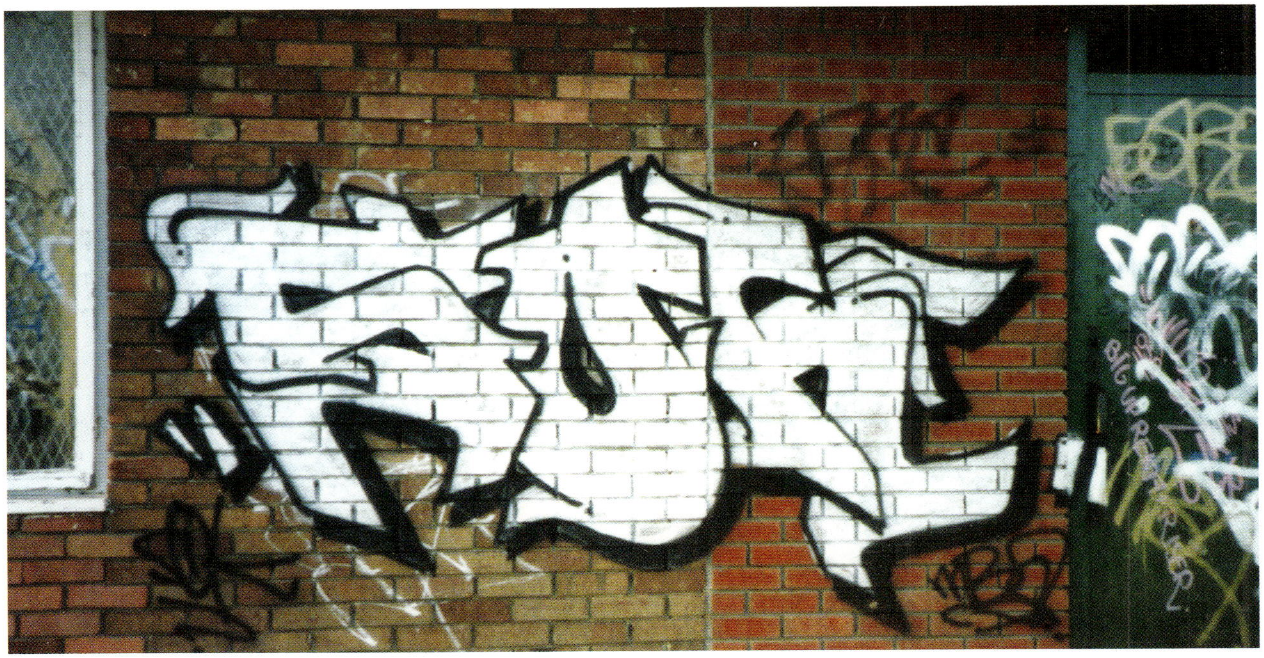

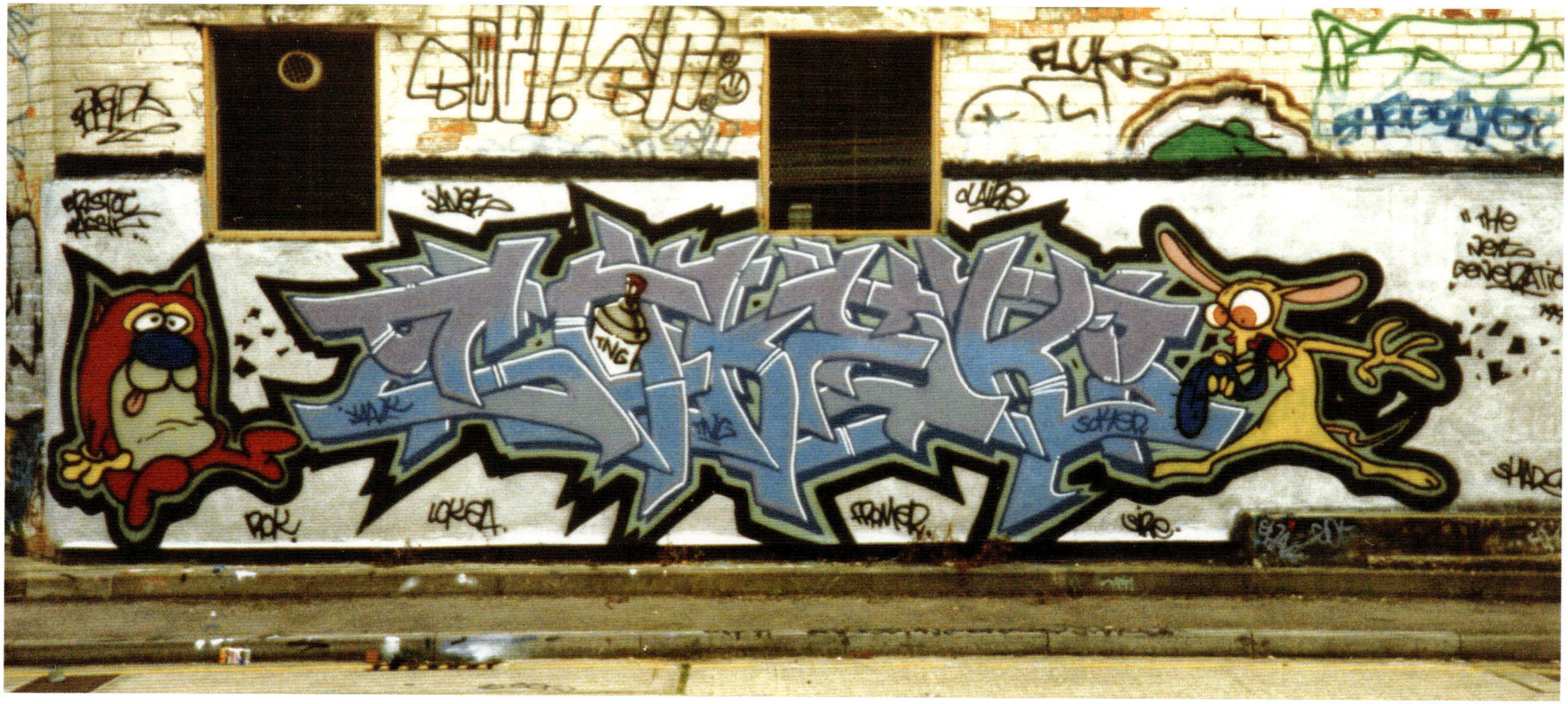

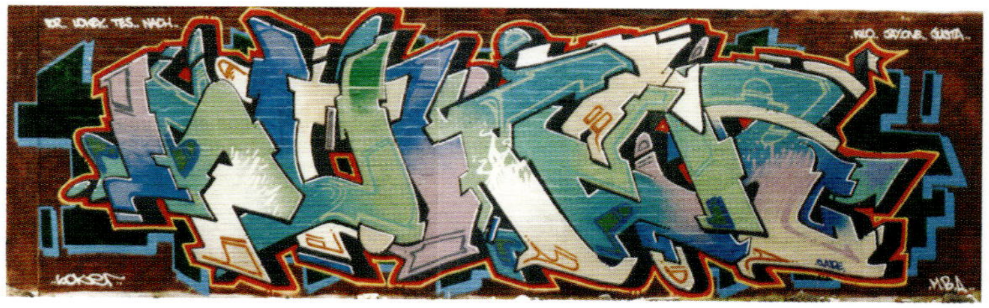

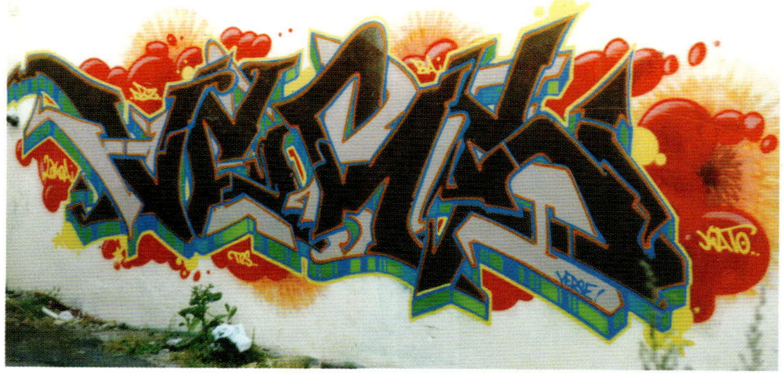

of what they do. The letters in a writer's tag are the skeleton that lies beneath every piece they paint. The way each letter joins the next is what gives form to their style. Finding a tag that feels right, that you can re-work into countless variations, is essential. Some writers stick with their first tag for life, others, like Soker, take their time finding the right one.

"For the first two years I probably changed my tag every couple of weeks, I had fucking loads, but then I was round my mate Tame's house one day – and at that time there were loads of pairs of writers with matching names – and he came up with Rok, so I started writing Sok, which came from the *Rockem Sockem* boxing robots game. I liked it because I could write it and link the letters all in one go, and I could write it so fast. Then after a while three letters just wasn't substantial enough to paint, so I extended it into Soker, and once I'd got used to it I liked the sound of it, and I liked the shapes of the letters."

The template thus created, Soker set his sights on both perfecting his style for his own satisfaction, and – perhaps more importantly – on that original, old-school goal of 'burning the competition.' The drive to attain recognition, and the admiration of those he in turn respects, is still a major part of what qualifies his creative flow.

"I've been sketching and painting for going on 20 years now, and every time you do a piece you want it to be better. I look at people like [Danish graffiti writer] Swet,

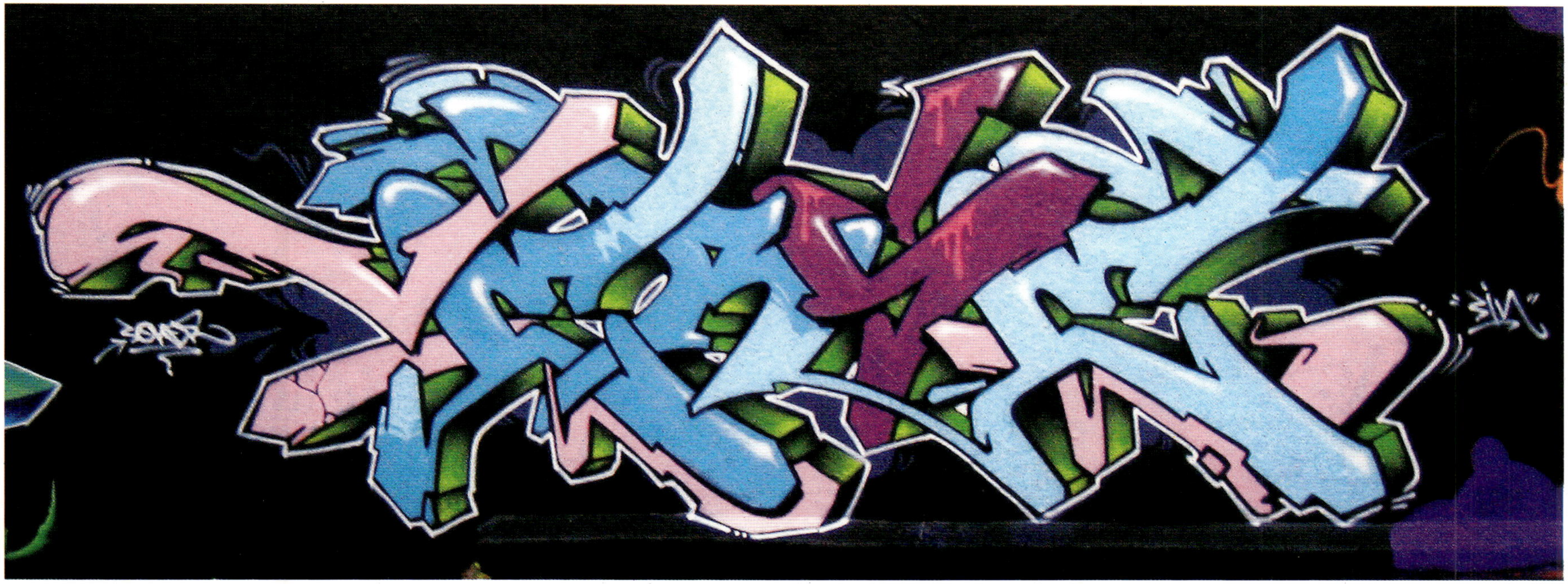

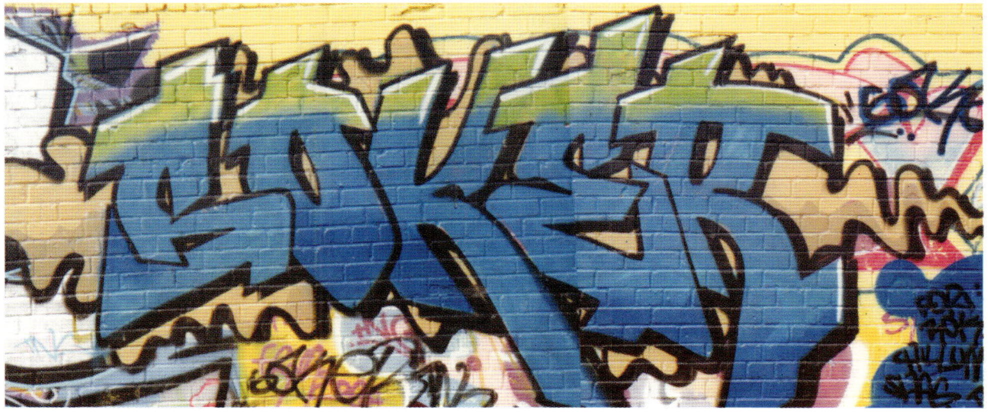

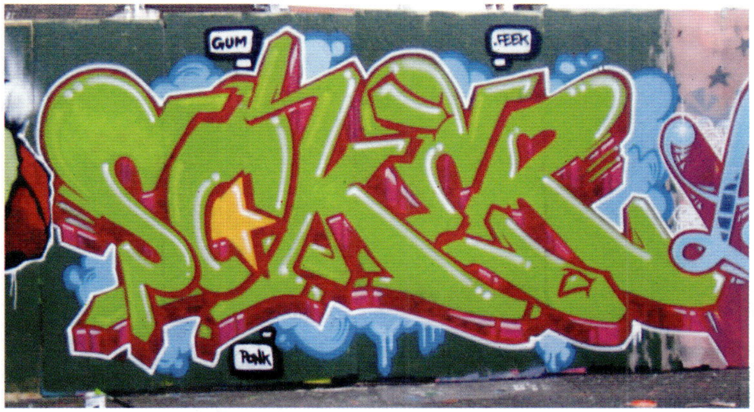

Top: Bringing the Verse alter-ego up-to-date, Bedminster skate park, 2008

Middle left: Early '90s Soker quickie in a classic New York style, 93/94

Middle right: Funky green bouncer from 2006

who are at the top of the pile as far as letter writers go, and for me that's where I used to want to be. But realistically I just want to get my name known again and be back up as a well-known and established writer in this country. I'm not looking to make any real money out of it or anything, for me it's just about getting back on the scene and getting my name back out there. I want to be appreciated and loved!"

The years have given Soker a frankness and sense of self-irony that has found him welcoming the younger generation of Bristol graffiti writers in a non-judgmental way (while, of course, still wanting to out-paint them). Their openness and enthusiasm have in turn refreshed his enjoyment of a scene which, in some bigger cities, can be cliquey to the point of becoming oppressive.

"What I like about it, more now than how it used to be, is that it brings you together with people. It puts you in a situation where you can get on with a lot of people that you wouldn't necessarily get on with in your day-to-day life. Getting back into graf over the last few years has opened a lot of

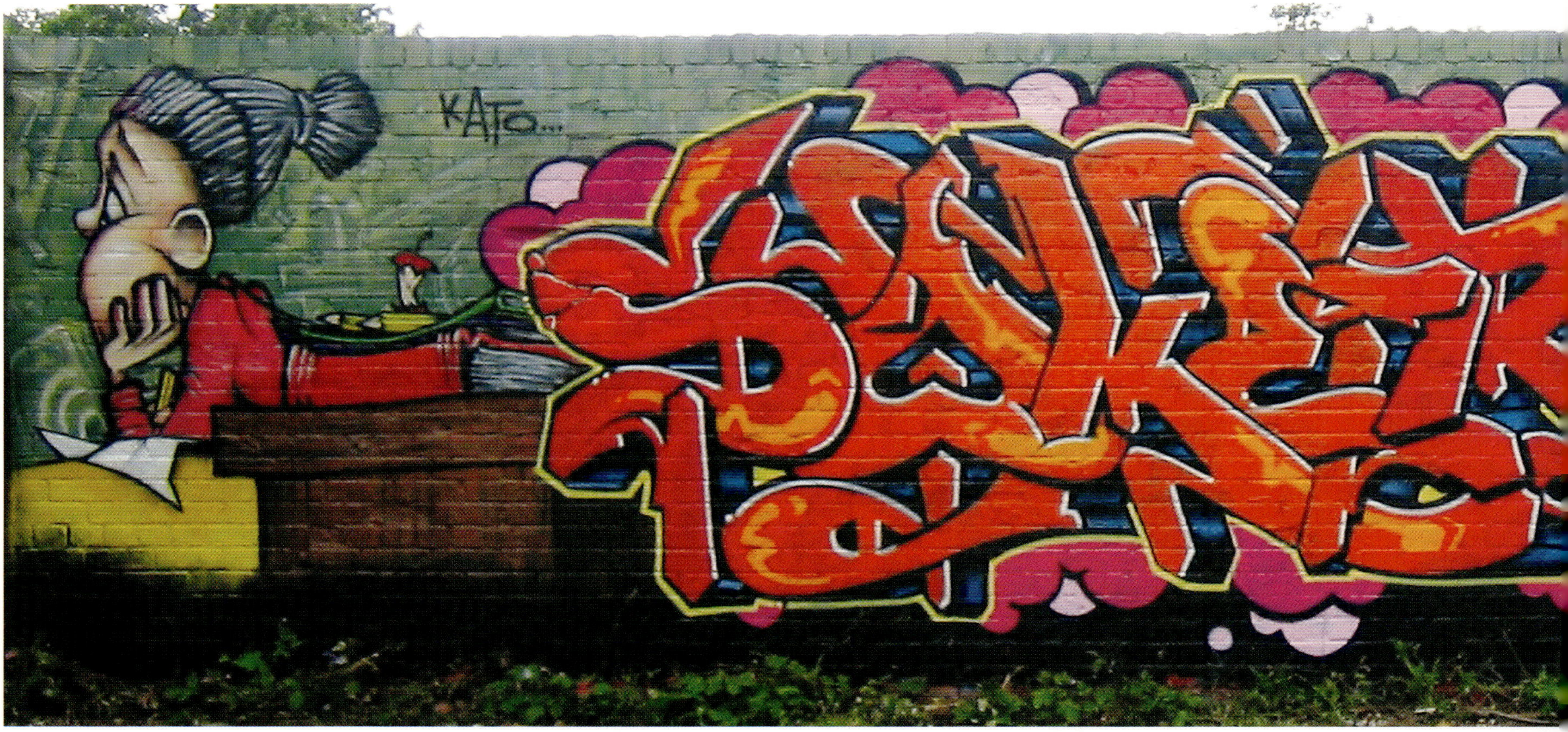

Above: After school style burner with Kato, 2007

Top right: 'Epok' piece by Soker (for Epok KTF) at Riverside Park hall of fame, Bristol, 2008

Middle right: At the old army barracks, 2008

Bottom right: Clever use of white emulsion on a collaboration with Cheo, 2008

doors and given me a lot of opportunities. I've met a lot of people, and I've got a lot more going on in my life."

Soker is perhaps mindful of his own negative experiences as a young writer, struggling to gain acceptance in an already established and hierarchical scene. Ironically, the events of Operation Anderson, which saw many writers retiring prematurely, in fact allowed a second generation of graffiti writers to come through and build their confidence on the walls of the Barton Hill Dug Out.

"It took me a while to get into it because I was in a little group at school and we were never really accepted, because we were younger and people thought we were toys, so it took a while to get any recognition. Going down Barton Hill Youth Club used to scare me to begin with, being a young pup around all these older writers I looked up to. TUB and all those lot were painting down there, they were all 17 or so at the time, and it was quite a frightening prospect. But after Operation Anderson it all went quiet, and a lot of writers dropped off, so we started to go down a bit more. I got to know John Nation, and he'd sort us out a bit of paint here and there."

After the rash of busts in 1989, the challenge was to ride out the wave of negativity that swept across the Bristol graffiti scene. Among those who embraced this challenge, three writers had a huge influence on Soker. Kato, a close and supportive friend, introduced him to Cheo and, perhaps more importantly, Inkie.

"I started in about '88. That's when I did my first outline on paper, and I was at the same school as Kato. One day I saw him coming out of the gym and I asked him to do me some sketches, and we went to the History block and he drew me some characters. Apart from Kato, my two biggest heroes at that time were Cheo and Inkie. Inkie was a massive influence purely because at that time he was different, he was so clever in how his letters worked."

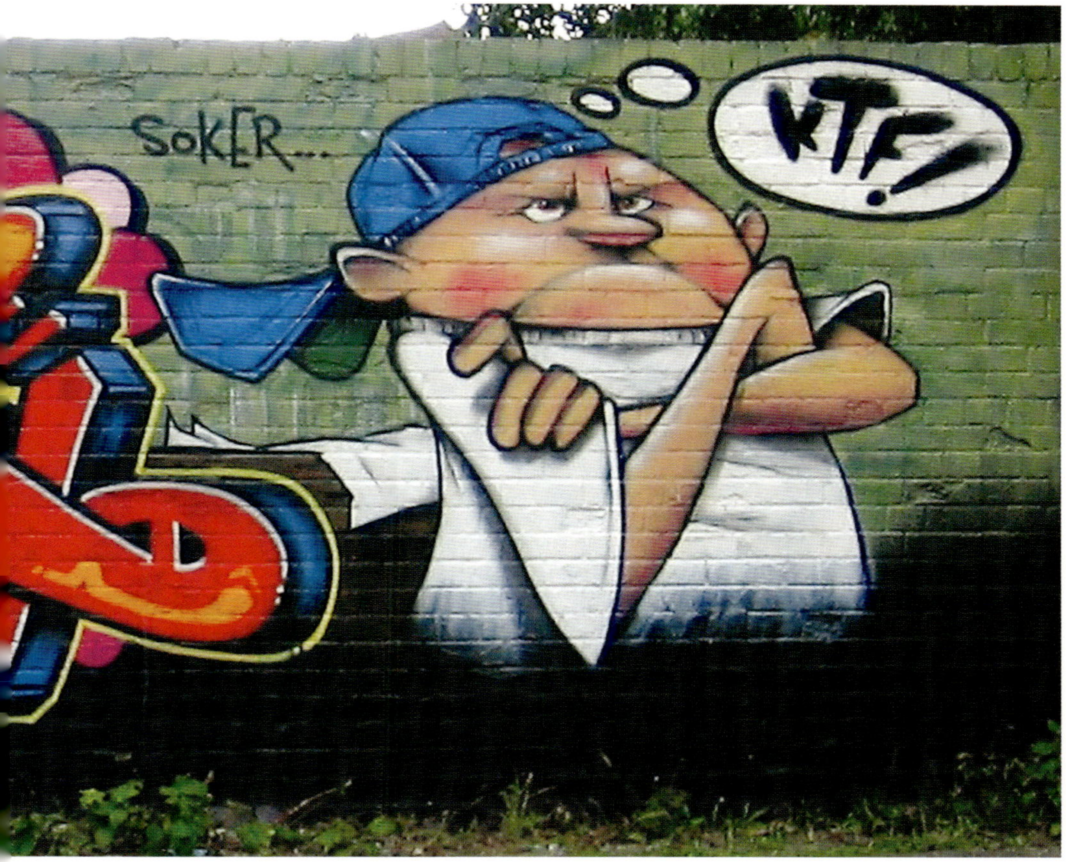

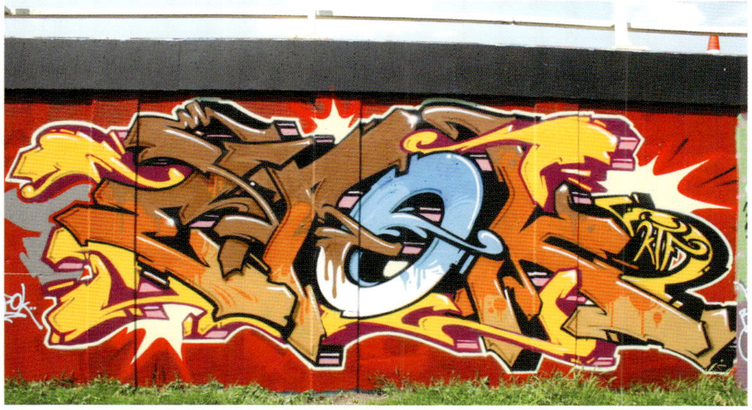

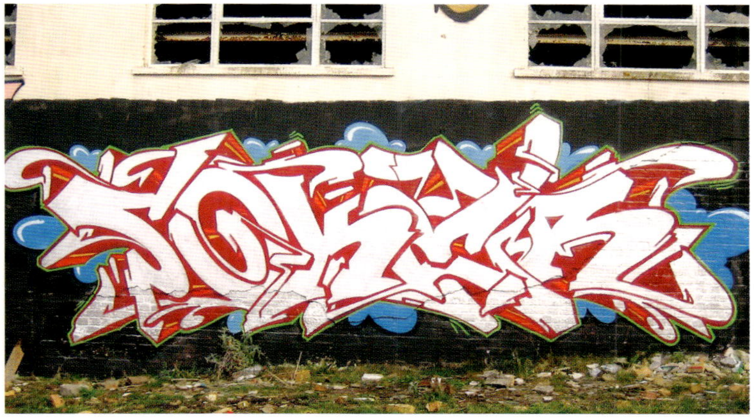

After Operation Anderson and the onset of rave culture, a small nucleus of graffiti fanatics painted harder than ever before to keep alive what was essentially a fading Bristol scene. Alongside ex-TUB stalwarts Tes and Sorse – plus new recruits like Justa and some kid called Banksy – Lokey, Kato and Soker kept the faith and kept the pieces coming under the moniker of DBZ.

"I don't expect anyone to suck us off for what we've done or anything, but at the same time I think we did play quite a big part in the Bristol graf scene. At one point it almost died on its arse, and we played a big part in picking it up again and bringing it back."

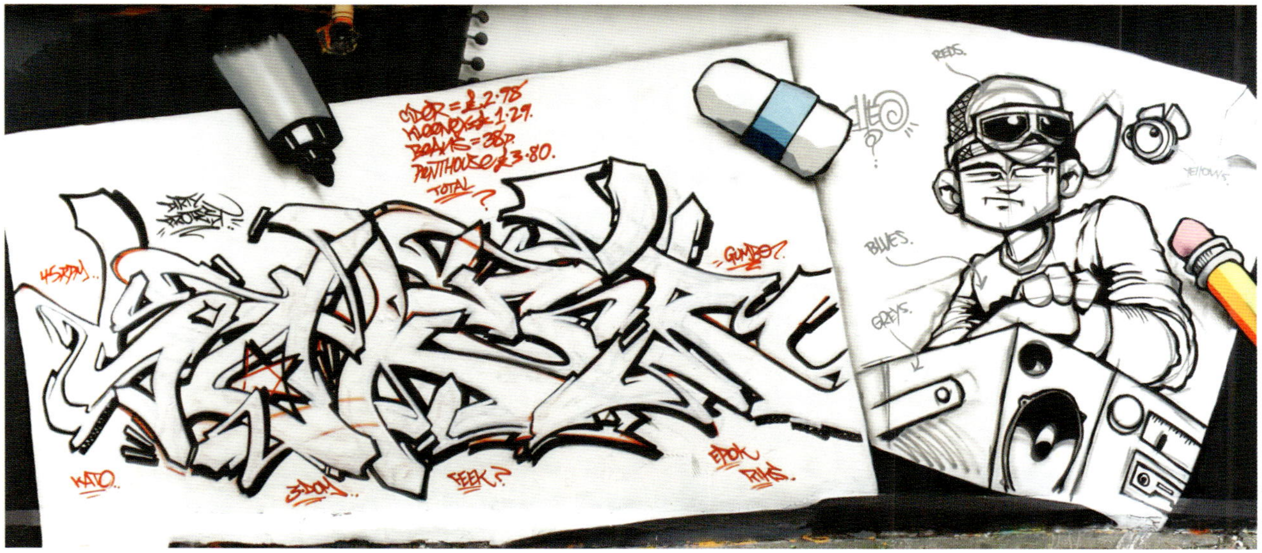

Right: Blue and pink never go out of fashion, 2008

Middle left: Mark up for main pic piece

Bottom: 'Verse' piece with Feek at Riverside Park hall of fame, Bristol, 2008

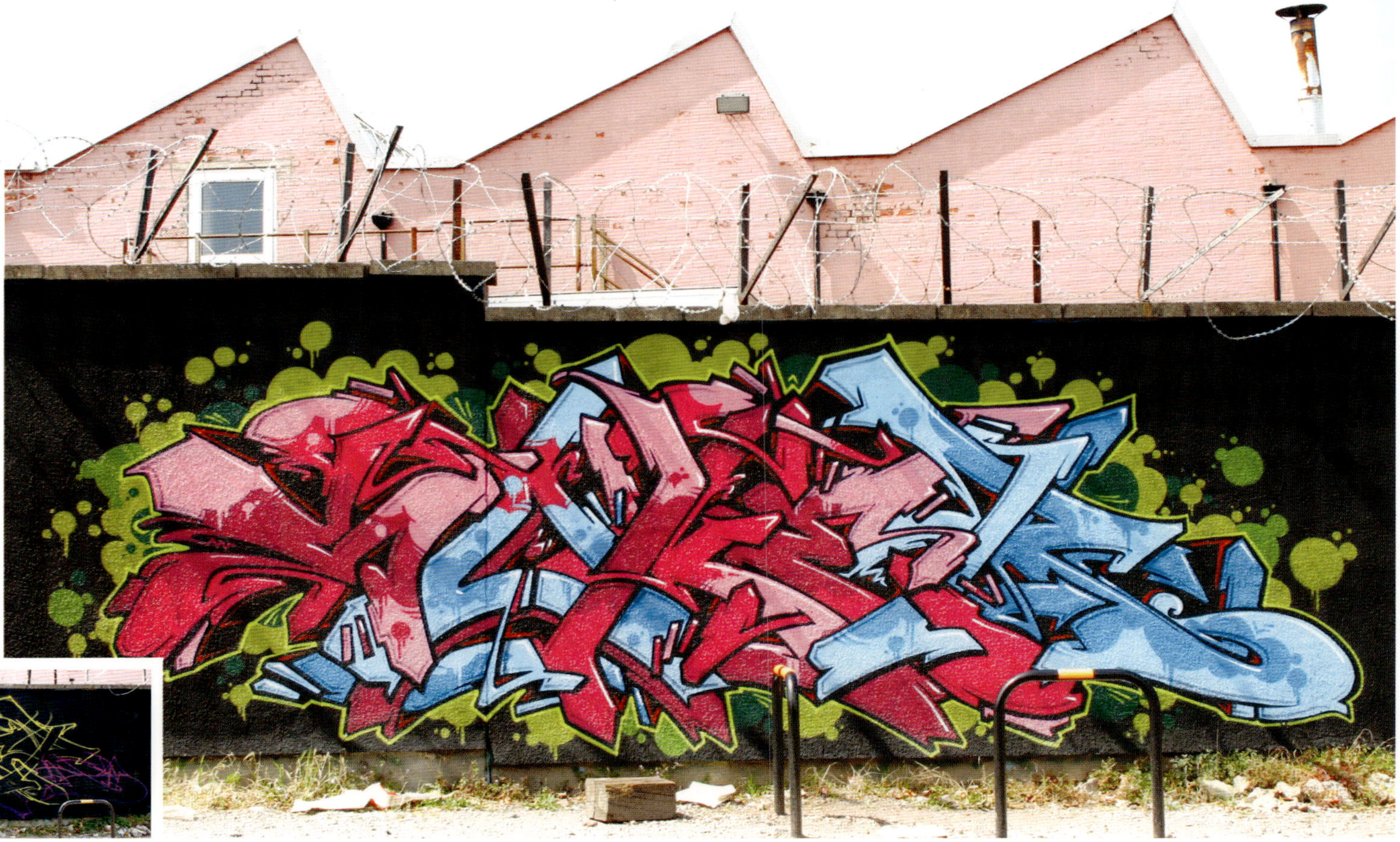

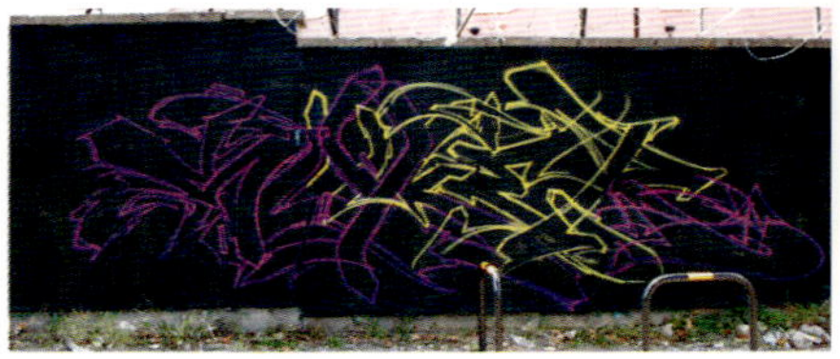

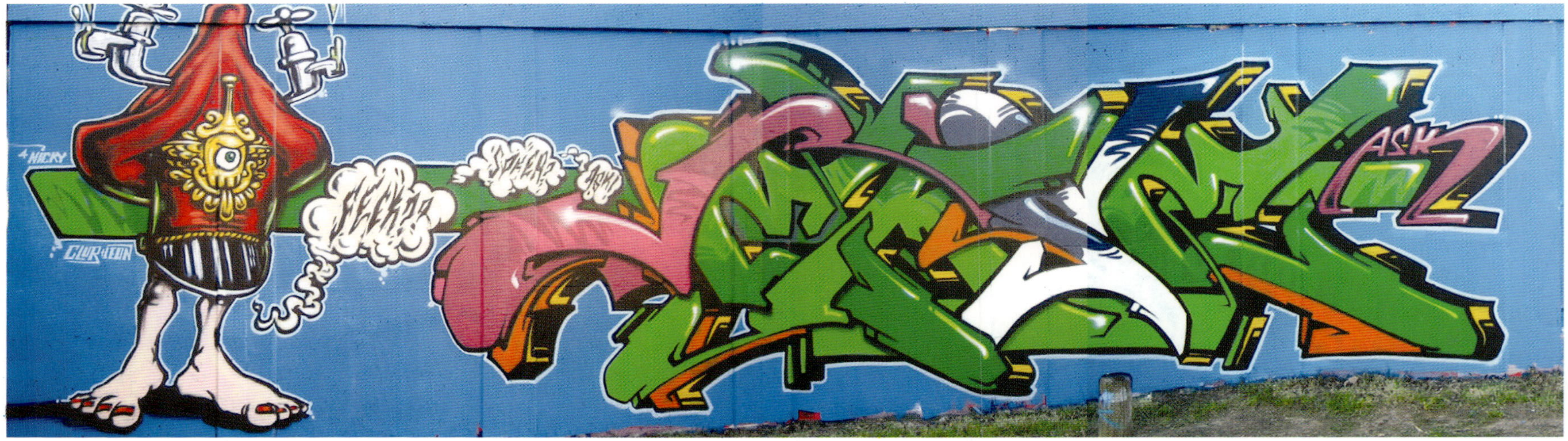

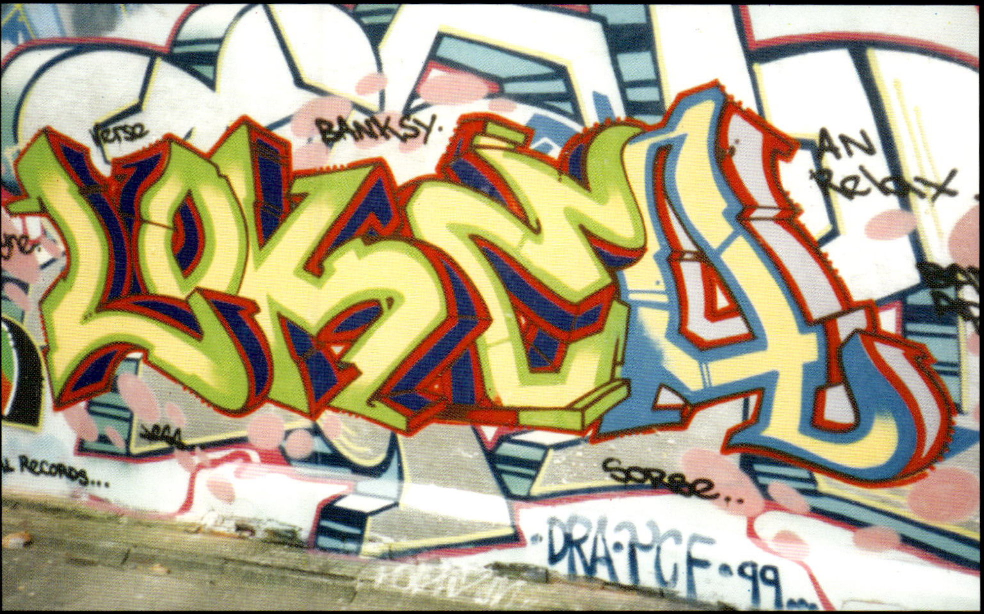

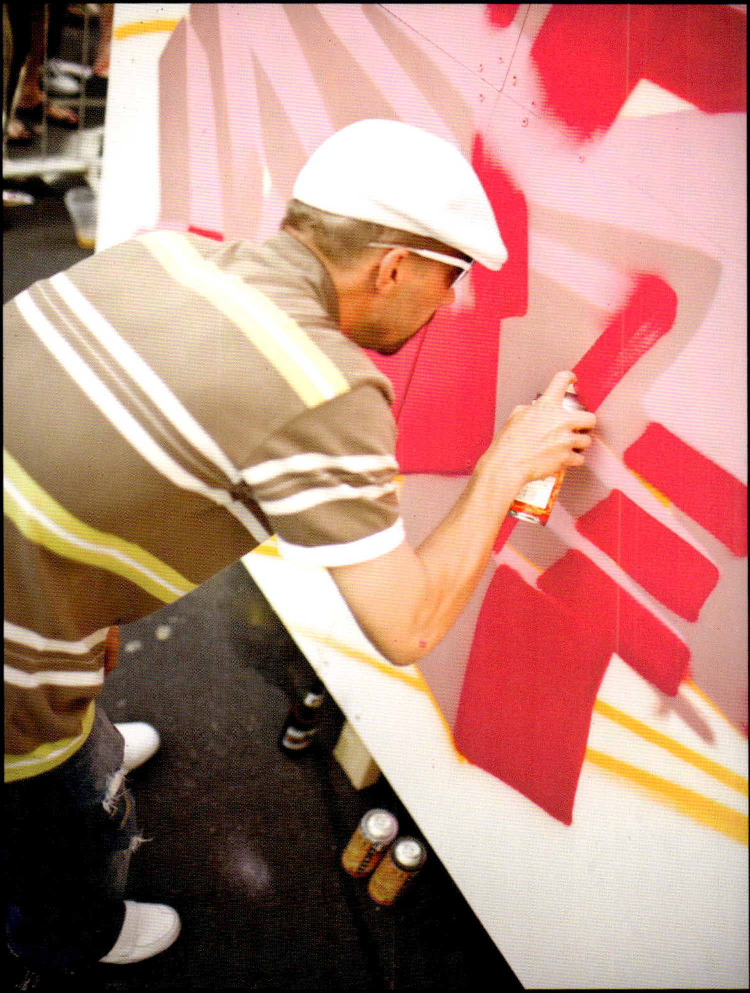

Top left: Bedminster skate park, 1997

Above: Lokey gets busy

LOKEY BA/DBZ

• Amongst Bristol's second wave of graffiti writers, Lokey is the youngest of the veterans, and was lucky enough to have been in the right place at the right time. A seasoned old timer who's still in his early 30s, he grew up among the Kingswood hip hop scene that nurtured the likes of Deed, Cheo, Kato and Soker, and went on to be a member of Bad Applez and The Dry Breadz.

Tell me about your first experiences of hip hop and graffiti. How old were you?
"I got into graffiti when I was nine, in 1987. I remember meeting some kids at the local park who had been to America and they brought back pictures of graff and early electro tapes and that. They were saying, 'yeah, you've got to have your street name, you've got to have your alias', and I just thought, 'wow! I want to be a part of this.' Then when I went to senior school I met people who had the same interests as me. We'd go on school trips to London in the first and second year, and we'd bugger off down the train lines instead of going round the museums."

What was your first crew?
"There were quite a few of us, about 15 or 20 of us, who all used to go out bombing together. The crew was called JFK (Just For Kicks). Then that changed to TSC – which stood for Too Stoned to Care, 'cos we were all smokers. There'd be like 10 or 15 people sat in a room smoking and doing outlines round my mate Tame's gran's house."

Do you remember seeing much graffiti around Bristol at the time?
"The only things I'd see around Bristol back then were the odd little thing by 3D, or stuff by Inkie, and then Shabs and Chaos."

Who were your early influences? Were they other graffiti writers who lived in the area?
"Yeah, Tame and Soker were a big influence on me because we were always designing together. I also knew all the Kingswood lot that used to go down the Dug Out in Barton Hill. I used to live one road over from Cheo, and with him being a few years older my mum didn't mind me crashing round his house on a Friday or Saturday night, so I

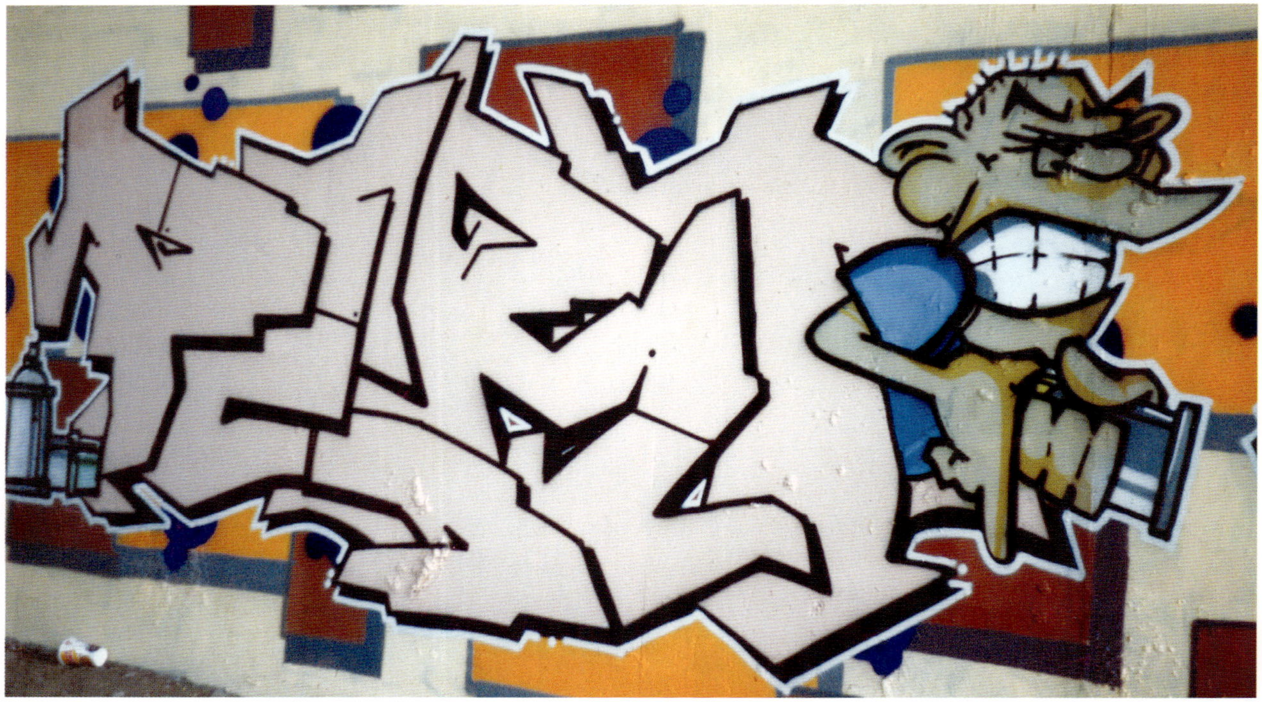

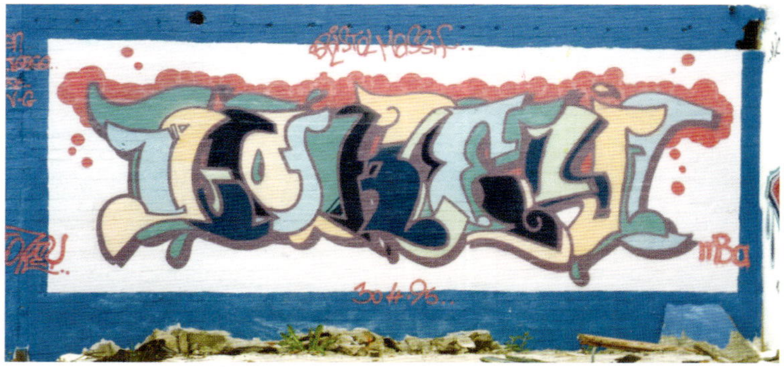

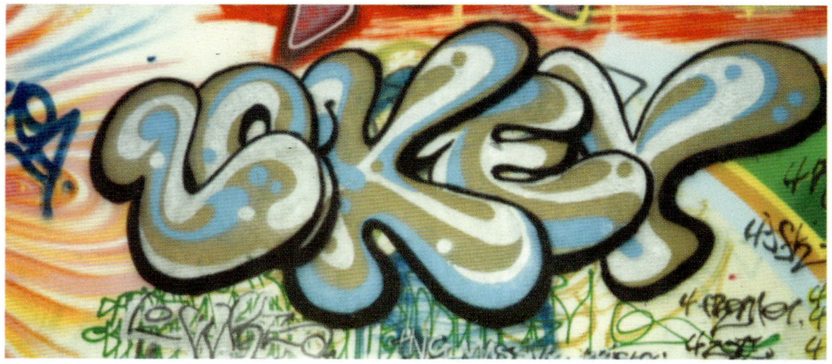

got to know Chome, and Chaos and Shabs and Remer. I was tiny, just a young kiddy."

What were your first experiences of painting illegally? Were you tagging, painting letter pieces, or doing characters?

"I was into painting letters from the off. My first tag was Sera. I stuck with that up until '91, when I started writing Lokey. When we were at school we were mostly just painting tags and dubs, it would be that kind of thing where someone would turn round and say 'I've got some pocket money, I'm going to buy some chrome' and someone else would buy a can of black. It would end up with about four or five people jumping on and doing one piece quick, getting covered in paint and getting drunk for the rest of the night."

I'm assuming you've been arrested for painting. How old were you when you first got caught?

"I was 13 when I first got nicked by the cops for tagging. Luckily enough they put my in the car and took me home to my mum, rather than to the police station. The next time I think I was 18 or 19, and me, Tame, Task, Soker and one or two others all decided (we were drunk out of our faces) that it'd be a good laugh to pile down town and tag the centre. Little did we know that we were being watched all the way. By the time we got to the centre there were two riot vans and fucking police dogs waiting and they circled us, which was no fun. But we all just ended up getting cautions because we all said we done it all. It was like 'no, he didn't do nothing, I done it all.' It's how we always worked when we'd been nicked for stuff before."

Did you nick paint? Any favourite spots for racking that you can remember?

"Yeah, we used to go down to Euro Graphics and they'd do that thing where they'd walk you round the shop, but while they were walking one or two people round, everybody else would sneak underneath the counter and go and thieve all the paint. But we also worked out what the delivery day was, and once or twice we did nick whole boxes (36 cans) from the back of the van while the driver was taking stuff up into the shop. It was all that Buntlack Rose Pink and Apple Green, and all those lush colours. I've still got a can of Rose Pink."

Lokey has quite a ring to it. How did the name come about? Are you a fan of Norse myths and legends?

"I got fed up with trying to get the letters

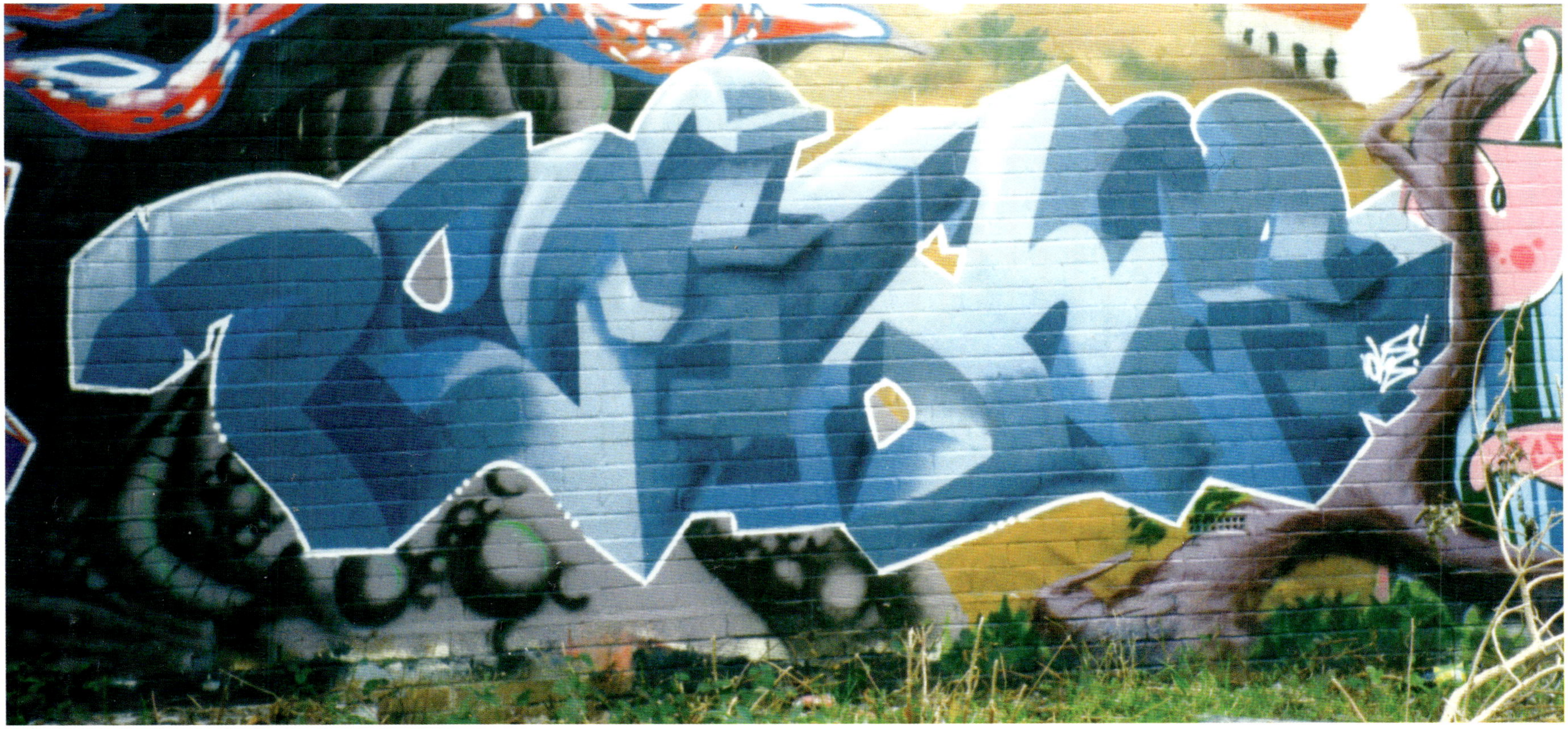

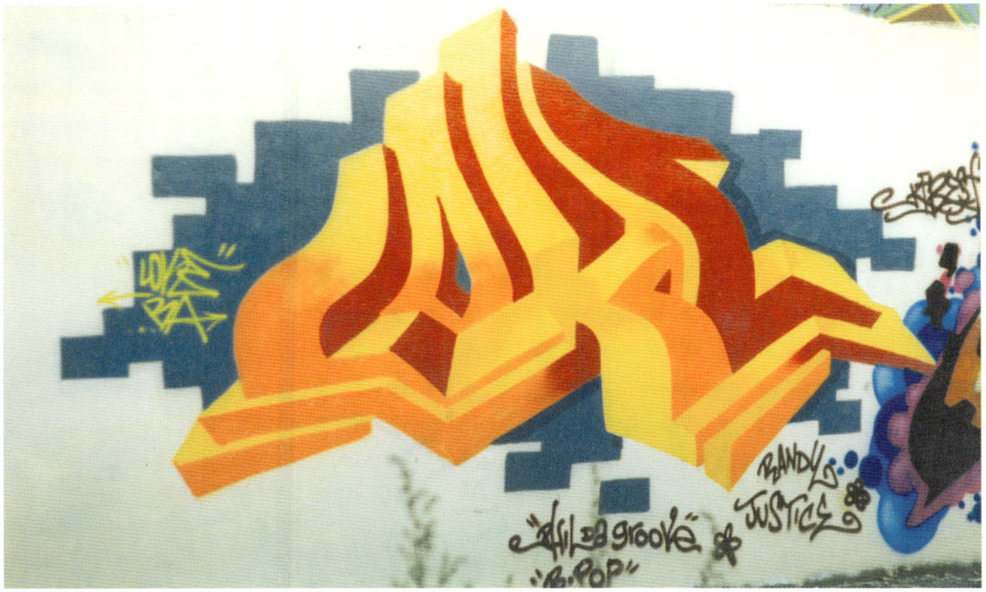

in Sera to work right together and one night I was trying to think of a new tag, and there was a band at the time called Low Key – a 'New Jack Swing' group – and I thought 'hmm, I like the sound of that.' It's got a few meanings: there's the Norse god of mischief and destruction, but then it also means 'quiet' and 'low profile', which tied in with how I was looking at things. I didn't want to be out in everybody's face, I just wanted to plod along, doing me own little thing. I just ended up dropping the W because six letters was just a bit too many."

Growing up with graffiti, you've seen a lot of changes. What's your take on the contemporary graffiti scene?

Opposite page. Top left: 'Pert', 1998

Middle left: Brislington warehouse, 1996

Bottom left: Simple, funky style. early '90s

This page. Top: Second 3-D piece, Radstock, 1997

Left: Millionaire's Club hall of fame, 1998

Top right: Custard Factory in Brimingham, Fresh 2000

Middle right: 'Burnin' Ambitionz', 1999

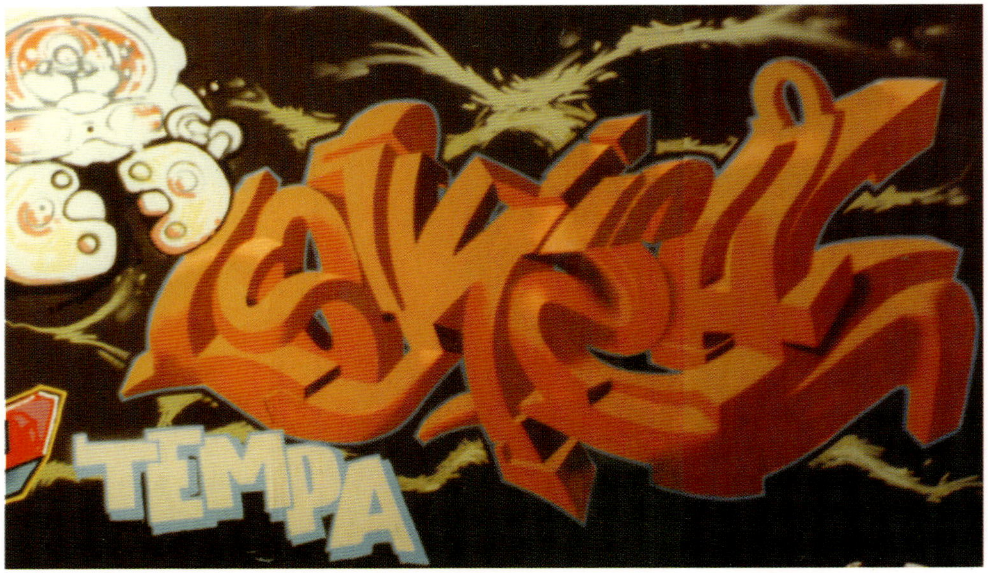

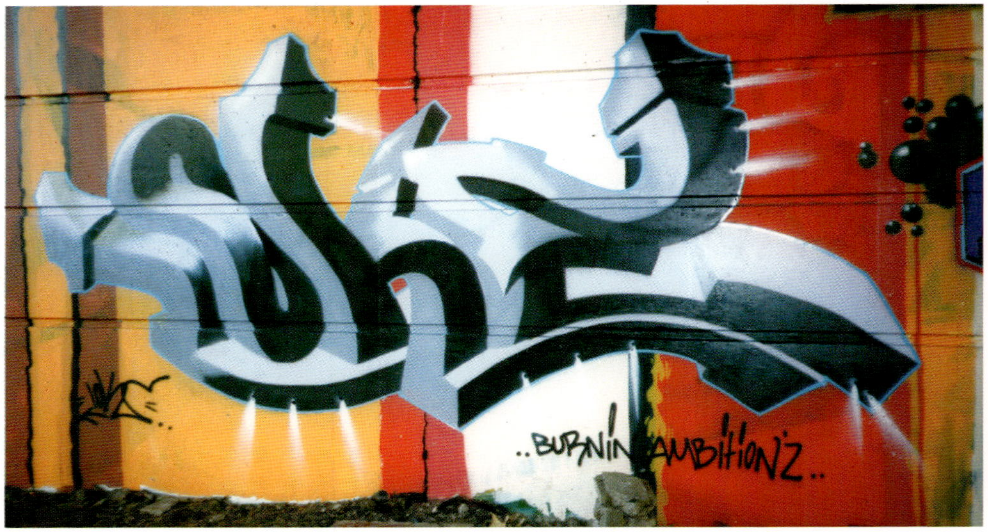

"Graffiti's totally changed. The politics are still the same, but the whole scene's changed. It's better on the one hand, because it's more acceptable now – but there are so many writers that there's a lot of mediocre painting being done. There are a few exceptional writers in Bristol, but then there's those people in the middle who do all the damage and keep giving it a bad name. There's so much more getting done on the streets. I understand it, because that's where it comes from, it comes from the streets, obviously. It might go into the galleries, but it always goes back to the streets."

You guys were always known for being able to pull off burners with rubbish paint back in the day, and for mixing your own colours. What is your take on the changes in paint technology?
"The paint now is fucking heaven. The consistency is so much better now, compared to what it used to be like. We used to have to mix between cans to get the shades we wanted. I wouldn't even dream of using Car Plan now. Good paint can make a shit piece look good, because it goes on the wall tidy; whereas back when it was shit paint, you had to know how to use it to put it on the wall. The colours in the can wouldn't match the lids – one can would be thick, and the next would be watery."

Why did you to switch from a 'traditional' style of painting to rendering letters three-dimensionally?
"I got sent a postcard with a Daim piece on it, and it just blew me away. At the time everything was beginning to look the same. There are only so many styles of arrows you can do, there's only so many things you can do with 2-D letters. I just thought Daim's stuff was the next step. So I started off by making my 2-D pieces 3-D, which I found quite easy to do. It was still semi-wildstyle, but in 3-D. If I draw a piece out in 3-D, I can see straight away how it would look from behind, or from above, almost as if I'm preparing to do a sculpture."

The crews you painted with seem to have the same members but more than one name. What's the difference between Bad Applez and Dry Breadz?
"DBZ was more the illegal thing, but Bad Applez was just me, Kato and Soker, and we did youth workshops and commissions: painting shop shutters and stuff."

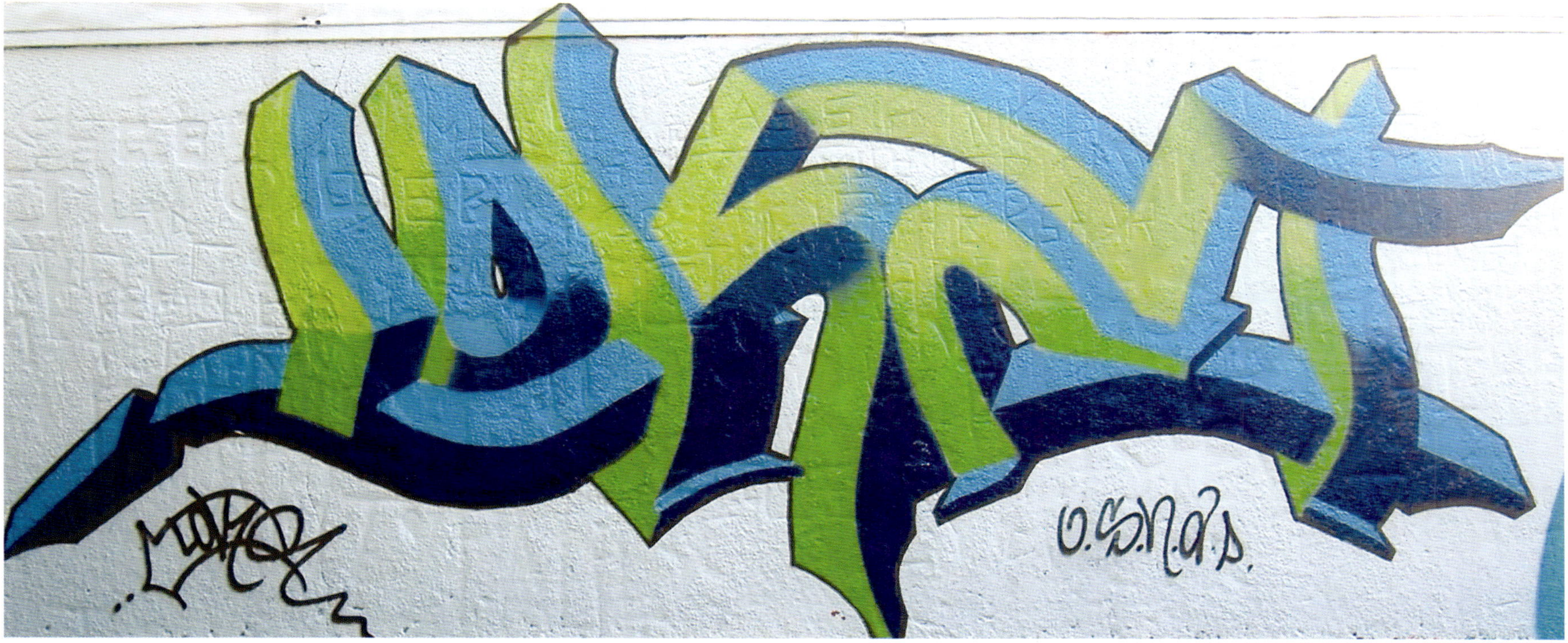

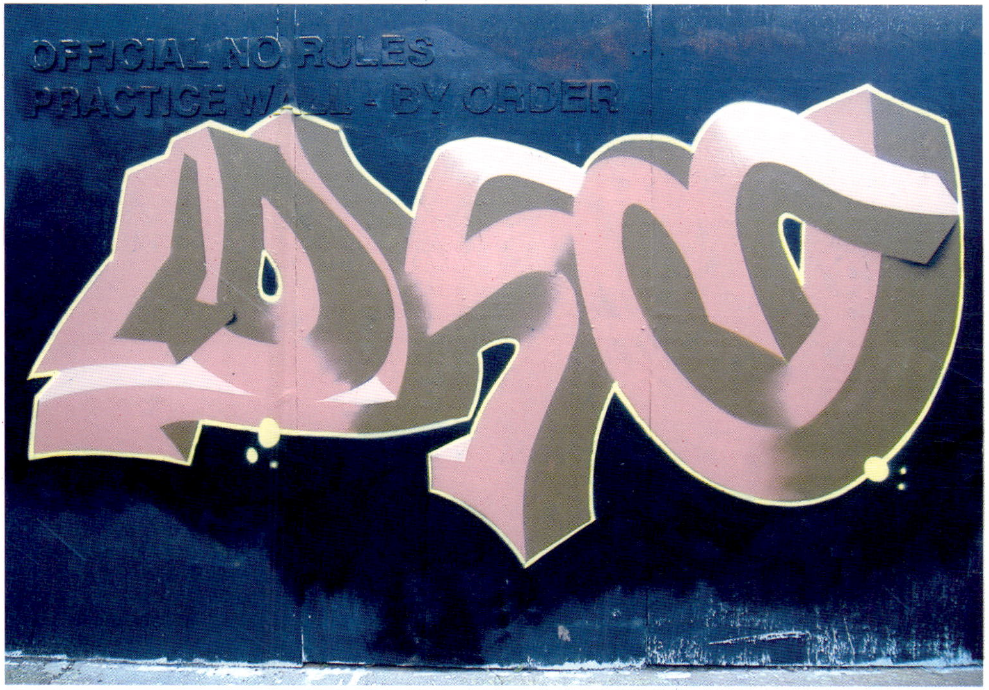

Top: Reviving the 3-d, 2008

Bottom: Ashley Road, 2008

Each of you guys has taken a few years off from painting at one time or another. Was there any particular reason why you had a break?

"My girlfriend died not long after Walls on Fire, and I just stopped writing after that. I was still watching what was going on, but it stopped being my main priority. I had always drawn my outlines with her sat with me; she'd come out with me when I went painting, she'd sit down for the whole time I was painting with a flask of tea. She'd make my reefers for me. I went from painting once a week, to once a month, to once every six months. That was the reason I fell off graffiti. My muse was gone. And going through my old sketchbooks when I started again was painful, because all my outlines were dedicated to her. Her name was on every page."

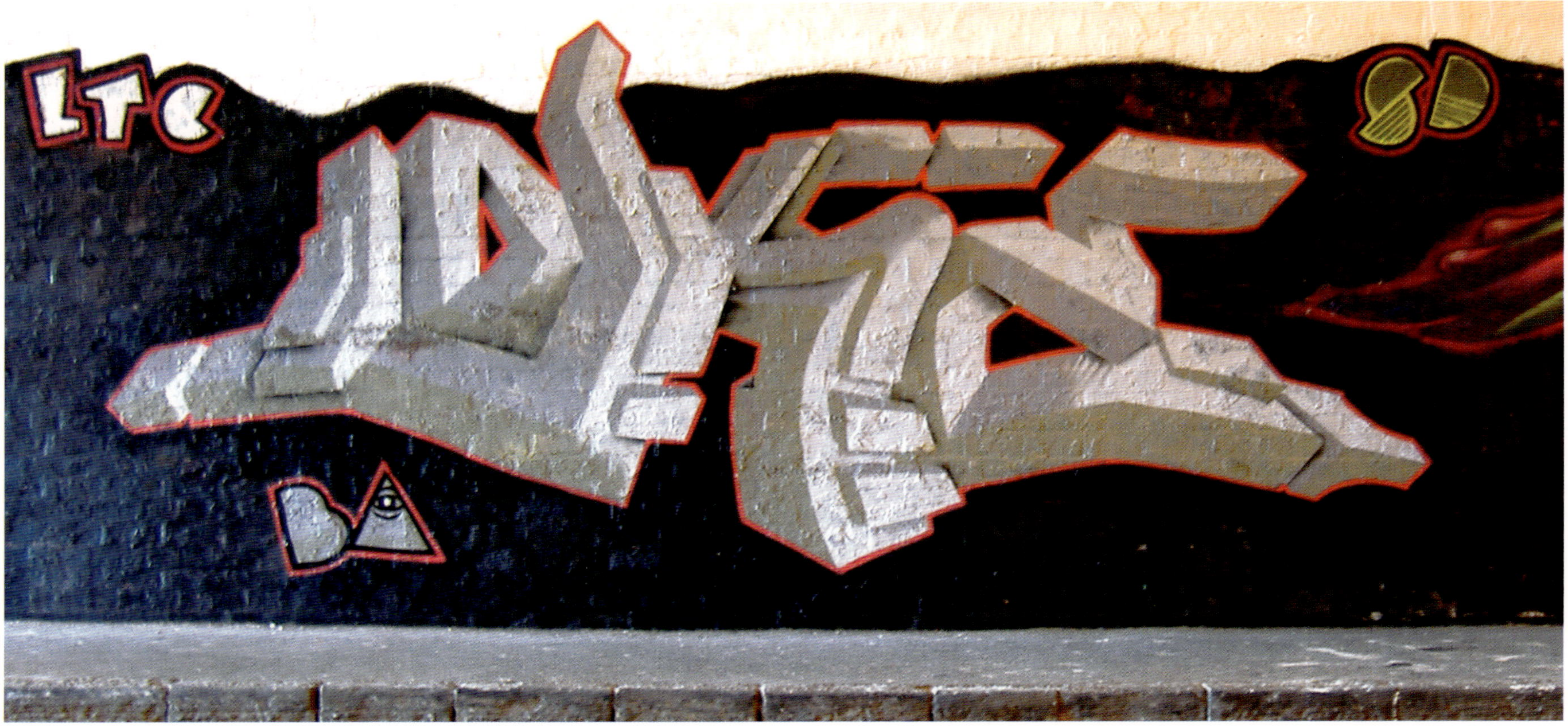

Top: At the all-weather St.Werburgh's tunnel spot, 2008

Bottom left: With Cheo, Cargo, London, 2008

Bottom right: Stokes Croft, 2008

Opposite page: Lokey print for threenine.com

How did it make you feel when you started painting again?
"When I painted my first piece after starting again, I felt like I hadn't had a break. I'm embracing it, it's fun, I love painting! Everybody gets on better now, but before everybody was in their own little groups and nobody talked to each other."

Is it still the all-consuming passion that it used to be?
"Totally. I wake up and think about graffiti, I don't leave home without me sketchbook, pens, and nozzles. My room's covered in it. I turn on my computer and it's full of graffiti. I suppose it's like a hobby that's taken over my life again."

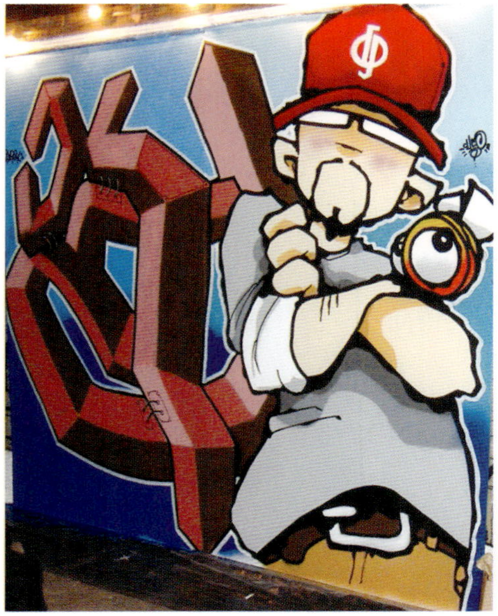

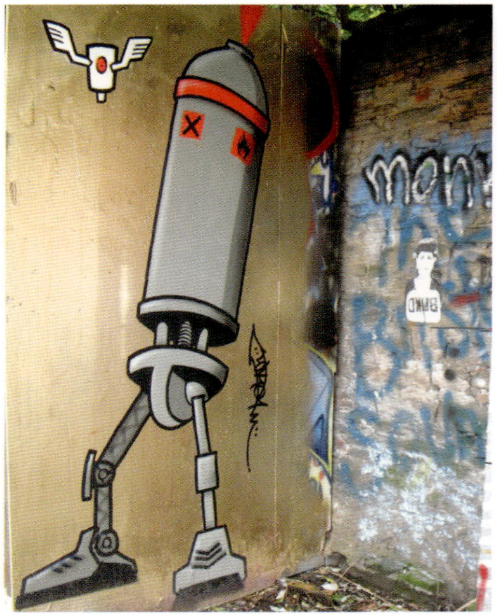

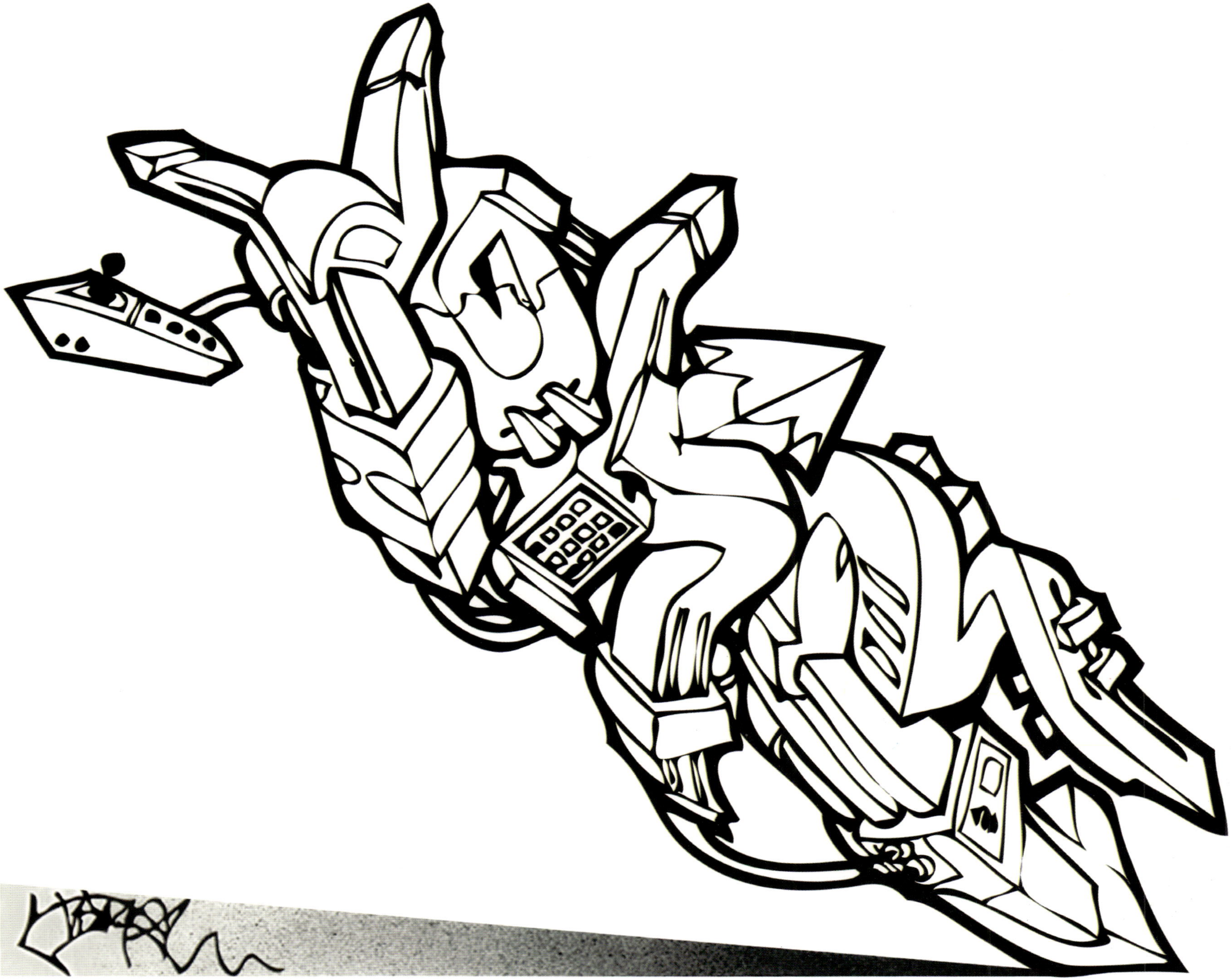

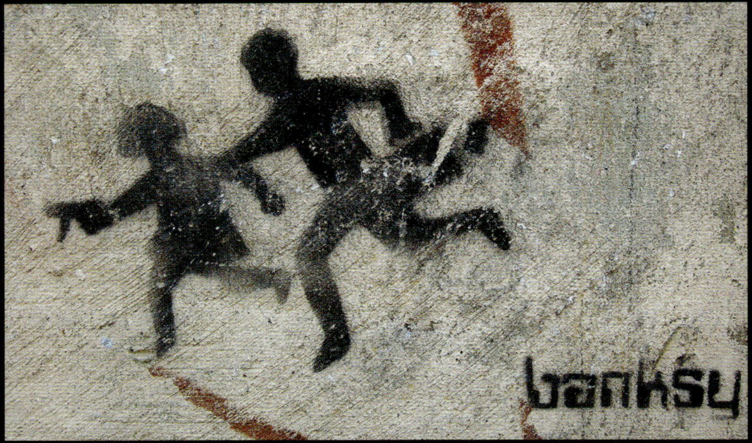

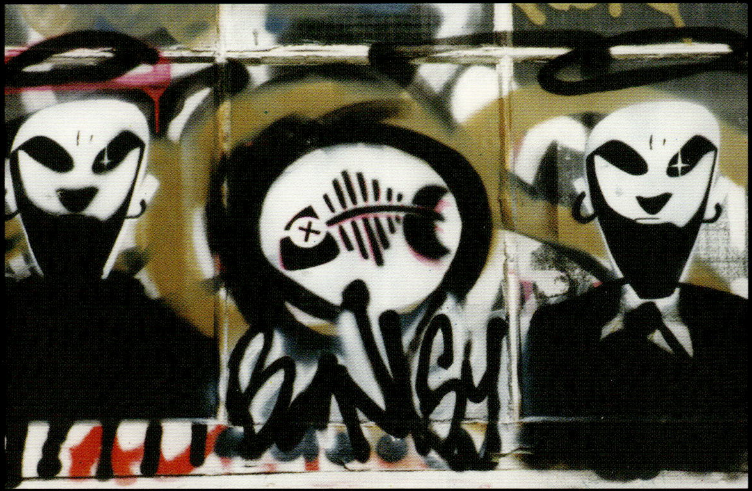

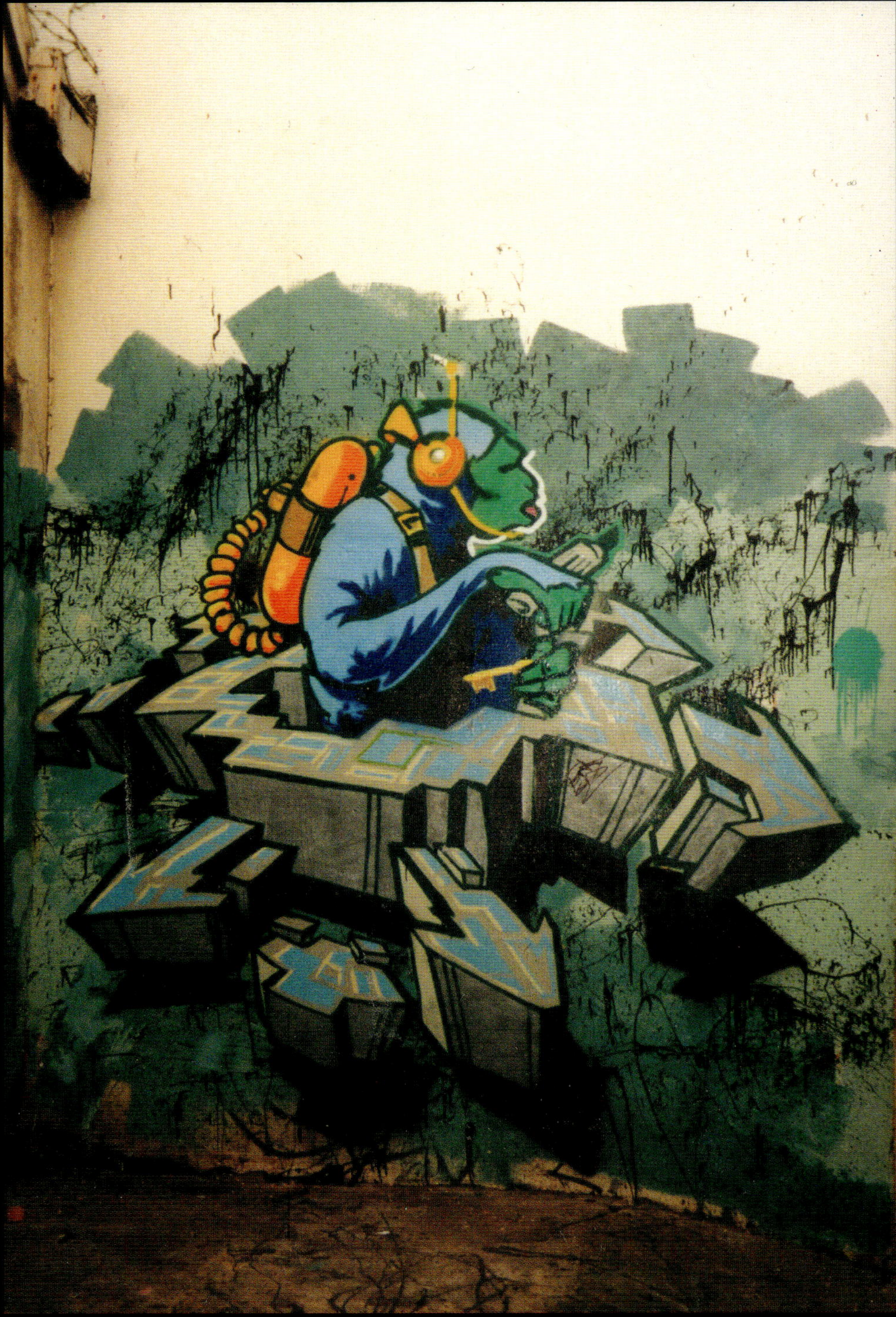

Top left: Robbing banks, early version of the bastardised 'children crossing' stencil, c.1996

Top right: Space monkey, Millionaire's Club hall of fame, c.1997

Middle left: Very early stencils with freehand tag, Barton Hill Youth Club, early-mid 90s

BANKSY

• **"I'd heard there was a graffiti hall of fame somewhere in Barton Hill, but my dad was badly beaten up there as a kid and had his trousers stolen, so he'd always put the fear of God into me about the place.** By the time I'd worked up the courage to cycle over and check it out, I was so terrified I actually remember choosing my best pants for the occasion, just in case.

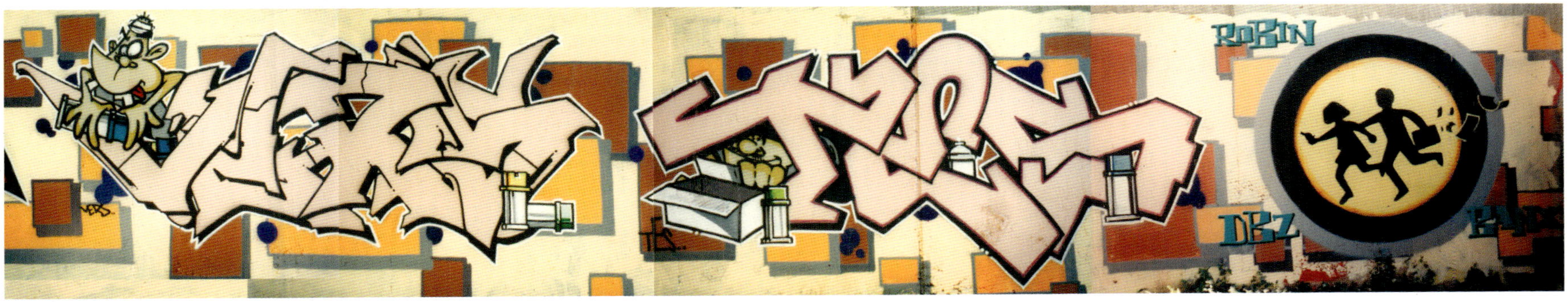

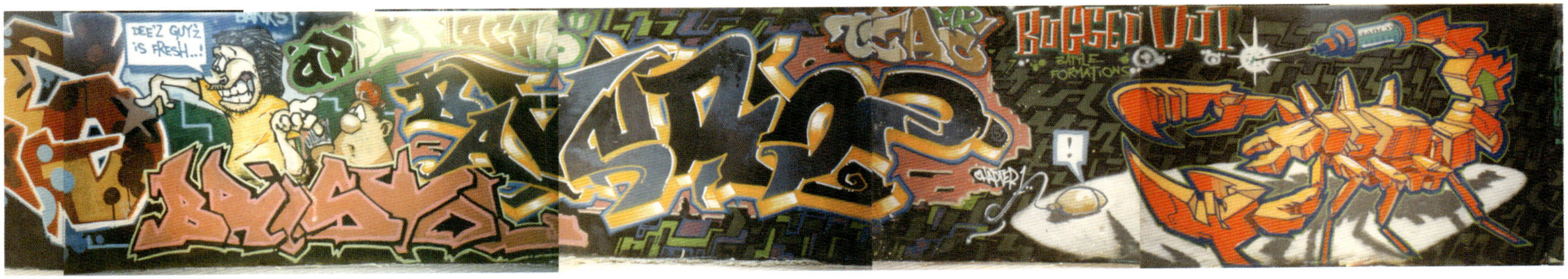

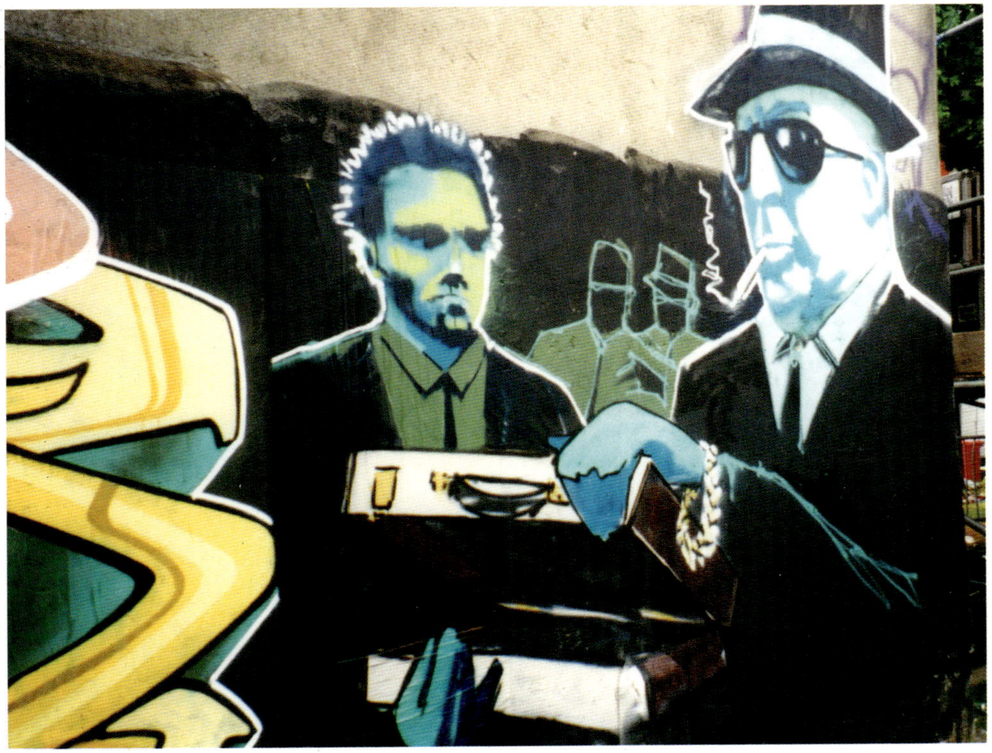

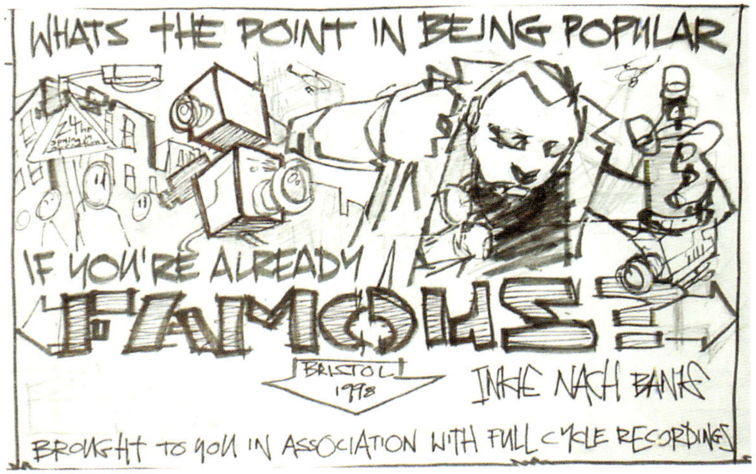

"Of course it turned out to be the most inspiring stretch of concrete in Bristol and I made a pilgrimage there every weekend. What it showed us was very powerful – that there was a choice between compromising and following our own strange little dreams. Barton Hill Youth Club spawned

Top: Vers (aka Soker) Tes, Robin Banx, Dry Breadz crew, Esso garage, 1997

Middle: Nach, Lokey, Vers, Banksy in 'Bugged Out Battle Formation,' Dry Breadz crew, 1997

Other captions, next page

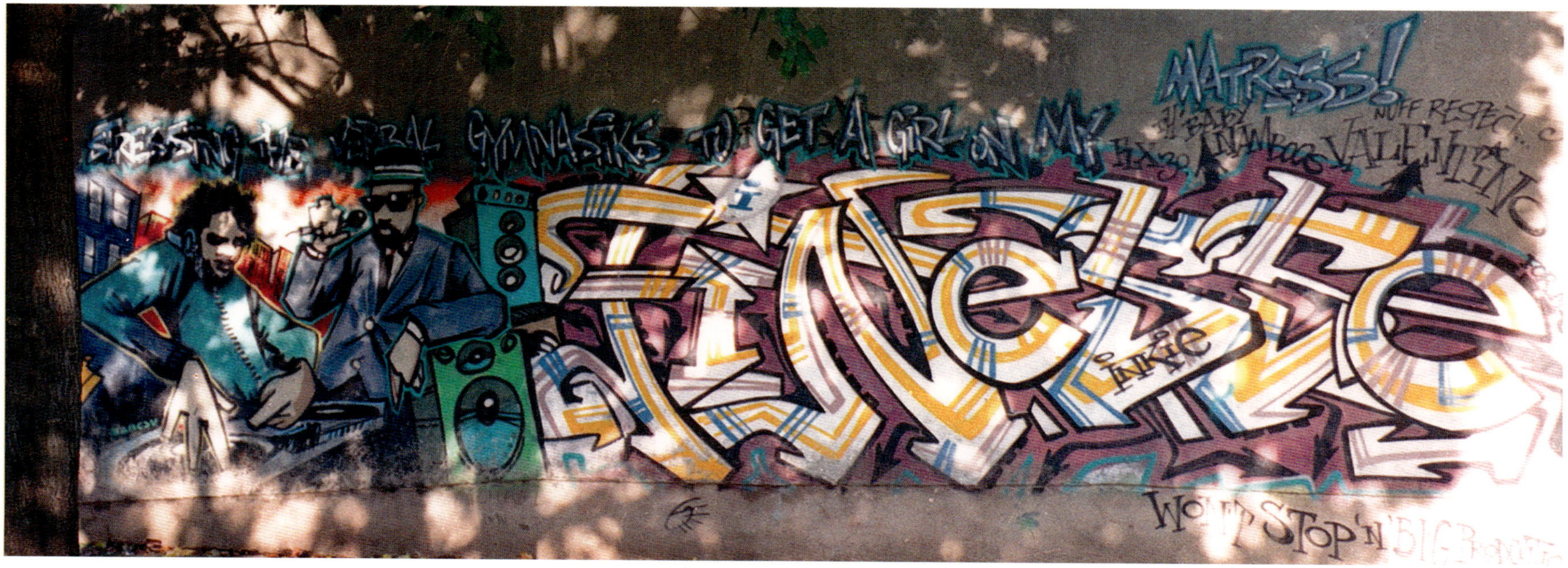

Top: 'Finesse' Banksy and Inkie, Grosvenor Road, St.Paul's Carnival, 1998

Far right: Sketchbook spread (for Lokey) stencil spray paint and paint pen, 1997

Middle: 'Heavy Weaponary' ('hello' added by unknown) c.1997

Left: Monkey with chainsaw, c.1997

Middle bottom: Bar code tank rubber stamp, 1998

Previous page. Bottom left: Selling off the ghetto to the highest bidder, a premonition of gentrification. Painted with Inkie, Lokey and Will Barras, see page 52) 1999

Bottom right: 'What's The Point In Being Popular If Your Already Famous?' sketch for Full Cycle Records commission wall that was never painted, 1998

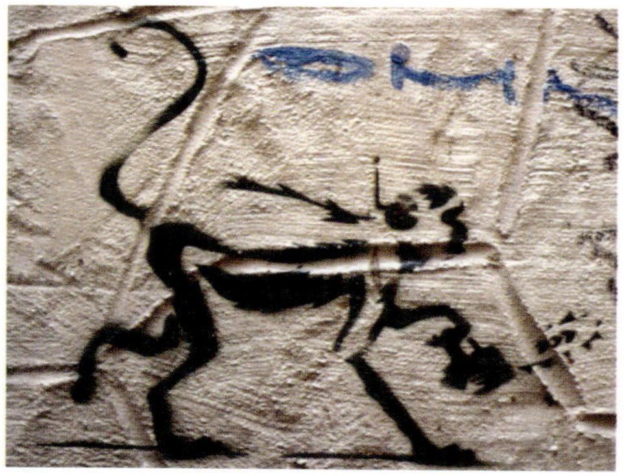

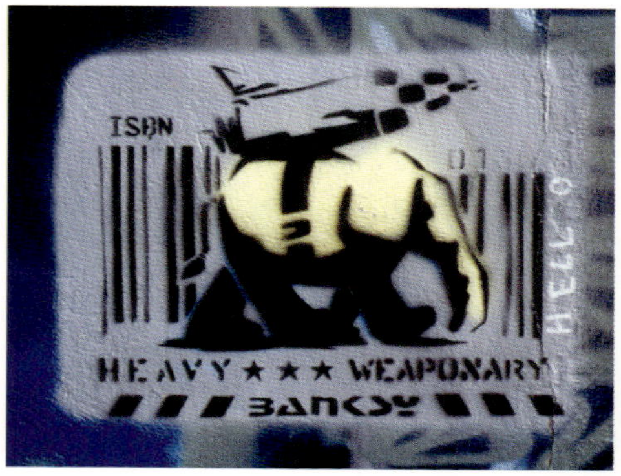

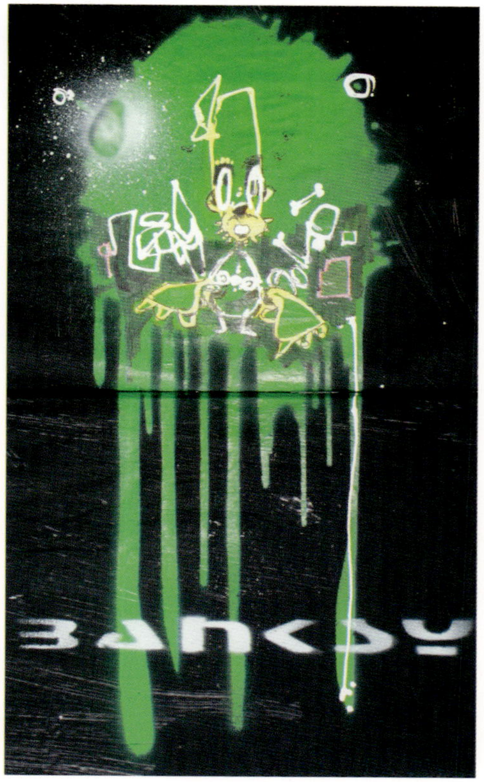

a flood of artists and musicians, many of them have had an impact across the city and far beyond. It might sound a little crazy, but I think John Nation, that shouty red-faced little social worker who made it all happen, has had more impact on the shape of British culture over the past twenty years than anyone else to come from the city. And I bet none of the cops who arrested him can say that."

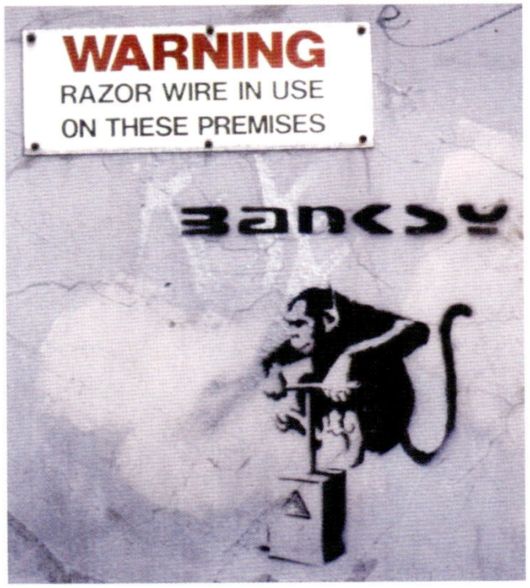

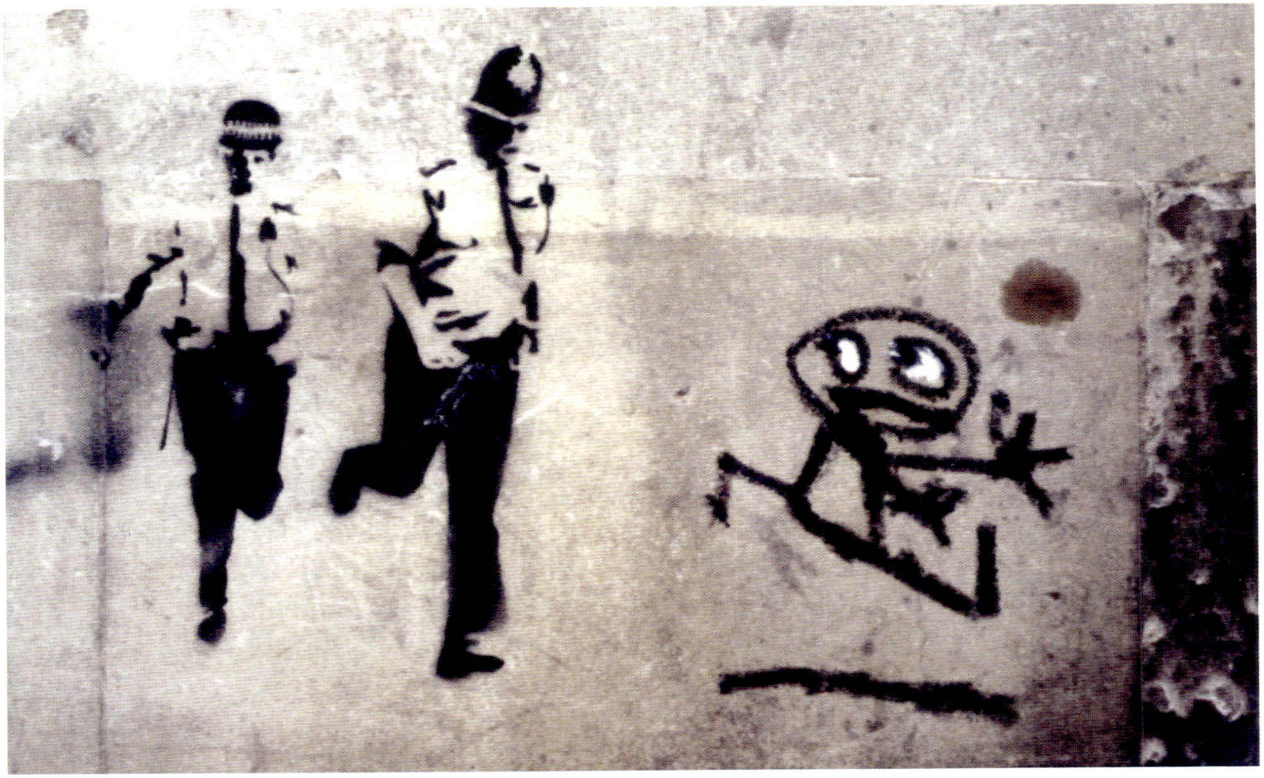

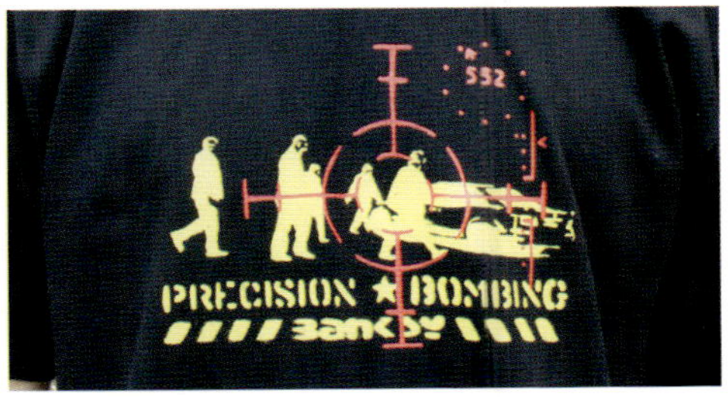

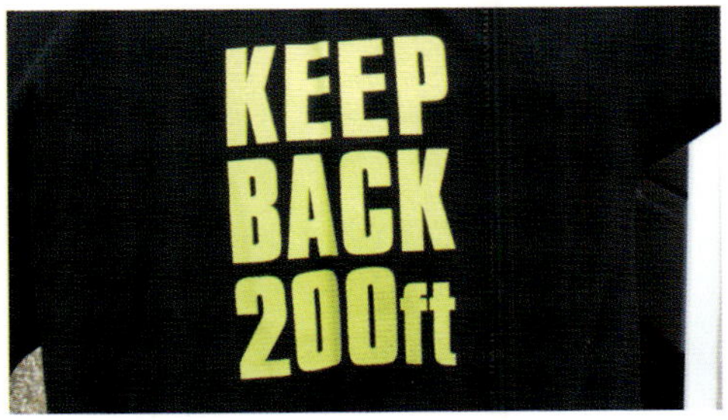

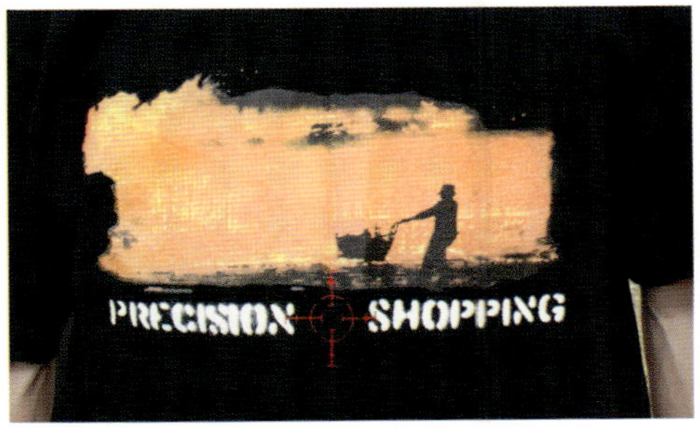

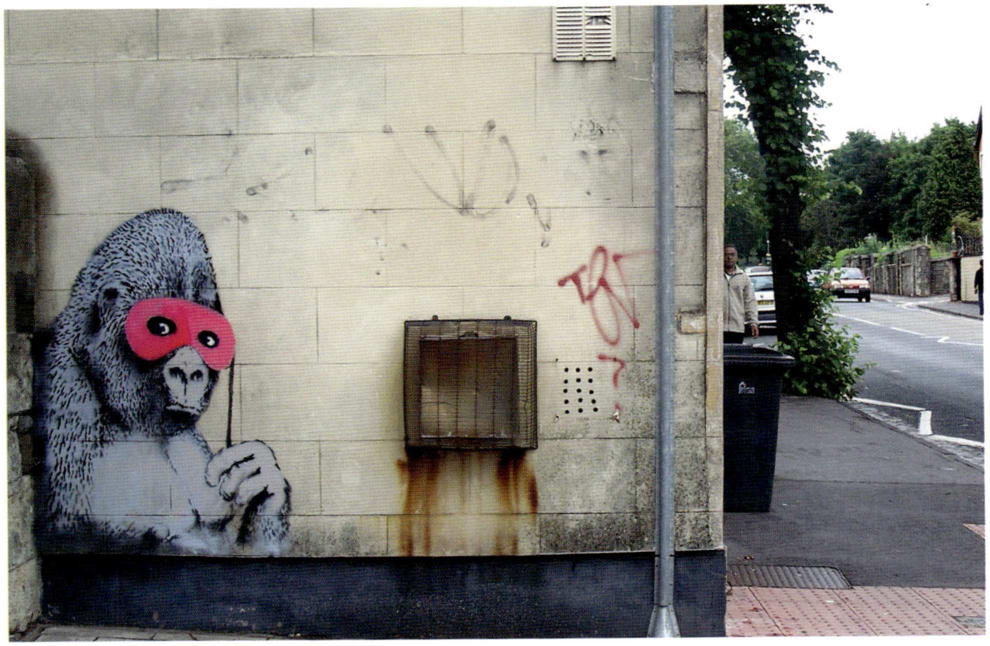

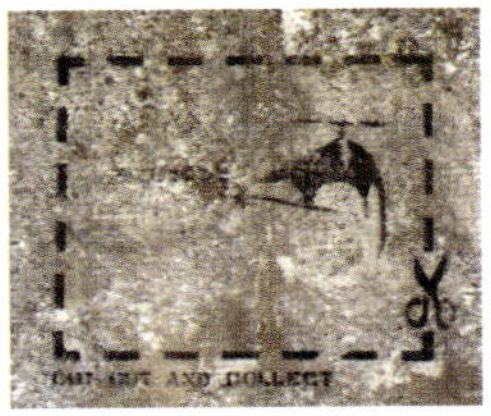

Top right: 'Crimes of the Innocent', Bridewell police station wall, Broadmead, c.1997

Bottom right: 'The Perfect Disguise', Stapleton Road, Easton, c.1997

Left, top-to-bottom: Uncontrolled detonation, c.1997; 'Precision Bombing' T-shirt, 1998; 'Keep Back 200ft' ('Precision Bombing' T-shirt, back); 'Precision Shopping' T-shirt (test print, never issued) 1998

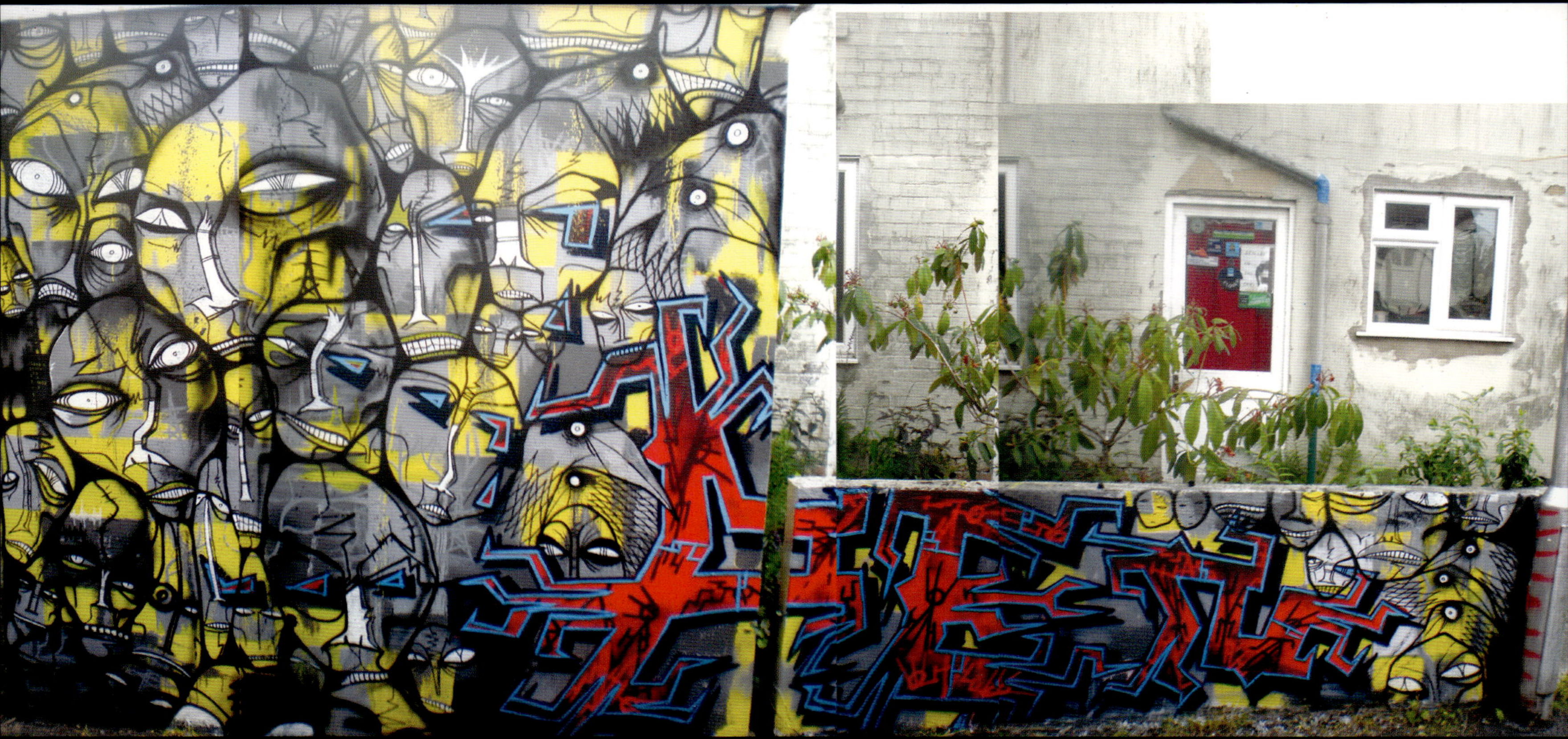

Above: Something to scare the children! Pen and Boswell (aka Warp) Frome, 2008

Right: 'Chain' (aka Vermin) Brislington warehouse, mid-90s

SOULS ON FIRE

• **Under the banner of Souls On Fire, Warp, Vermin and Pen have painted some of the most twisted and darkly humorous graffiti to have graced Bristol's walls.** Individually and collectively their work strikes a sharp chord, its honesty and originality peering out of the wall at you from whichever angle you approach it.

When and where did SOF form - and who came up with the enigmatic name?
Warp: "I'm pretty sure I came up with the name in about 92-93. Souls On Fire was a banner for a progressive graffiti group

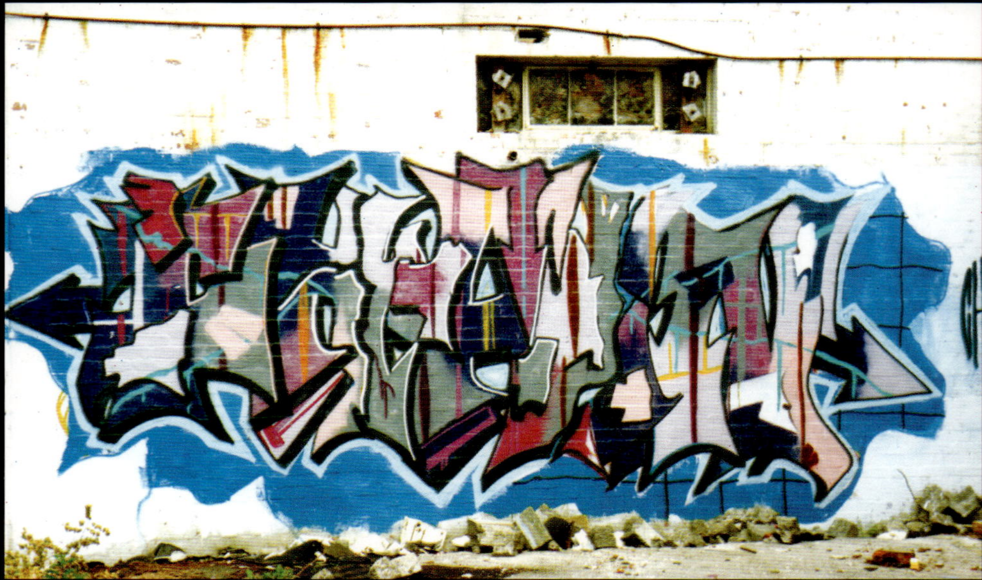

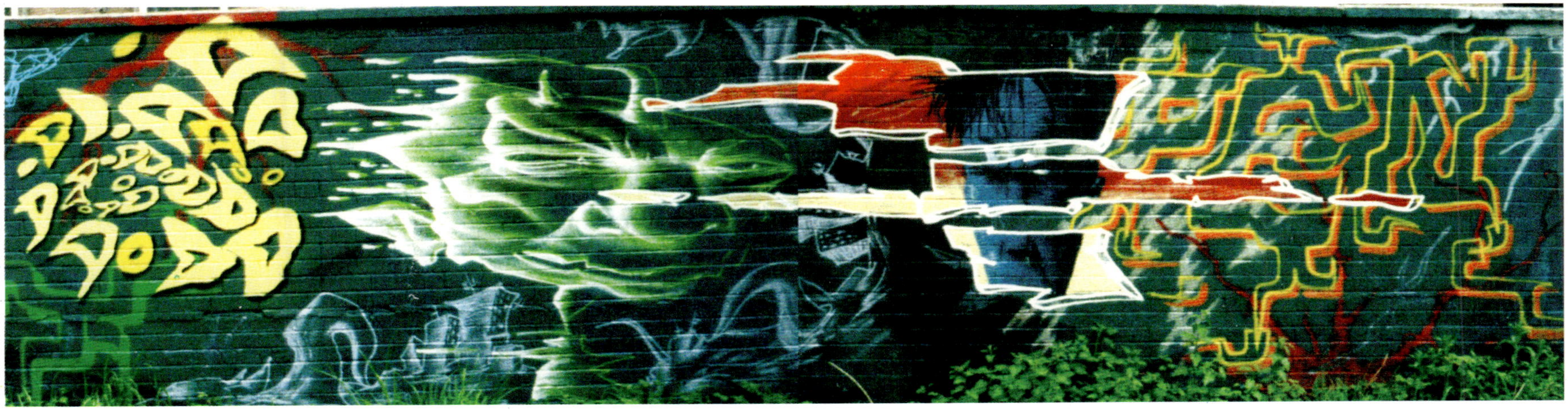

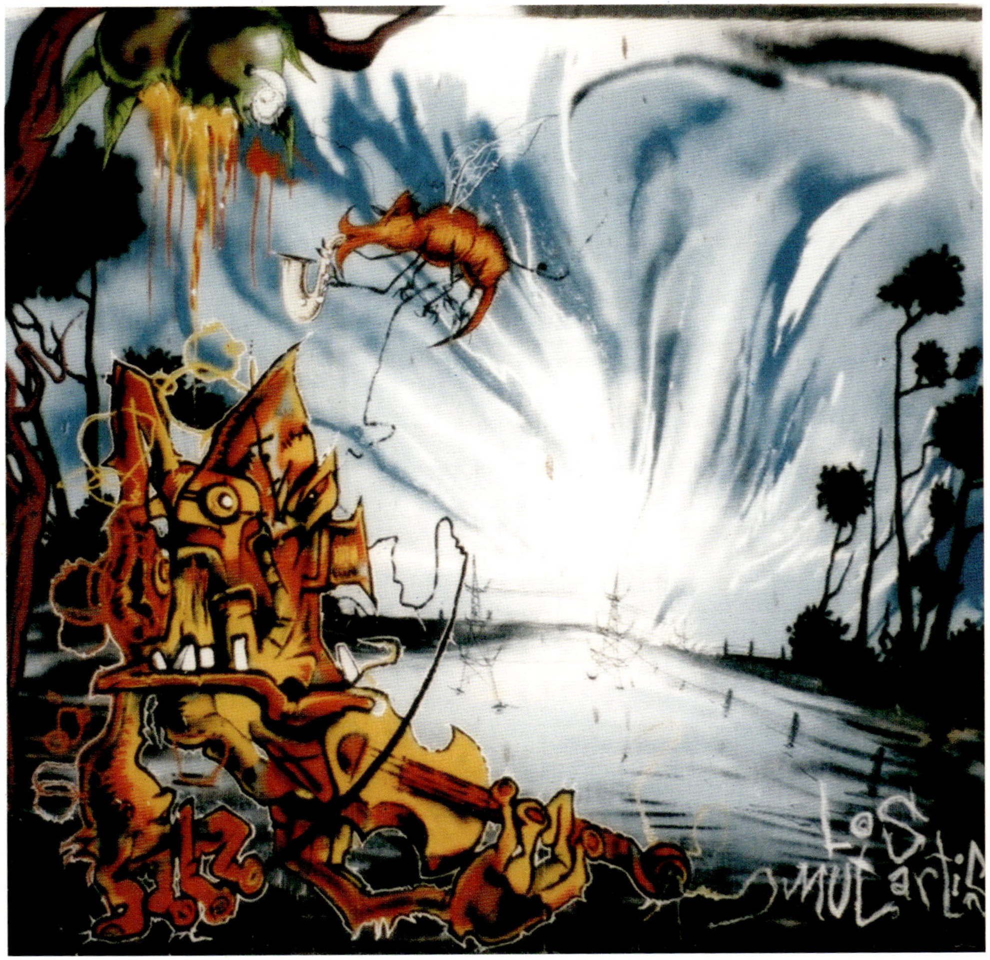

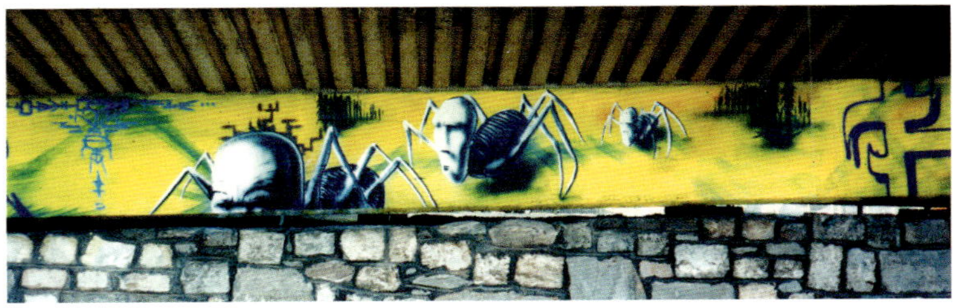

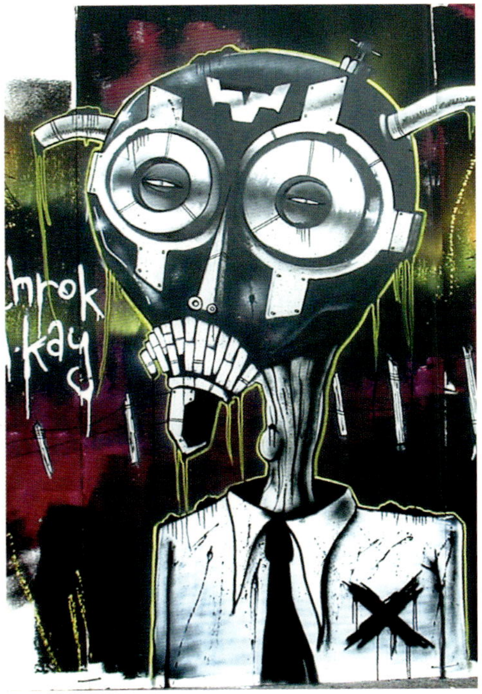

Top: Pen, Warp and Rowdy, Radstock, 1997

Bottom Left: Warp from 2006

Middle right: M32 hall of fame, 2000

Bottom right: Warp, Frome 2008

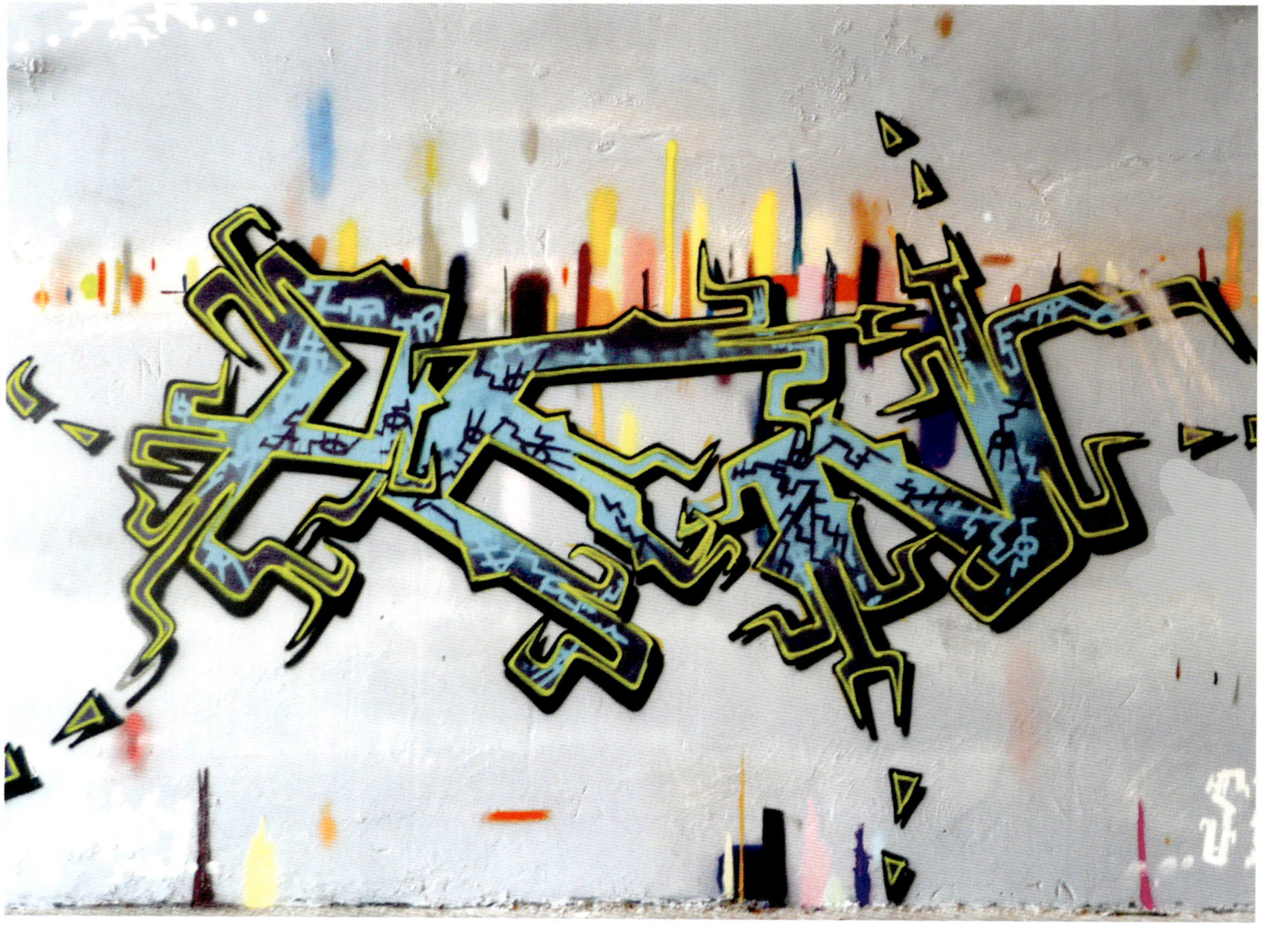

primarily consisting of Vermin, Rowdy, Pen and myself. The name was chosen for its elemental qualities – the 'Soul' is to show that the work came from the inside, as a means to artistic progression."

When did you come to Bristol to paint? What were your first impressions?

Pen: "I remember myself and Rowdy doing a trackside and bombing in Bristol in '92. We used to scope out graff spots looking for new stuff, but it seemed that every piece we found was flaking off the walls and old."

Warp: "Painting in Bristol was always an adventure. I remember going to the (Barton Hill) Dug Out quite a lot in the days of Shab, Inkie and everyone, and being pretty stunned by the work going up there. I did a bit myself in the end, it was a bit rudimentary at the time, but I was progressing. I remember doing a piece with a pretty twisted face on it, and a couple of evenings later I saw the piece on the HTV West news, with the presenter Richard Wyatt squatting in front of it. That made me chuckle."

Who else was painting in Bristol at the time, and where did you meet them?

Pen: "We'd met Kato a few years before in Bath, but the first person we met in Bristol was Tes, while painting in Barton Hill. That led to meeting Soker, Lokey, and Kato again."

Warp: "We did a few productions with them and hooked up with Turo and Shimz a few times. We also met Paris and Acer from Fantastic Super Heroes."

Did the free party scene mess up the graffiti scene for a few years? Or did

Above: Pen and Rowdy, St.Werburgh's tunnel, 2008

Right: Brislington warehouse, 1996

Opposite page: Top: Warp, Brislington warehouse, 1995

Bottom: Section from 'Planet Farmyard' production, 1996

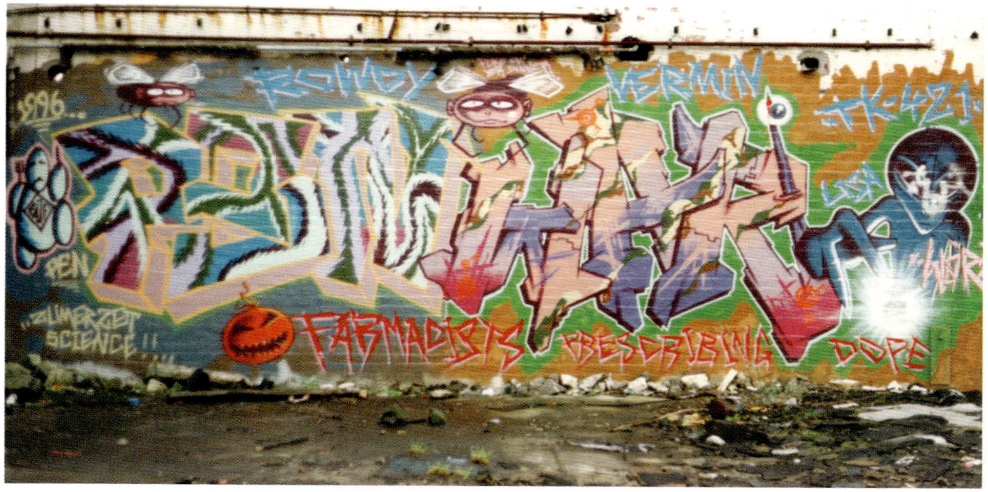

you guys embrace that scene?

Warp: "Yes, I think it probably did, as almost no one seemed to be painting at the time. I do remember dropping a couple of bits in warehouse parties here and there. But I was more into punk and hip hop around that time – I didn't really favour house music that much, so I concentrated more on painting walls when there wasn't that much going on. I remember our crew dropping productions on top of faded, decaying pieces that had been painted years back. What a different time: pieces only seem to last a matter of days in Bristol these days!"

Pen: "I went to a few parties at the time and did some bombing at a few. It was fun at the time, and quite underground. I think it did have an effect on the Bristol scene because potential writers were influenced by other things rather than graff. Then again, a lot of the decline was also due to the notorious busts which occurred. But as the party scene became commercial, the graff scene picked up again. I think these things come in cycles, graffiti had a popular spell in the '80s and is now popular again. Maybe the trend will die again in the future? Who knows? But the passionate artists will always stay in the game."

Souls On Fire have a very distinctive and – dare I say it? – dark style. Was it always like that, or did it evolve from more traditional styles?

Pen: "Our styles definitely evolved from traditional styles. I don't personally see our art as being massively dark, but it does have an edgy/comical twist to it. I enjoy playing with colour schemes, and I quite often concentrate on backgrounds and push the abstract side of things."

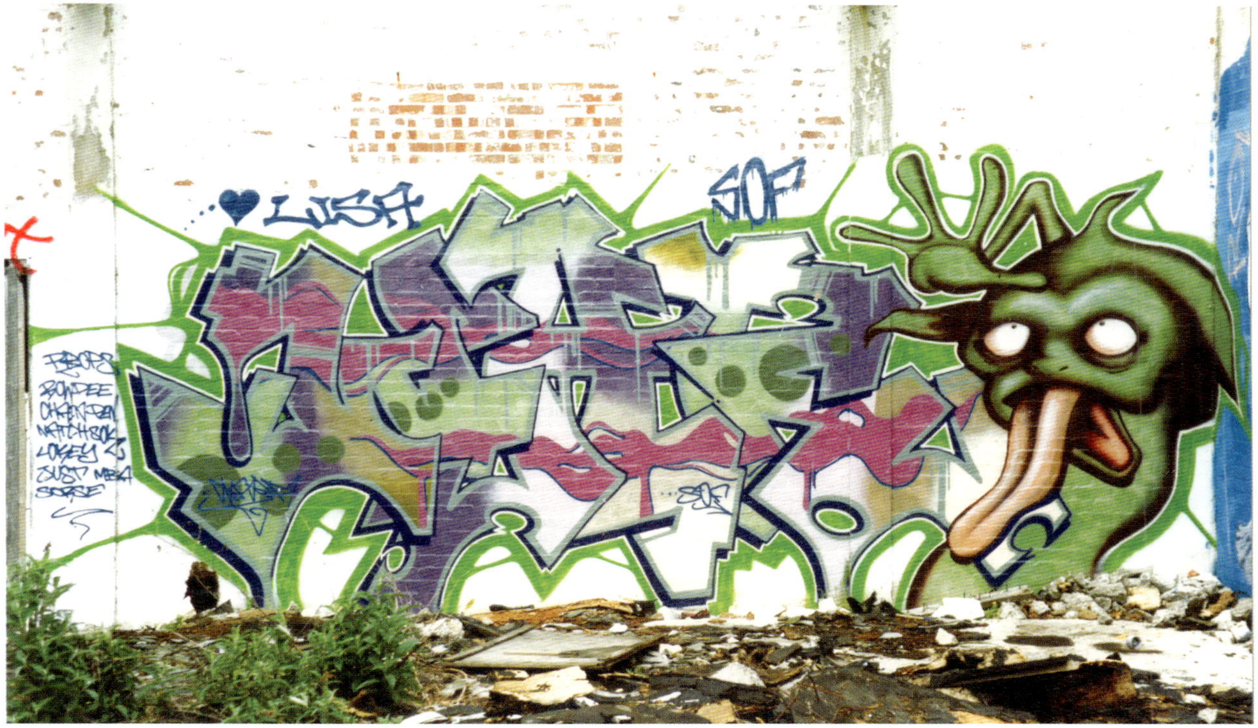

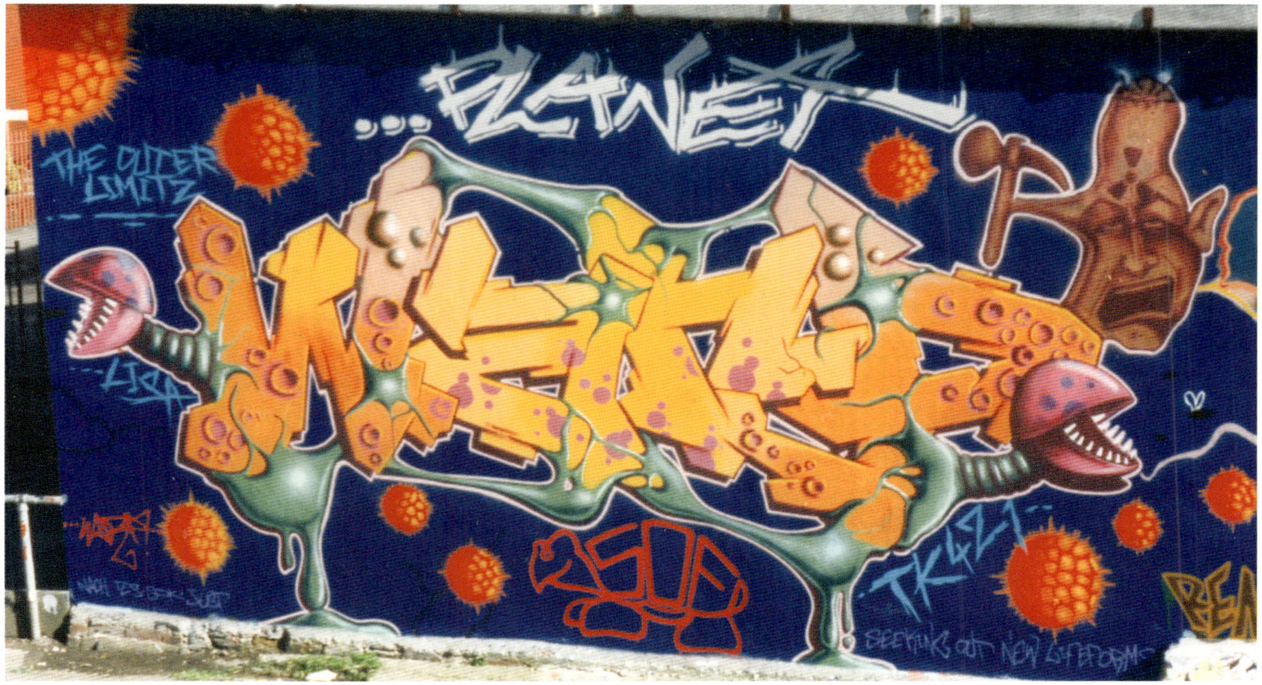

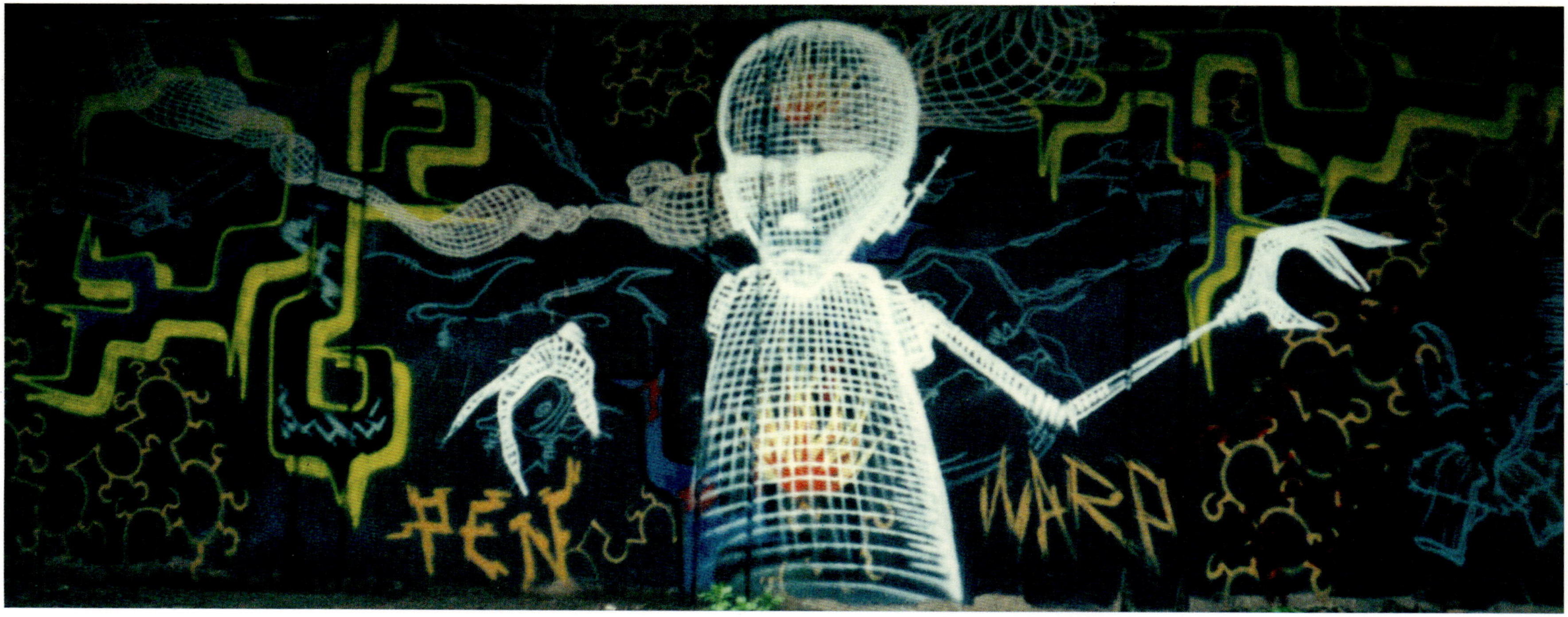

Top: M32, 1999

Above: Leicester jam, 1996/7

Warp: "I would say the productions have become heavier over the course of time, and perhaps more expressive in their rawness. I wouldn't necessarily say it's dark, although compared to a lot of other graffiti work it could be seen that way. We tend to approach our productions like a band making a track, each artist acting like a cog in a machine."

Your work is unlike that of any other crew I can recall. Did being from outside the city give you a unique take on graff?
Warp: "Yes, I think so; we weren't so caught up in the fashion side of graffiti. I was the only graffiti artist in the village for a good while, which helped my style evolve in an independent way. Our work has a weirder edge because of its more rural origins, the energy of the countryside, which we enjoyed bringing into the big city."

Pen: "Coming from the sticks gave us an underdog feeling when visiting the city, we felt that this was where the 'proper graff' was being done. I think that, as well as a massive passion for art, pushed us into being more imaginative in our concepts, styles and way of thinking."

Should art have a social purpose? Is your work dark because it's angry?
Pen: "Personally I don't think there are any rules. Whether you want to do graff to send a message, or if you're doing it strictly for yourself, it's all good. Being creative in any shape or fashion is a great thing."
Warp: "For me, art is a way of getting things out of my system, and it's not necessarily pretty or with deep meaning. I think there is emotion in the work, which viewers may pick up on. The work is angry at times but I think this is countered by a dark sense of humour. There is a lot of fluffier, happier stuff out there, which is good: people need uplifting stuff like that. But I think our stuff can be uplifting in a different way. It can make you think, and it doesn't offer you any easy-fix, happy pill."

Can you describe a few highs and lows in the life of the crew?
Pen: "The biggest high was when we broke through. We were painting non-stop. A low was when our crew broke down in 2000 due to internal disagreements, leading to Rowdy taking his own path and all of us throwing SOF to the dogs; but as a result we became more individual, which ultimately shaped us into the looser, more laid-back current collective."

Have drugs had an impact on your work?
Warp: "To a degree. Early on I was

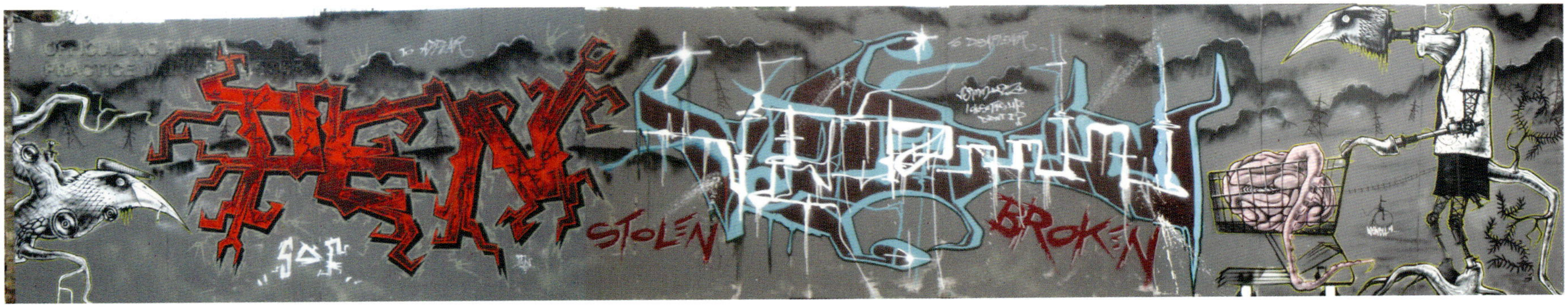

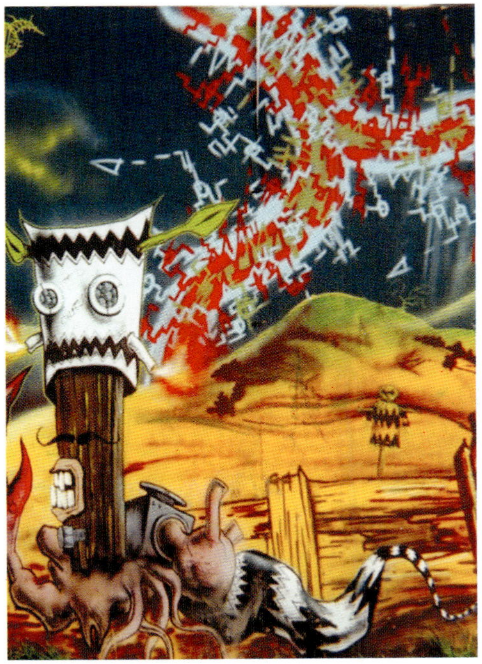

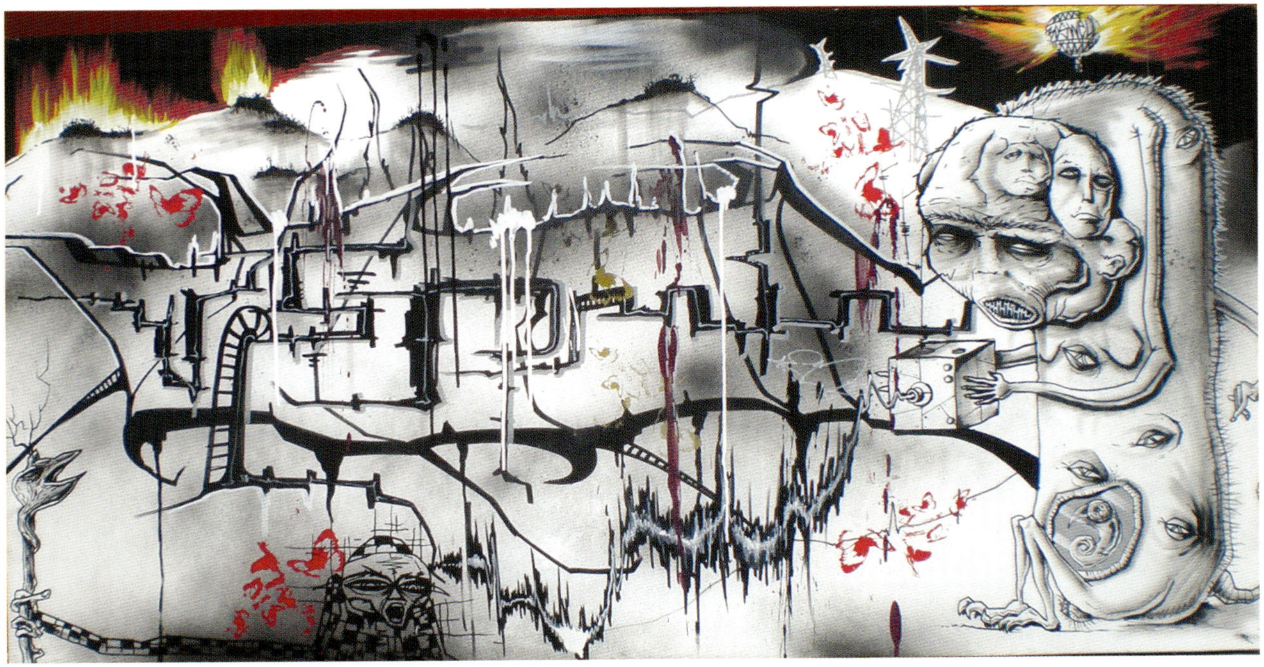

influenced by psychedelic drugs, which probably helped to unlock my imagination to a certain extent. Some people have said that our work has a druggy vibe, but primarily it is work from the imagination and not necessarily fuelled by drugs."

Pen: "I think drugs do open your mind to different thought processes, which can influence your work, but everything in life does that. Too much drug use can make you a lot less productive in the long run."

Has your work ever provoked strong reactions from members of the public?

Warp: "I remember this crazy woman who painted crosses over my characters because she believed they came off the walls, came to her house and drank her blood at night. I was also attacked by a pissed loony at Bedmo [Skate Park]. I had a pot of emulsion hurled at me, which exploded on the wall. And more recently, after I'd finished a piece in an alley in my local town, a woman showed her disapproval by threatening to run me over. Apparently she found the work aggressive. She said it scared her kids."

Can you say a few words about the present-day SOF?

Pen: "These days the approach to creating productions has loosened up considerably. We have a mostly freestyle approach to painting and building deep, atmospheric worlds out of layers of chaos."

Top: Ashley Road, 2008

Above left: Pen and Warp, Glastonbury Festival, 2006

Above: Vermin and Warp canvas, 2007

Top right: Vermin and Warp, c.1996

Bottom right: Vermin and Boswell (aka Warp) 2007

Opposite page. Top: Glastonbury Festival, 2004

Bottom: 'Child Falls on Dirty Syringe' spray paint, marker and photocopy on board, 2001

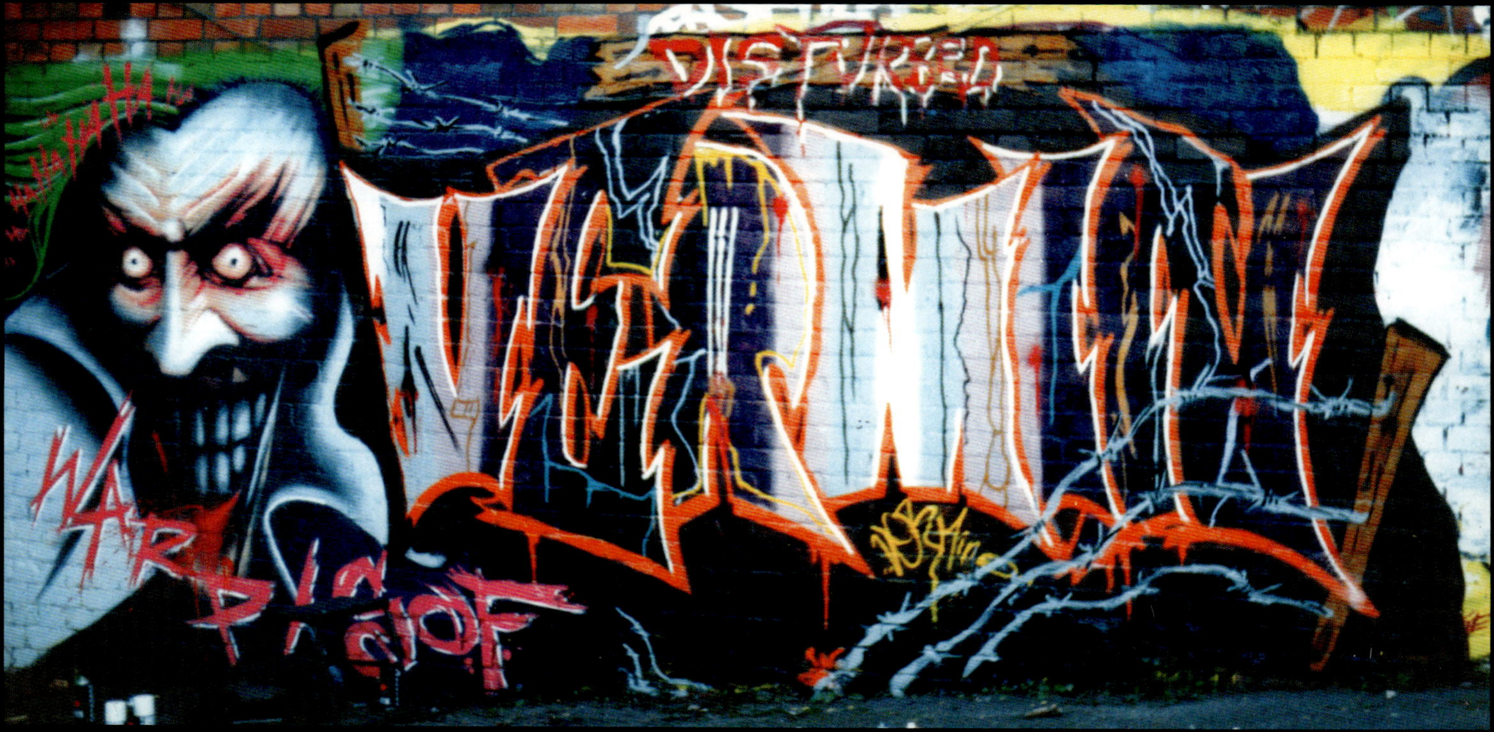

VERMIN SOF

• **"The cracks started to appear from a young age. When I think back now, being a sensitive person with an over inflated ego there were always going to be problems.** Visiting Bristol in 1988 when I was 14, I found the graffiti movement overwhelming. I visited Barton Hill and was in awe of the TUB painters, but felt too shy to converse – although I do recall taking some flicks on my camera, then going on 'free shopping' missions in the city, and coming back home on the bus to Radstock with cans of Buntlack paint and trying to paint the same as I'd seen in a makeshift hall of fame. Souls On Fire started in 1992 alongside the free party scene, when I was enjoying doing graffiti and taking drugs.

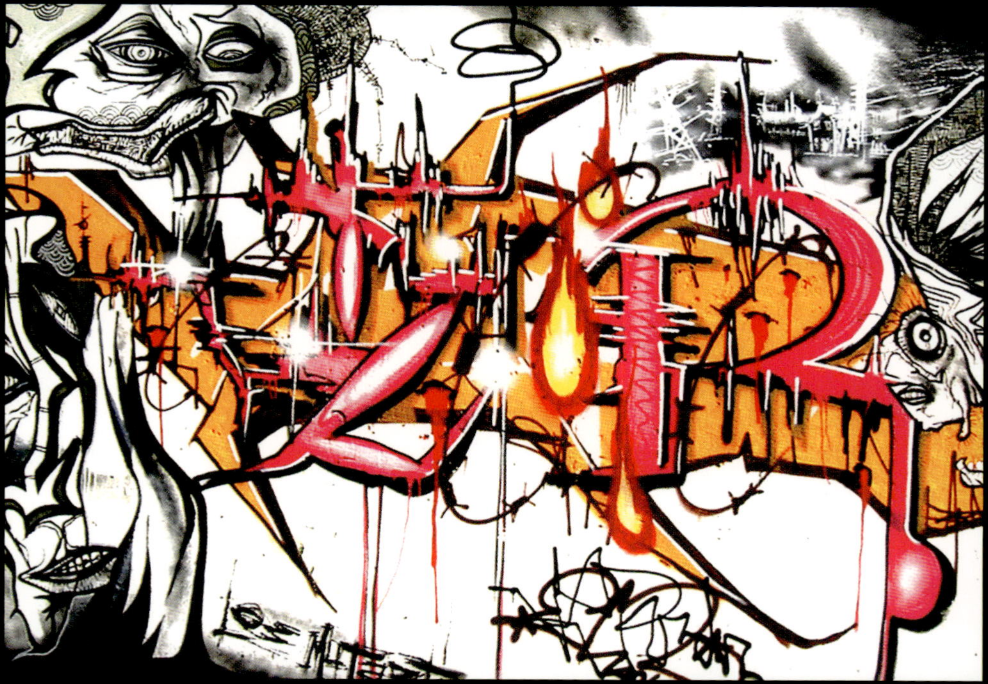

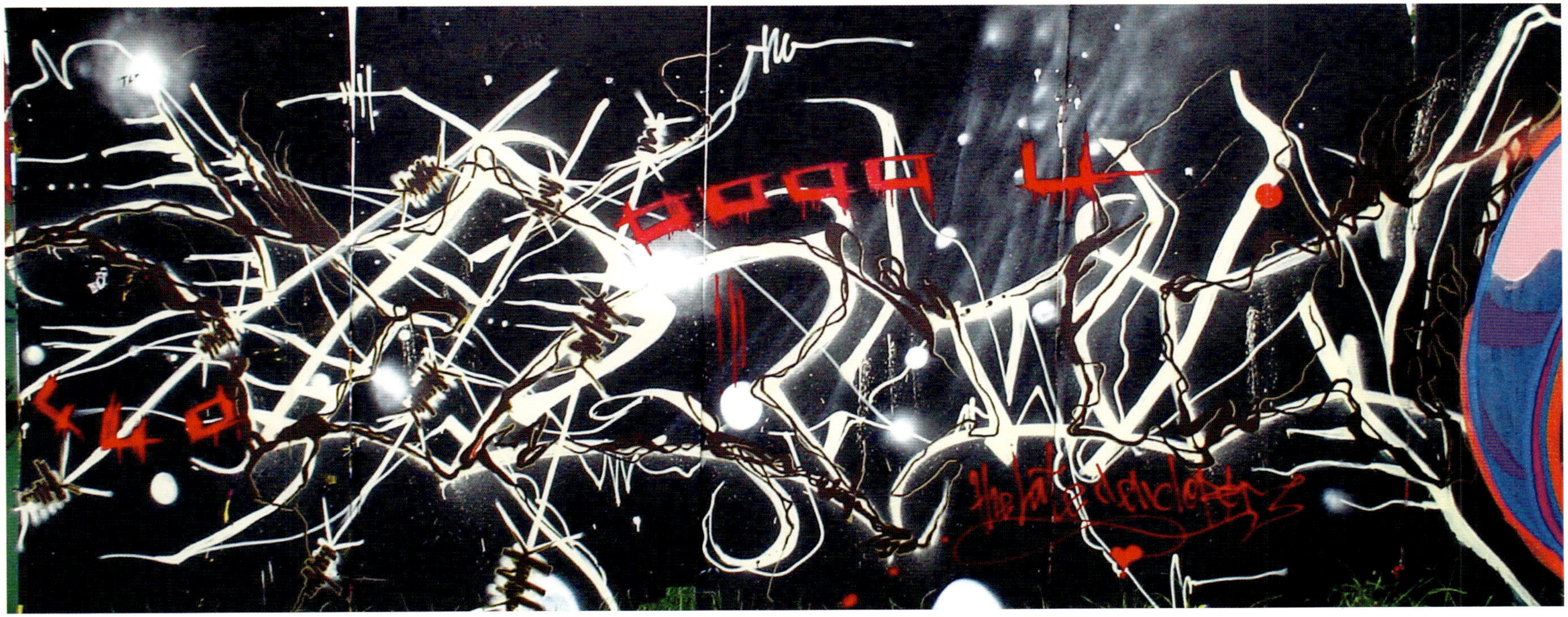

"I felt that 1996 was the golden year for Souls On Fire, and it was a pleasure to be the first crew to paint Bedminster top to bottom with the infamous Planet Farmyard piece. Another notable Bristol crew around that time – whom we befriended, travelled and painted with – was MBA, who later became Bad Applez. Along with writing Vermin, I started to add titles or sayings to my work, like 'disturbed', 'inbred', 'no shame', 'Dr Jelly casualties', 'farmyard rock 'ard', and 'demons destroying my sanity'. Sometimes I didn't even know what I was writing; they were just words to fill the gap.

"My drug addiction started to escalate uncontrollably by 1997. I had to take time out to reassess where I wanted to go with graffiti. At painting events such as Walls On Fire, I remember feeling uncomfortable because of my addiction – and in need of new directions. In 1999 I felt I had found my place as an artist. With SOF I had painted with my peers and I was ready to move into a new stage of social awareness. I was influenced poetically by music, it had taught me to be honest with myself and to be serious about what I was doing. My new painting style mixed dark, heavy elements with autobiographical, poetic words about my experiences and hopes for the future. Unfortunately for me, this brought rejection from other graffiti artists. I felt angry and questioned myself. The self-doubt had taken hold of my insecurity as a painter under the name Vermin, a name which represented my inner beauty. I felt the graffiti scene had no place for me any more, and I relied on taking drugs (heavily and daily), hardly sleeping and getting 'the bends' for a solid four months. I stared into Rodney Matthews books for hours on end, sketching for 24 hours solid, trying to

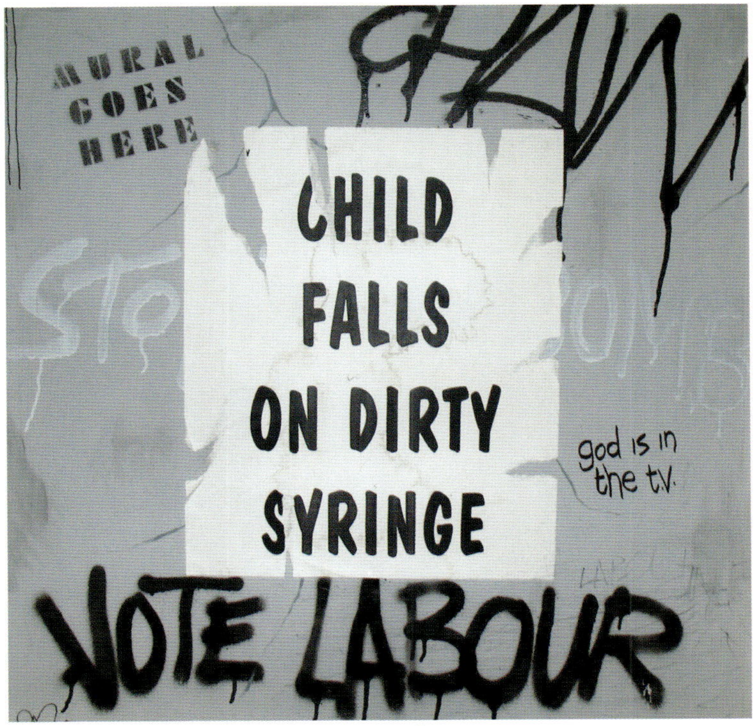

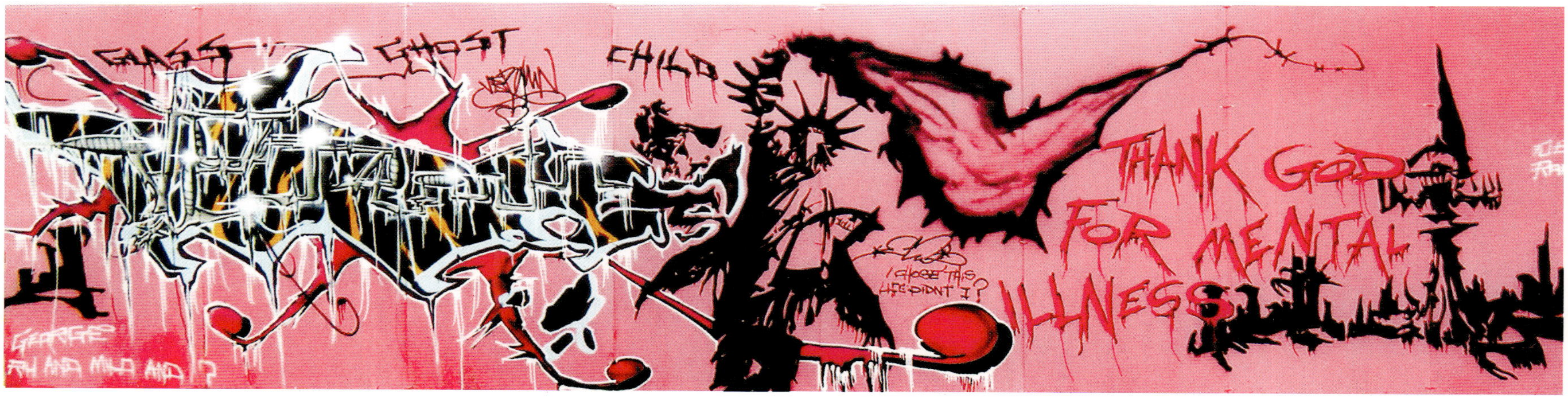
GHOST
CHILD
THANK GOD FOR MENTAL ILLNESS

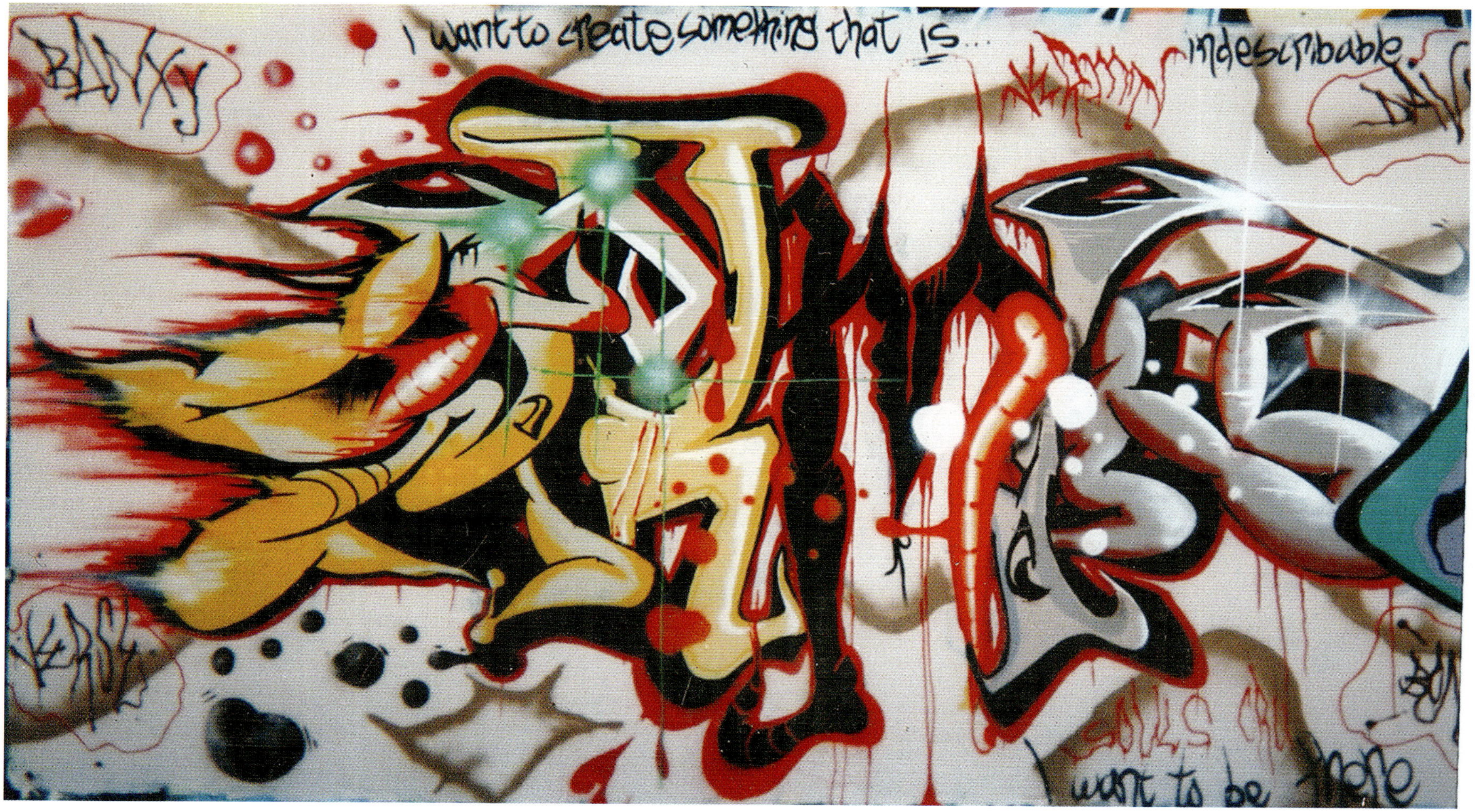
i want to create something that is... indescribable.
I want to be

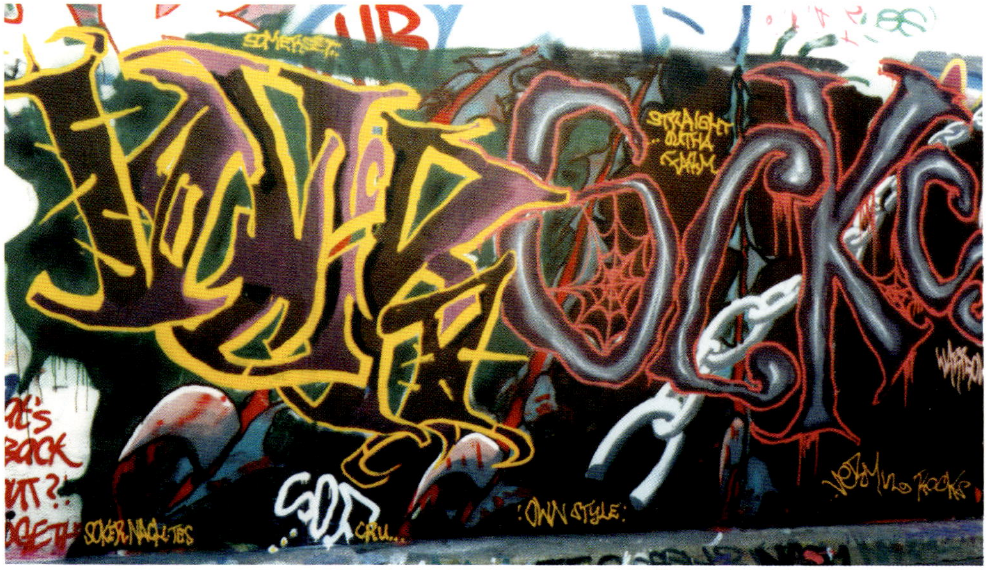

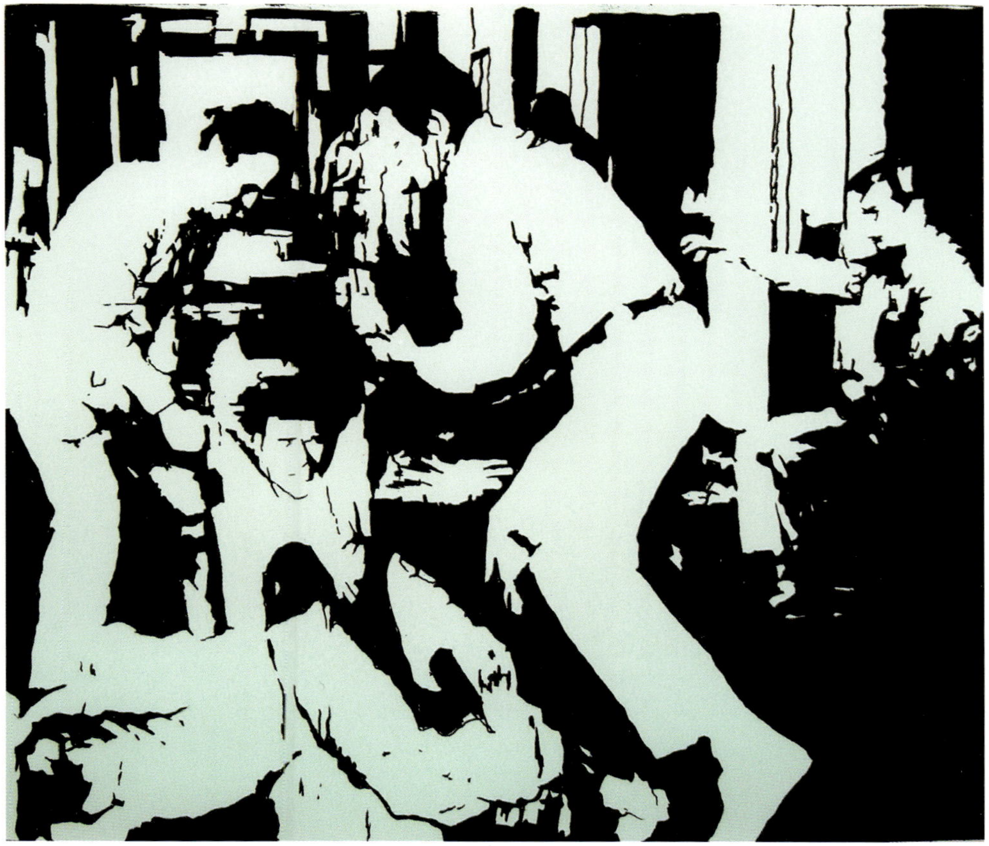

understand elements of his style to help create my own letterforms – only to come down and realise I hadn't sketched at all.

"In August of the same year, five of us decided to hit the fun-filled town of Newquay for a Bank Holiday weekend. I carried enough drugs for the five of us for three days. They weren't supposed to be taken by one person in one night, but that's what I did. Everyone around me became police and I was under close scrutiny, immersed in paranoia. At one point I sat, alone, and looked out across the ocean. I saw what I thought was a ship full of my contemporaries sailing away. Not only had I missed the boat, I had missed my last ship home. That weekend my life unfolded in front of me. I had reached an understanding of all the work I had put on walls and the meanings behind it. I didn't even realise it at the time, but I had observed my whole future in the space of three days and had witnessed the mechanics of the universe.

"I was admitted to a secure unit, where my psychosis lasted three months. My mind consisted of graffiti, war, fire, numeracy, space, and a non-existent religion structured around coincidence and chance. The fact that I was discharged by a Doctor Jelly added to the truth. It was a magical time, but the next seven years spent dealing with the aftermath of these experiences have tested me so much that I haven't been able to paint graffiti.

"Now older and wiser, I truly believe that personal expression should have a place in society in whatever form it requires. The social voice of freedom is something to be embraced. Graffiti isn't done for the viewer; it's a reflection of what is happening on the inside. If it's hard to understand, I think that says it all."

Opposite page. Top: 'Thank God For Mental Illness' Glastonbury Festival, 2008

Bottom: 'I Want To Create Something That Is Indescribable' Bedminster skate park, 1998

This page: Top: 'Verock (Straight Out Tha Farm)', 1996

Bottom: 'A Moment From The Cornwall Asylum', 1999

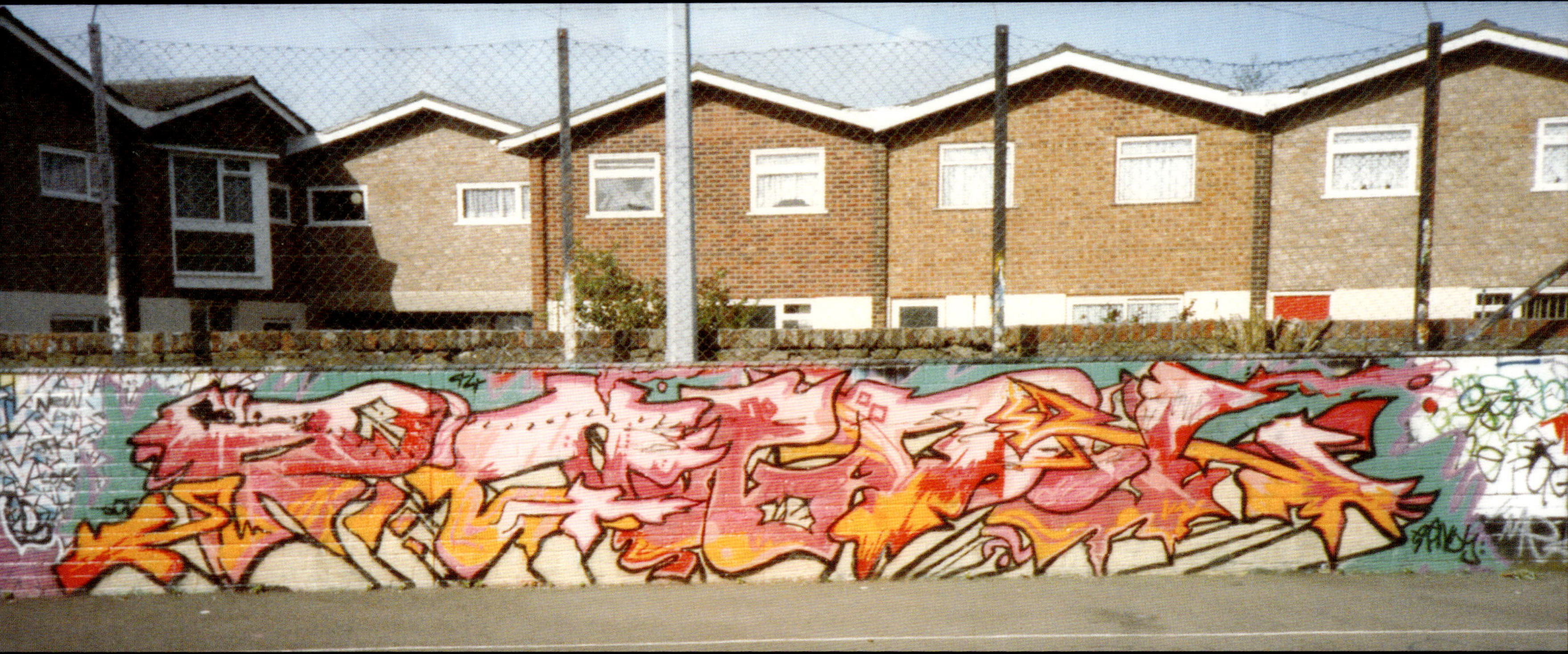

Top: 'Rowdy' Barton Hill youth club, 1994

Bottom: Rowdy, Warp, Pen and Chain (aka Vermin) front wall of Barton Hill youth club, c.1995

ROWDY

• **A West Country graffiti veteran with over 20 years' writing behind him, Rowdy stands virtually alone as an artist who continues to paint illegally as often, and as prominently, as possible.** His work is sometimes hard for people to digest. Angry and awkward, it is a far cry from the slick, familiar styles of a lot of his contemporaries. He seems to be making a conscious statement about the society we live in, and how it alienates outsiders – or, indeed, anyone who does not accept its received norms and values.

"If you do work that's polished and nice, it just blends in with everything else. I don't feel that comfortable with what's going on around me, I feel that needs to be

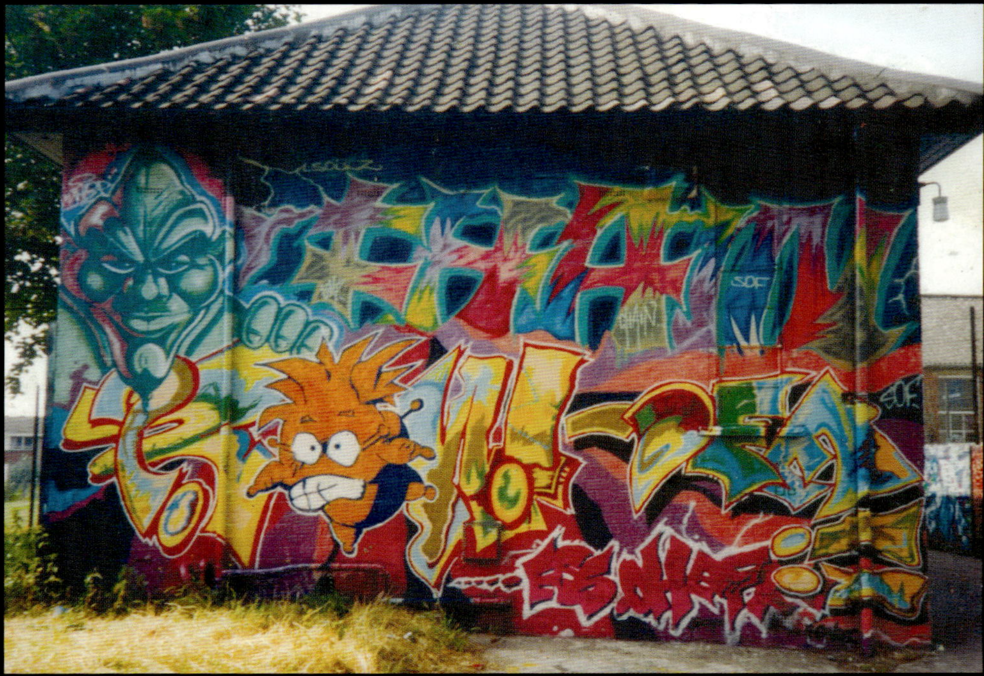

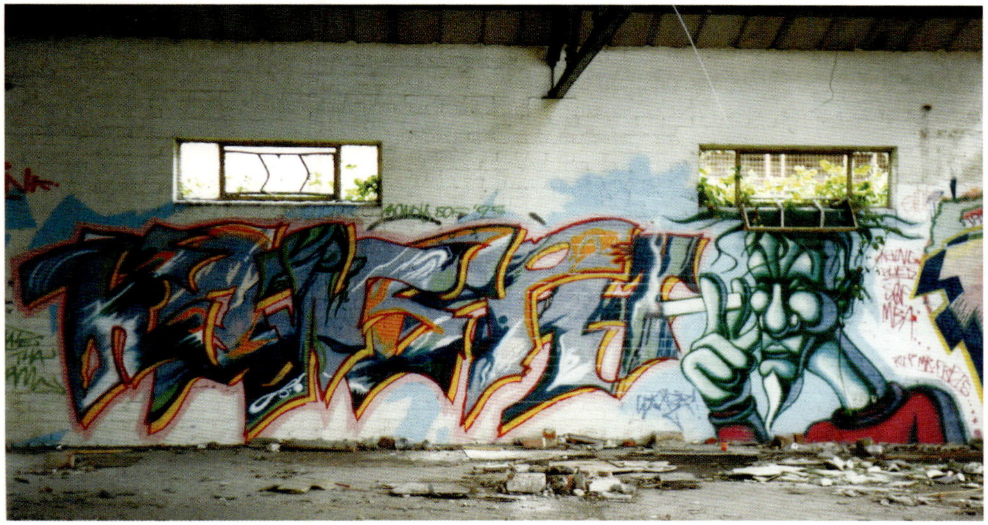

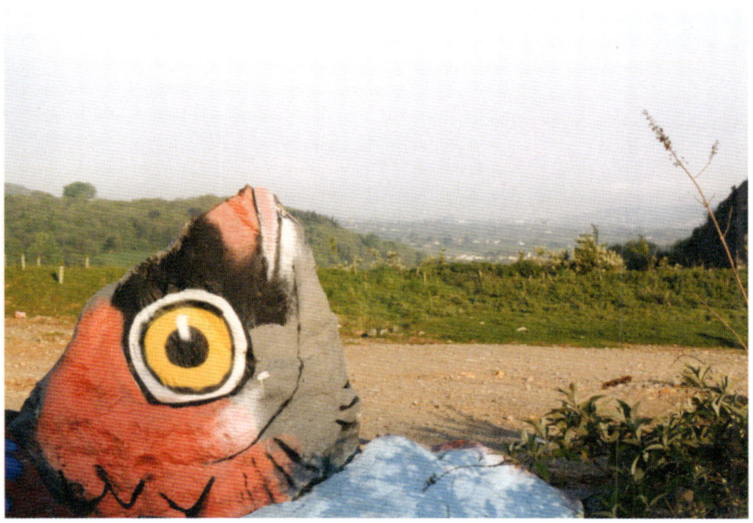

Top: 'Rowdy' Barton Hill youth club, 1994

Bottom: Rowdy, Warp, Pen and Chain (aka Vermin) front wall of Barton Hill youth club, c.1995

looked at. We see 'beauty' so much on TV, in film, and advertising, that young girls, for example, feel guilty about what weight they're supposed to be, about having the 'right' sort of products. I feel 'beauty' is very much to the detriment of our society.

"To celebrate ugliness, weirdness and oddballs is not such a bad thing; there are plenty of them around, so there's no point in pretending they're not there, even though TV and advertising does a pretty good job of it. They become misfits and there's a stigma towards them and they get told they're not going to fit in with the beautiful, cool people. Graffiti sometimes panders to that and is a victim of it itself and we need to look at that. A lot of people feel under-valued and manipulated, so I think it helps to make the kind of art that challenges and throws something back against the whole system."

The seeds of Rowdy's political leanings were sown way before he started writing graffiti, and he looks back on the days before hip hop as an important time, when an awareness and social conscience were instilled in him. Margaret Thatcher was in power and we had never had it so bad.

"The political content in my work has always been there. Before New York graffiti reached London, I used to travel there on the train and see political messages daubed on the track sides, so I remember that being the precursor. Plus in the early '80s I was going on CND marches with my mum, so it was obvious to me that something wasn't right in terms of Thatcherism and the state of the country. I needed to question that even from a young age. There were a lot of issues at stake: where I lived was an old mining area, and you had the miners' strike going on, then the area lost its railway infrastructure. I just watched all this decline, followed by the 'yuppie element' that crept into Thatcher's 1980s."

Rowdy started writing graffiti in 1987, whilst growing up in "a small town near Bristol" - he is vague about even this most basic of details, as he is constantly mindful of not accidentally incriminating himself. "I still believe in keeping some things under wraps. Plus I never had to take the rap and face the consequences of all the piecing I did in my formative years, and I want to keep it that way, really."

Those formative years were spent painting with his first crew in relative seclusion, at a rural spot they had claimed as their own, away from the heat of urban policing and all the hassle that comes with it for young, hungry, obsessed writers. It was here that he also first came into contact with the travellers' scene and its freer, almost chaotic approach to living - a way of life which sowed the seeds for the fledgling rave culture.

"The first place we used to paint was an old railway track. We basically had what was an illegal hall of fame running for a few years, and we had people from around Bath, Frome and Radstock getting down to it there. That was in 1986/87, and that convinced me that I could make pieces in my own area. Then in 1989/90 we started painting an old train works where they used to park up wagons and repair trains. There was a big warehouse that we'd paint, and we had a big travellers' scene down

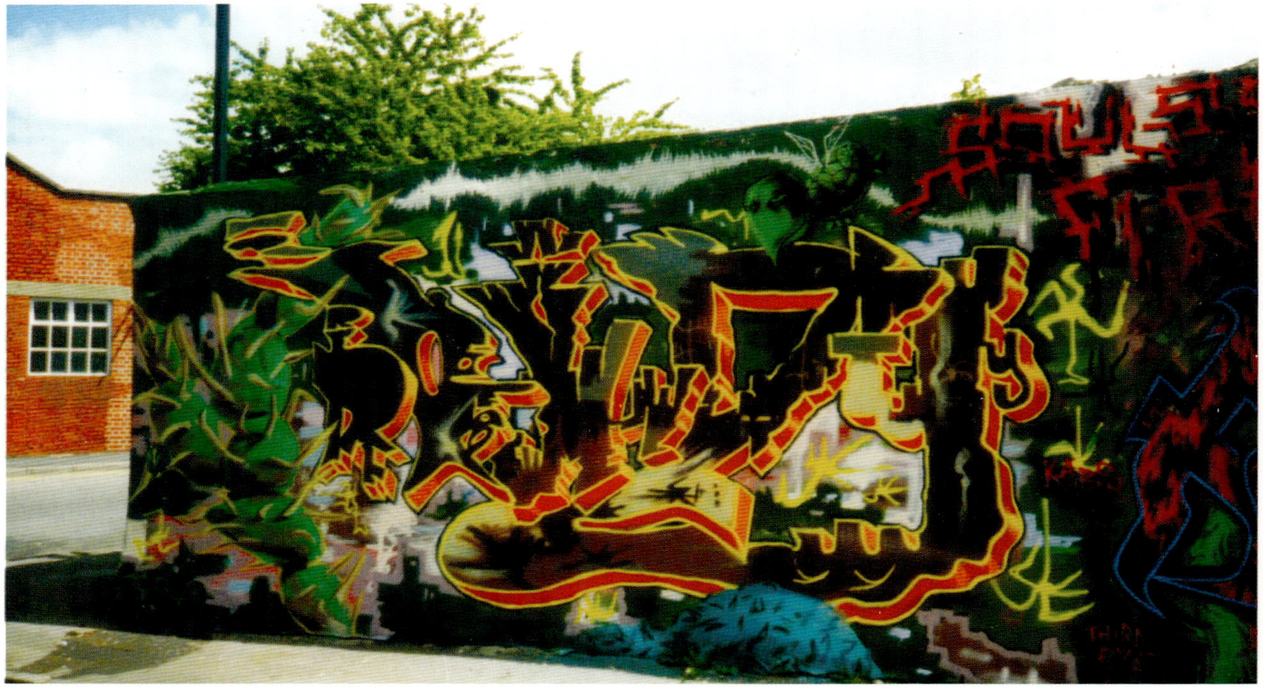

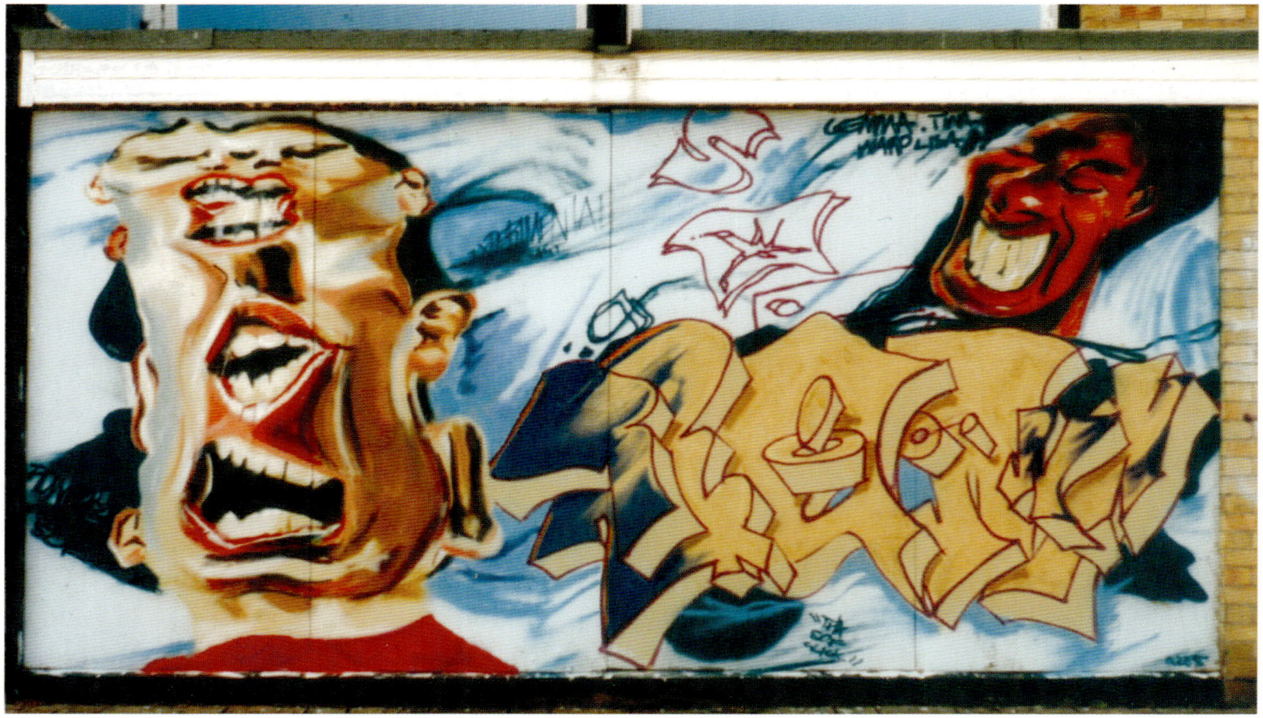

there as well, and that's when it started to get quite anarchic. That whole vibe, with the buildings getting smashed up and people making big fires, was mixed in with the graff. We held that place down for quite a few years. It was a place for hatching plans for free parties, and there were drug users and dealers there. That became like my second home."

While making regular visits to Bristol in the late 1980s and becoming aware of what was going on in places like Barton Hill and Bedminster Skate Park, Rowdy and his crew Souls On Fire continued to maintain a comfortable distance from the city, dropping pieces and then getting out again. In hindsight, remaining on the periphery of the illegal Bristol scene at this time was a very shrewd move, as the shit was about to hit the proverbial fan.

"In '89, when things were peaking at Barton Hill, we were just starting to make loose contacts with people there. After Operation Anderson, though, activity just seemed to plummet quite quickly. We knew about the heat BTP [British Transport Police] brought on people, and although we had done track sides and the odd train, it really didn't seem worth the bother painting trains that weren't going to run. And there were plenty of other places to get up, anyway. We had more of a creative drive to do artistic work, and hang out in places where we could smoke a few joints and just really relax and push the art."

In some ways Operation Anderson had the desired effect in Bristol, for a while at least, and Souls On Fire (along with one or two other crews) stepped into the void left by the mass police crackdown.

"It felt like we were some of the only people painting at that time, so we were

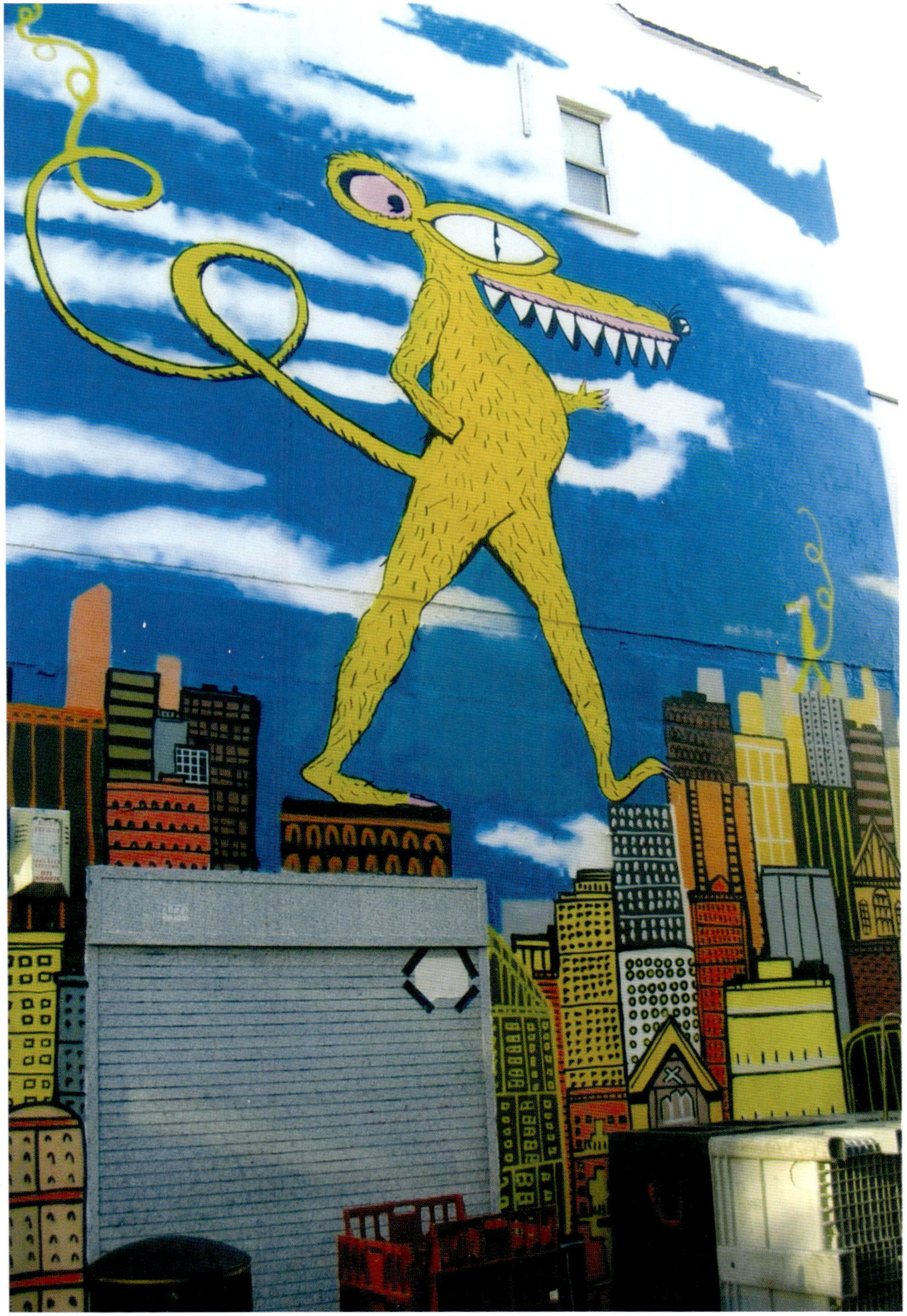

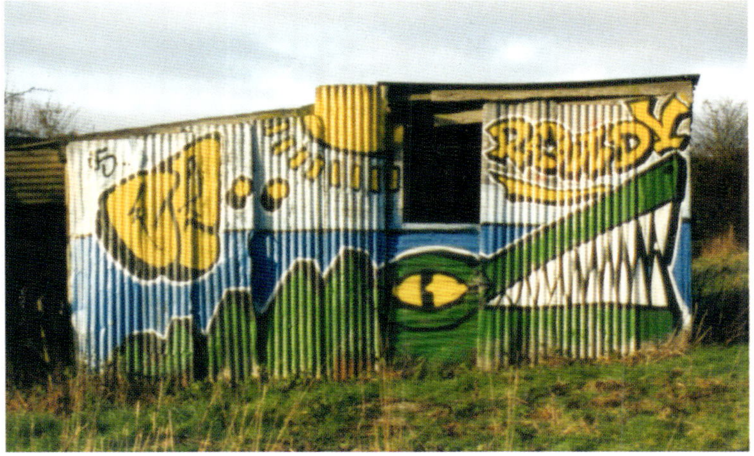

picking up where other people had left off, and we started reclaiming the spots like Bedminster Skate Park and Barton Hill Dug Out. Then in the mid 90s we started painting the Brislington warehouse and developed links with MBA and those guys. It seemed like there was so much up for grabs. We started bringing more people into the fold from places like Bath and Swindon and we were selling *Graphotism* from the very early days when it was still black and white, just doing a lot behind the scenes to re-introduce graffiti back into Bristol."

Ironically, despite being a major player in Bristol in the mid 90s, Rowdy still hadn't made it his home, and although he was making his presence felt on the city's walls, he still had other fish to fry out in the sticks. "I used to go and hang out in quarries. We had this place that people from all over would go to swim and chill out; it was like an alternative beach resort, that was our place to kick back. It'd been in the back of my mind to do something there, but I wanted to do it in the right manner, and I'd been looking at Andy Goldsworthy's stuff, so I started thinking about doing a graff take on that. I went and found some

Opposite page. Top left: Easton, 1999

Bottom left: 'Hall of Mirrors' style Frome, 1995

This page. Left: 'Ratodile' walking tall, London, 2007

Top right: The distinctive crocodile character welcomes visitors to Bristol, M32 Bristol approach, 2006

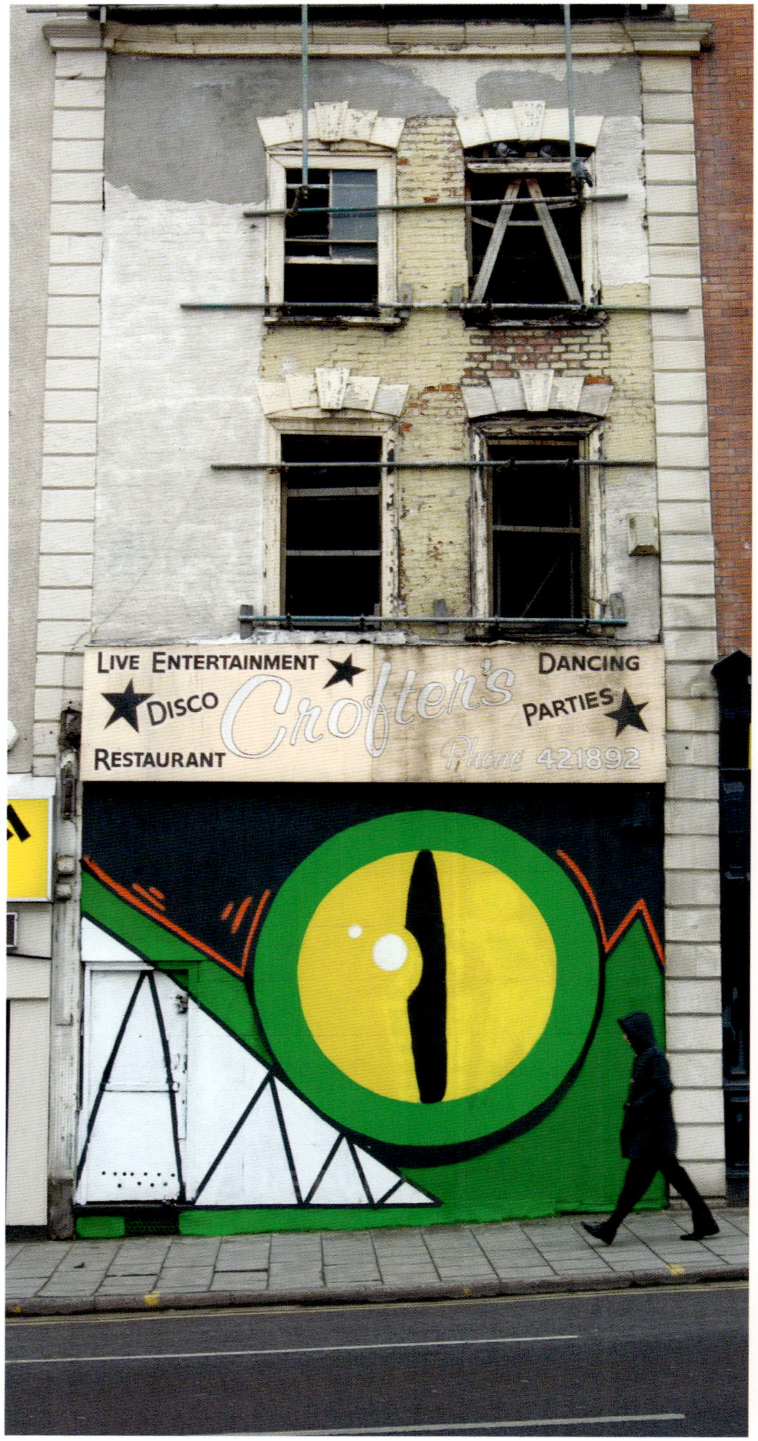
LIVE ENTERTAINMENT
DANCING
DISCO
Crofter's
PARTIES
RESTAURANT
Phone 421892

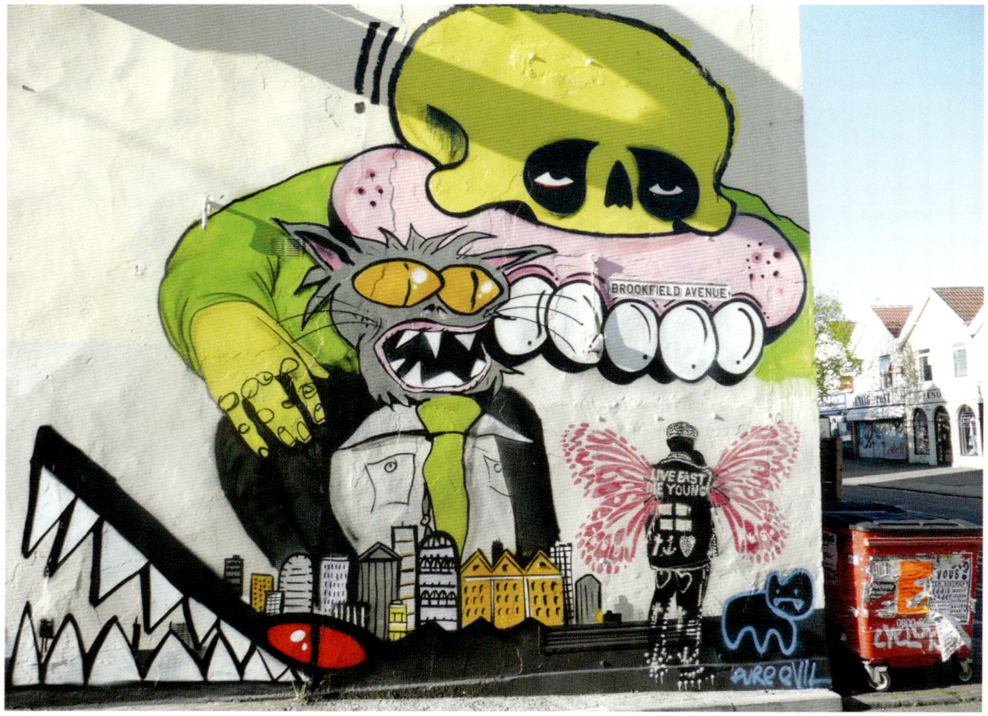
BROOKFIELD AVENUE

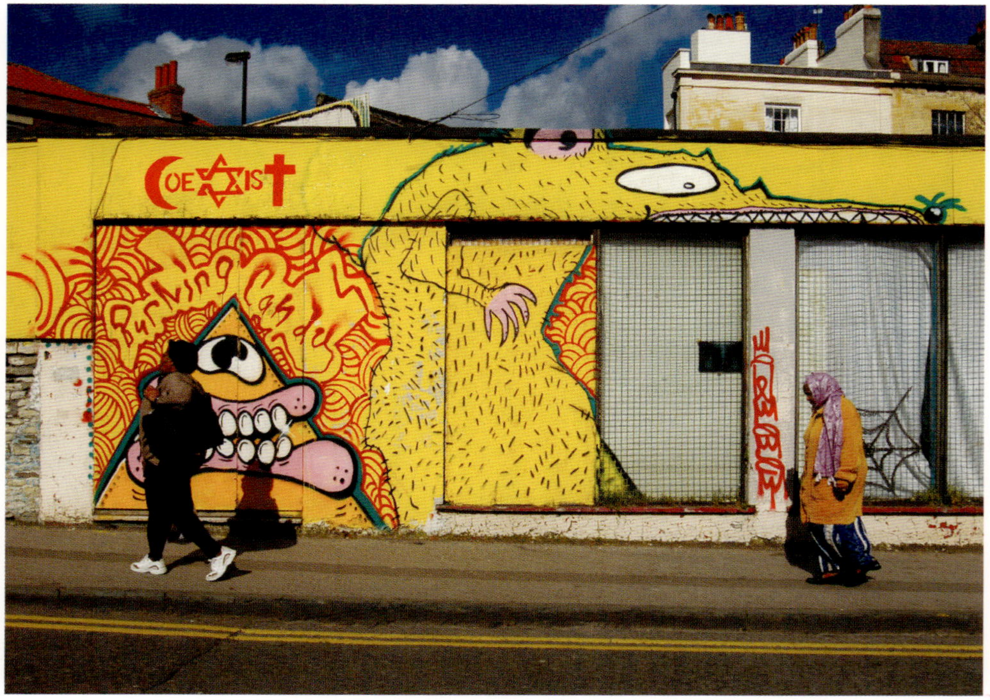

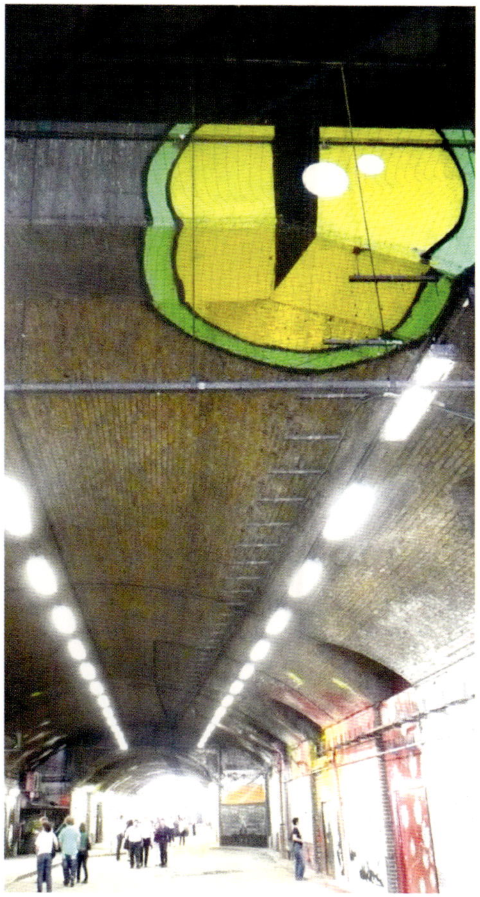

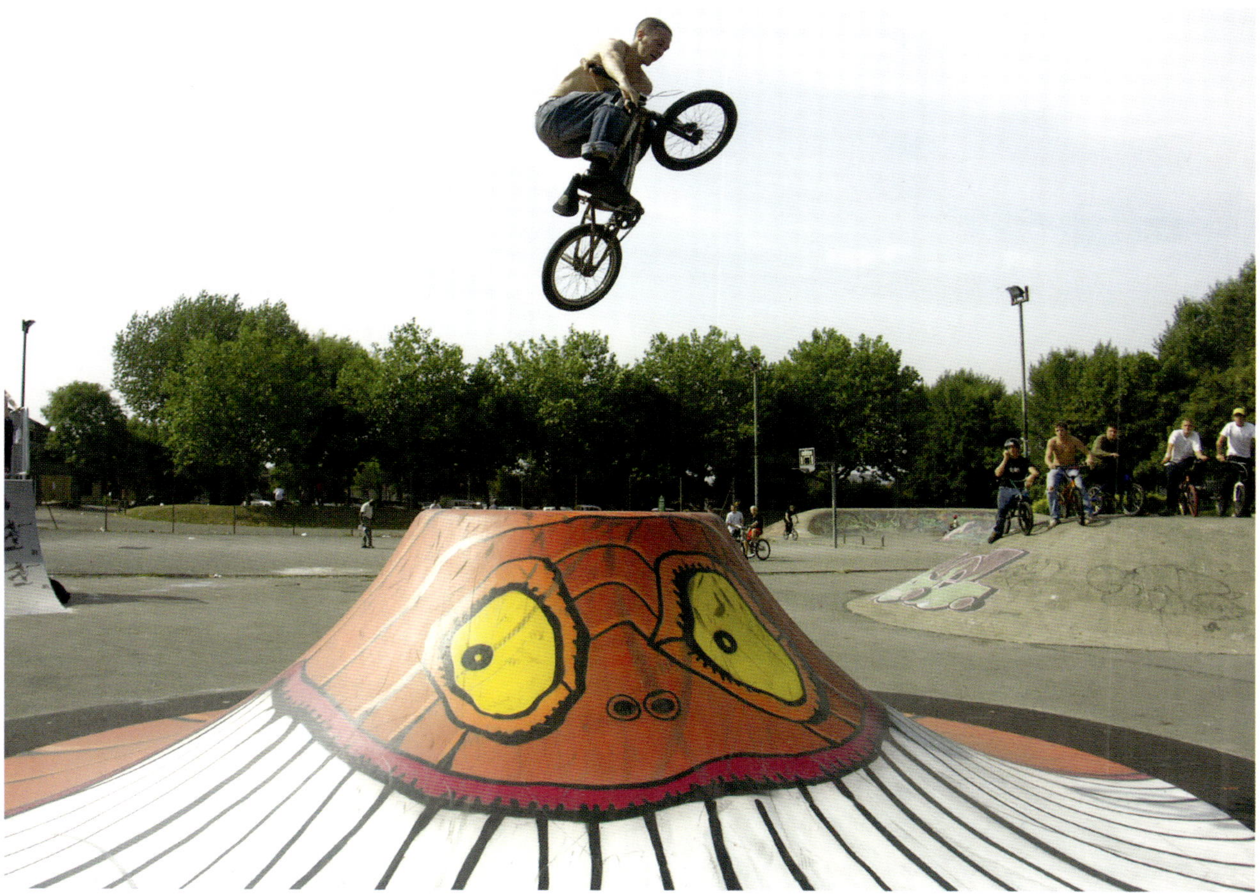

rocks that I liked the look of and covered them in masonry paint and just started painting on them, just experimental vibes. I hit three or four different quarries over about four or five years, trying to do things on quite an epic scale, trying to work with the space as much as possible. I enjoyed that headspace of having a huge area to hang out in on my own. With rock paintings you can physically get into the space, climb on them. It was something I discovered and nurtured for myself. It's totally different from painting in the city."

Rowdy finally made Bristol his home at the turn of the millennium, and the intensity of urban life seems to have impacted heavily on his approach, sharpening his political teeth and giving his work a more explicit purpose. "I arrived in Bristol in 2000. My graff had arrived a lot earlier, but I had always thought that coming to a city when I was younger would have meant getting in even more trouble, and I liked just keeping that distance. There's more surveillance in the city, so we used to just creep in and out, you know?

"But I moved here in the end because it seemed the smart thing to do, it gave me a chance to get a bit more involved. If I really had something to say, then stripping it back to statements and hitting petrol stations with quick hits seemed to me to be a very good way of doing it. I like using the slightly more hardcore vibe of graff to really push out messages and to get people thinking, to try and echo people's feelings. Sometimes it's quite hard to get that into a big painting but you can do it with a quick, snappy statement."

This need to make a point boldly, simply, and perhaps with a touch of wit for light relief, is most obvious in what might be seen as Rowdy's mascot (or 'spokesmanimal', if you like), The Croc. Baring its huge teeth in an unnerving

Opposite page. Left: 'Stokes Croc' Stokes Croft, Bristol, 2008

Top right: Collaboration with Burning Candy crew and Pure Evil, Gloucester Road, Bristol, 2008

Bottom right: Burning Candy (Sweet Toof and Cyclops) collaboration, Ashley Road, Bristol, 2006

This page. Top left: Croc eye oversees Cans Festival, London, 2008

Top right: Toothy grin, St.George's Park, Bristol, 2005 (pic by Craig, Body English)

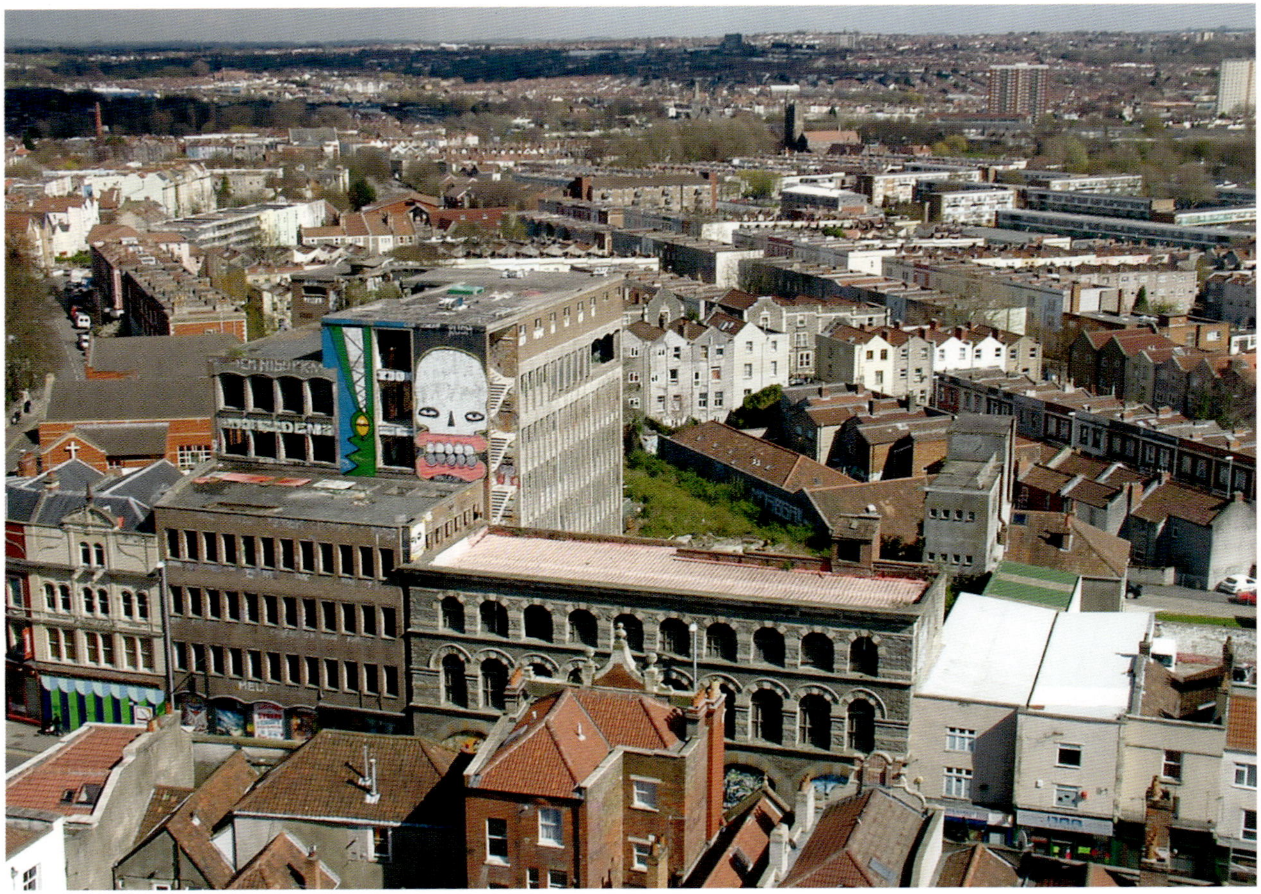

Above: Jumbo Croc and Burning Candy skull, Westmoreland House, Stokes Croft, Bristol, 2007

half-grin, The Croc has grown with each new manifestation, the largest of which (to date) pokes vertically above the city skyline at the top of Westmoreland House, an abandoned multi-storey blot on the landscape right in the heart of Bristol.

"It's taking it right back to that whole prehistoric thing. Crocs have got a presence and you have to be respectful towards them. So it's not all fun and cuddly, it's got that sharp element to it. It reminds people that there's nature out there, and they should treat it with some respect."

Painted in broad daylight over one memorable weekend, alongside a giant skull with false teeth by Cyclops and Sweet Toof, Rowdy's three-storey crocodile looms large like a kind of talisman, giving the metaphorical finger to the Council and the forces of law and order that would have us believe that they have the city locked down and under control.

"We had a standoff with the police down there. They had phone calls from the public about the graffiti going up, but they wouldn't come inside the disused buildings, for health and safety reasons or whatever. So we held our ground, and carried on painting. It had always seemed to be the perfect place to make a statement. I used to keep looking at the top and thinking, 'that whole wall needs to be taken out'. But I couldn't find anyone to do it with – until I started painting with Cyclops and Sweet Toof, and they were thinking big like I was. We did half of it upwards with roller poles, and half as a lean-over, where we stretched 20-30 foot roller poles as far as they'd go, standing on ladders as well. It just started getting more and more attention on that spot, and that's when it feels great. It's so in your face, a lot of people can see it from a lot of different angles. You can't miss it!"

Not fitting in, breaking the rules (society's and graffiti's), remaining in his own creative space. These traits seem to have defined Rowdy's work, be it with Souls On Fire, with loose collective The Farm Yardeez, or more recently alongside Before Chrome. He taps directly into graffiti's potential to be the true outsider art, and to force people to stop and think.

So long as the next generation of writers are born of the street and cut their teeth by writing their names on walls, graffiti's continued integrity, according to Rowdy, appears to be assured.

"It's just people writing their names, it's a natural thing to do – kids write on their school desks, everyone can make a mark that's their own. What tagging allows you to do is to get comfortable with making your mark in the public arena, and start being disobedient. People make taggers and young writers scapegoats for things that are going wrong in the community, when they need to look at relationships breaking down, alcoholism, and so on; there are other, much more serious ways that society is fucked. If you have a clean city with no tags, you're just going down the road of [George Orwell's] 1984."

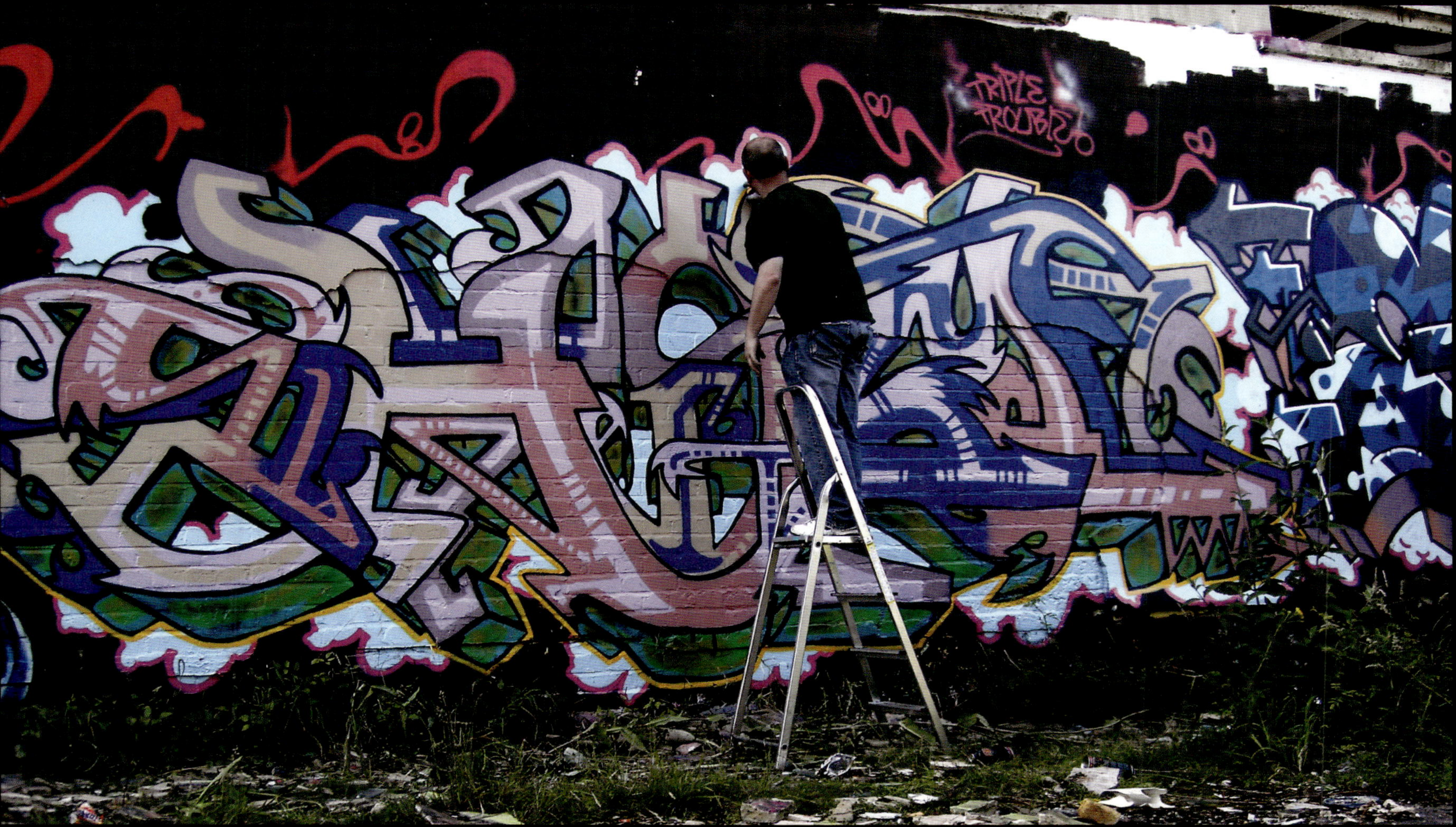

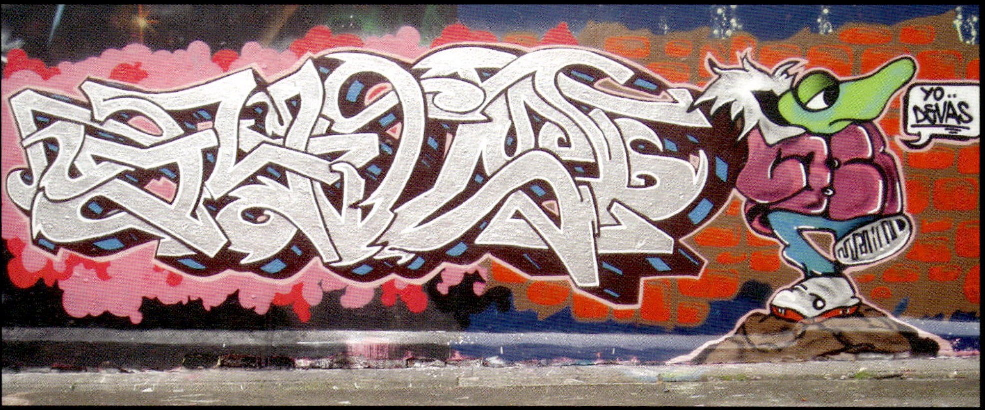

SHIMZ AWOL

• **Shimz lives for graffiti. His crew's name, AWOL (A Way Of Life), says it all.** Shimz is an old-school master, a wildstyle craftsman who translates the traditional New York aesthetic in a fresh and personal way. His juxtaposition of colour, form and line undergo constant reinvention, all the while remaining unmistakably his own. No two Shimz pieces are alike, yet they could

Top: Shimz adds the finishing touches, 2008

Left: Bode lizard in a goose-down jacket gives the shout out to Devas, Bedminster skate park, 2007

Top right: Punchy pastels amongst the drab grey tower blocks, 2008

Bottom right: Shimz FCK (Fried Chicken Crew) Quick track side, 2002

Opposite page. Top: Big and broad, 1999

Left: Brightening up some out of town steel, 2006

Middle right: Shimz FCK hand style

Bottom right: Shimz Bue big track side, 2000

never be mistaken for anyone else's work: no mean feat for a veteran of 20 years of graffiti writing.

When did you start writing, and which part of the city did you grow up in?
"I've been into graff since about '88/89. I grew up in a rough part of Bristol called Hartcliffe, a.k.a. Brownsville. When I was growing up, one by one each of my mates found a new best mate: Mr Brown - smack or heroin. I chose hip hop instead. Hip hop has always been there as far back as I can remember, and I love the original four elements: breaking, MCing, DJing and, of course, graffiti."

Can you describe some of your earliest memories of putting your name up?
"I used to ride miles on my BMX with pockets full of markers and stickers, just to get my tag up everywhere and to look for new pieces around town. If you came across a new piece, that was a serious buzz. The mystery was the best bit, because people didn't know who was who and who was writing what back then. Nowadays, you don't have to pinch the nozzle from your mum's polish to put on your can of spray paint. The tools are all there, ready for the younger generation of writers."

What inspired you to start writing, and whose work did you admire?
"Seeing *Style Wars* on TV for the first time when I was really young - that made me go cock-eyed. I'm what you'd describe as a traditionalist, and what influenced me in my youth was the 'golden' era of New York subway graffiti: Seen, PJay, Duster, all those sorts of writers. That's why I like to paint what is, in my eyes, proper graffiti

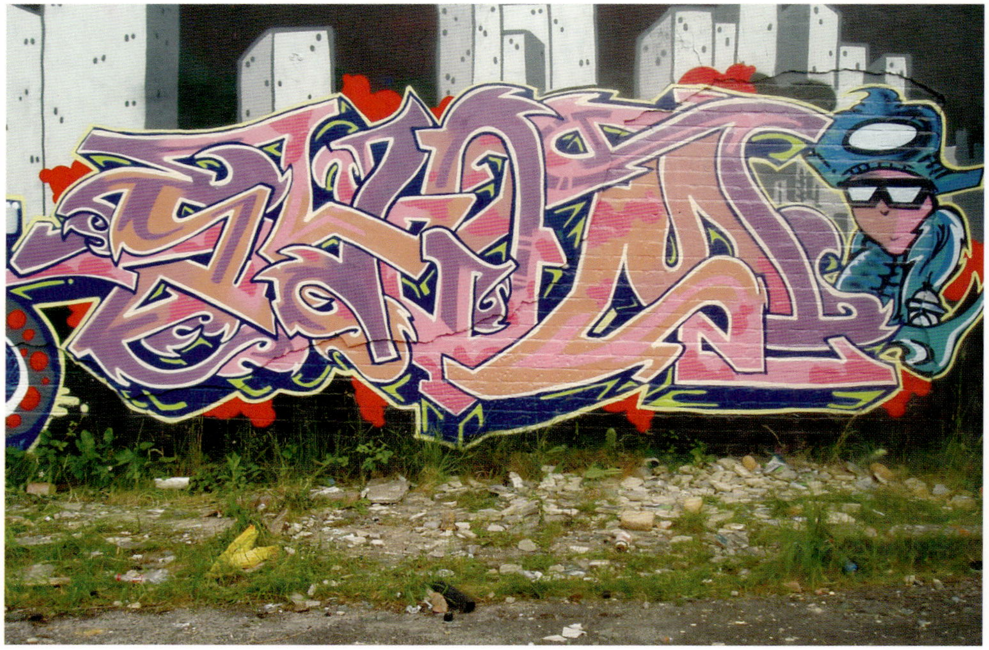

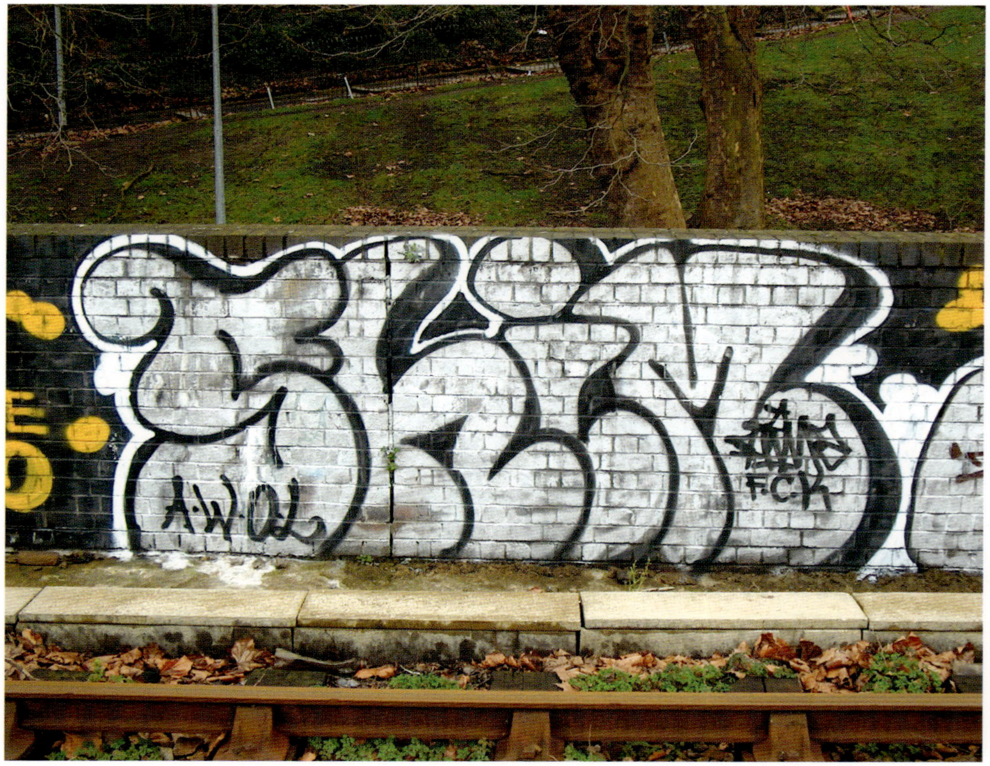

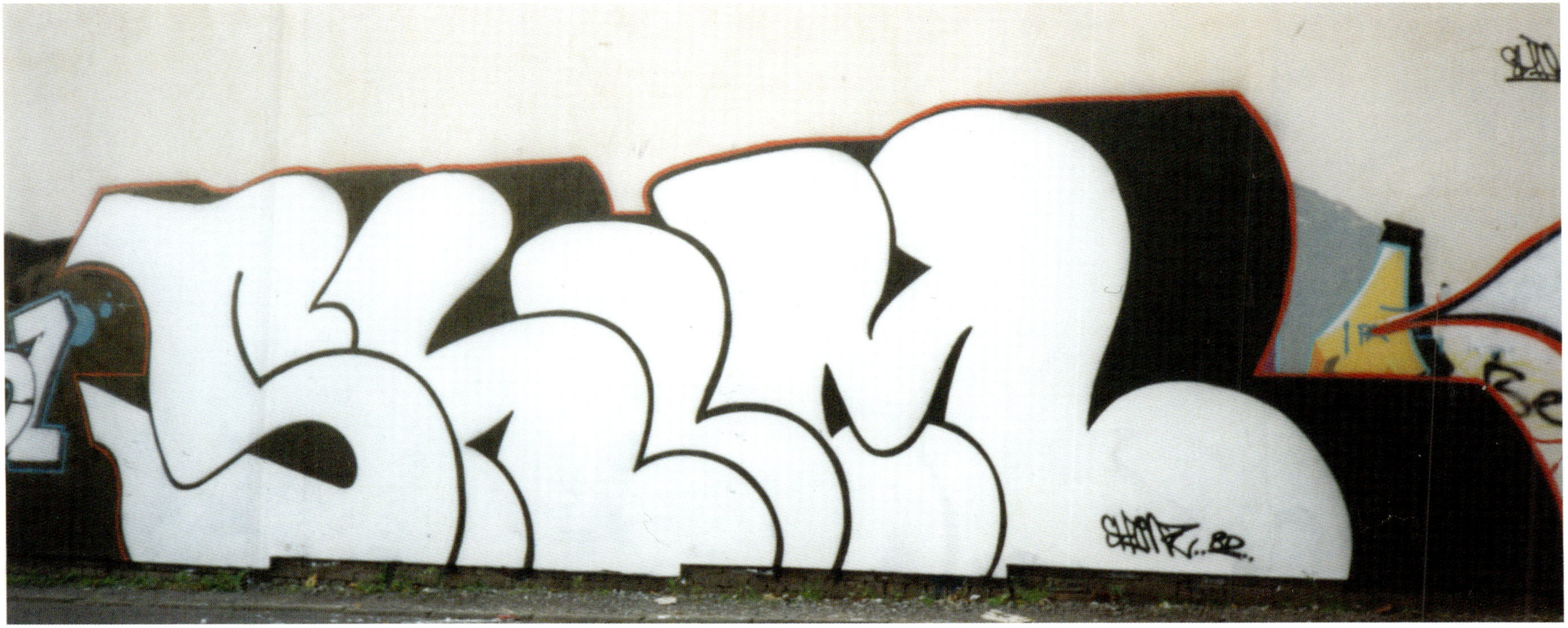

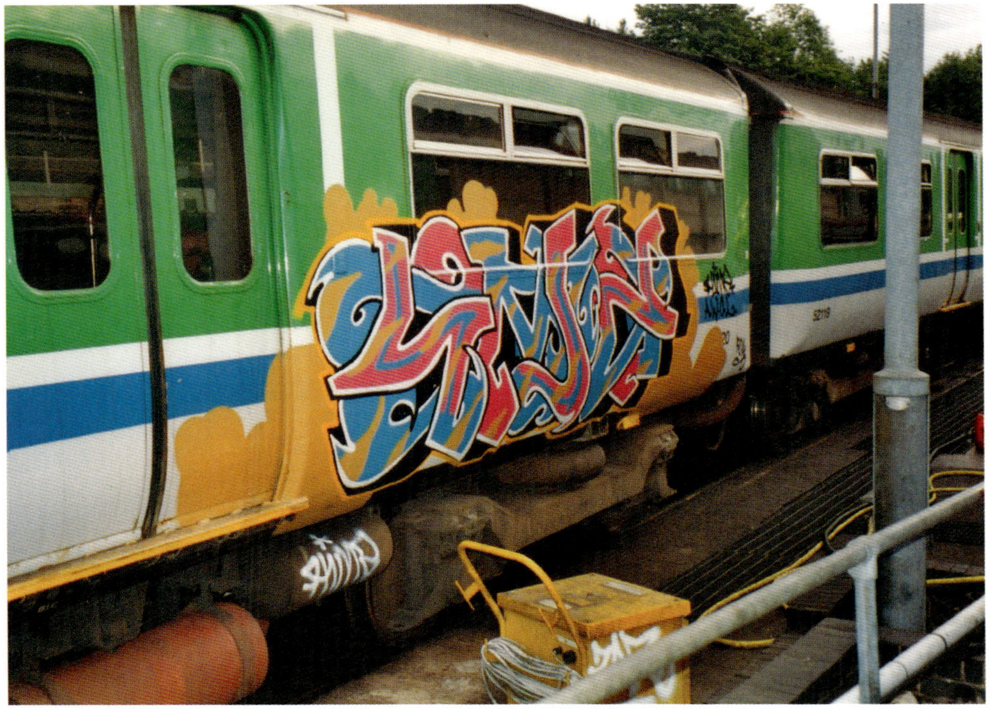

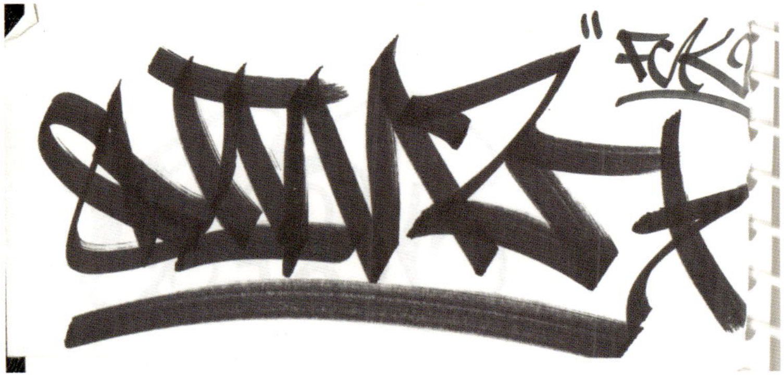

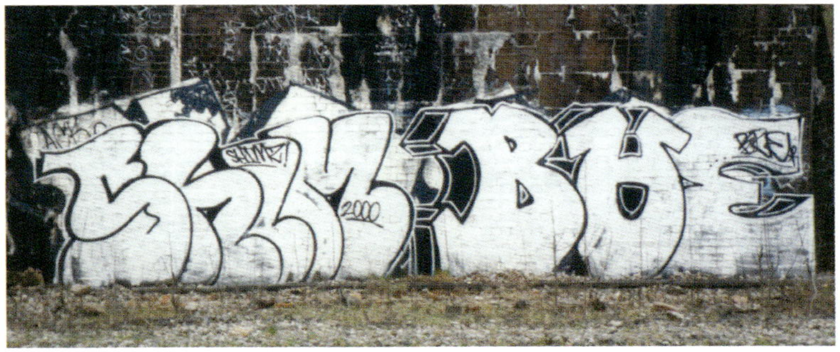

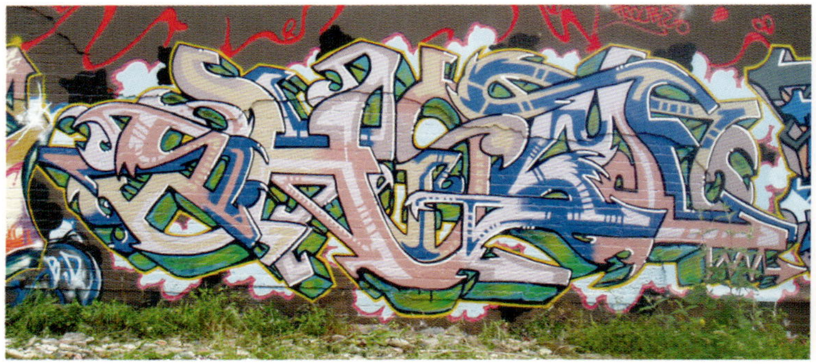

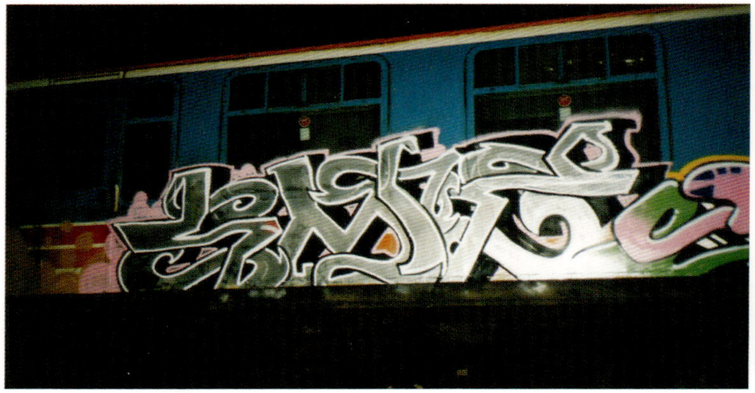

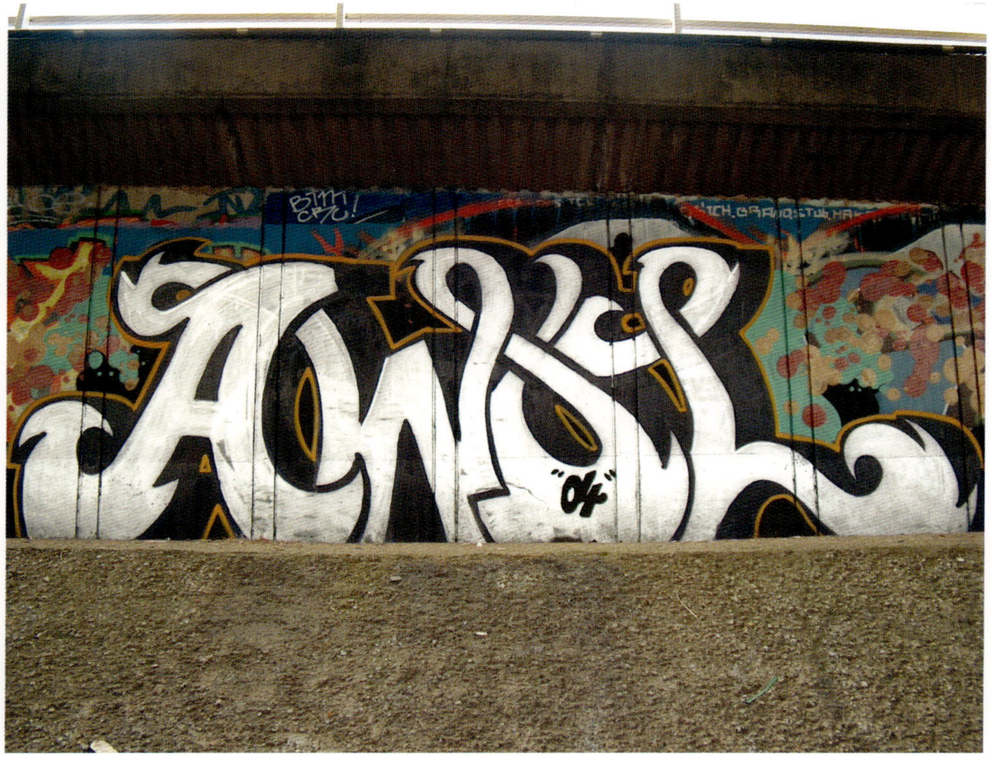

Top right: 'AWOL (A Way Of Life)' M32 hall of fame, 2004

Top left: Flaming styles, 2008

Left: SMZ panel piece, 2002

– wildstyle letter forms with good balance – not some deformed, twisty thing. [German writer] Can 2 is a big influence on me, because his flow is just so good. He's got his own style. When you talk about style, it's not about opening a book, seeing the latest craze and then copying it: it's all about what's you, what's coming from you. There are 26 letters in the alphabet, so it's about how you can best portray those 26 letters. I've also been inspired by Bristol writers, such as Turo, Bandito, 3D, Chaos, Shab, Risky, Teao, Inkie and Tes."

How long have you been painting trains?
"I painted my first train in about '93/94. As with anyone doing their first panel, it came out quite badly; but like anything else, you learn from your mistakes."

There's never been a big train-writing scene here. Have you ever painted trains in Bristol?
"I have attempted to do some, but it's always come on top [turned out badly]. And if you do manage to get away with something, it's very hard to get pictures, and you'll never see it running again. Painting trains is a lost cause in Bristol. It's never really been a train-painting city. People come to Bristol and think they can live like London writers, but London's a big city, it's ten times bigger than Bristol. You can get away with a lot more up there. I don't live too far from the train yards now, and it would be nice to go and paint trains here, but it's just a waste of time. So I travel outside of Bristol to have a nice little go in the 'playground', as I like to call it."

Are you still painting trains nowadays?
"I try to go and do something at least once a month. Graffiti's my true love, whatever I'm painting on, but after a while I find myself still seeking that buzz. There's something else that you need that you don't get from painting walls, and that's what you get when you paint steel. It's the whole concept of planning a night, from who I'm going to go out with all the way through to executing a piece on the train and then waiting to get your pictures when the sun comes up. That's all part of it. It can take a whole weekend and you get very little sleep."

Painting trains is a risky business, especially nowadays. What motivates you to keep going back to the yards?

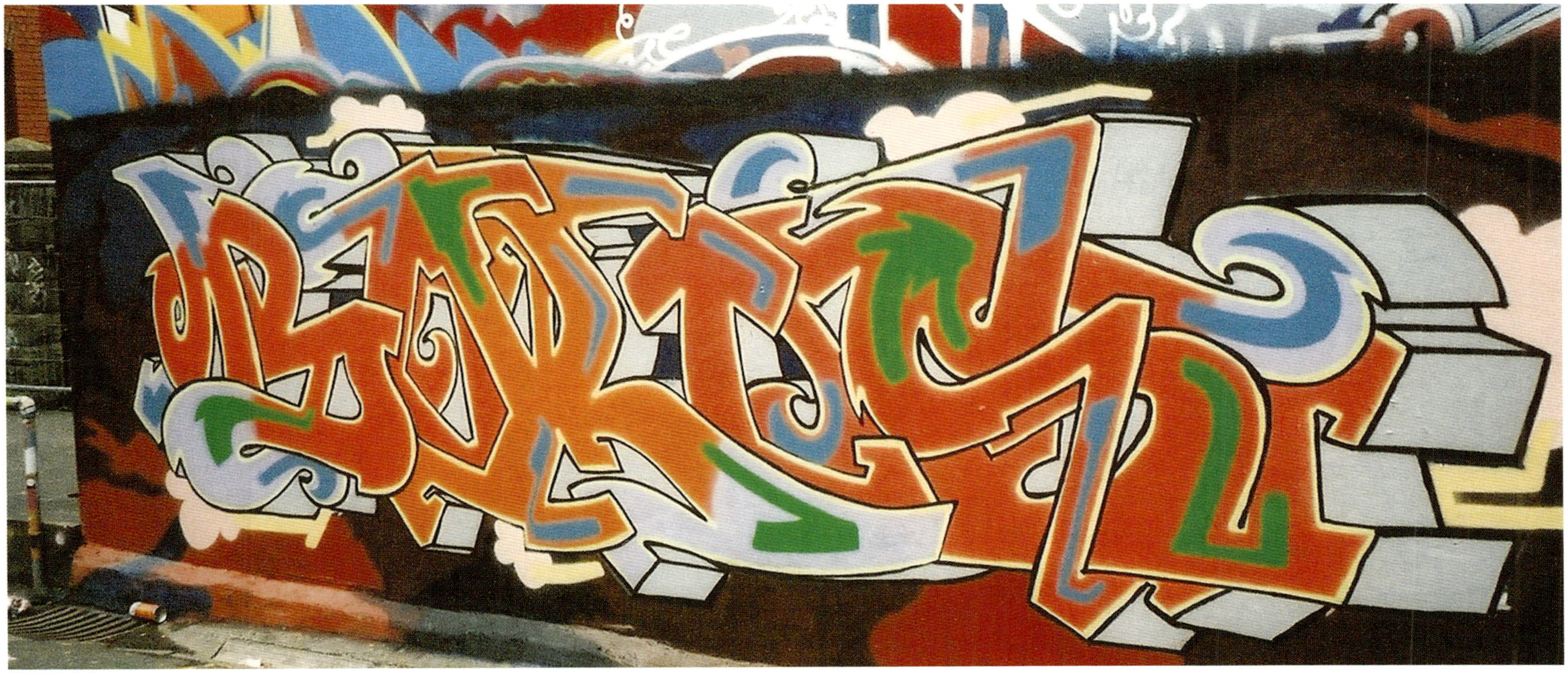

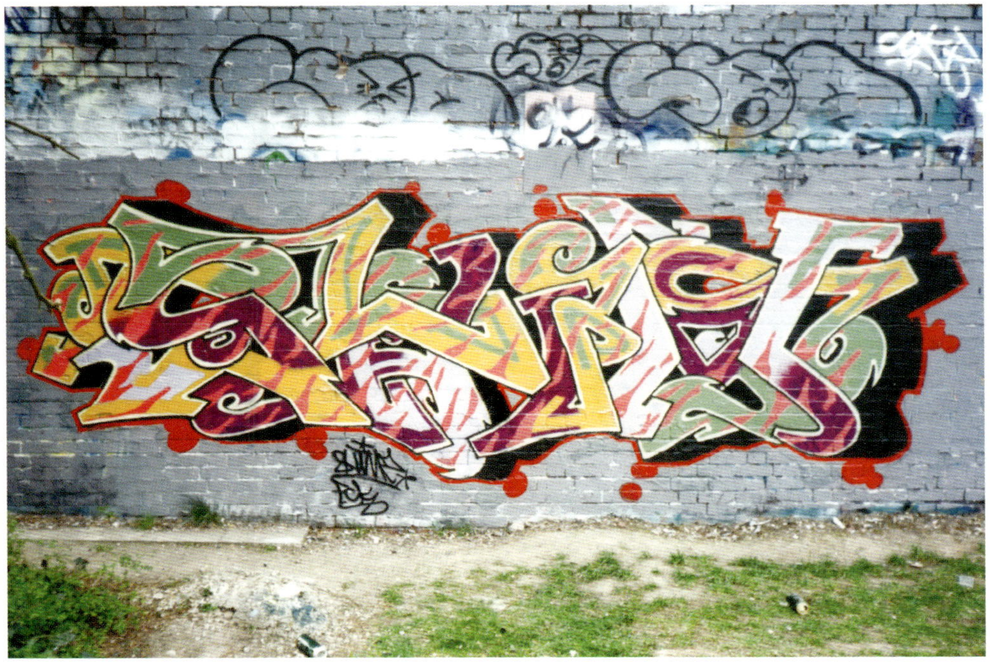

"I don't do this for the fame, I do it for the love of it, what I get out of it myself. Then if anyone likes it, that's a bonus. I don't go out there intentionally trying to impress anyone; it's just for me. That's just how I am. That's how I've always been, really, it's always been a part of me."

What are the downsides of going out on those missions?

"It can involve a lot of waiting around and you can get very impatient. And sometimes the weather can be a factor. You can go out with the best of intentions and be half finished when the good old British weather brings down the rain, and wet steel is not a good surface to paint on. What you're painting can end up looking very messy."

Top: 'Boris,' Bedminster skate park, 2005

Bottom: Anti-camo tiger style, 2005

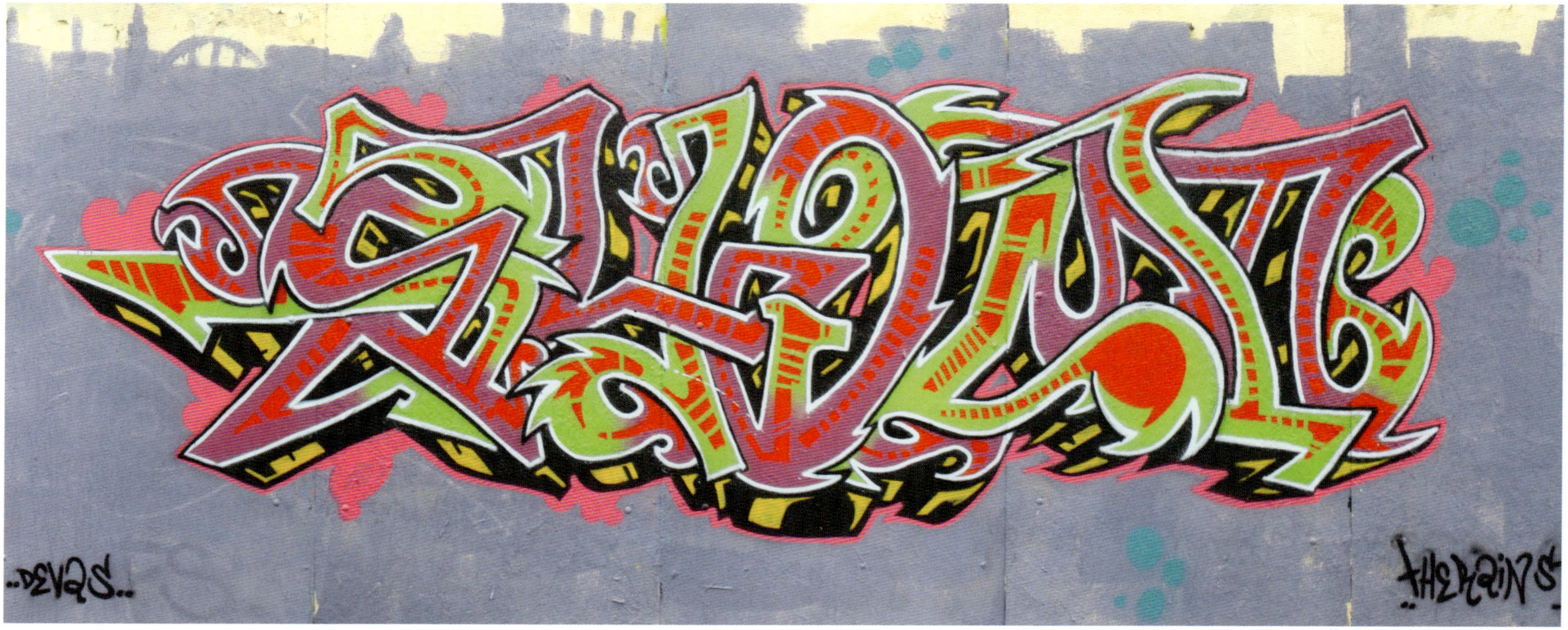

Top: City at dusk, how to make colours bounce, 2004

Bottom: Shimz over Paris, 2001

How do you avoid getting caught?
"Luck comes into it, but you can always take proper precautions. It helps if you're not doing stupid things when you're in the yards, like making a lot of noise - but that's just common sense. And I always keep a clean house and never post anything on the internet. I've only ever been busted once and no charge was brought because they couldn't prove anything."

You've painted all over the UK, how does Bristol measure up to other places?
"Bristol has a good atmosphere: it's laid-back and chilled compared to some cities I've painted in, although there will always be 'haters' in every city. It's simple, really: haters equal masturbators. I'll paint with anyone, as long as they're cool and don't have a big ego."

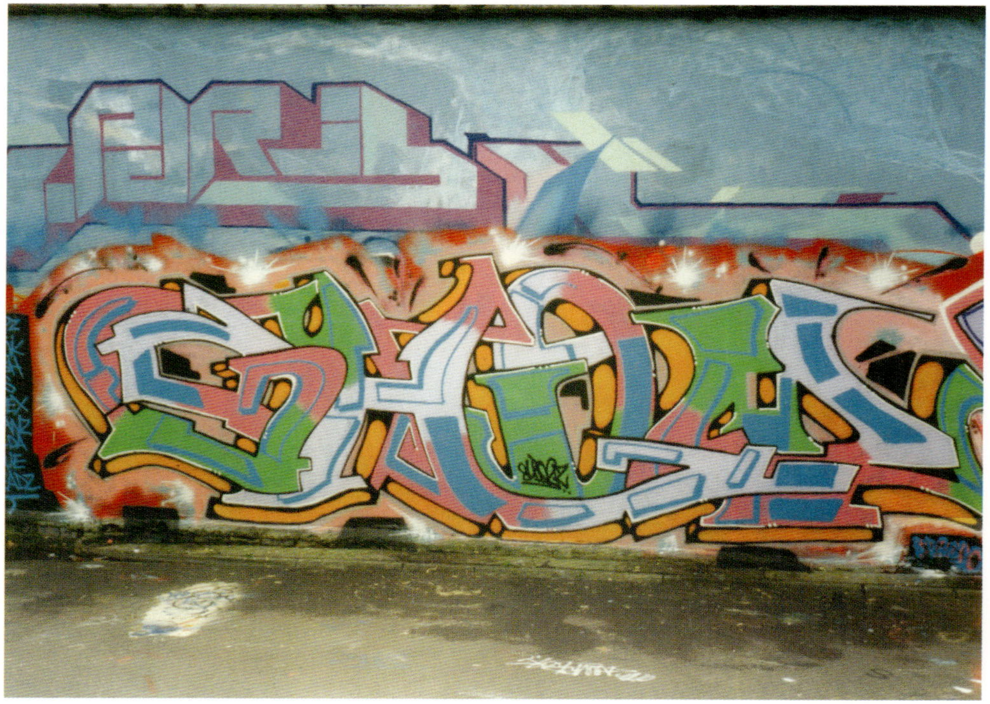

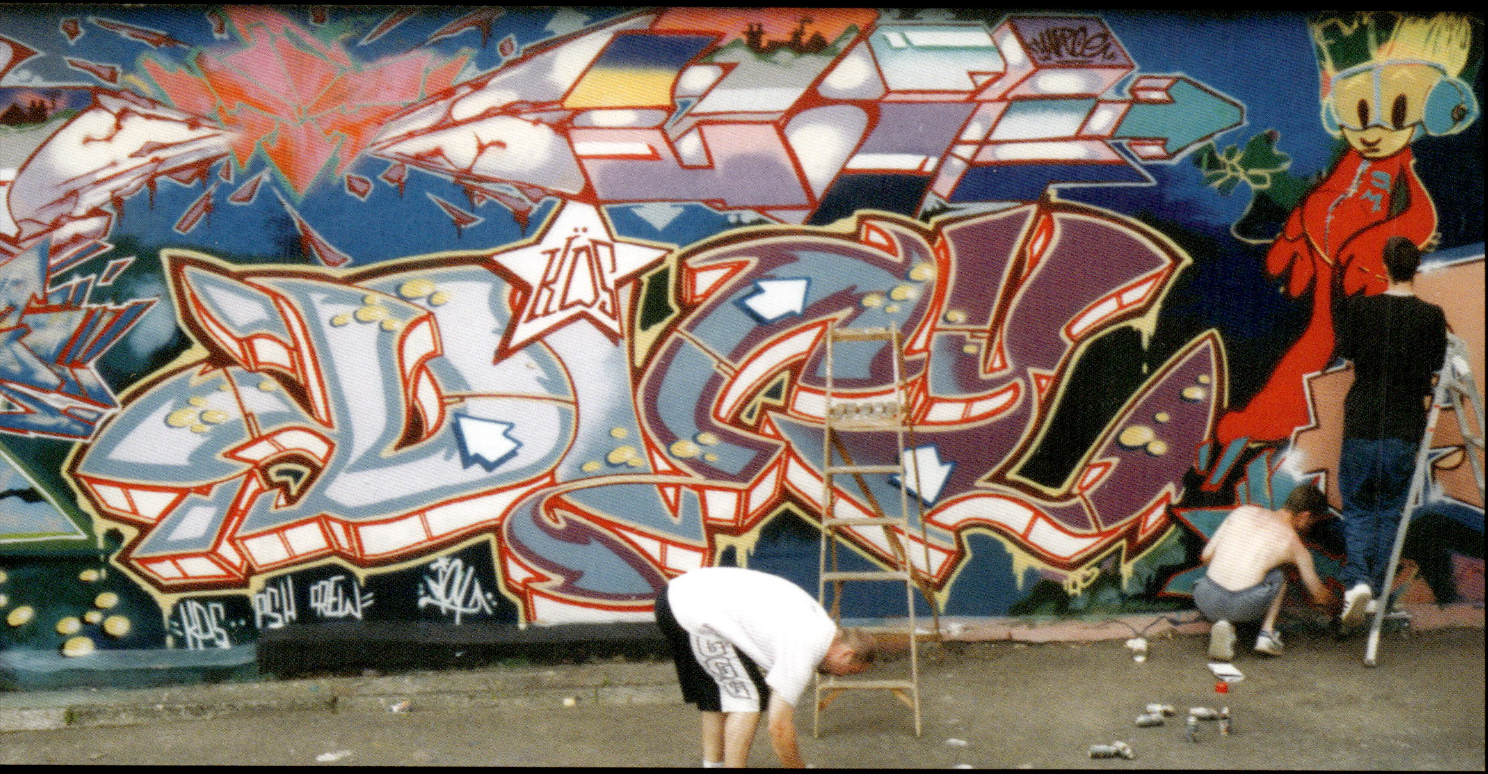

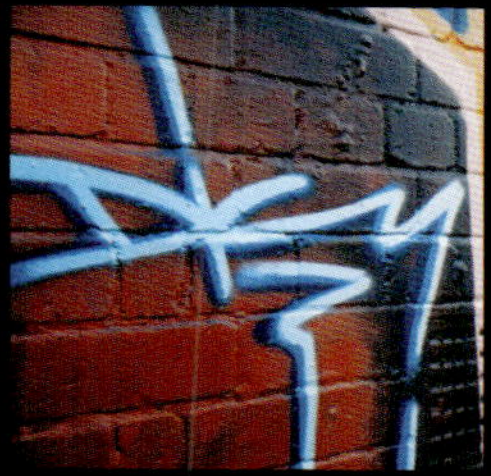

Top: Bedminster skate park, 1997

Left: Dicy and Feek celebrate St.Patrick's Day, 2008

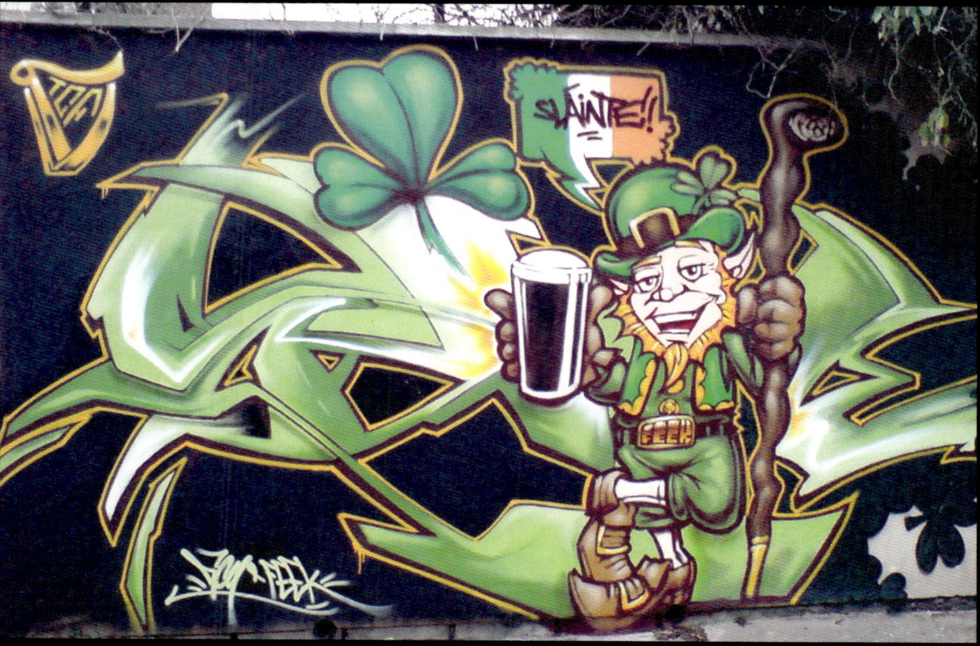

DICY TCF

• **Dissecting and reinventing classic graffiti aesthetics, Dicy's creativity finds form in both punchy, wall-based pieces and looser mark making, on canvas and in print.** With his graffiti/skate clothing line Kuldesac, Dicy was one of the first graffiti writers in Bristol to explore the potential of working with the art form in a commercial context. A multi-talented individual, he has also worked hard behind the scenes in Bristol, supporting other artists by arranging exhibitions and events and providing commercial outlets for their work – most recently through his art print project Let Them Hang.

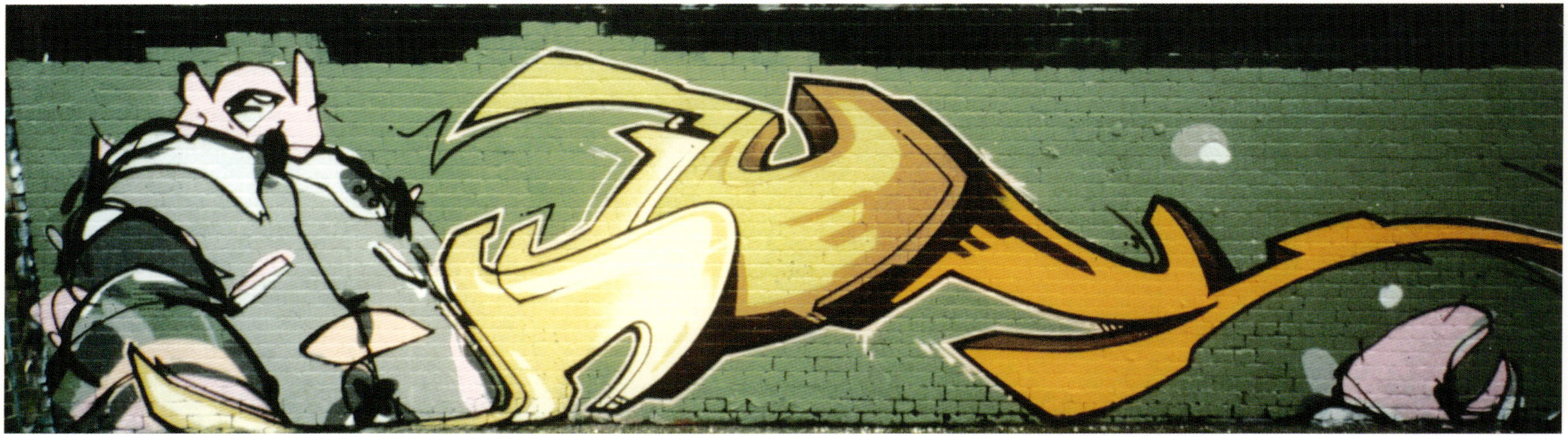

Top: Dicy and Mr. Jago, Bedminster skate park, 2005

Right: Promotional canvas for 'Run' club night, mixed media 2007

Left: Screen print and spray paint on canvas, 2007

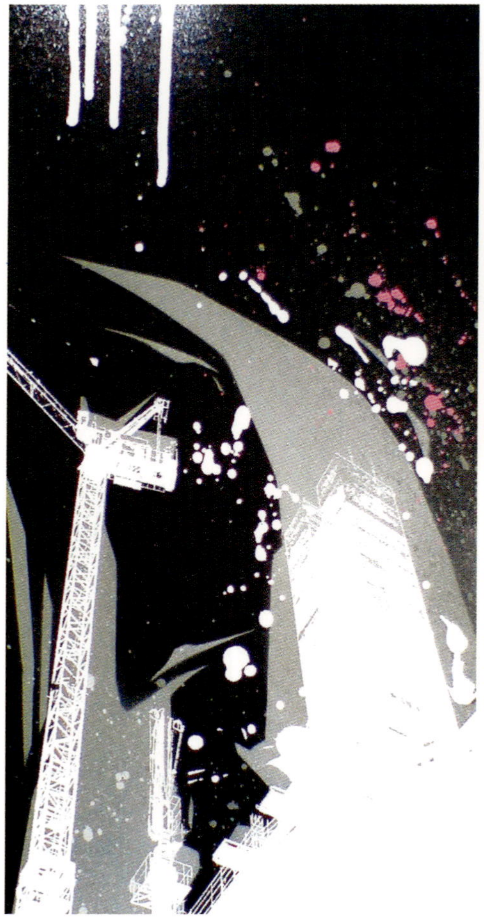

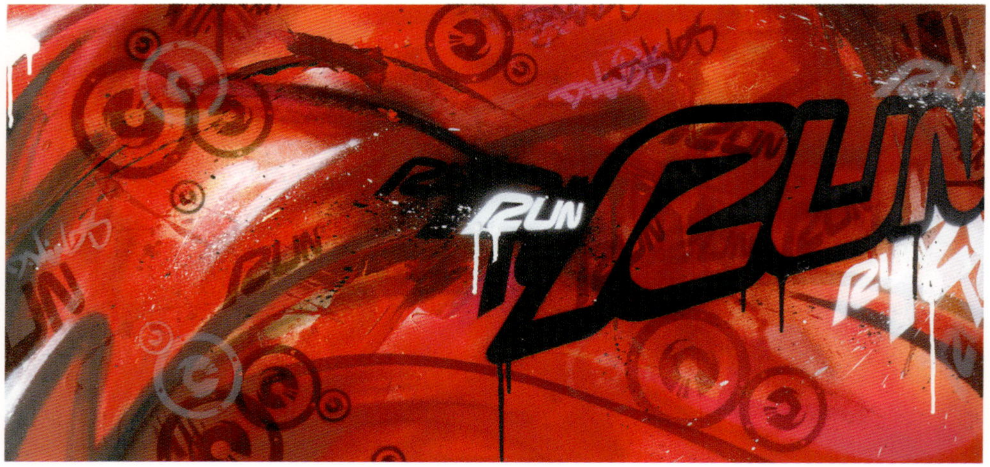

What first brought you to Bristol?
"I came to college at Bower Ashton in '89, but I had already been coming to Bristol for a couple of years to come to the skate 'fun days' they used to have at Bedminster skate park. Because of the strong skate scene in Bristol and the graff I saw at the park, I chose Bristol as my first choice for college... and got in! The first person I saw painting here was Inkie, doing a piece at the skate park – straight onto brick, no emulsion!

"I got into graff after watching *Style Wars* on Channel 4, but my first few years were spent mainly just tagging. Then from '87 to '89, before I moved away from Wolverhampton, my graff picked up a pace as things hotted up on the Midlands bus routes. The buses were so bombed, it was unreal. We used to travel on buses all day across the Midlands doing tags inside and out. The back outside panel was the dopest spot; they used to sell specially made devices in a graff shop in Birmingham, to

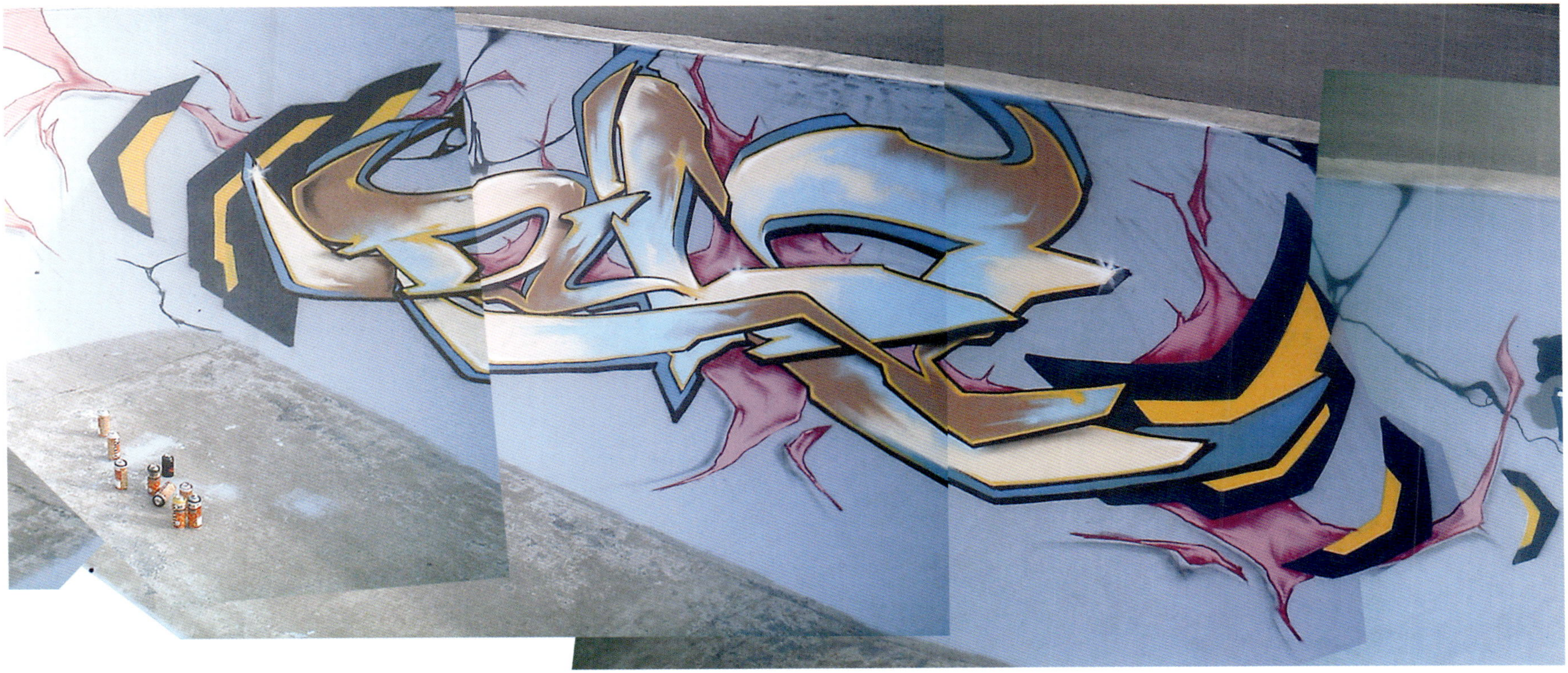

Above: Yate skate park, 2006

jam the mechanism in the window latch so the driver's alarm didn't go off downstairs when you opened it. You'd get someone to hold your waist while you leaned out with your plastic camera pot full of ink and did the biggest tag possible. The other massive thing at the time was stickers, everything from single tag stickers to huge elaborate penned pieces. They used to ride for weeks, man. And you'd spend lots of time on the tracks, or travelling on the rail network looking for trackside walls. Colour pieces started to emerge more and more, especially in the Walsall area."

Were there any Midlands writers who particularly influenced you?

"A big name who really influenced me and my crew (me, Beta, Part – who later became Toasters – and Nia) was Tazroc. And in the two years while I was doing my art foundation course, I would go to the Selly Oak Hall of Fame around the corner from college every lunch time. Writers like Juice, Rough and Chu used to be up there a lot."

How did the Fantastic Super Heroes come about?

"I spent most of my three years at uni skating, raving and DJing, while keeping a close eye on the graff scene. It seemed like Barton Hill was the main place, but MBA and SOF were painting Bedmo now and again. Then I got to hear about the warehouse in Brislington, and started going up there and dropping a few dubs. Then I met Paris painting one time at Bedmo, and he really got me painting full time. While I was setting up small parties and club nights, like-minded people from all sides of the hip hop scene started to hook up – all the Aspects boys, Vinyl Matt, Paris, myself, Acer, Turo, Azlan and many more. It became almost an open family for a time, with people adding themselves under the banner FSH.

"More of Paris' friends arrived from Hull, and the TCF crew, which was already well established up north, moved here. So basically the graff element of FSH became TCF, mainly through friendship and painting."

You, Feek, Mr Jago, Will Barras and Paris all went to Bower Ashton. Do you think this helped to nurture the scene, and perhaps inject a new lease of life?

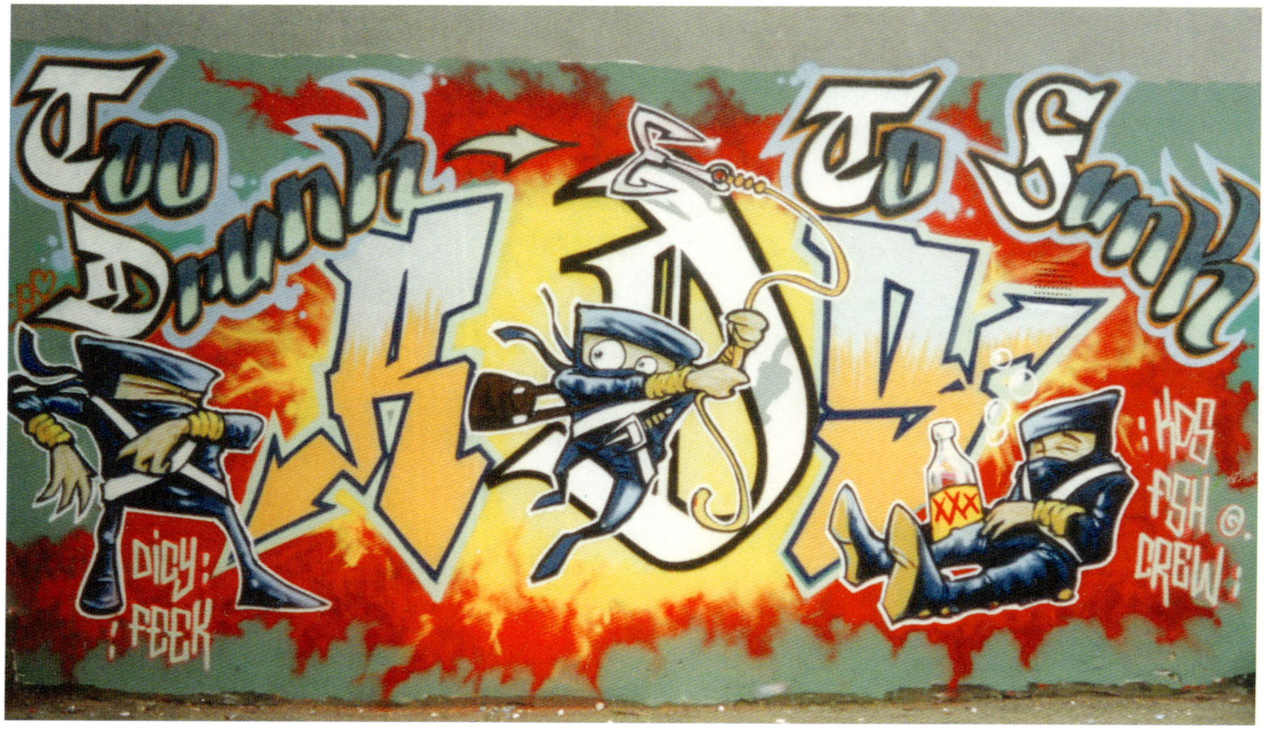

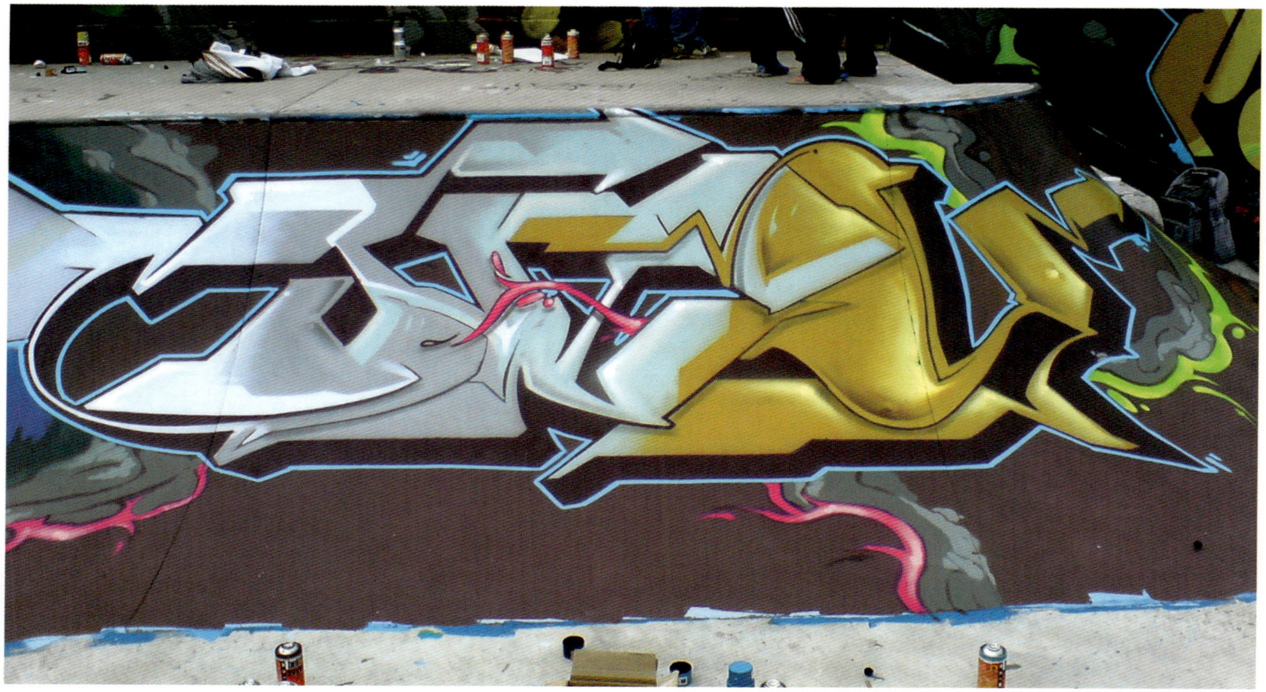

"College was definitely a very important factor. There were lots of creative minds at Bower Ashton, and that helped push the scene within the city. Graffiti at the time started to buzz again, with lots of new writers emerging, especially those coming to college from around the UK. After the big busts in Bristol at the end of the Eighties, illegal graffiti was on the rise again."

You were the first writer in Bristol to set up a company producing graffiti T-shirts, hoodies and stuff. How did that come about?
"I definitely learnt a lot about business at college, even though I didn't follow what I studied directly. After leaving and getting so involved in all the scenes around me – skating, hip hop and music – I just wanted to use my design and graff skills to create a brand that basically summed up my lifestyle. And so the Kuldesac brand was born: it initially started as a T-shirt label, later developing into an umbrella label for club nights, parties, and events."

You used to DJ a lot, and Kuldesac was a successful club night for a while. Can you expand on the relationship between art and music?
"Music has always been a love of mine. I grew up surrounded by it, and then I got into electro in my mid-teens. It was always a big thing, sitting down for hours doing outlines listening to Mike Allen on UK Fresh on the radio."

How did you get involved in Walls On Fire, and what are your memories of that weekend?
"I got involved through knowing Banksy, and I sorted out sponsorship money for

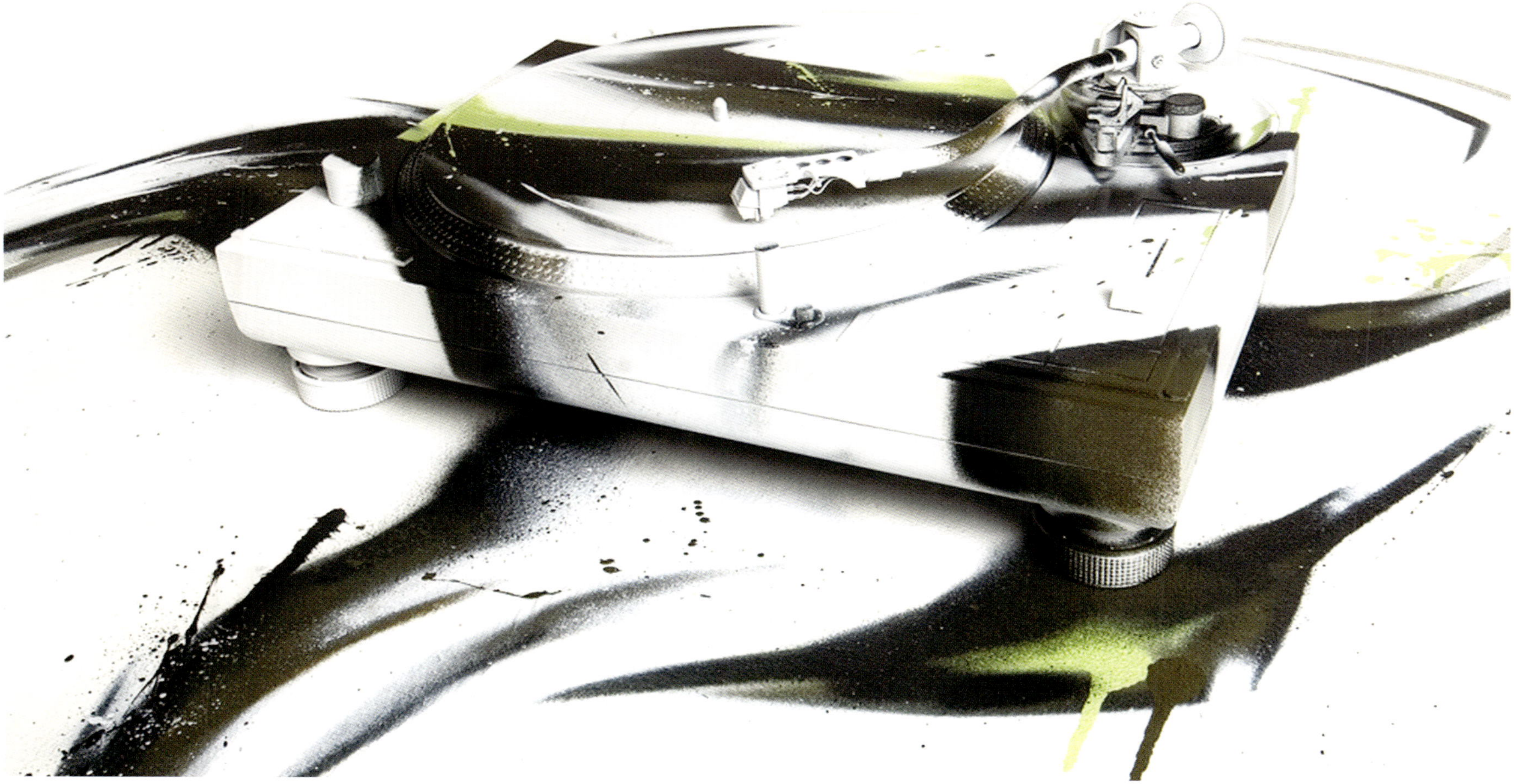

some of the paint through the record label Wall Of Sound and my own brand Kuldesac. Feek and myself produced and sold the T-shirts for the event. It was one of the biggest graff events the UK had ever seen."

What about your the graffiti jams at the Urban Games in London?

"I was involved with a company called Board X, who used to put on snowboard events in Battersea Park in the winter. They decided to do a summer 'urban sports' event, the Urban Games. It was the UK's first proper event covering skating, BMX and all aspects of hip hop culture, especially graff. For four years on the trot I organised the huge graff jams around the whole perimeter of the event on Clapham Common, bringing together writers from all over the UK as well as a few foreign visitors. It was the hardest event I have ever organised, but over the years it had some great results."

Do you have any enduring memories of painting at festivals? Is it something you particularly enjoy doing?

"Glastonbury was always good, although it tended to be a massive labour of love. It was real good working with Banksy, he certainly was a man with lots of ideas. But the amount of work we tended to put in, painting all day and into the night most days, didn't seem worth it for the ticket once the festival opened! The first Glastonbury was the best production we painted: two 50ft long, 20ft high scaffold walls, one either side of the Dance Stage. Those were painted by Banksy, Feek, me, Paris and Eko. I remember getting well

Oppsite page. Top: 'Too Drunk To Funk' Dicy and Feek, Bedminster skate park, 1995

Bottom: Skate park in Devon, 2007

This page: Customised Technics deck for 420 Recordings compilation, 2006

Top: Kuldesac logo, 1994

Middle: Numskullz piece, 2002

Right: Kuldesac t-shirt designs, 2004

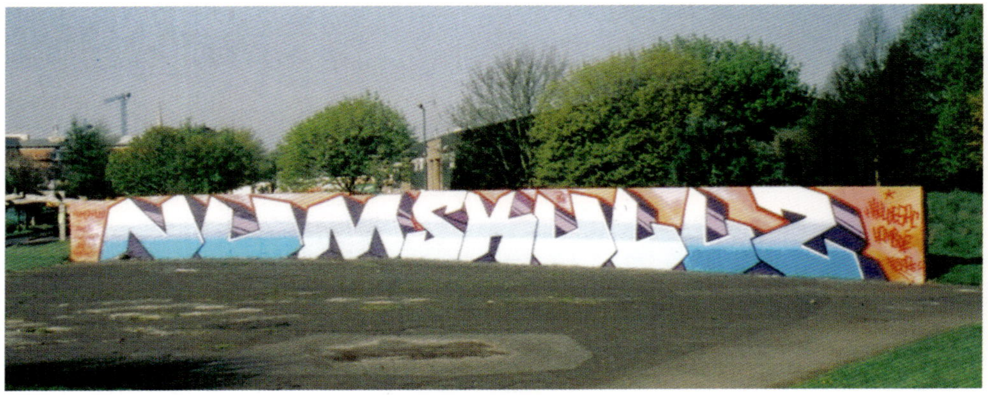

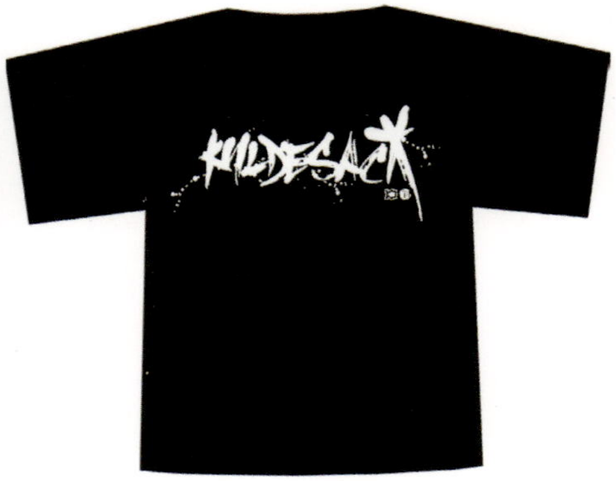

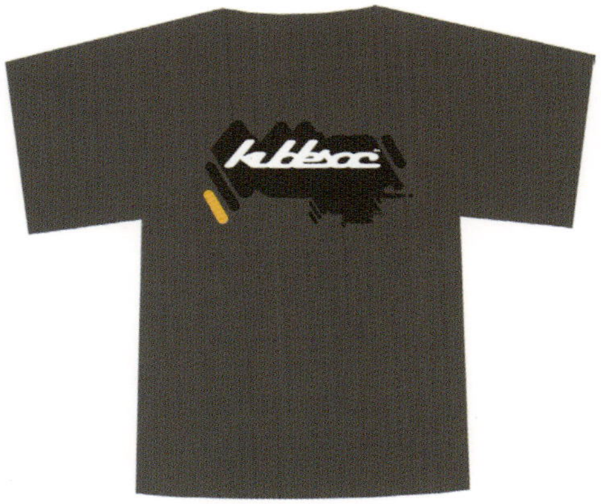

pissed off with people once the Dance Tent was in full swing; they were falling against it, pissing against it and standing in front of it, not even realising it was there!"

What is your take on the current commercialisation of the graffiti scene?
"People have been saying that graff has gone commercial for a long time now: we were doing commissions for big corporate companies ten years ago. I believe it's got to happen, you've just got to try and stay in control of the work you are doing for them. If we weren't doing graff work for big companies, we'd all be doing 9 to 5 jobs. You've just got to be careful how you do it.

"As far as how things are with the art market, it is pretty crazy; but I think a lot of it is good, and it's about time too. It's time people recognised graff as a relevant art form – but as far as people paying crazy money goes, that's how the art world works. I think things will settle down and the true artists will shine through – those that have put the time in and have the love for the scene and have their roots in it. That's not to say that people can't come along and get into it, but they shouldn't expect to be earning money from it. It's got to be about the art initially, not the money."

There seems to be a considered balance in your work between the tight, graphic approach, and the looseness of chucking paint about.
"I've just always enjoyed creating exciting, dynamic imagery – whether it's a piece on a wall, a painting on a canvas or a sketch on a sheet of paper. I was taught at college to experiment with different mediums to get a finished effect, and I definitely think my Art Foundation course opened my eyes to different things: paint, screen-printing, spray paint, wood, whatever. I really love the tightness of certain graffiti (especially my own!), but I also love the freedom of loose paint. The idea of being locked away in a massive studio with lots of paint and canvas, and going wild – that's heaven to me. But I also know that I'd then have to drop some sharp dynamic shit over the top, just to finish it off!"

A lot of your work stems from the classic aesthetics of 'traditional' graffiti. Do you think there are 'right' and 'wrong' ways to balance angles within letter forms?
"Because I grew up with graffiti when I did, I do have an idea of correct angles and pure styles. That said, things have developed an awful lot in 25 years, and I do enjoy some of the more modern styles. But you'll always get me buzzing more off a classic outline. I recently saw a sketchbook by Ryder from Swindon, and it was full of pencil drawings that rocked: classic forms and shapes that you just can't beat."

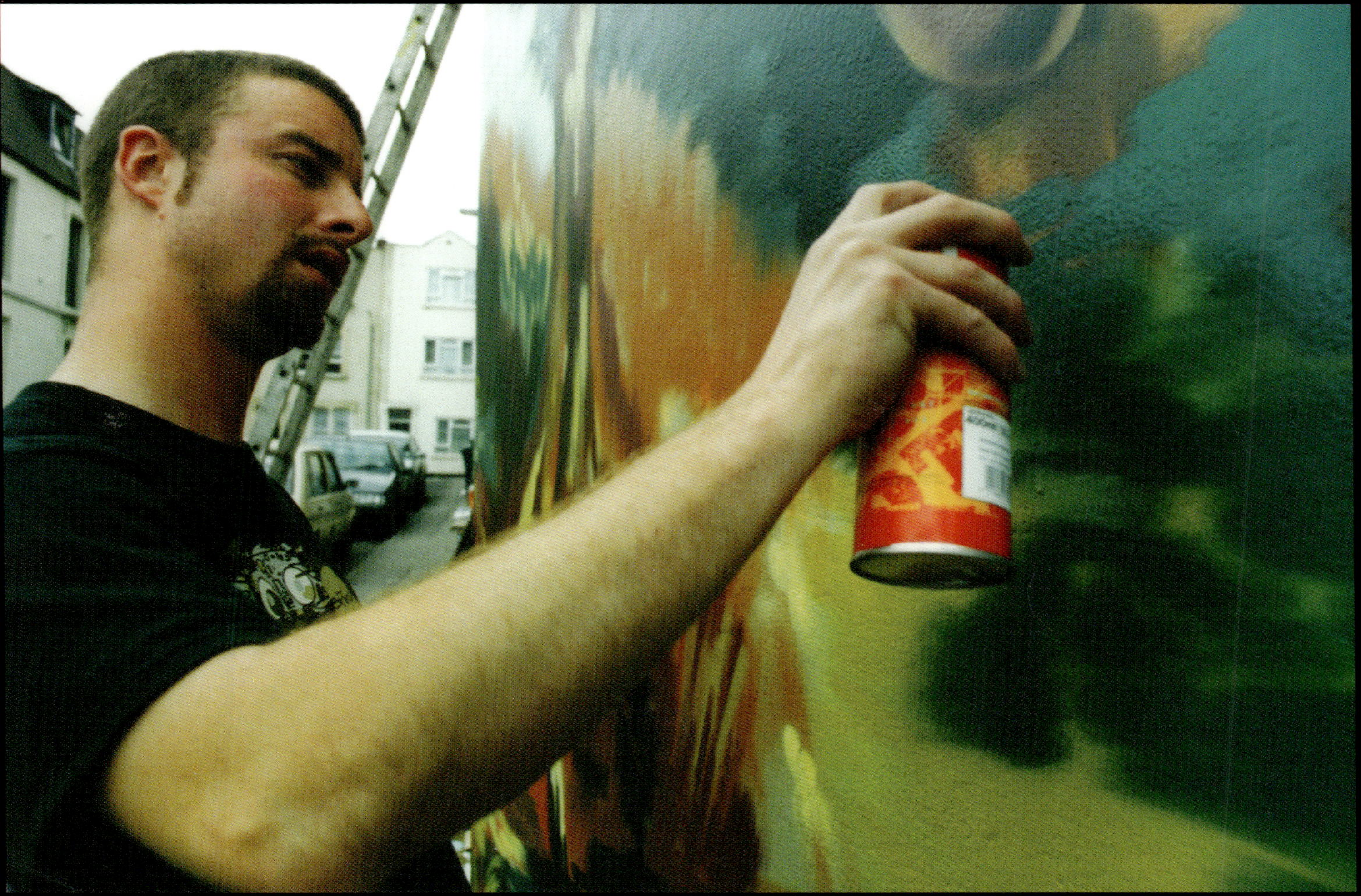

Left: Paris painting the Herbert's Bakery wall, 2002

PARIS TCF/WSSK

• Paris is the renaissance man of Bristol graffiti, equally at home with a roller or a mouse in his hand as he is wielding a spray can – or a needle and thread, for that matter. It was the latter which brought him to Bristol in 1996, to study Fashion and Textile Design at the University of the West of England.

"The course was a ticket to ride that got me out of Hull, out of the North and out of a potentially pretty bleak future. I was lucky enough to get a place at college. The North and the South, they were completely different worlds. I was interviewed for my course looking out onto the Suspension Bridge and Clifton, and I'd never seen anything like it before. This city still inspires me today, it's like nowhere else, it's got something about it. And the mix of cultures and the music scene back then in '96... I was inspired by it all."

Soon, fellow Hull writers Xenz and Eko had joined Paris in Bristol, tapping into the city's thriving hip hop scene. Showcasing their work at 1998's Walls On Fire event, the trio ruffled a few local feathers.

"Bristol's pretty territorial: any city is, I think, especially its graffiti scene, which can be ruled by tradition. The graffiti scene's the same the world over: if you know the right people you'll get to paint the right spots, and be looked after. And that's what came to pass."

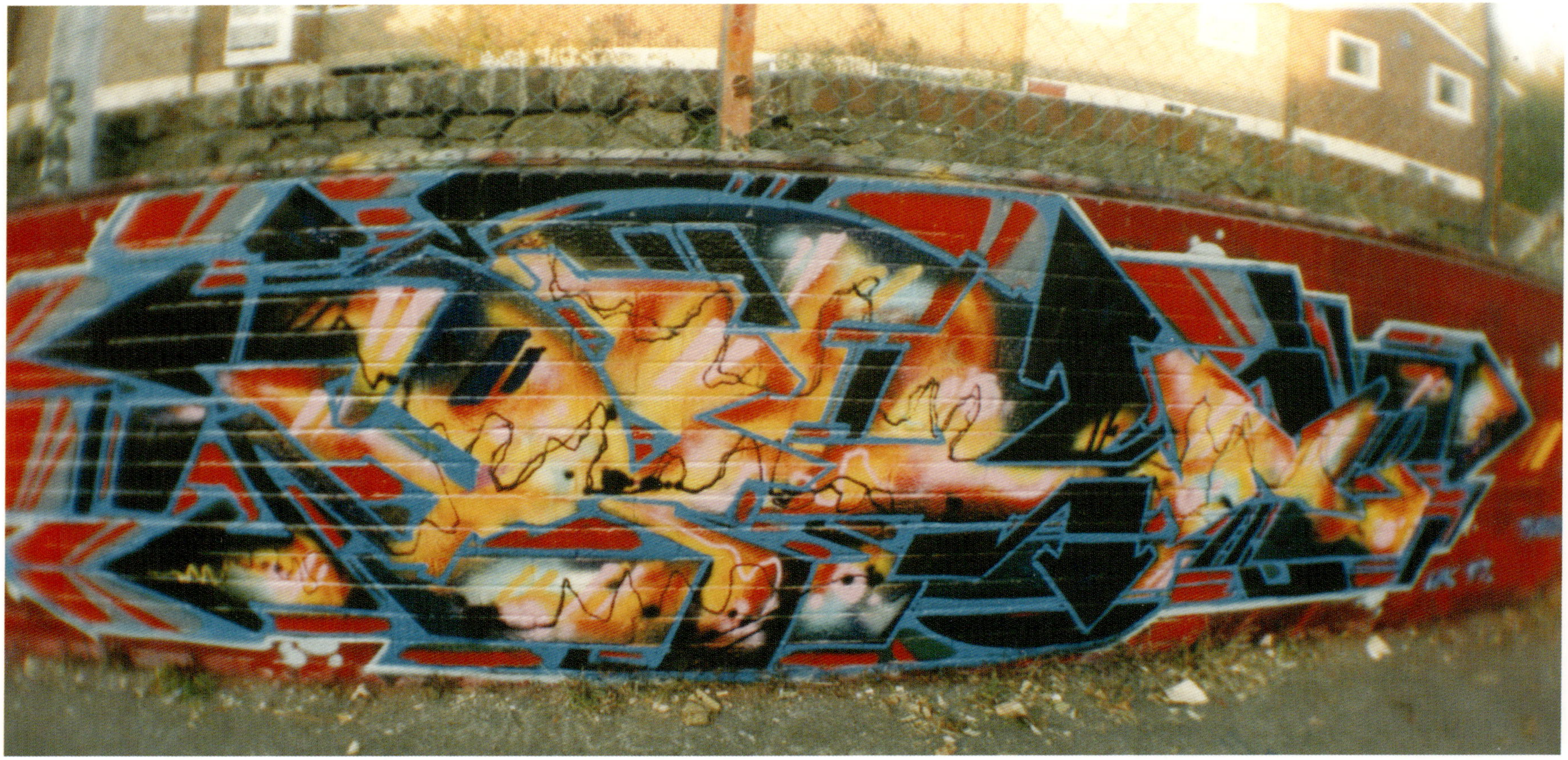

As teenagers in Hull, Paris, Xenz and Eko formed the TCF Crew [Twentieth Century Frescoes], honing their skills in abandoned warehouses in the area.

"When I first met Eko and Xenz and started doing graffiti, we were all starting out at art college in Hull, on the HND course in the early 90s. That was where I learnt about all this stuff that had gone on in the past: art movements and styles. At the same time that I was taking all that in, we were getting early issues of [seminal graffiti magazine] *Graphotism*, and I was still learning graffiti. I didn't see *Style Wars* until 1996. There was no way of getting stuff in Hull!"

That was until arts promoter Martin Jones (also Goldie's manager at the time) had the bizarre idea of hosting the World Graffiti Championships on the seafront in Bridlington, on TCF's home turf.

"Bridlington was on our doorstep, and it was like a black hole had opened up. All this amazing shit poured in from Bristol, from LA, New York, and Paris, and it was all happening in a sleepy seaside village, 20 miles from Hull. I was really young and it was just an absolute explosion, like someone lifting up the top of your head and pouring so much stuff in. The Bristol pieces [by Inkie and Cheo] left a huge mark and inspired the Hull styles."

The seeds of migration had been sown and education was the vehicle. Paris, though, was left somewhat deflated by his subsequent experience of graduation, albeit with a first-class degree. "College was like some utopia where you could just paint and draw anything you wanted to. But you come out and realise there are no jobs doing that. After college I had no intention of getting a full-time job, I wanted to pursue my art but college didn't really give me a grounding to sell my work. That was the main task, and that's what I've been doing for the last ten years: trying to make a living as an artist and carving out a career. And graffiti's part in that has been

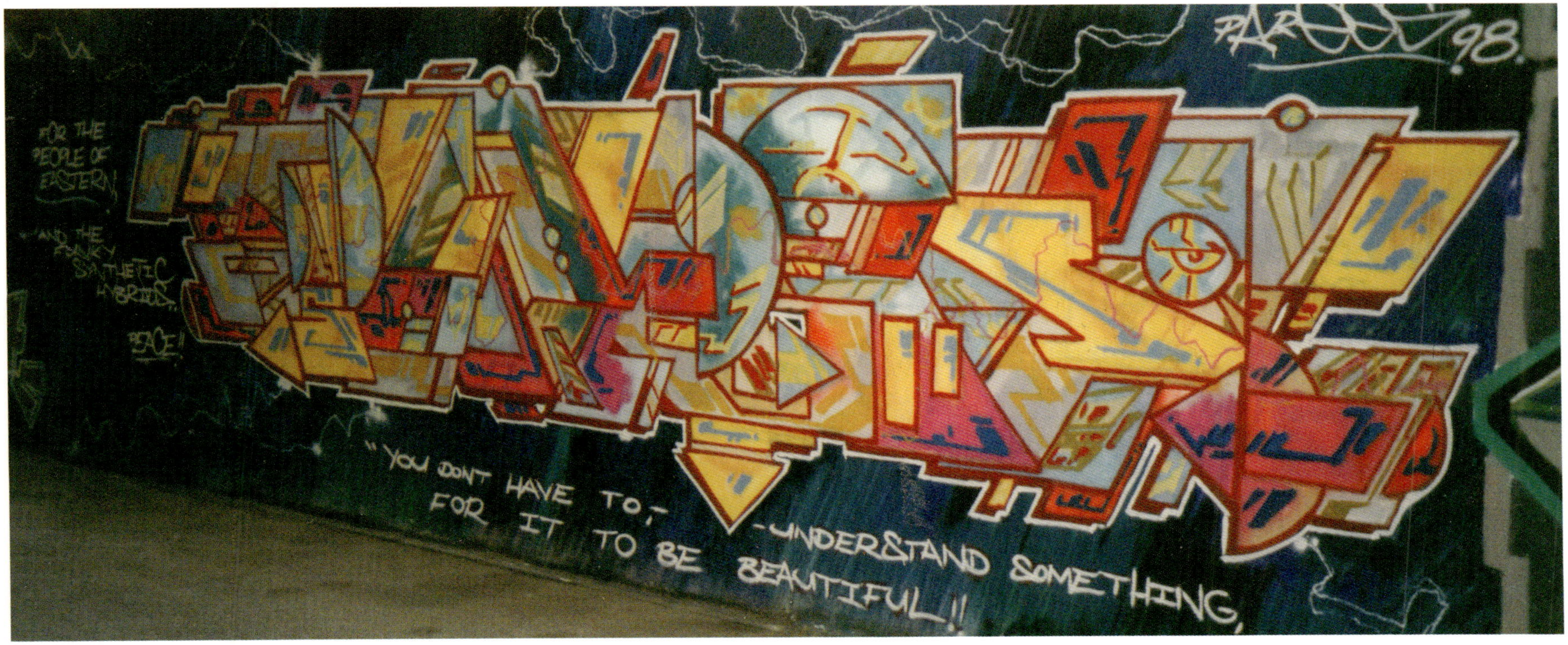

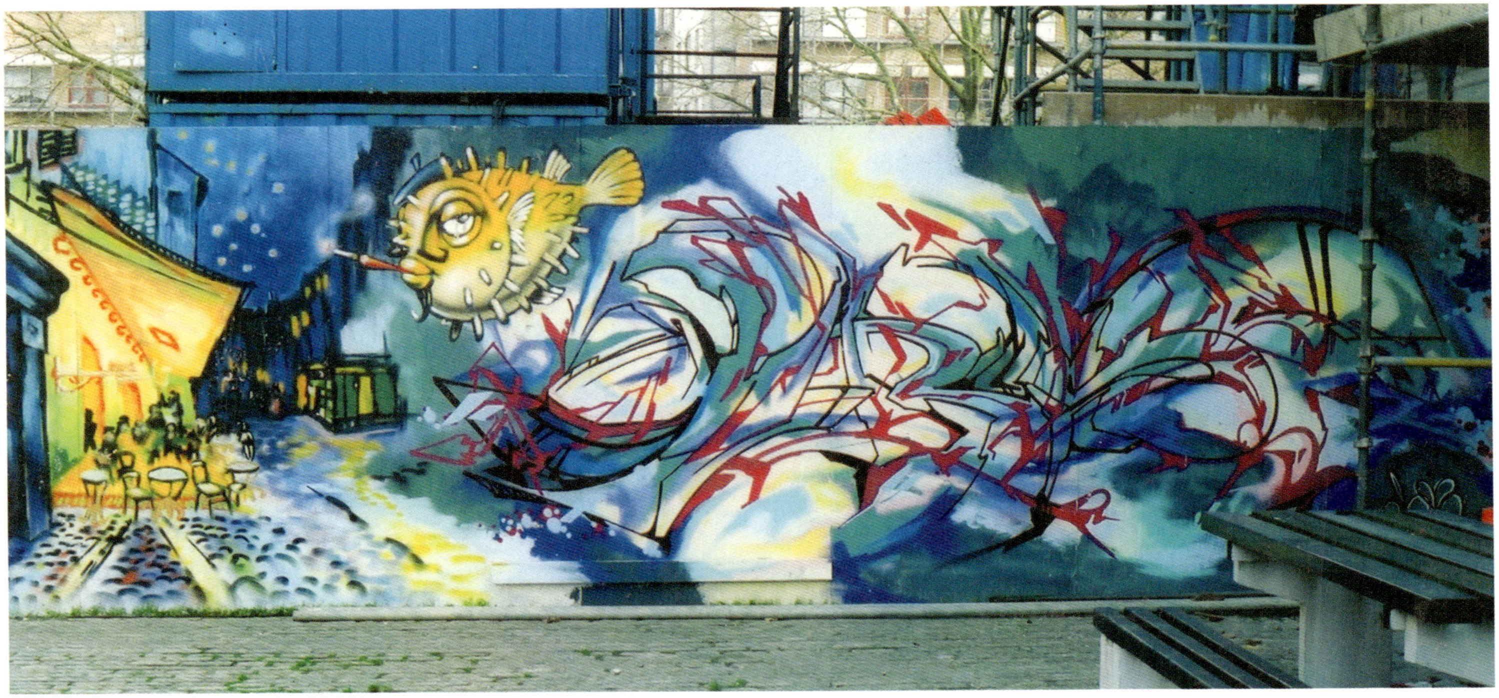

Opposite page. Top: RFM Rocking the wildstyle flow, Barton Hill youth club, 1997

Above: Various logos, 2004-5

This page. Top: 'You Don't Have To Understand Something For It To Be Beautiful' Millionaire's Club hall of fame, 1997

Left: Paris gets all Parisian, dockside, 2001

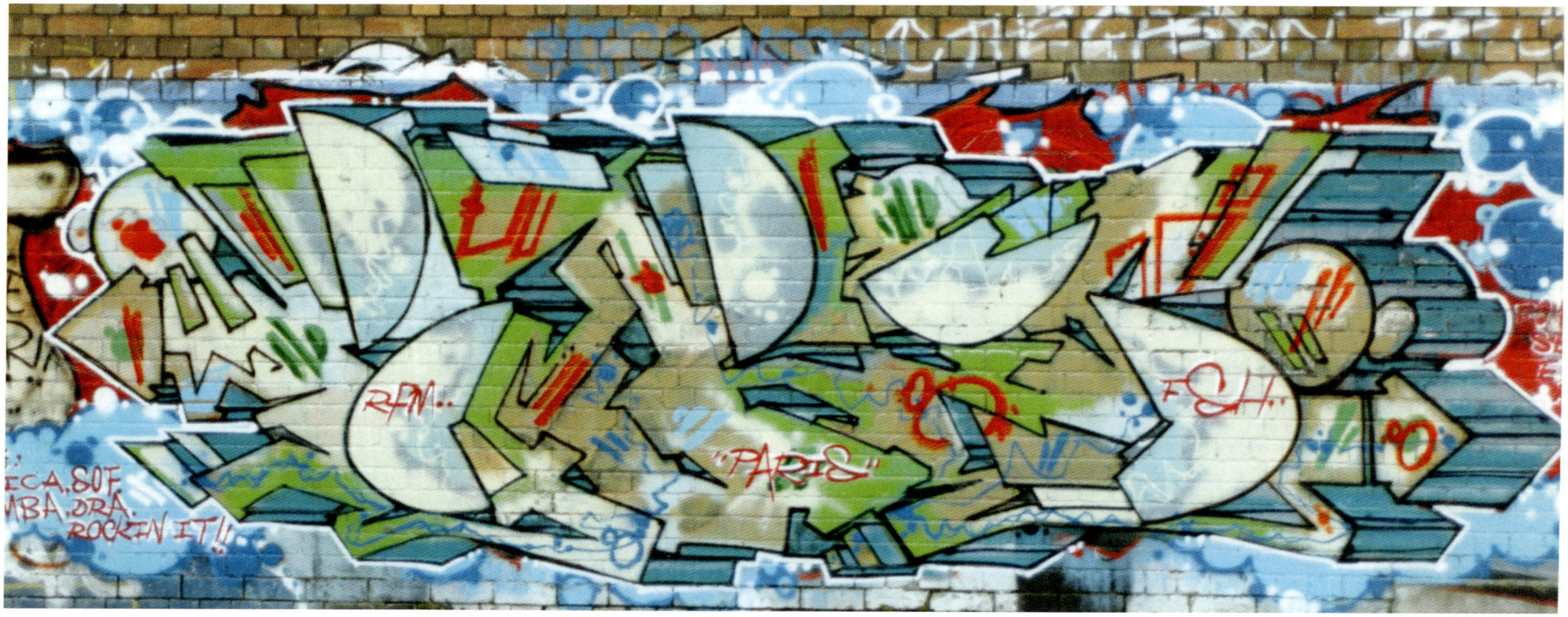

Above: Burning brick, 1996 first Bristol piece

constant. I've spent most of the time since I graduated reaching that point. And now I'm making a living out of it."

Over the last ten years, Paris has continued working alongside members of TCF, in Bristol and across the UK and Europe. He's painted some of the country's most adventurous graffiti productions, as well as constantly exploring new media, forms and influences. "Graffiti within the confines of hip hop can be quite limiting. Hip hop is its own ruling body, and nowadays 'hip hop graffiti' is very proscribed. So in the last five years I've kind of moved away from that – not as a reaction against it, more a natural progression, wanting to look at new things.

"All through my life, I've always checked things out and moved on from anything that didn't seem to be developing. I'm still painting and I'm still doing graffiti, so nothing's changed there, but I've always tried to reach as broad an audience as possible, not just a small subculture."

Paris's understanding of the evolving graffiti scene spans everything from the pre-graffiti painting of revolutionary Russian propaganda trains to innovative, influential pieces by Scandinavian graffiti writers. Clearly a lifelong student of the arts, his awareness of graffiti's place in the broader sweep of art history is inspiring. It's also visible in his huge, eclectic body of work. This includes screen-printing, logo design, type design and painting, as well as large-scale street pieces. "Graffiti is a response to what's going on around you. Mine is about whatever I'm looking at and soaking up at any given time."

In Paris's more recent, typographic-style pieces, simplification has become a way to camouflage letters – the opposite of most wildstyle letter painting. "Doing something simple is much more difficult than doing something over-complicated and flashy," he says. "When I look back at my sketchbooks all those styles are in there: the big 3-Ds and arrows, the wrapped-up letters with folds and stuff. Now I'm stripping my stuff down and peeling back the layers to create what I see as 'style' in its purest form. I'm also taking on board typographic influences, like Italian and Swiss logos for example. Lots of other aspects are coming into play, but of course the graffiti's still there. I think probably the closest relative to the graffiti I'm doing now is stuff that's happening in Scandinavia. It has that same aesthetic of simplicity."

He may have his detractors among the hardcore graffiti fraternity, but Paris seems to be on a personal journey of stylistic exploration. With maturity comes self-

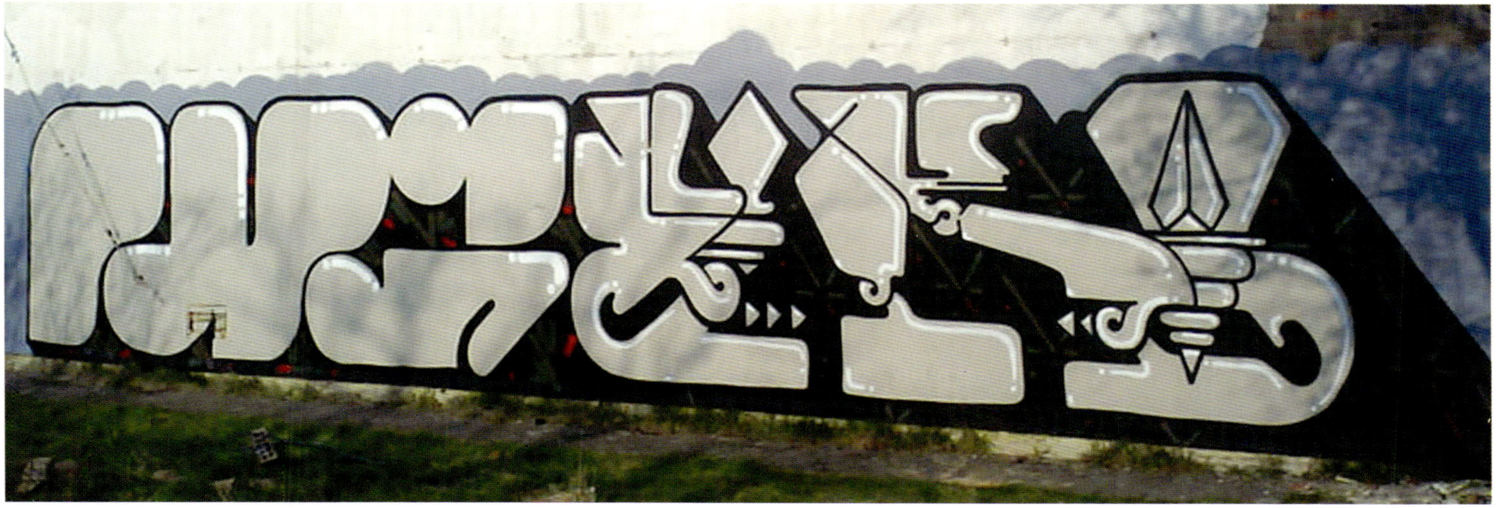

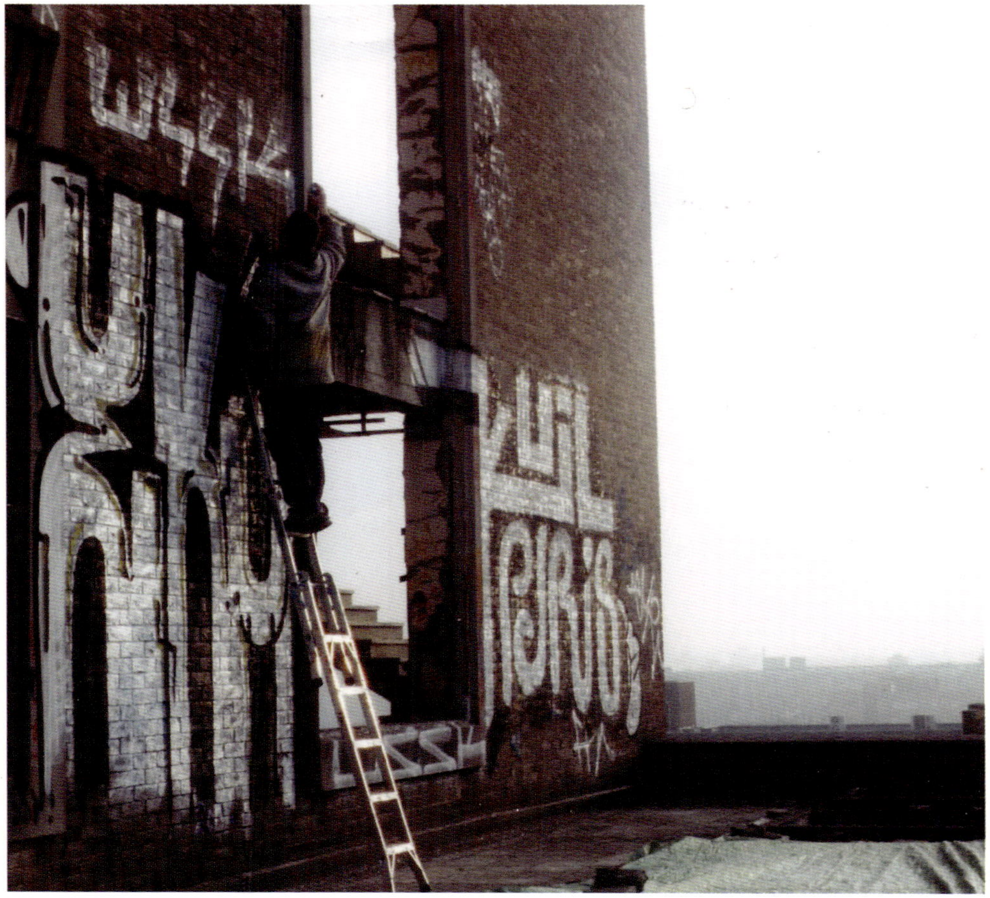

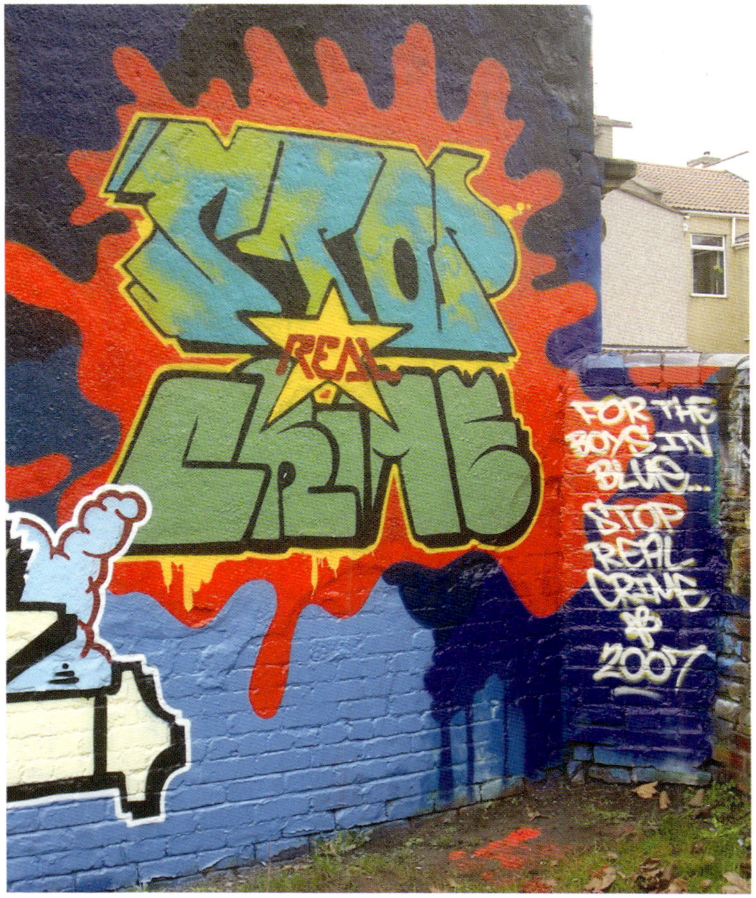

Top: Paris and Eko, side-by-side, 2006

Bottom left: Westmoreland House, Stokes Croft, 2005

Bottom right: 'Stop Real Crime' Paris tells it like it is, Bedminster skate park, 2007

Top right: Abstract organics, computer graphics, 2000

Bottom right: 'Show' Bedminster skate park, 2004

assurance and clarity of artistic vision. "These days I try and keep things simple and a little bit Zen, in that I just try to focus on my craft by pushing and exploring it. I couldn't really care if people like what I'm doing or not, I don't do it for that anymore. I'm doing it to appease my own fetishes with letter forms and styles."

Over the last few years, his involvement with the experimental WSSK (Wet Shame Crew), alongside Eko, Mudwig, and Eh? has seen Paris expanding his creative output even further to include banner-making, short film production and even poetry.

"With the Wet Shame stuff, we're consciously not looking at what's going on with street art and what other people are doing. We work off each other and we look at the past. There's so much to take from the past. In every era, there were people making letter forms that absolutely rocked. Then I look at what's going on in design and fashion today, and I wonder where it's going, a lot of it's rubbish. For us, it's about finding inspiration from the past – but picking our sources very carefully.

"I'm now doing textile-based work again, and doing a lot of printing. And I'm looking at patterns, styles and motifs that have always inspired me. It's feeding into my graffiti and my graffiti's feeding into my design work, graphics, logos, stuff like that. Now it's all coming together. All my different working methods are blending and forming into new styles. I'd like to think it's a formative style. In the last two years I've made a real effort to take one style – a flat graphic style – and really push it and push it. I'm really happy with it, so I'm going to keep doing that."

Since graffiti was first recognised as a new art movement in late 70s New York,

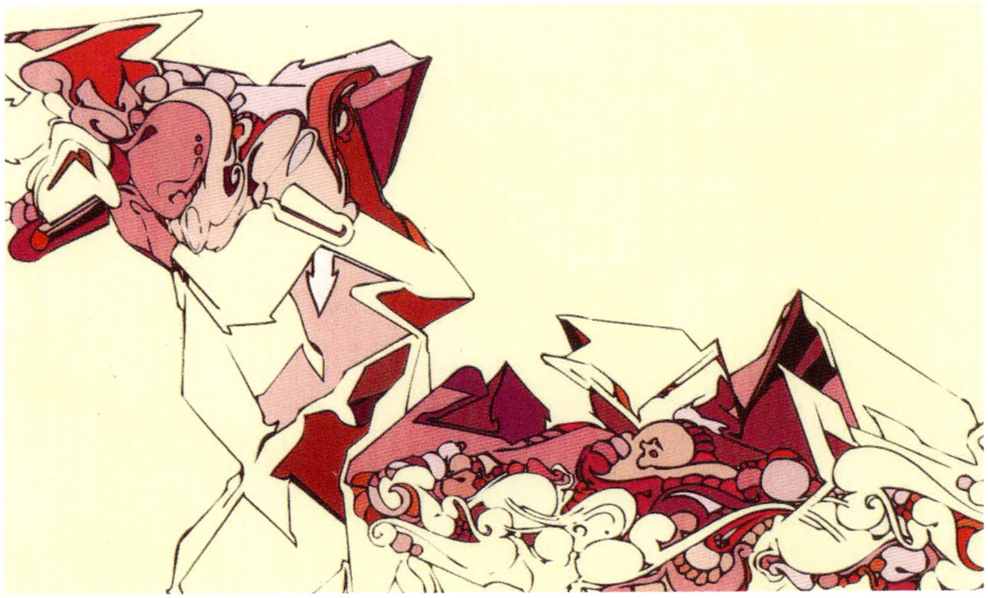

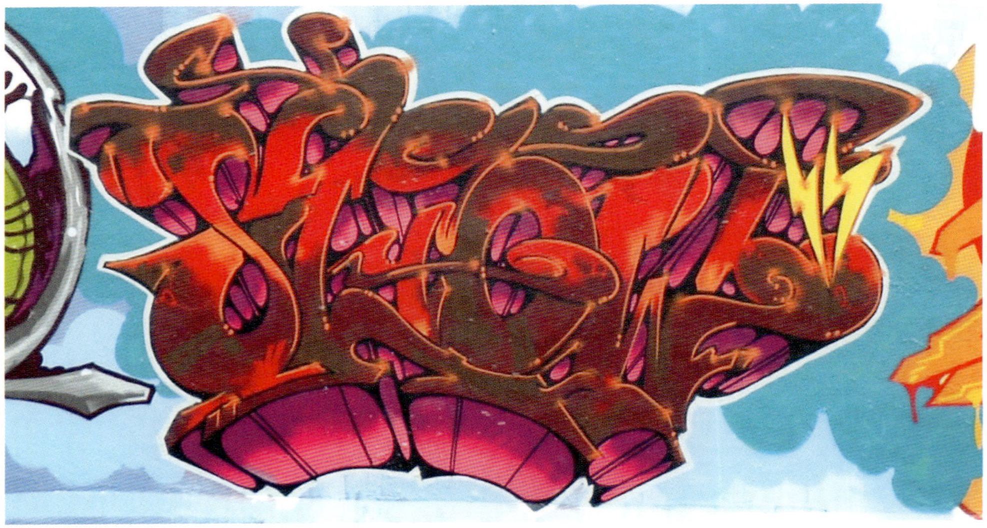

it has enjoyed an uneasy relationship with the fine art world and the galleries. Many would argue that 'real' graffiti can never be displayed in a gallery, and that selling street art is selling out. For Paris, this is a redundant argument. "We need to move on from that. That argument is as old as graffiti itself. There's a bigger picture. Personally, I've never been able to spray paint on a canvas like I would on a wall outdoors. Spray paint in general is almost too large and has too much energy to be contained within the confines of a canvas. Unless you go into someone's house and

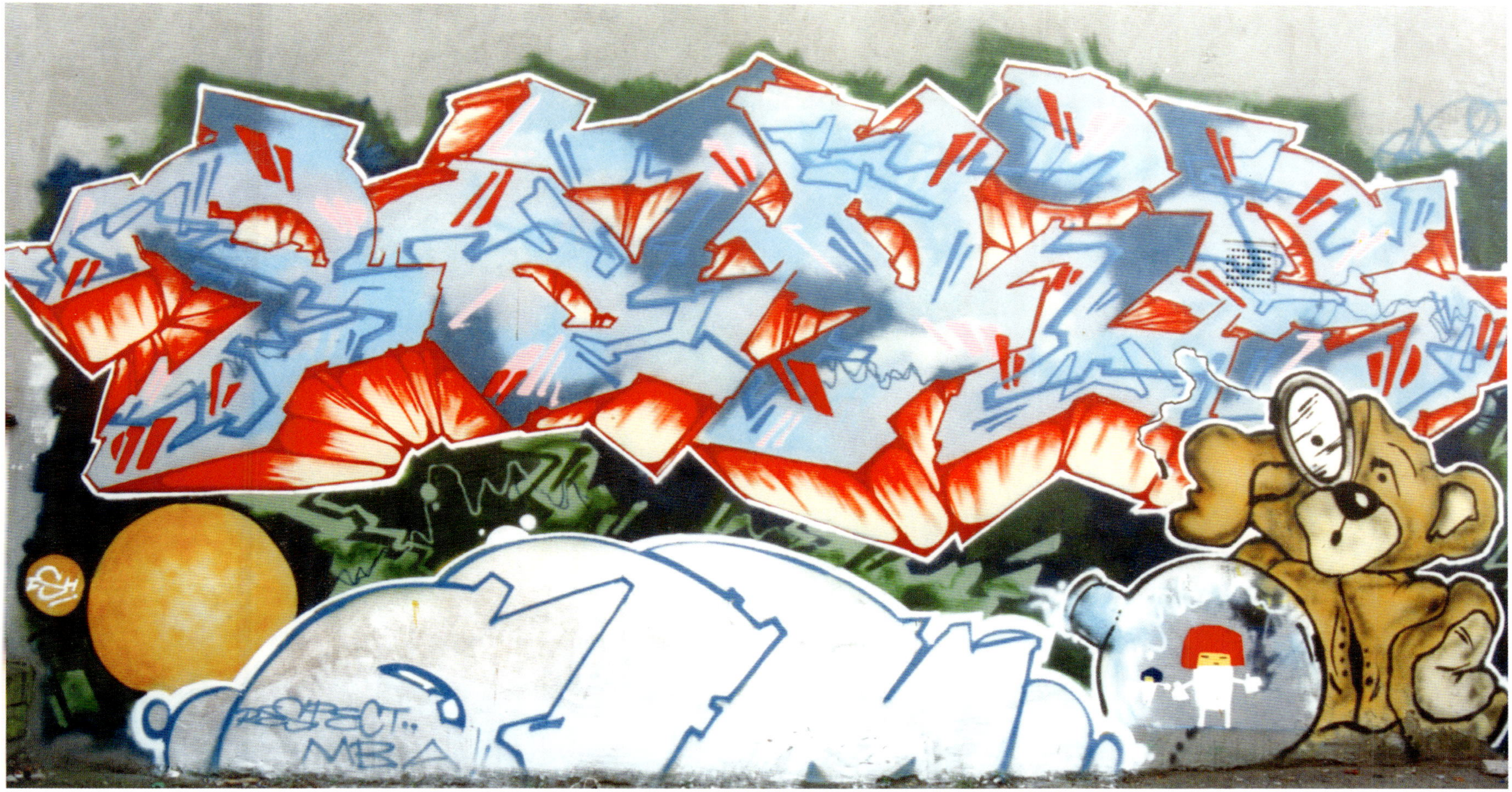

paint onto the walls, you're not really going to get that same feel, and even then you're not going to get the same effect as street graffiti. Whenever you take it onto a canvas you're almost creating an installation. When you're dealing with a gallery show you're creating a specific feeling.

"Graffiti is part of a broader street culture, and when it goes onto a canvas you've got to react with that. Your work's got to change and grow, and that's what I like to think my work has done. What I do on canvas is not what you'd see on the street: it contains elements of it but it's completely different. If you paint on a scrap of wood in the street, it's still a scrap of wood in the street, but if you move it into a gallery, it becomes a piece of art. Dada was the first graffiti to move into a gallery – Duchamp signed his name on a toilet and it became a piece of art!"

Paris strives to convey this passion, and self-belief to the young people he works with on youth arts projects in Bristol and beyond. As well as a crucial source of income that has enabled him to continue developing as an artist, it's something he feels duty-bound to do. "I feel I've got to do it. I came out of the inner-city and now I'm lucky enough to live the life I do. I see it as my way of giving something back, because I can communicate with young people. It's good research, you find out what's going on in their heads and I'd hate to be dislocated from that. It's the same with painting on the streets, you get to know what's going on in society at the deep end. I'd hate to lose that and be painting in some kind of bubble. I'd like to be doing it all over the world. Passing on knowledge to the next generation is the key."

Above: Burning blues and reds (incorporating existing Stephan Platez stencil into the piece) Bedminster skate park, 1997

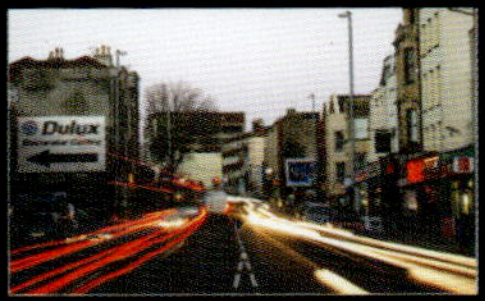

Top left: View up Stokes Croft, source image for painting on the right, Stokes Croft, Bristol, 2008

Far right: 'Making Headlines' portrait of Trigga Don, mixed media on board, 2008

Bottom right: 'B-boy Ooze Dez (Physical Jerks)' mixed media on board, 2008

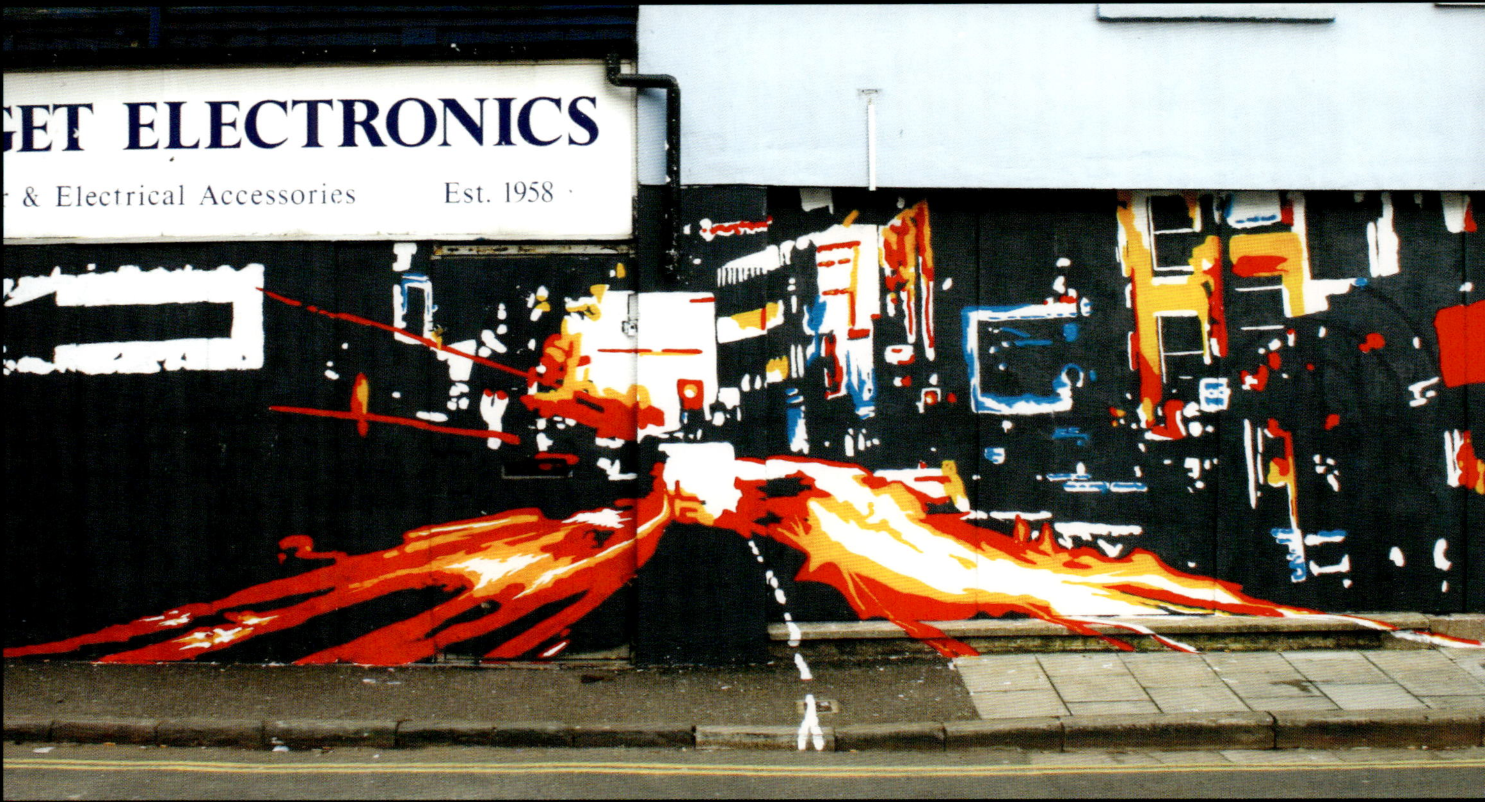

ACER TCF

• **Acer's bold, graphic letterforms are consistent in their diversity: at turns geometric, curvilinear, symmetrical and abstract.** Raised on a diet of early 90s rave flyer design and skateboard graphics, he became a meticulous draftsman who copied every angle and serif of his favourite logos by hand before he ever saw a single piece of graffiti. Having always counted the camera alongside the spray can as his tool of choice, Acer's more recent work utilises both to take him away from the graphic and into looser, more experimental territory.

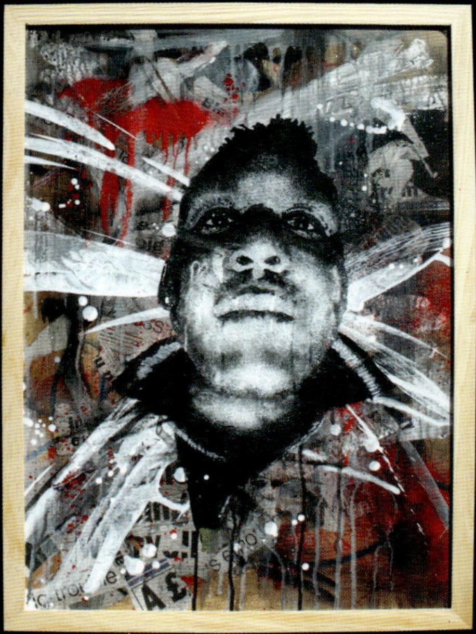

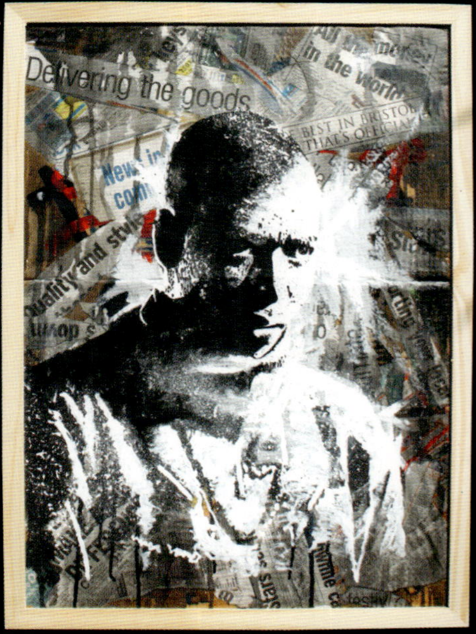

Starting from the beginning, what was your first tag and when did you first put your name up on a wall?
"There were all these rave DJs, like Slipmatt, Donovan 'Bassline' Smith, Groove Rider; and we heard all these cool names and it was like, 'right let's choose our DJ names' and right from the start I chose DJ Ace. Then one day - in around '94 - I saw spray cans for a pound a can at Millards (Auto Supplies) and I bought a can of gold and a can of silver. I met up with my man Greg whose tag was Code, and we went out and wrote Ace and Code everywhere around Bishopston, Horfield and St. Andrews. We went mad, writing on anything and everything: front doors, cars, people's houses. It's kind of embarrassing to think about it now."

What was your first experience of seeing actual pieces?
"The first time I saw pieces was down at Bedminster Skate Park, in '95, maybe '96, and I remember seeing this K with drips coming off it, and I met a skater who had a T-shirt on with the K on it and I said 'hey, I've seen that at Bedminster' and it turned out it was Dicy. He said 'yeah, that's me, that's my thing' and I said 'I write Ace.' He was like, 'oh, OK and you write everywhere, right?' He kind of put me straight, and was like 'Nah, not like that, like this.' So we swapped numbers and one day he rang me up and said 'let's go and paint a proper piece' and we went down to Bedminster."

So I take it Dicy introduced you to what was going on in Bristol at the time?
"Yeah, through Dicy I met Paris up at Brislington warehouse, which was the first place I saw proper graffiti being painted. And that's where I got my influences. I was doing a Photography BTEC course by then, and I was taking photos of pieces up there by the likes of MBA, SOF, Sake and his crew, Turo, Shimz, and all those guys. That was my only link to graffiti, we had no Internet, we had no magazines dedicated to it, as far as I was aware, but I had my camera.

"That was also when I learnt that there was not just a graffiti world but a whole culture based around graffiti. I knew nothing about hip hop culture, I was too busy going raving!"

You were in good company... Did they teach you the mechanics of letter design and how to structure a piece?
"Dicy and Paris showed me their work and told me how to go from a tag to a bigger piece, rocking a background and how to take it to the next level. I realised then that there was more satisfaction in painting something that had been properly thought out, but I already knew how to plan a piece, because I'd been copying all these skate and rave flyer logos."

I guess it must have been a real inspiration to be taken under the wings of these older graffiti writers?
"Mate! Paris showed me his black book and it was just bursting at the seams with photos of all his stuff from Hull, and I'd never seen anything like it. I'd never seen these styles before and I'd never seen colours be used like that. I feel privileged

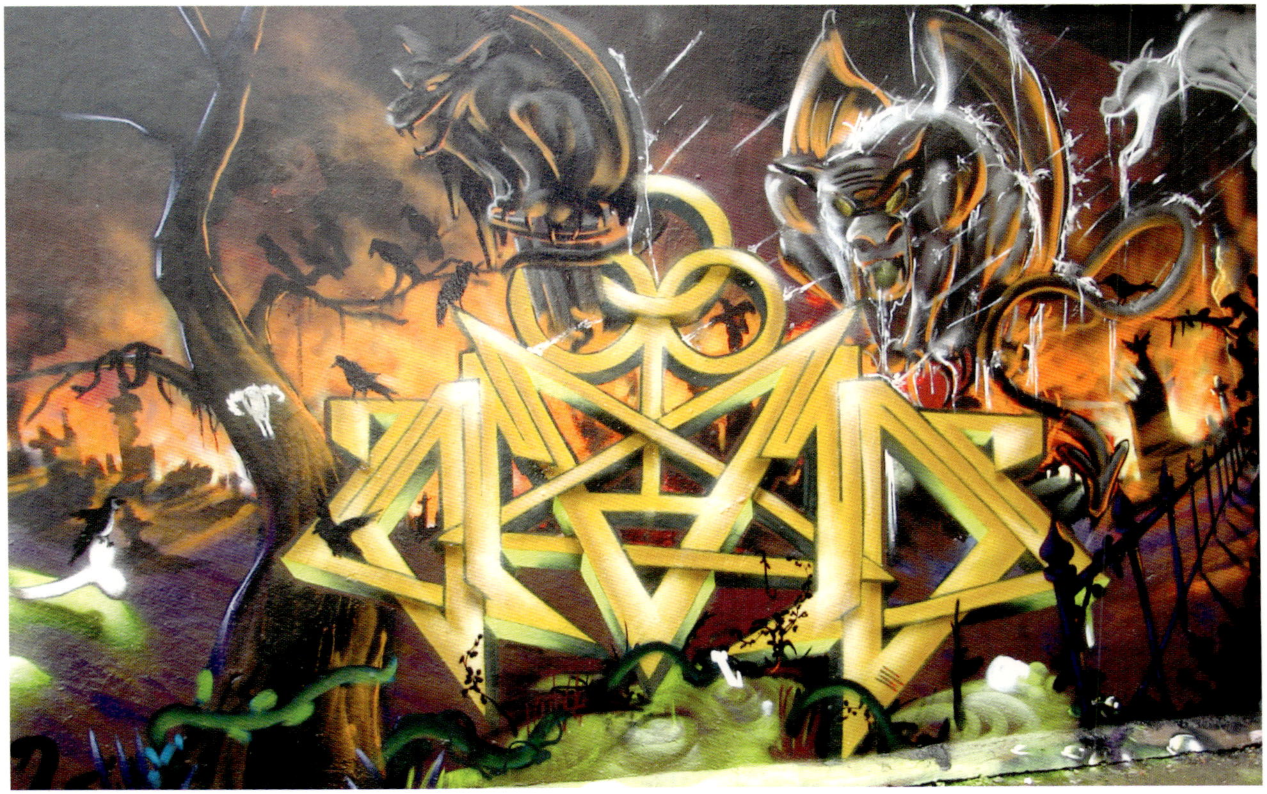

Above: Hallowe'en style, Acer and Xenz, Bedminster skate park, 2006

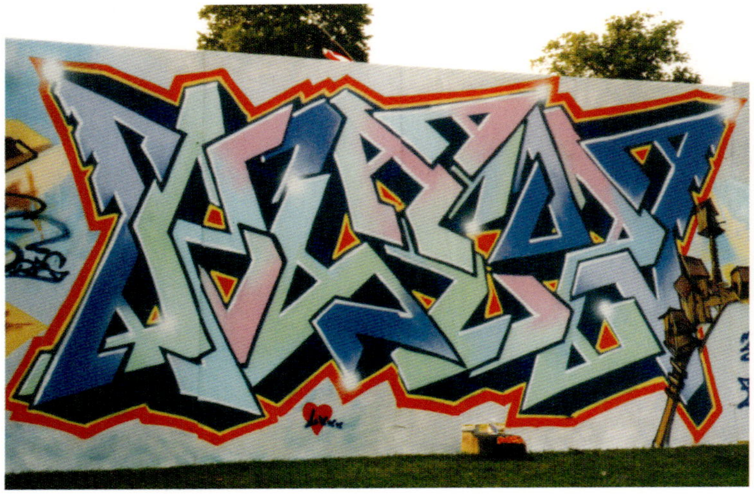

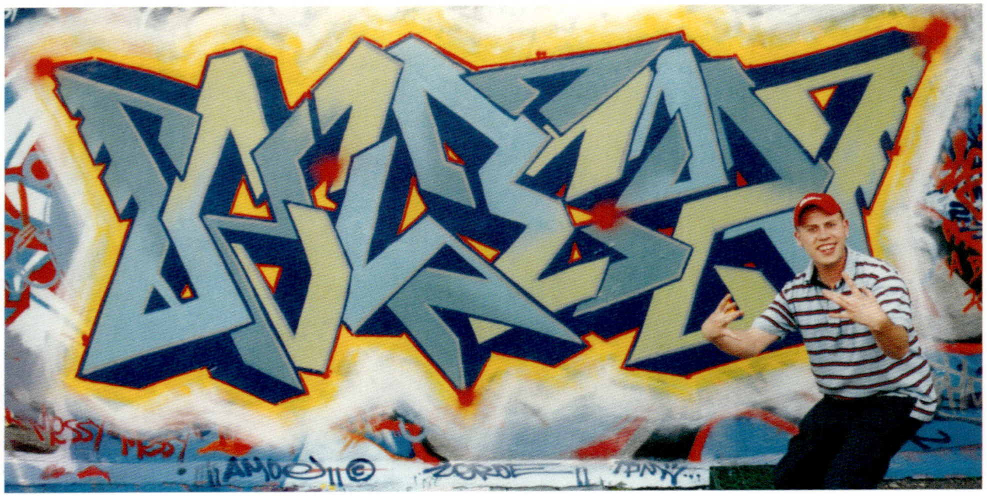

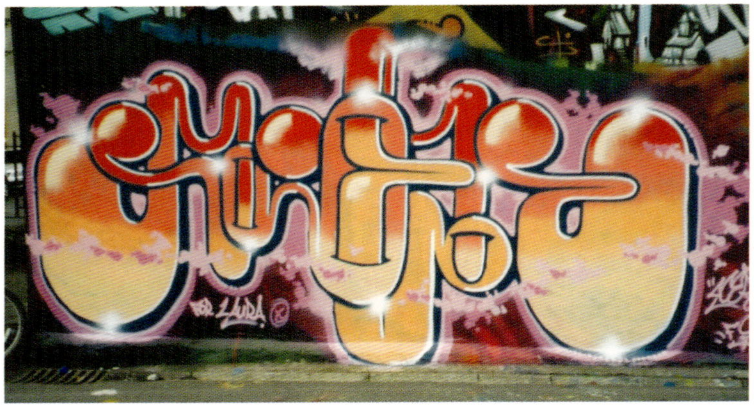

This page. Top right: Bubba (MC with Aspects) strikes a pose at Bedminster skate park, 2002

Top left: A to the power of ten, Urban Games, 2002

Above: Curvilinear Acer piece Bedminster skate park, 2003

Opposite page. Top: Symmetry in the undergrowth, Montpelier Park, 2006

Left: Triangulation style, Bedminster skate park, 2002

Right: Heartfelt symmetry, Riverside Park, 2008

to have been part of the last generation to understand what it was like to not have graff on tap, because back then you had to meet people and get shown stuff."

Can you tell me how you got involved with FSH (Fantastic Super Heroes) and how the collective came about in the first place?

"I met Paris's flatmates, Bubber and El Eye, from Aspects - who were Earthbound Aspects at that time - and they were part of FSH, and I was just initiated into the crew, basically. It was around the time FSH started and I was just made to feel a part of it. It was like a new door had opened. There was Dicy doing Kuldesac, DJ Vinyl Matt (aka Awkward) - who actually came up with the name for the crew - there were B-boys, MCs. We were doing nights at Cosies, and Scott Fury was putting on US hip hop acts at the Thekla. There were so many different creative minds involved that it just sort of happened. FSH became the creative link between everybody."

What sort of spots were you guys painting at that time? Were there many Halls Of Fame running?

"I painted Brislington warehouse a couple of times before it disappeared, and once that happened it had a mad effect. It seemed like the competition level had sort of evolved from that spot and because it was gone the wall space became limited again. There was just Bedminster (skate park) and Barton Hill Youth Club. So people started looking for new spots, and it pushed us, because one spot was gone and it had been the biggest one that we had. That in itself spawned links between Bristol writers, because we then hooked up with the SOF lot - who were out in Somerset - and we would go out to paint with them and they'd then come to Bristol and paint here. Those links started being made, and it was a real privilege to paint alongside all those people."

Looking at your pieces from back then - especially after you and the other FSH writers joined TCF - it looks like you were embracing the experimentation and boundary-blurring that was prevalent in certain crews at the time?

"It's something I came to understand coming up in the late 90s. The way we were painting then was to paint letterforms, but to use different stuff with them. We took influences from the old school but it was about breaking barriers, doing something different, doing something new with it, taking it in a different direction. Eko and the other Hull guys were always onto that, taking letterforms into another dimension. For me it's about not worrying so much about the letterform, but just making a visually interesting shape."

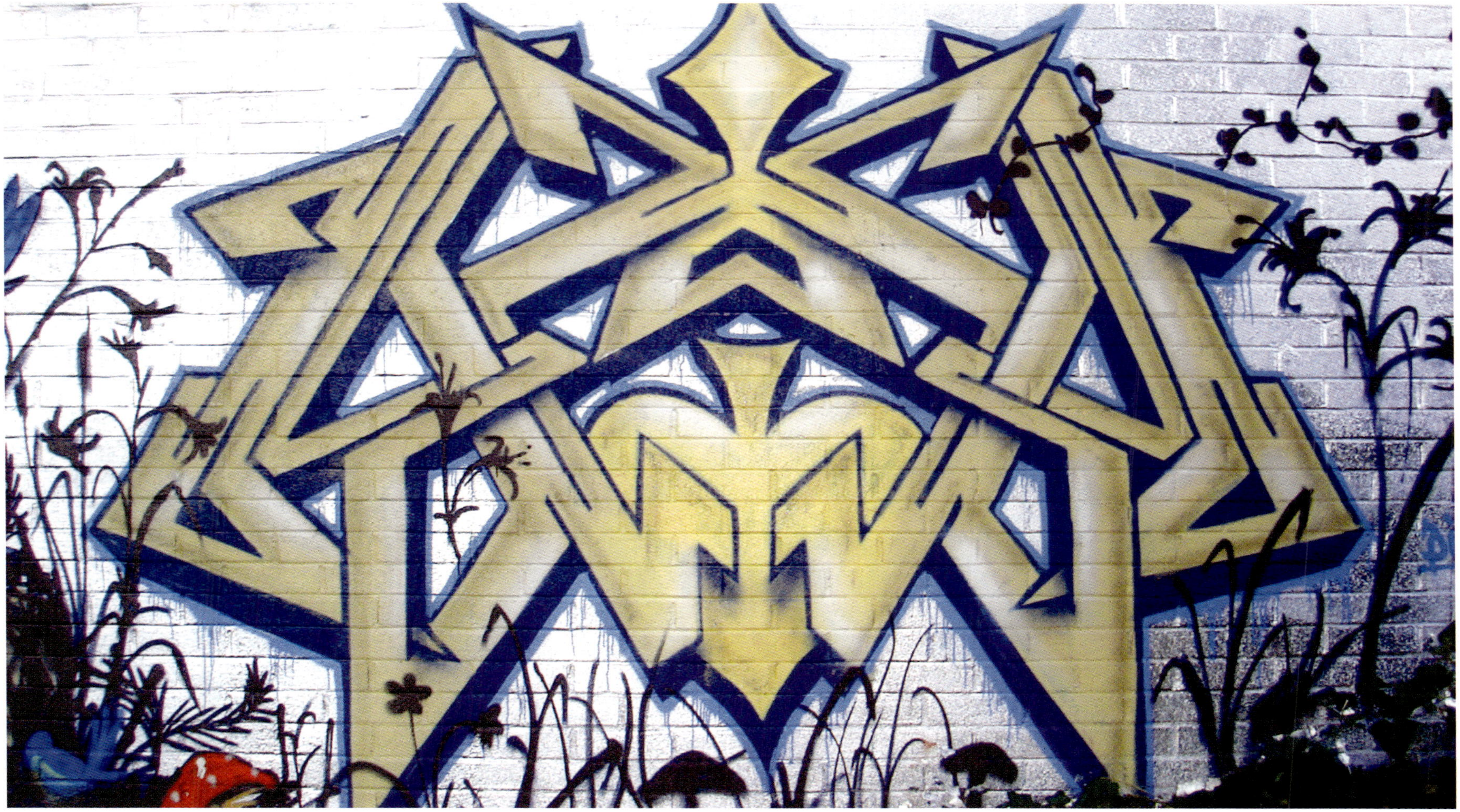

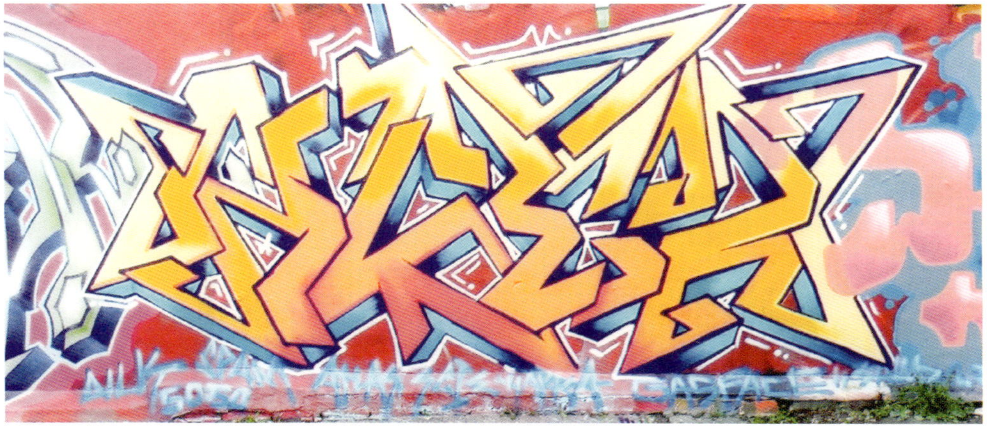

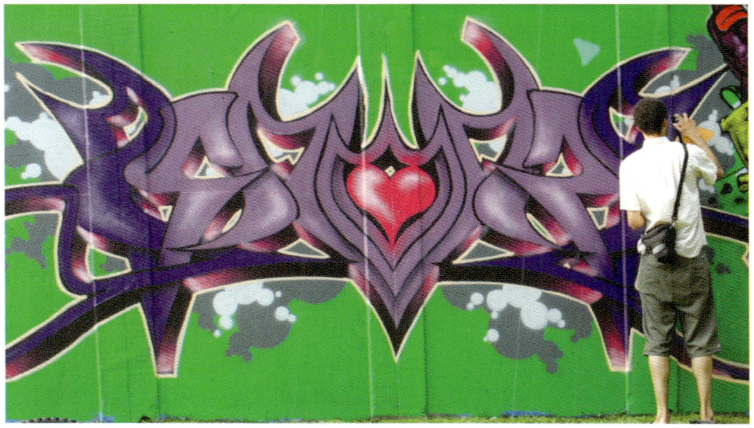

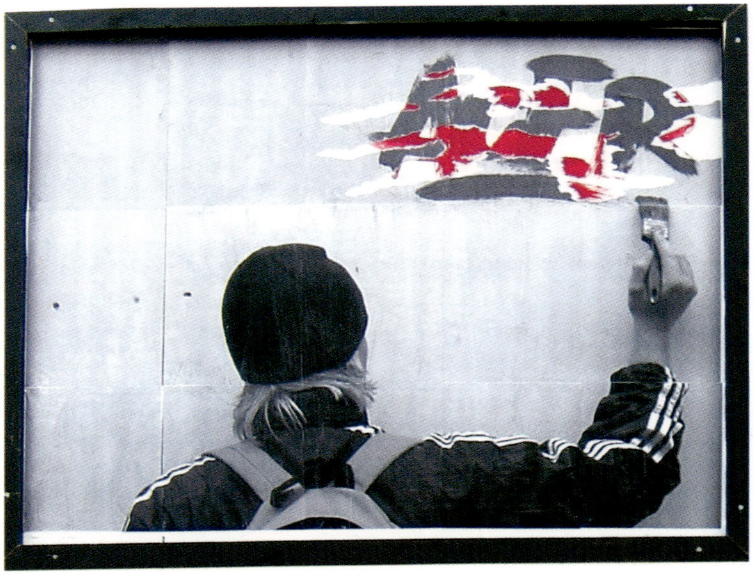

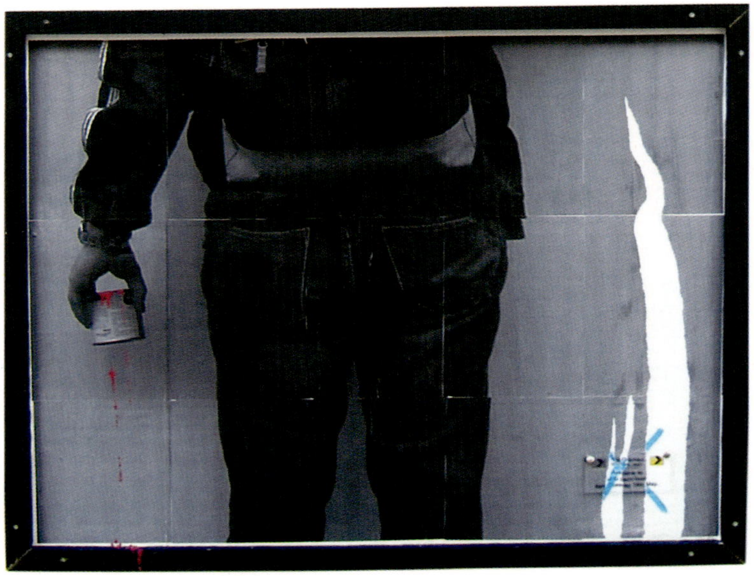

Above: Acer reinvents himself photographically, Jamaica Street, 2007

Opposite: Acer fans at a ramp-back quick block style, St. George's park, 2008

What is it that appeals to you most about painting as part of a crew?
"It's always been about a community thing, it's about meeting up with friends, and painting a good piece, obviously. And the actual day, you know? The only time I get to see a lot of these guys now is when we're all painting together. We used to do a kind of 'Sunday Social' with everybody coming out to paint on a Sunday. Now we're all older and have different commitments, but we still make an effort to paint with each other as regularly as possible."

Everyone's kind of doing their own thing now, aren't they? Is there a creative overlap between the crew's members outside of social painting?
"The great thing about being in a crew like TCF is that whilst we all come together and paint as a collective, we all also have separate projects that we work on and we help each other out. It's a way of communicating with friends. It's great having personal connections with all those people with their fingers in different pies. We're all doing different professional jobs now, and we can draw on those things when we work with each other."

Can you talk about the kind of work you're doing now and how it ties in with your painting?
"For a while now I have been working with young people in Bristol and I'm kind of passing on the same positive experiences that I had, you know: being taught how to do my thing and how to hone my craft, and perfect what I do, so now I try and pass that on. It wasn't a traditional mainstream route, but I learnt a lot from growing up through the graffiti subculture; and a lot of those skills that I learnt aren't necessarily arts-based; there are a lot of different things that I learnt through the culture that I try and pass on to disaffected youths and people that haven't got direction. It's not just graffiti, it's stuff I learnt through DJing, from being around MCs, and even breakdancing and skateboarding: they're all positive outlets for young people that aren't recognised as 'mainstream education.' Passing those things on and promoting them as positive outlets for their energies is what interests me. So really I can thank graffiti and I can thank Bristol's influence on me, as a young up-and-coming writer, for enabling me to do the job I do now."

More recently photography's played a big part in your work. It's quite a radical departure from the more technical, letter-based pieces.
"I think what it comes down to is there's one main source of inspiration for me and it's always been photography, it's always the buzz of making a photograph and making an interesting image. Now I'm trying to push that and make that image into something I want to paint, or create a new image from.

"It's kind of gone full circle now, I want to try different things; I want to push what I'm doing. I'm not as bothered about painting letterforms, and getting my 3-D totally right anymore. I'm almost at a point now when I look at some of my graffiti pieces and I just want to smash them up, make them look different. Ruin them. I guess that experimentation is what's driving me to do different things – taking it away from the traditional. I don't necessarily want to keep it real; I want to keep it new, keep it interesting for myself."

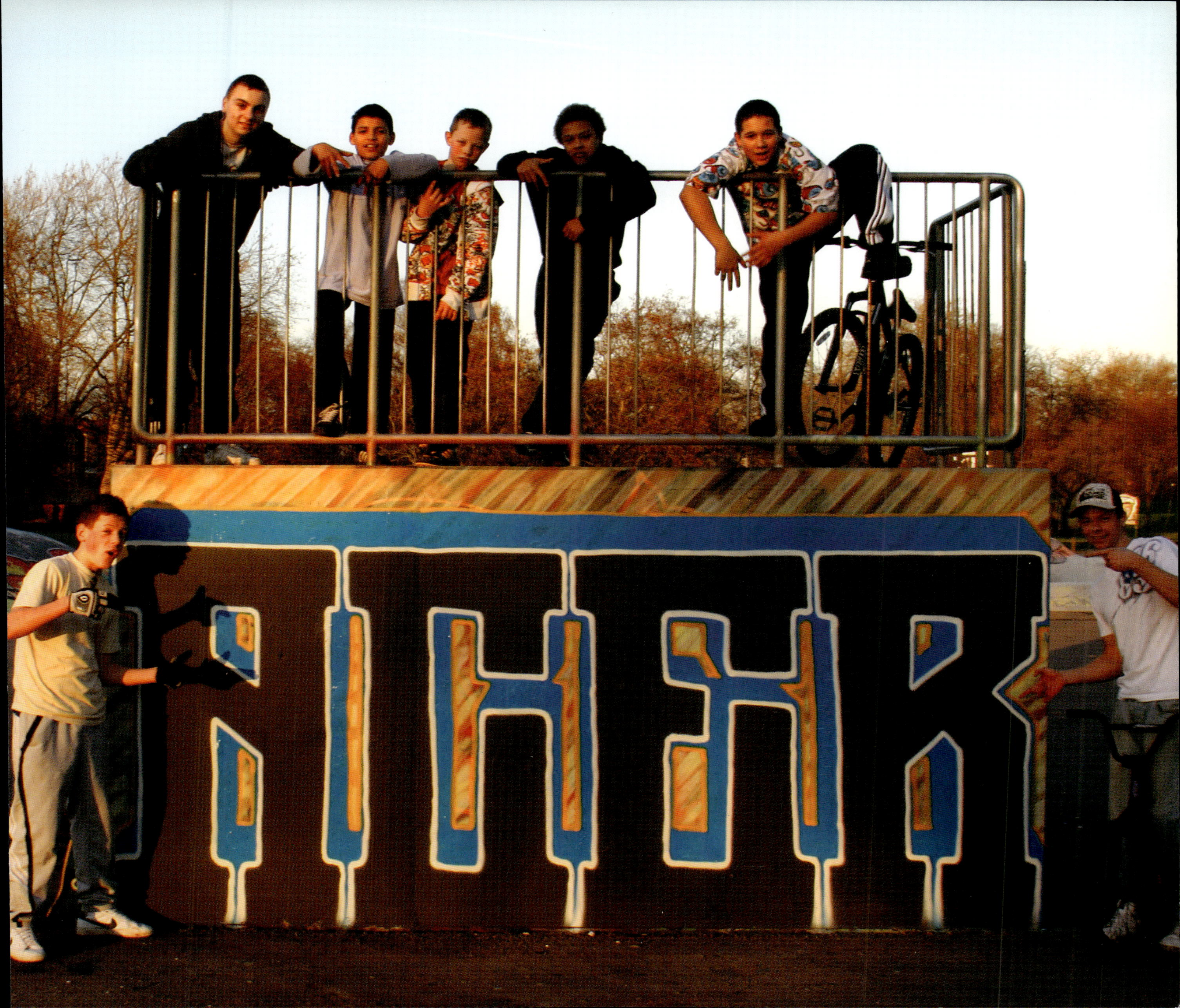

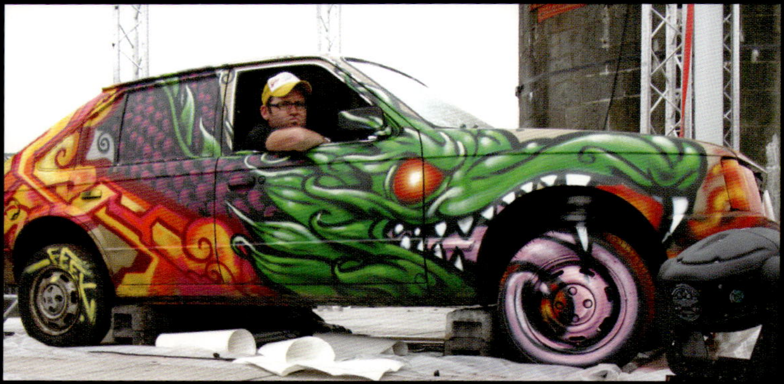

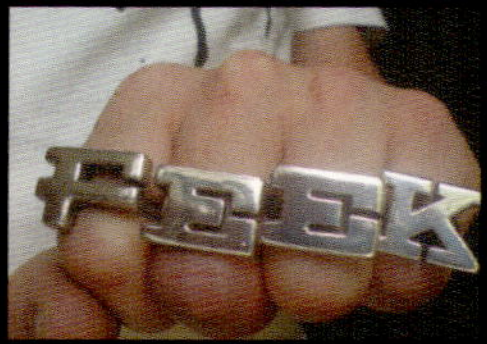

Top left: Feek in a customised Vauxhall, 360 Festival, 2008

Right: Beware of the dog! Angry mutt, 2004

Above: Remember the name, four finger Feek rings

FEEK TCF

• **A member of the ten-strong Twentieth Century Frescoes, Feek's characters bring a gnarly and often humorous dimension to the crew's pieces and productions.** As a long-time skater and cartoonist, his work rarely falls into the category of most 'traditional' graffiti character painting. Feek's subject matter is extremely diverse, yet always executed in his own unmistakable style. A hugely influential and confident can-wielder, he is never without something original and different to bring to a day's painting. He is also a master improviser. I once watched him paint a suitably moody French puffer fish - complete with cigarette and beret - in about ten minutes, using only a small plastic kid's toy for reference. His character designs and models also make regular appearances in the work of Bristol's best-known animation company, Aardman, the creators of Wallace and Gromit.

When and why did you come to Bristol?
"I came here in 1993 to go to art college. I came from the carrot-crunching land of Suffolk, accompanied by Mr Jago. We both got accepted onto the illustration course at

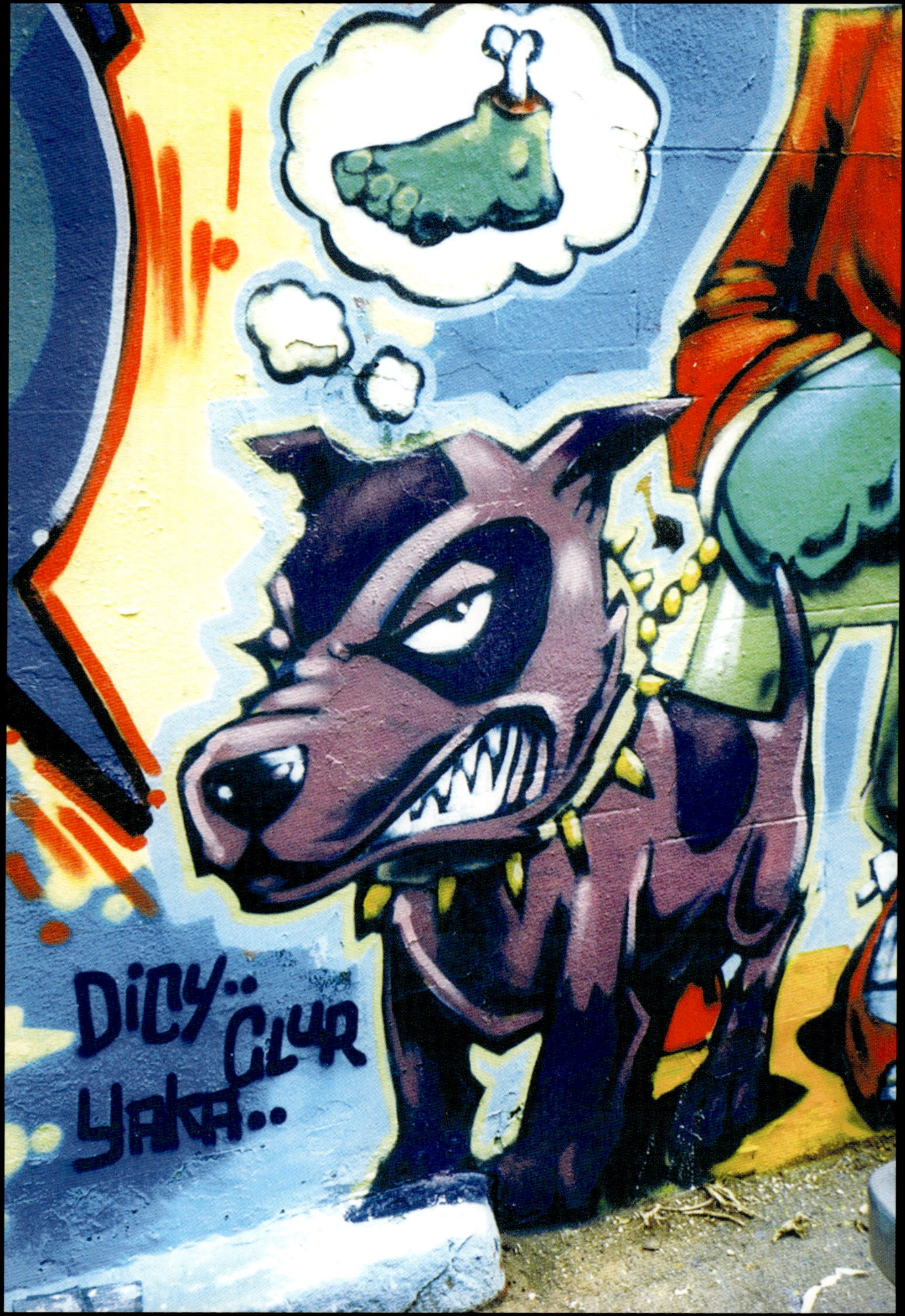

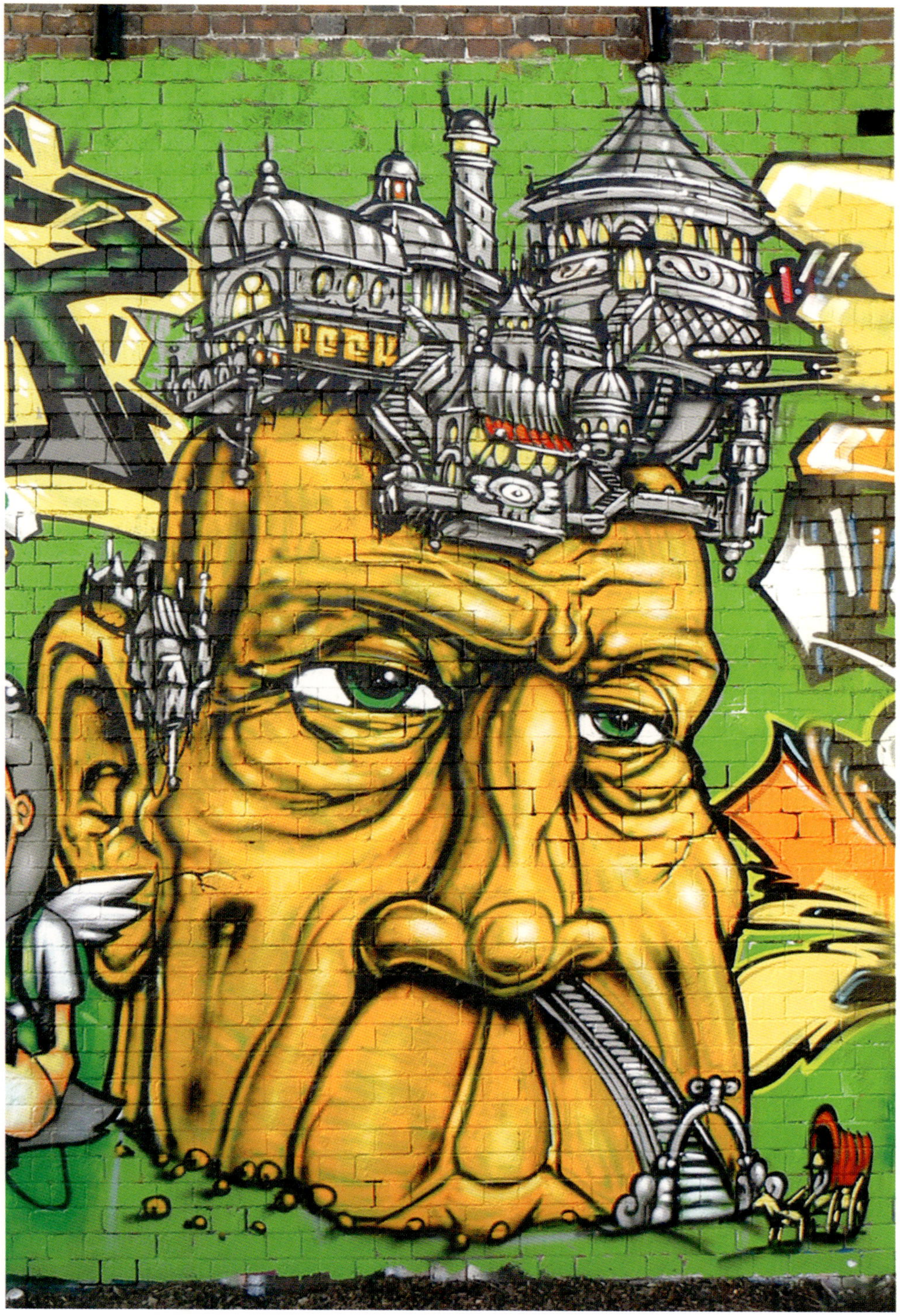

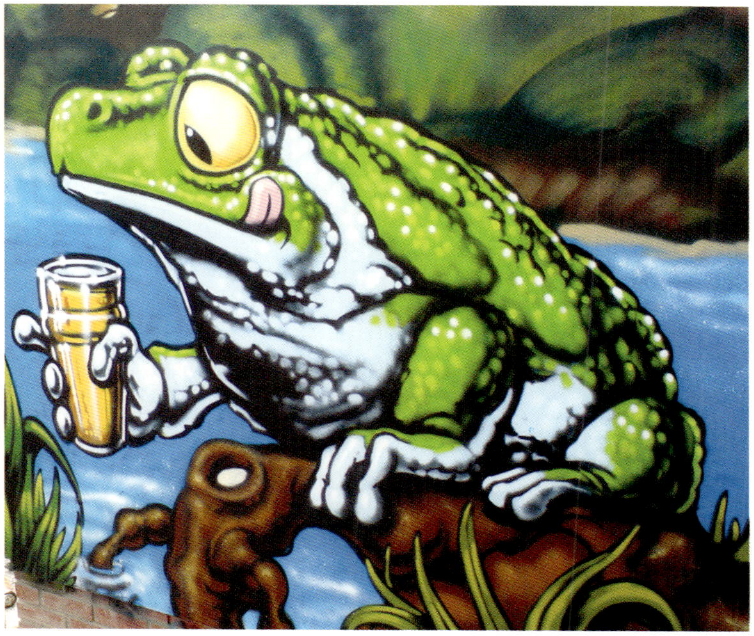

Bower Ashton, chiefly on the strength of our sketchbook work."

Did you have a distinct style before your started painting, or did it evolve after you picked up a can?
"I think I always drew in a certain way. Spray paint was a way of drawing big and quick, which really appealed to me."

Who were the first writers you met up with when you got here? Did you form a crew right off or was it an organic thing?
"The first person I really got involved with in terms of painting in Bristol was Dicy. We met down at Dean Lane [Bedminster] Skate Park, through a love of skateboarding and smoking cheap rocky hash. He got me into painting, showing me the basics. We painted a lot as Dicy and Feek before we got involved with the FSH (Fantastic Super Heroes) crew."

Left: A lot on his mind, Roxe Jam, Cardiff, 2008

Above: When water isn't enough. Thirsty frog, Duke Of York pub, 2008

• FEEK

Right: Bass robot, mixed media on canvas, 2003

Left: Robot tune digger, ballpoint pen on paper, 2006

Below: Drunken B-boy lets off a stinker, 2007

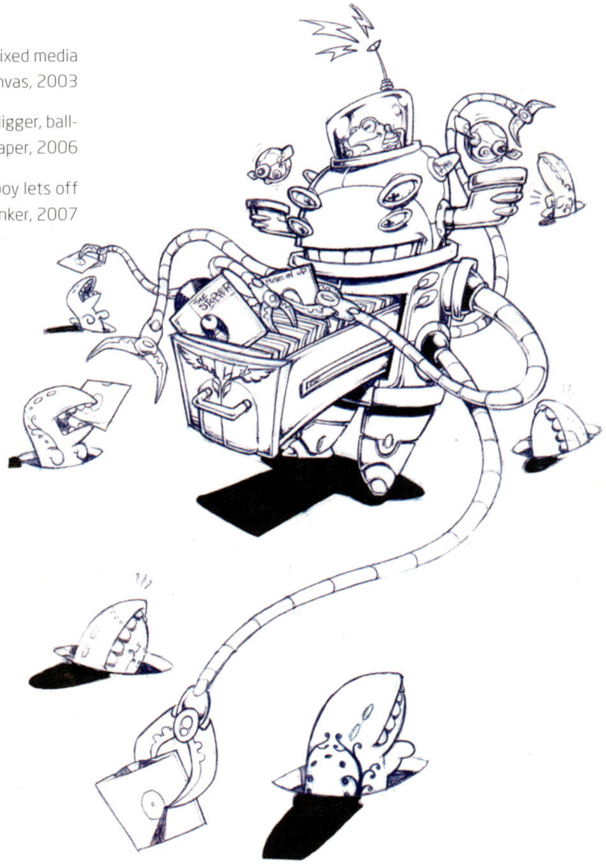

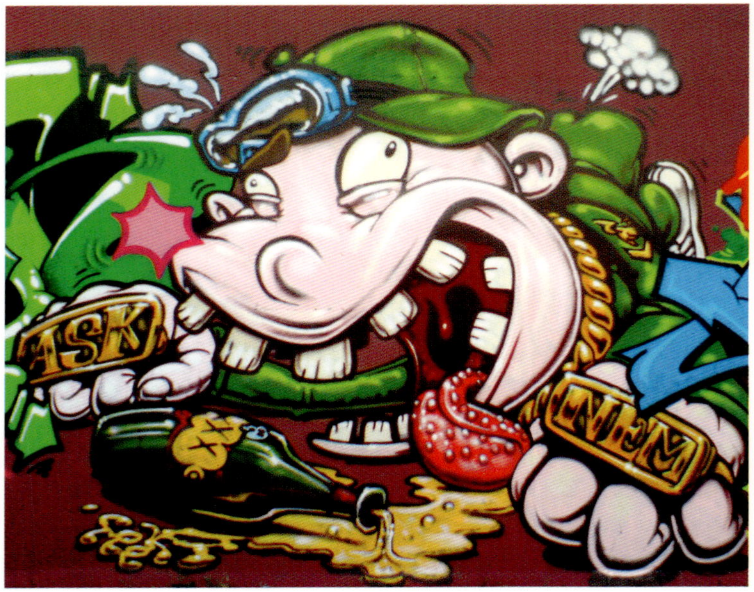

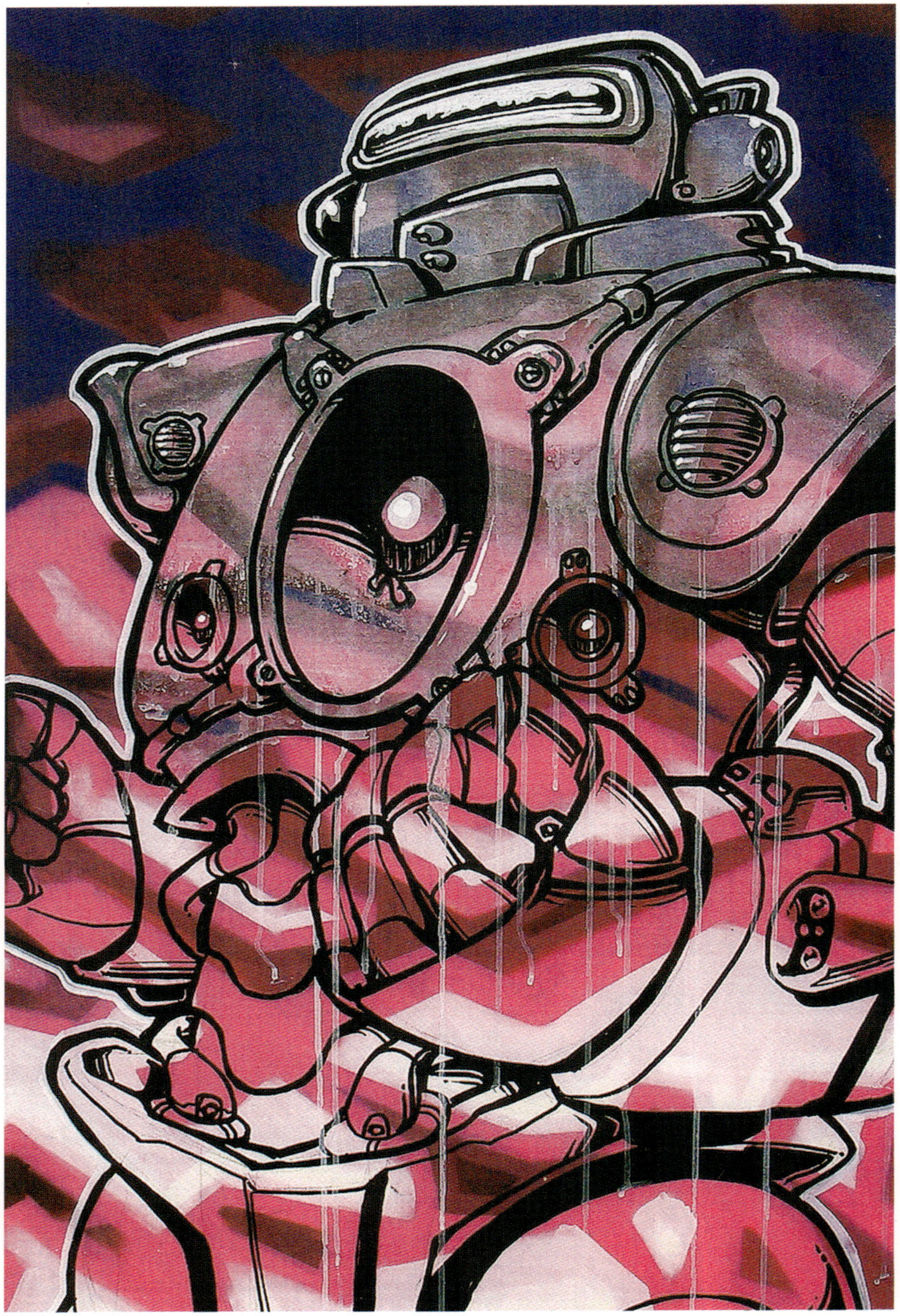

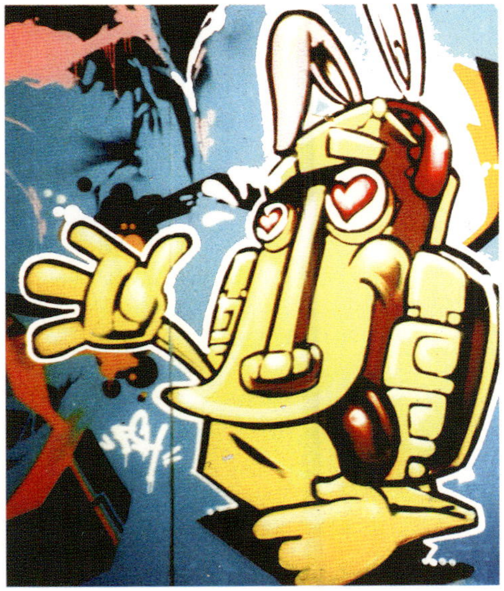

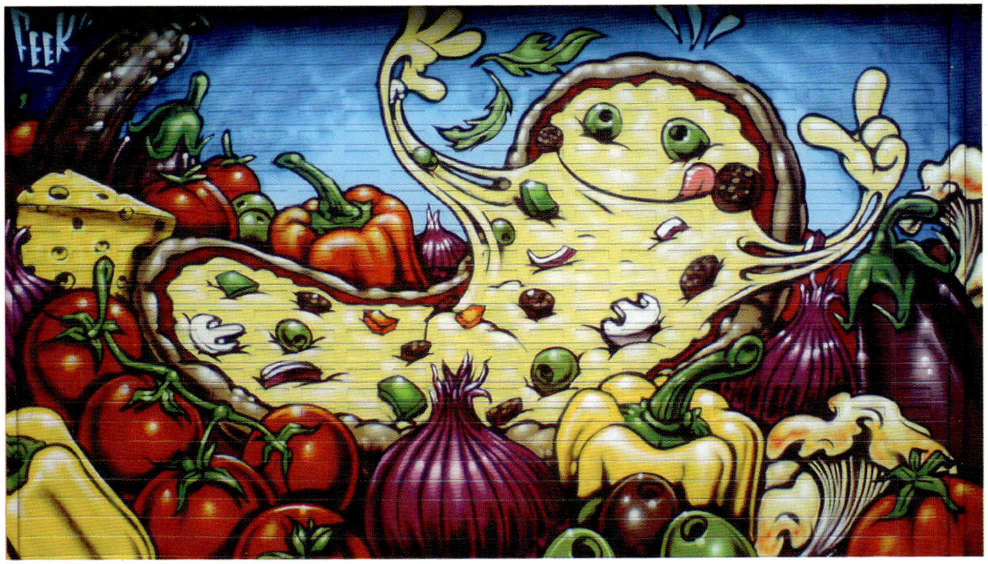

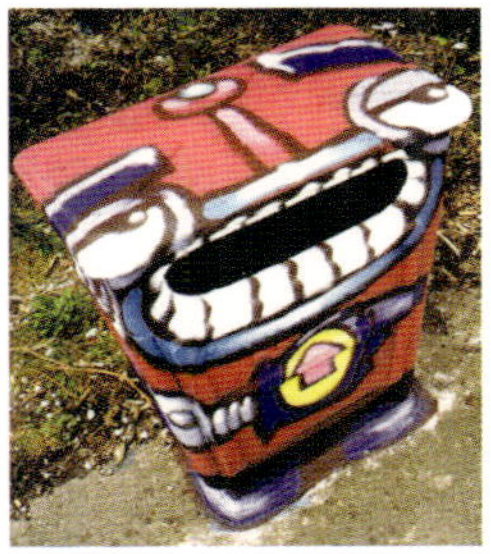

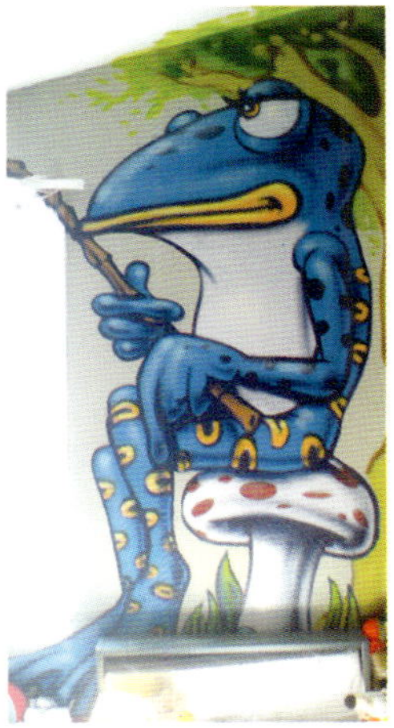

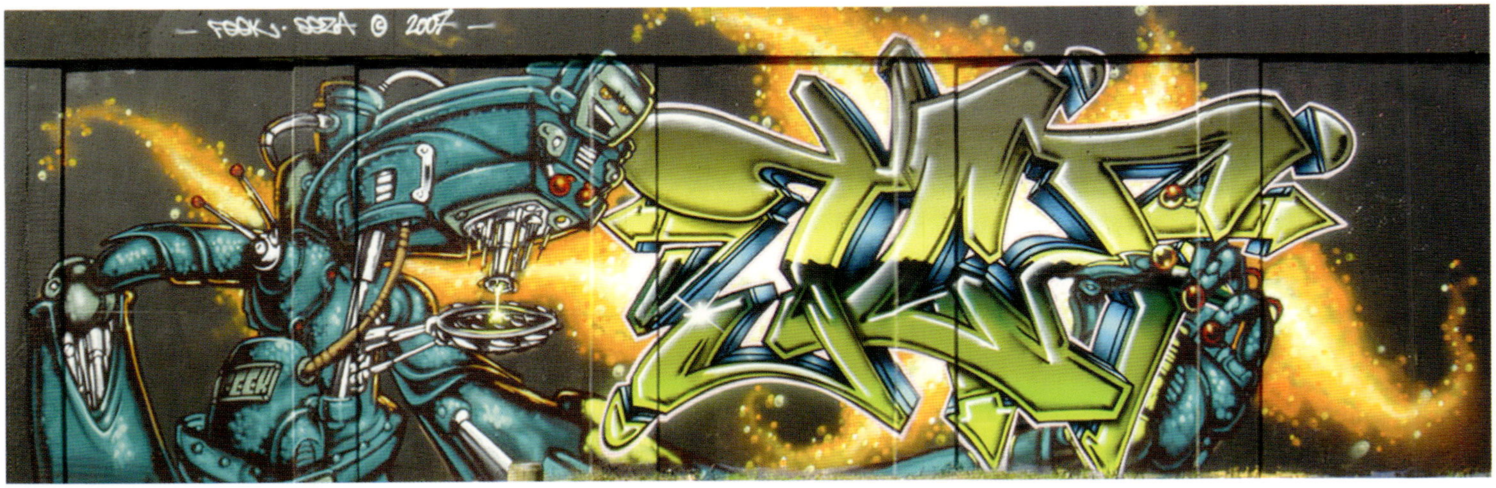

Top right: Robo-bin, Montpelier, 2000

Above: Mellow frog, 2004

Far left: Love-struck Easter Island head, 2002

Middle top: Pizzeria shutters, Montpelier, 2008

Bottom: Feek and Seza, Riverside Park, 2007

Are there any cartoonists that you emulated as a kid? Did you grow up on comics?
"I used to love comics, for sure, and especially the work of artists like Bill Sienkiewicz and his *Elektra: Assassin* series, Dave McKean of course, and 2000 AD artists like Mike McMahon (who used to draw the best Judge Dredd) and Simon Bisley, who really raised the bar for British comics. I used to do a comic strip for RAD skateboard magazine. It was a fairly cheesy affair called End Zone drawn in black and white with the obligatory birthday set of Rotring pens. The pay wasn't great but I used to get a lot of free skate stuff."

Do you prefer painting to drawing? What are the main differences?
"For me, drawing is the basis of what I do. I find abstraction difficult, I kind of paint definite 'things'. I never draw enough though, that's my problem."

How did you find the scene in Bristol when you arrived? Was it a buzzing place to live and paint, was there a strong creative community?
"Kind of, yeah. Certainly when the FSH thing started happening, with graffiti

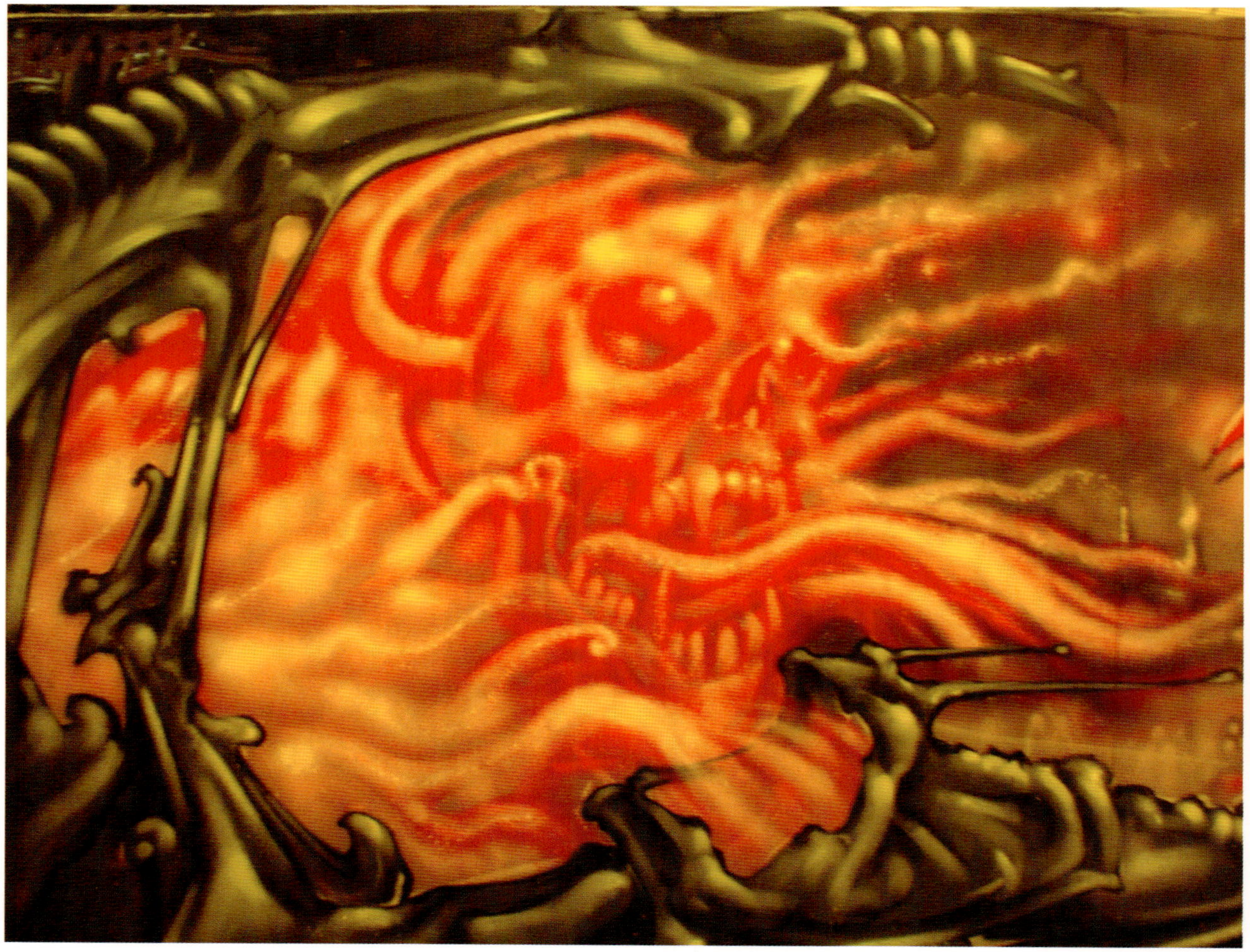

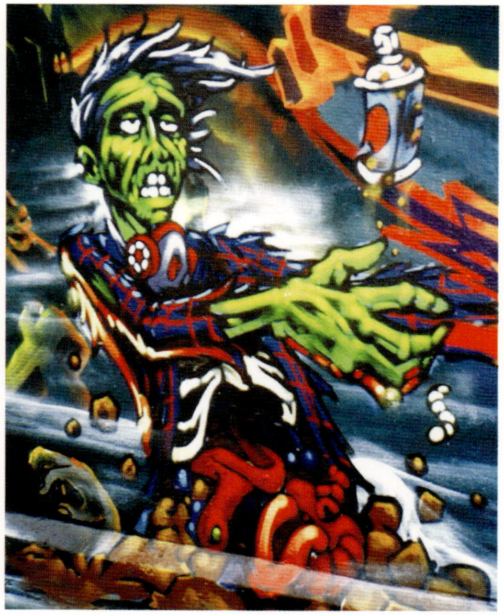

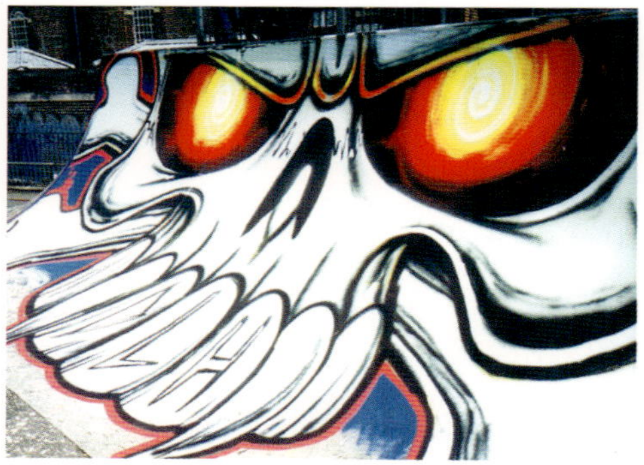

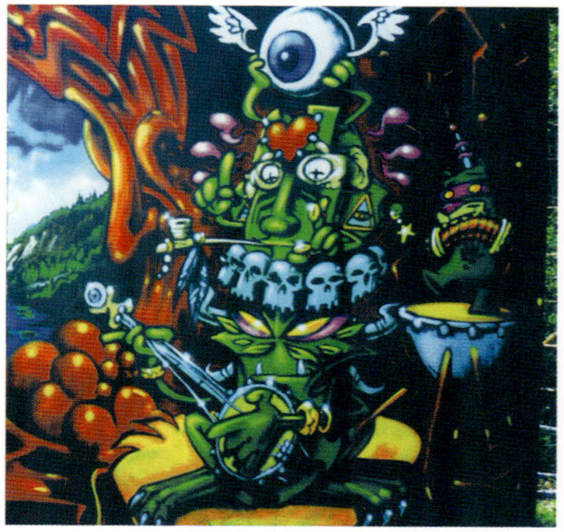

Above: Flaming skull, 2006

Top right: Zombie writer loses his grip, Bedminster skate park, 2005

Middle right: 'DLH' skull (Dean Lane Hardcore) Bedminster skate park, Dean Lane, 2005

Bottom right: Character totem, Glastonbury Festival, 2005

writers, MCs, breakers and DJs all in one crew, it really felt like something big, you know? Meeting up with the Hull crew though – Paris, Eko and Xenz – was a revelation. That's when the production burners really started happening. You just knew that when you where painting with those guys, your shit was gonna look good!"

Walls On Fire seems to have really re-invigorated Bristol.
"Yeah, it was great, despite the miserable weather! There were so many great writers there, I felt really proud to be a part of it."

Have you ever painted much illegal stuff? Any memorable stories you can recall?
"Some things, for sure. You should never mix booze and paint! Dicy and me got gripped at Redland train station (in Bristol) doing a piece under the bridge. We were finished as well, but decided to walk out to the front of the station. Dicy was swinging the pot of emulsion around and accidentally

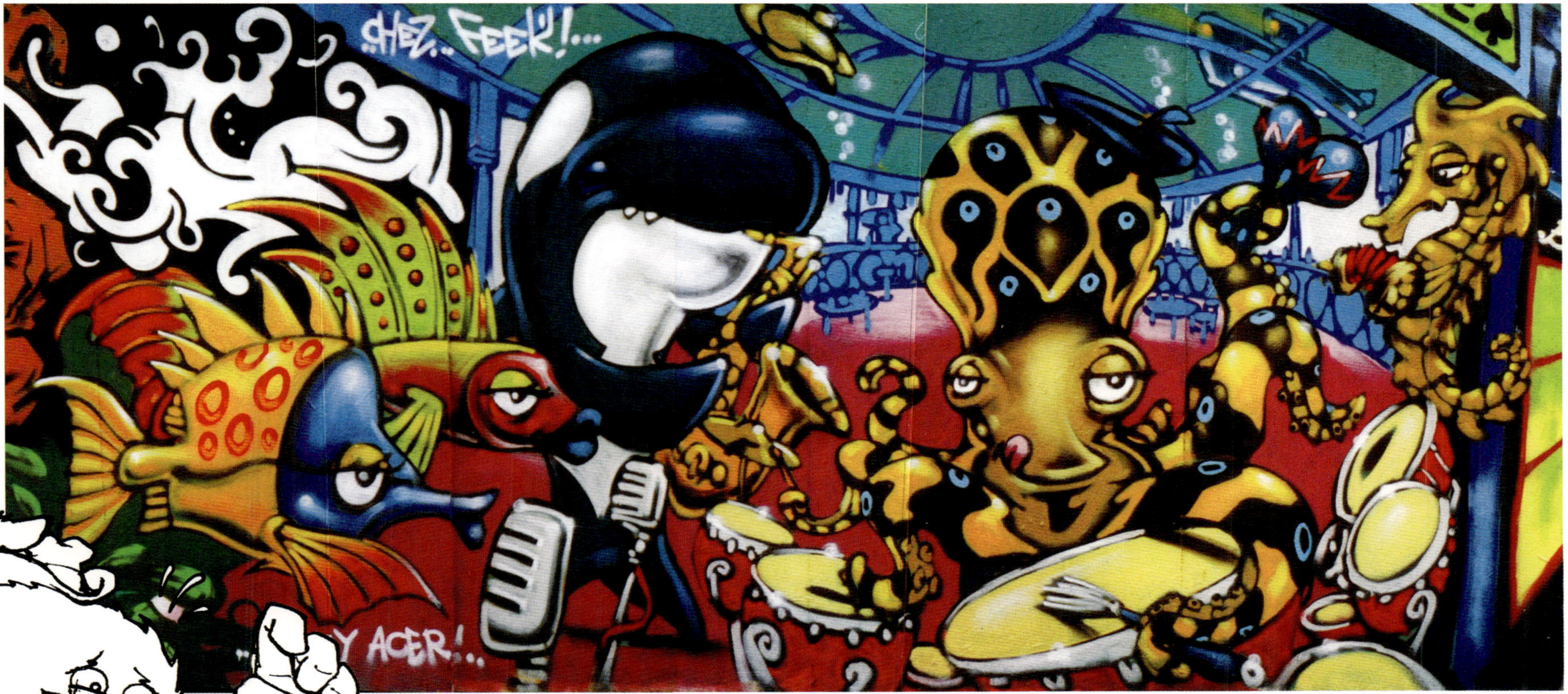

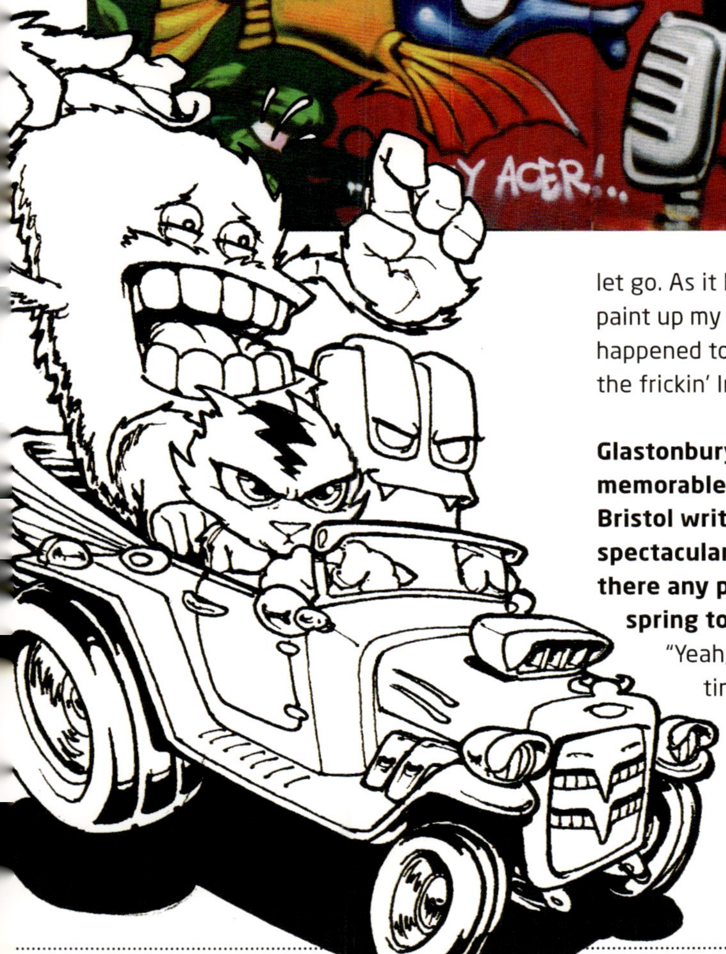

let go. As it hit the deck and sprayed paint up my entire body, a police car just happened to roll round the corner: luck of the frickin' Irish!"

Glastonbury Festival has hosted some memorable collaborations between Bristol writers, often messy and spectacular in equal measures. Are there any particular occasions that spring to mind?
"Yeah, we seemed to do them all the time. Banksy was responsible for the biggest one that we painted. It consisted of two pieces either side of the stage in the Dance Tent, both 16ft high by 32ft wide. Before we could paint, though, we had to build the wall! It was a bloody mammoth job, two weeks' solid work. That boy was always ambitious though."

Ziml described painting with the crew as like playing in a band. Can you give me an insight into the dynamics of TCF?
"It's more like being in the day room at a mental hospital when we all get together to paint. It's always well funny."

The days of TCF productions gracing Bristol walls on a regular basis seem to have passed. How hard is it to get everyone together these days?
"It's tricky because everyone is busy, but great fun when we do."

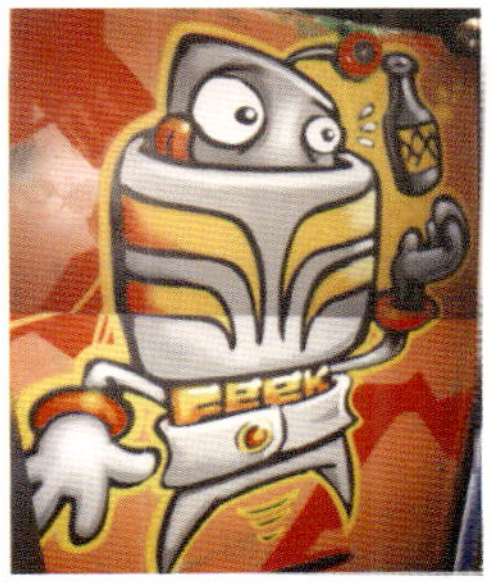

Top: 'Chez Feek' sub-aqua band, dock side, 2001

Above: Thirsty alien, Elbow Rooms, 2003

Far left: Monsters in a hot rod, illustration, 2007

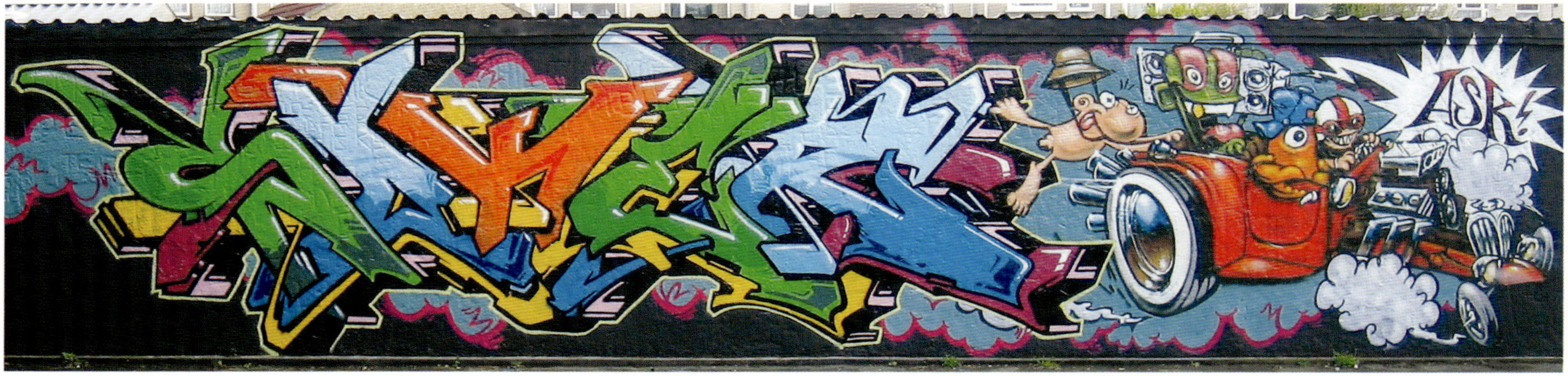

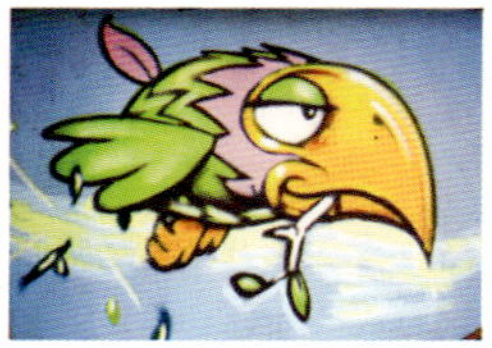

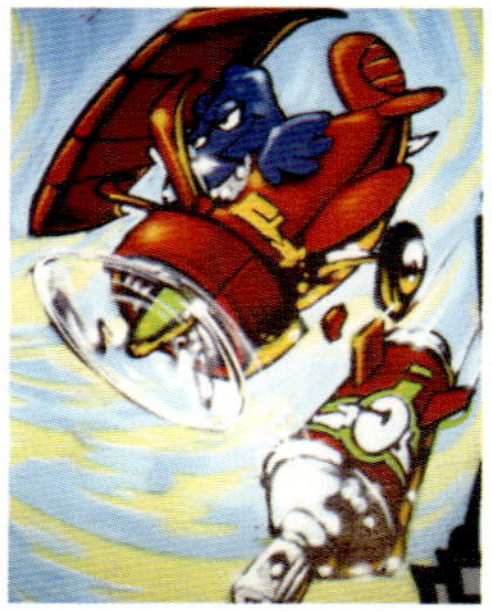

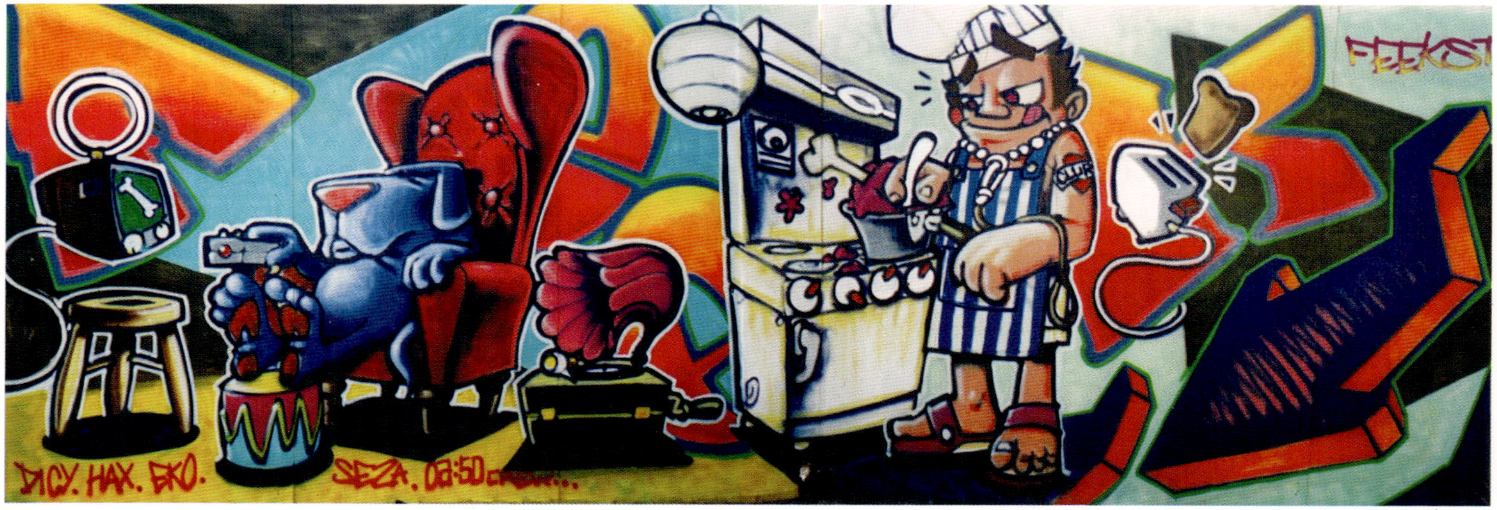

Top: Soker and Feek, dragster action, Champion Park, 2008

Middle left: Dopey bird heads for the nest, 2006

Above: TCF bomb the city, 2005

Above right: Dog's dinner, Urban Games, London, 2000

Bottom right: Little red, Bedminster skate park 2004

Has the passion for graffiti stayed with you? Do you make a living from your art in some way?

"I love painting and I think I will always do it. I would love to paint solidly as a job, and there are periods when I do. I also do a lot of sculpture, model making and set building, to supplement my graff and illustration work. Working three-dimensionally is a fantastic challenge in itself, and I love that, really frying your brain trying to create something."

Any artists - graffiti or otherwise - that you admire and are inspired by?

"Eko. I've said it before and I'll say it again: the man is a genius, and effortlessly so."

Is humour important to you? Your characters often make me smile.

"Laughter is the best medicine. I think some of my best pieces have been where I've nailed the technique and the humour to the same degree. That doesn't happen very often though!"

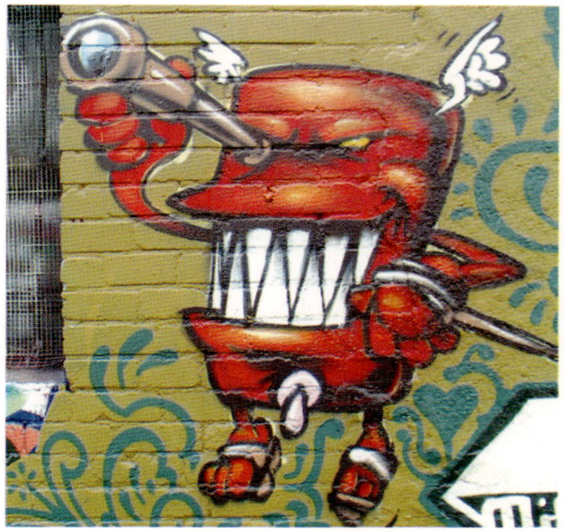

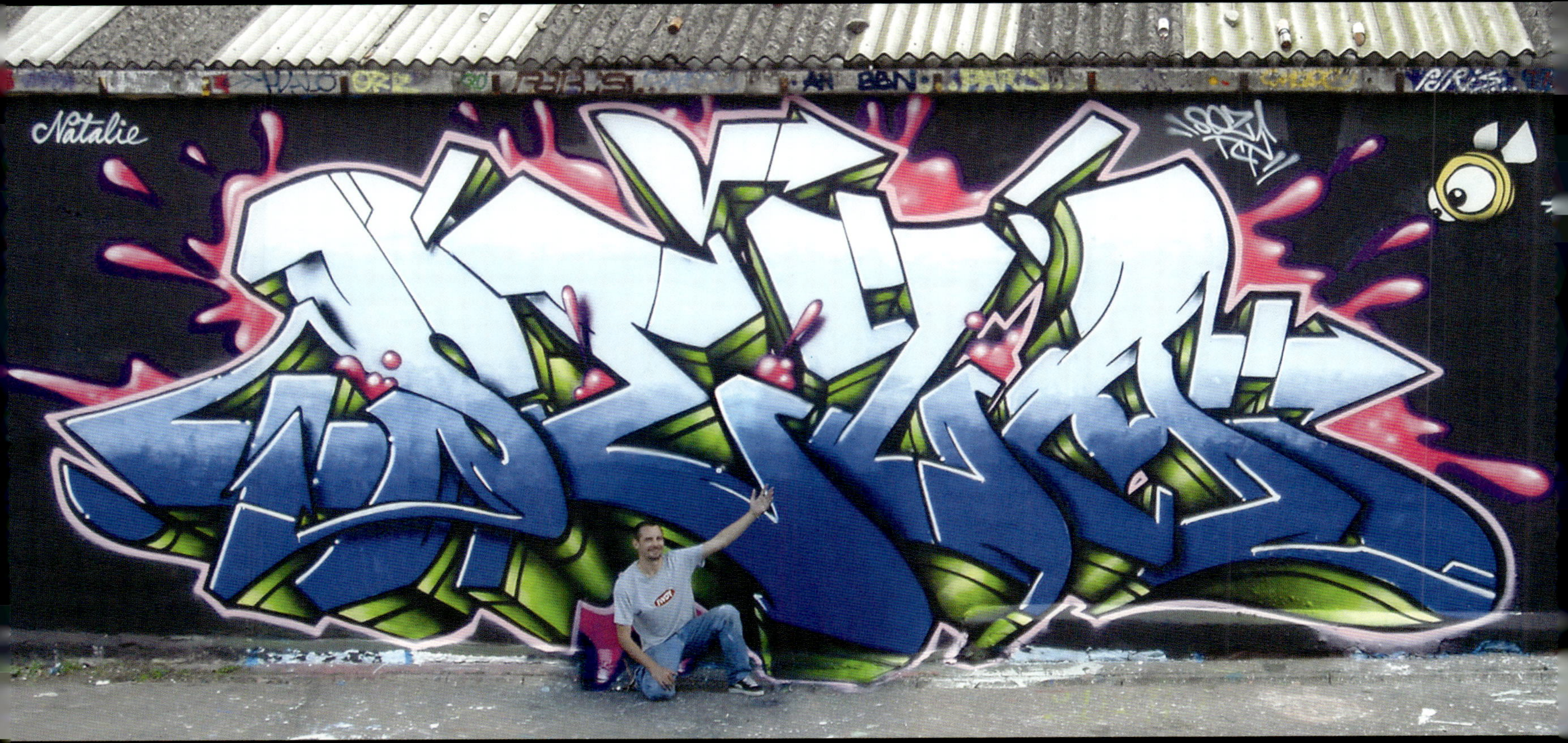

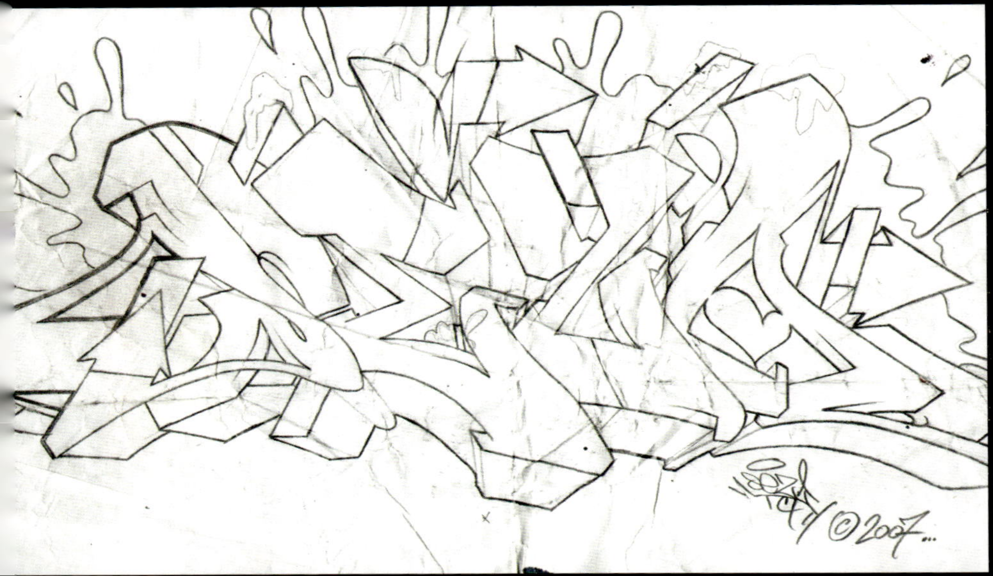

SEZA TCF

Above: Jumbo style, Bedminster skate park, 2007

Left: Sketch for jumbo piece

• A graffiti veteran with more than 20 years of writing behind him, Seza has a finely-tuned style that owes much to the golden era of New York subway writing - and yet he remains fresh, evolving constantly from one piece to the next. His burners jump off the wall with a vibrancy and an urgency that leave you in no doubt: Seza is as passionate and as hungry to burn the competition as ever.

How did you come up with the name Seza? Was it just a good combination of letters?

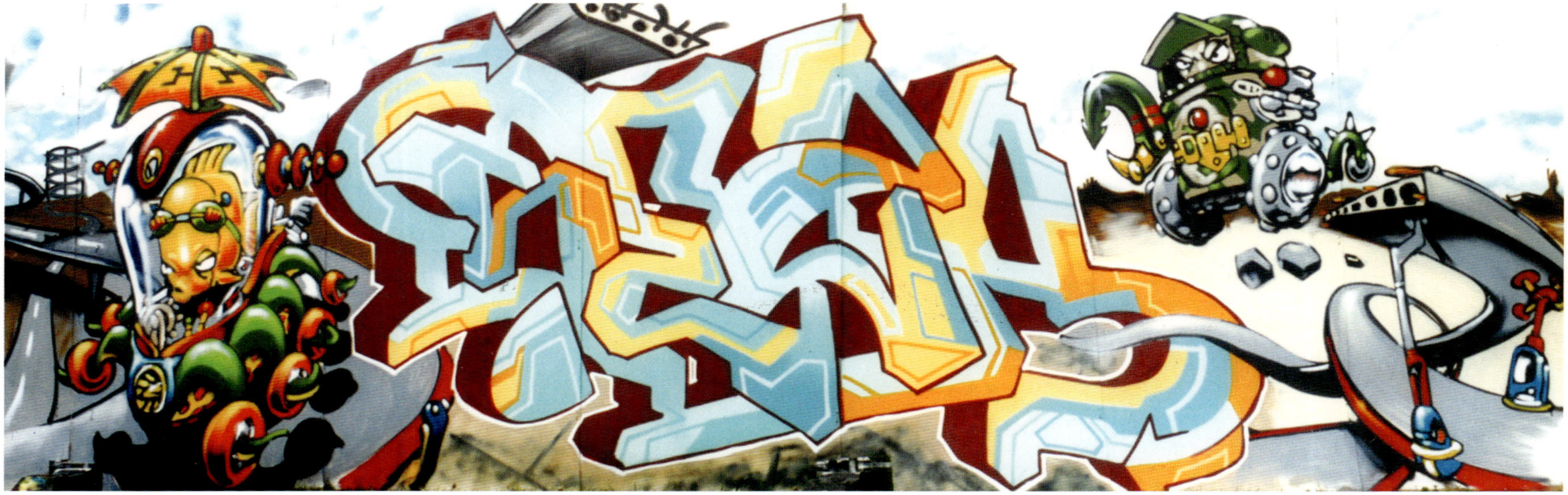

Above: Feek and Seza, 2002

"Ever since I was a kid I loved the Asterix books and I always liked the Roman stuff, so it came from Caesar. But I wanted to break it down to four letters, and I wanted to have an S in there, so I wrote it Seza. It's also good to have an 'E' in there, too. E is probably the baddest letter in the whole alphabet. Nowadays I get bored of it because I must have done 5,000 Seza pieces, or whatever, but I think you can tell a Seza piece when you see one. Even if I paint a Rusk piece or a Babylon piece, you can still see that same style there."

When and where were you introduced to graffiti?

"I grew up in Cardiff in South Wales, and when I was at school, in around '83/'84, the whole hip hop thing came in. Suddenly, all my mates were all spinning on their heads on bits of lino or trying to rap. For me, because I'd always liked art, the natural thing was to get into graffiti. My best mate's dad worked in an auto garage, and he came home one day with loads of tins of spray paint. That afternoon we did little mini pieces on the side of his mum's garage. She went crazy on us. Then we started going out on the evenings destroying all the streets and alleyways near his house with little throw ups and one-line pieces and tags. After that, we started doing colour pieces as well, although the standard was obviously pretty dreadful. We were also tagging on the trains and buses round Cardiff, on the backs of seats on the top deck, that sort of thing."

Were there many other people painting in Cardiff then?

"There were a lot of good crews in South Wales at the time: there was The Elite, who turned into Second To None (not to be confused with Second To None, the original breakers from London), they did some fantastic stuff. Then there was the Hard Rock Concept, and TMB (The Melody Boys)."

Do you have any lasting memories of painting from back then?

"Do you remember the kids' TV programme *Get Fresh*? We got asked to do that. It was being filmed at Cardiff Ice Rink, and they set up a load of boards and painted New York subway trains on them ready for us to piece on. That was fantastic - not only did we get our stuff on the TV, but they also gave us boxes and boxes of Buntlack, the majority of which we took away with us after we'd finished. We had all the fresh colours, the pinks and the ice blue and the lime green and all the stuff you couldn't get in the car paints at the time. That inspired me to do better, bigger, bolder, brighter, more complex stuff."

When did you move to Bristol, and what brought you to here?

"I moved up to Bristol in '95 for various reasons. I was getting a bit bored and I wanted a change, there was shit stuff going on, a lot of people were getting into heavy drugs and I didn't want to get sucked into that. I used to visit my sister - who came to college here - and I always liked the city. In the mid-'90s it was very vibrant, in terms of the music and art.

"From about '90/'91 I'd dropped off writing a bit, what with the rave scene coming on, but by the time I got to Bristol I was ready for a change, and one of the first things I wanted to do was get back into writing again."

How did you come to join TCF?
"I'd not been here long when I hooked up with Paris through one of my mates, then I met Eko and Xenz at Walls on Fire, where I was painting as well. I got chatting with them and from there we made plans to go out and paint together. We went up to London and painted at Urban Games in '99, and from that point I was in TCF. I think that was when I met Ziml as well. We all painted a wall together and at that point TCF became the five of us: myself, Paris, Ziml, Eko and Xenz."

TCF took large-scale painting to the next level in Bristol. What is it that sets the crew apart?
"For me it's a big part of my life, as big as the graffiti itself. I think we're a little bit different from a lot of other crews in how we work together. We've got ten members in the crew and they're all very creative, highly artistic people. We're well known for painting large production walls that have one single overall composition to them. So you've got lots of different pieces sat on a background, all interacting with one another, which gives one overall feel or look to the wall. We've never consciously tried to achieve that, but it's the nature of how we work together."

What are the logistics of painting a wall with so many artists involved?
"I think it's best when you're making a production if one person is driving it, has the vision and ties the whole thing together. Of course, if it's an enormous wall you can't do that and maybe two or three of you have to work together to create that unity. That said, problems can arise when you've got nine or ten people who all have very strong ideas and visions. Luckily, we've got one of the best writers in the world in our crew in Xenz. He's a master at directing productions, and it would be unfair to talk about this without giving props to him. But we've got other guys who can do it too - Feek can do it, I've done it, Paris can do it."

I know you've painted abroad a lot, and get invited to jams all over Europe. Has travelling and painting on the continent influenced how you paint?
"Massively. It's influenced everything, on so many different levels. It's a great experience to go out and meet other writers at the peak of their skills, and it's great to make international friends when graffiti is what we have in common. It's been important in terms of broadening my horizons and allowing me to see graffiti in other countries, but also to experience life in other countries. The way I paint comes from my thoughts and experiences of life and everything around me, so that any experience that affects me in quite a deep way - such as going away and meeting like-minded people - comes out in my work."

Are you a competitive writer?
"I've got a healthy sense of competition, so I'm always trying to outdo or burn other writers that I'm painting with, even if they're mates or part of the crew. You always want to burn whoever's painting next to you. For me, that's always one of the main elements of graffiti, whether you achieve it by making your name bigger, brighter, more complex or whatever."

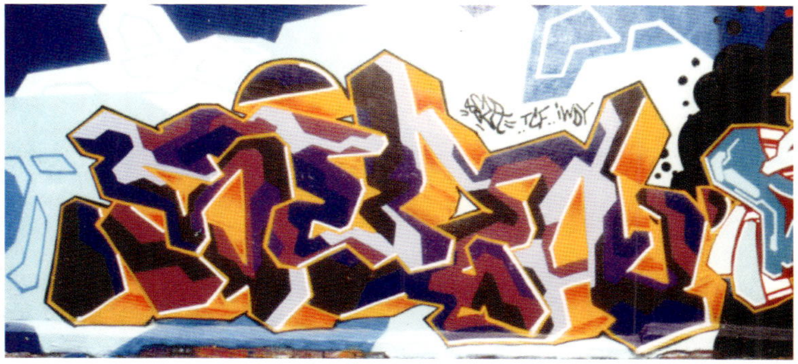

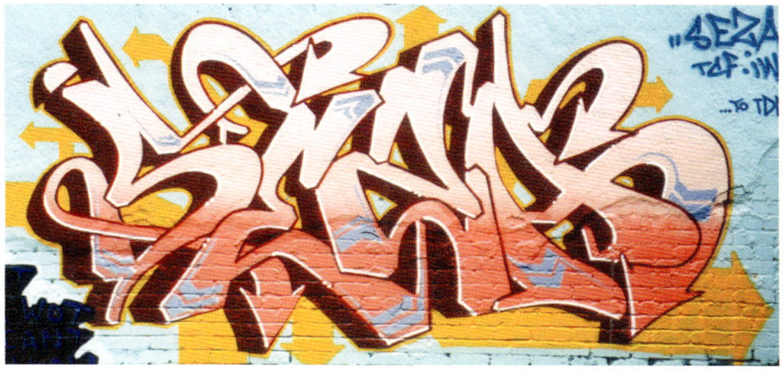

Top: Rocking the polygons, c.2000

Above: Multi-directional style, 2002

Your style has that classic New York feel. Did you consciously work on developing a pure wildstyle aesthetic?
"About three or four years ago I tried to strip every element back to basics and to the essence of what I love about graffiti. That's about style, outlines, the colour schemes or even painting techniques. With painting I used to do stuff with so much precision, but then I realised that in a photograph you can't even see some of the super tight stuff that you're doing.

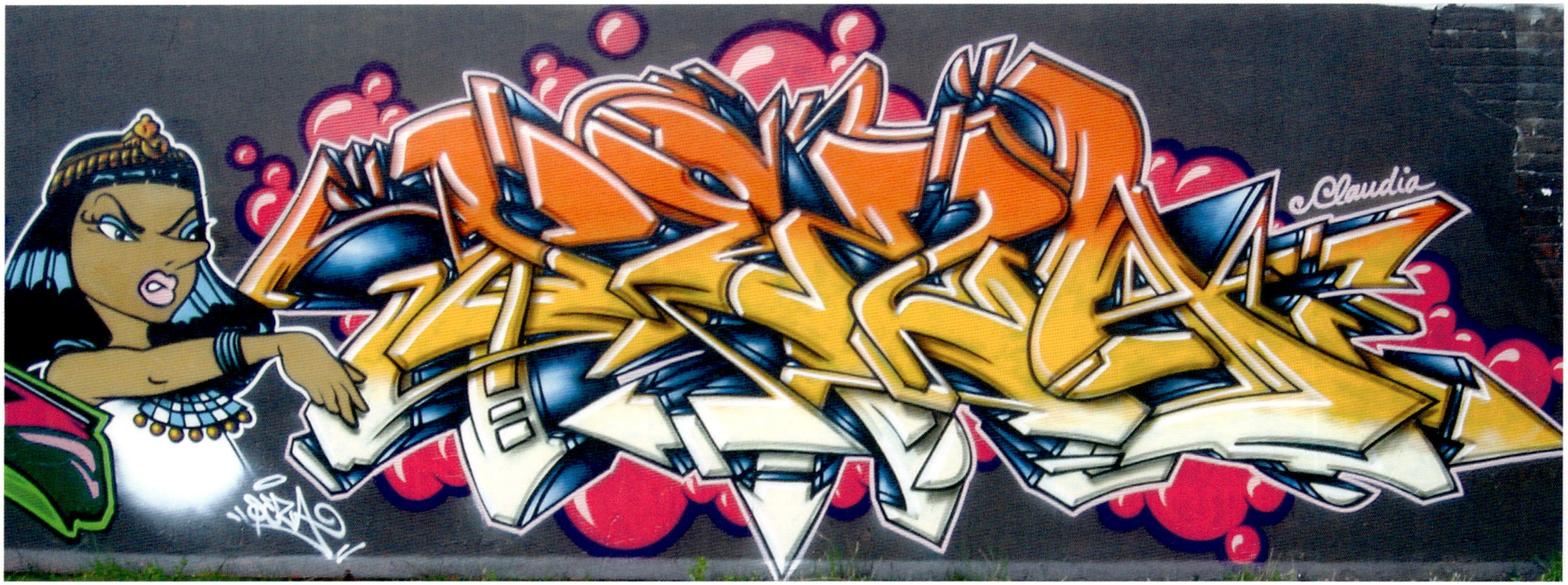

Above: 'Off with their heads!' Seza and Cleopatra show no mercy, 2008

Plus, by doing that tight stuff you're losing the core elements of graffiti, which are speed and energy – the free-flowing, one-hit part of it. If you try and repair and touch up a piece too much, it becomes a little bit sterile. I think graffiti can be painted quite fast: so long as it's got the funk and the flow to it, that's all that matters."

Spoken like a true purist. I've no doubt you have a strong sense of the importance of style, and the role that it plays in making a piece work?
"There's a famous quote from *Style Wars*: 'Style is the key to all forms of rocking.' Whether you're a B-boy rocking the floor, an MC rocking the mic, a DJ rocking the decks, or a writer rocking walls and trains, you've got to have style. Style has to be your own, but it also has to have that certain funkiness to it – or flavour, if you like – that makes graffiti rock. It was what captured my imagination when I first saw graffiti. The things that you can do with letters that make them so much cooler than reading a straight font – it's incredible. And that's what's always driven me to want to paint."

Style within graffiti is one of those concepts that good writers intuitively understand, and yet it's not that easy to explain to the layperson. Is it something that you can put into words?
"The only way I can really describe it is having an eye for aesthetics (and I'm not just talking about graffiti here), and knowing what makes a composition good or bad. It's the same when you look at letters – knowing what style is, and what has flavour, is about having that understanding. Then you can begin to recognise whether a piece has the right weighting, the right tilts to the letters, and so on. Take the way the letters lean, for example, you could think of a letter as crouching or ready to pounce, a bit like the movement of a human body.

"When you talk about the funk and the flow within letters, it's basically about creating movement and energy in letters. The funk is like a vertical bounce, so that the bottoms of the letters aren't all along the same horizontal line; the flow gives horizontal movement. It can go diagonally, or up and down as well, but it's basically the movement that is gained as you read through the word from left to right; it's how you move between the letters as you go from one to the next.

"When you couple those with the aesthetic qualities of the letters – the weighting of them, and so on – and you add that to the overall impact of how the whole word looks and feels, then you're getting close to defining how you achieve style within letters. A good writer can capture that flavour with both simple and complex

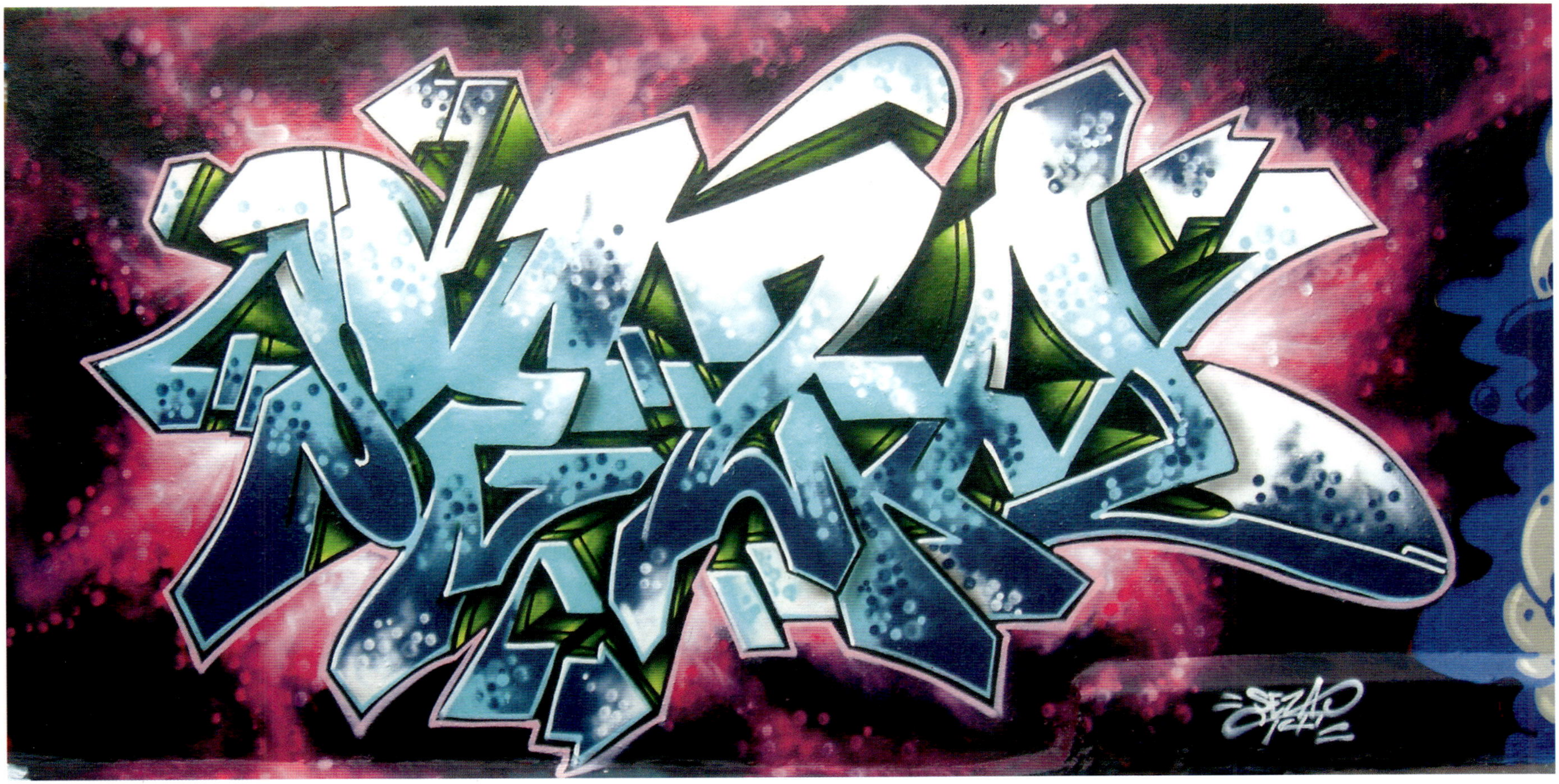

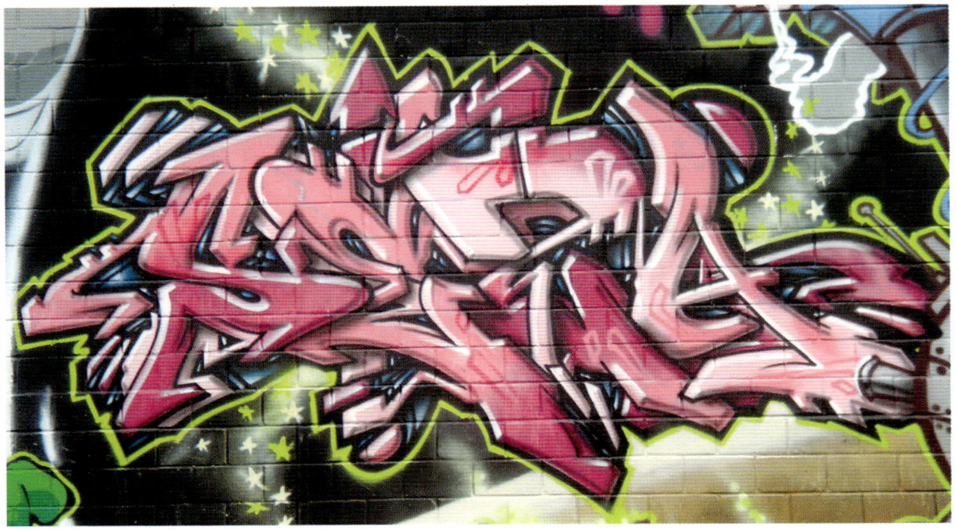

letterforms, and style will always win over technique."

You talked earlier about going back to basics and exploring the essence of traditional graffiti. How important is it to learn about the roots of the art form?
"Whatever graffiti you're doing, whether you're doing classical-style letters or crazy, bombed-out new styles or characters – whatever you're painting, it all comes from the same origins, you know? It all takes elements from the earliest, rawest forms of graffiti. You can always find inspiration from looking at classic old pieces, and I

Top: Bedminster skate park, 2007

Left: Double-layered, Switzerland, 2008

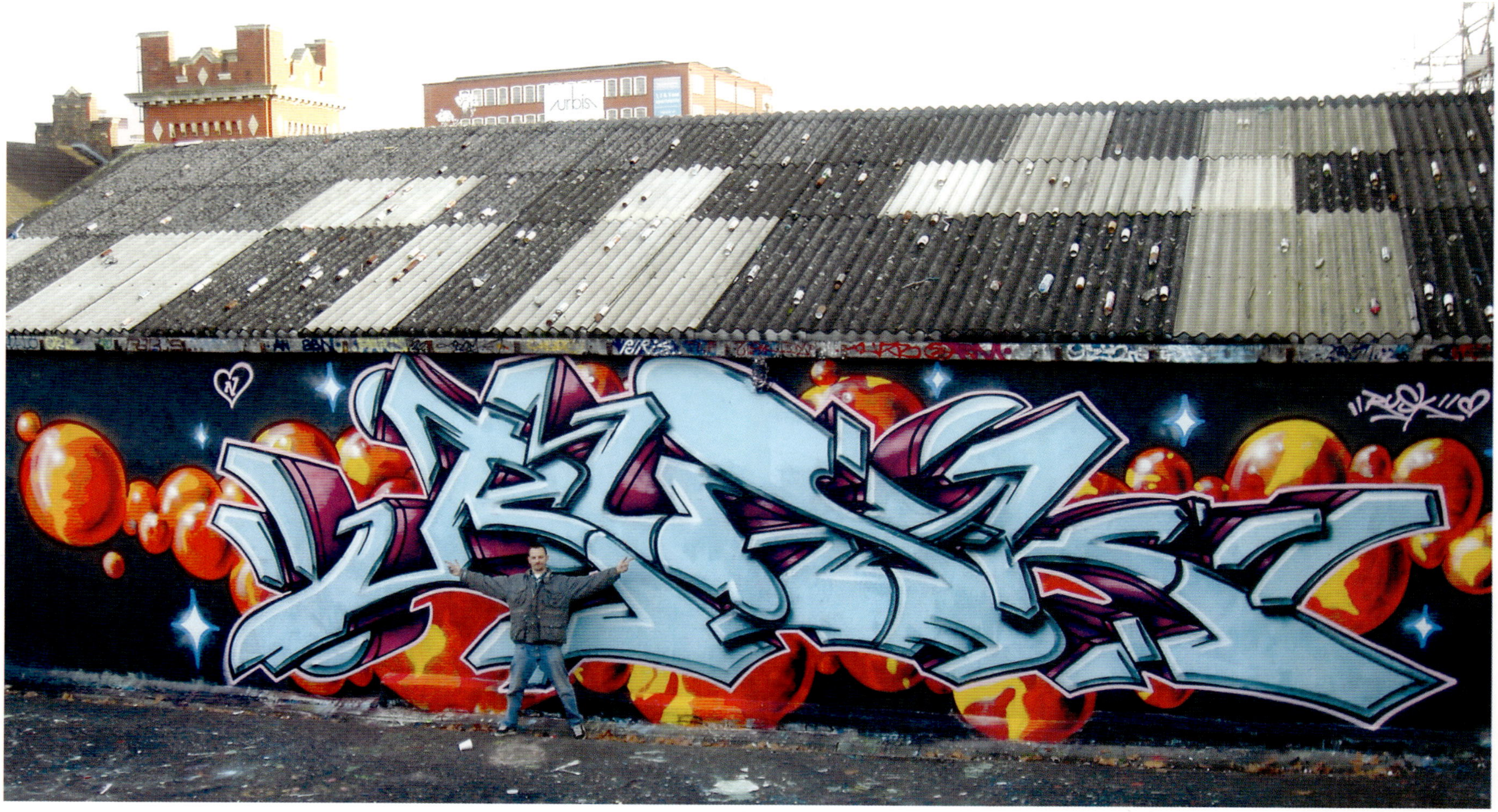

Above: "The next piece I do is going have an outline this wide!" Seza thinks big, 'Rusk' 2007

Right: Corsham 2007

Opposite page. Top: Anti-gravity chrome fill burner, 2007

Bottom left: Magic touch, 2007

Bottom right: X-ray special, 2007

don't think any writer should ever lose sight of the origins and history of graffiti. Everyone should learn about the writers from the 70s that started graffiti. There's the well-known ones like Phase 2 and Blade, but to see work by some of the other writers from the original crews of the early days of graffiti (such as King2 and Comet) is amazing! Check out Phase 2's book *Style – Writing From The Underground*, or the Fuzz One book: it's too much..."

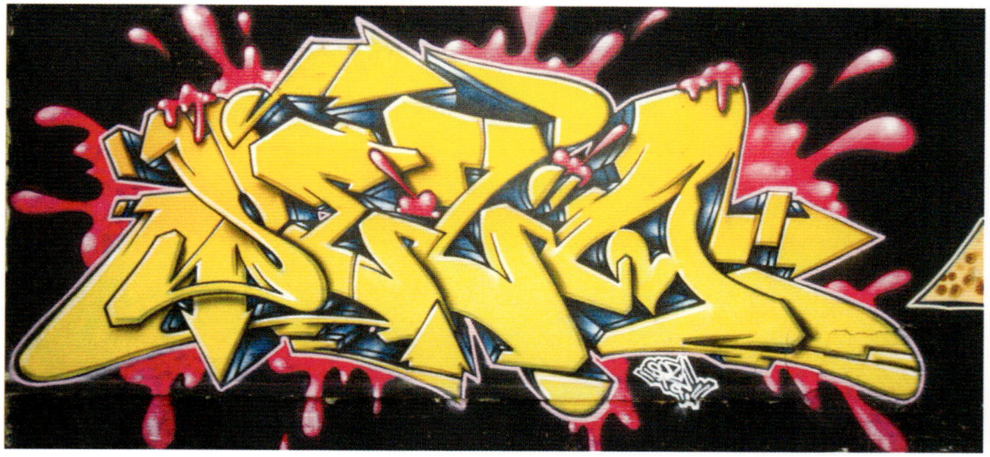

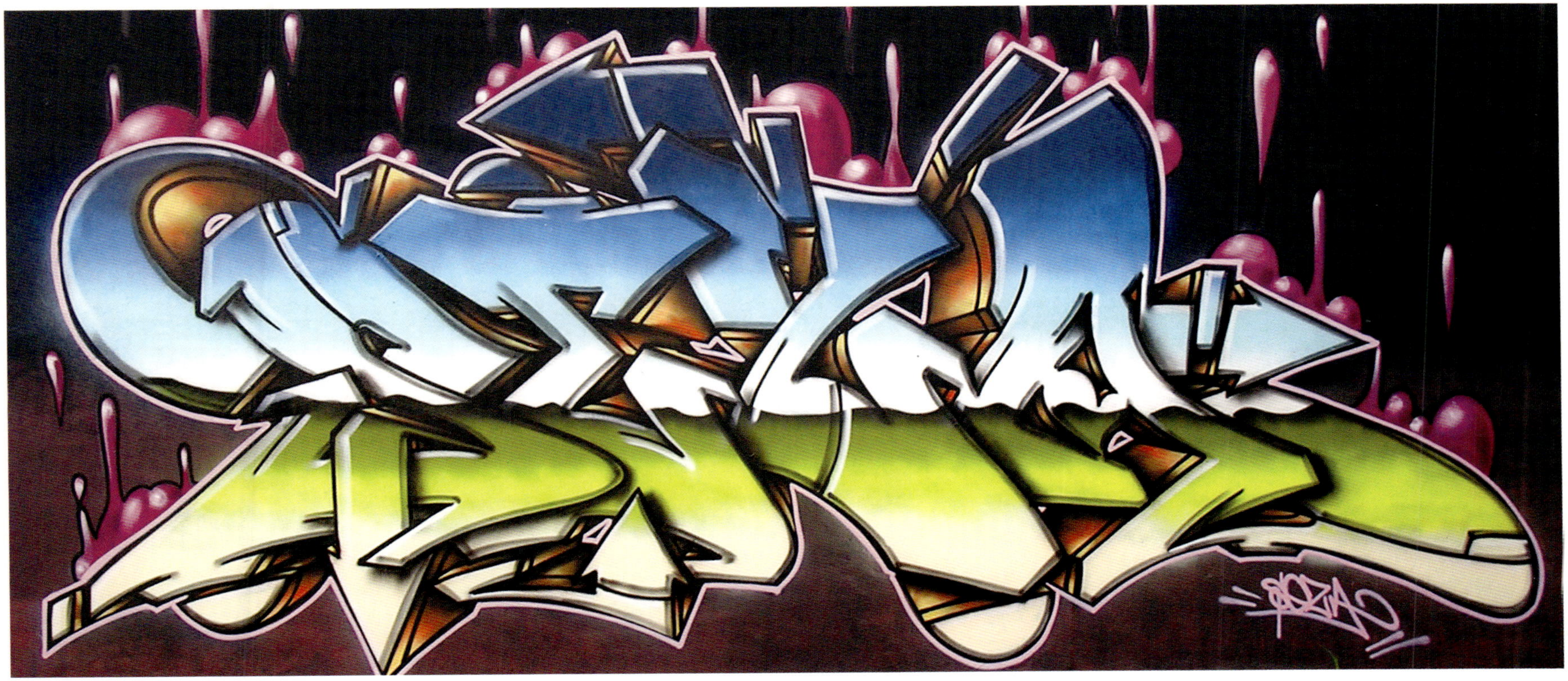

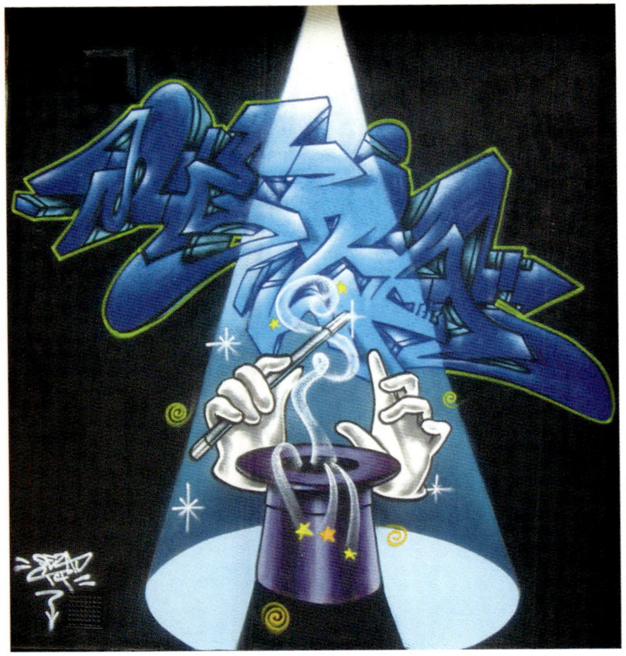

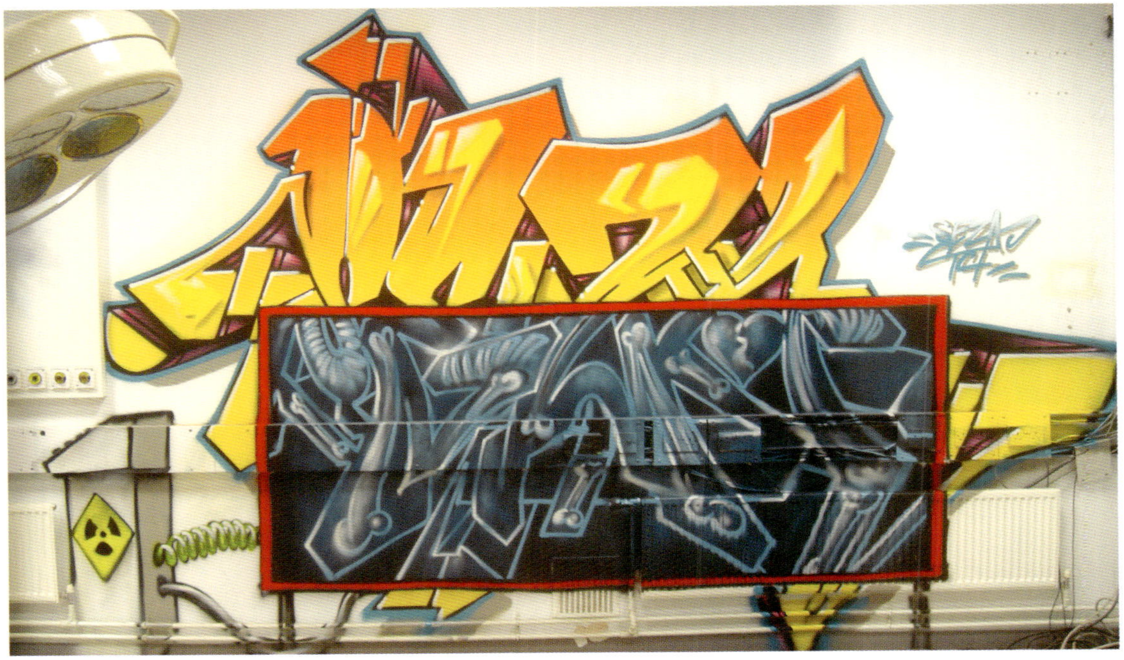

CHINA MIKE

Top right: 'Monolithic Journey' 2008

Bottom right: 'Sniff My Rose' 2007

Bottom centre: Sketchbook page, 1997

Bottom left: 'Construct' 2008

Top left: Sketchbook doodle, 2002

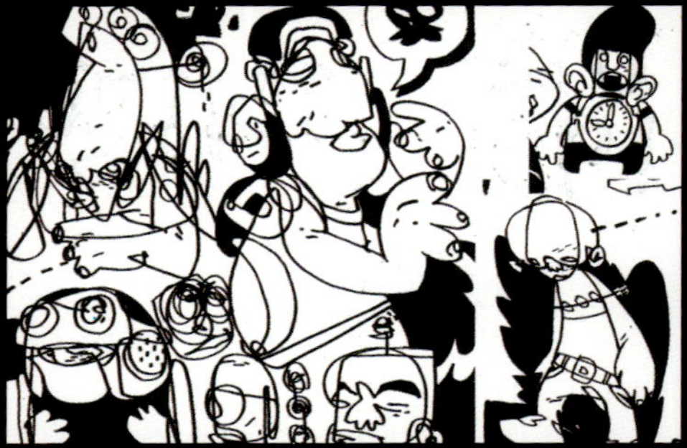

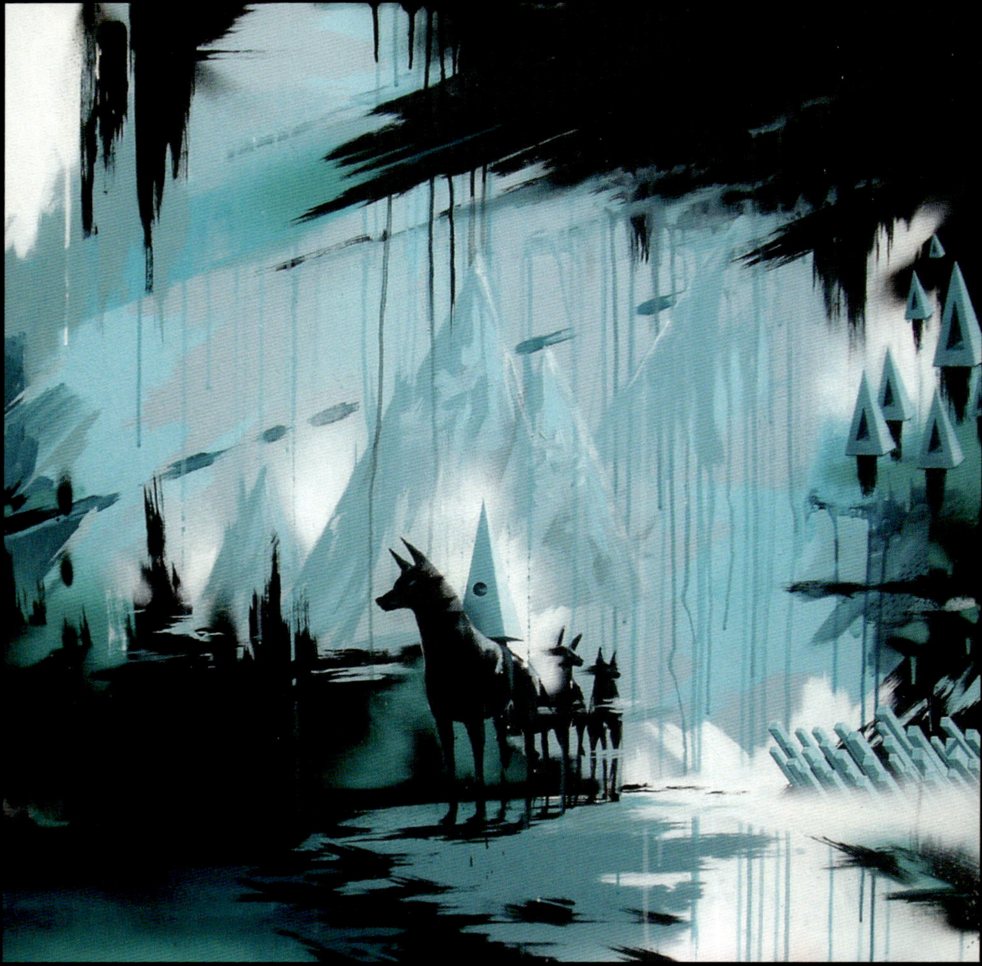

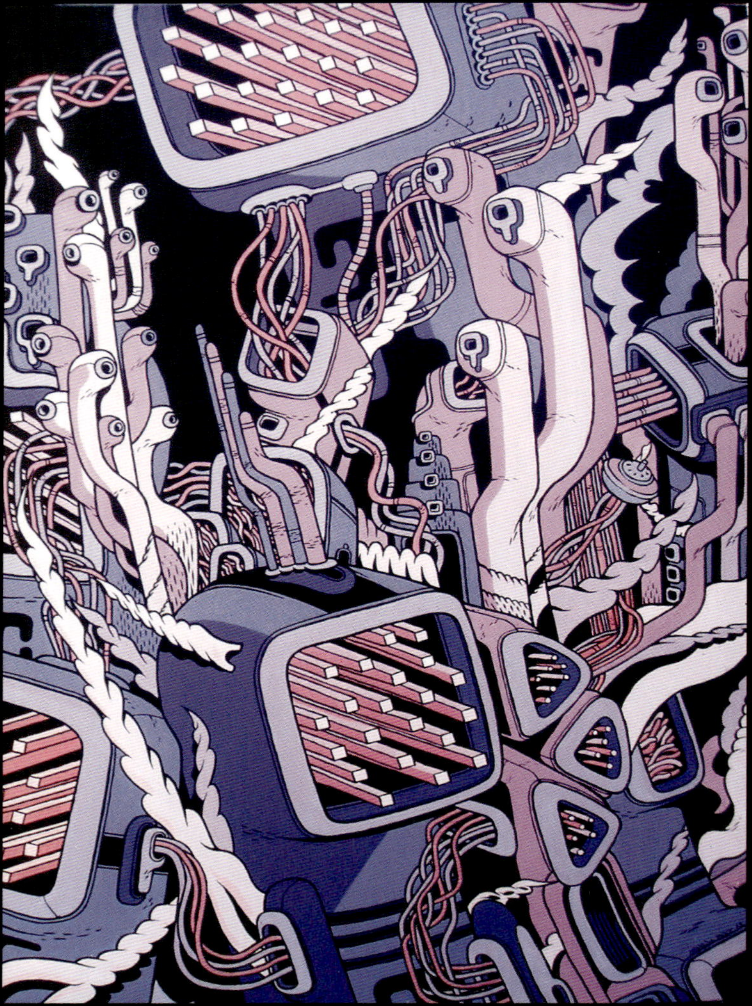

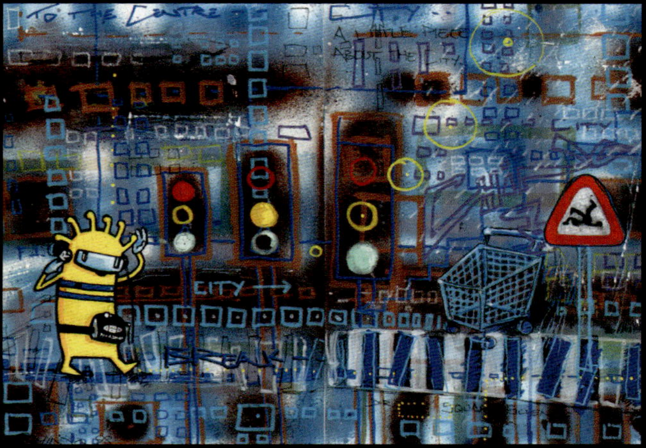

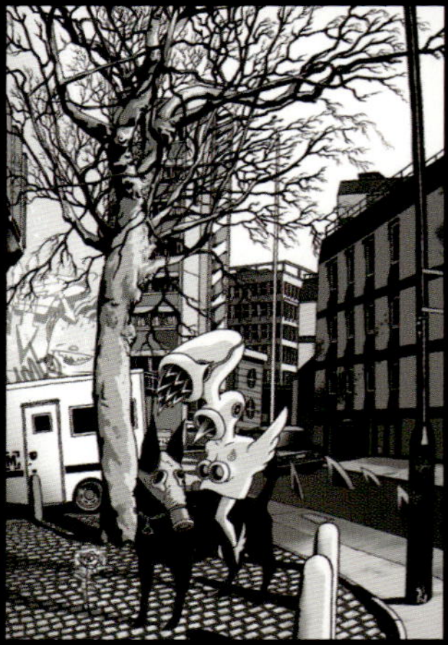

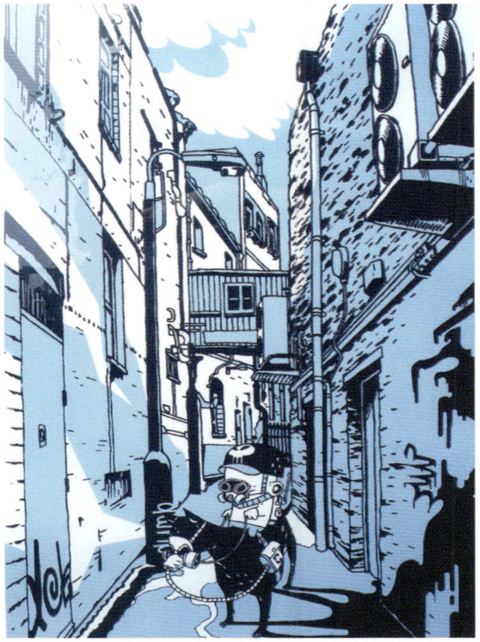

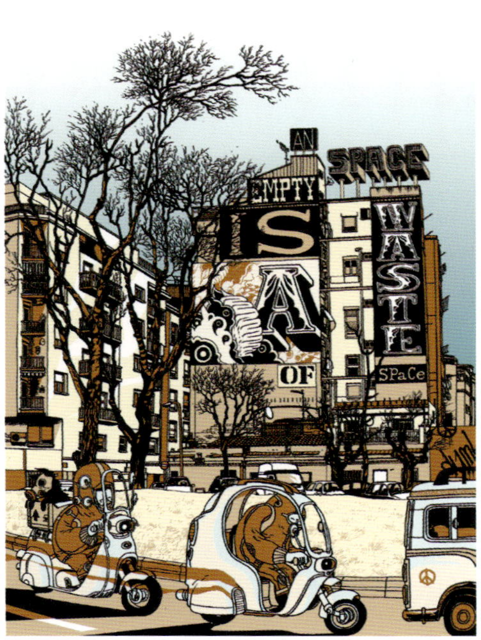

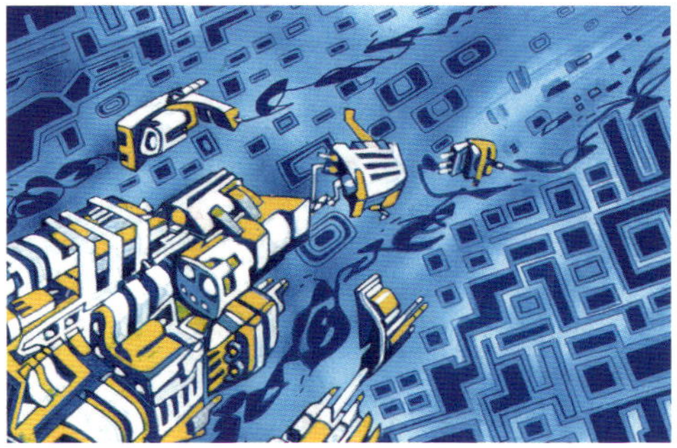

Top right: Sketchbook, 1999

Bottom right: 'All Bark No Bite' (detail), 2008

Bottom left: 'Night Walk' 2003

Top left: 'Black Dog' screen print, 2005

Top middle: 'Waste Of Space' 2008

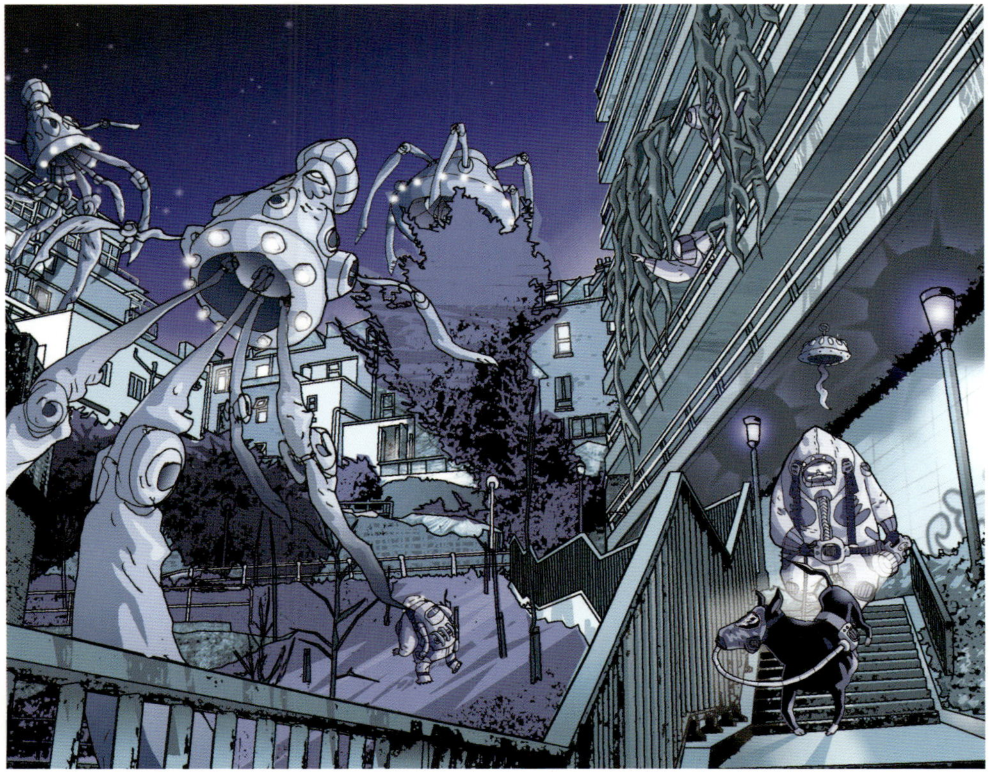

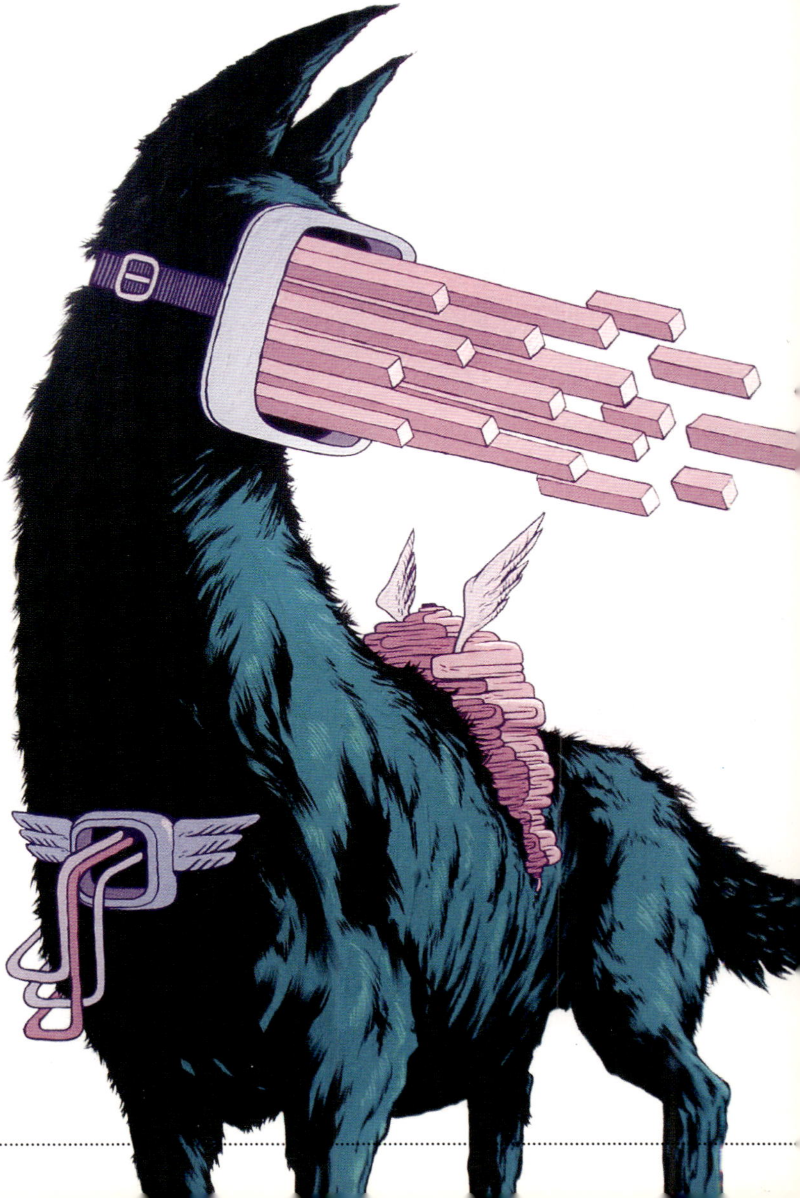

This page: B-boy and writer 2Keen expresses his take on pure, elemental hip hop

2KEEN ANTI CLONE

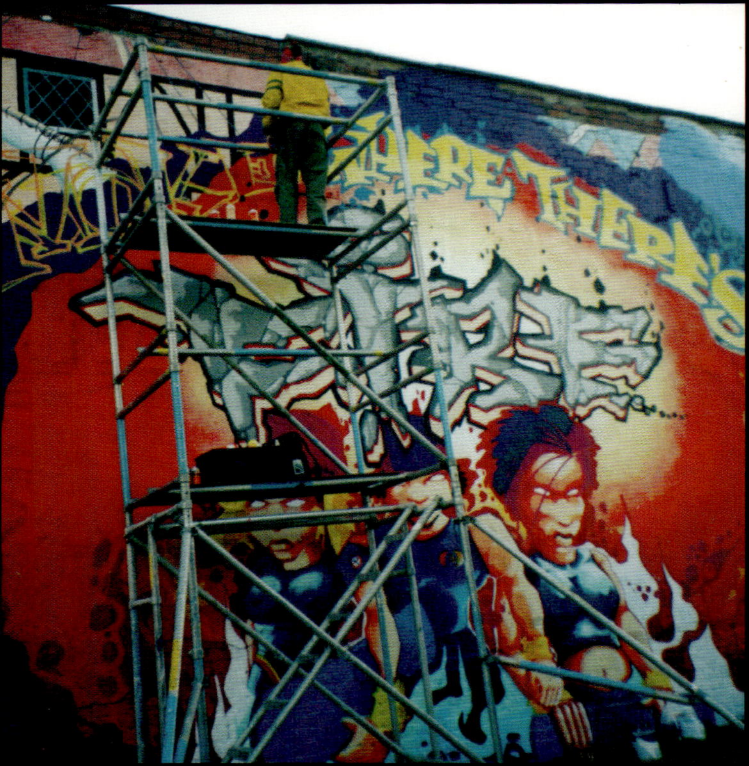

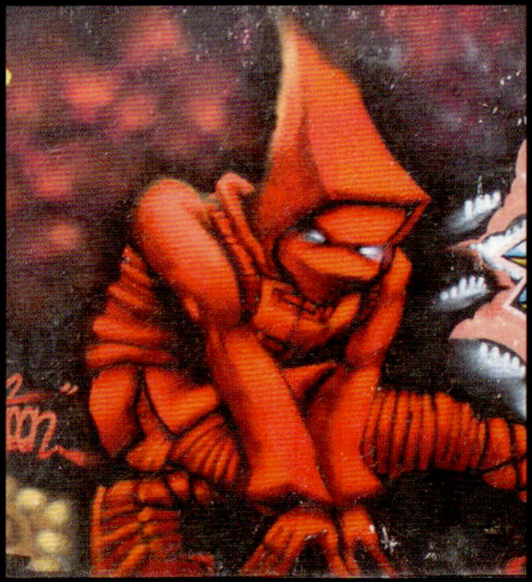

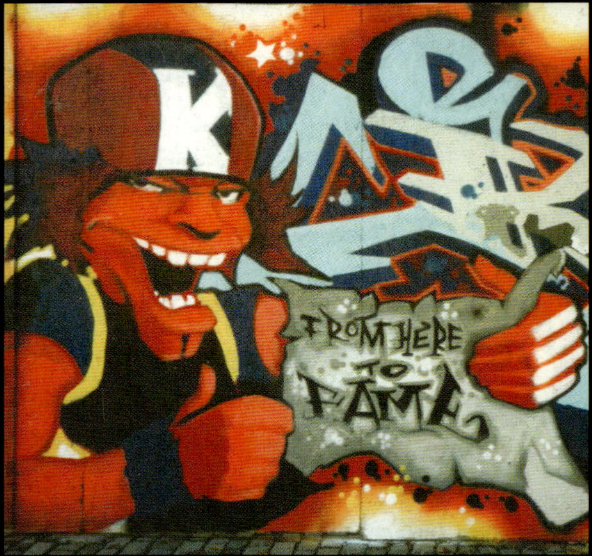

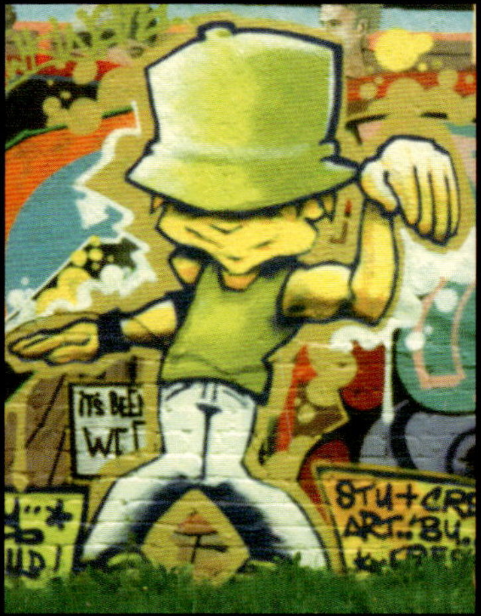

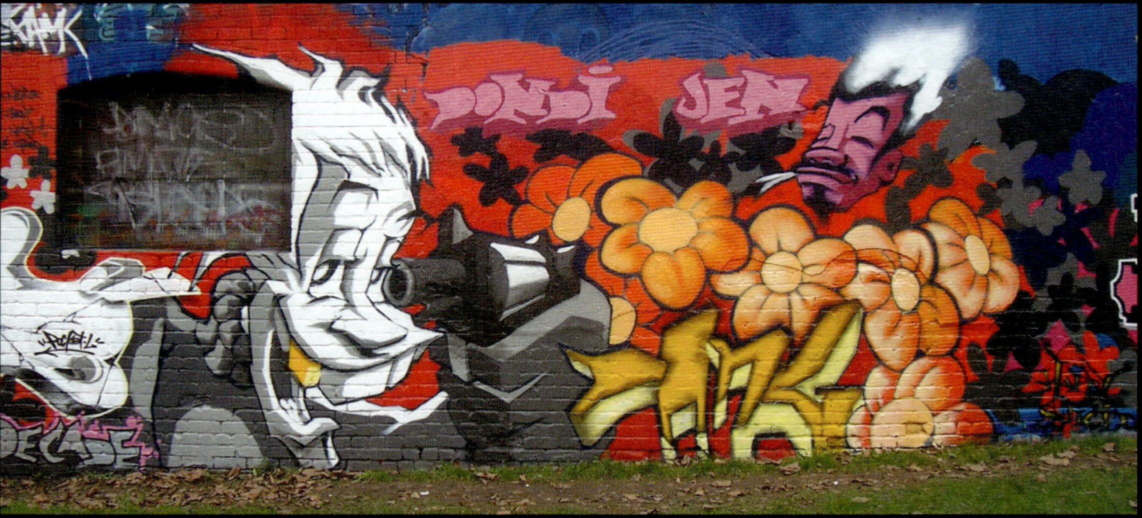

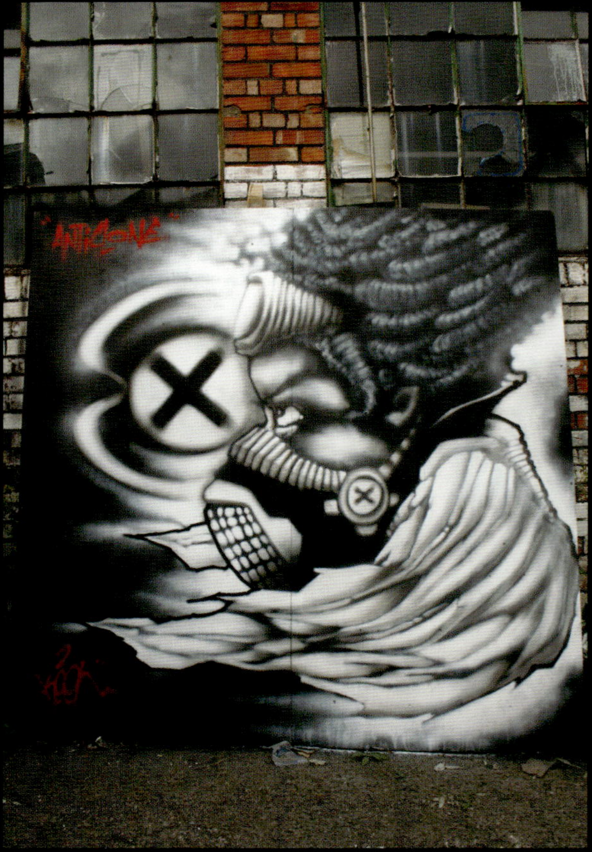

1998-2009:
The Renaissance

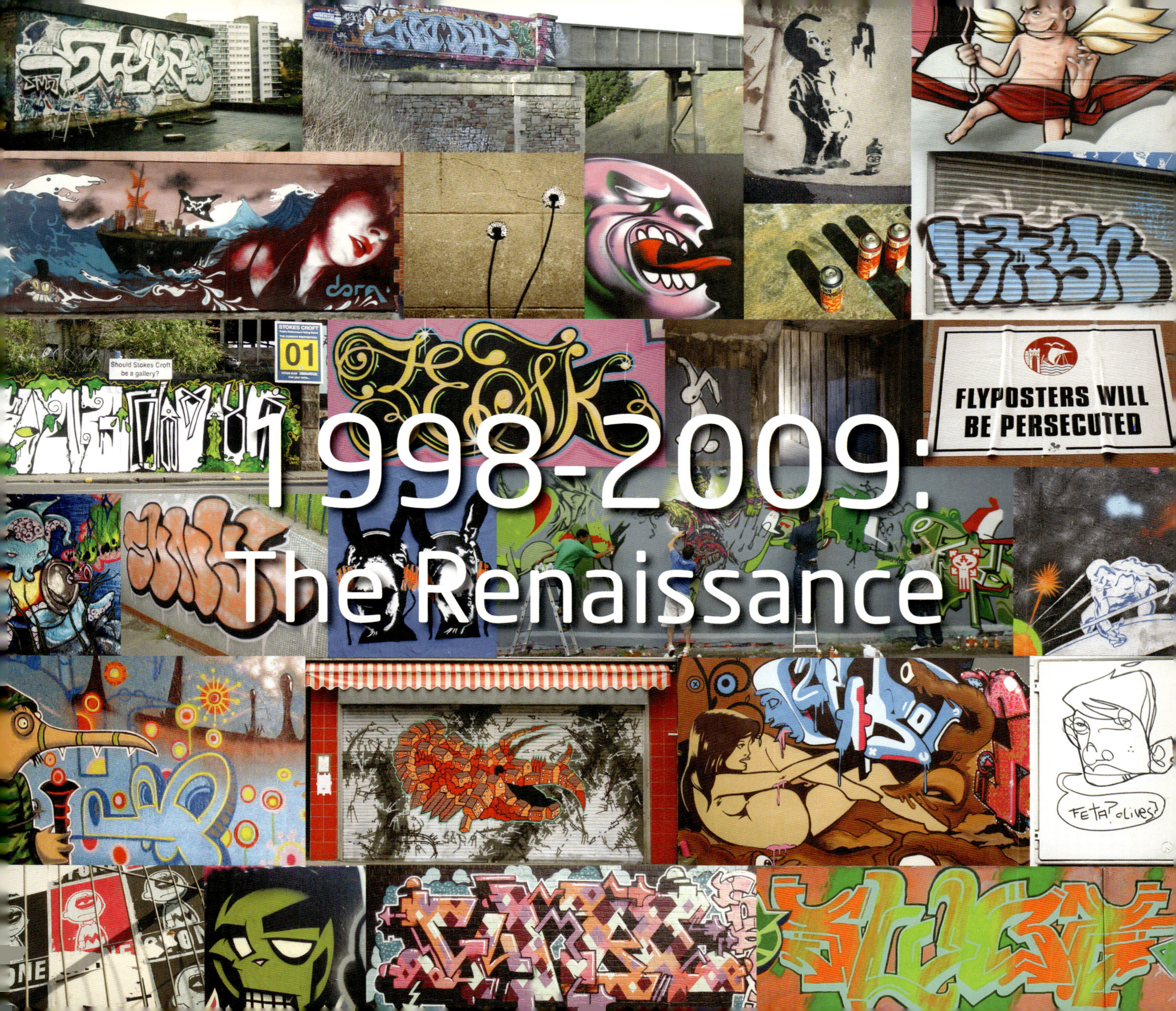

Right and middle: 'Every Picture Tells A Story' by Bad Applez/Dry Breadz, left to right: Pert (aka Lokey) Kato, Verse (aka Soker), Justa, Tes. Characters by Kato.

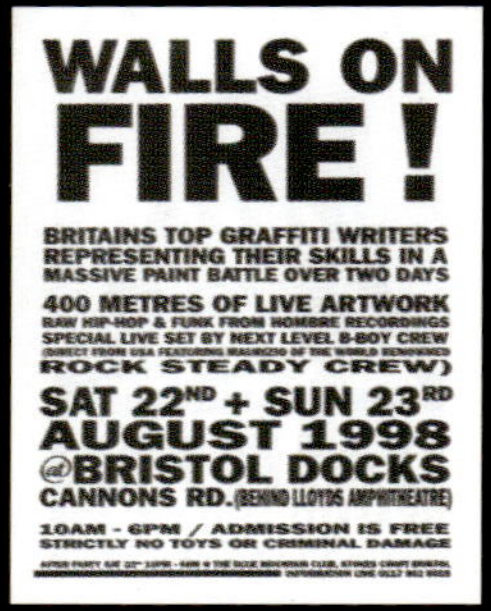
WALLS ON FIRE !

BRITAINS TOP GRAFFITI WRITERS REPRESENTING THEIR SKILLS IN A MASSIVE PAINT BATTLE OVER TWO DAYS

400 METRES OF LIVE ARTWORK
RAW HIP-HOP & FUNK FROM HOMBRE RECORDINGS
SPECIAL LIVE SET BY NEXT LEVEL B-BOY CREW
ROCK STEADY CREW)

SAT 22ND + SUN 23RD AUGUST 1998 @BRISTOL DOCKS
CANNONS RD. (BEHIND LLOYDS AMPHITHEATRE)

10AM - 6PM / ADMISSION IS FREE
STRICTLY NO TOYS OR CRIMINAL DAMAGE

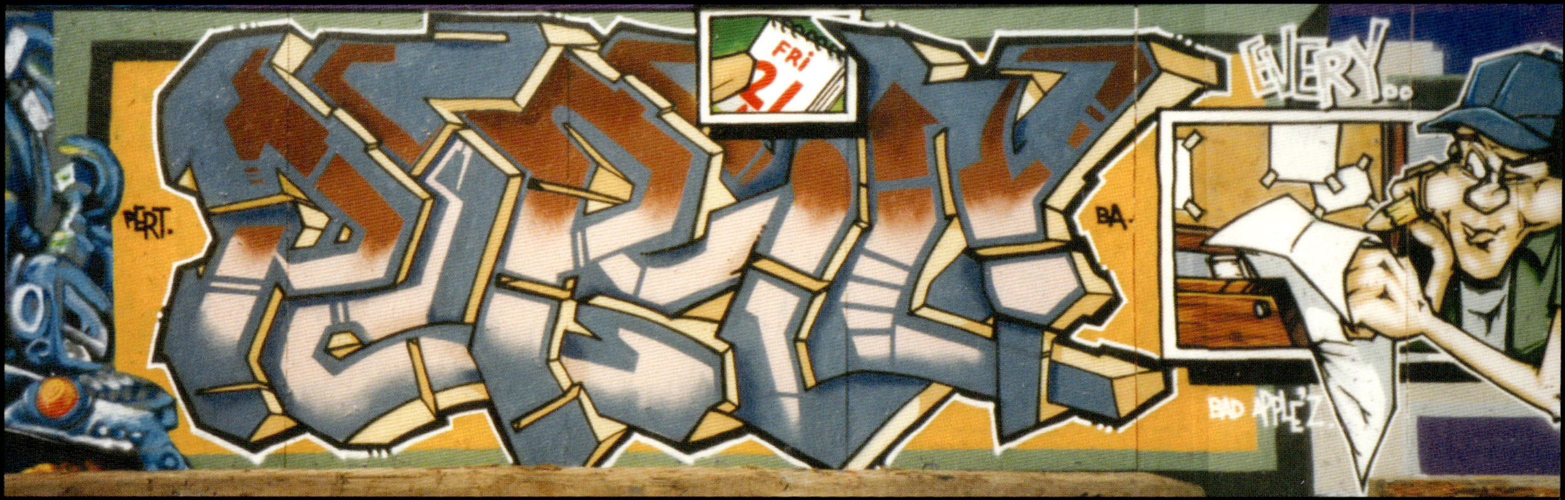

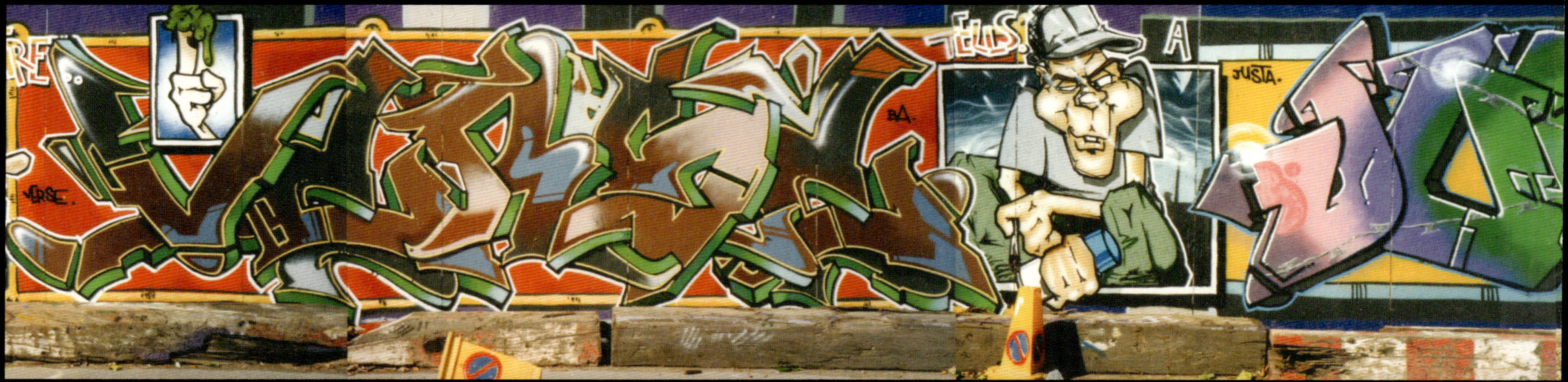

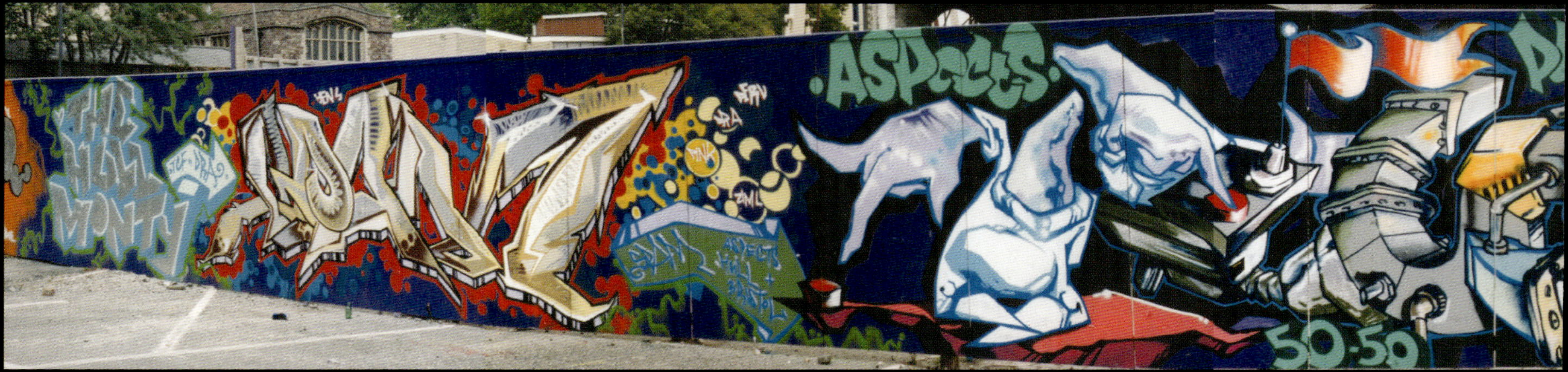

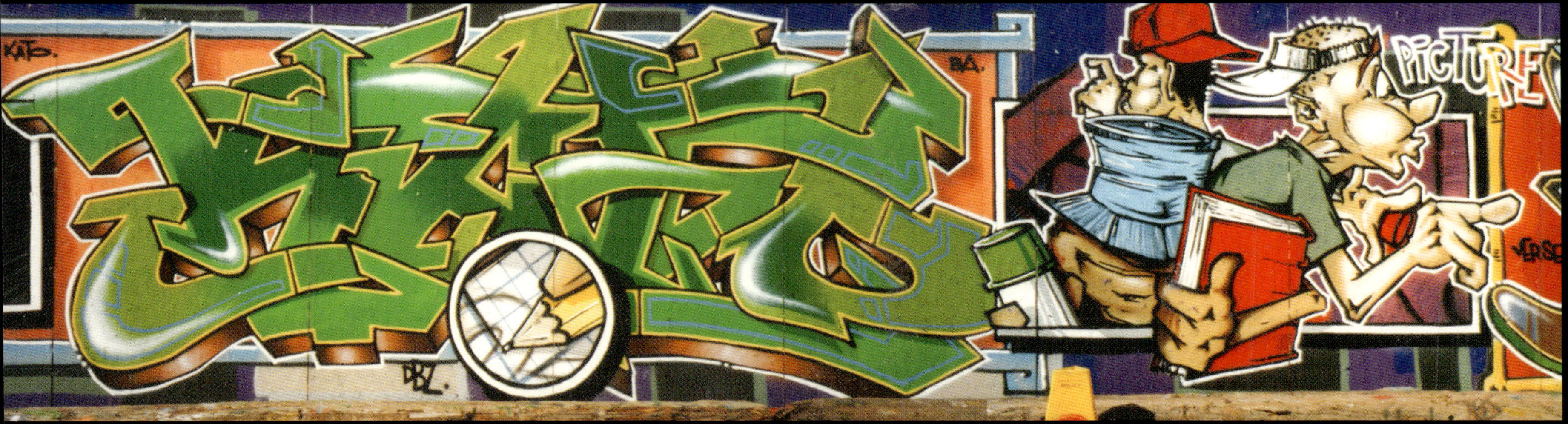
KATO.
BA.
DBZ.
PICTURE

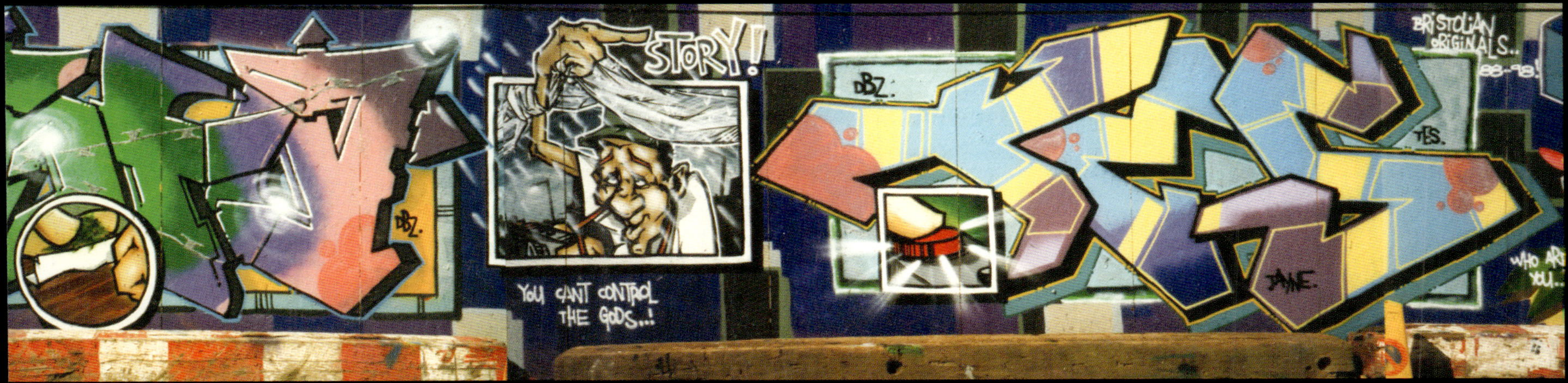
STORY!
YOU CANT CONTROL THE GODS..!
DBZ.
BRISTOLIAN ORIGINALS.. 88-98!
TES.
JAYNE.
WHO ARE YOU...

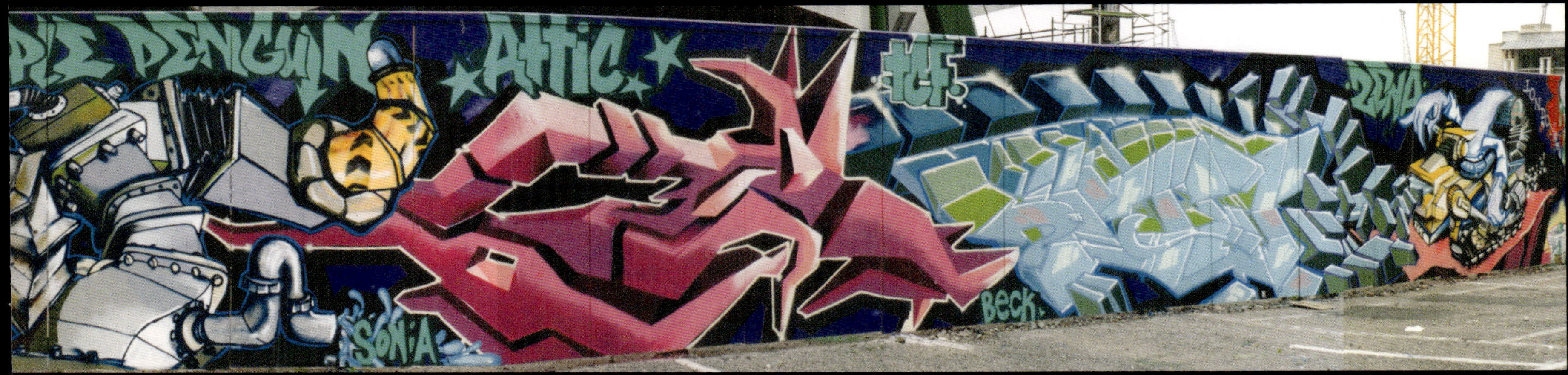
PENGUIN
Attic.
tcf.
Beck.
SONIA

Right: 'For Astek in The Scrubs' Banksy, lettering outline by Astek

Below: Inkie, character reading Mixmag with Roni Size front cover

Opposite page. Top left: Nick Walker

Top right: Shab saves the whale

Middle left: 'Direct Hit!' by Turoe

Middle right: Will Barras, Feek and Dicy (FSH)

Bottom: Completed FSH/KDS piece

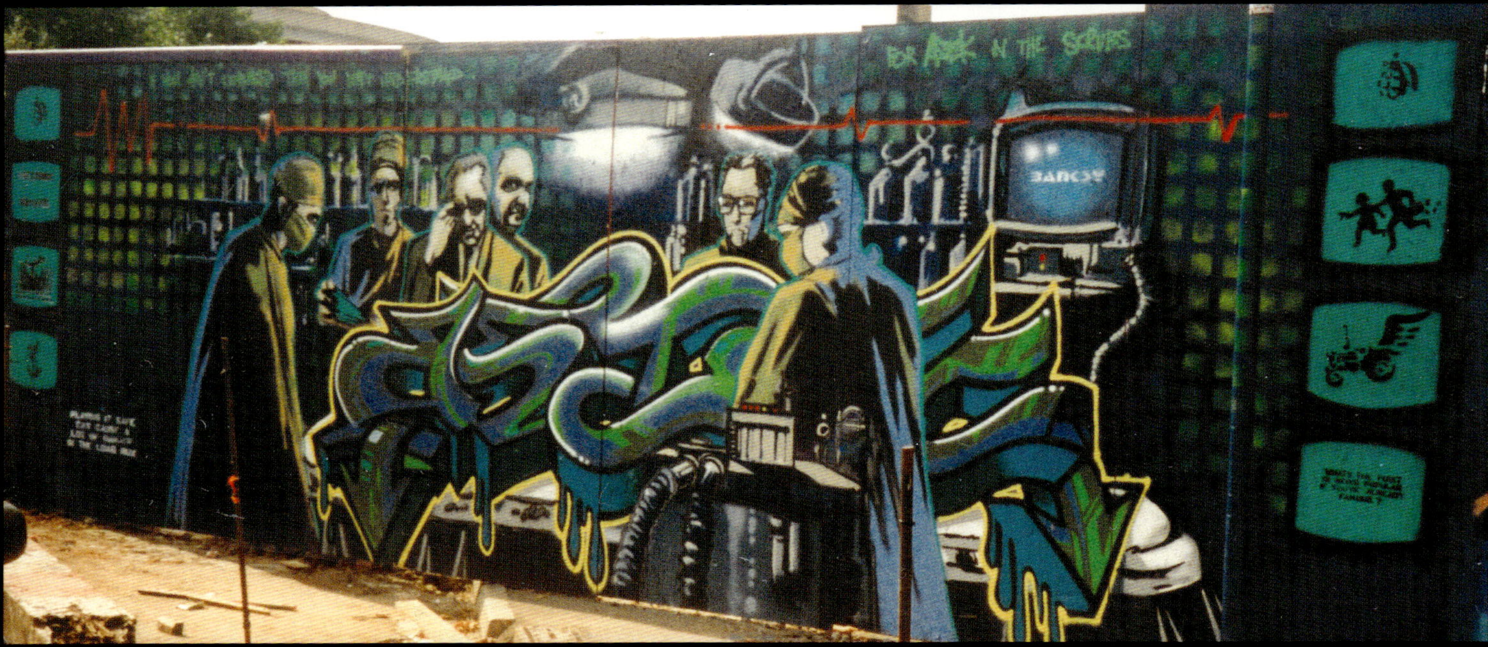

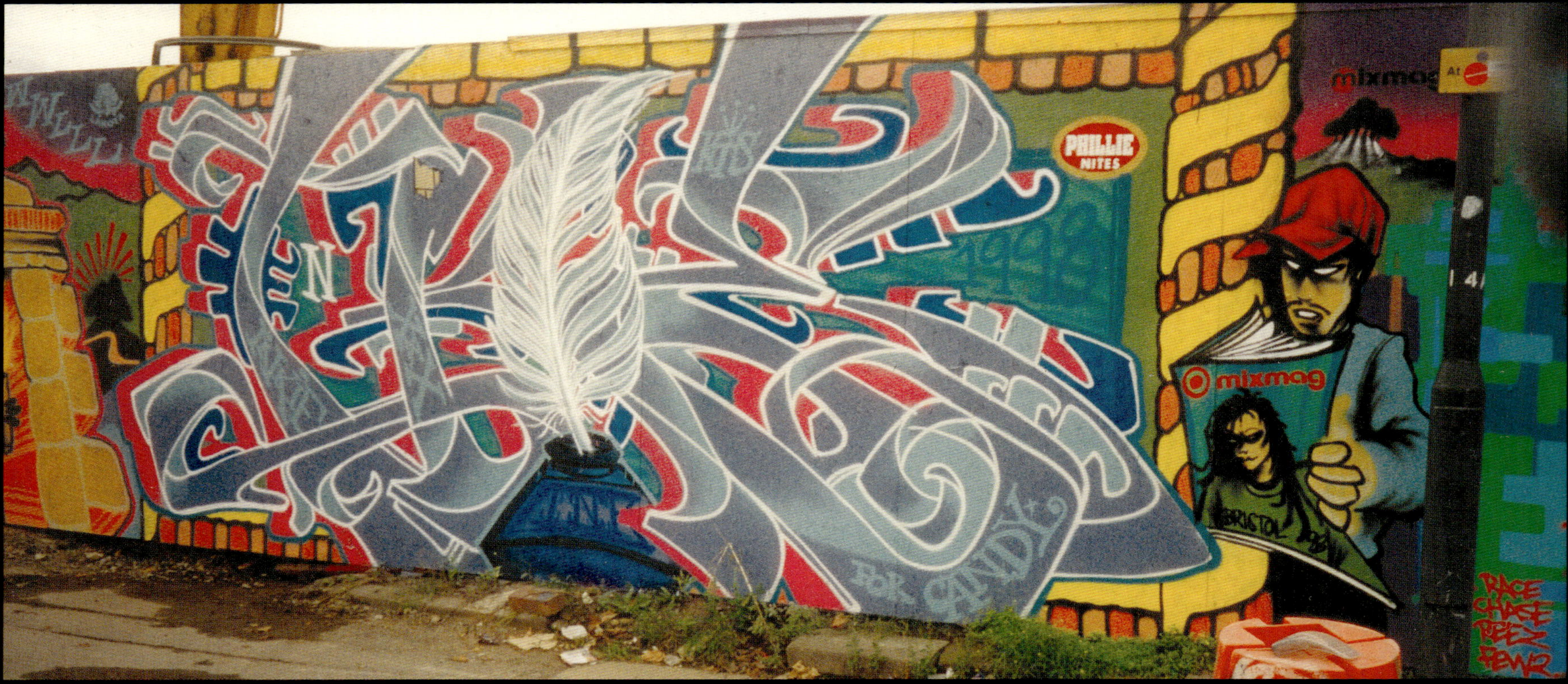

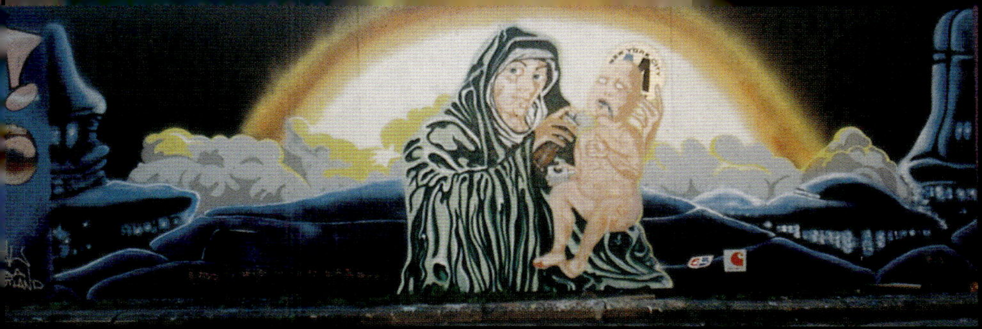

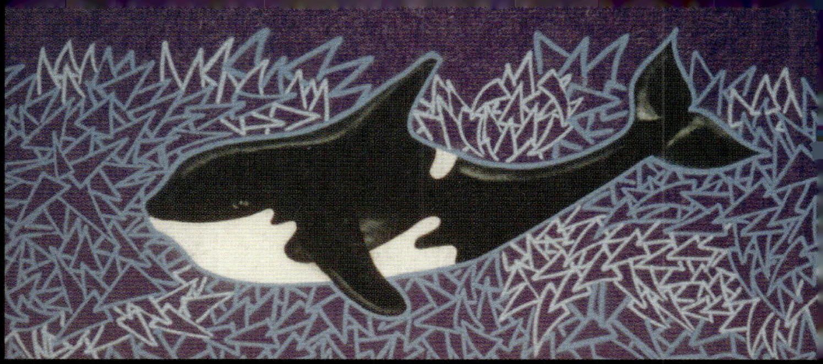

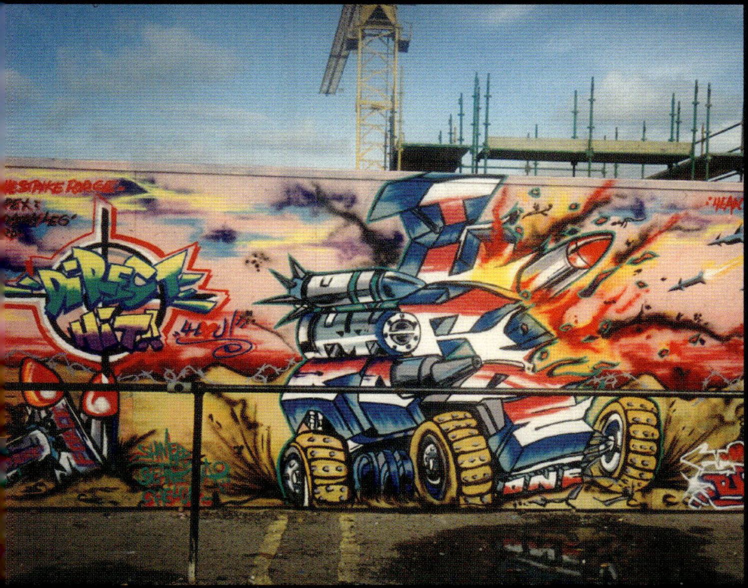

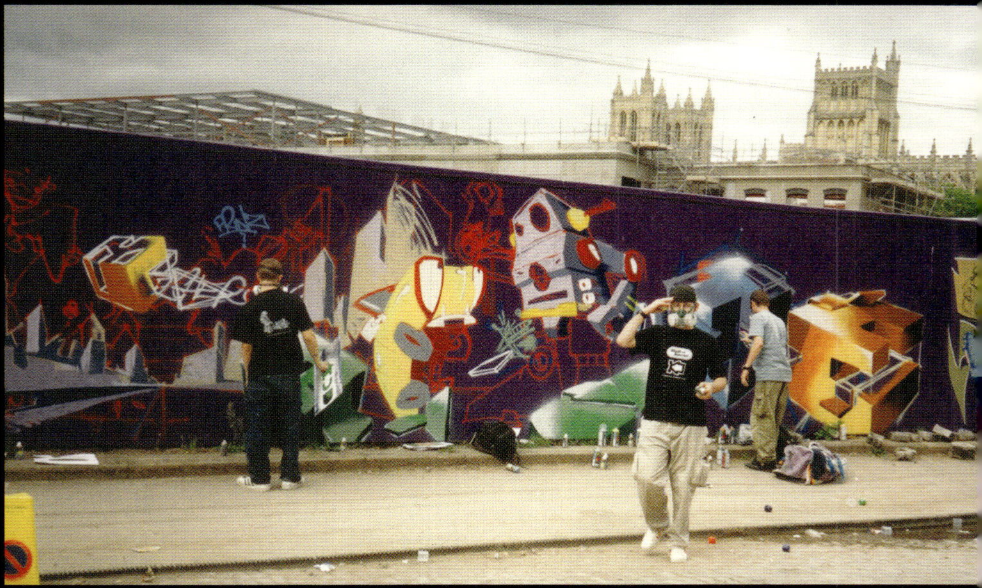

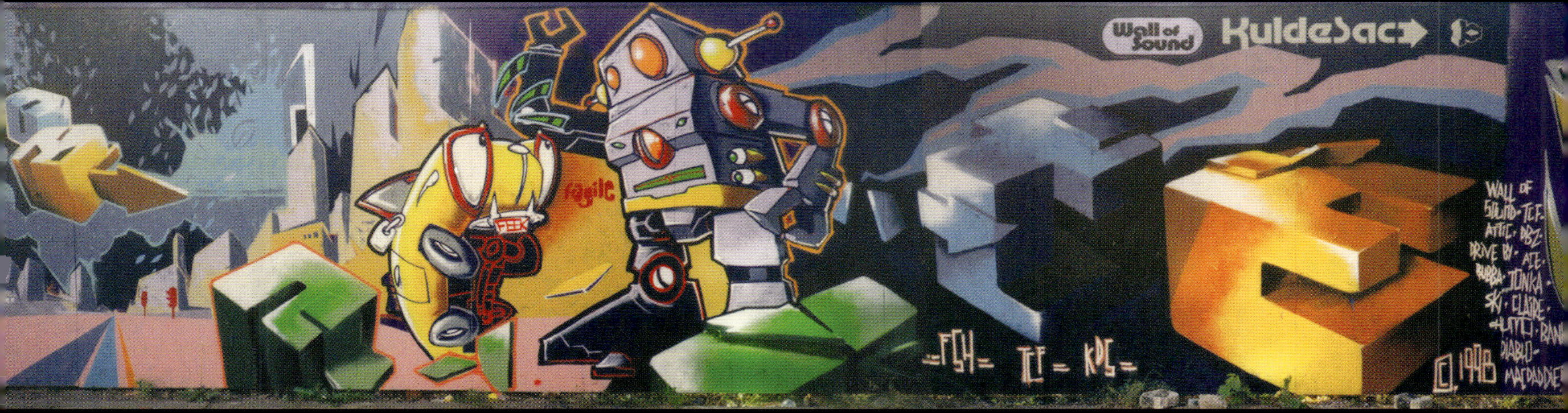
Wall of Sound
KuldeSac

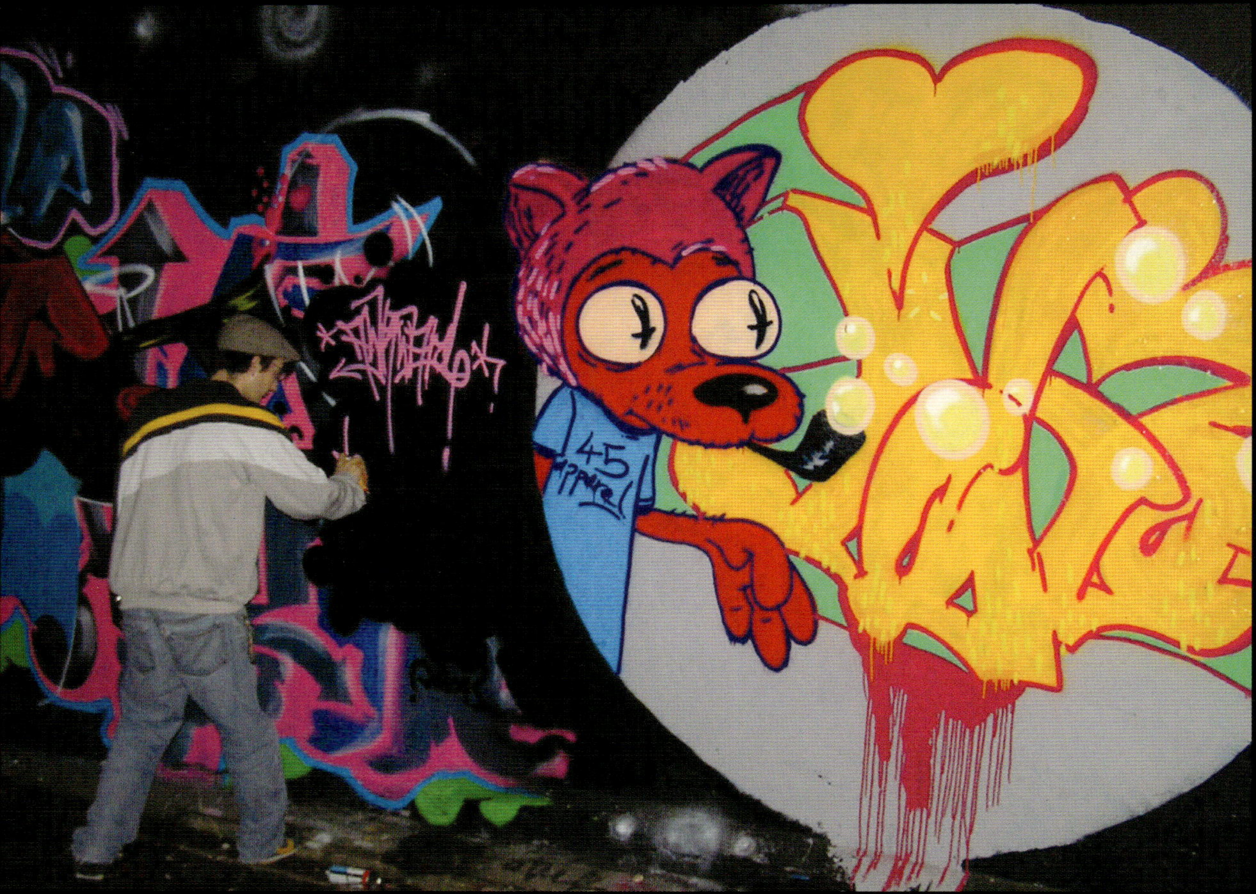

Above: Tagging 'Idiot' piece, Bedminster skate park, 2006

AWKWARD FSH

• A founder member of Fantastic Super Heroes, a hip hop / graffiti crew which also included Paris, Dicy, Feek and Aspects, Awkward is a true hip hop all-rounder who can turn his hand to any element of the subculture and master it in his own unique fashion.

Having grown up in and around hip hop, Awkward lives and breathes it in every creative move he makes – whether that's through B-boying, MCing, DJing, beat making or painting graffiti.

What are your earliest memories of seeing graffiti in Bristol?

"I'd say my oldest graff memories were of seeing the 3D piece outside Virgin Records in Broadmead. I began to fully appreciate the art form around the age of nine, when I was lucky enough to see the Arnolfini exhibition in 1985. I remember thinking that I wanted to do the same: paint my name in these weird new ways and shapes. Watching Bristol's B-boys and hearing the Wild Bunch play also had a massive impact on my perception of hip hop culture."

What was it like growing up with the scene itself evolving around you?

"I was a passive observer from about 1985 to 1992, just taking it all in, discovering and absorbing. I was too young to go to the clubs where it was all happening so I used to tune in to pirate radio and catch what was going on that way.

"To me, local hip hop, like the Wild Bunch or 3pm, was the same as any American group at the time: just as good if not better. The son of a friend of the family used to babysit me when I was young and he had local graff mags, radio tapes and records that I would always check out. That was definitely part of my foundation."

When did you first paint – and with whom?

"The first time I painted was at a graff workshop at the Hope Centre in Clifton. I wrote 'King'. It was terrible (I was only 11 or 12 at the time). That was the start of my on-off love affair with the art.

How did Fantastic Super Heroes come about? Who were the main members?

FSH was a crew that was founded in 1997 by [Bristol hip hop group] Aspects, some of the members of TCF crew from Hull who had recently moved down to Bristol, and myself. Ian from Aspects was at college with Paris from TCF and I'd met Ian while MCing live for One Cut and a band called Freestyle. After that it sort of snowballed into a 20-plus strong crew of MCs, DJs and graffiti writers which included Turroe, Stepchild, Acer, Azlan, my brother Phono Veins and Dicy to name but a few.

"I was always making more music, but I painted with them on occasion.
It was kind of a second renaissance for

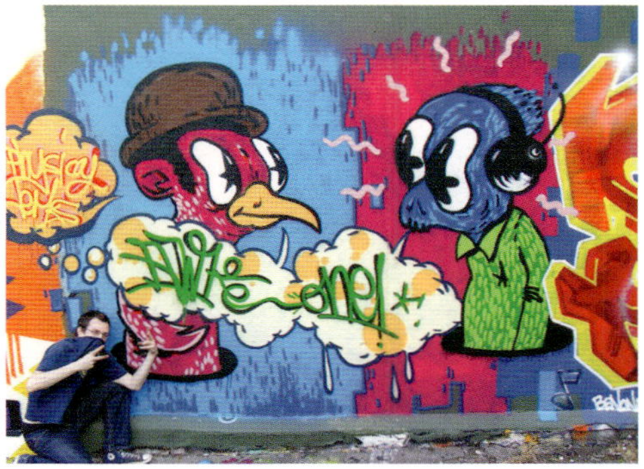

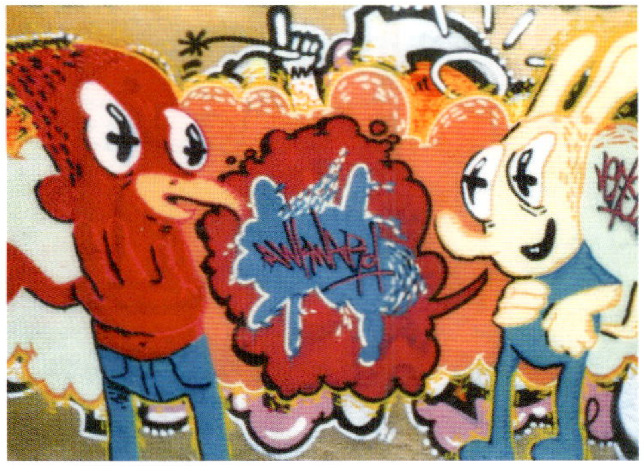

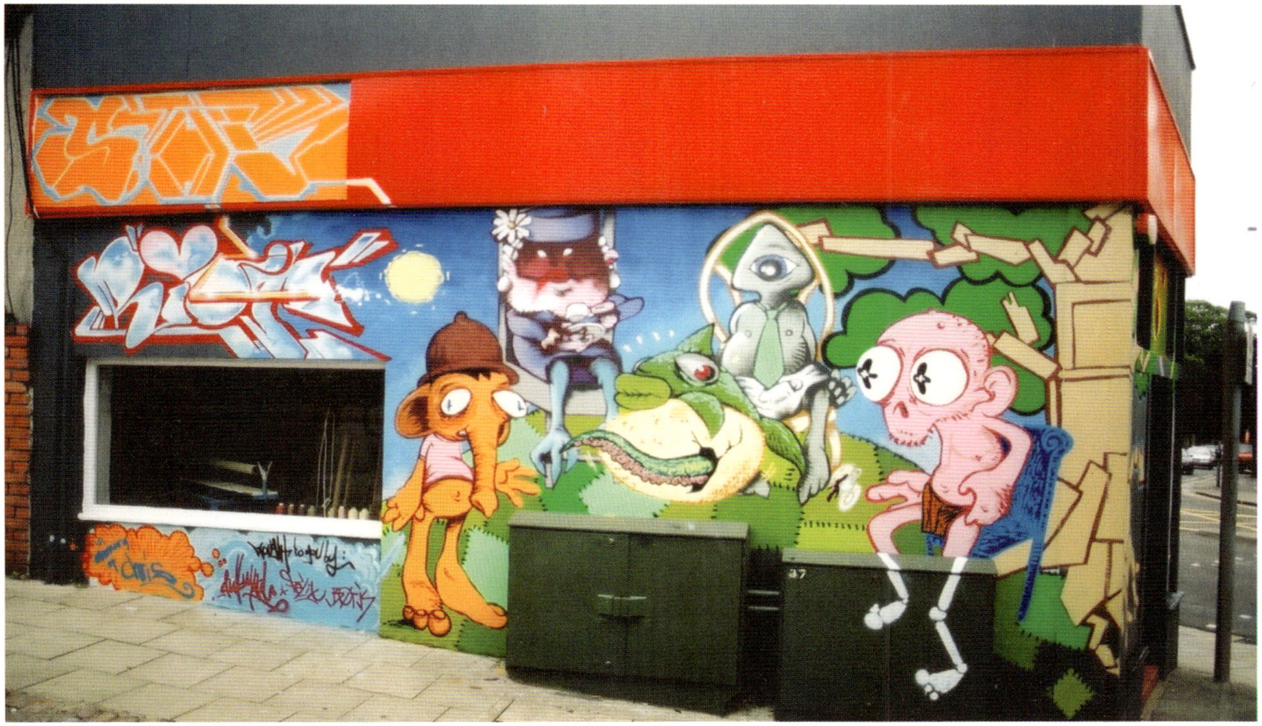

Top left and middle left: Awkward's distinctive conversational characters, 2008 and 2006

Right: 'The Tea Party' Awkward, FLX and Paris, Stokes Croft, 2005

hip hop culture in Bristol. The crew as a collective fizzled out around 2001 for various reasons, with everybody going off in different directions to bigger and better things."

Can you describe the evolution of your individual style? Did you copy comic styles as a kid?

"My style comes from the original B-boy character template, from the likes of New York legends Doze, T-Kid and Dondi. [Legendary comic artist] Vaughn Bode was definitely a big influence on my art. Ever since seeing versions of his characters in the book *Subway Art*, I had scoured the local comic shops in the hopes of finding the holy grail – some of the actual comics. In 1989 a lot of them were re-issued and I became a massive fan of Bode's twisted universe. At the same time, I was collecting *2000AD* solidly from '86 to about '94. I used to study artists like Ian Gibson and Brendan McCarthy, who also created unique stylistic universes. I used to copy Marvel and DC comics as well, along with *Judge Dredd* and some 80's Manga stuff. This sort of filtered down over the years, and although I did lettering as well, I found more enjoyment in character design and tag styles.

What in your mind are the main differences between drawing and painting?

Drawing utilises the pen, painting utilises paint, but I like to blur the distinctions.

Is it possible to nail something of the essence of how you draw and why your characters look the way they do?

I'm not sure. I like dynamic imagery, and I like to give my characters expression, as if they are mid-speech or mid-action. It usually just pours out and I'm stuck with what I've done. I don't really know where it comes from."

Your characters always seem to have speech bubbles. Do they have something to say, are they an outlet for your own opinions?

"Oh, they're definitely an outlet for my own opinions, good or bad. Sometimes it has to do with the look of the character; every now and then they talk back so I just write it down (laughs)."

What is your take on the state of graffiti these days and the mass

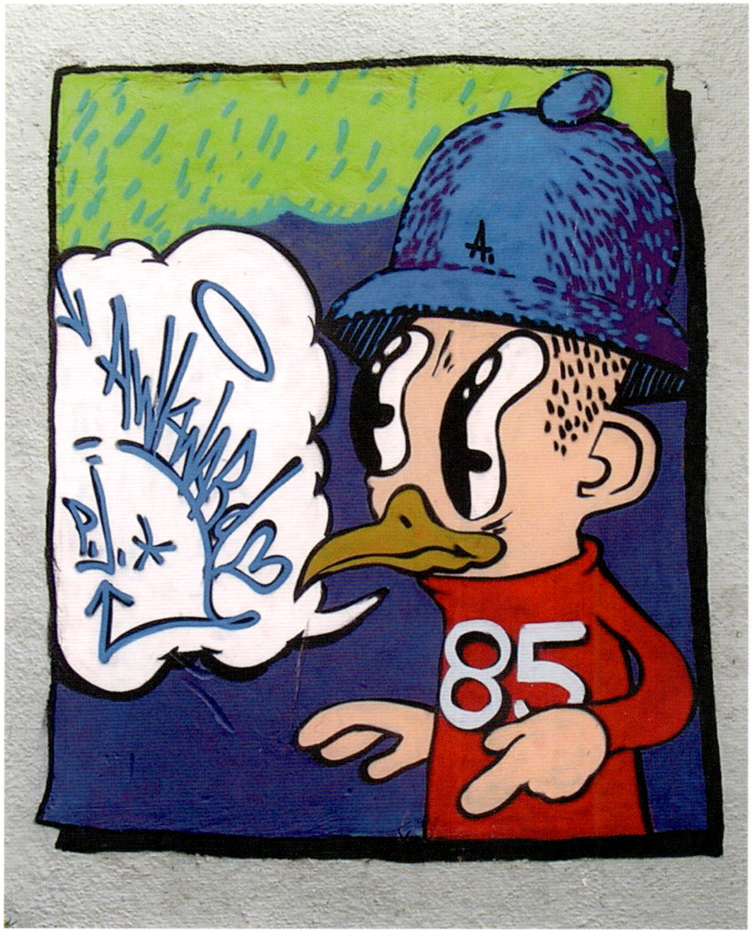

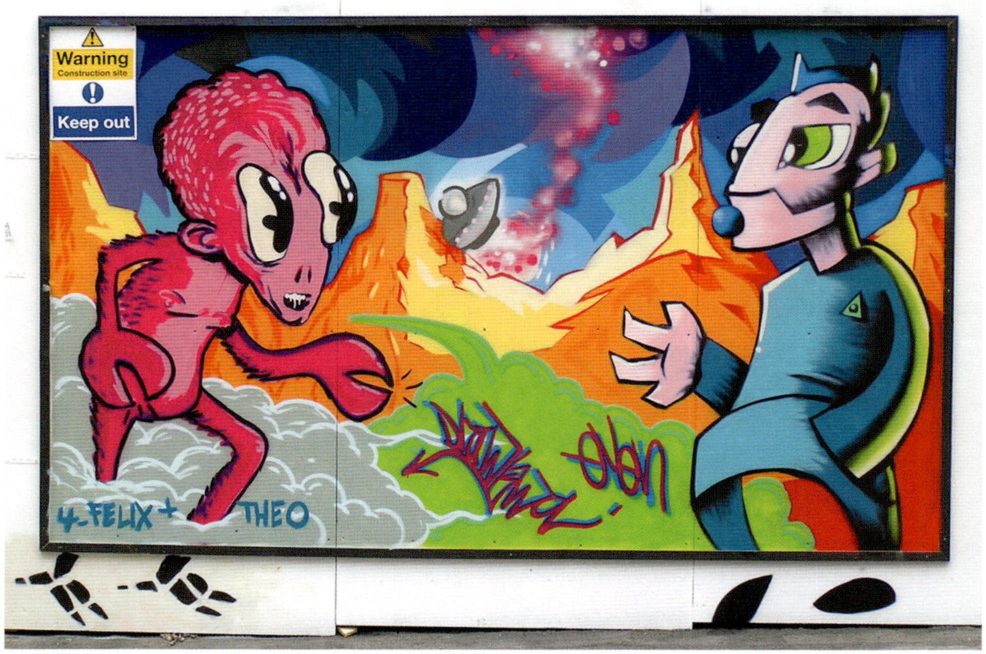

Above: Awkward, a classic B-boy

Top right: 'First Contact' Awkward and Even (aka FLX), 2007

marketing of the art form?
"The problem is that some people are not painting to create new art, they are co-opting the culture to further their own ends. A lot of people in the art world can't make the distinction between a 'toy' and a writer who has put in the effort to create an individual style. It's a kind of 'it looks like street art, it'll do' attitude.

"There seem to be a lot of chancers rushing in from both sides of the market. Art institutions are acting like Dondi, 3D and Futura 2000 never existed or hit the art markets hard during the 80s and 90s. These days you have these new champions of 'street' art trying to dictate the market, and the artists are following suit. Graffiti art is a part of hip hop culture whether you like it or not, it cannot be denied or covered up, but I think the art world likes it better when they can champion street art that exists without a so-called hip hop foundation – as if almost anybody can do it. That said, I think there is room for everything as long as the ethics are in place. Graffiti can go anywhere and, stylistically, look like anything it wants."

Do you think graffiti has a role to play in questioning systems of control and expressing individuality in an increasingly homogenised society?
"Yes, I think true hip hop culture is subversive. Our current system of control co-opts anything subversive, neutralises it and sells it back to us in a watered-down form in an attempt to make us forget the power of the original intent.

"Every time human beings create from consciousness, the governments, multinationals and their architects try their best to diffuse the flow of creativity by infiltration. I believe that the individual artist with their head on straight can navigate through the mass media and gain from it, but they are always swimming against the tide of mediocrity."

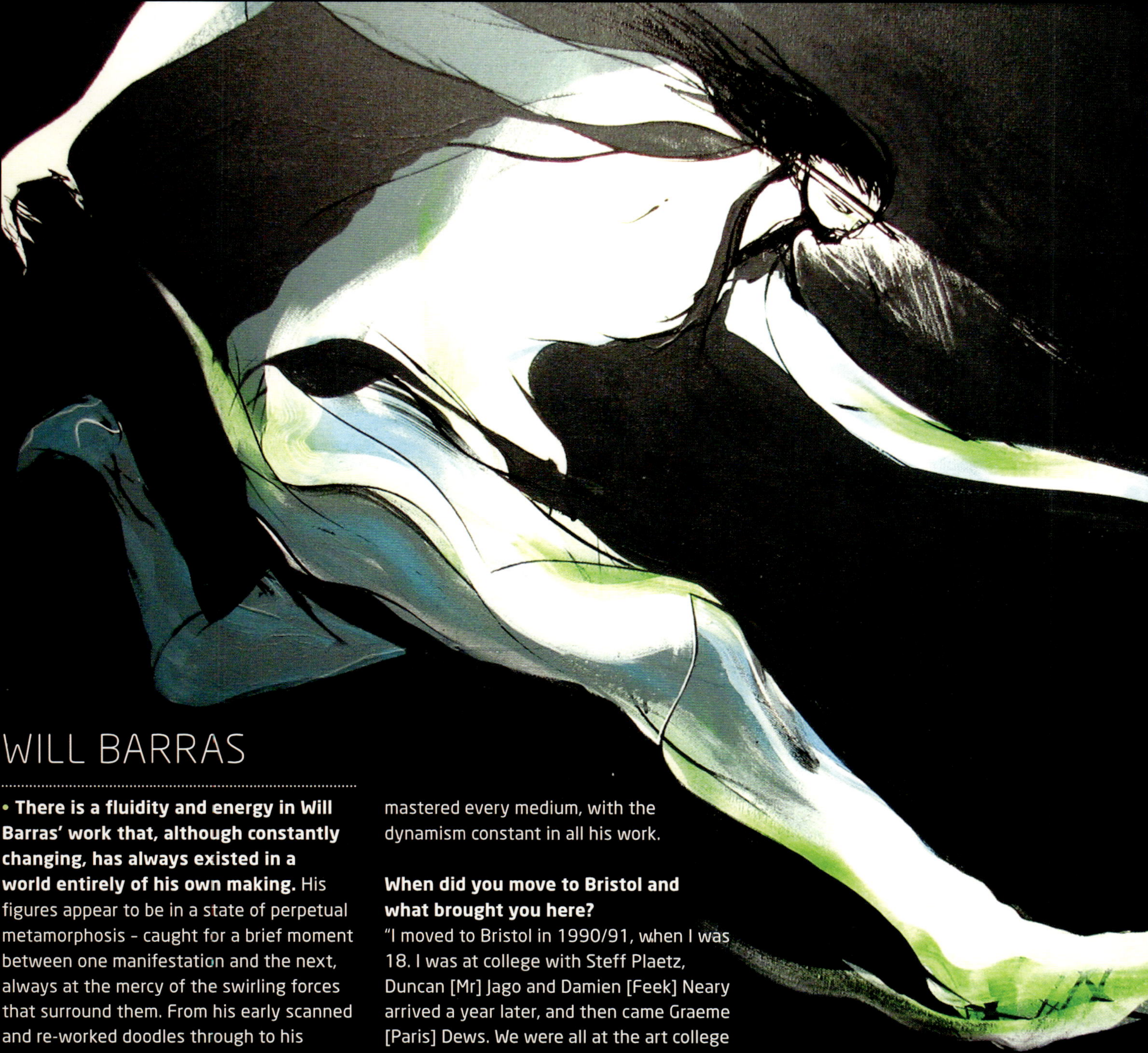

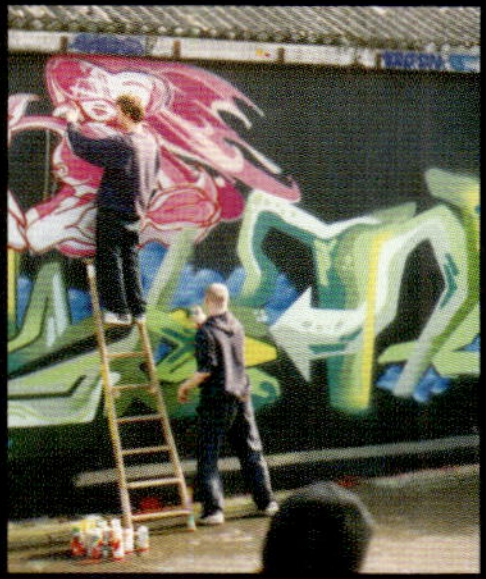

Left: 'Jesus Jogging' acrylic on canvas, 2007

Above: Will and Ziml, Bedminster skate park, c.1999

WILL BARRAS

• **There is a fluidity and energy in Will Barras' work that, although constantly changing, has always existed in a world entirely of his own making.** His figures appear to be in a state of perpetual metamorphosis – caught for a brief moment between one manifestation and the next, always at the mercy of the swirling forces that surround them. From his early scanned and re-worked doodles through to his recent, rich, mixed-media work, Will has mastered every medium, with the dynamism constant in all his work.

When did you move to Bristol and what brought you here?

"I moved to Bristol in 1990/91, when I was 18. I was at college with Steff Plaetz, Duncan [Mr] Jago and Damien [Feek] Neary arrived a year later, and then came Graeme [Paris] Dews. We were all at the art college at Bower Ashton.

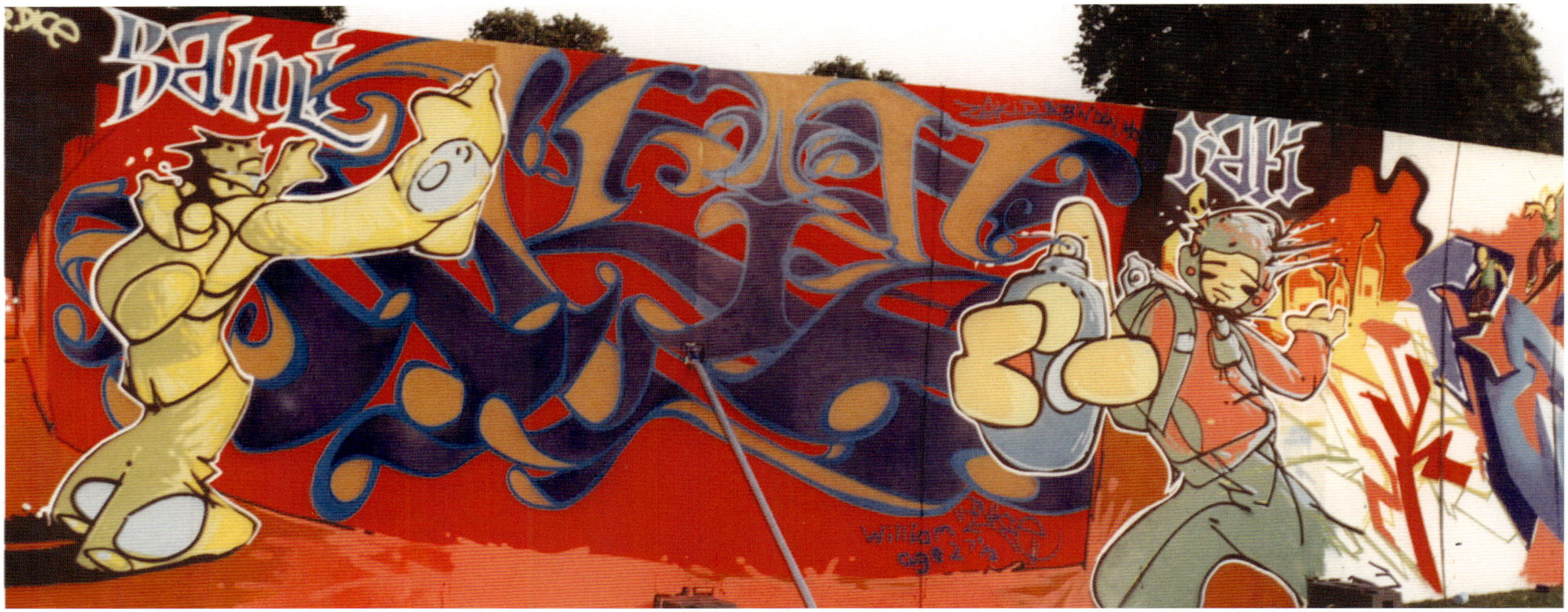

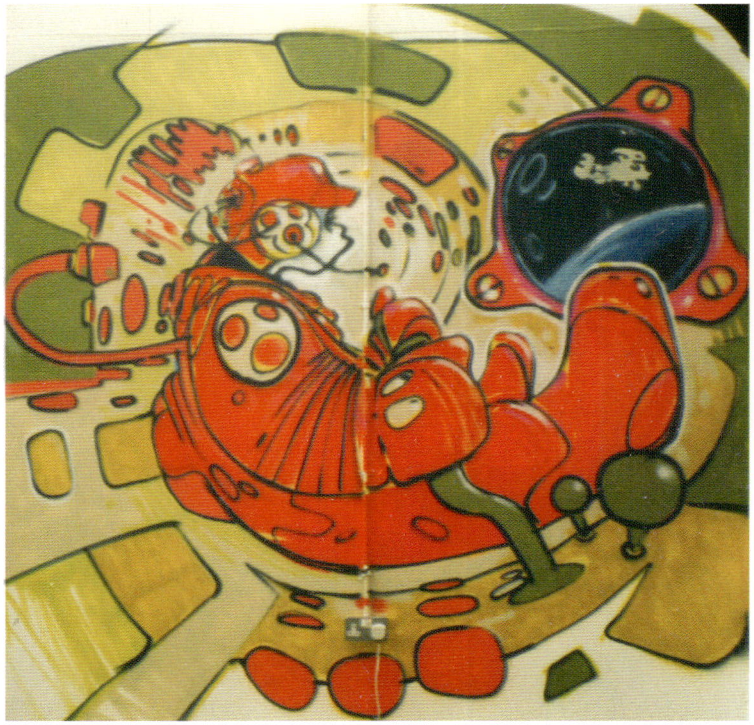

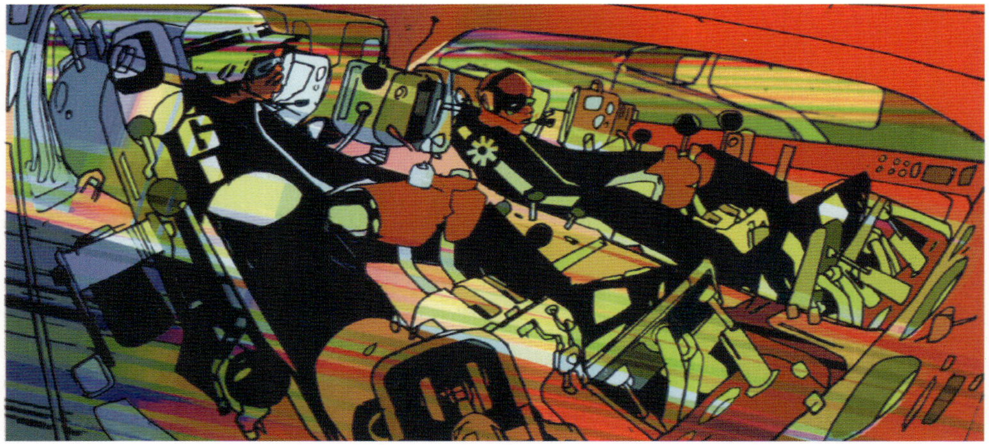

When did you first pick up a spray can?
"The first time I tried to do a spray painting was at the Walls on Fire event in 1998. I painted with Feek, Dicy and Acer, and they were always really encouraging and helpful. Along with Paris, they all gave me a push in that direction."

Do you find spray cans a sympathetic way to work, in relation to your 'swift and free' style?
"I really don't have much control over the can, so I try and harness my lack of control, but I think I prefer the versatile, liquid quality of paint and brushes. Then again,

that's probably because I'm crap with a can."

The first time you used a can was at Walls On Fire? That must have been pretty nerve wracking...

"I was really nervous about it, yeah. I remember I had a big bit of card, and everything I did was sprayed down a hard line, so I wasn't really doing any line work. I'd been doing illustrations for a few years, and Feek had started to get into doing graffiti and was getting really into spray painting. It was an amazing weekend, man. It was the first time I met Inkie and Nick [Walker]. It brought everybody together, like some of the older writers, and there were people from Birmingham as well, which is my hometown.

"It was a couple of years after I'd left college and I wasn't feeling like a student anymore, I was feeling more like I was someone just living in Bristol, and that was the first time I felt like I was a part of something that was happening in Bristol. It made me feel I belonged to the city. And this place has got such a strong identity, with the music and everything."

Did you feel a part of something significant in the late 90s?

"I think one of the key things was when Paris, Eko and Xenz turned up in Bristol, because they really shook it up. They had loads of energy, and they all had their aesthetic and idea about how to do what they wanted to do. They were going to paint the city, that was their whole thing. At the same time they were really encouraging, and they would be like, 'Come and paint with us.' I'd been just sitting indoors on my computer doing illustration work and I was starting to feel like I was back at the call centre, so I was really keen to try it."

Did your illustrational style develop when you were studying for your degree?

"No, I didn't draw all through my degree, I did videos and made an installation. I'd been hanging around with Duncan and Feek, and Duncan really inspired me to get drawing again. It seemed to be pouring out of him: he would just fill sketchbooks, which was amazing to see. So I switched onto that and I guess, in my own way, started drawing again. We'd go round to Duncan's house and he had decks and we'd smoke spliffs and draw. That was a lot of fun."

You did a fair amount of painting with the likes of TCF, Inkie and others. Weren't you tempted to make a go of it as a graffiti writer?

"No, I didn't throw myself into the graffiti thing: I didn't feel like that was what I was."

You say that, but some memorable pieces from that period were graced with your characters. I recall seeing you painting at St Pauls Carnival in 2000.

"I'd totally forgotten about that! I just rolled up at the carnival and painted something with Inkie and Banksy. That was exciting. They had the paint there already. They were like, 'Come on, put something up.' Inkie's really cool like that. That's the thing about Bristol, you can just go and do it. I don't know if it's like that in other cities."

You're one of those people whose work had a very distinctive flavour right from the start. Did anything or anyone in particular influence the way you work?

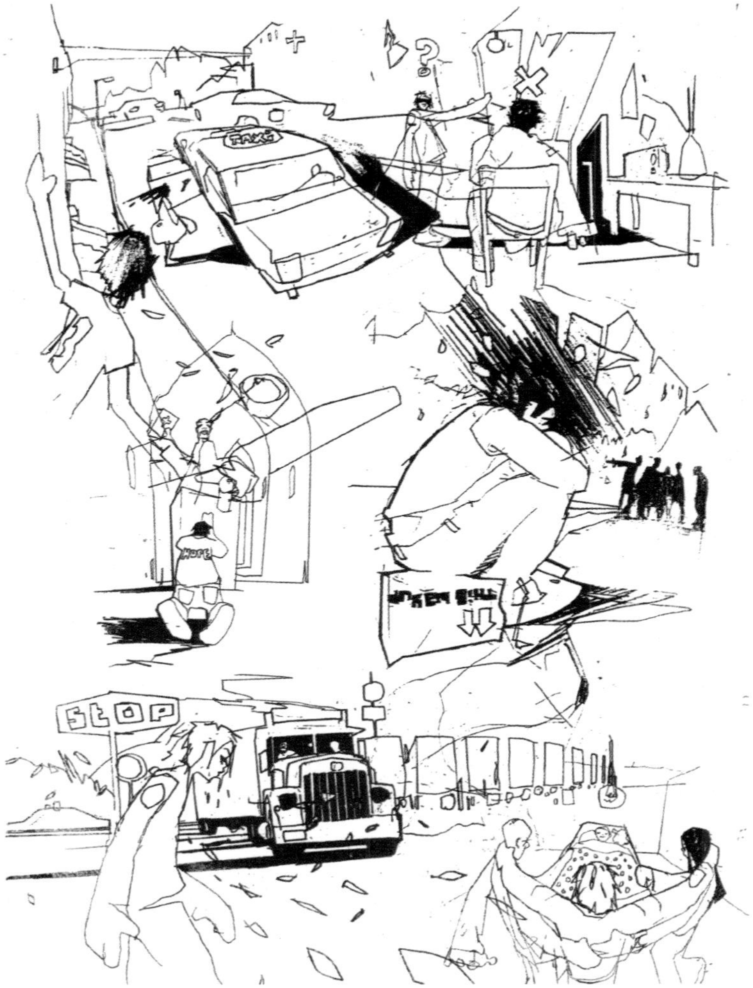

"I don't think I really copied anybody or looked at anyone else's work. I wasn't trying to draw like anybody else. My starting point was Duncan, really, and he was very much just drawing how he drew. There wasn't really that much to look at then; there was Jamie Hewlett, and Futura, I guess, with the Mo' Wax stuff. I just worked out my own way of drawing things. Initially, I just wanted to try and get work and I didn't want to work in a call centre

Opposite page. Top: Will Barras and Inkie, Urban Games, London, 2000

Left: In the cockpit, Custard Factory, Birmingham, 2000

Right: Bryan Gee and Jack Frost, for Knowledge Magazine, 1998

This page. Above: Sketch book page, 1998

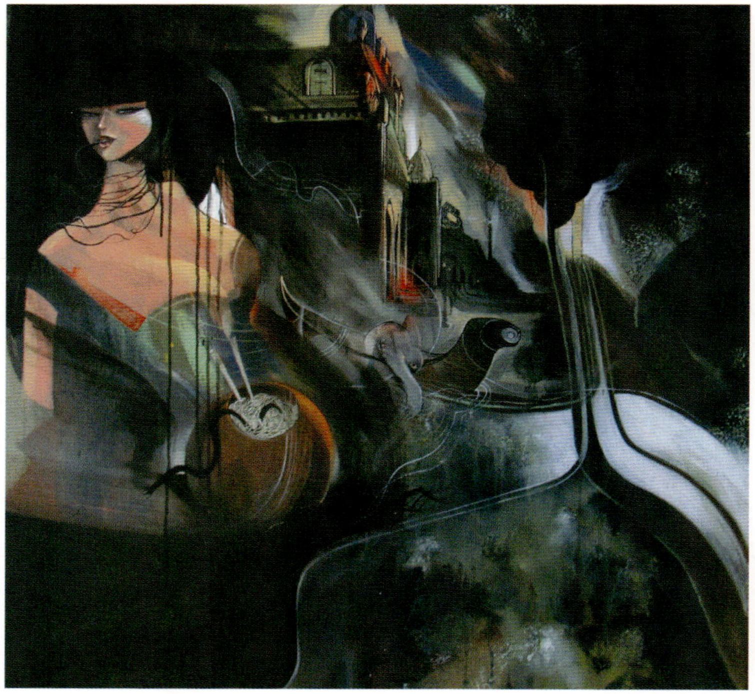

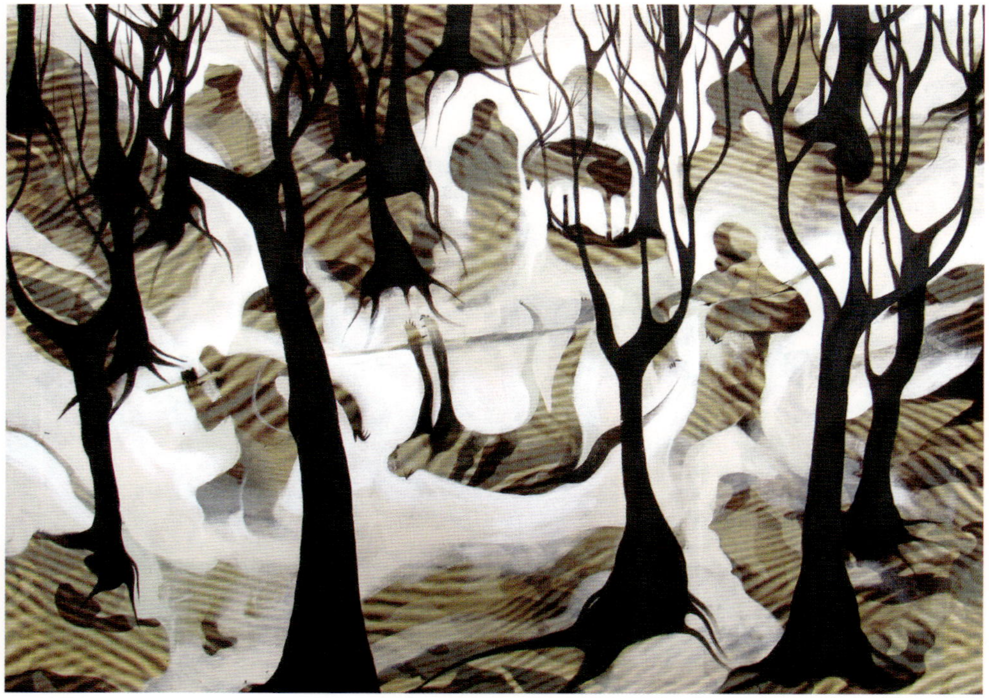

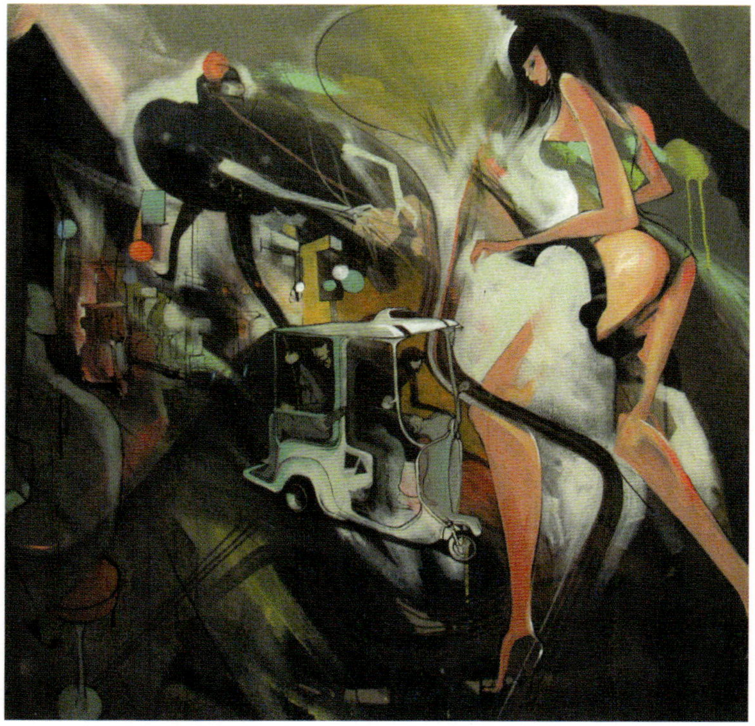

any more. It struck me that I could maybe start doing illustration work; so I really pushed that."

I remember seeing flyers and stuff that you were doing, a real mix of loose sketches and hard graphic colours.
"I was on my computer all the time, scanning stuff in and messing with drawings. I was just kind of fucking with them loads, using the Photoshop line tool. I still use it pretty much in the same way now. For a while I went in the direction of making things chunky and really digital."

When did things begin to take off for you commercially? Was there one particular job that got you noticed?
"I was going up to London once a week and trying to get work, just showing people my stuff. I went to see this guy called Pete Chadwick at a company called Zip. They were doing those *Hip Hop Don't Stop* compilations, and I just went in at the right time and they got me to do the artwork for those. At that time there was a resurgence in illustration, people were starting to move away from photography towards illustration. So from then on, it just kind of snowballed."

Did you feel like you were compromising by doing commercial work, or were you just happy not to temp anymore?
"Doing commercial work really pushes you in a certain direction, and you're not really doing your own stuff, but I was kind of happy to let people tell me what to do. I think that's made me a better draughtsman, because I've learnt to draw loads of different things, but it can also hinder you as an artist."

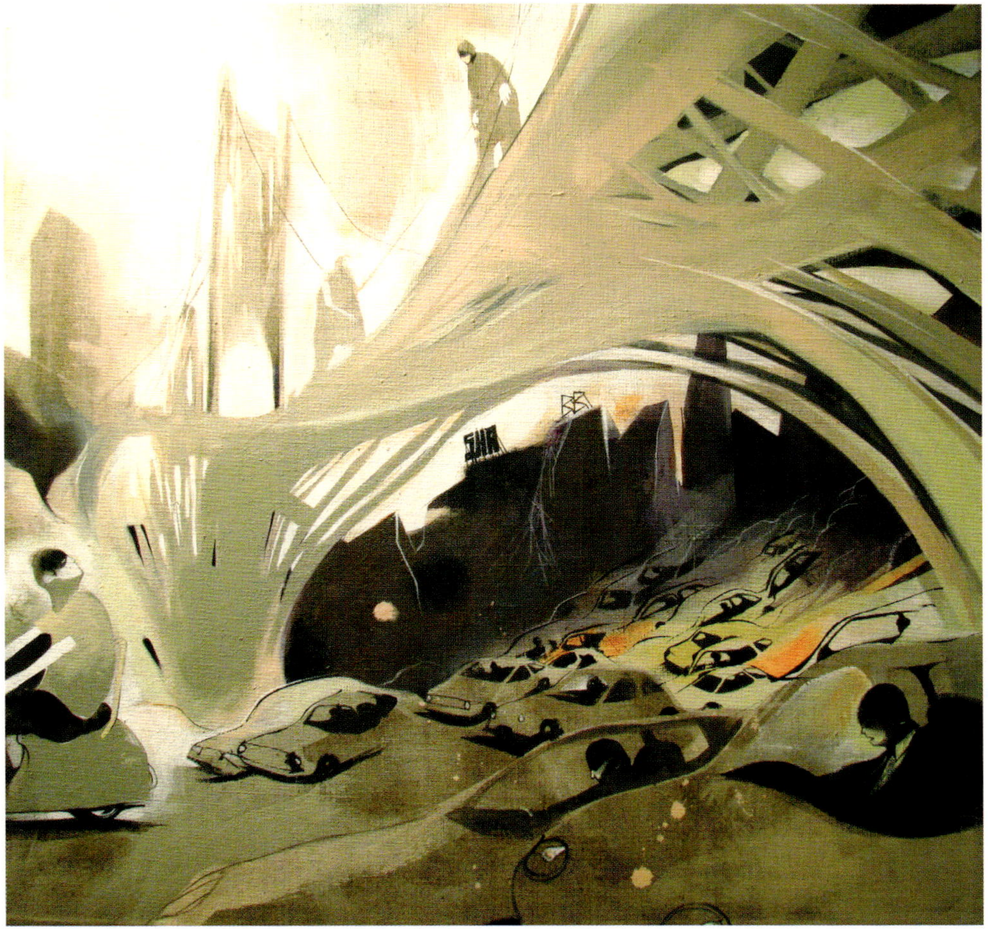

Apart from commercial jobs, I don't suppose there were too many outlets for the kind of work you were producing at that time?

"In the back of my mind was the idea that I wanted to do my own work – but I didn't think of it in terms of doing shows and canvases, like people do now. Then Dicy started doing that thing in his shop Alterior, where once a month people would put canvases in the window. I think that was the first time Duncan did canvases, and I did some the month after him. That was the start of us lot doing exhibitions in Bristol."

Can you tell me how the hook-up with the Scrawl Collective came about?

"Rick Blackshaw, who did the Scrawl Collective book, came to Bristol and met Duncan and me. As a result, I put my Shaft [Bristol club night] flyers in the book and we got loads of enquiries from that. We started doing bits and pieces with Rick and that pushed it another direction. Then the live painting thing came along."

What was the first major live painting event you were involved with?

"We went to Japan, to Osaka, and it was like a massive punk rock concert. We were at the back with this huge wall, and we were painting with Skwerm (David Ellis) and Kami and Pete Fowler. I remember doing something really small in the corner. Skwerm did this massive tree with speakers in it that was just fucking sick, and it really intertwined with Kami's stuff. It was just amazing: it blew my mind, man. It was like, 'Fuck, this is how it's done.' It was the first time I'd seen anybody doing big-scale stuff with paintbrushes. It was a real eye-opener, and from there it progressed."

Did that opportunity to work big again feed back into the way you were working?

"It really did. Everything got freed up, and it was all about doing proper pieces again. Slowly I started to learn how to use the paint and started buying proper brushes. I got into buying these ones with really long bristles, which is where that kind of really fluid line work comes from, and that in turn fed back into my pencil drawing."

Did your subject matter change when you started travelling and working with different people?

When I was in my twenties, we were all DJing at Cosies and I was playing hip hop, so the characters I was doing then were kind of hip hop characters. But I guess now I'm not so interested in that kind of thing anymore. I'm inspired by other artists and things that I see. Things have just kind of shifted now, and I guess they'll carry on shifting and going in different directions.

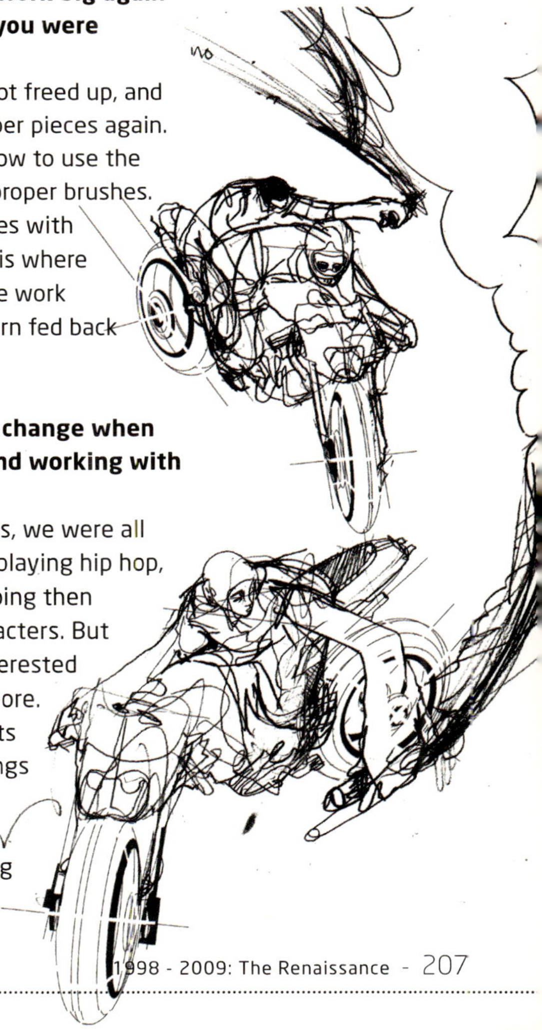

Opposite page. Top left: 'Worm food' mixed media on canvas, 2008

Top right: 'Hunt Henry' mixed media on canvas, 2008

Bottom left: 'Deep Sea Salvage' mixed media on canvas, 2008

This page. Top left: 'Bridge Over The River Ciao' mixed media on canvas, 2007

Bottom right: Sketch book bikers, 2007

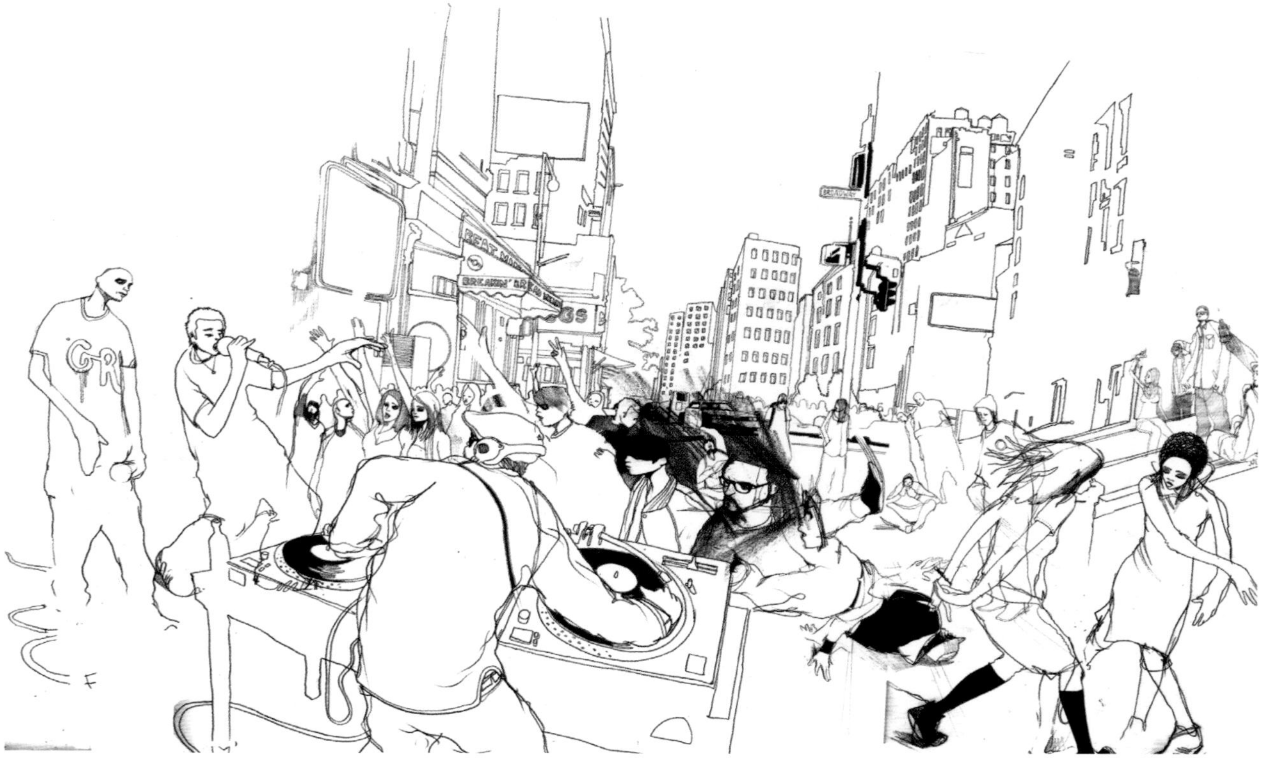

Above: 'Block party' pen on paper, 2008

You work in a wide variety of media. What are you most comfortable with?
"The great thing with acrylics and emulsion is that they're really versatile, they can either be totally watered down or super thick. Once you start messing around with all that – in fact, once you start messing around with all different media, like ink or spray paint – you just start learning different ways to draw. I do use spray paint – it can be quite atmospheric in an abstract sort of way."

Do you have a particular process for making a piece of work?
"It's a bit like playing the 'cloud game', where you're looking at shapes and deciding what they're going to be. While you're actually doing a painting, something emerges from it. It's nothing cleverer than that. Sometimes I go at something with a plan, I'll write a list of words, and I'll keep going back to it. It never really works out like that, but they're just there if your mind goes blank.

"But until I have a show and a deadline, I don't just sit there and paint single pieces. I kind of get a space and paint in it, so I'll have five canvases set up at once and I'll go across them in waves. The first marks are really fast and wet and loose, and then the next wave kind of focuses the painting, until it's been chiselled into a sort of scene, or until space is formed."

Looking back at the work you've produced over the last ten years, it seems to me that you're not someone who stands still for very long. Can you talk about how the way your work has changed?
"I used to do this thing where I'd put a load of colours down and I'd always make these shapes – like things that could be lighting, for example, or anatomical bone structures. They'd always be really loose, but they'd lend themselves to becoming figurative forms, or characters. Then I'd go at it afterwards with the outline, which is when it would all start to make sense.

"Recently, though, I've been drawing on the thing at the beginning rather than at the end, and covering the space so that it's a mess, and then painting into those spaces and pulling things in and out. It makes it look sort of like 50s illustration, because I guess they used to draw and colour it in afterwards."

Now that you are making much more of your own work and it's being well received, are you looking to leave commercial illustration behind you?
"I don't think so. I've really gained from doing the commercial work. On the whole it's been a good thing. It's given me the chance to do animation, which I love doing. I know that I'll always be doing commercial work in one shape or form. The thing is now that the briefs have become more open, and you're more often paid to just do your own thing. You just have to go in with your eyes open."

Does Bristol still hold a special place in your heart?
"Bristol is definitely where my formative years were spent. I don't think that if I'd moved to any other city, I'd be doing what I'm doing now. That's down to Bristol."

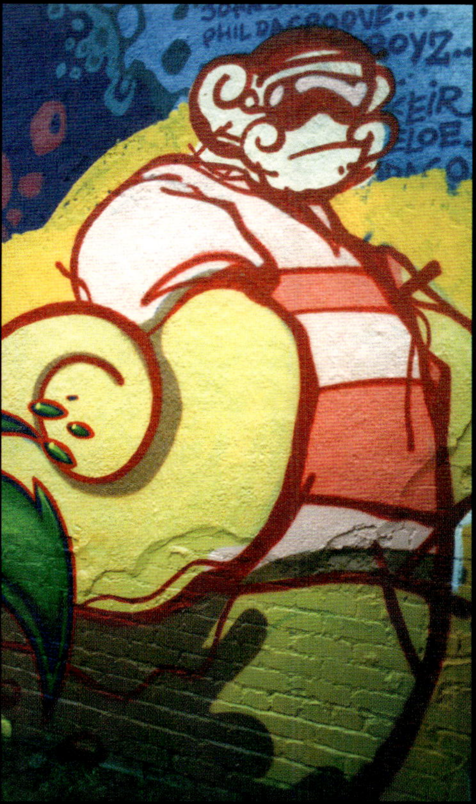

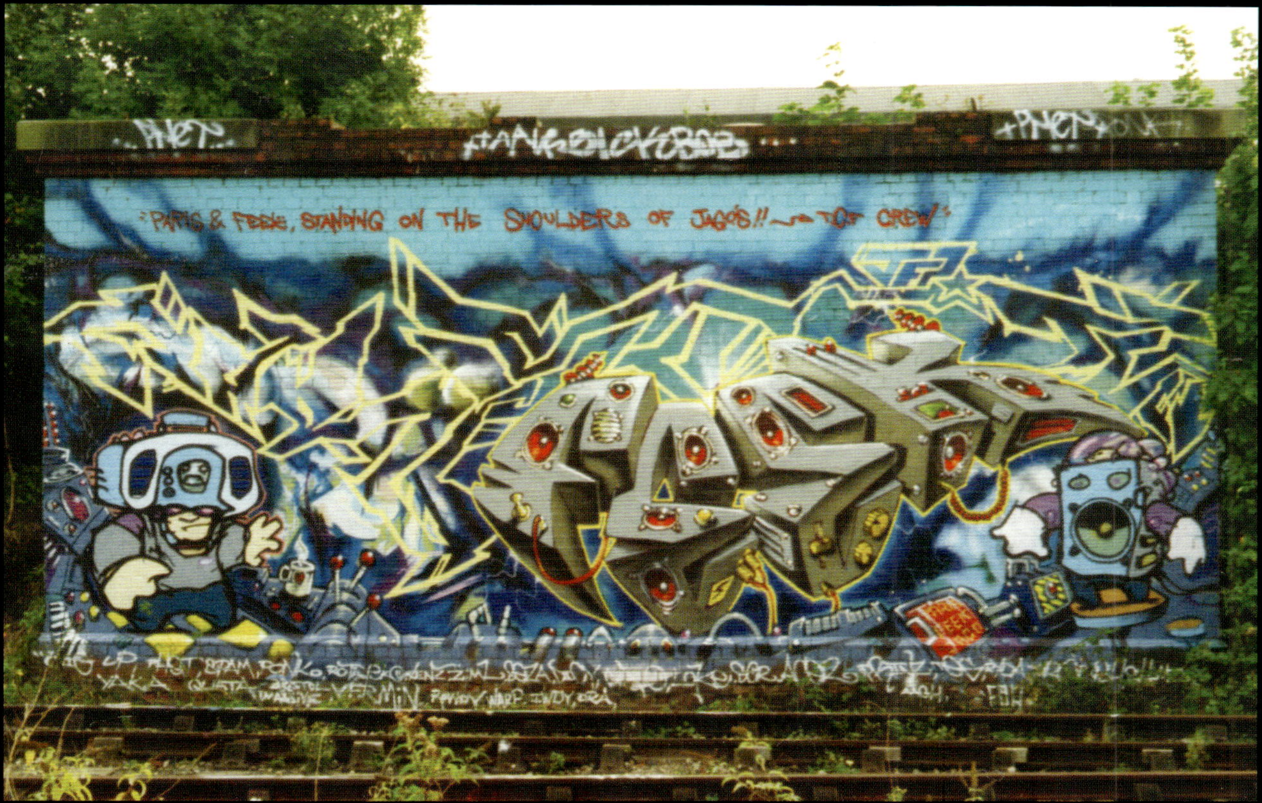

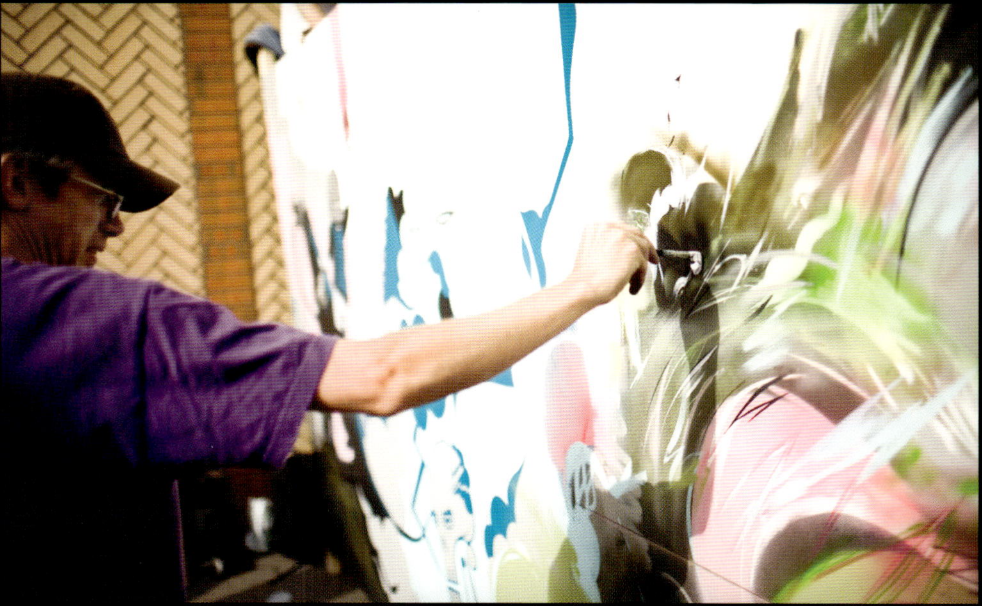

MR JAGO

• **Mr Jago's stylised robotic figures began life as scratchy sketchbook biro doodlings.** Over the years, they have continued to evolve as the vehicle for his creative experiments, to the point where their figures have melted and their forms have become secondary to his expressionistic, energetic mark-making. A craftsman whose work is as varied as it is unmistakable, Mr Jago's art exists both as a reflection of his early passion for hip hop culture – and in spite of it.

How did you first discover hip hop? I don't suppose there were too many

Top left: 'Monkey Man' c.2001

Above: 'Standing on the shoulders of Jagos' Feek, Paris and Mr Jago go track side, c.1999

Bottom left: Mr Jago at work

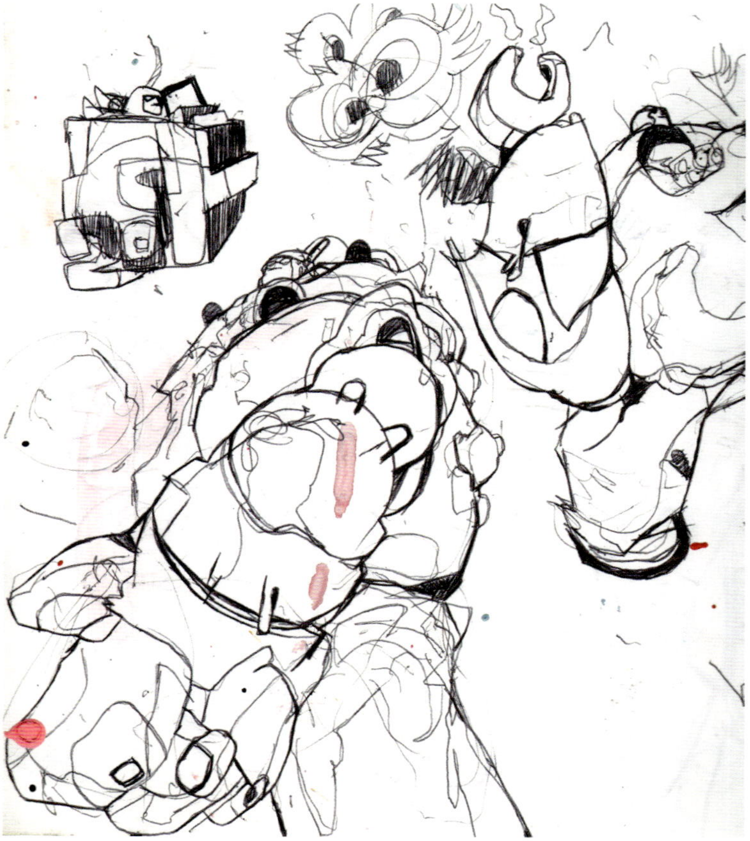

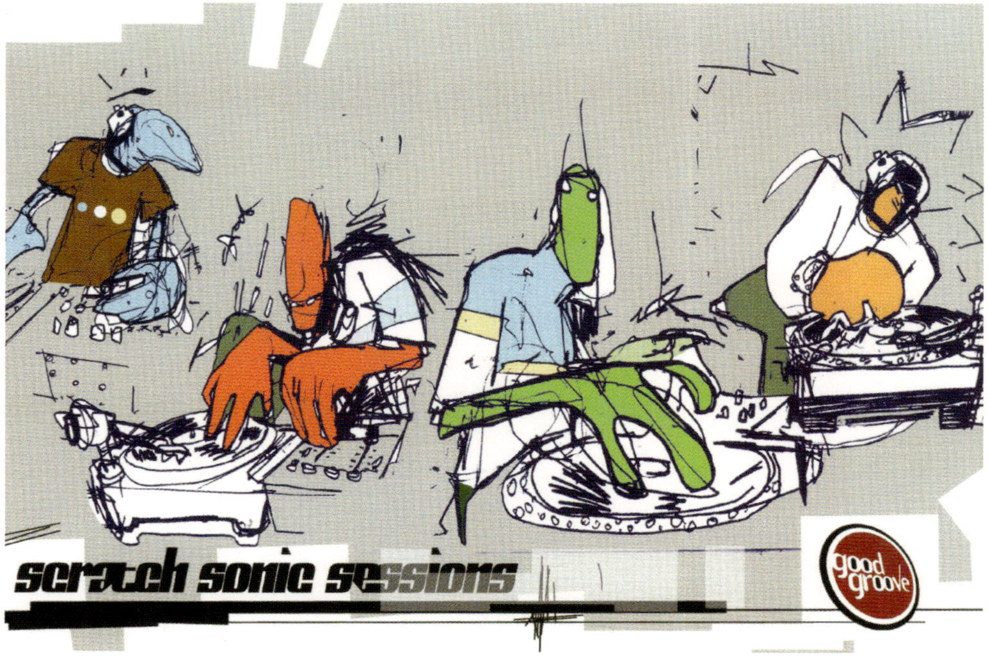

Above: Sketchbook robots, 2002

Top right: Scratch Sonic Sessions flyer, 2000

Right: Sketchbook page, 1995

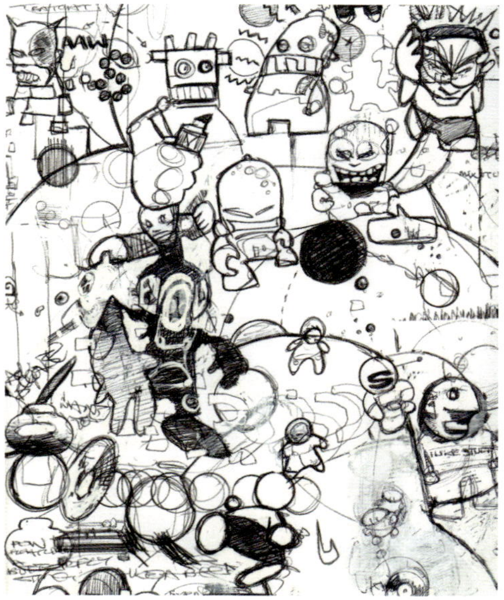

graffiti writers or sound systems in the wilds of Suffolk in the 1980s?

I remember first seeing it in Look In magazine. Do you remember Look In? I used to get it because my mum thought it was wholesome and good – I always wanted 2000 AD but I wasn't allowed. There was a double-page spread with Run DMC in there, and there was a Vaughn Bode character that Dondi did, which I copied. Run DMC were also on [kid's TV programme] Get Fresh. They didn't have any shoelaces in their shoes, and the presenter did the typical, 'Excuse me Run, why don't you have any shoelaces?' And he was like, 'So I can do THIS!' and kicked his foot up at the camera. I was thinking, 'These guys are terrifying, God they're so cool.' It was New York, straight to Suffolk.

"In my little town, we only got tiny bits of hip hop that floated down like that so we absorbed it that way and anything you got you really... well, it's like taking ten hours to eat a strawberry – you appreciated it a lot more because it was scarce. Maybe that's where my passion for it came from. It was like, 'I understand this culture, because it's the one thing that talks to me."

When did you first get your hands on some spray paint?

"I sprayed Breakdance Two Electric Boogaloo on one of my mum's old T-shirts with padded shoulders that she gave me. I made a stencil and sprayed that on there. I'd seen the first Breakdance film, which was better, but Electric Boogaloo just sounded better. I also had this vampire frog with the classic Vaughn Bode eyes and pointy teeth that i would do. I put that on a wall behind some trees in the park. But I got grassed up immediately and was made to clean it off. I didn't think I was doing anything wrong."

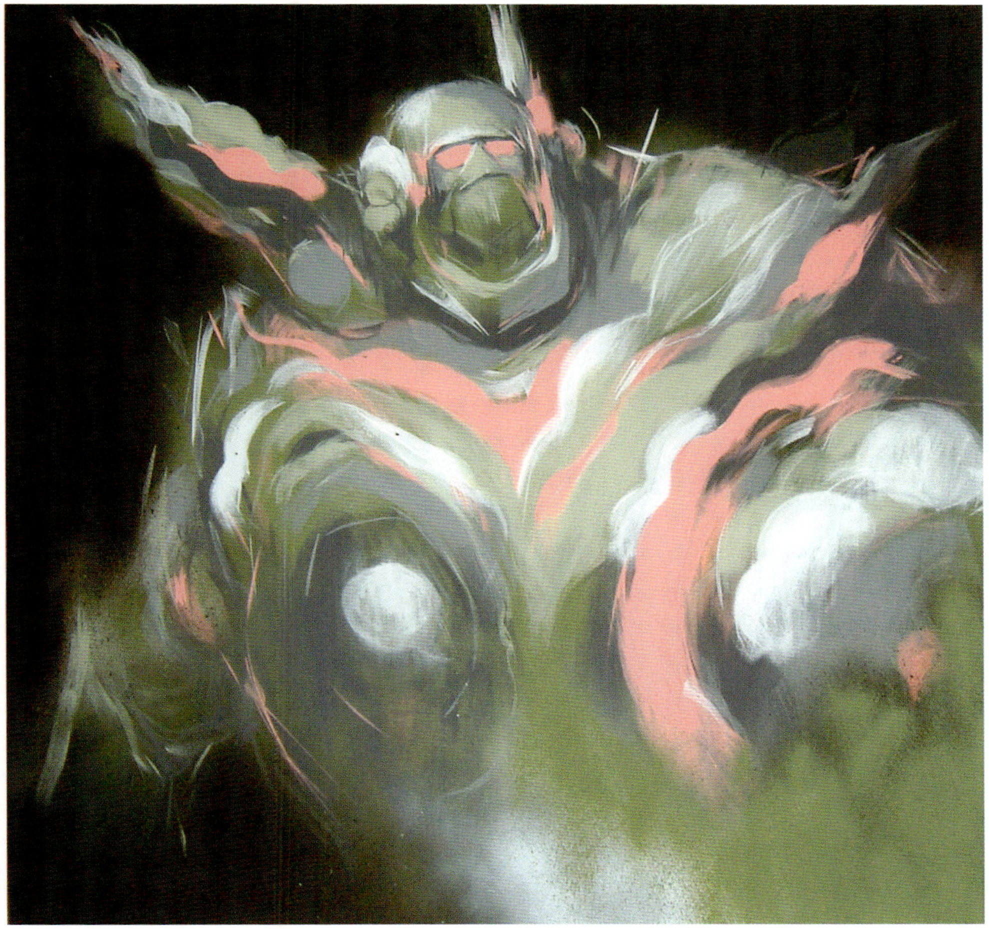

Left: 'Mosmun 1' spray paint and acrylic on canvas, 2007

What appealed to you about Bristol?
"Bristol had such a strong foundation. I was attracted to it because I grew up somewhere where hip hop was not acceptable. Even your own girlfriend goes, 'Well, if it's so good, how come it's not number one in the charts?' Not long after I got here, I found 3D's piece that was in Spraycan Art and I kissed it. I told him I had when I first met him. He was one of the reasons I came here. I saw Bristol as a hub for all that sort of shit, and I knew about it because I was reading about it in *Hip Hop Connection*, looking at Inkie's stuff in there. I was like, 'Wow!' I knew Bristol had it going on, I'd been reading about it for years."

When did you move here?
"I came here in 1991 to study illustration, even though I didn't know what illustration was. I knew it wasn't graphics, but I thought graphics was technical drawing, and I knew I was no good at that - so I applied to do illustration instead. I got a student loan and I thought, 'I'll buy a Technics 1200'. Then I got an HW International mixer. I was making mix tapes and stuff, and then I started DJing with Awkward. He was a kid, 15 or 16, and he was unbelievable at scratching even then. He played funk and hip hop: he had Funkadelic and things like that."

The hip hop subculture as a whole was obviously of huge significance to you.
I don't really feel involved in it now, but hip hop was so important to me. It's recycling, that's all it ever was: taking something from somewhere and making your own thing from it, then putting it back out there and saying, 'This is my take.'

How was your style of drawing received at college?
They didn't like what I was drawing. University was why I came here, but when I got here it wasn't what I wanted to do. I literally had one tutor say to me, 'Don't ever let me see this shit in this university ever again', in front of a room full of people who were on my course. I got very negative feedback, so I just did what I had to do to finish the course."

Never mind - I'm sure he's still there now, telling the next generation of successful illustrators the same thing. Did you find encouragement elsewhere?
"I was surrounded by everything that stimulated me. People would be coming round, and we'd be playing records, getting stoned and drawing. And I was just doodling in these books on lined paper. I worked with Will Barras doing shit phone jobs, and we just drew shit, and he made the jump before me and went, 'Right, I'm going to try and do this thing.'

"All of a sudden there's Will's work on a record cover in a record shop. So I started thinking, 'How can I get there?' I also

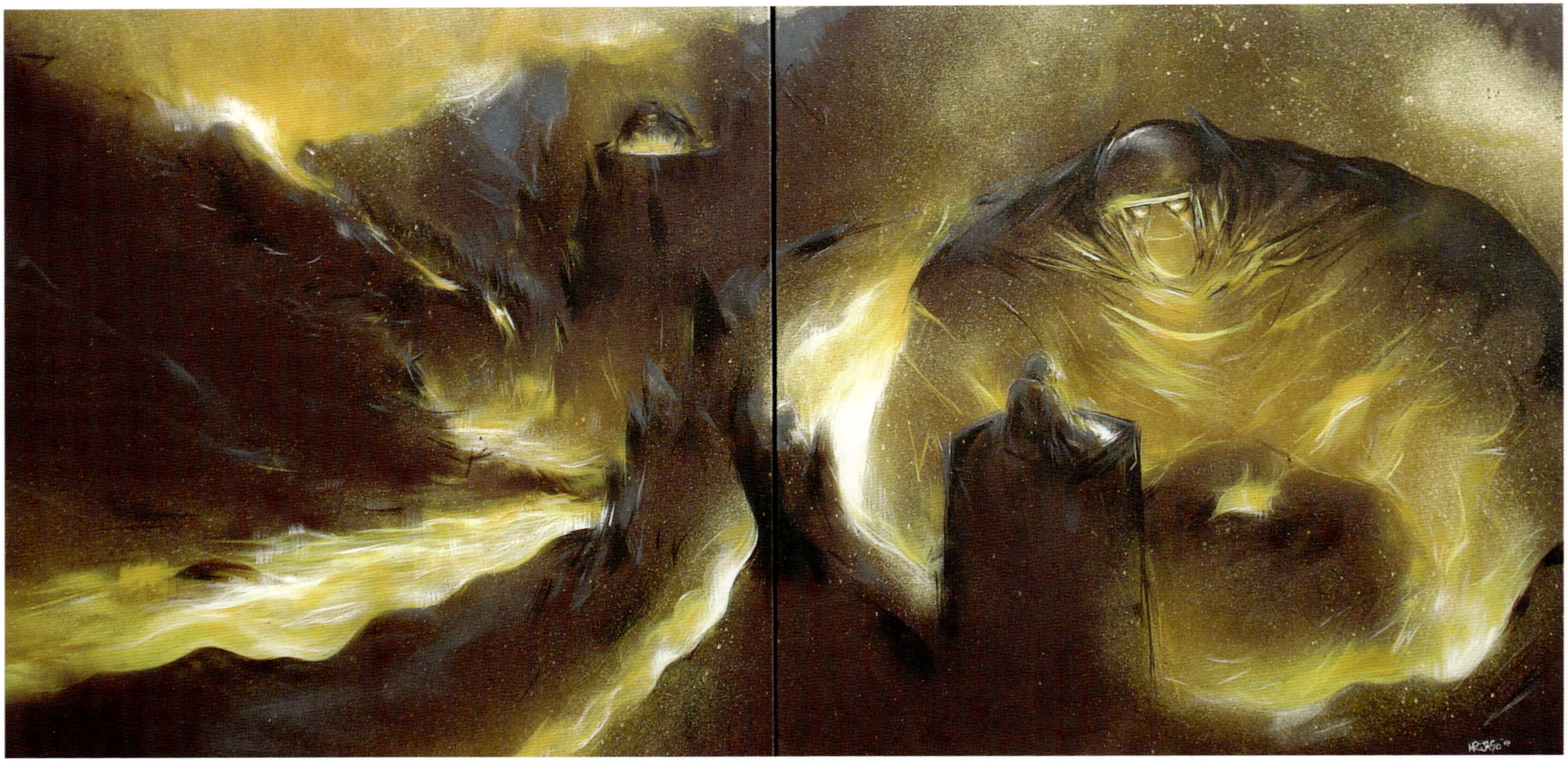

Above: 'Magma Maintenance' spray paint and acrylic on canvas, 2007

Opposite page. Top: 'Ramp Builder' spray paint and acrylic on canvas, 2007

Left: Xenz and Mr Jago collaboration, St.Paul's, 2007

Right: 'Untitled,' ink and gutta on silk, 2007

remember seeing Futura 2000's Mo' Wax record sleeve designs, and I fell in love with those immediately. It got me thinking, 'That's the ultimate thing I want to do.'"

How did you realise that ambition?
"I was fortunate enough to inherit £1,000, so I got a Mac, a scanner and a printer. I started scanning my drawings in and it was like, 'How can I make these look like a record sleeve?' I just started trying to get it out there; I was doing flyers and doing unpaid stuff for local magazines. I did a flyer for a night where Peanut Butter Wolf was playing, spent about 25 hours working on it and got paid a tenner."

How did your involvement with the Scrawl Collective come about?
"Rick Blackshaw came to Bristol to interview Will, and he said, 'Who else is doing stuff?' Will put him on to me. So I got included in the first Scrawl book, and when that hit the shops I had Nike phoning me up. Then I did a job for Levi's, I think. I just thought, 'I'm going to leave this job that's crushing me, I'm going to try and do this.' I got four and a half grand from doing one job when I was earning £400 a month, and all of a sudden I had all these people coming up to me, saying, 'Yeah, I really like that thing you did.' I couldn't believe it. I put myself out there and I got this immediate comeback of joy. It wasn't even about money. I just wanted to do the next one, and the next one and the one after that."

What was the first really big foreign painting job you did?
"After the first Scrawl trip to Japan where we painted with Kami, Sasu and David Ellis – I went to Taipei in Taiwan to do a job for a Japanese fashion designer, Yohji Yamamoto. They opened a department store and I went to paint as a performance thing. We had to paint these panels in four massive shop windows, in five days. I was totally making it up as I went along, just looking at my doodle book and thinking

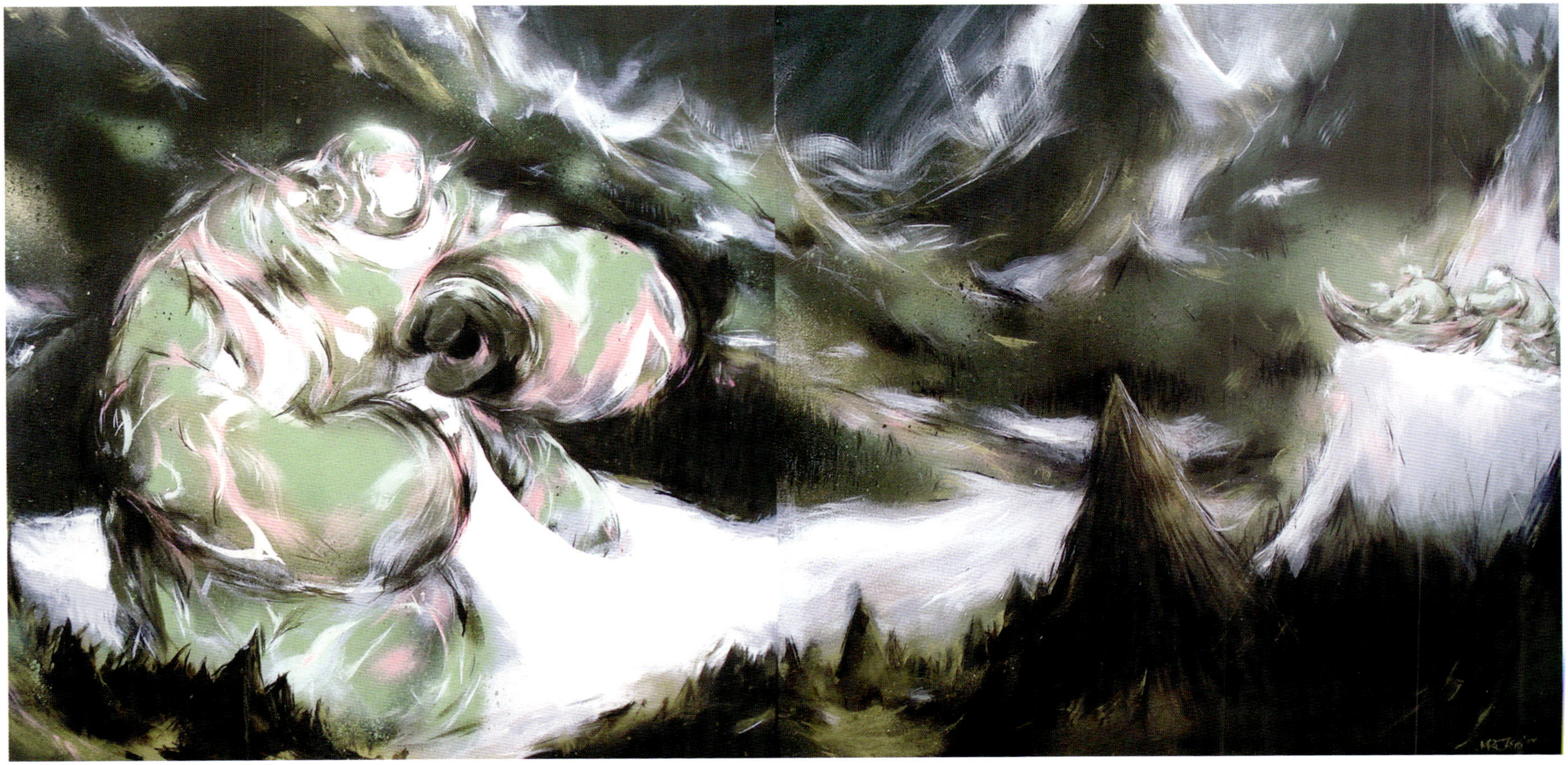

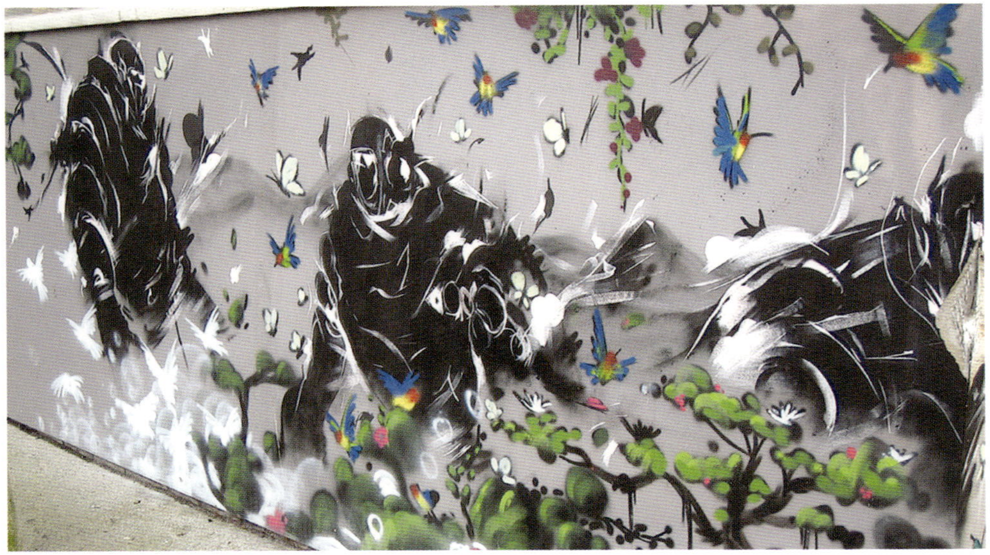

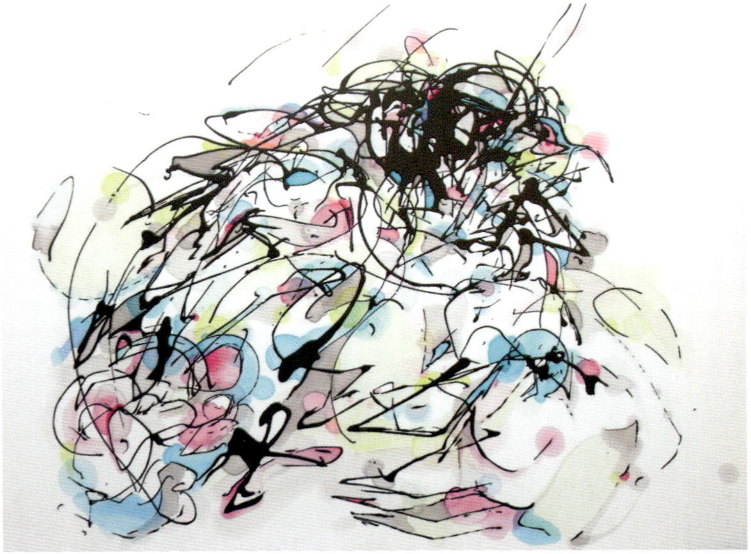

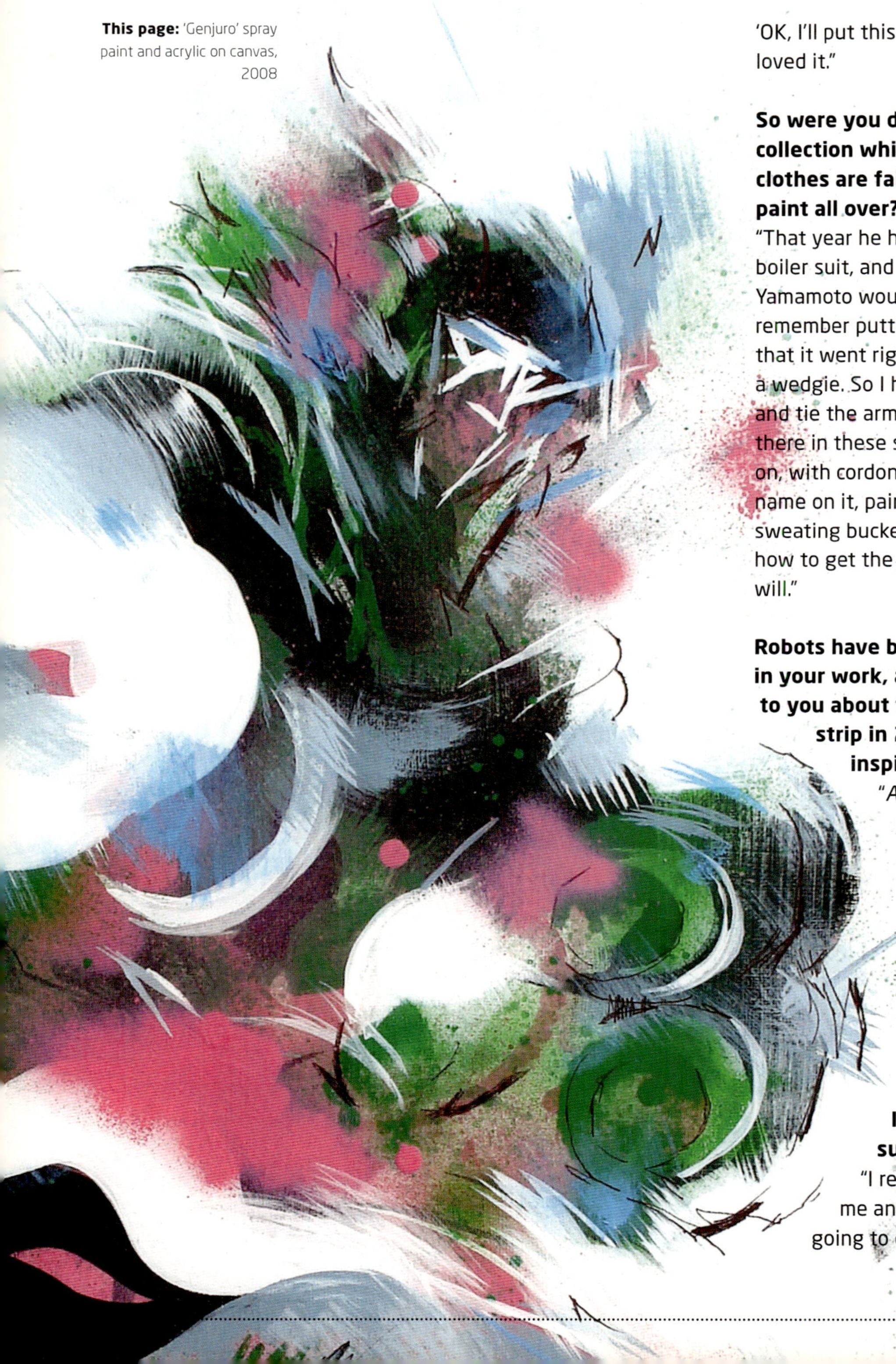

This page: 'Genjuro' spray paint and acrylic on canvas, 2008

'OK, I'll put this with that.' And they fucking loved it."

So were you dressed in Yamamoto's collection while painting. I imagine his clothes are fairly expensive to splash paint all over?

"That year he had designed a black silk boiler suit, and his 'team' were like, 'Mr Yamamoto would like you to wear this.' I remember putting it on and it was so tight that it went right up my arse and gave me a wedgie. So I had to take the top half off and tie the arms round my waste. I was there in these silken trousers with a T-shirt on, with cordon tape on the back with my name on it, painting in these windows and sweating buckets. If that doesn't teach you how to get the job done, I don't know what will."

Robots have been a constant theme in your work, and I remember talking to you about the ABC Warriors comic strip in 2000 AD. Was that an inspiration?

"*ABC Warriors* was absolutely amazing. It was quite punky, I thought. And *Star Wars, Return Of The Jedi*, it all felt like the same thing; but *ABC Warriors* had the ultimate style of bad-boy robots. It was growing up in the '80s: it was all of those influences."

Including graffiti as well, I suppose?

"I remember Eko coming up to me and saying, 'When are you going to do that stuff on a wall?' But because TCF were doing lots of productions and stuff, I would feel a bit embarrassed when I got involved. I always felt like the newbie. Spray paint wasn't really my medium, and I usually thought what I painted looked a bit clunky. But it was good fun, and that's what was nice about the social side of things in Bristol – even though I was never very confident with it. Everyone else's stuff would be so neat, and have like a continuous line or the same consistency to the paint. There didn't seem to be much mess coming into it."

You're using a lot of spray paint in your recent stuff. Is that what you mean by bringing mess into it?

"I like making a mess. I've started using spray cans much more and I'm not using them in the way I used to think you had to use them. I'll do things like scratch the paint off or rub it with my finger. I love it now I'm more confident, and I use it in a painty way; if it drips, it doesn't matter. There are certain ways to move your hand across a space: some of them are happy accidents, and some of them are much more definite."

Is there a reason why you paint?

"I think it's to prove to yourself that you can, it's just about being alive. My dad said to me, 'It's not about what you earn or what you own, it's what you leave behind that's important.' And that's about the best thing anyone has ever said to me. It took the pressure off. It's not an ego thing, you're just trying to tell your own version of your existence, to make your mark."

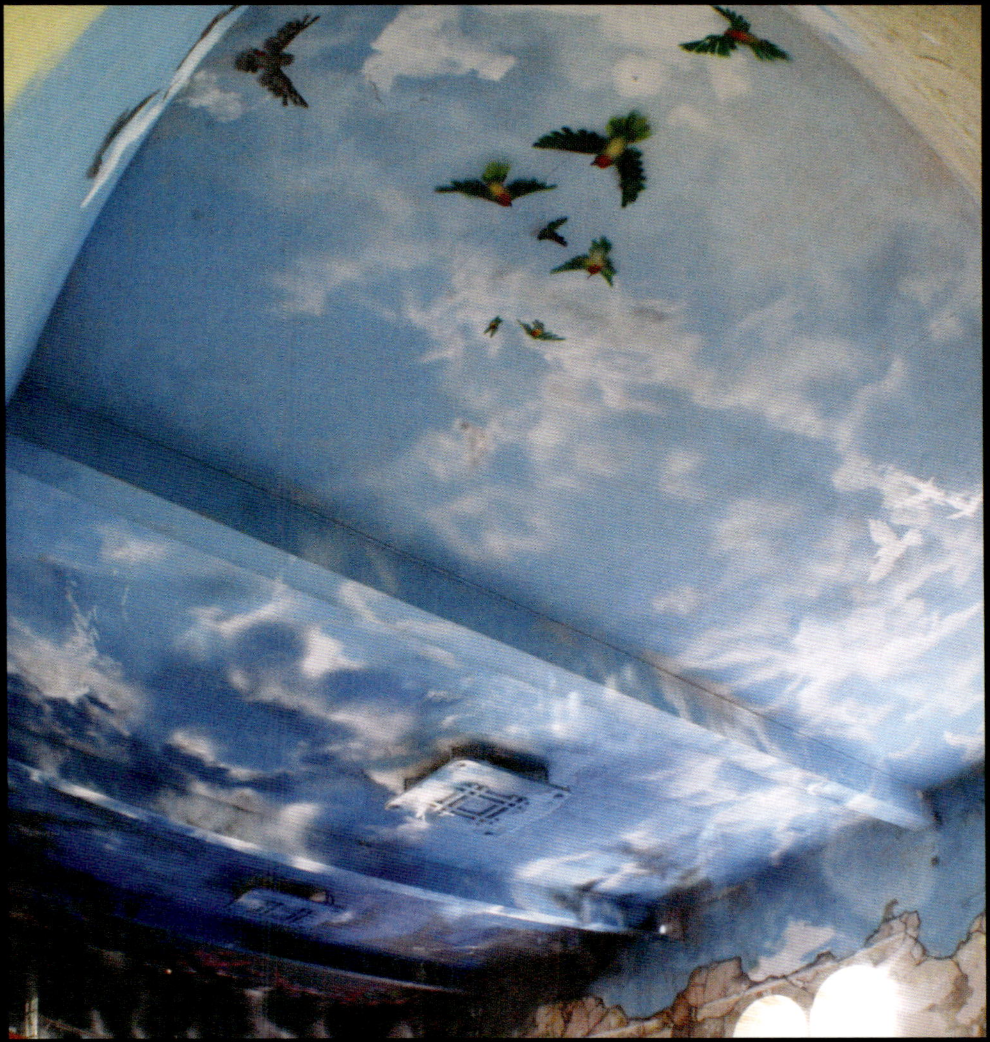

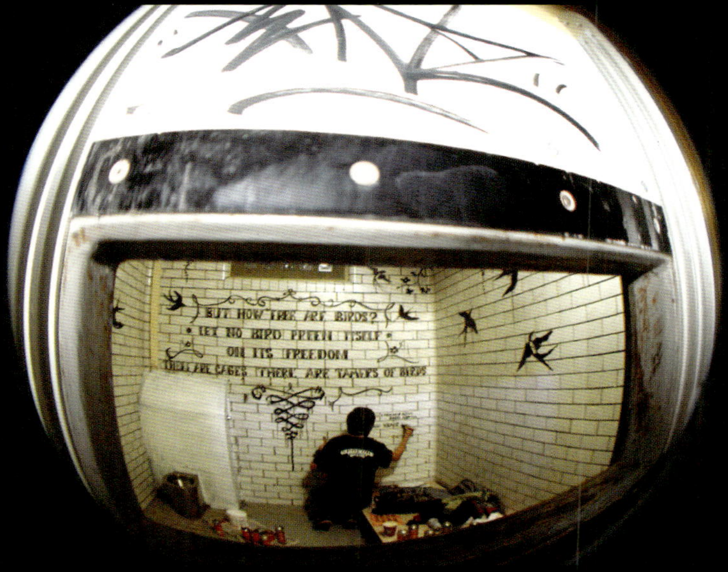

XENZ TCF

• **"The whole thing about graff is to be unique and stand out.** But I did that, in a way, by blending in. In about 1996 I stopped looking at graffiti, opened my eyes to the world around me and let the inspiration just flood out. If people only take their influence from graffiti then all they're going to produce is generic graffiti. I think it's really important if you're going to go out and make a mark that you think about it and put some other influences into it from outside the world of graffiti. People are so purist with it, but it shouldn't be like that."

Xenz is a creative free spirit who rarely paints from sketches, preferring instead to let his hand and mind wander across a surface to create scenes, landscapes and imaginary worlds. He has taken his art way outside the boundaries of 'traditional graffiti' to find his own, unique approach as much influenced by Turner's brooding

Top and bottom left: "I've always wanted to paint a giant ceiling." Pro Cathedral fresco, 2007

Above: Xenz decorates his cell for the 12 Days Of Xmas show in the old Bridewell police station, 2007

Bottom middle: Xenz T-shirt design

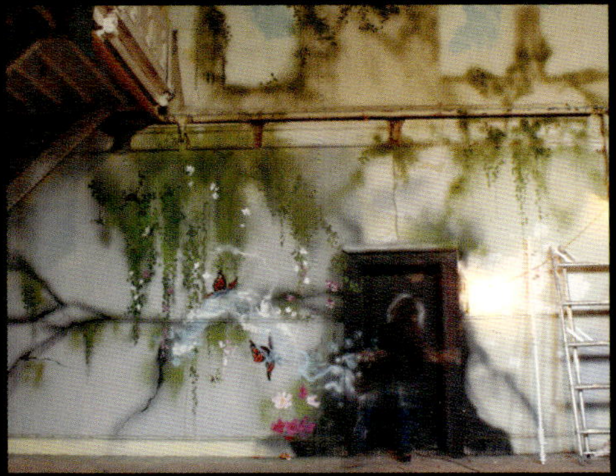

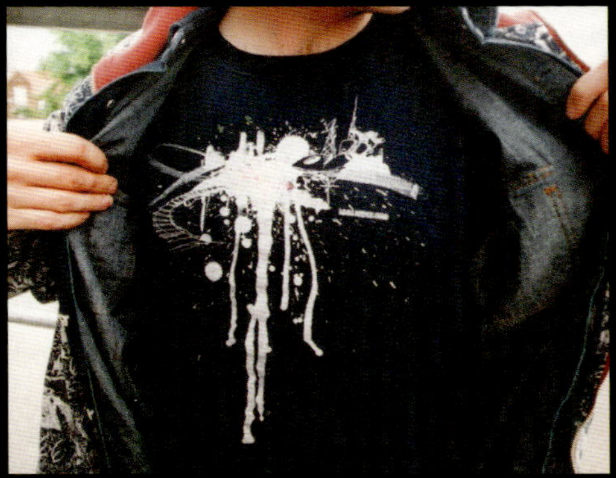

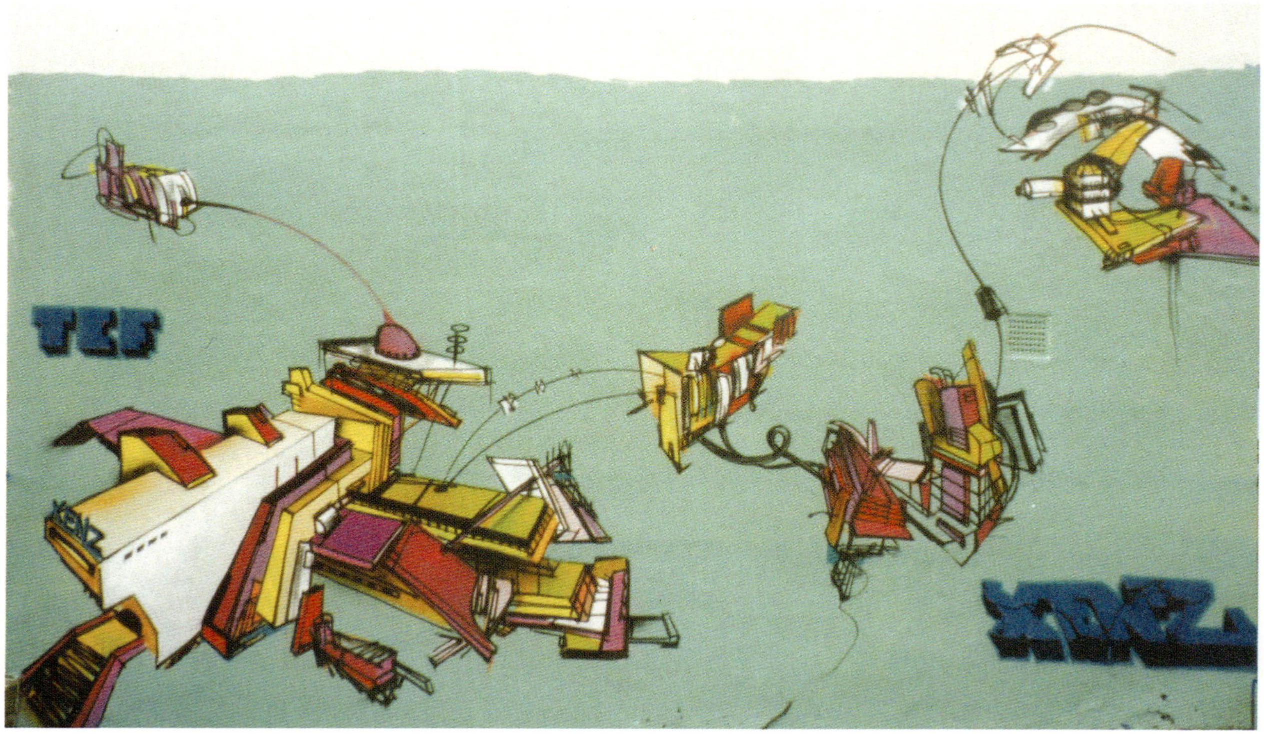

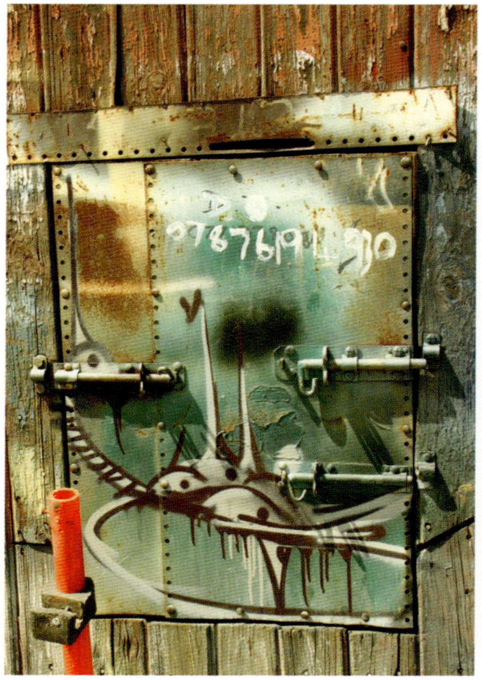

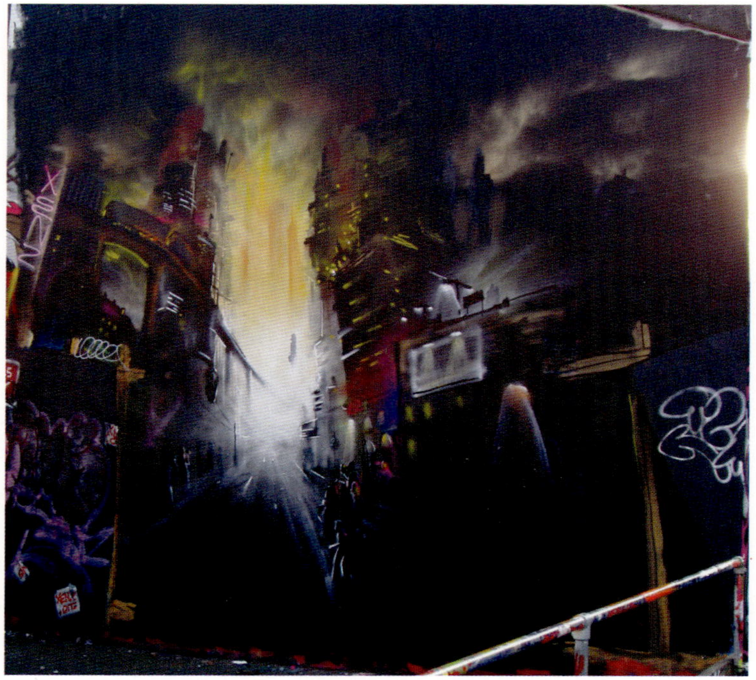

seascapes as by fantasy artists Rodney Matthews and Roger Dean. These days Xenz is essentially an artist who uses spray paint amongst other mediums, rather than a graffiti artist per se. However, to watch him propel paint at speed across huge spaces is to be left in no doubt where his roots lie.

"Once you start breaking down these barriers that are put in front of you – 'it should only be on a train', or whatever – if you start painting on anything you then start painting anything, and really exploring what you can do. When you're painting you're capturing light, almost, and that's just art. It's just exploring stuff and adding your own little twist. It comes from battling, you've always got to have that secret move. When I rock up to a wall people are nervous because they never know what's going to end up next to their work. Doing graffiti is about burning everything else in sight until only your work is worth examination".

This underlying impulse to burn the competition compels Xenz as much as the next graffiti writer. The need to continue to challenge himself and push the boundaries of his own style, however, have kept him driven and working in a huge raft of mediums.

"I'm a painter, an artist, I paint on anything and everything, with anything. Just because I can use a spray can better than a knife and fork doesn't eliminate computers, acrylics, oils, cameras, paintbrushes, or pencils. I think all I'm doing is using art's basic principles – but using them in my own way, using my own influences – the world around me, things I see and the way I see them. It's only the insular mindset of the purists which says that graffiti artists should never paint canvases or make money from art. People

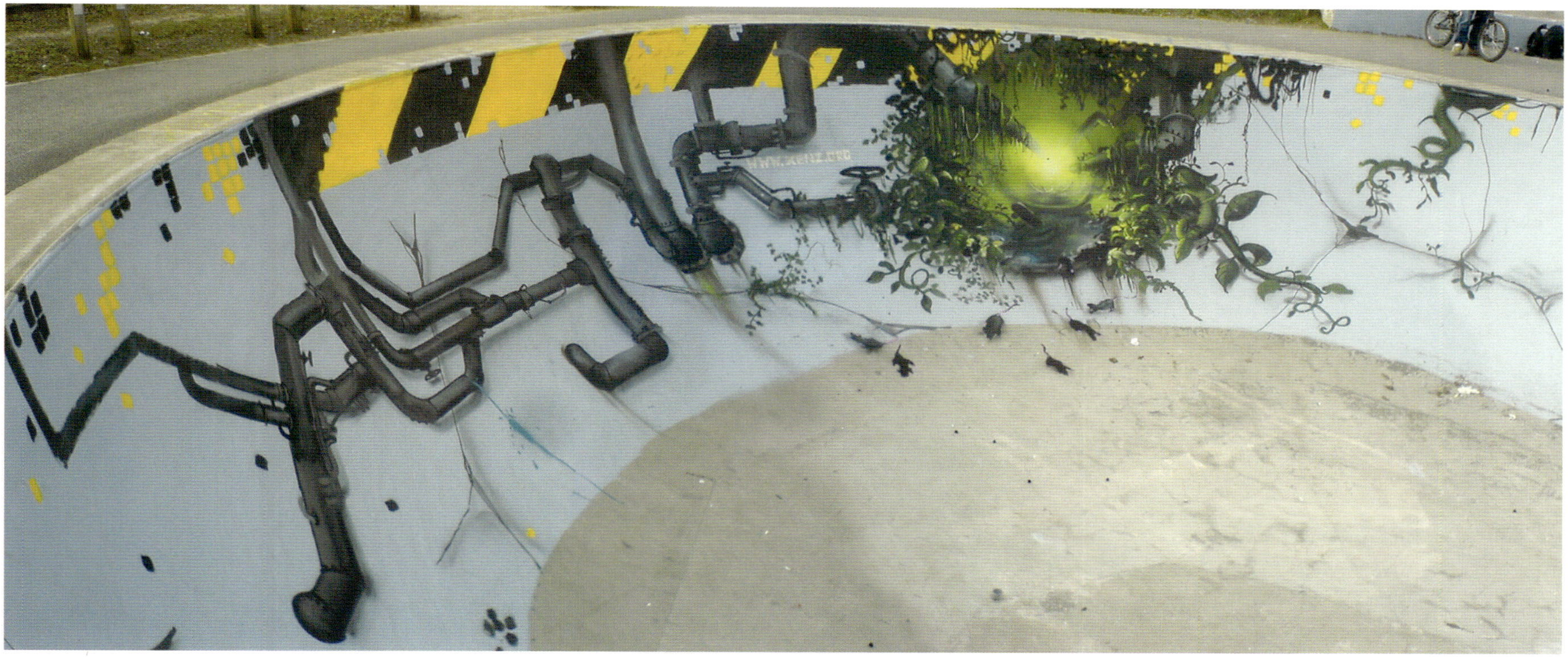

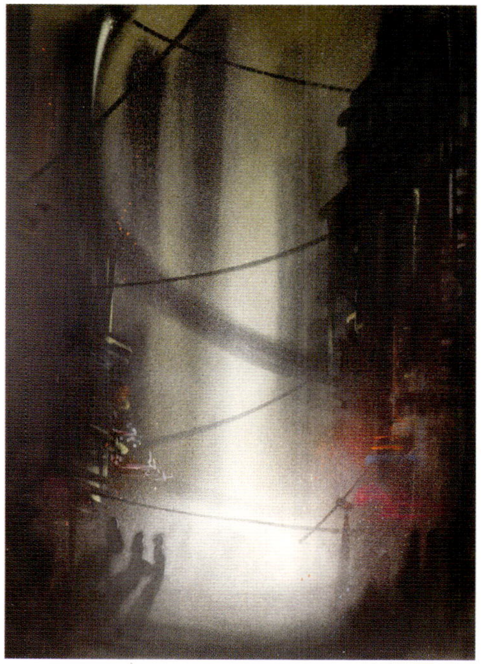

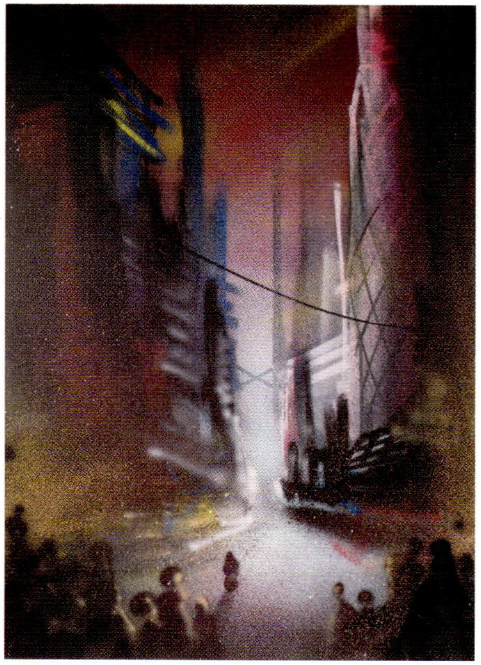

call me 'art fag', tell me I'm selling out or whatever, but it really doesn't interest me. It's something I've been doing since I was 12 years old and I'm now 33, and I haven't stopped. It's my identity now. I'm an artist - therefore, I'm going to make art."

As a graduate of the Hull warehouse scene and a founder member of the TCF Crew, Xenz's approach is typically experimental and wilfully at odds with trends within the graffiti scene. It's an attitude he shares with his contemporaries, for whom art was something to escape into as teenagers. Hull's bleak industrial landscape offered them ample opportunity to practise their painting skills, and a sombre physical environment against which to react, with colour and form.

"Hull had no direct graffiti influence or

Opposite page. Top left: Bedminster skate park, c.2000

Bottom left: Door panel, c.2001

Bottom middle: Bedminster skate park, 2007

This page. Top: A hole in the bowl, Yate skate park, 2006

Bottom left: 'Big City Of Dreams' spray paint on canvas, 2008

Bottom middle: 'This Town Is A Different Town' spray paint on canvas, 2008

Right and opposite page:
The Farm pub, Xenz, Busk and Bleach, 2008

strict graffiti rule book. We painted walls because it looked like fun. We weren't on a mission to emulate New York. We don't have a subway system. We basically did it our own way, with our own individual influences. It wasn't a vandalism thing, it was about expression. We had acres and acres of derelict northern industrial estates to practise in. Hull is all docks and things like that, and we'd always be playing around there when we was kids anyway, just going into all these abandoned buildings and breaking windows. It's just dereliction everywhere, so it was kind of a natural progression after seeing films like *Beat Street* and *Breakdance* to go back there. We were like 'right, let's go back in there and paint on the walls.' We didn't even feel like we were doing anything dodgy, it was all just experimenting with paint instead of going and doing something stupid like glue sniffing or whatever.

"The thing about Hull is it's always been about colour productions. It's never been a 'damage city' where it's like 'get up and go, attack the place.' It's more like everything's fucked anyway, the buildings are run down, so we were quite a hippy community, I suppose, just trying to survive in this dead-end city. Everyone was getting addicted to heroin or going to prison or just getting jobs building caravans or packing fish, but we wanted better and bigger. Doing graffiti was a real source of enlightenment in our lives; art in general was a whole new world. Instead of talking about growing different strains of weed, or whatever, we wanted to talk about Sonia Delaunay, or Marcel Duchamp. Then along came Seen and Dondi, and everyone was suddenly, 'wow! New York!' It really changed the way we were looking at things."

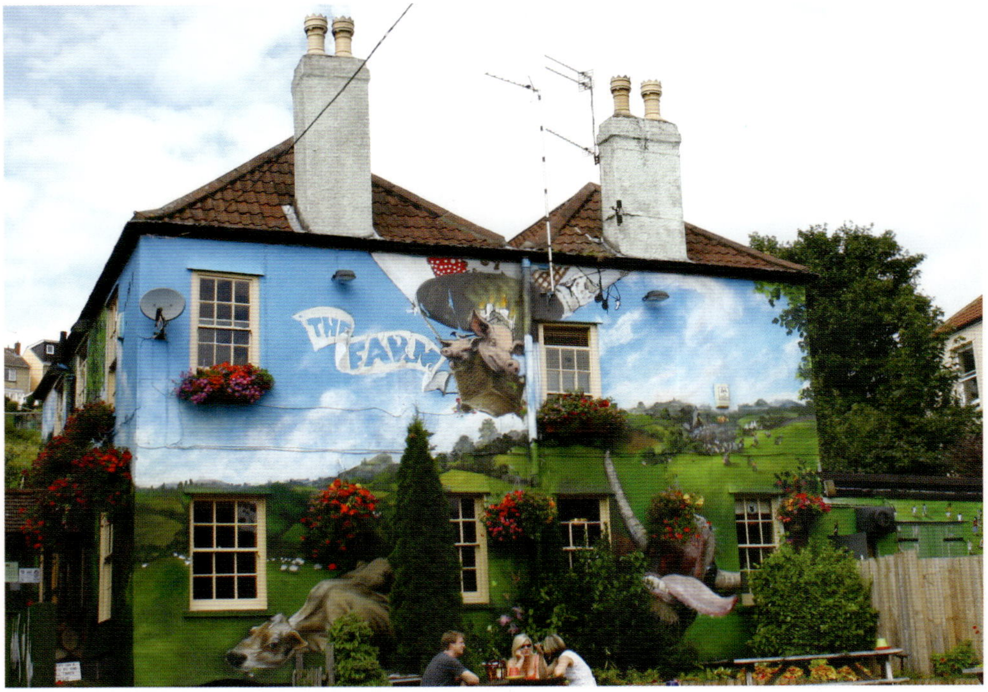

With TCF Crew's bonds built on firm and long-standing friendships, their graffiti quickly went from being something to show off about as teenagers, to a definition of who they were, giving them a shared identity and sense of purpose. That identity would ultimately see them leaving Hull to study art and spread further afield their idiosyncratic take on graffiti.

"In the same way that people started up bands at that time, we became that unified force – trying to take on the society we were in, to make our mark, and (to be honest) to impress girls. It was like 'yeah, we're that group, we do that!' I could do good stuff on my own but it was always better with two other people. It's like the old breakdance routines where some people would be good at the floor work and some people would be good at body popping. You get that respect thing, you get that buzz, where people dig what you're doing, then you just want to do more, bigger, better all the time. Then a few years later, when we'd all moved out of Hull and started meeting a lot more artists, we began to feel like we were exporting what we'd found and practising our little craft."

After studying art in Edinburgh, Xenz found himself visiting Bristol on an increasingly regular basis – until finally he settled here, reuniting with original TCF members Eko and Paris to make a big impression at 1998's Walls On Fire jam.

"When I finished college I'd come down to Bristol to visit Paris, because he was a good mate, but he was living at the other end of the country. I always found that whenever I'd come here the response to anything we were painting was just so invigorating, it was so alive with colour and positivity. Eventually I found myself

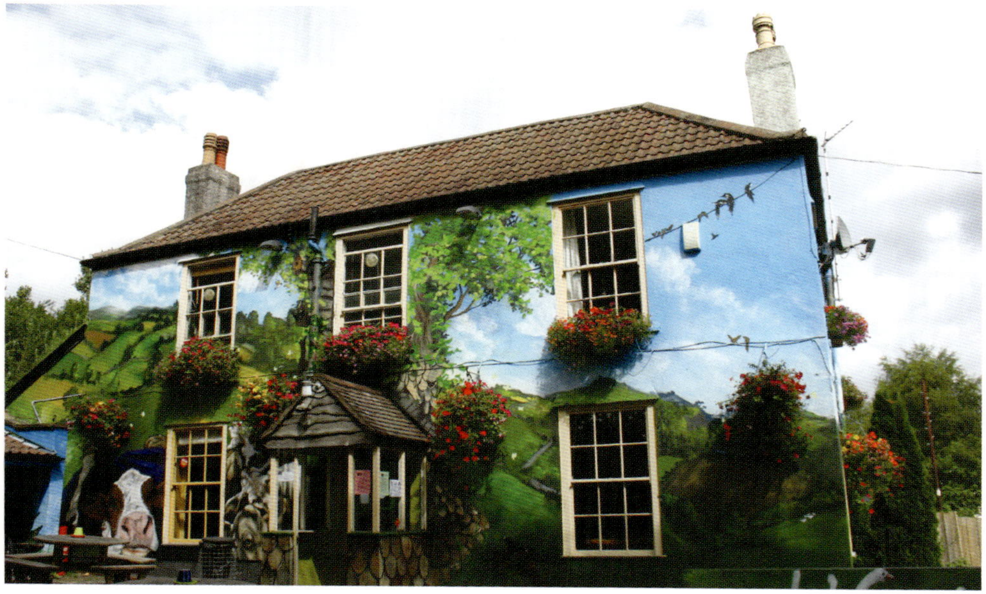

visiting more times than I was at home and so I thought 'maybe I'm going to stay down here, maybe I should find a flat?'.

"Walls On Fire was a great event - shame about the rain. Bristol was the epicentre of creativity in the mid-to-late 90s, a great place to be. Everyone was so friendly and happy... it was a buzz."

TCF made an enormous impact on Bristol, growing to a ten-strong crew whose huge productions set new standards in the city. Xenz's improvised scenes and landscapes became the glue that held these collaborative pieces together and gave them mood, space and atmosphere. It's no mean feat collaborating with so many artists on one piece, however, and ultimately Xenz is an artist on a mission with a singular vision.

"The way I work when I paint with other people, it's like I'm the drummer in the band. I do the background and the composition, I bring my 'look' to a wall, and that look is affected by the people who I'm working with - usually the people in the crew who introduce the letterforms. But it's not easy persuading a big group of egotistical maniacs to do it my way. Sometimes I think I should be in the army! It does make for a good photo, though.

"I prefer solo walls because then I only have to entertain myself and I'm quite erratic and ambitious. But it's not about ego for me - it's about scale, doing big stuff. The bigger the better, and really high quality as well - the best I can do."

Given a free rein, Xenz has become increasingly adventurous, creating ethereal pieces by playing with light and form in an impressionistic way, never quite focusing on any one point and taking the viewer's eye on an energetic journey. He has an intuitive understanding of the countless ways in which spray paint can be used, and has made its limitations (dripping, splatting, being caught by the wind) into strengths, harnessing the potential of paint made airborne by a high-pressure gas.

"Sprayed paint comes out in millions of colour particles like the dots on a big TV screen. I blend these dots until I'm happy with the colour. I feel like I'm painting a cloud that crashes into a wall and leaves a mark. Ever since I was a kid I've always seen something in splats of paint, and I've always seen things in clouds, like really vivid sculptures that I could make, almost like a hallucination. It's my imagination playing tricks on me. I've always tried to express that in my art, and the only way I can achieve that is by experimenting with mark-making, with splashes and scratches. If it's wood I'm trying to paint then the paint's got to live a bit like wood. And because I can spend a bit of time on my murals, I've learnt to do that. I practise and practise every day."

The process of constantly painting, of living and breathing your art, of dreaming about painting and then waking up and painting what you've dreamt, these feelings have been shared by artists and graffiti writers throughout history. After 20 years of solid painting, Xenz's style and approach stand on a bridge between the two: still ready to rock battle styles, whilst at the same time infusing his pieces with metaphors and subtle depth of meaning. And, like all graff writers, it started with the simple act of writing his name.

"I drew letters, but I just couldn't leave it as a simple block form; I just loved drawing buildings, so I combined landscape with perspective, but also used the X, the E, the N and the Z as compositional tools to draw the eye through the wall. Whether it looked like the letter Z or the letter N didn't really matter too much to me anymore. Instead, I started to use more symbolism, like bridges - or broken bridges, depending on my mood.

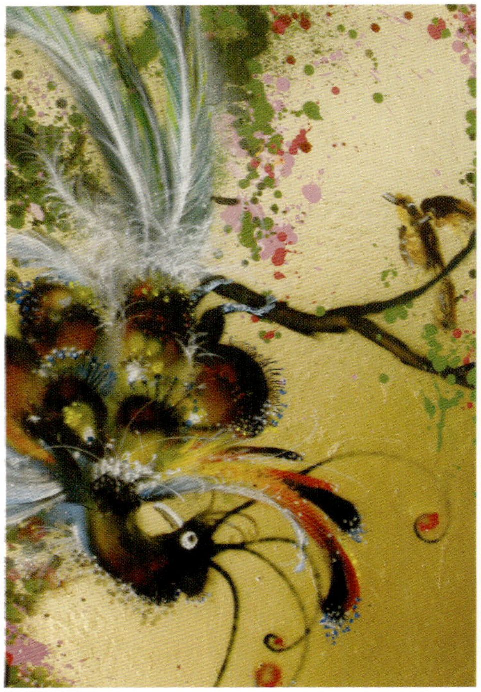

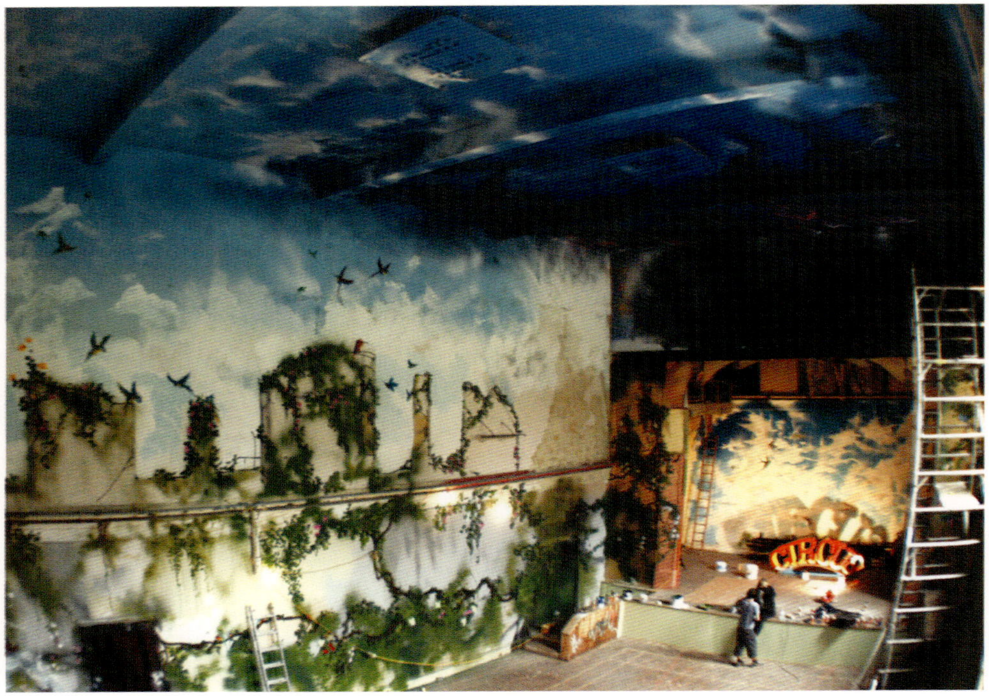

Left: 'Paradise Bird 2' mixed media on canvas, 2008

Right: Fresco for Invisible Circus, Pro Cathedral, 2007

I started to use birds and animals to give a scale to my work because I needed to exaggerate the drama in it, whilst still using the same principles used in graffiti to identify yourself. Like arrows, for example: if you're battling, the arrows are pointing outwards, or if it's in a jam they're pointing inwards, as if to say 'look at me.' These disciplines still interest me, and I still use them in my paintings now. For example, the bird motif, for me, describes how I picture myself in the art scene – beyond graffiti. As a graffiti artist, yes, but in the art scene as well. It's like, 'That's me there, on that branch, this is my favourite branch, these are my feathers, look at me!'"

Painting at graffiti jams and festivals across Europe over the last ten years has suited Xenz's process, with the act of painting almost becoming a performance in itself, its impact generated by a combination of scale and speed.

"I've always been impressed by magicians or comedians that can stand up and just release something really quickly, or perform a party trick, so what I'm thinking when I'm doing graf is, if anyone's watching me doing it, I want them to be so taken aback that they're like, 'how the fuck did you do that?' It's almost the reverse of what most people think of as graffiti, where it's done at night, at the top of a building, or wherever. If people are amazed by watching a piece evolve, from a blue square into a really nice dramatic sky with birds flying through it, then I'm glad. Turning round and seeing the delight in people's faces, that's an achievement to me."

Travelling has also given Xenz an insight into what can be done with graffiti as public art – how its long-held ambition to transform public spaces can improve the quality of people's lives in sprawling, depressingly homogenous urban spaces.

"I think we could really do with a lot more people being commissioned to paint a lot more walls. What I've noticed from painting abroad is that the councils get involved with the local artists, who are world-class graffiti artists. They commission them to paint their big buildings, and these works are going to stay there for as long as the buildings are there. That doesn't happen too much here. I'm taken aback sometimes by how much space a human being can cover with paint, with a bit of planning and a bit of foresight; and how much that can change the environment, can transform somewhere where you wouldn't even take a piss, into somewhere where you would want to sit and have a barbecue. I love that."

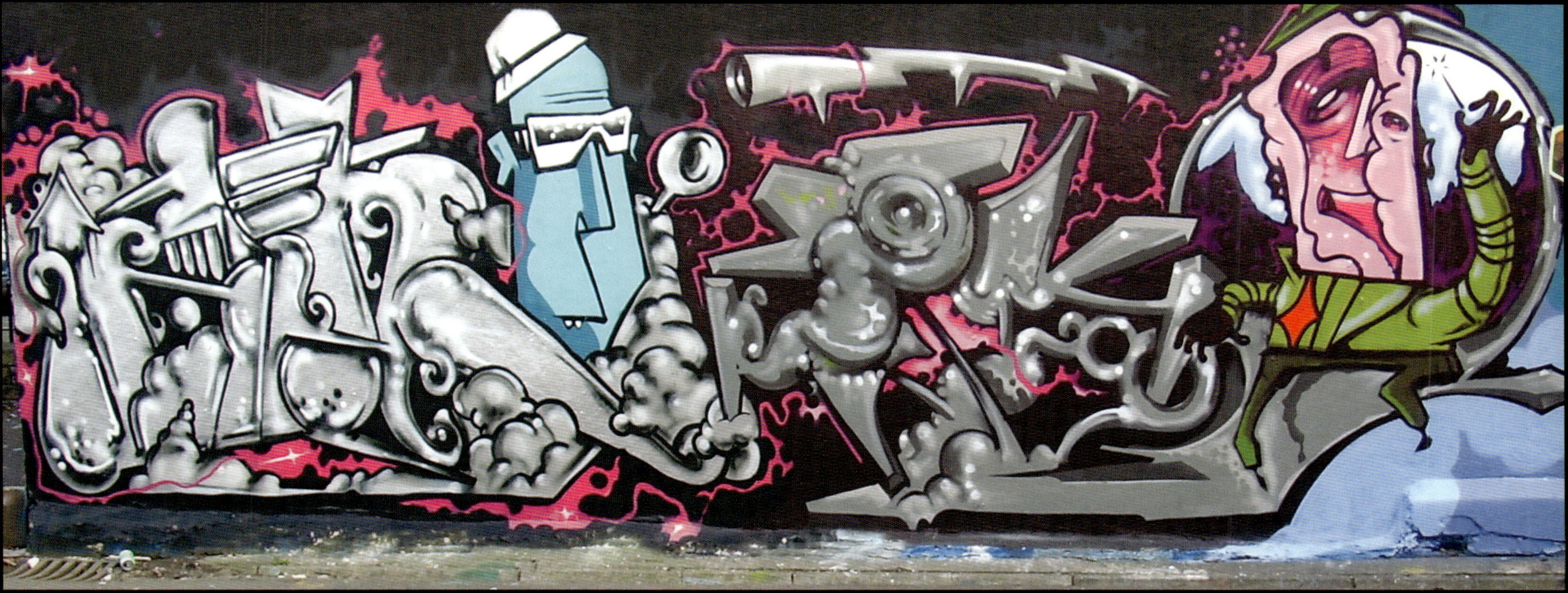

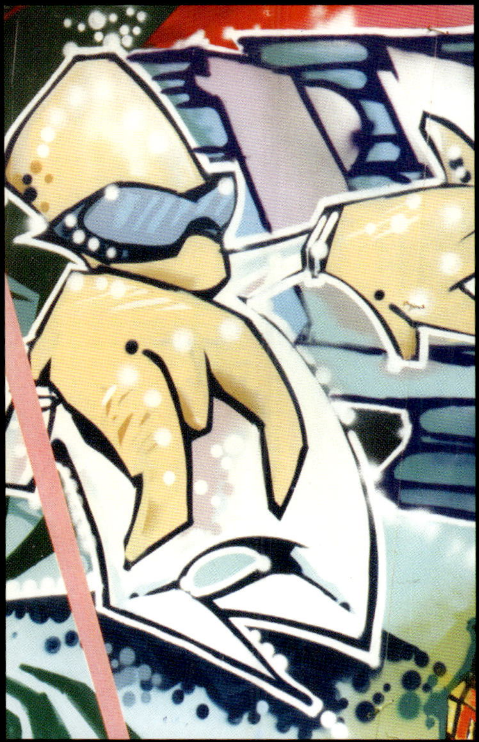

EKO TCF/DRA/IWDY/WSSK/EH?

• **Always evolving, always different, Eko's work is as unorthodox as it is playful.** The fact that he constantly surprises and remains unpredictable after more than twenty years of painting, drawing and designing is a huge testament to his talent and sheer hard work. From graffiti to record-cover artwork, whether painting for pleasure or producing commercial design, Eko's is a unique visual language, and his vocabulary is endless.

As a young graffiti writer painting in the Hull warehouses, did any of your contemporaries influence you?
"My friend Pinky, who's a well-known graffiti writer and artist, was my mentor in a lot of ways. He showed me that my starting points didn't have to be hip hop, that you didn't just take from one particular genre. He was making fucking amazing, brilliant, wigged-out individual work. He's an innovator and a free thinker. It was just so inspiring."

Hull is almost as far from Bristol as you can get in England. How did you become aware that there was some interesting graffiti being painted down here?
"I'd been to Bridlington in 1989 and was already active as a writer by then. Bridlington's about one hour north of Hull, and a whole coach load of us went. I'd been there and I'd watched Inkie paint. That was just awesome. The year before he'd done a graffiti jam in York, which is also our neck of the woods. In fact, I rang John Nation when I was a kid. I was going to come and visit. I was a proper nipper. I rang him and left a message on the Barton Hill answer phone.

Above: Two Eko pieces side-by-side, letters and characters by Eko, Bedminster skate park, 2005

Bottom left: Old-style Eko character, 1998

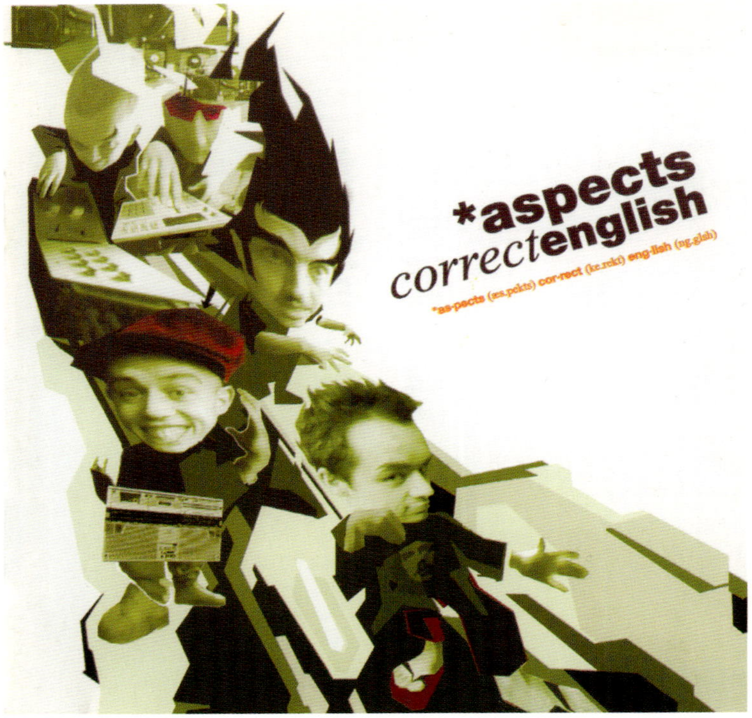

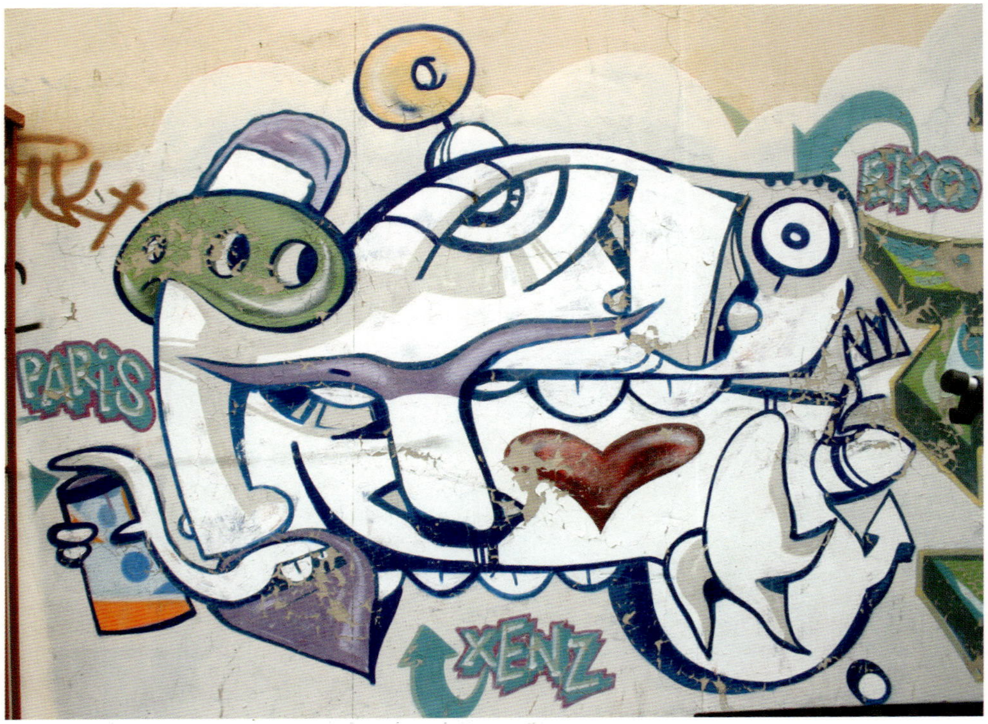

Above: *Correct English* by Aspects, illustration by Eko, design by Azlan, 2001

Top right: The three-headed creature that was the original TCF Crew, c.1998

I wanted to come and see the Dug Out, which was a weird request from someone so far from Bristol. So Bristol was already in my subconscious, already there in the back of my mind and in my knowledge of graffiti."

When did you first come down here?
"I just turned up at Glastonbury Festival in 1997 and painted some boards and stuff. That was an entirely new world, because I'd come from warehouse painting. The commercial side of it - the links between Bristol and the Festival, that was all new to me. There was a really great vibe about that, and I met Inkie for the first time, which was a massive moment. That was a big deal, actually meeting him - he was my hero, and he's a legend in the UK. He didn't influence me style-wise, but I sensed there was something about what he was doing which was completely original.

"It was also the first time I met Feek as well, which was awesome. I sort of fell in love with Feek instantly; he was just really positive. He'd only been painting for six months or something and it was one of the first things he'd done, so his enthusiasm for it was just beautiful and his characters blew me away."

What was it that made you decide to make Bristol your home?
"Paris was knocking around with Bubba Louie and El Eye out of Aspects, and they said, 'When we do a record, you're going to do our sleeve for us.' That's why I moved to Bristol. That was a real starting point for me because they bugged out on what they saw, and were really enthusiastic [about my work]. They were really welcoming and I liked that, because it was a creative community. It was all really new.

"At that point I was living in the moment. That's all I did. I lived and breathed graffiti and spray paint. That was one of the first moments when I'd actually thought about the future and thought, 'Yeah, that'd be something to aim for.' I was like, 'the weather's good, it's a new scene, I've done I don't know how many years of painting up North.' It was just brilliant. I moved to Bristol and just let rip."

When you moved here, you were mostly painting characters, weren't you? I've seen you paint letters as well. Do you think the two require a fundamentally different approach?
"You loosen up doing the characters,

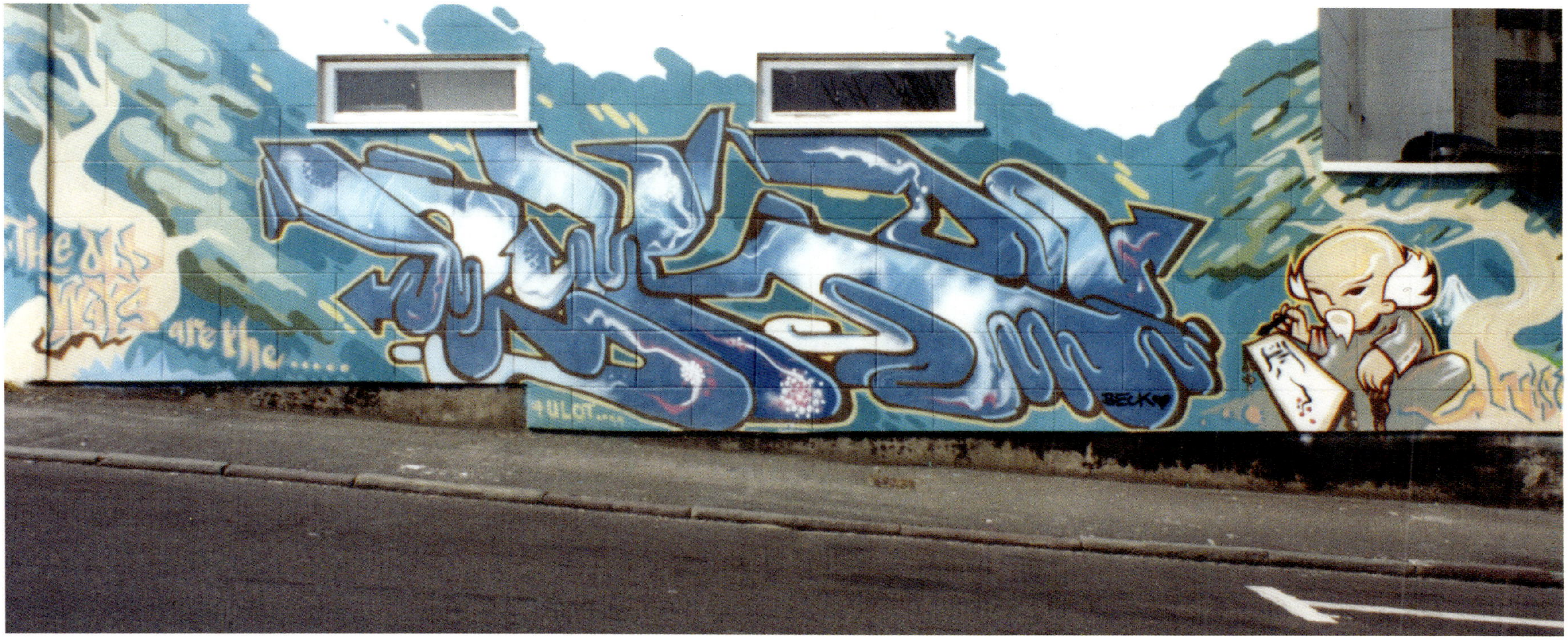

you've got a certain mentality you take on when you do them; and then you have to switch your brain to do lettering. They are interlinked, they have a lot of the same moves and grooves about them; but I used to separate the actual discipline of painting a character and painting a bit of lettering, so that I could do each of them well. At the bottom of my heart, I'm a purist in a way."

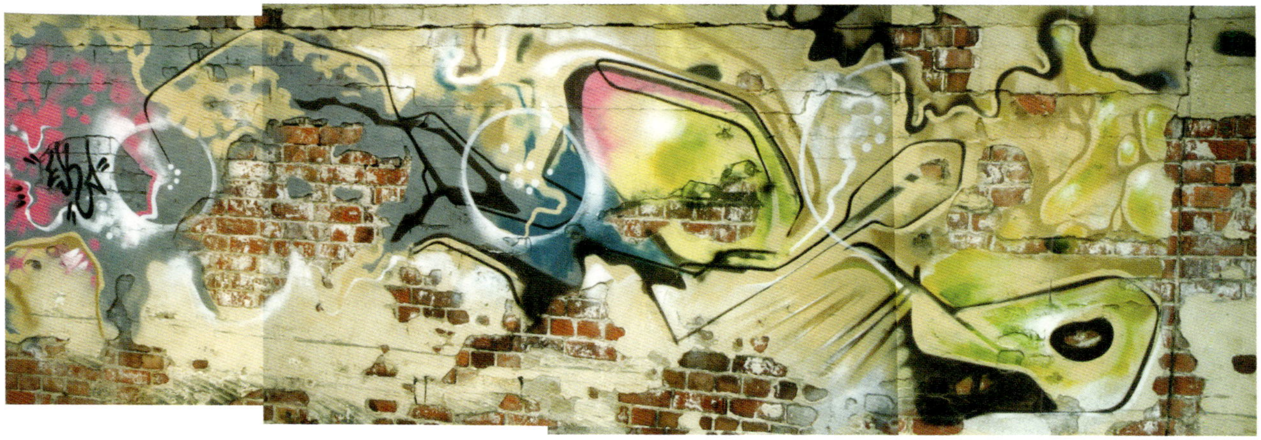

What was the creative climate like in Bristol after you arrived? The scene underwent something of a renaissance, didn't it?

"There was this mid-point, I guess about 1999-2000, where everyone was crossing over. There were people who were illustrators, like Duncan (Jago) and Will (Barras) who were wanting to paint walls, because they'd been around graffiti writers, and they were taking it from new angles and showing us what could be done. And there was a really nice equal, opposite process, where I was coming from a graffiti background and was starting to think about print and illustration. I was twisting that up in the same way that they were twisting up the painting on walls. That was really an important stage for me. I'd been painting for 15 years, they'd been drawing or doing illustration for however many years, and that was a really interesting period.

Top: 'The Old Ways Are The Wise Ways' Zen wisdom from Eko, St. Andrew's, 1997

Above: Eko freestyle incorporating exposed brick in the flow of the piece, 2000

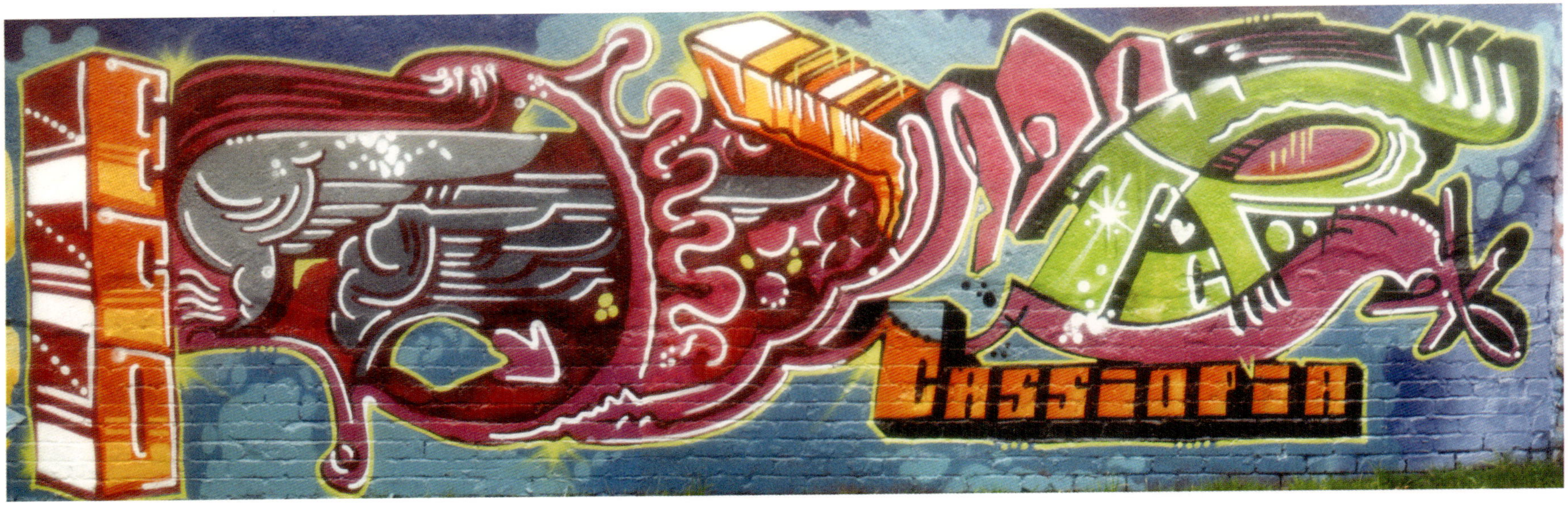

Above: 'Cassiopia' Eko lets the freestyle muse take hold, Bedminster skate park, 2002

Through my association with them, I got a renewed excitement for illustration."

You've pretty much painted everything in your time: not just letters and characters, but backgrounds, abstract forms and so on. Can you talk about the graffiti aesthetic as a whole, and what defines it?
"That's why I was drawn to this craft, because of the aesthetic of it. I don't want to lose that when I'm doing graff. That's important for me, and now it just happens, it's a part of my psyche. There are those shapes and angles that you only really get in graffiti. I could draw you a line and say, 'this is graffiti,' just by using certain lines. There are recurring angles in graffiti that, bizarrely, you don't see a lot elsewhere. You can look at an unorthodox piece of graffiti, something quite cutting-edge, and you could get the 'graffiti protractor' out and find that it'll still have those angles going on. I see them in Mr Jago's work especially. He's definitely got the protractor out."

The 'graffiti protractor?' So there are a certain set of angles inherent in all graffiti?
"Yeah, if you take it down to the bare essentials we're all making similar shapes – whether you're a purist, a bomber or whatever."

Looking at your work, it seems to be constantly changing and pretty far removed from 'mainstream' graffiti. I don't ever remember it looking generic or much like anyone else's style.
"I think that in a lot of ways I've transcended that visual language of graffiti. But it's still there, the angles are still there. I'm into moving forward and discovering stuff, but I'm always going to do graffiti – it's my first love, it's what enabled me to get to where I am and it's what excites me."

Is sketching an important part of your creative process? I guess sketchbooks are where new approaches evolve...
"It's absolutely everything. What my sketchbooks provide is a sanctuary. It's my way of calming myself and also of travelling, it's a transportation sort of thing. It's the same thing as reading a book, only these are my own words. So rather than picking up a book and reading it, I'm writing my own book in a way. Sketchbooks should be playgrounds, not places where you go and fine-tune things.

"I look at the sketchbook as being like a big well that goes down and down. I'm just drawing until I'm at the bottom on my own and all I can see is the page in front of me. I've forgotten everything and I'm there. It's like a meditation. That's where anything of value's going to come out: it's where you'll find the treasures."

Do the pages of your sketchbooks act as blueprints for your pieces when you paint on a wall?
"I find it really hard to draw something and reproduce it on a wall. That's partly because I've drawn it once, so why would I

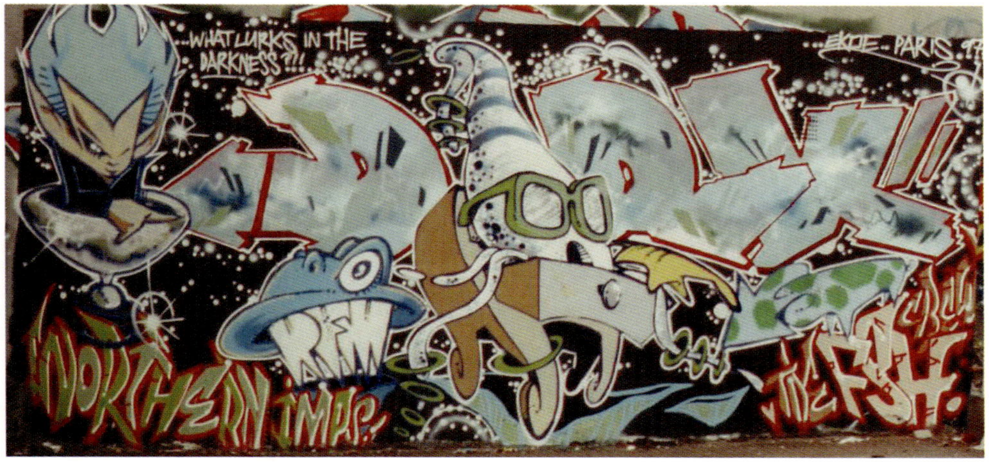

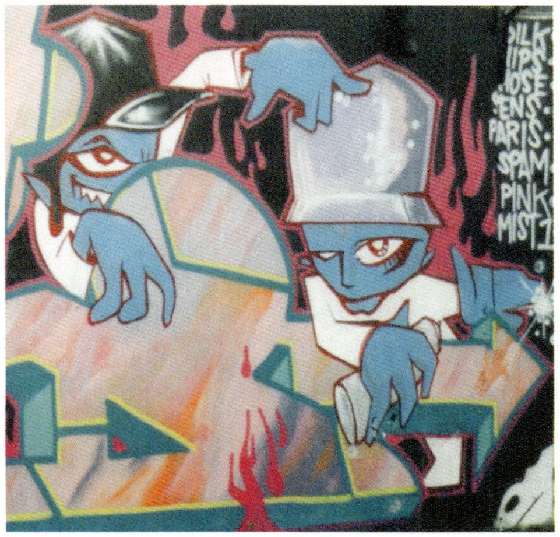

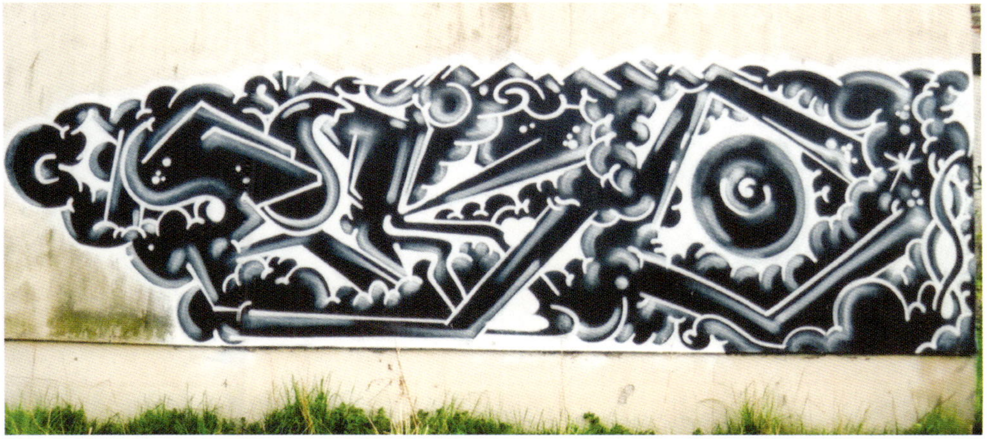

Top left: 'What Lurks In The Darkness' Eko and Paris, 1997, Bedminster skate park

Top right: 'Blue fiends', Millionaire's Club hall of fame, c.1999

Bottom left: Reversed-out Eko piece, 2005

want to draw it again? What I tend to do is use my drawing as a tone – to get a couple of shapes down, and a general idea. Then I forget about the drawing completely, and then you've got to look at it as a wall.

"I might have only half an E and a K, but then I change what needs to be changed so that it works with that space in front of me. It works for me because how I felt when I did the drawing is different to how I feel when I'm stood in front of the wall, and what works well on paper isn't necessarily going to work well on the wall.

Do you think that your dyslexia plays a part in how your mind works creatively? From what I can gather, it amounts to the brain being wired differently, affecting perception and interpretation among other things.
"Apparently, a lot of dyslexics gravitate towards art. What they find is that when you're dyslexic your brain has to work twice as hard to do everyday tasks, and so parts of your brain swell and get really strong and over-compensate. So when you're doing tasks like writing, your brain's working twice as hard, but when you're doing something that doesn't involve having to verbalise something, like drawing or problem-solving with shapes and colours, then your brain's over-developed. So it's not about 'intelligence', but when you're seven and you can't write and you can't read, it's really hard."

Looking back at your work over the last ten years, you seem to be one of the few artists from a graffiti background who doesn't have a specific style, or a fixed way of doing things.
"It's just too confining, and it kind of shoots you in the foot. This is why I struggle with making art sales. It can't happen because I move on too often. I move along and do something different all the time. It's hard for people to sell my work. Probably one of the only conscious things I do is to try to produce something different each time, because otherwise I'll just get bored of it. If I find something that works, I can't flog it and flog it, because my personality changes all the time."

And yet you've worked successfully for the recording and fashion industries

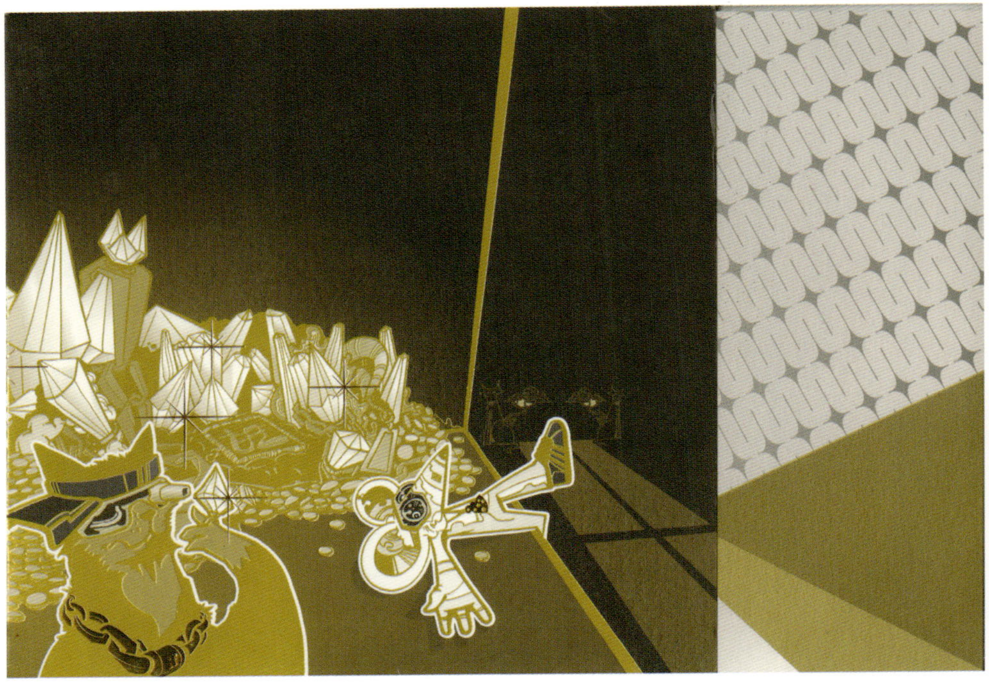

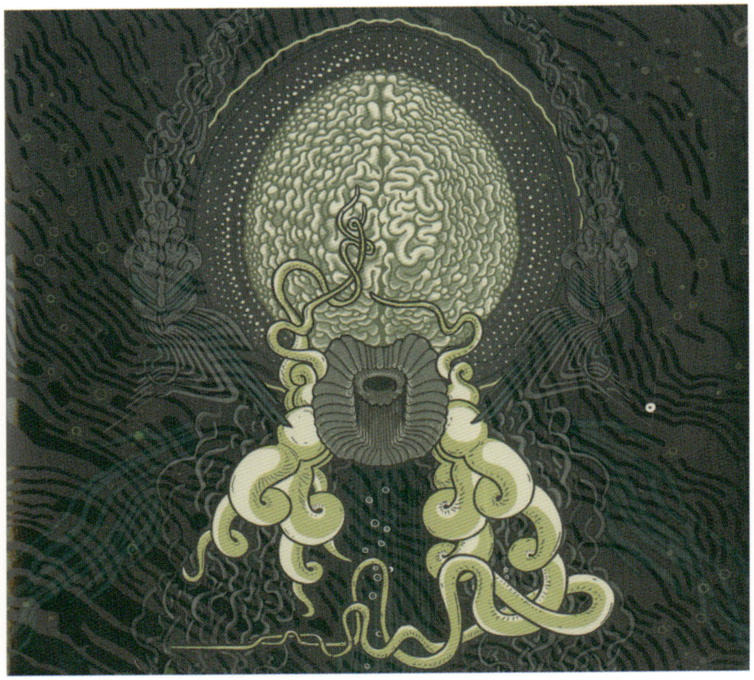

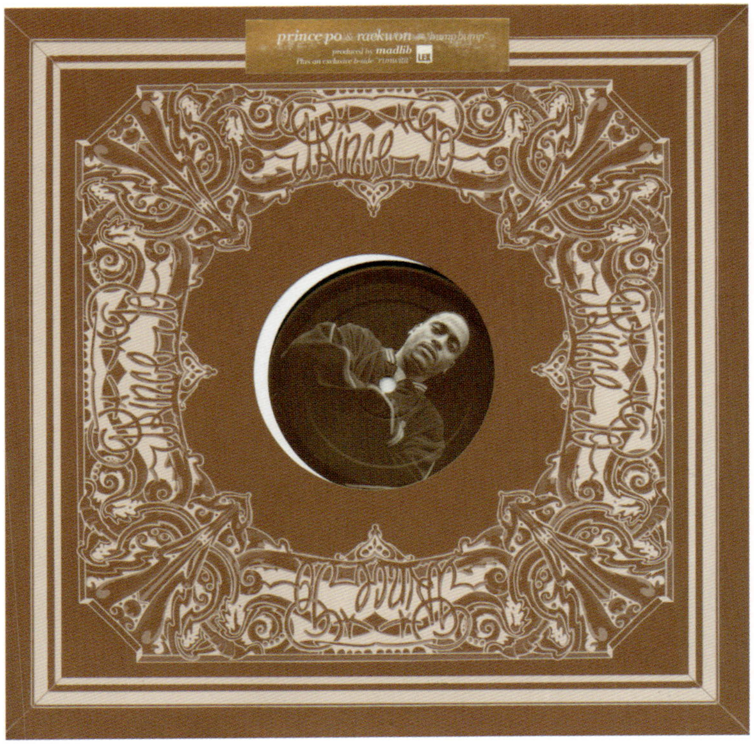
prince po & raekwon
produced by madlib

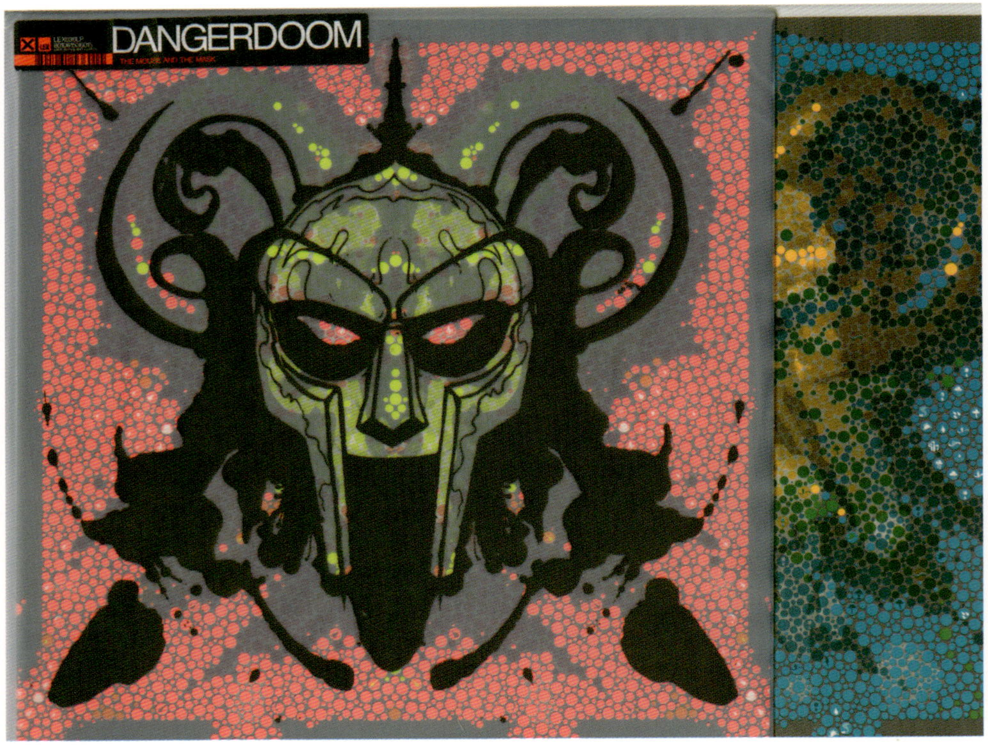
DANGERDOOM
THE MOUSE AND THE MASK

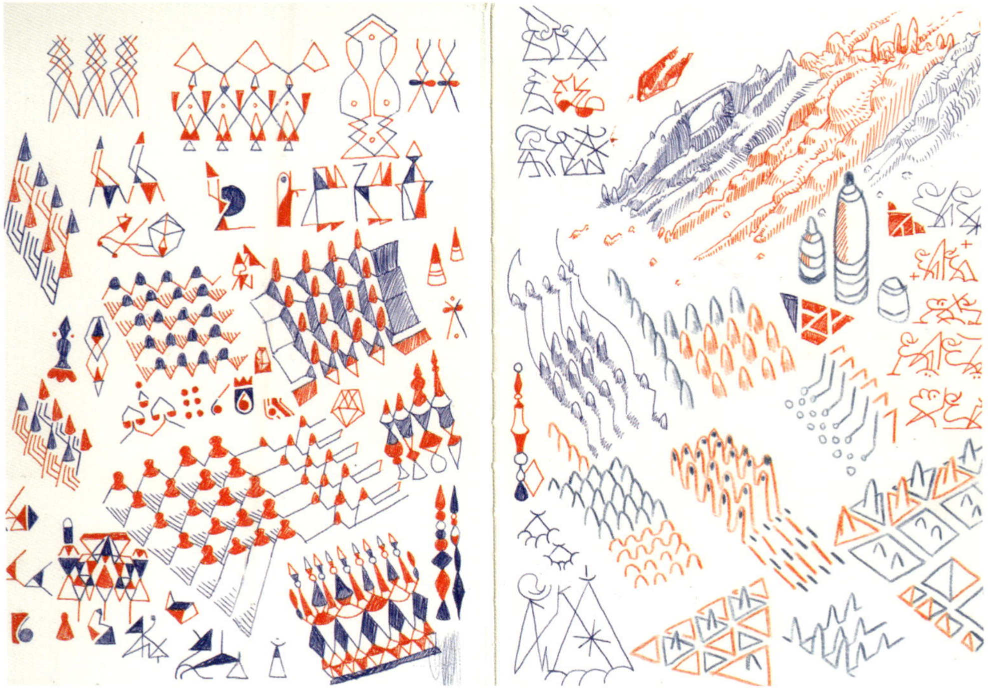

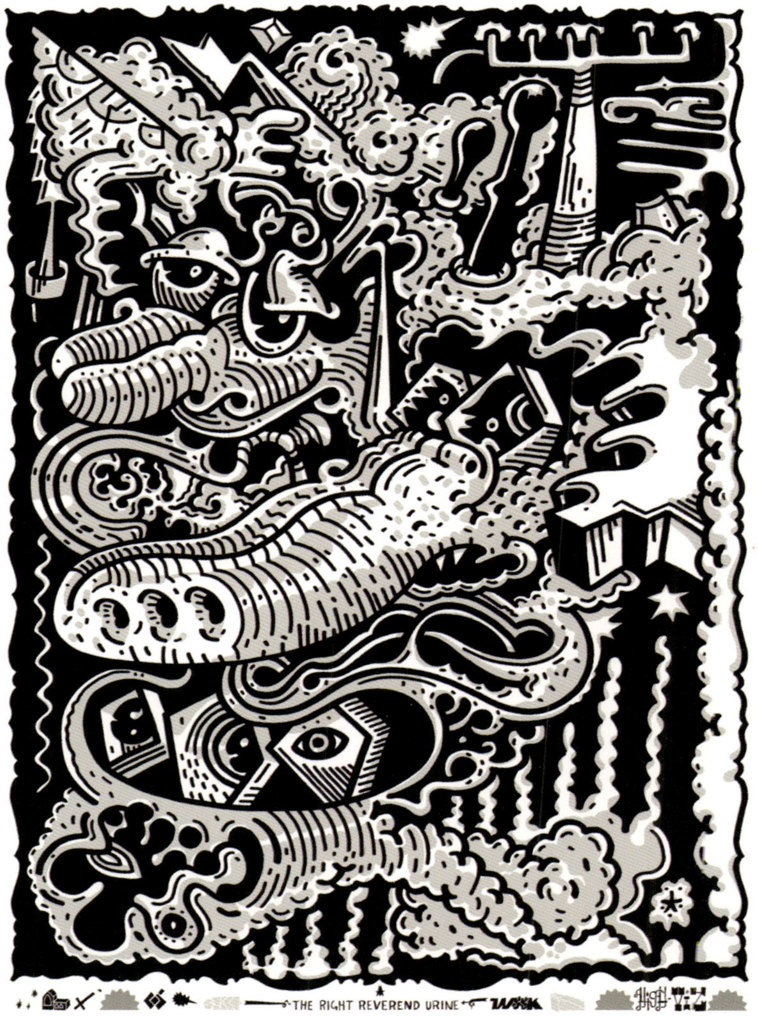

for a long time. Maybe it's only the art market that requires work we can always recognise, stylistically, as being by a particular artist?
"I think that's why commercial success with the record sleeves for Lex Records has been nice, because it relies on me not doing the same thing for each artist. I have to do something different each time, each with a distinctive style, and that works for me. At the same time, there's a lot of freedom, something you wouldn't get in another sector of design or illustration."

Do you think reinvention is the key to originality? It seems to be an undervalued quality in art and design these days.
"There's a difference between absorbing something – putting it through your own filter process – and looking at something and physically copying it. Everyone's got a different depth. I'm coming around to the idea that nothing's original except things that come out of technological advances. I feel like a bit of an old knob saying that, but part of me thinks it's probably the truth.

"Picasso said that being a genius is about how well you hide where you stole your ideas from. It's quite simplistic, how he put it, but you take ideas from stuff, and it's up to you how much you mix it up before you put it out again. It's reworking stuff to make it look original, which is what Picasso said. That's where the excitement lies."

Opposite page. Top left: *Ghetto Pop Life* LP by Danger Mouse and Gemini. Cover design by Eko with Eh? (Lex Records, 2003)

Top right: *Craft Of The Lost Art* LP by Shape Of Broad Minds. Cover design by Eko with Eh? (Lex Records, 2007)

Bottom left: *Bump Bump* by Prince Po and Raekwon. Cover design by Eko with Eh? (Lex Records, 2004)

Bottom right: *The Mouse And The Mask* LP by Dangerdoom (Danger Mouse and MF Doom). Cover design by Eko with Eh? (Lex Records, 2005)

This page. Top left: Sketchbook spread, 2008

Top right: 'Right Reverend Urine' illustration, 2006

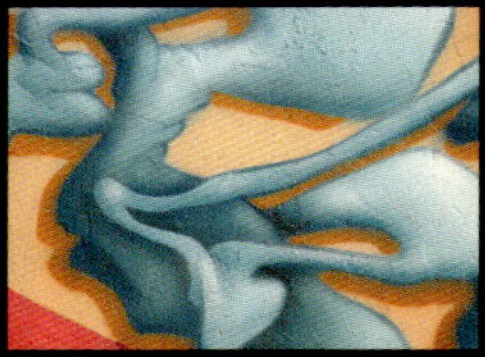

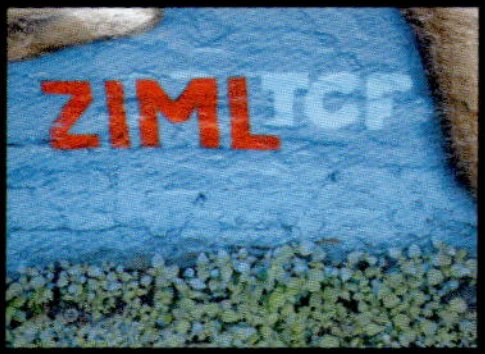

Right: Jumbo size piece, 2007

Bottom right: Ziml at work

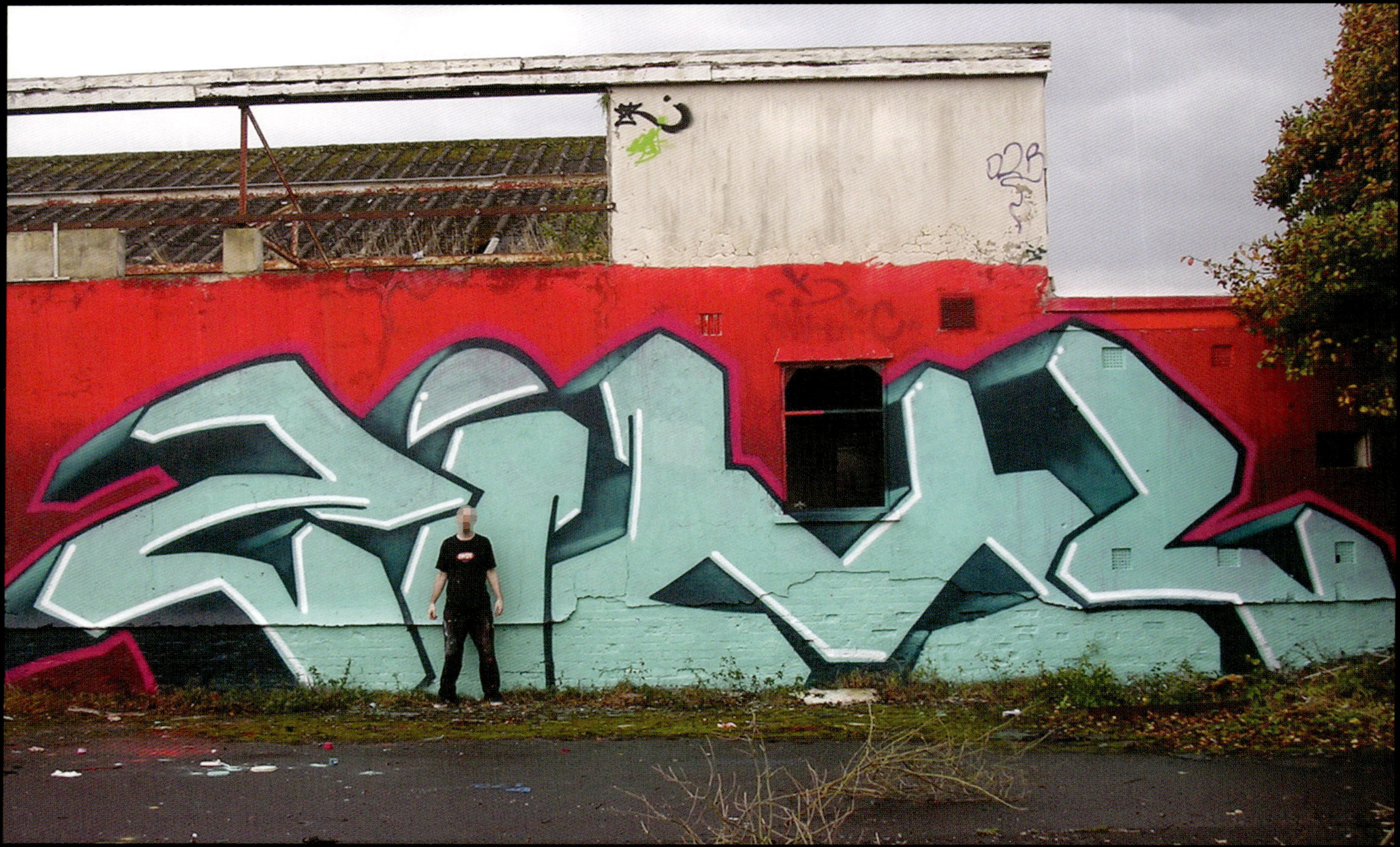

ZIML TCF/DRA/IWDY

• **Ziml is like a mad professor, an obsessive technician whose graffiti is experimental and futuristic.** And yet, at the same time, he focuses almost solely on the original icon of the art form: the word, the name, the tag, the artist's alter ego. Ziml's graphic language of choice is wildstyle, created by New York graffiti pioneers to make their letters overlap, bounce, interconnect and, most importantly, rock the sides of the subway cars they stole a ride on.

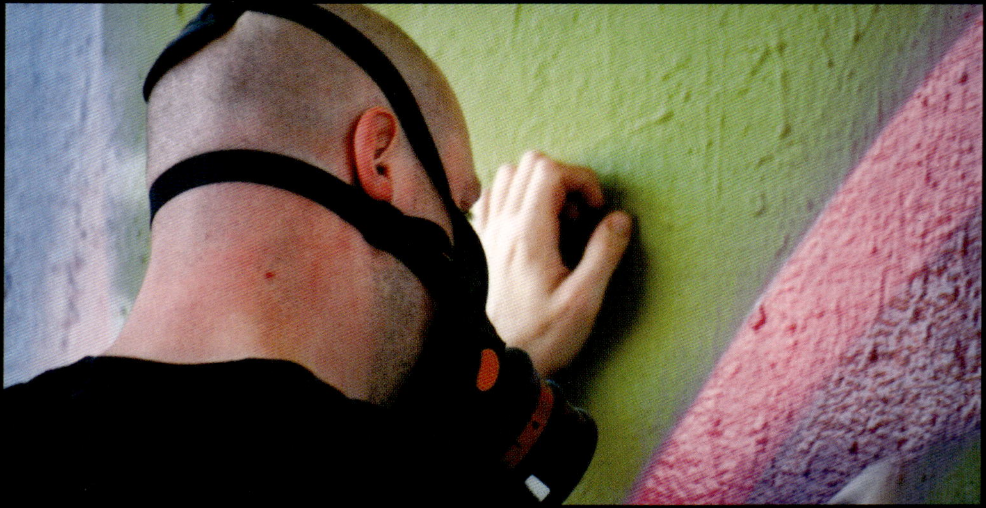

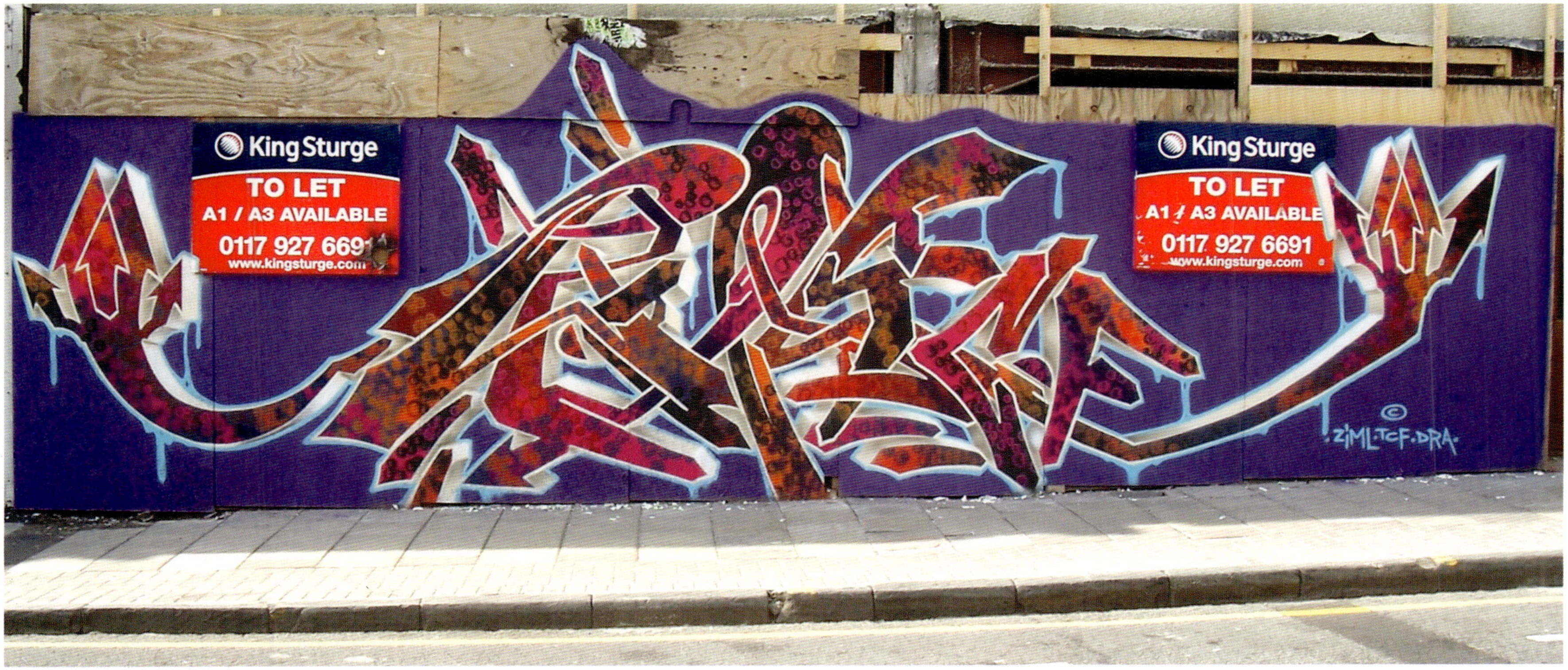

Above: Burner with tridents, Gloucester Road, 2007

"I fuck with my letters, so they're still recognisable but I've pushed the possibilities of what they can be. I'm asking, 'what constitutes a letter?' It's almost like: 'it's that letter because I say it's that letter'. That then takes you into the broader realm of how you actually perceive a word. When you look at a word, you don't really read each letter: you almost create a pictogram, or a symbol, which is made up from those shapes. But to me the letters are still the most important things, and if you strip away the accessories they should stand up on their own. I'm dressing pieces up with various bits and pieces; the connections and the arrows, they're like little formulas, little aesthetic additions."

Painting wildstyle pieces demonstrates a writer's mastery of style on a complex level, in a context where words mutate into something more abstract. Ziml's pieces are a storm of juxtaposed forms that jostle, intertwine and interact in different ways.

"It all comes down to style and movement. When you're making a wildstyle piece, you're painting something that has impact and power, energy and dynamics - but in a static object. There's this kind of universal flow that is applicable to all this shit. Sometimes the letters have degraded to the point where their identity is getting tenuous, the letters are all still in there but they're pushed to the limit of intelligibility."

Having the right letters in a tag - letters that work together and that a writer feels comfortable painting - are essential to the evolution of a personal lettering style. Ziml's idiosyncratic tag is indicative of his unconventional approach, and its evolution hints at his progressive way of working.

"I used to write Smell but I got so sick of doing the S every time that I changed it round and turned it into a Z, which made it a bit more interesting. From then on, it was a little bit like doing plastic surgery: it became more exciting to write and to look at each time, through the evolution from Smell to Zmel, to Zee-Mell to Ziml."

Ziml's style is constantly changing, and these days - apart from the structural elements - few of what you would recognise as traditional graffiti letter shapes remain. But solid 3-D effects and connections between letters and arrows (he has devised his own, where two painted parallel to one another interlock to create a third) are part of a unique visual dialect,

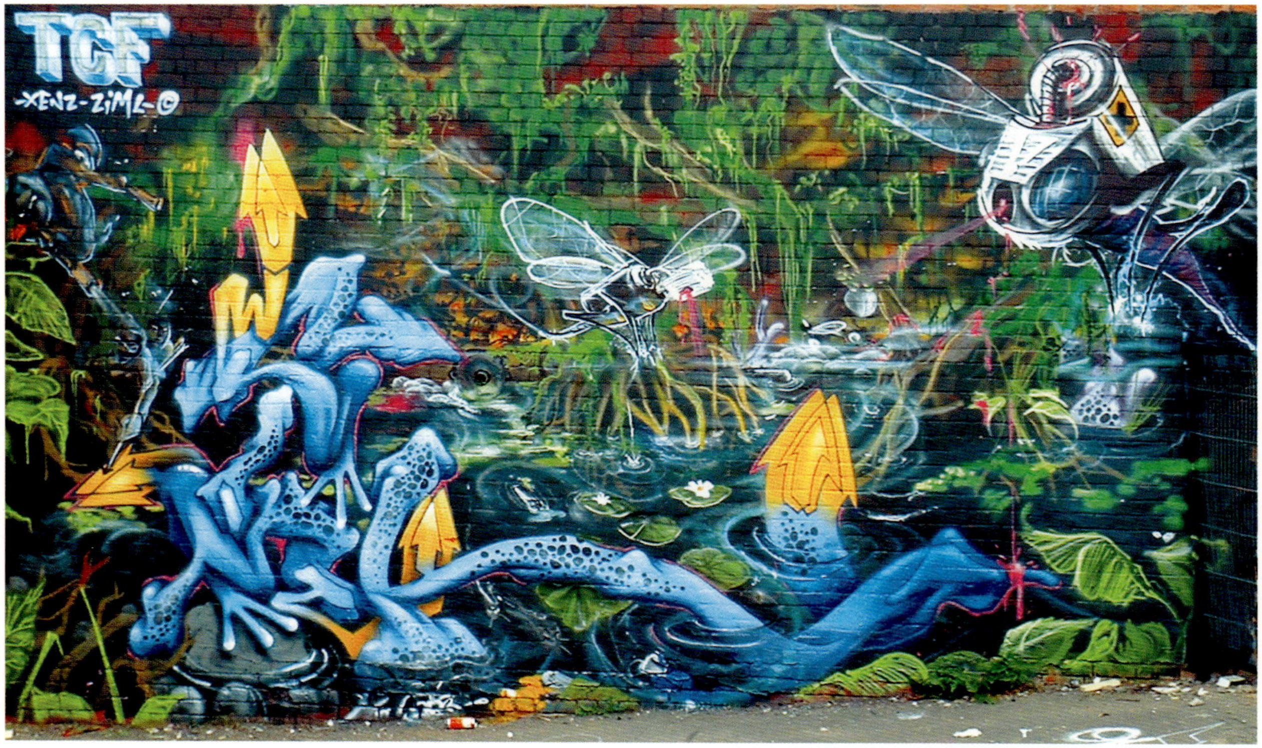

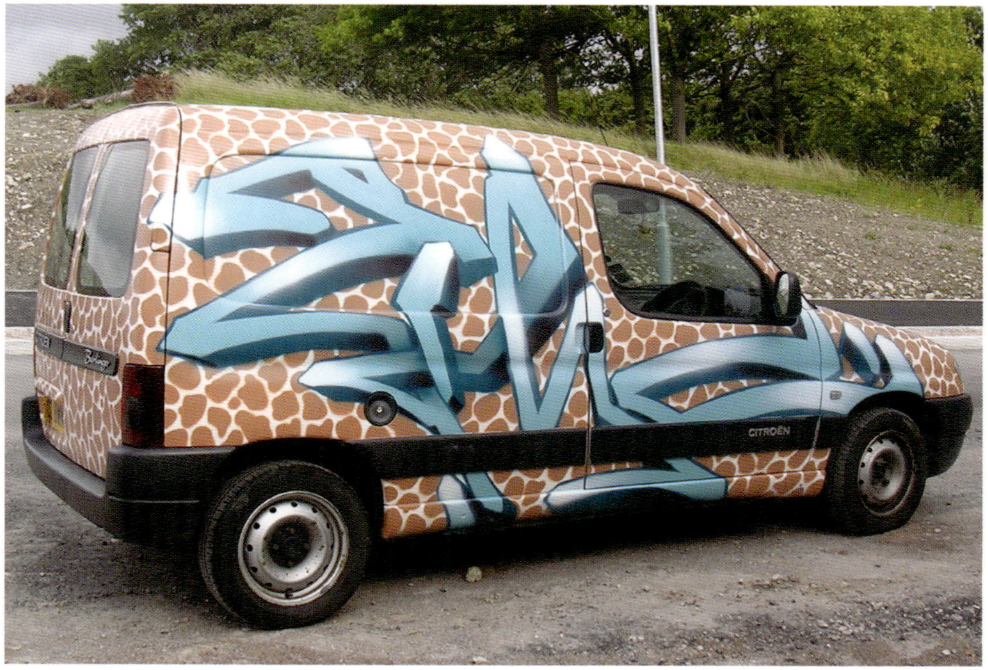

Above: Xenz and Ziml in the swamp, Bedminster skate park, 2004

Right: Patterned van, 2008

Opposite page. Top: The 'Zimulator' making his mark on society, Bedminster skate park, 2004

Left: 'Smell: Edward Skin Up Hands,' 1996

Middle right: Customised Adidas, Angelus Leather Paint, 2005

Bottom right: 'Blue 3D' Acrylic on canvas, 2004

born from countless long nights doodling, designing and painting in Hull.

"In Hull we were cranking out pieces at a massive rate - and we had no idea whether people were seeing them or not, so we got to the point where we were only doing it for ourselves. We were doing it to do each other's heads in, to see how stupid we could be, and from that grew an attitude of not needing validation from other people. Me and (old school Hull writer) Pinky started doing these drawings where you'd literally draw as fast as you could with the word (you were designing) in your head. We weren't trying to construct some complex style, we were just doing these totally bugged out scribbles that would contain the essence of the word.

"We'd sit there and say 'what's the most fucked up thing I've drawn? No one would ever paint that shit - right, that's what I'm off to paint!' We had this total freedom, this total abandonment of the rules of graffiti. I was always a letter writer but I didn't allow myself to be constrained by having to conform to one thing or another. Basically you could pretty much have a mental breakdown on paper so long as it had an outline, a band and a 3-D!"

An enduring connection exists between the graffiti scenes of Bristol and Hull and for Ziml it goes back nearly 20 years to the days of fanzines, packs of photos swapped by post, and the seminal World Graffiti Championships held in Bridlington in 1989.

"It was a key moment. It created a lot of connections between people - there were these A5 flyers, designed by Inkie, that were dished out to everyone at Bridlington. When you traded packs of photos with people, they would be in there. [Pioneering Hull writer] Equal was already in touch with John Nation

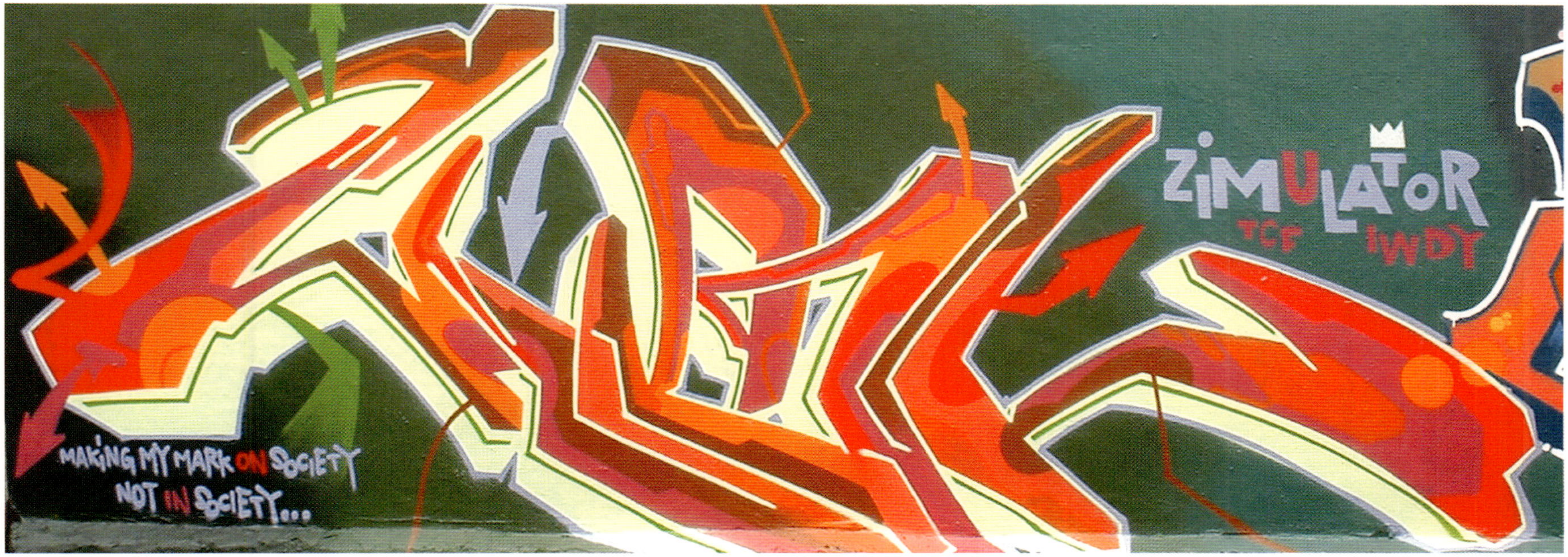

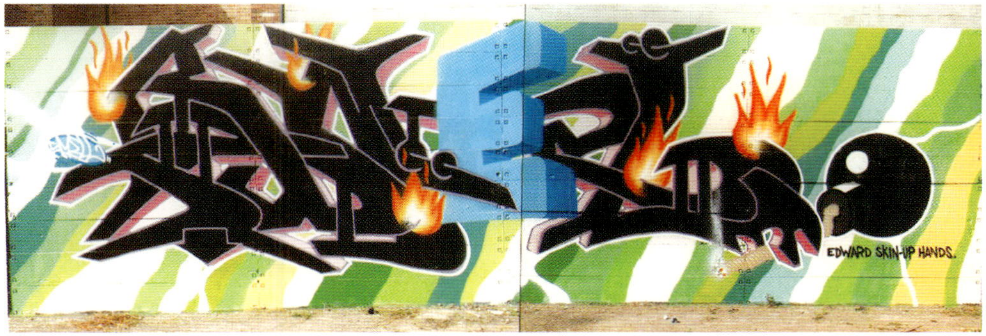

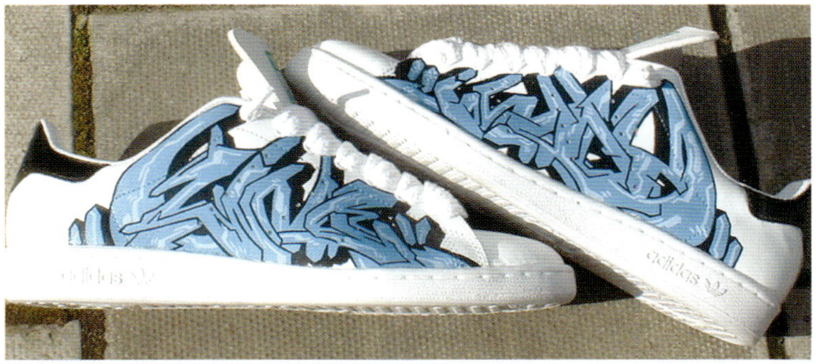

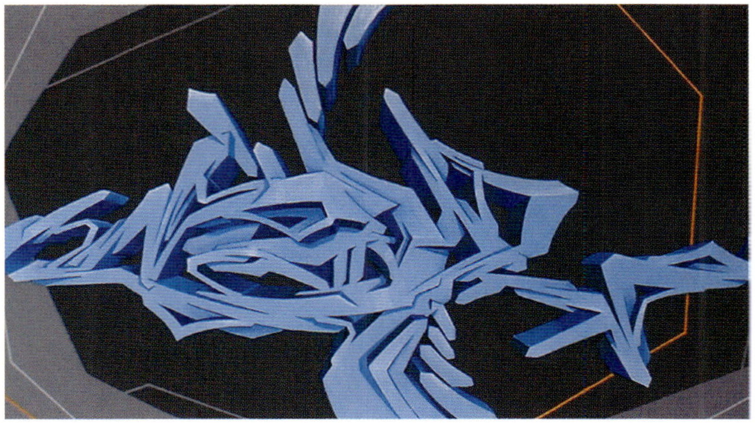

by this time, and I got his address from this card. I was sending him all this crazy stuff, and I started receiving these packages of high-quality shit back from him. John was a pioneer."

The seeds had been sown, and ten years later Ziml moved to Bristol and found himself living and painting with old Hull rivals TCF – who historically had been at war with his crew, DRA.

"In Hull there was this whole east/west thing going on. DRA were on one side of town and TCF were on the other, so I couldn't ever imagine being in TCF. But after being in Bristol for a while and painting with them I just wrote it in on a piece, because by then I was in TCF, it just made sense. The Bristol scene was there to be penetrated, but we didn't have any grudge or malice, like 'we've got to take over the city'. There was nothing like that, it was more, 'I need space to paint so I'm going to take it'."

These days Ziml is still based in Bristol

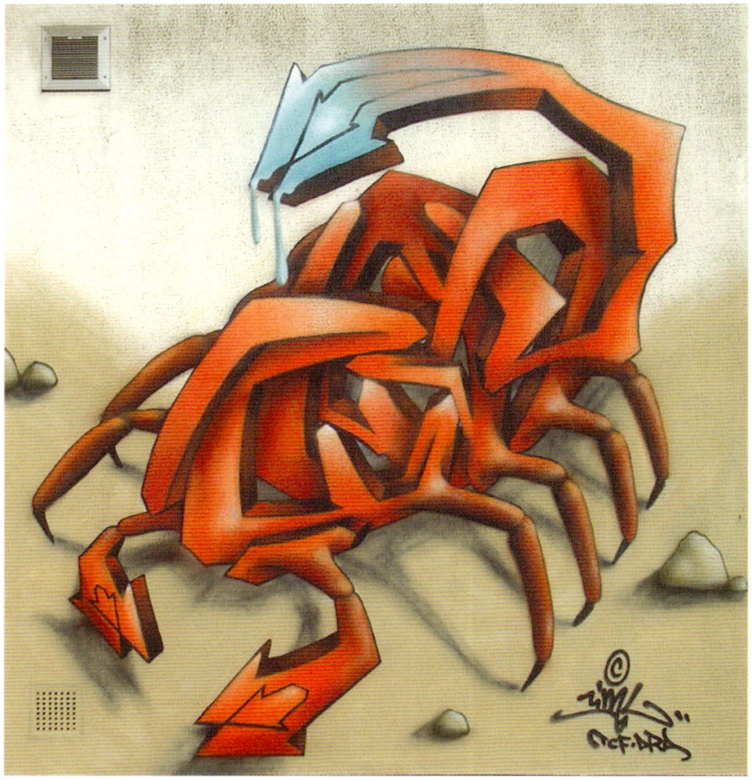

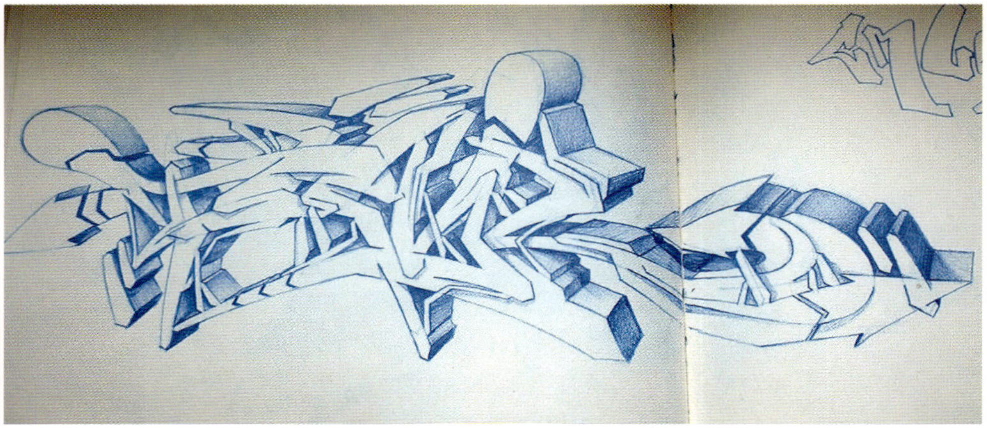

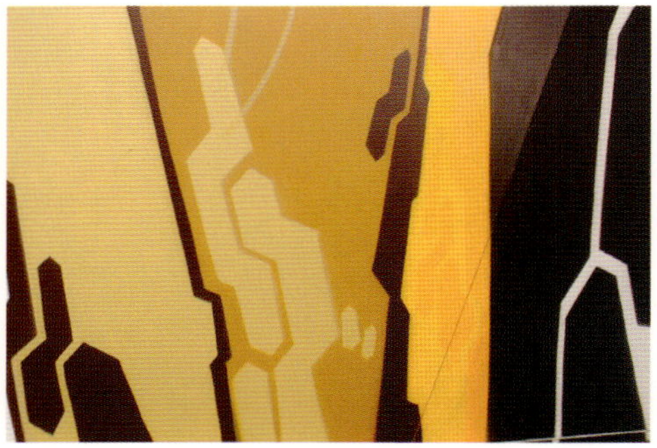

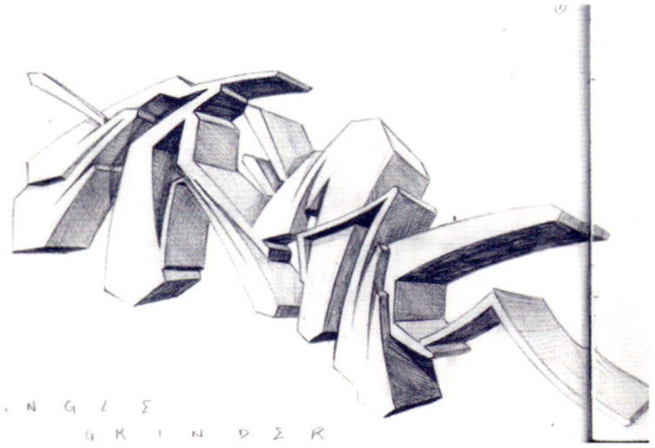

This page. Top left: 'Scorpio' 2007

Top right: Blue pencil sketch, 2004

Right: 'Angle Grinder' sketch, 2004

Middle: Detail, 'Strongbow Rooms' 2005

Opposite page. Top: Originality is the key. Ziml lets the biters know, 2004

Below: 'The Zimulative System,' Anatomy of a piece, old Bristol General Hospital, 2007

and, while continuing to explore and develop new forms in his pieces, he's also finding an increasing number of commercial vehicles for his work.

"I now make a living purely as an artist and designer. Sometimes I do what you might call 'graffiti' jobs, painting graffiti letters as part of a commission; other times I might be doing T-shirt designs with letters. I also do sign writing and set painting, which uses a lot of the materials and skills I developed from graffiti; and I work in print design, more specifically for screen-printing. I also work customising trainers, as a completely separate part of my career, and have designed and brought out production trainers with a very well-known brand.

"I'd say overall that graffiti has helped me develop a lot of traditional art and design skills, but through a non-traditional route. I have an interesting working life, doing really varied work that challenges me. I work in a whole load of different disciplines at different times, so I've always got a mix of stuff on the go. I'm constantly thinking up new things I want to make happen, and I always enjoy new challenges. For me it's about the buzz of making something new and interesting happen, and solving the problems that that poses."

Ziml remains consistently hungry and focused. He appears to take great pleasure in ensuring that the outcome of each visual experiment he undertakes is fresh, precise and, most importantly, has style.

"Overall you can sum up what I do with the words 'technical', 'creative' and 'fun'. Most of what I do has an underlying theme of wanting to get up and have an impact, which comes from being involved in graffiti since I was 12 years old. I don't want it to be me personally in the spotlight like a performer or celebrity though. I like my various outputs to be in the spotlight, with me watching anonymously from the sidelines."

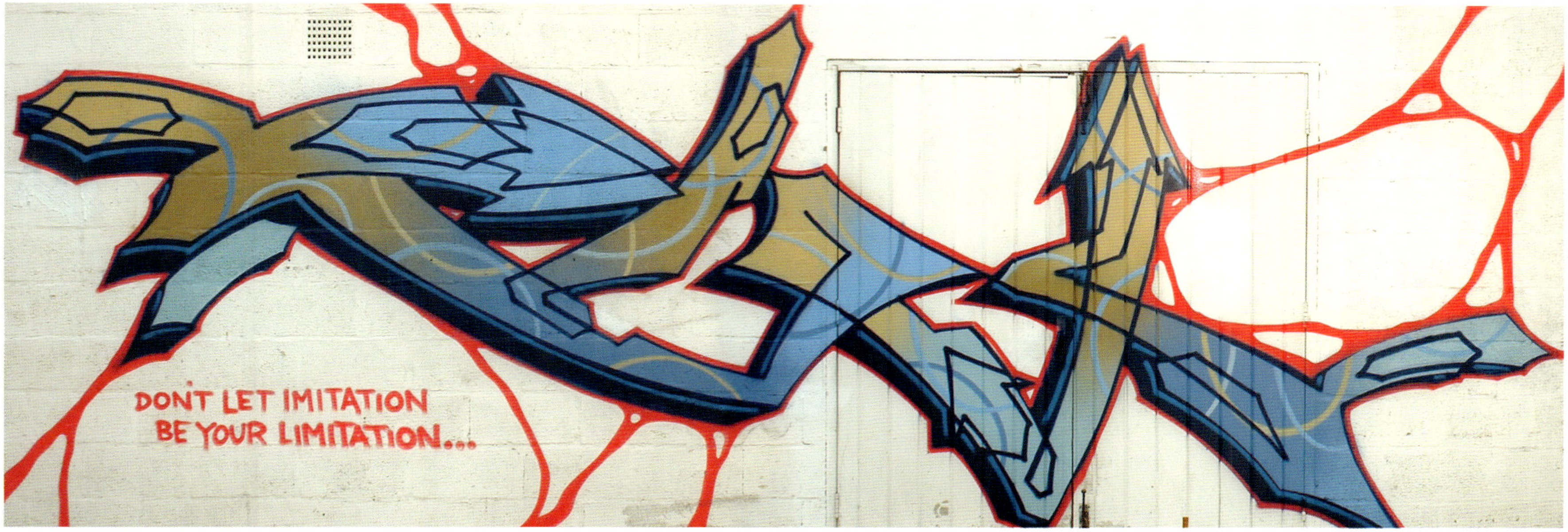
DON'T LET IMITATION
BE YOUR LIMITATION...

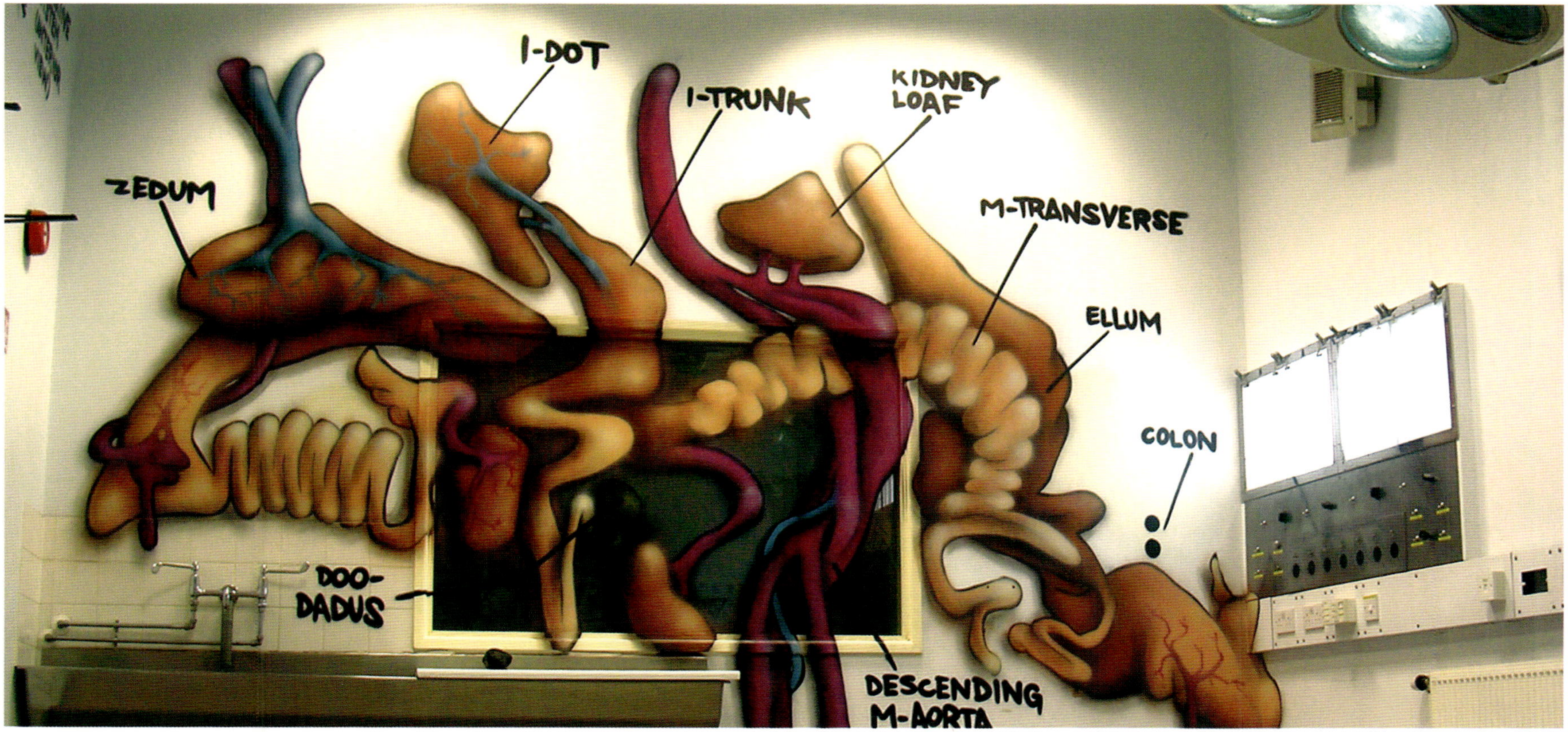
I-DOT
I-TRUNK
KIDNEY
LOAF
ZEDUM
M-TRANSVERSE
ELLUM
COLON
DOO-
DADUS
DESCENDING
M-AORTA

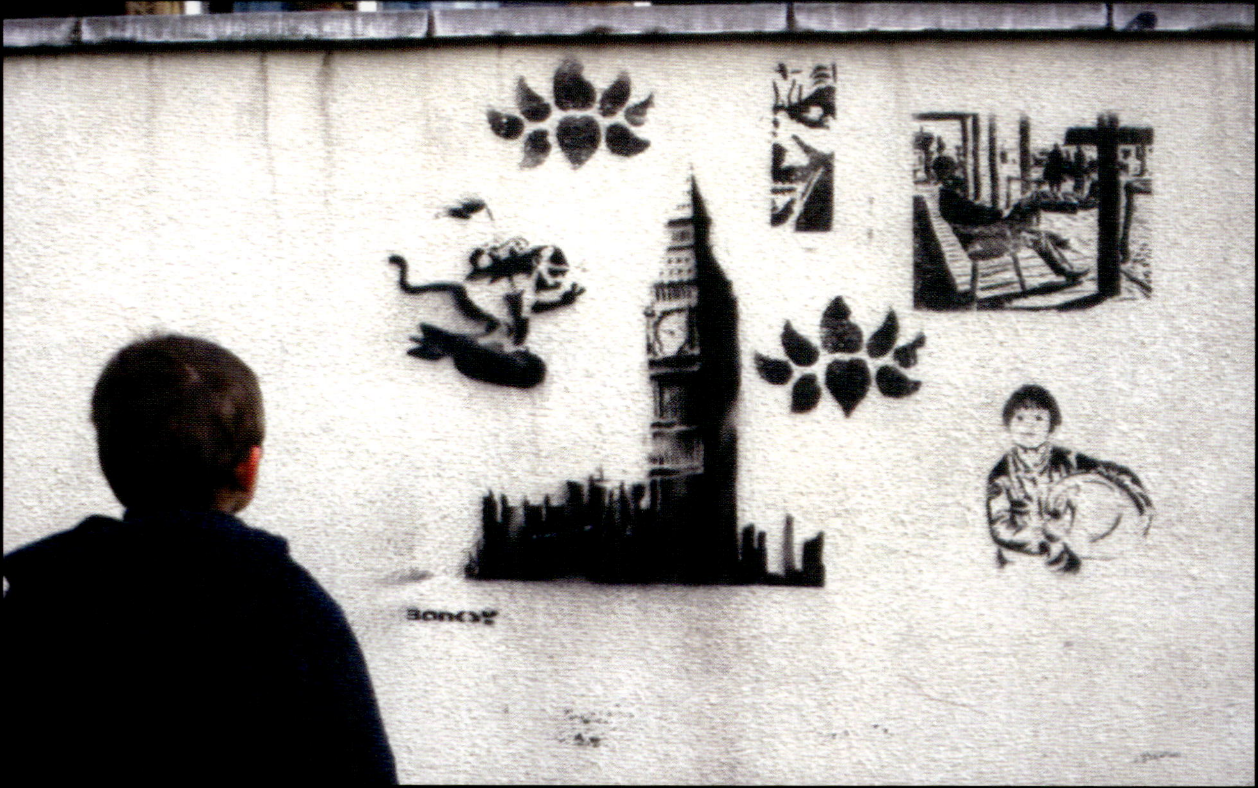

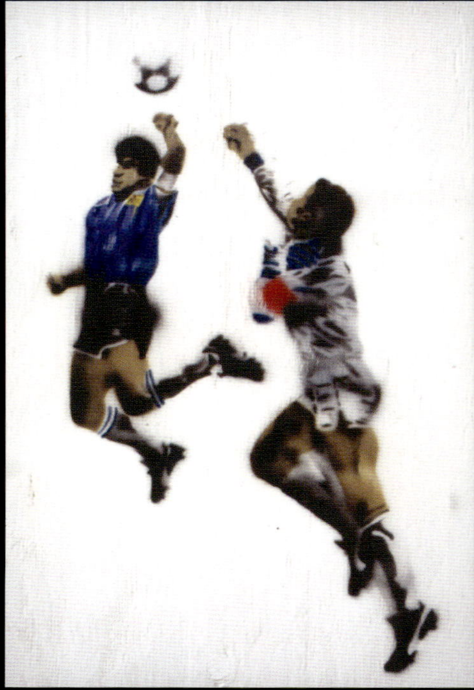

This page. Above: Stencils congregate. Only the Banksy piece was on this wall one week earlier, 2000

Top right: 'The Hand Of God' by Jeff Row, 1999

Opposite page. Top left: 'Mad Dogs For Englishman in the Middle Of The Daily Sun' Jeff Row 2000

Top middle: Rulers of the Earth, Jeff Row, 1999

Top right: 'Why Did The Monkey Fall Out Of The Tree?' Jeff Row, 1998

Bottom left: 'Charlie's Well Fit' Jeff Row, 2006

Bottom right: 'Bryter Layter' Jeff Row 2000

STENCILS ARE FOR EVERYONE BY JEFF ROW

• **"My dad taught me that as a rule we should never generalise, but I really do believe that Bristolians genuinely love the city's stencil culture.** Whilst stencilling on the streets of Bristol, I have been nicked twice, hit round the head with a house brick, and lifted off the ground by my throat by an extremely large member of the Bedminster builders' guild, asking if it was me who wrote on his Transit van (and pointing to a Demz tag).

"However, I believe that on the whole Bristolians very much enjoy these little bytes of an unknown person's psyche that are dotted about their city. They are private snapshots of the artist's loves, hates, joys and sorrows, made public to get these matters off their chests and to enable us to share in them for a fleeting moment as we walk to work, stare out of a bus window or wobble back from the pub.

"They may have no effect on us whatsoever as we view them. An image of a rat holding a paintbrush may slip in and out of our message centres leaving no trace, just as quickly and pointlessly as me telling my girlfriend last Saturday's football results. Then again, these images might bring a smile to our faces, or give us a welcome breather from worrying about our mortgage or the fact that we're late for work again. They may even provoke disdain, a mental shake of the head, a negative reaction, but a reaction nonetheless.

"Sometimes, however, we – the viewer – connect with the stencil. It strikes a chord with us and reflects our own thoughts and feelings. If one of my stencils can make one person feel that they are not alone in thinking a particular thought or emotion, can make them say to themselves, 'They're talking about my life there', then I have done my work for that day, brought one more loose soul closer to the collective consciousness that I like to call humanity.

"Now I reckon, and indeed hope, that there will be scores of freehand graffers reading this and thinking, 'My pieces do all that, and I bet you only stencil because you can't use a spray can properly.' You may well be right. A lot of Bristol's freehand graff simply takes my breath away. The

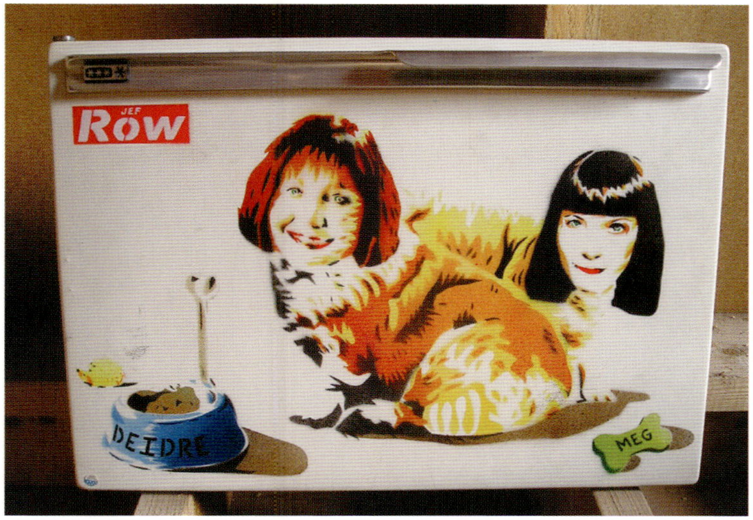
JEF
RÖW
DEIDRE
MEG

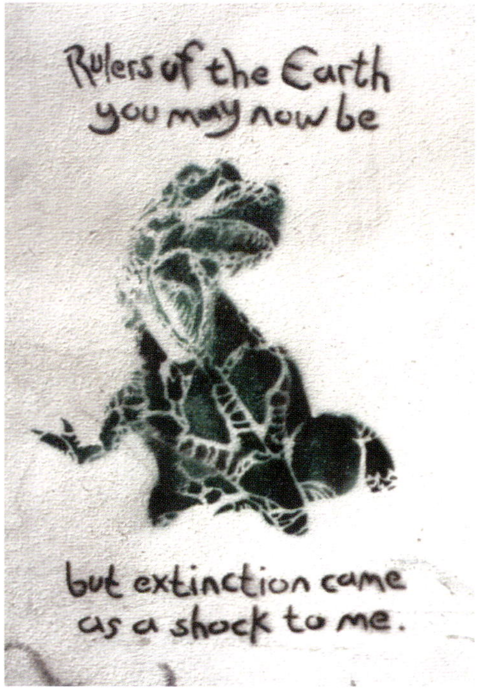
Rulers of the Earth
you may now be
but extinction came
as a shock to me.

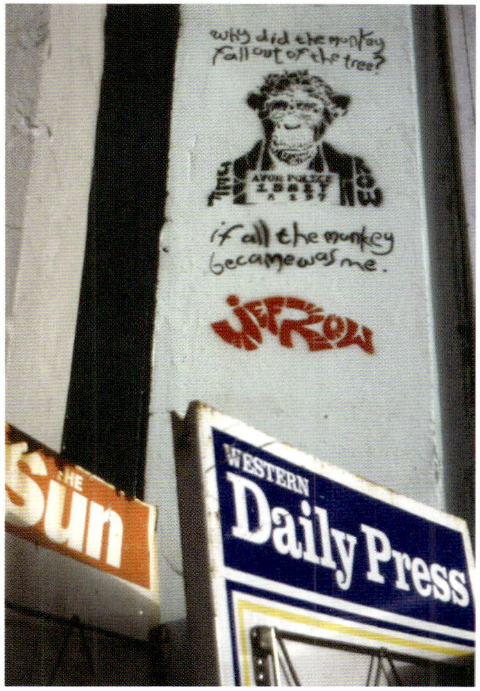
why did the monkey
fall out of the tree?
if all the monkey
became was me.
JEF ROW
THE Sun
WESTERN
Daily Press

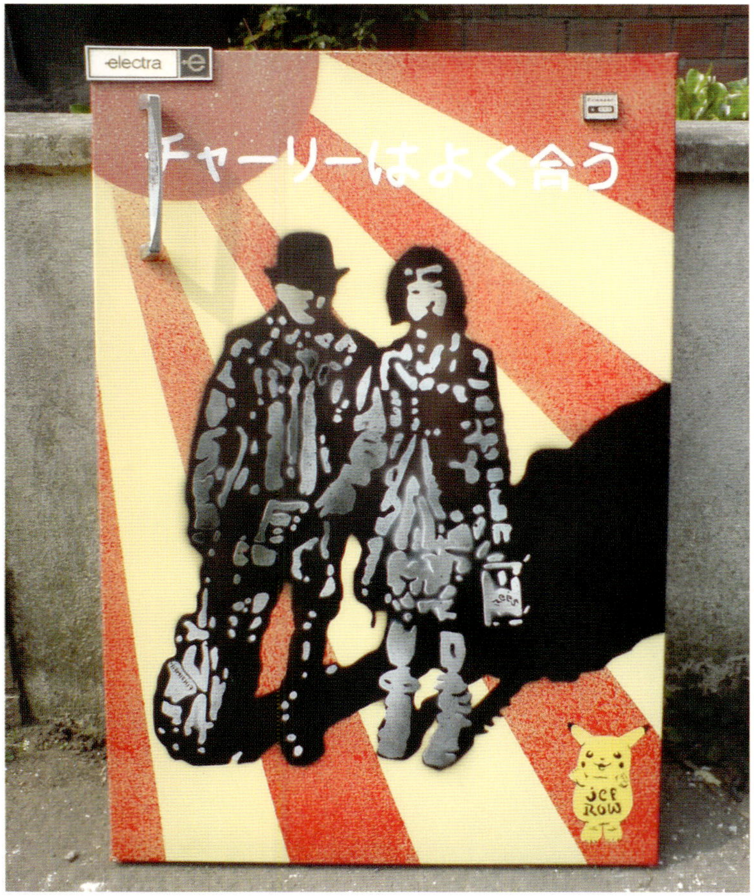
electra
チャーリーはよく合う
JEF
ROW

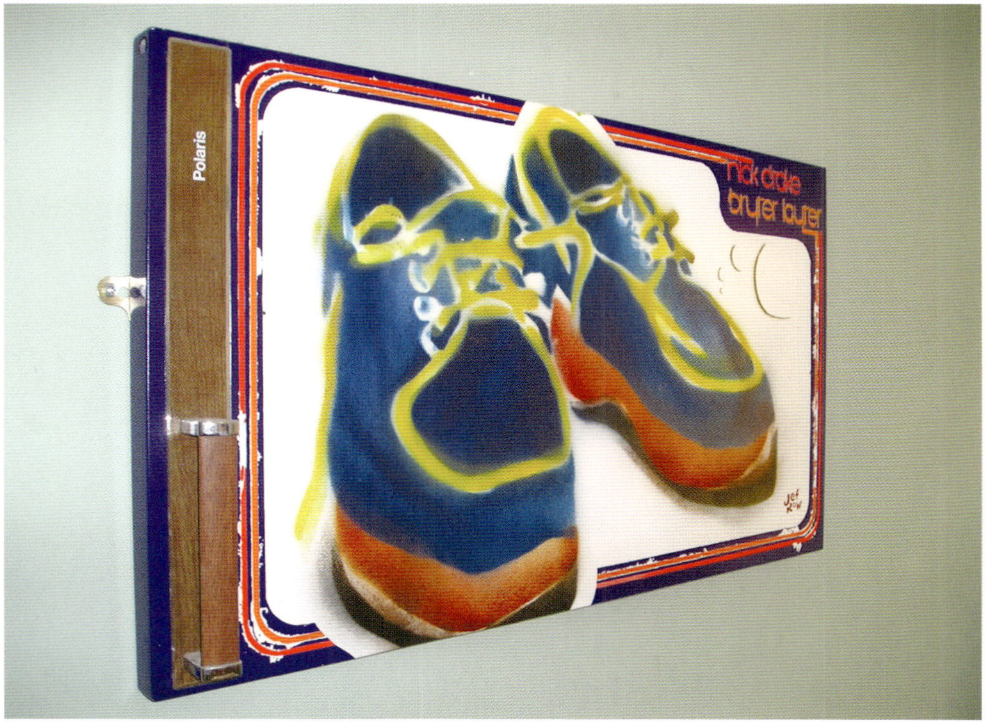
Polaris
nick drake
bryter layter
JEF
ROW

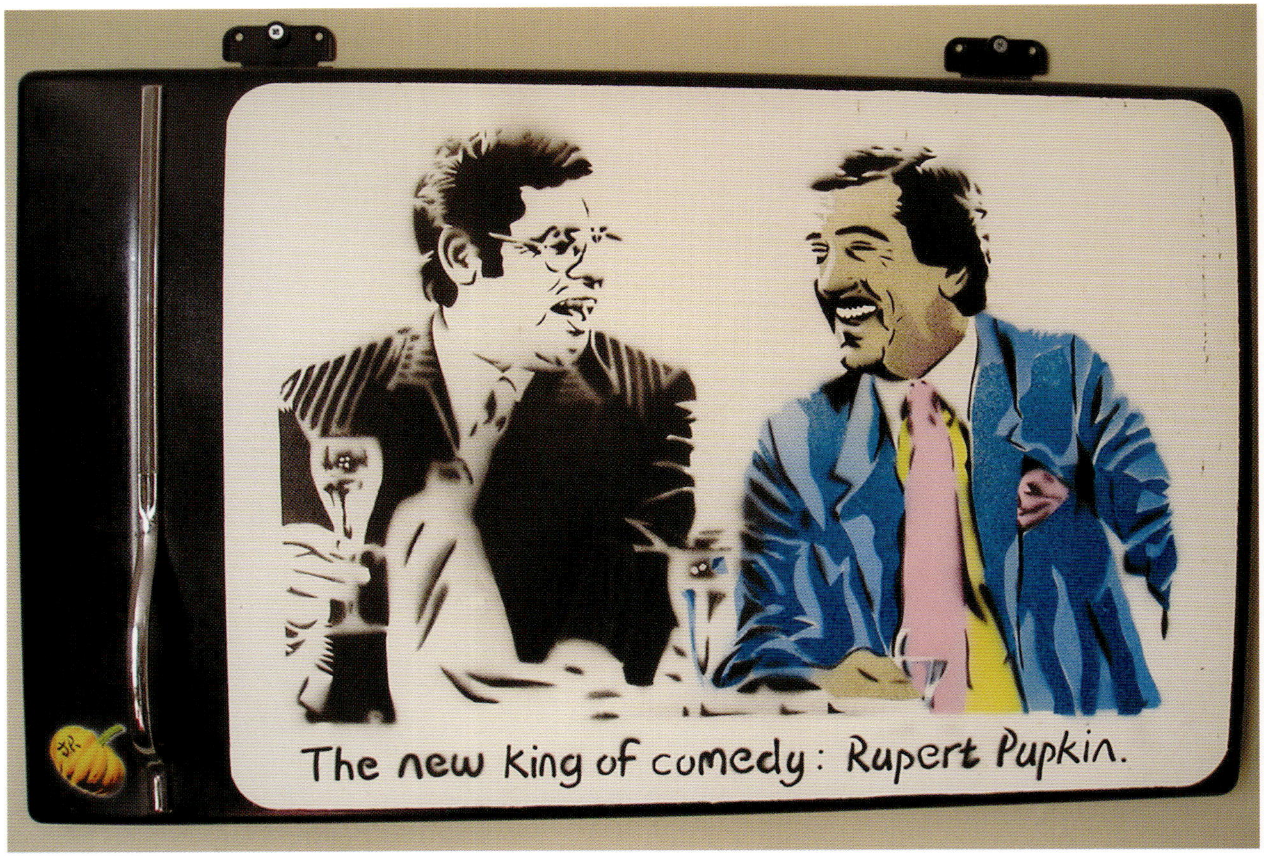

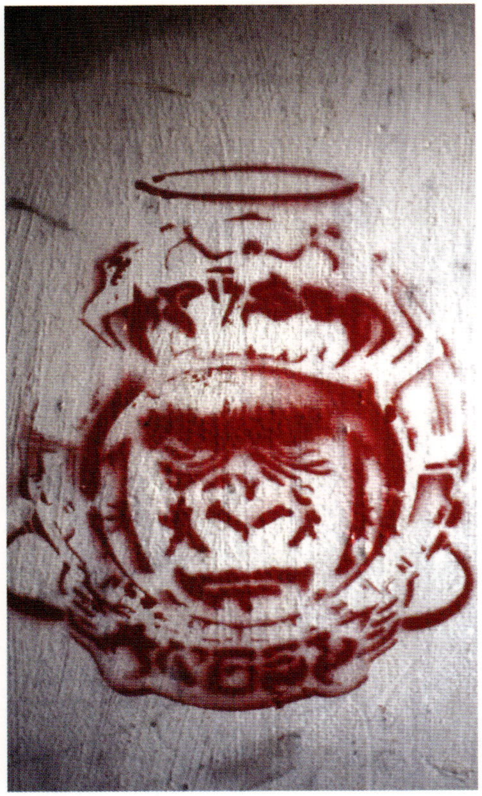

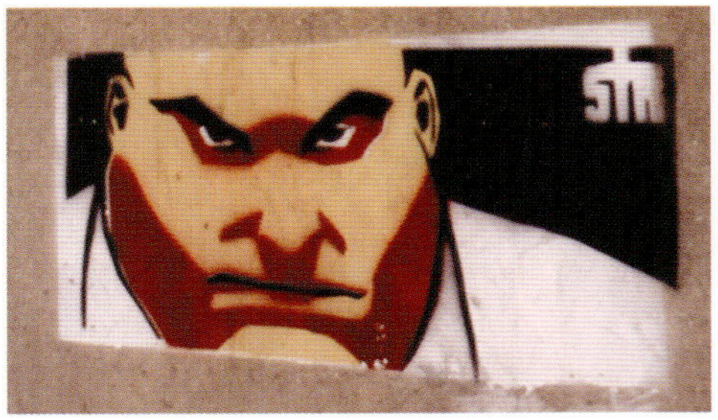

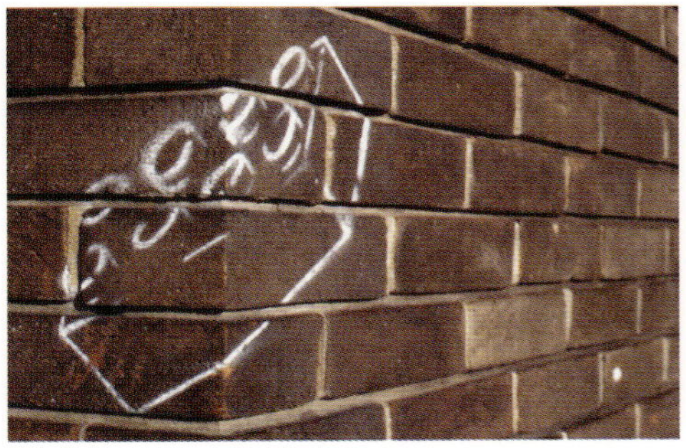

Top left: 'The New King Of Comedy' 2000

Top right: 'Apish Angel' Nick Walker, 1999

Middle right: 'Kingpin' by STR, Lawrence Hill, 1999

Bottom right: Lego brick on brick, by Arse, 1999

TCF Crew and friends transport us into fantastic and beautiful landscapes from this world and others. I take my hat off to these artists, their skills with an aerosol outreach mine and I know that Bristolians, other earthlings, and probably even visiting aliens all cherish their creations.

"However, most freehand graffiti is letter-based and therefore simply does not speak a language understood by the majority of the population. I believe it's all valid (and I have painted using these forms), but on the whole it only allows the public at large to glean fleeting pleasures from it. After all, a colourful wall is surely better than a blank, grey one. But the fact remains that most freehand artists write or piece just one word – their name or tag – and most of the time they do it to gain street fame and the respect of their peers.

"There is nothing wrong with this, and many stencil artists do sign their work and therefore crave some level of notoriety. Many such artists have come from backgrounds where they began life as taggers, and deep down they love the thought of people they have never met discussing their latest creations. I know I do, so maybe we aren't that different after all. The thing that sets stencils apart from other forms of graffiti (aside from the fact that they can be created by just

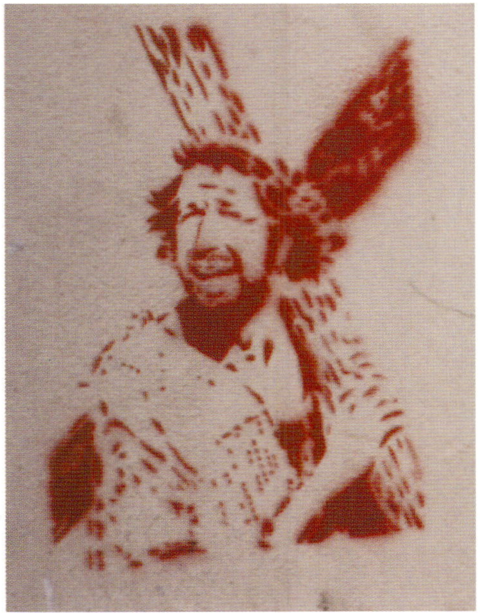

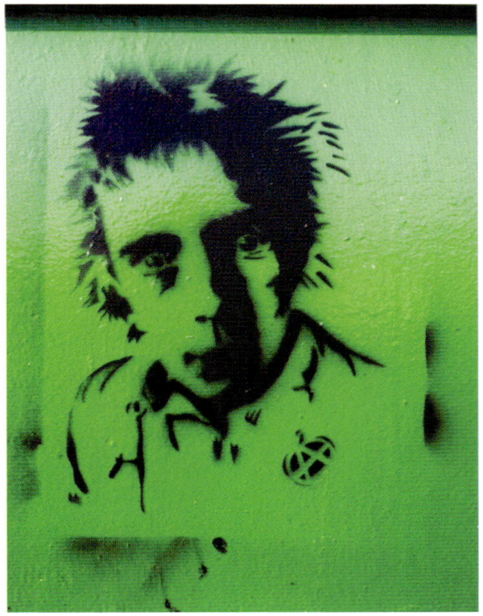

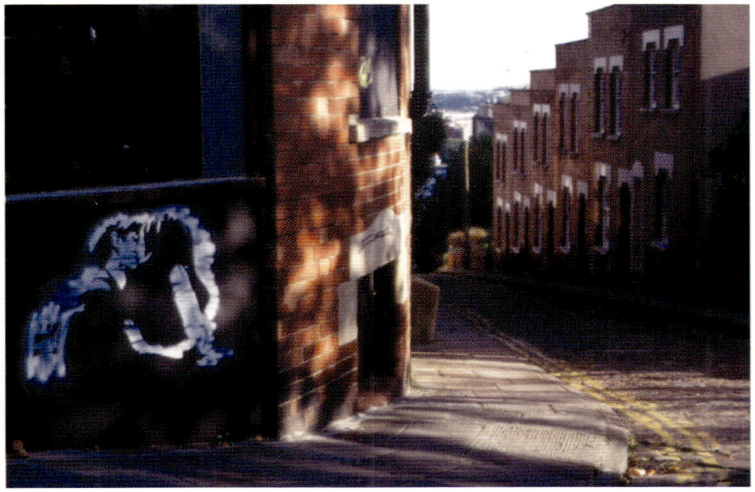

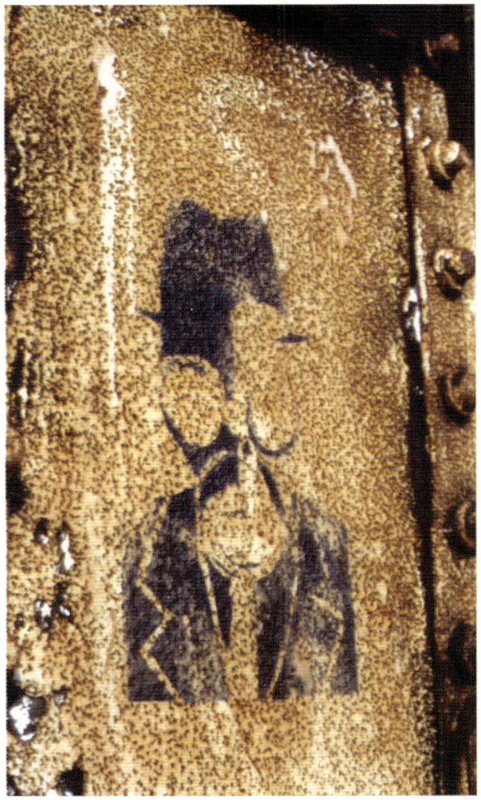

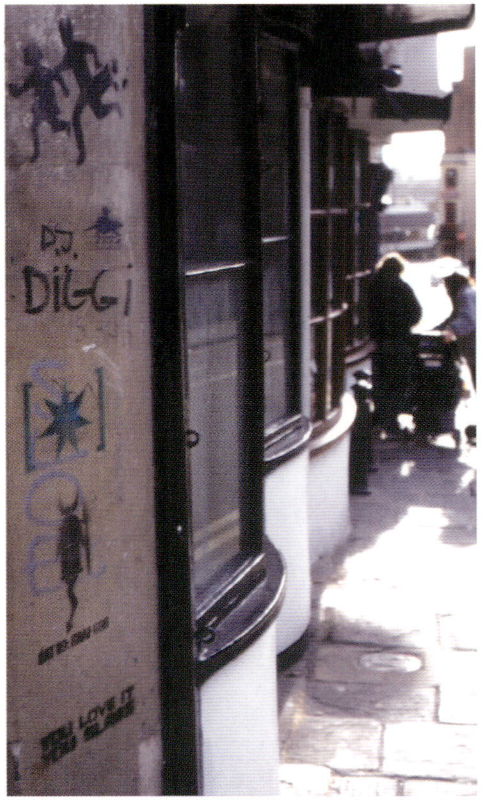

about anybody and understood by just about anybody) is that they have a whole separate creative stage in their evolution. By this I refer to the gathering and copying/drawing of the image to be stencilled, and the subsequent cutting out stage, where a style is fashioned. It is this last stage that really interests me. What possesses a person, once they have decided they have something to share with the rest of us, to go through all that painstaking work to do so? Not only that, but how and why do they choose the images and styles they do to get these gems of information out onto the streets and into our heads?

"One thing is for sure, the results are seldom boring, often mystifying, sometimes very clever and always in the form of images and text that any mind from any walk of life can decipher. What those minds then do with this information, and whether or not the viewer and artist connect in any way as a result, is purely subjective. But then, that's art for you, innit."

Top left: Happy Christmas Bedminster' by Jeff Row, 1999

Top middle: Johnny Rotten, by Jez, 1999

Top right: 'Kiss,' Kingsdown, 1999

Bottom left: Gasface, old prison gate, Bedminster, 1999

Bottom middle: Various artists, Colston Street, 1998

Right: 'AAGH' Dog 'Avin a go' on his head, 2005

Far right: 'Bobble' pen and pencil on paper, 2006

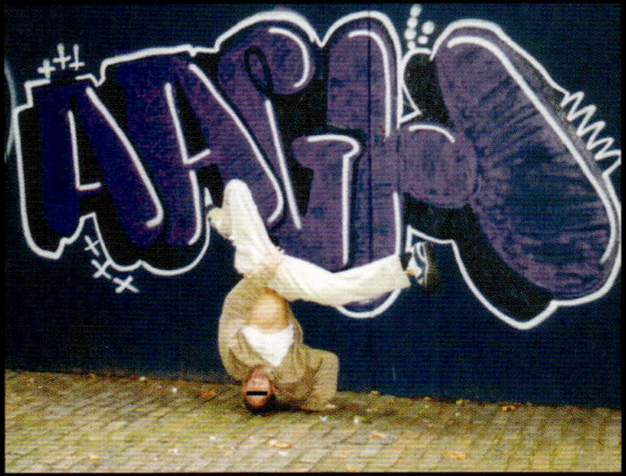

DR DOG AAGH

• **Dr Dog (aka Spam) moved to Bristol from Hull in the late 1990s.** Finding a kindred creative spirit in Sickboy, together they formed the genre-bending AAGH crew. Dr Dog's twisted take on graffiti is as odd as it is humorous, and bears little resemblance to anything that came before it – or, for that matter, anything that has been painted since.

The Hull warehouse scene was a fertile breeding ground. Which writers had a real impact and were important to you?
"Pinky, Detour, Elite, Eko, Perv, Admass, Ziml and the DRA and RFM crews."

What made you take the long journey south from Hull to Bristol?
"I went to Inkie and Banksy's Walls on Fire jam in 1998 and just really liked the attitude of Bristol and its fair people – laid back, but plenty going on. I fell in love with the place. Paris had already made the maiden voyage down from the northern hemisphere, so word had spread like wildfire amongst the hoi polloi of Kingston-upon-Hull."

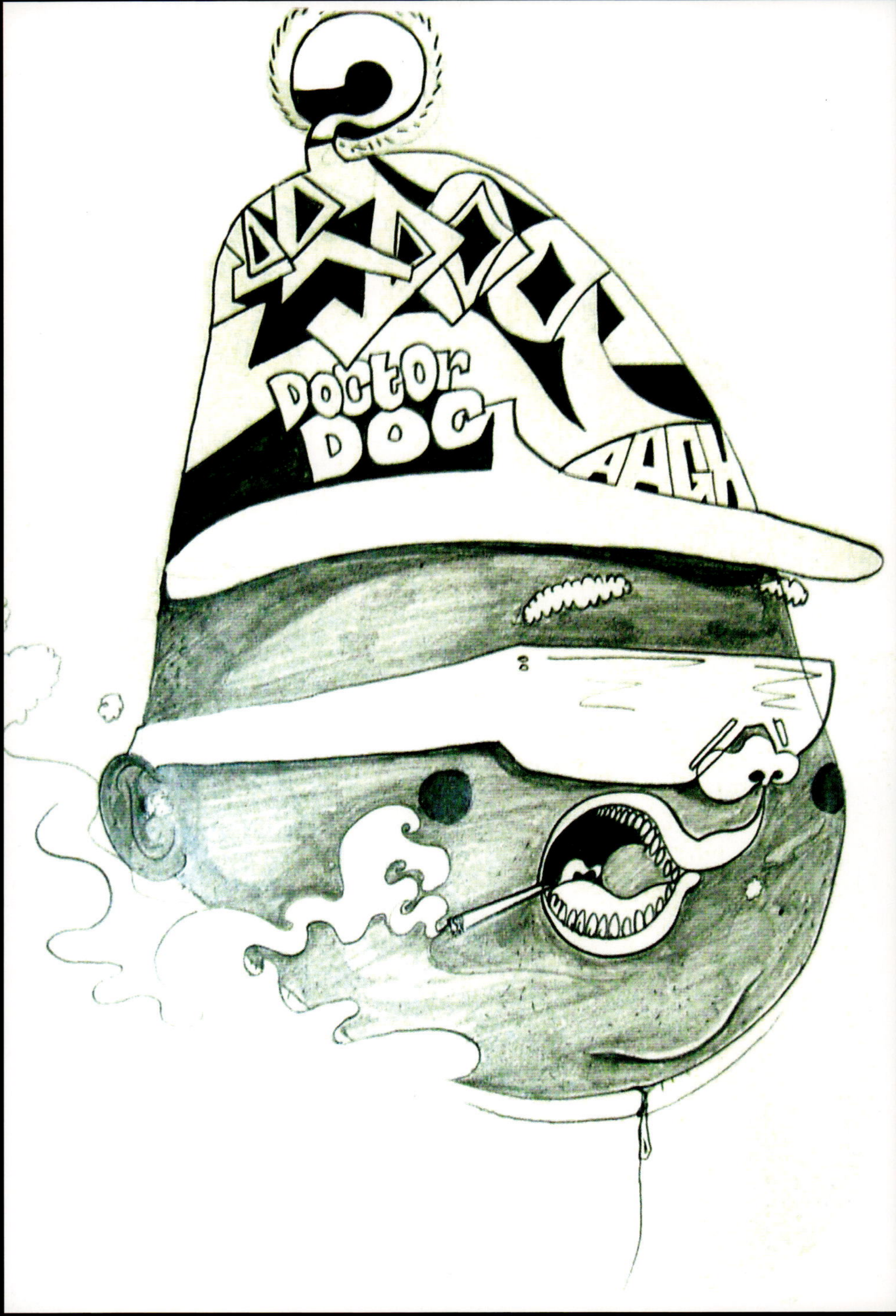

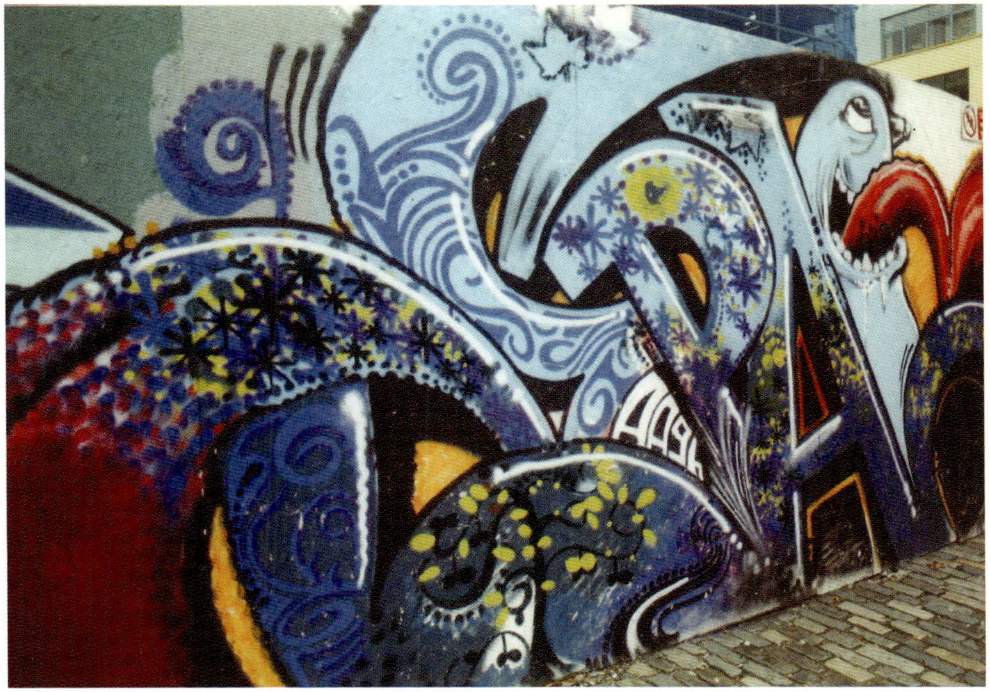

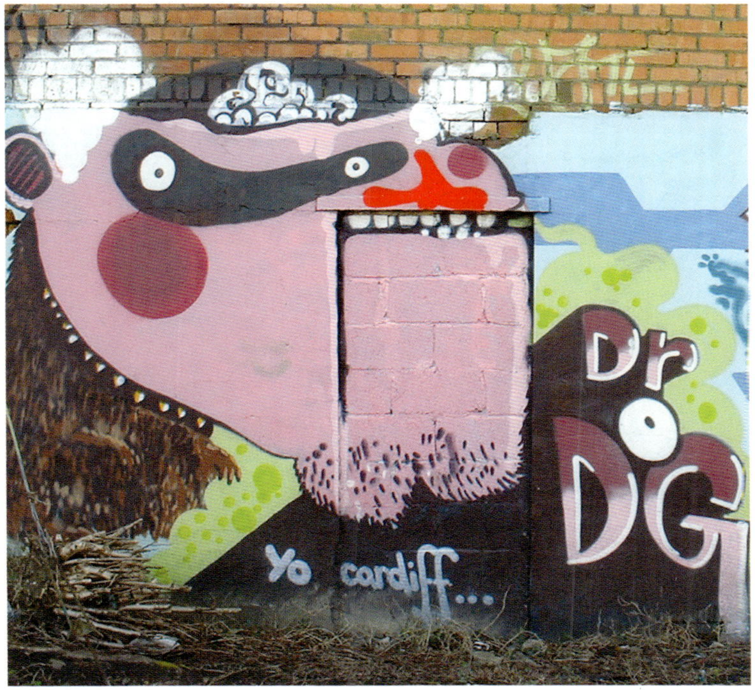

How did the AAGH name come about?
"It stands for '(H)Ave-A-Go Heroes' and was just one of those classic Northern local newspaper headlines that seems to get recycled over and over. Manchester and Hull are just full of 'have-a-go heroes,' so it just seemed perfect for us two then! The way we would say it was 'ave' so then it looked like a comic-style 'AAGH!'"

The name seems to reflect the attitude and mindset of the crew, somewhere between just having a laugh and being totally passionate about what you do.
"I guess a lot of writers would have thought our style was pretty 'gay', but we didn't really give a fuck. I believe people have to follow their own path, cut their own groove, express themselves in the way they feel sets the right tone. We painted pieces together, really talked a lot and philosophised about what we were doing. We wanted to have something fresh. The idea of a new 'bazaar' or 'carnival' style was something that got bandied about, and we just went out and tried to do something different, to make our pieces interesting. Even if you were just centimetres away from the wall, you could see we had tried to create a narrative."

Which other writers expanded the ranks of AAGH?
"We met Ponk and he was just a junior guy like us, and he fitted in well with the crew. So really that was the core of it, just us three, sketching until the sun came up and tagging, smoking, drinking and going to the Thekla, Lakota, Platform One, Dojo and all the other great clubs in Bristol. Then over the years, we just invited people who were funky and fresh - Sums, Nylon, and some lads Sickboy knew from Manchester; Dabl and Vagina. Sober was a local, and a junior guy like us. More recently O'Tick and Iron Elephant have joined."

Are you a dedicated believer in the power of, and need for, bombing?
"Bombing and tagging is what keeps it all fresh, keeps it real, away from the Cans Festival and Shoreditch and back onto the dark and sinister backwaters of suburban Grimehampton city centres. I won't front like I'm a bomber/tagger, but I have painted a couple of trains and scaled a few buildings and whatnot. Some tags are just shit though, like a dog has rubbed its egg pipe on the wall in too much of a rush. It's like: kid, get some STYLE before you defile!"

What's the difference between Spam and Dr Dog?

Top left: 'Spam' Bristol harbourside, 2001

Top right: 'Yo Cardiff', 2004

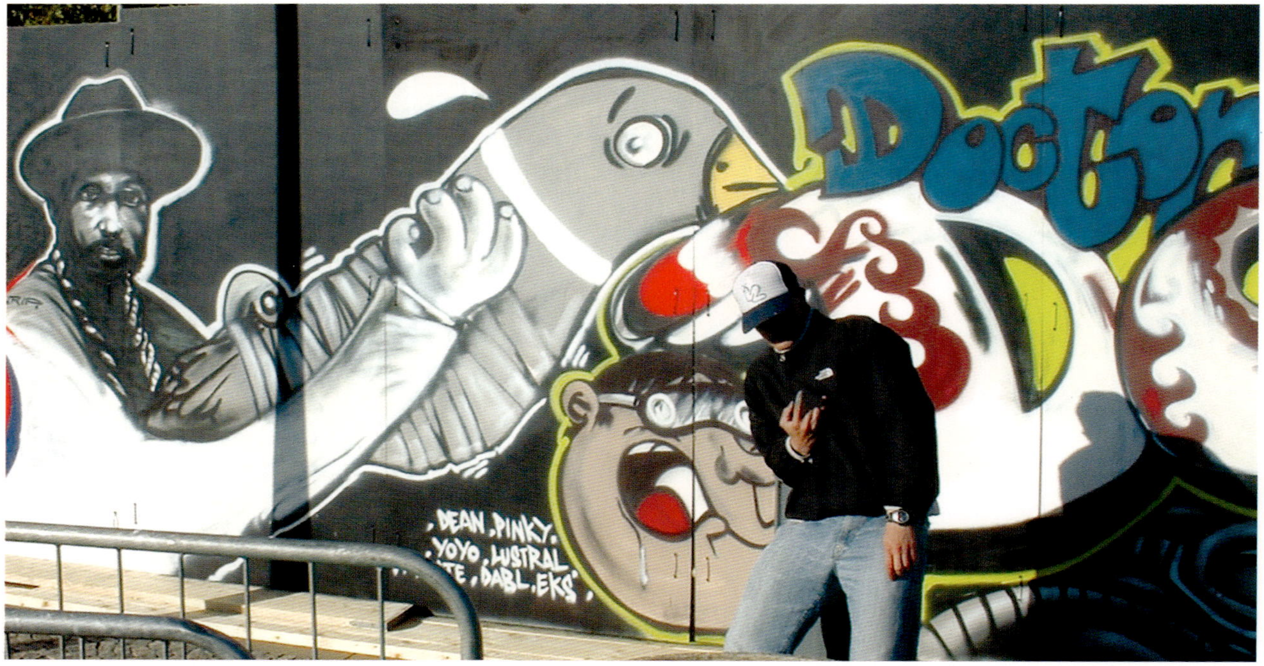

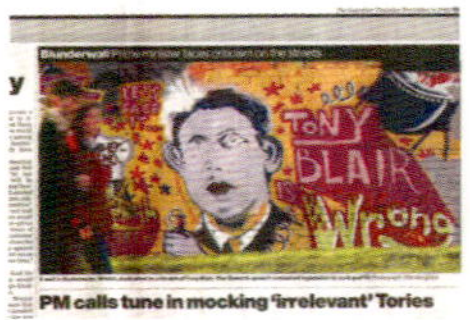
PM calls tune in mocking 'irrelevant' Tories

Top: Liverpool, 2004

Right: 'Let's Face It…Tony Blair Is Wrong' (which made it into The Guardian newspaper, above) Bedminster skate park, 2003

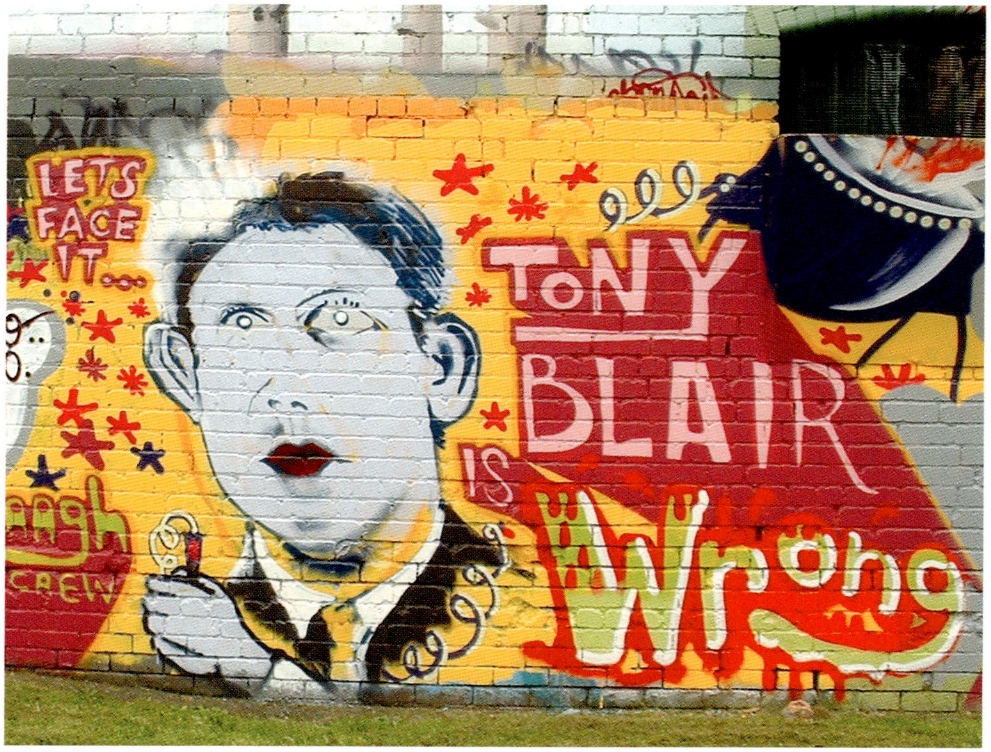

"One you can eat, the other one is God Rd. backwards."

You seem to have an irreverent, humorous take on graffiti. Where did your unique style stem from?
"I've always had writers around me saying, 'just do some crazy shit kid', so don't blame me if I end up painting Jam Master Jay bumming a taped-up pigeon."

Graffiti, in the loosest sense, has changed so rapidly in the last ten years. Is it still possible to have a single definition of style?
"Style is the key to all forms of rocking. Graffiti style these days is really going a long way from where it used to be. Os Gemeos, The Birds, Twist: they're all just really bad (meaning good). Just think what it will be like in another 20 years! I can't believe it really, I love it, there is so much crazy shit going off like fireworks all around the world. Just look at South Korea and Japan and how they have grown in confidence over the 10-15 years they have been rocking. Now you can see their style. Style is just people. That's why people bite, they just see people they want to be like."

What it is that makes Bristol such a creative city, that continues to breed and attract so much diverse talent?
"Bristol is just well nice. It's full of great, lovely people who've always got a smile on their faces. They're not in too much of a rush to meet their maker. It has lovely cider, drugs and sun. You have got it all and there's just too much going on there. I will always think of it as my second home."

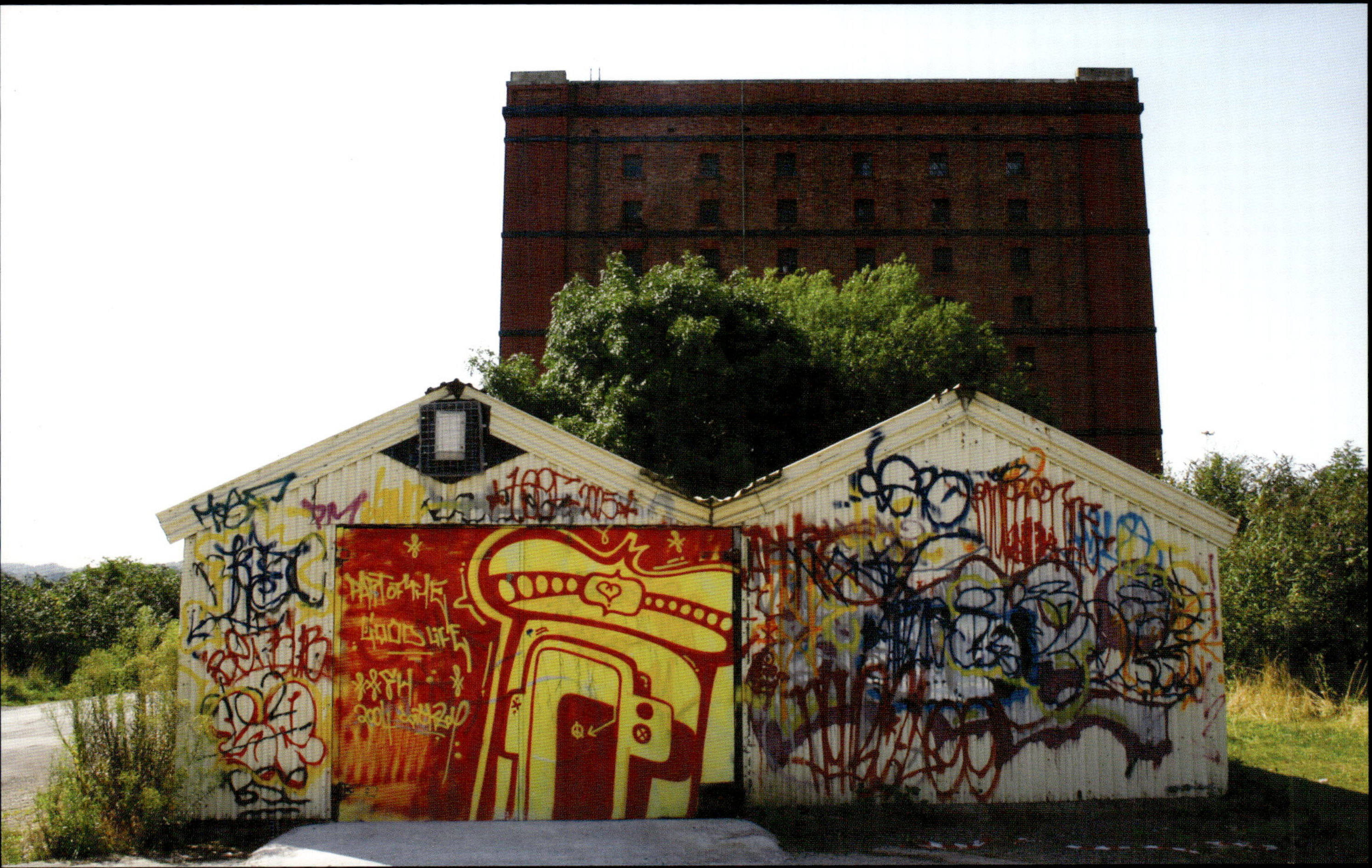

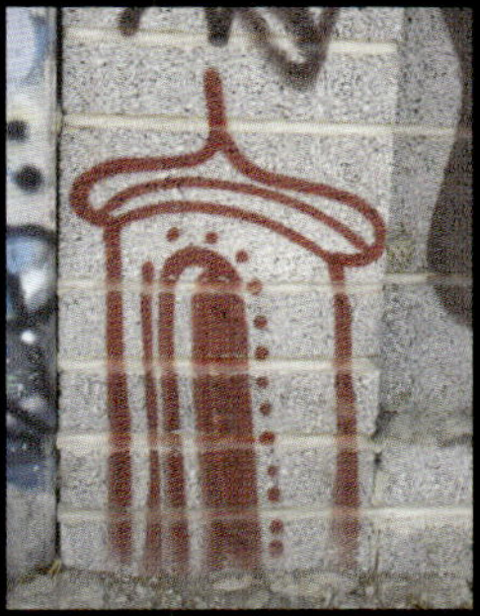

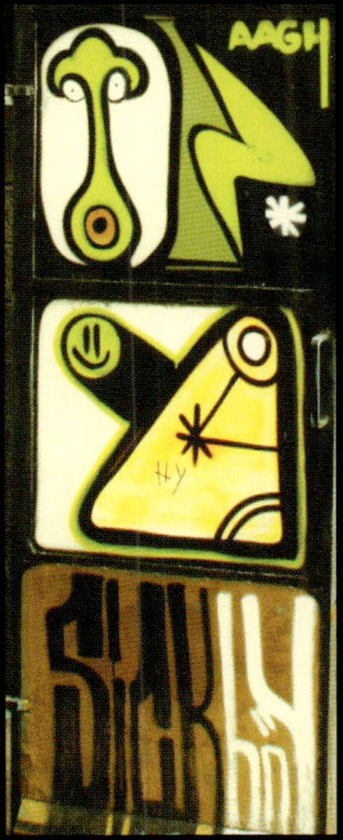

Left: 'Part Of The Good Life' temple in the shadow of the CREATE Centre, 2004

Top: Early temple, c.1999

Above: The green door, quick styles, 2006

SICKBOY AAGH

• **If ever there was a fitting tag, it is Sickboy's.** Like an inappropriate joke that nonetheless makes you laugh, his work conveys a melancholic humour – and a sadness that is occasionally hilarious. His colours are celebratory, yet his subjects are often brooding. Riddled with symbolism that references both popular culture and the deeply personal, his work is accessible and beguiling.

How did you first get into graffiti? Do you remember the first pieces you saw?
"When I was 14 I used to go round to my mate Neil's house and get up to all sorts of mischief. We used to nick weed from his brothers' room and he had a bit of a graffiti shrine on his wall. He also had all this paraphernalia: spray paint, markers, nozzles. He had a piece of paper with a hundred New York fat caps laid out on it and it said '100 New York fat caps, Neil: DO NOT TOUCH!'"

So did you nick some of Neil's brother's paint?
"Yeah, and Neil said, 'Do you want to go out and try doing some tags?' So we got some spray paint and I did this really naïve Snoop-E thing. I hadn't realised, but Neil had already locked down a tag style. It was really stylish, and he said, 'Do you want to learn how to do it?' So we made up a new tag for me there and then, which was Ridl. He wrote it for me, then I went home on the bus and on the way I went through a whole A4 pad, writing RIDL RIDL RIDL

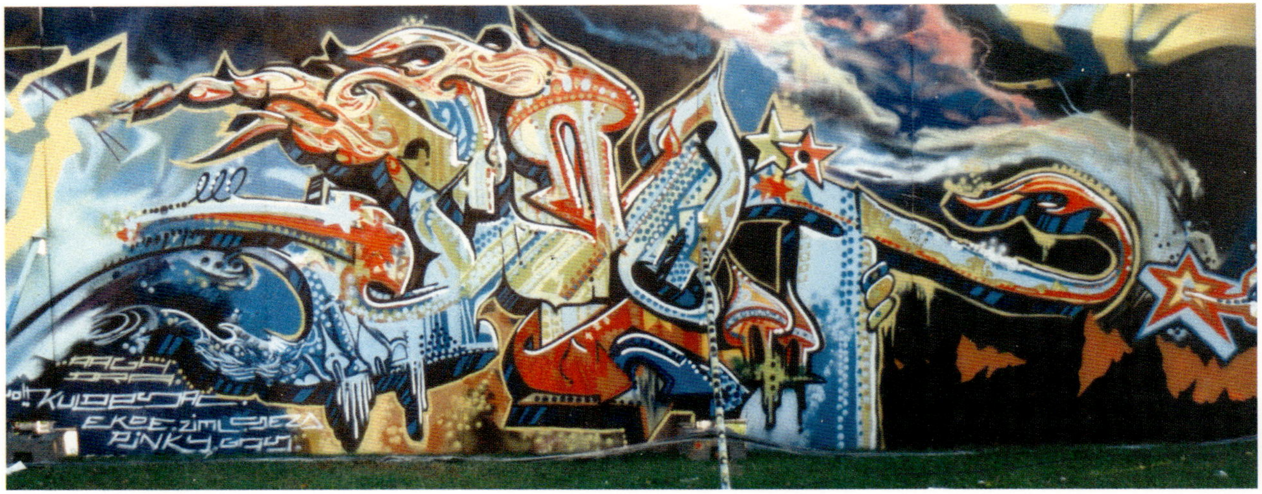

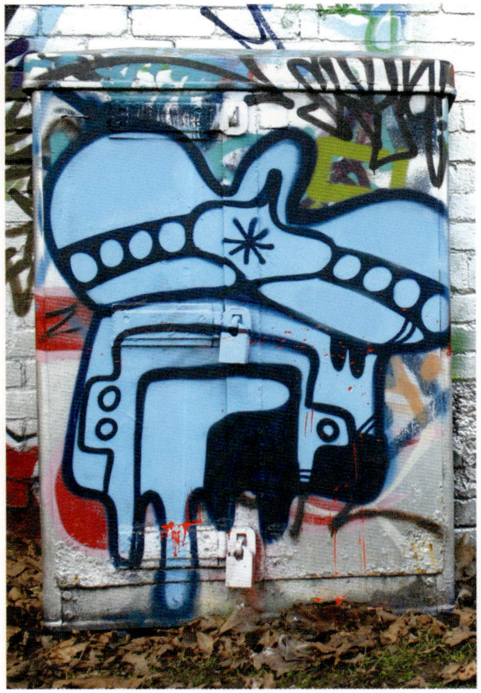

Top left: Phet piece incorporating temples, Urban Games, London, c.2000

Top right: Blue temple, Bedminster skate park, c.2004

Opposite page: A selection of sickly characters from 2006

RIDL RIDL RIDL with a green pen – and it still looked bollocks. But when I got off the bus at the other end I wrote it on a bin. I thought I'd mastered style.

"I woke up the next morning and was just buzzing about it, and I was like, 'Hey, we've got to do more stuff!' We formed a crew called the FX Crew, which stood for FREAX, copying that New York thing of using the first and last letters with your throw ups."

So were you going into Manchester and bombing? I remember seeing lots of pieces around Hulme in the early 90s.
"I'm from Warrington, which is outside of Manchester, and I was never really part of the Manchester graffiti scene, because I was just a kid. But I was going into Manchester a lot at the time, and I was really awestruck by it. Back then you were embarrassed to say what you wrote. I'd just go along with my little bit of paper to see Kelzo painting in Hulme, and I'd be like, 'Oh, can you sign this?' Hulme basically was the Manchester scene, and they were having these big graff jams with people coming up from London – people like Diet, Teach, Arize, and all those sorts of people. But for me it was all about tagging, I wasn't bothered about the pieces."

Where did you learn to paint pieces?
"I had my own little hall of fame. This school got knocked down near where I lived, and I approached this guy and asked if I could paint there. I told him it would be like a community mural, and then I just did my own thing. I remember doing this piece in silver, outlining it in black, then putting the second outline on with a pen, on a brick wall: just fucking mental. Then I did loads of smiley acid faces coming off the white outline.

"By then I had started writing Phet, which was supposedly short for amphetamine. I liked the letters and what the name implied, in terms of adrenaline and painting quick, but I wasn't going into Manchester and making a name for myself. It wasn't until I went to Stockport College and hooked up with some of the writers there that I started painting halls of fame and track sides and stuff."

What was it that brought you to Bristol? Had you heard about the graffiti scene down here?
"No, not at all. My dad was living in Somerset, running a business and commuting on the weekends, and he suggested Bristol as a good town to look at for going to university. I didn't even know where Bristol was then, so I came and had a look, and liked the vibe of it. I also happened to see Walls on Fire going on."

That must have helped. So did you start going out and putting up pieces after you arrived?
"By the time I came down to Bristol, I had this really bastardised graffiti thing that I was doing, and I did a lot of tagging but not much piecing at first. Back then you needed to have nice letters to be a 'name.'"

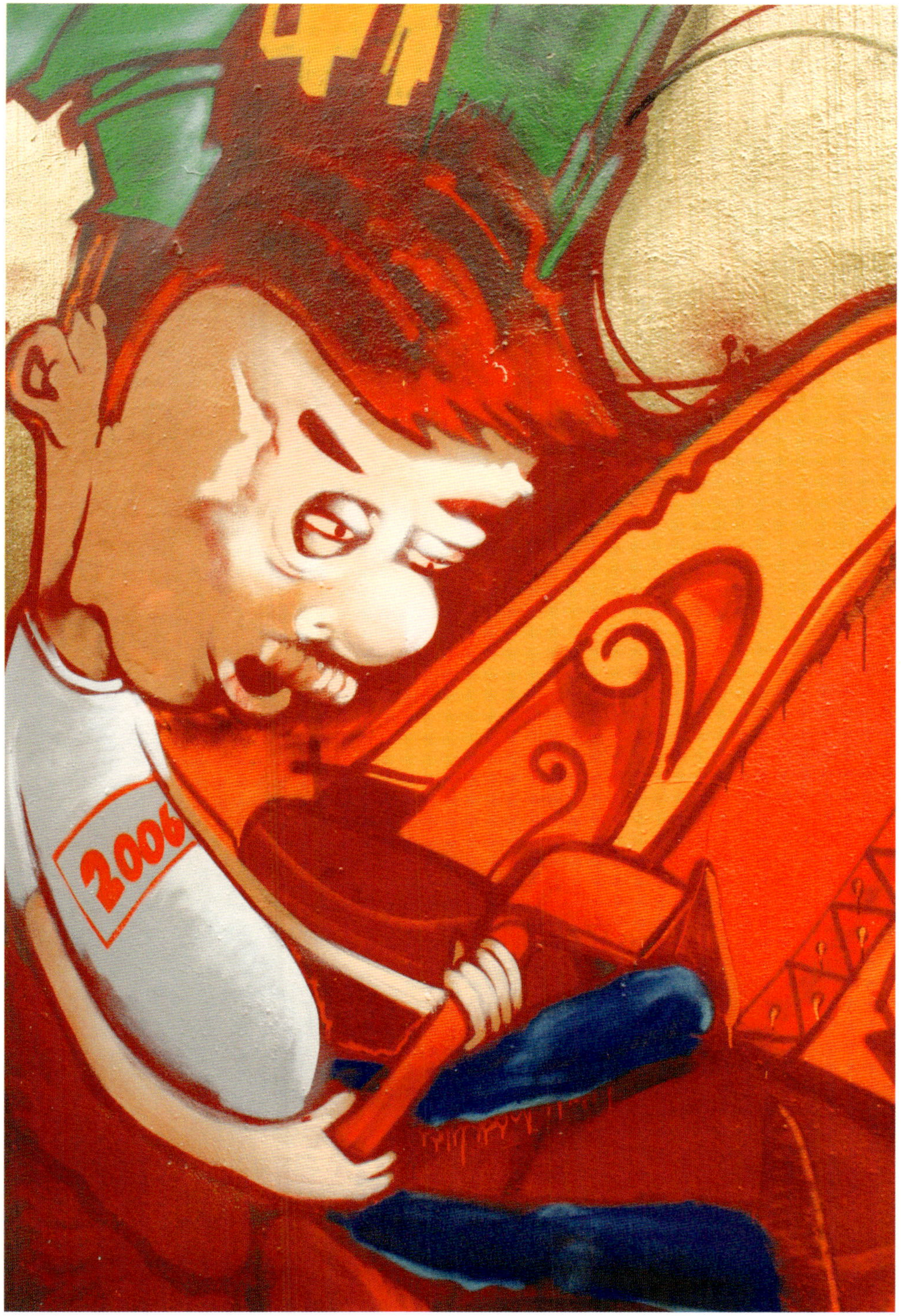
2006

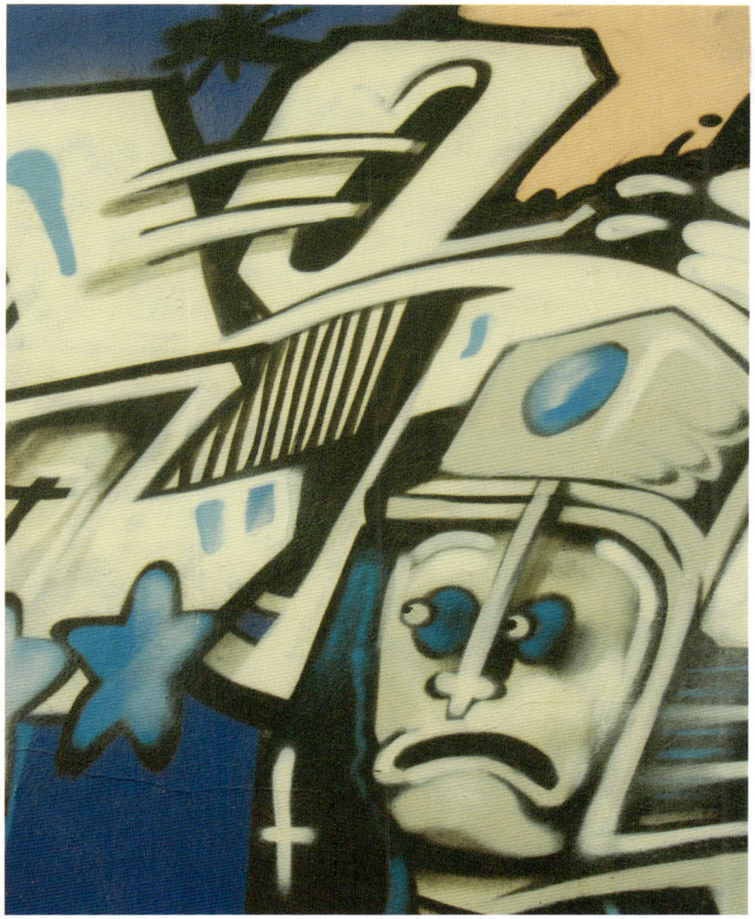

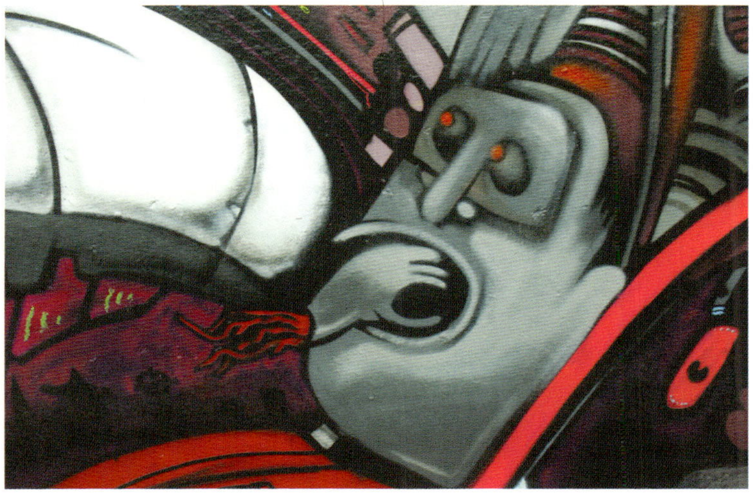

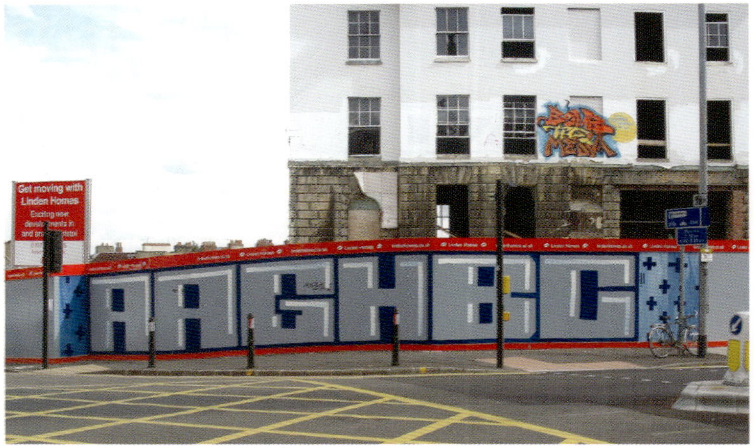

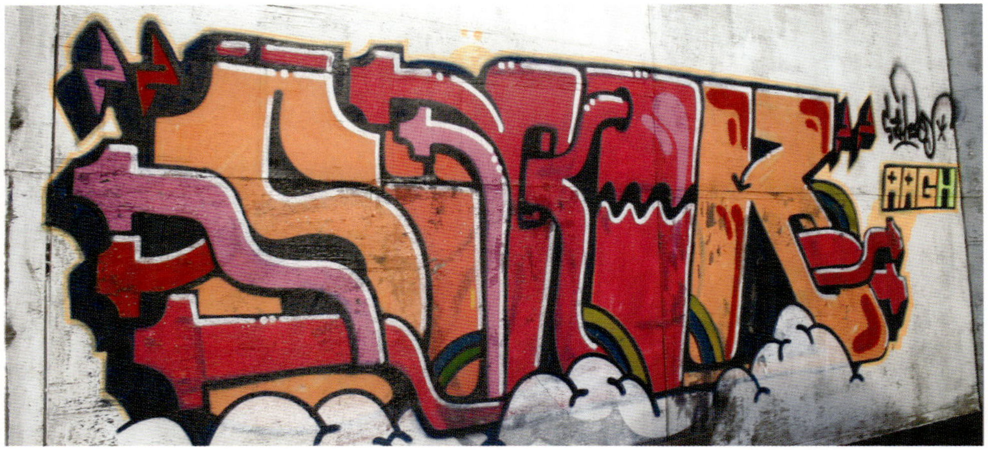

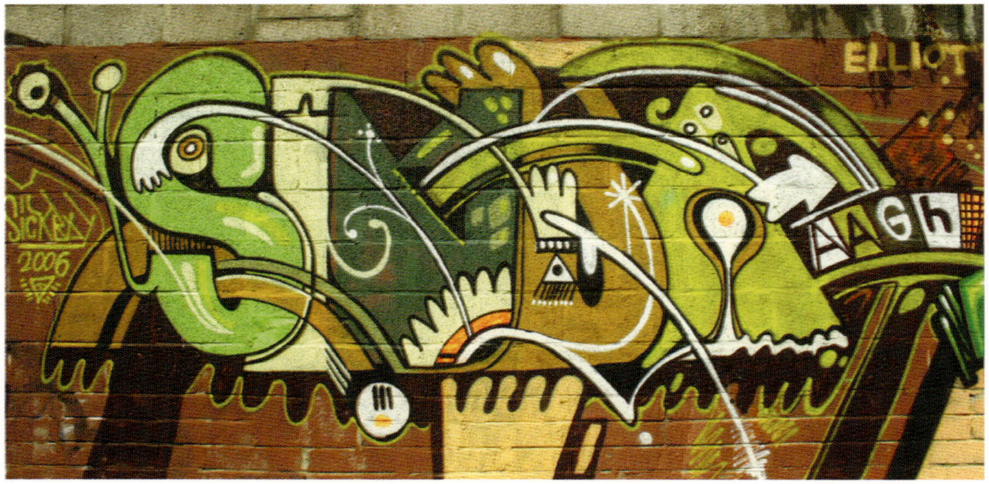

Top left: 'AAGHBC' Stokes Croft, 2008

Top right: 'Sick' 2006

Right: In memory of Elliot, 2006

Who were the first writers you met after you moved here?
"I'd already met Paris when I met Kelzo up in Hulme, and then never saw him again until I got to Bristol. I bumped into him in Cosies [wine bar]. He had a folder with all these outlines and I thought, 'Fucking hell, this guy's good.' Then I met Eko and Xenz, and they took me under their wing, really."

So this would have been around the same time as you hooked up with Spam (Dr Dog) and started AAGH. Was that a meeting of similar creative minds?
"We just influenced each other. It was like a cartoon style, and we were into this whole idea of 'free style'. Whereas Paris, say, would go to a wall with a sketch, we'd go with nothing and just vibe off each other. We thought what you needed to do was to take the ambience of the day and put it on the wall. We thought that was a bit more arty. AAGH stands for 'Ave A Go Heroes,' so we were having a bash at anything."

Fun being one of the central things, I guess?
"Yeah, that was completely it. If you take the elements of a piece – fill-in, outline, second outline, highlight – we'd swap it around. The highlights wouldn't be white, they'd be black, the outline wouldn't be touching the fill-in, or there wouldn't be a fill-in at all. We were just playing with those elements. And that probably pissed some people off, they probably thought, 'Who the fuck are those weirdos?'"

Was it a reaction to the pieces other people were painting at the time?
"TCF were breaking boundaries and stuff, and I think me and Spam were just, 'Well, they've done that, it's really clean, really slick; we can just get messy with it.' Drips were ok, you know? Spam would do things like the Queen Mother with a massive willy in her mouth, and the veins were just really crudely done, but I think I was a bit more precious about making things look like a burner. We did some nice pieces back then. I was doing sort of carnival-style stuff, quite brightly coloured pieces, and Spam was just off the wall, but it worked, somehow."

How did Sickboy come to replace Phet as your tag?

"There was this ramp at Bedminster Skate Park and I wrote 'Sick Toys,' like it was going to be another crew or something, and I just quite liked it. Then I did the same piece I'd done on the ramp on a bridge in Hotwells, and changed the 'T' for a 'B' and dropped the 'S.'

"It's a bit of a mouthful compared to most tags. There are some pretty long-winded ones around now that I can think of, but usually it's about having a name that you can put up quickly and letters that combine to make a well-structured piece. It's that thing of trying to go against the grain – everyone had four-letter tags, and there weren't many seven-letter ones. So I did that and then realised that it's quite difficult to put up seven-letter tags, it does take quite a long time. I don't worry so much about putting up tags anymore, I just tag all the time, but back then it was, 'shit! It's got to be done really quick.'"

How did the red and yellow temple come about?

"I'd been getting into Hundertwasser's architecture and 'natural art'. It was after a visit to Barcelona, and seeing Gaudi's stuff, all his flowing lines and onion domes on top of the buildings. I was seeing the graff around Barcelona, and there was also this style of letters – Nach did it, and Nemer did it – with this sort of onion dome thing added to letters. I just took that, and turned it into a logo. Also, I just thought 'Sickboy is too long to write, I'll just do this temple thing and see how it goes.' I think I must have been losing the plot or something, because I went out and did it during the day in some really hot spots. It was just like,

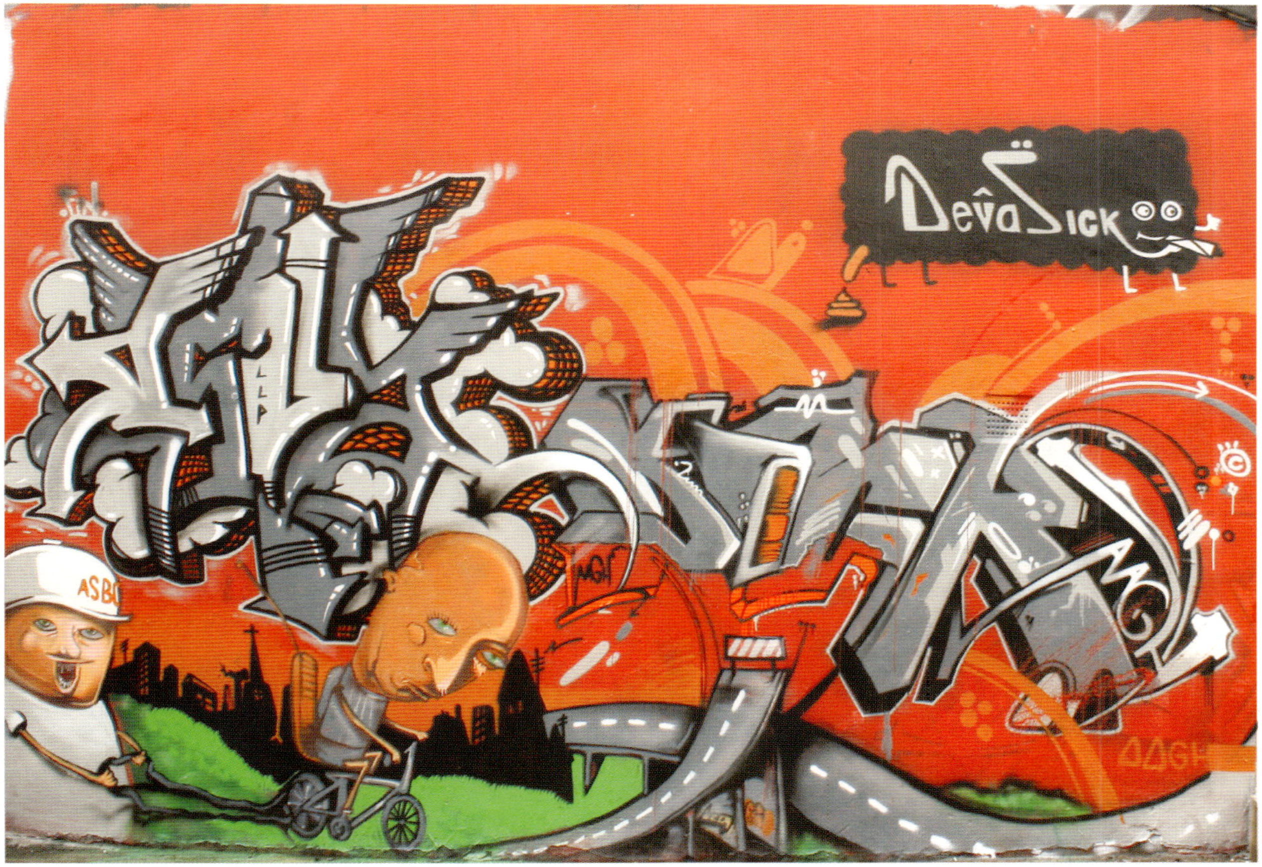

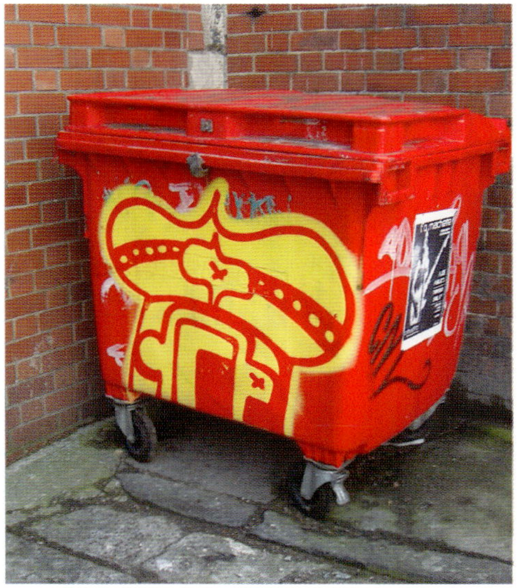

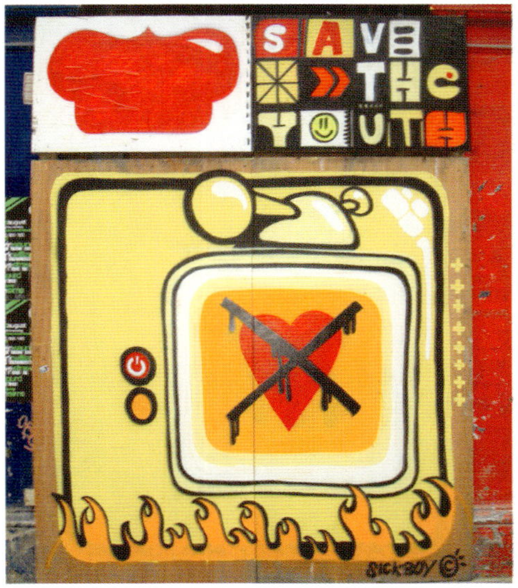

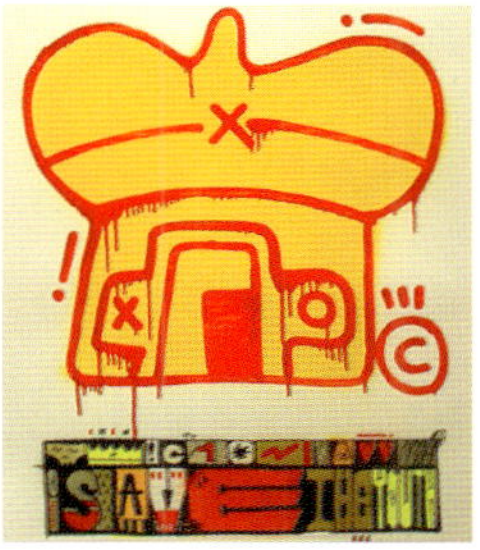

Top: Sickboy and Devas, Bedminster skate park, 2006

Bottom row: On bins, hoardings and paper, the ubiquitous temple in various forms

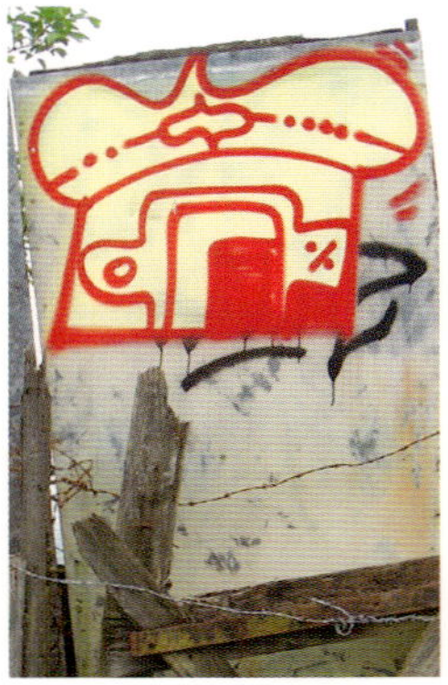

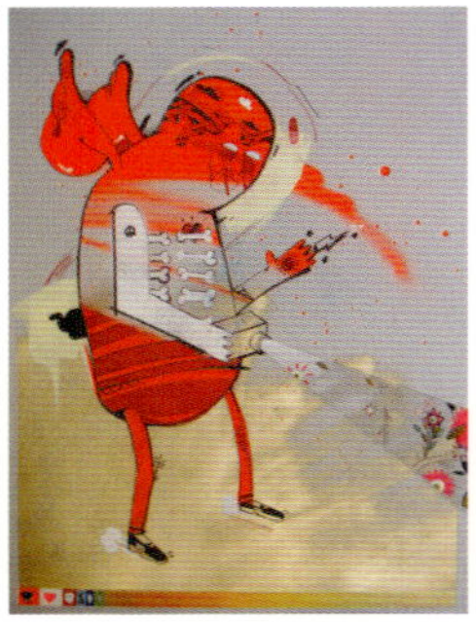

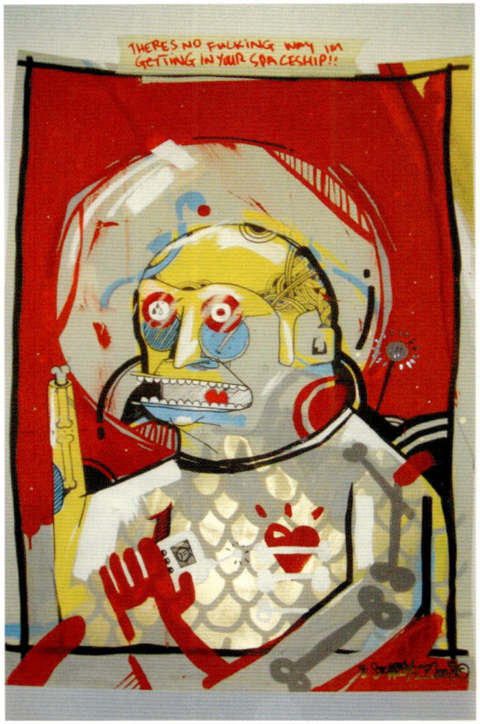

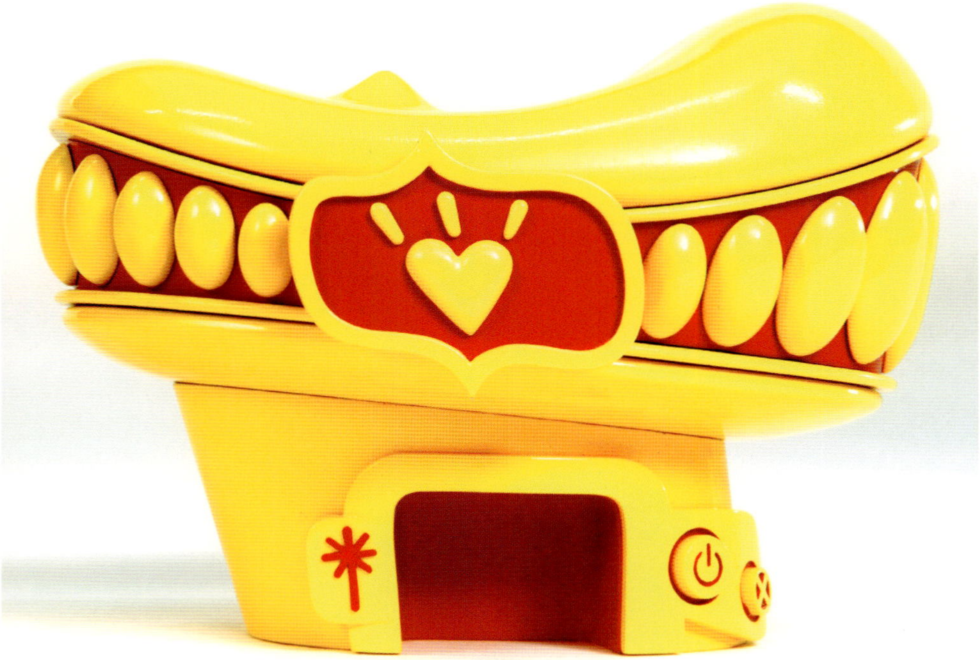

Top left: Ashton Court, 2005

Left: 'Step In The Light' mixed media on paper, 2008

Middle: 'There's No Fucking Way I'm Getting In your Spaceship' mixed media on paper, 2008

Right: 'Pimp Pad' 3-d temple, 2008

balls out. After I did the first one, I thought, 'sweet, I'm quite buzzing', and then I just did one on a bin, and it fitted nicely. I had that thing of thinking, well, if anyone stops me all I'm doing is painting on something that's full of fish bones and cans of beer. I know the company that make the bins don't want their logo going over, but I thought it was probably better than painting on an old building which somebody owns. Best of all, you can get the thing, unlock the wheels and drag it round the corner, paint it and then put it back on the street."

There wasn't really that much of an illegal graffiti scene in Bristol at the time. Was that your motivation?

"I think it goes back to understanding from the very beginning that it had to be illegal and it had to be to do with tags. It was about putting up your name, and getting fame for that. I think when you hide it all in a hall of fame, although it's outside you're still restricted to a sort of gallery. It's better to see something by surprise going down the street, rather than thinking, 'I'm going to Dean Lane Skate Park to check out what pieces are up.' It's much more fun to be like, 'Bang! that's a new one, he's been busy!'"

At Bedminster skate park you did those intricate letter-based pieces. You seem to have moved away from those now.

"When I was doing the letter thing, I was trying to make sure that it wasn't just letters. I was still conscious that you've got to make it so that everyone can enjoy a little bit of it, but through getting into doing printing and doing stuff for Pictures on Walls, and sort of taking myself more seriously as an artist, I realised that print needs a different approach – it has to be to the point. It's like poster art, you have to get it straight away. The way for me to do that with my art is to take one section and turn it into a piece, and that's fed into what I'm doing now on the street."

Was moving to London a career move?

"I got arrested, and got a £5,000 fine and 300 hours' community service so I couldn't really paint illegally any more, Bristol was just getting too small. Plus I was coming to London more to do things. I think I moved at exactly the time things started really going up, you know? There's loads of space, loads of places to paint. I'm a new person."

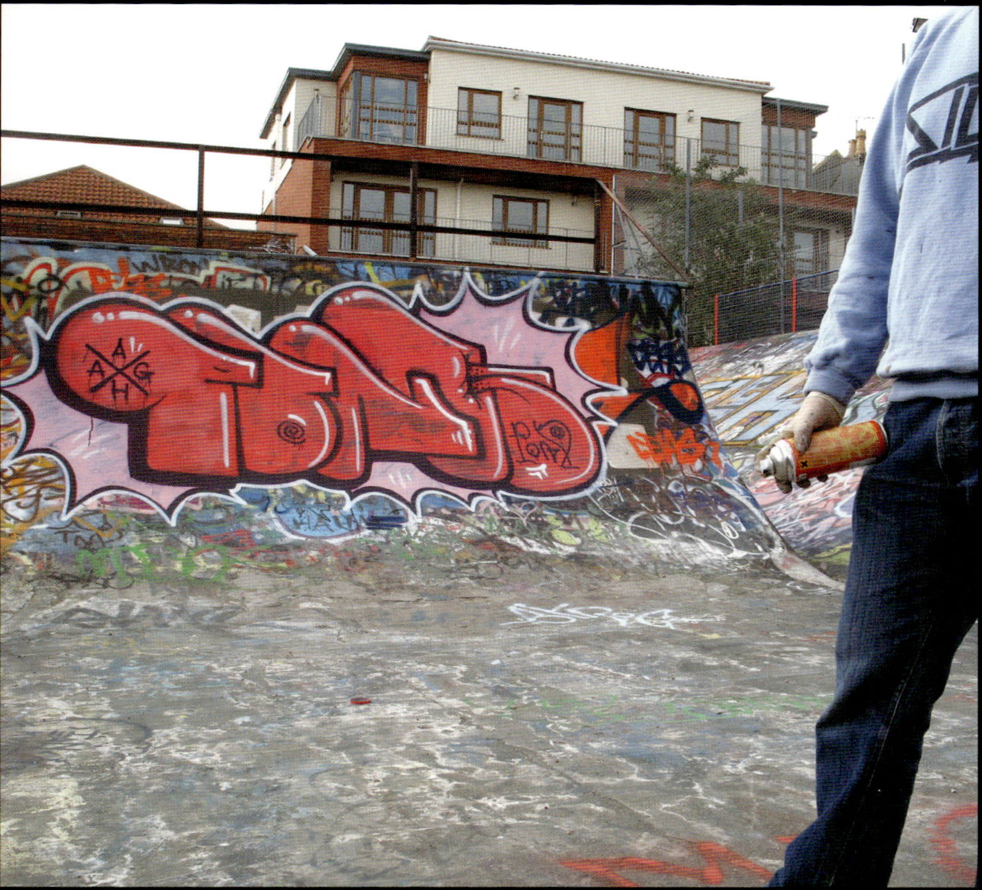

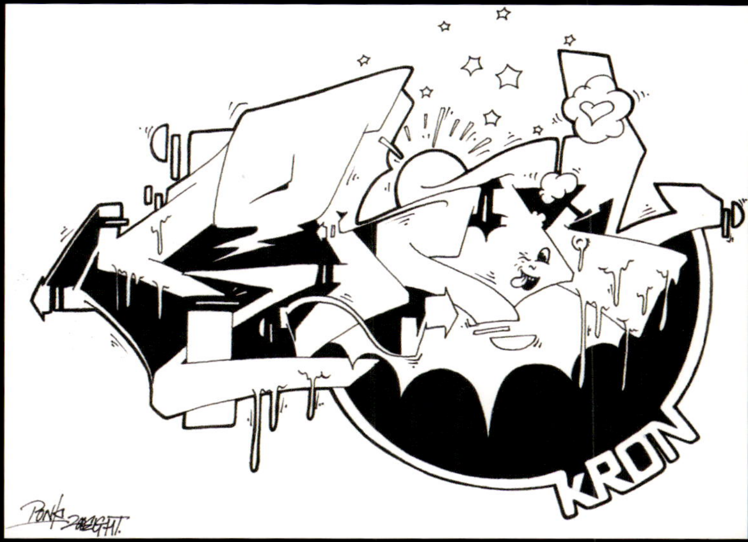

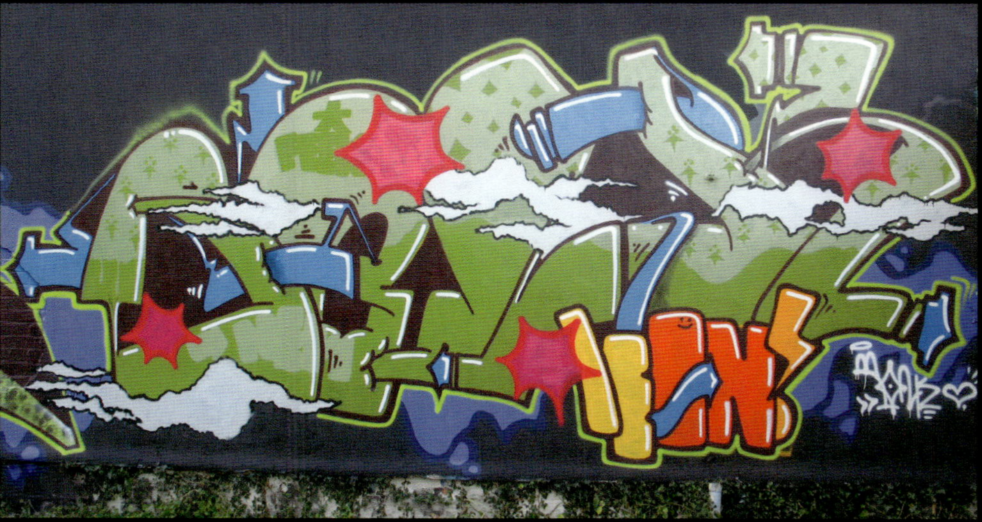

Top left: Bedminster skate park, c.2006

Top right: Pen on paper, 2008

Bottom left: Ponk Leon, 2008

PONK AAGH/TCF

• **You can spot a Ponk piece from 100 yards away, and yet every one is unique and idiosyncratic and has a rhythm all of its own.** He is a prolific graffiti writer whose work owes little to the classic, some would say generic, New York styles that even now dominate so much of graffiti lettering. Awkward angles, wonky letters, and occasionally bizarre additional elements all go towards making his work highly distinctive, playful and humorous. Not an easy trick to pull off whilst maintaining a definite sense of style.

When and why did you move to Bristol? Were you painting before you got here?
"I came to Bristol in 2000 to start to paint and to get involved. I'd been painting bits and pieces in London - just a few toy track sides. I was learning. I was doing things at school in the late 80s, but not seriously, just sketches in school books.

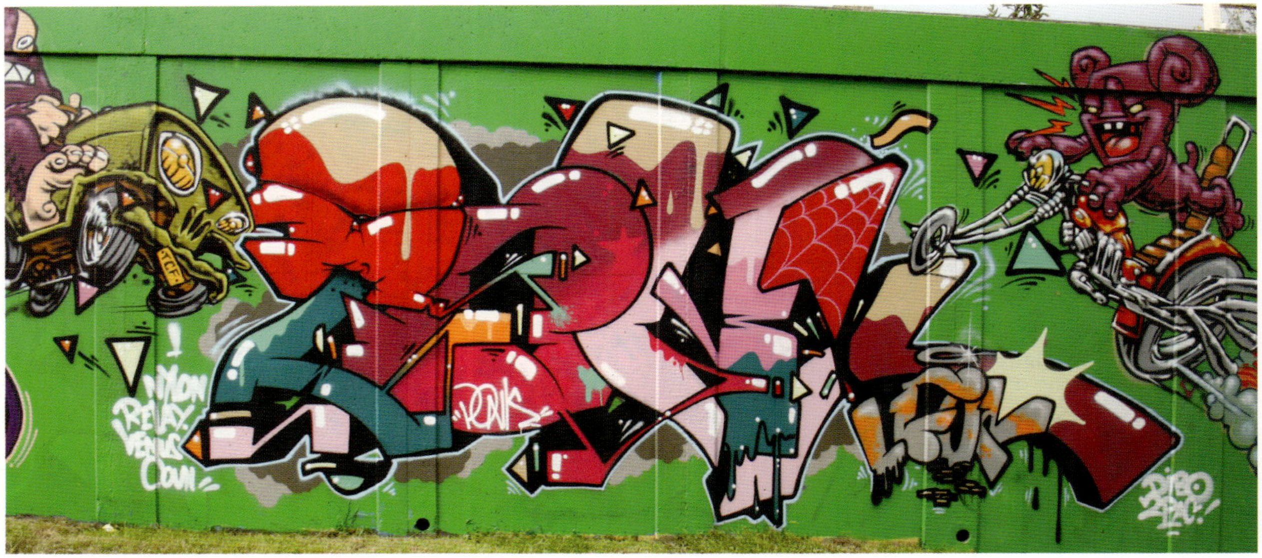

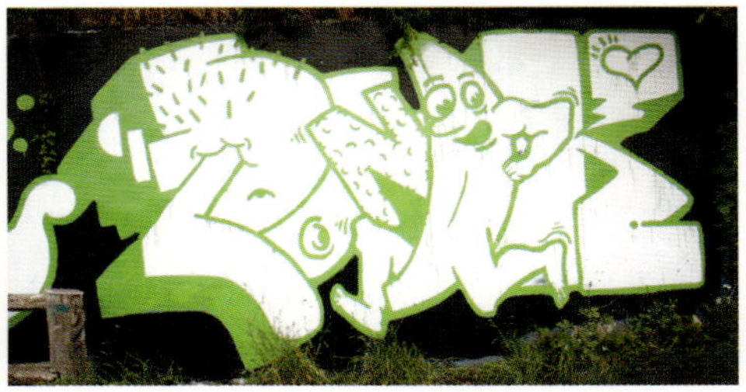

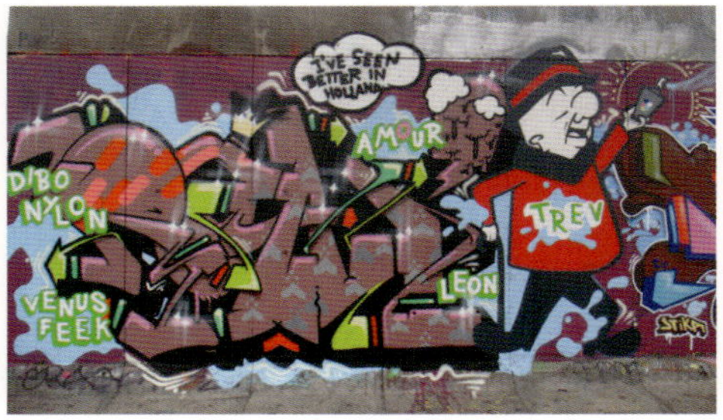

Top left: Rocking the multi-coloured tortilla chips, Ponk and Feek, Riverside Park hall of fame, 2008

Top right: Banana man by the river, 2008

Right: 'I've seen better in Holland,' 2008

TCF were painting some big productions back then. Did you start painting with them as soon as you arrived?
"When I got here, I was just running around putting tags up, really, but I was keen to learn to paint with Feek and his crew. I knew what it would mean to paint with them, because I was aware of what TCF were doing at the time. That was their heyday, in some respects. Feek was painting with Paris, Eko, Xenz, Ziml and all those guys, and they were doing these crazy, full-on productions, the likes of which nobody had seen in Bristol at the time. Then I met Spam and a few others and we painted an old abandoned building somewhere in Bedminster. That's when I got to know Sickboy, and started hanging out and painting with him and Spam."

Your style seems to have much more in common with European, or Scandinavian graffiti than traditional styles. Did you find Spam and Sickboy kindred spirits, stylistically speaking?
"When I was just starting I was looking at the obvious magazines, things like *Graphotism*, and seeing all these generic, US-influenced pieces. There were a lot of good things happening in London, a lot of good people painting, but it was in a very classic, traditional graffiti style. Spam and Sickboy were doing much freer, more artistic things from the beginning. It was still about understanding what graffiti was, but it was so much looser and more expressive, not constricted by ideas of how a piece should look.

"Spam was all over the place, doing crazy characters and Sickboy was more illustrative, doing characters, using different colours and taking influences from outside graffiti. That made me think about their influences and got me looking at other stuff. In eastern Europe, there were a lot of styles that you were beginning to see through the internet. Eastern European styles seem to be more organic, not focused so much on structured letter forms, a lot looser and freer.

Those new styles took me a while to get my head around, with each letter contradicting the last one and bulging and squashing each other. They were a reaction to more traditional styles, and I guess they made graffiti more playful?
"That was always a big thing, me and Sickboy would always try and do pieces that were more fun. And we'd have fun while painting them – using fat caps to outline, for example, so it was faster and more expressive. It was about letters that didn't look right, and people were adding doo-dads [chunks coming off letters] and other new forms, not just arrows or blocks of the letter or cracks in the letter – things which up until then had been the only 'accessories'. People started putting in faces and hands, and squirts of sperm, or whatever else, really.

"There were faster styles, more like train styles, coming through onto walls. We were expanding on that, it was a more European train style with bubbly letters, much freer. We were taking that ethos to a wall and

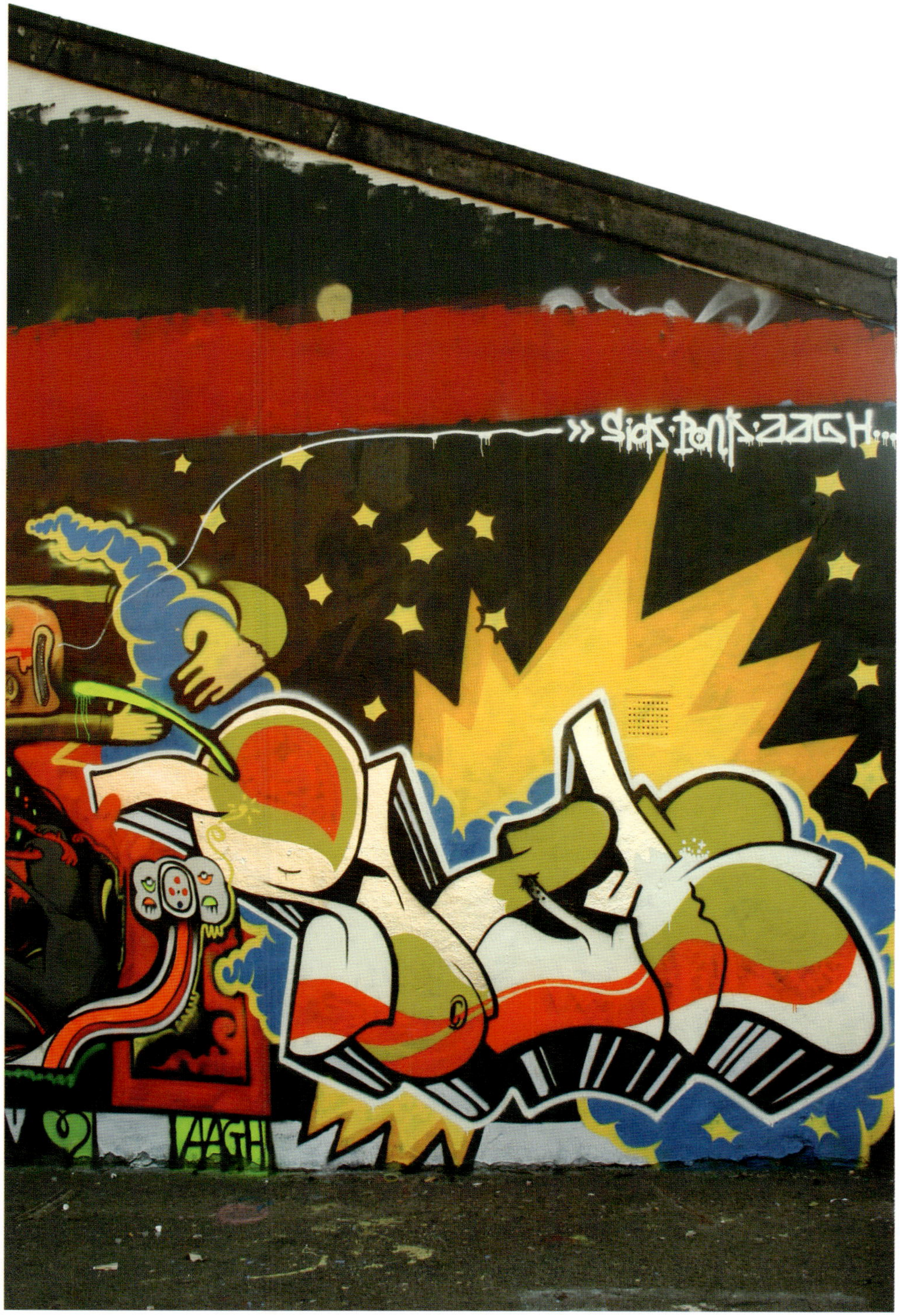

Left: Bedminster skate park, 2006

then were able to take time on it, but still giving it that feeling, that flavour and that movement in the letters.

"We were wanting to go out and do illegal things. That's something I'll always look at within graffiti, and I think that's where a lot of the more expressive things come from. It has to be quick, but at the same time it has to look good. So certain styles are developed in order to make it work in a shorter space of time. That's why the illegal side of graffiti is so important, because it affects everything else down the line. I'll change the shape of the letters in my tag regularly, and the style of my tag affects the look of my pieces. I try to consciously do that, to make sure that the shapes of the letters in my pieces don't always look the same."

The new styles included the traditional elements of a piece, though – outlines, highlights, 3-Ds or shadows, and so on. "We tried not to include those elements sometimes, not even to have that structure to doing a piece. So we wouldn't put a 3-D on, for example, or we'd put highlights in a different colour, or in the wrong place. Or we'd make them more random – not just a line next to the outline, but a squiggly line on the other side, or going all over the place. It gave pieces more flavour. Obviously, you're still using those traditional elements – but you're playing with them a bit, not being so rigid with it.

"It's a case of not necessarily making a piece symmetrical, or not making it balance. Instead, you have letters up and down and all over the place, and arrows coming out of places they wouldn't normally. It's about having a bit more fun, playing around with the structure a bit."

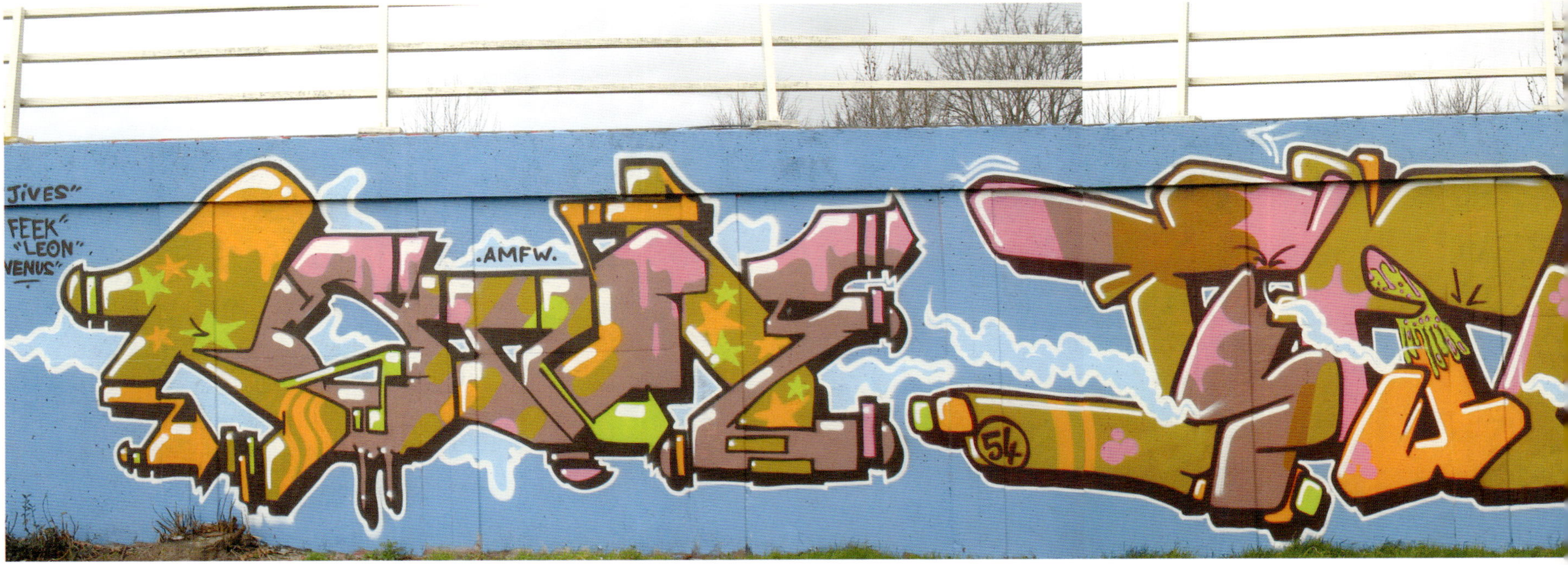
JIVES"
FEEK"
"LEON"
VENUS"
.AMFW.

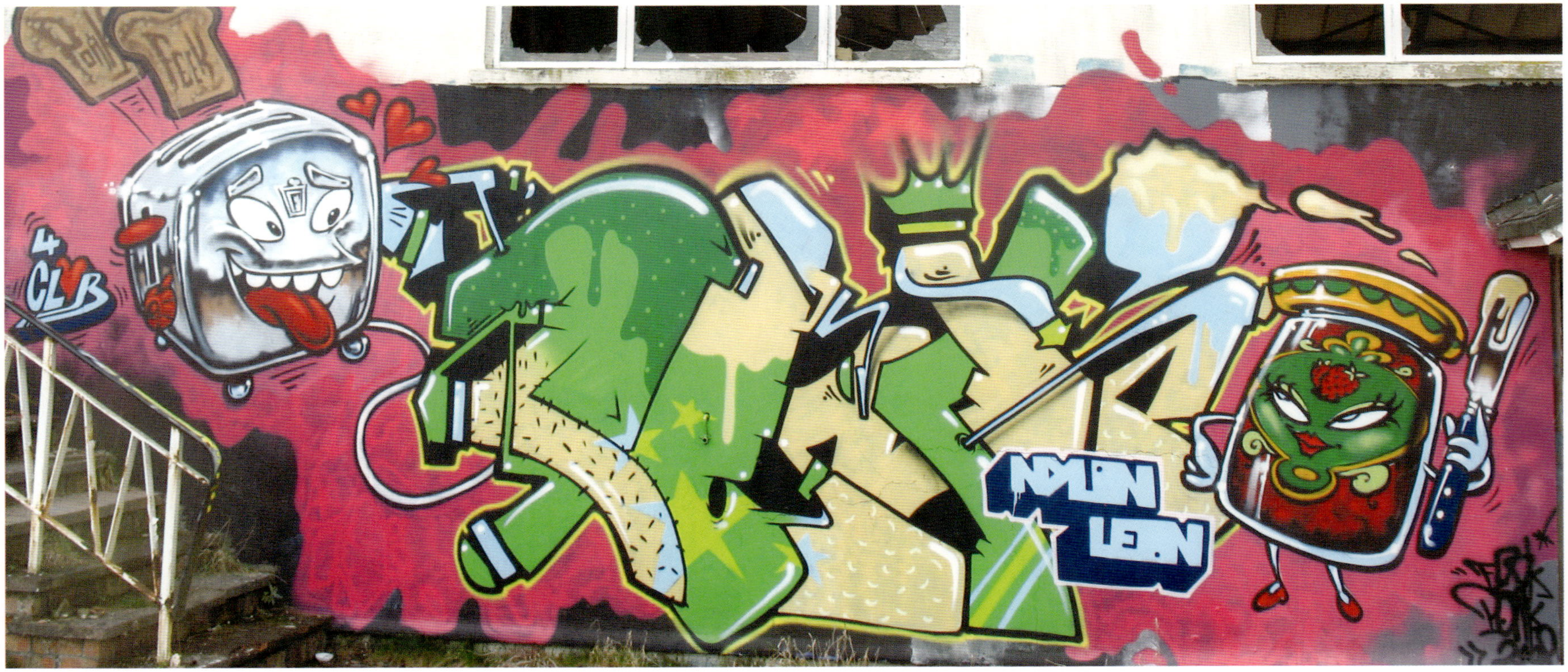
NYLON
LEON

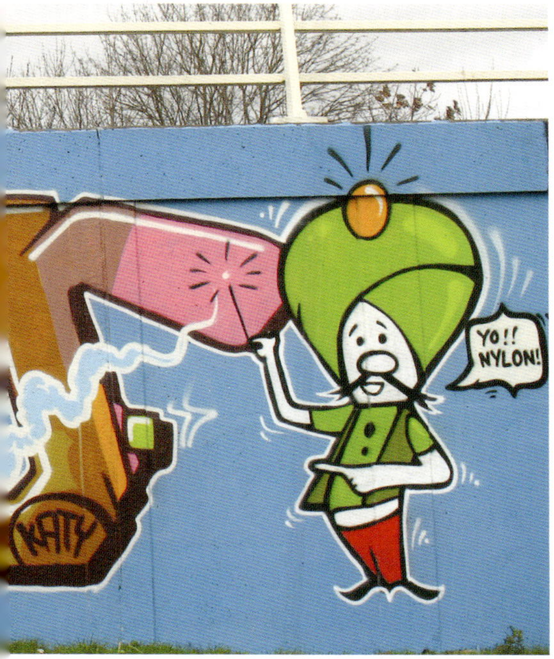

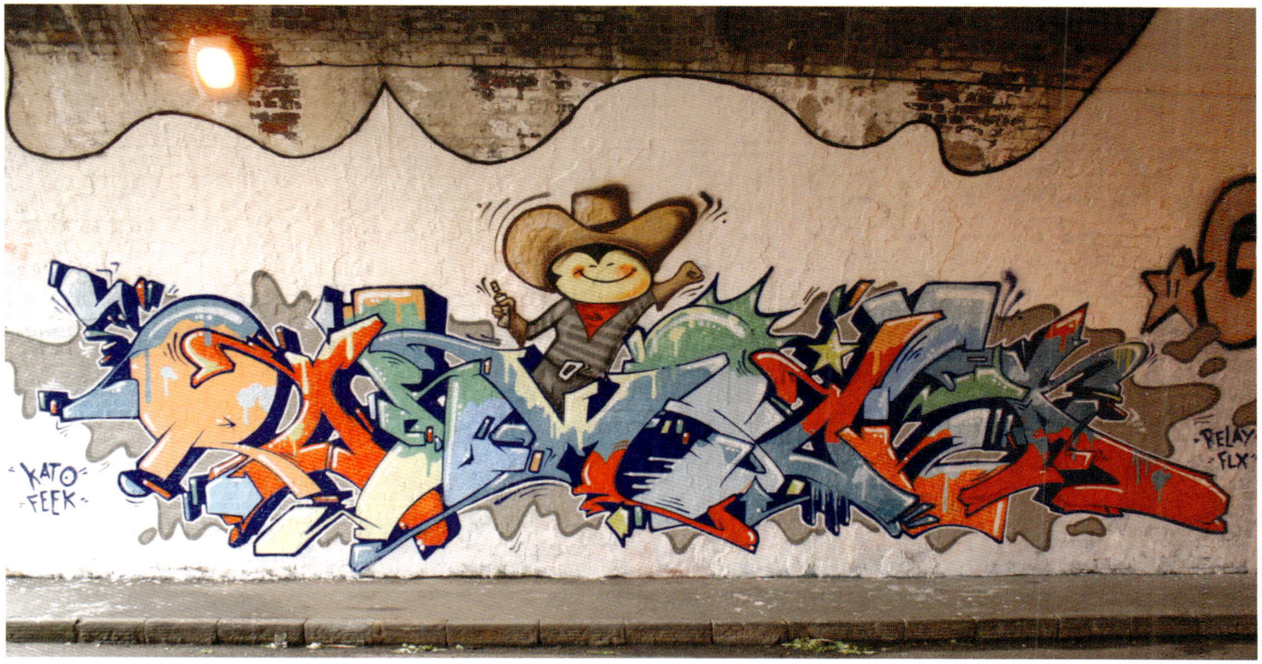

Your pieces also have a lot of humour. How did that aspect of it come about?
"When you begin to work with people like Feek, who can bring humour in, it can be fun. It's not so cool, not so hip hop, not so street and gangster and all the rest of it - which isn't how graffiti artists are anyway, in their day-to-day lives. They're not living in the projects or council estates, and yet their pieces will often reflect that sort of style, which is a load of shit. We all have our own version of what 'cool' is, but I don't think you need to lie to yourself - I think it's better to be a bit more true to yourself."

You've painted abroad a lot. How did that come about?
"That was partly due to the internet, and being able to meet people and talk to them in that context. I've met a lot of people from other countries. It's all very well seeing photos, but they don't ever do a piece justice. So when you actually see these pieces being painted and see the level of skill and style, you realise that no matter how good you thought you were before, there's a million people doing the same - but better, faster and more skilfully than you'll ever do. And that's inspiring, it pushes you to want to do more, and bigger, and better.

"Going away has definitely influenced me. I've got friends now in Spain, France, Germany, Portugal and Poland and they come here as well. I've got good friendships with all these people, through the Internet, e-mailing, sharing photos on Fotolog and things like that. I've learnt loads from those people and it's helped me progress and pushed me. So it's been essential for me."

Are you a competitive writer, concerned with 'burning the competition' and being at the top of the pile?
"I don't think so, but I'm definitely competitive with myself. I'm never happy with my last piece, I always think, 'oh, I should've done that,' or, 'I could've done that if I'd had more time.' I'm always struggling and fighting myself to find a reason why I'm doing it anyway in the first place, and also what I'm going to do for the next piece, or the next colour scheme. I always want to step it up on some level, and to progress."

Your pieces appear to be meticulously planned out. Do you sketch a lot, and take a lot of time preparing to paint?
"I do try to draw every day, and I'll always doodle while I'm at work. Sometimes I try to draw just with a black pen, not sketching or cutting back or anything. A lot of the time my drawings look unfinished, but I'll always find elements of little things that I like. I find it's a freer way of doing things and

Opposite page. Top: Ponk and Piro, Riverside Park hall of fame, 2008

Bottom: Ponk and Feek, 2007

This page. Above: Ponk and Soker go alternate letters, St.Werburgh's tunnel, 2008

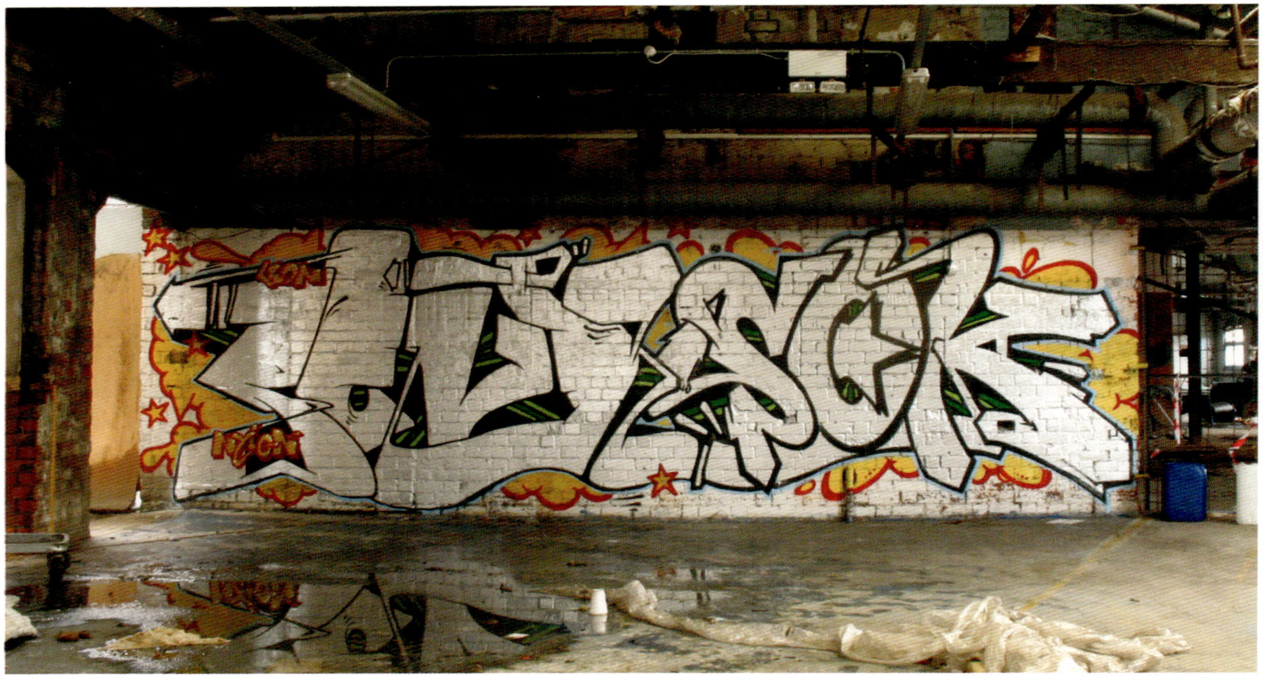

Above: 'Ponk Sok' 2007

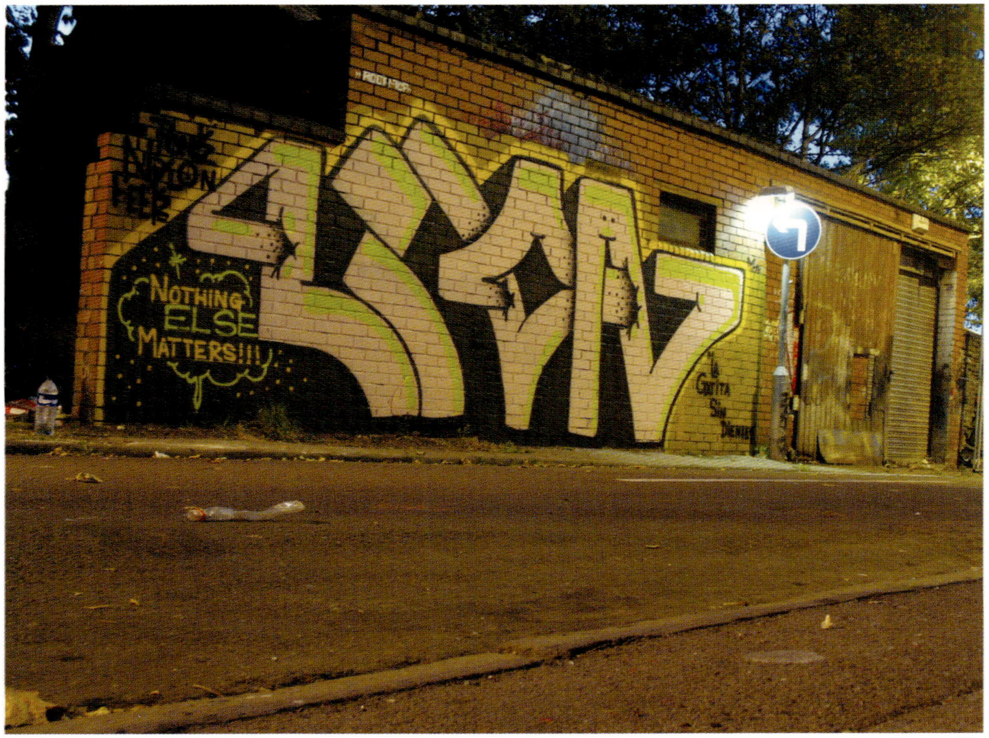

Right: 'Leon (Nothing Else Matters) Easton, 2008

Opposite page. Top left: Bedminster skate park, 2008

Top right: 'Your just a grass wiv a badge' Bedminster skate park, 2005

Left: Ashley Road, 2008

Bottom right: It's all in the detail. Haka gets his pink on.

coming up with ideas. I very rarely bring a sketch to a wall to do a piece, but I'll always remember little bits, even subconsciously, that become little additions to my pieces."

So the drawing becomes a bit like practising a musical instrument to the point that you can improvise?
"You have to make those first lines count, which is why I want to draw this way. I suppose it is practising, really. I've learnt that from Paris and Eko: they always do their sketches with a black pen. Those first initial lines are the lines: you can't rub them out and start again. You get a much freer sense of what you're trying to do or what you want to do."

How do you feel about doing commercial work?
"I'll do the work if someone asks me, and if I think I'm capable of doing it. I work full-time, so it's not really possible for me, but if a job comes up I'll take a couple of days off and do it for the money, and for the (leftover) paint.

"About five years ago I tried to do the whole making-money-from-painting thing, like doing canvases and workshops, but I was signing on and getting housing benefit, and without doing that I wouldn't have been able to do it. It's a very difficult thing to do unless you're really on it. I did a fair amount of canvases, I sold some and had some exhibitions, and I struggled by, but after six months I realised it wasn't what I wanted to get out of doing graffiti. I didn't want to sell it. I don't really agree with that on some levels. I felt it was my own private little world, exclusive to me, and I didn't want to make it mainstream – I didn't want to be part of the machine."

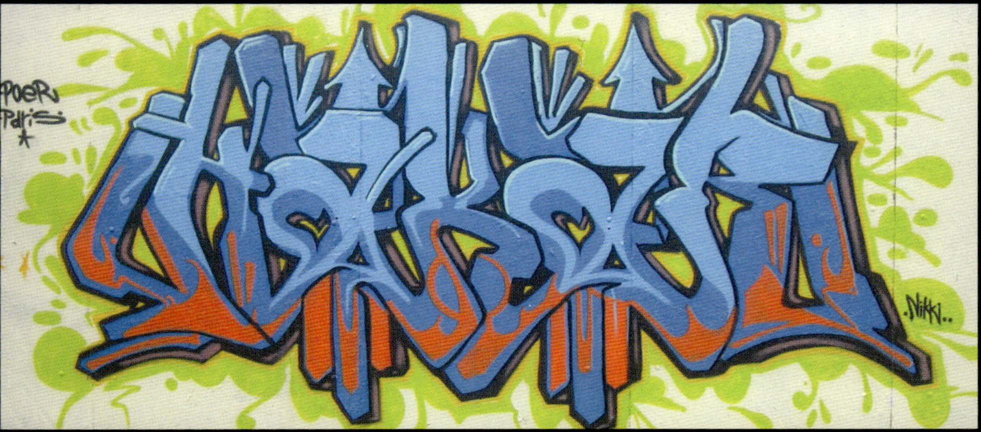

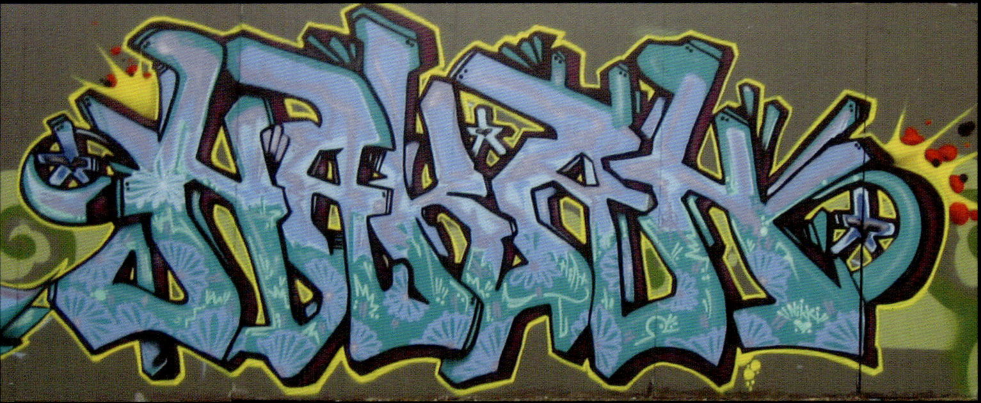

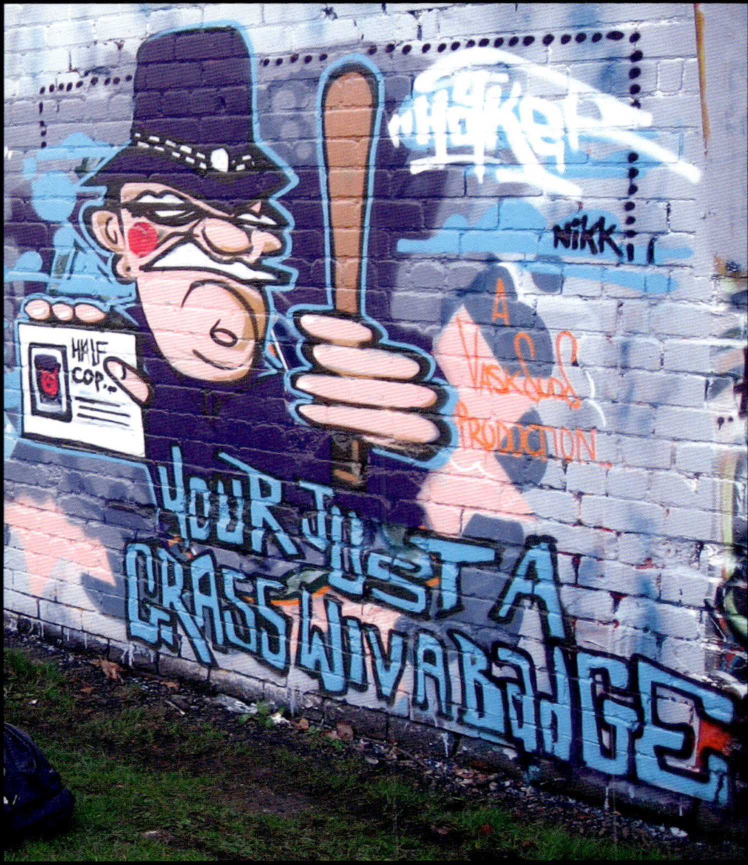

HAKA BTM/PM/KTF

• **Haka's pieces have an organic, bouncy feel and distinctive quality of line that is consistent throughout his characters, letters, and backgrounds.** He has his own curvilinear take on the art form that is both relaxed and dynamic at the same time.

Your style doesn't sit comfortably in any category, such as 'classic' or 'European.' Is that a conscious decision?
"I've been progressing my letters in my sketchbooks for many years, but actually taking it to a wall is the point where you think 'right, it's got to be my very best work every time.' I always like to give as much as I can to the wall and put as much as I can into my letters, to give them flow, character, symmetry, and I like to use serifs. I put in whatever I feel makes up what I am as Haka, and I've fallen into a style where people can recognise my work from looking at it, which is a nice thing, but I'm always looking to take it beyond that.

"I think everyone in the world is born with their own individual style, even if someone says they can't draw, if they were told to do a picture they'd still do it in their own style. Then it's up to you how much you choose to follow it or take inspiration from other people. It's that constant evolution of growing up with your style and evolving as a person that changes how you perceive your surroundings. That plays a big part subconsciously in how your letters, or whatever you're painting, comes out on a wall."

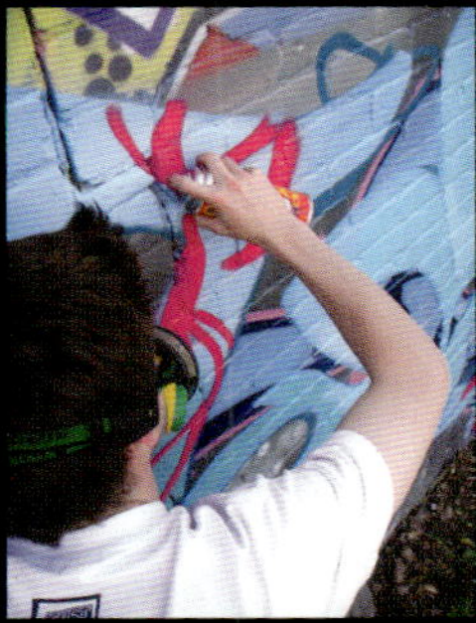

Do you have a particular approach, or process, that you adopt when painting a piece?
"There's a formula you create to step into a wall, and the movements you flow with become like second nature to you, because

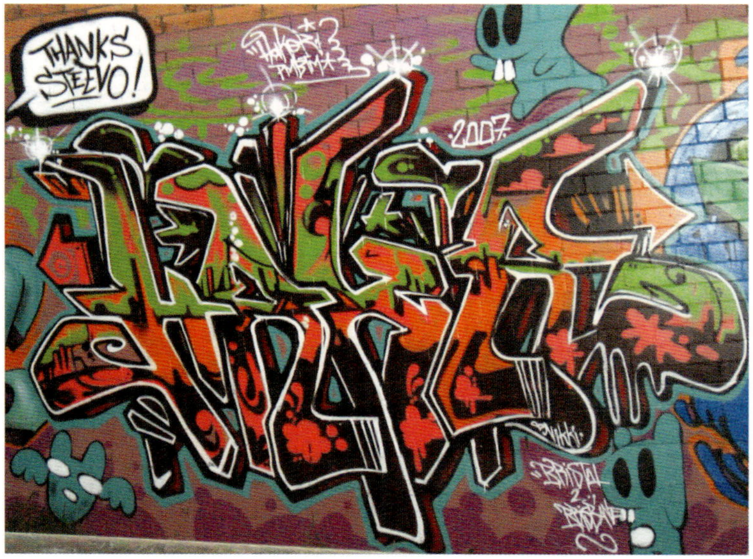

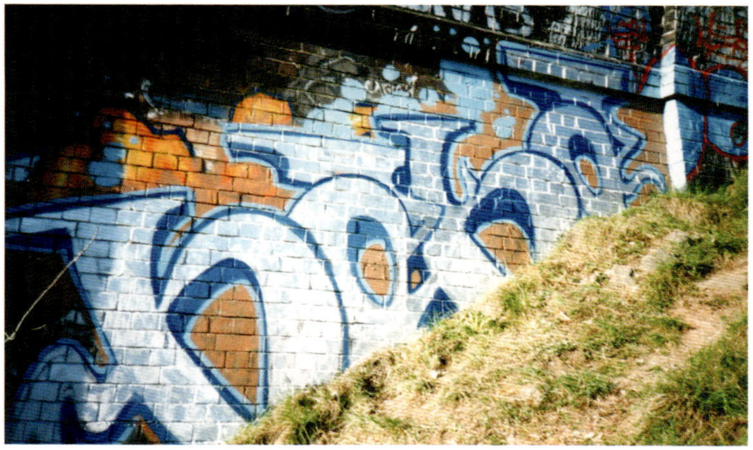

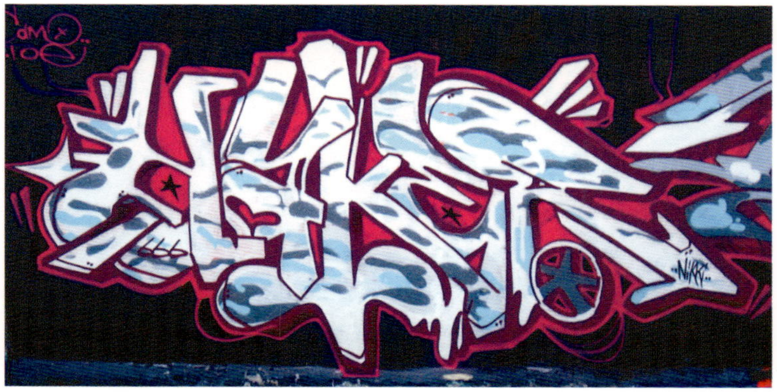

you know the structure of your letters off by heart. I've drawn mine for the last seven or eight years, and I've always liked free-styling, or taking a sketch and adjusting it to the wall to make it suit its surroundings."

The levels of concentration involved in painting a piece can sometimes be quite intense. Do you have to be in the right frame of mind to paint?
"When I get into the zone I'm really set free and my mind goes elsewhere, me and [crew-mate] Stubz always used to describe it as 'cloud stepping' where you could be anywhere in the world, but when you're in the zone and concentrating on your art, time, or anything other than what you're drawing or painting isn't really relevant. That time it takes up we called 'cloud stepping' and that comes from an old UK hip hop artist called Lewis Parker, who made loads of references to it."

How, and when did you first get into graffiti?
"I got into skating first, with a group of older kids from school, and I thought they were cool – they were from a crew called The Bath Pimp Stars! They told me I needed a tag to be a skate boarder. So I came up with some letters and wrote them on stickers and started sticking them around school. I hooked up with a couple of my friends and we went and started doing a couple of our first pieces around our local area, with car paint on garage doors.

"Then I started knocking around with Stubz and DSK Crew, which was Wrecker, Kid Kier, and those guys, and we met up down at the spot under the M32 one time. They were the boys who sort of said 'come on, you can put together something nicely with a bit of emulsion behind it.' From there me and my mate Driz did our first full colour piece down under the M32. It was okay, but my outlines were a bit shaky. It was dark blue with orange bubbles and a red 3-D."

Were there any older writers who gave you pointers or were an influence?
"The first person who taught me how to paint characters was Acer (TCF), I met him maybe like a year down the line, after doing a few little things with a couple of my friends. He started to school me a bit and I showed him my sketches and my outlines, and he was quite critical to begin with, and always picked up on things like if one of my characters looked too much like a Vaughn Bode's, he would be the first one to say, which was what I needed.

"Acer was always my biggest critic: he'd say 'you need to tighten up, you need to do this, you need to do that, watch your colours.' He really helped me, he gave me a bit of discipline when it came to structuring my pieces, he definitely made a big impact on the standard of my artwork. Paris (TCF) always looked out for us, and was always enthusiastic, and Shimz to an extent as well. He was very excited about what was going on with the younger scene."

Your work embraces influences from different places. Which artists from outside graffiti do you most admire?
"I did a graphic design HND course, and I had a very anal teacher, who was very much into typography and it sort of got drummed into me that you had to have a type style that represented something and I think I applied that to my graffiti. We went off on a college trip to Prague, and it was over there that I got really influenced by

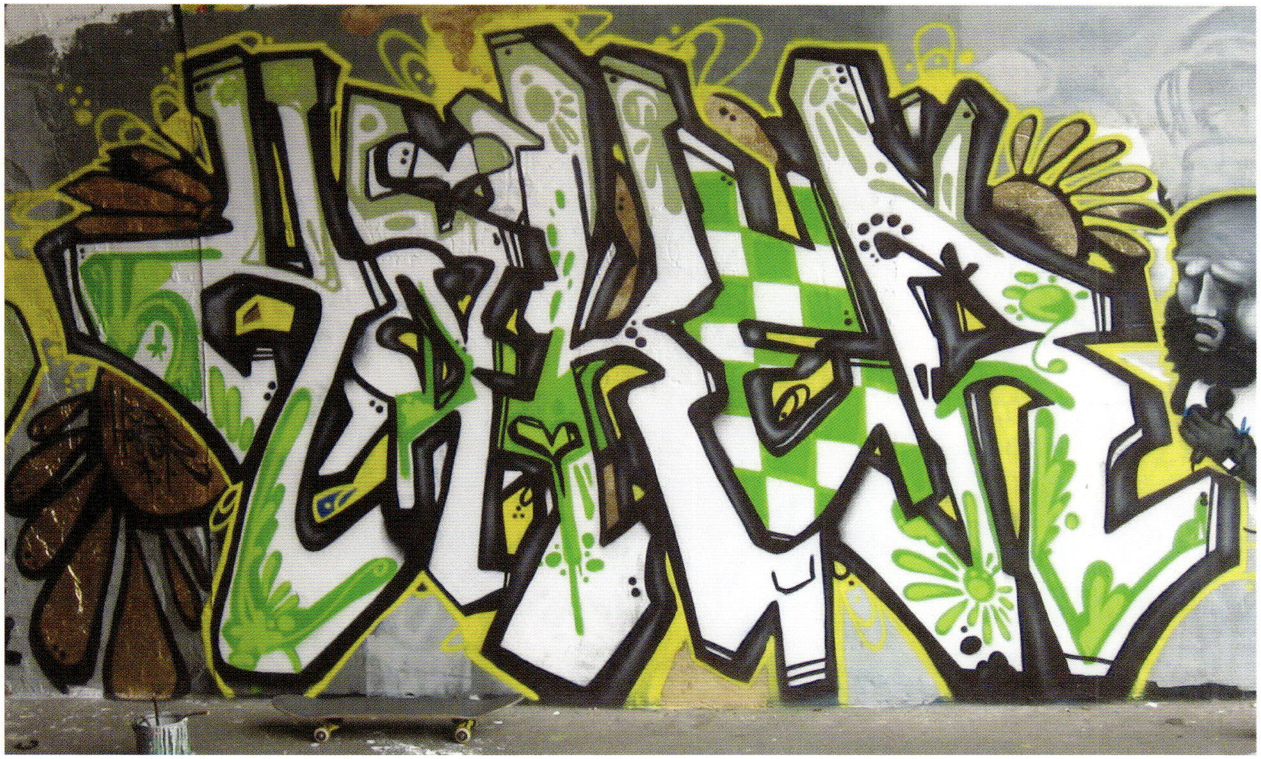

Alphonse Mucha. We went to his gallery and from there a lot of Art Nouveau came into my work. I started working on borders and also female characters. While we were in Prague I went off – saying I had a friend there – but I actually hooked up with one of the founders of the Prague scene, a writer called Pois, and he took me in and showed me around and we painted together, and that was my first piece of published graffiti – it was in a Czech graffiti magazine."

I know you've painted with lots of different people over the years, but who were your first crew?

"BTM, the founder members were myself, Scie and Driz, and back then we were smoking quite a lot of weed, so we came up with the name Burn Too Much, which had two sides to it – burn too much weed, and also burn too many walls. Being 15 and stoned we thought that was really clever. Then there was little Syan, who was my apprentice, and I schooled him in the same way as I was schooled by Acer, I passed on a bit of knowledge to him, and helped him with some of his earliest pieces.

"We were doing track sides and street bombing – mostly one line hollow throw ups, not too much tagging. I was always concerned with getting something a bit more up. I had this certain throw up that I practised quite a lot, and I wouldn't tag them, I'd leave it more as a kind of street logo. It contained a love heart and I was with this girl at the time, and the idea was that I was spreading the love throughout the city, so every time she saw my stuff she'd know the love heart was for her. Cheesy shit! I did a piece on my girlfriend's route home, which was like a motorway spot. I was going to a free party one night, and had some chrome and black with me and so I decided to do a big blockbuster with her name on it, so I did a big Nikki piece right there on her way home and didn't tell her about it. I just said 'you might want to look out of your window under that flyover.' It was five six-foot square letters."

Graffiti can make a personal statement in a public space, which is strange when you consider the inherent anonymity involved in illegal painting.

"A lot of my stuff would refer to things that were going on in my life at the time, and in some sort of weird fucked up way every time I look at a piece of mine I think about where I was in my life, and what state of mind I was in. I can trace back to where I was when I painted it and think of the circumstances I was in, and that was how I expressed myself at the time, through graffiti, and a lot of the things I was trying to achieve were channelled through that."

Which productions or collaborations are you especially proud of?

"We were the first people to do the M32 spot end-to-end, it was St Patrick's Day so a lot of Guinness got drunk. There were writers from all over England that all came together. And although it's never been classified as a legal spot and people have been arrested there, it just goes to show that if you've got that many people working towards the same goal, and you look like you're being professional and organised, people tend not to bother you."

Opposite page. Top left: Australia, 2007

Middle left: Uphill track side, c.2002

Bottom left: New camouflage, Bedminster skate park, 2006

This page. Above: Haka and Kye One, St.Werburgh's tunnel, 2008

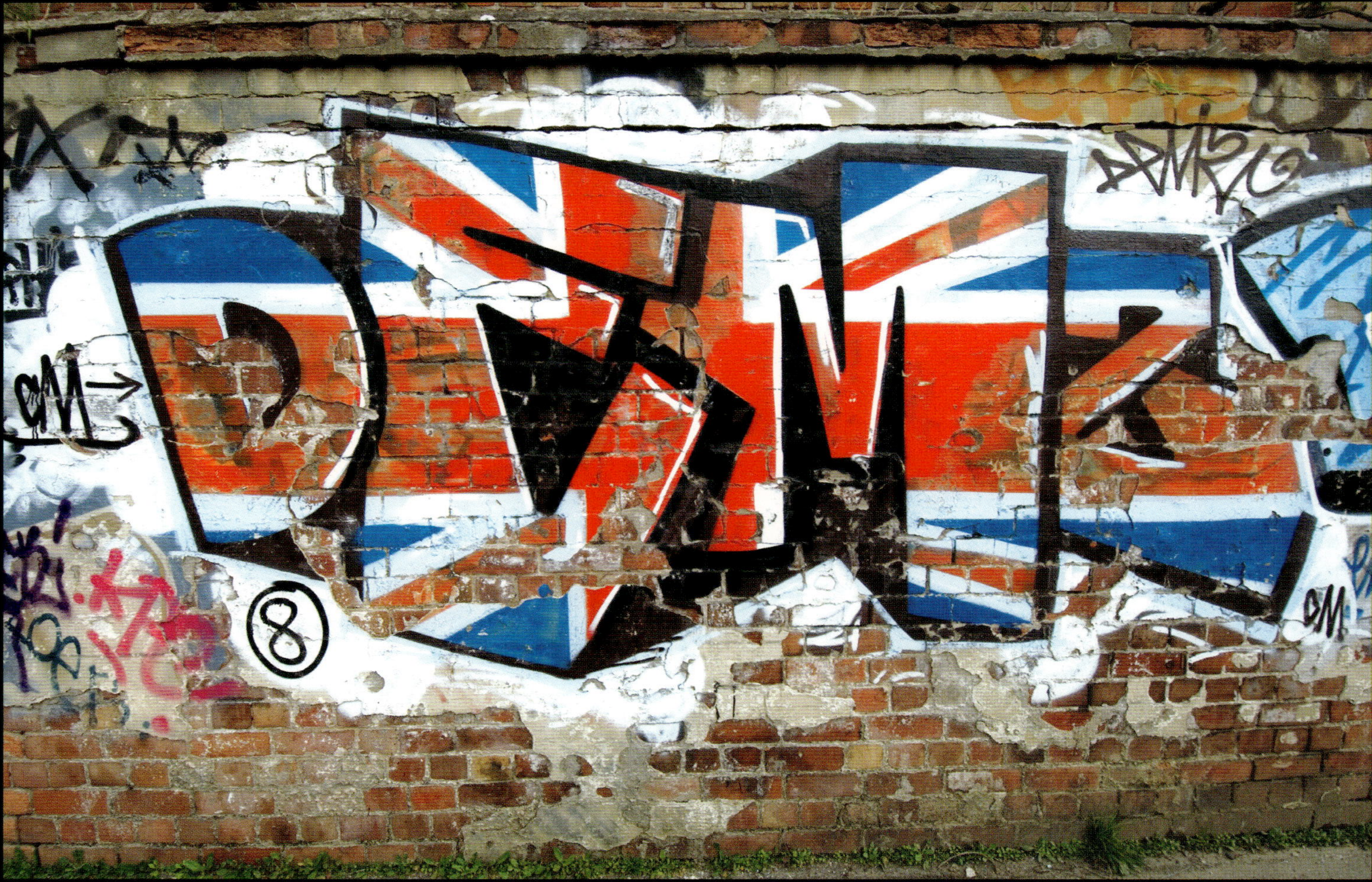

Above: CM crew in effect, Westmoreland House, Stokes Croft

Above right: The distinctive Union Jack fill, behind Temple Meads station

DEMZ CM

• **"I don't see myself as no big writer, I haven't even done that much graff, I just did my little corner of the world when I was younger, and had fun with my friends.** I just enjoyed it and had a good time."

Demz's self-effacing summary of his time painting illegal graffiti in Bristol belies the fact that many local writers hold his audacious achievements in high regard. Yet he does not consider his work to be especially noteworthy or even worth documenting and he is even less concerned by people's opinions of it - or of him.

Can you recall your earliest memory of seeing graffiti in Bristol?
"I remember when they built At-Bristol they had that massive production, Walls on Fire. I must have been eight years old or something - and just thinking 'how have they done that?' I liked every single piece, just because it was there. It blew my mind."

Why did you first pick up a can of paint?
"I started writing on my own, just vandalising things at first, before I got into graffiti. I was going out with pens and spray cans and writing things. I didn't have a tag. We always used to go round as kids and go into derelict buildings, just smashing things up, and I'd take a can of spray paint and just fuck some things up with it."

Can you remember your first attempt at painting a piece?
"My mate Dowz had this kind of lettering

style, and the two of us used to skip school and go to this building. It's not there any more – like everything in Bristol that was good, it's been made into a block of luxury flats. We'd just go and smash windows and shit. I had a can of paint and I tried to do this outline. It was possibly the shittest thing known to man, probably the worst piece of graffiti in Bristol history."

So you would consider yourself to have been a toy when you started out?
"I think all writers should work their way up from being toys. These days, writers just come out and they go down on the lines, find a style and take it – and then they think they've got style. Before they've even got can control they've got style. I think everybody should be a toy for a good amount of time. Just be a toy and accept the fact, and respect other people's graff. Then as you paint more, you'll get better."

Back in the day, biting was the worst crime you could commit. But we were all influenced by other writers.
"Taking influence from people is one thing, but if you see somebody that's never been a toy, you think, 'where's this come from?' The reason I was such a big toy is because I never had anyone to school me. When I was younger I came up in the lapse in Bristol graffiti when there was no illegal stuff and TCF were doing big projects. When I started looking at graff properly I saw that people like DMS were doing stuff, and they did smash the track-sides, but you had to know about graff to know they were up."

When did you start to venture out onto the train tracks?
"Around 2003. That was about the time I started painting with Numb. I knew him from when I was about 12, we used to smoke weed together. We started stealing Plasti Kote and painting on the streets around Montpelier, because it was between where we both lived. Montpelier's got a train line going through it, so from then we got into track-sides. We got well into that because it's so much fun, it's an easy vibe. There were fences and that, but it weren't that hard.

"Every weekend we'd go down the lines and each time we'd get a bit further and bomb out all our paint on the lines. Then we'd walk back through Easton with our pens and the dregs of our paint and we'd bomb all the way back to Montpelier. We were doing tags, throw ups, and attempting pieces. Our stuff was a bit weird, a bit off-key, not deliberately, but we didn't have a direct influence from any one style."

For teenagers who live and breathe graffiti, it can be deadly serious. Did you ever fight over graffiti?
"Me and Numb used to be well into that sort of thing. Think about it from a 15-year-old's perspective: if all you do is put all your effort into painting graff, and spending your days robbing paint, and then somebody goes over your piece, it don't seem mad to hit them, it seems completely natural. Especially if they come to your area – then, it's like, 'Go on then! Go over me, watch what happens!' That's just how it is, and when you're young you've got that mentality. You don't give a fuck about next week, you just care about today and you care about your graff. Even now I look back and think it was stupid, but that's just graffiti. Any illegal scene is always going to have an element of violence to it. The problem is that if the toys see older writers getting violent, they'll grow up with the same attitude themselves."

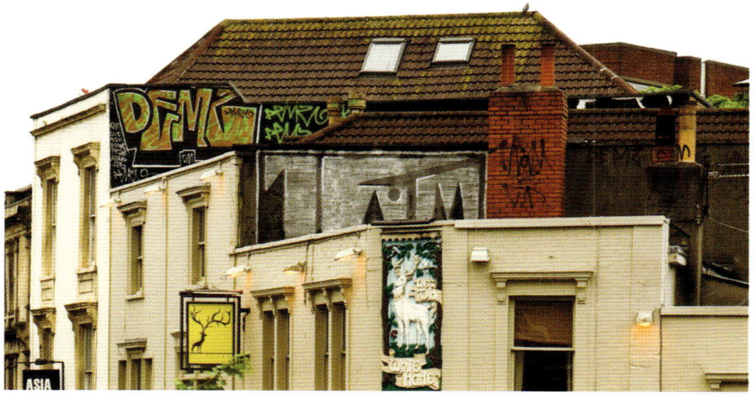

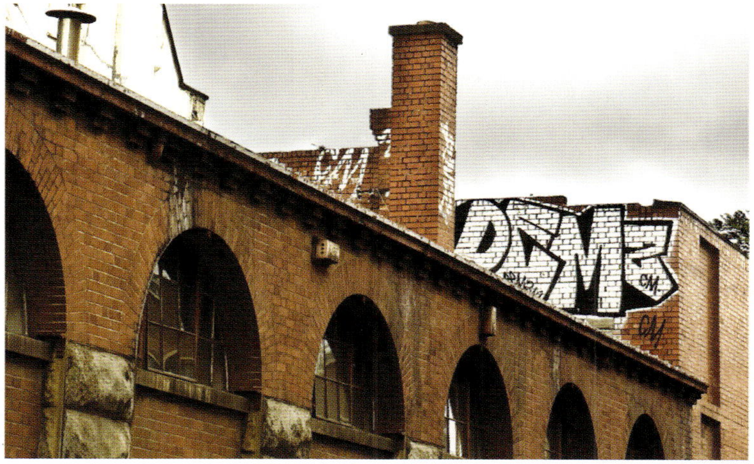

Top: Demz and Prom take to the roofs, Park Row

Above: Chrome roof top, Jamaica Street

Tell me about Crew Mess. Was that something you started?
"No, it was Niso and Adapt that started the crew. It's more like a friendship than a crew. I didn't know them before, but we became good friends through graff, and we used to chill every weekend. I never went to school that much, so I didn't have friends outside of graff. For a long period of my life all my friends were writers, whereas the rest of

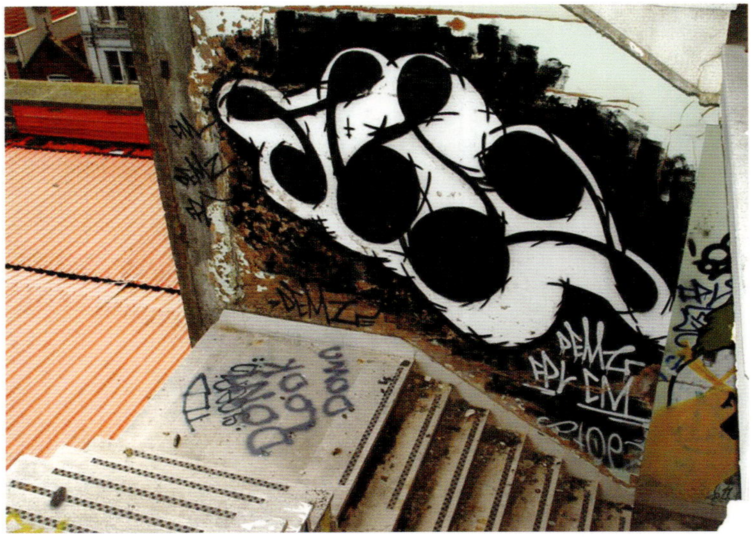

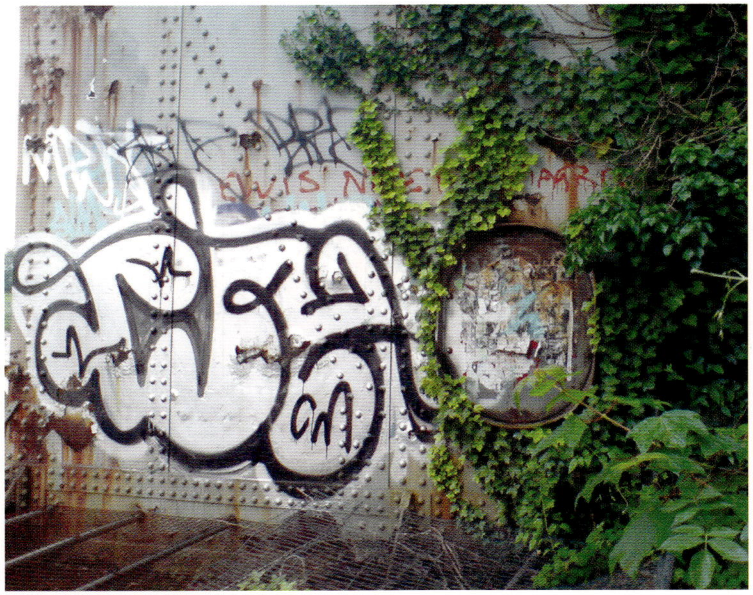

Top: Westmoreland House's staircase is not for the faint hearted

Above: Bridge quickie, behind the CREATE Centre

Right: Westmoreland House chrome and black

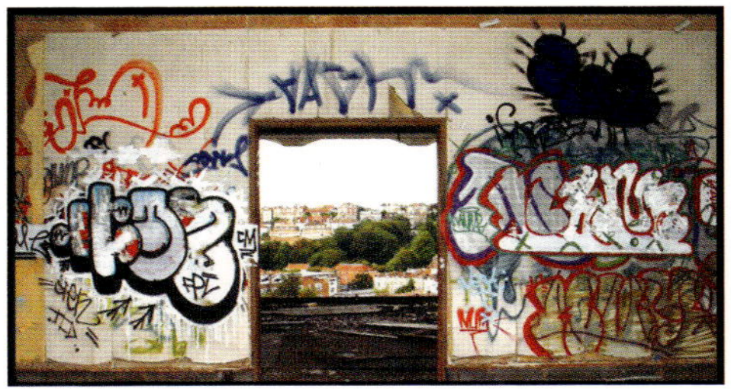

them would have mates that they'd take drugs with, or they had birds, or whatever."

A part from track-sides and rooftops, did you have any particular spots that you enjoyed painting?
"Our crew would never paint halls of fame. I think that made us different. Even people who were out bombing would go and paint places like Bedminster skate park, or the M32. I never liked halls of fame, I always thought, if you could get every piece that's ever been painted in them and spread it around the city, how much nicer would the city look?

"We used to paint derelict buildings, and I'd get really annoyed if people went over my graff, especially when piece writers would come and paint in our buildings. They would treat it like a hall of fame, but it's not, man. It's different,you have to climb in, or whatever, you have to make an effort. Buildings are different. I've seen people injecting heroin between their toes. That ain't a hall of fame vibe. You don't see that nowhere else. You see some crazy shit in derelict buildings."

What makes you want to paint?
"For me it's just about personal enjoyment. It's having something to do that isn't just getting hammered every weekend. I paint for the moment, for the memory and that, and I haven't taken photos of any of my graff. Well, maybe the odd [train] panel. But I haven't got photos of any of my rooftops, or any of my track-sides."

Style had been the preoccupation of graffiti writers since the 1970s, but around the Millennium things changed. Do you think style is important?
"Other people in the crew were into style and it rubbed off on me. I like style and I like people who have a good style, but it's how you use it more than anything. I see it like this: if you do a throw up on a shutter, that's going to take you two minutes, but if you manage to pull off a colour thing, or something that looks tighter and better, you've upped what can be done. If someone's done something better and taken more time to do it, then I'll rate them more for doing that, because they've obviously put more effort into doing it. In that sense I do rate style."

Did you consciously adopt a kind of 'anti-style', or did it just come from bombing hard and fast?
"Looking back I'd say most of my graff was regrettably lacking in style! It was more about getting up and doing letters that people could read. You get a style from doing things quickly. My hand style was so wack when I started writing, but you progress. Most of the rooftops were just done fast, I wasn't really that bothered."

Are there any writers you've painted with who have been an influence?
"When I started writing with Adapt and Niso, after Numb got caught, those two were definitely an influence both style-wise and on how to paint. Adapt don't even paint no more, but when he had a mission, it was a proper mission. Then after Adapt, I started painting with Prom, and we did some rooftops together, although I did most of them on my own, really. I'd do track-sides on the weekend with everyone else, then go and do rooftops during the week on my own."

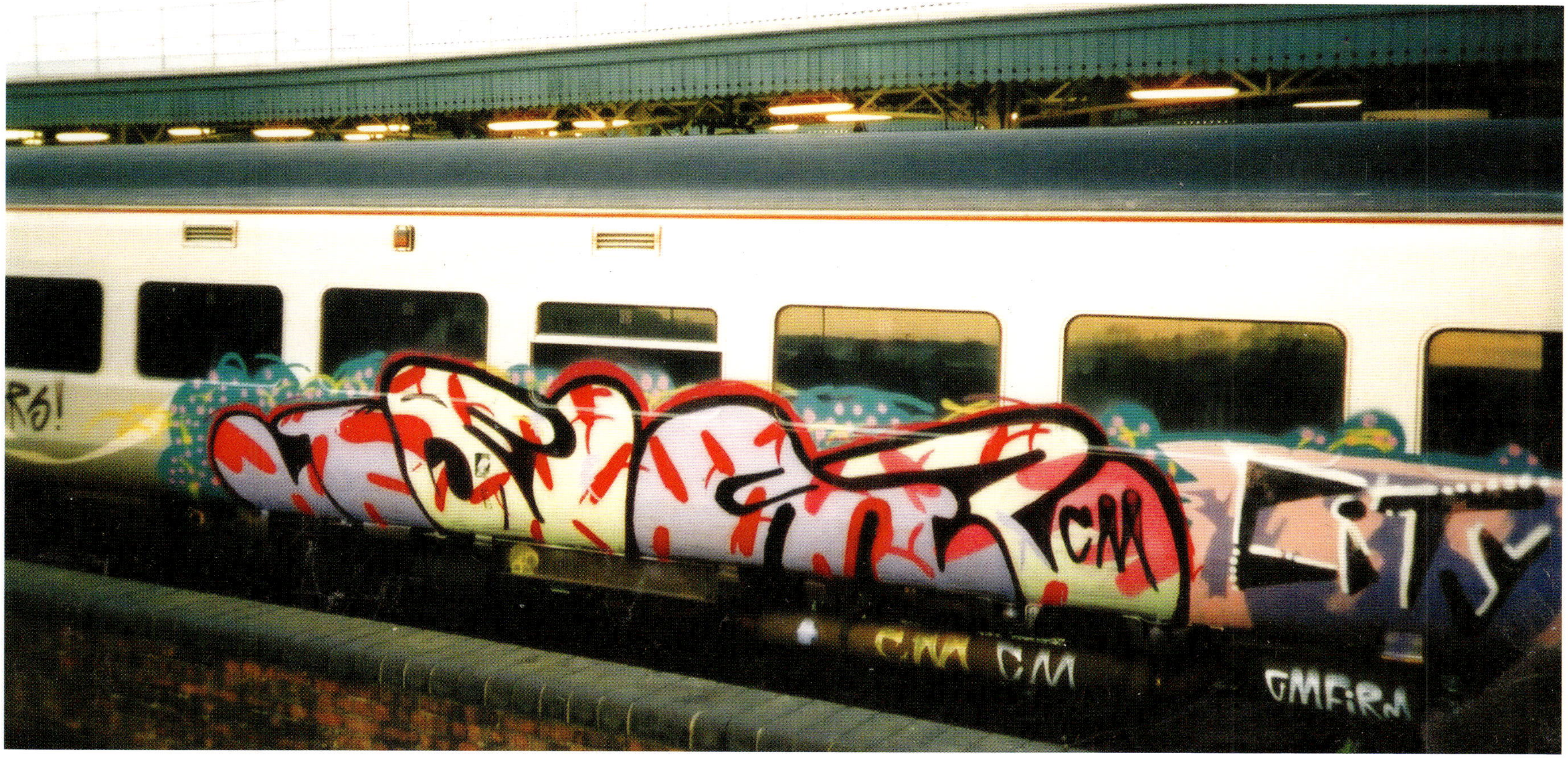

Above: 'The next train on platform 5 is the Demz inter-city express'

I'm glad you brought up the subject of rooftops, that's probably what you're best known for. How did you do it?
"Everyone has their own way of painting anything. I'd just walk around looking up – nearly getting run over about 100 times a day – and I'd just look for a way to get up, look for a back alley. Or look for scaffolding and think, 'well, if that's there, how can I get along and get onto the next rooftop? If I can get up there on that, how can I get from there to there?' Every time I did one, it would get me thinking about the next one – I'd look across and think, 'oh fuck, if I go across there I can get a little bit further.' It's not rocket science."

And once you're up there, is it actually easier to paint a rooftop than, say, a wall on a street? They don't point CCTV cameras upwards, after all…
"Completely. If you paint on the street, anyone can come up to you and be like, 'Oi, what the fuck are you doing?' But on a roof, you can put up a piece on a main road without too much risk from police, cameras or other people. Once you've done it, it does look better as well, because it's up high. And in Bristol they last longer, because the Council can't have a squad of people going around on cranes cleaning off graff."

I guess these days there's a lot to be paranoid about if you're an illegal writer?
"I think smoking too much skunk at a young age made me paranoid, and graffiti just kept the paranoia there. I'm paranoid about everything. What's really scary is when your paranoia comes true. A lot of times I'd think, 'Was that a CID car? Oh, I'm just being paranoid.' But what if it was? That's the thing about paranoia: you never know whether it's justified until it's too late."

What about the British Transport Police? It seems as though they almost take it personally that people are

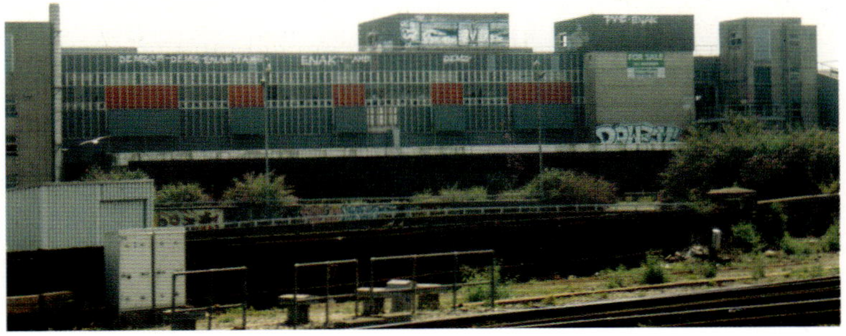

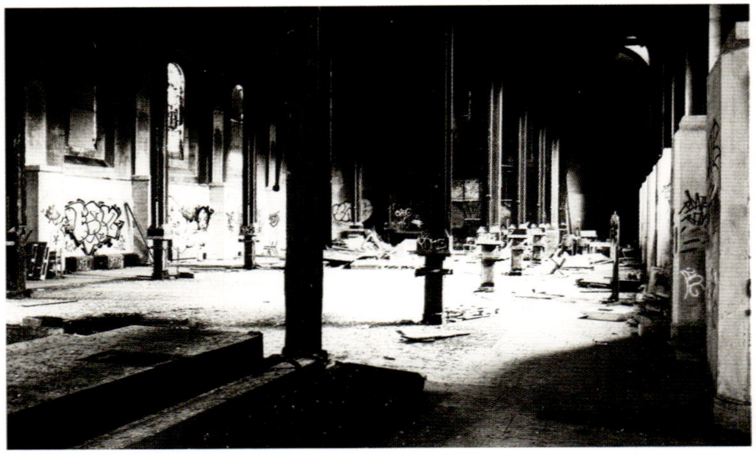

Top: Demz and crew hit the old Royal Mail building at Temple Meads

Above: The old Waldorf School, Pro Cathedral Lane

hitting trains and track-sides.
"The thing about Bristol is that it's a really small city, and if you live in a bigger city you can be anonymous. But in Bristol the BTP have specific people they want to catch and they do take it personally, and a lot of people do write things about them. I never did myself, I couldn't see the point. I don't hate them, they're just doing their jobs. Some of them are alright, some of them are complete fucking bastards, but the majority of them are quite polite."

I guess it goes with the territory. As long as there's illegal graffiti being painted there are going to be people whose purpose in life is to stop you.
"You just have to accept it – there's no point getting angry about it. At the end of the day you're painting graff, and they're getting paid to stop you. If you don't want your house raided, don't paint graff: it's that simple. They can only hold you for 24 hours, unless they're going to remand you in custody, so fuck it! What's 24 hours of your life? How many teachers or people you work for fuck you around for way longer than that? My advice is, if they put you in a cell, just try and sleep. Or, if you really hate them, do a massive shit on the floor."

It's a vicious circle, isn't it? The more people they arrest, and the more the press demonise graffiti writers, the more appealing it becomes to any teenager who wants to rebel.
"For a few years, there was a lapse in illegal painting in Bristol. But as soon as we started bombing there was this crackdown, Operation Compass – and after they started that operation, so much more graff got done on the streets of Bristol. Now they've started a new one to combat the effects of the last one! They put reports in the newspaper to portray it as a bad thing, but I bet kiddies are looking at that and thinking, 'There's kids going out and doing that? I should be doing that!' And at the same time their nans are reading that thinking, 'My house is going to get vandalised, it's not safe to go out.'"

Graffiti seems to have become a convenient scapegoat. Harsh sentences for graffiti writers are an attempt to prove some kind of point, I guess?
"Some friends of mine moved down to Bristol from up North, and they couldn't believe somebody had an ASBO for graffiti here – which basically meant that you can't carry anything that you can commit criminal damage with. I could walk down the street naked and if I really wanted to commit criminal damage I could. That's ridiculous, what's that about? It's a load of shit."

The Council and the police have really got the bit between their teeth over graffiti in Bristol. It's like they see the city as a World Heritage Site. I'm not sure they recovered from the mistakes of Operation Anderson 20 years ago.
"The Council brought Colin Saysell [Detective Constable, British Transport Police] in to deal with the 'graffiti problem' in Bristol. He arrived at the end of Operation Anderson and got trained up by the people that made those arrests. Colin's got anti-graffiti passion."

Passion? It almost sounds like you respect him?
"I respect him a lot, he's dedicated to what he does. I'm not joking, he's a fucking cunt, but he's dedicated to what he does and he hates graff as much as I like graff, probably more. I know that, deep down, he's got a bit of admiration for writers. All the Anti- Graffiti Squad get into graff, because they see so much of it, I know they like it. And they're getting paid for what they do, they wouldn't exist if we didn't exist. We fucking made them. Colin Saysell, and Ali Ross – they're a product of Bristol graffiti, it made them who they are. They need to think about this. Their salary for the last year has been paid because we paint graffiti. If it weren't for us they'd be regular police dealing with drunken bastards and crackheads on the street. We've given them a good job, so they should be fucking thankful for that."

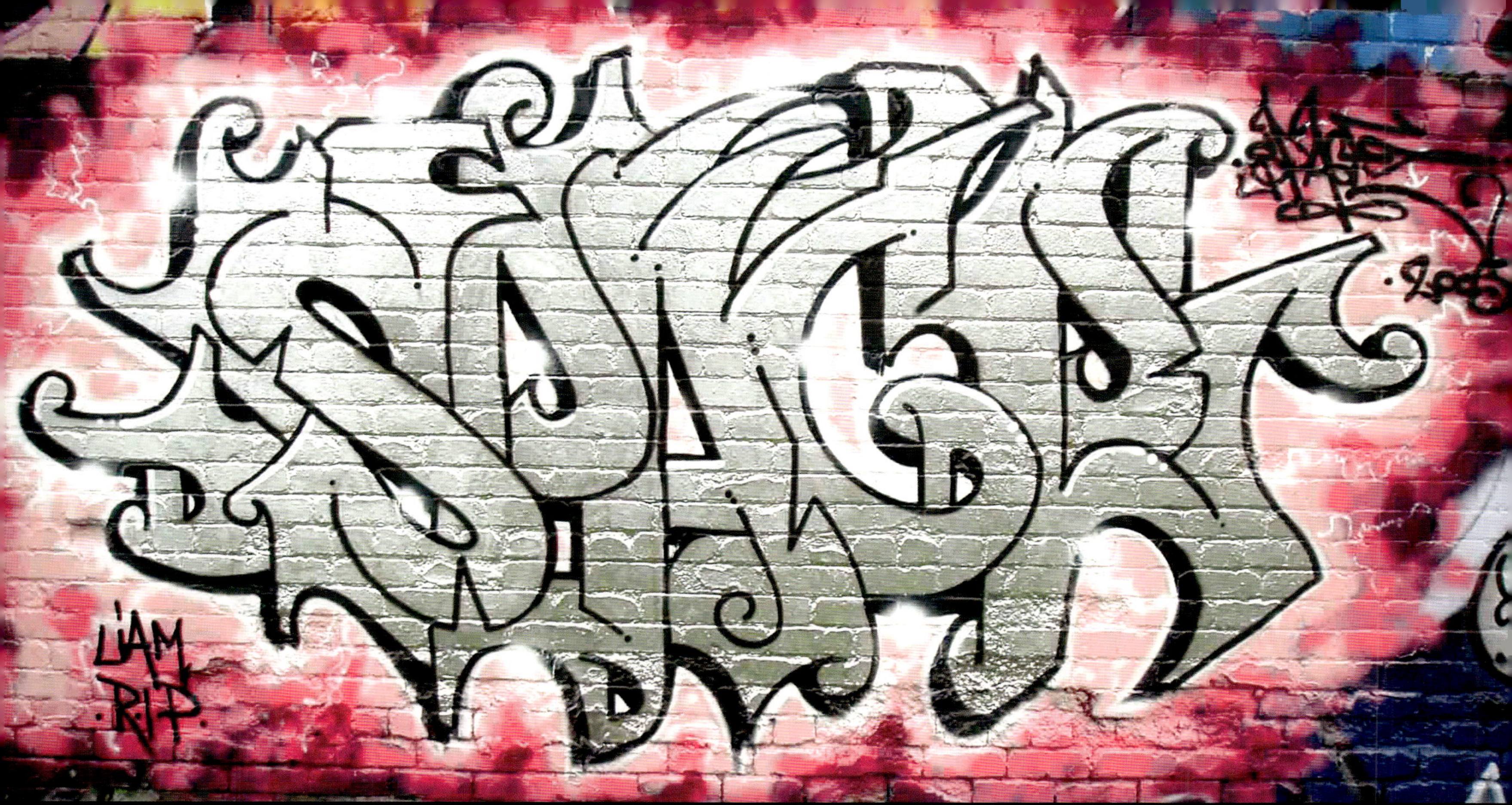

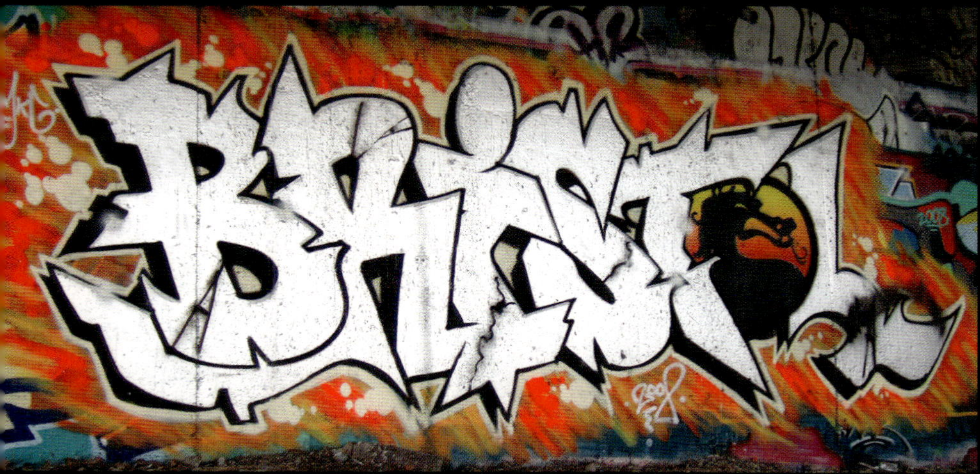

Top: 'Liam RIP' in memory of a friend, 2005

Bottom left: 'Bristol' 2008

SPACE

• **Space is a dyed-in-the-wool graffiti purist whose pieces are both readable and complex.** He is a wildstyle fanatic with a strong sense of tradition and some definite ideas about what constitutes style. A strong believer in the medicinal power of hip hop, Space also teaches graffiti to young people as a form of alternative education at schools and youth centres in Bristol.

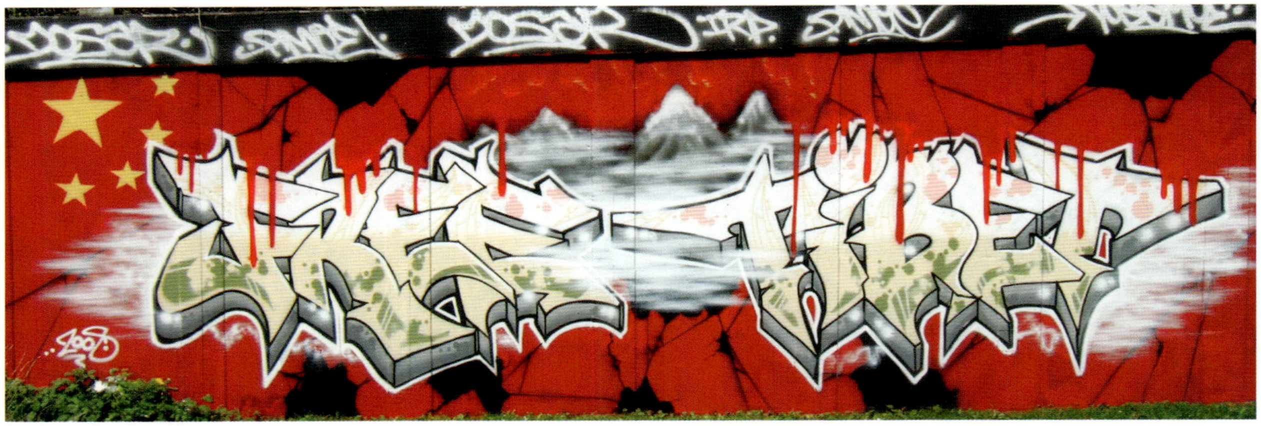

Above: 'Free Tibet' blood in the mist, Riverside Park hall of fame, 2008

opposite page. Top right: Burning black, Riverside Park hall of fame, 2008

Bottom right: MK= Most Kredible, Riverside Park hall of fame, 2008

Where do you remember first seeing graffiti in Bristol?
"For me, it all started from seeing graff on the M32 in Eastville, on the wall along the back of the Millionaires' Club. Shimz was the one that first caught my imagination. His pieces twist and turn, he's wild with his letters, and it's perfectly balanced. What he did was completely pure. It looks how graffiti should look. The colours he mixed were so distinctive they were gritty and disgusting but they shone like nothing I had ever seen. No one had his colours. I wanted to do what he did.

"Then, through a good friend I met the West London legend Infoe One, from KTC. He was an originator of so many styles, a true pioneer. There are a few people reading this who will understand what I mean when I say that Infoe One is a true king. Infoe is my hero. He taught me the ethics of graffiti, and I'm very lucky and grateful. So I got into both pieces and bombing. While I spent my money on Montana and Hicote for pieces, I stole Plasticote from B&Q to do my tags and throw ups. It was all about getting them up in central Bristol for people to see and recognise. A lot of my early bombing was shameful in terms of quality, but my name was out there and that's what you desire more than anything else when you start."

Is there a formula or set of rules that you adhere to for making a piece work?
"For me, it's all about letters. I was never much into characters, although I did like to paint them now and again to complement a piece. But all I really care about is wildstyle. That's what I love the most: wildstyle and awesome colours. Infoe taught me many secret techniques for attaining perfect balance in each individual letter and in the piece as a whole. I learned that graffiti was very much about mathematics, calculating angles and distributing the energy and direction of letters."

Are you a crew writer or do you prefer to paint solo?
"I've pretty much always painted on my own, pieces and bombing alike. I mostly just stayed away from other writers. However, I have painted with a few people: Lev2, DVS One, Adapt and Logoe."

Can you tell me about your experiences of getting arrested for graffiti?
"Getting busted wasn't very good. It was when they first brought CCTV to Bristol and I didn't realise how effective it could be. I was on my mountain bike dropping some tags on Denmark Street, when I got hounded by police cars. They gave chase and blocked me in. It was over. I was arrested and charged with criminal damage, and that's when they took my name. Once they've taken your name they have a piece of you. I can never write Space again."

Have you had any near misses, or been chased much?
"One time I got away from [Colin] Saysell [Bristol graffiti cop]. I'm painting the Millionaires' wall, when I hear a Welsh voice behind me say, 'It's not your lucky day, lad.' I'm backed against a wall with Saysell and some other copper in front of me, asking me what I write. I bide my time with some lies. Then, while he's looking in my bag at all my paint, I see an opportunity to flee. He's looking at the ground. I turn and I'm gone. He gives chase, but I'm a big runner, no one's catching me when I'm running. I'm through the M32, into Tesco. Off with my jacket and my hat. Do a shop. Walk home."

Do you do anything to encourage up-and-coming graffiti writers?
"I do my best to nurture the younger generation, both directly and indirectly. One of the greatest compliments I have ever been paid was that a big bomber – someone who hit Bristol pretty hard – said that I was the one that inspired him to smash the streets. When he was at school he would see my throw ups in the centre of Bristol, and a few years later he proceeded to destroy the town and dwarf anything I ever did. So for him to say that meant a

lot to me. I think a lot of younger writers are inspired by the sheer quantity of what goes up. Their peers get up all across the city, sadly sometimes with little or no style. This means that if a young person is inspired to paint, he will aim to do the same. I hope that through the work I do with young people, I can inspire and pass on the skills, techniques and styles I have been taught for proper piecing and painting walls. Graffiti is a vocational thing, and it's all about passing on the knowledge."

Do you feel that graffiti is a part of hip hop, or is it self-contained?
"I think you have to love hip hop to paint graff. Pure graffiti has a very distinctive look about it. You know when a writer is a hip hop head by looking at their work. You can certainly tell when they are not.

"Just because someone has painted something on a wall, that doesn't make it graffiti. It has to have certain things about it to make it graffiti: blazing colours, rocking letters, a certain energy. A lot of the more abstract artists don't have that quality. That's what makes what they do street art, and what I do graffiti. A stencil is not graffiti. It's neither more or less valid, but it isn't graffiti."

Did your experience with older writers influence the work you do these days?
"I was taught by Infoe One and followed the likes of Shimz and Soker in terms of style. I think anyone can see that, and I intend to carry developing in that direction. I like to encourage young writers to paint traditional graff and pass on the heritage. As the art form evolves, it seems that there are fewer people painting 'proper graff'. I'd like it to stay alive."

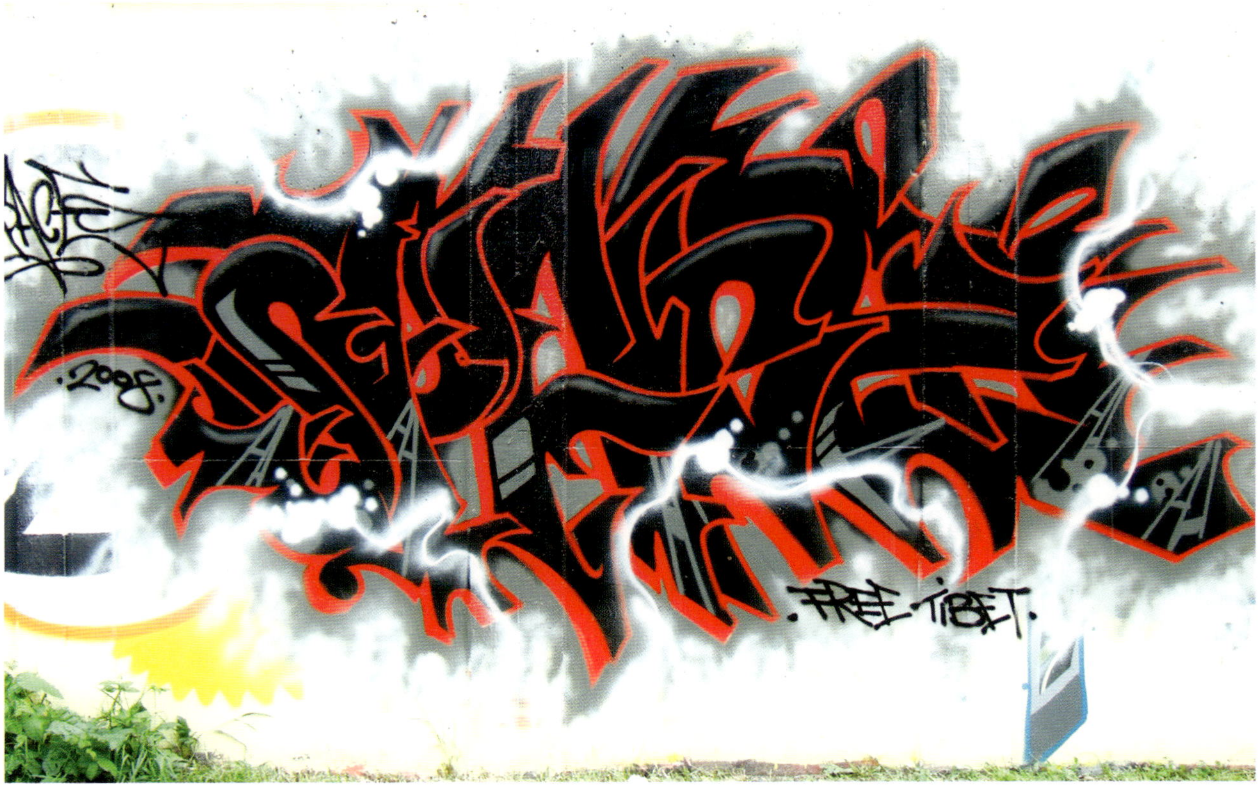

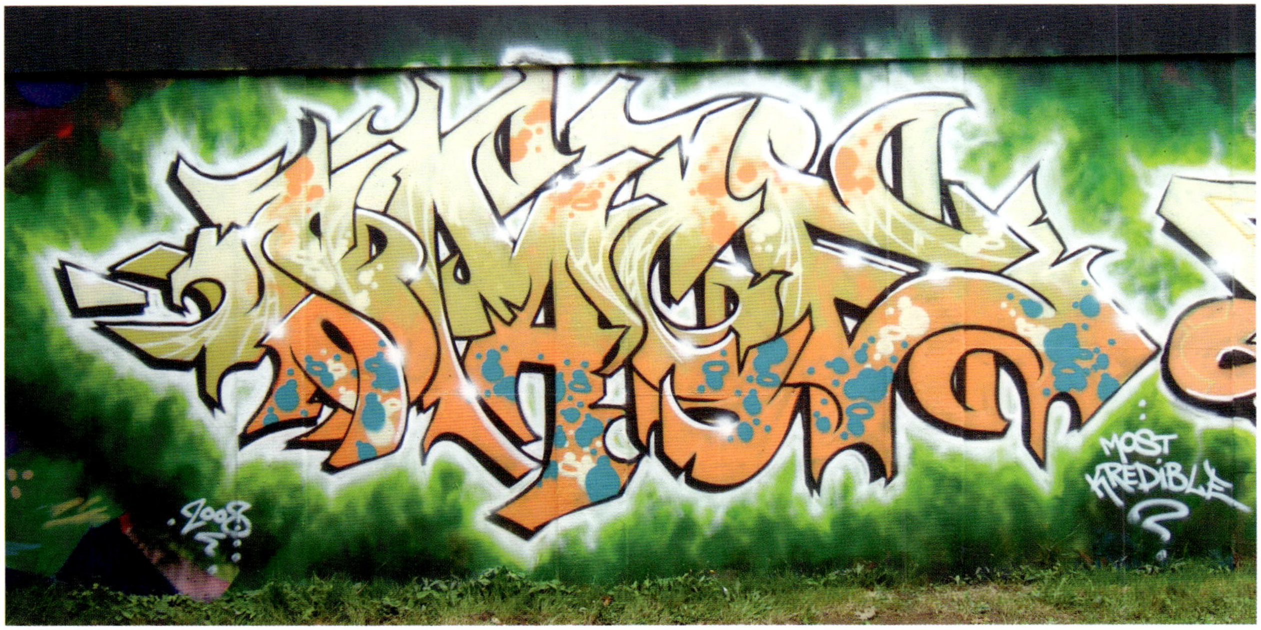

CHEBA

Right: A Cheba canvas goes on sale for 50p at the Cube, at the time Banksy canvases go for five figures...

Middle: Live painting at *Banksy's Bristol* book launch in London

Below: Piece at Walls on fire 2 at the Bristol Festival.

Below: Weapon of Choice exhibition Guernsey

Opposite page. Top Left: 'Chebastein' screenprint

Above: A laser cut skateboard

Bottom: Bombing Welshback 2002 and a more recent Cheba and Lokey take on the Krylon logo in Stokes Croft

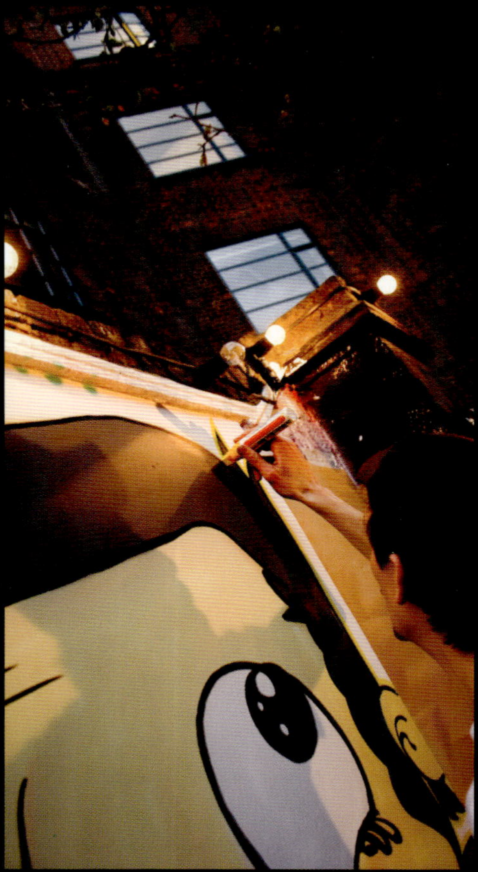

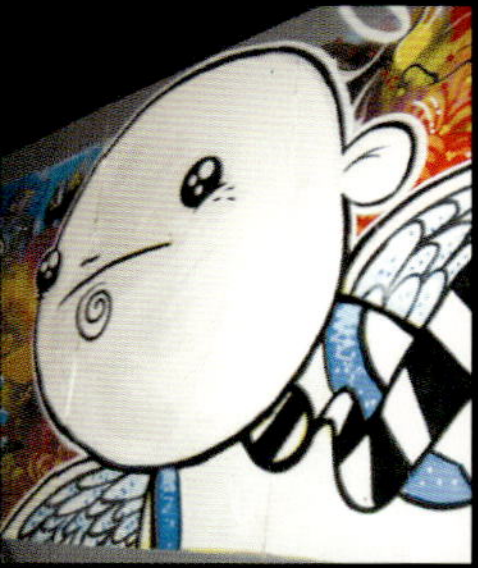

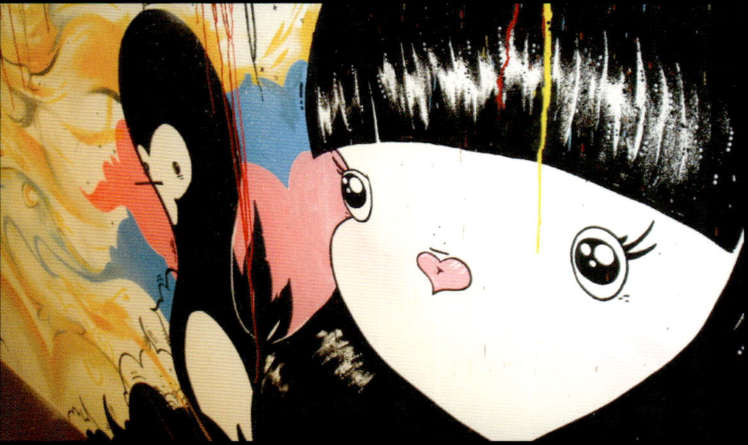

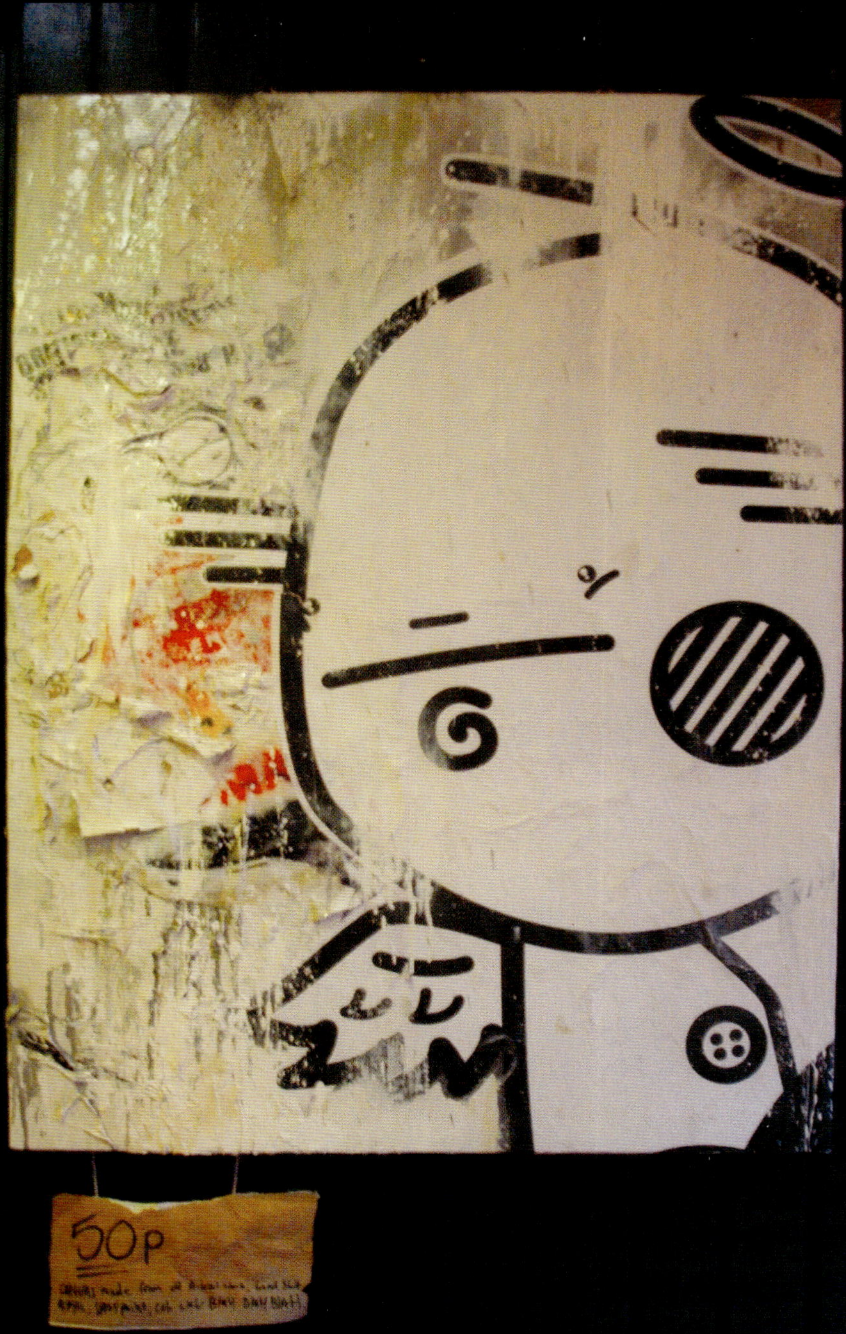

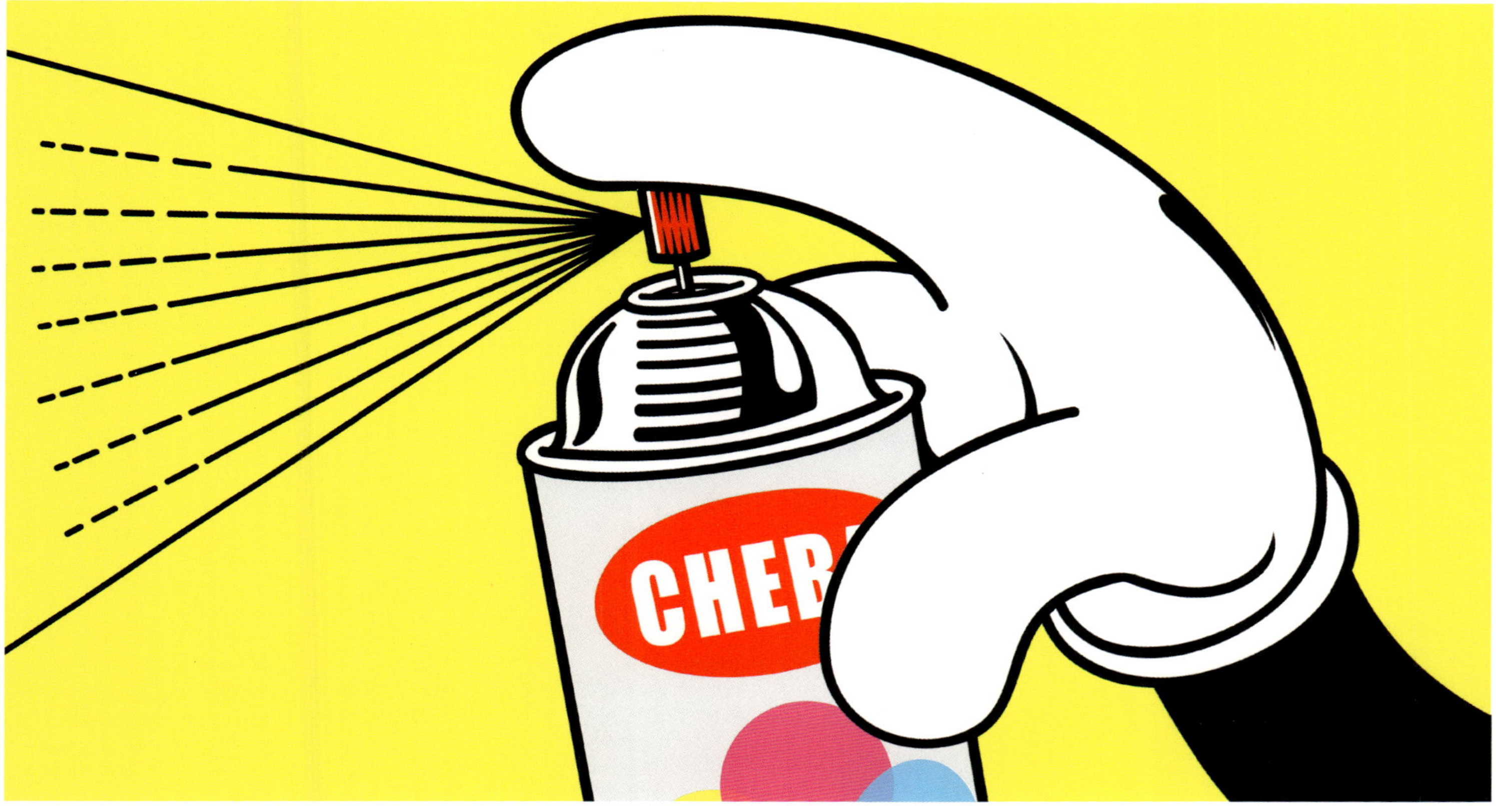
CHEB

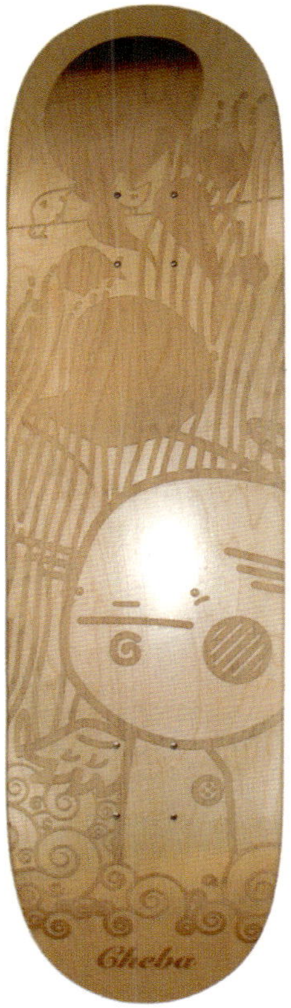
Cheba

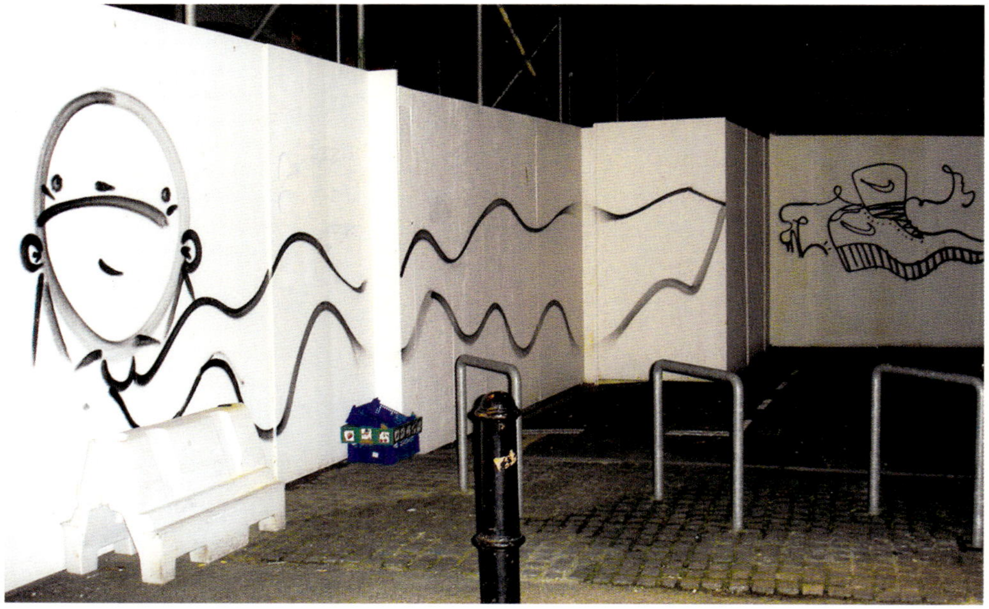

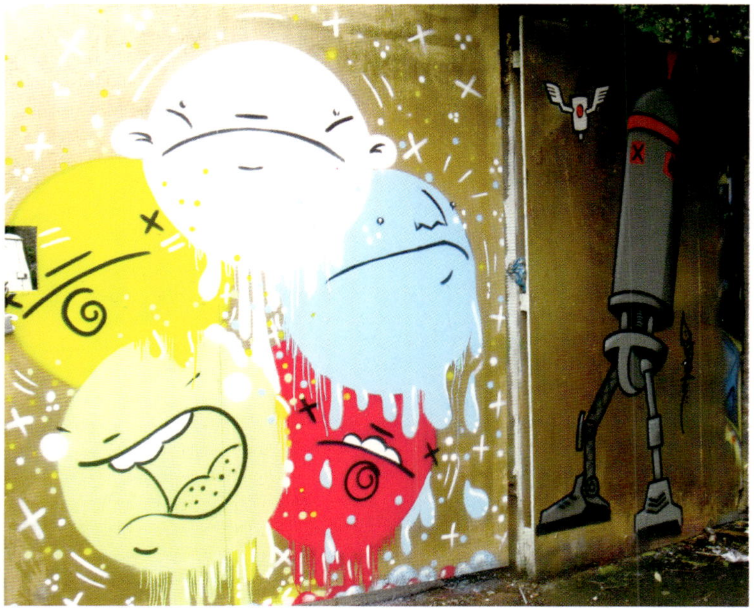

MUDWIG WSSK

Below: 'Dogs' digital image, 2006

Top right: 'Mudwig Engines,' Bristol 2004

Bottom left: Mudwig's train set, Bristol, 2003

Bottom right: 'Shame UK' with Paris, Berlin, 2004

• **Müdwig defines his current work as "Anti-beau Situationist landscape stroke-art",** but thinks that to everyone else it just looks like cottage cheese thrown at some photographs.

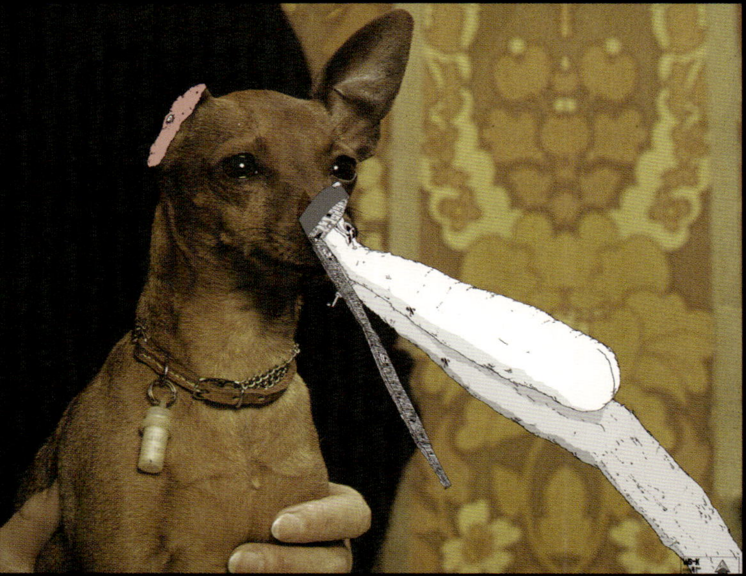

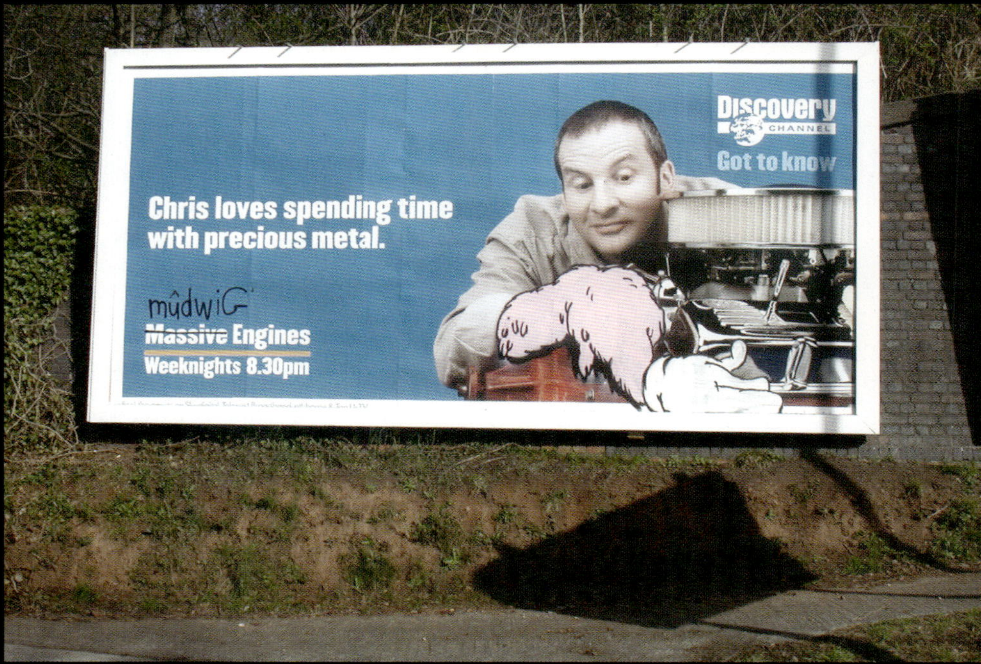

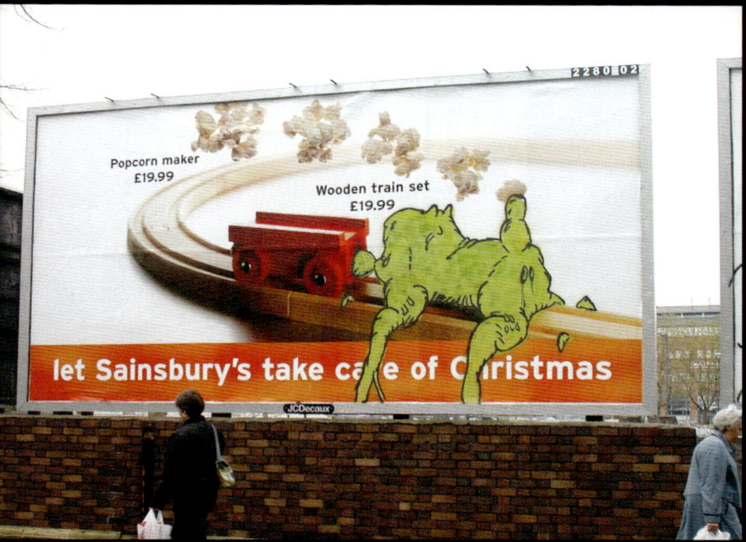

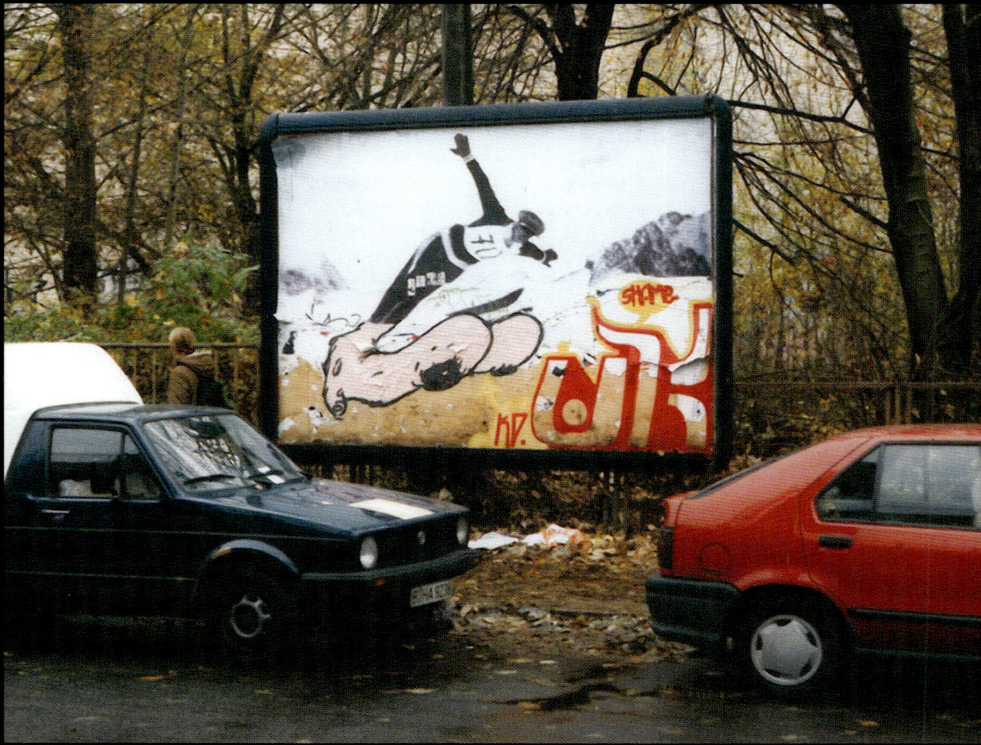

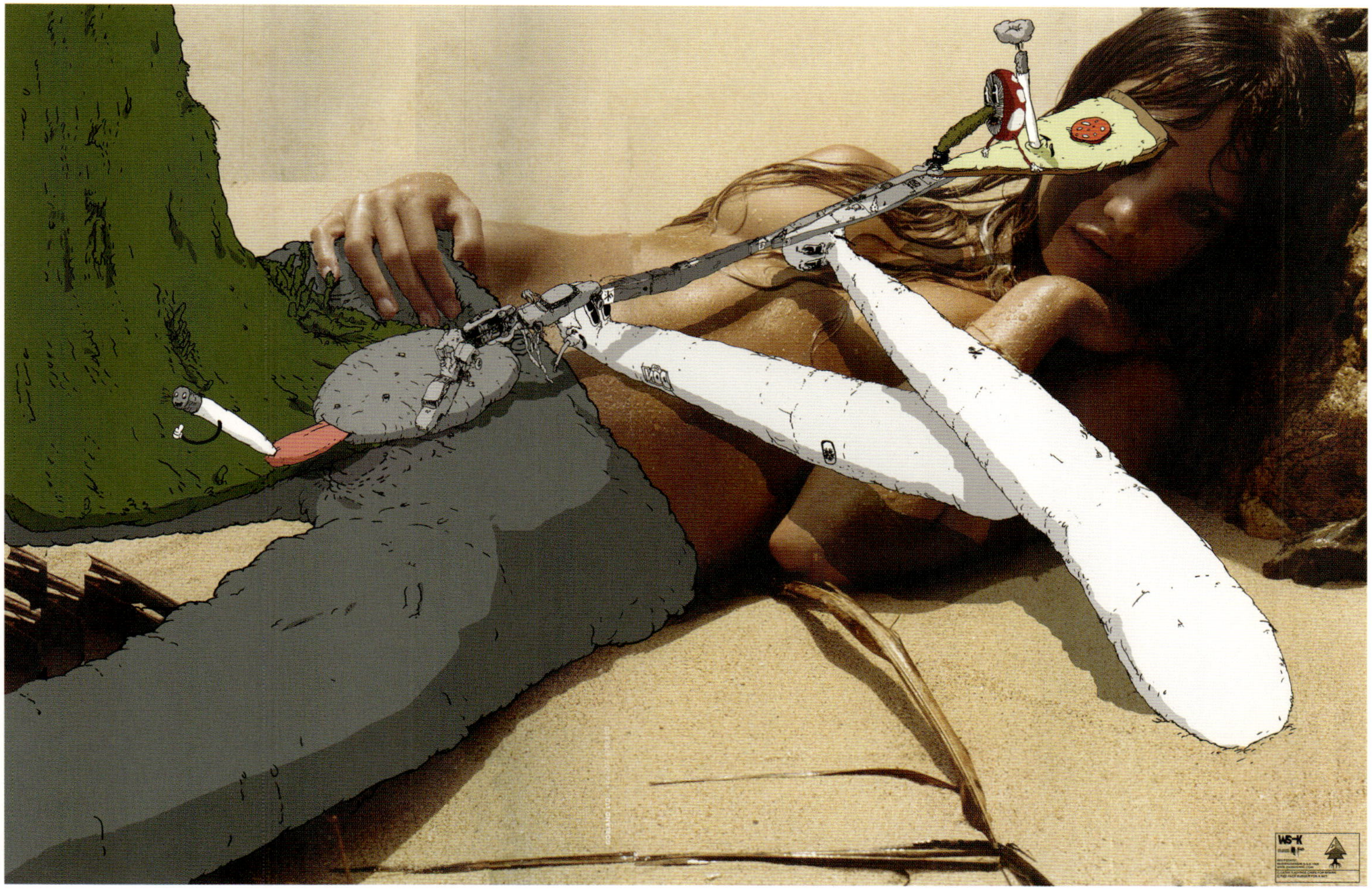

Left: 'Calvin' digital image, 2008

Below: 'U144' digital image, 2008

Bottom: 'Seggy 5' digital image, 2008

Bottom left: 'Lorealegs' Bristol, 2003

Bottom right: 'Green wheels' Bristol, 2003

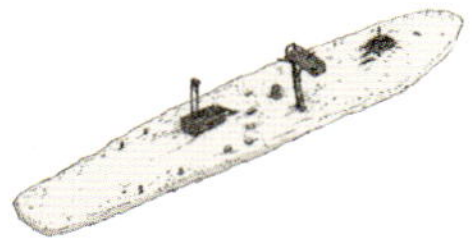

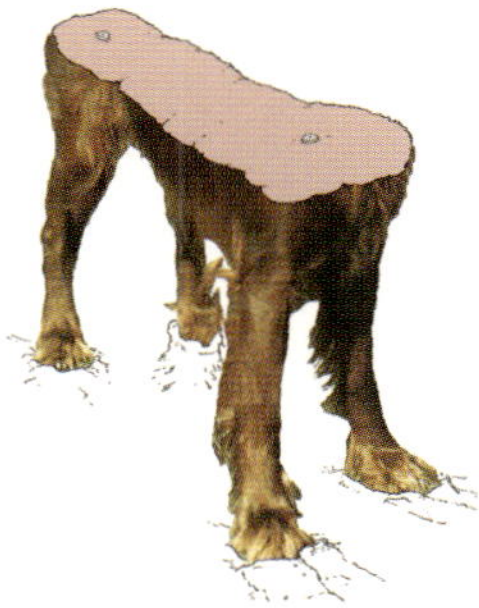

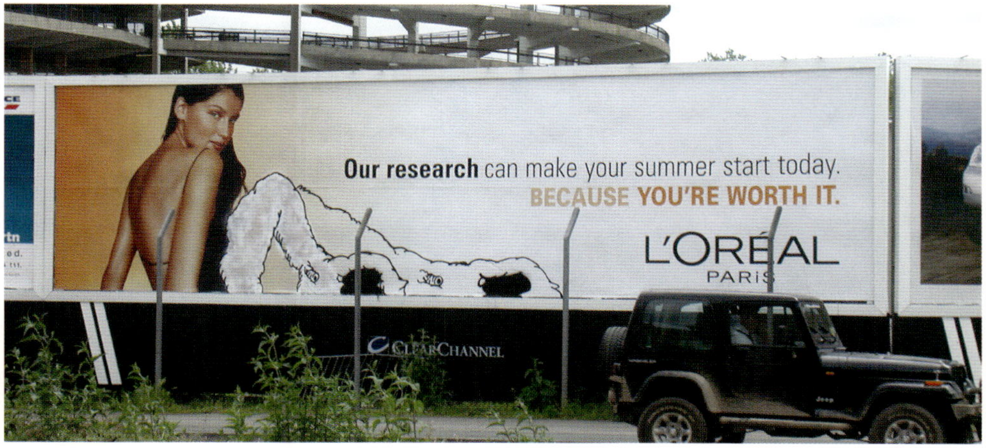

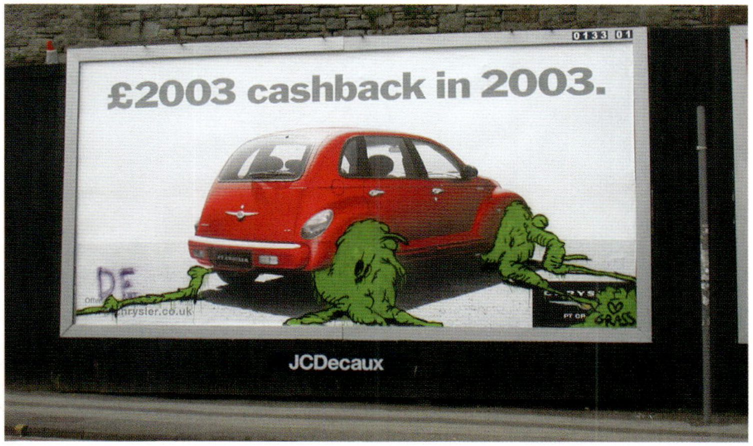

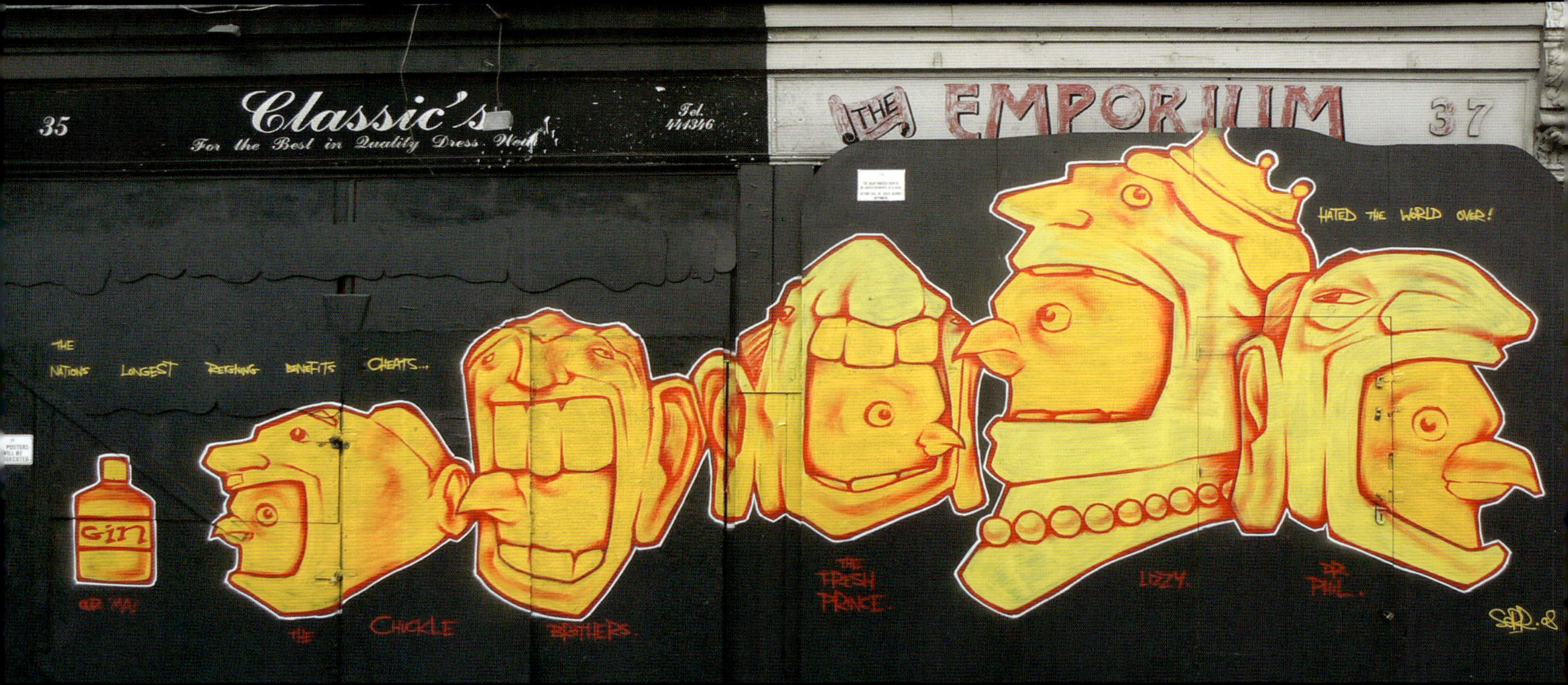

Above: 'Nation's Longest Running Benefit Cheats' Sepr doesn't have much time for the monarchy, Stokes Croft, 2008

Middle: Five heads in one

Right: 'Panda' mixed media on canvas, 2008

Opposite page. Top: Pigs might fly, Sepr and Atak (aka Song) Stokes Croft, 2008

Middle: 'The War On Terravision' St.Werburgh's tunnel, 2007

Bottom: 'Battle Of The Century', 2007

SEPR

"I have a hunger for something that has no real physical purpose; it's just expression, I guess, and wanting to do something and maybe not knowing why. When people ask me why I've painted something, I don't really have an answer - and I like that. There's just a thirst for it. That's what stops us from just surviving, or just being alive."

Amongst the younger generation of Bristol graffiti artists, Sepr's work stands alone in both its subject matter and style. Growing up in Filton, on the northernmost edge of Bristol, he was isolated from what was going on in the rest of the city until he was old enough to explore it on his own.

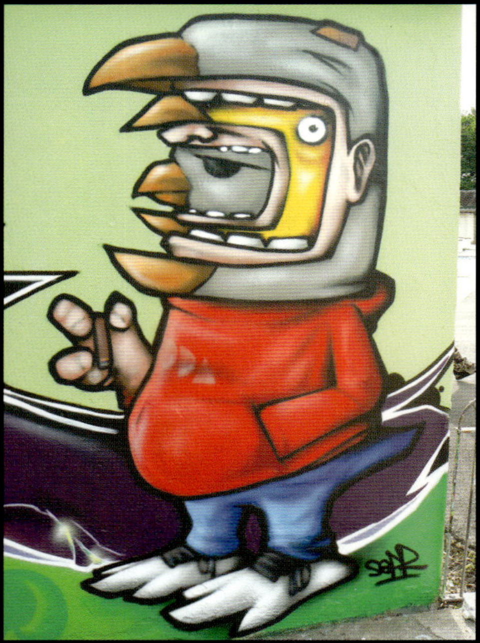

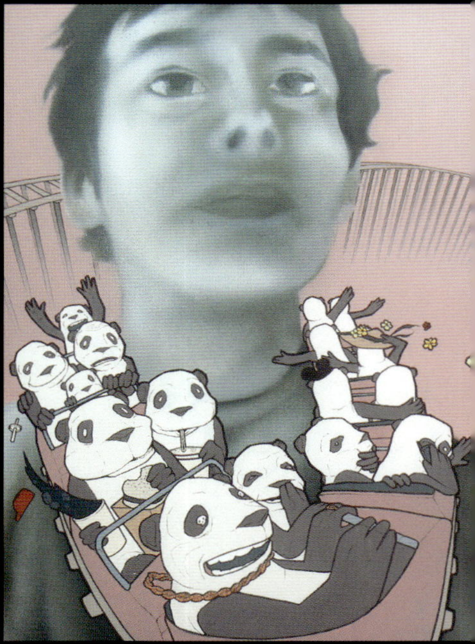

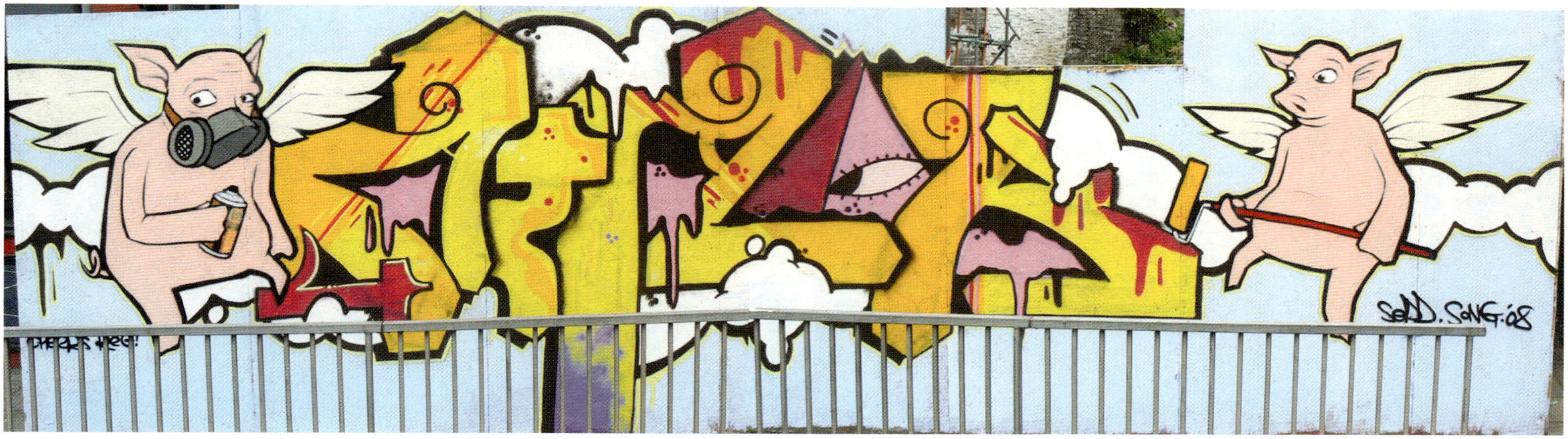

Add to this his musical background – punk, rather than hip hop – and the origins of Sepr's individual style start to become clear.

"Graffiti was just a mystery to me, I didn't know anyone that did it, I didn't know how to do it – but I just thought it was well exciting. I didn't know about any of the books or videos, or anything like that, so it was what I saw around about. I was amazed at how good it was, especially when I tried it myself and realised how hard it was.

"I was seeing a girl who lived in Easton, so I'd get the train there from Filton. I saw all the track-side stuff and I started to get properly excited about it. Also, I used to go and see my dad in Brislington, so on the way back I'd go past Barton Hill Youth Club, and I'd see the pieces on the front of the building by people like Bad Applez and FSH and all those guys."

Like most writers, Sepr's starting point was painting lettering. What drew him in, though, was more a lack of confidence than a particular interest in letterforms or traditional approaches to graffiti. "I started doing letters because I thought that characters were too hard. I just couldn't do them for ages, I didn't know any techniques or anything. I tried it a couple of times and it was a disaster. I got into doing different styles of writing, but my excitement with lettering faded over the years."

Without friends who shared his new-found passion, Sepr's style evolved not from street bombing and tagging, but from sitting at home drawing for hours on end. The connection between drawing and painting remains central to his thinking, the main difference being the scale and speed afforded by working with spray paint.

"If you draw or use brushes, it can be tedious. Spray paint's much more immediate – you can do the side of a building in a day. If you tried to paint that amount of space with brushes it'd just be a nightmare."

For Sepr, the medium comes first. It's the technique of graffiti, rather than its associated subcultures, that he is drawn to. An individual with strong views, he sees graffiti as an opportunity to provoke thought and raise issues that need addressing. It's something that owes more to his involvement with a punk band with whom he plays drums than to hip hop or

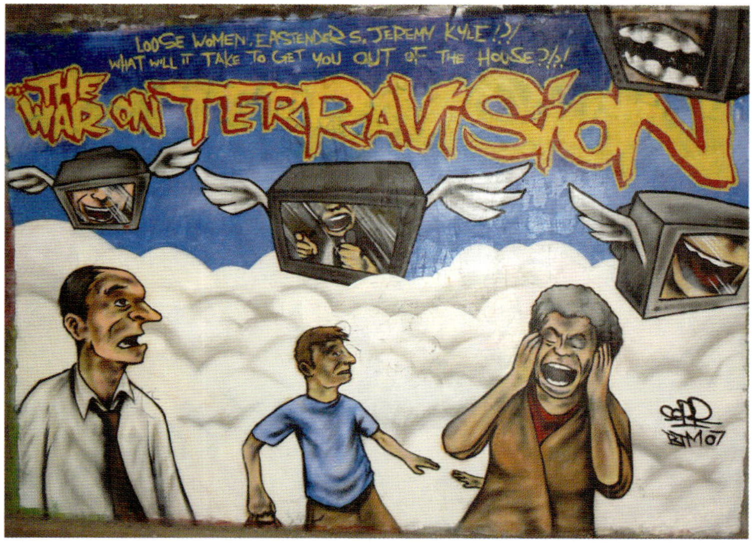

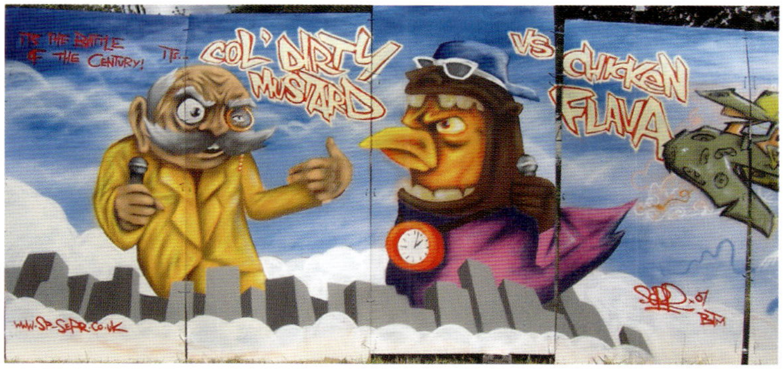

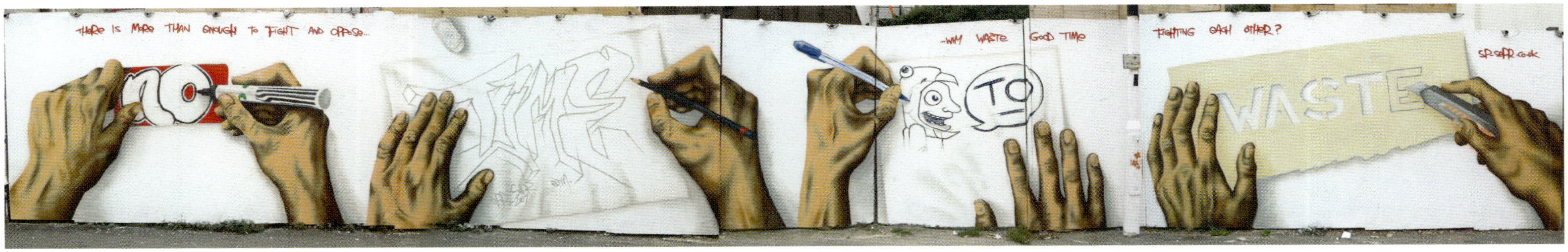

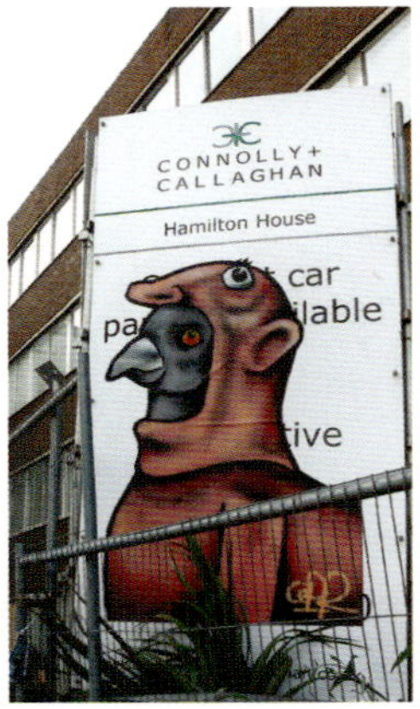

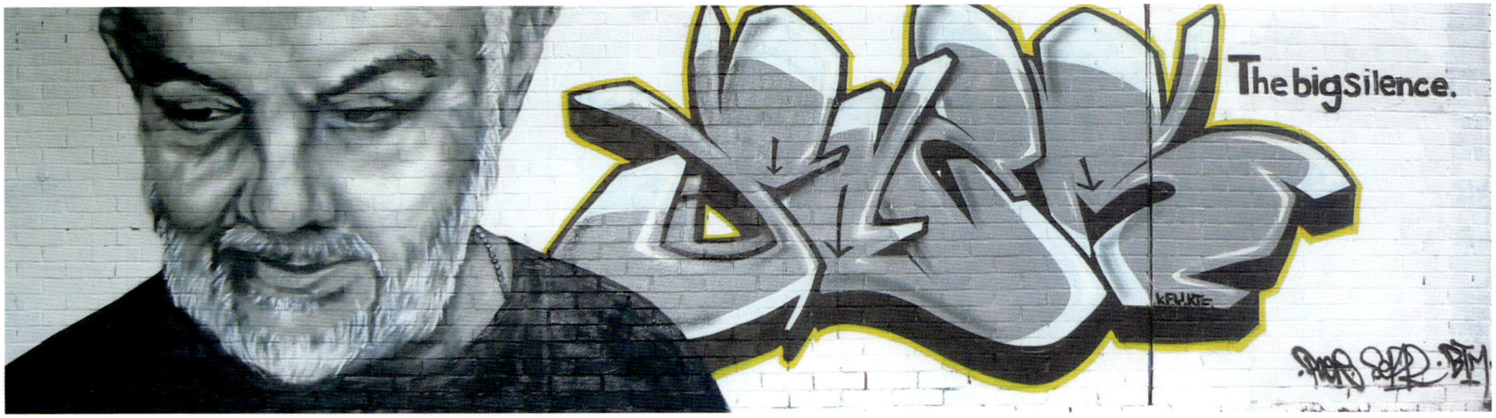

Top: 'No Time To Waste (Why waste good time fighting each other?)' Sepr's call for unity, Jamaica Street, 2007

Above left: 'Pidgeon Head' Stokes Croft, 2007

Middle: 'The Big Silence (John Peel RIP)' Sepr and Poer, Montpelier Park, 2007

graffiti. "One of the things I learnt from being in a punk band is that if you're going to be putting stuff out there it should say something. People like Rowdy, whose pieces have some sort of meaning, something that people can relate to: that's pretty cool, it's quite inspiring. And then there's Banksy, of course. He inspired me when he was first getting big in Bristol."

A hungry young artist, Sepr's output over the past few years has been phenomenal. As well as its consciousness-raising element, another facet of his work is a love of natural, flowing organic forms and all aspects of nature. Once again, this stems from a passion for drawing and exploring forms through creative experimentation.

"I was seeing things like Xenz's paintings of flowers and trees and I thought they were amazing, they blew me away. So I thought I'd give it a go. I knew I could draw better than I could do lettering, so I just thought, 'Fuck it, I'll try to paint what I already draw.' But I don't know why I started doing flowers, really. I suppose it's just that nature is endless."

Like Xenz, Sepr is perhaps best described as an artist who uses spray paint, rather than a graffiti artist in the 'traditional' sense. Despite collaborating with letter-writers on productions with crews BTM, ODA and KTF, his vision extends far beyond what can, at worst, be a stifling and conservative subculture.

"The thing with graffiti is that people can take it too seriously in ways that aren't important. Life is too short. There's a lot of wicked reasons to be painting and there's a lot of fucking awful stuff going on as well, and all the negative stuff just helps the police. It just makes their jobs so much easier."

Nonetheless, with the current scene in Bristol so vibrant and diverse, Sepr finds himself with plenty of good reasons to paint and ample opportunity to do so. There has never been a better time to be painting on the walls of Bristol, and people's attitudes towards graffiti seem to have matured with the art form itself.

"It's nice to do things that benefit communities, especially in areas where there may be problems. It's good to do something positive, even if that means that the graffiti purists are going to look down on it. Painting and drawing is great, but when you can do it on a large scale in public, that's what exciting about graffiti. It's just freedom to express yourself."

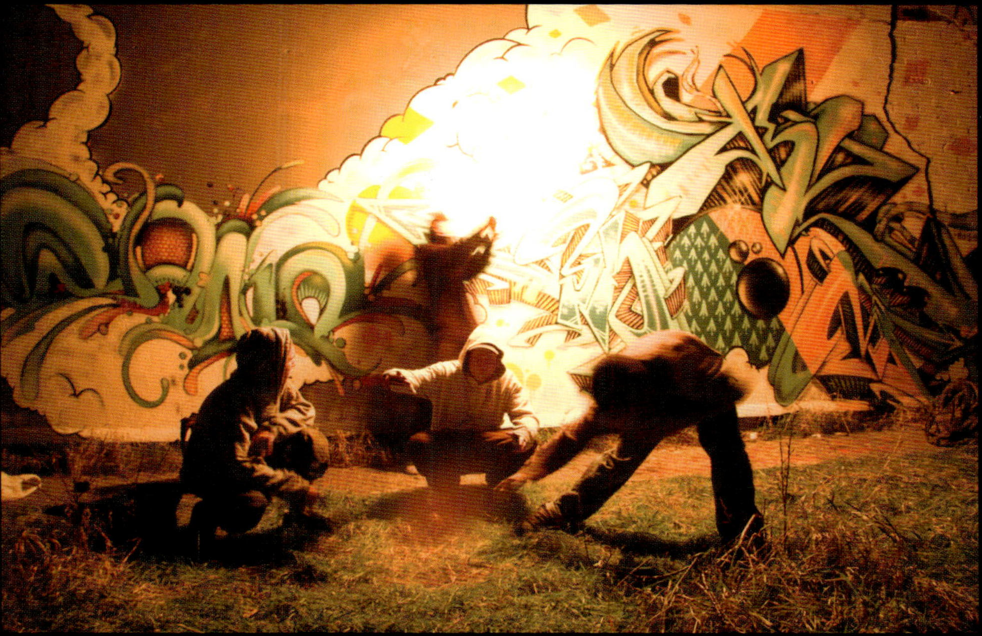

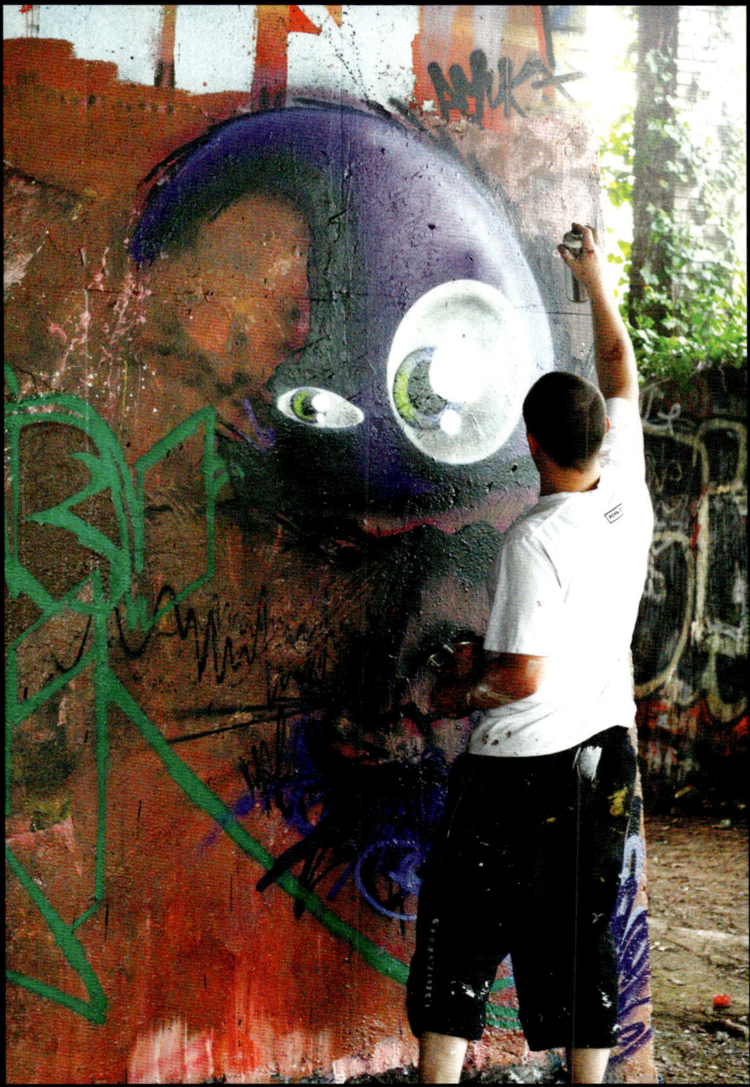

Top left: Step into the light crew portrait

Above: Mag1c at full stretch

JUST ANOTHER CREW

• JAC are amongst a handful of crews in Bristol whose productions consistently work as a single entity, rather than a collection of pieces painted side by side. Together, Mag1c, 3Dom, Deltron and Voyder's work embraces everything from photo-realism and 3-D letter painting to odd, off-key characters and occasional social commentary – all combined with the traditional New York ethos of making everything you paint bounce and burn as hard as possible.

What brought you to Bristol and how did the crew get started?

Voyder: "I came here for university to study Quantum Electrodynamics. I changed to Fine Art after a year, which suited me better. That was in 2004. I met Mag1c on the first day and we went and did a piece."

3Dom: "I was doing illustration but I changed to another course. I could just tell from looking at you lot that you were writers, you looked scrappy as fuck."

V: "It's the paint on the hands that gives it away."

3: "I think they asked if I wrote and we went out and painted. I hooked up with these boys, went out on some crazy missions, did some tags and some horrible dubs."

How did you start out painting?

3: "I think I'd seen *Subway Art* in the library and thought, 'This is perfect for what I want to do.' I went out and got some Car Plan. I didn't know anything about paint, or caps. I was just completely naïve, toy to hell. I went to a spot near some bridge and did a piece with some mates."

V: "2001 was when I did my first ever painting. My mate from college got me into it. He had some graff mags, and started making some stencils. He introduced me to this whole world, and I just thought, 'splendid: that's amazing.' I immediately went out and started trying to paint stuff."

What kind of reception did you get from the established Bristol writers when you started painting here?

3: "We kept getting lined out and I didn't

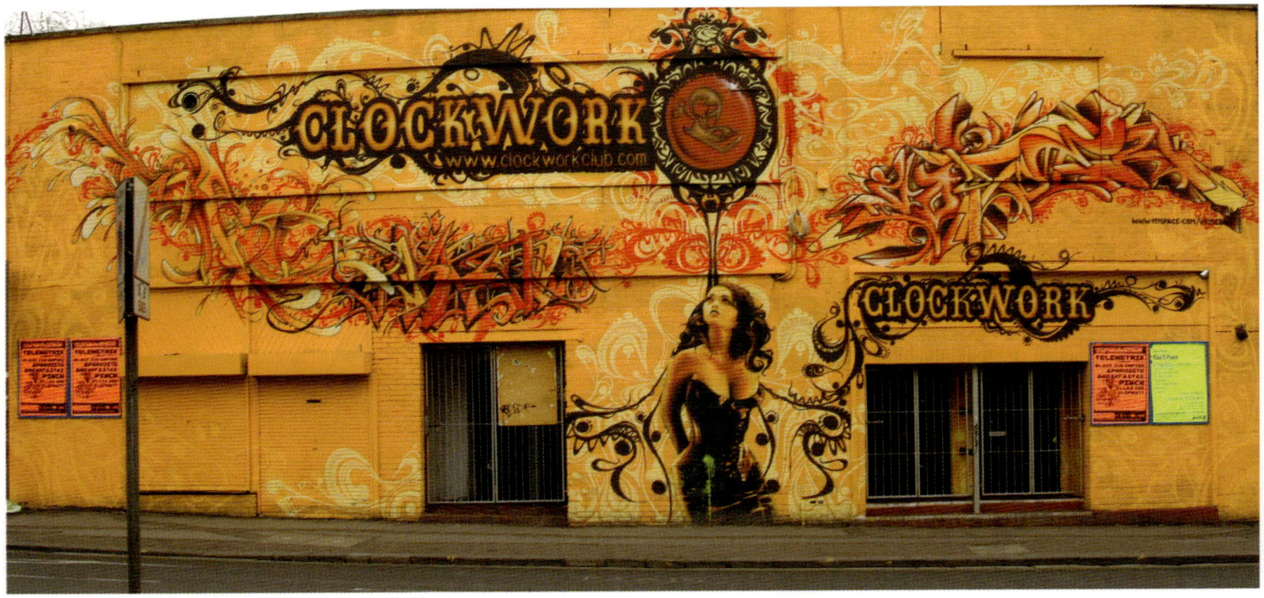

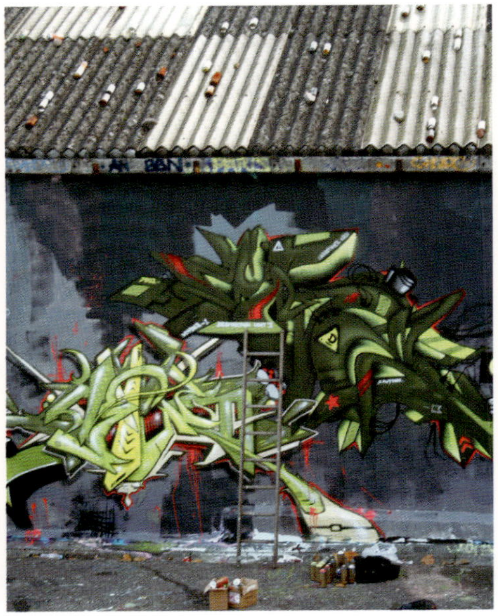

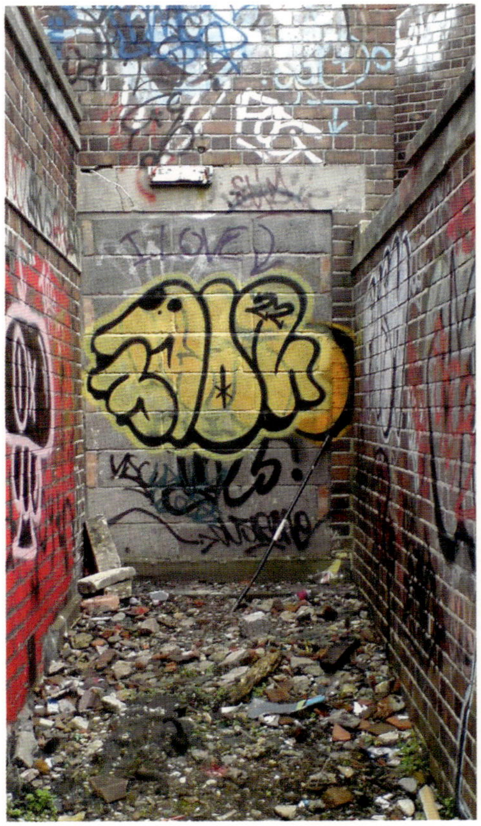

Above: Clockwork night club, Stokes Croft, 2008

Top right: Work in progress, Bedminster skate park, 2007

Bottom right: 3Dom dub, 2007

Opposite page. Top: Heat seeking styles. Voyder, Mag1c, 3Dom, Deltron, 2008

Middle right: Mag1c on gold, 2008

Bottom right: Voyder, Koh Phangan, Thailand, 2008

Left: Green Mag1c character, 2007

know why that was. I was completely fucking stupid, didn't know what I was doing. I just came to Bristol from a small town and was unaware I was stepping on people's toes."

V: "You don't think it's going to piss anyone off to start with."

3: "I didn't know about beef. We didn't know there were rules and regulations. I was the only writer in my town, I never had someone there to be my mentor and to tell me what's right and wrong, I just had to teach myself. We got a lot of hate and I took it to heart. But at the end of the day, it made us better writers because we had to prove something and show that we weren't going to stop just because someone was hating on us. Life's too short to dwell on that kinda stuff."

V: "It was probably quite a good thing."

3: "It was, it humbles you. That changed the whole way I looked at things, it made me sit down and sketch out designs and work on what my style was going to be. It helped my style develop and pushed it to where it is now."

V: "We started going mad doing illegal stuff. We were in a fresh city, we thought, 'it doesn't matter, we can do whatever we want.' I had already been in a bit of trouble before I got here, but I was like, 'it's a new city, we can just go mental.' We did some pieces that took us a good three or four hours and people would go and put a line through it."

What kind of illegal work were you doing when you first started bombing in Bristol?

V: "A bit of anything. I didn't care, I was a student at the time so I was getting drunk all the time, but it's really bad, you go out the next morning..."

3: "...Pens, paint and alcohol – so many nights have ended up in chaos. It was a case of anything we could do, mainly street stuff."

V: "We started getting into stickers,

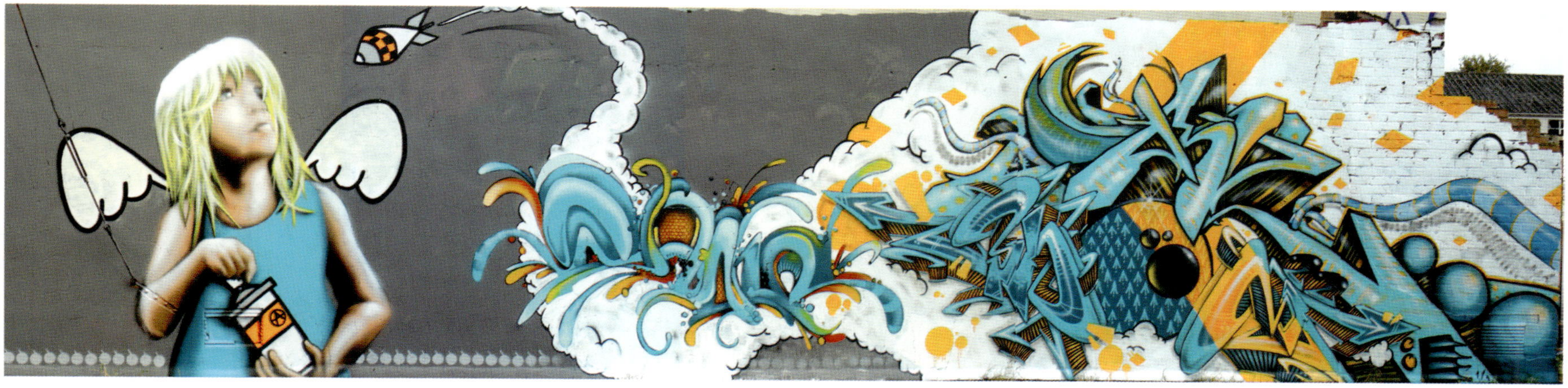

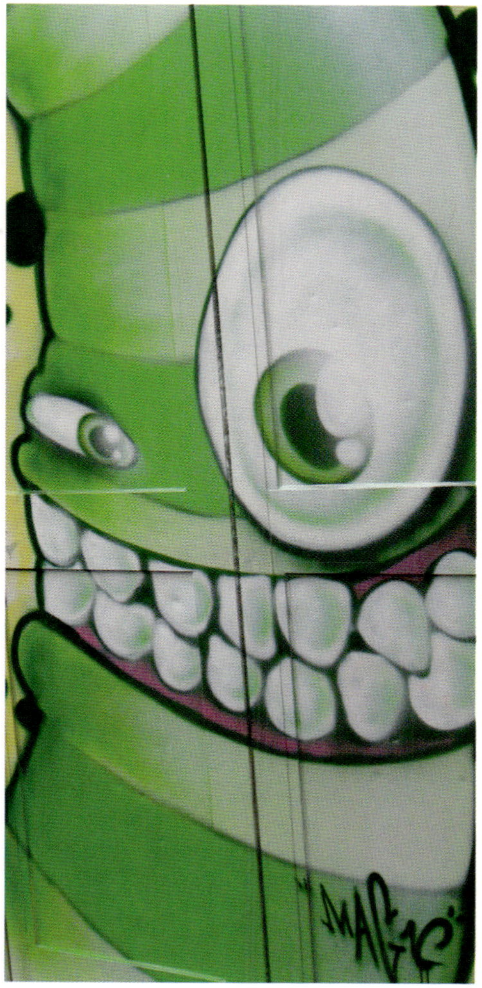

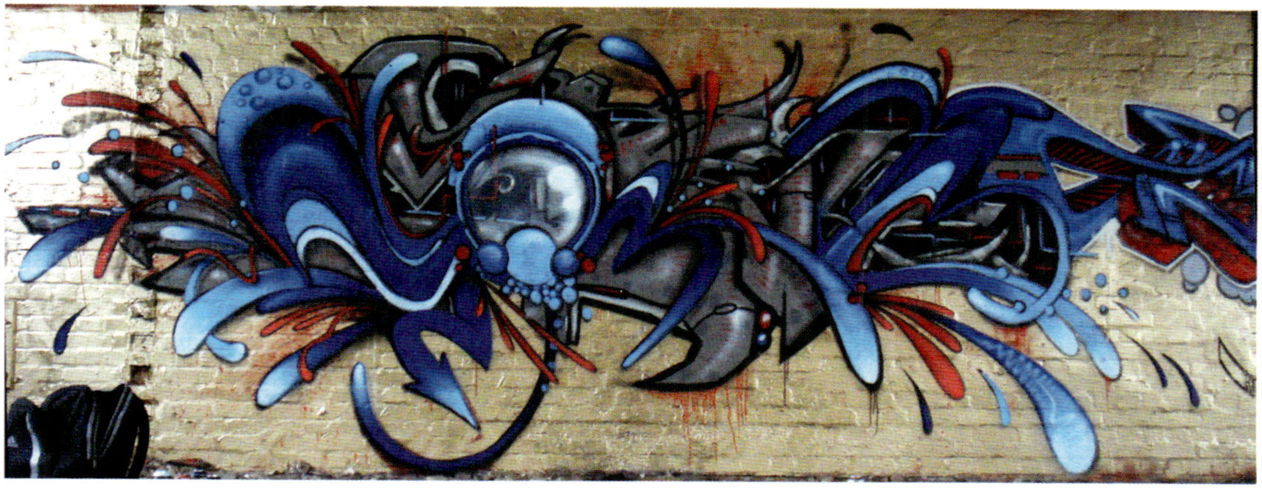

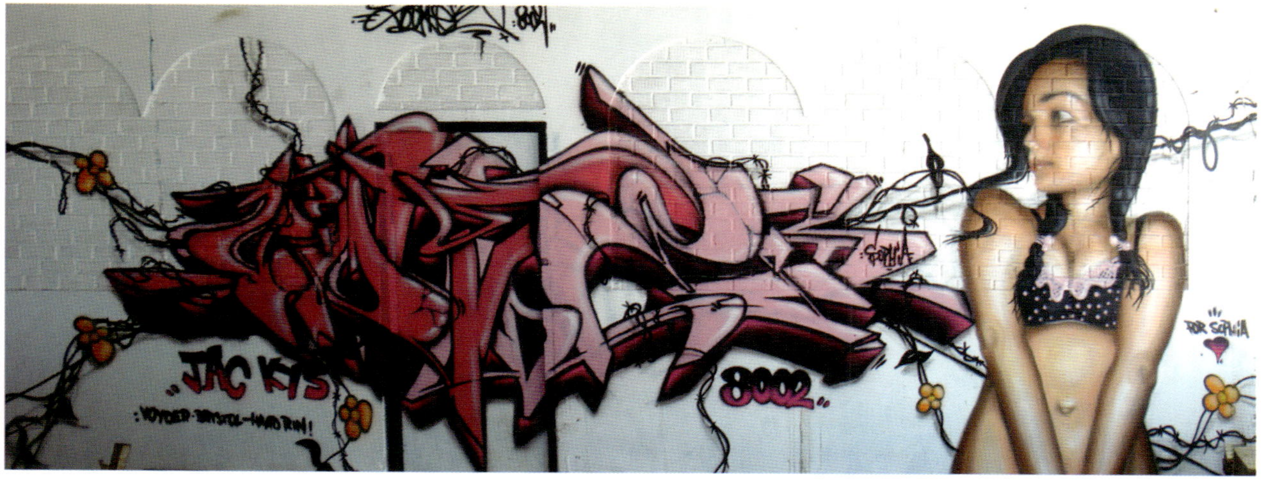
JACKYS
8002
FOR SOPHIA

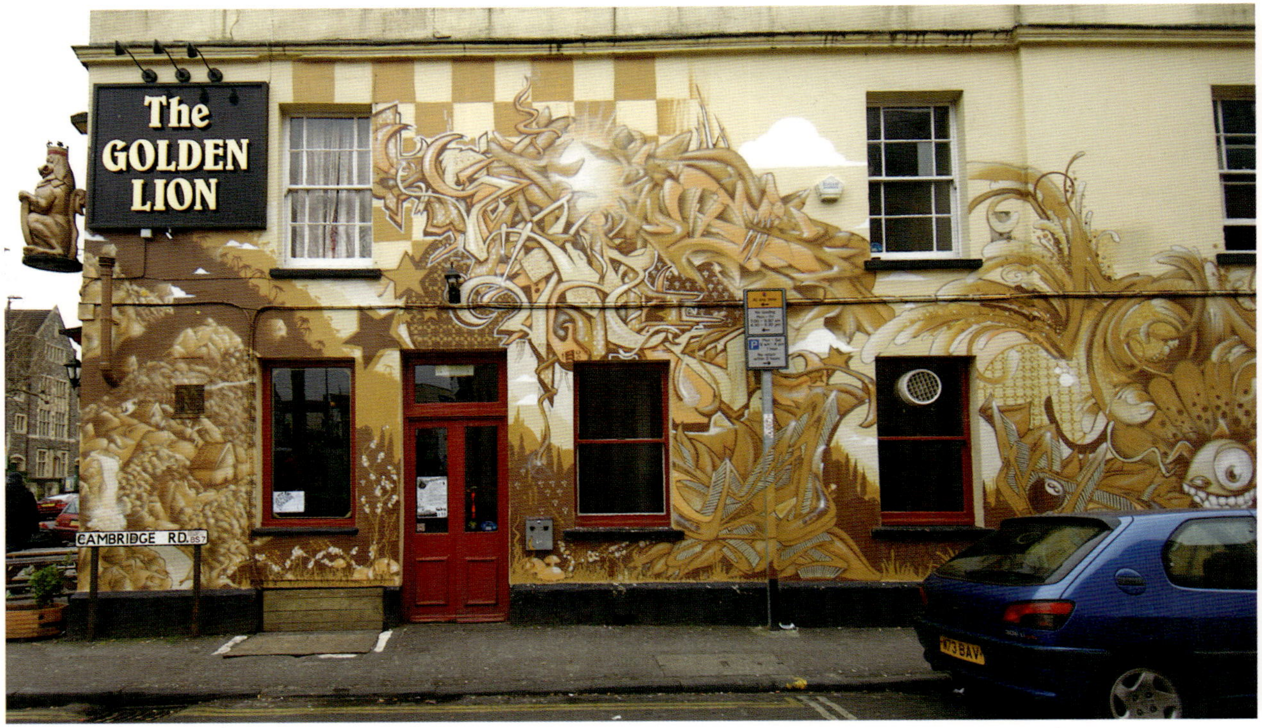

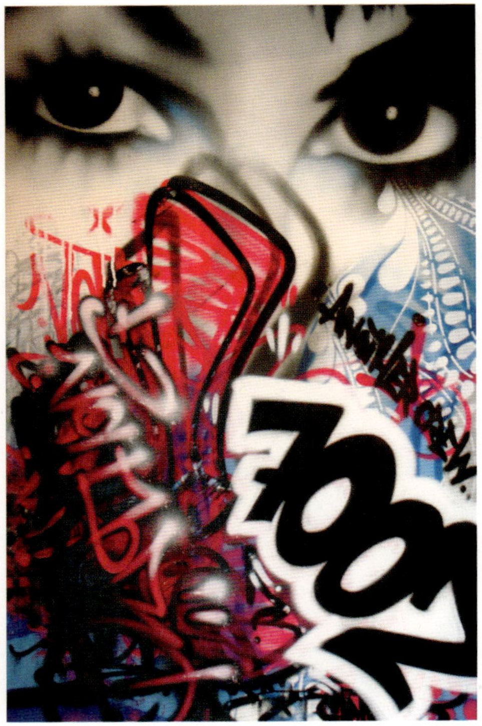

Above: Golden Lion pub, Gloucester Road, 2008

Top right: '7002' by Voyder, spray paint on canvas, 2007

posters, making pictures in frames and sticking them up with No More Nails; just anything we could think of."

Who were the first Bristol writers who gave you the time of day?
V: "I think Paris, probably. I remember we met him in St Pauls. Me and Mag1c were stood admiring this piece and he walked along and said that he'd painted it, and I said, 'You're Paris, then?', which he denied! But I think we mentioned some of the things we'd done and he gave us a little bit of positive feedback, which really helped."

You come across as an old-style crew who work together on a production to create one single, cohesive painting.
V: "Totally, and I think that's when we come out with our best stuff. I think we try and make a wall rather than just four separate pieces. It's always about the overall thing. And that takes a lot more work: it's not just about your ideas, you've got to work with other people."
3: "I think that's to do with all being at the same level when we first met. We all had the same mentality and wanted to do the same sorts of things."

How do you find working in a context where anyone can come up and comment on what you're painting?
V: "It's good working in the streets and getting feedback from the public. You go from doing illegals and thinking everyone hates you to doing something for the community. In Bristol graffiti is really well understood in that way."
3: "You get someone coming up and asking if you can put their daughter's name up or whatever: and that's cool, it really makes their day. You get so many positive comments. I've never really had bad responses."

You both paint characters and letters. Do you have a preference?
V: "I don't really see my characters as characters because I'm painting from photos. I've never been able to draw characters. A character to me is something with exaggerated features. With photorealism I could be painting anything - it could be a photo of a building. It's a different discipline to painting characters in the traditional sense. With my letters, I've always wanted to push them to be wildstyle and that's how I see them, although I don't know if they are. It's my

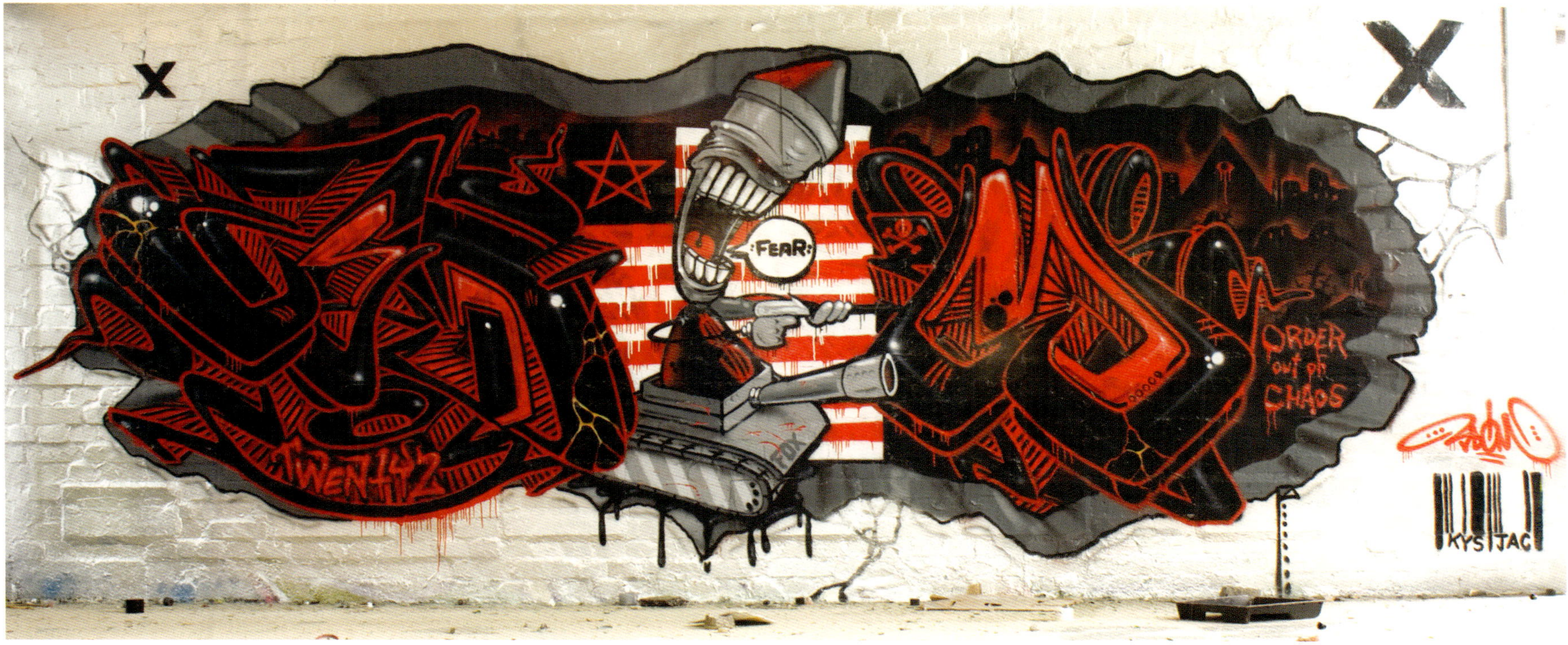

Top: 'Order Out Of Chaos' 3Dom, 2008

own breed of wildstyle, I suppose. With the photorealism it's a really different process, and I love it because it's all shading and I enjoy that. But I get bored of stuff quickly so I have to switch or I get stale."

3: "I started painting characters, and I'd always drawn cartoons. Then, after seeing *Subway Art* and some graffiti mags, I remember seeing Shok 1's organic 3-D stuff and that was like 'holy shit!' That got me wanting to paint 3-D letters, I wanted it to be alive and like a solid object on the wall. Seeing wildstyle letters that looked like they were dancing on the wall, I wanted that effect - but I wanted it to be 3-D as well. I got so into doing letters that after a while I completely forgot I could even draw characters. It's only in the last year that I've been getting back into doing characters."

I know you've all travelled and painted a fair amount. Do you think it has changed how you think about painting?

V: "Meeting new people and painting in a different country is brilliant. You see so many different styles that you start getting influenced in all these different ways; you're using different types of paint, dealing with different legal attitudes. I think painting in the same place all the time makes you go a bit stale. I love travelling anyway, and it gives it some purpose rather than just being on holiday."

3: "You might not speak the same language, but through graffiti you have an instant connection with people when you're abroad. It's like an instant community and a way of meeting new people and they'll put you up or whatever and you can do the same for them. I think travelling is fundamental to the growth of graffiti and to the evolution of styles."

V: "We painted at a jam in Amsterdam and it was so good to be around other people who are all painting in different ways. We went to Sleeping Giants in Brighton as well, and that was brilliant. There was a complete mixture of styles there, which was amazing. And it de-mystifies things, you watch these pieces coming together and you think, 'Oh, that's how he gets that effect.'"

With innovations in paint technology, modern writing's become much more technical. Is it something you embrace?

V: "Graffiti is a really nerdy thing. People have got all their different caps, and all the technical shit, and I love that geekiness about it."

KTF

KTF (Keepin' Things Fresh). Members: Epok, Poer, Siren, Sepr, Riks and Ryder. Also featured on these pages: Kai One (LP)

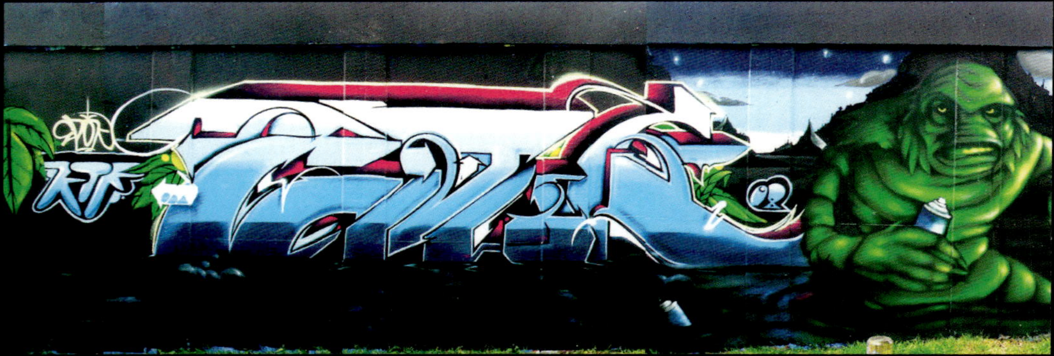

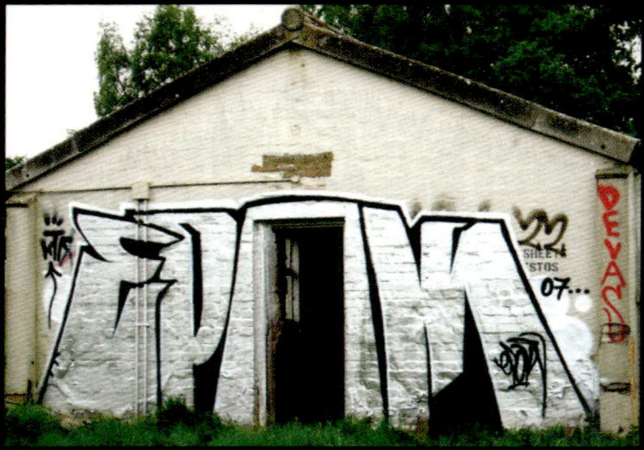

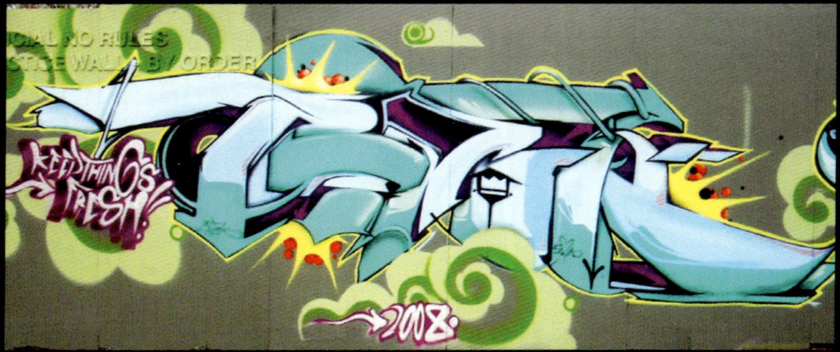

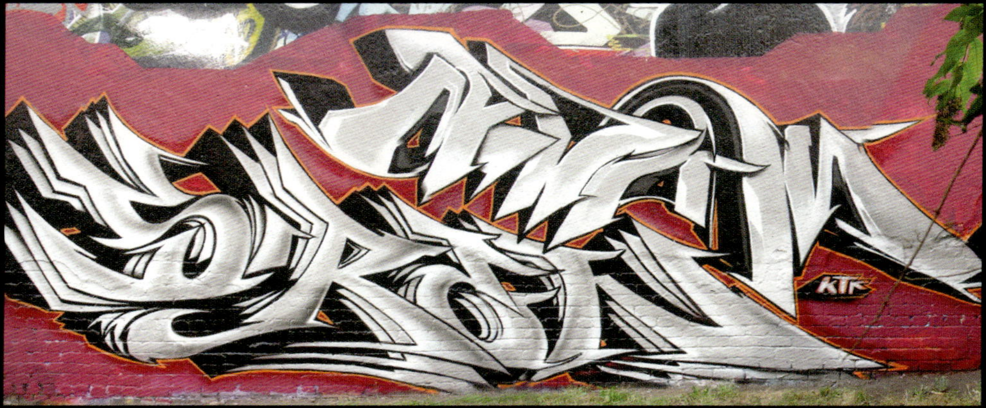

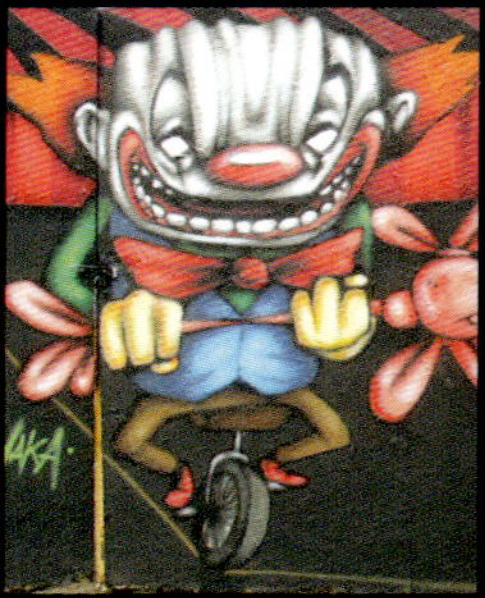

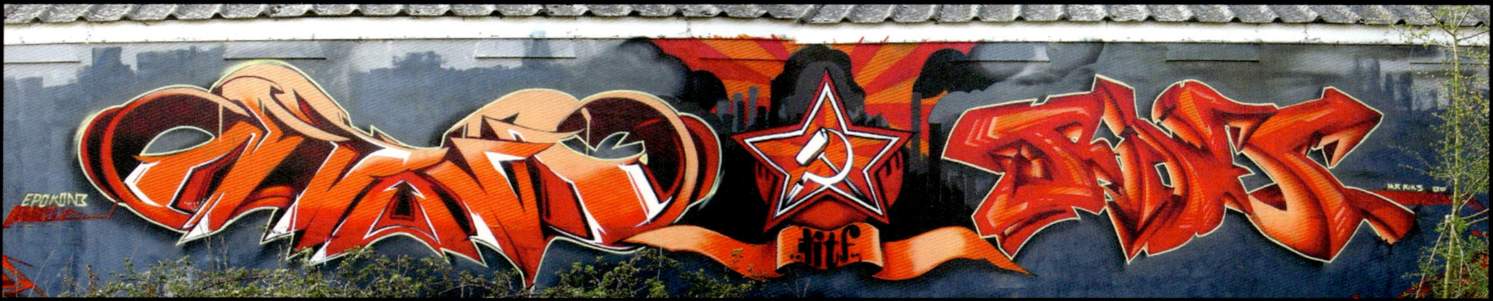

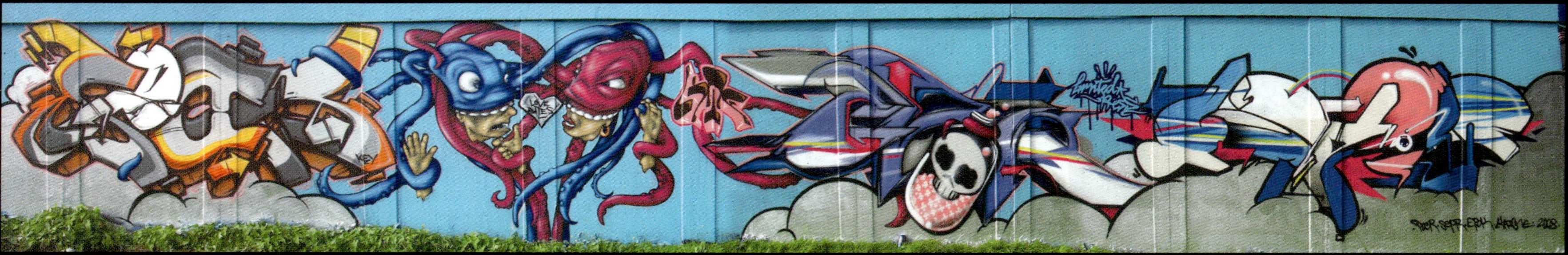

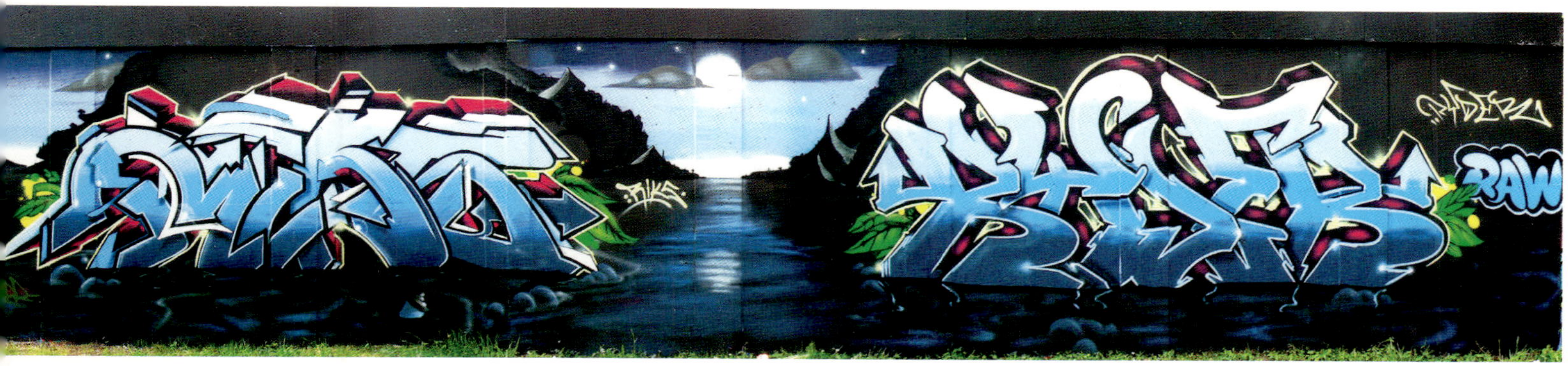
RAW

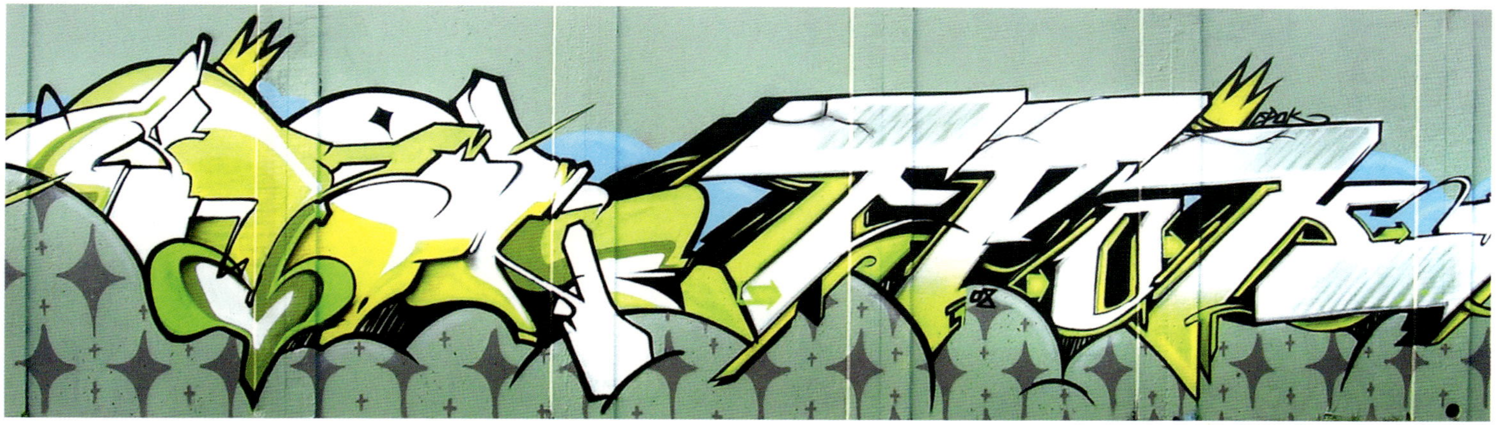

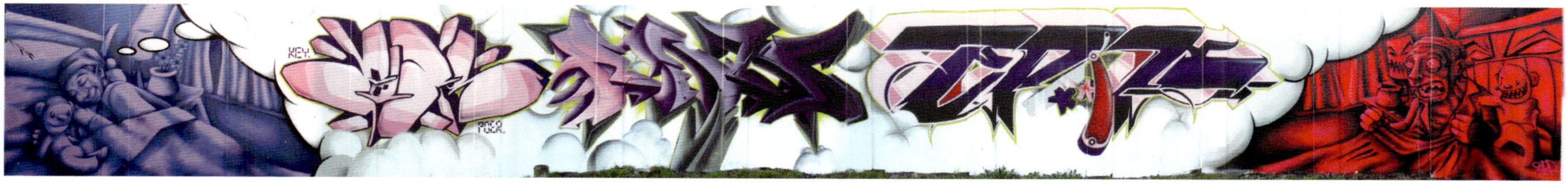

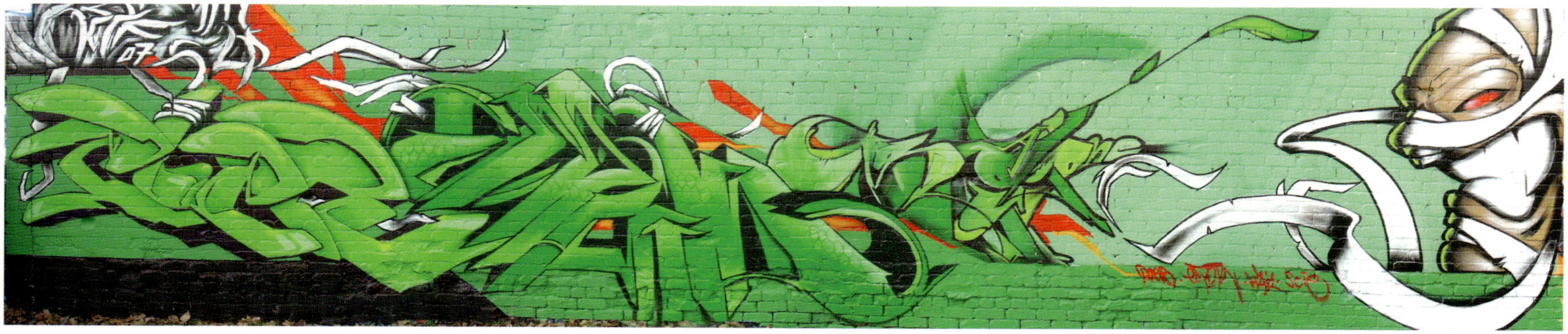

This spread: The work of RichT, Sums and 45 RPM.

WHAT COLLECTIVE

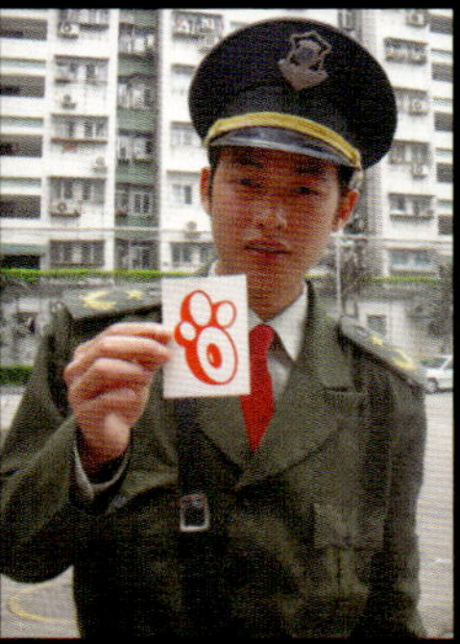

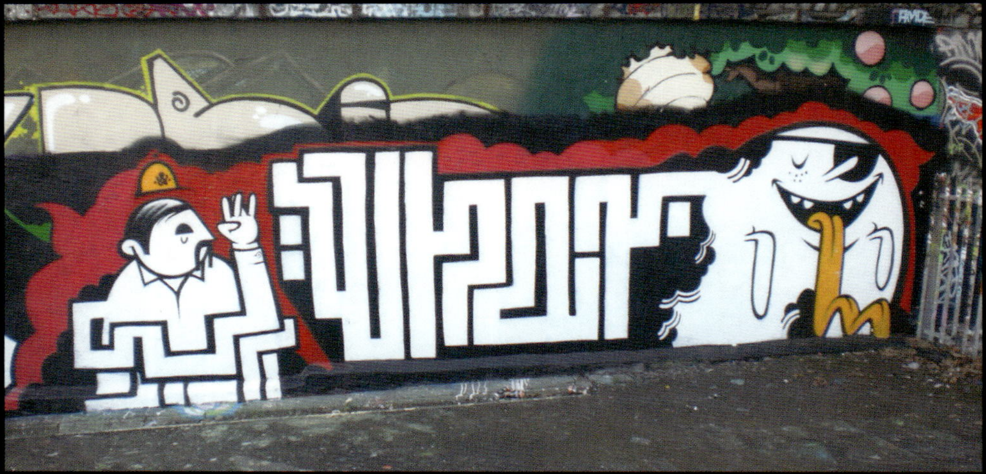

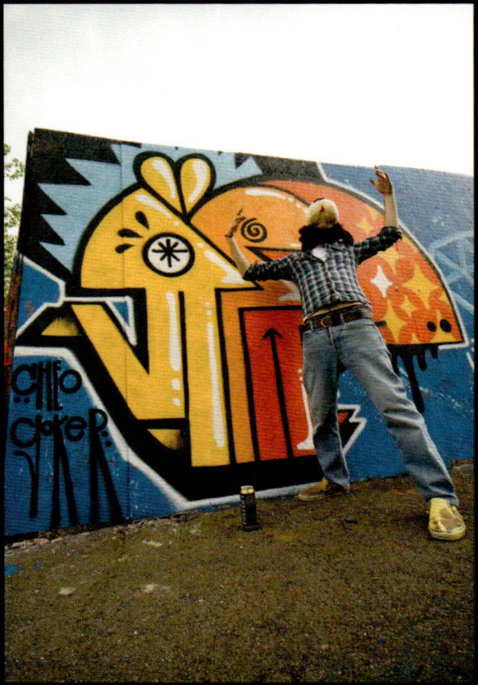

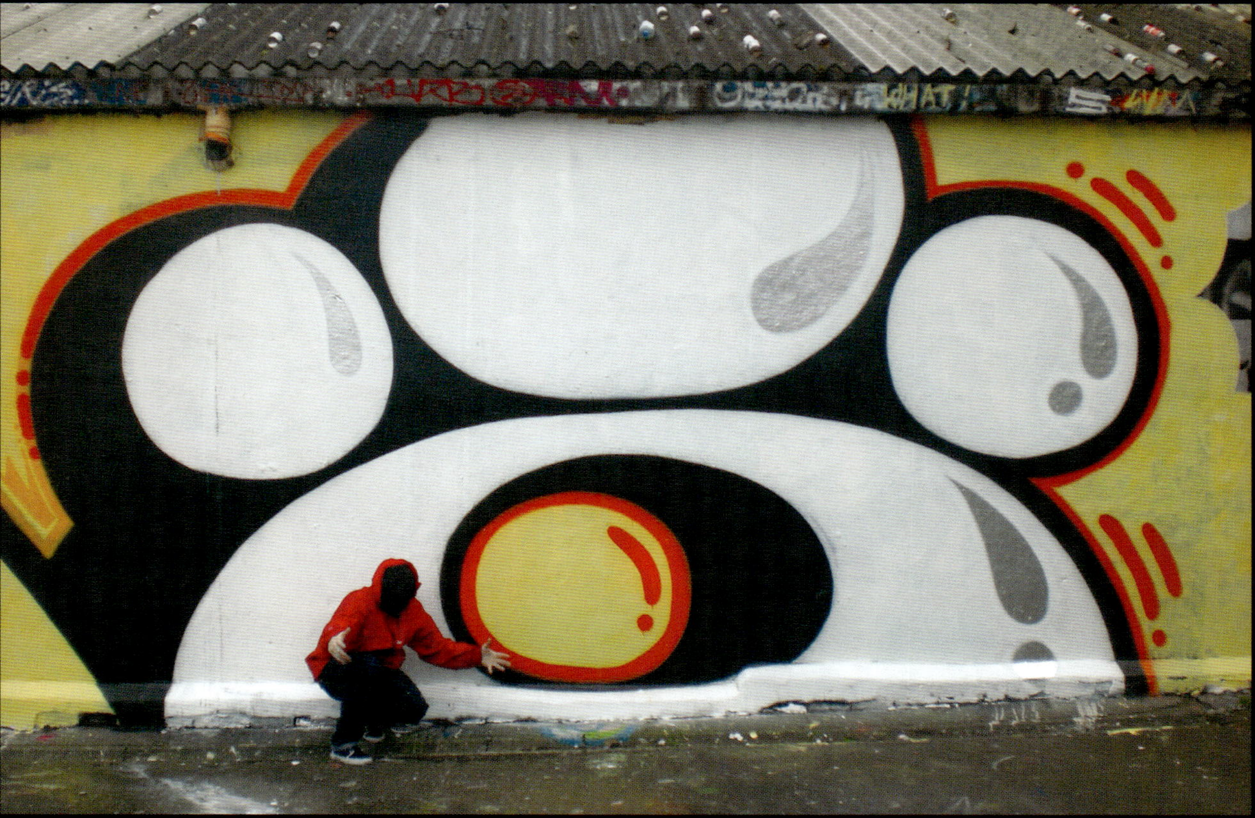

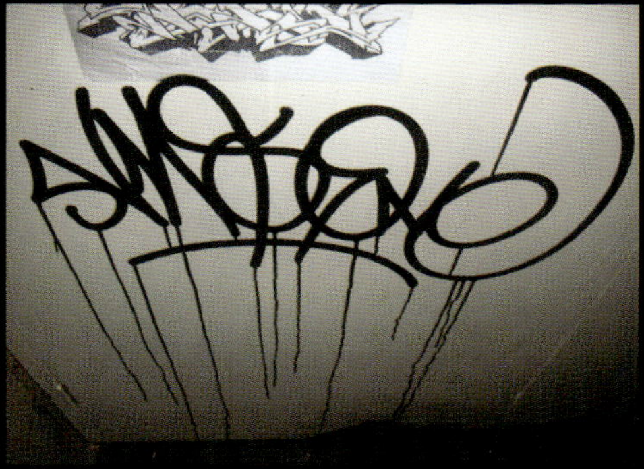

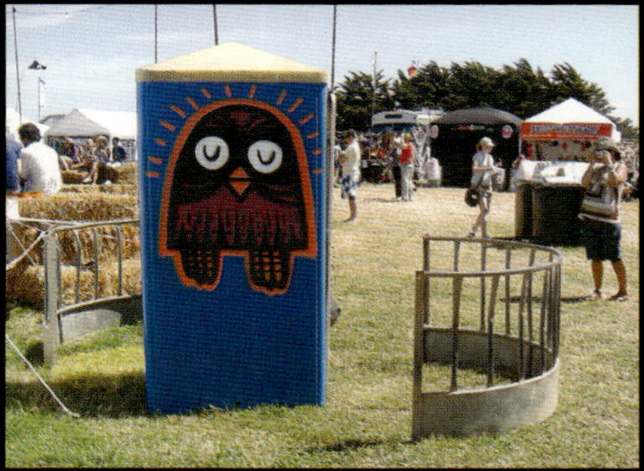

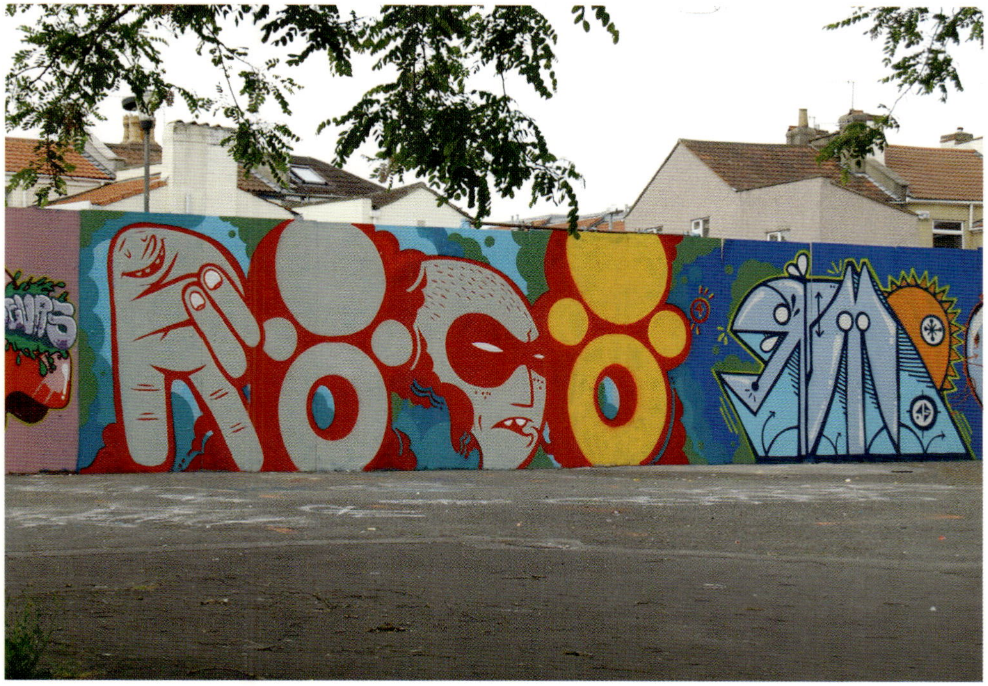

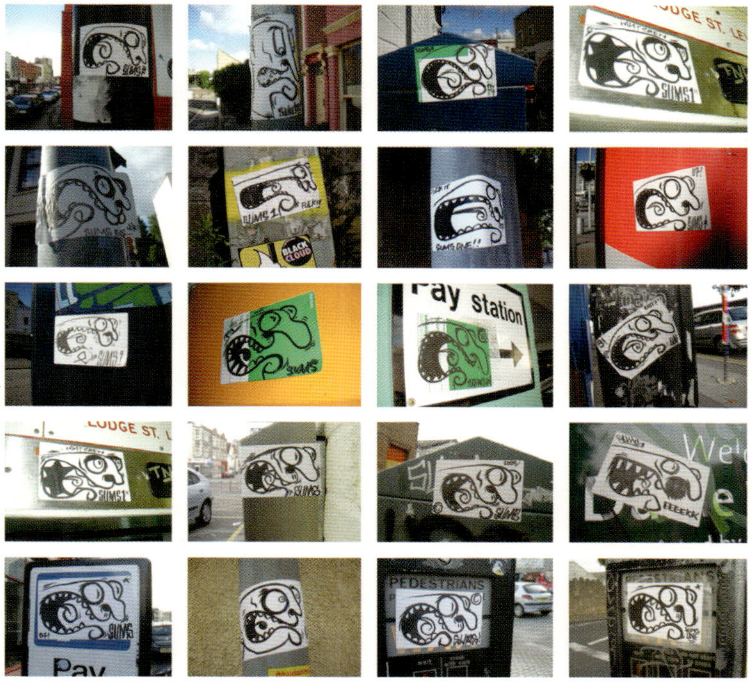
Pay station
PEDESTRIANS

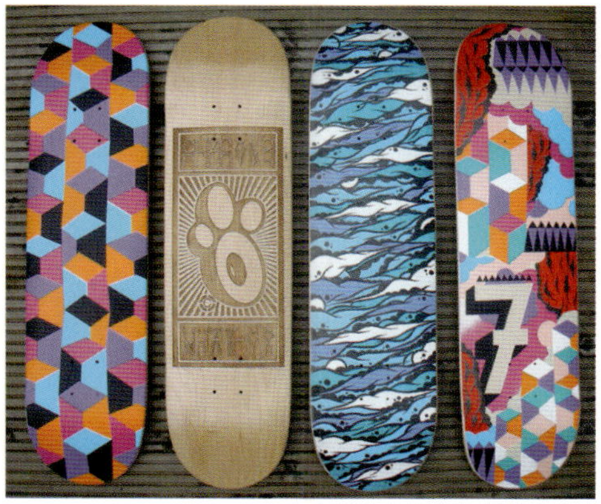

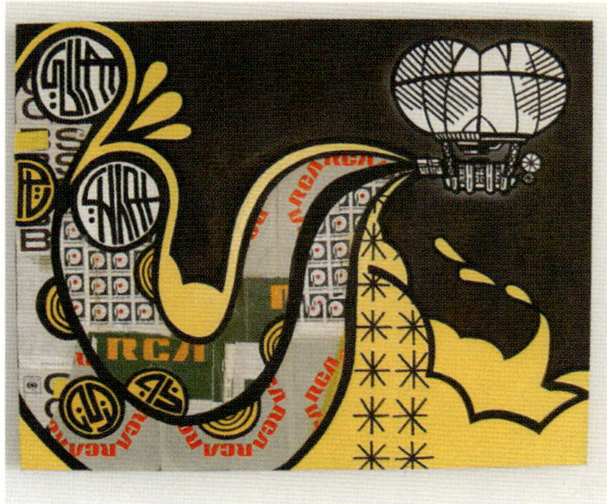

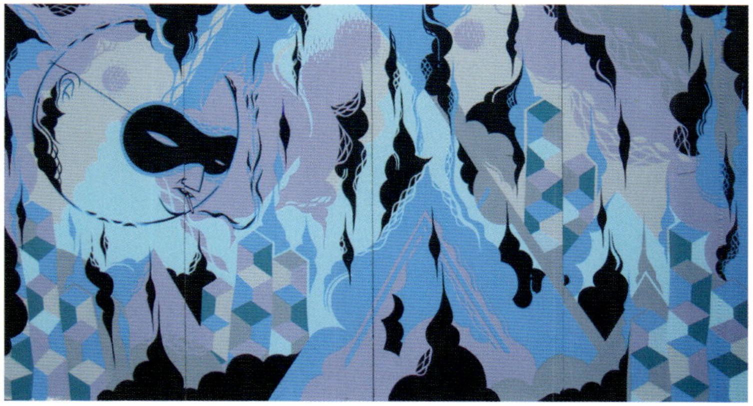

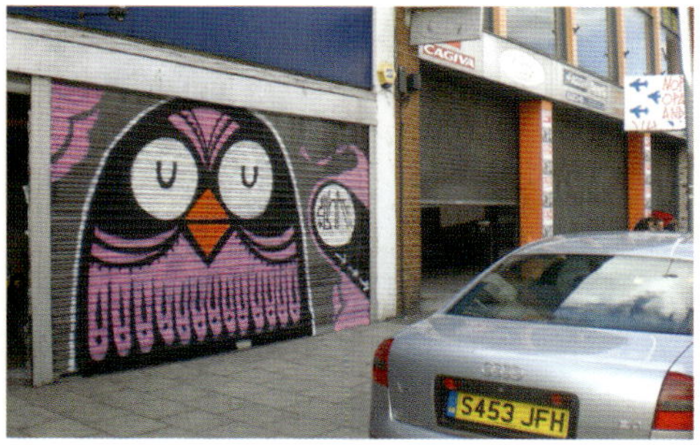
S453 JFH

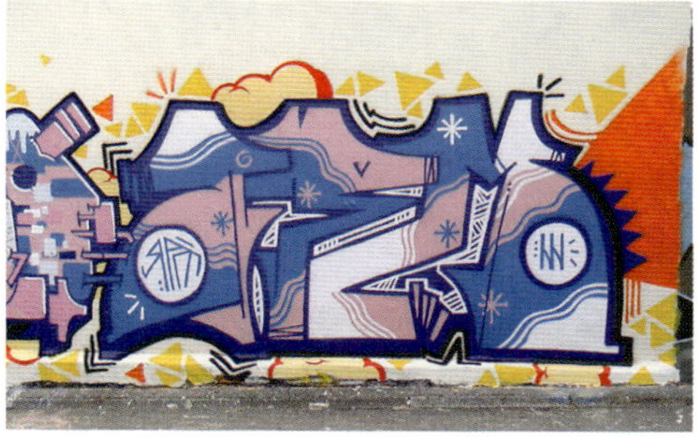

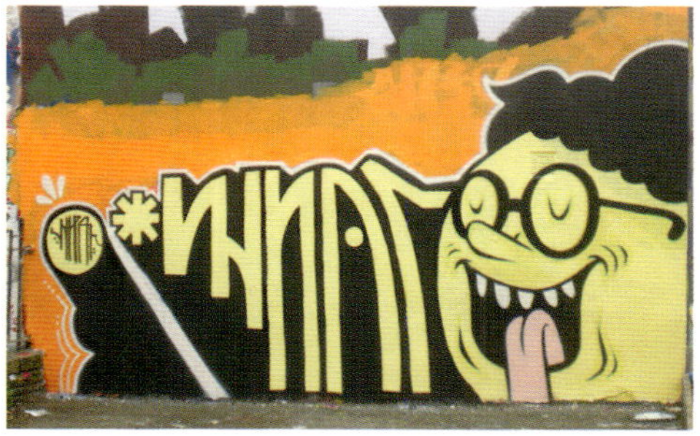

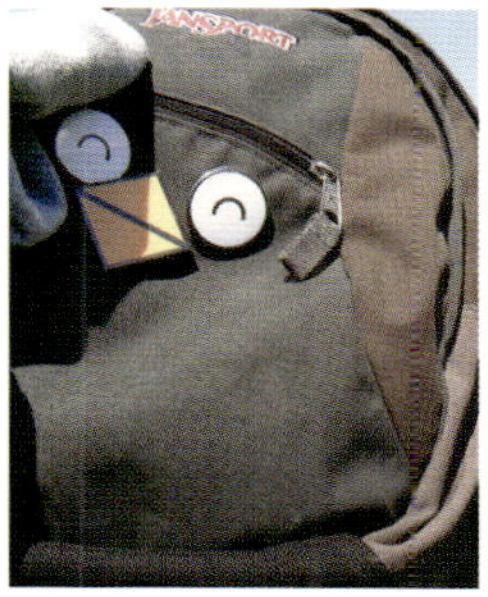

Right: 'Stop that train!' after hours antics

Right top to bottom: Hitting panels in the yards

Opposite page. Top left and right: Keeping the crew name alive, on brick and on steel

Middle: Bored to death

Bottom: 'Be One' on the cycle path

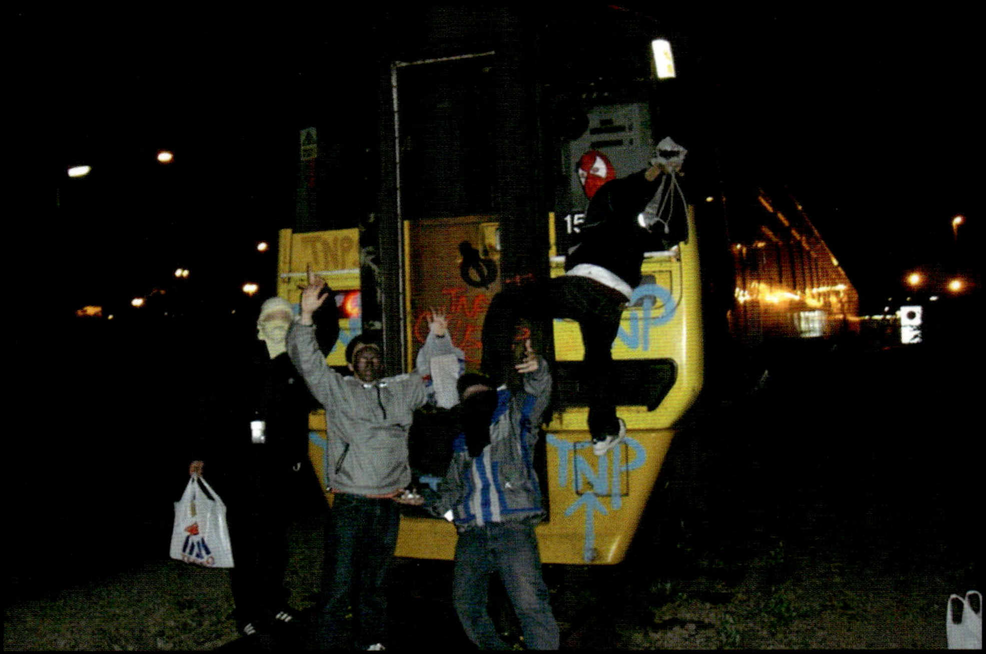

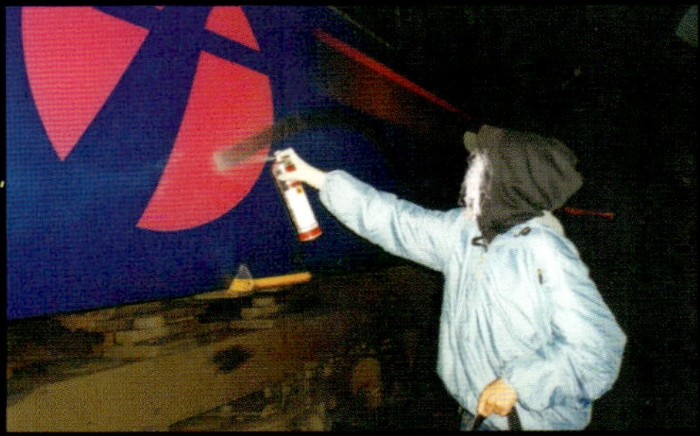

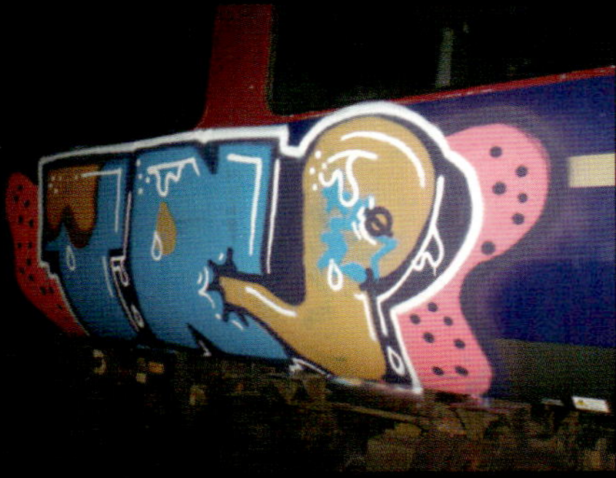

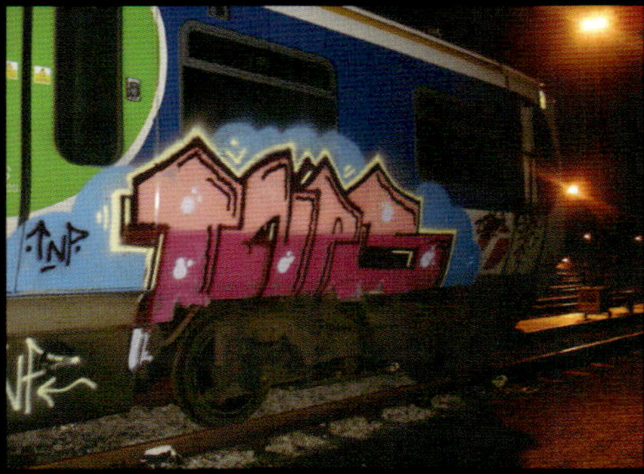

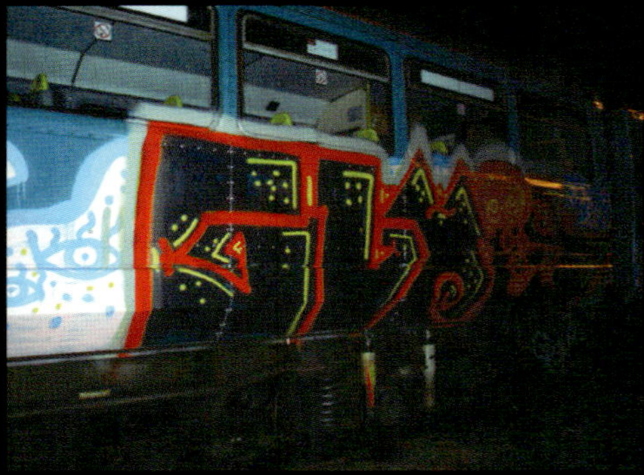

TNP

"TNP has always been a 'fuck you' sort of crew – to anyone and everyone. Some people love it, some people hate it. They just have to deal with it."

TNP's interests are much the same as those of many other young men in Bristol – or any city, for that matter. What sets them apart from the rest of the lads in the pub on the night when I finally catch up with them, is a shared passion for painting graffiti. And by that I mean real, proper, illegal graffiti – street bombing, tagging, painting trains. It is their common interest and what brought them together, from all across the city, in the first place. They harbour no ambitions to achieve greatness or widespread recognition for what they paint, it's just something they do, for the buzz – and usually after plenty of cider.

"Big up cider, that's graff juice. Cider and graffiti are the two things we've all got in common. Without cider there'd be no graffiti in Bristol," say TNP, who speak to me as a crew. As the empty glasses mount up the conversation around the table inevitably turns to graffiti, the one subject on which they all seem to agree.

"It's just something we do for a laugh. I don't like to think too deeply about it. As soon as you take it too seriously, it's not fun anymore. You can see in our work over the last few years what we think about it: what we've painted has just got more and more stupid, and I think that's brilliant."

TNP stands variously for Toys Need Punishment, Take No Prisoners, Take No Pride or Tits Not Personality. Whatever is the bluntest or daftest seems fair game; and a game, albeit a risky one, is ultimately what it is. It's reckless recreation,

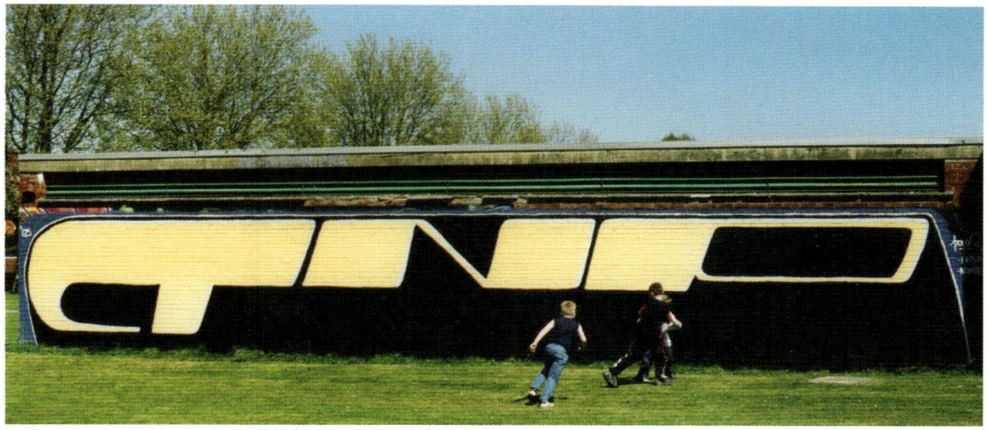

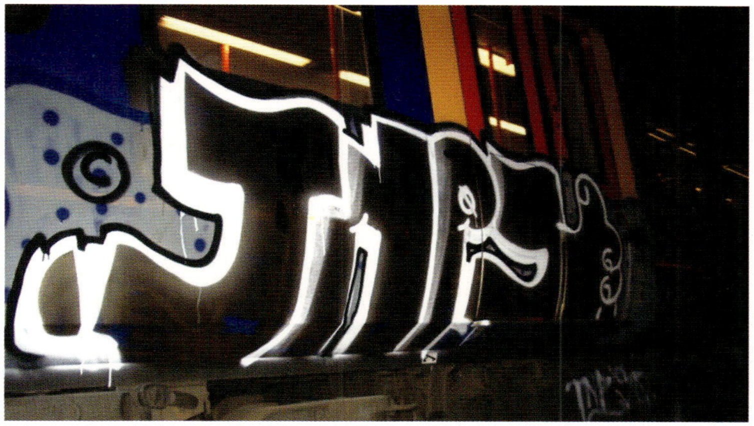

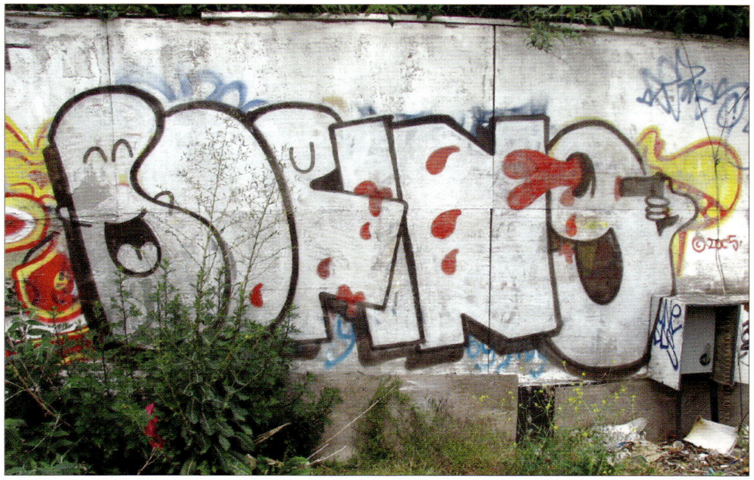

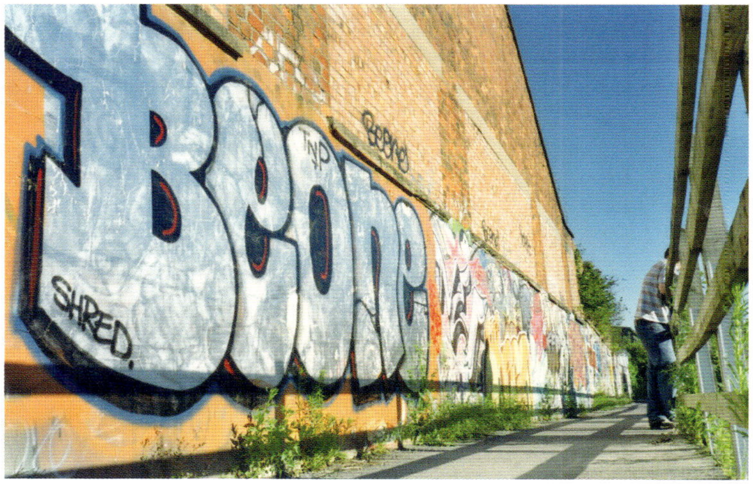

adrenalised escapism for the young and the young-at-heart.

"Every bloke's got that thing where they don't want to grow up, whether you're Jeremy Clarkson or some graff writer from Bristol. Whether you like to drive a big car really fast or paint your name on something, it's not dissimilar."

TNP was formed in 2002 by Nomad, Polar and old-school veteran Tes. Formerly of TUB, KTS and DBZ, Tes has always had an irreverent attitude towards the wider graffiti scene, and it's something he instilled in the new TNP recruits as their numbers grew.

"Our main influence has always been Tes. He's got less serious as he's got older, and that's brilliant. He still thinks the same stuff about graffiti as we do. We don't even like the graffiti 'scene' to be honest, we like painting, but all the bollocks that goes along with it is just rubbish."

Within a couple of years, TNP's ranks had swollen with younger writers hell bent on taking things back to basics – back to the streets and back to the train yards. Bristol has never been an easy city in which to paint trains, but TNP rose to the challenge.

"When us younger ones came in it sort of all went a bit crazy, painting everything and anything. When we first started doing trains none had been done in Bristol – that we knew of, at least – since Omni was doing them in the late 90s. We'd been asking people 'what about doing trains?' and all we'd hear was 'no, don't ever do it, there's no way you're ever going to do this.' So we went in blind. There was no information from anyone, we just had to go and do it for ourselves. I think if I'd known back then what I know now, we could have got away with doing so much more, whole cars and everything, because the BTP (British Transport Police) weren't expecting it.

"One time, when we'd just about finished, we had to hide and watch the BTP come into the yard looking for us. Then a couple of days later I was in bed with a hangover and my mum opened my bedroom door with the Evening Post in her hand and asked, 'what's all this about?'"

However, years of policing trains, stations and the yards where they are parked overnight have given the BTP plenty of time to hone their skills – evading capture has had to become an exact science. What's more, Bristol's local constabulary now deploys its own

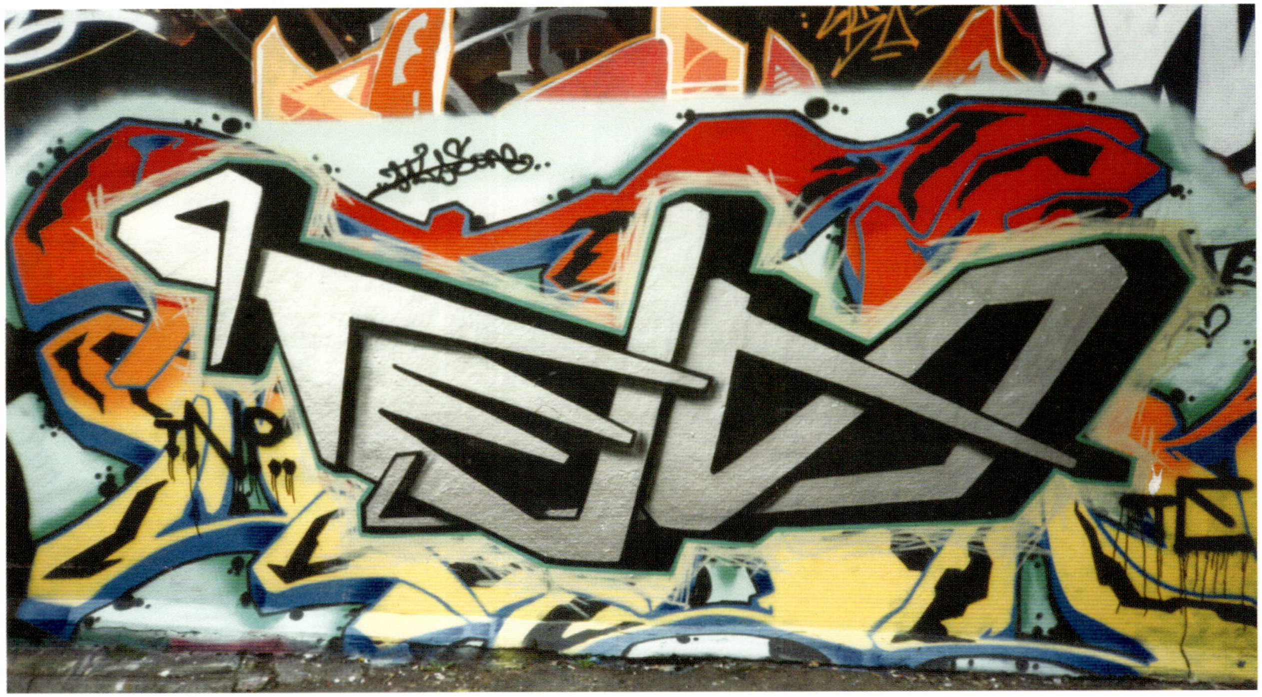

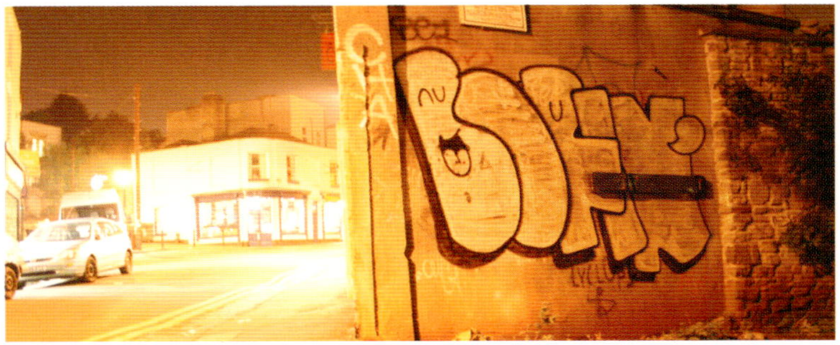

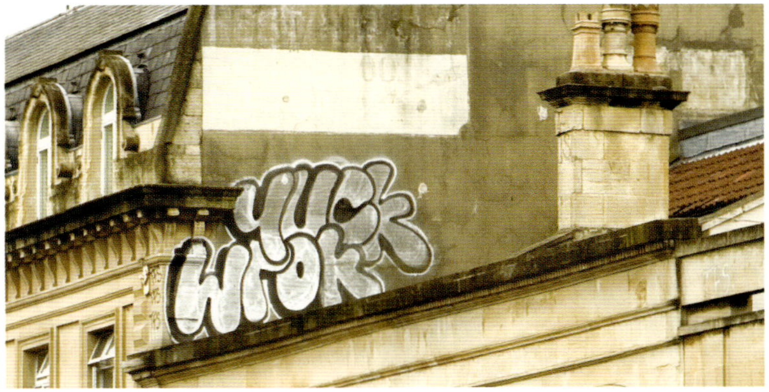

Anti-Graffiti Squad to work alongside the BTP. These days, extreme precautionary measures must be taken by any writer wishing to avoid capture in a city where CCTV is the least of your worries.

"If you're going to paint illegally, paranoia is something that you're definitely going to have to deal with. You're always living with the fact that your door might get kicked off at six in the morning. That's just something you have to put up with and learn to deal with. You just keep painting and if something happens, it happens; the more you think about it, the more paranoid you get.

"Of all the people that I know that have been gripped [caught] recently, none of them have been caught painting graff. They've all been done through intelligence. Intelligence! What the fuck's that about? Bristol is seventy five per cent sell-outs and snitches. It's too local, everyone knows everyone's business; everybody lives in each other's pockets."

PCs, camera phones, and posting photos online are all potentially as risky as having marker pens, paint, and sketches, if confiscated and used as evidence. The modern technologies that have allowed graffiti writers to record and share their pieces globally have, ultimately, sent illegal painting in Bristol further underground than ever before.

"Mobile phones and the Internet are the worst things that have happened to graffiti: they're bait. Every website you go on is traceable, every text message you send is traceable. Any writers who put footage up on YouTube are just stupid. Why would you do that? The net is too dangerous. We don't even take photos anymore. Publicity, as far as we're concerned, isn't necessary; we're not bothered about it. Actions speak louder than words."

All of which has left TNP operating at a grass roots, word-of-mouth level, where pieces have to be seen in the flesh and photographs of painted train panels are closely guarded gems, rarely seen by anyone outside the crew.

Old school notions of fame and new school methods of achieving it – such as the internet – are laughable and irrelevant within this small circle. They paint, it seems, to please no one except themselves.

"When we're out doing it, it's just 'how much of an effortlessly funky thing can we paint on this wall?' And 'can we see it on our way to work?' That's always a good one."

Doing the work itself brings its own rewards. "Doing a train panel: that's a proper night, that's memories. I can look at a photo and remember that night. I can look at it and remember ten different stories from that one night. That's why I do panels. I don't care if it runs, I don't care if anybody sees it. It's not for the fame, I don't care about fame. People who do it for fame are sell-outs."

"What you've got to understand about panels is that they're painted by people who don't expect their graffiti to be seen, they don't want people to know they've done it. It's a little bit bizarre!"

No more bizarre, you might argue, than painting in a city where the Council appear to condone the illegal work of one particular graffiti artist, whilst demonising all the others; where graffiti is regularly front page news, but a youth-on-youth stabbing barely makes the fifth column of page three.

"It's to make the public feel safe, it's propaganda. They do it to make people feel safe when really they're not. No one's safe. There's much worse stuff, like paedophilia and knife crime, and they're cracking down on graffiti. What's the point? Graffiti's a victimless crime. Its fucking stupid how anything by Banksy gets left up but everything else gets buffed."

With everyone from Bristol City Council to Audi and Adidas repackaging graffiti for their own purposes, it is little wonder that TNP - and countless other crews - are cynical about the meteoric rise in popularity of so-called 'street art.'

"Outside Foot Locker there's a stand and it's got (legendary New York writer) Cope 2 on it, and there's all these trainers - like on each stop on a subway line - and it says 'Cope 2: King of the 4 Line'. It's fucking gay. They're happy to use graffiti to sell products and to make loads of money from it, but the people who do it can go to prison for it.

"It's just another thing we do for a crack on the weekend and in some little art gallery in London there's some guy stuck onto the side of my neck like a leech, making money off what we do.

"People who are passionate about graffiti can see clearly that this whole 'art fag' scene is built on the back of people who do real graffiti, who put their neck on the line and get in trouble for it. The art scene just feeds off it and makes money, while all the real writers are still getting in the shit. There are people who claim to be a part of this, just to make money from it, yet they're nothing to do with it. It's bullshit."

There will always be crews like TNP, and they are the first to point out that they are neither the greatest nor the most prolific in Bristol. But even if the police rounded up every single teenager in Bristol with a marker pen or a spray can tomorrow morning, their younger brothers, nephews and cousins would be stood in the wings waiting to pick up the baton and make their mark on society.

Ultimately graffiti is an expression of free will, of being able to make choices beyond those that are rigidly prescribed by the systems that we are forced to live within. 'Anti-social behaviour' is a constructed concept that suggests that society as a whole shares the same values - and that individual expression is all well and good as long as it doesn't upset anybody else's sense of order.

"Everyone should do what the fuck they want - graffiti or whatever, just do what you want, because - without getting too deep - who's to tell you what to do? Why is one human being superior to another? If your thing is painting and a certain group of people don't want you to do it: fuck them, just do what you want."

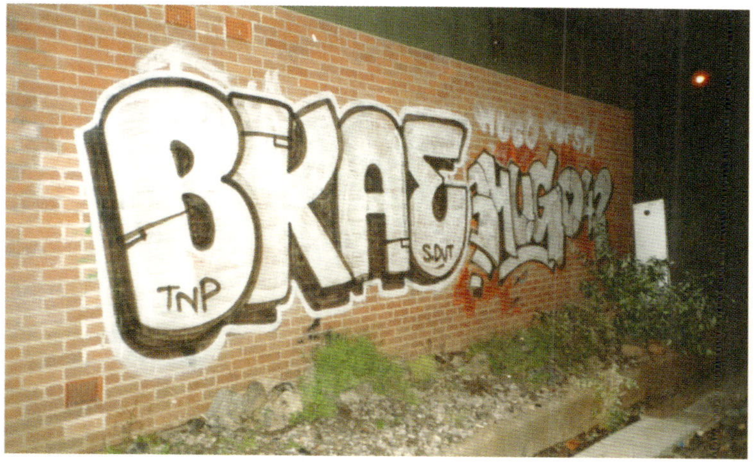

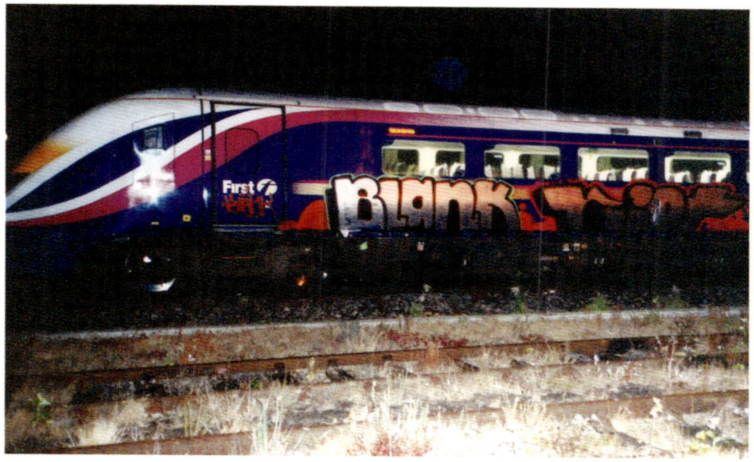

Opposite page. Top: Old school writer and founder member of TNP, Tes

Middle: Another borin' night

Bottom: Yuck and Wrong get high in Clifton

Top: B-Kae track side

Bottom: Blank and Riot go inter city

This spread: Filthy Luker's inflatable objects make their presence felt in urban and rural spaces alike, utilising the environment to make his point and to raise a smile

FILTHY LUKER

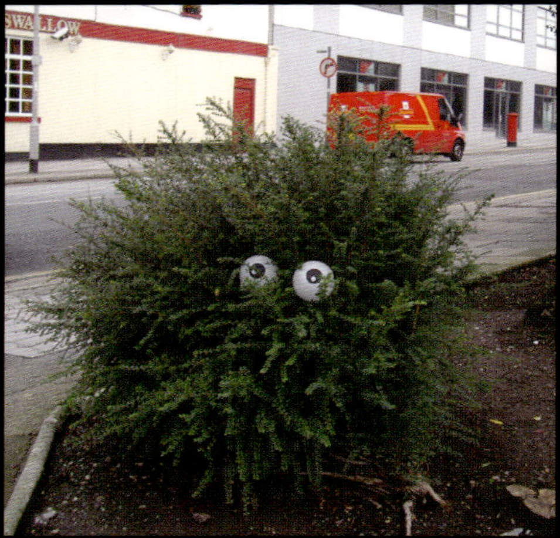

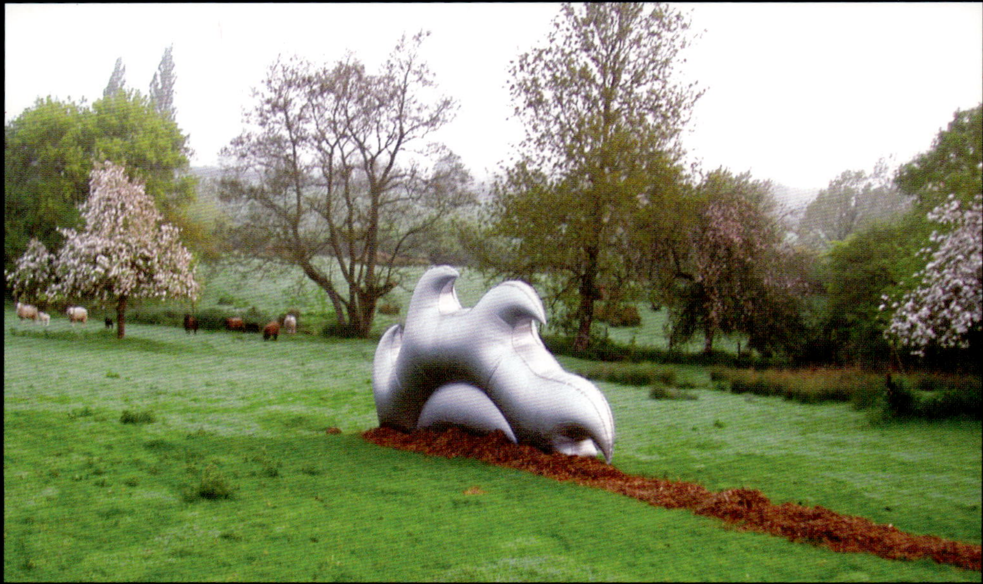

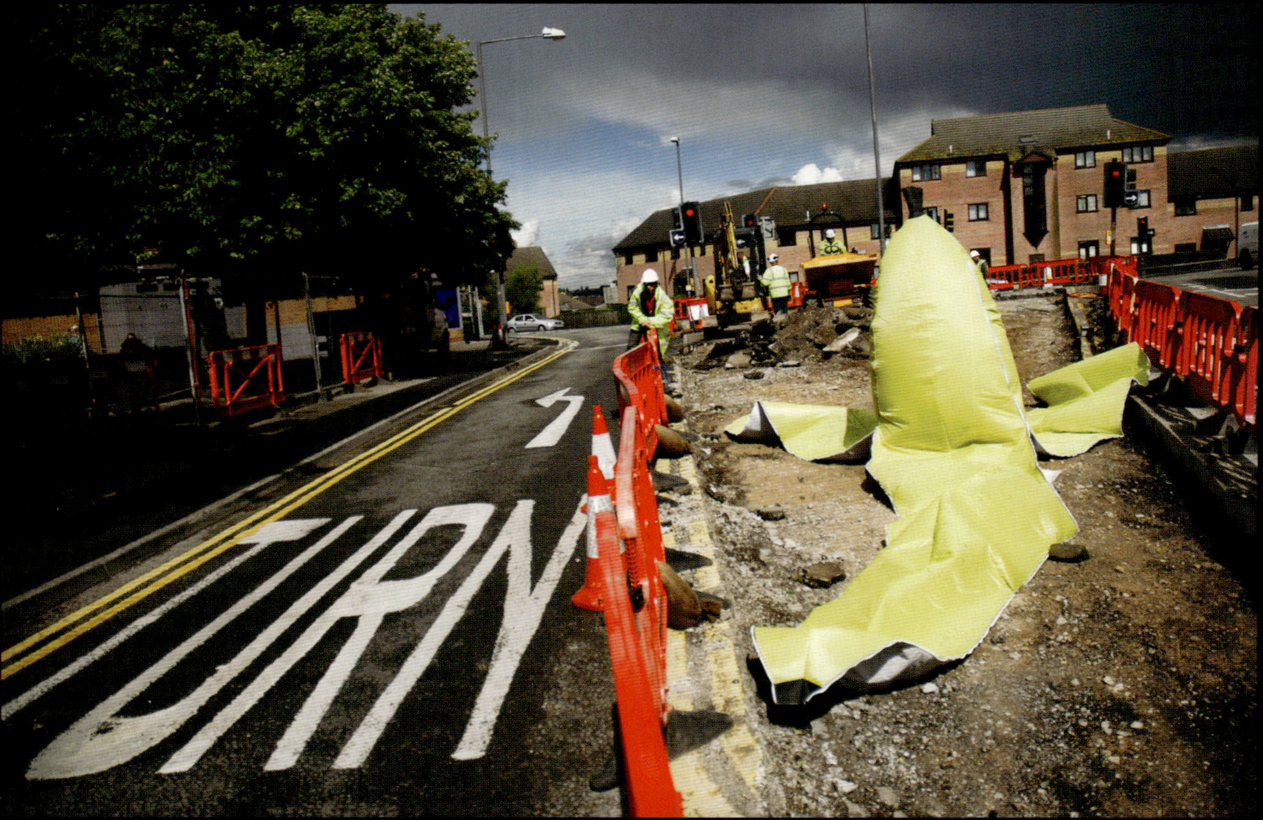

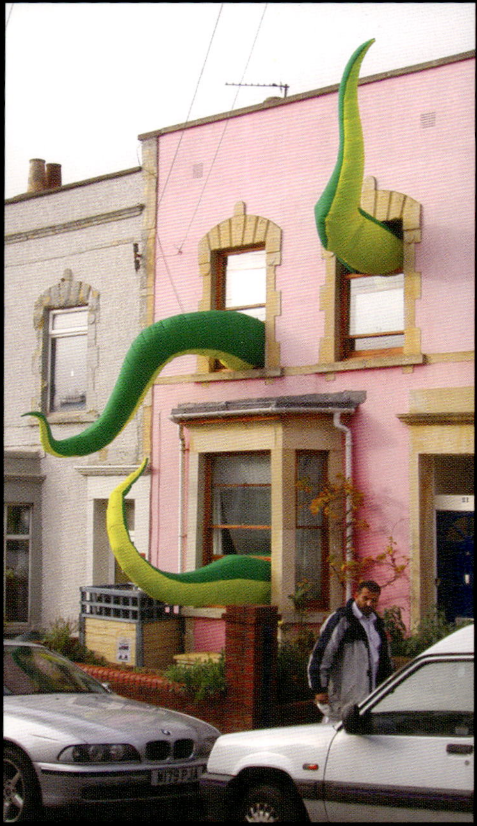

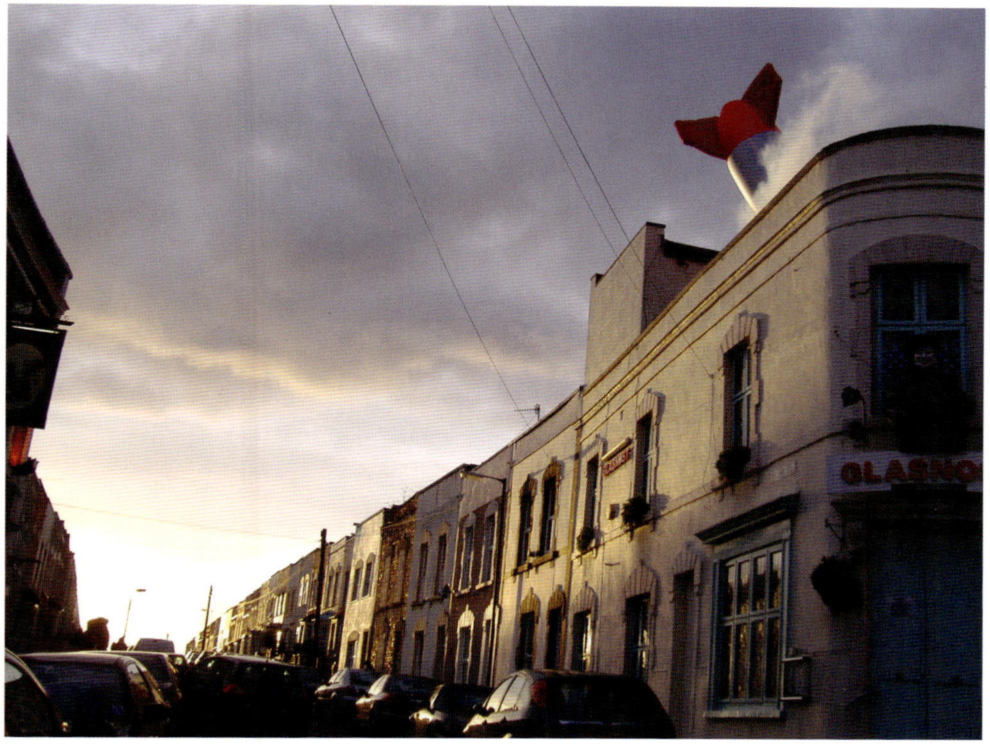
GLASNO

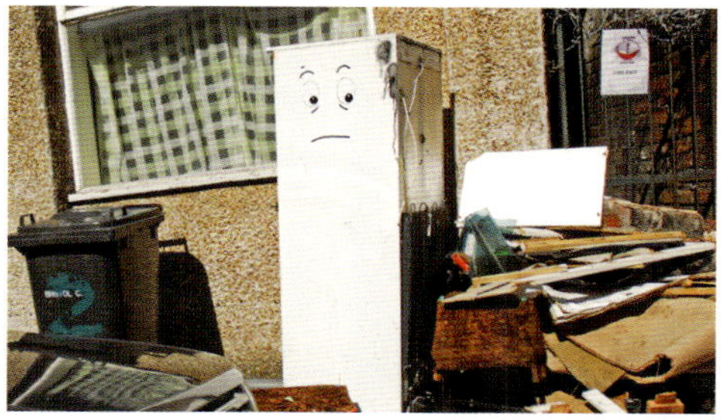

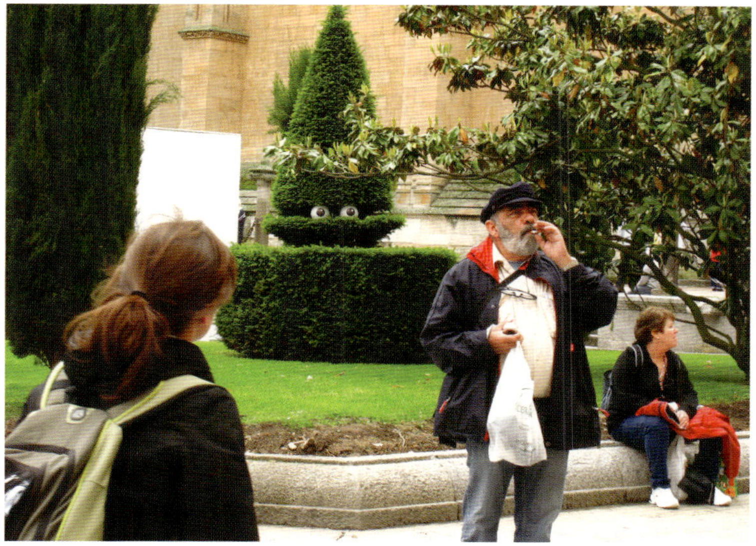

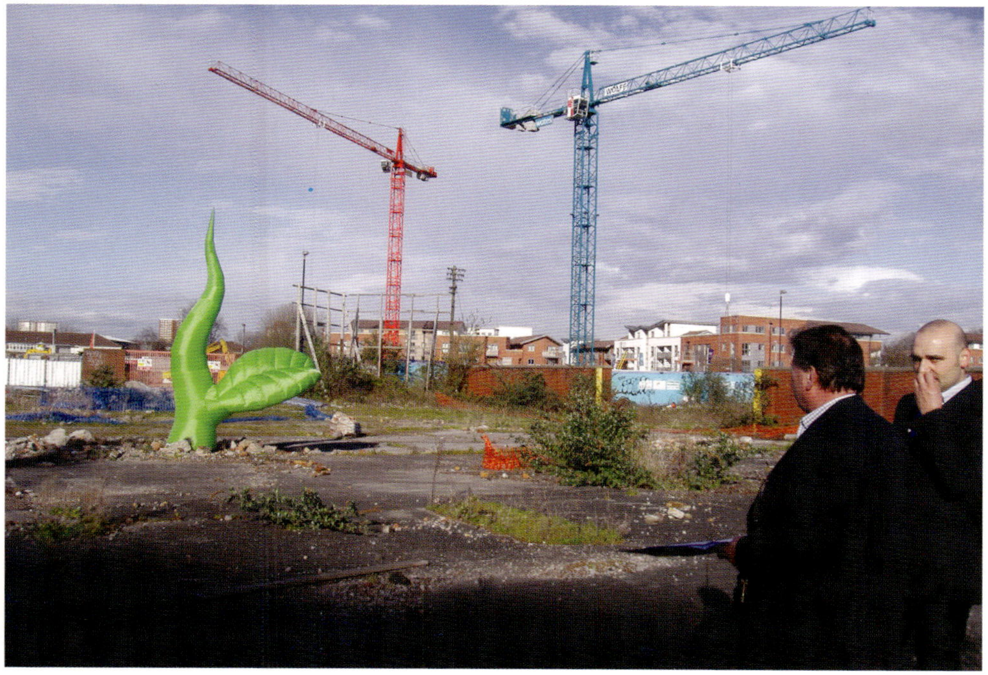

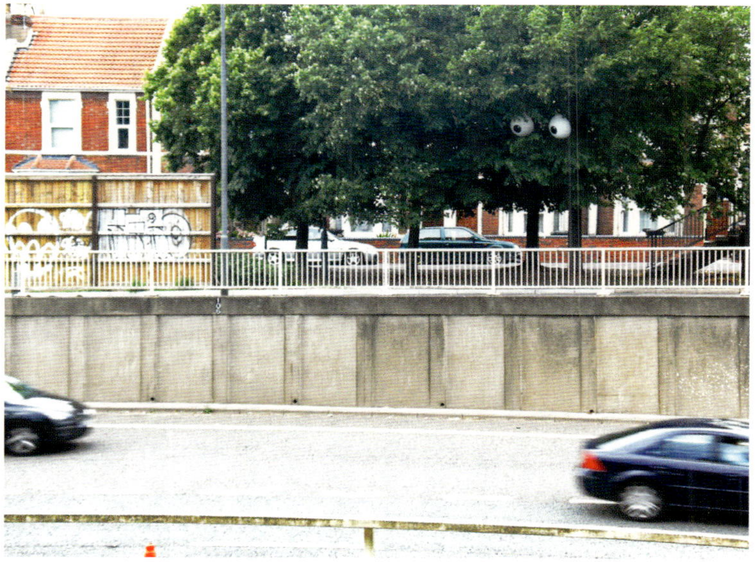

This page: The work of female writer Milk is bold, graphic and most of all fun

MILK

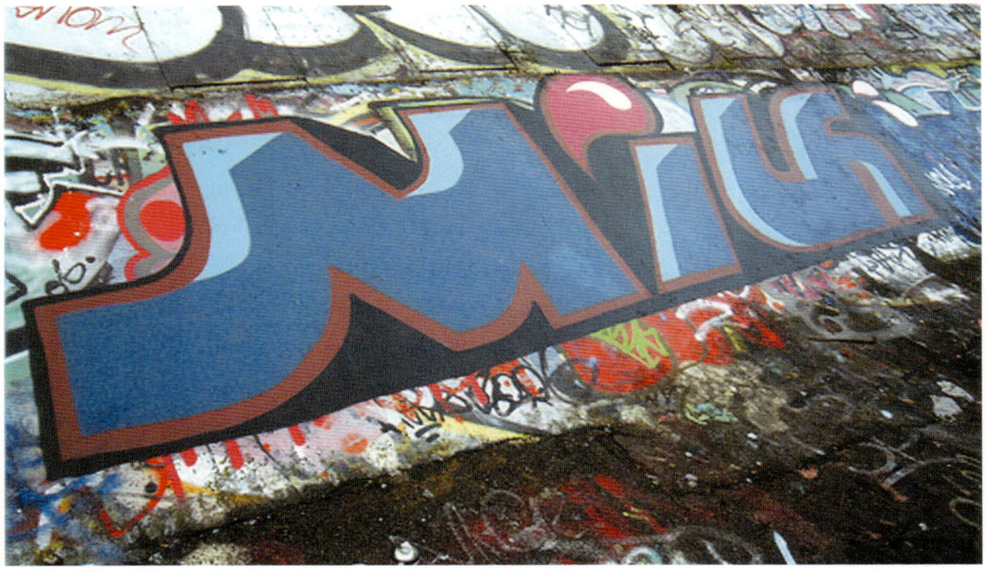

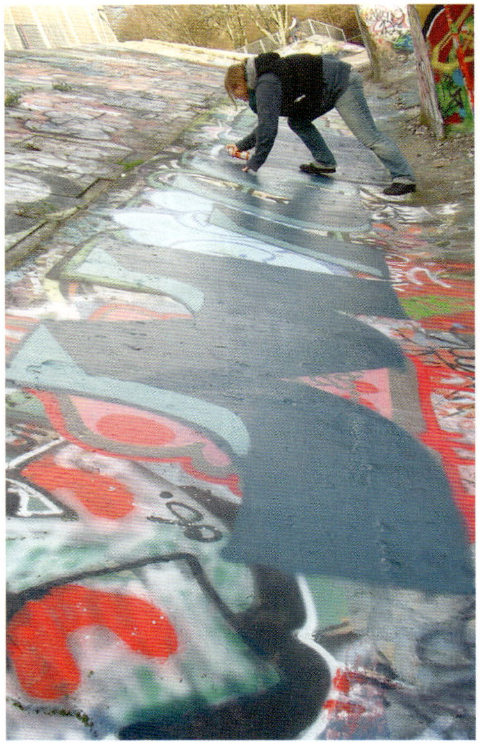

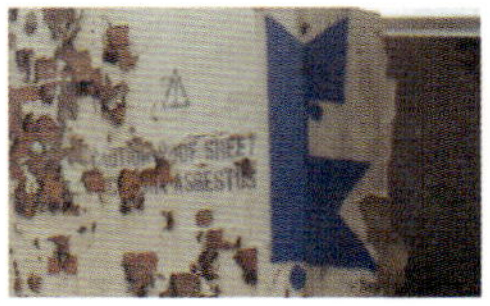

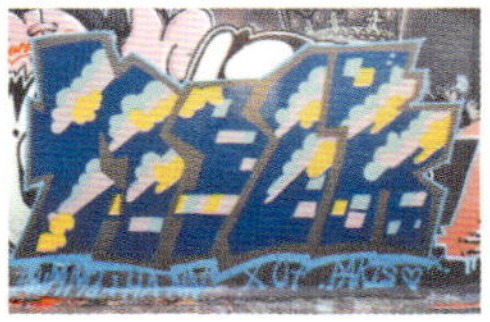

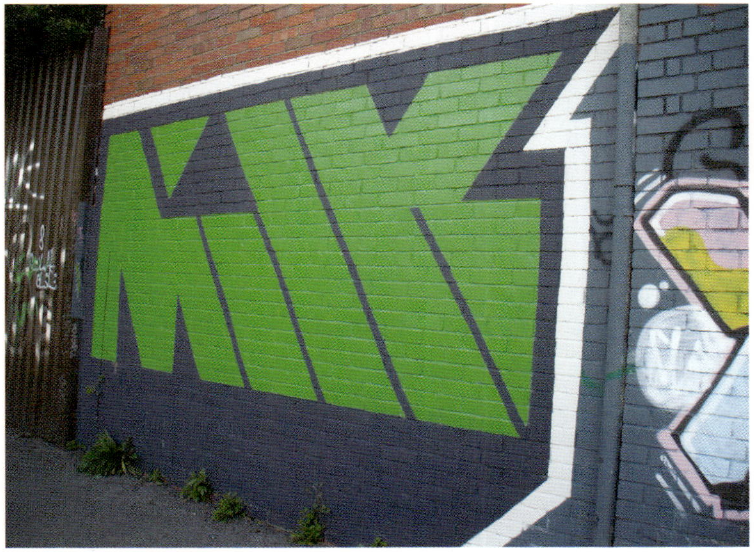

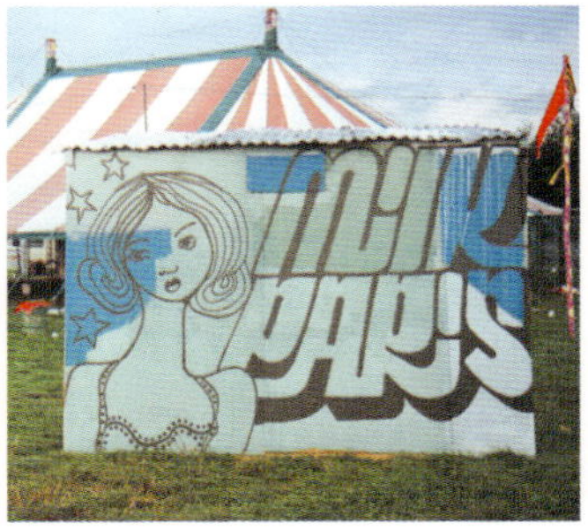

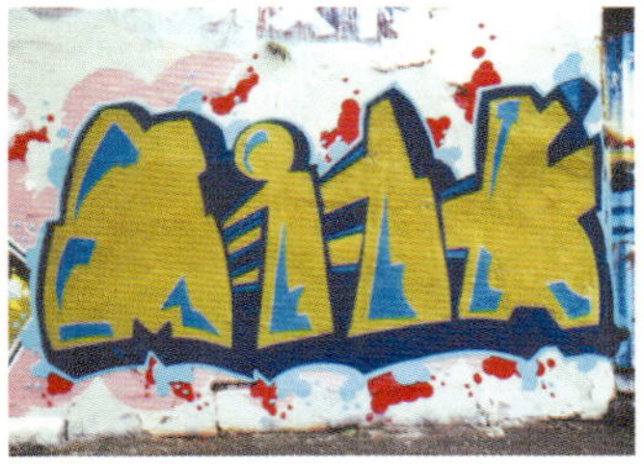

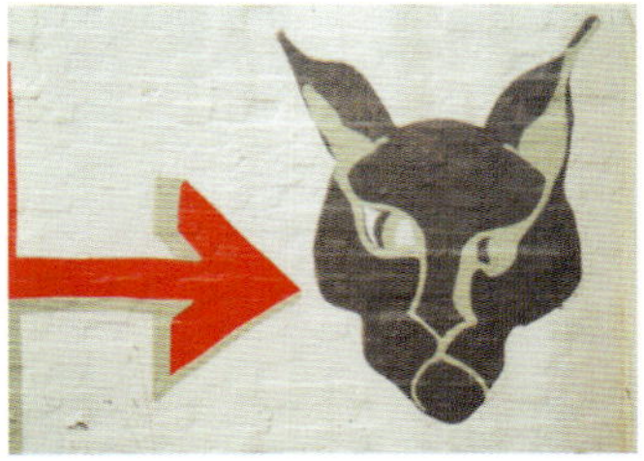

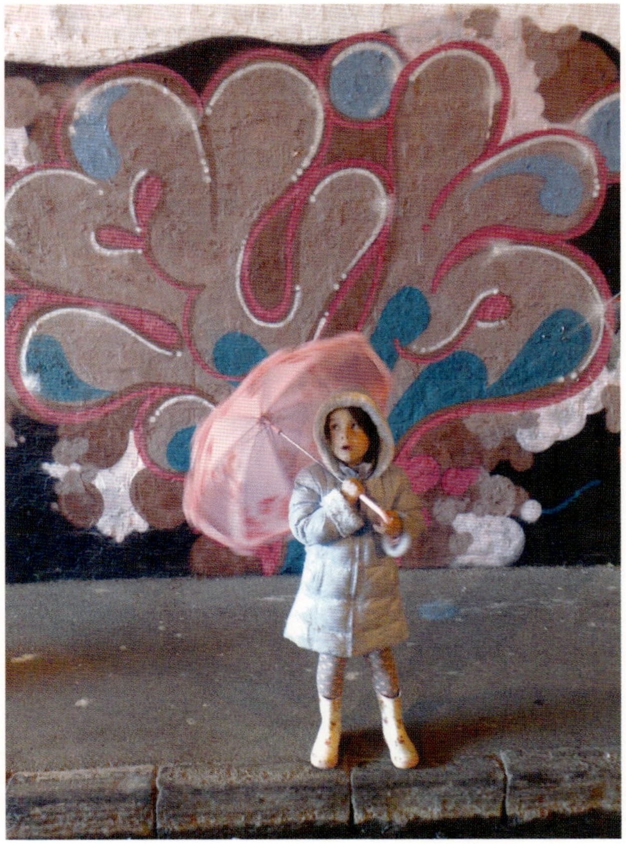

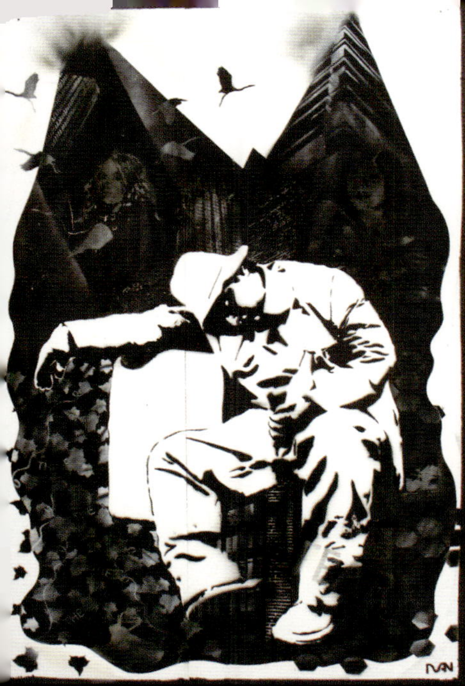

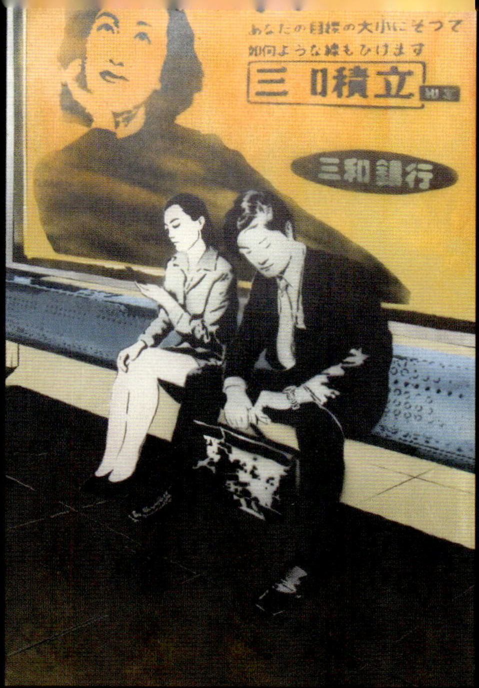

DAN

This page: Intricate and poignant stencils by Dan

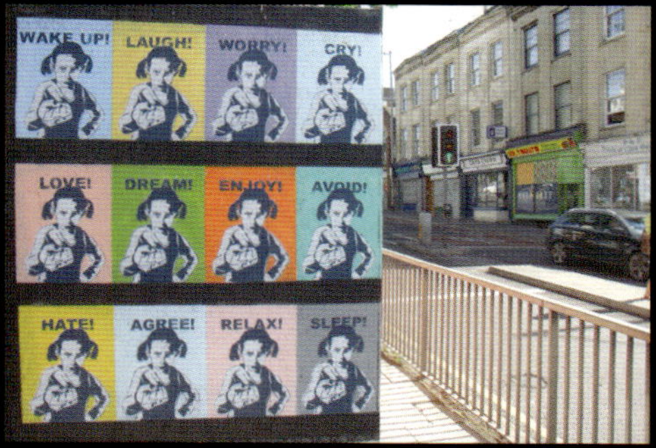

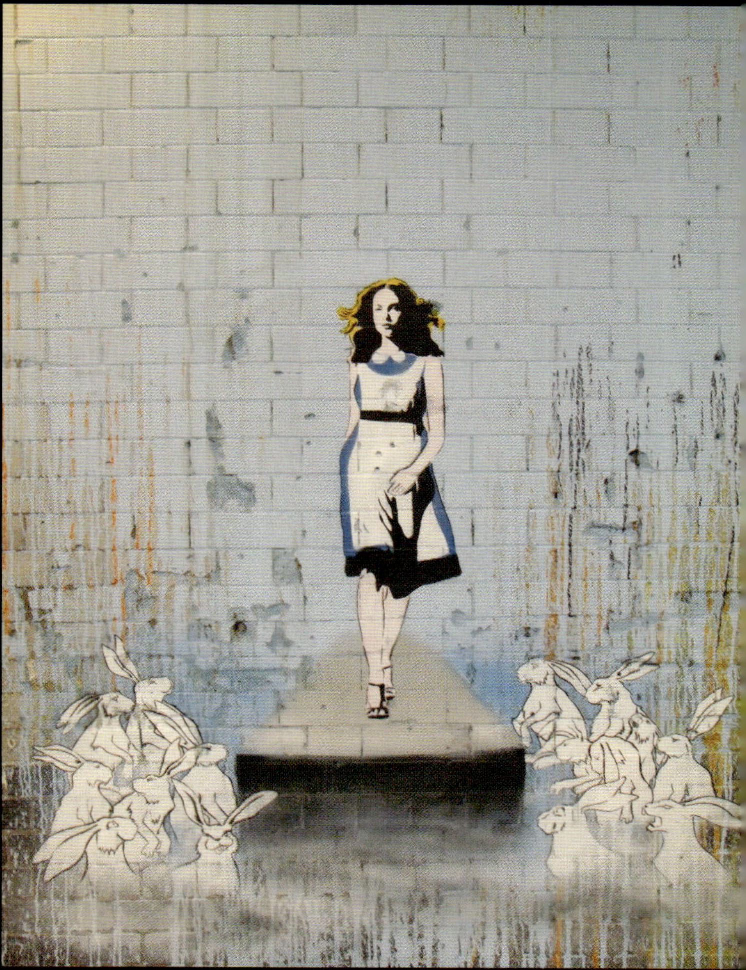

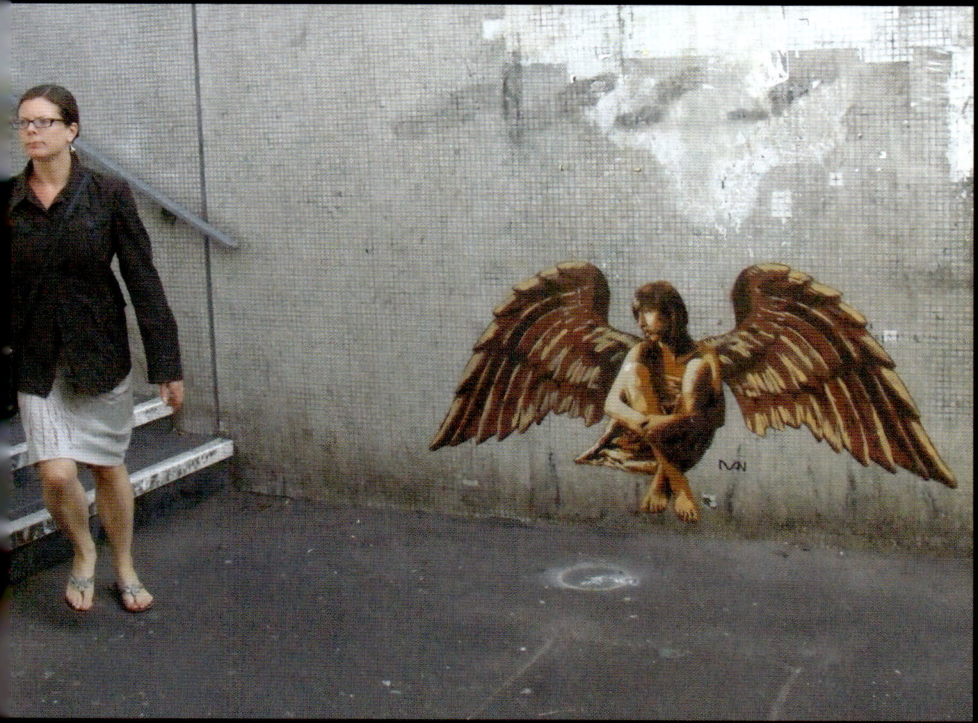

CREWS AND LINKS

CREWS

AAGH: 'Ave A Go heroes
ASK: After School Klub
AWOL: A Way Of Life
BA: Bad Apples
BTM: Burn Too Much
CIC: Crime Inc Crew
CM: Crew Mess
CMA: Criminally Minded Artists
DBZ: Dry Breadz
DP: Dirty Protest
ESR: East Side Rebels
FCK: Fried Chicken Crew
FSH: Fantastic Super Heroes
GK: Gruesome Krusome
JAC: Just Another Crew
JFK: Just For Kicks
JKC: Junior Krime Childs
KTF: Keepin' Things Fresh
KTS: Kane The System
MBA: Mind, Body and Art
MK: Mortal Kombat
NOT: Ninjas Of Tag
OGOG: Original Gods Of Graffiti
OMBD: Original Member Brain Dead
PM: Past Midnight
RDA: Real Deal Artists
SINSTARS/SIN: Strength In Numbers
SOF: Souls On Fire
TCF: Twentieth Century Frescoes
TCP: Tee-Cut Posse
TNP: Toys Need Punishment
TUA: The Ultimate Artists
TUB: The United Bombers
WSSK: Wet Shame Crew

ARTISTS

2 KEEN: www.myspace.com/_fromhere2fame
3D: www.massiveattack.co.uk
ACER: www.flickr.com/photos/acertcf
ANDY COUNCIL: www.andycouncil.co.uk
www.andycouncil.blogspot.com
AWKWARD: www.myspace.com/awkward
www.awkwarduk.blogspot.com
BANKSY: www.banksy.co.uk/
CHEBA: www.flickr.com/photos/cheba
www.myspace.com/cheba_bristol
CHEO: www.cheo.co.uk/
www.flickr.com/photos/dirtyprotest
CHINA MIKE: www.chinamike-art.co.uk
DAN: www.dan.eu.com
DEED: www.hairyparents.com
DICY: www.letthemhang.co.uk
DORA: www.okdora.com
DR DOG: www.flickr.com/photos/dr_dog/
EKO: www.flickr.com/photos/ecobandodo/
FEEK: www.flickr.com/photos/feekertron
FILTHY LUKER: www.filthyluker.deviantart.com/
www.filthyluker.org
FLX: www.flxdesign.co.uk
HAKA: hakerbtm@yahoo.co.uk
INKIE: www.inkie.co.uk
JODY: www.digital-fire.co.uk
JUST ANOTHER CREW: www.myspace.com/voyder
KATO: www.flickr.com/photos/catobristol
KTF: www.tymedesigns.com
www.markmywordsprint.com
LOKEY: www.flickr.com/photos/jerforceone/
MILK: www.321milk.com
MR.JAGO: www.mrjago.com
MUDWIG: www.dasmudwig.com/
NICK WALKER: www.web.mac.com/nickwalkerz
PARIS: www.grahamdews.com
www.kuildoosh.com
SEPR: www.sp-sepr.co.uk
SEZA: www.flickr.com/photos/seza
SHIMZ: www.flickr.com/photos/42855071@N00
SICKBOY: www.thesickboy.com
SOKER: www.flickr.com/photos/soker
SOULS ON FIRE: boswell66@hotmail.co.uk
SPACE: www.spaceonedesigns.co.uk
TURO: www.myspace.com/properbristolhiphop
www.flickr.com/people/22851794@N08
WHAT COLLECTIVE: www.flickr.com/photos/whatcollective
www.flickr.com/photos/sumsthepaw
www.flickr.com/photos/richt
WILL BARRAS: www.willbarras.com
XENZ: www.xenz.org
ZIML: www.fromstore.com

PHOTOGRAPHERS

LIL PETE: www.fao2.co.uk
BEEZER: www.beezerphotos.com
IYERS: www.flickr.com/people/i_y_e_r_s/
PAUL WHITFIELD: www.2020photo.com/
SARAH CONNOLLY: www.flickr.com/photos/knautia/
TELBERT JAMES: www.telbert.blogspot.com/
FRANK DRAKE: www.pyramidfoundation.org
LAURA THORNE:
www.flickr.com/photos/79513319@N00/
GINA LUNDY: www.ginalundy.co.uk
JULIAN MONAGHAN: www.guerrillagalleries.com/
CRAIG BODY ENGLISH:
www.bodyenglishtheartistsweb.co.uk/
KAREN DEWS: www.k148.co.uk/
BEN MASON: www.osnap.co.uk
ALICE LOWNDES: www.flickr.com/photos/alicelowndes

BRISTOL GRAFFITI ON DISPLAY AND FOR SALE

www.art-el.co.uk/
www.1loveart.com/
www.filthymodernart.com/
www.threenine.eu/
www.guerrillagalleries.com/

BLOGS

http://bristolgraffiti.wordpress.com/
http://bristolgraffiti.blogspot.com/

ACTION

www.prsc.org.uk/
www.bristol.indymedia.org/
www.btp.police.uk/